THE
ARCHAEOLOGY
OF SOCIETY IN
THE HOLY LAND

For my loving wife and best friend
Alina
and for
C. Paul Johnson
patron and friend, one who embodies the best of America

THE
ARCHAEOLOGY
OF SOCIETY IN
THE HOLY LAND

Edited by THOMAS E. LEVY

Facts On File®

AN INFOBASE HOLDINGS COMPANY

Archaeology of Society in the Holy Land

Facts on File, Inc.
460 Park Avenue South
New York, NY 10016

Library of Congress Cataloging-in-Publication Data

The archaeology of society in the Holy Land / edited by Thomas Evan Levy.
    p.   cm.
   Includes bibliographical references and index.
   ISBN 0–8160–2855–9
   1. Palestine – Social life and customs.   2. Palestine – Antiquities.
   3. Palestine – Civilization.   4. Excavations (Archaeology) – Palestine.
   I. Levy, Thomas Evan.
   DS112.A73   1995
   933–dc20   94–35170

Facts on File books are available at special discounts when purchased in bulk quantities for
businesses, associations, institutions or sales promotions. Please call our Special Sales
Department in New York at 212/683–2244 or 800/322–8755.

The satellite image maps were produced by City Cartographic, London Guildhall University
by Gareth Owen under the direction of Don Shewan.

The relief shading was illustrated by using the software package 'Mountains High Maps'™
Copyright 1993 Digital Wisdom, Inc.

10 9 8 7 6 5 4 3 2 1

Printed in Hong Kong

CONTENTS

LIST OF CONTRIBUTORS   vii
ACKNOWLEDGMENTS   ix
PREFACE   x
     Thomas E. Levy
PREHISTORIC CHRONOLOGICAL FRAMEWORK   xiv
     Ofer Bar-Yosef

I APPROACHES TO THE PAST

1   SOCIAL CHANGE AND THE ARCHAEOLOGY OF THE HOLY LAND   2
     Thomas E. Levy and Augustin F.C. Holl

2   POWER, POLITICS AND THE PAST: THE SOCIAL CONSTRUCTION OF ANTIQUITY IN THE HOLY LAND   9
     Neil Asher Silberman

3   MAN AND THE NATURAL ENVIRONMENT   24
     Avinoam Danin

4   THE CHANGING LANDSCAPE   40
     Paul Goldberg

5   PEOPLE OF THE HOLY LAND FROM PREHISTORY TO THE RECENT PAST   58
     Patricia Smith

II STONE AGE ADAPTATION, EVOLUTION AND SURVIVAL

6   SOCIAL CHANGE AND THE ARCHAEOLOGY OF THE HOLY LAND: PREHISTORIC LITHIC PRODUCTION THROUGH TIME   76
     Augustin F.C. Holl and Thomas E. Levy

7   THE LOWER PALEOLITHIC OF ISRAEL   93
     Naama Goren-Inbar

8   THE ORIGINS OF MODERN HUMANS   110
     Ofer Bar-Yosef

9   THE FORAGERS OF THE UPPER PALEOLITHIC PERIOD   124
     Isaac Gilead

10   COMPLEX HUNTER/GATHERERS AT THE END OF THE PALEOLITHIC (20,000–10,000 BP)   141
     Nigel Goring-Morris

11   THE FIRST SETTLED SOCIETIES – NATUFIAN (12,500–10,200 BP)   169
     François Valla

III FARMERS, PRIESTS AND PRINCES: THE RISE OF THE FIRST COMPLEX SOCIETIES

12   EARLIEST FOOD PRODUCERS – PRE-POTTERY NEOLITHIC (8000–5500)   190
     Ofer Bar-Yosef

13   EARLY POTTERY-BEARING GROUPS IN ISRAEL – THE POTTERY NEOLITHIC PERIOD   205
     Avi Gopher

14   CULT, METALLURGY AND RANK SOCIETIES –CHALCOLITHIC PERIOD (CA. 4500–3500 BCE)   226
     Thomas E. Levy

15   PLOUGH AND PASTURE IN THE EARLY ECONOMY OF THE SOUTHERN LEVANT   245
     Caroline Grigson

16   EARLY BRONZE AGE CANAAN: SOME SPATIAL AND DEMOGRAPHIC OBSERVATIONS   269
     Ram Gophna

17   SOCIAL STRUCTURE IN THE EARLY BRONZE IV PERIOD IN PALESTINE   282
William G. Dever

18   THE DAWN OF INTERNATIONALISM – THE MIDDLE BRONZE AGE   297
David Ilan

19   ON THE EDGE OF EMPIRES – LATE BRONZE AGE (1500–1200 BCE)   320
Shlomo Bunimovitz

20   THE IMPACT OF THE SEA PEOPLES (1185 – 1050 BCE)   332
Lawrence E. Stager

21   THE GREAT TRANSFORMATION: THE 'CONQUEST' OF THE HIGHLANDS FRONTIERS AND THE RISE OF THE TERRITORIAL STATES   349
Israel Finkelstein

22   THE KINGDOMS OF ISRAEL AND JUDAH: POLITICAL AND ECONOMIC CENTRALIZATION IN THE IRON IIA–B (CA. 1000–750 BCE)   368
John S. Holladay, Jr

23   THE KINGDOMS OF AMMON, MOAB AND EDOM: THE ARCHAEOLOGY OF SOCIETY IN LATE BRONZE/IRON AGE TRANSJORDAN (CA. 1400–500 BCE)   399
Øystein S. LaBianca and Randall W. Younker

24   SOCIAL STRUCTURE IN PALESTINE IN THE IRON II PERIOD ON THE EVE OF DESTRUCTION   416
William G. Dever

25   BETWEEN PERSIA AND GREECE: TRADE, ADMINISTRATION AND WARFARE IN THE PERSIAN AND HELLENISTIC PERIODS (539–63 BCE)   432
Ephraim Stern

26   THE IMPACT OF ROME ON THE PERIPHERY: THE CASE OF PALESTINA – ROMAN PERIOD (63 BCE–324 CE)   446
James D Anderson

27   CHURCH, STATE AND THE TRANSFORMATION OF PALESTINE – THE BYZANTINE PERIOD (324–640 CE)   470
Joseph Patrich

28   ISLAM AND THE SOCIO-CULTURAL TRANSITION OF PALESTINE – EARLY ISLAMIC PERIOD (638–1099 CE)   488
Donald Whitcomb

29   SETTLEMENT AND SOCIETY FORMATION IN CRUSADER PALESTINE   502
Ronnie Ellenblum

30   BETWEEN CAIRO AND DAMASCUS: RURAL LIFE AND URBAN ECONOMICS IN THE HOLY LAND DURING THE AYYUBID, MAMLUK AND OTTOMAN PERIODS   512
Myriam Rosen-Ayalon

31   THE INTRODUCTION OF MODERN TECHNOLOGY INTO THE HOLY LAND (1800–1914 CE)   524
Ruth Kark

32   CONCLUSION: A MASS IN CELEBRATION OF THE CONFERENCE   542
Norman Yoffee

BIBLIOGRAPHY   549
INDEX   605

IV   CANAAN, ISRAEL, AND THE FORMATION OF THE BIBLICAL WORLD

V   LOCAL KINGDOMS AND WORLD EMPIRES

VI   THE RISE OF CHRISTIANITY AND ISLAM IN THE HOLY LAND

LIST OF CONTRIBUTORS

Thomas E. Levy is Professor in the Department of Anthropology and on the faculty of the Judaic Studies Program at the University of California, San Diego. Prior to this, he was assistant director at the Nelson Glueck School of Biblical Archaeology, Hebrew Union College (1987–92) and the W.F. Albright Institute of Archaeological Research (1985–87), both in Jerusalem. Research and teaching interests focus on anthropological archaeology, ethnoarchaeology, nomadism and the archaeology of Syro-Palestine. He has directed excavations at Gilat, Shiqmim, and Nahal Tillah in Israel and conducted ethnoarchaeological research in Cameroon. Author of numerous scholarly papers, he recently co-edited (with A.F.C. Holl) *Spatial Boundaries and Social Dynamics – Case Studies from Food-Producing Societies* (Ann Arbor: International Monographs in Prehistory).

James Anderson recently completed his PhD at the University of Newcastle-Upon-Tyne, England. His thesis focused on the dynamics of Roman military organization in the western periphery of the empire. His primary field work has been carried out in England and Israel.

Ofer Bar-Yosef is currently the George G. and Janet G.B. MacCurdy Professor of Prehistoric Archaeology, Department of Anthropology, Peabody Museum, Harvard University. He has been involved in numerous excavations throughout Israel, as well as those at Karain and Öküzini caves in Southwestern Turkey. Most recently he initiated a new research program at Hayonim Cave in northern Israel.

Shlomo Bunimovitz is a lecturer in archaeology at both the Department of Archaeology and Near Eastern Cultures, Tel Aviv University, and the Department of Land of Israel Studies, Bar-Ilan University. He is currently co-director of the Tel Beth-Shemesh excavations and was assistant director of the excavations at Shiloh and the Land of Ephraim survey.

Avinoam Danin is Professor of Botany in the Department of Evolution, Systematics and Ecology at the Hebrew University of Jerusalem. His main areas of interest are those of desert vegetation, specifically in Israel and Sinai, and the use of biogenic weathering of limestone for palaeoenvironmental investigations and the protection of archaeological monuments from biodeterioration. Publications include *Desert Vegetation of Israel and Sinai: An Analytical Flora of Eretz Israel.*

William G. Dever has been Professor of Near Eastern Archaeology and Anthropology at the University of Arizona since 1975, specializing in Syro-Palestinian archaeology. Prior to this, he was director of the W.F. Albright Insitute of Archaeology, Israel (1971–75) and of the Nelson Glueck School of Biblical Archaeology (1967–71). He has directed excavations at Gezer, Shechem, Kh. el-Qom, and Be'er Resisim, Israel and is widely published in his field of Near Eastern Archaeology. He is author of *Recent Archaeological Discoveries and Biblical Research* (Washington University Press).

Ronnie Ellenblum completed his PhD in the Department of Geography at the Hebrew University of Jerusalem, where he is now a lecturer. His primary research focuses on the Crusader period in Syro-Palestine. Recently, he was post-doctoral research fellow at the Sorbonne, Paris.

Israel Finkelstein is Professor of Archaeology at Tel Aviv University and is, at present, co-director of the Megiddo Expedition. He has directed numerous expeditions and excavations and is a member of the editorial boards of *Tel Aviv*, Journal of the Institute of Archaeology, Tel Aviv University, the *Monograph series* of the same institute and that of *Qadmoniot*, Quarterly for the Antiquities of Eretz-Israel and Bible Lands. He is co-editor with N. Na'aman of *From Nomadism to Monarchy: Archaeological and Historical Aspects of Early Israel* (1994) and with S. Bunimovitz and Z. Lederman of *Shiloh: The Archaeology of a Biblical Site* (Monograph Series of the Institute of Archaeology, No.10, Tel Aviv University, 1993) and editor of *Archaeological Survey in the Hill Country of Benjamin* (1993).

Isaac Gilead is Professor of Archaeology at Ben-Gurion University of the Negev, and was recently a chairman of the Department of Bible and Ancient Near Eastern Studies. His primary fields of research are the Middle and Upper Paleolithic and Late Neolithic and Chalcolithic in the Levant, with field work especially in the Negev and Sinai.

Paul Goldberg is currently a geologist at the Texas Archaeological Research Laboratory, University of Texas at Austin, working on sites in Texas, Israel, England, South Africa and Turkey. Until 1991, he was Associate Professor at the Institute of Archaeology, Hebrew University of Jerusalem. A pioneer in the use and development of the technique of micromorphology in archaeology, he is a co-editor of the journal, *Geoarchaeology*.

Avi Gopher teaches at the Institute of Archaeology, Tel Aviv University. He has participated in the excavation of Neolithic sites since 1976, most recently conducting field projects in the Menashe hills, the coastal plain and the Judean Desert in Israel.

Ram Gophna is currently Professor of Protohistory at the Institute of Archaeology, Tel Aviv University. His areas of research focus on Protohistory of the Near East; Chalcolithic and Early Bronze Ages and Settlement Archaeology. His most significant excavation sites have been Tel Poleg, Tel En Besor, Tel Tsaf and Tel Dalit.

Naama Goren-Inbar is an Associate Professor in Prehistoric Studies at the Institute of Archaeology, Hebrew University of Jerusalem. She specialises in the areas of Levantine prehistory, paleoecology, early hominid behavioral patterns and lithic technology.

Nigel Goring-Morris is a lecturer in Prehistoric Archaeology at the Institute of Archaeology, Hebrew University of Jerusalem. From 1990–93, he was in charge of Prehistory at the Israel Antiquities Authority, and has recently begun a major project at the Pre-Pottery Neolithic settlement of Kfar Hahoresh near Nazareth, Galilee. Main research interests focus on the development of man/land relationships during the Upper Palaeolithic, Epipalaeolithic and Neolithic periods.

Caroline Grigson manages the Museums of the Royal College of Surgeons of England, London. She specialises in the study of the remains of animals from archaeological sites in the Levant and in Britain. Her particular areas of study in the Levant are the changes in the relationships between people and the environment, and the use of domestic animals and plants, during the social transformations implicit in the transition from the late Neolithic to the first urban societies.

Augustin F.C. Holl is Maitre de Conférence at the University of Paris, Nanterre. Over the last ten years he has conducted a long-term archaeological and ethnoarchaeological project in the Cameroon portion of the lake Chad basin, as well as being involved in the Northern Negev research programs at Shiqmim, Gilat and Nahal Tillah in Israel.

John S. Holladay, Jr teaches the Archaeology of Syria-Palestine at the Department of Near Eastern Studies, University of Toronto. In 1977 he launched a major multidisciplinary investigation of Tell el-Maskhuta, near Ismailia, which continued until 1985, as part of the university's Wadi Tumilat Project in Egypt. His main research interests are pottery, functional architectural analysis based on cross-cultural and ethnographic perspectives, social archaeology, and strategies for stratigraphic excavation and interpretation.

David Ilan is a PhD candidate at Tel Aviv University, and the G.E. Wright Scholar at the Nelson Glueck School of Biblical Archaeology at the Hebrew Union College-Jewish Institute of Religion, Jerusalem.

Ruth Kark is Associate Professor of Geography at the Hebrew University. She has written and edited several books and numerous articles on the historical geography of Palestine and Israel and has recently completed a manuscript on *American Consuls in the Holy Land*. Her research interests include the study of concepts of land, land-use, and the patterns of land ownership in Palestine in the 19th and 20th centuries, urban and rural settlement processes and characteristics, and the influence of Western civilizations on the Holy Land.

Øystein S. LaBianca is Professor of Anthropology and Associate Director of the Institute of Archaeology at Andrews University, Michigan. For the past ten years, he has been co-director of the Madaba Plains Project, Jordan, and prior to that was anthropological consultant to the University of Toronto's Wadi Tumilat Project. Publications include *Sedentarization and Nomadization* (Andrew University Press, 1990).

Joseph Patrich is chairman of the Department of Archaeology, University of Haifa and co-director of the Combined Caesarea Expeditions. Between 1981 and 1991 he carried out excavations and surveys of hermitages and caves in the Judean desert, and excavated the Byzantine town of Rehovot-in-the-Negev, and Beth Loya in the Judean Hills.

Myriam Rosen-Ayalon is Leo A. Mayer Professor of Islamic Art and Archaeology, the Hebrew University of Jerusalem. She specializes in Islamic art and archaeology, focusing on Iran and Palestine, with particular interest in Jerusalem and the period of the Middle Ages. Since 1985 she has been involved with the Ashkelon excavations, and in 1992 she won the Schimmel Prize for Archaeology.

Neil A. Silberman is a contributing editor to *Archaeology Magazine*. His recent books include *Digging for God and Country* (1982); *Between Past and Present* (1989) and *A Prophet from Amongst You: The Life of Yigael Yadin* (1993).

Patricia Smith has been associated with the Hebrew University since 1969 and is at present Head of the Dental Division of Anatomy and Embryology, with particular responsibility for research and teaching in biological anthropology. Research projects carried out in Israel, Africa, Australia, North America and Europe, have encompassed the evolution of human dentition, as well as the skeletal biology and evolution of past populations in the Near East.

Lawrence E. Stager is the Dorot Professor of the Archaeology of Israel in the Departments of Near Eastern Languages and Civilizations, and of Anthropology at Harvard University. He is Director and Curator of the Harvard Semitic Museum. From 1973–86 he taught at the Oriental Institute in the University of Chicago. He has led major archaeological expeditions to Idalion (Cyprus), Carthage (Tunisia), and Ashkelon (Israel), where he is currently directing the Leon Levy Expedition. His many publications have focused on the archaeology and history of Canaanites, Phoenicians, Philistines, and Israelites. At present, he is working on three books dealing with everyday life among the Israelites, kinship and kingship in ancient Israel, and a history of the cosmological aspects of Jerusalem.

Ephraim Stern is the Bernard M. Lauterman Professor of Biblical Archaeology at the Institute of Archaeology, the Hebrew University of Jerusalem and the editor of the *Qadmoniot* journal. In 1994 the Israel Museum awarded him with the Scheimel Prize for the Archaeology of the Holy and Bible Lands. Publications include *The Material Culture of the Land of the Bible in the Persian Period* (Aris and Philips/Israel Exploration, 1982), which won the 1984 BAS Publication Award for the Best Scholarly Book on Archaeology, and his recent monumental edited volume, *The New Encyclopedia of Archaeological Excavations in the Holy Land* (Simon and Schuster, 1993).

François Valla is Chargé de Recherche, CNRS, Paris. Specializing in the Natufian culture, he has published two books: *Le Natoufien, une culture préhistorique en Palestine* and *Les industries lithiques de Mallaha (Eynan, Israel) et du Natoufien dans le Levant*, as well as co-edited *The Natoufian Culture in the Levant* with O. Bar-Yosef.

Donald Whitcomb is a Research Associate at the Oriental Institute, University of Chicago. He specialises in Islamic archae-ology, one of his major interests being the use of archaeological data to address historical questions in the development of early Islam. He has conducted excavations at Aqaba, Jordan and Quseir al-Qadim, as well as surveys in Iran, Syria, Oman and Saudi Arabia. He is editor of the *Encyclopedia of Islamic Archaeology*.

Norman Yoffee is Professor and Chair of the Department of Near Eastern Studies, University of Michigan, also holding appoint-ments as Curator of Near Eastern History in the Museum of Anthropology and Professor in the Department of Anthropology. His recent publications include two edited volumes; *Archae-ological Theory: Who Sets the Agenda?* (co-edited with A. Sherratt, Cambridge University Press, 1993) and *Early Stages in the Evolution of Mesopotamian Civilization: Soviet Excavations in Northern Iraq* (co-edited with J. Clark, University of Arizona Press, 1993).

Randall W. Younker is Assistant Professor of Old Testament and Biblical Archaeology, and Director of the Institute of Archaeology at Andrews University, Michigan. He is currently a PhD candidate at the University of Arizona, where he received his MA in Near Eastern Archaeology in 1987. At present he is directing excavations at Tell Jalul for the Madaba Plains Project.

ACKNOWLEDGMENTS

The idea of writing a book for Leicester University Press (LUP) grew out of discussions in 1989 between Graeme Barker of the University of Leicester and Alec McAulay, formerly of LUP. I am grateful to both of them for taking the initiative, and especially Alec whose trust in me and friendship helped push this book to completion. When I joined the faculty of the University of California, San Diego (UCSD) in July of 1992, I thought that the only real way to bring this project to completion was to mount a meeting where all the contributors could assemble and be locked together for over 50 hours, under the skies of southern California. In fact, this book would never have seen the light of day had it not been for the international symposium held at the University of California, San Diego (UCSD), 29–31 January 1993, entitled *The Archaeology of Society in the Holy Land – New Perspectives on the Past*. The bulk of the funds for the symposium came generously from the C. Paul Johnson Family Charitable Foundation (Chicago) and the UCSD Judaic Studies Endowment. I am grateful to Paul Johnson and his family for their continued support of my research endeavors, their deep friendship, and willingness to join in with me on some challenging endeavors. I would also like to thank my colleagues in the Judaic Studies Program at UCSD, David Noel Freedman, Richard Elliott Friedman, David Goodblatt, and William Propp for their enthusiastic support of our symposium. Additional support for the symposium was given by the Glickman Family Foundation, and the Deans of Humanities, Stanley Chodorow and Social Sciences, Michael Rothschild, of UCSD and Jerry Katzin. Special thanks also to Ofer Bar-Yosef, Neil Silberman, Lawrence Stager and William Dever for all their pre-publication help.

In the Department of Anthropology at UCSD, special thanks go to Don Tuzin, then Associate Chancellor, for his help and to Guillermo Algaze for his friendship and support. Thanks also to those University of California colleagues who served as moderators at the symposium: Guillermo Algaze, Brian F. Byrd, Elizabeth F. Carter, David Noel Freedman, Richard Elliott Friedman, Hassan Kayali, Michael E. Meeker, James J. Moore, Alden A. Mosshammer, William H. Propp, and Carol Sussman. Laurel Manen, program representative of the UCSD Judaic Studies Program, did a marvelous job in helping to organize the symposium and in producing the beautiful graphics used. I would also like to thank the symposium participants, most of whom are old friends, teachers, and colleagues who I got to know over a beautiful 14-year period of living in Israel.

At Pinter Publishers in London, the owners of Leicester University Press, I would like to thank Frances Pinter, who has stood solidly behind the project from its inception. The Pinter production team has been wonderful. I would like to thank Vanessa Harwood, the managing editor, who has been a great help in organizing the nuts and bolts of this project; Patrick Armstrong production director, for the excellent work in designing this book and the copy editor, Jane Holden, for ensuring the readability of this volume. When I began work on this project I was the Assistant Director of the Nelson Glueck School of Biblical Archaeology (NGSBA) at the Hebrew Union College-Jewish Institute of Religion (HUC-JIR), in Jerusalem. I would like to sincerely thank Avraham Biran, the NGSBA Director, Alfred Gottschalk, President of HUC-JIR, and Paul M. Steinberg, Vice-President of HUC-JIR, for providing me with the freedom to carry out this work and all my other research projects in Jerusalem.

Photographs and illustrations have been supplied by a variety of sources and are referenced in the text by the individual authors. To all of these sources I am grateful. Special thanks to Catherine Commenge and Jean Perrot, Centre Recherche Français de Jerusalem; Zev Radovan, Garo, and Werner Braun, photograpers in Jerusalem; the Israel Museum; Israel Antiquities Authority; Zev Herzog, Tel Aviv University; Israel Exploration Society; the British Museum and the Oriental Institute, University of Chicago. Apologies for any photographs which appear without proper acknowledgement; any oversights will be corrected in future editions.

I would also like to thank my Negev friend and colleague, David Alon, for teaching me so much about the symbolic significance embeded in the archaeology and people of the Holy Land.

Finally, I am grateful to my wife Alina; without her love and support throughout this project I would never have completed it. To my sons Ben and Gil, and yes our canine boxer, Sandy, I thank them for providing comic relief and affection during the different stages of this work in Jerusalem and San Diego.

Thomas E. Levy
San Diego
June, 1994

PREFACE

Thomas E. Levy

It was June and you could hardly hear yourself think for the blare of the cicadas chirping in the hot Israeli Mediterranean sun. The rickety bus had just collected a fresh-faced group of us from the Lod central bus station and dumped us on the top of one of the most important ancient cities in the Holy Land – Tel Gezer. On the way up to the crest of the mound, we passed a number of Bedouin encampments set precariously along the Terra Rossa valley bottom which led up to the French Trappist monastery at Latrun. Only 22 years earlier, fierce fighting between the newly established state of Israel and the Jordanian Arab legion took place at this junction. The momentous events of the 1967 Arab–Israeli Six Day War were only four years old and the remains of military trenches and barbed-wire could still be seen around the mound. It was 1971 and I was about to have my initial experience in American Biblical Archaeology in Israel. That evening, we had our first introductory lecture concerning the historical importance of the site and its relationship with a number of important events mentioned in the Hebrew Bible. The lecturer was young, dynamic and able to weave the biblical narrative and the archaeological remains found at Gezer into a tantalizing story which made the past live for all of us that night. The Bible in the Book of I Kings 9: 15–17 explains that King Solomon had fortified four monumental cities and that evening we were shown tangible archaeological evidence of one of Solomon's gates discovered in the archaeological strata at Tel Gezer. When four a.m. rolled around the following day, the students couldn't wait to get out to the site to find more tangible proof which would illustrate the events mentioned in the Bible.

That evening after finishing a delicious meal prepared by the Tanour family, our Palestinian cooks, another staff member gave a lecture concerning the changing shapes and wares of pottery found in the archaeological sequences of the Holy Land. As each pottery vessel type was discussed in minute detail, interest began to wane in the audience. As far as the lecturer was concerned, the societies whose people had actually made and used the tons of pottery that were being recovered each season at the site had little to do with the material culture we were working so hard to retrieve. We could not see the Israelite behind the artifact. As the endless list of dates and pot types were paraded in front of the mass of students, an almost catatonic state engulfed the group. Although only 17 years old at the time, I had attended other lectures by American archaeologists such as Lewis Binford at UCLA some months earlier. At that time the passion of the New Archaeology, a more

scientific discipline grounded in anthropology, was in the air in California and students there were infected by the excitement and potential that archaeology had for revealing the dynamics of ancient societies. The Biblical Archaeology of the early 1970s was aimed primarily at identifying people and places mentioned in the Bible. Here at Tel Gezer, after our second lecture in the dust of the Holy Land, the thrill was gone.

The problem facing us that hot summer evening focused on the dichotomy between historical Biblical Archaeology practiced by American scholars, and the developments in theory that were emerging in the departments of anthropology in the United States where archaeology was generally taught. Since my participation on the Gezer excavation over two decades ago, this philosophical dichotomy has been vigorously debated in the Syro-Palestinian archaeological literature. However, it is only recently – in the past five years or so – that substantive change has come to the way archaeology is done in the Holy Land. Today, Israeli, Jordanian, American, European and a growing group of Palestinian archaeologists are discovering new and exciting ways of linking history, broad anthropological theories of culture change, and archaeology. The proof is in this book, which I hope will be of interest to colleagues and students working all over the world – not only in Near Eastern archaeology, but in world archaeology, ancient history, anthropology, social theory and other disciplines. The shift in the scientific paradigm of archaeology in the Holy Land is evident in that some of those very same lecturers that addressed the mass of student workers at Tel Gezer have now written chapters for this volume.

The issues that are discussed here go beyond the specific geographical boundaries of the troubled land that all of the contributors to this book deeply love. I believe the underlying factor responsible for the leap away from the historical particularism of earlier eras in Syro-Palestinian archaeology is the increasing importance within our discipline of interdisciplinary research bridging the gap between ethnohistory, anthropology and archaeology. In the remainder of this preface, I would like to outline how this approach leads to the kinds of problem-oriented studies which are presented in this book.

Interdisciplinary archaeology in the Holy Land

One of the underlying themes of this volume is the overall concern of the contributors with long-term problems of

Fish-Eye View of Jerusalem (photograph: © Garo)

humanistic interest rooted in identifying the trends and processes of socioculture change in the Holy Land. The emphasis on a long term diachronic perspective which imbues many of the papers presented here is linked conceptually to the *Annales* school of French historiography (Braudel 1972) which is described by Levy and Holl in the introduction to this volume. Another unifying theme in our approach to the past is the reliance on integrated interdisciplinary research. The majority of scholars who are represented here are active field archaeologists and all utilize what can be termed a contextual approach to archaeology. This approach is based on principles from the work of Karl Butzer, but with some modifications (cf. Butzer 1982; Hodder 1987; Levy 1993).

Contextual archaeology, as proposed by Butzer (1982) and followed by our contributors, centers on the human ecosystem which emphasizes the interdependence of cultural and environmental variables. The human ecosystem serves as an organizational framework for discussing different scientific approaches needed for understanding the processes of cultural and environmental interaction. Human ecosystems are composed of the atmosphere, hydrosphere, lithosphere, and biosphere. They differ from other biological ecosystems because information, technology, and social organization play a more controlling role. As Butzer (1982) points out, the ability of human groups to carry out purposive behavior gives them a power to manipulate the environment on a scale that other biological systems cannot. Thus, human societies can:

1. match resources with cultural needs and objectives;
2. transform natural phenomenon to meet these needs; and
3. plan, i.e., think about these processes objectively without actually implementing them (Butzer 1982: 32; Bennett 1976).

An essential assumption in contextual archaeology is the assumption that the environment not be considered as a static variable. Instead, the natural and cultural environment must be viewed as a dynamic factor in the analysis of all archaeological contexts, in much the same way that the *Annales* school views time as a dynamic. As Butzer (ibid.) emphasizes, the basic ingredients of archaeology are artifacts and their context, ranging from food and tool residues to sediment and landscape constellations. Within this framework, context is taken from the Latin verb *contexere* which means 'to weave together' or 'to connect'. Seen from this perspective, the context of archaeological materials is the key database for reconstructing the past. The main components of Butzer's contextual archaeology (archaeobotany, archaeozoology, geoarchaeology and spatial archaeology) are not new. What is innovative in Butzer's approach is the effort to integrate fully these and other disciplines with the general goal of understanding the human ecosystem.

What is not emphasized by Butzer, however, is the need to examine human ecosystems in their specific cultural environment. Thus, I would join with Hodder (1987) in calling for a more through examination of the role played by symbolism, ideology, and religion in shaping the evolution of societies. In addition to geosciences, environmental archaeology and archaeometry, there is a need to emphasize anthropological theory in the context of history to achieve an understanding of the past. In the culture area of the Holy Land this can be achieved by utilizing ethnography and ethno-historical documents, on the one hand, and biblical studies and ancient history on the other. This model for a contextual archaeology of the Holy Land is presented in the flow chart in Figure 1. The key to integrating this interdisciplinary approach is the ability to measure change in the underlying properties of interest to all interdisciplinary participants in the research program which focuses on the human ecosystem. These properties include space, scale, complexity, interaction and stability. By monitoring change in these attributes of the data – obtained mostly through the methods of archaeology – it is possible to isolate those processes responsible for change in human ecosystems and, consequently, social evolution. Each of the chapters in this volume deals with these properties.

Space, scale, complexity, interaction and stability all have anthropological and archaeological meaning because they incorporate temporal and spatial dimensions. These concepts are defined by Butzer (1982: 7) in regard to human ecosystems in the following way:

Space Cultural and environmental phenomena are rarely distributed evenly in space. Thus, human groups, geomorphic features, climate, and biological communities are amenable to spatial analysis (i.e., Hodder and Orton 1976).

Scale Cultures are established, maintained and/or changed by processes that operate at a number of spatial and temporal scales which may be periodic or aperiodic. Spatial analysis in archaeology, as used by the contributors, helps to define small, medium, and large-scale archaeological phenomena, clusters, and patterns of past cultural activities.

Complexity Cultures and environments are not homogeneous but vary in size and levels of complexity. To define them, different spatial and temporal approaches must be used.

Interaction Most ecosystems have an uneven distribution of resources. Consequently, human and non-human communities interact internally, with each other and with the natural environment at different scales, with different degrees of proximity and at changing rates.

Stability Human and other living communities are affected in different degrees by negative feedback from

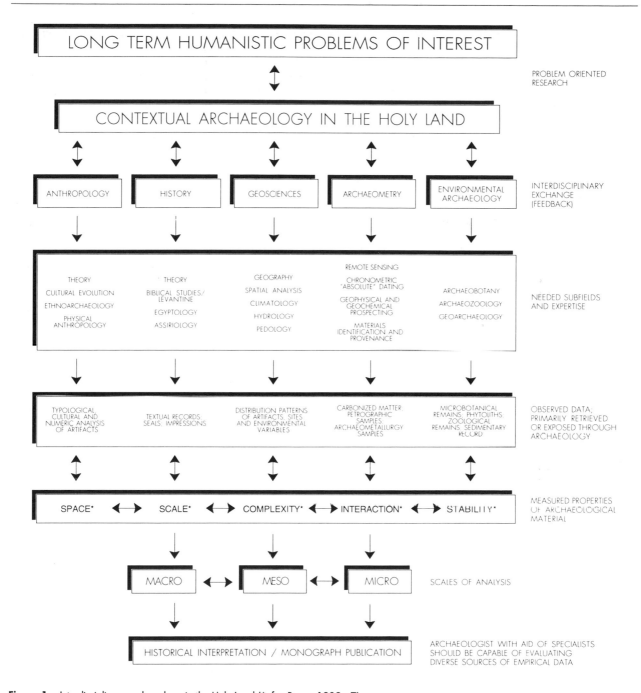

Figure 1 Interdisciplinary archaeology in the Holy Land (*after Butzer 1982–7)

internal processes or external inputs to their local environment. Thus, human societies are constantly in a process of readjustment. These readjustments may be minor, major, short term or long term.

Finally, as shown in Figure 1, spatial analysis provides the general framework for analyzing past human social and ecosystems and for integrating interdisciplinary archaeological research. These levels of resolution comprise:

Macro level The macro level is between sites within a region. Studies at this scale focus on all large-scale archaeological and environmental distributions dispersed across landscapes. The macro or regional scale gives us the first glimpse of the social organization of a society. In social evolutionary terms, we refer to the family-level group, the local group, and the regional polity (cf. Johnson and Earle 1987).

Meso level   The meso level examines within-site distributions of artifacts and structures and the developmental history of the site. A site can be defined as the geographic locale that contained a set of human activities and is often associated with sets of structures or activity areas; sites may be cities, domestic settlements, pastoral camps, food or material processing locales, ceremonial centers, cemeteries, industrial complexes or seasonal foraging camps (cf. Clarke 1978: 11).

Micro level   The micro level is within and between structures, and activity areas found on sites. At this level of resolution, personal and household space is examined. A structure is any small-scale construction or selected unit that contained human activities or is a consequence of those activities. These include natural shelters, rooms, houses, graves, granaries, silos, shrines, etc. (cf. Clarke ibid.). Activity areas are the loci of socio-economic activities at the household and community level.

Most of the chapters in this volume focus on the macro scale of investigation, primarily because our interest is in fleshing out the dynamics of the structure and changes affecting the larger issue of past social organizations which existed in the Holy Land (cf. Holl and Levy 1993). To monitor these changes, different chronological schema have been used by the contributors. A brief summary of some of these chronological issues is provided in Figures 2 and 3 – for the prehistoric periods by Ofer Bar-Yosef and for the historic periods by me.

Prehistoric chronological framework (by Ofer Bar-Yosef)

The chronology of the prehistoric sites and cultural entities in the country is based on a combination of methods including the means used to affirm the relative chronology and the radiometric chronology. Relative chronology encompasses the geological stratigraphy and site stratigraphy. The study of faunal bio-zones, often amalgamated assemblages of mammals and micro-mammals clustered as community associations, are ordered with the new species as those that determine the relative age (e.g., Tchernov 1981, 1986). The so-called 'absolute' chronology is based on radiometric readings such as ^{14}C, K/Ar, ^{40}Ar/^{39}Ar, Electron Spin Resonance (ESR) and Thermoluminescence (TL) with the addition of Amino-Acid Racemization (AAR). The ^{40}K/^{40}Ar dates are matched with the paleomagnetic sequence (that records the past position of the magnetic pole and its excursions) and create a good yardstick for ordering late Pliocene and Lower and Middle Pleistocene sites. Unfortunately not all Lower Paleolithic sites in the Levant contain, or were covered by, volcanic tuffs or lava flows and, in some cases, late demagnetization has hampered the use of the paleomagnetic scale. Middle Paleolithic sites are currently dated by ESR and TL but the results should conform to what is known about the relative bio-stratigraphy.

The radiometric method is essential for dating Upper Paleolithic, Epipaleolithic, Neolithic and Chalcolithic sites. The use of this method requires information about the dated material (charcoal, seeds, bone, carbonates) and the exact archaeological context. The latter is not divorced from an understanding of site formation processes, which in these periods include varied human activities such as building, digging, leveling, dumping, the collection and reuse of dead wood, etc. Currently the archaeological sequence back to about 10,000 years ago can be calibrated to conform to calendar years (Stuiver and Braziunas 1993). It is important to note that the use of the conventional conversion to BC dates is essentially wrong because it consists of subtracting 1950/2000 *calendrical* years from a date which is given in *radiocarbon* years. It is well known that radiocarbon years, when matched with calendrical years, lose about 1000 years per 10,000 years. In the near future, archaeologists will have to deal with the implications of the calibration curve.

The terminology used in the literature on Levantine prehistory can be rather complex for those readers who are not familiar with the dynamic research in the region. The terms and the numerous changes to them are a result of the large number of schools of archaeology which operate in the region. There is no other geographic region in the world where so many different schools participate in uncovering the past. We should, therefore, be patient and accept this situation in which the same cultural entities, lithic assemblages or specific layers in sites are named differently by different schools.

The present chart (Figure 2) is an effort to incorporate the most frequently used terms and the general chronological position of the industry/cultural entity along a radiometric time scale. The first column presents the subdivision of the Quaternary era. The second column illustrates the dates and the conventional subdivision of prehistoric periods as used in the book. The third column presents the most commonly used terminology in the southern Levant, while the fourth column is a partial list of terms used by various authors either in this book or in other literature on Jordan, Syria and Lebanon. There are more terms in the literature, especially labels coined from the 1930s to the 1960s. The curious reader can find them by reviewing the numerous references that follow each chapter; with this table it will be possible to place older names in their current context.

GEOLOGICAL PERIOD	ARCHAEOLOGICAL PERIOD AND APPROXIMATE AGE B.P.	LITHIC TRADITIONS AND CULTURAL ENTITIES	ADDITIONAL/ALTERNATIVE TERMS
	1.7 Ma 1.5 Ma	non-biface occurrences	Oldowan
LOWER PLEISTOCENE 730,000	LOWER PALAEOLITHIC	Early Acheulian Tayacian Upper/Late Acheulian Acheulo-Yabrudian Mugaran Tradition	Tabunian / Shemsi Industry { Acheulian facies { Amudian = Pre-Aurignacian { Yabrudian facies

MIDDLE PLEISTOCENE
 	
130,000
	300/250,000
	
	MIDDLE PALAEOLITHIC
	
	47/45,000
		Mousterian Tabun D type
		              Tabun C type
		              Tabun B Type
			Hummalian
			"Levalloise-Mousterian"

UPPER PLEISTOCENE	UPPER PALAEOLITHIC
	
	20/18,000
		Transitional Industry = Emiran
		              Early Ahmarian }
		Levantine Aurignacian
		
		              Late Ahmarian }
			Ksar'Akil Phase A
			Ksar'Akil Phase B
			Levantine A
			Aurignacian B
			                  C = Alitian
			Masraqan

	EPI-PALAEOLITHIC 10,300 8,300 B.C. uncalibrated	Kebaran Geometric Kebaran Early Mushabian Late Mushabian = Ramonian Natufian Early Late Harifian (in the Negev and Sinai)	{ Nebekian { Qalkhan { Nizzanan Madamaghan Hamran Epi-Natufian in Syria

HOLOCENE	EARLY NEOLITHIC (ACERAMIC)
	
	7,500 5,500 B.C. uncalibrated
		PPNA - Khiamian
		            Sultanian
		PPNB - early
		            middle } Tahunian
		            late
		            final - PPNC
			Mureybetian
			
			Ghazalian

	LATE NEOLITHIC (CERAMIC) 5,200?	PNA { Yarmukian { Lodian = Jericho IX PNB Wadi Rabbah	Sha'ar Ha-Golan Jerichoan Early Chalcolithic
	CHALCOLITHIC 4,500–3,500 uncalibrated	Ghassulian Beersheva	Golan Nahal Patish Nahal Grar

Figure 2   Prehistoric chronology for the Holy Land (O. Bar-Yosef)

BRONZE AGE		
Early Bronze Age	I A-B	3500-3000 BCE
Early Bronze Age	II	3000-2700
Early Bronze Age	III	2700-2200
Middle Bronze Age	I A	
(EB IV-Intermediate Bronze)		2200-2000
Middle Bronze Age	II B	1750-1550
Late Bronze Age	I	1550-1400
Late Bronze Age	II A	1400-1300
Late Bronze Age	II B	1300-1200
IRON AGE		
Iron Age	I A	1200-1150
Iron Age	I B	1150-1000
Iron Age	II A	1000-900
Iron Age	II B	900-700
Iron Age	II C	700-586
BABYLONIAN AND PERSIAN PERIODS		586-332

HELLENISTIC PERIOD	
Early Hellenistic period	332-167
Late Hellenistic period	167-37
ROMAN AND BYZANTINE PERIODS	
Early Roman Period	37 BCE - 132 CE
(Herodian period, 37 BCE - 70 CE)	
Late Roman period	132-324
Byzantine period	324-638
EARLY ARAB TO OTTOMAN PERIODS	
Early Arab period (Umayyad and Abbasid)	638-1099
Crusader and Ayyubid periods	1099-1291
Late Arab period (Fatimid and Mameluke)	1291-1516
Ottoman period	1516-1917

Figure 3   Chronological table for the historical–archaeological periods (source: *The New Encyclopedia of Archaeological Excavations in the Holy Land* 1994)

In dating later prehistory, BP radiocarbon dates are given in large fonts while the conventional BC dates are in small fonts. The sole abbreviations used are PPNA, PPNB, PPNC and PNA that, following Kenyon's Jericho sequence, designate Pre-Pottery Neolithic A, B and C and Pottery Neolithic A and B respectively.

General historical chronological framework

The general chronological framework used by the contributors in dealing with the periods spanning the Early Bronze Age through to the British conquest of Palestine in 1917 CE is presented in Figure 3. Following the Chalcolithic period, the importance of radiocarbon dating diminishes and relative chronologies become more important. These are based primarily on typological studies of pottery sequences obtained through careful regional studies of stratified assemblages. When these regional sequences are compared, it is possible to build a general temporal framework for the entire Holy Land. From the Early Bronze Age onwards, ca. 3000 BCE, the historical chronology of the Holy Land is based primarily on that of Egypt (cf. Stager 1992). As Mazar (1990: 28) points out, Egyptian artifacts found in the Holy Land – including royal inscriptions, scarab seals, and other finds – and artifacts exported from the Holy Land to Egypt and discovered in dated contexts provide the basis for our historical chronological framework. This is due to the close role that Egypt played in the history of our region from the beginning of the Early Bronze Age to the Iron Age and later periods. The general framework presented here follows the one recently published in *The New Encyclopedia of Archaeological Excavations in the Holy Land* (Stern 1994). However, some of the contributors may use more fine grain divisions of this framework, depending on the questions they address in their respective chapters.

PART I

APPROACHES TO THE PAST

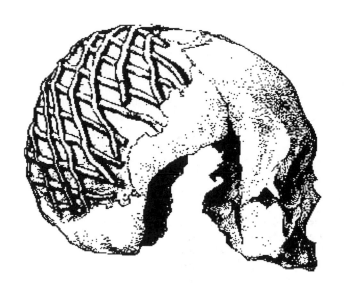

1

SOCIAL CHANGE AND THE ARCHAEOLOGY OF THE HOLY LAND

Thomas E. Levy

Augustin F.C. Holl

Introduction

Standing at the base of the mountain of time in the Holy Land, we look up from the slopes of prehistory, to the foothills of Biblical history, and on to the peaks of the classical and recent past. How can we provide an explanatory spatio-temporal framework wide enough to comprehend such variety in this part of the world spanning a period of over one million years? One of the most useful paradigms for this task is the conceptualization of history put forth by the proposals of the *Annales* school of social and economic history developed by French historians (Bloch 1966; Braudel 1972; Febvre 1920; 1949 [1973]; Le Roy Ladurie 1974; Lombard 1971; 1974; 1978). Some of the reasons the *Annales* school is so relevant for archaeological research in the southern Levant, with its immense sweep of time, are the *Annales'* stress on generalization and its quest for broad insights which go beyond an examination of unique phenomena. The growth and establishment of the *Annales* school climaxed with the publication of Fernand Braudel's book in 1949, entitled *The Mediterranean and the Mediterranean World in the Age of Phillip II* (Stoianovich 1976). The recent 'discovery' of the *Annales* school by archaeologists from all over the world points to its utility as a theoretical framework especially suitable to archaeological research (cf. Barker 1991; Bulliet 1992a, 1992b; Duke 1992; Fletcher 1992; Jones 1991; Knapp 1992a, 1992b; Moreland 1992; Smith 1992a, 1992b; Snodgrass 1991; Vallet 1991).

The *Annales* stand for a number of concepts which make their paradigm very appealing for archaeological research. First, the *Annales* school has advocated a move away from the study of unique and particular aspects of history to achieve wider insights into human history. Secondly, the *Annales* platform explicitly calls for interdisciplinary collaboration with all the disciplines concerned with human society (Bintliff 1991: 5). The *Annales* school has tried to adapt data and concepts from a wide range of fields including economics, linguistics, sociology, anthropology, psychology, and the natural sciences for the study of history (Stoianovich 1976: 19). This kind of intellectual foraging is remarkably similar to the way archaeologists work, drawing on a wide range of disciplines to analyze and interpret their data. On the world archaeology scene, the recent publications of John Bintliff (1991) and A. Bernard Knapp (1992a) show the keen interest in an *Annales* approach to archaeology today. In Syro-Palestine, the pioneering work of Lawrence Stager (1985a, 1985b; 1987) has shown how the *Annales* paradigm can be applied to the study of ancient Israel.

One of the advantages of an *Annales* framework is its notion that different historical processes operate at different temporal levels. Too often, Syro-Palestinian archaeologists have worked according to what Robert Asher (1961: 324) refers to as the 'Pompeii premise', the 'erroneous notion, often implicit in archaeological literature ... [that archaeologists recover] ... the remains of a once living community, stopped as it were, at a point in time'. In fact, we rarely encounter 'instantaneous occurrences' fossilized in the archaeological record (Smith 1992a: 27). Instead, the archaeological record usually reflects the accumulation of repeated activities carried out in the same place through time, with little evidence of the individual. According to Binford (1986: 474), the archaeological record represents a reality 'that living, breathing persons have in fact never directly experienced'. Two connected issues may however be considered at this juncture: space and time contexts of actual behaviors and material products; and the pace, scope, and rhythms of transformations. From this perspective, one of the important legacies of processual archaeology is the emphasis on problem oriented research strategies which was already advocated posthumously by Marc Bloch (1949) in *Apologie pour l'Histoire ou le Metier d'Historien*. According to Bloch, and in contrast to the positivist research tradition which was predominant, the historian must design well-defined research problems, formulate different kinds of hypotheses, and use the available data to test the accuracy of his reconstruction. Thus, the problem of the perception of time and space

Plate 1 Overview of Temple Mount, Jerusalem (photograph: © Werner Braun)

frameworks by archaeologists lie at the heart of the recent efforts to make Syro-Palestinian archaeology a 'secular' discipline removed from the historical particularism which characterized Biblical Archaeology up until the last decade. Archaeological data, unlike textual evidence, is thus best suited for providing a more generalized picture of human behavior which was carried out within the constructs of ancient social and economic institutions. The chapters in this volume reflect this more generalized view of time.

The Braudelian temporal framework

In tackling the broad stretch of prehistoric and historic time in the southern Levant, Braudel's (1972) framework of time provides the needed integrated temporal processes which tie this trajectory together. In Braudel's *The Mediterranean*, an explicit formulation of the *Annales* paradigm is presented. He shows that historical time (and we would add prehistoric) is dominated by three major groups of processes which operate contemporaneously but at different levels through time. These time scales include:

1. Short-term processes (*evenements*) such as narrative political history, events, the acts of individuals.
2. Medium-term processes (*conjonctures*) which include the processes of change in social and economic history; economic, agrarian, and demographic cycles; the processual history of eras, regions and societies; and world views and ideologies (*mentalites*).
3. Long-term processes (*la longue duree*) which cover geohistory and the environmental framework that enables and constrains social evolution; the history of civilizations and societies; technology; and world views (*mentalites*).

As Bintliff (1991: 6) suggests, reality is observed when we reveal how a particular region underwent change as the final result of an inner dialectic between these different processual time scales. Braudel's framework of time can be modeled in an appealing way for archaeologists as is displayed in Figure 1.

The temporal dynamics of these time frames can be summarized as follows. *Evenements* or events are the traditional domain of historians who focus on the study of records of human activities and individual human personalities which highlight political history, events and individuals. Because of the nature of archaeological data, archaeologists have failed for the most part to operationalize *evenements* into an explanatory tool. *Conjonctures* or medium-term structures are characterized by cycles of socio-political, agrarian and demographic change. These are processual cycles which operate over periods of centuries or generations and have been referred to as the *moyenne duree* by Hexter (1972: 504, n. 31). Perhaps the most famous notion of Braudel's is the *longue duree*, or dynamic of long duration, which Febvre (1949 (1977): 37) sees 'as a guiding force, channeling, obstructing, slowing-down and checking or, on the other hand,

History of events   Short term (episodic) — *evenements*
      Individual time
         Narrative political history; events; acts of
         individuals.

Structural history   Medium-term structures (cyclical) —
         conjunctures
      Social time
         Processes of change in social and
         economic history; economic, agrarian, and
         demographic cycles.

         Processual history of eras, regions, and
         societies.

         World views, ideologies.

      Long-term structures of the 'longue duree'
      (structural)
      Geographical time
         Geohistory and environmental framework
         which enables and constrains social
         change.

Figure 1 Braudel model of time (after Bintliff 1991; Braudel 1972; Knapp 1992a)

heightening and accelerating the interplay of human forces'. Some of the long-term forces may include the natural environment with geological, climatic, and geomorphologic constraints (see Danin, Goldberg, this volume), and the social environment with dominant and slowly changing controls over production, technology, and ideologies.

Both the *longue* and *moyenne duree* are, for Bintliff (1991: 7), 'beyond the perception of past individuals, they act as structures – from which has arisen the term structural history for this model – which form constraining and enabling frameworks for human life, (both) communal and individual.' Concentration on these structures of time make the *longue* and *moyenne duree* of particular importance to archaeological researchers where the individual frequently escapes recognition in the archaeological record. These multiple, hierarchical time scales represent aspects of a continuum and provide archaeology with an heuristic framework for conceptualizing time and change in prehistoric, protohistoric, and historic societies (cf. Fletcher 1992; Knapp 1992a: 10; Smith 1992a). Depending on the research interests and periods involved, scholarly studies of ancient societies will concentrate on one aspect of Braudel's model.

The *Annales* paradigm and archaeology in the Holy Land

The 'New' or Processual Archaeology and 'Post-processual' schools of archaeology which have had such a great impact on the scholarly community from the United States and Europe, have been of little concern for the majority of researchers working in the Holy Land. The most noted exceptions are those archaeologists contributing to this volume. The 'new' or processual archaeology, with its science-based ahistorical orientation was rejected by the majority of archaeologists working in Palestine. This is because Palestinian archaeology has been practiced for the most part by scholars who view all dimensions of the archaeological record through the lens of the Bible when investigating all aspects of the past. An in-depth survey of the reasons for this 'denial' of outside archaeological theory in Syro-Palestinian archaeology are discussed by Dever (1992).

As we approach the year 2000 and look at where our field is going, perhaps the most positive aspect to evolve out of Syro-Palestinian archaeology's view of the developments in 'new' archaeology was the adoption of multidisciplinary projects which included specialists in archaeozoology, archaeobotany, geology, anthropology, archaeology, epigraphy, and other fields. The result of this organizational change in research has been the production of vast amounts of essential environmental and non-environmental data from these projects. Unfortunately, while these organizational changes may have appealed to granting bodies such as the National Endowment for the Humanities and the National Geographic Society in the United States, in truth there has been very little cross-fertilization between the researchers involved in these projects or the production of truly interdisciplinary studies. A case in point are the Gezer volumes which offer little synthesis of the vast quantities of published data (cf. Dever 1986; Gitin 1990). Notable exceptions are the interdisciplinary studies published by the archaeological projects in the Madaba plains (La Bianca 1990), Shiqmim (Levy 1987), Izbet Sartah (Finkelstein 1986) and Idalion (Stager and Walker 1989). As Paul Goldberg (1988), a long time geological specialist involved in archaeological projects in the Levant, points out, if specialist reports do not fit in with the archaeologist's historical perception of the archaeological record the 'interdisciplinary' input is usually ignored.

After more than 100 years of scientific archaeological investigation in the Holy Land, there is an immense body of historical, archaeological, and environmental data which is amenable to the different scales of analysis advocated by the *Annales*. For all of its virtues, the *Annales* has been subject to detailed criticism (Clark 1985; Chartier 1988; Hufton 1986; Le Goff and Nora 1985; Schneider 1977; Sherratt 1992; Stone 1985). However, some of the positive aspects of the *Annales* paradigm which are related to Syro-Palestinian archaeology can be summarized as follows:

1. Braudel's framework offers a concise model for archaeologists to consider how change occurs in different temporal contexts. Braudel's framework of time is the type of 'classic' model (e.g. Clarke 1968) which is especially applicable to investigations which combine archaeological and historical data. This is because the Braudelian model provides a framework for viewing change which is influenced by different processes of time.

2. As mentioned above and by numerous scholars, the nature of archaeological data *usually* precludes the identification of the individual in the archaeological record. Consequently, we are drawn to Braudel's medium- and long-term structures of change. In Dever's (1992: 366 I) recent *Anchor Bible Dictionary* summary of Syro-Palestinian and Biblical Archaeology, he highlights how examination of the more general aspects of a society, such as the domestic dimensions of ancient cultures, including religion, can illuminate the dynamic nature of ancient societies. In his own archaeological studies of Canaanite and early Israelite religion, which combine textual and archaeological data, Dever (1987) has shown how Israelite religion, which the Hebrew Bible proclaims as supposedly Yahwistic, was something much more complex. By focusing on the general distribution patterns of Canaanite cult objects in Israelite sites, Dever uses archaeology to show that the folk religion of Israel was highly syncretistic and included popular cults that were highly influenced by the Canaanite fertility religions (ibid.). Thus, by moving away from a desire to isolate individual historical events, Dever (1987) has isolated the dynamics of a medium-term process which affected Israelite society at large. While the intellectually stimulating developments of processual archaeology have blossomed and evolved with little impact on Syro-Palestinian archaeology, the renewed concern with history advocated by 'post-processual' archaeology (cf. Hodder 1986) on the world scene demands that we reconsider how to integrate the vast quantities of archaeological and ethnohistorical data into a synthetic view of the past.

3. John Cherry (1987: 146) has suggested that archaeology may be viewed as 'political geography in the past tense'. From the perspective of the southern Levant, geography is a prominent, perhaps the prime mover variable in the long-term social evolution of the region. Palestine's geographical setting and makeup present the long-term structure which has enabled and constrained cultural developments in the region. Located on the land bridge connecting Asia and Africa, near the cradle of humankind in Africa's rift valley and the centers of ancient Near Eastern civilizations, geography has been a determining factor on the prehistory and history of social change in this region from the beginning over one million years ago until today. As A. Mazar (1990: 1) points out:

> The geographic location of the country determined its important role in the history of the ancient Near East. On the one hand, Palestine formed a bridge between the two ends of the Fertile Crescent – Egypt on the south and Syria and Mesopotamia in the north; on the other hand, it was compressed between the Mediterranean Sea on the west and the desert to the east. This unique situation was a basic factor in

Palestine's history and cultural development. More than any other country in the ancient world, Palestine was always directly or indirectly connected with other parts of the Near East and the eastern Mediterranean.

Thus, it is the geography of place which determines the Holy Land's place on the post-Bronze Age periphery of civilizations, empires and superpowers. Although environment is viewed as critical factor in social change, we follow Shmuel Eisenstadt (1988: 239) and resist the 'temptation to view environmental boundaries as independent of social ones'.

According to Dever (1992: 364), the future of archaeological research in the Holy Land may be linked to many of the conceptual developments made by the *Annales* school:

> Archaeology does not, of course, possess the extensive written documentation that can be sifted through by historians of the *Annales* school, nor can it perhaps ever write really fine-grained individual history. But archaeology today is ecological and focuses on setting; it turns up masses of obscure artifactual data that reflect the daily life of ordinary individuals; and it is unique among all disciplines in its sensitivity to cultural change over very long periods of time. Thus, there is good reason to believe that Syro-Palestinian archaeology has scarcely begun to fulfill its potential for writing social and economic history on a much broader scale than formerly thought possible. The tools are at hand, because the very multidisciplinary, ecological, and systemic approaches noted above already point promisingly in the right direction.

The optimism reflected in these remarks for a broader socio-economic view of cultural change in the Holy Land is hopefully realized by the contributors to this volume. While each of the prehistoric and historical archaeologists involved in this endeavor may not utilize the vocabulary of the *Annales*, they all employ many of the qualities outlined above that make it possible to write a social archaeology of the Holy Land today which can be subsumed into the broad definition of the *Annales*. These approaches include an interdisciplinary approach to the past, the analysis of cultural systems, and an emphasis on cultural ecology and the paleo-environment.

According to Birnbaum (1978: 230), 'contemporary' *Annales* historical analysis is based on five platforms:

1. to establish distinctive temporal periods;
2. to identify the major lines of development with each period;
3. to identify and measure regularities specific to each development;
4. to recognize innovation and the emergence of new structures within and between eras;
5. to propose a range of elements that helps to isolate and explain continuity or change within and between periods.

Given the vast sweep of time in our region and the different intellectual orientations of the numerous scholars involved

in this project, it was thought best to leave paradigm names out of the guidelines to authors. With such a vast array of scholars, it would have been a recipe for disaster to suggest that each one write according to 'prehistoric', 'biblical archaeology', 'new biblical archaeology', 'processual', 'post-processual', '*Annales*', 'contextual', or another other school of thought. All of these terms are loaded with conceptual and intellectual baggage which could easily be manipulated in a small group, but would cause chaos in a large number of contenders. Instead, all the contributors were asked to organize their chapters along *Annales* guidelines without utilizing the term *Annales*. The following themes are addressed differentially, depending on the time scales and periods studied by the different researchers.

Major transitions

Based on accumulated knowledge from archaeological and historical sources, the major cultural and/or historical transitions for each of the main periods of Palestinian archaeology are identified. To summarize the temporal trajectory of human occupation in the Holy Land, the human occupation of the region has been divided up into 22 traditionally accepted general chronological periods spanning the Lower Paleolithic to the modern nineteenth and early twentieth centuries. This corresponds to *Annales'* position of identifying the major lines of development in a given period of time.

Pattern and process

By concentrating on changing patterns of settlement (identified archaeologically), the dynamics of change in adaptation, social organization, and economic organization can be garnered. As each of the archaeologists are advocates of interdisciplinary investigation, regional cases studies depicting settlement change through time were requested which integrate environmental and cultural variables so that the magnitude of social organization and interaction in a given period can be identified. Thus, maps depicting the family group, local group, and regional polity level of social integration were requested to highlight changing socio-economic behaviors through time in the broad environmental and cultural context of Palestine and the ancient world (cf. Johnson and Earle 1987: 22–23). Discussions of changing organization in settlement pattern on the family, local and regional level are related to Braudel's medium-term *conjonctures* of time connected especially to the history of a region and the cycles of economic, agrarian, and demographic change.

Innovations and technology

Contributors were asked to identify major innovations in areas such as technology, subsistence strategies, trade, and industrialization so as to identify the emergence of new structures within and between periods. From a materialist perspective, these topics relate to structural change in the organization of production systems in societies. By looking at the transmission of innovation or its local independent development which are manifest in the archaeological record, it is possible to monitor how social groups acquire, maintain, and lose power. These factors are of immense importance for understanding how socio-political systems evolve. This follows Birnbaum's (ibid.) point that the 'contemporary' *Annales* strive to recognize innovation and the emergence of new structures within and between eras. By studying the control of production, it is possible to monitor changes in power relations in societies through time and the rise and collapse of different social systems.

Religion and ideology

In examining religion and ideology, the emphasis here is on the role of cult and/or religion in society. By using material culture which reflects religion and/or ideology, contributors were asked how these dimensions of culture enforce, modify, and/or destroy existing social organizations. Some of the questions asked include: what is the scale of investment in cult/religious facilities? Is there evidence of differential participation of segments of the society in ritual activities? Do other religions or cults exist in the society? Is there a state religion versus a popular one and how does this influence the organization of society? From an *Annales'* perspective, religion and ideology (collective belief systems), and world views reflect and transform human life. This view was not developed by Braudel but by other *Annalistes* such as Bloch (1939/40), and constitutes what Febvre (1920) formalized with the term *mentalites*. According to Bintliff (1991: 11), Bloch's view has dominated '*Annales*' scholarship since the 1970s as "anthropological history". Bloch examined the social and economic context of a *mentalite* as appropriate explanatory conditions for its origin and role in history, exploring the effect of human concepts of the logic of everyday life (e.g. through the realities of health and hygiene, diet, and the class basis for certain ideologies).'

Social organization

In an effort to develop a common terminology for discussing the archaeological manifestations of past social organizations in the southern Levant, contributors were asked to utilize the terminology of neo-evolutionary cultural typology developed by Service (Bands–Tribes [Segmentary Lineages]–Chiefdoms–States; 1962) and Fried (Egalitarian–Rank–State; 1967). Although elements of this model, in particular Service's notion of 'Chiefdom', have recently come under fire (cf. Yoffee 1992), the clear definitions associated with these terms are of great utility

for the '*grande* perspective' covered in this volume. More important are the problems associated with social organization evolution for the contributors:

- How do institutions associated with social reproduction change through time?
- Can changes be seen in stratification systems through time?
- Did maladaptive social structures emerge during the period?
- How do different kinds of exchange systems relate to kinship organization?
- How did ritual and political power work together to produce new social organizations?

From an *Annales'* perspective, the dimension of time (*evenements, conjonctures, longue duree*) used to analyze these problems will color the identification of the processes responsible for social change in the southern Levant.

In dealing with state societies, Yoffee (1992) has suggested an important alternative model to social evolutionary typologies based on the study of power. For the purposes of identifying archaeologically the evolution of state societies, Yoffee (ibid.) views the dimensions of power as the key to understanding the evolution of social complexity. Thus, power has three dimensions: economic power, societal power (including ideological), and political power. The state depends on the interplay between these dimensions of power and emerges by combining economic control over production, 'the segregation and maintenance of the symbols of community boundary, and the ability to impose obedience by force'. Like many archaeologists, our use of the *Annales* paradigm can be viewed as an intellectual foraging expedition, unlike Yoffee who has presented a rare, independent archaeologically-based model for the evolution of social complexity. However, as this volume deals with over one million years of culture change, in a region which lacks evidence for pristine state evolution, the impact of geography, the shifting control over local production organizations, and center–periphery relations may ultimately give us a generalized picture concerning the processes of culture change in the Holy Land. An *Annales* approach provides us with a more general framework for examining the full range of societies which evolved in the southern Levant.

Processes of change

To fulfill the ultimate goal of this volume, the explanation of culture change in the Holy Land over a period of some one and a half million years, the contributors were asked to summarize 'why' the major transitions identified in their period occurred. By trying to answer 'why' these transitions happened, a clear link is made with the settlement pattern data, innovations and technology, religion and ideology, and social organization. This is where Braudel's tripartite 'wedding cake' of time is brought out, and, depending on the period under review, the processes of change related to events, cycles, or the *longue duree* are summarized as the determinants of change.

Center—periphery

A central motif in the archaeological history of Palestine is its location on the periphery of the major states and civilizations of the ancient Near East. Following the Chalcolithic period, cultural evolution in Palestine becomes intimately connected and affected by change in those centers of civilization. Consequently, in dealing with post-Bronze Age Palestine, social evolutionary theories are of less utility. Instead, an examination of the changing relationships of power, both within the societies of the Palestinian periphery and in the political centers of the ancient Near Eastern empires holds more promise (cf. Champion 1989; Rowlands, Larsen, and Kristiansen 1987). Toynbee (1954) had long ago indicated the tendency for new and dynamic societies to emerge on the fringes of old and declining ones, which is certainly reflected in the rise of Israel's United Monarchy. However, simple center—periphery equations will not take us very far in gaining new insights concerning social change. Through a careful consideration of change in center—periphery relationships, combined with studies of shifts in power on the local and pan-regional level set against the backdrop of the long-term structure of the Levantine environment, the contributors will hopefully produce a new social archaeology of the Holy Land.

These topics are in fact the bare bones of 'contemporary' *Annales* historical analysis applied to over one million years of human occupation in the southern Levant. They represent the threads which can be used to weave a coherent picture of social evolution and socio-economic change in this part of the Mediterranean. An *Annales* perspective seems most useful for this enormous

undertaking precisely because archaeologists are interested in the diachronic issues of origin, growth, diffusion, transformation, and the processes which frame these developments (cf. Knapp 1993, 1992a: 13).

In summing up the *Annales* and archaeology, R.W. Bulliet (1992b: 132) has said

> There is ultimately nothing in the *Annales* school that can take archaeologists much farther intellectually than they have already gone . . . like the failed bumblebee that defied the predictions of the aeronautical engineer that its wing area would be insufficient to bear it aloft, this effort at interdisciplinary cross-fertilization flies, and buzzes, and makes honey.

The *Annales* school will work for the archaeology of the Holy Land because it advocates a comparative and interdisciplinary approach to the past which utilizes historical, archaeological, and ethnohistorical sources to build a social archaeology. Unlike the 'New Archaeology' which was ahistorical and based on building general laws of human behavior, an *Annales* perspective tries to embrace the whole of human activity in a given society (*histoire totale*, Forster and Ranum 1975), which by default demands a concern with historical documents. Finally Braudel's *longue duree*, which emphasizes the impact of physical geography as providing the 'enabling' and 'constraining' factors in human history, is indeed the key for understanding Palestine's internal and external evolution over the past circa one million years.

Acknowledgments

The authors would like to thank Fitz John P. Poole and Guillermo Algaze of the UCSD Department of Anthropology for their erudite and very useful comments on the *Annales* school and this paper.

2

POWER, POLITICS AND THE PAST: THE SOCIAL CONSTRUCTION OF ANTIQUITY IN THE HOLY LAND

Neil Asher Silberman

The history of archaeological exploration in the Holy Land is not necessarily a story of scientific adventure with a happy ending, though that is how the tale has usually been told. Most of the works on the history of research in the Land of the Bible have been written by participants in the process, who have presented their own scholarly contributions, or those of their contemporaries, as the culmination of a long scientific struggle to reach an ever more accurate or objective understanding of the past (for some representative examples, see Besant 1895; Bliss 1907; Macalister 1925; Albright 1949: Chapter 2; Wright 1962: Chapter 1; King 1983; Moorey 1991). While these historical studies have certainly offered competent accounts of refinements in excavation technique and have recorded the most significant discoveries, they have rarely placed the work of archaeologists in the Holy Land in a broader social or political context (with a few notable exceptions, such as Glock 1985; Broshi 1987; Larsen 1989). This is an essential challenge, for the archaeological exploration of the Holy Land has, throughout its history, been closely connected to modern western attitudes toward the Bible, great power competition, and the development of modern nationalism in the Middle East (Silberman 1982, 1989, 1991). The story of pilgrims, early explorers, pioneer cartographers and famous excavators in the Land of the Bible should, therefore, be seen not only as a steady accumulation of archaeological knowledge but also as a process of continual historical reinterpretation deeply influenced by modern social, economic, and political change.

Archaeological interpretations, like other scholarly understandings of society and culture, are necessarily formulated in a contemporary context. As such, they cannot help but embody contemporary ideologies and social ideals (Trigger 1984; Leone et al. 1987; Tilley 1989). The assumptions by which an archaeologist connects a burnt layer with an historically recorded invasion or migration, how he or she explains the significance of a certain distribution of seeds or bones; or how an excavator identifies the function of a certain room or building are all necessarily founded on the scholar's most basic perceptions of the logic of the world. Many social historians suggest that such perceptions are subject to dramatic transformation. Recent studies on the origin of modern concepts of race, progress, nationalism, labor specialization, gender roles, and even the idea of the autonomous 'individual' have linked them to specific changes in economy and social organization in the Industrial Age (among many, Foucault 1973; Anderson 1983; Larkin 1988). Thus it might be argued that archaeologists' interpretations, often based on contemporary social concepts, can reveal as much about the societies in which they are members as about the ancient societies whose cultures they attempt to explain.

There is another point worth bearing in mind in any consideration of the history of archaeology. Artifacts, architecture and settlement patterns, however well documented and dated, possess meaning only *within* a culture. The aim of archaeologists – particularly anthropologically-oriented archaeologists – is to understand the role played by the pottery, tools, architecture and landscape in the societies of ancient times (Hodder 1982). Yet excavated artifacts and preserved archaeological sites can also be seen as the material components of the society that discovers and studies them. As museum pieces and tourist attractions they possess a social significance naturally quite distinct from the function for which they were originally designed (Van Keuren 1984; Ettema 1987; Fowler 1987). Thus, a recently discovered Iron Age juglet from Jerusalem would have quite a different meaning for a Byzantine pilgrim, an early nineteenth century antiquarian, or a late twentieth-century ceramic specialist. The history of archaeology in the Holy Land should, therefore, also be seen as a complex process of reinterpretation. And any serious study of this process must concern itself with not only *which* innovations or interpretations took place at which time, but also *why*.

From pilgrimage to exploration

It is impossible to determine when ruins or excavated artifacts were first recognized as a source of evidence about

Plate 1 University of Chicago Excavation Team at Megiddo, 1926
(photograph: Courtesy of The Oriental Institute of The University of Chicago)

the Holy Land's past cultures, but the many editorial comments in the Old Testament relating to *tells*, tombs, and 'high places' and the demonstrated continuity of temple sites at Bronze and Iron Age cities (as in Yadin 1972: 67–105; Kempinski 1989: 169–88) indicate what might be called a proto-archaeological consciousness. Certainly some antiquarian investigations must have preceded the construction of the monumental Herodian enclosures around the Temple Mount in Jerusalem and the Cave of Machpelah in Hebron. Yet there is no evidence until a much later period of the use of ancient material remains to formulate an independent understanding of the past. Venerated ancient or biblical sites became the stage setting for a ritualized reenactment, in which the pilgrim or supplicant did not challenge or rewrite the historical tradition. The object was, instead, the internalization – and material illustration – of a sacred history.

Even after the destruction of the Temple in Jerusalem in 70 CE, many of the most important biblical sites of the Land of Israel were never completely lost or forgotten. The tradition of Jewish pilgrimage to sites of biblical importance continued (Mazar 1975: 237–9). With the acceptance of Christianity as the official religion of the Roman Empire in the fourth century CE, the province of Palaestina became the 'Holy Land' for an enormous mass of faithful and many of its biblical sites (of both Old and New Testaments) were imbued with a corresponding holiness (Wilken 1992). A new Christian tradition of pilgrimage to biblical sites in the Holy Land was established and encouraged on a truly massive scale (Hunt 1984). The efforts of Constantine's mother Helena can, in fact, be seen as the first efforts at what might be called archaeology. In contrast to the earlier practice of preserving and embellishing historical sites whose significance or location was never in question, Helena sponsored extensive excavations in Jerusalem and Bethlehem to discover the sites of Jesus' nativity and tomb (Hunt 1984: 28–49). These, and dozens of other shrines established at sites of supposed or uncovered antiquity, became the focal points of an elaborate geographical representation of biblical history. And although the purpose was religious, the historical-geographical understandings of the Byzantine period, in literary works such as the *Onomasticon* of Eusebius and in the archaeological evidence of the siting of Byzantine churches, continue to be an important tool in the modern identification of ancient sites.

The era of Byzantine pilgrimage added another important element to the constellation of antiquarian interests that we have come to identify as 'archaeology'. For the first time – as far as we know – moveable archaeological artifacts began to take on a significance, at least partially, independent of the place where they were found (Hunt 1984: 128–54). Bones of saints, garments and shrouds of New Testament figures, and virtually every sort of relic associated with famous biblical personalities were dug up, bought, sold, and highly prized for their spiritual and healing power. By the end of the fourth century, the export or 'translation' of relics from the Holy Land had reached enormous proportions. Ancient bones, stones, and pottery became objects of interest and veneration in churches, monasteries, and private chapels throughout Europe (Brown 1981). This international market in relics was encouraged by church officials, for it became an important source of revenue for the monastic and religious establishments in the Holy Land. And the inherent value of these relics and the frequent conflicting claims to possession of identical relics led to an ever greater emphasis on the objects themselves.

Recent archaeological discoveries in Jordan have revealed the extent to which the Christian historical landscape of the Holy Land survived that far-reaching social and political transformation of the Muslim Conquest (Schick 1988). And with the advent of Islam, the Qur'anic versions of biblical traditions encouraged Muslim interest in many of the ancient sites of the country as well (Le Strange 1890; Duri 1990). The establishment of the Crusader Kingdom in the twelfth century ushered in a new era of antiquarian interest. Yet what was sought was not a new understanding of the Holy Land's history but a continuing search for biblical identifications – conveniently fitted in to the standard pilgrim's itinerary (Grabois 1982). The continuing trade in relics and seasonal religious tours conducted under the auspices of the various monastic orders can be seen as manifestations of economic and political connections between certain European cities and the trade networks of the Holy Land (Geary 1990). However, in the period we have come to call the European Renaissance, a new motivation and mindset began to influence the contemporary understandings of the archaeology of the Holy Land.

As representatives of the various European merchant cities sought to negotiate with the Mamluks and their Ottoman successors for trade concessions and access to the eastern spice routes, the purely religious interest in the Holy Land began to give way to a more down-to-earth curiosity about its peoples, plants, and ruins (Bliss 1907: 121–72; Rodinson 1987: 31–44). Biblical traditions were less immediately useful than factual information that might lead to the discovery of profitable commodities and offer a chance to corner the market in their trade. Botanists, such as the French physician Pierre Belon du Mans and the German Leonhard Rauwolf, in the sixteenth century were pioneers in a study of the natural history of the Holy Land that would reach culmination with the encyclopedic studies of Palestinian flora, fauna, and geology of Carsten Niebuhr and Friedrich Hasselquist in the late eighteenth century. New historical insights were also developed. The rise of antiquarianism in Europe sparked a new, secular interest in the monuments and geography of ancient Mediterranean civilizations and such explorers as Laurent

Figure 1 A 15th-century view of Jerusalem, combining information gleaned from pilgrims' reports with artistic imagination. From Hans Schedel, *Liber Chronicarum* (Nüremburg: 1493)

D'Arvieux (1658–65), George Sandys (1610–11), Richard Pococke (1738), and François Volney (1783–85) avidly recorded and in some cases collected examples of Greek and Latin inscriptions, coins, pottery and classical statuary (Bliss 1907: 141–71). The scholarly understanding of the history of the Holy Land in the post-biblical periods was, for the first time, independently expanded through the study of material artifacts.

This expansion of knowledge was tied not only to commercial and geographical curiosity but also to a new perception of the world that made the acquisition of new information not only desirable, but imperative (Lach 1977; Harvey 1990: 240–59; Greenblatt 1991). The successful expansion of transoceanic navigation to the New World and around the Cape of Good Hope to India and the Far East required concepts of time and space dramatically different from those of the Middle Ages (and, for that matter, of Antiquity). While terrestrial and coastal landmarks had always provided dependable sensory cues and measures of motion, the trackless expanses of the world's oceans required a more abstract method of orientation. And thus – to put it very simply – arose the concept of terrestrial space as a geometric grid and progressive time as a uniform scale. The portolan map and the clock became two of the most distinguishing artifacts of this new era. The coldly transcendent grids of time and space by which new geographical entities and new universal histories would eventually be created would challenge the power of the preexisting traditions of the Catholic Church, of African and Asian kingdoms, of Native American chiefdoms, of Dar al-Islam, and of Am Yisrael.

In this period of Holy Land exploration, we can see the beginnings of an inquiry not based on participation in a shared ritual or tradition. The goal for the merchant venturers and explorers became filling the empty latitudinal and longitudinal grid of 'Palaestina' – to use the Latin scientific terminology – with a wide variety of empirically observed plants, animals, mountains, valleys, rivers and native inhabitants. Likewise a time scale stretching from Creation to the present had to be filled with epochs, cultures, and historical events. In place of the pilgrim's subjective experience of 'reliving' or 'rediscovering' famous biblical sites came a concerted effort to construct an 'objective' history and natural geography of Palestine. And in contrast to the pilgrim's image of the Holy Land as a self-contained biblical realm, this new method of representation made it possible to equate Palestine's flora, fauna, modern cultures and antiquarian curiosities with those of other ancient lands.

The 'new' Holy Land

The tradition of Holy Land pilgrimage was, of course, not destroyed by the scientific spirit. Though affected by shifting political and economic conditions, a steady stream of pilgrims from Europe continued through the Late Middle Ages and into the early modern period, under the supervision of the Franciscan order in the Holy Land (Simon 1980; Jacoby 1986). It was the theological impact of the Reformation, far more than the intellectual ferment of the Renaissance, that marked a major turning point in this movement. While Catholic pilgrimage continued, the Protestants of north-western Europe transformed the Holy Land from a place to a metaphor. 'The Promised Land' became a religious ideal – a divinely-sanctioned model for millenarian communities established in Europe (Cohn 1970: 252–80) and for religious colonies founded in the New World (Lowance 1980). This metaphorical vision of 'new' American Jerusalems, Bethlehems, Hebrons, and Nazareths carved from a wilderness populated only by savages would have unique power when Protestant scholars and divines experienced their first jarring encounter with the 'old' Holy Land.

Great power conflict at the very end of the eighteenth century made that confrontation inevitable. England's strategic interest in the Middle Eastern trade routes toward India, American maritime commercial interests in Turkey and North Africa, Imperial Russia's southward expansion, and the attempt in 1797–99 by the French Republic to conquer Egypt all contributed to an intensifying scramble by the western powers to establish territorial spheres of influence in the Middle East. Traditional religious attachments to the Holy Land offered an obvious point of entry and, in the early decades of the nineteenth century, the Palestinian provinces of the Ottoman Empire were visited by an unprecedented influx of western traders, explorers, missionaries, adventurers and military men (Herold 1962; Marlowe 1971; Silberman 1982: 10–27).

Many of the new visitors, however, were not the traditional Holy Land pilgrims, nor were they scientists of a strictly secular bent. Their political allegiance and religious orientation made them instinctively hostile to the

Holy Land's icon-filled shrines, which were zealously maintained by Catholic and Orthodox churches – and their French and Russian benefactors. Most prominent among many were the explorations of Ulrich Seetzen (1809), John Burkhardt (1810–12), John Silk Buckingham (1816), and Charles Irby and John Mangles (1817–18). Because their interests were at least partly religious, they were all eager to visit sites mentioned prominently in the Old and New Testaments. And the result was a new kind of pilgrimage, which furthered the Protestant nations' imperial ambitions by challenging the traditional view of the Holy Land's past (Ben-Arieh 1979; Silberman 1982).

Typical of this new breed of skeptical pilgrim was a Cambridge don named Edward Daniel Clarke, who accompanied the British fleet after the defeat of Napoleon at Acre in 1799. Vowing 'not to peer through the spectacles of priests', Clarke attempted to locate the 'true sites' of biblical history through a first-hand comparison of modern topography with the scriptural sources (Clarke 1817: vols. 4–5). In practical terms, Clarke's call for the discovery of the 'true' biblical landscape and restoration of the 'Sacred Geography' can be seen as the first step in the creation of a new and politically significant geographical entity. As more western explorers gained familiarity with the language and topography of the country, the techniques of 'Biblical Geography' were considerably refined (Ben-Arieh 1979). Its recognizable, modern form took shape during the 1838 exploration of Sinai and Palestine by Dr Edward Robinson, an American Biblical scholar, and Eli Smith, an American missionary long resident in Beirut (Robinson 1841). During the course of an exhausting three-month trip from Egypt to Lebanon, Robinson and Smith identified dozens of modern villages and landmarks with sites mentioned in the Bible, speculated on the ancient landscape of the country, and formulated a system of linguistic rules by which they believed that ancient Hebrew geographical names had been gradually transformed into modern Arabic. It is a system that is still, at least in its basic outlines, used by historical geographers (see, for instance, Aharoni 1967: 106–12).

Robinson and Smith's linguistic presumptions were deeply influenced by contemporary German and French comparative philology, with their theoretical emphasis on linguistic 'degenerationism' (Poliakov 1971: 71–105; Said 1978: 123–48; Stocking 1987: 20–5). That theory, which Robinson had studied under the philologists Gesenius and Rödiger (Albright 1932: 18; Ben-Arieh 1979: 85), posited the existence of several original, primitive languages (suggestively named for the migrating sons of Noah: Hamitic, Semitic and Japhetic), each of which had undergone progressive distortion and grammatical deterioration over the centuries (Poliakov 1971: 188–92; Stocking 1987: 23–4). The present geographical terminology of Palestine, Robinson believed, was the result of 'a truly national and native tradition', which was

Figure 2   James Silk Buckingham, early 19th-century author, politician, and pioneering British explorer of the Holy Land. From his memoir, *Travels in Palestine* (London: 1821)

'deeply seated in the genius of the Semitic languages', through which the transformations from Hebrew to Aramaic to Arabic could be traced (Robinson 1841: vol. I, 255). Since the exact location of many places mentioned in the Bible had been obscured by the change or replacement of their names during the intervening centuries, the study of the historical geography of Palestine was, in Robinson's words, a hunt for buried treasure, 'a first attempt to lay open the treasures of Biblical Geography and History still remaining in the Holy Land; treasures which have lain for ages unexplored, and had become so covered with the dust and rubbish of many centuries, that their very existence was forgotten' (Robinson 1841: vol. I, xi).

Although 'the dust and the rubbish' represented a history certainly no less complex or meaningful for the country's inhabitants than that of the biblical periods, it became, for Robinson and his successors, merely an obstruction that had to be swept away. The impact of this kind of historical geography was not merely academic. Through the replacement of the existing landscape of natural features and traditional landmarks with a list of archaeological sites (verified by scholarship, not faith) a 'new' Holy Land was effectively defined. This project was continued and expanded with the researches of Stanley, Ritter, Guérin, and the British-sponsored Survey of Western Palestine (for extensive bibliographical references, see Ben-Arieh 1979). All of these surveys followed the linguistic lead of Robinson and Smith in compiling an encyclopedic list of Arabic place-names and their relationship to biblical localities. The tangible modern consequences of historical geography in creating modern political realities are often not, however, fully recognized. The boundaries of the 'Land of the Bible' as determined by the Survey of Western Palestine, rather than any existing Ottoman political divisions, served as a basis for the delineation of the shape and extent of Mandatory Palestine after World War I (Ra'anan 1976: 40–1, 97–141). And through the official adoption of Hebrew and Biblical place-names, linguistically and historically approved by the British Mandatory Government (Government of Palestine 1929) and later by the Names Committee of the Academy for the Hebrew Language in the State of Israel (as followed, for instance, in Hareouveni 1979), the contemporary geography of the Holy Land, on maps and in the public consciousness, was dramatically transformed.

Imperial struggles, imperial histories

Although the Holy Land lacked the monumental architecture and colossal statuary found in Egypt, Mesopotamia and the Aegean, the early history of its archaeological exploration is marked by repeated attempts at excavation by individuals seeking religious relics or ancient works of art. The first of the diggers on record was the French adventurer Laurent D'Arvieux, who reported the discovery of a colossal statue – which he mistakenly identified as the image of the Philistine god Dagon – at Gaza in 1659 (Dothan and Dothan 1992: 7). The haphazard tradition of digging was taken up again at the beginning of the nineteenth century when Lady Hester Stanhope, in a determined search for treasure, uncovered the torso of a Roman statue at Tel Ashkelon (Silberman 1984). In 1856, Louis-Félicien De Saulcy led some companions on a tour of the Dead Sea region and dug up a few tombs in the Qumran cemetery and removed a portion of the mosaic floor from the Byzantine chapel at Masada. In 1863, he returned to loot the 'Tombs of the Kings' in Jerusalem (Silberman 1982: 63–72). Yet these isolated episodes of archaeological plunder – and certainly there were countless others that went unrecorded – did nothing to advance an independent understanding of the history of the Holy Land. Far more influential for the future of archaeology were the systematic excavations of Charles Warren around the Temple Mount in Jerusalem (1867–70), which were the first to devote themselves primarily to careful, accurate recording rather than to the harvest of museum-quality artifacts (Warren 1876).

The pace and intensity of nineteenth-century western archaeological advancement was, not surprisingly, closely tied to political and economic developments. The increasing involvement of the various western powers in the internal affairs of the Ottoman Empire was

Figure 3 In the course of subterranean explorations in Jerusalem for the British-sponsored Palestine Exploration Fund (1867–70), Captain Charles Warren of the Royal Engineers collected important information on the history of Jerusalem and the construction of Herod's Temple. From *Illustrated London News*, April 24, 1869

accompanied by their establishment throughout the empire of a wide variety of religious, educational and diplomatic missions (Tibawi 1961, 1966; Hopwood 1969; Wallach 1975). By the end of the nineteenth century, all of the major powers had established permanent national archaeological societies devoted to the exploration of the Holy Land (Silberman 1982). First among these was the Palestine Exploration Fund, established in London in 1865 under the patronage of Queen Victoria and the Archbishop of Canterbury. It was followed by the German Palästina Verein in 1878, the École Biblique et Archéologique (founded in 1890 by the French Dominican order), and the short-lived American Palestine Exploration Society (1870–75) and the much longer-lived American Schools of Oriental Research (established in 1900). It is interesting to note that the geographical distribution of the various societies' activities closely reflected their nations' spheres of interest in the Holy Land. The British work concentrated on sites in the south and in Sinai, in strategic proximity to the Suez Canal; the Americans initially concentrated in Transjordan, which remained, by agreement with the

British, an American preserve. The French Dominicans concentrated in Jerusalem, with its many church establishments and religious associations. And German activity centered in Galilee and the Jezreel Valley, conveniently close to the Haifa-Dera'a spur of the Hijaz Railway, built under the supervision of German engineers. The pursuit of archaeology had by that time become a national, rather than individual, undertaking. At times of political crisis or tension in Europe, the competition for particularly noteworthy antiquities such as the Mesha Stele and the Shapira 'Deuteronomy' (see Window 1) became matters of national prestige.

At the turn of the century, the character of archaeological work in the Holy Land underwent a methodological revolution with the beginning of stratigraphic excavations at some of the country's most prominent *tells*. The earlier work of Augustus Pitt-Rivers in England and Heinrich Schliemann at the mound of Hissarlik in Asia Minor demonstrated the character of stratified archaeological deposits, and the excavation of Palestinian mounds became the source of a new understanding of the progressive development of ancient civilization, not merely rich mines of relics and isolated monuments. This long range perspective was apparent in the excavations conducted by W.M.F. Petrie and Frederick Bliss at Tel Hesi (1890–2), R.A.S. Macalister at Gezer (1902–09), Gottlieb Schumacher at Megiddo (1902–05), and Ernst Sellin at Ta'anach (1902–10) and Jericho (1910–14). Yet it should also be stressed that each of these excavators identified a different element as the primary motive force in ancient Palestinian history (Silberman 1993). Petrie, a fervent adherent of the eugenic theories of Sir Francis Galton, saw in the destruction levels of Tel Hesi, a millennia-long saga of the triumph of active races over the more passive ones (later expressed clearly in Petrie 1912). Schumacher and Sellin, the excavators of Megiddo, Ta'anach, and Jericho, were interested in distinguishing 'Babylonian' influence in the material culture of Palestine as evidence for a natural process of cultural domination by a complex culture over its less sophisticated neighbors (Sellin 1905: 29–33). And in the version of Palestinian history devised by Macalister on the basis of his excavation of Gezer, the sequence of various 'Semitic' and 'non-Semitic' periods underlined what he considered to be an eternal and inevitable conflict between 'East' and 'West' (Macalister 1912).

The archaeological interpretations of these scholars in the era of high imperialism can still be clearly seen as metaphorical validations of the contemporary European penetration of the Middle East. Yet there is another important element to note in this period of growing archaeological professionalism: it was an era in which many older attitudes, understandings, and approaches to the past were finally and quite decisively discredited as mistaken, primitive, or naive. The peoples of Palestine – Jews, Muslims and Christians – had traditionally regarded the material remains of the past as an inseparable part of the landscape. In the tombs of the saints scattered on hilltops and valleys, in the names given to natural features, in favorite epics and legends, and in favorite places of pilgrimage, they participated in a subjective relationship to antiquity (Canaan 1922; Vilnay 1973–8). Whether celebrating the ceremony of the Holy Fire on the Saturday before Easter in the Church of the Holy Sepulchre, converging on the shrine of Nebi Musa in the spring time, or flocking to the Tomb of Rabbi Simeon Bar Yohai in Meiron on Lag Ba-Omer, the connection to the past was a highly-ritualized reenactment of a repertoire of familiar historical motifs. Yet these traditions were now valuable to the archaeologists only in so far as they were seen to represent the fossilized customs of antiquity.

The 'golden' age

The conduct of archaeology in the Holy Land changed dramatically with the British conquest of Palestine during World War I. Within only a few years of the establishment of an efficient, centralized colonial government and the improvement of transport and communications throughout the country, the Holy Land became one of the most active centers of excavation and archaeological research in the world. This was due in large measure to the regulatory efforts of the Palestine Department of Antiquities. As an autonomous unit of the Mandatory Government, it was patterned after similar departments in other British colonies. By the provisions of the Antiquities Law of 1928, the director of the department was authorized to set standards for historical significance in a published list of protected archaeological sites. The director was also empowered to specify permissible methods of archaeological investigation, in setting standards for the issuance of excavation permits. Research facilities were also improving. The construction in Jerusalem in 1935 of the Palestine Archaeological Museum (later known as the Rockefeller Museum, after its American donor) greatly facilitated the work of the Department of Antiquities by serving as its headquarters – with modern storerooms, laboratories, study galleries and public exhibition halls.

The period between the two World Wars is often called the 'golden age' of excavation in the Holy Land (Moorey 1991: Chapter 3), and that description is certainly accurate, if only in terms of sheer scale of activity. Among the most important foreign-funded archaeological projects carried out during this period were the excavations of the Palestine Exploration Fund at Ashkelon (1920–1); the University of Chicago Oriental Institute at Megiddo (1925–39); the University of Pennsylvania at Beth Shean (1921–33); the American Schools of Oriental Research at Tell Beit Mirsim (1926–32); W.M.F. Petrie at Tel Jemmeh (1926–7), Tell el-Farah (south) (1928–30), and Tell el-Ajjul (1937–8); and the Welcome-Marston Expedition at

Figure 4   The Palestine Exploration Fund Survey of Western Palestine (1875–81) effectively delineated a new territorial entity — modern Palestine — through its extensive mapping work. From Claude Conder, *Tent Work in Palestine* (London: 1878)

Plate 2   The Mecha Inscription or 'Moabite Stone', discovered in 1868, was the object of fierce rivalry between British, French, and German archaeologists. From Heron de Villefosse, *Notices des Monuments provenants de la Palestine et conservés au Musée de Louvre* (Paris: 1879)

Lachish (1932–8); the excavations of the British School at Samaria (1931–5), and the joint British-American expedition to Gerash (1925–35). During this period, the chronological range of archaeology in the Holy Land was considerably expanded with the important prehistoric researches of Dorothy Garrod in the caves of Mount Carmel (1929–32) and the excavations of the Metropolitan Museum at the medieval site of Montfort (1926).

These large-scale excavations were of a distinctly different character than the excavations conducted before the war. Large professional staffs – instead of a single supervisor – were now employed to conduct controlled and increasingly standardized excavations, with the publication of excavation reports also gradually assuming a standard form. Work methods were made more efficient with the development of a far more articulated hierarchy of skilled and unskilled labor, and the gradual abandonment of the custom of paying *bakshish*, special cash payments, to native excavation workers for the discovery of special finds. Indeed, the economic factor is rarely taken into account in tracing the history of Biblical Archaeology. It is ironic that the 'golden age' of Palestinian archaeology took place precisely at times of serious unemployment and recession – in the periods 1922–4 and 1926–8 (Halevi 1983) – for, in certain respects, the 'goldenness' of that

golden age was made possible by a steep drop in the going wage rates for Jewish laborers and *fellahin*.

As in the previous period of archaeological history, certain distinctive philosophical trends can be distinguished. Following a series of consultations between the directors of the major foreign archaeological schools in Jerusalem in 1922, a two-tiered system of chronological terminology was devised in which the cultural-historical epochs, named for ethnic groups or religio-cultural phenomena – Canaanite, Israelite, Hellenistic, Roman, Byzantine, Arab – were somewhat uneasily nested within broader technological stages, known in Europe as the Stone, Bronze, and Iron Ages (Gitin 1985). It should be noted that the compromise between ethnic history and universal progress implicit in this new terminology reflected a subtle theoretical divergence within the discipline.

On the one hand was the universal, humanist emphasis of James Breasted, founder of the Oriental Institute of the University of Chicago, who saw the study of the ancient

Plate 3   Sir William Matthew Flinders Petrie (1856–1942) was one of the founders of stratigraphically-based archaeological excavation in Palestine. Photograph courtesy of the American Schools of Oriental Research

civilization of Canaan – though certainly interesting as a cultural crossroads – clearly secondary to that of the great cultural centers of Egypt, Anatolia and Mesopotamia. From the start, in his program for the Oriental Institute, Professor James Breasted had been motivated by a guiding philosophical image in which the modern nations of the West were the true inheritors of Ancient Near Eastern civilization. And, in pursuit of the ideal proclaimed in the art deco-style relief placed over the main portal of the Oriental Institute building in Chicago (with its vision of the Old World offering its wisdom to the New), Breasted was not interested primarily in specific biblical questions but in a secular gospel of technological and cultural advancement. In excavating the site of Megiddo, the Chicago team concentrated on city planning, architecture, political administration, institutionalized religion and military engineering, which were precisely the elements that Breasted most prized as being characteristic of western civilization (Larsen 1989).

In contrast to this Breastedian progressivist vision was the biblical romanticism of William Foxwell Albright, the spiritual father of American Biblical Archaeology. Unlike Breasted, with whom he carried on a long polemic (as in Albright 1964), Albright saw the spiritual history of the Holy Land as its great contribution to human civilization; material culture was useful primarily as a chronological aid and a verification of the accuracy of the biblical accounts (Albright 1940). Albright utilized ceramic and stratigraphic evidence to construct a socio-religious history of the peoples of the Lands of the Bible, arguing adamantly for the essential historicity of the patriarchal narratives and the biblical accounts of sudden, militarily coordinated Israelite conquest (Albright 1949). Albright's unique mix of faith, philology and potsherds was carried on for decades by his students and scholarly heirs. His successors in the directorship of the American School of Oriental Research in Jerusalem, Nelson Glueck and G. Ernest Wright, made the excavation of biblical cities and the modern examination of Canaanite and Israelite material culture personal acts of piety (King 1983; Dever 1980a).

Beyond its ideological component, there was another element that aided the continuation and spread of this brand of archaeological investigation. While the large expeditions of the Oriental Institute, the University of Pennsylvania and the British School of Archaeology (which were dependent on a small professional staff and a huge force of local workers) became too expensive in periods of prosperity and rising wages, Albright-style excavations, based on the active participation of scholar-volunteers from a broad consortium of universities and theological schools across America and Canada, proved far more adaptable to the changing economic and political fortunes of Palestine.

The archaeology of new nations

The authority of foreigners to set the agenda for the study of the Holy Land's past was sometimes challenged. In 1863, the Jewish community of Jerusalem urgently appealed to the Sultan to call a halt to DeSaulcy's excavations in the 'Tombs of the Kings'; Muslim public opinion consistently resisted any attempts to excavate in the vicinity of the Dome of the Rock and al-Aqsa; and, toward the end of the nineteenth century, the Ottoman Government insisted on appointing an official commissioner (even though most were ill-qualified and unmotivated) to supervise all foreign excavation projects (Silberman 1982). Yet it was only in the early decades of the twentieth century that active archaeological interest began to spring up among the inhabitants of Palestine, both as a sign of new intellectual influences and as a symptom of intensifying national self-consciousness.

The Jewish community was the first to engage in independent archaeological research (Shavit 1987). With the birth of the Zionist movement in the nineteenth

Plate 4 The American excavations at Samaria (1908–10), directed by George A. Reisner, introduced sophisticated recording methods and artifact card files that would be used by nearly all subsequent excavations in the Holy Land. From the Matson Collection and Episcopal Home

century, enormous political support for the ideal of a Jewish State had been derived from a skillful evocation of images from antiquity. As was the case in the crystallizing nation-states of central and eastern Europe, where many of the early Zionist leaders were born and educated, the potent constellation of ancient religious traditions, common territorial aspirations, and historical persecutions were adduced as ample justification for modern sovereignty. Yet even more direct links between modern Jewish settlers and the land of Zion were ultimately to be provided by the excavation of tangible monuments and artifacts. In December 1912, the Society for the Exploration of Eretz-Israel and its Antiquities was founded by a group of Jerusalem and Tel Aviv teachers. They modeled their new organization closely after the example of nationalistic European antiquarian societies and undertook the first locally-initiated excavations, at the ancient synagogue of Hammath Tiberias, in the winter of 1920–1 (Brawer 1965). Subsequent excavations of the Society at the 'Third Wall' in Jerusalem (1925–8), the ancient synagogue of Beth Alpha (1929), and the

necropolis Beth Shearim (1940) sparked widespread interest among a significant segment of the Palestinian Jewish community, who came to see archaeology and historical geography as a powerful nationalistic activity (Broshi 1987). The establishment of a Department of Archaeology at the Hebrew University of Jerusalem in 1935 facilitated the professional training of local Jewish archaeologists.

With the establishment of the Palestine Oriental Society in 1920, a small number of Christian and Muslim scholars began to investigate the folklore and customs of the country, as an outgrowth of foreign anthropological interest in the survival of biblical customs and as an expression of emerging Palestinian cultural nationalism. This activity was actively encouraged by W.F. Albright, who gathered around him a circle of enthusiastic local Christian and Muslim scholars to collect and write about Palestinian folklore (Running and Freedman 1975: 86–7). Field archaeology, however, held an insignificant place in the Palestinian nationalist movement. It was conducted entirely in the context of foreign expeditions and by the Christian and Muslim officials of the Department of Antiquities.

Archaeological activity in the Holy Land was almost entirely halted during the Arab Rebellion of 1936–9 and during World War II. The 1948 War and the *de facto* partition of the Holy Land between the Hashemite Kingdom of Jordan and the State of Israel created a new situation, ending the possibility of direct archaeological cooperation across the border for all but foreign nationals. As a result, two distinct national traditions developed, each a natural outgrowth of local intellectual and cultural life. In Jordan and the West Bank (officially annexed to the Hashemite Kingdom in 1950), the Department of Antiquities continued, until 1956, to be directed by a British archaeologist, Gerald Lankaster Harding. For the most part, large-scale activity in Jordan was conducted by foreign expeditions, among them, the American Schools of Oriental Research at Tell Balata (1956–64); the British School of Archaeology at Jericho (1952–8) and Jerusalem (1961–7); and the École Biblique at Tell el-Farah (1946–60) and Khirbet Qumran (1951–6). The manuscript discoveries at Qumran and in its vicinity (1947–56), initially made by unauthorized bedouin digging, were stored and studied by an international committee of biblical scholars at the Palestine Archaeological Museum. Yet in the summer of 1956, in an atmosphere of increasing nationalistic pressure, Harding was removed and the Department of Antiquities would henceforth be directed by Jordanian nationals.

In the State of Israel, a Department of Antiquities was organized in July 1948 as a branch of the Ministry of Education and Culture, and soon thereafter the first Israeli excavation was conducted, under the supervision of Benjamin Mazar at Tel Qasile near Tel Aviv. During the

1950s, the Israel Exploration Society became a national organization, coordinating the efforts of public and academic bodies involved in excavation, sponsoring public lectures and congresses on archaeological subjects, and promoting the participation in excavations by volunteers from all over the world. This period also witnessed the crystallization of a unique Israeli style of large-scale, architecturally based excavation – beginning in the Hazor excavations directed by Yigael Yadin (1955–8). As an increasing number of *tells* were excavated, participation in archaeological excavations came to be a national ritual for Israeli schoolchildren, soldiers, senior citizens and foreign visitors. Nowhere else in the Middle East or the eastern Mediterranean was the message of national rebirth conveyed so effectively – through excavated sites like Hazor, Arad, Beersheva, Megiddo, and Masada, and through evocative artifacts like the Bar Kochba Letters and the Dead Sea Scrolls.

In June 1967, war once again dramatically changed the character of archaeological excavation in the Holy Land. With Israel's military occupation of the West Bank, all antiquities in the area came under the control of the Archaeological Staff Officer. In the years following the Six Day War, large-scale excavations were conducted on both sides of the Jordan, examining levels from the Paleolithic to the Ottoman period. Their far-reaching results and historical insights comprise a significant proportion of the material of this book. Even more significant in the post-1967 period was the initiation of intensive regional surveys, which introduced to the archaeology of the Holy Land the study of ancient demography and settlement patterns.

In the 1970s and 1980s, large international consortia were organized to undertake multinational excavations at important sites such as Tel Hesi, Lahav, Akko, Caesarea, Tel Miqne, and Tel Dor (for an excellent survey, see Wolff 1991). At the same time, archaeological institutions in both Israel and Jordan expanded greatly. In Jordan, the establishment of departments of archaeology at the University of Jordan and the University of the Yarmuk, the Government's growing concern with cultural resource management, and the initiation of major international projects at sites such as Pella, Gerash, and Petra signaled a period of intensification of archaeological activity (Hadidi 1982, 1985). In Israel, teaching departments of archaeology were established at Haifa, Ben-Gurion, and Bar-Ilan universities – joining the efforts of the older institutes in Jerusalem and Tel Aviv.

The post-1967 period was also distinguished by bitterly argued political and ethical issues relating to the pursuit of archaeology in the Holy Land (Silberman 1990). Although the Hague Convention, to which Israel was a signatory, explicitly prohibited the removal of cultural property from militarily occupied areas, both foreign and Israeli archaeologists mounted extensive excavations in the occupied territories that, according to some critics, went far beyond the legitimate and permitted function of protecting immediately endangered archaeological sites. In early 1993 Israeli and Egyptian negotiating teams finalized plans for the return of archaeological materials removed during Israel's occupation of the Sinai. The situation on the West Bank, however, remained as uncertain as the areas's future status. Despite the vast amounts of new archaeological data that were accumulated in excavations, and intensive surveys and new historical insights gained for understanding the prehistoric, biblical, classical and early medieval periods, relatively little effort was made to preserve or protect archaeological remains from the later Islamic and Ottoman periods, which were of direct relevance to the area's Muslim and Christian inhabitants.

Thus arose what seemed to be an inevitable development in the history of archaeology all over the world. The pursuit of the past through excavation had always been both a symptom of and factor in the crystallization of modern national consciousness. While the leaders of the Palestinian national movement had never shown any great interest in archaeological interpretation, the rapid expansion of West Bank universities in the 1980s led to the emergence of a distinctive approach to Palestinian archaeology. A new generation of Palestinian graduate students and foreign-trained archaeologists began to study and uncover the remains of the late Islamic and Ottoman periods in village contexts (Glock 1983, 1987). It remains to be seen whether this research trend represents a dramatic new approach to the study of traditional Palestinian culture or whether these are just the first steps taken along the well-trodden path of archaeological nationalism.

Modernizing the past

The conduct of archaeology in the Holy Land was only belatedly affected by the theoretical revolutions of the American 'New Archaeology' (Dever 1980a, 1985). During the 1950s and 1960s, in the absence of serious theoretical discussion about the objectives and social function of foreign expeditions in a changed Middle Eastern reality, methodological refinement of excavation techniques became a primary goal. Kenyon's excavations at Jericho and the American excavations at Shechem and Gezer were distinguished by their attempts to distinguish ever more precise stratigraphic units, and pottery and artifact types. This led to a much-publicized, though largely inconclusive, methodological debate with Israeli archaeologists over their much greater use of architectural analysis (Dever 1973). The adoption of such scientific innovations as radiocarbon dating, chemical provenance studies, geological, botanical and faunal analysis, and increasingly complex data processing – had, by the 1960s, made excavations in Israel and Jordan among the most technologically sophisticated in the world. Yet in the 1970s, under the growing influence of American 'New Archaeology', scholars working in Israel and Jordan became increasingly concerned with questions of social evolution and adaptation, rather than traditional culture history.

As a growing proportion of funding for archaeology in the region came from non-religious sources, biblical and even specific historical questions were being gradually supplanted by new research questions about agricultural efficiency, economic profits, specialized production and regional population growth. This change in emphasis can, of course, be seen in a wider context, for it neatly parallels the imperatives of modern economic development that have become so pressing in the closing decade of the twentieth century (Miller 1980; Patterson 1986, 1987). In recent years, as Middle Eastern peoples and economies have been drawn into the western industrial world system, cities have grown up, and *fellahin* and bedouin have been transformed into workers, it might be argued that these far-reaching modern changes have influenced – if not completely determined – the interpretation of archaeological finds in terms of complex social interaction and economic development.

And so the process of reinterpretation continues. Archaeology in the Holy Land can never completely avoid being influenced by contemporary preoccupations and ideologies because it is, and has always has been, a powerful social, religious and political activity. Future generations of archaeologists must recognize their responsibility to the general public as well as to their scholarly colleagues. Images from the past have enormous potential for encouraging either hatred or understanding, for establishing either a shared or a conflicting heritage. It is, therefore, inevitable that archaeology in the Holy Land, in its reconstruction of ancient landscapes and societies in the midst of modern economic challenges and continuing political conflicts, will continue to play an important role in shaping the Holy Land's present and future – as well as its past.

FAKES, FORGERY AND SUICIDE – THE STRANGE CASE OF MOSES WILHELM SHAPIRA

Of the many tales of academic controversy and international competition that punctuate the history of archaeology in the Holy Land, the 'Shapira Affair' is certainly one of the most tragic. The central character, Moses Wilhelm Shapira, was a Jewish immigrant from Kiev who settled in Jerusalem in 1856, and set himself up as an antiquities dealer. Self-educated in antiquarian matters, he gained a fame throughout the scholarly world as a purveyor of high quality archaeological artifacts to institutions and wealthy collectors all over the world.

Shapira had greater ambitions than mere profit. He was anxious to gain scholarly legitimation. In the years following the 1868 discovery of the famous Mesha Stele (bearing a royal Moabite inscription of the ninth century BC), Shapira offered for sale an extensive collection of pottery vessels bearing Moabite inscriptions, some of which he attempted to translate. He reported that these unique artifacts came from the same region as the Mesha Stele and sold a large collection to the Prussian Imperial Museum.

In the wake of the Franco-Prussian War of 1870, however, antagonism and suspicion ran high between the two nations. The skepticism of the French archaeologist scholar Charles Clermont-Ganneau toward his German counterparts led him to investigate the origin of the Moabite pottery. When he discovered that the unique vessels that the Germans had purchased were worthless modern forgeries, the public reputation of Moses Shapira (who was apparently an unwitting dupe of a con man) suffered a serious blow.

Shapira was determined to regain his good name and to obtain an archaeological discovery whose significance was beyond dispute. In 1878, according to Shapira's account, he was approached by several bedouin who sold him a collection of parchment fragments bearing ancient Hebrew characters, which they claimed to have found in a cave near the Dead Sea. Shapira initially kept the discovery secret. He worked hard on a translation and eventually identified it as a portion of the Book of Deuteronomy with striking differences from the standard biblical text.

For most biblical scholars of the time, the scripture was considered divinely inspired and unchanging. Shapira's discovery of an early variant text of Deuteronomy (which he dated to around 800 BC) challenged the conventional wisdom in a daring and heretical way. At first, he succeeded in persuading German scholars of the value of the ancient manuscript fragments. Then, making his way to London, concluded a deal to sell 'The World's Oldest Bible' to the British Museum for the astounding sum of one million pounds sterling.

Unfortunately, the episode ended in humiliation and personal tragedy for Shapira. In the midst of the public excitement, Clermont-Ganneau, Shapira's old nemesis, came to London, examined the fragments, and declared them to be forgeries. He counted among his reasons the impossibility of ancient documents surviving in the relatively wet climate of Palestine, and, of course, the many glaring differences from the traditional text. The scholarly support for the self-educated Jewish antiquities dealer quickly crumbled. The British Museum hastily called off the deal and Shapira became an international laughingstock.

Yet the verdict was premature. Less than 70 years later, the discovery of the Dead Sea Scrolls disproved some of the main contentions against the authenticity of Shapira's manuscript fragments. Though his dating was certainly far too early, the possibility that the ancient text might have been written by members of a Jewish sect in the late first or early second century AD could not be entirely ruled out. But further investigation was impossible. Soon after Clermont-Ganneau's public accusations, Shapira's scroll fragments were sold at auction for a pittance and eventually disappeared. Shapira himself, paying the price for challenging the scholarly consensus, was shattered. He took his own life in a cheap hotel in Rotterdam in the spring of 1883.

PUNCH'S FANCY PORTRAITS.—NO. 152.

MR. SHARP-EYE-RA.

SHOWING, IN VERY FANCIFUL PORTRAITURE, HOW DETECTIVE GINSBURG ACTUALLY DID MR. SHARP-EYE-RA OUT OF HIS SKIN.

Figure 1.1 *Punch's acerbic cartoon on the Shapira Affair. September 8, 1883*

FROM LEGEND TO MONUMENT: MEGIDDO AND ITS EXCAVATORS (1852–1967)

Tell el-Mutesellim, 'the mound of the governor', is perhaps the most-excavated and most thoroughly studied site in modern Israel. Identified as the ancient Canaanite and Israelite city of Megiddo, it was also mentioned in the Book of Revelation as the site of the world's final, apocalyptic battle. 'Armageddon' is a Greek variant of the Hebrew name *Har Megiddon*, 'the hill of Megiddo'. The impressive 15-acre site has been excavated in three distinct phases of exploration – by German, American, and Israeli expeditions – and its ruins have yielded an enormous mass of data about the cultural, economic and political development of the city from the Neolithic to the Persian period. Indeed the exploration of Megiddo can be seen as a microcosm of the history of archaeology in the Holy Land.

A hundred and fifty years ago, Tell el-Mutesellim was not a biblical landmark but ruin-strewn pasture familiar only to the shepherds of the nearby village of el-Lajjun. That situation began to change with the 1838 visit of a bookish American biblical scholar, Edward Robinson, who identified the mound as the likely site of the ancient city of Megiddo, on comparison of ancient descriptions with the modern topography. Robinson's identification, widely accepted by scholars, was the first step in the construction of a modern archaeological monument.

Great Power politics eventually entered the process. Following Kaiser Wilhelm II's visit to Palestine in 1898, German activity in Haifa and in the western Jezreel Valley increased dramatically. German agricultural colonies were established in the vicinity of Tell el-Mutesellim and German engineers supervised the construction of a railroad line. The Kaiser was also anxious to further German scholarly activity and, in 1903, he provided funds for the excavation of ancient Megiddo – under the supervision of Dr Gottlieb Schumacher, an experienced explorer and architect.

Born to pious parents in the German Templer Colony in Haifa, Schumacher was anxious both to develop the country's future and to explore the remains of its past. Directing excavations on behalf of the *Deutscher Palästina Verein*, the 'German Palestine Society', he followed the example of his countryman Heinrich Schliemann, who had pioneered the archaeological exploration of Middle Eastern mounds in his excavation of ancient Troy, in Asia Minor. At Megiddo, Schumacher likewise hired large numbers of native workers to drive an enormous trench through the center of the *tell*.

The best known finds from these early excavations clearly reflect Schumacher's theological interest. He interpreted Middle Bronze Age infant jar burials as remains of child sacrifice, saw a colorfully painted incense stand as evidence of pagan worship, and identified the structural stone columns of an Iron Age structure as *massebot*, or religious monuments. Eager to show that the ancient Hebrew prophets' condemnations of idolatry reflected an authentic historical reality, Schumacher used the site of Tell el-Mutesellim as a source of biblical illustration, not independent research.

After World War I, and the British conquest of Palestine, Megiddo became the focus of a quite different archaeological investigation. Professor James Breasted of the Oriental Institute of the University of Chicago initiated a 14-year program of excavations, beginning in the summer of 1925. Dr Clarence Fisher served as the first director of the excavations, which were carried out with the labor of skilled workers from Egypt, not unskilled villagers from Lajjun (see Plate 1, p. 10). The core staff of American scholars at first bivouacked in tents, but eventually moved into an imposing stone 'dig house' furnished with running water, electricity, and modern appliances. Despite the transfer of directorship from Fisher to P.L.O. Guy and then to Gordon Loud, the interpretive focus of the excavations remained firmly fixed on a characteristically progressive vision of the past.

Breasted had been motivated by a guiding philosophical image in which the modern nations of the West were the true inheritors of Ancient Near Eastern civilization. Instead of concentrating on specific biblical religious questions, the American team traced the city's urban life, technology, political administration, institutionalized religion and military engineering from the Neolithic to the Persian period. The emphasis was on Megiddo's connections with the rest of the Fertile Crescent, not on either Israelite monotheism or Canaanite paganism.

After the establishment of the State of Israel, new themes in

Figure 2.1 Dr. Edward Robinson (1793–1863), the first modern scholar to identify Tell el-Muttasellim with ancient Megiddo. From Claude Conder, *Palestine* (New York: 1872)

Megiddo's history were addressed. Excavations by the Institute of Archaeology of the Hebrew University, directed by Professor Yigael Yadin in 1960, 1966 and 1967, focussed particularly on the Solomonic period, and Megiddo's role as a military and administrative center of the Israelite Kingdom. Following his discovery of an impressive eight-chambered gateway at Hazor that closely matched those of Gezer and Megiddo, Yadin reexamined the archaeological remains of Megiddo to search for additional evidence of Solomon's extensive building activity as recorded in I Kings 9: 15.

Yadin's excavations were unlike any that had gone on at Megiddo before. Muscle power was supplied by archaeology students of the Hebrew University, not Egyptian workers, or local *fellahin*. The surrounding landscape was also quite different; as a result of the 1948 War, Megiddo now lay close to the barbed-wire and thickly-mined border between Jordan and Israel. It was little wonder, therefore, that questions of military engineering and administration dominated the research agenda. Although a number of scholars contested the specific details of Yadin's reconstruction and stratigraphy, none denied that some of the fortifications and administrative buildings at Megiddo should be ascribed to the biblically-attested rebuilding by Solomon. Thus, in the 1960s, Tell el-Mutesellim entered its third modern incarnation: as a site of national history.

Today, the restored and signposted archaeological site of Megiddo is the third most popular National Park in Israel (after Caesarea and Masada), with almost four million annual visitors. School children, foreign tourists, and families on weekend excursions receive a full color brochure to guide them through the excavated ruins and to explain briefly

their historical significance. And it is enlightening to note the incorporation – even homogenization – of the various interpretations that have accumulated over the years. Indeed every structure that has, at some time or other, been even hypothetically linked to Solomon is highlighted by the National Parks Authority.

Yet we should not so casually dismiss this imaginative modern presentation of ancient Megiddo as a mistaken 'popular' version of history. Public understanding of the past – however mistaken or garbled – is one of the most powerful outcomes of archaeological work. The mound of Megiddo, like every other archaeological site, is at least partly a mirror. In excavating its ruins, scholars have always focused on their own societies' most deeply felt political, religious and social concerns.

Plate 2.1   Dr. Gottlieb Schumacher (1857–1924), architect, explorer, and director of the early German excavations at Tell el-Mutasellim. From his *Tell el-Mutasellim* (Leipzig: 1908)

3

MAN AND THE NATURAL ENVIRONMENT

Avinoam Danin

Introduction

Israel and Jordan are situated at a transition zone between the extreme desert areas of the Saharan type in the southern and eastern parts of the east Mediterranean countries and the relatively mesic Mediterranean zone in the north. The boundary between the dry and the relatively moist parts is influenced by the special topography of the two countries with the longitudinal depression of the Jordan, Dead Sea, and Arava rift valleys influencing the local climatic conditions. This boundary has changed its position, as part of global climatic changes, several times since prehistoric times. The climatic changes during the evolutionary history, the edaphic and climatic diversity, and the long history of human activity in the area have led to high diversity of the flora and vegetation of Israel in a rather small geographic area (ca. 440 km long and maximally 120 km wide)

Flora

There are 2682 plant species within Israel's boundaries on the vegetation map in an area of 29,600 km², as derived from the data on plant distribution in Feinbrun-Dothan and Danin (1991) and in Danin (1992: 43). This number includes some 200 species that occur in the Mt. Hermon area and are absent from the other districts of Israel. The number of species is high as compared with that of many other countries (Table 1).

The high species richness of the country, expressed as species to area, is related mainly to three factors:

Table 1   Species richness of the flora of several countries

Country	Species	Area km²	Species/100 km²
Israel	2,682	29,600	9.06
California	2,325	63,479	3.66
Sinai	889	61,100	1.45
Greece	4,200	132,562	3.17
Italy	5,600	301,100	1.86
Britain	1,666	229,850	0.72

Notes: California is in fact Californian coastal area; Britain is the British Isles. Information for countries 2 and 6 is from Johnson and Raven (1970: 127); for countries 4 and 5 from Pignatti (Personal Comment).

1. Its position in a meeting zone between plant geographical regions, each with its typical flora.
2. The existence of the many habitats needed to support these species. The wealth of habitats derives from the climatic transition between the relatively moist area in the northern part of the country and the desert in the southern part. Topography is a second factor in creating the warm climates of the Jordan to Arava rift valleys and the relatively cold climate of Mt. Hermon. In a similar way other highlands and lowlands have local climatic influence which increases Israel's habitat diversity and hence plant species diversity. The geomorphological structures are relatively small but the number of rock types is high. As a result, many soil types develop in a small area (Dan and Raz 1970) increasing the diversity of habitats available for plants.
3. A long history of human activity of cultivation and grazing by domestic animals led to strong stress on the existing flora and enabled the introduction of many alien species. Many of the latter occupy synanthropic habitats (i.e., growing in habitats created by human activity. Zohary 1973; Danin 1991a: 95).

According to Eig (1931–32: 1), Zohary (1962; 1966; 1972), Feinbrun-Dothan (1978; 1986), and Danin and Plitmann (1986: 43), the flora of Israel is divided into seven groups, the distribution of which is:

1. Mediterranean (M) species, which are distributed around the Mediterranean sea.
2. Irano-Turanian (IT) species, which also inhabit Asian steppes of the Syrian desert, Iran, Anatolia in Turkey, and the Gobi desert.
3. Saharo-Arabian (SA) species, which also grow in the Sahara, Sinai, and Arabian deserts.
4. Sudano-Zambesian (S) species, typical to the subtropical savannas of Africa.
5. Euro-Siberian species, also known in countries with a wetter and cooler climate than that of Israel; growing mainly in wet habitats and along the Mediterranean coasts.
6. Bi-regional, tri-regional and multi-regional species that grow in more than one of the regions mentioned above.
7. Alien species from remote countries; these plants propagate without human assistance. The principal countries of origin are the Americas, Australia, and South Africa.

Four plant geographical territories have been delineated in Israel (Eig, 1938: 4; Zohary 1962):

Plate 1 Dead Sea and Salt Deposits (photograph: © Garo)

1. Mediterranean
2. Irano-Turanian
3. Saharo-Sindian
4. Sudano-Decanian enclaves.

Zohary (1966) renamed some of the phytogeographical regions; he regarded parts of Eig's Saharo-Sindian as Saharo-Arabian and Eig's Sudano-Decanian as Sudanian. Eig's Sudano-Decanian enclaves in the Dead Sea area became a 'territory of Sudanian penetration' (Zohary 1966).

In a recent analysis of the plant geographical territories of Israel and Sinai (Danin and Plitmann 1986: 43), a new plant geographical map of the area was composed. In that map the Mediterranean territory (see M in Danin and Plitmann 1986: 43), is rather similar in extent to that of Eig (1931–32). All other territories are regarded as 'complex territories' where the second most frequent chorotype is in parentheses (i.e., in the M(M–IT) the most frequent chorotype is the Mediterranean [M] and the second one is the bi-regional M–IT). These complex territories are the following: M(M–IT), SA(M), SA(IT), SA(S), IT(SA), and S(SA) (for explanation of the abbreviations see above). On a large scale map one can see two main domains in Israel: the Mediterranean – including the M and the M(M–IT) territories, and the Saharo-Arabian – including the SA(M), SA(IT) and SA(S) territories. The area that the IT(SA) and the S(SA) territories occupy in Sinai is more prominent than in Israel.

A new phytogeographical analysis of Israel and Jordan is presented in Figure 1. The data used for this map is predominantly from Feinbrun-Dothan and Danin (1991). The flora of each of the 31 districts of Israel and Jordan was analysed and the bars presented in the bargraphs in Figure 1 are those of the following chorotypes in order, from left to right: M, M–IT, IT, SA, Thrm (= thermophilous, including Sudanian, Tropical and Subtropical), and Oth (= other chorotypes).

Bar graphs of districts 1 through 5 display the distribution of chorotypes in the districts of the coastal plain. There is a gradual decrease in the percentage of Mediterranean (M) species from north (1) to south (5); a relatively constant proportion of the M–IT chorotype and an increase of the desert (SA and IT) and thermophilous species.

Bar graphs of districts 6 through 12 and 17 through 20 are of the Mediterranean territory of Israel and display a rather similar phytogeographical spectrum, with M and M–IT chorotypes being the most prominent ones. In most of these eleven districts the percentages of the IT, SA and thermophilous species are negligible.

Most of the desert districts display a rather mixed spectrum except for the extreme desert ones (16 and 25) where the SA chorotype has the highest percentage. This mixed spectrum indicates that the environmental conditions are neither too dry nor excessively moist, thus enabling the coexistence of species from various chorotypes. The high percentage of M and M–IT species in districts 13, 14, 21, 22, 23, and 24 may be explained by the geographical proximity of these districts to the boundary of the Mediterranean region. The high percentage of the latter species in the Negev Highlands was attributed by Danin and Plitmann (1986: 43) to the presence of many relicts (Danin 1972: 437) of moister climates in crevices of smooth-faced outcrops of limestone and in wadis.

The districts east of the Jordan river display patterns that are similar to those of the area west of the Jordan. When comparing the bar graphs from north to south, the Mediterranean ones (26 through 28) display the predominating chorotypes of the M and M–IT. The highest peak in the study area, Mt. Hermon, is rather exceptional having a high percentage of Irano-Turanian species. This fact will be discussed later in the vegetation section. As in the coastal plain of Israel, the north to south gradient is associated with moderate but clear changes in the flora. There is a gradual decrease in the percentage of the M and M–IT chorotypes and an increase of the IT, SA, and thermophilous species. The nearly unimodal phytogeographical spectrum of the Mediterranean districts is prominently different from that of the desert ones such as Edom (31).

Whereas the north to south gradients in the floristic composition in areas with small differences in mean annual rainfall is moderate, the gradients in west to east transects are much more abrupt. The floristic differences between the districts of the main mountain range and the area east of it display, floristically, the rain shadow effect. This is evident when districts 6 or 7 are compared with 18, district 10 with 21, 12 with 22, and 15 with 16. In all these cases the more drought resistant species that belong to the IT and SA chorotypes and the thermophilous species display a higher percentage at the rain shadow, whereas the M and M–IT chorotypes have a lower percentage.

Plant growth forms and the environment

When studying the ways of plant adaptations to the environment one can draw some conclusions from the physiognomy of vegetation. In this intuitive way one may regard the plants that look typical to various climatic zones of the country as adapted to these zones. Thus, evergreen trees and shrubs dominate the rocky and stony highlands of the relatively moist part of the country; semi-shrubs are the dominants in most plant communities of the semi-steppes and steppes of the Judean Desert and the Negev Highlands. Spiny trees give the main impression in the warm parts of the country in the Jordan – Arava rift valleys and the southern Coastal Plain.

When the list of species that occur in each part of the

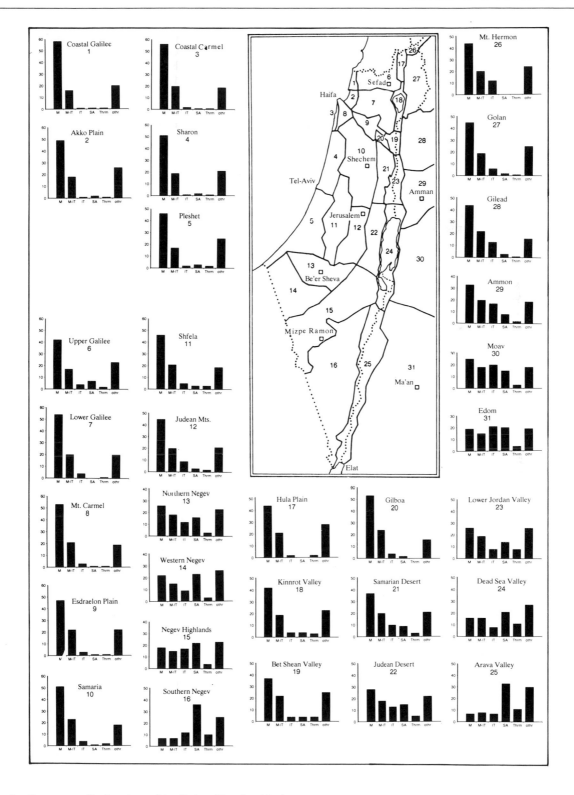

Figure 1 Phytogeographical analyses of the districts of Israel and Jordan

country is analysed, other features of the vegetation become prominent. The distribution of trees and shrubs versus annuals and herbaceous perennials along the precipitation gradient was analysed by Danin and Orshan (1990: 41). The persistent plants (trees and shrubs) keep living and active stems above the ground throughout the year whereas the ephemeral plants have no such organs during the harsh dry summer. The renewal buds of the latter are either in the seeds or in bulbs, corms, rhizomes, or at the top of thick roots at or slightly below the soil surface. The percentage of persistent plants in the flora of the geographic subdivisions of the country decreases up to 150 mm mean annual rainfall; above this value the percentage remains more or less constant (see Figure 2). The percentage of ephemeral plants is reciprocal to that of the persistents. However, from other curves presented by Danin and Orshan (1990: 41), it is evident that the proportion of herbaceous perennial plants (hemicryptophytes and geophytes) in the flora is positively correlated with the mean annual rainfall. The curve expressing percentage of annuals as related to the rainfall is more or less curvilinear with the highest percentages occurring between 200 and 500 mm of rainfall. The distribution of life forms is also correlated with mean annual temperatures, but less significantly.

The analysis of changes in leaf attributes in the vegetation of 22 plant communities along the precipitation gradient (Keshet et al. 1990: 151) showed the following results:

> The average leaf size increases with increasing precipitation; there is a prominent tendency for a change in leaf color from green in the moister part to glaucous or whitish (due to tomentosity) in the moist part of the gradient; malacophyllous, sclerophyllous and winter deciduous plants are more frequent in the moist part of the climatic gradient.

Most semi-shrubs in the dry and moist parts of the country are evergreen with two types of leaves – small and often hairy summer leaves and relatively large and less hairy winter leaves. This dimorphism fits well with the limiting seasonal environmental factors – paucity of solar radiation in winter when there is sufficient water in the soil, and high intensity of radiation in the warm and dry summer.

Vegetation

The vegetation can be dealt with, as the flora, in two parts – that of the mesic Mediterranean part of the country and that of the dry steppe and desert areas with prevailing Saharo-Arabian species. The description of the vegetation follows this subdivision and the categories in the key of the vegetation map (see Figure 3).

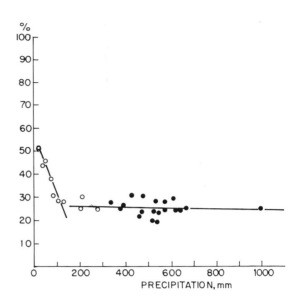

Figure 2   Distribution of persistent species in the flora of 27 districts in Israel as related to precipitation. Full dots are for the districts with mean annual rainfall higher than 300 mm

Vegetation of the mesic part of Israel

1.   Maquis and forests

The mountains of Judea, Samaria, Carmel, Galilee, and lower elevations of Mt. Hermon were covered in historical times by forests or maquis of evergreen trees dominated by *Quercus calliprinos* on hard limestone with Terra Rossa soil. Soft marly chalk lands with Light Rendzina soil were dominated by woodlands of *Pinus halepensis* and *Arbutus andrachne*. The shape, density, and to a certain extent even the composition of the vegetation in this area was influenced by human activity during the last millennia. Clearing woodlands for agricultural purposes, leaving the land fallow for long periods, and the burning of areas to increase the quality of the vegetation by pasture plants were the main components of the history of land use in this area. At present, and it seems that for a long time throughout history, large parts of this area look like mosaics of formations, syngenetically related, and created following various kinds of disturbance by human activity and by natural causes. The components of these 'mosaics' are successional formations of herbaceous communities, semi-shrubs communities, and taller shrubs and trees. These develop in areas that were covered by woodlands, destructed and then recover from destruction, passing through different stages. The stage of herbaceous formations is relatively short, due to the poverty of the soil in phosphorous on most types of Terra Rossa and other nutritional problems on the Rendzinas (Rabinovitch 1979).

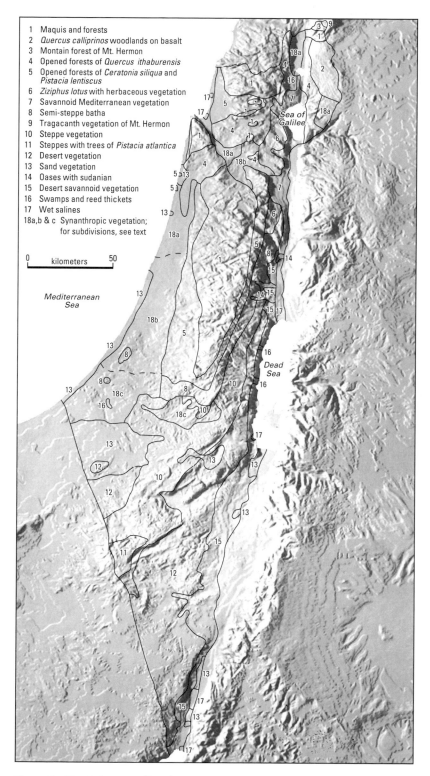

1   Maquis and forests
2   *Quercus calliprinos* woodlands on basalt
3   Montain forest of Mt. Hermon
4   Opened forests of *Quercus ithaburensis*
5   Opened forests of *Ceratonia siliqua* and *Pistacia lentiscus*
6   *Ziziphus lotus* with herbaceous vegetation
7   Savannoid Mediterranean vegetation
8   Semi-steppe batha
9   Tragacanth vegetation of Mt. Hermon
10   Steppe vegetation
11   Steppes with trees of *Pistacia atlantica*
12   Desert vegetation
13   Sand vegetation
14   Oases with sudanian
15   Desert savannoid vegetation
16   Swamps and reed thickets
17   Wet salines
18a, b & c Synanthropic vegetation;
         for subdivisions, see text

0   kilometers   50

Mediterranean
Sea

Sea of
Galilee

Dead
Sea

Figure 3   Vegetation map of Israel

Land use (mainly after Dan et al. 1975) varies according to soil and topography. Rocky slopes are used mainly as pastoral areas; deep soils are planted with fruit trees, either non-irrigated (mainly in the Arabs farms) or irrigated (mainly in the Jewish farming). The common cultivars are olives, grapes, and various deciduous fruit trees such as apples, plums, peaches, etc. Cereals and pulses are cultivated on shallow soils in this area.

2.   *Quercus calliprinos* woodlands on basalt

The woodlands on basalt of the Golan and a small patch in northeastern Galilee differ from those on Terra Rossa by the absence of semi-shrub communities from the successional stages of vegetation recovery after destruction. The herbaceous communities prevail in the area for a long time after destroyed areas are left fallow. This seems to be related to the higher phosphorous content of the soil on basalt (Rabinovitch 1979). Much of the oak woodlands appear in aerial photographs as squares of tree lines at the margins of grassland areas. This is the result of management of the area. The farmers of the past (we do not know when it started) left trees to function as wind breaks, and as a source of wood and other products of the natural vegetation. The tree layer differs from that on Terra Rossa by the absence of many calciphilous trees and shrubs. Of the herbaceous companions the most interesting are the annual grasses with large seeds – the wild progenitors of wheat (*Triticum dicoccoides*), barley (*Hordeum spontaneum*), and oats (*Avena sterilis*). The high vulnerability of this type of vegetation to fire hazards is reflected in the adaptations of many species. Most trees and shrubs of this area will sprout from the base of the trunk after the above ground is burnt. Seeds of many annuals have some mechanism to penetrate the soil, where they are protected from the high fire temperatures.

Large pastoral areas support herds of cows. Areas with deep soils are planted with apples and grapes – both known for their high fruit quality.

3.   Montain forest of Mt. Hermon

Mt. Hermon is the mountain in the region and, with its peak at 2800 m in Lebanon and Syria, it creates a set of environmental conditions that differ from the rest of the country. Precipitation in much of the area falls as snow, due to low temperatures at high elevations. Wind velocity on its slopes is rather high. The vegetation altitudinal belts prominent in Mt. Hermon are evergreen maquis dominated by *Quercus calliprinos* from 200 to 1200 m, mountain forest dominated by deciduous trees, such as *Quercus boissieri* and *Q. libani*, from 1300 to 1700 m. Many perennial grasses and other herbaceous plants are among the companions. The vegetation here is under strong pressure from grazing by domestic animals and cutting of lignified plants for fuel. At elevations higher than 1800 m the spiny cushion plants dominate (cf. category 9).

Rocky areas close to the Druze villages at the foot of Mt. Hermon are used as pasture for sheep and goats. Small areas in the valleys near these villages are planted mainly with apples that are famous throughout the country for their high quality.

4.   Open forests of *Quercus ithaburensis*

Tree canopies are far away from each other due to the large distance which separates oak trees in these woodlands. *Q. ithaburensis* dominates in habitats drier than those where *Q. calliprinos* is dominant. A rather common feature of the vegetation of this category is seen in the vicinity of Tivon in the Lower Galilee. The Tabor oak prevails on most slopes of hard Eocene chalk with dark Rendzina soil, whereas *Q. calliprinos* is the dominant on north-facing slopes that get lower solar radiation, and hence are moister and cooler than other slopes. The Tabor oak is accompanied by plenty of herbaceous plants and the few semi-shrubs found in this community are of *Majorana syriaca* and not *Sarcopoterium spinosum*, which is the common companion of *Q. calliprinos* (Aloni and Orshan 1972: 209). Stony and rocky slopes are used as pastures for cows. Deep soils of the valleys among the hills are cultivated with a high diversity of cereals, cotton, sunflowers and other such crops.

The Tabor oak was dominant in woodlands that developed on the red sandy-loam soil known as Hamra. The parent material of this soil is the coastal sand dunes that were enriched by airborne silt and clay during a long pedogenetic history. The clay layer of the soil is typically rich in tree roots. The companions are mostly herbaceous, some of them are rather rare. However, due to the successful development of irrigated citrus orchards on this soil, most of its area is cultivated at present.

Large areas of the Tabor oak woodland form an altitudinal belt in the Golan below that of *Q. calliprinos* – between sea level and ca. 500 m above sea level. In much of the area the trees are found emerging from piles of stones gathered in the Middle Bronze age. Herbaceous plants, such as wild wheat, barley, and oats, accompany the oaks and cause a high vulnerability to fire hazards. The tree seedlings are protected from fire among the stones collected by humans, and thus stone piles distribution patterns influence the woodland architecture. The few arboreal companions are *Pistacia atlantica* that occupies the same habitat as the oak, and *Ziziphus spina-christi* and *Ziziphus lotus* that grow in the once cultivated land, i.e., not on stone piles. Much of the area of this category in the Golan functions presently as pasture, supporting large herds of cows. Deep soil in the plateaux areas of this category are used for cultivation of cereals, cotton and occasionally for vegetables and fruit trees.

The slopes of northeastern Galilee to the rift valley are populated with an opened woodland that resembles the latter type of Tabor oak woodland but is dominated by

Pistacia atlantica and *Amygdalus korschinskii*, with grasslands dominated by wild wheat, barley, and oats. This community develops in areas drier than those dominated by the Tabor oak.

5. Open forests of *Ceratonia siliqua* and *Pistacia lentiscus*

This type of vegetation occupies Terra Rossa soils at the lower elevations of the main mountain ranges, below 300 m and above sea level. It is more drought and heat resistant than the communities dominated by *Quercus calliprinos* and has a similar position in the aridity sequence of communities as those dominated by the Tabor oak. The typical companions change according to soil type and climatic conditions. One of the important companions in rocky situations at Mt. Carmel is the wild olive – *Olea europaea* var. *sylvestris* – which looks similar to the cultivar but has much smaller fruits (see Plate 2). The finding of olive stones (seeds) in the prehistoric site (Pottery Neolithic, E. Galili, personal communication) in the Mediterranean sea near Mt. Carmel, leads us to thoughts about domestication and use of wild plants thousands of years ago (Zohary and Spigel-Roy 1975: 319). Wild olives seem to have been included in the epipalaeolithic diet as discovered by Kislev et al. (1992: 161). The important companion in the southern Shefela is *Rhamnus lycioides* which replaces the two dominants in even drier sites. Land-use in this area is rather similar to that of category 1, but with larger areas of cultivated deep soil in the wider valleys.

The carob-pistachio woodlands which have developed on calcareous sandstone (Kurkar) close to the Mediterranean coast are mosaics of small patches of the intact community covered by maritime sand. The depth of sand, its texture and age greatly influence the composition of the vegetation developing there through soil nutrient and moisture regime (Kutiel et al. 1979/80: 20; Danin and Yaalon 1982: 101). It is possible to display in this area some 10 stages of vegetation changes – from the pure wind blown sand through gradual establishment of plants that are adapted to mobile sand, poor soil to dark soil rich in humus and clays – covered by the woodland that reoccupies the area.

6. *Ziziphus lotus* with herbaceous vegetation

The relatively dry and warm area of basalt hills in the southeastern Galilee is still populated with a grassland dominated by wild wheat, barley and oats. The drier and warmer environment here is evidenced by dominance of *Stipa capensis* in dry microsites or over large areas in relatively dry years. An even better indicator is the lignified dominant – *Ziziphus lotus*. Taller trees that grow in moister areas with this *Ziziphus*, and mentioned above, do not grow here. Prominent phenomena in this area are the nests of harvester ants. They can be detected from afar by

Plate 2 *Olea Europaea* — the wild progenitor of the cultivated olive, in rock crevices, upper Galilee (photograph: A. Danin)

the 'crowns' of the milky thistles (*Silybum marianum*) which are several times taller than the plants of the grassland around them (Danin and Yom-Tov 1990: 209). The oily body, situated below the pappus base at the tip of the achene of this thistle, functions as an ant-attractant. After removing the oily body inside the nest, the ants discharge the large intact achenes with their hard and smooth surface, into the refuse zone around their nest. Here the thistle enjoys a high level of nutrients and aerated soil rich in organic matter, and hence overtops the possible competitors that grow in the grassland. Being a successful competitor for soils rich in nutrients makes the thistle pre-adapted to the ruderal habitat that was existing, to a small extent, before the expansion of humans. The thistle is rather successful on marking stations of male gazelles (these are heaps of their droppings), in the shade of trees where the droppings of animals that use the shade to escape from high solar radiation accumulate, and in similar habitats (Danin and Yom-Tov 1990: 209). Most authors of floras covering the Mediterranean region regard this plant, and several others that are associated with nests of harvester ants, as ruderals or synanthropic (Danin 1989: 449).

Much of the area of this category functions presently as pasture, supporting large herds of cows. Deep soil in the plateaux areas of this category are used for the cultivation of cereals and cotton.

7.   Savannoid Mediterranean vegetation

The warm stony-rocky slopes in the rift valley below sea level are dominated by *Ziziphus spina-christi* and grassland of wild wheat, barley and oats; most of the deep alluvial soils in this area are cultivated under irrigation at present. *Z. spina-christi* dominates in savannas in Africa where it is accompanied by Sudanian perennial grasses. The fruits of this tree are palatable, and fall when ripe. The dry fruits are eaten in Israel by gazelles and ibexes that excrete the hard-coated seeds far away from the mother plant. The environmental conditions here enable the growth of the tree, but its companions are the Mediterranean grassland plants. Therefore, the term used here is 'savanna-like' (savannoid) vegetation. The activity of ants and gazelles discussed above can be seen here as well.

The relatively high winter temperatures in the rift valley, which enable the successful growth and even dominance of the thermophilous *Ziziphus* trees, enable the cultivation of several summer vegetables, such as tomatoes and eggplants, in winter. Intensive irrigated agriculture is typical for much of this area along the Jordan Valley.

Acacia albida, a relatively rare Sudanian tree in Israel, forms patches of savannoid vegetation in a few places in the Beth-Shean, Esdraelon, HaElla Valleys, and Pleshet. The thick coated fruits, that are not open when ripe, are rare in Israel and the few formed on a few trees in each population contain only 1–2 seeds. It is suggested that the tree arrived in Israel a few million years ago from Africa and established itself in a few isolated places where it propagates mostly vegetatively at present (Halevy 1971: 52).

8.   Semi-steppe batha

The communities dominated by semi-shrubs at the boundary of the Mediterranean zone, where mean annual rainfall is 300–400 mm, are regarded as semi-steppe bathas. There are several communities dominated by Mediterranean plants such as *Sarcopoterium spinosum* that dominates bathas in more mesic parts of the country (category 1 in this account). Others, such as *Artemisia sieberi*, dominate steppe areas in the Negev, Sinai, Jordan, and eastwards to Afghanistan. Many plants that play an important role in the seral communities in fallow fields at the center of the Mediterranean region grow here in their primary habitats, where no disturbance is needed to enable their growth. *Sarcopoterium spinosum*, which becomes etiolant and dies in the shade of trees and shrubs in the

Plate 3   Semi-steppe batha dominated by *Sarcopoterium Spinosum* and *Thylaea Hirsuta*

course of plant succession in category 1 (see above), has no such competitors here. There are many more examples of such plants.

Stony and rocky slopes in this unit are either afforested or used as pastures for sheep and goats. The deep soil in the valleys is used for cereal cultivation.

9.   Tragacanth vegetation of Mt. Hermon

The most prominent formation of vegetation developed on the windward slopes of the peaks (above 1900 m) of Mt. Hermon is dominated by shrubs that look like spiny cushions. This formation is also known as tragacanth vegetation, a name derived from a large group in the genus *Astragalus* – section *Tragacantha* (regarded at present as the independent genus *Astracantha* Podlech). Many species of this group and of the genus *Acantholimon* are components of the cushion-plants formation all over the Middle East. The spiny cushion seems to have some biological advantages that make it adapted to the harsh conditions of this habitat; these are: cold winter with high velocity winds, precipitation mainly as snow, dry summer, high pressure from grazing by domestic animals. Because of the short growth season and the harsh environment only very few annuals accompany the cushion plants.

There are other vegetation formations in the high altitudinal belt of Mt. Hermon. Wind velocity on the slopes that are in the wind-shadow of small local ridges or crests is rather low. Hence, snow accumulates there and covers the soil with a layer that may reach a depth of 10 m for a few months. Water drainage from the slopes of this area is through karstic systems and not through wadis, as in many parts of the country. On these slopes and depressions other types of vegetation are found.

Land use here was restricted in the past to grazing and cutting of lignified plants for pasture; at present, much of the area is protected by law, being part of a nature reserve.

Vegetation of the dry part of Israel

The two principal patterns of distribution of vegetation in the dry part of the country are related to wadis. Wherever the plants grow all over slopes and depressions the pattern is regarded as 'diffused' (mode diffus *sensu* Monod 1954: 35). In extremely dry deserts, where vegetation is restricted to wadis that receive additional water supply, the pattern is 'contracted' (mode contracte *sensu* Monod 1954: 35).

10. Steppe vegetation

Semi-shrubs grow in a diffused pattern in most of the area of the Negev Highlands and the Judean Desert with 80–250 mm mean annual rainfall. Edaphic conditions may influence the pattern of distribution because it is through the soil and rock that plants obtain their water and nutrients. Hard and fissured limestone and dolomite get much of the rainfall available to the semi-shrubs growing there because water infiltration is good and the soil is leached. Accumulated deep in the soil, this water is protected from direct evaporation by rocks and stones. The most common dominants are *Artemisia sieberi*, *Noaea mucronata*, *Helianthemum vesicarium*, *Thymelaea hirsuta*, and *Gymnocarpos decander*. The phytomass produced by annuals in the plant communities developing here is always rather small when compared with those of fine-grained and deep soils. The latter types hold much of their water close to the soil surface, thus losing much of it through direct evaporation. The minute quantities of salts (8 ppm) carried by clouds and later by rain from the Mediterranean sea remain in the soil and accumulate there (Yaalon 1963: 105). The soil may be too dry or too saline for the growth of annuals in regular or dry years. Nearly monospecific communities of semi-shrubs exist, each of them best adapted to the specific local saline conditions (Danin 1978). The most common dominants under these conditions are *Reaumuria hirtella*, *Reaumuria negevensis*, *Salsola damascena*, and *Bassia* (*Chenolea*) *arabica* on chalk and marl derived soils and *Anabasis syriaca* and *Hammada scoparia* on loess derived soils. However, in moist years there is a wealthy development of annuals, although in patches with high salinity there are mono-specific patches of salt-resistant annuals. Showy geophytes such as species of *Tulipa*, *Iris*, *Ixiolirion*, *Ranunculus*, and *Anemone* may bloom in high quantities in the steppes in moist years.

Sandy soils are leached efficiently by water that infiltrates to a depth that is protected from direct evaporation. The vegetation of these soils differs under dry and wet conditions from that of other soils (see category 13).

Outcrops of smooth-faced hard limestone support plants that may differ from those on the other soil types. The hard rocks do not absorb water and through runoff much water is concentrated in the few crevices and soil pockets of these rocks (Danin 1972: 437). The relatively

Plate 4 Steppe dominated by *Artemisia Sieberi* on slopes and *Hordeum Spontaneum* in the valley

high quantities of water available in this habitat enable these rocks to function as a refugium for plants of the Mediterranean region that existed in the area when the climate was moister (such as in the Neolithic or several times during the Pleistocene). Isolated populations of dozens of Mediterranean relicts are found in this habitat in the Negev and the Judean Desert. The semi-shrub *Sarcopoterium spinosum*, and the geophytes *Narcissus tazetta*, and *Sternbergia clusiana* are representative examples of this phenomenon. Several species that were discovered as new to science and many species that were not collected before in the steppe areas of the Middle East are confined to this habitat.

Land use in this area can be dealt with in two different modes of management. The traditional Bedouin agriculture totally depends on rainfall. Raising of goats and sheep is the traditionally typical way of life in this area since biblical times. The Hebrew word confined to this area is Midbar – the grammatical root of which is derived from pastoral life. Much of the Judean Desert belongs to this category. In this area the prophet Jeremiah lived; much of his prophecy was influenced by the shepherd's life in the Judean Desert. Small areas of cereals are cultivated in regular and rainy years. Barley is the main crop in most areas and years. Wheat is cultivated in moist years and habitats with relatively high amounts of available water. The Jewish agriculture depends much on irrigation. Kibbutz Sede Boqer used the ways of water harvesting of the ancient agricultures discovered in the Negev (Evenari et al. 1971). They built up a dam to store the water that floods in local wadis after rainstorms. They irrigate their fruit trees with this water, thus decreasing the need for water to be pumped from the northern part of the country.

11. Steppes with trees of *Pistacia atlantica*

Most of the area of this category is covered by steppes dominated by *Artemisia sieberi* and accompanied by the showy semi-shrub *Helianthemum vesicarium* which has here its highest diversity of flower color in all its populations of Israel. Together with tulips and other showy geophytes, the blooming plants in a rainy year make the steppe of the Central Negev Highlands look like an unbelievably beautiful garden. This category differs from the previous category by the presence of some 1400 adult trees, most of which are of *Pistacia atlantica*, and some are of *Amygdalus ramonensis* or *Rhamnus disperma* (Danin and Orshan 1970: 115). These trees are found in affinity to outcrops of smooth-faced rocks. The high yields of runoff water from these rocks to their crevices enable successful germination and the establishment of seedlings, even out of wadis. In places with large enough outcrops of limestone the seedlings may develop into trees; some are several hundreds of years old. Wadis with such outcrops in their catchment area support large trees. Rare relicts, such as the vines of the Mediterranean maquis *Prasium majus* and *Ephedra foemina*, and endemic plants, such as *Origanum ramonensis* and *Ferula negevensis*, occur in these rocks too.

Apart from the remnants of ancient agriculture found in the wadis this area is protected from destructive land use by humans. Being close to the international border human activity is minimal here.

12. Desert vegetation

Shrubs and trees are confined in this category, including the southern and eastern Negev, to wadis. However, on the boundary of the category with the steppes the typical semi-shrubs *Anabasis articulata* and *Zygophyllum dumosum* grow in a diffused pattern. Chalk and marl outcrops are populated with the halophyte communities of *Suaeda asphaltica*, *Salsola tetrandra*, and *Hammada negevensis*. The nearly monospecific communities of semi-shrub halophytes are accompanied by a diverse assemblage of herbaceous plants that grow on the leached soil.

Areas with a low amount of available water are populated with contracted vegetation. At the head of wadis, annual plants grow; one of the interesting plants of this community is *Anastatica hierochuntica* – the famous Rose of Jericho. This plant is a lignified annual, the seeds of which are not dispersed when becoming ripe unless there is an event of strong rain that opens the entire plant and splashes the seeds. This mechanism is regarded as a strategy that enables water gauging by the mother plant before dispersing the seeds. The religious beliefs associated with this plant are related to its spread after being dead for even dozens of years. A lower section of the wadi gets higher quantities of water and supports small and short living semi-shrubs such as *Pulicaria incisa*; further down, larger semi-shrubs such as *Anabasis articulata* grow. A section dominated by shrubs such as *Retama raetam* prevails further down the wadi system. In the lowest section of the wadi system, trees – mostly acacias or tamarisks – may be found. The nature of plant com-

munities and the sequence of their occurrence along the wadis are in close affinity to rock and soil types, which greatly influence the moisture, salinity, and nutrient regime in the wadi systems (Lipkin 1971). There are different plant communities in wadis on flint pebbles, flint rocks, limestone outcrops, magmatic rocks, or marl. An example of the diversity of plant communities in such an area near Hazeva is discussed by Rudich and Danin (1978: 160).

Land use in this category is minimal. Apart from small areas irrigated near the few settlements and irrigated ornamental gardens in the urban areas, there is not much influence here. Phytomass production is low and its consistency is such that pastoral life cannot depend on most of this area.

13. Sand vegetation

Sand dunes or sand fields occur in Israel on the Mediterranean coastal plain, in the Western Negev as a continuation of Northern Sinai sands, a few valleys of the Northern Negev, and in the Arava Valley. In each of these areas there is a different climatic regime, sand texture is different, and hence the vegetation and processes of its development differ.

Sands carried by the Nile River from Africa to the Mediterranean are transported by currents in the sea and deposited on the coast. When dried, the sand is transported inland by the common westerly winds. Devoid of fine-grained particles the plant-less sands become populated by the perennial grass *Ammophila arenaria*. Its seedlings are capable of growing above the mobile sand that covers them. In time, when growing bigger, this grass decreases sand mobility in its close vicinity and leads to the formation of phytogenic mounds below it. Airborne fine-grained material is incorporated into the sand near the plants, thus leading to amelioration of its moisture regime. *Artemisia monosperma* is the dominant on stable sand that, in its first few years, may cause the formation of mounds. In the course of time new *Artemisia* plants establish themselves among the mounds and the area becomes flat. Dust accumulation becomes efficient once the vegetation covers more than 30 per cent of an area. The moisture regime of the soil becomes better as additional quantities of dust and humus accumulate at upper soil layers. The response of vegetation is an increase in species diversity and phytomass production. At a certain stage the maquis plants succeed in growing in the shade of the *Retama raetam* shrubs and, in the course of time, replace them. When much of the area is covered by shrubs of *Pistacia lentiscus* and *Calicotome villosa*, the trees of *Ceratonia siliqua* develop in their shade on a humus-rich soil. In the southern coastal plain the succession does not go much beyond the *Artemisia monosperma* with *Retama raetam* stage.

Mobile sands in the Western Negev are dominated by the grass *Stipagrostis scoparia* that grows above the sand that covers the plant and constitutes phytogenic mounds. The sand has a finer texture than the coastal sands and, therefore, has a relatively good moisture regime. Airborne silt and clay become incorporated into the upper soil layers that soon become populated by filamentous cyanobacteria (Danin et al. 1989: 55). Being drought resistant, these blue-green algae flourish in the fine-grained upper layers of the sand and bind the soil grains, thus decreasing their mobility. Stable sand supports communities of *Artemisia monosperma* and desert plants such as *Noaea mucronata* and *Panicum turgidum*. The north to south gradient in the Haluza sands displays an increasing proportion of mobile sands that are organized as longitudinal dunes, whereas large parts of the northern sands area are immobile sand fields covered by the microphytic crust. In Sinai, west of the border, overgrazing, cutting of lignified plants and destruction of the microphytic crust by continuous trampling has led to reworking of the sand and to the light color of this area in the satellite image (see Plate 5). Before 1948, when there was no difference in management between the two sides of the Israeli-Egyptian border, no such boundary could be observed in aerial photographs (Noy-Meir and Seligman (1979: 113).

The patch of sandy areas in the eastern Negev, some 20 km west of the Dead Sea Valley, is in three valleys that are filled with Neogene sandstone. The typical dominant of these sand fields is *Anabasis articulata*. The soil is sandy loess in most of the Yeroham-Dimona valley, and harbours the spectacular reserve of *Iris petrana* which grows also in the eastern Rotem-Yamin plain in much smaller quantities. In this valley the soil is more sandy, *Calligonum comosum* is dominant in places where the depth of sand above the solid sandstone or siltstone is 1–5 m; *Anabasis articulata* is dominant in places where the depth of sand above the solid rock is 10–100 cm; and lignified annual *Anastatica hierochuntica* develops on outcrops of the solid rocks where no semi-shrubs grow.

The sands of the Arava Valley are derived from the weathering of Nubian Sandstones in Edom. The relatively high water table in the Arava enables the successful development of *Haloxylon persicum* in sites where sand is sufficiently deep. Most stands of this plant in Israel became intensively irrigated agricultural areas. This soil is easy to leach and was found to be good for growing, in winter, crops that are regarded as summer crops in other parts of the country. Sand mobility is high in a few places but most of the sandy areas are stable. The common semi-shrubs growing in the sandy areas are *Hammada salicornica* and *Salsola cyclophylla*. In wadis crossing the sandy areas there are large *Haloxylon* plants as well as occasional *Tamarix aphylla* trees covered by sand mounds that may reach a height of 5 m or even more.

Intensive irrigated agriculture is practiced in many settlements, both in the desert and non-desert areas.

Plate 5 Satellite image of SW Israel and NE Sinai, highlighting overgrazing in the light areas (numbers 1, 3–6)

14. Oases with sudanian trees

Three main oases were marked in the vegetation map (Figure 3) – En Gedi is the southern most, Jericho (Plate 6) and Auja are further north. The main features of the environment in these patches are the high temperatures typical of the rift valley and the high quantities of fresh water available throughout the year. Most springs in the dry part of Israel, that are not marked on the map, may be recognized from afar by the presence of date palms (*Phoenix dactylifera*) that are regarded as part of the typical flora of this habitat (Danin 1983). Many more tree species typical of the Sudanian savannas are found in these oases. Such are: *Acacia raddiana, Acacia tortilis, Calotropis procera, Moringa peregrina, Balanites aegyptiaca* and *Ziziphus spina-christi*. The long and continuous existence of these fresh water springs, and the additional springs that existed along the rift valley in the past, may have helped the development of this northern extension of many species which have their main area of distribution further south of here.

Plate 6   Oblique satellite image of Jericho oasis area (prepared by J. Hall)

Plate 7   Desert savannoid vegetation. *Acacia Tortilis* in the Arava valley near Hazeva. Tree density indicates high water table

Relatively large date groves are planted in the vicinity of the fresh water springs or on sites with a high water table in this category. The high winter temperatures and the scarcity of events of low temperature ensure the regular growth of summer vegetables in these areas in winter. This kind of land use typifies the area of the following category as well.

15.   Desert savannoid vegetation

Savannoid vegetation where *Acacia* trees are accompanied by desert semi-shrubs is the main feature of large parts of the Arava and the Dead Sea Valleys. The upper soil layers support in wadis the typical desert vegetation (as described in category 12) with *Anabasis articulata*, *Hammada salicornica*, *Zygophyllum dumosum*, *Retama raetam*, and *Lycium shawii* as the principal contributors. *Acacia gerrardii* subsp. *negevensis* is confined to the areas that are at a relatively high elevation, such as the upper tributaries of Nahal Paran. *Acacia raddiana*, which is less resistant to low temperatures, is the dominant at lower elevations, and *Acacia tortilis*, which has the highest demands for high temperatures, grows in the southern Arava or below sea level in the northern Arava and Dead Sea Valley (Halevy and Orshan 1972: 120) (see Plate 7). The density and size of trees depends much on the water regime of the specific wadi and that of the deeper soil layers. Tree density is relatively high in the vicinity of Hazeva, En Yahav, and Yotvata where there is a high water table and a few springs flow from geological faults (such as En Hazeva, En Tamid, En Mashak, and En Yahav). Many *Acacia* trees are much larger than expected from the ca. 50 mm of mean annual rainfall that fall on this area. In a few places there are species such as *Nitraria retusa* and *Alhagi graecorum* which are indicators of a high water table. In other places such as the water divide of the Arava, near Beer Menuha, there are only a few small *Acacia raddiana* trees in the entire area that supports only a few semi-shrubs in the few wadis.

16.   Swamps and reed thickets

The large swamp areas with diverse vegetation that existed in the country at the beginning of the century have been drained and only small nature reserves, such as that of the Hula Lake, remain. Fresh water springs still flow and a small number of species that produce high quantities of phytomass are rather prominent throughout the country. The most common indicators for the flowing water are *Phragmites australis*, *Arundo donax*, *Arundo plinii*, and *Typha domingensis*. Large areas of swamps in the Hula Valley supported *Cyperus papyrus* which had reached here its northernmost station. Several rivers of the Coastal Plain that supported riparian vegetation in the past have now become sewage canals and their polluted water has destroyed most of the rivers' vegetation that existed in the past.

17.   Wet salines

Wet salty soils occur in places where springs of salty water rise or in sites where the water table is close to the surface and the evaporating water leaves salt in the upper soil layers (Danin 1981: 269). In arid regions, a salt crust may be formed at the soil surface and plants may grow only in small wadis where leaching takes place. Most plants growing in the desert salt marshes are perennials that establish themselves in the rare events of leaching. The typical plants of desert salty soils are *Suaeda monoica*, *Suaeda fruticosa*, *Suaeda vermiculata*, *Nitraria retusa*, *Seidlitzia rosmarinus*, and a few species of *Tamarix*.

Small areas of wet salines occur along the Mediterranean coast mainly near Akko, where the geological structure enables the penetration of salty water inland and its mixing with fresh underground water. The vegetation here is more diverse than in the desert areas and contains also many annual species in microhabitats that are better leached than in the desert.

18. Synanthropic vegetation

There are records of human activity in the Middle East starting hundreds of thousands of years ago. Humans had gathered fruits and plants as many animals do today. Unlike today, these activities did not interfere and did not change the vegetation and the natural conditions. The lists of plants found in the excavations of archaeological and prehistoric sites do not differ much from those of the present day flora of Israel. There is no clear evidence supporting the idea (as brought by Zohary 1983: 287) that the present flora of Israel is composed of plants which escaped the intensive human activities of the last millennia. This is not to say that human activity has had no impact on the vegetation – such an impact was discussed above in terms of the sandy areas of the western Negev. Dozens of species that belong to the flora of remote countries succeed in growing in habitats made by humans at present. The degree of affinity to human-made habitats (synanthropy, cf. Danin 1991a: 95) in the flora of several habitats in Israel can be summarized as follows:

1. Overgrazing in areas such as the Judean Desert, Negev Highlands, and the Galilee do not open niches for the true synanthropic plants that develop in urban areas at present. The flora of this area has experienced the stress of grazing by herbivores, such as ibex, gazelle, and such like in evolutionary times. Thus it seems that grazing is not a factor that may enable the penetration of invader colonizing species from remote countries.
2. Fire is also one of the natural evolutionary factors leading to the development of plants that belong to the natural flora of an area. Here the number of synanthropic invader species is relatively small.
3. Roadsides at present, in the way they are constructed and managed, function as an important habitat for invaders. The spraying of roadsides with herbicides that control the development of winter annuals, that are typical to Israel's mesic part, leave an opened niche for the establishment of plants that germinate in late winter when the herbicides have already became inactive. Several adventive species from the genera *Sorghum*, *Panicum*, *Conyza*, *Amaranthus*, and *Xanthium* belong to this group (Danin 1991b: 392).

Category 18 is further divided into three subcategories according to the remnants of trees found in the intensively cultivated areas: in 18a it is trees of *Quercus ithaburensis*, in 18b the tree is *Ziziphus spina-christi*, and in 18c it is *Acacia raddiana* and *Ziziphus spina-christi* (Danin 1988: 129).

Concluding remarks

This then is the present day vegetation pattern of the southern Levant. For human subsistence activities in the region, the Mediterranean region provided lush herbaceous vegetation which promoted raising herds of domesticated herbivores. Annual grasses with large seeds such as wheat, adapted to local environmental conditions, were domesticated and function at present as one of the basic sources of food for humankind. Pulses were domesticated too from wild species growing at present in this area. Olives, the fruits of which have been used since prehistoric times, still grow as an important component in the maquis covering the mountainous parts of Israel. Desert and steppe areas of the country did not provide much subsistence for human activity beyond the basis for extensive pastoral life in these areas. Fresh water springs at present support wild date palms, as they probably did in the past. Such populations could have been the primary populations used for the domestication of dates.

The most effective environmental factors influencing the boundaries and the extent of the vegetation zones are the climatic ones. While rainfall patterns may have shifted these vegetation zones some dozens of kilometers in the east–west direction in the rainshadow of the central mountain range of the country, they shifted even hundreds of kilometers in the north–south direction towards Sinai. However, the general vegetation make-up is believed to have stayed about the same as it is today.

Although human activity imposed a strong pressure on plant life as human populations grew, the flora of the country has remained about the same throughout history, except for changes in the proportions of plant populations. The proportions of plants sensitive to a certain kind of pressure decreased whereas the proportions of resistant plants increased. Thus, very few plant species are known to have become extinct during the Holocene, even if woodlands gave place to herbaceous vegetation in certain places or vice versa.

HUMAN USE OF PLANTS

Plants offer much to the people who obtained the know-how of their usage. There are edible plants such as those which helped communities of gatherers to sustain their living in all parts of Israel. From this group there are plants with edible roots, leaves, stems, fruits and seeds. On the other hand there are poisonous plants that one should be aware of. Some of these plants can be used to hunt animals or to cure various illnesses and thus may function as medicinal plants. Plants have other qualities that are very useful to humans, for example, there are plants that supply the raw materials for building shelters, mattresses, ropes, for starting fires, and for feeding fires, and plant indicators for drinking water, for soil types, and animal nesting places (Danin 1983).

One of the most interesting inventions of human beings — found on all continents, and occurring rather early in our evolution — is the making of ropes and strings from wild plants. The wealth of findings of this kind in caves in Nahal Heimar from the Neolithic period are an example of proof of the long history of this activity. I was taught how to make ropes by Mr. N. HaReuveni, who had learnt it from a Bedouin in the Negev. Using the same method

and trees have thin fibers that can be used after a short treatment. Such are *Thymelaea hirsuta* (one of the best sources for fibers to make rope of any diameter), *Colutea istria*, and *Acacia* species.

In order to make a rope, take five long date palm leaflets and split them into fine fibers; twist the fibers and keep twisting them, always in the same direction (Plate 1.1a). After sufficient twisting, the bundle of fibers will bend and the two parts will start winding around each other (Plate 1.1b). The point of bending should be held firm, either by another person or by stepping on it (Plate 1.1c). Continue twisting the fibers in the same direction at the same time, so that the two bunches

Plate 1.1 Making a plant fiber rope. (a) Twisting palm leaflet fibers (b) The bundle of fibers bends and the two parts start winding around each other (c) Further twisting of the fibers while the rope is held firm (d) Adding new fibers to lengthen the rope

in Central America I could compete with a local Amer-Indian on the speed of preparing a rope, using the same method, from the bark of local trees. The qualities of a plant that are necessary for it to serve as a source of raw material for a rope are that it will have long, thin, strong (not easy to tear), and twistable parts, such as stems, leaves or bark. Cattail (*Typha*), Papyrus (*Cyperus papyrus*) and other *Cyperus* species, *Juncus* spp., most palm species, and *Agave* (introduced from America) have long fibrous stems or leaves that can be split into thin fibers. The bark of a few shrubs

of fibers are wound around each other. Add a small quantity of more fibers as soon as the two parts become shorter than 15 cm. The additional fibers are folded in a 'V' shape, and each arm is added to one part of the rope (Plate 1.1d). The two parts are tied together when the rope is the desired length. There is a quicker method, by which the fibers are twisted while sliding one hand against the other. In this way, an expert can prepare one meter of rope within two minutes. However, it is difficult to explain the method in words.

PLANT INDICATORS FOR POTABLE WATER

The availability of water is critical for human survival in most parts of Israel and the neighboring lands. Plants which prefer or require a high water table, or even running water, may serve as good indicators for the kind of water they may use. Thus, one can distinguish between plants indicating fresh water, slightly saline, or saline water. In fact many of the plants growing in saline substrata indicate a rather broad range of salinity and not a narrow range as do fresh water plants. Fresh water plants are: *Typha* spp., *Arundo* spp. *Cyperus* spp., *Mentha* spp., *Saccharum* spp., *Platanus orientalis, Rubus sanguineus*, and *Salix* spp. Fresh to slightly saline water is indicated by the presence of *Phoenix dactylifera, Polpulus euphratica, Phragmites australis, Polypogon monspeliensis*. The following plants grow in fresh to saline water: *Juncus* spp., *Tamarix* spp., *Alhagi graecorum, Imperata cylindrica, Nitraria retusa*. Saline water is found in the places where the following species grow: *Arthrocnemum macrostachyum, Sarcocornia fruticosa, Sarcocornia perennis, Suaeda monoica, Halocnemum strobilaceum, Zygophyllum album, Limonium angustifolium*.

Springs may be located from a distance as green patches in landscapes that are poor in vegetation, for example springs in the extreme desert areas of the Arava Valley (En Tamid, En Rachel, En Hazeva) or the Negev Highlands (En Avdat, En Aqev, En Ziq). Green patches of springs are very prominent on the steep slopes of the Golan, above En Gev and Tel Katzir, and in other places in the northern part of the country.

Springs in extreme desert areas may also be located as one walks along dry sections of a wadi that has a fresh water spring at its upper course. Stems or leaves, parted from the plants that grow near the water and carried away by the streams, may be deposited on plants or rocks downstream. Identifying these plants may help in finding drinking water upstream.

Cisterns used to collect water from a large catchment area may be tended by people living in the area and cleaned periodically of any plants that grow near by. Abandoned cisterns, on the other hand, may function as a habitat for the establishment and growth of wind-dispersed trees that prefer wet habitats. Such are the *Tamarix nilotica* trees that spread millions of minute seeds, some of which may fall on wet soil in or near a cistern. Many of the ancient cisterns in the Negev Highlands may be identified from a distance by the tamarisk trees growing there, far from a wadi which is the common habitat for tamarisks.

4

THE CHANGING LANDSCAPE

Paul Goldberg

Introduction

The Holy Land possesses a rich history of human occupation which extends over hundreds of thousands of years during the Quaternary. This is an extensive history, and over this time span peoples clearly interacted with their natural environment and surroundings. This is particularly true of the geological environment and former landscapes, which were quite dynamic during this period, and served as the local and regional substrate over which former human activities took place.

In order to fully appreciate changes in human development and behavior – including the hows and whys – it is essential to be aware of the types of landscapes that existed in this area and how they have changed. This chapter attempts to characterize the variety and development of Quaternary landscapes in Israel, and to depict how they may be interpreted in terms of large-scale paleoenvironmental changes. It will also try to show that landscape changes can have the effect of influencing the preservation, occurrence and distribution of archaeological and prehistoric sites in the region, and their temporal continuity. This in turn places constraints on our understanding and interpretation of the archaeological record. By developing an awareness of the changing landscape, the archaeological record can be better understood.

Present geographical setting

Since this topic is extensively covered in Chapter 3, only a brief overview will be presented here.

Israel is located between the subhumid Mediterranean zone in the north and the arid and semi-arid area of the Negev Desert in the south. The entire region is characterized by relatively short cool, rainy winters and long, hot summers. Most precipitation falls between mid-November and mid-March, and varies from up to ca. 1000 mm in the Galilee and Golan Heights in the north, to less than 50 mm in the southern Negev. Temperatures show local variations, with the coolest mean annual temperatures in the mountainous areas of the Galilee and Golan in the north and Judean Mountains in the center, and the Central Negev Plateau in the Negev; the warmest temperatures are in the Jordan Valley and Arava which are parts of the Syrian-African Rift (Atlas of Israel 1970).

Physiographically, the area is constrained on the west by the Mediterranean and on the east by the rift valley, which is distinguished by the presence of the Kinneret (Sea of Galilee), the Dead Sea and the Jordan River (Figure 1). From west to east one encounters successively the coastal plain which ranges from 0 to ca. 150 m asl (above sea level), the low foothills of the Shefela rising up to ca. 400 m, and the central mountainous area of Judea and Samaria that reaches up to ca. 800 m (Orni and Efrat 1971). Other upland regions are found in the Galilee, the Golan, and the Central Negev Highlands. General lowland areas are found in the Coastal Plain and the Western Negev region.

Soil types reflect climatic variations, and localized effects of topography and bedrock. The effects of climate are particularly important and striking (Table 1). Soils in the semi-arid and arid areas of the Negev are characterized by less leaching, and greater accumulation of soluble salts and carbonates. In addition, soils from the northern and western Negev are strongly affected by aeolian inputs of silt and clay originating from the south and west. Hence, in moderate hilly areas in the center and north, one finds noncalcic *terra rossa* soils on calcareous parent material and brown Mediterranean soils on basalts; on comparable parent materials in the arid south, one finds shallow and calcareous lithosols and arid brown soils (Dan 1988). In low plateaus and plains in the north, vertisols, red sandy loams (locally called *hamra*), and dark brown soils occur, grading to loessial arid brown, serozem soils toward the south.

Former landscapes and their association with archaeological sites

In this section various aspects of former landscapes and palaeoenvironments in Israel will be described, concentrating on those that are associated with major archaeological and prehistoric sites. (In this paper I will use the term 'archaeology' in a broad sense to include both prehistory and archaeology from historical periods.) Since many papers in this volume are concerned with specific archaeological periods (e.g., Lower, Middle and Upper Paleolithic Periods), this site information will be presented for each geological environment. This is in preference to describing, for example, individual Mousterian sites from

Plate 1 Overview of the 1968 excavations at Tabun Cave, Mt. Carmel, Israel (photograph: © Paul Goldberg)

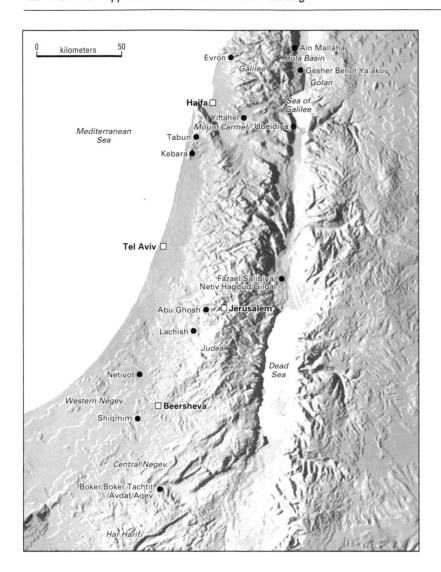

Figure 1   General map of the area showing principal locations and areas mentioned in the text

all over the country from various environments, which is both difficult to comprehend and dreary.

Lacustrine environments

Lacustrine deposits and environments are limited primarily to the area of the rift valley, which has served as a locus of geological deposition and archaeological settlement throughout the course of the Quaternary, and exhibits a wide variety of temporally diverse lacustrine and fluvial sediments. Here a number of relatively large lakes existed sporadically throughout the Quaternary, continuing to today with the presence of the Dead Sea and Kinneret. Smaller, more ephemeral lakes can be found in the Western Negev, extending into Northern Sinai.

Jordan Valley

The earliest lacustrine deposits in the Jordan Valley known

to occur in association with archaeological material is that from the 'Ubeidiya Formation. These sediments are best exposed at the site of 'Ubeidiya south of the modern Kinneret (see Figure 1) (Tchernov 1987; Bar-Yosef 1989a; Bar-Yosef and Tchernov 1972; Bar-Yosef and Goren-Inbar 1993). In all, there are about 190 meters of alternating limnic and fluviatile members (Picard 1965; Picard and Baida 1966).

At 'Ubeidiya, the lacustrine units are composed of soft chalks, marls, oolitic limestone, and laminated clay, whereas the fluviatile units consist of conglomerates, sands, silts, clays and interbedded fresh-water chalks (Plate 2). Although in total, four distinct lacustrine and fluvial units were recognized (Li, Fi, Lu, Fu), there are noticeable lateral lithological variations throughout the formation. These indicate that in the area of the prehistoric site, deposition was associated with fluviatile deltaic and lake margin environments in an expanding and contracting lake. The

Table 1 Major soil types in Israel and their relation to climate and topography (modified from Dan 1988)

TOPOGRAPHY	Substrate	CLIMATE					
		Humid	Subhumid	Semi-arid	Midly arid	Arid	Extremely arid
Plains, plateaus and undulating areas	Gravel or stones with fine material		Stony dark Brown soils		Stony light Brown soils	Stony Serozems	Regs
	Sand	Hamra		Quartzic dark Brown soils	Quartzic light Brown soils	Sand dunes and Sandy Regosols	
	Silt (loess and alluvial)			Grumic dark Brown soils	Loessial light Brown soils	Loessial Serozems	Alluvial soils
	Clay (aeolian and alluvial)		Grumusols	Grumic dark Brown soils	Natric Grumusols		
	Basalt	Basaltic Brown Mediterranean soils	Basaltic Grumusols		Natric Grumusols		
Mountains	Basalt	Basaltic Lithosols and Protogrumusols					
	Hard limestone and dolomite	Terra Rossa				Brown Lithosols	
	Chalk or marl	Pale Rendzina				Rendzinic desert Lithosols	Saline Calcareous desert Lithosols

final, fluviatile phase (Fu) appears to mark the final regression of the lake. Sometime after its deposition tectonic movement caused the folding, faulting and tilting of the 'Ubeidiya Formation.

Palaeontological and palaeobotanical data from the two lowermost units (the bulk of the archaeological material is limited to the lower fluviatile member, Fi), suggest a moist Mediterranean climate during accumulation of the 'Ubeidiya deposits (Bar-Yosef and Tchernov 1972; Picard 1965).

No direct dating of the 'Ubeidiya Formation is available. The most recent study of the biostratigraphic evidence of fossil mammals places it about 1.0 to 1.4 million years old (Tchernov 1987; Bar-Yosef 1989a). Preliminary paleomagnetic research had indicated that at least some of the deposits display reversed magnetic polarity, although these results have recently been questioned (D. Braun, personal communication, 1991).

Overall, then, during the time of the deposition of the 'Ubeidiya Formation there is evidence for a repeatedly fluctuating lake whose deposits were covered and interspersed with fluvial sediment, all of which was deposited under a Mediterranean climate, somewhat moister than today's.

Similar types of sediments crop out in the Hula Valley (the northern segment of the Jordan Valley). Here, in the Gesher Benot Ya'akov area about 35 km north of the site of 'Ubeidiya, steeply dipping beds of lacustrine chalks and marls occur with some peat (Mishmar HaYarden Formation of Horowitz 1979; see also Picard 1965). These are rich in molluscs and contain a few vertebrates and some flakes that are reminiscent of those at 'Ubeidiya, indicating that the same lake continued this far north.

These deposits at the Gesher Benot Ya'akov were covered by at least one flow of lava, and later faulted, a phenomenon which continues until recently (Goren-Inbar and Belitzky 1989). The area was then occupied by the Hula Lake, whose expansions and contractions reflected general climatic conditions: at pluvial times the lake expanded south, and during drier intervals receded northward toward the center of the lake in the Hula Basin. The shores of this lake, and the streams which fed into it, were frequently occupied (Stekelis 1960; Goren-Inbar and Belitzky 1989). The earliest lacustrine layers were rich in molluscs dominated by *Viviparus apamea*, and contained Acheulian artifactual assemblages that seem to share affinities with Africa (Goren-Inbar et al. 1992; Bar-Yosef 1987; Goren-Inbar 1990).

The dating of the Acheulian layers at Gesher Benot Ya'akov remains imprecise. The Benot Ya'akov Formation unconformably overlies the Yarda Basalt which has been recently dated to between 800,000 and 880,000 years

Plate 2 Steeply dipping sediments of the 'Ubeidiya Fm. These are primarily lacustrine chalks (Li member) on the left and become more fluvial to the right (Fi). The entire formation was tilted during a major tectonic phase that affected the entire central Jordan Valley

Plate 3 White marls of the White Cliff Member of the Lisan Fm. abut against bedrock in the area of Ein Boqeq, west of the present day Dead Sea. Above and left are remnants of strandlines left by the Lisan Lake as it retreated from its maximum of −180 m below sea level

before present (Goren-Inbar and Belitzky 1989). Thus, it is younger than 800,000 years old.

Two prominent and widespread lakes that were precursors to the modern Dead Sea are the Lisan Lake, and its predecessor, the Samra Lake. These lakes extended from the Sea of Galilee in the north to Hazeva, south of the present-day Dead Sea. Numerous exposures generally reveal a predominantly detrital Samra Formation, overlain by chemical sediments of the Lisan Formation. The latter, in turn, consists of two basic units, the Laminated Member and the younger White Cliff Member (for details see Horowitz 1979: 148; Begin et al. 1974, 1980; Kaufman et al. 1992). Of these, Lake Lisan and its deposits are of greater interest since it is more widespread, complete and associated directly or indirectly with archaeological sites. We note in passing, however, that recent [230]Th/U dates show the Samra Lake to have existed between at least 350,000 years ago to about 63,000 years ago, with fluctuations in lake level (Kaufman et al. 1992).

In the Lisan Formation, the Laminated Member (ca. 26 m thick), is comprised of alternating fine laminae of white chemical precipitates (aragonite, gypsum, calcite and halite) and darker clastic components (quartz, dolomite, clay minerals, and detrital calcite), whose proportions change laterally throughout the basin (Begin et al. 1985). In contrast, the upper White Cliff Member typically has a greater proportion of chemical sediments compared to detrital ones.

The Lisan Formation (Plate 3) has been dated by radiocarbon (Vogel and Waterbolk 1972) and Uranium-series methods (Kaufman 1971; Kaufman et al. 1992). Both have yielded roughly comparable results which show that the lake began 63,000 years ago with the deposition of the Laminated Member. At about 36,000 years ago deposition of the White Cliff member began, and lasted to

about 15,000 or 17,000 years ago. During this period, the lake probably attained its maximum extent at an altitude of −180 m asl (its present elevation is ca. −400m). Furthermore, a recent compilation of radiometric dates on algal stromatolites, oolites, and organic matter in the Lisan marls imply that fluctuations of lake level did take place over the last 30,000 years (Begin et al. 1985). As discussed below, the final stages of lacustrine deposition and retreat of the lake are more closely pinpointed by the distribution and stratigraphic position of prehistoric sites.

The study of both the diatoms and the sediments demonstrate an increase in salinity through time, although overall salinity was less than that of the present Dead Sea (Katz et al. 1977). This is interpreted by Begin et al. (1974) to represent a general trend toward climatic aridity, with greater precipitation/evaporation ratios at the base of the Lisan Formation, some 63,000 years ago.

Understandably, few prehistoric sites are found in direct association with the lacustrine Lisan sediments themselves. Most of the sites or isolated artifacts have been recovered in stream channels, with associated freshwater springs and lush vegetation.

In the area of the Lower Jordan Valley near Wadis Fazael and Salibiya (see Figure 1), several prehistoric sites are associated with sediments that are contemporary with the Lisan Formation (Bar-Yosef et al. 1974; Schuldenrein and Goldberg 1981). In Wadi Fazael, for example, the *in situ* Mousterian site of Fz I occurs at an altitude of ca. −185 m, within sediments that interfinger with the Lisan Formation. Further upstream and well above this elevation, Upper Paleolithic and Epipaleolithic sites occur within alluvium that interfingers or rests upon the Lisan Formation (Bar-Yosef et al. 1974; see below).

In Wadi Salibiya, ca. 7 km south of Wadi Fazael, Epipaleolithic sites (Kebaran and Geometric Kebaran – ca. 17,000–13,500 years ago) are generally found between −

180 m, and −193 m and −203 m (Hovers and Bar-Yosef 1987; Hovers 1989). The location of these sites appears to indicate that the Lake Lisan was roughly at this maximum elevation until the end of the Geometric Kebaran (ca. 13,000 years ago).

Natufian sites are situated at lower elevations in topographic lows developed on the Lisan marls as the lake retreated; the lowest are located at −215 and −230m in the Salibiya basin. Geomorphic and palynological evidence suggests that climatic conditions were wetter during the Geometric Kebaran and Early Natufian, and became increasingly arid during the late Natufian (Schuldenrein and Goldberg 1981; Leroi-Gourhan and Darmon 1987; Baruch and Bottema 1991). This drying period has been tentatively correlated with the 'Younger Dryas' (Goldberg and Bar-Yosef in press), a major climatic event marked by global cooling.

The rather rapid retreat of the Lisan lake left behind a generally flat valley bottom with a few small basins and freshwater pools or small lakes. This is also reflected by the faunal assemblages of the Early Neolithic sites of Gilgal and Netiv Hagdud in the Salibiya basin. There, numerous remains of ducks and the water mole, *Arvicola*, were uncovered in archaeological deposits dated to 10,100–9400 BP (Noy et al. 1980; Bar-Yosef 1987).

Negev lakes

Lacustrine sediments in the Negev are rare, tend to occur over areas of a few km², and are related more to factors of local drainage, such as in interdunal depressions in northern Sinai; these appear to be associated with Upper Paleolithic and Epipalcolithic sites (Goldberg 1977, 1986; Goldberg and Bar-Yosef 1982).

In the Nahal Sekher area of the Western Negev (Figure 2), migration of dunes led to the blockage of the stream channel, resulting in the formation of a playa (Yair and Enzel 1987). Radiocarbon dates of post-playa carbonates indicate that the playa formed before 11,000 BP (Magaritz 1986). This dating is bolstered by the occurrence of Epipaleolithic sites within the sands (see below and Goring-Morris and Goldberg 1990).

Streams and terraces

Fluvial landscapes of the early Pleistocene (roughly equivalent to the 'Preglacial Pleistocene' of Horowitz 1979) were different from today's although virtually none have been found in association with prehistoric sites. Sediments from this interval – consisting primarily of gravels – are most widespread and best known in the southern part of the country, although Plio-Pleistocene fluviatile sediments occur in the central Jordan Valley near 'Ubeidiya (e.g., Erq el Ahmar Fm; Tchernov 1975).

The HaMeshar Formation for example, consists of extensive conglomerates deposited in a complex fluvial system 'that indicates a westward drainage, which began at the foot of the Central Negev Highlands, where the HaMeshar Formation wedges out, and proceeded toward the Southern Negev Plains and Sinai' (Horowitz 1979: 116) (Figure 3). In other words, the drainage system led westward from the Transjordanian Plateau and flowed into the Mediterranean. Its exact age is not known but is considered early Pleistocene by Horowitz, since it rests upon Pliocene sediments and is eroded by streams which flowed into the present-day Dead Sea Basin. Patches of some early Pleistocene deposits are also known near Bethlehem (Bethlehem Conglomerate), in the coastal plain and in the area near Eilat (Horowitz 1979); these have not been dated.

Middle Pleistocene fluvial deposits are generally represented by more patchy occurrences. In the Jordan Valley, near Gesher Benot Ya'akov, for example, outcrops of the Hazor Gravels occur, which clearly underlie the Benot Ya'akov Formation but whose age is not known. Further south, near 'Ubeidiya, the Nahariyim Fm. crops out, consisting of interbedded gravels and reworked brown clay soils; it post-dates the 'Ubeidiya Fm. and is covered by the Yarmuk basalt, dated to about 700,000 years ago (Horowitz 1979). Some Acheulean artifacts are found associated with it.

During the end of the Middle Pleistocene and onset of the Late Pleistocene, fluvial landscapes begin to resemble those of today. This is also when temporal and stratigraphic resolution improves dramatically, aided by the relative abundance of *in situ* archaeological sites and by the ability of techniques to date objects in this range. This period is typified by alternating periods of deposition and erosion, with an overall increase in relief and deepening of valleys, particularly in the southern part of the country. Alluvial deposits are best exhibited in streams in the Negev, and in wadis that flow into the Jordan Rift. In the north, the landscape is much less dynamic, and most valleys are filled with Holocene alluvium and colluvium that contain exceptional sites (Garfinkel 1987). The abundance of sites along stream courses is not particularly surprising since, as today, water must have played an important part in trying to subsist in these marginal environments.

Alluvial sediments in the Central Negev

A wealth of prehistoric sites can be found in the Nahal Aqev/Nahal Avdat areas of the Central Negev Highlands (Marks 1976; 1983) (Figure 1). This area is situated along the edges of an incised chalky plateau, with *in situ* Mousterian, Upper Paleolithic, Epipaleolithic and Neolithic sites found at successively lower elevations between 500 and 400 m asl (see window 1).

The *in situ* early Mousterian site of D-35 is situated in an eroded terrace remnant that overlooks the spring of Ein Aqev in Nahal Aqev. Lateral facies changes within the silty gravels show that prehistoric occupation took place at the margins of the former channel, which received both alluvium and colluvial scree from the valley walls. Contemporary travertine deposits have yielded Uranium-series dates of between 75,000 to 85,000 BP (Schwarcz et al. 1979). The geomorphic and palynological evidence point to substantially wetter conditions at the time of occupation (Horowitz 1979; Goldberg 1986).

This gravelly unit was subsequently eroded by down-cutting of the stream sometime between 75,000 and 50,000 years ago, leaving behind a surface which today can be found about 30–40 m above the valley floor. The erosional remnant, which can be observed in both Nahal Aqev and Nahal Zin as a semi-continuous surface or as isolated patches of gravel, was followed by a period of deposition coeval with Upper Paleolithic occupation in the area, beginning about 47,000 years ago. These deposits, associated with Upper Paleolithc sites, are widespread over an area of several square kilometers between Nahals Aqev and Avdat. These sites include the site of Boker Tachtit, which exhibits a technological transition from Middle to Upper Paleolithic (Marks 1983), and a series of sites/occupations collectively known as Boker; the latter have been dated to between ca. 37,000 and 25,000 years ago (Marks 1983). These sites generally occupy environments that are associated with perennial water sources that are present in this area. The geomorphic setting, sedimento-logical evidence, and fossil pollen collected from these sites imply a climate wetter than today's (Horowitz 1979; Goldberg 1986).

After deposition of these 'Upper Paleolithic' sediments, another phase of erosion took place in which the stream cut down vertically to the level of the present channel; this erosion post-dates the youngest Upper Paleolithic occupation level at Boker.

Western Negev/Northern Sinai

Similar situations occur in the Western Negev area, where alluvial sequences are augmented by the deposition of sand dunes and aeolian dust (Figures 1, 2) (see section on aeolian landscapes below). This area is characterized by a relief that is gentler, and more rolling than that of the Negev Highlands. Consequently changes in the fluvial landscape tend to be more subdued.

No *in situ* Middle Paleolithic sites have so far been recorded in this area, although several relatively fresh Middle Paleolithic artifacts have been recovered from massive, well-rounded gravel deposits in Nahal Nizzana, Nahal Sekher and Nahal Besor/Beersheva. These eroded fluvial remnants once belonged to depositional surface that in Qadesh Barnea, eastern Sinai for example, was over 15 m higher than the present channel. As at Nahal Zin, the deposition of these gravels is ascribed to a climatic regime noticeably wetter than today's (Goldberg 1986).

Upper Paleolithic sites in Nahal Nizzana and Nahal Besor, on the other hand, are associated with massive,

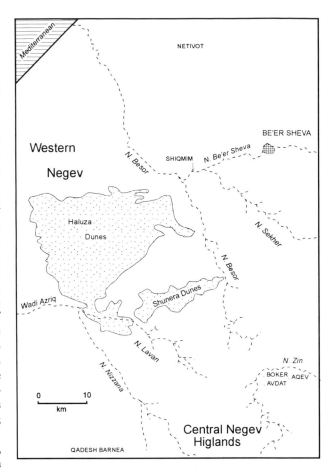

Figure 2 Map of the western Negev and Central Negev Highlands showing location of drainages, dunes and localities discussed in the text

areally widespread fluvially reworked loessial silts, sands and clays, that display some gleying from high groundwater (Goldberg 1986; Goring-Morris 1987; Goring-Morris and Goldberg 1990). These sediments are found in terrace remnants that are a few meters thick. They were deposited by low energy, perhaps perennial, streams, with local ponding conditions (Sneh 1983), under distinctly wet climatic conditions. Many of the Upper Paleolithic sites have been dated to between 35,000 and 25,000 years ago, bolstered by additional dates from pedogenic carbonate nodules in several localities (Goodfriend and Magaritz 1988; Magaritz 1986).

Epipaleolithic sites are found within sedimentary units that either overlie the Upper Paleolithic silts, as in Nahal Besor, or are inset into eroded Upper Paleolithic sediments, as at Qadesh Barnea, E. Sinai. The latter case indicates a period of erosion and downcutting took place between the two periods, ca. 23,000 to ca. 15,000 years ago. In addition, in many locations sediments associated with Epipaleolithic sites tend to be somewhat sandier. As discussed below, this reflects the expansion of sandy dunes

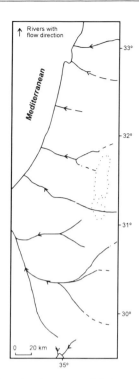

Figure 3 Map illustrating the westward drainage of streams during early Pleistocene time (modified from Horowitz 1988)

during and after the hyper-arid phase associated with the Late Glacial maximum at ca. 18,000 years ago (see below; Goring-Morris and Goldberg 1990).

Widespread erosion and downcutting of Late Pleistocene silts took place over most of the area of the Western Negev. This is particularly striking in the Nahal Beersheva. Here the Chalcolithic site of Shiqmim (ca. sixth millennium BC; Figure 4; Plate 4), is situated next to the present-day Nahal Beersheva channel. The latter in turn has incised close to 20 m below the top of the Late Pleistocene silts that ceased to be deposited about 10,000 years ago (Figure 4). Recent excavations at the site demonstrate that the site is interstratified with at least 2–3 m of alluvial sands and silts that rest upon 3–4 m of well-rounded gravels that contain Chalcolithic material (Goldberg 1987). This demonstrates the possibility that the Chalcolithic inhabitants were able to exploit the aggrading fine-grained alluvium of Nahal Beersheva for cultivating their fields using floodwater farming (Levy 1986).

The Northern Negev/Southern Shefela

Alluvial sediments in the Northern Negev/Southern Shefela region (see Figure 1), consist of Holocene gravels, sands, silts and clays that contain pottery dating to the Early Bronze (EB), Middle Bronze (MB), Late Bronze (LB), Iron Age and Byzantine periods (Rosen 1986 a, b). During the EB for example, the finer grained units, were considered to

represent floodplain deposition, in association with ponding and weak soil formation. During the Iron Age, on the other hand, the presence of angular, poorly sorted gravels and sandy silts suggested short-distance transport, as in the case of colluviation of hillslope materials derived from Tel Lachish following the destruction of the site and abandonment. The latter would result in neglect of agricultural fields and eventually bring about soil erosion.

Colluvial settings

In the northern, more humid part of the country a number of archaeological sites, mostly Neolithic and younger tend to be associated with colluvial deposits. Many of these are located along footslopes in which the archaeological remains interfinger with colluvium. Since these situations tend to be localized and relatively abundant (e.g., Ain Mallaha, Hatoula, Abu Ghosh, Yiftahel), it is not possible to discuss them in detail. Suffice it to state that the environmental conditions responsible for such colluviation are poorly known, although some may have been related to the destruction of vegetation caused by humans around semi-sedentary and sedentary settlements (Bar-Yosef et al. 1974).

Aeolian landscapes

Loess and loessial deposits

Accumulations of aeolian silt (loess) are widespread in the northwestern Negev and in the Beersheva Basin (see Figure 2). These deposits, which are 25–30 m thick (Horowitz 1979: 127), consist primarily of calcareous silt, and become increasingly rich in clay from south to north. This, coupled with study of the heavy minerals of loess and modern atmospheric dust (Ginzbourg and Yaalon 1963; Ganor 1975), and studies of pollen (Horowitz 1979), suggest a source of the dust from central and northern Sinai.

As stated above, abundant Upper Pleistocene silty fluvial deposits – containing numerous Upper Paleolithic and Epipaleolithic sites – also occur in this region. The petrography and overall aspect of these water-lain deposits is identical to that of the aeolian deposits. This indicates that both are genetically related and that as the loess accumulated on the ground it was being contemporaneously reworked into nearby drainage systems. Several authors (Horowitz 1979; Issar and Bruins 1983; Goldberg 1986) have independently argued that both aeolian and fluvial accumulations of these silty deposits are tied to more moist, equable climates. Horowitz and Sneh (1984) have even suggested year-round rainfall during the period of accumulation.

The age of these loess deposits is not precisely known. For the relatively intact Netivot section, Bruins and Yaalon (1979) suggest that deposition began about 140,000 years ago and continued to the beginning of the Holocene,

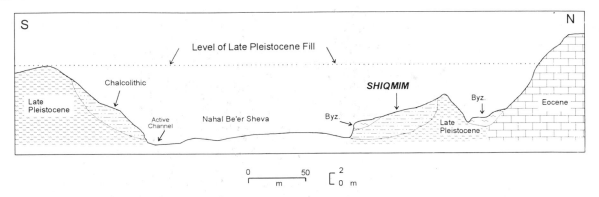

Figure 4 Cross-section across Nahal Beersheva at the Chalcolithic site of Shiqmim. Note the three different alluvial fills: Late Pleistocene fill, which contains Upper Paleolithic and Epipaleolithic sites, the mid Holocene fill associated and coeval with the site of Shiqmim, and the latest one dating to the Byzantine Period. Also note the amount of erosion and downcutting of Nahal Beersheva between the time of deposition of the Late Pleistocene fill and the occupation of Shiqmim. This vertical lowering of ca. 18–20 m took place during a span of about 4000 yr

although in the Central Negev Plateau near Har Harif abundant Chalcolithic material is buried under ≅10 cm of true loess (Goldberg 1986). Elsewhere in the Negev, most loess and loessial deposits do not seem to contain artifacts older than Middle Paleolithic, although some handaxes have been found at the northern end of the Central Negev Highlands eroding out of silty deposits (Goring-Morris, personal communication).

In sum, it seems that during much of the Late Pleistocene the northern and western Negev was the locus of accumulation of large amounts of aeolian dust emanating from the west that was being washed out of the atmosphere and being reworked into the fluvial system. This was associated with noticeably wetter climatic conditions.

Sandy deposits

Significant amounts of aeolian sandy deposits are generally limited to the areas of Northern Sinai and the Western Negev (see Figures 2, 5 and 6), with lesser amounts distributed along the coast in the more northerly part of the country (see section on coastal environments below). In the south, modern and subrecent dune accumulations cover much of the area, except where anticlinal ridges poke up through the sand cover. The sands are disposed primarily as linear dunes which are oriented southwest to northeast or west to east, depending upon locality, and generally cover deflated silty alluvial or aeolian deposits associated with Upper Paleolithic sites (see above). These sandy terrains, particularly where sand cover is thin, provide a good habitat for foraging and grazing.

Prehistoric sites are relatively abundant in this area, and provide a good chronological framework. Most of this information is based on recently published surveys and detailed excavations of prehistoric sites in association with exposures in the Nahals Nizzana, Shunera, Sekher, and Beersheva (Goring-Morris 1987; Goring-Morris and

Goldberg 1990). Results from these surveys and excavations show that most of the dunes rest unconformably upon vast silty alluvial deposits that contain Late Mousterian through Upper Paleolithic sites (see above and Window 1).

The first occurrences of sandy deposits resting upon this Upper Paleolithic 'undercoating' are found in northern and eastern Sinai, and are dated to about 25,000 years ago. In Qadesh Barnea, E. Sinai, for example, the Upper Paleolithic site of Qseima I (ca. 25,000 years old) was excavated from well-sorted aeolian sands that exhibit aeolian festoon cross-bedding oriented NW–SE. However, as one moves toward the Nahal Beersheva drainage to the northeast, the initial arrival of dune sand from the west becomes successively younger. In Nahal Nizzana, for example, the 20,000 (?) year old site of Azariq XIII is situated at the base of the dune complex. In the Shunera area, 15 km further to the east, the earliest sites at the base of the dunes overlying fluviatile silts with Upper Paleolithic implements date to ca.16,000 to 20,000 (?) years ago. In Nahal Sekher, ca. 50 km east of this, aeolian dunes occur in association with Epipaleolithic sites that are about 14,500 years old (Goring-Morris 1987; Goring-Morris and Goldberg 1990).

It would appear then that, based upon the timing of the movement of the dune sand prior to its stabilization, the period of ~25,000 to 18,000 years BP is one characterized by increasing aridity. Dune mobilization on a much more local scale can be documented for later periods in the Holocene, such as the Neolithic, Chalcolithic and Byzantine (Goring-Morris and Goldberg 1990), generally tied to overall aridity for the Western Negev/Eastern Sinai. However, as has been discussed elsewhere (Goldberg 1986; Goldberg and Bar-Yosef 1990), geomorphic changes associated particularly with Byzantine settlements are not assuredly related to paleoclimate alone; intensive settlement and human

Plate 4 The Chalcolithic site of Shiqmim situated in Nahal Beersheva, ca. 18 km southwest of Beersheva (see Figure 2). The rounded hillocks in the upper part of the photograph are eroded remnants of Late Pleistocene sediments. The site is adjacent to Nahal Beersheva (upper right hand corner), which has cut down into about 18−20 m of sediment before the site was occupied about 6000−7000 years ago. The flat area adjacent to the stream in the upper right hand corner of the photo is comprised of fluvial silts with remains of Byzantine pottery. These silts represent an additional phase of stream aggradation and are ubiquitous in the Western Negev. It is not clear whether they are related to the effects of climate change or Byzantine land use practices

activity in the Negev at this time may have been in part responsible for these changes.

Finally, it should be noted that during this dry phase sites tend to be small and probably represent ephemeral occupations. Major archaeological occupations of this vast sandy plain took place immediately after this arid phase (Goring-Morris and Goldberg 1990; Goldberg and Bar-Yosef in press).

Coastal settings

The coastal zone consists essentially of two major parts. The northern part extends from the Lebanese border in the north to the southern edge of Mount Carmel, and is characterized by a relatively narrow coastal plain which abuts against a rocky, mountainous terrain to the east. The southern zone extends into northern Sinai. It is generally broader, becoming increasingly wide toward the south, and is comprised of greater and more extensive quantities of sand. These are transformed into dunal terrains further inland (see above).

In both parts, Pleistocene coastal landscapes are represented by cemented calcareous sandstones (locally called *kurkar*) and reddish sandy loams (*hamra*) (Horowitz 1979; Neev et al. 1987). These have been examined from numerous exposures and from hundreds of boreholes (e.g., Issar 1968; Gvirtzman et al. 1983/4).

Typically, the calcarenites occur as longitudinal ridges that span much of the coastal plain, and extend well into the Negev. In all, they exhibit several regional trends,

becoming increasingly older eastward; increasingly close together towards the north, and lower in elevation toward the south (Schattner 1973). The ridges tend to form small divides with small, poorly drained, swampy channels between them (so-called *marzeva*).

The *hamra* share roughly the same distribution as the *kurkar*. These non-calcareous, sandy soils contain small amounts of red, iron-rich clays, and are low in organic matter (Yaalon 1967; Dan 1988).

Evidence for occupation coeval with the accumulation of *hamra* comes from the Evron Quarry, in Western Galilee (Figure 1; Issar and Kafri 1972; Ronen and Amiel 1974; Haas 1970). Middle Acheulean artifacts are associated with both alluvium, and grey and reddish clayey soil units. The presence of rhinoceros, hippo, and horse, for example, indicate locally marshy conditions probably surrounded by a steppic landscape. Nevertheless, more decisive studies of dating and paleogeography, and the origin of the sediments and soils is needed.

To the south, individual *hamras* with Middle Paleolithic and Epipaleolithic artifacts occur (Farrand and Ronen 1974). Although Mousterian artifacts occur in an Upper Pleistocene red loam (the 'Mousterian Hamra') its exact age is still unknown, and may represent more than one soil forming event that began during the Last Interglacial. Only one Mousterian occurrence has been systematically excavated in this *hamra* (Ronen 1977).

Several Epipaleolithic sites are found in a younger *hamra* unit situated along a *kurkar* ridge that is commonly closest to the sea (Bar-Yosef 1970; Saxon et al. 1978; Ronen et al. 1975; Ronen and Kaufman 1976). Most of the sites are ascribed to the Kebaran and Geometric Kebaran cultural complexes (Bar-Yosef 1981), but no radiocarbon dates are available.

Although most researchers accept that the *hamras* represent some type of fossil soil (paleosol), their exact origin and environment of formation (as well as those of the *kurkar* ridges) are still a subject of discussion (Farrand and Ronen 1974). For example, whereas much of the clay fraction is essentially wind transported (Yaalon and Ganor 1973), it is still not clear whether their formation is best interpreted in terms of past climate fluctuations, former positions of sea level, or the original mineral content of the underlying *kurkar* (e.g., Horowitz 1979). Moreover, while some are readily interpretable in terms of soil forming processes (Yaalon and Dan 1967; Karmeli et al. 1968; Dan et al. 1968), others are clearly sedimentary in origin (personal observations at Evron Quarry). Their regional stratigraphic and chronological position are still problematic, in spite of numerous attempts to understand them (Issar 1968; Issar and Kafri 1972; Gvirtzman et al. 1983/4).

The *kurkar* is equally enigmatic. In addition to the lack of suitable material to date, the environment of deposition of the sands is still difficult to interpret (Issar 1968; Yaalon

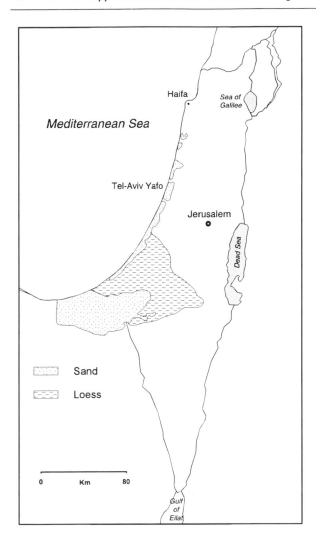

Figure 5   Map of Israel showing distribution of loess and sandy dune deposits. The latter occur in both the western Negev and along the coast

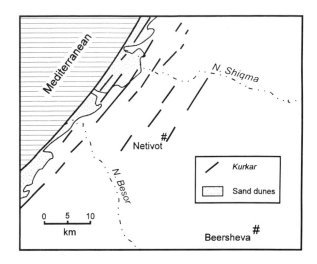

Figure 6   Map of the Netivot area schematically illustrating the distribution of *kurkar* ridges (both exposed and covered), and the location of modern coastal sand dunes, which have a broader areal distribution than that of fossil sands

1967; Yaalon and Dan 1967; Gvirtzman et al. 1983/1984). For example, it is still not clear which of the sandstones are continental in origin (aeolian or beach) or shallow marine, nor whether the sandstones and loams form during periods of marine transgressions or regressions, or both (see Farrand and Ronen 1974).

In sum, in spite of their prevalence, the *kurkar* and *hamra* units provide little unequivocal paleoenvironmental data. The best that can be stated at present is that people occupying the coastal region during the Pleistocene would have observed a sandy landscape which was periodically stabilized by vegetation probably during periods of wetter climate; this resulted in the formation of reddened soil horizons that commonly were locally eroded and redeposited. They would have also noted the rising and lowering of sea level in response to retreat and advance of the ice sheets in the northern latitudes.

Caves

Although caves represent small landscape features, they are particularly important in Israel because they are a primary locus of prehistoric activity. Moreover, as sediment traps, they commonly have relatively long and complete stratigraphic sequences that can contribute to our understanding of the conditions outside the cave. Finally, their well-preserved human remains directly reflect upon the origin of modern humans (Valladas et al. 1987; Valladas et al. 1988; Stringer et al. 1989; Bar-Yosef et al. 1992). Although there are many caves in the area, the most prominent are Tabun, el-Wad, Skhul, Kebara, Qafzeh, Hayonim, Amud, Zuttiyeh, Rakefet and Emireh. Only the succession at Tabun and Kebara will be discussed here, since they have been excavated relatively recently. Hence, their stratigraphy – including dating – is better understood. Moreover, stratigraphic succession at Tabun most clearly reflects the effects of paleogeographic changes that took place outside the cave, including changes in sediment source that appear to be tied to eustatic changes of sea level. Kebara was chosen because it illustrates the complexity of depositional and post-depositional processes that take place in these caves (Laville and Goldberg 1989; Goldberg and Laville 1988; Bar-Yosef et al. 1992).

Tabun

Et-Tabun Cave is situated on Mount Carmel, about 22 km south of Haifa (Figure 1). Facing northwest, it overlooks the coastal plain which is composed of alluvial clays that overlie and abut against a number of *kurkar* ridges.

Essentially, the deposits can be broken down into a lowermost unit consisting of silty sands grading up to sandy silts (with Upper Acheulean, Acheulo-Yabrudian and Mousterian industries) (see Plate 1). These are overlain by stratified burnt layers containing Mousterian implements. These interdigitate with an overlying red clay unit containing abundant rockfall (Garrod and Bate 1937; Jelinek et al. 1973; Jelinek 1982; Goldberg 1973, 1978; Goldberg and Nathan 1975; Bull and Goldberg 1985).

The textural analysis of the sediments points to primarily one episode of deposition for the lowest unit: sand was blown into the cave from the neighboring coastal plain, probably during a relatively high stand of an interglacial sea level. Within this unit, the upward increase in the silt to sand ratio reflects a regression of the sea, since the silt essentially represents suspended aeolian dust. The middle unit is anthropogenic, and represents periodic burning episodes (Jelinek et al. 1973). Its composition of red clay and stones show that the roof had begun to open at this time allowing the soil mantle (*terra rossa*) to be washed into the cave from the chimney.

The chronology associated with these events is still being debated. Initial interpretations suggested that the entire sequence began in the Last Interglacial (Farrand 1979; Goldberg 1978). However, recent considerations would assign the Acheulo-Yabrudian to Isotope Stage 6 and the Upper Acheulean to an earlier time (Bar-Yosef 1989b; Grün et al. 1991).

Kebara

Kebara Cave, like Tabun (see Figure 1; Plate 1) is situated on the western flank of Mt. Carmel. The temporal succession at Kebara is much shorter, with Middle and Upper Paleolithic, Kebaran and Natufian industries. Burnt flints from the Mousterian units have been dated by TL from about 60,000 to 45,000 years ago (Valladas et al. 1987); charcoal from the lowermost Upper Paleolithic sediments dates to about 42,000 years ago (Bar-Yosef, personal communication).

The Kebara sediments are generally fine-grained organic rich silts and clays, marked by a number of burnt, ashy horizons, particularly in the Middle Paleolithic units (Meignen et al. 1989) (see Plate 2.1; Window 2). The lowermost deposits in these units consist of brownish grey silts that are generally sterile (Goldberg and Laville 1988). The uppermost layers with Mousterian contexts fill irregular depressions in the underlying sediments, and appear to represent sediments that have been reworked by biological and geological activity. Burrows are widespread throughout all the deposits and are expressed by circular holes, or by masses of homogeneous, loose, crumbly sediments. These upper sediments appear to interfinger laterally with red, calcareous, silty clays that represent *terra rossa* clays originating from Mt. Carmel. The dip of many of these deposits to the rear of the cave, indicates subsidence of the sediment into solution cavities developed in the bedrock.

The Upper Paleolithic sediments, siltier and less organic-rich, tend to be finely laminated, particularly in the upper part. These appear to be a result of deposition by runoff from outside the cave and are associated with greater effective moisture, possibly tied to a wetter climate (Goldberg and Laville, 1988). Like the Mousterian deposits, they are also burrowed. Such burrowing, particularly at the boundary between the Middle and Upper Paleolithic units, obscures the contact between them, and helps account for the 'transitional' nature of the industries of these units (Laville and Goldberg 1989).

Most of the sediments (*terra rossa,* quartz silt and sand) within Kebara originated from outside the cave, and were either blown in or transported by runoff. The latter is shown by the lamination of the deposits with Upper Paleolithic artifacts. Colluviation is probably responsible for the deposition of much of the non-laminated sediments, but many of the original sedimentary structures and fabrics have been modified by post-depositional processes, such as rodent burrowing or earthworm activity, or diagenesis (phosphate mineral transformations) (Weiner et al. 1993). The effects of anthropogenic sedimentation are illustrated by the numerous burnt layers, and the overall organic rich nature of the Mousterian deposits in particular.

Post-depositional transformations of the deposits are delineated by subsidence of the deposits into subsurface swallow holes; a phenomenon which took place a number of distinct times during the infilling of the cave. In addition, secondary mineral transformations are widespread (Weiner and Goldberg 1990; Weiner et al. 1993). Most of these involve the precipitation of various phosphate minerals associated with dissolution of bone or phosphate-rich solutions derived from guano. These mineralogical transformations have important archaeological implications that relate to the distribution of bone within the cave. At Kebara the distribution of bone appears to be a result of both human activities and post-depositional modifications (Bar-Yosef et al. 1992; Weiner et al. 1993).

In sum, both of these studies, and other works not discussed (e.g., Sandler et al. 1988), reveal that much of the sediment in Israeli caves has been influenced by conspicuous anthropogenic and biogenic activity and modification. In terms of deposition, this is shown by the presence of hearths and organic-rich layers. Bio-anthropogenic activities are also prominent post-depositional agents, which foster actions such as trampling, and extensive burrowing. The latter is widespread in most caves including Tabun, Kebara, Hayonim, Nahal Heimar, and Rakefet. These biological influences, along with diagenetic mineralogical transformations, hamper our ability to decipher the paleoclimatic meaning of these cave sediments. As a consequence the paleoclimatic signal appears to be weak and possibly non-existent (Goldberg 1990).

Discussion

This summary has attempted to provide an indication of the types and changes of landscapes and geological environments that existed in Israel during the Quaternary Period. Admittedly, this has been an eclectic summary, and has tended to emphasize the more recent part of the Quaternary where resolution is greater. The reader should therefore consult the references for further details. Nevertheless, in spite of this brevity, certain points should be apparent or deserve emphasis.

First, within this relatively small area one notes a wide variation in types of past and present landscapes, including lacustrine, fluvial, aeolian and coastal environments. However, when examined from the standpoint of the entire Quaternary (i.e., about 2 million years), it is evident that indications of past changes are spotty, both regionally and temporally (Figure 7).

The Rift Valley, for example, has long been a site of lakes, ever since its formation in early Quaternary times. The evidence for such lakes is found in 'Ubeidiya, the Hula Depression (Gesher Benot Ya'akov) and along the central and southern Jordan Valley (Lakes Samra and Lisan), including the modern Sea of Galilee. However, when the temporal distribution of these phenomena – even with uncertainties of dating – is examined, it is apparent that various lakes were in existence for less than half the total time of the Quaternary (see Figure 7). Lacustrine situations in the Negev are even more ephemeral features and appear only in the Late Quaternary.

A similar condition arises for fluvial settings, which are more dynamic landscapes marked by periods of deposition and erosion, whereby previously deposited materials are removed and reworked. Alluvial deposits are also patchy in their spatial and temporal distribution, and large gaps exist where apparently nothing was accumulated or at least we have no geological evidence. Although this view is influenced to some extent by the difficulties of dating such deposits, it seems that with the exception of Upper Pleistocene fluvial deposits in the Negev there is not much evidence for fluvial landscape development since the time of deposition of the widespread Lower Pleistocene HaMeshar gravels there (Figure 7).

Even if more complete stratigraphic sequences could be found, many deposits, particularly fluvial ones, are not particularly environmentally diagnostic. With the absence of fauna or flora, they generally do not provide information that can be translated into paleoenvironments. For the early and middle Pleistocene, for example, the stratigraphic occurrence of fluvial deposits is more useful in reconstructing the geological history of the area (including tectonic uplift – e.g., 'Ubeidiya and HaMeshar Fms.) and reconstructing paleogeographic changes in the fluvial system, than in inferring paleoenvironmental changes. The stratigraphically localized fauna and flora at 'Ubeidiya (Fi

member), however, do provide some indications of a Mediterranean climate during its accumulation.

Thus, for the Lower and Middle Pleistocene many gaps exist in the evidence, and stratigraphic sequences tend to be of unknown duration. Therefore, for these earlier periods, erosion has filtered to some extent our view of human development. As a result, we tend to get a jagged, punctuated view of cultural transition during these earlier prehistoric times.

This uneven record is less of a problem for landscapes of the Upper Pleistocene, whose deposits are fresher, more complete and there is much greater temporal and stratigraphic resolution. This is particularly true for the Upper Paleolithic and later Periods. During these past 40,000 years we can observe almost intact remains of the former landscapes and environments, particularly alluvial, aeolian, and lacustrine. It is also a period in which there is abundant supplementary paleoenvironmental information acquired from other disciplines, including zoology, palynology and paleobotany, and geochemistry.

For the Upper Paleolithic and Epipaleolithic, for example, the evidence indicates wetter conditions between ca. 40,000 to ca. 25,000, and 14,500 to ca. 12,500 years ago with the intervening period being marked by drier conditions (Goldberg 1986; Goldberg and Bar-Yosef in press; Goldberg in press). In the Jordan Valley this is illustrated by the pollen data and alluviation associated with high Lisan Lake levels. In the Negev and Sinai, this is implied by the widespread occurrences of high water tables and alluviation, and the broad distribution of Upper Paleolithic and Epipaleolithic sites in the region. It is also supported by isotopic evidence from carbonate nodules from the Negev and coastal regions.

The Pleistocene/Holocene transition (ca. 12,000 to 10,000 years ago) is particularly well represented in the northern half of the country and is characterized by a shift to drier conditions and increased temperature at about 11,000 years BP. A colder and drier spell is inferred from 11,000–10,000 years ago, the span generally correlated with the 'Younger Dryas' (Baruch and Bottema 1991)). Evidence for a Holocene wetter period is restricted to the Jordan Valley where abundant Pre-Pottery Neolithic sites with fauna, pollen and plant remains are recorded (Bar-Yosef et al. 1991). In the Negev, little stratigraphic information is extant, and most prehistoric occurrences are surface sites, or in locally mobilized dunes.

For most of the later Holocene, there is little stratigraphic information in the Jordan Valley. In the Western Negev, on the other hand, the substantial amount of Chalcolithic alluviation points to wetter conditions about 6000 to 7000 years ago (Goldberg 1987); carbon isotope data on snails (Goodfriend 1990) and faunal data from this site support this conclusion as well (C. Grigson, personal communication).

The coastal zone and nearby surroundings are relatively

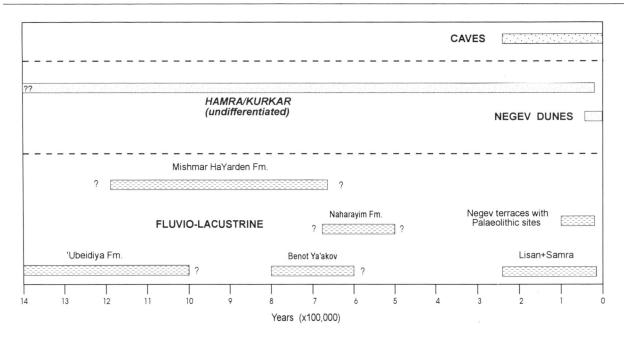

Figure 7 Chart showing temporal distribution of landscape features and deposits during most of the Quaternary in Israel. Noteworthy is the lack of continuity of any of the environments. Although the 'kurkar/hamra' bar is long, most of the accumulations cannot be temporally differentiated and they are distributed in time in a much more punctuated fashion

rich in remains of former human occupation as represented by caves, *in situ* sites in *hamra*, and by surface scatters. However, these contexts also suffer to some extent from a certain lack of stratigraphic continuity.

In caves, the possibility of monitoring and documenting culture change more closely is potentially greater since they represent more of a closed system, and, as such, they tend to retain whatever materials accumulate there. Caves are also typified by relatively rapid rates of deposition which can provide greater temporal resolution. This resolution is also aided by the relative abundance of materials (both organic and inorganic) that can be dated with a variety of techniques, such as radiocarbon, uranium series, thermoluminescence and electron spin resonance. Their temporal capabilities match the apparent time span of most of the Israeli cave sequences.

Information teased from cave sediments, however, can have limitations. For one, occupation of caves in Israel seems to be relatively recent, with apparently no remains of occupation earlier than 200,000 years ago. Although Tabun and Oumm Qatafa may be somewhat older than this, most contain Middle Paleolithic and later industries that are probably younger than 150,000 years; however, the dating of these earlier deposits is still open to question. As such, most extant cave deposits represent about less than 10 per cent of Quaternary time.

In addition, although caves have the potential for registering long cultural sequences and transitions, they are not immune to post-depositional modifications. This is the case at Kebara and it is visible at other caves in the area

(e.g., Hayonim, Rakefet, Amud). Thus at Kebara, although the change from Middle Paleolithic to Upper Paleolithic can be roughly bracketed to between ca. 47,000 and ca.41,000 years ago (Bar-Yosef, personal communication), the stratigraphic relations between these two cultural identities have been blurred by post-depositional modifications in the form of biological activity (burrowing) and slumping (Laville and Goldberg 1989).

One of the only other localities in Israel where a similar transition has been observed is at the site of Boker Tachtit in the Nahal Zin (Marks 1983). Elsewhere in Israel, this transition does not appear to be visible because in many localities, particularly the fluvial landscapes of the Negev, erosion was taking place and there is no sedimentary record from this time interval.

As is always the case with empirically derived data such as those presented here, the above assessment should be viewed as a tentative working document that needs to be continually updated as more information accumulates. The above statement is true for all periods, although there is a greater chance of finding new information in the younger deposits simply because they are fresher and there are more of them. For example, recent unpublished investigations by D. Braun (Hebrew University) have uncovered new and exciting information on Plio-Pleistocene sediments in the Central Jordan Valley area.

Future work in the study of ancient landscapes and environments should continue in all sectors of the country and time periods. In particular, however, and as ironic as it may sound, much more work is needed in the northern half of the country, particularly for the Late Pleistocene and Holocene. Here, geological and archaeological reconnaissance work has been hampered by several factors. Principal among them is the general youth of the valley fills (i.e., early half of the Holocene) which have concealed many sites, as at Yiftahel, for example. Similarly, exposures tend to be poor in this region and much of the landscape has been disturbed by modern agricultural practices that have decreased the visibility of sites and the geomorphic and stratigraphic contexts in which they are found.

For these historic periods, greater attempts should be made to gather and freely incorporate other paleoenvironmental data (e.g., pollen, fauna) as is routinely done in prehistoric research, where, ironically, there are far fewer material remains to work with. Baruch's (1986) attempt to integrate pollen data with historic land use practices is very notable in this regard and should be expanded.

Finally, and most important, we need to develop new ways of looking at evidence of existing landscapes and their associated sites. This can be done at all scales, including the regional scale (e.g., the site and its drainage basin), the meso-scale (the site in relation to its immediate surroundings, i.e. few $km^{2)}$, and the micro-scale (e.g., the significance of a certain layer: geologic vs. anthropogenic).

One relatively new technique that has proven very effective in sorting out geological and anthropogenic effects at all of the above scales is micromorphology, the study of sediments and soils using petrographic thin sections (Courty et al. 1989) (see Window 2). Micromorphology is directed at the interface between geological, pedological and anthropogenic processes (in their broadest senses) that operate and come to focus at an archaeological site. By being able to recognize these factors, we are in a stronger position to fully understand the types and distribution of human activities at a site, and assess patterns of behavior and their relationship to the geological environment. This should help contribute to answering broader scale problems related to changes in settlement patterns, technological transitions and aspects of social organization.

Acknowledgments

Over the years I have benefited greatly from discussions and collaboration with Ofer Bar-Yosef who has been instrumental in helping me gather much of this information. I would also like to thank Tom Levy for his support and interaction, and for the invitation to participate in this volume. The helpful comments of Jessica N. Johnson are appreciated for their value in improving the quality of the manuscript for which I bear full responsibility.

OBSERVING LANDSCAPE CHANGES

Much of this chapter discusses the landscape and how it has changed during the last ca. 2 million years of Quaternary history. But how can changes in the landscape actually be monitored or inferred?

Researchers commonly investigate these changes by working at various scales of inquiry both in the laboratory and in the field. These scales range from the study of satellite imagery of portions of a subcontinent, down to the microscopic study of soils and sediments (see Window 2). Whereas both laboratory and field analyses are necessary, the bulk of the evidence of geomorphic change is based on observations made in the field.

Field evidence is different in every location. For example, in the arid area of the Western Negev (Plate 1.1) many exposures along the major drainages (e.g., Nahal Nizzana, Nahal Lavan, Nahal Shunera, Nahal Sekher) show remarkably similar indications of landscape change, encompassing both shifts in fluvial regimes and dune migrations. At these localities, readily observable, are discrete Upper Paleolithic sites sealed within the silty stream deposits. Net accumulation of this silty alluvium is not taking place at the present time, and instead, erosion and downcutting through extant

Pleistocene and Holocene deposits is the rule. In addition, depending upon locality, these silts commonly contain one or more distinct bands of calcium carbonate ($CaCO_3$) nodules. These have been dated by radiocarbon to several discrete periods as for example, ca. 13,000, 28,000, and 37,000, years ago. These soil

Plate 1.2   Nahal Zin looking southward towards Avdat and the Central Negev Plateau from Sede Boker. The beige colored hill in the center right of the photograph displays the remnants of stream gravel, as well as the Mousterian site of D–6. About 35 m lower than this, on the west side of the Zin channel and next to the dirt road is a flat terrace containing alluvial silts and gravel and the Upper Paleolithic site of Boker Tachtit. The site of Boker is hidden behind this hillock

Plate 1.1   Nahal Shunera, western Negev. The lighter band in the middle ground are with fluvial silts which locally contain Upper Paleolithic material in them. These are overlain by a longitudinal dune marked by a long ridge under the sky line, and contain late Upper Paleolithic, Epipaleolithic and Neolithic sites upward

nodules not only indicate a period of landscape stability during which the nodules formed below a stable surface, but they also signify climatic conditions wetter than today's, since under the present day arid regime it is too dry for them to form.

Overlying these fluvial silts are aeolian sands which represent fossilized dunes that arrived in the area from the direction of Sinai to the north and west. These are several thousand years younger, since they contain late Upper Paleolithic and Epipaleolithic sites. It is generally believed that sand mobilization and dune formation take place under arid conditions, thus pointing to a shift to greater aridity.

Another situation can be seen in the Nahal Zin area of the Central Negev, although there are no dunes present. Within the Nahal Zin are accumulations of fluvial gravels and silts situated at different elevations within the basin (Plate 1.2). These former abandoned floodplains or *terraces* contain discrete, *in situ* artifact scatters or sites which provide some indication of the time at which the stream was flowing at that elevation. For example, we note the occurrence of the Mousterian site of D-6 associated with fluvial gravels at an elevation of ca. 406 m above sea level (asl). This is perched well up above the present-day channel, which is about 370 m asl at this location (see Figure 1.1; Plate 1.2); its age is not known, but from other stratigraphic information in the area, an age of ca. 80,0000 years is not unreasonable. Along the channel adjacent to this site, it is possible to see an extended accumulation of gravels and silts which parallel the present channel and have a distinct terraced, tread and riser morphology. This accumulation is ca. 10–12 m thick, and rests a few meters above the present-day active channel of Nahal Zin. Within these fluvial deposits are several Upper Paleolithic sites (Boker and Boker Tachtit complexes, excavated by Prof. A. E. Marks of Southern Methodist University), that range in age from ca. 45,000 to 25,000 years old. The geometry and ages of these terraces

between aggradational/depositional mode to degradation/downcutting mode over only a few thousand years.

Other examples of geomorphic transformations include changes in sea level and lake levels, and the deposits associated with them. Evidence of former sea levels in Israel is expressed as erosional notches and deposits of gravelly fossil beach deposits. The former are best known from the Mt. Carmel area where several platforms at various elevations have been cut into the bedrock (e.g., at ca. 40 m, 60 m, 79 m and 120 m a.s.l.) by the sea. On the sandy coastal plain and coast, former positions of the sea are indicated by the presence of numerous longitudinal sandstone ridges, locally called *kurkar*. Several ridges have been recognized, and although the exact ages and processes of formation have yet to be precisely determined, they do become progressively younger in a westward (i.e., shoreward) direction.

Evidence of former Quaternary lake deposits and lake levels are well exposed in several localities in the Jordan Valley. These include the ca. 1.4 million-year old 'Ubeidiya Formation encompassing a Lower Paleolithic prehistoric site, lacustrine

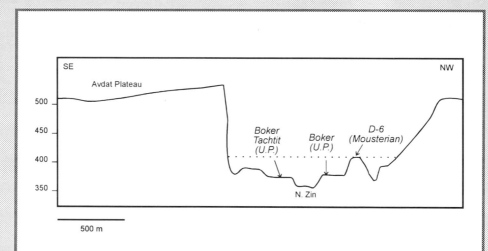

Figure 1.1 Cross-section through Nahal Zin in the vicinity of the Middle Paleolithic site of D-6 and the Upper Palaeolithic sites of Boker and Boker Tachtit, illustrating the surfaces and terraces shown in Plate 1.2. Note the difference in elevations of the landscapes during Middle Paleolithic and Upper Paleolithic times and the amount of lowering that took place between them

clearly show that sometime after 80,000 years ago, Nahal Zin cut down to the level of the present channel and then began to refill itself about 45,000 years ago with the accumulation of alluvium; with Upper Paleolithic sites. This represents a vertical difference of over 35 meters. Sometime after 25,000 years ago the stream began to down cut once more to the level of the present day channel.

In sum, these different terraces (though the story is actually a bit more complex than discussed here) clearly show the dynamic nature of the terrain, and how the landscape can shift repeatedly

deposits in the Hula Valley, and the deposits associated with precursor lakes to the modern Dead Sea. Of these, the most prominent is that of the Lisan Lake, whose bright, eroded marls are prominent features in the Jordan Valley from Hazeva in the south, to the Kinneret in the north. Lake Lisan was in existence roughly from ca. 65,000 to 14,000 years ago, at which time it began to retreat rather rapidly. As it did so, it left behind numerous bouldery strandlines that marked temporary stillstands of the lake, similar to those produced during shrinkage of the Dead Sea in recent years.

MICROMORPHOLOGY

Micromorphology involves the microscopic study of soil, sediments and archaeological materials such as plaster, cements, daub, pottery, and floors. Like petrography in the geological sciences, it utilizes the petrographic thin section, which is a 30 μm thick slice of soil or sediment mounted on a glass slide. It is usually prepared from an undisturbed, oriented block of material collected in the field, which is dried in the laboratory and then

Plate 2.1 The west profile of Kebara Cave showing numerous ash layers formed during Middle Paleolithic occupation of the cave. Thermoluminescence dates on burnt flints show that these deposits are between 48,000 and 58,000 yers old. In the upper left part of the profile are numerous burrows which formed at the end of the Middle Paleolithic occupation of the cave

particular attributes or 'features', which help reveal the overall history of the soil, sediment or material being studied. These features can be classified into three principal types: *sedimentary*, concerning the origin and sources of the sediment, its mode of transport, and types of chemical precipitates such as in travertine or speleothems; *pedologic*, referring mostly to post-depositional modification by mechanical, chemical or biological processes acting principally in the upper part of the deposit; and *anthropogenic*, relating to human activities that produce elements, such as charcoal, ash, bone, pottery, and plasters.

Although micromorphology is practiced in the laboratory, it can be applied to the study of landscape changes, notably Quaternary sediments and fossil soils (paleosols). Although field observations are invaluable, they are not always diagnostic. For example, in the Negev desert, calcium carbonate nodules are quite widespread in Late Quaternary alluvial and aeolian silt deposits, and are readily observable. However, it is not always clear whether they formed *in situ* or were secondarily deposited, i.e., reworked from pre-existing soils. This is more readily evident in thin section, where a reworked nodule which has been transported will have a sharp border in relation to the surrounding matrix; a nodule formed in place will tend to have a gradational contact with the matrix that it impregnates.

In the last decade, micromorphological applications in archaeology have become more widespread. Not only can the origins of construction materials (bricks, mortar, plaster) be recognized (e.g., ash, straw, charcoal), but also the conditions of manufacture can be determined, such as firing conditions. In addition, studies of composition and fabrics can disclose human activities such as clearing, tilling and stabling that might not be apparent from field evidence.

impregnated under vacuum with epoxy or polyester resin. The hardened block is then trimmed with a rock saw; the slice is mounted on a glass slide, and then ground to the proper thickness.

Thin sections are typically viewed with a petrographic microscope, utilizing polarized light. With this type of illumination it is possible to make a broad range of observations relating to the mineral and organic composition of the coarser (coarse silt size and larger) grains, their abundance, size, and shape. For the finer fraction (fine silt and clay) that comprises the matrix, it is possible to examine the manner in which these constituents are organized in the sample, or the 'fabric'.

Observations of all these elements and how they may have been modified, enable the recognition of

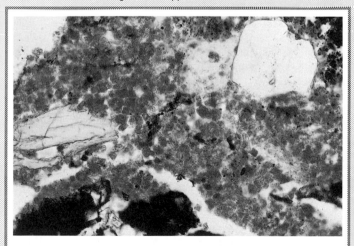

Plate 2.2 Photomicrograph of one of the Mousterian ash layers in Kebara Cave. The ash displays rhombic crystals of calcite that are characteristic of wood ash. The large yellow fragment at the left is a piece of bone, whereas the clear, circular grain in the upper right is quartz which originated on the coastal plain outside the cave. Field of view is *ca.* 1.4 mm

5

PEOPLE OF THE HOLY LAND FROM PREHISTORY TO THE RECENT PAST

Patricia Smith

For approximately the first million years of settlement, the archaeological record for Israel shows that people were hunters and foragers, with limited technological resources, and needing a high degree of physical fitness and strength for survival. The climatic changes occurring during the Middle and Upper Pleistocene modified selective pressures operating on the human populations of Israel and surrounding regions. Marked shifts occurred in the distribution of African versus Asiatic biotypes and the human populations may have moved with them. If early hominids did not retreat south in response to cold spells, they would have had to cope with changing food resources and increased seasonality in their availability. Climatic change would also have affected the ability of these early hominids to survive. Many of the long-term physiological and morphometric adaptations favorable to survival in a hot climate are disadvantageous in a cold climate. Under such conditions both population movement and the development of new adaptive strategies may have occurred. Indeed, it has been suggested that the early Mousterian populations of Israel did not, in fact, adapt to changing climatic conditions, but migrated as did many of the other mammals. According to the proponents of this hypothesis, population replacement rather than evolutionary trends *in situ* account for the phenotypic changes recorded in the Mousterian of Israel.

The technological explosion that began in the Upper Paleolithic was associated in Israel with a marked change in subsistence strategies, causing a major shift in dietary adaptations and behavior. Hunting patterns changed, partly in relation to the changing biotype and partly in relation to new technologies. Grinding stones, querns and mortars appearing in Kebaran and Natufian sites are indicative of new ways of preparing food. The advent of agriculture and animal domestication in the Neolithic, produced a further shift in the pattern and intensity of selective pressures, that accelerated in response to the new developments of the Chalcolithic and recent periods. The characteristics that make a successful hunter are not necessarily those that make a successful farmer, tradesman or statesman. Deficiencies in body size and physical fitness are less critical for survival, and can be compensated for by improved technology, the use of pack animals and servants or slaves.

The development of agriculture and animal domestication in the Neolithic, greatly modified the relative quantity and availability of food staples utilized, while the introduction of pottery at the end of this period facilitated new methods of food preparation, and specifically the preparation of soft, boiled foods. These changes further modified selective pressures affecting human populations. However, the advantages of a more reliable food supply were partially offset by the associated increase in disease rates. The aggregation of large numbers of people in permanent or semi-permanent settlements facilitated the spread of disease. The absence of adequate methods of sewage and garbage disposal resulted in an increase in pests as well as contamination of water supplies. Use of stored foods meant greater susceptibility to infection through food spoilage or contamination from pests, as well as a reduction in its vitamin content. Husbandry involving closer contact with animals, increased the risk of infection from animal-borne disease, while milk consumption exposed people to tuberculosis and brucellosis. This scenario of changing environmental pressures constitutes some of the selective pressures operating on the Holocene populations of Israel. However, Israel has also been the scene of repeated migrations, that have contributed to admixture and/or population replacement at various times. The evolutionary trends that have taken place in the populations of Israel, in relation to changing adaptations, need to be examined critically and distinguished from change through gene-flow in all periods.

Population diversity and microevolutionary trends

This synopsis of the prehistoric and historic populations of Israel will focus on two main topics: first, the extent of population diversity in the Middle Paleolithic, and second, microevolutionary trends and population displacement associated with changing adaptations and cultures in the Epipaleolithic to recent periods. Two groups of hominids, one identified as Neandertals and

Plate 1   Male burial at Gilat, late 5th millenium B.C.E. (© T.E. Levy)

one considered the prototype of Upper Paleolithic Cro-Magnon *Homo sapiens sapiens*, have been found in Mousterian contexts in Israel. This contrasts with the situation elsewhere in the world, where there is no evidence of the coexistence of both types. In Europe all hominids found in association with Mousterian industries are of the Neandertal type. In Africa all hominids associated with the equivalent Middle Stone Age industries are considered early examples of *Homo sapiens sapiens*. Thermoluminescence and ESR dates suggest that *Homo sapiens sapiens* in Israel antedated most if not all of the Neandertals there by some 30,000 years. This raises the question of the nature of the relationship between them, and between them and later populations in the region – a question that is crucial for our understanding of the origins of modern humans.

The second topic dealt with here is the extent and pattern of change in the populations of Israel over the past 12,500 years, and its relation to shifting environmental pressures and population movements. Although it lies on the periphery of the fertile crescent, archaeological investigations have made Israel one of the richest sources of information on the social, cultural and technological changes associated with the advent of plant and animal domestication in the Neolithic. The wealth of skeletal remains from the Natufian to recent periods provides an unequaled diachronic series for the investigation of microevolutionary trends. During this critical period a revolution occurred not only in the external environment of people, but also in their internal environment as food resources and methods of food preparation changed. In addition to the changes in physical activity, degree of mobility and skills associated with these innovations, population size began to increase. This increase in fecundity, imposed an additional burden that specifically affected women. More frequent childbirth meant increased metabolic demands on women, in order to cope with pregnancy and lactation, as well as greater investment in childcare. The increased group size and degree of sedentization, adoption of new foods and methods of food preparation, affected stress levels, specifically in relation to nutrition and disease. Increased trade and warfare also contributed to changes in the genetic make-up of the populations, so that the biological record helps to identify the faces behind the contrasting cultures and religions for which we have written records, and to differentiate between cultural diffusion and population change.

The earliest inhabitants of Israel

Lower and Middle Pleistocene Hominids

Numerous Lower Pleistocene and Middle Pleistocene sites have been found in Israel (Bar-Yosef 1980, 1992 and in

this volume; Goren, this volume) but only very fragmentary human remains have yet been identified and few of them are in good stratigraphic contexts (Figure 1). At 'Ubeidiya the earliest levels have been dated to *ca.* 1.4 million years BP and two pieces of parietal bone and one temporal fragment were uncovered by a bulldozer, and two teeth – an upper lateral incisor and third molar – were found during the excavations carried out there between 1960 and 1963. Tobias (1966) described these fragments as indistinguishable from those of recent populations and chemical tests have confirmed that they are younger than the associated Cromerian fauna (Molleson and Oakley 1966).

An early date has also been claimed for three crania found in association with handaxes and other Acheulean implements as surface finds near kibbutz Hazorea (Anati and Haas 1967). However, since the crania resemble those of recent *Homo*, and show no archaic characteristics, their attribution to the Acheulean must be considered dubious. It is hoped that they will be dated directly in order to establish their provenience.

Other finds, while still fragmentary, do however demonstrate the presence of archaic hominids in Israel during the Middle Pleistocene. At Gesher Benot Ya'akov, two femur shafts mixed in with the faunal collections from the site, were identified as human (Geraards and Tchernov 1983). Once again their provenience is unclear, but they were found in association with faunal remains characteristic of the Terminal-Middle Pleistocene and they exhibit the thick shafts characteristic of early *Homo*. Other human remains from Middle Pleistocene deposits in Israel are a tooth and femur shaft from Tabun E (McCown and Keith 1939) that, in size and shape, fall within the range known for archaic *Homo* elsewhere.

The partial skull from the Zuttiyeh cave, also known as 'The Galilee Skull' (Keith 1927), provides more specific information on the morphology of early *Homo* in Israel. It may be between 250,000 and 300,000 years old (Bar-Yosef 1992). It comprises the frontal bone, small portions of both nasal bones, the frontal process of the right maxilla, part of the right sphenoid and zygoma. Primitive features include thick brow ridges and extreme width of the greater wing of the sphenoid (Plate 2). However, as recognized by Keith (1927), the Galilee skull also has a number of neanthropic features. These include a bulging and relatively high forehead giving a frontal angle of 62.5° (it is 65° in Tabun 1 and 55° in Gibraltar), high flat maxilla and slender zygomatic process. In his 1927 paper, Keith identified the cranium as female, because of its neanthropic characteristics, but after examining the Mount Carmel finds, McCown and Keith (1939: 256) concluded that the Galilee skull was probably that of a male. Its neanthropic characteristics were attributed to the fact that it was more advanced along the evolutionary scale than European hominids of the same period and very similar to

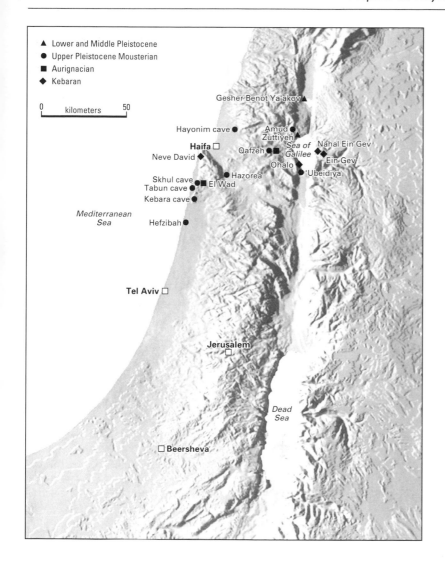

Figure 1 Map showing Pleistocene sites with hominid remains

Legend:
▲ Lower and Middle Pleistocene
● Upper Pleistocene Mousterian
■ Aurignacian
◆ Kebaran

0 kilometers 50

Map labels: Gesher Benot Ya'akov, Hayonim cave, Amud, Zuttiyeh, Haifa, Qafzeh, *Sea of Galilee*, Nahal Ein Gev, Neve David, Ohalo, Ein Gev, Hazorea, 'Ubeidiya, Skhul cave, Tabun cave, El Wad, Kebara cave, *Mediterranean Sea*, Hefzibah, Tel Aviv, Jerusalem, *Dead Sea*, Beersheva

the Mount Carmel skulls, especially Skhul IX. In a more recent study Vandermeersch (1981a) suggested that the Galilee skull was ancestral to early *Homo sapiens sapiens* represented at Skhul and Qafzeh. Suzuki (Suzuki and Takai 1970: 189) and Trinkaus (1992), however, considered Zuttiyeh as possibly ancestral to Neandertals, but emphasized that any attempt to classify it could only be tentative since it is so incomplete.

Upper Pleistocene Hominids

The Mousterian

For the period *ca.* 150,000–50,000 BP, the number of well-preserved fossil hominids that have been excavated in Israel is exceptionally large. All were found in caves or rock shelters located in the North of Israel (see Figure 1). They include 10 partial skeletons and additional fragmentary remains from Skhul (McCown and Keith 1939),

one individual, a second mandible and isolated teeth from Tabun (McCown and Keith 1939), a minimum of 14 individuals from Qafzeh (Vandermeersch 1981b; Tillier 1989), two individuals and isolated bones and teeth from Wadi Amud (Suzuki and Takai 1970; Rak et al. 1992), two individuals and numerous teeth from Kebara Cave (Bar-Yosef and Vandermeersch 1991; Smith and Arensburg 1977; Smith and Tillier 1989) and isolated bones and teeth from Hayonim Cave (Arensburg et al. 1990).

The specimens from Skhul and Qafzeh have been dated to around 92,000 BP (Schwarcz et al. 1988 and 1989) and have been generally classified as *Homo sapiens sapiens*. Those from Amud and Kebara have been dated to *ca.* 58,000 BP (Valladas et al. 1987) while layer C from Tabun, in which both the female skeleton (C I) and male mandible (C II) were found, may date to as early as 150,000 BP (Grün and Stringer 1991; Grün et al. 1991).

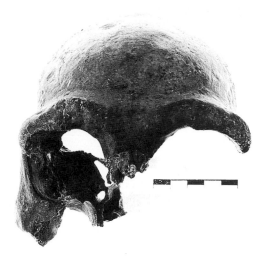

Plate 2   Frontal view of the Galilee skull

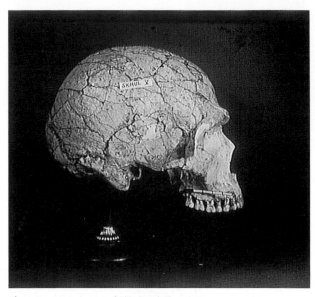

Plate 3   Lateral view of Skhul V skull

The hominids from the Tabun, Amud, Kebara and Hayonim caves show many similarities to Mousterian hominids from Iraq and Europe, and are generally classified with them as *Homo sapiens neandertaliensis*.

The recognition of two different hominid groups in Mousterian context in Israel can be traced back to McCown and Keith (1939). Writing of the Tabun and Skhul specimens, McCown and Keith (1939) refer to them as different 'breeds' of humanity, 'but breeds of the same stock' (1939: 265). Discussing the distinctive characteristics of the Tabun woman they state, 'We find it very hard to believe that these are mere individual anomalies; they have all the appearance of intrinsic structures of morphological value' (1939: 373).

The distinctive morphometric features of the Tabun female have now been identified in the Amud, Hayonim and Kebara specimens, but not in the hominids from Qafzeh who resemble those from Skhul (Plates 3 and 4a–b). They include details of cranial form and orbital torus development; angle formed between the cheekbones and maxilla; angle formed by the cranial base; relation of the mandible to the maxilla; mandibular angle; anterior posterior dimensions of the alveolar bone and dental morphology. In the postcranial skeleton the most distinctive feature is pelvic form and, specifically, the dimensions of the pubic element that is flattened caudo-cranially in the Neandertal group. Other major differences include the morphology of the limb bones (Plate 5) and bones of the extremities, that suggest differences in muscle development and function between the two groups of hominids.

Many of these differences result from very early divergence in developmental pathways, that are genetically determined. A good example of this is the significant difference present in the morphology of the deciduous teeth that begin development early *in utero* (Zilberman, Skinner and Smith 1992), while according to Tillier (1992), most of the differences in head shape and facial morphology appear in childhood (Tillier 1992). Current studies now in progress further suggest that Neandertals also differ from *Homo sapiens sapiens* in the internal structure of their bones.

Trinkaus (1992) has recently summarized the evidence for morphometric differences between the two groups of Mousterian hominids. He agrees with other researchers in concluding that these differences may reflect functional adaptations, and so presumably behavioral differences between them, despite the similarities in lithic assemblages and diet suggested by the archaeological record.

The provenience of all these specimens, except for those from Tabun, is good. At Tabun however, Garrod (Garrod and Bate 1937: 61–64) was uncertain as to whether the Tabun female found in level C was contemporary with these deposits or intrusive from level B. The skeleton was found 35 cm below the surface of C, in an area where the distinction between the two levels was poor. The male mandible from Tabun was found at a lower level, some 1.2 m beneath the surface of C. While the Tabun C male mandible could be accommodated within a generalized early *Homo* lineage, the Tabun female is very definitely Neandertal and similar to the Kebara Neandertal. If the Tabun female is indeed over 150,000 years old, then she would predate any Neandertal yet known, and we would have to assume biological stasis for the 100,000 years that would then separate her from the other Neandertals in Israel. Direct dating of the Tabun human remains is necessary to resolve this issue.

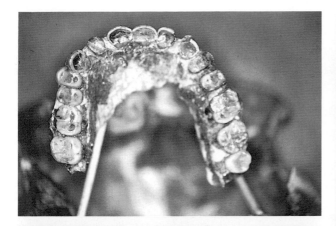

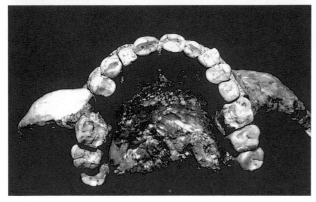

Plate 4a–4b Upper dental arch of Tabun CI (4a) and Skhul IV (4b): note difference in length/breadth dimensions of the dental arch and incisors

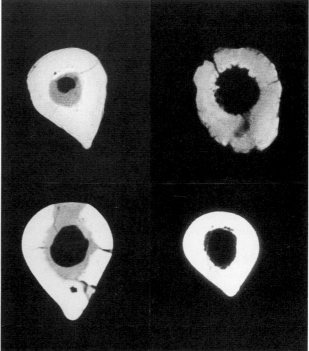

Plate 5 Cross-section of femurs seen on c–t scan

At the present time there are two schools of thought regarding the genetic relationship of the two groups of hominids. Many see the Amud-Tabun-Kebara-Hayonim group as part of a widespread Western Asian Neandertal group present also in Iraq and in the Crimea (Trinkaus 1983) and related more closely to European Neandertals than to the Skhul-Qafzeh hominids in both skeletal and dental traits (Stringer et al. 1984; Smith 1989a; Trinkaus 1983, 1992; Vandermeersch 1992). Other researchers such as Arensburg (1991) and Corrucini (1992) have emphasized the similarity of the two groups. The issue is complicated by the fragmentary nature of many of the specimens. For McCown and Keith (1939) the anatomy of the pelvis, hand and foot bones, and teeth were the most distinctive features of the Tabun female. These features are shared by Amud and Kebara, and Neandertals from Europe and Western Asia (Endo and Kimura p. 313 in Suzuki and Takai 1970; Rak 1991; Trinkaus 1983). They are not present in any of the specimens from Skhul or Qafzeh in which these parts of the skeleton are represented, not even in Skhul IX, whose very incomplete cranium shows a number of primitive features (McCown and Keith 1939; Suzuki and Takai 1970; Corrucini 1992).

Israel is the only place where remains of both Neandertals and *Homo sapiens sapiens* have been found in association with Mousterian artifacts. However, there is no evidence of simultaneous presence, much less of interbreeding between the two groups described here, since they are separated by over 30,000 years and appear to be associated with different climatic conditions. It is, theoretically, conceivable that the Israeli Neandertals were descended from the local Skhul-Qafzeh and/or Galilee prototypes. However, a more plausible and parsimonious explanation for the replacement of early *Homo sapiens sapiens* in Israel by Neandertals was proposed by Vandermeersch (1981b) and elaborated upon by Bar-Yosef (1992). Vandermeersch (1981b) proposed that the Neandertals in Israel represented the southern advance of European Neandertals following their retreat from Europe during cold phases of the last glaciation, and is related to the observed climatic and faunal changes that took place in the region. At the same time, the *Homo sapiens sapiens* populations in Israel moved south to Africa, so the two were not in direct contact for any length of time. Trinkaus's studies of limb proportions and estimates of body mass in Mousterian hominids give some support for this hypothesis, with the Neandertals having relatively short extremities and greater body mass which would give them an advantage in cold weather (Trinkaus 1983, 1992).

But if the Tabun specimens really do date to *ca.* 150,000 BP, other possibilities must be considered. These include the possibility of displacement of an early local Neandertal population in Israel by early *Homo sapiens sapiens* as they migrated out of Africa in a warm phase; evolution *in situ* of early *Homo sapiens sapiens* to a Neandertal form, or the sumultaneous presence of Neandertal and sapiens populations in Israel throughout the latter part of the Upper Pleistocene.

Sites with late Mousterian and transitional industries are known, especially in the Negev and Sinai (Bar-Yosef 1992), but they have yielded no human skeletal remains. There is then no skeletal evidence to show how long the Neandertals survived in Israel or their possible contribution to later populations. No specifically Neandertal traits are, however, present in Upper Paleolithic or recent populations. This I would suggest indicates that the Neandertals did not contribute to the modern gene pool, and so presumably did not interbreed with early representatives of *Homo sapiens sapiens*.

The Aurignacian and Kebaran

Aurignacian and Kebaran sites with human remains, like those of earlier periods in Israel, are located in the northern third of the country (see Figure 1). Fragmentary Upper Paleolithic remains were found at Qafzeh by Neuville and Stekelis in 1933 and briefly described in Vandermeersch (1981b: 26). They comprise the frontal bone and part of the nasal bones of an adult male and two fragments of a mandible (H. 2). Teeth and fragmentary bones have also been found in the Aurignacian deposits at El Wad and Kebara (McCown and Keith 1939) and more recently at Hayonim (Arensburg et al. 1990). However, the most complete skeletal remains from the Upper Paleolithic are those from the early Kebaran (*ca.* 19,000 BP). They comprise a female from Nahal Ein Gev, on the eastern shore of the Sea of Galilee (Arensburg 1977), and at least four partial skeletons from Ohalo on the southwest shores of the Sea of Galilee (Nadel and Hershkovitz 1991, Hershkovitz et al. 1992). Additional remains dating to circa 13,000 BP have been recovered from Ein Gev I (Arensburg and Bar-Yosef 1973), Newe David (Kaufman 1989) and Hefzibah (Ronen et al. 1975).

The human remains from Ohalo have not yet been described in detail, but preliminary observations by Hershkovitz (1992) on the male skeleton indicate that this specimen was similar to the Natufians in morphometric characteristics, but resembled European Upper Paleolithic CroMagnons, especially in orbital configuration and degree of robusticity. The same applies to the cranial features of the female from Nahal Ein Gev (Arensburg 1977), although her postcranial skeleton appears to have been extremely gracile, even in relation to the more recent Natufian females. The male frontal from Qafzeh, whose exact age is unknown, is long and only slightly curved, and looks somewhat more primitive than the Ohalo skull. It has marked superciliary eminences, measuring some 16 mm in height, that fan out above the central portion of the orbits, and are directed upwards and outwards. The mandibular fragments from Qafzeh 2 consist of the right and left sides of the corpus and molar teeth. Corpus thickness at M1–M2 and molar tooth size lie within the range of values found at Ohalo, and molar tooth size is similar.

Morphometric parameters of the bones and teeth found in Aurignacian context at El Wad and Kebara can similarly be accommodated within the range of variation known for the later Natufian period. Despite the retention of some primitive facial characteristics of the orbital region, discussed in Arensburg (1977), Upper Paleolithic and Kebaran skeletons so far known from Israel resemble the Epipaleolithic Natufians in stature, head form and tooth size.

The paucity of human skeletal remains for the Early Upper Paleolithic in Israel, precludes any attempt at directly analyzing the extent of change taking place in this dynamic period. However, the fossil record for Europe and North Africa provides two different models against which to evaluate the probable rate of change in the Israeli Upper Paleolithic sequence. In Europe, marked changes occurred between the Early and late Upper Paleolithic, with late Upper Paleolithic and Mesolithic populations significantly shorter, with smaller teeth and jaws than those of the early Upper Paleolithic populations (Frayer 1984). In North Africa, however, little change seems to have occurred over the same period. Ibero-Maurasian Epipaleolithic populations from Taforalt and Afalou were as tall as early Upper Paleolithic Europeans with even larger jaws and teeth, reminiscent of those of Skhul and Qafzeh. In the Nile Valley, represented by Wadi Halfa and Jebel Sahaba, large bodied and large toothed robust populations survived until as recently as some 7000 years ago (Smith 1979, 1988).

The similarity present between the Kebaran populations of Israel and the Late Upper Paleolithic populations of Europe in stature, head form and tooth size, suggests that they may have been exposed to similar selective pressures. The observed reduction in tooth and body size and robusticity in European Upper Paleolithic populations has been related to changing selective pressures associated with new behavioral and dietary adaptations that occurred towards the end of the Pleistocene (Frayer, 1984). The archaeological evidence suggests that even more drastic changes in technology and food staples occurred in the Israeli Upper Paleolithic sequence (Bar-Yosef 1980; Belfer-Cohen 1991: Goring-Morris this volume). The stability of North African and Nile Valley populations may, in turn, reflect the lack of major changes in subsistence strategies in these regions.

The advent and consequences of agriculture: Terminal Pleistocene and Holocene populations

The Natufians provide a good starting point from which to study the changes that have taken place in the populations of Israel as hunting and foraging activities were replaced by farming, pastoralism, the development of urban societies and increased trading. These changes were associated with marked shifts in selective pressures operating on populations. The characteristics needed for success in hunting are not necessarily those most advantageous in farming or herding, while minor genetic differences can affect not only the ability to utilize new foods but also disease susceptibility. It is not then surprising that marked microevolutionary changes have taken place in the populations of Israel, even within the relatively brief time span represented by the past 12,500 years.

Arensburg (1973) suggested that the Natufians and their descendants formed a 'core' population in Israel that could be traced down to recent periods, but was added to, or temporarily displaced at certain times. I have adopted his assumption as my working hypothesis in this analysis of Natufian to recent populations from Israel. The provenience of the specimens studied is given in Figures 2–4. Unfortunately, the number of specimens available for analysis varies from period to period, and some samples were too small for reliable analysis. Descriptive statistics for cranial measurements in different periods and cultures are shown in Table 1 and their relative distance from one another is plotted in Figure 5. Some estimate of the extent of diachronic trends in the teeth and jaws can be seen in Figure 6 (see p. 73). Between the Mousterian and Natufian periods, head size, jaw size and tooth size reduce. From the Natufian to recent period, tooth size reduces more than any other parameter studied here. In order to identify the presence of 'outlier' groups and the significance of the differences between them and the core population, two tests were employed. One provided a robust test for the comparison of samples of unequal size (Brown and Forsythe (1974a, 1974b); one provided for the simultaneous comparison of a number of samples (the Bonnferonni test described in Miller 1981). Except for basion-bregma height, which may be affected by environmental factors, all variables chosen were those considered to have a high component of hereditability. A detailed summary of the evidence for this is given in Keita (1988).

Natufian populations

The most dominant feature of the Natufian period is the increasing reliance placed on foraging, with cereals gaining ever increasing importance in the diet. This adaptation affected behavior as well as nutrition. Three distinct phases of the Natufian have been recognized on

the basis of the archaeological findings (see Bar-Yosef and Valla 1991, Belfer-Cohen 1991; Valla, this volume, for detailed summaries of the archaeological evidence) and human remains have been found at numerous sites (see Figure 2). At El Wad, Hayonim and Eynan, the human remains date to all phases of the Natufian. At Kebara and Erq el Ahmar they appear to be restricted to the lower phase, and at Hatoula, Nahal Oren and Shukbah they date to the upper phase (Valla 1987).

The Natufians are characterized by low to medium stature, large, low, dolichocranic (long and narrow) skulls; short, broad faces, short mandibles with wide rami, an anteriorly flattened dental arch and marked alveolar prognathism (Plate 6; Arensburg 1973; Crognier and Dupouy-Madre 1974; Ferembach 1961a, 1977; Keith 1934, McCown 1939; Smith et al. 1984; Soliveres 1988; Vallois 1936).

The teeth are relatively broad bucco-lingually with large lingual tubercles and Carabelli's cusps. The second premolars and both the upper and lower second molars are reduced mesio-distally. Lower second molars are generally four cusped (<90 per cent) and upper second molars have reduced or missing hypocones. In addition, there is a high frequency of congenitally missing third molars, relative to other populations of comparable tooth size, especially at Hayonim (Smith 1991). Since congenital absence of third molars is an inherited condition, the high prevalence at Hayonim is evidence for consanguinity between the people buried there. Belfer-Cohen et al. (1991) correctly state that the incidence of third molar agenesis at Hayonim is similar to that found in modern small-toothed populations. However, it must be remembered that the frequency of congenital agenesis is inversely related to tooth size. The incidence of agenesis in Natufians from other sites, or indeed from populations with similar tooth size to the Natufians, averages less than 5 per cent compared to the 21 per cent at Hayonim.

Intersite differences and diachronic trends in the Natufians are relatively few. Ferembach (1961a) reported that the Natufians from Eynan had larger skulls and mandibles and were taller than Natufians from other sites. She postulated that this was due to nutritional differences between Eynan and other sites. Soliveres (1988) has now analyzed the entire series from Eynan, and her results confirm those of Ferembach's earlier study. Head length at Eynan appears to be slightly greater than at El Wad or Hayonim, and mandibles are slightly larger. Stature estimates at Eynan were also reported by her and by Belfer-Cohen et al. (1991) as greater than those of Hayonim, El Wad or Nahal Oren. This conclusion should, however, be regarded with caution as there were intact femora from only two individuals at this site. The additional estimates were derived from femur shafts – and the error of estimate involved is several centimeters.

Smith (1989b, 1991) suggested that most of the

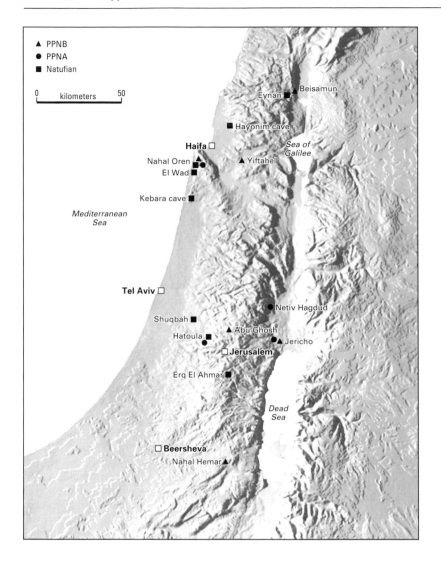

Figure 2 Map showing Natufian and Neolithic sites with human remains referred to in text

available measurements from Eynan may have been derived from skeletons from the earliest phase of the Natufian, so that the apparent intersite differences might be due to diachronic trends within the Natufian. The paper by Soliveres (1988) confirms that indeed most of the measurable specimens from Eynan do date to the earliest phase, but they still appear to be larger than early Natufian specimens from Hayonim and El Wad. The largest Natufians appear to be those from Erq el Ahmar and Eynan, followed by Hayonim and El Wad and finally by Shukbah and Nahal Oren. The first group have the longest largest skulls and mandibles, the second group have rounder skulls and mandibles with short thick ascending rami, and the third group are the most gracile.

Between and within sites, the only significant diachronic trend that can be traced is a reduction in ramus width and increase in dental disease over time (Smith 1991). Both appear to be related to changes in the diet, indicating a shift to more cariogenic foods that require less vigorous chewing. This finding is corroborated by the archaeological evidence in the form of number of grinding implements, sickle blades and remains of cereals.

Neolithic populations

Considerable differences in adaptations are present between the various phases of the Neolithic (10,300–6500 BP), and between contemporaneous sites in different ecological zones. Sites with published human remains are, however, few. Specimens from Israel, the West Bank and Jordan discussed here include, from north to south Yiftahel (Hershkovitz et al. 1986), Horvat Galil (Hershkovitz and Gopher 1988), Beisamoun (Ferembach 1978; Soliveres 1978), Nahal Oren and Abu Gosh (Arensburg et al. 1978) Hatoula, Jericho (Kurth and Rohrer Ertl 1981) Nativ Hagdud (Belfer-Cohen et al. 1990), Ain Ghazal (Kafafi et

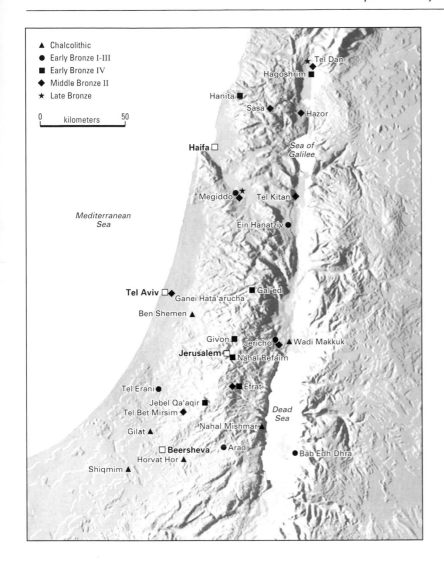

Figure 3 Map showing Chalcolithic and Bronze Age sites with human remains referred to in text

al. 1990; Rollefson and Simmons 1985; Rollefson et al. 1985), Nahal Hemar (Arensburg and Hershkovitz 1988) and Basta (Schulz 1987, Schulz and Scherer 1991). Most of these specimens are fragmentary and cranial sample sizes available were too small for detailed statistical analysis. They are, therefore, excluded from the plots shown in Figure 5. For the mandibles and teeth, sample sizes are larger and the Neolithic values for these variables are included in Figure 6.

For the PPNA there is one skull from Jericho for which measurements have been published by Kurth and Rohrer-Ertl (1981). An additional PPNA skull from Hatoula is now being studied and there are some jaw fragments with teeth from Hatoula and Netiv Hagdud (Belfer Cohen et al. 1990). The PPNA skull from Jericho is long and narrow and falls within the range of measurements seen in the Natufian. The Hatoula skull most closely resembles that from El Wad. The PPNA mandibles from Hatoula are gracile, and tooth size slightly smaller than in the Natufians.

The PPNB specimens span some 1500 years but the skeletal finds are too fragmentary for evaluation of diachronic trends in this dynamic period that is associated with animal domestication. The PPNB crania from Nahal Hemar, Abu Gosh and the plaster skulls from Jericho and Beisamoun, appear to be shorter and broader than those of the Natufians. Facial measurements are available for very few specimens and are extremely variable. They suggest a more elongated face than that characteristic of the Natufians and this is substantiated by comparison of the mandibles. These tend to be longer with greater ramus height than is characteristic of the Natufians. At the present time sample sizes are too small for definite conclusions, but the underwater excavations being carried out by U. Galili at Atlit and Neve Yam may change this picture. Kurth and Rohrer-Ertl (1981) suggest that head moulding may have

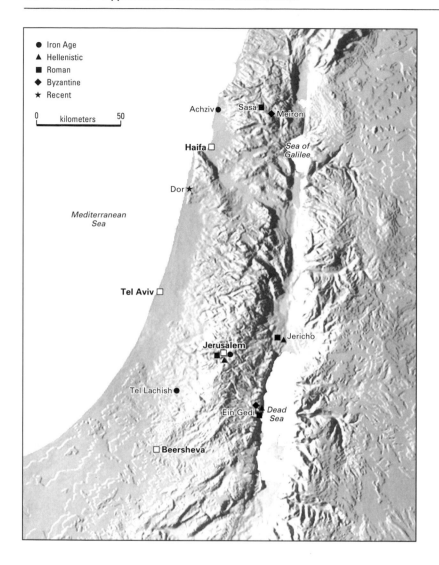

● Iron Age
▲ Hellenistic
■ Roman
◆ Byzantine
★ Recent

0   kilometers   50

Achziv●   Sasa■
              ◆ Meiron

Haifa □   *Sea of
                    Galilee*

Dor ★

*Mediterranean
Sea*

Tel Aviv □

                 ■▲ Jericho
Jerusalem
■□●
▲

Tel Lachish ●

Ein Gedi ◆   *Dead
           ■   Sea*

□ **Beersheva**

Figure 4   Map showing Iron Age to recent sites with human remains referred to in text

been practiced at Jericho, and Strouhal (1973) reported that one of the plaster skulls examined by him showed evidence of *intra vitum* head moulding. However, most of the illustrations provided by Kurth and Rohrer-Ertl (1981) show clearly that considerable post-mortem deformation had taken place in the Jericho skulls.

Stature in PPNB samples appears to have been similar to that of the Natufians, although the PPNB specimens from Abu Gosh and Beisamoun appear to have been more robust than even the largest Natufians (Arensburg et al. 1978, Soliveres 1978). At Jericho, Kurth and Rohrer-Ertl (1981: 449) report on male stature in the PPNA as 167 cm and in the PPNB as 171 cm. Male stature in the terminal phase of the PPNB at Ain Ghazal (Rollefson's PPNC) was reported as 170.8 cm (Kafafi et al. 1990; Rollefson and Simmons 1985; and Rollefson et al. 1985: 108, Schulz (1987) and Schulz and Scherer (1991) described the terminal PPNB sample from Basta as gracile. The

specimens from Basta and Ain Ghazal also appear to have more dental disease – especially calculus and caries – than those from the PPNA or early PPNB sites previously described.

People in the Neolithic also show an increased frequency of ante-mortem tooth loss from severe dental attrition in comparison with the Natufians. Since this condition increases with age, this means either that people lived longer or that the diet became more abrasive (probably from increased carbohydrate consumption) between the Natufian and Neolithic periods. Evidence for such a change in diet between the Mesolithic and Neolithic populations of Abu Hureyra in Syria has now been published by Molleson and Jones (1991), based on SEM studies of tooth wear.

The differences in stature and skeletal robusticity within the Neolithic may also be related to differences in environmental stress and changing lifestyles. Dental hypoplasia, which is one estimate of environmental stress, is present in less than 50 per cent of Natufians and PPNB samples, affected over 90 per cent of the PPNA sample from Hatoula, and appears to increase again towards the end of the PPNB. If the situation at Hatoula proves to be reflected at other PPNA sites, this may indicate a temporary increase in environmental stress in the initial stages of plant domestication, followed by a temporary amelioration of conditions in the earlier phases of the PPNB through the addition of other crops such as legumes, and the beginning of herding. The findings from Basta and Ain Ghazal suggest, however, that the improvement was temporary, and that by the end of the PPNB the quality of life of most people was deteriorating. Recent excavations at Lod, Neveh Yam and Nahal Zohoriya have yielded PN skeletons that are now being analyzed. The results will show if the poor health suggested for the terminal PPNB continued into the PN.

The Chalcolithic and Early Bronze Age: proto-urban and early urban communities

The Chalcolithic–EBI provide the earliest population samples of fully fledged farming communities yet published from Israel. Like the earlier periods discussed, this is again a period of transition in which societies increased in complexity and size, and in which regional differences may have become ever more pronounced (Levy, this volume).

Statistical data presented here for the Chalcolithic and EBI, are based on specimens from Ben Shemen (Lacombe 1980), Nahal Mishmar (Haas and Nathan 1973), Jericho (Kurth and Rohrer Ertl 1981), Megiddo (IIrdlicka 1938), and unpublished specimens from Arad, Gilat, Shiqmim, Horvat Hor and Wadi Maqoch, shown in Figure 3. In contrast to the earlier periods, where skeletal remains were concentrated in the Northern part of the country, many of these sites are from the Judean desert and Negev. However, preliminary studies have shown that they resemble both the Chalcolithic sample from Byblos on the Lebanese coast described by Ozbek (1974) and the Early Bronze I–II samples from Bab-edh-Dhra in Jordan described by Krogman (1989). This suggests that there were no major genetic differences between populations living in different parts of Israel and those on its northern and eastern borders at this time.

The urbanized populations of the EBII and EBIII are poorly represented by human skeletal remains. In addition to the small sample from Tel Erani, studied by Ferembach (1961b), some EBIII specimens were found at Lachish, but were pooled with the Middle Bronze Age series from the same site for analysis (Giles 1958). The situation with regard to skeletal remains is somewhat better for the EB1V. Sites with human remains examined for this study include Jebel Qaaqir, Givon, Nahal Refaim and Efrat (see Figure 3).

Stature shows little or no change between the Natufian and Chalcolithic to EB periods, averaging 168 cm in males and 155 cm in females. Head form also shows little alteration in shape, but a slight reduction in size (see Table 1 p. 70; Plate 7). Mandibular dimensions decease slightly, but the main difference seen is in tooth size (Figure 6). Tooth size in the Chalcolithic-EBI sample is significantly smaller than that of the Natufians or Neolithic samples in bucco-lingual dimensions, and decreases even further in the EBIV (Figure 6). Dental hypoplasia reached an exceptionally high level in the Chalcolithic, affecting some 90 per cent of individuals studied. These data suggest an exceptionally high level of environmental stress in infancy and childhood. It has not yet been determined to what extent this was diet-related, or reflects an increase in disease load in the wake of increased sedentism and population density. The frequency of dental hypoplasia decreases slightly in the EBIV, suggesting some amelioration of environmental stress at this time.

Middle Bronze populations: the evidence for population displacement

Most of the MBII samples that have been studied are dated to the MBIIB or MBIIC. Specimens studied here are derived from Efrat, Nahal Refaim, Tel Dan, Ganei HaTa'arucha, Megiddo, Sasa and Hazor (see Figure 4). They show significant differences from all of the earlier populations in this region in craniofacial characteristics. In the MBII samples the head is shorter and wider, with a high rounded skull and shorter broader face and nose than in any of the earlier or most of the later populations inhabiting Israel. Statistically significant differences are present in five out of the seven measurements shown in Figure 5, and the direction of change found differs from that to be expected as the result of microevolutionary trends or environmental factors affecting growth and development. The MBII samples studied here then represent an intrusive group, and their characteristics suggest that they originated from a damper and/or more temperate climate than that of Israel. Determination of their exact point of origin is now planned, using DNA analysis.

Late Bronze to recent populations: cultural diffusion versus migration

From the MBII to recent periods the archaeological and written records suggest very rapid change as well as considerable admixture. Space limitations preclude a detailed discussion of all the population samples associated with the different cultures identified, but a brief overview is presented here. For the Late Bronze Age

Table 1   Cranial measurements for human populations in different periods in the Holy Land

	Basion-nasion length			Porion-bregma height			Biasterion width			Cranial length			Cranial breadth		
	N	M	SD	N	M	SD	N	M	SD	N	M	SD	N	M	SD
Mousterian	—	—	—	2	114.5	—	2	127.0	—	2	199.0	—	2	145.5	—
Natufian	4	97.5	8.1	27	114.5	9.6	3	109.0	6.0	27	191.6	8.3	26	135.7	6.6
Neolithic	—	—	—	2	115.5	1.0	—	—	—	9	183.2	8.2	11	146.9	8.3
Chalcolithic	5	96.6	2.8	15	116.4	6.8	10	106.2	6.8	22	186.5	5.8	21	136.8	5.1
MBI	10	102.7	4.8	12	120.8	7.0	12	108.7	8.3	15	186.9	7.8	13	136.1	4.9
MBII	5	104.4	2.8	3	126.0	5.1	7	112.0	4.0	7	183.7	3.9	7	139.5	5.6
Iron															
Achziv	4	102.7	1.7	4	116.5	0.5	5	116.0	4.1	5	189.2	3.9	5	141.8	5.4
Jerusalem	—	—	—	—	—	—	—	—	—	5	181.4	—	4	135.0	—
Lachish	26	101.0	3.8	—	—	—	—	—	—	322	184.5	5.8	327	136.8	5.1
Hellenistic–Roman															
Samaritans	25	100.2	5.7	20	116.4	4.0	21	109.1	6.4	22	181.9	6.2	22	136.8	4.4
Jewish	9	96.2	8.2	8	113.1	7.6	13	115.8	9.3	18	182.2	8.4	19	143.8	4.6
Ottoman	17	105.1	4.0	17	118.4	5.1	17	109.8	3.8	18	183.6	5.4	17	140.0	5.8

	Basion-bregma height			Nasal breadth			Nasal height			Minimum frontal width			Nasion-prosthion height		
	N	M	SD	N	M	SD	N	M	SD	N	M	SD	N	M	SD
Mousterian	—	—	—	2	29.0	—	2	54.0	—	2	102.0	—	—	—	—
Natufian	9	138.9	8.0	3	24.0	3.6	2	47.5	0.7	23	96.7	6.1	3	68.6	4.0
Neolithic	—	—	—	3	25.3	1.5	3	48.0	4.5	8	103.3	7.9	5	68.8	5.4
Chalcolithic	13	133.0	5.1	17	25.1	1.8	15	51.8	3.7	20	91.9	3.7	10	69.1	6.2
MBI	11	134.7	9.7	12	22.8	1.2	12	49.8	12.7	14	94.5	4.0	13	68.7	3.6
MBII	5	141.2	4.2	8	23.7	2.2	8	49.1	1.5	7	102.7	16.7	7	61.8	6.3
Iron															
Achziv	4	132.7	4.0	3	25.6	2.0	4	50.0	1.1	3	96.3	5.5	1	67.0	—
Jerusalem	—	132.7	—	—	—	—	—	—	—	8	97.1	—	5	68.0	—
Lachish	268	133.8	5.0	26	25.0	1.5	26	52.8	3.2	319	95.5	4.2	98	70.1	4.3
Hellenistic–Roman															
Samaritans	20	130.6	4.9	10	25.0	1.3	10	50.1	2.5	21	93.4	6.4	9	66.5	3.0
Jewish	13	128.2	7.9	9	24.3	1.9	8	50.7	3.0	20	98.9	8.7	6	67.5	5.0
Ottoman	17	137.2	5.6	18	24.0	2.1	20	53.2	3.5	17	97.9	4.0	17	69.4	7.9

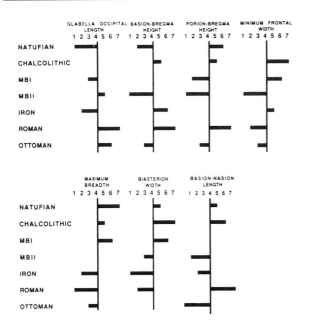

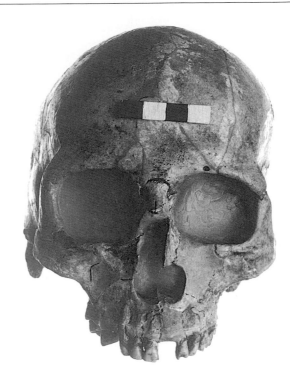

Figure 5 Deviation of different measurements from the common mean (vertical line) are shown as horizontal lines on a scale from 1 to 7. Deviations to the left indicate values smaller than the mean; deviations to the right indicate values larger than the mean. The absence of a horizontal line indicates that the sample mean and group mean were identical

Plate 6 Frontal view of skull from Eynan (Natufian)

there are a few specimens from Megiddo (Hrdlicka 1938) and Tel Dan (Arensburg 1973) that appear to be intermediate in physical characteristics between the MBII and the Iron Age Phoenicians from Achziv. They are, however, too few for detailed analysis and were omitted from the statistical calculations.

The Iron Age is represented by Phoenicians from Achziv (Smith et al 1993), a small sample of First Temple Jews from Jerusalem (Arensburg and Rak 1985) and the large Iron Age sample from Lachish (Risdon 1939). The Iron Age Phoenicians from Achziv most closely resemble the Late Bronze Age sample from Megiddo, followed by the MBII samples, whereas Iron Age Lachish more closely resembles the 'core' population represented both by the pre-MBII populations and by the more recent Arab population. The First Temple Jews from Jerusalem appear to lie between the two, but the sample is too small for rigorous statistical analysis (Plate 8).

For the Hellenistic, Roman and Byzantine periods there are skeletal remains of Jews from sites ranging from the Judean desert in the South to Sasa and Meiron in the North. Of the numerous publications on these populations, that of Arensburg et al. (1981) is the most detailed. Sites with human remains measured for this study are shown in Figure 4. In addition, there is a Samaritan sample from a late Hellenistic site at Wadi Daliya (Wadi ed Daliyeh;

Krogman 1974). The Wadi Daliya sample was remeasured for this study and some of the measurements are shown in Table 1. They have remarkably small, narrow heads and most closely resemble the local Arab population. In contrast, the combined Jewish Hellenistic-Byzantine group are, like the MBII sample, an outlier group, characterized by relatively short, broad skulls and faces. They differ from other populations of historic periods discussed here who are characterized by relatively narrow heads and long faces. The distinctive features of the Jewish population from Israel from the Hellenistic through to the Byzantine Period were also commented upon by Arensburg et al (1981). They differ markedly from the Samaritan skulls from Wadi Daliya, which are exceptionally small, but fit into the general shape pattern of the core population and are intermediate between Iron Age Lachish and the Arab population from the Ottoman period.

Conclusions

The data presented above indicates that major evolutionary changes have taken place in the past populations of Israel. The depth of our understanding of the factors associated with these changes is constrained both by the samples available for analysis and our ability to reconstruct their lifestyles. Thus, the morphology of the earliest populations in this region is still unknown and the 'Galilee' skull

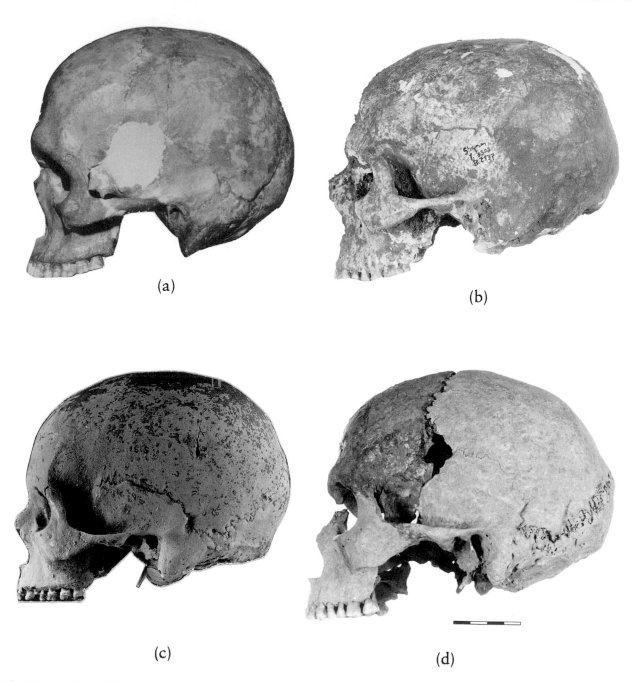

Plate 7   Lateral view of skulls: a) Natufian from El Wad; b) Chalcolithic skull from Shiqmim; c) EBIV skull from Jebel Qa'aqir: d) EBI skull from Kabri. Not all to same scale

provides only a tantalizing glimpse of the peoples associated with the Acheulean culture. The Mousterian samples, while more numerous, are still too few in time and space to provide a detailed record of the evolutionary changes and interactions that led to the emergence of the Upper Paleolithic populations. There are still numerous unanswered questions regarding the relationship of Neandertals and *Homo sapiens sapiens* Mousterian hominids in Israel and those elsewhere in the world. In spite of these deficiencies, the Mousterian hominids do provide a starting point from which to estimate the pattern and rate of change that has occurred in different skeletal parameters.

Stature is at its maximum in the early *Homo sapiens*

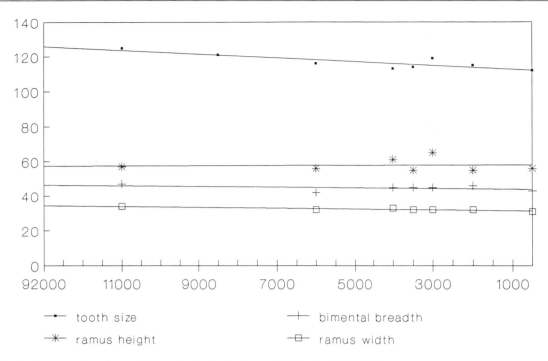

Figure 6 Diachronic trends in the mandible and tooth size for the samples described in Table 1

sapiens from Skhul and Qafzeh (180 cm in males), while from the Kebaran to recent periods it averages 168 cm in males, with only slight fluctuations. This reduction in stature is generally associated with increased environmental stress that acted to depress growth. However, the plasticity of the available gene pool has been drastically demonstrated by the marked secular trend in stature in modern Israeli populations.

Unlike the change in stature, the changes in head form – especially in head length, facial height and bizygomatic breadth – continue through to the Early Bronze Age. They result in decreased head length and increased head height so that the skull has become more globular. However, head length and head width ratios change only slightly so that most of these early Holocene populations remain dolichocranic. Figure 5 shows the extent of differences in morphometric characteristics of the skull in populations from different periods in Israel, in relation to the pooled mean of all samples studied. As can be seen, the Natufian, Chalcolithic and EBIV samples group together and separate out from the much more heterogeneous samples from the MBII and later periods. The changes occurring in the mandible are similar in timing and extent to those that have occurred in the skull. Size and robusticity decreased markedly between Mousterian and Upper Paleolithic populations. In later periods, the Natufian mandible with a broad ramus and acute gonal angle, was replaced by a thinner ramus with an obtuse gonal angle and thinner

corpus. However, the only parameter to show continued reduction until the present time is tooth size (Figures 5 and 6). From the MBII to recent periods, there is considerable fluctuation in all other parameters discussed above. Between the Natufian and the MBII it is possible to trace unidirectional microevolutionary trends in the skull, mandible and teeth. From the MBII onward, there are numerous fluctuations in all measurements, suggesting greater heterogeneity in the peoples inhabiting Israel and masking, to a greater or lesser extent, evidence of microevolutionary trends in the skull and mandible, although tooth size continues to reduce.

The extent and timing of changes in the skull, mandible and teeth have not all taken place at the same time, and in some periods, notably in the MBII and Roman-Byzantine periods, a sudden change and apparent reversal has taken place in cranial but not dental parameters. The long-term trends can be related to long-term selective pressures, that have acted to reduce skeletal robusticity and tooth size, whereas the sudden changes seen in MBII and Jewish populations indicate the introduction of a different population group. Smith (1989c, 1991) and Smith et al. (1984) have proposed that the pattern of microevolutionary change that characterizes the Israeli sequence, can be related to increased levels of environmental stress in Holocene populations following the adoption of agriculture.

Obviously, many more samples are needed before any

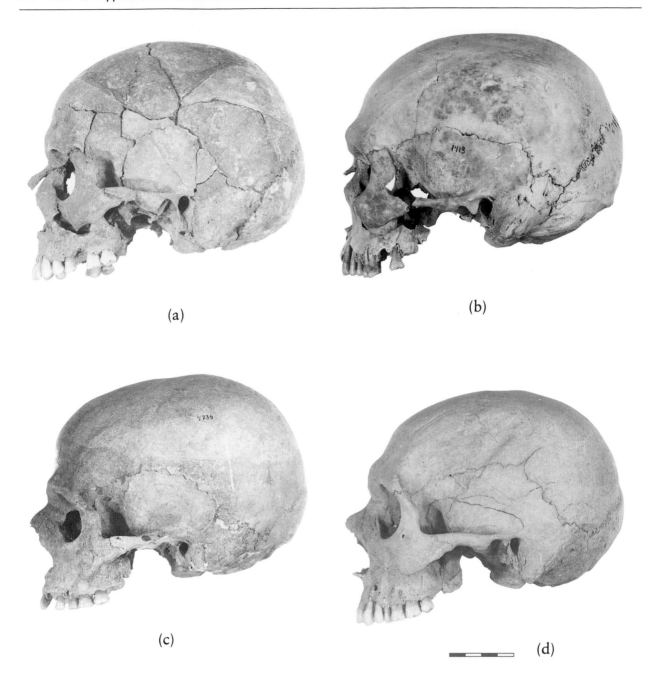

(a)

(b)

(c)

(d)

Plate 8 Lateral view of skulls: a) MBIIB from Sasa; b) Late Hellenistic skull from Ein Gedi; c) Iron Age skull from Achziv; d) Arab skull from Dor. Not all to same scale

attempt can be made to map the full extent and pattern of regional and temporal diversity within Israel, or the connections between populations in Israel and neighboring countries. Hopefully, the additional samples will become available through continued excavations. At the same time the new techniques available such as c-t scan imaging and DNA analysis of fossil bone, will improve the scope of research and enable the anthropologist both to ask new questions and to answer old ones with a degree of reliability undreamt of in the past.

PART II

STONE AGE ADAPTATION, EVOLUTION AND SURVIVAL

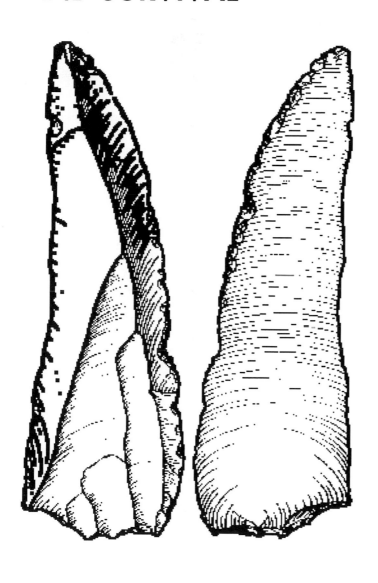

6

SOCIAL CHANGE AND THE ARCHAEOLOGY OF THE HOLY LAND: PREHISTORIC LITHIC PRODUCTION THROUGH TIME

Augustin F.C. Holl

Thomas E. Levy

Introduction

During the last decade, there have been some major shifts in archaeological research; one of the most important concerns the greater emphasis on various attempts to model and explain the dynamics of prehistoric social systems, and the development of methods, theories and techniques to recover the 'meaning' of things uncovered in archaeological contexts. Social archaeology, seen as based upon a body of explicit interpretive theory, is a relatively new subject (Renfrew 1984: 4). It is now accepted that:

> in studying the human past it is not enough simply to reconstruct what happened. Reconstruction is indeed one of the legitimate concerns of the historian and the archaeologists, and a necessary preliminary to further analysis. But we need to know more. We need to understand in some sense *how* it happened. We have to discern some pattern, to identify some simplifying principles. We have to decide what is significant for us. . . . Increasingly we are coming to appreciate that a social approach is a particularly rewarding one. (Renfrew 1984: 3)

The purpose of this chapter is highly ambiguous as it refers to at least two different but definitely connected aspects of archaeological research. The first aspect concerns the history of the discipline on the world scene and how it has been implemented in fieldwork and research programs (Daniel 1981; Trigger 1984, 1990); the second concerns the theories, models, ideas and subsequent narrative on the nature and the fabric of past social systems presented by different scholars and generations of researchers to make sense of the various kinds of archaeological data recorded.

In this chapter, we will focus mainly on the second aspect, neither in terms of scientific history *per se* nor as a synthesis of the long and complex archaeological record of the Holy Land; instead we have chosen to address some selected issues congruent with the theories and models expected from archaeological research on the eve of the third millennium AD. In this perspective the concept of 'social change' is but a convenient proposition for the study of social evolution as long-term history.

The need for a new framework for the study of past social systems results from several difficulties encountered in different attempts made during the last 30 years to generate genuine theories of cultural evolution (Renfrew 1984). The debates have, however, succeeded in clarifying some of the issues of contention. In general, it appears that deterministic models of social evolution based on the simplified idea of a prime-mover – environment, technology, demography, etc. – have partly failed to give satisfactory explanations for the diversity of social systems even within similar environmental and technological contexts; they have not explained the *why* of some amazing and strong similarities between different kinds of social systems within different ecological, technological and even political contexts, at different times and places. As considered in this chapter, 'social change' therefore refers to holistic transformations of human societies in different time scales and spatial contexts. Complicating the goals of social archaeology are the different approaches used to recover and study pieces and scatters of material evidence fossilized in the archaeological record. The history of prehistoric and archaeological research in the Holy Land is thus shaped by conflicting paradigms which have been used as important frames of reference for fieldwork and the

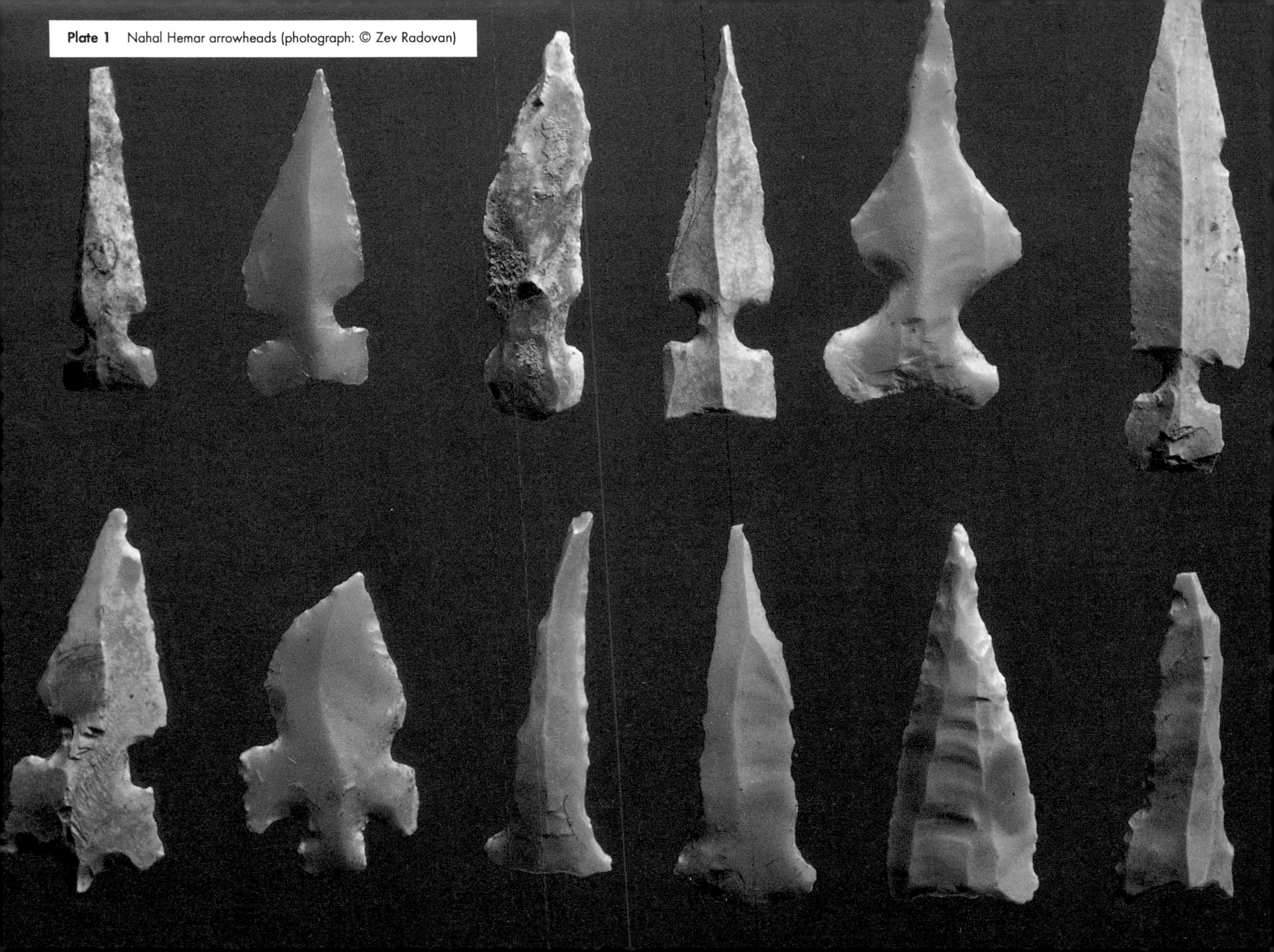

Plate 1 Nahal Hemar arrowheads (photograph: © Zev Radovan)

analysis of material evidence, and consequently the explanatory models constructed to make sense of the record at hand (Bar-Yosef and Mazar 1982; Dever 1992).

Archaeological knowledge as an evolutionary process

At the theoretical level, 'archaeological evidence' is an ambiguous conceptual category, which is always submitted to a continual process of definition and redefinition as new classes of data are included within the realm of archaeological investigation. Thus diversity and range of material remains is open-ended and what may have been considered yesterday as irrelevant, such as minute chips of bones and even tiny fragments of stone, may be considered today and tomorrow as highly important for the understanding of the dynamics of prehistoric societies. The same is true for the sets of ideas, theories, models and scientific expectations of archaeologists and the wider audience. It therefore appears almost axiomatic that, without variation, conceptual change would be impossible. The process of knowledge seeking is characterized by tensions and paradoxes (Popper 1991; Kuhn 1990); what is considered today as scientific archaeology in the global world of learning had emerged at some specific time and place in particular social circumstances, and has been shaped by different aims and purposes. Academic archaeology, with its endemic theoretical and methodological debates, its organization into complementary and/or competing 'demes' or 'schools of thought' and its various curricula, starts to become intelligible if considered in evolutionary terms:

> that science is a social institution functioning in various societies is neither controversial nor an especially interesting assertion. That scientists form social groups as small and tightly knit as research teams or as large and loosely structured as those that grow up around a particular subject matter is not especially controversial, but one of the messages of this book is that this demic structure of science is extremely interesting. (Hull 1988: 15)

The above point of view is extremely interesting as it may clarify the ideas which have shaped the development of archaeological research in the Holy Land in its role in either supporting or countering different assumptions about the past of this area of the world. Changing truths, theories, models and explanations are often interpreted by professional scientists as normal signs of progress in the clarification of the fundamental issues of their disciplines; this comfortable attitude has been seriously challenged by many scientists and scholars (Edelman 1992; Gould 1991; Hull 1988; Kuhn 1990; Mayr 1982; Moorey 1992; Prigogine and Stengers 1984). Kuhn (1970) for example

has convincingly argued that paradigmatic changes in scientific explanations result from complexes of interacting factors, not only reducible to progress in interpretation.

> What occurs during a scientific revolution is not fully reducible to a reinterpretation of individual and stable data. In the first place, the data are not equivocally stable. More important, the process by which either the individual or the community makes the transition from one theory to another is not one that resembles interpretation ... given a paradigm, interpretation of data is central to the enterprises that explore it. This enterprise can only articulate a paradigm, not correct it. Paradigms are not corrigible by normal science at all. (Kuhn 1970: 121)

Explanation may be roughly considered as a restatement of something – an idea, a concept, an event, a theory, a doctrine, etc. – which, in terms of current interests and assumptions, satisfies because it appeals to a specific *world view* and thus supersedes older or rival sets of ideas (Wilk 1985; Hall 1984a; Holl 1990). If archaeological knowledge is considered as a dynamic interplay between all the components of scientific investigation and belongs to a particular kind of evolutionary process of selection, then we may be in a position to understand some aspects of the current development of archaeological science in general, and more specifically the archaeology of the Holy Land. First, we will be in a position to realize that archaeology is not simply a straightforward record of discoveries; second, that the data recorded in fieldwork and processed by different researchers are variable mixtures of empirical facts, scientific theories, social and ideological assumptions; and, third, we will understand why scientists challenge certain tenets and take others for granted.

In the perspective outlined above, archaeology is definitely a historical science characterized by the singularity of past human experience which cannot be reenacted, the master concept being *contingency* (Gould 1991; Chapter 1). The reconstruction of the past, must, therefore, be considered neither as an unattainable 'past in itself' nor as a series of 'past as-known', but mainly as an open synthesis dependent upon the scientists' minds, and the intellectual and social framework within which their research aims and purposes are conceived and dispatched; debates among scientists are instrumental for the improvement of our knowledge of the past and are necessary to select the most accurate syntheses among many. The past can therefore serve diverse and multiple purposes; it can be 'past as charter' or 'past as bad example' (Wilk 1985: 319). Consequently, far from being a refuge and an escape from the present tormented world, the past assumes specific roles in the present – in cultural, social and political spheres. As members of a research field committed to studying the past, archaeologists *de facto* assert firmly that there is a connection between past and present, and that this feature is highly relevant and important today and certainly tomorrow.

According to both Wilk (1985) and Hall (1984b), there is no need for archaeologists to be defensive about explicitly or implicitly drawing on their personal, cultural and political experience in their professional work:

> I think we should drop the pretense of absolute objectivity. Further, I suggest that drawing on present experience and interests is hardly 'unscientific' and that it strengthens, rather than weakens, our work. The connection between present and past is a source of power, the power to offer legitimacy or attack. . . . Rather than condemning those who 'pervert' the past to their own political purposes, we should acknowledge that there is *no* neutral value-free, or non-political past − that if we take the present out of the past we are left with a dry empty husk. (Wilk 1985: 319)

In this regard, it does not seem to be controversial that 'archaeologists are not impassive and neutral conduits passing on the past to a wider audience but active and motivated participants in an industry the business of which is creating versions of the past' (Smith 1992). In this context, archaeology obviously does not occur in a social vacuum.

Archaeology and social change

There are diverse and sometimes conflicting views about the aims and methods of archaeology; however, such a general discussion is beyond the scope of this chapter. The long sequence of the archaeological record from the Holy Land, which starts with early occurrences of Lower Paleolithic through to the present, offers an opportunity to discuss some major issues concerning the tempo and modes of change of past social systems. Accounts of the evolution of human societies are almost always shaped after the format of hero tales in folklore, as a struggle for survival against blind forces of mother nature, the outcome being the development of civilization − control and then domestication of plants, animals and nature, the emergence of cities, states, empires; and, finally, human domination over everything. All general textbooks in prehistory and archaeology seem to be based upon this narrative which appears to be a genuine *genre littéraire*. Following Isaac (1989: 101), we are seriously worried and embarrassed by such a strong bias. Is it possible to avoid falling into this trap? At first glance, the position taken by Glynn Isaac (ibid.) for the research field of paleo-anthropology is partly relevant for our purpose:

> I have got used to the idea now − and would counter-argue that provided the fit between the stories and empirical evidence is improvable through testing and falsification, then this is indeed science. − If any of the rest of the scientific community is inclined to snigger at the embarrassment of the paleoanthropologists (here archae-ologists) over all this, pause and reflect. I bet that the same

basic findings would apply to accounts of the origin of mammals, or the flowering plants, or of life . . . or even the big bang and the cosmos. (Isaac 1989: 101)

However, we are not condemned to follow this strict anthropogenic narrative if we take seriously into account the very nature of historical sciences, in which *singularity* and *contingency* play a major role in the fabric and evolution of human social systems (Gould 1991). In this perspective, the long-term transformations which occurred in past social systems were certainly unpredictable for prehistoric peoples. Depending on actual circumstances, what may appear as a minor fluctuation near a bifurcation point may have produced unexpected and grand scale consequences which finally resulted in a profound change of the whole system (Prigogine and Stengers 1984). Hypotheses testing is therefore the main possibility to assess the congruence of our narratives on the evolution of past social systems.

Social change refers to the archaeological study of social dynamics; the issues concern a wide range of topics and can be addressed from different points of view such as analysis of settlement patterns, subsistence systems, patterns of social organization, etc., at different time scales. In this chapter, we will focus on lithic technology of paleolithic hunter-gatherer societies and its connections with patterns of mobility of prehistoric hunter-gatherer societies.

Paleolithic lithic technology and socio-economic dimensions

It is common knowledge that stone artifacts from the Paleolithic were manufactured, used, and discarded by mobile hunting and gathering societies who, depending on time and place, later adopted food-producing economies. This general statement is probably true, but it is useless in terms of operational research. Stone artifacts, sometime associated with animal bones, are the most common archaeological items to be found in Paleolithic sites; the major research problem is *how* to infer behaviorally-significant information from this category of data, beyond the necessary but insufficient morphological, technological, and stylistic classifications. An archaeological artifact, a stone tool for example, is

> a product of patterns of behavior, and the form of that object may be a result of the combined effects of constraints imposed by the raw material, technology, intended function, traditional and stylistic preference, ideological considerations, and so forth, plus a certain amount of random variability. (Close et al. 1979: 11)

Generally, in archaeological fieldwork, it is concentrations of discarded material which are found in sites and collected. The sampling techniques used to collect the data recorded are therefore important to assess the reliability of our inferences about past social systems. Lithic assemblages are often distributed among several localities within the same study area, they may vary from one site to another, share some similarities or be totally different, or be made from the same or different categories of raw material. It is these different kinds of variability which are interesting; we can no longer simply assign stone tools to discrete functional classes and then use the range of classes and relative frequencies of tools as indices of activities conducted in past social systems. It appears increasingly clear that variability in stone tool technologies is not explained solely by the functional requirement of activities (Eder 1984; Shott 1986; Torrence 1983, 1986). Lithic technologies are integrated in a larger set of interacting components which condition the way they are organized within cultural systems. If we intend to shed some light on the dynamics of prehistoric societies of the Holy Land, we need to learn not only to apply the appropriate questions to our static data, but to frame our queries in a manner which will yield the adequate information. In order to explain the variability of stone tool assemblages, we must understand the organizational principles of lithic technological systems, and their interaction with both the settlement patterns and systems of mobility of prehistoric hunter-gatherer societies (Kaufman 1986, 1988). The topic is a very large one and will be addressed through the formulation of an interpretive theory, the transport-cost model for foraging societies.

The transport-cost model for foraging societies

The transport-cost model for foraging societies may be summarized as follows: in any kind of hunter-gatherer society, transportation of items of material culture places heavy constraints on the organization of the foraging-settlement system. Thus, we may expect diverse strategies in the development of technological systems which will result in alleviating these constraints; sequences of these alleviating mechanisms which may appear optimal may later be selected and included in the cultural repertoire of foraging societies and may be directional in the long run, and/or time and place specific. According to Shott (1986) and Eder (1984), ethnographic evidence shows that elements of technology are related to the settlement mobility of forager societies in numerous situations. Mobility places constraints upon technology mainly by imposing carrying costs. Consequently, with the same transportation system, the size and diversity of the equipment and the technology cannot increase indefinitely even if there are functional demands to meet. In this regard,

> the response to constraints imposed by settlement mobility should involve a limit on the size of the tool inventory or

even a reduction in its size if increasing mobility reduces the overall transport capacity of the group. Tools may also become smaller and lighter and assume a greater range of uses; that is, tools should become less specialized and more multifunctional in character. In addition, tools should be designed to enhance their portability. (Shott 1986: 20)

Mobility can therefore be considered as a critical variable in the technological organization of foraging societies. There are, however, different kinds of mobility connected to environmental and social parameters which may need to be understood according to their dominant characteristics, along with their actual duration and relative frequency (Binford 1980, 1982). Depending on the existing climatic patterns, which may have been more or less predictable, and the time scale under consideration, the lithic technological system – procurement of raw material, manufacture of stone items, use, recycling and discard – of any prehistoric foraging society is intimately connected with the actual economic and subsistence strategies. A foraging system combines in varying degrees residential and logistic kinds of mobility, and both vary in duration of each actual stay at one place, and frequency of moves in any specific time unit (a day, a week, a month, a season, a year). Theoretically, at the general level, it is possible to consider that logistic mobility is more connected with task-specific demands – procurement of raw material, hunting stand, butchering sites, etc. – while residential mobility is more related to global maintenance activities and other numerous and undifferentiated activities of daily life – food preparation and consumption, craft activities, building of dwelling facilities, etc. – these two components being articulated to each other by the efficiency of the transportation system actually developed – leather bags, baskets, etc. Thus, we may expect different degrees of variability in site lithic assemblages belonging to similar spatial and/or temporal frames of references. The same place may be settled at different times by the same or another group of hunter-gatherers for different activities; it may be reoccupied regularly or not at short-term intervals of time. The result is a palimpsest of lithic material which is the normal archaeological situation. An archaeological study of lithic assemblages cannot simply be based on the important but inaccurate experimental research on lithic technology, whatever strict and controlled experimentation protocol may have been implemented. We need to devise research methods which are congruent with the very nature of our archaeological data base; it is therefore lithic assemblages from sites which are the basic unit of analysis.

The above discussion of our preliminary interpretive model suggests some interesting expectations which may be important if we wish to achieve a deeper understanding of paleolithic lithic assemblages. To mention but a few of these expectations:

1. The problems of the scheduling of multiple sets of activity within the same time-budget of foraging societies (Marks 1983; Halstead and O'Shea 1989; Torrence 1983; Wobst 1983).
2. Actual responses to risk and uncertainty in the implementation of strategies of procurement of the needed raw materials.
3. Long-term patterns of transformations of stone tools inventories.

Such expectations can only be dealt with within a new analytical framework, based on space/time as major variables. Lithic assemblages may therefore be considered as actual technological testimony of human behavior on the studied site, and their variability within any time/space frame of reference may suggest the range of possibilities attempted in the past.

Considered from the perspective outlined above, the dynamics of lithic technology is somewhat similar to non-equilibrium systems following a non-linear path of transformations (Nicolis 1989, Prigogine and Stengers 1984; Prigogine 1988), even if it appears to be directional. In this regard, it is the variability of stone tool assemblages which is the rule, and recorded variations may be considered as fluctuations. The range of fluctuations may be wide or narrow depending on actual circumstances. Fluctuations may be near a bifurcation point, that is near a radical and unpredictable change. A minor fluctuation may produce unexpected and grand scale transformations, as it may be boosted and amplified by feedback with other components, that invade the whole technological and even social system. In studies of paleolithic lithic technology, the development of the Levallois technique, the blade and bladelet debitage techniques and the production of microliths are examples of fluctuations as they have often been recorded in earlier chronological contexts in different parts of the world, well before their generalization within some specific space/time contexts (Bar-Yosef 1980: 116). The approach to lithic technology proposed here highlights the importance of *contingency* in the evolution of human societies as it is the random interaction of relatively independent dynamic components which shapes the unpredictable evolutionary pathways of human social systems.

On the making of stone tools and archaeology

Due to the subtractive nature of the process of manufacture of stone tools, a linear and sequential model is easy to frame. The process starts with the selection and procurement of raw materials. The selected cobbles or blocks are then processed following some sequences of knapping and some specific by-products are discarded and abandoned on the site. Different classes of stone items are thus produced and used to perform different tasks; some items are function-specific some

others are not. Consequently, depending on the quantity of labor invested in the production of items, some artifacts produced with the minimum quantity of labor have been classified as expedient tools, that is tools made to face immediate demands (Binford 1982), and those manufactured with much more attention, to face future needs, have been termed curated tools. This last category of the lithic inventory is often studied more seriously as it is considered to contain important technological, stylistic and cultural information which may disclose some major aspects of paleolithic foraging societies. The concept of *chaîne opératoire* is very useful regarding the study of technological know-how of prehistoric hunter-gatherers but it has to be coupled with attempts to understand the *patterns of management* of selected raw materials. At a general theoretical level the dichotomy between expedient and curated tools is important, but it often results in the neglect of assemblages dominated by expedient tools which are equally important for the understanding of the dynamics of past foraging societies.

Within the space/time approach, it is the spatial distribution of lithic assemblages and their degrees of variability which is relevant as a starting point. Raw material procurement sites may be located near rock outcrops or close to a river course if cobbles are collected. Alternately, the location of procurement areas may shift from one place to another according to the actual distribution of cobbles. Such sites are often littered with thousands of primary flakes or blades with cortex, secondary flakes and blades, and cores and chunks, if the manufacture of tools and preforms is carried out on the spot. In the first case, the lithic workshop is located on the raw material procurement site; it may however occur that the manufacture of tools is carried out elsewhere, in a specific locality or within the settlement of the foraging group. Tools are used in daily life activities and when worn out they may be recycled, they may sometimes be lost within the site territory, and/or purposely discarded. Theoretically at least, paleolithic sites can be arranged following the relative proportions of diverse classes of stone items within the landscape – with site assemblages dominated by debitage by-products and waste at one extreme of a continuum, and those with discarded tools at the other. The number of possible combinations between these extremes seems infinite, as changing patterns of settlements may complicate the matter. In summary, lithic technology as a dynamic system may at least be partitioned into four interacting components:

1. the search for and selection of raw materials unevenly distributed in the physical environment,
2. the range of tasks to be performed within the changing economic, subsistence and social requirements,
3. the development of a flaking technology, and
4. a tool repertoire,

Table 1 Frequency distribution of sites per chronological periods according to different authors

Study areas	The Levant (Bar-Yosef: 1980)		Mount Carmel (Olami: 1984)		Negev/Sinai (Goring-Morris: 1987)		Northern Negev (Levy: 1987)	
	n	%	n	%	n	%	n	%
Lower Paleolithic	13	12.02	1	0.52	–	–	–	–
Middle Paleolithic	36	33.33	50	26.45	–	–	–	–
Upper Paleolithic	–	–	5	2.64	23	7.54	–	–
Epipaleolithic	59	54.62	10	5.29	282	92.45	–	–
Neolithic	Many		105	55.55	–	–	11	15.06
Neolithic/Chalcolithic	–	–	9	4.76	–	–	–	–
Chalcolithic	–	–	9	4.76	–	–	54	73.97
Early Bronze Age	–	–	–	–	–	–	8	10.95
Total	108	–	189	–	305	–	73	–

all the mentioned components being submitted to random drift and cultural selection.

The quality of our data base on paleolithic foraging societies of the Holy Land depends on the sampling techniques used by different generations of researchers to collect and publish information from archaeological sites (Bar-Yosef 1980; Bar-Yosef and Valla 1991; Bar-Yosef and Vandermeersch 1989; Goring-Morris 1987; Marks 1976, 1977; Ohel 1986, 1990; Olami 1984; Phillips 1987; Ronen 1984; Vita-Finzi and Higgs 1970). Several criteria are often useful in order to have a realistic estimate of the degree to which the information published in archaeological reports matches the potential information available from the global sampling universe of sites. Among these we can mention a few simple criteria such as site size, areal sample size, total number of artifacts; and complex criteria like average density, density of stone items, density of debitage and waste, clusters of classes of artifacts, etc.

Depending on the nature, the aim of the research and the frame of reference used by authors of archaeological reports, different and complementary information on prehistoric societies of the Holy Land may be gleaned (Table 1). A recent synthesis of the prehistory of the Levant (Bar-Yosef 1980) was framed to highlight some of the important achievements of prehistoric research in that part of the world. Olami (1984) offers the result of his archaeological survey in the Mount Carmel area. Goring-Morris (1987) has published in-depth studies of Late Upper Paleolithic and Epipaleolithic foraging societies of the Negev based on survey, excavation and integration of earlier research. And finally Levy (1987) provides information based on systematic survey, integration of earlier works, and excavations. Each of the selected examples presents a particular trend of the frequency distribution of archaeological settlements through time (Figure 1).

For example, information on the regional distribution of archaeological sites in the Mount Carmel area (Olami 1984) can be used for a preliminary exploration of the changing patterns of settlements through time, from the Lower Paleolithic to the Chalcolithic Period (Table 2, Figure 2). Sites have been recorded according to their nature: cave sites, *in situ* open-air sites, quarry and alluvial sites, displaced material and undetermined occurrences. Based on these survey data alone, the former idea of Paleolithic hominids as cave dwellers becomes partly intelligible, as shown by the shift which occurred during the Neolithic period with the increased number of open-air settlements relative to cave sites (Figure 2). Considered from the perspective of fluctuating densities of settlements, it also appears that there have been two major periods of intense settlement, the Middle Paleolithic and the Neolithic period as suggested by the bi-modal distribution curves. Many other interesting hypotheses can be formulated from the data collected from grand scale surveys such as the one cited above, and can be used to focus on narrower problem-oriented research strategy.

Approaches to Paleolithic lithic assemblages

The earliest series of stone tools collected in the Holy Land belong to the Acheulean period and every type of environmental zone, from the Sinai and Negev deserts (Phillips 1987) to lake shore and caves, was occupied (Bar-Yosef 1980: 109–110). Lithic assemblages are characterized by varying proportions of core tools, choppers, chopping tools, bifaces, cleavers and picks; but flakes and informal tools are predominant. According to Bar-Yosef (1980), a feature common in Lower Paleolithic assemblages is the lack of standardization of forms among the tool groups and tool kits changed very slowly during this long period of more than one million years. Middle Paleolithic sites are more numerous and their lithic assemblages present much more variability than during the former period; it lasted from *ca.* 100,000 BP to *ca.*

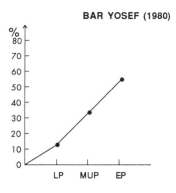

BAR YOSEF (1980)

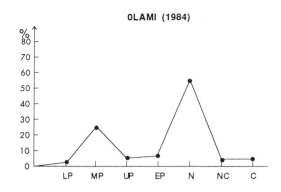

OLAMI (1984)

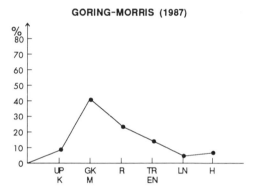

GORING-MORRIS (1987)

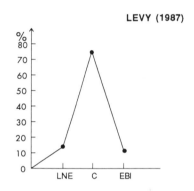

LEVY (1987)

Key: LP — Lower Paleolithic; MP — Middle Paleolithic; UP — Upper Paleolithic; EP — Epipaleolithic; K — Kebaran; M — Mushabian; GK — Geometric Kebaran; R — Ramonian; TR — Terminal Ramonian; EN — Early Natufian; LN — Late Natufian; H — Harifian; N — Neolithic; LNE — Late Neolithic; NC — Neolithic/Chalcolithic; C — Chalcolithic; EBI — Early Bronze Age I

Figure 1 Some frequency curves of the distribution of archaeological sites in the Holy Land

40,000 BP. Basically, the lithic technology is geared above all toward the manufacture of tools on flakes and blades, with an important proportion obtained through the use of the Levallois debitage technique. The formal tool repertoire is expanded to include different kinds of scrapers, burins, borers, knives, notches, denticulates and points. Some bifaces are attested in the earliest levels of some sites such as the cave of Tabun (Olami 1984: 108–109). The four Mousterian facies recorded in the Holy Land are more an artifact of the Bordian typological type list than a genuine understanding of the vexing problem of the variability of Middle Paleolithic lithic assemblages. Upper Paleolithic assemblages are characterized by the development of blade/bladelet debitage technique and greater techno-typological variability among site assemblages. Settlements seem to have been relatively small and it is inferred that 'small mobile bands of hunter-gatherers formed the basic social units during that period.' (Bar-Yosef 1980: 118). Finally, the Epipaleolithic is characterized by the predominance of microlithic

components used for composite tools such as the bow and arrow, and lasted from ca. 18,000 BC to 8,000 BC.

From the above short summary of lithic assemblages of the Holy Land, the crudest level of variability observable at this point of our discussion is temporal change. During the Lower Paleolithic, unretouched flakes are predominant and core tools are the major category while flake tools appear to have contributed only marginally to site assemblages. During the Middle Paleolithic, with the generalization of the Levallois technique which has been recorded in Late Acheulean contexts, the technology shifted toward the manufacture of different classes of flake tools, and some of them, such as Mousterian points, were certainly hafted as spears. During the Upper Paleolithic a new shift occurs with the development of the blade/bladelet debitage technique. The technology is highly standardized but at the same time there is greater variability between site assemblages. During the Epipaleolithic, the miniaturization of stone implements occurred with the production of microliths for composite tools.

Table 2 Nature of prehistoric localities in the Mount Carmel area after Olami (1984)

Nature	Cave		Open–air		In situ	Q	D	A	Und	Total
	n	%	n	%	n	n	n	n	n	%
Lower Paleolithic	1	2.27	–	–	–	–	–	–	5	6	1.95
Middle Paleolithic	18	40.90	32	15.17	10	22	54	15	6	125	40.71
Upper Paleolithic	–	–	–	–	–	–	–	–	–	5	1.62
Epipaleolithic	6	13.13	4	2.75	4	–	3	–	4	17	5.53
Neolithic	12	27.27	93	64.13	93	–	11	9	2	127	41.36
Neolithic/Chalcolithic	–	–	9	6.20	9	–	–	–	–	9	2.93
Chalcolithic	2	4.54	7	4.82	7	–	–	–	–	9	2.93
Undetermined Period	–	–	–	–	–	–	–	–	–	9	2.93
Total	39	14.33	145	47.23	123	22	68	24	17	307	–

Key: Q = Quarry site, D = Displaced material, A = Alluvial occurrence, Und = Undetermined

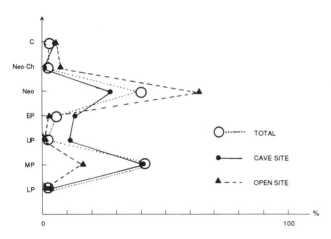

Figure 2 Distribution of prehistoric sites (open vs. cave) in the Mount Carmel region (after Olami 1984)

Such changes are often explained in general adaptive terms combined with a natural drift; however, models presented by Torrence (1983) and Marks (1983) are more specific and interesting. According to the 'time-stressed environment' model of Torrence, in ecologically specialized zones with a limited range of relatively mobile and unpredictable resources, the acquisition of needed food is under strong pressure. Therefore, the efficient use of time will be favored by such behaviors as the scheduling of resource exploitation or by increasing the speed and efficiency of critical activities such as capturing and pursuing prey. Such strategies will be implemented through the development of an embedded procurement of raw material, the manufacture of tools integrated within other activities or within specific parts of the time-budget. In the same vein, Marks (1983) has presented a model to explain the Middle–Upper Paleolithic transition in the Levant, as attested by changes in lithic technology. The model is based on the hypothesis of

increasing aridity which resulted in greater mobility of hunter-gatherer groups, and less continuous and repeated use of the same territory: 'increased mobility, with less and less security as to the predictability of available flint sources near any one site probably was met with additional "economizing behavior"' (Marks 1983: 92). With careful selection of raw material, and the production of preformed cores suitable for the manufacture of elongated blanks, the Upper Paleolithic blades were therefore technical solutions devised to cope with this new situation.

Both models presented above share several implications even if the sequences do differ: environmental change – time stress – economizing behaviors – adapted new lithic technology. Both models have been devised to explain the development of lithic technology during a particular time sequence of the prehistoric record, and cannot be expanded to the long-term evolution of the Paleolithic record, a possibility offered by our preliminary interpretive model, the transport-cost model. It can easily be observed that, on average, the size and bulk of individual stone tools decreases from the earliest times of the Lower Paleolithic to the Epipaleolithic. At the beginning we have relatively heavy Acheulean core tools, then less heavy but still large flake tools of the Middle Paleolithic, which are followed by tools on blades and bladelets from the Upper Paleolithic and, finally, microlithic tools during the Epipaleolithic. In the long term, the transportability of stone tools seems to increase.

The observed long-term pattern may be explained as follows: an above all expedient technology lacking any standardization and related to very mobile foraging strategy was predominant during the Acheulean. This appears to have been a period of moving peripatetic groups, not focused on specific places, following the patterns of group choice. In this regard, Acheulean groups seem to have merged at some localities which were visited at a specific time of the year – Central Place Foraging – and then split into smaller social units following dominant individuals, males or females. In such a strategy, the major portion of tool kits may have been manufactured for immediate need or for short-term purposes and then discarded after use. Tools were, under exceptional circumstances, curated for future needs. With low densities of population and large tracts of unsettled territories, the Acheulean system was basically territorially unbounded and space-expansive; the technological system evolved very slowly and the whole complex lasted for more than one million years.

During the Middle Paleolithic, depending on the nature of the site and the episode of occupation, a punctuated and unstable equilibrium between expedient and curated technologies seems to have existed for the whole period. The large range of variation in number of formal tools recorded in Middle Paleolithic assemblages suggests a greater degree of intersite differentiation within the same foraging system, and a combination of residential and logistic kinds of mobility, with multiple occupations of the same places for longer periods of stay. Variability in the occurrence of formal tools, often collated under the term Mousterian facies, may have resulted from the addition of multiple activities executed at the same place at different times by the same group of foragers, in patterned succession by different but linked groups with varying technological know-how, and/or the superimposition of the same set of activities at roughly regular intervals on the same site. The emergence of the habit of burying the dead at some sites such as Skhul, Tabun and Qafzeh (Bar-Yosef and Vandermeersch 1989) suggests that during the Middle Paleolithic some notion of territoriality emerged among early *Homo sapiens*. On average, some Middle Paleolithic sites seem to have been more intensely settled, even if the quality and quantity of information published do not allow very definitive conclusions (Bar-Yosef 1980). The mobility pattern may have been structured on some base camps and special purpose sites, such as flint procurement sites (Phillips 1987), within bounded but as yet unknown territories. The lithic tool kits were more easily transportable from one place to another.

During the Upper Paleolithic, the all blade and bladelet debitage technique succeeded in alleviating constraints on the transportability of stone tools; but these tools were more and more specialized and function-specific. The consequence of this transformation was greater variability between site assemblages, some being dominated by flake debitage while others are mostly composed of blades/bladelets. If the sea level was about 100 meters lower than today (Vita-Finzi and Higgs 1970), large parts of the coastal plain were probably included within the economic and social territories of Upper Paleolithic hunter-gatherers. It is therefore hypothesized that major settlements, which may have fulfilled the role of base camps, may have been located on the coastal plain. In this scenario, sites recorded today which appear to be relatively small would have belonged to micro-bands who camped in the

territories of smaller groups after the initial split of larger bands. If, as suggested here, marine resources may have been collected by Upper Paleolithic foragers along with terrestrial mammals, the model of 'time-stressed environment' will have to be modified or even discarded. It is the transport-cost of stone tools which is at a premium, if the distribution of raw material in the landscape was highly skewed.

During the following Epipaleolithic, lithic technology became very standardized; items produced are small sized objects which are combined with wood and bone for the manufacture of composite tools, thus enhancing their portability. The sizes of sites are moderate on the average, suggesting a high frequency of mobility made possible by the existence of highly curated and portable technology (Goring-Morris 1987; Bar-Yosef 1980). However, the long-term perspective presented above suggests some interesting views which can be tested at different levels with site assemblages.

Socio-technological structures of lithic assemblages

The concept of socio-technological structure refers to the interaction between the dynamics of hunter-gatherer foraging systems and the organizational principles of stone tool production as manifested by the procurement and selection of raw materials, manufacture of tools, use, recycling and discard (Kaufman 1988; Wendorf and Schild 1992; Torrence 1983; Mitchell 1988). The study of these structures may be operationalized through the use of six criteria:

1. of tools to debitage and waste
2. the ratio of cores to waste
3. the ratios of cores to primary waste (unretouched flakes and blades with cortex)
4. tool diversity
5. tool versatility
6. degrees of equipment flexibility.

The different ratios may signal the relative importance of stone knapping in each site assemblage and their distribution in the landscape relative to known sources of raw materials may give some accurate pictures of the territorial ranges of Paleolithic foraging groups.

Tool diversity indicates the number of distinct tool classes or categories in a site assemblage; if grouped into activity sets we may gain some knowledge about the range of activities carried out at each site and assess their space/time compatibility within the actual foraging systems.

Tool versatility denotes 'the number of tasks to which tool classes can be applied. It may vary across tool classes and values can be calculated by class or in the aggregate for complete technological inventories' (Shott 1986). This preliminary definition poses no theoretical problem, but in practice, assigning specific functions to tools using shape as determining criteria is a very difficult problem, very close to circular reasoning. However, we can devise a classification of elementary task applications based on types of physical motions (Leroi-Gourhan 1971) such as hammering, chopping, knapping, cutting, scraping, sawing, piercing, etc. Then, tools belonging to each assemblage are partitioned into non-exclusive classes under these different headings. If we assign one mark for each heading under which a tool appears, some tools, such as Acheulean bifaces appear to be very versatile or multifunctional while others, such as burins, are exclusively task-specific. It is the sum of the marks over all the tools in an assemblage which gives the index of tool versatility. There is, however, one problem resulting from the fact that unretouched flakes and blades are not integrated in this scheme, even if it appears that they may have played an important role as expedient tools. In the long-term perspective, it appears that the degree of tool versatility decreases in general from the Acheulean to the Epipaleolithic, as multifunctional tools are replaced by more specialized ones, with a later shift toward the manufacture of microlithic components for more complex tools. A comparison of tool diversity to tool versatility carried out for the Saharan desert (Holl 1989) has shown that the lower the diversity, the higher the versatility.

The degrees of equipment flexibility are measured in site assemblages by the differences between tool versatility and diversity. This measurement is based on the simple fact that in lithic assemblages exclusively composed of specialized tools, versatility is equal to diversity. In such situations it may be inferred that lithic assemblages do not offer any possibility to grasp the reaction of prehistoric peoples to unexpected task demands. However, the flexibility of tool kits based on the patterned occurrence of groups of tools pertaining to different sets of activities performed at different settlements within the same space/time social units can be used as an approximation of socio-technological structures developed by prehistoric societies.

As hunter-gatherer strategies always combine different kinds of moves at different time scales to meet subsistence and social demands, residential, logistic and semi-logistic patterns of mobility may thus interact to produce prehistoric settlement systems. With due understanding of the site formation processes and their patterned distribution within each regional unit, it is possible to extend the study of socio-technological dimensions of Paleolithic lithic assemblages beyond simple typology. In this regard, research must be carried out using multiple and complementary criteria such as the regional distribution of sites, site sizes, areal sample studied, total density of artifacts, tools, waste, number of debitage categories, different ratios, tool diversity, versatility and

degrees of equipment flexibility, raw material selected, etc. Such an approach will show that the Acheulean period was characterized by a high degree of mobility, connected to the existence of an above all expedient lithic technology, and settlement strategies in a relatively unbounded space seem to have been poorly structured. During the Middle Paleolithic, residential and logistic mobility seems to have emerged as a structured pattern within bounded territories, with specific base camps and special purpose sites. During the Upper Paleolithic, territories seem to have been larger with a greater differentiation between summer and winter camping areas, and site assemblages witnessed greater variability thus suggesting a greater diversity of activity sets and technological know how (Gilead, this volume Chapter 9). During the Epipaleolithic, the legacy of Upper Paleolithic continued for the early phase of the period but was followed by a shift toward smaller territorial units (Goring-Morris 1987). Due to the reduction of the size of stone tools, composite tools, and the high degree of portability of the technology, the average frequency of moves from site to site seems to have been quite high. At this time subsistence-settlement systems were highly structured within a more 'planned' foraging strategy. Stone tool manufacturing sequences appear to have been relatively free from the locations of raw material procurement areas. The Natufian culture, which has emerged as a pan-regional phenomenon with relatively bulky dwelling facilities and storage features, is probably the outcome of the process of territorialization of hunter-gatherer societies which later culminated with the development of settled and sedentary Pre-pottery Neolithic A and B groups (see in this volume: Bar-Yosef, Chapter 8; Bar-Yosef and Valla 1991; Goring-Morris 1987; Goring-Morris, Chapter 10; Valla, Chapter 11).

The space-time approach as exploratory model

The general ideas discussed above can be contextualized to make sense of the empirical record at hand in one selected study area, the Late Pleistocene settlements of the Negev and Sinai studied by Goring-Morris (1987). The important discussions by different researchers (Goring-Morris 1988; Henry 1988; Marks 1988; Speth 1988; Valla 1988) have highlighted some issues needing further clarification and elaboration. The most important point, however, is that the research carried out in these areas is based on an explicit theoretical approach which can be tested using a scientific methodology. In this chapter, we will focus on the spatial dimensions of the prehistoric record.

The prehistoric record at hand ranges from the Terminal Upper Paleolithic (*ca.* 30,000–17,500 BC) to the Harifian (*ca.* 8,500–7,500 BC), organized into seven

Table 3   Late Pleistocene prehistoric sites of the Negev and Sinai after Goring-Morris (1987)

Period/Culture	n	%	Uncalibrated radiocarbon chronology
Terminal/Upper Paleolithic and Kebaran			
ca. 17,000–13,500 BC	23	7.54	ca. 20,000–17,500 BC
Geometric Kebaran	63	20.65	ca. 14,000–11,500 BC
Mushabian	60	19.67	ca. 13,500–10,500 BC
Ramonian	74	24.26	ca. 11,500–10,500 BC
Terminal Ramonian/Early Natufian	37	12.13	ca. 11,000–8,500 BC
Late Natufian	21	6.88	ca. 9,000–8,000 BC
Harifian	27	8.85	ca. 8,500–7,500 BC
Total	305	–	ca. 20,000–7,500 BC

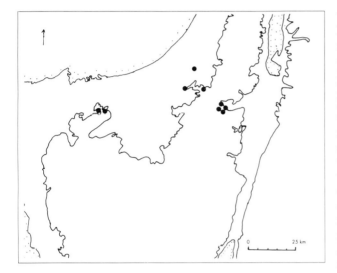

Figure 3   Terminal and Upper Paleolithic (after Goring-Morris 1987)

taxonomic units (Table 3). The frequency of sites in each unit varies from 21 for the Late Natufian to 74 for the Ramonian. As far as the regional distribution of settlements is concerned, Terminal Upper Paleolithic sites are organized into two major clusters (Figure 3) and three relatively isolated occurrences, all of them situated along the 300 m contour line. The maximum territorial extent measures 150 km, site clusters being located at about 100 km from each other, while isolated sites are at some 25 km from each over (Table 4). Surprisingly enough, mid-distances between neighboring sites measuring 12.5 km match the average site-territories of tropical hunter-gatherer societies (cf. Bailey 1991). Kebaran settlements are distributed in a territory measuring 200 km in maximum extent, with one cluster in the center and two isolated and remote sites (Figure 4); distances between nearest occurrences in the center vary from 10 to 15 km (Table 4), while isolated sites are located 100 km apart. Geometric Kebaran sites are distributed in a larger

territory, the maximum extent being 230 km (Table 4, Figure 5); isolated sites are located on the periphery while numerous clusters have been uncovered in the central area. Distances between nearest clusters vary from 10 to 20 km, while major settled areas are located at 140 to 150 km from the core area. Mushabian settlements, including Nizzanian Assemblages (Figure 6) have been uncovered in two major areas within a territory measuring 175 km in maximum extent (Table 4). The Nizzanian sites are relatively equidistant from each other, 20 km from one to the nearest, in a territory measuring 50 km in diameter, while 'Classic' Mushabian sites are organized into dense clusters 20 to 30 km distant from each other in the core area, with major settled areas located at about 100 km from each other. The Early and Late Ramonian sites follow a general pattern of distribution similar to the Mushabian one, within a less extensive territory measuring 150 km. There is, however, one important difference, as highland situated above the 600 m contour line is settled during the Ramonian (Table 4, Figure 7). During the Terminal Ramonian and Early Natufian, the settled territory was extended, measuring 230 km; the distances between settlements in the center vary from 20 to 70 km, while nearest sites and clusters of sites are located at 10 to 20 km from each other. The distance between major settled areas varies from 100 to 120 km, and a linear pattern of distribution of settlement occurred in the highland of the eastern part of the study area (Table 4, Figure 8). Late Natufian settlements are distributed in a territory measuring 210 km in maximum extent; in the core area, nearest sites and clusters are situated on average at 20 to 50 km from each other, while major settled areas are situated at 100 to 120 km from each other (Table 4, Figure 9). Finally, Harifian sites are found mostly in the core area, in a territory measuring 170 km in maximum extent. Distances between nearest sites and clusters vary from 10 to 50 km, while major settled areas are situated 110 km apart (Table 4, Figure 10). The distribution pattern of sites into clustered and isolated settlements may have resulted from the high degree of mobility of small

Table 4 Theoretical territorial ranges of Late Pleistocene settlements in the Negev and Sinai

Territorial ranges	Site territorial range (km)	Site cluster territorial range (km)	Major settled territorial range (km)	Maximum territorial range (km)
Terminal Upper Paleolithic	25	50	100	150
Kebaran	10–15	30	100	200
Geometric Kebaran	10–20	40	140–150	230
Nizzanian	20	30	30	50
Mushabian	20–30	40	100	175
Ramonian	10–20	30–50	100	150
Terminal Ramonian/Early Natufian	10–20	30–70	100–120	230
Late Natufian	20	30–50	100–120	210
Harifian	10–15	40–50	110	170

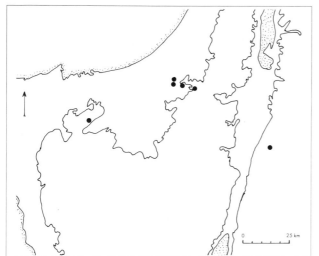

Figure 4 Kebaran sites (after Goring-Morris 1987)

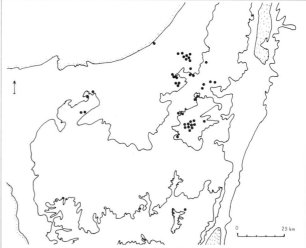

Figure 6 Mushabian sites (after Goring-Morris 1987)

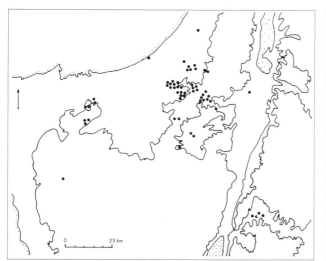

Figure 5 Geometric Kebaran sites (after Goring-Morris 1987)

Figure 7 Early and Late Ramonian sites (after Goring-Morris 1987)

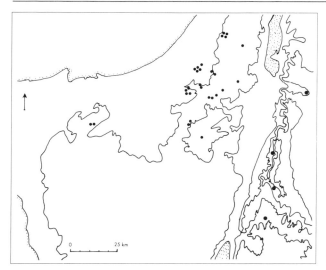

Figure 8 Terminal Ramonian and Early Natufian sites (after Goring-Morris 1987)

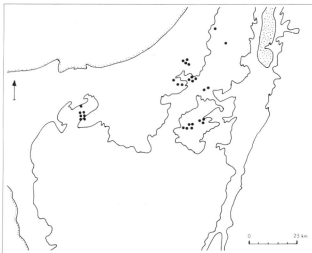

Figure 10 Harifian sites (after Goring-Morris 1987)

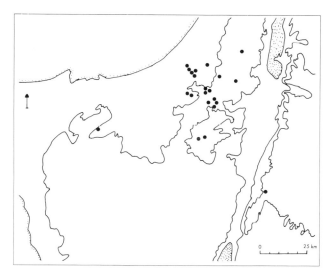

Figure 9 Late Natufian sites (after Goring-Morris 1987)

groups of hunter-gatherers which, depending on the actual circumstances, may have shifted their settlement from one place to another within the same seasonal drainage. In this process, depending on the flexibility of their social systems, some individuals may have moved from one group to another, some groups may have merged for some specific social and economic circumstances. The variability of lithic tool kits and even the areal extent of settlements may have, therefore, resulted from the combination of these factors.

In general, the changing patterns in the regional distribution of settlements can be considered from a wide range of research perspectives which aim to explain the observed variations. If we considered the total number of settlements for each taxonomic unit, there is a nested hierarchy of spatial units: the sizes of site-territories, ranging from 10 to 25 km, present the lowest degree of variation; site-cluster territories range from 30 to 70 km, major settled areas had territories ranging from 100 to 150 km, and, finally, regional territories ranging from 150 to 230 km attest for the maximum degree of variation (Figure 11). As the Mushabian was partly contemporaneous with the Geometric Kebaran, it is far from clear how both taxonomic units had shared the same territory, with overlapping distributions of settlements, for millennia. It may be argued that, following a pioneer stage of settlement during the Upper Paleolithic and Kebaran, with sites located in only four or five areas, Geometric Kebaran and Mushabian groups of the Negev and Sinai were progressively merged through marriage and other kinds of alliance. The result of this combination of different lithic traditions and social systems generated the peak of Epipaleolithic occupation, which occurred during the Ramonian, characterized by higher degrees of site clustering in some favored localities (Tables 5 and 6) and the extension of settlements to 14 or 15 areas. From the Terminal Ramonian/Late Natufian onwards, there seem to have been in-depth transformations of the relations between societies and their territories and landscape, as only six or seven areas were settled (Figure 12).

When available, data on the surface extent of settlements show that Kebaran sites were on average the smallest, ranging in size from 5 m^2 at Shunera XVII to 75 m^2 at Azariq I, while Late Natufian sites were the largest, their sizes varying from 10 m^2 at Shunera XIV to 5000 m^2 at Rosh Horesha (Table 7, Figure 13). However, if major

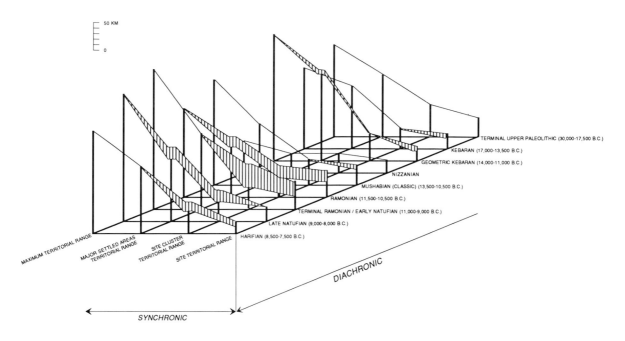

Figure 11   Diagramatic model of nested territorial units of Late Pleistocene hunter-gatherer societies of the Negev and Sinai

Table 5   Patterns of distribution of Late Pleistocene settlements in the Negev and Sinai

Cluster size	1	2	3	4	5	6	7	8	9	10	Total
Terminal Upper Paleolithic	3	1	—	1	—	—	—	—	—	—	8
Kebaran	3	—	1	—	—	—	—	—	—	—	6
Geometric Kebaran	6	7	2	1	—	2	—	1	—	10	62
Nizzanian	4	1	—	—	—	—	—	—	—	—	6
Mushabian	4	2	1	1	2	—	2	—	1	—	48
Ramonian	6	5	2	1	1	—	—	1	—	1	49
Terminal Ramonian/ Early Natufian	8	2	2	2	—	1	—	—	—	—	33
Late Natufian	6	2	2	1	—	—	—	—	—	—	20
Harifian	5	2	1	1	2	1	—	—	—	—	32

settled areas are considered, there are important variations from one area to another (Table 8, Figure 14). Larger settlements were preferentially located in the Azariq area, which was inhabited from the Upper Paleolithic to the Ramonian, followed by the Mushabi area, which was settled from the Kebaran to the Ramonian, abandoned during the Late Natufian and resettled during the Harifian. The Shunera area was inhabited during the whole Late Pleistocene, while the Lagama area was abandoned during the Late Natufian and resettled during

the Harifian. It therefore appears that each local area witnessed a specific dynamic of settlement which needs to be understood. The fact that settlements from the same area have been presented as summer camp (Mushabi XIV/2) and winter base camp (Mushabi V) highlights the difficulties of assigning the general distribution of settlements to seasonal variation in animal and plant biomasses alone, in an ecotonal situation such as that of the Negev and Sinai foothills which may have been a patchwork and a mosaic of different kinds of resources.

Table 6 Patterns of sub–regional distribution of Late Pleistocene settlements in the Negev and Sinai

Parameters	Number of settled areas	n	Min.	Max.	Mean	Range	Standard deviation	Coefficient of variation
Terminal Upper Paleolithic	5	7	1	2	1.40	1	0.48	0.34
Kebaran	4	5	1	2	1.25	1	0.43	0.34
Geometric Kebaran	15	58	1	9	3.42	8	2.38	0.69
Mushabian	14	48	1	8	3.38	7	2.13	0.63
Ramonian	15	77	1	13	5.00	12	3.44	0.68
Late Natufian	7	16	1	5	2.28	4	1.48	0.65
Harifian	6	21	1	5	3.50	4	0.95	0.27
Total	21	232	1	13	3.54	12	2.70	0.76

Table 7 Settlements sizes during the Late Pleistocene in the Negev and Sinai

Parameters	n	Min. (m^2)	Max. (m^2)	Mean (m^2)	Range	Standard deviation	Coefficient of variation
Terminal Upper Paleolithic	6	30	200	81.33	170	60.08	0.73
Kebaran	5	5	75	47.20	70	23.86	0.50
Geometric Kebaran	25	10	100	48.00	90	26.87	0.55
Mushabian	20	15	150	70.50	135	41.94	0.59
Ramonian	16	5	200	52.50	195	53.58	1.02
Late Natufian	6	10	5000	960.83	4990	1813.85	1.88
Harifian	13	25	600	260.38	575	191.72	0.73
Total	91	5	5000	145.09	4995	522.10	3.59

Some other aspects, such as matrimonial network, kinship, friendship, enmity, etc., may also have been instrumental in the formation of the archaeological record of Late Pleistocene foraging societies of the Negev and Sinai. Studying these social aspects from the archaeological record is a very difficult task; however, research on lithic assemblages alone, even if they are framed to consider stylistic dimension, will have to be backed by systematic analysis of spatial behaviors, however incomplete our data base may be. With this, it seems appropriate to close this discussion with a quote from Goring-Morris (1988: 85), who has spent most of his adult life studying the late Pleistocene foraging societies of the Negev and Sinai deserts:

> The material record of prehistoric groups, however imperfect and differentially preserved, does exist and warrants attempts at not only description but also interpretation and model building of economic and behavioral systems. The stone tools assemblages are out there on the field, organic preservation, both faunal but more especially vegetal remains, is frequently poor. Differences in the size and distribution, and composition of the lithic assemblages are documented and to my mind beg interpretation, however tentative and inherently biased.

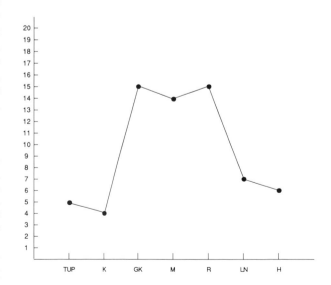

Figure 12 Number of settled areas

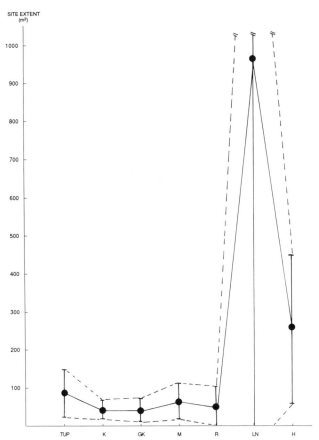

Figure 13 Mean and standard deviation of settlement size

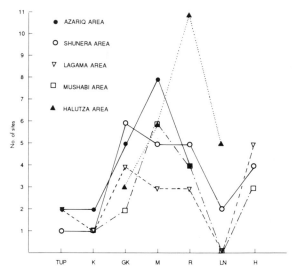

Figure 14 Long-term dynamic of settlement in some selected areas

Table 8 Long-term dynamics of Late Pleistocene settlements in some selected areas of the Negev and Sinai

Areas	Azariq		Shunera		Lagama		Mushabi		Halutza	
	n	Extent Range (m²)	n	Extent Range (m²)	n	Extent Range (m²)	n	Extent Range (m²)	n	Extent Range (m²)
Terminal Upper Paleolithic	2	44	1	40	2	56−177	—	—	—	—
Kebaran	2	40−75	1	5	1	—	1	56	—	—
Geometric Kebaran	5	50−100	6	—	4	80	2	25	3	—
Mushabian	4	40−150	5	25−80	3	—	6	50−150	6	—
Ramonian	4	20	5	80−100	3	—	4	120	11	—
Late Natufian	—	—	2	10−25	—	—	—	—	5	—
Harifian	—	—	4	25	5	75	3	85−350	—	—
Total	21	20−150	24	5−100	18	56−117	16	25−350	25	—

7

THE LOWER PALEOLITHIC OF ISRAEL

Naama Goren-Inbar

This chapter is concerned with the manifestations of the Lower Paleolithic cultural entities, identified in Israel. It focuses mainly on the Acheulean Industrial Complex – that archaeological entity of longest duration of which in this author's view all the local Lower Paleolithic occurrences are components (Goren 1981a; Bar-Yosef and Goren-Inbar 1993). The discussion revolves around several aspects of the lithic assemblages ascribed to this period, from which some insight may be gained regarding various rudimentary behavioral patterns of Lower Paleolithic hominids. It is assumed that examination of the Acheulean lithic tradition, and its complex pattern of time-dependent variability, may contribute to an understanding of processes of cultural change which must have occurred during this immense span. Though discussion is essentially limited to Lower Paleolithic occurrences within the region of Israel, it necessarily draws on relevant information obtained throughout the entire Levant.

The Lower Paleolithic, considered to have lasted for over a million years, is the longest of all prehistoric periods. Its beginning in the Levant is documented in the site of 'Ubeidiya, dated to 1.4 Ma (Eisenmann et al. 1983; Tchernov 1988) and its end is assumed to have taken place around 0.128 Ma, with the onset of the Upper Pleistocene period.

Although the makers of Lower Paleolithic Acheulean artifacts elsewhere in the world are unanimously considered to have been *Homo erectus* (Leakey 1971), no direct evidence was found for this notion in Israel. The very few Hominid skeletal remains from this period, recovered from sites in Israel, are insufficient for a reconstruction of a whole skeleton (see Smith, this volume). These remains include two isolated teeth found at 'Ubeidiya (Tobias 1966), two leg bones from Gesher Benot Ya'akov (Geraads and Tchernov 1983) and a skull fragment – the 'Galilee Man' – found at Zuttiyeh (Turville-Petre 1927; Keith 1927). The Zuttiyeh skull is regarded by some authorities as perhaps belonging to an ancestral form of modern Levantine hominids (Vandermeersch 1982; Trinkaus 1991) whereas others view it as representing the earliest Levantine Neanderthal form (Klein 1989). The prevailing consensus, that the history of anatomically modern man is as old in the

Levant as in Africa (Grün et al. 1990), further complicates the issue of Lower Paleolithic hominids' taxonomic status.

The Levantine record from the Lower Paleolithic has furnished a considerable body of archaeological data, consisting of lithic assemblages frequently with associated faunal remains. Still, the extent of the data available for study of this period is limited. For various reasons, discussed at length elsewhere (Bar-Yosef 1975; Clark 1975; Gilead 1970a; Hours et al. 1973), the number of archaeological occurrences dating from the Early and Middle Pleistocene is relatively small. For the same reasons, foremost among which is the damage caused by geomorphic processes, stratified and dated Lower Paleolithic sites are even scarcer. Furthermore, the complex geological structure of the Dead Sea Rift on one hand, and the rapid sedimentation rate characteristic of Israel's coastal plain, on the other, preclude correlations between rock-stratigraphic units from both these regions in which most of Israel's Lower Paleolithic sites are located. Considering the fact that only a fraction of the recovered material has been adequately published, the fragmentary nature of the available evidence is well accounted for (Bar-Yosef and Goren 1980; Goren-Inbar 1988). However, surface finds collected – sometimes by amateurs – from various sources (such as deflated sites and small scatters) are rather more common and indeed form a major part of the published data.

Study of the Lower Paleolithic, in Israel as well as other regions, is further complicated by lack of an appropriate methodological framework. Even the criteria for the very definition of an Acheulean site have never been properly formulated. As a direct result of this inadequacy of criteria, a multitude of occurrences – such as those recently documented in Jordan, Syria and Lebanon – each consisting of but a few items, have been introduced in the literature as Acheulean sites. Despite their meagre contents, these findspots are frequently compared in various publications, with sites of a. far larger order, abounding with thousands of Acheulean items. By these standards, regions such as that of Mt. Carmel (Olami and Gilead 1979) should by rights be regarded as encompassing several hundreds of sites! The lack of a uniform methodological framework is even more evident

Plate 1 Excavation overview of Gesher Benot Ya'akov

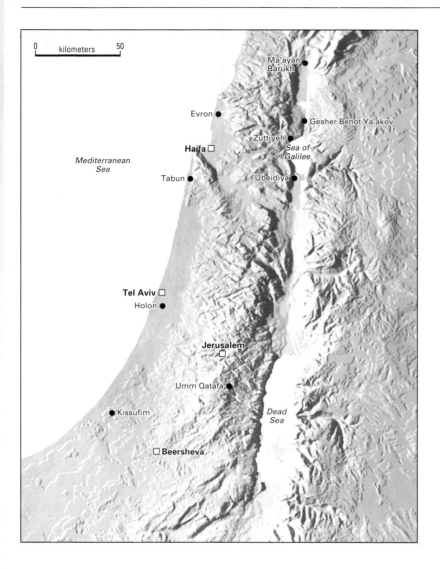

Figure 1 Distribution map of selected Acheulean sites mentioned in text

with regard to the analysis of lithics. This domain displays a multitude of approaches, each emphasizing different aspects of the material and focusing on different results. This situation does not allow for effective comparisons between assemblages and renders any generalizations difficult.

Given the great antiquity of the period under consideration, its long duration and the relative scarcity of data, topics such as subsistence strategies, models of adaptation or indeed any inferences of structural or cultural traits reaching beyond the actual evidence of the material remains, should be treated with far greater reticence than is perhaps necessary when discussing later periods. From the above, it should be clear that the following discussion is a factual, primarily lithic-oriented account of Lower Paleolithic manifestations that refrains, quite deliberately, from too far-reaching conclusions.

Among the Acheulean sites (most of them from Israel, but some from Lebanon, Syria and Jordan) described below in some detail, greater emphasis is placed on Late Acheulean occurrences, which represent the final manifestation of the Acheulean Industrial Complex in the Levant. It is in this stage, that the acceleration in the tempo of cultural change is most evident. An attempt is made to view individual sites against the broader background of the entire Lower Paleolithic sequence in the Levant, and to relate them to an up-to-date chronological framework, notwithstanding its fragmentary nature.

The discussion is illustrated by two case studies treated in somewhat greater detail – the sites of 'Ubeidiya and Gesher Benot Ya'akov, both located in the Dead Sea Rift (see Figure 1). These sites are of utmost importance for prehistoric research as they constitute rich sources of data suggestive of hominid modes of living during the Lower and Middle Pleistocene.

Needless to say, opinions expressed in this overview reflect the author's point of view, alone.

History of research

During the early decades of this century, prehistoric research in Israel was dominated by European research orientations, which tended to place greater emphasis on the investigation of cave sites where stratified sequences could be expected to be found, than on open-air sites. Consequently, of the five Lower Paleolithic sites known in Israel at that time, three – Umm Qatafa (Neuville 1951), Zuttiyeh (Turville Petre 1927) and Tabun (Garrod and Bate 1937) – were of the former type, and the other two – Gesher Benot Ya'akov (Stekelis et al. 1937, 1938) and Baq'ah Rephaim (Arensburg and Bar-Yosef 1967) – belonged to the latter type. In later years, more archaeological occurrences from this period were identified, many of them exposed in the course of cultivation and construction activities.

Following a shift in research orientations during the 1960s towards regional research (Goren 1981b), extensive fieldwork took place in the Negev and in Sinai, which nevertheless yielded no Lower Paleolithic occurrences. However, in the coastal plain and the northern parts of the country, numerous surface finds were detected as well as many additional sites, frequently much disturbed by various recent activities (Gilead 1975).

Chronological and classificatory schemes

Several temporal divisions have been proposed for the Lower Paleolithic sequence in the Levant. These subdivisions, most of them threefold ones as those suggested for the corresponding period in Africa and Europe, were based mainly on typological criteria while stratigraphical considerations were rarely heeded.

Garrod's (Garrod and Bate 1937) division, based on the 24-meter-thick Lower Paleolithic deposits of Tabun cave, postulated a sequence whereby the Tayacian cultural entity was succeeded by Upper Acheulean ones. Both her subdivision as well as Neuville's (1951) scheme, based on his study of Umm Qatafa where Tayacian, Middle and Upper Acheulean levels were identified in stratigraphic sequence, have evidently been strongly influenced by European prehistorical percepts, reflected in the adoption of both European terminology and European typology.

Gilead's (1970a) division of the Lower Paleolithic in the Near East, into Early, Middle and Late Acheulean phases, encompassed only assemblages comprising a bifacial component and was based 'neither on chronological nor on faunal grounds, but on cultural differences' (Gilead 1970a:4). His subdivision of the Late Acheulean, which he considered more diversified and widespread than the other

phases, was likewise based on techno-typological criteria. He recognized within the Late Acheulean material four distinct groups – those of Ma'ayan Barukh, Evron, Yiron and an Acheulean of a Yabrudian Facies (ibid.).

Another scheme, based on the Syrio-Lebanese data (Hours et al. 1973), conceives of the entire Lower Paleolithic as a sequence of manifestations of the Acheulean Industrial Complex – the Early and Middle Acheulean, followed by the Tayacian and culminating in the Late and Final Acheulean (the latter encompassing the Yabrudian, pre-Aurignacian and Amudian). This framework was later revised twice, the first time (Hours 1975) to include the Para Acheulean, the Early/Middle and Middle/Late Acheulean and the Tayacian, and the second time (Hours 1981) to include the Early, Middle and Recent Lower Paleolithic, followed by the Developed Recent Acheulean.

These recurrent revisions, dependent on the ever-changing nature of constantly accumulating data, clearly demonstrate the pressing need to formulate solid criteria which will allow clearer identification and easier clustering of the diverse Lower Paleolithic entities.

NOTE: In order to avoid confusion in nomenclature, the term 'Late Acheulean' is employed below with regard to all the cultural entities stratified above Tabun F – including all the lithic assemblages correlated and compared with the Mugahran Tradition (Jelinek 1981) of Tabun.

Dating

The antiquity of the Lower Paleolithic and the nature of Levantine sedimentary deposits, preclude application of the most common radiometric dating technique of C-14. While enormous progress has been made recently in the application of other radiometric techniques to archaeologically-relevant material – particularly those of ESR and T/L but also those of uranium series (^{230}Th/^{234}/U), potassium argon (K/Ar) and Argon/Argon (^{39}Ar/^{40}Ar) (see Figures 2, 3) – these are still very much restricted to Upper Pleistocene sites and thus far yielded only preliminary results for terminal Middle Pleistocene occurrences (Grün and Stringer 1991 and references therein).

The stratigraphic context of a site and its depositional character are highly significant to the choice of dating technique to be applied. It is frequently the case that whereas an archaeological horizon cannot be directly dated for technical reasons, another part of that depositional sequence (such as volcanic rock) does allow application of some dating method. Indirect as such chronological information is, as regards the archaeological horizon itself, it is nevertheless of considerable importance. Thus in Berekhat Ram (Feraud et al. 1983; Goren-Inbar

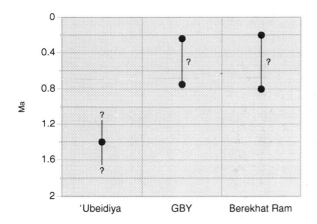

Figure 2 Estimated age (indirectly dated) of Lower Paleolithic sites (date derived from: Eisenmann et al. 1983; Feraud et al. 1983; Mor 1986; Moshkovitz and Magaritz 1987; Goren-Inbar et al. 1992a)

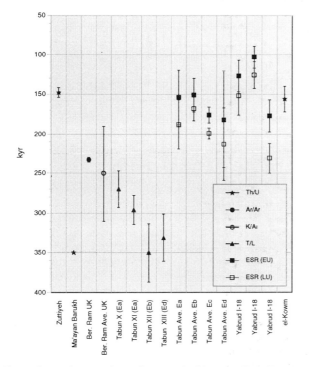

Figure 3 Radiometric dates of Lower Paleolithic sites (data derived from: Feraud et al. 1983; Grün et al. 1991; Hennig and Hours 1982; Mercier 1992; Mor 1986; Porat and Schwarcz 1991; N. Porat, per. comm., 1992; Schwarcz et al. 1980)

dating of a basalt flow, the Yarda Basalt, underlying the Benot Ya'akov Formation and a paleomagnetic study of the relevant stratigraphic sequence, showed the Formation's age to be younger than 0.9 Ma and younger than 0.73 Ma, respectively (Goren-Inbar et al. 1992a).

Most of the Lower Paleolithic sites, however, are not (or cannot yet be) radiometrically dated. In certain cases, estimations of age can be inferred from biological data as in the case of 'Ubeidiya, where chronological determinations were based on the retrieved paleontological material that was, in turn, dated by comparison to radiometrically-dated assemblages from elsewhere (Tchernov 1988 and references therein; see Figure 2).

At present, the limitations of radiometric methods being as they are, an eclectic approach seems the only practical one by which to address the problem of chronological determinations for Lower Paleolithic sites.

The cultural entities of the Lower Paleolithic

The identification of the Lower Paleolithic cultural entities of the Levant, is based on a variety of typological and – to a lesser extent – technological criteria. Thus, the constantly ongoing accumulation of data leads to frequent changes in terminology and to what may be described as somewhat 'restless' dynamics of nomenclature. Furthermore, the greater emphasis during the last few decades on regional research, accompanied as it was by a tendency to reconstruct isolated local sequences and label them, led to the build-up of a plethora of cultural entities.

The following paragraphs present short descriptions of these entities (see also Table 1 p. 99).

The Tayacian

The Tayacian, identified in Israel in two sites only – in layer G at Tabun and at Umm Qatafa layers E, F and G – was detected at both these caves in the lowermost part of the cultural sequence, and was defined as a cultural entity devoid of bifaces (Garrod and Bate 1937; Neuville 1951). It was termed 'Tayacian' due to the resemblance of the assemblages to the European Tayacian ones, being 'poor, both in quantity and quality . . . [and] consist[ing] for the most part of small flakes and chunks of flint, more or less extensively utilized' (Garrod and Bate 1937: 86).

These assemblages, elsewhere also termed 'Tabunian' (Howell 1959), are characterized by the presence of flakes, waste products and cores, by rare retouched artifacts, and by the absence of bifaces and products of the Levallois Technique (Neuville 1951).

The resumed excavations in the deepest layers of Tabun cave (Jelinek 1975: Bed 80; 1981: Beds 90A–90J), yielded no similar assemblages. Instead, the recovered material

1986), the broad chronological context of the site was established once the two basalt flows directly underlying and overlying it, were dated to *ca.* 800 ka and *ca.* 233 ka, respectively (Plate 2 p. 98). Such 'deduced' chronological information is of even greater significance when the stratigraphical sequence has been paleomagnetically investigated. Thus, a combination of radiometric (K/Ar)

Plate 2   Berekhat Ram. Top: Upper Kramim Basalt; bottom: Lower Kramim Basalt. The flint artifacts are bedded between the two flows

seemed to constitute a typological mixture of the finds from Garrod's layers G and F, featuring bifaces, scrapers and a variety of flake tools such as burins and notches. This assemblage was assigned by the excavator to the Late Acheulean, due to the presence of whole and broken bifaces as well as by-products of their manufacture.

Tayacian levels have also been identified in Bezez, Lebanon, though sample sizes were too small (Copeland 1983). Indications were found to the presence of bifaces, Levalloisian items, notches, denticulates and various other retouched flakes. These lithic assemblages differ both technologically and typologically from those of Umm Qatafa, Tabun or Yabrud IV, and as they were recovered from levels stratified below the Acheulo-Yabrudian layer C, they were regarded as younger than the Tayacian assemblages from those sites and were claimed to be 'some sort of residue of an Acheulo-Yabrudian industry like the one that is in itself so well seen in the overlying layers' (Copeland 1983: 205).

The Acheulo-Yabrudian and Yabrudian

The Levantine Acheulo-Yabrudian and Yabrudian entities are most extensively represented at Tabun Cave (Garrod and Bate 1937; Garrod 1956; Jelinek 1981) in layer E, which attains a thickness of at least 4.50 m. However, it was the site of Yabrud I, where the archaeological layers were interstratified with archaeologically-sterile ones, which enabled a more clear-cut distinction between them (Rust 1950). Adopting Rust's terminology, Garrod (1956) abandoned her original identification of Layer E at Tabun as 'Upper Acheulean', proposing instead that it be regarded as an Acheulo-Yabrudian and Yabrudian sequence.

This entity was characterized by the presence of asymmetrical convergent scrapers (*déjeté* or *Winkelkratzer*), transversal scrapers, thick blanks, high frequencies of

plain striking platforms and items with Quina and demi-Quina retouch. Assemblages of similar characteristics were retrieved in Zuttiyeh (Gisis and Bar-Yosef 1974), Hummal Ib (Besançon et al. 1981), Jerf Ajla (Schroeder 1969), Yabrud I (Bordes 1955) and Adlun (Copeland 1983). Reexamination of the Acheulo-Yabrudian, Yabrudian and Acheulean lithic assemblages from Layer E at Tabun (Jelinek et al. 1973; Jelinek 1975) convinced Jelinek that, contrary to previous notions, the two cultural entities could not be distinguished from one another on the basis of any other techno-typological criteria but the presence (in the Acheulean) or absence (in the Yabrudian) of the bifacial component. He consequently argued that the entire sequence should be regarded as representing a single cultural entity: the Mugharan tradition (Jelinek 1981, 1982).

Excavations in Adlun, Lebanon (at the Bezez Cave and at Zumoffen rock-shelter) led to identification of three Yabrudian variants within the Bezez C sequence, each located in a different area of the site. One of them was found to be characterized by the presence of racloirs, another by the presence of bifaces, and the third was declared a less typologically distinct facies (Copeland 1983; Kirkbride et al. 1983). A Yabrudian complex, clearly characterized by a distinct blade component, was identified at Abri Zumoffen as well (Garrod and Kirkbride 1961), in addition to an Amudian sequence.

The Amudian and Pre-Aurignacian

Distinct assemblages, recovered from within Acheulean and Yabrudian levels, were reported from Tabun as well as from Yabrud and Adlun. The assemblage from layer E at Tabun, notable for the presence of blades and blade tools, was originally termed 'pre-Aurignacian' (Garrod 1956) following Rust's (1950) taxonomy. Later, it was found to be associated with bifaces and scrapers (Garrod 1956), and labelled 'Amudian' (Garrod and Kirkbride 1961). Though Garrod viewed this particular assemblage as an intrusion of non-European origin within the sequence, she nevertheless argued that the entire contents of this level were indicative of the fact that the technique of blade production was in use by the Acheulo-Yabrudian and Acheulean occupants of Tabun: 'Nous avions trouvé, en effet, des grattoirs sur lames, des burins, et quelque lames grignotées jusq'à la base de la couche F, mais toujours isolés et en petit nombre' (Garrod 1956: 46).

A comparison between the Tabun E Amudian assemblage and the 'Pre-Aurignacian' one from Yabrud I (layer 15) shows that the two differ in tool-type frequencies, the former featuring a high frequency of backed knives and low frequencies of endscrapers and burins, thus resembling the Amudian of Abri Zumoffen and the 'Beach Industry' there. These assemblages contain scrapers, bifaces and products of the Levallois Technique,

Table 1 Cultural entities of the Levantine Lower Paleolithic (based on references mentioned in text)

Acheulo-Yabrudian and Yabrudian	Amudian Pre-Aurignacian	Tayacian Tabunian	Hummalian	Samoukian	Shemshian
Tabun E	Tabun E	Tabun	Hummal Ia	Nahr el Arab	Yabrud IV
Yabrud I	Yabrud I	Umm Qatafa		Fidio III	
Zuttiyeh	Bezez	Bezez		Mchaïrfet es Samok	
Bezez C	Zumoffen	Ras Beiruth		Idris IIIa	
Zumoffen	Hua Fteah				
Masloukh					
Hummal Ib					
Lion spring					
C spring					

though their presence, especially in Adlun, is minimal (Copeland 1983).

Both Garrod (1956) and Jelinek (1981) assigned the complex sequence of Tabun E to the Last Interglacial, in disagreement with the much younger age ascribed for the Amudian/'Pre-Aurignacian' by Bordes (1955, 1977). While their chronological considerations differ (the stratigraphy of the Lebanese coast for Garrod, and the global climatic oscillations for Jelinek), their notion of the antiquity of these assemblages proved to be in greater accord with recent radiometric dates, although these indicate yet older ages (Grün and Stringer 1991; Grün et al. 1991). A list of radiometric dates obtained for the Late Achaeulean sequence, is presented in Figure 3.

Several approaches have been advocated with regard to the observed variability within the Late Acheulean lithic assemblages. While Rust and Garrod conceived of the sequence of Yabrud I and Tabun in terms of discrete and different traditional entities, Jelinek and Copeland preferred a somewhat less clear-cut distinction. Thus, Jelinek (1981, 1990) explains all the observed variability of Tabun E as reflecting coexistence of three 'facies' of the same tradition – the Mugharan. Advocating a functional approach, he interprets the observed variability in terms of climatic oscillations, so that an increase in biface frequencies is attributed to cooler conditions, and decreased frequencies or complete absence to warmer ones. Interestingly, Copeland (1983) suggests a similar interpretation for the observed variability at Adlun, where the spatially-organized facies were viewed as task-specific areas.

Two additional models were proposed in an attempt to account for the variability within the Late Acheulean lithic assemblages from Lebanon and Syria. The first unilinear model (Copeland and Hours 1978; Hours 1979) based on the sequence in Tabun or Yabrud I, views the Mousterian as probably deriving, by a continuous process, from Late Acheulean entities. A second, later, model (Copeland and Hours 1981) is a regionally oriented scheme, interpreting lithic variability in terms of cultural diversity arising from

geographical factors, and explaining the pronounced element of overlap apparent in the lithics in terms of contact zones between the various entities (Copeland and Hours 1981).

At present, however, there is wide agreement – generated by awareness of the drawbacks of the available data – that the inherent complexities of the Late Acheulean entity are yet beyond full understanding.

Other Late Acheulean Lithic entities

In the course of the last 20 years, several Late Acheulean entities have been documented outside the boundaries of the Levantine coastal plain. Of importance are the Samoukian, the Hummalian and the Yabrudian of el-Kowm, all of them identified in Syria and assigned to the latest phase of the Acheulean complex. The Samoukian (Copeland and Hours 1978; Hours 1979) is characterized by the presence of bifaces, cores, choppers, products of the Levallois technique and a high frequency of flake tools. It is considered as a distinct facies of the Late Acheulean, contemporaneous with the Yabrudian and thus with the Mugharan. The Hummalian (identified at Hummal site 1a), likewise identified as a Late Acheulean entity (Besançon et al. 1981), nevertheless shows such a striking techno-typological similarity to the Mousterian assemblages of Tabun D, as to yet leave room for certain doubts regarding this attribution (and see excavators' note (ibid. 41) describing the Yabrudian level as located some 75 cm higher than the Hummalian, albeit not in the same section of the pit).

All Late Acheulean entities share two common features. They are all stratigraphically located above Acheulean levels and below Mousterian ones, and they are all characterized by the presence of bifaces, in varying quantities, in their inventories. Lithic assemblages ascribed to the closing phases of the Acheulean Industrial Complex display far greater diversity than those assigned to its earliest stages. This phenomenon denotes the emergence of a pattern which is to be very typical of all prehistoric cultures to follow (see, for example Isaac 1972): a lengthy period marked by absence of any significant change is terminated with an outburst of diversification in both the typological and the technological aspects of the material culture.

Discussion

Stratigraphical considerations – the position of layer E at Tabun and other Acheulo-Yabrudian layers elsewhere directly between Acheulean and Mousterian levels – as well as certain techno-typological similarities (i.e., presence of the Levallois technique; high scraper indexes) between the Mousterian and the Mugharan, led prehistorians to view the latter as a transitional phase, either tightly-linked with the Middle Paleolithic sequence (Garrod 1956; Copeland 1983), or virtually constituting its earliest manifestation (Jelinek 1981). While Copeland's opinion was based on the wide-range evidence of the stratified assemblages from Tabun and Adlun, Jelinek's evaluation rests on the fact that 'the composition of the Yabrudian Facies, . . . typologically, is strikingly similar to the Quina Mousterian of the Middle Paleolithic of Western Europe' (Jelinek 1981: 272).

The current state of knowledge does not seem to confirm either Jelinek's or Copeland's views concerning the Mugharan's transitional status and hence its Middle Paleolithic affinities. The sheer thickness of the relevant layers at Tabun appears to negate such an assumption, as it quite evidently attests to a very long history of sediment accumulation and to a lengthy occupational sequence, repetitively interrupted.

Furthermore, techno-typological comparisons between Late Acheulean and Mousterian assemblages clearly indicate that the latter are typically devoid of a bifacial component (handaxes and cleavers). In the case of Tabun, for example, of the few handaxes recovered from the Mousterian layer D, 'the majority were found at the base of the layer and [were] undoubtedly derived from Ea' (Garrod and Bate 1937: 77). In the light of this, Schroeder's (1969) assignment of unit 'Yellow 2' in Jerf Ajla, Syria, to the Mousterian, is rather questionable, as the presence of bifacials in that unit would seem to indicate Yabrudian affinities.

Since the Levantine Mousterian likewise lacks the chopping-tool component characteristic of all Late Acheulean entities, it is only the presence of Levalloisian items and flake tools (particularly scrapers) which remains the common feature for both entities. It seems, therefore, that at least until more solid criteria are established for differentiating between the Lower and Middle Paleolithic – criteria that are needed equally with regard to these periods in Southwestern Europe – the Late Acheulean should be regarded as a Lower Paleolithic entity whereas the Mousterian as a Middle Paleolithic one.

Technology, innovations and the process of change

The impression of considerable complexity emerging from an overall assessment of even the earliest manifestations of Lower Paleolithic material culture, preclude their attribution to a 'beginners' stage. The principal factors responsible for the appearance of each type and each technology – whether functional, traditional or others – may be largely a matter for speculation, but the complexity typical of this entity and of its African analogues, is nevertheless striking (Bar-Yosef and Goren-Inbar 1993).

Lithic assemblages such as that from 'Ubeidiya attest to the existence of a 'standardized' tool-kit, repetitively produced throughout an immense span of time. This technologically complex tool-kit is characterized by careful selection of specific raw materials for the production of distinct tool types. The various tool types can be demonstrated to be each the end-product of a different and quite independent modification strategy. Thus, when the arbitrary distinction (Leakey 1971) between flint chopping-tools and flint polyhedrons is ignored, both types are clearly recognized as products of the same process of manufacture, differing from the technological sequence employed for the manufacture of limestone spheroids which, in turn, is distinctly unlike that used to produce basalt quadrihedrals, trihedrals, etc.

Two prominent strategies of artifact production are the Levallois and the Kombewa techniques. The use of these advanced procedures – each of which is of a clearly distinct nature and each of which is applied equally to different raw materials – implies an impressive scope of planning as well as directedness towards very specific end-products. Although both techniques are commonly ascribed to an African origin, nothing can be firmly established regarding their earliest appearance, at least until more data is available from Africa and Euroasia (Goren-Inbar 1992). Thus, at Gesher Benot Ya'akov, certain ancient reduction processes such as those reported from 'Ubeidiya for the production of spheroids or heavy duty scrapers disappear altogether, clearing the scene for these two novel technologies and their products (cleavers and a variety of other bifacial tools).

At a certain point, postdating the times of Gesher Benot Ya'akov, the diversity typical of raw material selection is replaced by a rather simplified pattern, characterized by an exclusive use of flint. The technological and typological heterogeneity, otherwise characteristic of the Late Acheulean, is definitely not reflected in the patterns of raw material utilization.

On the techno-typological level, however, the Late Acheulean and specifically the Mugharan Tradition, clearly exhibits coexistence of several distinct technologies, expressed by a variety of retouch techniques (regular,

Plate 3   Berekhat Ram — the earliest reported piece of art (figurine)

Quina, and Demi-Quina) as opposed to the previous dominance of regular retouch, and by the appearance of a blade technology alongside the simpler flake technology. These features frequently coexist with the Levallois technique, though not at every Late Acheulean site.

The appearance of several technologies and typological features, later to become widespread, is reported from the Lower Paleolithic. All the traits considered typical of the Middle Paleolithic, whether the Levallois technique, the laminar technology or the 'Upper Paleolithic' tool types, have been shown to occur during the Lower Paleolithic at the various sites described above. The Levallois technique, identified at Gesher Benot Ya'akov, Berekhat Ram and all other Late Acheulean sites, has evolved during Mousterian times into the most common technological feature of the Levantine Middle Paleolithic. 'Upper Paleolithic' tool types were reported from Acheulean assemblages (Goren-Inbar 1985) and from the controversial 'Pre-Aurignacian'/ Amudian entity, discussed above. This pattern – initial sporadic manifestations of a feature gradually increase in frequency, eventually attaining prevalence, and then gradually subside again – is typical of all prehistoric cultural entities.

Any attempt to discuss processes of change during the Lower Paleolithic, or to identify innovations that occurred in its course, is necessarily rather pretentious in light of the extremely fragmentary nature of the evidence. The Lower Paleolithic record cannot possibly be regarded as an accurate documentation of a sequence of events, but at best as furnishing some fragmentary information. All the evidence accrued – mainly through typological comparisons, both qualitative and quantitative (Gilead 1970a; Bar-Yosef 1975; Clark 1975) – does not amount to a comprehensive description from which specific change processes may be inferred. While the range of behaviors linked with lithic artifacts may well reflect only part of a wider array of hominid behaviors, lithic assemblages nevertheless constitute most of the preserved material evidence and thus are the best available indicators of change in this domain.

Processes of change pertaining to the lithic assemblages are a complex issue, probably best dealt with on a hypothetical level. In light of the intricacy of the processes of assimilation and diffusion of ideas, and considering the drawbacks otherwise affecting research into this question, the need for high-quality data is doubly clear. Lower Pleistocene data indicate that there is a minimal change through time and no functional influence on the tool-kit. By contrast, Middle Pleistocene times, and especially the Late Acheulean period, are characterized by a complex repetitive pattern particularized by inter-entity contacts and by a correspondingly high degree of variability in technological-typological features. The factors suggested to have affected this variability vary from paleoclimatic fluctuations through geographical factors, to diversity of social structure or of function. Be the responsible factor what it may, the rate of change was clearly more rapid, and thus the processes of change more evident, in the Middle Paleolithic record.

Evidence of another pattern of change arises from comparisons of lithic assemblages from the Lower and Middle Pleistocene, indicating a shift from multiplicity (as in the 'Ubeidiya assemblages) to paucity (as in Late Acheulean ones) of reduction strategies. This process later culminates, in the Mousterian of the Upper Pleistocene, in what seems superficially as predominance of a single reduction sequence. Intriguingly, the narrower array of reduction sequences witnessed in the Late Acheulean assemblages is accompanied by increased diversity in tool-types, reflected particularly in the diversity within the flake tools. These developments coincide with an increasing standardization, in both the final form and the location of the retouched edges, as well as in the type of retouch.

These developments bear the stamp of a long and continuous process which is documented far beyond the boundaries of the Levant.

Future goals and research orientations

Notwithstanding the relative scarcity of sites and the drawbacks affecting the available data, the Lower

Paleolithic holds considerable potential for future research, affording as it does a wide range of, as yet, insufficiently-studied subjects.

As clearly demonstrated by research endeavors elsewhere, greater effort should be invested in study of various site-formation processes. Results such as those obtained in the investigation of the Upper and Middle Paleolithic sequences at Kebara Cave (Bar-Yosef et al. 1992), indicate the central role of post-depositional processes in the formation of a site. Greater awareness and better understanding of such processes are bound to improve our understanding of the implications of the obtained information. Various procedures of taphonomic research, such as that employed for identification of different zones of bone diagenesis through infrared spectrometry (Weiner et al. 1993) can contribute significant insight into the subject under study. Greater emphasis should also be placed on investigation of such aspects of the retrieved material as its density, and its spatial distribution. The latter aspect was indeed treated, to some degree, by many researchers of the Lower Paleolithic, but still awaits more strenuous efforts.

Insufficient as the lithic evidence may be for a comprehensive reconstruction of hominid modes of living during the Lower Paleolithic and for an adequate evaluation of hominid behavioral capacities, none the less, lithic assemblages remain the major source of information available for these purposes. It is the very drawbacks affecting this data, which call for a greater emphasis on the methodological aspects of the treatment of lithics. Greater sophistication in the analysis of lithics, welcome as it is, is of little consequence unless accompanied by adherence to a uniform methodological framework – the absence of which was commented upon above. Only when this essential prerequisite is fulfilled will the results of lithic analyses be reliable enough to allow inferences regarding hominid behavioral traits and manifestations of their higher capacities (Plate 3).

Acknowledgments

This study was partially supported by the L.S.B. Leakey Foundation, the Irene Levi Sala Care Archaeological Foundation, the National Geographic Society, the Hebrew University, the Basic Research Foundation administered by the Israel Academy of Sciences and Humanities, the Dorot Foundation and by an anonymous donor. I wish to thank A. Belfer-Cohen and Y. Cohen for their help and suggestions. Figures 1–3 were drawn by G. Hivroni; Figure 1.1 was drawn by J. Ogden; Figures 2.1–2.3 were drawn by Z. Vitelzon and G. Hivroni; Figure 2.4 was drawn by L. Zeiger and Figure 2.5 by J. Moshcovich. Plates 1.1 and 1.2 are included by the kind permission of O. Bar-Yosef; the photograph in Plate 2.2 was taken by N. Slapak.

'UBEIDIYA

The site of 'Ubeidiya is located in the Central Jordan Valley, a segment of the Dead Sea Rift, some 3.5 km south west of Lake Kinneret, about 190 m below msl (see Figure 1). It is embedded within a Pleistocene formation which was identified towards the end of the last century as a malecological locality (Blanckenhorn 1914) characterized by an abundance of the gastropod species *Melanopsis*. An accidental find of mammalian bones in 1959, followed by the discovery of stone artifacts at the type locality, led to the initiation of an archaeological and geological research which began in 1960 and continued until 1974 (for details see Bar-Yosef and Goren-Inbar 1993). Lately, three additional field seasons (1989–1990, 1992) took place at the site (Debard et al. 1989).

Geological study of the 'Ubeidiya Formation (Schulman 1962; Picard and Baida 1966a, 1966b) indicated that the type locality of 'Ubeidiya Hill was the most extensive exposure of this formation, other exposures located elsewhere in the Central Jordan Valley being fragmentary and small, as well as devoid of stone artifacts. Investigations of the formation at the type locality were carried out by means of geological trenches extending over a total length of more than 1000 m. Though the bottom of the formation has never been reached, a composite cross-section of all trenches enabled researchers to identify a complex sedimentological sequence *ca.* 150 m thick, overlain unconformably by younger Pleistocene formations (for details see Horowitz 1979; Bar-Yosef and Goren-Inbar 1993). Various geological phenomena characteristic of the formation, were attributed to post-depositional

Plate 1.2   'Ubeidiya — chopping tool (flint), spheroid (limestone) and biface (flint)

Plate 1.3   'Ubeidiya — Chopping tools (flint) and spheroids (limestone)

Plate 1.1   'Ubeidiya — post depositional tectonic feature (the anticline's core)

tectonic activity which disrupted the original bedding of the layers, tilting them in dips of up to 90° (Plate 1.1).

The composite depositional sequence exposed in the site as well as the paleontological data, were indicative of a freshwater lake environment (Bar-Yosef and Tchernov 1972; Tchernov 1973, 1975, 1986). Four members have been identified in the formation, two for each of the two main depositional environments — a lacustrine environment (Lu and Li) and a fluvial one (Fu and Fi).

Over 60 archaeological horizons have been identified at 'Ubeidiya, making it the richest Lower Pleistocene site in Southwest Asia. Most were embedded in Member Fi, within a variety of sedimentary environments ranging in grain-size from conglomerates to clays. Stekelis's (1966) preliminary investigations at the site, and his techno-typological examinations of the

Table 1.1 'Ubeidiya — typological classification of lithic assemblages (minimal sample size = 65)

	Choppers	Bifaces	Polyhedrons	Discoids	Spheroids	HDS	Scrapers	Varia	N
I-27	13.39	0.89	1.78	1.78			15.17	66.96	112
I-26 a	31.25	0.36	0.36	1.47	0.73		12.13	53.67	272
I-26 b1	27.88	1.44	3.36	1.92	0.48	1.44	18.26	45.19	208
I-26 b2	35.13	7.20	5.85	0.45	2.70	2.25	9.90	36.48	222
I-26 b/c	10.97			2.43			9.75	76.82	82
I-26 c	28.08	4.87	5.15	2.86	2.25	7.16	12.03	37.53	349
I-26d	32.65	7.14	7.14	1.02	4.08	4.08	11.22	32.75	98
III-34	39.00		7.80	0.70	2.12	3.54	11.34	35.46	141
II-24	28.30		19.81	1.88	8.49	7.54	9.43	24.52	106
II-26	30.54	1.47	5.41	2.46	5.41	0.98	4.92	48.27	203
II-36	20.71	4.14	2.36	1.77	2.36	1.77	9.46	57.39	169
K-25	13.84				9.23		15.38	53.84	65
K-26	4.73		2.95		1.18	1.18	17.75	72.18	169
K-28	3.57				1.02		16.32	79.08	196
K-29	37.68	4.34	9.27	2.60	17.10	0.86	5.79	22.31	345
K-29 VB	18.55	0.51	4.63	2.57	5.15	1.54	20.61	46.39	194
K-30	28.47	42.03	11.52	0.67	3.05	0.67	4.47	8.81	295
K-30 VB	21.11	22.22	5.55	3.33			15.55	32.22	90

Table 1.2 'Ubeidiya — frequencies of flake tool types

	Scrapers		Notches		Denticulates		Awls		L.T. Flakes		Total	
	N	%	N	%	N	%	N	%	N	%	N	%
I-27	17	18.47	25	27.17	20	21.73	10	10.86	20	21.73	92	99.96
I-26 a	33	18.43	66	36.87	25	13.96	22	12.29	33	18.43	179	99.98
I-26 b1	38	29.23	24	18.46	16	12.30	19	14.61	33	25.38	130	99.98
I-26 b2	22	21.35	30	29.12	7	6.79	18	17.47	26	25.24	103	99.97
I-26 c	42	24.41	56	32.55	20	11.62	18	10.46	36	20.93	172	99.97
I-26 b/c	8	11.26	23	32.39	13	18.30	11	15.49	16	22.53	71	99.97
I-26 c/d	6	17.14	14	40.00	7	20.00	2	5.71	6	17.14	35	99.99
I-26 d	11	25.58	18	41.86	3	6.97	1	2.32	10	23.25	43	99.98
II-36	16	14.15	37	32.74	26	23.00	16	14.15	18	15.92	113	99.96
II-26	10	9.17	43	39.44	12	11.00	18	16.51	26	23.85	109	99.97
II-24	10	28.57	10	28.57	7	20.00	4	11.42	4	11.42	35	99.98
III-34	16	24.61	12	18.46	15	23.07	12	18.46	10	15.38	65	98.98
K-29 VB	40	30.76	23	17.69	16	12.30	20	15.38	31	23.84	130	99.97
K-29	20	20.83	26	27.08	13	13.54	11	11.45	26	27.08	96	99.98
K-30 VB	14	32.55	9	20.93	8	18.60	5	11.62	7	16.27	43	99.97
K-30	14	35.00	7	17.50	7	17.50	3	7.50	9	22.50	40	100.00
K-26	30	19.73	33	21.71	42	27.63	25	16.44	22	14.47	152	99.98
K-25	10	22.22	9	20.00	11	24.44	7	15.55	8	17.77	45	99.98
K-28	32	17.11	54	28.87	40	21.39	31	16.57	30	16.04	187	99.98

lithics, produced finds suggestive of 'Ubeidiya's resemblance to the site of Olduvai Gorge and thus indicative of its great antiquity. The occupants' tool-kit was found to be composed of chopping tools, polyhedrons, discoids, spheroids and sub-spheroids, bifaces (including trihedrals and quadrihedrals), heavy duty scrapers and a variety of flake tools (Plates 1.2, 1.3). Stekelis noted consistent associations between certain tool types and specific raw materials: chopping tools, polyhedrons, discoids and flake tools were made habitually on flint, bifaces

on basalt and spheroids as well as heavy duty scrapers on limestone (Stekelis 1966: Stekelis et al. 1969).

The most impressive paleontological assemblage obtained from the different layers of the site showed outstanding diversity — as many as 66 different bird species and 56 mammalian species, originating from diverse biogeographical provinces (Tchernov 1986, 1988, and references therein). This array, which very likely represents only part of a much larger and more diversified inventory, attests to a wide range of

Table 1.3 'Ubeidiya — typological classification of bifaces (mimimal sample size = 7)

	I-26 b2		I-26 c		I-26 d		II-36		K-29		K-30		K-30 VB		(Chapter IV) I-15	
	N	%	N	%	N	%	N	%	N	%	N	%	N	%	N	%
Proto Biface			4	23.52			1	14.28					2	10.0	25	29.06
Irregular Ovate	3	18.75	4	23.52	4	57.14			3	20.00	30	24.19	9	45.0	15	17.44
Pick			2	11.76					2	13.33	5	4.03			10	11.62
Double Pointed Biface															5	5.81
Square Butt Biface							5	71.42	3	20.00	27	21.77				
Cleaver			1	5.88									2	10.0	5	5.81
Quadrihedral	2	12.5	1	5.88							4	3.22	1	5.0		
Trihedral	11	68.75	5	29.41	3	42.85	1	14.28	7	46.66	58	46.77	6	30.0	26	30.23
Total	16	100.0	17	99.97	7	99.99	7	99.98	15	99.99	124	99.98	20	100.0	86	99.97

ecological niches and to the optimal conditions around the paleo 'Ubeidiya Lake.

Introduction of new excavation techniques by Bar-Yosef and Tchernov (Bar-Yosef and Goren-Inbar 1993) enabled lateral exposure of the layers, and allowed detailed observations of the unique living floors, constituting one of the most prominent features of the site. These living-floors, two of which (1–15 and 1–26) have been extensively exposed (Gilead 1993; Bar-Yosef and Goren-Inbar 1993) are one- to two-pebbles-thick and dotted with stone artifacts and faunal remains. A few burned flint pieces identified on some of them (Bar-Yosef and Goren-Inbar 1993) can be interpreted as attesting to the use of fire and would thus suggest rather advanced modes of adaptations.

All the lithic artifacts from the 1960–1974 seasons underwent a detailed attribute analysis which included typological, technological and stylistic attributes. Some of the typological data are presented in Tables 1.1–1.3.

> NOTE: in all illustrations and tables relating to 'Ubeidiya, Roman numerals refer to trenches and Arabic ones to specific layers in trenches; the smaller the numeral, the older the layer it represents.

Inter-layer variability in typological composition, which seemed particularly evident with regard to bifaces, was initially taken (Stekelis 1966) as evidence for the presence at the site of two successive cultural entities, regarded as local variants of two distinct traditions: the Oldowan Industrial Complex (characterized by absence or scarcity of bifaces) and the Abbevillian tradition (featuring large quantities of bifaces). Stekelis accordingly distinguished between an 'Israeli variant of the Oldowan tradition' (IVO II), further subdivided into three phases (I–III), and an 'Israeli variant of the Abbevillian tradition' (IVA), which he considered to have postdated IVO II. Further finds (Bar-Yosef and Tchernov 1972), which clearly indicated

that IVO II levels were stratigraphically overlying IVA levels as well as underlying them, could not be reconciled with Stekelis's model, suggesting instead contemporaneity of the two traditions, similar to that proposed in Leakey's (1971, 1975) model for Olduvai.

The results of attribute analyses conducted on the entire lithic assemblage were eventually employed to examine several hypotheses pertaining to the possible source of the reported variability in typological composition. The lithic assemblages included in these examinations were sampled in a manner to represent both different points along a temporal axis and various depositional environments.

The analyses showed no time-related differences in typological composition between the various assemblages, which would seem to imply that the previously reported absence of certain tool types from some assemblages merely reflects insufficient sample sizes. The assemblages were found to be typologically characterized by an essentially unchanged type-inventory, predominated by core tools, notches, denticulates and scrapers. Typological frequencies were also found generally close across assemblages, the notable exception being the increased or decreased frequencies of few specific tool types in certain layers (such as the abundance of bifaces in layer K-30 and that of spheroids and sub-spheroids in layer K-29) (see Table 1.1 p. 104).

The technological analysis demonstrated that each of the examined attributes (amount of cortex, type and angle of striking platform, number and pattern of scars on the dorsal face, etc.) showed a similar pattern of distribution throughout the entire stratigraphic sequence and across the various depositional environments. Stekelis's observation regarding preferences of specific raw materials for the production of specific tool types was found to hold for all assemblages (Figure 1.1). No such preferences were detected regarding the size of pebbles or cobbles selected for modification, and the typically-wide size distributions were found to be temporally transgressive for all artifacts. Taken together, the technological evidence is incompatible with any hypothesis proposing to deduce from the lithic evidence the presence — either contemporaneously or in succession — of two distinct cultural entities at the site.

Currently, the specific pattern of typological variability apparent in the 'Ubeidiya assemblages is similarly viewed as the variability identified in several other Acheulean assemblages (i.e., Olorgesailie: Isaac 1977; the Mugharan assemblages from Tabun: Jelinek 1981, to mention only two), where a dichotomy was observed in the frequencies of bifaces and scrapers — some assemblages featuring higher frequencies of bifaces, and others larger proportions of scrapers. Until more information has accumulated, the available evidence seems to accord best with non-explanatory stochastic approaches to this issue, such as the 'random walk pattern' hypothesis, advocated by Isaac (1972, 1977).

In conclusion, all lines of evidence seem to indicate that the lithic assemblages of 'Ubeidiya are a manifestation of a single continuous tradition, forming part of the Acheulean Industrial Complex.

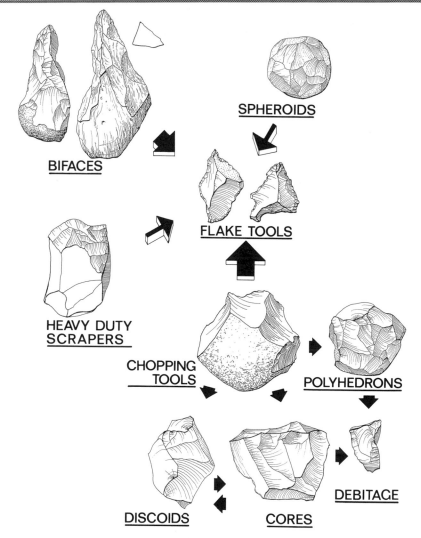

Figure 1.1 'Ubeidiya: schematic model of the typological components (the relative contribution of each type of raw material to the flake)

GESHER BENOT YA'AKOV

Gesher Benot Ya'akov is an open-air, water-logged Acheulean site, located in the Dead Sea Rift — the northern extension of the Red Sea— East African rift system, some 2 km south of the former shoreline of the Hula Lake, in northern Israel (see Figure 1).

The site, situated along a section of the course and of both banks of the Jordan River, is embedded in the Middle Pleistocene Benot Ya'akov formation (Horowitz 1979 and references therein), characterized by the presence of the fossil gastropod species *Viviparus apameae*. It was investigated by Garrod, Stekelis (Stekelis et al. 1937, 1938; Stekelis 1960) and Gilead (1968, 1970a, 1973), and was among the first Levantine sites to undergo interdisciplinary

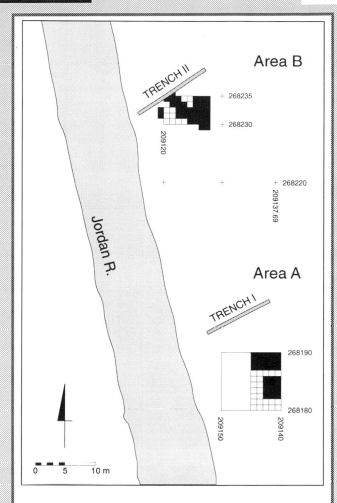

Figure 2.2   Gesher Benot Ya'akov. Detailed map of the study area

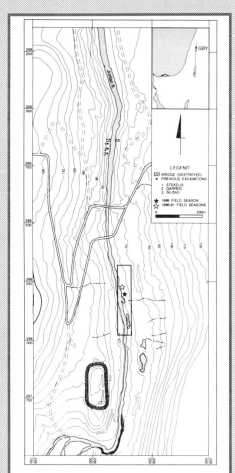

Figure 2.1   Gesher Benot Ya'akov. Location map of previous and recent excavations

investigations of its geological and paleontological aspects as well as its prehistorical ones (for references, see Goren-Inbar and Belitzky 1989).

Investigations of the site's vicinity were resumed following the discovery of previously unknown exposures of the Benot Ya'akov formation (Goren-Inbar and Belitzky 1989). Following a geological/archaeological survey, excavations at the site were resumed in an area located on the eastern bank of the river, south of the previously excavated area. The 20–25 meter-thick lacustrine-fluvial deposits investigated in this area (Figure 2.1) represent a fragment of a sedimentary sequence, deposited in the Benot Ya'akov Embayment as well as in the Hula Basin *sensu stricto*, and document part of the Middle Pleistocene depositional history of a freshwater lake (Goren-Inbar et al. 1992a). The severely deformed deposits were folded, faulted and displaced by tectonic movement, and formed an anticline at the excavation area.

The excavations (Figure 2.2) revealed the existence of at least seven archaeological layers of diverse characteristics, of which three were exposed in two excavation areas yielding varied lithic and paleontological assemblages (Figure 2.3; Plates 1, 2.1). Well-preserved organic material was recovered from most of the depositional units (Goren-Inbar et al. 1992a, 1992b), comprising fruits, seeds, bark and wood (Plate 2.2) and — most notably — a wooden plank with manmade polish (Belitzky et al. 1991).

Analysis of the lithics demonstrated utilization of three kinds of raw material — basalt, flint and limestone. Some preference for basalt for the production of bifaces was demonstrated, though small numbers of handaxes made of flint or limestone were also retrieved (Goren-Inbar 1992: Figures 6.4, 6.5). These finds seem to negate Stekelis's observations regarding the exclusive use of basalt for the production of bifacial items, which would appear to imply that his observation is valid only for the area excavated by him. Flint was found to have been used extensively for the manufacture of flakes and flake tools, and limestone pebbles were occasionally modified into chopping tools.

Technological examinations of the abundant lithic material indicated that most if not all the stages of the reduction process of bifaces took place *in situ*, as attested by the presence of large cores and characteristic by-products (*éclat de taille de biface*) of the biface production.

Evidence was found, for the first time in the Levant — though similar finds were reported before from the Maghreb (Dauvois 1981) — for the coexistence of the Kombewa and the Levallois

Plate 2.1   Gesher Benot Ya'akov — the recent excavations (Layer 11—6, level 4)

techniques, both of which are unanimously regarded as clearly indicative of fore-planning. The former technique, previously reported from this site as employed for the manufacture of cleavers (Gilead 1970b), was found to have been used quite extensively for the production of handaxes as well (Goren-Inbar and Saragusti in prep.) (Figures 2.4, 2.5). The latter technique was found to have been applied to flint rather more often than to basalt, for the production of cores, flakes and cleavers.

Analyses of the lithics

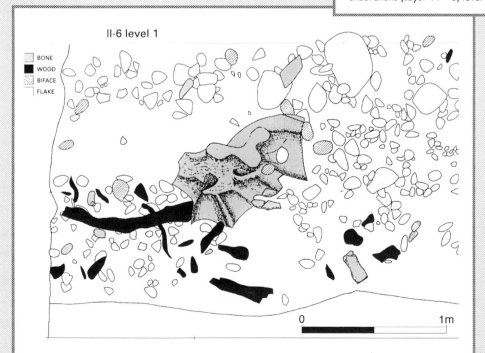

II-6 level 1

☐ BONE
■ WOOD
▨ BIFACE
☐ FLAKE

0   1m

Figure 2.3   Gesher Benot Ya'akov. Detailed distribution map of Layer 11—6, level 1 (partial)

demonstrated that Stekelis's attribution of African affinities to the site — on the basis of certain typically 'African' features such as extensive use of basalt, presence of the 'block on block' technique and the high frequencies of cleavers within the bifaces — is in need of thorough review. Nevertheless, the extensive use of the 'African' Kombewa technique does not permit us to abandon this notion altogether.

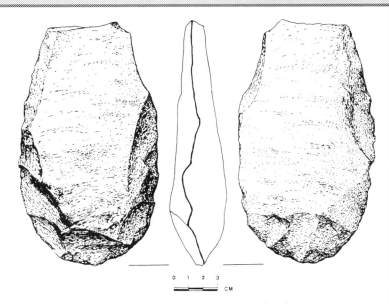

Figure 2.4   Gesher Benot Ya'akov. Kombewa a cleaver (basalt)

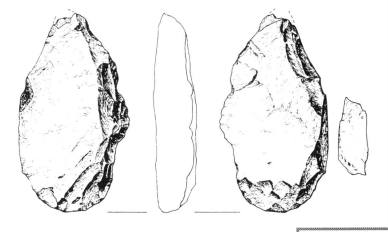

Figure 2.5   Gesher Benot Ya'akov. Kombewa a handaxe (basalt)

Plate 2.2   Gesher Benot Ya'akov — a wood fragment and associated basalt handaxe (Layer 11—6)

8

THE ORIGIN OF MODERN HUMANS

Ofer Bar-Yosef

Introduction: the debated issues and the Mousterian chronology

The origin of modern humans, whose earliest fossils were recovered in Middle Paleolithic deposits, has been in recent years at the center of a lively debate. Both the dating of the fossils, their attribution to one or two populations and their archaeological contexts are under constant revision (Figure 1). The rival evolutionary models that try to accommodate the evidence and explain 'when' and 'where' modern humans, as defined by their morpho-type charcteristics, emerged are dubbed the 'multiregional evolution' and the 'out of Africa' models. The relevance of the Levantine fossils and their lithic industries to this intriguing argument is discussed in various publications (e.g., Vandermeersch 1981, 1992; Bar-Yosef 1989a,b, 1992; Grün and Stringer 1991; Marks 1991; Tillier 1992; Trinkaus 1989, 1992; Wolpoff 1989). In brief, the main controversies emerge from the following observations:

1. Nuclear and mitochondrial DNA indicate that it is quite possible that modern humans came out of Africa sometime between 400,000 and 60,000 years ago.
2. A few fragmentary skeletal and rare isolated skulls, defined as archaic *Homo sapiens*, were dated to about 100,000 years ago in south and east Africa and could be considered as the predecessors of modern humans.
3. The morphological and metrical variability among the Middle Paleolithic human fossils in the entire Near East and especially in the Holy Land is larger than the recorded variability among Middle Paleolithic fossils in Western Europe. Among these there are those that were named 'Proto Cro-Magnons' (uncovered mainly in Qafzeh and Skhul) and were assumed to be the ancestors of the European Cro-Magnons (e.g., Vandermeersch 1981, 1989). Others were classified as Neanderthals although they differ from those of western and central Europe (e.g., Trinkaus 1984).
4. The earliest Levantine Upper Paleolithic assemblages reflect a rapid change of flint knapping technique that is cautiously dated to around 47–45 ka BP. From 38–35 ka BP blade technologies fully dominate most of the Upper Paleolithic sequence. The poor conservation of early Upper Paleolithic sites precludes conclusions concerning changes in subsistence, mortuary practices or even intra-site distribution of faunal and lithic remains.
5. Most Middle Paleolithic faunal assemblages reflect hunting of small and medium-sized animals and opportunistic scavenging of large bovids, while Upper Paleolithic animal bone assemblages were largely the result of hunting and trapping. Such differences can be interpreted as gradual innovation or improvement in tool use but may indicate the introduction of new techniques.

Needless to say, other scholars have suggested alternative interpretations. The advocates for regional continuity in the Levant also view the European sequences as demonstrating similar continuity (Clark and Lindly 1989; Clark 1992) in spite of overwhelming evidence to the contrary (e.g., Harrold 1989).

In recent years, the chronology of the Levantine Mousterian has been the subject of major controversy. Alternative chronological frameworks which indicated the much older age of Qafzeh (Bar-Yosef and Vandermeersch 1981; Tchernov 1981) were criticized (Jelinek 1982a) but were supported later when Thermoluminescence (TL) and Electron spin resonance (ESR) readings became available (Valladas et al. 1988; Schwarcz et al. 1988, 1989). The older age of Tabun D and E (Bar-Yosef 1989b) gained support from the ESR dates (Grün and Stringer 1991). However, new TL dates (Mercier and Valladas in press), indicate that the Tabun sequence is even older and suggest that Tabun D is about 270–300,000 years old (see opening paragraph, Chapter 4). The ESR ages for Tabun C are supported by the ESR and TL dates for Skhul as about *ca.* 100–120,000 BP (Figure 2). The ages for Kebara layers XII–VII are between 60–64 and 48,000 BP (both TL and ESR) and for Amud cave, with the same industry, ESR dates are around 47–55. Similarly, Tor Farj in Jordan provided dates at the same range of 60–50,000 BP (Henry, personal communication). Considered together with the stratigraphic evidence, it seems that the Levantine Mousterian lasted from about 270,000 (or 180,000) BP to about 47–45,000 BP (Figure 2).

Paleoclimate and chronological uncertainties

The late Middle Pleistocene and Upper Pleistocene paleoclimatic sequence is based on studies in the caves of the Lebanese coastal range, the Galilee and Mt. Carmel as well as the valley basins. Incorporation of the data from both inland and coastal sites is attempted here based essentially on the Lebanese shoreline evidence (Sanlaville

Plate 1 Overview of Kebara Cave excavation (courtesy of Ofer Bar-Yosef)

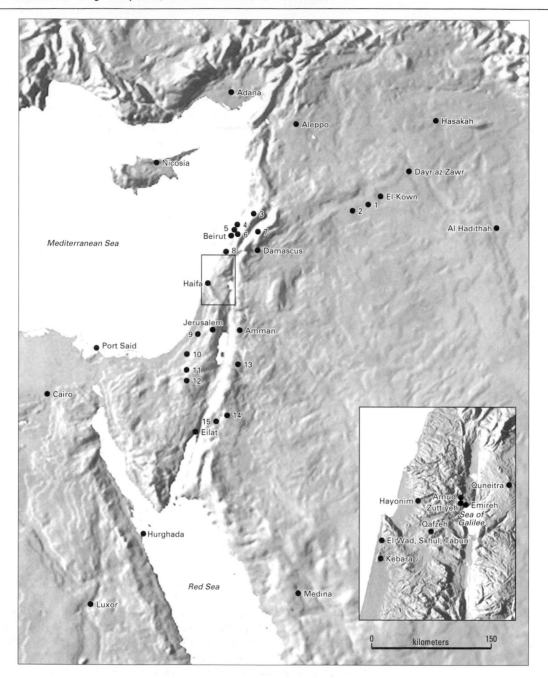

Figure 1   A map of Middle Paleolithic sites in the Levant: (1) Douara; (2) Jerf Ajla; (3) Keoue; (4) Nahr Ibrahim; (5) Ras el Kelb; (6) Ksar Akil; (7) Yabrud; (8) Bezez; (9) Shukbah; (10) Fara II; (11) Rosh Ein Mor; (12) Ain Aqev; (13) Ain Difla (14) Tor Faraj; (15) Tor Sabiha

1981), the reinterpretation of the Tabun cave sequence (e.g., Bar-Yosef 1989b; Grün and Stringer 1991), the TL and ESR dated Mousterian sites (Qafzeh, Skhul, Kebara, Tabun; see Figure 2), and the Negev and Transjordanian sites (Goldberg, this volume; Goldberg 1986; Henry 1986).

The Lebanese coast, where the mountains descend directly into the sea, provides a series of sites that are

directly linked to the Pleistocene marine stratigraphy. Coastal abrasion with episodal and sporadic depositional events left a series of clear-cut marine terraces, dunal accumulations and beach-rocks. Sanlaville's detailed studies (1981) defined a sequence of marine terraces of both transgressive and regressive character, ranging in altitude between 20 and 8 m above sea-level, named

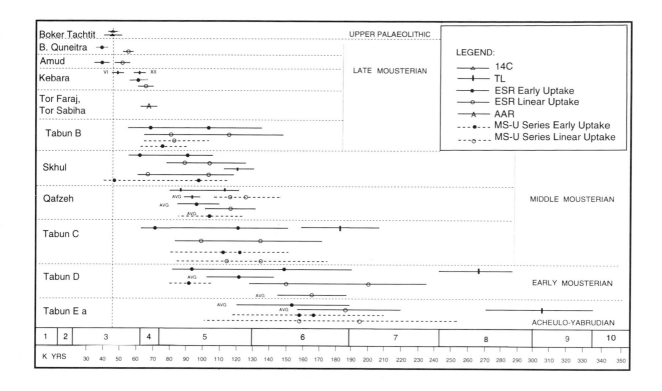

Figure 2 Distribution of ^{14}C, TL, ESR, amino acid racemization (AAR), mass spectrometer Uranium series (MS–U) for early Upper Paleolithic and Middle Paleolithic sites. The vertical line marks the approximate age for 7 the beginning of the Upper Paleolithic. Note the descrepency between the the ESR and TL dates for Tabun C, D, and Ea; acceptance of these dates means that the Mousterian sequence began earlier than previously accepted

Enfean I and II and Naamean. Only the Enfean II shoreline deposits contained the *Strombus bubonius* Lmk. a West African molluskan species which usually designates the Tyrrhenian faunas in the Mediterrranean basin. This Senegalese species, penetrated to the Western Mediterranean at least during Isotope Stage 7 and never reached the southern Levant due to the dominant sandy environment of its shoreline. Instead, the Tyrrhenian fauna is considered to be represented by *Marginopora*, a foraminifera that inhabits warm sea water, probably not more than 30 m deep. Sandy deposits that contain this species and identified in Mt. Carmel between the 6m and the 45m beaches, were tentatively correlated with Tyrrhenian shorelines of the Western Mediterranean (Horowitz 1979).

Enfean I and Enfean II shorelines were uncovered inside and in front of the caves of Ras el-Kelb, as well as Bezez and Abri Zumoffen, near Adlun (Roe 1983). A transgressive shoreline deposit without *Strombus* shells was identified at Abri Zumoffen. This 12 m beach is overlaid by lithic assemblages of the Mugharan Tradition (Amudian and Yabrudian). Although it was assigned to the Enfean II on the sole basis of altimetric considerations, it is suggested to re-date it to post-Enfean I (Bar-Yosef 1992b),

which would correlate it with Tabun cave, Layer E, or Isotope Stage 9 or 7.

The geological studies in Tabun cave, which lies 45 m above sea level, clarified the site's stratigraphy (Jelinek 1982a,b; Farrand 1979, 1982) and made it into a general cultural yardstick. The lower part of the sequence (Garrod's layers G, F and half of E – 'Tayacian/Tabunian', Upper Acheulean and Acheulo-Yabrudian) are predominantly sandy, and resemble the modern dune sands of the Mt. Carmel shoreline (Farrand 1979). The upper part of Layer E (Acheulo-Yabrudian) becomes increasingly silty, while the deposit of Layer D (Mousterian) resembles loess, presumably from the Sinai and Egyptian deserts (Farrand 1979). The lower sandy unit in Tabun (Garrod's Layers G, F and part of E) contains evidence for at least two slumping events, apparently caused by the lowering of the water table which could hardly be a local event. Such major changes could have been during each of the Pre-Middle Paleolithic glacials and interglacials when the shore of the Mediterranean reached the steep escarpment of Mt. Carmel, perhaps earlier than Isotope Stage 9 or 7. The repeated retreat of the sea could have caused these slumping phenomena (Isotope Stages 11–10, 9–8 and 7–6?).

The accumulation of the more silty upper Layer E and the 'loessial' deposit of Layer D are taken to indicate that the source of the sand (i.e., the shore) was further away from the cave at this time. These conditions could be correlated with the continuous deposition of the *kurkar* ridge, 2 km west of the cave and the *hamra* formation, that indicates a woodland landscape. Such wetter conditions (Horowitz 1979) could be correlated with wet phases of Stages 8 or early 6. At that time the Negev highland sites were occupied by the Early Mousterian 'Tabun D type', as both the geomorphological and the pollen evidence indicate.

The Negev Mousterian sites have so far provided very few clues for their dates. The stratigraphic position indicates that Mousterian sites existed in this desert area before the deposition of the massive, well rounded gravels interpreted as the results of higher and more sustained discharges under a climatic regime wetter than today's (Goldberg 1986). In the current interpretation it will be Isotope Stages 5d–5a. This reconstruction is supported by the U-series dates of fossil travertines from the Ain Aqev area (Schwarcz et al. 1980) and by the few pollen samples from adjacent Mousterian sites (Horowitz 1979). Thus, sites like Rosh Ein Mor would be better placed in Stage 6, a suggestion which is supported by their overall lithic resemblance to Tabun D (Munday 1979).

During the Last Interglacial, the *Strombus* assemblage, a cluster of West African mollusks, penetrated into the Eastern Mediterranean basin – an event which could have happened only during the warmest interglacials. This is the reason why the Enfean II shoreline in Lebanon is related to Isotope Stage 5e and covered by industries that can be included in the 'Tabun C type (see below), such as Ras el Kelb, Bezez and Naamé. The dry and warm conditions which characterize the second half of an interglacial may explain the faunal assemblage collected in the lower Mousterian layers in Qafzeh cave. The TL and ESR dates for these layers range from 92–115 ka (see Figure 2) and indicate that the burials were probably done over a period of at least 20,000 years during Stage 5. Recent dates from Skhul suggest a similar interval although the exact provenience of dated flints and teeth is unknown.

The dry and cold conditions of Stage 4 are probably responsible for the erosion in the main chamber of Kebara cave (Bar-Yosef et al. 1992). This was followed by the rather rapid accumulation of Mousterian layers approximately 4.5–5 m thick, rich in hearths, bones, charcoal and lithic artefacts dated to 65/60–48 ka by TL and ESR. In Unit XII an almost complete burial of an adult male, classified as a Neanderthal, was uncovered in 1983 (Bar-Yosef et al. 1988; Bar-Yosef and Vandermeersch 1991). The lithic analysis (Meignen and Bar-Yosef 1991) indicates that the assemblages of Kebara are similar to the

'Tabun B' industry and probably to Amud cave as well as Tor Faraj and Tor Sabiha (Henry 1986), two rock-shelters, located in the hilly area of southern Jordan.

In wadi terraces in the Negev and elsewhere, the erosional phase which followed the accumulation of the gravelly unit indicates arid conditions (Goldberg 1986) during 75–65 ka. In Nahal Besor, the site of Fara II (Gilead 1988), which is embedded in silts, suggests that the return to somewhat wetter (and possibly cold) conditions took place before the beginning of the Upper Paleolithic. This is also indicated by the deposits which underlie Boker Tachtit. The lithic industry from Fara II is made of cobbles and shaped by predominantly unidirectional convergent preparation. An additional open air site is Biqat Quneitra, located on the basalt plateau of the Golan, where rich lithic and faunal assemblages were recovered (Goren-Inbar 1990). ESR dates provide an age of about 53 k yrs (Ziaei et al. 1990) to the industry which is dominated by the radial and convergent preparation. Finally, no clear evidence for a climatic break marks the onset of the Upper Paleolithic. A summary of the chronology of Middle Paleolithic sites is presented in Figure 3.

The hominids

Middle Paleolithic human fossils from Levantine sites form one of the largest samples in Eurasia. Better known are the various burials uncovered in Tabun, Skhul, Kebara, Qafzeh and Amud (Plate 2). Isolated bones and teeth were found in these sites as well as in El-wad, Geula and Hayonim caves.

Morphologically the Levantine homonids, as mentioned above, are divided into two groups; the first is known as 'western Asia neanderthals' or Mediterranean Neanderthals while the others are classified as 'Proto-Cro-Magnons'. The first group includes the skeletons from Tabun, Kebara and Amud, the second those found in Skhul and Qafzeh (Plate 3). It is worth mentioning that the hominids from Shanidar cave, in the Zagros mountains, are also classified as Neanderthals (Trinkaus 1984). The two groups are differentiated morphologically (e.g., Smith, this volume; Tillier 1992, Trinkaus 1992; Vandermeersch 1992 with references) although they do share some common features.

The Skhul-Qafzeh group has higher skulls with flatter faces than the Neanderthal group. The mandibular gap between the ramus and the last molar is reduced or absent. Their legs were longer, although there is little indication that they were taller than the other group. Comparing the Skhul and the Qafzeh skeletons the latter are the more remote from the Neanderthal group, resembling the more modern *Homo sapiens*. Due to their 'transitional' characteristics, the first researchers, McCown and Keith, interpreted the entire sample as a local population. It was

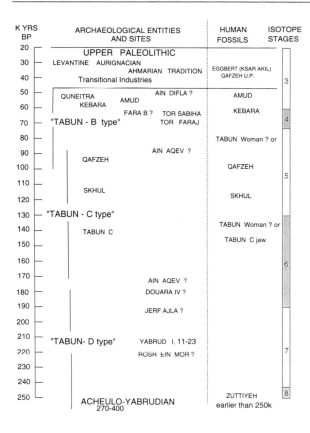

Figure 3 A composite chronological table based on the dates from Figure 2, that indicates the overlapping between ESR and TL dates. As yet undated sites are indicated by a question mark. The chronological position of the hominids is noted in the far-right column. Note the two possible dates for the Tabun Woman (from Layer C)

only later that the woman from Tabun was grouped with the West Asian Neanderthals.

Similar differences were noted in the metric attributes of the teeth that happen to be smaller among the more modern populations. The local Neanderthals have short more prognathic faces. Differences in the length and angles of limb bones are interpreted as reflecting unknown behavioral differences between these two groups (Trinkaus 1992). These morphological charcateristics developed since infancy as shown by Tillier (1992). Only further archaeological investigations will be able to document whether it is the nature of the behavioral differences that is reflected in the bones of these humans while living in the Levant or if Neanderthal morphology is of foreign origins.

Major transitions

The transition from the Lower Paleolithic to the Middle Paleolithic is generally considered to be not well defined. Several scholars have suggested including the Acheulo-

Yabrudian in the latter period. Recently, with advanced lithic studies, additional stratigraphic evidence and TL and ESR dates, it seems that the Acheulo-Yabrudian should be ascribed to the Lower Paleolithic. The known geographic distribution of the Acheulo-Yabrudian sites covers solely the northern and central Levant and, in spite of intensive surveys, none of its typical stone tools were found in the Negev and Sinai or in the region of southern Jordan. Therefore the southern distribution of this entity is delineated as an east–west boundary which is not ecological or climatic. The hypotheses that some of the Negev Mousterian sites are older than currently viewed and thus contemporary with the Acheulo-Yabrudian, or that a few Late Acheulean assemblages are contemporary with the Acheulo-Yabrudian require further testing.

The end of the Middle Paleolithic is marked by the transition to the Upper Paleolithic (Marks 1990). When both periods are compared across Europe and Western Asia this transition can be defined as a revolution. Several major features went through significant changes which are not so obvious when we compare the latest Mousterian to the Early Upper Paleolithic. Similar to other revolutions, the change is better demonstrated when a slightly later period is examined, after the revolution took place. In the case of the European sequence, the proliferation of antler and bone tools, mobile art objects and the cave art in the southwestern corner of the continent, are well known. In the Near East, it is more the ephemeral character of the Upper Paleolithic sites that indicates higher mobility – the evolved blade technology, the appearance of grinding tools, the modest use of bone and antlers mark the shift. That the change was rapid is clearly demonstarted by the 14C dates. Until 48–46,000 BP Mousterian industries are dominant while from 42,000 BP onwards blade industries are the basic stone tool-kits. This is well expressed in the few excavated and recorded sites.

The Levantine Upper Paleolithic began with two versions of a 'Transitional Industry' – one in the central Levant in Ksar Akil, Lebanon (Ohnuma 1988; Ohnuma and Bergman 1990) and the other in the Negev, namely in Boker Tachtit (Marks and Kaufman 1983). The transition from the Mousterian to the Upper Paleolithic in Ksar Akil is characterized by the continued use of the unipolar Levallois core reduction strategy. Similar unipolar convergent blanks, which in the late Mousterian times were shaped into racloirs and points, were modified into end scrapers, chamfered pieces (an end scraper in which the working edge was obtained by a transverse blow) and burins. The study by Ohnuma and Bergman (1990) indicates that prismatic, unipolar cores dominate the earliest assemblages of Ksar Akil (XXV–XXI) with diminishing numbers of Levallois cores. This industry directly evolves into the full-blown blade based Ahmarian.

Marks and Volkman (1986), while reanalyzing the Mousterian assemblages of Ksar Akil, demonstrated that

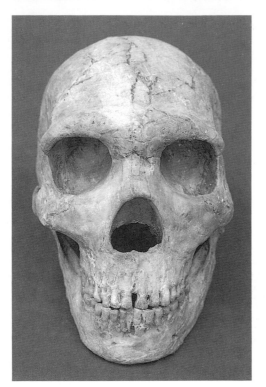

Plate 2 The skull from Amud cave (The Israel Museum, Jerusalem)

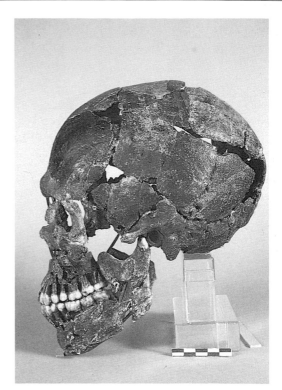

Plate 3 A skull from Qafzeh cave (photograph: B. Vandermeersch)

a trend to radial preparation is well expressed in the latest Mousterian assemblages and, therefore, they could not have been the technological origin of the unipolar and bipolar Early Upper Palaeolithic Transitional Industry. However, it is worth mentioning that there is a stratigraphic gap in Ksar Akil between the Middle and the Upper Paleolithic and the samples of the earliest Upper Paleolithic assemblages (XXV–XXIV) are quite poor.

Settlement Pattern

The information concerning the number of Middle Paleolithic sites is incomplete although many are known from surface scatters. Many sites have been destroyed by erosion and are now found as isolated pieces incorporated in gravel and alluvial/colluvial deposits. Moreover, the clustering of all Mousterian sites into one entity ignores their temporal range which, by the new chronology, is much longer than suggested in most of the summaries published before 1989. If the current TL and ESR dates get further support in the future, the Mousterian period lasted at least from about 180,000 BP (or more) to about 47–46,000 BP.

Prehistoric sites of hunter-gatherers are generally classified in relation to the pattern of mobility of the group. On the whole, two kinds are well explored in the

literature : (a) sites that designate residential moves and (b) sites of logistical moves(Binford 1980). In the Near East, Mortensen proposed two models known as circular and radial mobility. The first means that the entire group moves while the second accepts the notion of a base camp and stations for task forces within the surrounding territory. In reality, the two models were probably mixed together as the subsistence strategies depend on the ability to predict the placement of various resources. The accessability, predictability and reliability of the dispersed resources could have been different from year to year, especially in the eastern Mediterranean where the distribution of the rains depended on several storm tracks. During some years the main storms would come through North Africa, making the southern part of the country richer and lusher; in other years, the rain was mostly distributed towards the northern region. In both cases areas along the coastal plain from the Galiliee to Judea would have been wetter that any other area. This means that survival in Mt. Carmel was always feasible. In addition, one has to take into account as limiting factors the neighboring groups and competition with other predators. Although we know very little about the vegetal diet of the Mousterian, it seems from the example of Kebara cave to be rather limited (see Plate 1.1 in Window 1 p. 122). We therefore employ here the typology of camp-sites as devised for modern humans but with reservation.

On the basis of their known contents, Mousterian sites can be defined as (a) hunting/gathering ephemeral camps, and (b) kinds of base camps. The first class is often represented by low frequencies of artifacts relative to the excavated volume, sometimes a large number of curated pieces, and a paucity of primary chipping that is expressed in the rarity of cores. In other cases, when the sites were hunting stations, most of the tools were produced locally and many pieces can be refitted (Gilead 1988). The list of ephemeral sites will include in Mt. Carmel the sites of Tirat Carmel, that was perhaps a quarry site (Ronen 1974), Sefunim cave that could have served as a hunter's shelter (Ronen 1984), and perhaps Geula cave (Wreschner 1967), although only a small portion of the cave remained after the modern quarrying activities. In the lower layers of the Qafzeh cave the remains of a range of special activities have been found, including building fires, and human burials. A special case are the rock-shelters found in the Judean desert (Neuville 1951) for which we do not possess the entire assemblages (although Erq el-Ahmar layer H provided the same limited assemblage as Sefunim). Several plateau sites in the Avdat area (Munday 1979) served as a basis for reconstructing, with Rosh Ein Mor, the settlement pattern for the Negev Highlands (Marks 1981). Fara II was both a quarry site and a hunting station; Quneitra possibly served as a hunting station on the edge of a seasonal pond (Goren-Inbar 1990).

Base camps or intensively used sites include Tabun cave (see opening photo Chapter 4), Qafzeh layers XV–VII where numerous animal bones, mostly of large- and medium-sized mammals were found (Bouchud 1974), Kebara cave (Bar-Yosef et al. 1992), El-Wad G–F (Garrod and Bate 1937), Amud cave (Suzuki and Takai 1970; Hovers et al. 1991) and probably some levels at Hayonim cave. If well preserved, these sites contain the remains of numerous hearths (see Window 1: Kebara cave, Plate 1.1) and the seasonality evidence would indicate repeated occupations during the year. In the case of Kebara cave, gazelle were hunted during summer and winter (Lieberman and Meadow 1992) and legumes collected in the spring. It is still premature to ascertain whether the Mousterian groups were sedentary in the same sense as the Natufian, but they stayed for longer periods in what seems to have been a relatively small territory of several hundred square kilometers.

Site size and intensity of occupation (artifacts per cubic meter) are difficult to discuss due to insufficient published information. However, it should be stressed that several sites lend the impression of having been used relatively quite often. For example, in Tabun Cave a total of 8 m accumulated between 270/180–50/60 ka (layers D–B, without the accumulation in the chimney which was about 3 m thick). This sequence, besides slumping and minor gaps, includes a major erosional phase between D and C. In Kebara about 4 m of ashes and fine sediments were deposited from 60/65 to 48 ka (see Chapter 4). In Ksar Akil an accumulation about 18 m thick represents a time span from *ca.* 45 ka to 20 ka (based on ^{14}C). Of course, there are many sites in which the intensity of use is less impressive and a gradual change can be observed as one moves into semiarid/arid regions or high altitudes.

The distribution of Mousterian sites with the thicker deposits in the Mediterranean coastal belt was already noted by S. Binford (1968) who suggested human groups were moving across the countryside in an east–west direction following the main wadi courses. Studies of tooth increments of gazelles (Lieberman and Meadow 1992) indicate that even among the cave sites located on the west-facing slopes of the coastal ranges, the season of occupation differs from one locale to the next.

When the intra-site patterning is examined it becomes obvious that there is no use of stones in hearths for cooking or providing warmth. Small round-oval hearths were uncovered in Qafzeh and Kebara. A large hearth, 5 m in diameter, was reported from Douara Cave (Syria), layer IV (Akazawa 1987).

The available evidence concerning the spatial distribution of artifacts within the archaeological horizons of the Mousterian is rather scanty. Spatial analysis in Rosh Zin suggested to Stevens and Hietala (1977) a pattern of repeated occupations in which Levallois points, burins, end scrapers and notches were usually aggregated in the same area over the total thickness of the site (*ca.* 1 m) within the excavated block (45 m^3). A certain patterning is suggested in Kebara where the area of the hearths and distributed ashes contain a few artifacts while all the bones, the lithics and the small debitage are laid around, towards the rear part of the cave. Infrared Spectroscopy demonstarted that the areas without bones did not contain bones. The small percentage of burnt bones (Speth in Bar-Yosef 1992) is the same as in later periods, thus it does not preclude cooking over the fire.

Innovations and technology

There is evidence for the use of fire during the Late Acheulean, but the better preserved information comes from Middle Paleolithic deposits. Mousterian hearths, when intact such as in the lower layers at Qafzeh and Kebara are generally small (30–60 cm in diameter). However, it should be mentioned that a large hearth was uncovered in Douara Cave (Akazawa 1987). These features differ considerably from the ashy deposits of Layer C in Tabun Cave (Jelinek 1981, 1982a,b; Garrod and Bate 1937) that are interpreted as being the result of brush fires. Micromorphological evidence suggests that different types of combustibles (e.g., wood, grass) were burned in the various hearths in Kebara (see Window 2 in Chapter 4).

Branches of Tabor oak (*Quercus ithaburensis*) were the most commonly used (U. Baruch, personal communication). Phytolith analysis aimed at the identification of grasses is underway in both Kebara and Hayonim caves (A. Miller-Rosen, personal communication).

Due to the lack of well-preserved wood or bark objects, most of the information about the available technology employed by Mousterian groups is derived from lithic studies.

The new way in which Mousterian assemblages are currently examined is known as the *chaîne opératoire* approch (Geneste et al. 1990; cf. Hall and Levy, this volume). This is the dynamic process that exposes, when clearly analyzed, the choices made by humans. It begins with the selection and transportation of raw material, through the production of the blanks, the using and/or re-shaping and using of artifacts (Dibble 1987), to the final discard of utilized objects and other debitage elements. It is assumed, as based on the analysis of ethnoarchaeologically recorded operational sequences, whether in stone, pottery or metal, that the series of sequential decisions reflected in the analyzed operational chain are determined by the technical traditions of the studied human group. Aspects such as differential selection of raw material, methods used for the knapping, and the selection of the blanks for either use or retouch and use, are derived from the technical habits of the given population. On the basis of ethnographically and historically studied groups, it is assumed that the methods used for tool manufacturing among prehistoric groups were transmitted orally or through imitation from one generation to the next. However, in a prehistoric social entity, either synchronically or diachronically, individuals possess the knowledge of several, interrelated techniques from which they are able to choose a certain mode or modes. Each of the modes is defined as the existing options through which a preconceived object can be produced and later used, while taking into account the presence of constraints such as the quality, availability and accessibility of raw material. When choices, methods and modes are recurrent, they cluster into what archaeologists characterize as the expression of a social group (Geneste et al. 1990).

In the case of the Levantine Mousterian, the study of the various Levallois methods indicate that Levallois core reduction can be achieved by either radial, unidirectional or bidirectional removals (Plate 4). In addition, the distal and lateral convexity of cores can be obtained either by radial flaking or by unidirectional *éclat débordant* ('lateral core-edge flake'; see Boëda 1988). Variations can be identified at each stage of the operational sequence and may occur in numerous combinations. The best way to study these sequences is by refitting and through tedious replicatory experiments.

Although F. Bordes employed quantitative analysis of assemblages as the basis for defining 'cultures', his famous

Plate 4   A radial Levallios core from Kebara cave (photo: Kebara archives)

type-list is used by most researchers in a reduced version. Progress in understanding site formation processes made it clear that the percentages of retouched pieces, debitage (unretouched blanks often longer than 2.5 cm), debris and cores in an excavated assemblage reflect a wide range of activities including: the type of occupation, different activities such as retooling, curation of selected artifacts, and production of an expedient industry nature which is a result of the quality and/or abundance of raw material. Middle Paleolithic prehistoric groups are now better defined on the basis of their operational reduction sequence, their exploitation of raw material, and the choices made in shaping certain retouched pieces. The premise of the 1970s – that under the same environmental circumstances different groups will produce similar lithic industries because function and raw materials are the dominant factors – is not accepted any more. In the same place and from the same abundant raw materials the Mousterian artisans of Mt. Carmel succeeded in producing different industries.

The definition of the Levantine Mousterian is based on the Tabun sequence and has been roughly subdivided into three phases labelled 'Tabun D-type, Tabun C-type, and Tabun B-type' or 'Mousterian Phase 3,2,1' (Copeland 1975; Jelinek 1982a,b; Bar-Yosef 1989a,b; Meignen and Bar-Yosef 1991). The basic morphological chartcteristics of the assemblages are as follows:

1. 'Tabun D-type'. Blanks, blades, and elongated points were predominantly removed from Levallois unipolar convergent cores, and more rarely from bipolar cores, with minimal preparations of the striking platforms. Elongated retouched points, numerous blades, racloirs and burins are among the common tool types. Rare

Plates 5 and 6   Two Levallios points from Kebara cave (photographs: Kebara archives)

bifaces occur in Tabun Cave (that could have been a mixture with Tabun layer E). This industry is found in Tabun D, Abu Sif, Sahba, Rosh Ein Mor, Nahal Aqev 3, Hayonim cave, Jerf Ajla, and Douara layer IV (Plate 5).

2. 'Tabun C type'. The blanks, often ovaloid flakes, sometimes large, were struck from Levallois cores, through radial preparation or from bi-polar cores. Triangular points appear in small numbers (Plate 5). This industry is common in Qafzeh (Boutié 1989), Tabun layer C, Skhul and Naamé (Fleisch 1970).

3. 'Tabun B type'. Blanks were mainly removed from unipolar convergent Levallois cores with small frequencies of radial preparation. Broad based points, often short, thin flakes and some blades are common. The best examples for this industry are Kebara units VI–XII, Tabun B, Amud and Bezez B (Meignen and Bar-Yosef 1991).

The suggestion to see 'Tabun B type' and 'Tabun C type' industries as two facies of the same entity (Ronen 1979) was not well established and the new technological analyses, together with the radiometric dates, make this proposition untenable (Meignen and Bar-Yosef 1991).

I, therefore, suggest referring to the stratigraphic sequence of Tabun as a scale and as a basis for correlation with other sites and industries (see Figure 3). In sum, this would place the Late Acheulean in Stages 9 and 8, the Acheulo-Yabrudian as well as 'Tabun D type' assemblages in Stages 7 and 6, the 'Tabun C type' (Qafzeh, Skhul) will be in the early part of Stage 5 (130/110–90/80 ka) and 'Tabun B type' from about 90/80 ka to 47/45 ka.

Additional refinement is urgently needed as well as a better dating resolution for the Early Upper Paleolithic.

The Levantine Mousterian differs markedly from the Mousterian facies in the Zagros and the Taurus mountains, although the industry of Karain Cave (in southwest Turkey) has a more substantial component of radial Levallois preparation (that differs from the Zagros assemblages). The number of retouched pieces in these assemblages is higher than in the Levant, perhaps due to constraints of raw materials.

Stone tools were produced mainly for maintenance activities (preparing wooden spears, digging-sticks, scrapers and knives for hide working, etc.) and procurements tasks (e.g., stone spear (Shea 1988) heads for hunting, butchering knives, and so on). Unfortunately, most of the direct evidence concerning Middle Paleolithic diet still comes from the analysis of the preserved animal bones. Rare finds from sites such as the Kebara and Douara caves indicate that we are missing the vegetal menu. By comparison with other low to mid-latitude hunter-gatherers, it can be assumed that their diet was based primarily on fruits, seeds, leaves and tubers. In Douara cave, near Palmyra, the fruits of the *Celtis* sp. (Akazawa 1987) were found. Legume seeds, mostly various species of vetch, occur in all the Mousterian layers in Kebara (E. Lev, personal communication), indicating the presence of humans in the cave in springtime and the exploitation of carbohydrates at the time of seasonal stress.

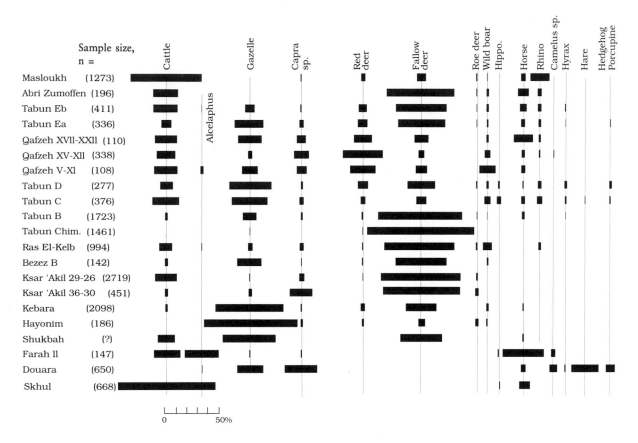

Figure 4   Frequencies of animal bones from Acheulo-Yabrudian and Mousterian sites from the coastal mountains of the Levant (based on the table in Bar-Yosef 1989a).

It is quite possible that the differences between Middle and Upper Paleolithic humans were in the ways in which vegetal resources were collected and prepared for food. Carbonized plant remains from Ohalo II – a Late Upper Paleolithic (19,000 BP) waterlogged site on the shores of the Sea of Galilee (see Goring-Morris, this volume) provide important data concerning diet. This assemblage supports the contention of a wide ranging use of plants, encompassing more than 35 species. Sporadic grinding stones in several Upper Paleolithic contexts substantiate this observation.

Other sources of information concerning the Mousterian economy are the faunal reports that record both hunted and scavenged animal species. The frequencies are given here in Figure 4 (from Bar-Yosef 1989a). Only a few published studies include counts of body parts. The main phenomena in the Mousterian assemblages can be better understood when compared to the Acheulo-Yabrudian, as reflected in the bone counts (NISP):

1. One-third of the mammalian bones in Acheulo-Yabrudian contexts such as Masloukh cave, Abri Zumoffen and Tabun layer E are of large animals (*Bos primigenius*, rhinoceros and equids).

2. Large mammals are predominant in the two open-air Mousterian sites – Farah II (Gilead and Grigson 1984) and Biqat Quneitra (Davis et al. 1988). It was suggested that such bone collections reflect opportunistic scavenging (Bar-Yosef 1989a).

3. The dominance of fallow deer, gazelle, roe deer and a few other relatively small mammals in Kebara and Amud caves are indicative of intentional hunting (Speth and Tchernov in Bar-Yosef et al. 1992).

4. The tendency to consume medium and small mammals, reptiles and birds continued, without apparent change, at least from the Late Mousterian through the Upper Paleolithic. The interpretation that these assemblages represent the results of hunting and trapping now requires further examination in order to find out what were the techniques employed. Different trapping methods could mean different rates of success and, therefore, changes in work load.

The overall conclusion that hunting techniques developed during Mousterian times is in accordance with similar situations in a Mediterranean environment in coastal Italy

(Stiner 1991). In prime situations where scavenging was a time and energy saving strategy, the Mousterian people took advantage of the available carcasses.

Symbolic behavior

Human burials from the Middle Paleolithic provide one of the earliest views of human ideology in the Levant. The suggestion to view Mousterian burials as depositional accidents was refuted (Belfer-Cohen and Hovers 1992). Perhaps the most important observation that should be stressed is that in the active formation processes which characterize the Levantine cave-sites, not one skeleton – whether animal or human – would remain intact unless well covered. The evidence for intermittent occupations of humans and hyaenas is obvious when micromorphological analysis is used as a tool for deciphering the micro site formation processes. The evidence for such alternate occupations was uncovered in each of the properly examined sites such as Kebara and Hayonim caves (see Goldberg, this volume).

There are no demonstrable differences between the burials left by Middle Paleolithic modern-looking hominids (Skhul and Qafzeh) or the local Mediterranean Neanderthals (Tabun, Kebara and Amud). It is worth mentioning that we often assume that the hominids were buried in their own camps, whether occupied repeatedly (like Kebara) or ephemerally (like the lower layers at Qafzeh). This requires further detailed examination that our archaeological analytical tools are not yet able to produce.

Conclusions: processes and change

The chronology of the Middle Paleolithic fossils which contribute to the recent debate is presented in Figure 2 (see Smith, this volume). I have placed the woman from Tabun in the context of Layer B, where it seems, in view of Garrod's hesitations, to better suit the current interpretation. Fossils with the 'Tabun C type' industry are those of Skhul, Qafzeh, and Tabun II (the mandible). Fossils with the 'Tabun B type' are Kebara, Tabun I, and Amud. Currently we have no human fossils associated with the 'Tabun D type' industry. Uncovering additional human remains will facilitate the testing of the hypothesis that the archaeological assemblages included in this entity, or an earlier one (such as a Late Acheulean of Levallois facies), were produced by an in-coming African or a local population.

Superficially, there seems to be a correlation between certain lithic industries and the fossils. However, the reader is reminded that there are early manifestations of blade industries (in Stage 6 and 5e) in the Levant and Western Europe (Jelinek 1990; Otte and Keeley 1990) which are not necessarily associated with modern looking hominids. Making blades by removals from flat shaped unidirectional cores is an invention that is repeated several times. It is only with the appearance of prismatic cores, at the beginning of the Upper Paleolithic, that both the invention and the needs come together to play a driving role in the newly shaped lithic assemblages. In sum, the association between the fossil hominids and the archaeological assemblages indicates that modern-looking, hominids such as those from Qafzeh and Skhul, produced Mousterian industries which show no hints of developing into characteristic Upper Paleolithic industries. Therefore, we may conclude that the transition from Middle to Upper Paleolithic was mainly a socio-economic and cultural revolution unrelated to the morphological differences that are observed among the human fossils. It is possible to hypothesize that this cultural shift occurred within the descendents of populations similar to the Qafzeh-Skhul group although no fossils from the end of the Levantine Mousterian are available. Only additional human relics will enable the testing of this hypothesis.

CASE STUDY: KEBARA CAVE

Kebara cave is located on the western escarpment of Mount Carmel (Plate 1.1). It was first excavated by F. Turville-Petre in 1931 who stripped off the historical deposits (layer A), an Early Natufian layer that contained several skeletons in a central burial ground, a few cremated fragmentary skeletons and a rich lithic and bone industry. Layer C was a thin deposit with a microlithic industry later called Kebaran. Layer D was assigned to the Aurignacian, while layer E was allocated to an earlier Aurigancian. The lithic industries were dominated by carinated and nosed scrapers with many more blades and El-Wad points in Layer E. M. Stekelis excavated from 1953 to 1965 uncovering some Upper Paleolithic layers but dedicating most of his efforts to the Mousterian. In one of the early levels he uncovered the relics of an infant attributed to the Levantine Neanderthals.

The last series of excavations (1982–1990) were co-organized by the author and B. Vandermeersch with an interdisciplinary team. Most of the excavations were carried out in the Mousterian layers (units V–XIII) where bedrock was found below several sterile, mostly water-laid layers (units XIV–XV). The Upper Paleolithic was excavated over a limited surface (units IV–I). These layers correspond to Turville-Petre's E and lower D and were dated to 42,000–28,000 BP. One of the most striking discoveries was a Mousterian burial of an adult. However, the team of researchers was interested in the following questions that illustrate several potential research avenues in Middle Paleolithic sites:

1. What were the processes responsible for the preservation of hearths and ash lenses within the Mousterian layers and what happened to these hearths through time while diagenic processes were active?.
2. What were the agents and processes that resulted in the accumulation of different bone assemblages in various parts of the cave? How do the frequencies of cut marks, gnaw marks, charring and fragmentation patterns reflect the varying roles of anthropogenic, biogenic and natural processes?
3. What were the operational reduction sequences employed in manufacturing the lithic industries, including the ways in which artifacts were used as viewed through micro-wear and edge-damage microscopic studies?

Traditional geological analyses (by H. Laville) and micromorphology (by P. Goldberg) as well as the use of Infrared Spectrometry (by S. Weiner) enabled the excavators to understand some of the site formation processes and answer, in part, some of the more specific questions outlined here.

The Mousterian layers inside Kebara cave reflect two major occupational episodes (Goldberg and Laville 1991). The first occupations (Unit XIII) contain hearths and ashes, with very few artifacts, that had accumulated in the central part of the cave. Following an erosional gap of unknown duration, repeated occupations accumulated about 3.0–3.5 meters of sediments, mostly of biogenic origins. Tl dates indicate that this sequence is encapsulated in the time interval of about 60–48,000 BP (Valladas et al. 1987). Although the entire surface of the cave was not excavated, it seems that during the early times the Mousterians occupied the interior portion of the chamber and, as

time passed, they moved their center of activities towards the entrance. One should keep in mind that the shape of Kebara is similar to other karstic caves in the region. This means that the original entrance is a limestone threshold that slopes towards the interior swallow-hole. Thus, the deposits which accumulated indoors had an initial dip inwards and those in front of the dip line sloped outwards.

The interior of the cave was gradually filled by materials brought by humans such as firewood, lithics, hides, animal tissues, plants gathered for consumption and bedding as well as the ephemeral use of the cave by hyenas, together with blown-in dust and sand. Near the entrance, washed-in colluvial red soil with some angular fragments became mixed with the residues of the late Mousterian occupations. It was only after the slumping of the swallow-hole, which caused the folding, faulting, erosion and

Plate 1.1   Kebara cave: a general view (photo: Kebara archives)

redeposition of sediments from Unit VII, that more colluvial material was washed into the cave.

The hearths are often visible as white ashy deposits and indicate two phases in hearth use (see Goldberg, this volume). First a rounded or oval fireplace was established, and later the white ashes were distributed over a larger surface creating an irregular ashy lense. The best preserved hearths were uncovered mainly in unit XIII, the lowermost occupational deposit, where occupations seem to have been more ephemeral than in Units XII–VII. The many hearths in Kebara contain very few bone fragments and the number of charred bones is minimal. However, there were a large number of burned lithic pieces in the hearths which enabled their dating by TL. The absence of small stones or cobbles indicates that there was no warmth banking. It seems that cooking or parching methods did not differ considerably from those found in the residues of Upper Paleolithic hearths in Kebara. Numerous carbonized seeds of vetch were found in the blackish lower level of many hearths. This kind of organic data allows us to reconstruct the season when these hearths were used. April and May would be the time when legumes are available in patches on the slopes of Mt. Carmel.

The distibution of bones within the excavated area is of particular interest at Kebara. Bone concentrations were exposed in the central area and masses were found near the northern wall, especially closer to the area under the chimney. Both were dumps, but the differences between the artifacts reflected a different use of the space. While the central area was the main living space, the piles near the wall included more waste flakes and exhausted cores. Within the central area the spatial distribution of bones and lithics including small debris, reflects an intentional arrangement, with hearths and ashes located towards the cave's entrance while most of the lithics and all of the bones are dispersed towards the rear part of the cave. This spatial distribution was repeated in the upper Mousterian layers, and was truncated by a diagenic front, which means that the entire southern portion of the cave in the Mousterian is devoid of bones.

The importation of flint nodules for the production of blanks is clearly demonstrated by the ability of the excavators to reconstruct the entire core reduction sequences from the excavated lithics. Most of the assemblage is made of flint with only one well-shaped basalt pebble, which probably served as a grinder, that was brought in from the Mt. Carmel area.

One cannot study the Kebara lithic assemblages in isolation. They are best understood by comparisons to the Tabun cave lithic sequence. Tabun Cave (see opening photo, Chapter 4), which is located 13 km north of Kebara, shared a similar environment. As explained above, the Mousterian layers D, C and B at Tabun, as defined in Garrod's excavations, help up identify the sub-divisions of the Levantine Mousterian. The unidirectional convergent method of core preparation characteristic among the Kebara assemblages resembles that reported from Tabun B (Copeland 1975). The Levallois flakes in Kebara are always the dominant group and the Levallois points are short with a broad base and their striking platform was often shaped in the form of 'chapeau de gendarme' (Plate 5). Most of the artifacts in Kebara were not retouched. Extensive study of edge damage demonstrated that tools were used for a variety of activities and motions, including butchering, wood working, etc., while the Levallois points were used as spear points and butchering tools (Shea 1989).

The spatially and temporally uniform cut-marks and burning signs on the animals bones enable us to assess the role of humans who transported animal parts into the cave. These pieces were processed and the bones were discarded, generally close to the north wall. Evidence of carnivore gnawing and depletion of soft epiphyses and upper limb elements are the results of attritional processes operating on these bones after they had already been abandoned by humans. These conclusions do not preclude the occasional denning of hyenas within the cave, especially during the Upper Paleolithic. In addition, an increase (from the Mousterian to the Upper Paleolithic) in the proportion of immature gazelles and fallow deer and the decline in the proportion of very old gazelles, as well as an apparent shift in the sex ratio of gazelles from mostly females to an equal or perhaps even male-biased sex ratio, were observed. These shifts may reflect changes in the seasonality of site occupation or perhaps even more fundamental changes in the technology and organization of animal procurement.

The remains of two almost complete skeletons were uncovered during the excavations of the Mousterian layers in Kebara: KMH-1, an infant, and KMH-2, an adult (Plate 1.2). The exact disposition of the infant bones is not well known although the almost complete skeleton indicates that it was probably a burial. The adult skeleton was an intentional burial. The position of the ribs, which are well preserved, indicate that the body was placed in a narrow pit with vertical sides. Thus the thoracic cavity was conserved in almost original form and many of the finger bones from the left hand were found in it and the abdomen area. The two hands were folded over the chest and the belly. Little is known about the legs. The left one dissolved by the diagenic processes and only the proximal end of the femur remained. The right leg was missing altogether but the reasons are unknown. As the skeleton was not disturbed it seems that perhaps a human agent removed the leg. The most conspicuous absence was that of the skull, which was removed after the flesh decayed. This removal caused minimal disturbance. The right upper third molar fell from the dry socket. The jaw was slightly pushed towards the thorax, but the fragile hyoid bone – the oldest ever recovered from a Paleolithic site – was found in place (Arensburg et al. 1989).

The morphological features of KMH-2 include archaic traits on the jaw and the iliac blade. Neanderthal features are observed on the mandible, the upper limbs and the pelvis. The morphometrics of the hyoid, the ribs and the vertebral column fall within the range of variability of modern humans. KMH-2 can be affiliated with the Amud-Tabun-Shanidar group rather than with the Skhul-Qafzeh skeletons. Moreover, it has a special place among the first group by being the most robust individual known from the Levant.

Plate 1.2   The burial from Kebara (photo: Kebara archives)

9

THE FORAGERS OF THE UPPER PALEOLITHIC PERIOD

Isaac Gilead

Introduction

Rene Neuville (1934) was the first to reconstruct the cultural succession of the Upper Paleolithic period in the early 1930s, after enough assemblages had been studied. Garrod (1957; Garrod and Bate 1937) accepted the essence of his scheme. This sequence of six phases (see Window 1), the classical sequence, was for many years the starting point for discussing the Levantine Upper Paleolithic (Table 1). Only a few new sites and assemblages were discovered before the late 1960s (for research history, see Gilead 1991). Since the late 1960s, however, archaeologists have discovered numerous new Upper Paleolithic sites in the arid and semi-arid zones of the southern Levant: in the central Negev (Marks 1981; Goring-Morris 1987; Gilead 1981, 1993), in Sinai (Bar-Yosef and Belfer 1977; Gilead 1983; Gilead and Bar-Yosef 1993; Phillips 1988), and in the Transjordan. (For main results of the different projects; see Garrard and Gebel 1988.)

Since the rich assemblages uncovered by the early excavators came from stratified cave sites, the chrono-logical-stratigraphical ordering of assemblages was the main objective of their research (Garrod and Bate 1937; Neuville 1934, 1951). They reconstructed the culture history relying on recognizable and unique tool shapes: index fossils. For example, the presence of the Emireh point indicated that an assemblage was of the transitional phase; the El-Wad point, when common, dated the assemblage to the early phase of the Antelian, etc. (see Window 1, p. 138).

This approach was due, among other things, to the nature of the sites. The old assemblages were found within relatively thick deposits of caves and rock-shelters, that were disturbed by later settlers and by natural post-occupational modifications. This prevented studies of behavior since 'living floors' were not (or could not be) defined.

The recent research is different since it concentrates more on open air sites, some of which were covered a very short time after abandonment. Thus, the chances for recovering 'living floors' are better than in the cave sites where post depositional disturbances are more common. Moreover, most of the new sites are in arid zones and the recent human activities hardly affected them. The continuous and extensive occupation during the recent millennia probably obliterated many Upper Paleolithic open-air sites in the less arid parts of the Levant.

The occasional concentration of many Upper Paleolithic sites in small territories, and in primary *in situ* contexts, has stimulated settlement pattern studies (Window 2, p. 139) as well as the attempts to reconstruct aspects of social organization, which play an important role in the recent research. The regional nature of the research also results in paying more attention to the various aspects of paleoenvironments. Efforts to study the paleo-microenvir-onmental variability and the successive surface modifications, encourage the collection of evidence by numerous disciplines, much more than in the early stage of research.

The new assemblages display an impressive techno-typological variability that the traditional unilinear scheme, based as it was on the study of limited tool types, could not explain. Many assemblages seem to differ in important techno-typological attributes from the previously known assemblages. It is also worth noting that different assemblage types overlap in space and time, a rare phenomenon in Levantine Paleolithic record.

Subsistence resources and environments

The core area, the Mediterranean zone, stretches along the coast and the Galilee-Judean mountains (Figure 1). It is the most humid part of the southern Levant. Many of the famous Upper Paleolithic cave sites are situated here, e.g., El-Wad, Kebara, Hayonim, Qafzeh, and Erq el-Ahmar. Along the high elevations of the Gilead, Moab and Edom mountains in the Transjordan, is another, narrower strip of the Mediterranean zone. It is separated from the main one by the Jordan Valley.

Plate 1 Typical bone and flint tools from the Upper Paleolithic period (photograph: © Zev Radovan)

Table 1 The classical sequence of the Levantine Upper Paleolithic (after Gilead 1989)

Phase	Flint tools	Sites and Levels	Ksar Akil	Phases
VI — Kebaran	Numerous truncated and pointed bladelets	Kebara B Hayonim C Nahal Oren 9	1 4	Kebaran
V — Atlitian	Polyhedral and truncated burins	El Khiam E El-Wad C Nahal Ein–Gev I	6 7	Levantine Aurignacian C
IV — Upper Antelian	Aurignacian endscrapers, few El-Wad points	Erq-el Ahmar B El-Wad D, Hayonim D Kebara D, El-Khiam F	8 9 10	Levantine Aurignacian B
III — Lower Antelian	Aurignacian endscrapers, many El-Wad points	Erq el-Ahmar D El-Wad E Kebara E	 11–13	 Levantine Aurignacian A
II — Unnamed	Pointed blades, endscrapers, burins	Erq el-Ahmar E,F Qafzeh D	15	Ksar Akil Phase B
I — Emiran	Emireh points, Levallois tec., Blades	El-Wad F–G Et-Tabban B Qafzeh E	21 25	Ksar Akil Phase A

The marginal area extends to the south and east of the core area, i.e., Sinai, the Negev, the southern and eastern Jordan, and the Syrian desert (Figure 1). The most recent research has been conducted here, mainly in the south. The vegetation of the area is rather sparse, mainly bushes, due to the low annual average rainfall, ranging from 100–350 mm.

The role of the vegetation in human diet during the Upper Paleolithic period is practically unknown. Danin (1983: 124–6), for example, provides a list of numerous edible wild plants that the Bedouins use in the marginal areas. These include edible leaves and/or herbaceous stems, bulbs and roots (fresh or roasted), juicy plants and spices. Naveh (1984: Table 3.2) compiled a list of 70 edible plant species near Sefunim Cave, in Mount Carmel. In the marginal area the vegetation is sparse compared to that of the core area. The vegetal mass in the latter is and was denser, more diversified and, hence, more predictable for gatherers' subsistence.

Ethnographic analogies (e.g., Lee 1968) suggest that vegetal food played a more important role in the Levant compared with its role in Europe. Unfortunately, the botanical evidence is too scanty. Macrobotanical remains are very rare in the Levantine Upper Paleolithic sites, so it is not easy to establish the nature of the vegetal diet. The only evidence of vegetal remains consists of charcoal samples from El-Wad E and D (Bankroft 1937), and from sites in the central Negev (Liphschitz and Waisel 1977: Table 1) and southern Sinai (Phillips 1988). Bankroft identified oak, tamarix, and olive at El-Wad. The charcoal remains of the Upper Paleolithic central Negev sites consist of six *Pistachia*, three *Olea*, and two *Tamarix* trees. The few wood samples from southern Sinai consist of *pistachia* and *quercus*.

About 1400 *pistachia* trees grow today in the central Negev and hundreds in southern Sinai (Danin 1983: 102–4). These are the relicts of a larger population of such trees that existed there during the Upper Pleistocene. The *pistachia*, and other nuts and fruits, were probably one of the main staples of the local Upper Paleolithic inhabitants. Some of the limestone tools in the site, discussed below, were probably tools to grind them. The poor preservation of vegetal remains and their scarcity in the archaeological record is a major limitation in Upper Paleolithic studies.

A key resource of the Upper Paleolithic inhabitants of the Levant was meat, mostly of medium to large ungulates. The Upper Pleistocene mammalian fauna of the Levant witnessed no dramatic changes and most of the now extinct ungulates survived until the late historical periods. The most important meat sources of the Upper

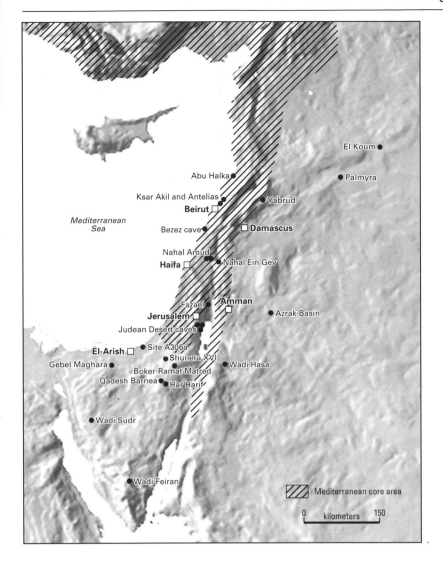

Figure 1 The Upper Paleolithic of the Levant. Diagonal lines= Mediterranean core area

Paleolithic were the bovids (mainly gazelles, cattle and ibexes), cervids (mainly red deer, roe deer and fallow deer), and the equids (horse and onager). The faunal assemblages in the sites clearly indicate this (Table 2).

There are more ungulate species in the core area than in the marginal area. Of the three species of the cervids, for example, none is reported from the marginal area during Upper Paleolithic times. The gazelles, on the other hand, while typical dwellers of the arid marginal zones are also common in the core zone. Moreover, the smaller territories and the higher densities of the gazelles, and probably other herd animals, in the core area compared with their larger territories and low densities in the marginal zones, indicate that the biotic richness of the core area was greater and its resources of meat more diversified and predictable (Bar-Yosef and Belfer-Cohen 1989: 450–1).

The role of smaller mammals, reptiles, fish, and snails in the Upper Paleolithic diet is not clear yet. They are either absent or marginal in the Upper Paleolithic bone assemblages. Tchernov (1984: 409, 416) lists a few elements known from Upper Paleolithic cave contexts such as the huge (1.20 m long) legless lizard (*Ophisaurus apodus*), including many burnt bones, and the lizard *Agama*. The tortoise (*Testudo graeca*) is also present, and could have been preserved live for extended periods. Pigeons and bats were probably also meat resources. Avnimelech (1937: 87, 91) suggested that mollusks from the Upper Paleolithic levels of Qafzeh (*Levantina caesareana*, *Unio sp.*) and Erq el-Ahmar (*Levantina hierosolyma*) were eaten.

The faunal assemblages of the cave sites in the core area consist, as expected, of bones of a diversified range of animals, mainly ungulates (Table 2). Generally, the most common species hunted were gazelle and fallow deer (*Dama mesopotamica*), along with cattle and goats. In

Table 2   Selected megafaunal assemblages from Levantine Upper Paleolithic sites (from Gilead 1991: Table II)

	Ksar Akil VI–IX	Qafzeh 8–9	Kebara E	Kebara D	El-Wad F–C	Erk el-Ahmar D	Erk el-Ahmar B
Gazella	X	X	X	X	X	X	X
Alcelaphus	X	X	X	X	X	—	—
Capra	X	X	X	X	X	X	X
Dama	X	X	X	X	X	—	—
Cervus elaphus	X	X	X	X	X	X	—
Capreolus	X	X	X	X	X	—	—
Procavia	—	—	X	—	X	X	—
Equus	X	X	X	X	X	X	X
Sus	X	X	X	X	X	—	X
Bos	X	X	X	X	X	?	?
Hystrix	—	—	—	—	—	—	—
Martes	X	—	—	—	X	—	—
Meles	X	—	X	—	X	—	—
Vormela	—	—	X	—	X	—	—
Hyenids	—	—	X	X	X	X	X
Canis	X	—	X	—	X	—	X
Ursus	X	—	—	X	—	X	—
Vulpes	X	—	X	X	X	—	—
Felis chaus	X	—	X	—	—	—	—
Felis silvestris	X	—	X	—	X	—	—
Panthera pardus	—	—	—	—	X	—	—

X = present; — = absent; ? = large bovid.

addition, there are pigs, carnivores, birds, rodents and reptiles. It is likely that owls introduced some of the bones of the smaller mammals, birds, and reptiles, while the Paleolithic hunters brought to the sites all or most of the larger mammals.

The Upper Paleolithic sites of the marginal area yielded very few bones. In Ein Aqev (central Negev), for example, the bones of ibex, gazelle, and equid were too few for detailed study (Tchernov 1976: 70). Only in the southern Sinai sites do the faunal remains seem to be more frequent and better preserved (Phillips 1988: 186–7). They include bones of *Gazelle sp.*, *Sus scrofa*, *Equus hemionis*, *Bos premigenius*, *Capra ibex*, *Vulpes sp.*, *Canis lupus*, *Felis sp*, and *Haliaetus rocifer* (African fish eagle). This relative abundance is probably because the sites were near perennial ponds or marshes. The differential distribution of the bones in these sites suggests that one of them was a butchery site of an onager and that another site was a base camp.

Ostrich egg shells are common in the sites of the marginal area. In Qadesh Barnea 601, for example, there were hundreds of fragments on the living horizon (Gilead and Bar-Yosef 1993). Although less common in the other sites, the evidence indicates that it was a more important component of the diet in the marginal zones, and less available in the core area.

The Upper Paleolithic faunal assemblages are similar in nature to the other Middle Paleolithic (excluding hippo-

potamus and elephants) and Epipaleolithic assemblages. They suggest a subsistence economy of extensive gathering of the available resources scattered over the landscape, rather than any specialized foraging. The faunal assemblages, along with the small size of the sites, to be discussed soon, suggest that the Upper Paleolithic 'foragers' of Palestine congregated in small, highly mobile bands (Gilead 1988; Marks and Freidel 1977).

The composition of the faunal assemblages thus reflects primarily the nature of the environment and, to a lesser extent, climatic change. In Lebanon, for example, the fallow deer dominates the faunal assemblages, constituting two-thirds of the bone. To the south, in the Galilee and the Carmel caves, gazelles are also important since it was drier than in Lebanon (Gilead 1991: 114–15). In the marginal zone, the absence of deer and the dominance of ibex, gazelle and equids, reflect the available species, even when the climate was more humid.

There seems to have been no fundamental change in the subsistence economy throughout the Upper Paleolithic period, until about 13,000–12,000 BP (Gilead 1988). Moreover, the evidence for the 'Broad Spectrum Revolution' in the Levant is still too meager. The available data does not support the suggestion that the smaller resources (e.g., fowl, fish, mussels, snails) were added to the diet only after 20,000 BP (Gilead 1991).

The discussion in this section has emphasized that the resources of the core Mediterranean area are richer and more predictable than those of the marginal area. This dichotomy existed during Upper Paleolithic times as well. On this basis, one should predict that the core area of Palestine was more extensively inhabited during the Upper Paleolithic period. That this was not always the case is one of the interesting, and even somewhat enigmatic, aspects of the Upper Paleolithic period.

Paleoclimates of the Upper Paleolithic period

Bate (1937: 39–142), in her famous Dama-Gazella graph, was the first to attempt a reconstruction of the paleoclimatic sequence of the Paleolithic period, on the basis of archaeological evidence. Currently, paleoclimatic indicators other than fauna play the major roles in attempts to reconstruct past environments.

Palynological (Bottema and Van Zeist 1981; Horowitz 1979) and geomorphological (Goldberg 1986) studies of Late Pleistocene sediments during the last two decades have contributed immensely to the better paleoenvironmental recognition of the Upper Paleolithic period. The various isotopic studies (Gat 1981; Issar and Gilead 1986; Goodfriend and Magaritz 1988) add a new dimension to paleoenvironmental reconstructions. The available evidence suggests the following general sequence of climatic fluctuations during the Upper Paleolithic period (Gilead 1991).

Table 3 Climatic phases of the Levantine Upper Paleolithic

Phase	Years BP	O^{18} stage	Period
Climatic amelioration	post 13,000	1 early	Epi-paleolithic
C. Very dry, cold	22,000–13,000	2 late	Late Upper Paleolithic
B. Humid	32,000–22,000	2 early	Early Upper Paleolithic
A. Relatively dry	45,000–32,000	3 late	Middle to Upper Paleolithic – Early Upper Paleolithic
Very dry	75,000–45,000	3–4 early	Late Middle Paleolithic

The climate at about 55,000–40,000 BP, when the Middle to Upper Paleolithic transition occurred, is yet poorly known. It was probably wetter than today but still drier than Early and Main 'Würm' (Horowitz 1979). The time span between 45,000 to 34,000–32,000 BP seems to correspond to the later part of oxygen stage 3, when the climate was still relatively dry. This is our phase A of the Upper Paleolithic paleoclimate in the Levant (Table 3). Evidence from the caves suggests a damper phase during the time of the first Upper Paleolithic occurrences (Bar-Yosef and Vandermeersch 1972).

Phase B, between *ca.* 34,000/32,000–22,000 BP, broadly corresponds to the early part of oxygen stage 2. This is the most humid period of the Levantine Upper Paleolithic and this was especially so during its early part, until *ca.* 26,000 BP. The deposition of most of the Upper Paleolithic fine-grained aggradations in the wadis occurred during this phase. This signifies a climatic regime noticeably wetter than in phase A and today (Goldberg, 1986: 239). Water flowed more regularly in the wadi channels, in a few cases even forming local ponds and now extinct lakes (Begin et al. 1980; Gladfelter 1990).

Phase C, the last in the Upper Paleolithic sequence, started about 24,000–22,000 years ago and lasted till about 14,000–13,000 BP. It is the driest and coldest phase of the Upper Paleolithic period, and it broadly corresponds with the European maximum glacial and the later part of O^{18} stage 2. After 24,000 BP, the sea was about 120–130 m below its present level and the Levantine coastal plain was larger than today, especially in its southeastern part (Van Andel 1989: 736). The Hula pollen diagram (Bottema and Van Zeist 1981: 115–16) indicates that the vegetational cover near the lake changed

after 24,000 BP: Zone A-1 is less rich in arboreal pollen and suggests a forest-steppe vegetation.

There were, most probably, also short-term fluctuations that could have influenced human adaptations but the record is not yet complete enough to detect them. The relative abundance of settlements in the marginal zones at about 32,000 and 14,000 BP, for example, may be the result of such short term fluctuations, each about 1000–2000 years long.

The Middle to Upper Paleolithic transition

The earliest Upper Paleolithic phase, Neuville's (1934) Upper Paleolithic I, or Garrod's (1951) Emiran, was for many years one of the most criticized phases of the classical Upper Paleolithic sequence (Bar-Yosef and Vandermeersch 1972). The more recent detailed studies of the Lebanese assemblages, mainly from Ksar Akil 25–21, and the discovery of Boker Tachtit in the central Negev, suggest that some of Neuville's and Garrod's techno-typological observations are still valuable.

The radiometric dates of the transitional assemblages from the site of Boker Tachtit are *ca.* 47,000 BP and later. A specialized Levallois technique is common, resulting in elongated blanks for Upper Paleolithic tool types. The relatively high frequency of the Emireh points (Figure 2: 3–4), more than in any other known assemblages, is also worth noting. Marks and his colleagues now agree that Neuville and Garrod were substantially correct in maintaining that the Emireh point is a fossil guide of the transitional contexts (Marks 1983b: 86–7). Thus, it is fully justified to refer to the transitional contexts as 'Emiran' instead of the somewhat long taxon 'The Middle to Upper Paleolithic transition' (Gilead 1989: 232).

Marks (1983b) suggests that with the climatic amelioration at about 50,000 BP the Negev became open again to groups from the east, for at least seasonal occupations. The first settlers at Boker Tachtit used a specialized technique, a typical early Mousterian feature, and produced almost only blades and Levallois points. The larger area to be exploited under the somewhat better conditions demanded a more economic use of the flint cores to get the longer blades that dominate the late assemblages of Boker Tachtit. These were obtained by utilizing a single platform core for the production of long blades, another element known in the early Mousterian. This reduction strategy became the only one in use in the latest level of Boker Tachtit. Marks suggests that the transition from the Middle to Upper Paleolithic is a long-term shift from the Mousterian bi-directional Levallois cores to a single platform blade production – a response to the increasing residential mobility to exploit the newly improved environments. It is thus obvious that the Levantine Upper Paleolithic originated from the local

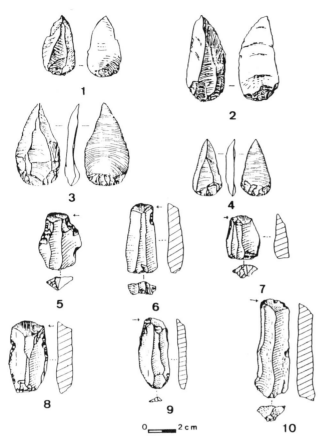

Figure 2   Fossil indices of the transition Middle to Upper Paleolithic. Emireh points, 1: Tabban B; 2: El-Wad F; 3–4: Boker Tachtit. Chanfreins, 5–8: Ksar Akil XXIV; 9–10: Ksar Akil XXV (from Gilead 1991: Figure 2)

Aurignacian, described below, is intrusive in the Levant, it is possible that the same Modern Humans who introduced the Aurignacian to western Europe also carried it into the southern Levant.

Both the paleoanthropological remains, when available, and the cultural evidence hint that local hominids, in more than one area, developed the earliest Upper Paleolithic traditions. In the Levant, the *Homo sapiens*, Neanderthals, or both, developed the Emiran and the Ahmarian traditions. The latter is, in fact, the earliest known Upper Paleolithic industry to be heavily dominated by the production of blade tools as well as blank blades and bladelets. In southeastern Europe, the Aurignacian and other Upper Paleolithic entities developed out of a local Middle Paleolithic tradition (Kozlowski 1988). In western Europe the Chatelperronian developed out of the local Mousterian by the Neanderthals (Demars and Hublin 1988). At about 40,000 BP, Aurignacian groups spread from their core area to both western Europe and the Levant.

The cultural assemblages of the Upper Paleolithic period

Archaeologists have extensively studied the technological and typological aspects of the Upper Paleolithic lithic assemblages during the 1970s and the 1980s (Gilead 1991: with bibliography). I do not intend to discuss this aspect in detail below, since only a brief summary is called for.

The true Upper Paleolithic, following the 'Emiran', may be divided into two main parts: Early Upper Paleolithic and Late Upper Paleolithic. The first starts after 45,000–40,000 years ago and ends at about 24,000–22,000 years ago. The Late Upper Paleolithic follows until about 14,000–13,000 years ago, including also entities currently labeled as Epipaleolithic.

The most important point to consider is that many assemblages, early as well as late, can be clearly divided into two groups. One group features a preponderance of blank blades and core blades (Figure 3) along with a profusion of pointed, retouched and backed blades/bladelets (Figure 4). Endscrapers and burins are relatively few. The second group consists of numerous blank flakes and numerous endscrapers, sometimes Aurignacian, and burins (Figure 5). Although the blade industries are the earliest, there is no doubt that both groups coexisted, from at least 32,000–30,000 BP, throughout the Upper Paleolithic period. The blade industries that developed out of the local Mousterian are referred to as the Ahmarian tradition (Figure 4), while the endscraper-burin assemblages are referred to as Levantine Aurignacian Tradition (Figure 5) (Gilead 1981; Marks 1981).

The best known Early Upper Paleolithic (38,000–30,000 years ago) culture of the Ahmarian tradition is the Lagaman of Sinai, and the Negev (Bar-Yosef and Belfer

Middle Paleolithic. This confirms Garrod's (1951, 1957) suggestion that the earliest Upper Paleolithic occurrences in Palestine developed out of the Local Levallois-Mousterian.

The scarcity of human remains in the Early Upper Paleolithic period obscures the identification of the Levantine Upper Paleolithic populations. Now it is implicitly taken for granted that the Modern Humans were responsible for the Middle to Upper Paleolithic transition since they lived in the Levant during both the Middle and Upper Paleolithic periods. The recent discovery, in Saint Cesaire, France, of a Neanderthal in an early Upper Paleolithic context (Lévêque, 1988) indicates that the Neanderthals manufactured early Upper Paleolithic flint tools. Hypothetically, such a scenario may be also applicable to the Levant since the Neanderthals inhabited the Levant in the Late Middle Paleolithic period and, thus, could have even produced the earliest Upper Paleolithic assemblages. If indeed the Levantine

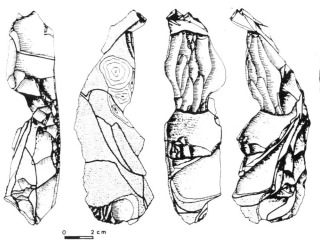

Figure 3 A partially refitted opposed platform blade core with the core-tablets. From Qadesh Barnea 601

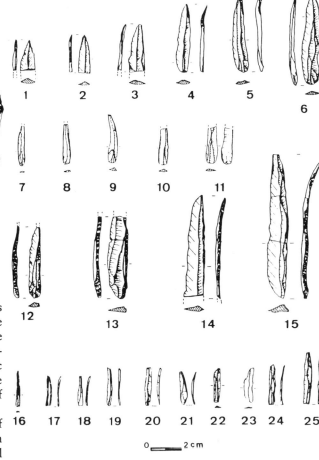

Figure 4 Typical tools of Ahmarian assemblages. 1—6: El-Wad points from Kadesh Barnea; 7—10: narrow retouched bladelets, and 11: ventrally retouched bladelet, from Gebel Maghara; 12—15: backed blades from Kadesh Barnea; 16—25: retouched bladelets from Fazael X (after Gilead 1991: Figure 5)

1977; Gilead 1983; Gilead and Bar-Yosef 1993; Phillips 1988; Marks 1983a). The best known culture of the Levantine Aurignacian tradition is the Levantine Aurignacian B of the caves in northern Israel (Belfer-Cohen and Bar-Yosef 1981). The recent radiometric dating of such assemblages in Units II–I of Kebara cave confirm their contemporaneity to the Lagaman (Bar-Yosef et al. 1992).

For the Late Upper Paleolithic period, the lumping of assemblages into cultures is less clear. The Ahmarian features usually a profusion of bladelet tools. A typical late Levantine Aurignacian assemblage with numerous endscrapers is from the site of Ein Aqev, radiometrically dated to 18,000–17,000 years ago.

Settlement patterns

The distribution of Upper Paleolithic sites in the southern Levant is very differential. Ronen (1975), who counted the number of sites in Palestine during the different prehistoric periods, noted that the number of Upper Paleolithic sites is significantly smaller than in either later or earlier periods. While 18 caves north of Jerusalem were inhabited during the Middle Paleolithic, only seven caves were inhabited in the same area during the Upper Paleolithic. The results of a major prehistoric survey in the Carmel area (Olami 1984) clearly demonstrated the different frequencies between the Middle and Upper Paleolithic sites. While there are only five Upper Paleolithic sites, all in caves (Figure 6a), there are 72 Middle Paleolithic sites, 12 in caves (Figure 6b).

The recent research in the marginal area suggests that the settlement here was more intense than in the core area. This is readily apparent when comparing the frequency of

sites in a typical core area habitat such as Mount Carmel, with a typical marginal area in the central Negev. While in the 232 km^2 of Mount Carmel there are only five Upper Paleolithic occurrences (Figure 6b), there are 14 such occurrences in the 55 km^2 of the Avdat area of the central Negev (Marks 1977: Fig. 1–6). That these figures do not reflect just different research strategies, which do indeed exist, is evident when comparing the figures of the Middle Paleolithic period in both areas: while there are 72 Middle Paleolithic occurrences in Mount Carmel (Figure 6b), there are only 21 occurrences in the central Negev (Marks 1977: Fig. 1–5).

The paucity of Early Upper Paleolithic sites in the core area, and their relative abundance in the marginal zones is not merely a problem of archaeological visibility. The deficiency of Upper Paleolithic sites in the core area is

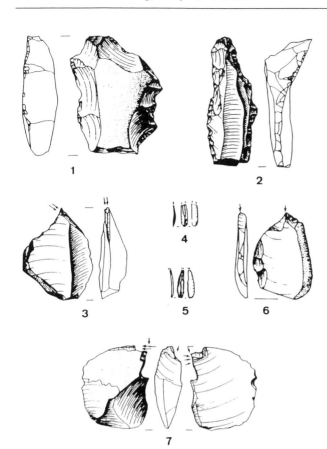

Figure 5 Typical tools of Levantine Aurignacian assemblages. 1–2: endscrapers; 3, 6, 7: burins; 4–5: *Lamelle Dufour* (after Gilead 1991: Figure 6)

(Bar-Yosef and Belfer-Cohen 1989: Fig. 3b). The archaeological data sometimes refute predictions that originate in environmental assumptions. The unexplained differential distribution of Upper Paleolithic sites in the core and marginal areas, contrary to the assumptions based on the richness of the environments, calls for a reevaluation of either the basic assumptions and/or the available data.

Not enough attention was devoted to the size of the living horizons in the cave sites, since the early digs emphasized the stratigraphy and not the spatial observations. In the Israeli caves, the Upper Paleolithic layers have a limited spatial extension compared with the Mousterian layers below and the Natufian above. This is well illustrated in Hayonim D, where the Aurignacian occupied only a small natural basin formed inside the Mousterian deposits, probably 40–50 m² (Belfer-Cohen and Bar-Yosef 1981: Figs. 1–3). A more recent illustration of the same comes from the new exvacations at Kebara Cave (Bar-Yosef et al. 1992: 519)). Upper Paleolithic hearths and ash lenses are not as common as those of the Middle Paleolithic period. The more pronounced scavenging activities during the Upper Paleolithic period also indicate that human use of the cave was more ephemeral than before.

Although the size of sites in the Negev and Sinai ranges considerably, they are generally small. The size of the Lagaman sites ranges between 16 to 117 m² (Gilead 1983: Table 1) and the largest *in situ* remnant is 26 m². In the Avdat Aqev area, the surface scatters of artifacts are larger, and the maximum size is 1,500–1,800 m², but deflation is the main factor behind the large sizes (Ferring 1976). The estimate is that about 250 m² of Sde Divshon are *in situ*, and this is probably the largest well-documented Upper Paleolithic site. Another large site is Abu Noshra II in southern Sinai, of which 172 m² were excavated (Phillips 1988: 187).

The spatial organization of Upper Paleolithic sites is poorly understood. In the few cases where preservation is reasonable, the most visible feature is the hearth and/or ashes (Goring-Morris 1988). The hearth was constructed mostly in shallow rounded, oval pits, as, for example, is the case for Lagama VI, VII, XVI (Bar-Yosef and Belfer 1977: Figures 19, 22b, 32b, c). What seems to be a recurring pattern is a number of hearths on one living surface, in a linear arrangement: Boker BE (Marks, 1983a: Fig. 2.3), Ein Aqev East (Ferring 1977: Fig. 4–5), or Shunera XVI (Goring-Morris 1987: Fig. 4–7). In some of the cases, e.g., Ein Aqev (Marks 1976: Figure 9–8, 9–9) wadi pebbles were aligned around the hearth or part of it. The Wadi Feiran sites also feature such hearths in addition to a large ash pit (180 × 230 × 35 cm), probably for roasting whole animals (Phillips 1988: 193).

There are hearths in cave sites too. Five small hearths in Hayonim D, four of them in a line, *ca.* 50–60 cm apart. The fifth, outlined by three stones, was next to a 'kitchen

intriguing since its biotic potential is, and was, higher than that of the marginal area. Why is the richness of the core area, its diversity and predictability of resources, not depicted in the archaeological record?

Neither the archaeological nor the environmental data offer an easy answer to this problem. Nothing supports the assumption that during the first 20 millennia of the Upper Paleolithic period the climate of the core area was too inhospitable (Ronen 1975: 424). The ability of Upper Paleolithic humans to adapt to the much colder environments of Europe negates such an assumption. Some of the sites in the more extensively settled marginal zones are within a distance of only a few days' walk from the core zone, which could have been reached easily if indeed its biotic potential surpassed that of the marginal areas.

Moreover, the marginal area was preferred even during the latest Upper Paleolithic (early Epipaleolithic). There are, for example, more Geometric Kebaran and Mushabian (*sensu lato*) sites in the marginal area than in the core area

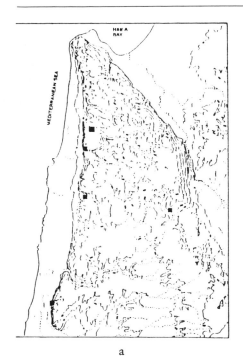

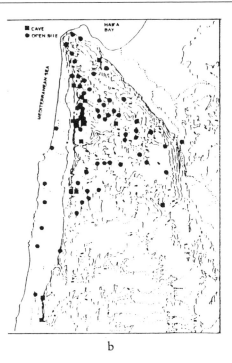

a   b

Figure 6 a: Middle Paleolithic sites in Mount Carmel (from Ronen, 1984, Figure 32.1). b: Upper Palaeolithic sites in Mount Carmel (from Ronen, 1984, Figure 32.2)

midden' with numerous bones (Belfer-Cohen and Bar-Yosef 1981: 21–22). Here – as in most of the other cases – the bones and artifacts were most concentrated near the hearths.

The interpretation of the hearths, and especially their linear arrangement, is not easy since it is hard to know whether each is a discrete temporal unit or they are all contemporaneous. A hearth, or a few hearths, in the open sites, may represent a light structure, a sleeping area, or other activity areas. In many cases, however, the hearth and its surroundings feature finds that do not support a specific task interpretation.

Marks and Freidel (1977) carried out a settlement pattern study of a more general nature of the central Negev Stone Age sites. They suggest that during the Upper Paleolithic and early Epipaleolithic periods (our Early and Late Upper Paleolithic) the settlement patterns were different from before (Mousterian) and after (Natufian).

The Upper Paleolithic settlements are ephemeral when compared with the others, without the pronounced inter-site variability of the lithic assemblages. The shift towards the mobile, general pattern of the Upper Paleolithic, the 'circular pattern', is evident also in the intra-site variability of the different levels at Boker Tachtit; coupled with the technological shift, it marks the onset of the Upper Paleolithic pattern (Marks 1983b).

The Mousterian and the Natufian settlement patterns in this area are different since they feature a number of large and intensively settled locales that were occupied for longer time spans. In addition, there are also small, very ephemeral sites that were used for special activities such as

flint quarrying, specialized hunting, etc. This pattern of a central site and its satellites that represent a settlement of a more sedentary nature – the 'radiating pattern' – is different from the 'circulating' pattern of the more mobile Upper Paleolithic groups.

Lieberman (in press) has recently studied the cementum increment in gazelle teeth from major cave sites in Israel. His study, that determines the season(s) sites were occupied, indicates that the Upper Paleolithic sites were only seasonally settled, while most Natufian and some Mousterian sites ('Tabun B') were occupied on a multi-seasonal basis. This further supports the suggestion that the Upper Paleolithic settlement system tended to be more seasonal while some elements of the earlier and later periods tended to a kind of sedentism.

The two settlement systems probably signify, among other things, two different hunter-gatherer social systems. The Upper Paleolithic circular pattern, smaller and more ephemeral in nature, represents small groups with a relatively simple social organization. The radiating pattern, especially in the Natufian, signifies larger residential units with a higher social complexity.

Non lithic objects of the Levantine Upper Paleolithic

Bone tools

The most important contribution of the Upper Paleolithic humans to the repertoire of artifacts is the bone tools (Figure 7). Bone tools were manufactured before, but seem

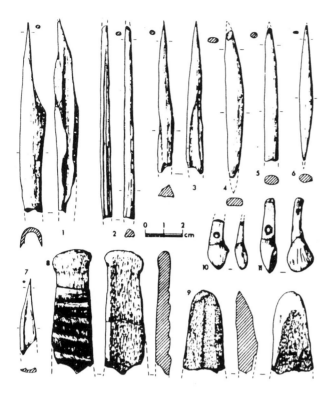

Figure 7 Bone tools from Hayonim D. 1, 7: awls; 2—6: points; 8: decorated haft (?); 9: polisher; 10—11: teeth pendants (from Belfer-Cohen and Bar-Yosef, 1981, Figure 6)

Paleolithic bone industries from Europe and the later local Natufian industry, the Upper Paleolithic assemblages are poor and monotonous, both typologically and technologically.

Most bone tools originate from Levantine Aurignacian layers, mainly Neuville's phase IV, and the first impression is that this craft was not practiced in the Ahmarian. It is, however, interesting to note that the only typical European Aurignacian bone tool, the base-split point, was recovered from the Ahmarian context of El Quseir D.

It is also worth noting that in most of the Levantine Aurignacian sites bone tools are either scarce or entirely absent even if animal bones were preserved. Ksar Akil and Hayonim D are rather exceptional. Another point to consider is that the sites that best represent the early Ahmarian are in the arid zones, where the preservation of animal bones, and consequently the bone tools, is extremely poor. In the Wadi Feiran sites where the preservation of bones is relatively better than in the other desert sites, there is a bone point in the site of Abu Noshra II (Phillips 1988: 187). In short, it is difficult to evaluate properly the significance of the association between bone tools and the Aurignacian.

Stone objects and ochre

The earliest stone objects originate from the lowest Upper Paleolithic layer (9) in Qafzeh cave: a flat mortar and a handstone of basalt (Ronen and Vandermeersch 1972, Figure 8). Stains of ochre are clearly visible on the rim of the quern-like stone, suggesting that it was a color grinder. A cobble with one extremity showing traces of ochre was reported from El-Khiam (Perrot 1951: 139).

Layer D at Hayonim cave yielded a relatively rich collection of basalt and limestone objects, many of which exhibit ochre stains (Belfer-Cohen and Bar-Yosef 1981: 34–5). There are several flat limestone slabs with ochre stains, incisions, and signs of cutting and pounding. In addition, there are a few limestone scrapers and a chisel, and three basalt rubbing stones – again all with ochre stains. The same site also yielded a unique grooved stone made of soft basalt, with several deep incisions. It could have been used as a shaft straightener or whetstone (Figure 8: 1).

In the south, two handstones and two grinding slabs made of porphyritic dike material were found in southern Sinai (Phillips 1988: 187). Limestone and basalt grinders, three of which were used for ochre processing, were recovered from Boker BE (Jones et al. 1983: 323–5). The Late Upper Paleolithic site of Ein Aqev produced three pieces of groundstone (Marks 1976: 268–70): a handstone (Figure 8: 4) and a fragmentary quern made of basalt, and a fragmentary limestone handstone. Although there were pieces of ochre in all the excavated layers of the site, ochre was not reported to adhere to

to be rather an exception in earlier periods. However, during the Upper Paleolithic times a large corpus of bone tools reflects a relatively standard industry in terms of types and of techniques.

The bone tools have a variable distribution in the sites, and they are most common in the caves of the Mediterranean zone. The largest assemblage is from layer D at Hayonim cave (75 items). There are also smaller quantities in El-Wad (7), Et Tabban (2), Umm Naquos (1), El Quseir (2), Masaraq an-Na'aj (2) (Belfer-Cohen and Bar-Yosef 1981), and in the Upper Paleolithic sites in Fazael (Goring-Morris 1980a).

Typologically, the points dominate the assemblages of bone tools (Figure 7: 2–6), including a base-split bone from El Quseir D. Awls (Figure 7: 1,7) are the second common type. In addition, there are also polishers (Figure 7: 9), spatulas, incised fragments (Figure 7: 8) and perforated teeth (Fig. 8: 10–11). Generally, the typological composition of the assemblages is monotonous. In Hayonim D (Belfer-Cohen and Bar-Yosef 1981: 30–1) the points (37 per cent) and awls (13 per cent) dominate, although there are also spatulas (4 per cent), polishers (3 per cent), worked antler (9 per cent) and other miscellaneous pieces (34 per cent). Compared with Upper

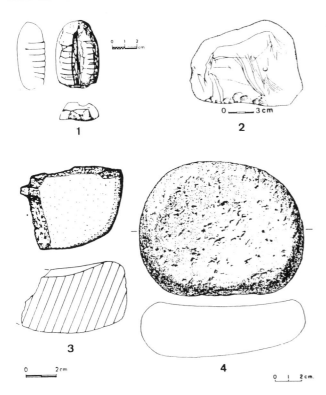

Figure 8 Upper Paleolithic stone objects. 1: basalt grooved stone from Hayonim D (from Belfer-Cohen and Bar-Yosef, 1981, Figure 7: 4); 2: incised limestone slab from Hayonim D (from Belfer-Cohen and Bar-Yosef, 1981, Figure 8C); 3: a fragment of a basalt grinding stone from Fazael X (from Goring-Morris, 1980b: Figure 14); 4: a basalt handstone from Ein Aqev (From Marks, 1976, Figure 9–28a)

these stones. Basalt grinders (Figure 8: 3) without ochre stains were also reported from Fazael X (Goring-Morris 1980a).

This suggests that substances other than ochre, maybe vegetal food, were ground as well. However, the presence of ochre in Upper Paleolithic occurrences and its association with grinding stones is prominent. Compared with the Middle Paleolithic period, ochre is very common in Upper Paleolithic sites. Along with pieces of raw ochre and smeared stones, stains of ochre were also found on flint artifacts, best exemplified in the Lagaman sites of northern Sinai (Bar-Yosef and Belfer 1977: 81). The flint artifacts were probably used to scrape or cut the ochre lumps, mainly in Lagama VII and XVI.

Ochre is rare in Levantine Mousterian sites. Wreschner (1980), who studied the distribution of ochre in Paleolithic sites and its significance, mentioned ochre in only two Middle Paleolithic sites: Qafzeh and Geula (where its association with human activities is not clear). During Upper Paleolithic times, on the other hand, the role played by ochre in the Levantine material culture is unequivocal. The Upper Paleolithic artisans were probably the first in

the Levant to grind the ochre into powder and produce liquid mixtures. The function of such mixtures is still obscure. The use of liquid ochre in burial ceremonies and for art work is one of the well-known attributes of the European Upper Paleolithic. Since burials and art works are virtually absent in the Levantine Upper Paleolithic, the function of ochre in the local sites is yet unknown. Its role in spiritual-cognitive activities and in decorating bodies and artifacts cannot be excluded. Ochre, however, could have been used also in mundane, daily, activities such as hide processing (Keeley 1980: 170–2). Whatever its use was, the Levantine Upper Paleolithic people were among the first to process red ochre on a regular basis and use it as a liquid pigment.

Shells

The use of sea shells, probably for personal adornment, is another innovation of the Upper Paleolithic humans in the Levant. Although they are not abundant, their presence in sites is more than accidental. In Gebel Lagama sites, isolated *dentalium* shells were recovered from Lagama IIIE, Lagama XI, and 82 pieces from Lagama X. The five *dentalium* pieces from the *in situ* context of site QB9 in Kadesh Barnea area are, in fact, the earliest shells in the Levant since they originate from an area where identical cultural assemblages were radiometrically dated to *ca.* 32,000 BP (Gilead and Bar-Yosef 1993). Site A306a in northern Sinai (Gilead 1984), 150 m from the sea shore, demonstrates that the southern Upper Paleolithic groups were familiar with environments closer to the coast, where *dentalia*, and other shells, could have been collected.

Late Upper Paleolithic assemblages with shells are Ein Aqev, featuring along with *dentalium*, *Nassa gibberula* (a few covered with ochre) and *Mitrella scripta* (Marks 1976: 235). A *dentalium* bead and other unidentified marine shell fragments were found in Ein Aqev East (Ferring 1977: 87). *Dentalium* shells and Mediterranean gastropods were also reported from the Late Upper Paleolithic sites of the western Negev (Goring-Morris 1986, 1987: Table X–2). In the Jordan Valley, numerous Mediterranean mollusks were found in the Fazael sites: in addition to *Trivia* sp., *Columbella rustica*, worth mentioning are the 220 *Dentalium* sp. fragments and the 61 *Mitrella gerdillei* fragments (Goring-Morris 1980a). Although reported, there seem to be less marine mollusks in the caves and rock shelter sites of the Levant (listed in Inizan and Gaillard: 1978: 303–4).

The presence of sea shells in Upper Paleolithic sites, especially in the sites of the Jordan Valley, Negev and Sinai, indicates a network for transporting raw materials over relatively long distances – up to about 100 km and maybe more. Shells, however, were not the only substance that was transported. Basalt, of which the grinders in Boker BE and Ein Aqev were made, is found about 25 km

Plate 2   The Upper Paleolithic burial of a woman from Nahal Ein-Gev I, before removal (photograph: courtesy of O. Bar-Yosef)

south of the sites. Moreover, the possibility that the basalt of the Negev sites originated either in the Transjordan or the Galilee cannot be excluded.

It is yet impossible to reconstruct the network behind the transportation of the above mentioned raw materials. The fact, however, that in some cases long distances are involved suggests that exotic raw materials were indirectly procured through exchange (gifts) with other groups closer to raw material sources. The frequencies and probable role of exotic materials in the Upper Paleolithic cultures were relatively restricted, especially in comparison with the succeeding cultures of the Natufian and the Harifian (Goring-Morris 1986: 176, 184).

Cognitive-spiritual aspects of the Levantine Upper Paleolithic

One of the main sources for studying the cognitive-spiritual aspects of culture is the burials. Unfortunately, they are very rare in the Upper Paleolithic sites of the Levant. Fragmentary and isolated human remains were recorded from a few Upper Paleolithic sites (Arensburg 1977): a complete prepubertal male skeleton and fragments of skull from Ksar Akil, fragments of a skull and long bones of a fetus from Antelias (cave sites near Beirut), two frontal bones from Qafzeh, fragments of humeri, ulnae and mandibles from Kebara, miscellaneous fragments of limbs, trunk, mandibles and isolated teeth

from El-Wad, and fragments of femur and teeth from Kebara. The scarcity of human remains and burials hinders the assessment of important issues related to social and spiritual aspects of life in the Upper Paleolithic period.

That burials were hardly found in Upper Paleolithic sites, is one of the noticeable characteristics of this time span. There are numerous burials in the preceding Mousterian sites, especially in the cemeteries of Qafzeh and Skhul, and there are hundreds of burials in Natufian sites. For the Upper Paleolithic period there are only three burials: in the Levantine Aurignacian site of Nahal Ein Gev I, in the Kebaran site of Ein Gev (Arensburg 1977), and the Geometric Kebaran site of Neve David (Kaufman and Ronen 1987).

It seems that the burial from Nahal Ein Gev I (Arensburg 1977) is the earliest among the three. It is of a woman, 30–35 years old, 1.56–1.58 cm high; lying on her right side, with legs strongly flexed towards the head (Plate 2). There were three bovid horns near her left shoulder. Strongly flexed bodies charecteize Natufian burials and later they became very common.

A comparison of this skeleton with Upper Paleolithic skeletons from Europe (Arensburg 1977) indicates some differences. Worth noting is the smaller cranial capacity, shorter length of skull, and mesocraniality. The comparison between the Nahal Ein Gev I specimen, the Kebaran one from Ein Gev I, and Natufian specimens shows a strong similarity. This similarity is behind

Arensburg's (1977: 214*) statement that the populations in the southern Levant in the Late Upper Paleolithic to the Neolithic are autochthonous.

The small sample of only three graves hampers discussion of Upper Paleolithic burial practices and their possible spiritual and social implications. The three burials are primary, with flexed individuals. Such burials are common in the Natufian times, when interment is very common. This suggests that some of the burial practices have their roots in the local Upper Paleolithic. The flexed fetal or sleeping position of the dead suggests that they were not supposed to be active in the after life. It is also worth noting that there were no personal adornments on the bodies.

The scarcity of Upper Paleolithic burials in the Levant does not seem to reflect bad preservation. It rather reflects that the practice of burial in habitation sites was not common (Ronen 1975). The higher frequencies of burials in the Levantine Mousterian and their abundance in the Natufian clearly contrast with the Upper Paleolithic data. The semi-sedentary or sedentary nature of Mousterian and Natufian settlements (Marks and Freidel 1977; Bar-Yosef 1983) on one hand, and the nomadic nature of the Upper Paleolithic settlements on the other hand (Gilead 1988), suggest that burials signify a stronger attachment to the habitation sites. If this is the case, the scarcity of burials in Upper Paleolithic sites is another indication of their ephemeral nature.

Works of art are another indicator of the spiritual aspects of the culture. In the Levantine Upper Paleolithic sites such works are virtually nonexistent. The few incised bones and stones mentioned earlier may have had some cognitive significance. Otherwise, there is only one art object, from the Levantine Aurignacian of Hayonim D (Belfer-Cohen and Bar-Yosef 1981: 36–7, Figure 8). This is an incised limestone slab with a line that resembles the back of an ungulate and its head, with many lines that give the impression of fore-legs and rear-legs (Figure 8: 2). Hovers (1990) has recently described another art object from a Kebaran site: a limestone pebble with mostly concentric incisions.

Both the Neanderthal and the Stone Age *Homo sapiens* had the potential capacity for symbolic behavior. This is confirmed in the Levantine Middle and Upper Paleolithic by the Mousterian burials and the ochre. The use of powdered ochre and marine shells in the Upper Paleolithic period further supports this suggestion. It is, therefore, of interest to note that in Europe works of art, including sculpturing and painting, are very common compared with their virtual absence in the Levant. In Palestine, art works become relatively abundant only in the Natufian, at *ca.* 12,000–10,300 BP.

A possible explanation of this discrepancy may be found in the functional approach to prehistoric art (Belfer-

Cohen 1988). If indeed arts reflect social stress in large groups of tribal societies, its scarcity in the Levantine Upper Paleolithic should not be surprising. The settlement pattern studies indicate that the size of the Upper Paleolithic social unit in the Levantine habitation sites was limited, and that the sites were ephemeral in nature. Only during the Natufian times, with the sedentism, larger social units and complexity, do the art objects became more common.

Summary

The Upper Paleolithic of Palestine has its roots deep in the local Mousterian traditions of the Middle Paleolithic period. The first true local Upper Paleolithic tradition (post 37,000) – the Ahmarian – features an overwhelming dominance of the retouched, pointed and backed blades and bladelets. At about 32,000 BP, or somewhat later, another cultural entity appeared and for 16 millennia coexisted side by side with the Ahmarian. This new tradition, the Levantine Aurignacian, in its classical manifestations is radically different to the Ahmarian. It features a poor blade technology and only a few blade tools. The dominant tools are either endscrapers, burins, or both.

Although it is possible that the local Aurignacian is a local development, the early dates of the Aurignacian in southern Europe suggest that the Levantine Aurignacian is an intrusion into the Levant. It probably diffused after 35,000 BP from southern Europe both to western Europe and the Levant.

The variability within the Ahmarian and the Levantine Aurignacian and the partial radiometric control hamper the subdivision of assemblages into more discrete units (cultures). It is, therefore, difficult to trace and explain the culture change through the many millennia and explain it.

Settlement pattern studies imply that the Upper Paleolithic social units were small and that their sites were ephemeral in nature. This suggests that the Upper Paleolithic societies in the Levant were foragers with a simple social organization. This is well reflected in the nature of their sites, and the scarcity of burials and art objects. Less favorable environmental conditions, especially during the Late Upper Paleolithic (after 24,000–22,000 BP), were at least partially responsible for this pattern.

The Upper Paleolithic inhabitants were the first to introduce into the Holy Land many new aspects of material culture that were never, or hardly, used before: bone tools, stone vessels, ochre and shells, probably for decoration and art. Thus they set the stage for the Natufian Revolution at the end of the Paleolithic period.

THE CLASSICAL SEQUENCE OF THE UPPER PALEOLITHIC CULTURES

The Upper Paleolithic of the Levant has been the subject of study for more than sixty years. Although somewhat arbitrary, this span consists of two periods: before and after the late 1960s. The excavations of the major caves and rock-shelter sites started during the earlier period; in the Wadi Antelias near Beirut, in Yabrud, north of Damascus, and in the Galilee, Mount Carmel, and the Judean desert. These large-scale projects provided ample evidence for constructing the culture history and the stratigraphic framework of the local prehistory in general and the Upper Paleolithic in particular. It is impossible to understand the current status of the Upper Paleolithic studies without referring to the research of this time span.

Neuville's first phase of the Upper Paleolithic, Phase I (Table 1), is also known as the Emiran (Garrod 1951). Typologically, it was characterized by the Emireh point as the index fossil (Figure 2). Technologically it features both the Levallois technique along with punched blades. The site of Boker Tachtit in the central Negev is the recent, most important, contribution to the understanding of this transitional phase.

Phase II is characterized by robust retouched blades and the absence of both the Levallois technique and the Emireh points. It was not found in the Carmel caves and since Neuville never published his Qafzeh material, the definition of this phase is illustrated by about 130 pieces only.

Phases III and IV were the best known phases of the classical sequence. Carinated and nosed endscrapers, burins, along with pointed blades — the El-Wad (Font Yves) points are the diagnostic elements of these assemblages. The carinated and nosed scrapers, similar to those of Upper Paleolithic assemblages of western Europe, are behind the term 'Aurignacian' (Garrod and Bate, 1937: 120–1) as a label for these assemblages. The division into two phases followed the observation that in the earlier assemblages the El-Wad points were significantly more common. Since a diagnostic artifact of the European Aurignacian — the split based point — was not used in the Levant, Garrod (1957: 440) preferred later to label these phases as 'Lower Antelian' and 'Upper Antelian'. In the

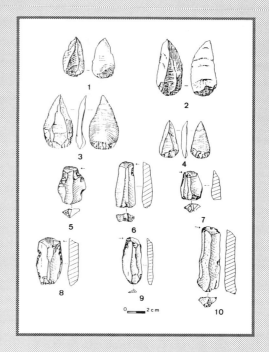

recent research such assemblages are labeled as 'Levantine Aurignacian'.

Phase V — 'Atlitian' according to Garrod — is characterized by the abundance of burins and the relative scarcity of the endscrapers that became very carinated, similar to bladelet cores.

The last phase of the sequence — VI — 'Kebaran', is best represented in layer C of the type site Kebara cave . The profusion of microliths was essential in the definition of the Kebaran, which included all the local microlithic industries before the Natufian, which was regarded as a Mesolithic entity. It is now recognized that the microliths, i.e., retouched bladelets, were also produced in early Upper Paleolithic times, ca. 32,000 years ago.

A CASE STUDY OF SETTLEMENT ARCHAEOLOGY: THE UPPER PALEOLITHIC SITES OF GEBEL LAGAMA

The classical research tended to concentrate more on aspects of typology and culture history (Window 1). Currently, scholars tend to add other dimensions, beyond the study of artifact assemblages and individual sites, and one of the most important approaches is the study of settlement archaeology, or settlement patterns. This approach does not consider the mere distribution of sites in the landscape or their relations to the various resources. It rather aims toward understanding economic and social structures of related site systems. The two main components of this approach consist of studying the location, size, and structure of sites on the one hand and, on the other hand, the nature of the cultural assemblages of the different sites and the way they interrelate.

Much attention has been paid to settlement pattern studies during the last 15 years. Worth noting is the study of Marks and Friedel (1977) who attempted to decipher the changing settlement systems of the Middle, Upper, and Epipaleolithic periods in the central Negev – covering a time span of about 70,000 years. Other studies attempt to interpret broadly contemporaneous sites, and such a case study is presented below.

In the Gebel Maghara ridge, northern Sinai, there were nine broadly contemporaneous Upper Paleolithic sites of the Lagaman culture, radiometrically dated to 32,000–30,000 years ago (Bar-Yosef and Belfer 1977). All the sites were concentrated in an area of only half a square kilometer (Figure 2.1) – an unprecedented phenomenon in the Levantine prehistory. The sites at the foot of Gebel Lagama are embedded in the top of sand dunes, further away from the local shallow wadi channel.

The small sites contain some tens to hundreds of artifacts, and were originally sites of about 2–4 m², in which two or three people were active. The sites of tens of square meters that contain thousands of flint artifacts, represent larger loci occupied by the local inhabitants during one or a few seasons.

A detailed analysis of the flint assemblages showed that there is a co-variation that is important in discussing the nature of the settlement patterns (Gilead 1983). It was observed that the number of blades in an assemblage correlates with their size: the longer the blades are, the more common they are, along with more El-Wad points (Figure 4: 1–6) and less microliths. An overall correlation between the typological and technological characteristics of the Lagaman assemblages suggests that the variability is due, on a very general level, to

the different tasks that were performed in the various activity loci.

To get raw flint chunks, a certain degree of mobility is required in the case of the Gebel Lagama sites. This mobility is also essential in hunting; an activity carried out by the 'Lagamans' as indicated by the few preserved bones. It is probable that the more mobile hunters imported the flints into

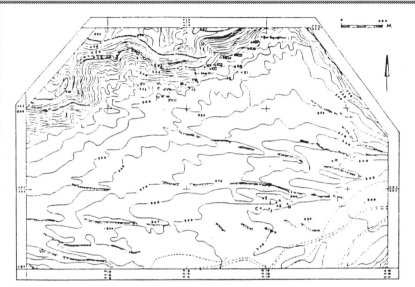

Figure 2.1 Location of Upper Paleolithic sites (III, V–VIII, X–XII, XV, XVI) at the foot of Gebel Lagama (from Bar-Yosef and Belfer, 1977, Figure 15)

the sites and knapped the longer blades for hunting tools – mainly the El-Wad points. Because of the scarcity of flint, the knappers continued to use the smaller cores to prepare smaller blades and microliths. This took place at different sites where other activities were performed. It is worth noting that ostrich egg shells were in sites where there was a higher frequency of microliths. It is not claimed that some locales were occupied by males and others by females. Nevertheless, it is suggested that in a few of the sites the activities of hunters were more pronounced.

While it was possible to trace variability in the case of the Gebel Maghara sites, it was not discerned in the sites of the Lagaman culture in the Qadesh Barnea area (Gilead 1983, Gilead and Bar-Yosef 1993). The Lagaman sites of the Qadesh Barnea area, radiometrically dated to about 31,000–32,000 years ago, were near a main channel, Wadi Qudeirat. Here, good quality Eocene flint is readily available – mainly nodules of scree found on the slopes next to the sites. In one of the *in situ* sites (QB601), the use of ochre was extensive and the surface of the occupation was littered with ostrich egg shell fragments. In another *in situ* occurrence (QB9) the use of ochre was minimal and the ostrich egg shells were rare. Despite the obvious functional difference, the lithic assemblages of the two were quite alike. This is due to the similarity in the retouched blades, the virtual absence of microliths and the more homogeneous size of the blank blades. The mean length of the rejected cores well illustrates the difference in the degree of core reduction between the Lagaman and Qadesh Barnea sites: 35–39 mm in Gebel Lagama and 54–58 mm in Qadesh Barnea.

It seems that the Early Upper Paleolithic microlithic assemblages were a response to raw material restrictions. That is why microliths were not a standard product in the Early Upper Paleolithic times. In areas where good quality flint is abundant near the sites, as in the Qadesh Barnea area, retouched bladelets were not produced, although blank bladelets were common. Only where flint was rare, as in the case of Gebel Maghara, were more microliths produced. The southern Sinai sites again illustrate this point. The sites are in a massif of metamorphic and granite rocks, and the closest sources of flint are 15–60 km away. The Early Upper Paleolithic sites are characterized by the dominance of retouched bladelets among the tools – about 45 per cent (Phillips 1988: Table 3).

Plate 2.1 Section of an Upper Paleolithic 'living floor' in the Qadesh Barnea site QB601 (courtesy of O. Bar-Yosef)

Plate 2.2 The channel and the Upper Paleolithic sediments in the Qadesh Barnea area. A typical setting of Upper Paleolithic sites in the marginal zones of Palestine (courtesy of O. Bar-Yosef)

10

COMPLEX HUNTER/GATHERERS AT THE END OF THE PALEOLITHIC (20,000–10,000 BP)

Nigel Goring-Morris

Introduction

The interval from approximately 20,000–10,000 BP in the Levant is commonly referred to as the Epipaleolithic period. When the broad outlines of the prehistoric sequence were described prior to the Second World War the number of known occurrences was extremely limited and the few microlithic assemblages of 'Upper Paleolithic Stage VI' (also known as the Kebaran) were of interest only in the largely chronological sense of being intermediate (or perhaps even an interlude) between the 'Paleolithic' and the newly defined 'Mesolithic' Natufian entity, as viewed from a basically Eurocentric perspective (Neuville 1934; Garrod 1932).

Pioneering, detailed studies of the earlier Pre-Natufian part of the period were conducted in the mid–late 1960s in the Mediterranean zones of the central Levant by Bar-Yosef (1970) and Hours (1976). Following Perrot (1968) and work in North Africa (Tixier 1963), they concluded that, together with the Natufian, it warranted a separate status, namely the 'Epipaleolithic'. With a few exceptions – e.g., Gilead (1989) who essentially returns to Neuville's original scheme – most researchers have adopted this terminology.

Since the late 1960s research orientations of this period have largely been conducted in areas that were until then largely *terra incognita* and peripheral to the Mediterranean zone, whether in Sinai, the Negev, southern Transjordan, or the Azraq, Palmyra, el-Kowm basins. This has resulted in a plethora of primary data, such that today some 700 or so distinct assemblages can be related to this time frame throughout the Levant, of which some 600 have been described in at least minimal detail. Supplementary palynological, geomorphological and allied research has demonstrated that this period coincided with the maximum of the last glaciation and its immediate after-effects, with the Levant as a whole undergoing rapid

changes in environment and landscape on a scale matched neither earlier nor later, in the Pleistocene.

With few exceptions and notwithstanding the obvious differences in the material culture between various regions within the area as a whole at different times, the conceptual framework in which the fieldwork of the past two and a half decades has been conducted does not seem to have kept pace with the proliferation of primary data. While some have adopted a splitters approach to taxonomic classification (e.g., Henry 1982, 1989; Goring-Morris 1987), others have tended to lump (e.g., Bar-Yosef and Vogel 1987; Bar-Yosef and Belfer-Cohen 1991). Yet others have adopted time-stratigraphic or purely chronological units (e.g., Aurenche et al. 1981; Besançon et al. 1975–7; Moore 1985; Garrard et al. 1994).

Such a situation is somewhat surprising given the increasing recognition that comprehension of the Epipaleolithic as a whole is crucial to comprehending the whys, hows and wherefores of the shift from mobile gatherer-hunter to settled farmer and herder, epitomized by Childe (1952) as the 'Neolithic Revolution'. Without the combination of environmental events and human responses (in respect of available techno-sociological mechanisms) during the preceding several millennia, it is unlikely that the shift would have occurred.

This chapter does not intend to provide an all-embracing alternative perspective to currently-accepted schemes; nevertheless, it seems pertinent to take stock of the framework within which research is currently operating. Thus the chapter first outlines the systematic and environmental milieus upon which investigation of the material remains is based. Short descriptions are then given of the various archaeological entities focusing on the dynamics of the chronological sequence, spatial/territorial aspects, and adaptive strategies of the populations occupying the changing landscape. Since the later part of the Upper Paleolithic and the Natufian (the later part of

Incised pebble from 'Early Kebaran' site of Urkan e-Rubb II, Lower Jordan Valley (photograph: courtesy of E. Hovers)

the Epipaleolithic) are dealt with in other chapters in this volume, they will only be referred to when relevant to the main thrust of this chapter. Finally, mention is made of what appear to be potentially promising avenues for future research of this period.

Paradigms, methodology and systematics

The approach adopted here is based upon a number of premises detailed elsewhere (Goring-Morris 1987). These include the assumption that various aspects of the most commonly preserved material remains, most especially the lithic assemblages, can be used to identify specific social groups in the landscape.

Most conspicuous, and the element almost invariably present, is the stylistic content − consciously or unconsciously invested by the knappers in the microliths − relating to specific aspects of morphology, metric dimensions, retouch and the specific techniques of manufacture (e.g., the microburin technique). As such they are the 'calling cards' or *fossiles directeurs* of specific population groupings. Other tool groups may be similarly diagnostic, but are not so numerous or not always so distinct.

The view advocated here is that Epipaleolithic knappers saw the finished product, i.e. the tool in its functional context, as the ultimate objective. Specific techniques of core reduction were adapted accordingly, and thus stylistic input is likely to be less marked at the level of blank manufacture than in the finished product. Since microliths are the most commonly produced items, due to their use in various combinations in composite tools (projectile points, knives, etc.), they tend to display a high degree of standardization. In the vast majority of assemblages only a very limited array of basic microlithic forms tended to be produced, albeit within a range of variability acceptable to the knappers. In general, uniformity tends to be greatest in smaller ephemeral occupations, presumably reflecting both the restricted number of knappers and the length of occupation of the site.

Other realms of material culture − such as marine mollusks, beads, exotics, bone tools, artistic endeavors, groundstone tools, installations (hearths and structures), internal spatial organization of occupations, etc. − may also be utilized as supplementary sources for identifying specific social groups. Indeed one of the primary differences distinguishing the Upper Paleolithic from the Epipaleolithic lies in the obviously more marked emphasis on stylistic elements of the material culture in the latter. Though undoubtedly present earlier during the Upper Paleolithic, they appear to be more subtle and difficult to isolate, perhaps partly due to the different chronological spans.

However, it should be stressed that almost all of the elements distinctive of the Epipaleolithic were already present to some degree in the Upper Paleolithic − microliths, marine mollusk ornaments, artistic endeavors, etc. − but on a much smaller scale. Other major distinguishing features include the clearly increased tempo of cultural change coinciding with and following the glacial maximum at *ca.* 20,000 BP, and increasing territorialism.

Raw material constraints for chipped stone tools are rarely of significance in the Levant, since sources (of varying qualities) are widely available throughout the region. Only in areas such as the southern coastal plain of Israel, southern Sinai and the basalt massifs of the Golan and Jebel Druze are flint sources absent (though rarely more than a day's walk away). It is, however, clear that some Epipaleolithic groups preferred specific types of flint, not always immediately available, e.g. chalcedony in the Negev and Sinai, lustrous white/blue/grey patinated flint for some Natufian groups, though the matter awaits systematic study.

The primary building block is the assemblage − a collection of artifacts from a defined area, whether 1−2 m^2 or several dunams, and of defined thickness. Such collections may be classified in terms of their integrity. Thus, small clusters of artifacts commonly deriving from a 5−8 cm thick surface, and sealed by under- and over-lying low-energy, sterile sediments, are pristine assemblages − often amenable to detailed spatial analysis. Where accumulation is slow or there is subsequent deflation or erosion, however, overlap and admixture of different assemblages may occur; given the re-use of the same localities during the course of the Epipaleolithic, such instances are quite common (e.g., the Negev, Sinai, and especially the Coastal Plain). Based upon comparisons with assemblages of greater integrity, various elements (usually the more distinctive microlithic forms) can be identified and separated. In caves and rock-shelters, where available area is necessarily restricted, repeated re-occupation over many millennia may blur separate occupations − the result of a combination of anthropogenic, biogenic and geomorphic processes. In such cases meticulous excavation may sometimes isolate living floors. Seeming mixtures, however, may also result from intergroup exchange mechanisms.

Currently, the most promising approach for grouping the assemblages, given the plethora of sites available, is to first define the smallest units in terms of material remains in time and space, and then to use these 'building blocks' to construct larger groupings at the level of cultural complexes and the like. This avoids the pitfalls of broadly-defined entities which necessarily assume a degree of association which may or may not be present − a problem seen in some definitions of the Kebaran, Mushabian and even Geometric Kebaran complexes, for example. Despite the ensuing difficulties for those interested in the broad overview of cultural historical developments who are not specifically versed in the intricacies of Levantine lithic technotypology, this approach is strongly recommended.

Occupation sites are viewed as being part of open systems: that is, the preserved remains were not necessarily (and indeed frequently were not) manufactured, used and discarded solely within the confines of the location where they were found. This is all the more valid for relatively mobile adaptations. Raw materials and finished products would be introduced and abandoned onsite, others would pass through the site, and yet others would be manufactured onsite for use and eventual abandonment elsewhere.

Nevertheless, based on the premise that the major typological classes do reflect broad functional categories in at least some instances, the general composition and frequency of tool types are considered to be partially representative of the range of tasks performed with knapped tools at or from the site. Unfortunately, prior to the late Epipaleolithic (Natufian), many of the more standardized knapped tools seem to be associated mainly with tasks connected with animal exploitation (hunting, butchering, hide processing, etc.), or with manufacturing tools to work with more perishable materials such as antler, bone, sinew, wood, fiber, etc. The overall role or input of tasks such as vegetal procurement and processing can often only be hinted at on the basis of site locations, plant distributions, broad ethnographic comparisons, and so on. Though some plant processing equipment is preserved, such items may also have been made from perishable materials.

A final proviso relates to animal procurement. Complete projectile points can also be made of perishable materials, whether, antler, bone or wood (an argument used elsewhere to explain the lithic composition of some Upper Paleolithic Levantine assemblages). However, there is virtually no direct evidence to indicate when trapping, snaring and netting of prey was initiated in the Near East.

The chronological framework

Radiometric dating has become a commonly-applied tool for ordering Late Quaternary prehistoric occupations over the past 30 years, further encouraged lately by the introduction of linear accelerator dating techniques.

Some 140 dates are available for occupations that do, or most probably should, fall within the interval under discussion and almost another 100 for the Late Epipaleolithic (Figure 1). However, many problems exist, not all of which can be adequately explained away as 'intrusions'. Currently it is not possible (or likely to be in the near future) to calibrate dates from this time period accurately, though recent evidence has been presented that C14 dates are consistently younger than the true ages, with a maximum difference of 3500 years at *ca.* 20,000

BP (Bard et al. 1990). This is particularly troublesome given the indications for a series of 'radiocarbon plateaus' about 12,500, 10,000 and 9500 BP (Lotter 1991), and there is also the likelihood of earlier plateaus.

Additionally, there are problems with the materials being dated – old wood, bone, etc. Even when what appears to be a consistent series of dates is derived from a single occupation horizon, the results on occasion seem to contradict the stratigraphic data. As dates accumulate it is becoming obvious that, while the central chronological spans of various archaeological entities can be more certainly defined, the crucial beginnings and ends become increasingly blurred. Some 45 percent of the available dates are suspect to some extent (whether clearly aberrant, too large standard deviations, in inverse stratigraphic order, etc.). In short, radiometric dating cannot yet replace solid stratigraphic evidence and detailed techno-typological seriation.

Food resources

On the basis of ethnographic parallels, plant foods are likely to have been more significant than meat in terms of the overall diet. Furthermore, vegetal foodstuffs probably reflect more accurately local ecological conditions in the surrounding landscape at the time of occupation.

Until recently recovery of botanical remains has been virtually non-existent due to the nature of Levantine soils. Recently, however, isolated but significant assemblages have been recovered, most notably from the Early Epipaleolithic of Ohalo II (Kislev et al. 1992) and the Azraq Basin; from the Late Epipaleolithic from Tell Abu Hureya (Hillman 1989b), Wadi Hammeh 27 (Colledge, in Potts et al. 1985) and Hayonim Cave; and, further afield in the Nile Valley, at Wadi Kubbaniya, *ca.* 17–18,000 BP (Hillman 1989a). Occasional macrobotanical remains have also been identified in the Negev and Sinai (e.g. Liphschitz and Waisel 1977; Bar-Yosef and Phillips 1977). Though few and far-between, all these permit at least a glimpse of the wide variety of seeds, nuts, berries, tubers, rhizomes, etc. that were present, known, and commonly exploited from at least the Early Epipaleolithic.

The situation regarding faunal remains is more promising in terms of numbers and sizes of assemblages, though reports in the past were frequently insufficiently detailed and emphasized larger mammalian species at the expense of smaller elements. There is little evidence to indicate major faunal shifts in the procurement of prey through the various regional Epipaleolithic sequences prior to the Natufian. The assemblages generally appear to reflect the natural mix of locally-available species – fallow deer are emphasized in the mountainous northern areas of Lebanon, mountain gazelle predominate in the rest of the Mediterranean zone, dorcas gazelle and ibex feature in the southern craggy regions, and goitered

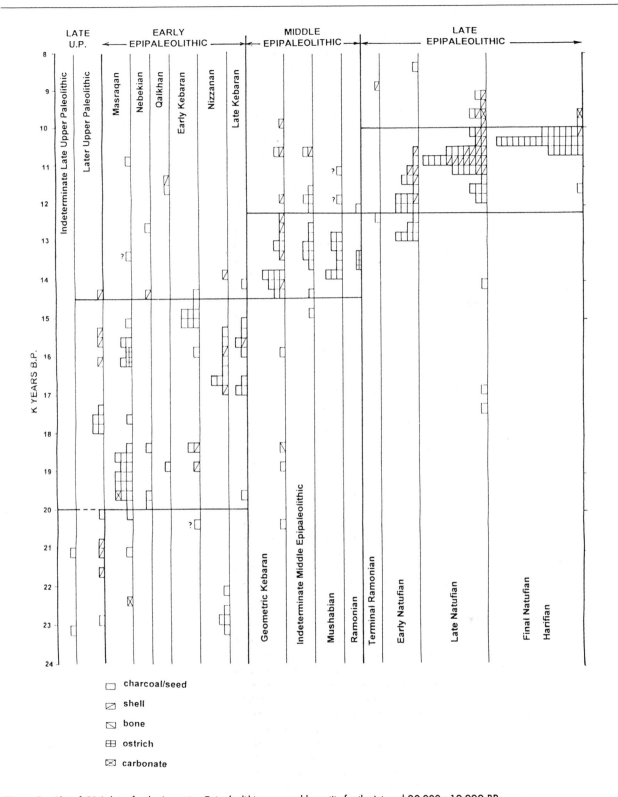

Figure 1   Plot of C14 dates for the Levantine Epipaleolithic arranged by entity for the interval 20,000–10,000 BP

gazelle and wild ass dominate on the eastern steppes. Other larger species hunted more sporadically include aurochs, hartebeest and wild boar. Smaller species were also taken on occasion, such as hare, fox, reptiles, tortoise, lizards and birds. Behavioral studies indicate that all of the larger species mentioned above, with the possible but unproven exception of goitered gazelle, are non-migratory and tend to be quite territorial within limited ranges. Many bird species, by contrast, use the Levant as their main migratory corridor between Africa and Eurasia, and so can provide valuable indications concerning seasonality.

The early Epipaleolithic – ca. 20,000–14,500 BP

Environmental background

Conditions during the Pleniglacial in the Levant were severe and undoubtedly had a major impact on human populations. The snowline was lowered, particularly affecting the habitability of large areas of the Lebanese and Anti-Lebanon Mountains, as well as areas such as the southern Sinai High Mountains. This is reflected in pollen diagrams throughout the Near East, which all display very low AP levels through to at least ca. 16,000 BP (Baruch 1994; Bottema 1987).

The global drop in sea levels to approximately 120 m below the present level would have almost doubled the size of the Israeli and northern Sinai coastal plain, and annulled the Gulf of Suez, while the much deeper Gulf of Aqaba would presumably have been almost entirely cut off from the Red Sea at the Straits of Tiran to form a virtual lagoon (Figure 2).

At the beginning of the period Lake Lisan, covering some 2850 km^2, probably continued its high stand at ca. -180 m, causing a major impediment to contacts across the Rift Valley in much of the central–southern Levant, though, following the glacial maximum at 18,000 BP there is some evidence for a major but temporary drop, the result of tectonics and/or changes in the rate of influx and evaporation (Begin et al. 1985; Yechieli et al. 1993). Lake Lisan would have displayed a north–south cline in terms of salinity.

Although details are scant, the inland basins on the Transjordanian plateau, such as el-Jaffar (1000–1800 km^2), Wadi Hasa, Azraq (4500 Km^2), and Wadi Sirhan, and north in Syria at Damascus, Palmyra, el-Kowm, etc. probably also sported shallow, year-round lakes.

Extensive dunefields rapidly advanced from the Nile Delta across the floodplains of northern Sinai and the western Negev (Goring-Morris and Goldberg 1991). Dune formation is also documented in the el-Kowm basin, at Umm el-Tlel 2, levels VII–V and IV (Molist and Cauvin 1990), while aeolian silts and loess accumulations are documented in the Azraq area at Wadi Jilat and Uwaynid (Garrard et al. 1994). Further south, in the Hisme, dunes were also active (Henry et al. 1983).

The steppic, Irano-Turanian zone in particular would probably have shrunk considerably at the expense of the Sahara-Arabian zone in the Negev, Sinai, and southern and eastern Transjordan and Syria, while the Mediterranean zone would also have been restricted to the lower lying areas.

Compared with previous conditions during the Upper Paleolithic, the impact of these environmental changes on the potentially habitable land available throughout the Levant, given the technological and social resources available would have been profound. In consequence human hunter-gatherer populations most probably retreated into a number of local and relatively isolated *refugia*, i.e., the Israeli and Lebanese coastal plains, and the fringes of the Rift Valley along the narrow shores of the central and northern portion of Lake Lisan (Plate 1); the fringes of the Negev highlands; southern Jordan; and around the shores of the inland basins. Such competition may have triggered the increasing emphasis on group identities and territoriality more noticeably expressed in the stylistic elements of the material remains. The frequency, intensity and nature of intergroup contacts are thus likely to have changed quite radically. The environmental changes brought about by the Pleniglacial could not be anticipated in terms of 'normal' annual variability, and hence 'insurance policies' such as the exchange mechanisms described for the Kalahari San, are probably not applicable in this instance.

Cultural sequence

The transition from the Upper Paleolithic to the Early Epipaleolithic remains poorly defined in terms of change in the material culture remains. Until now most assemblages assigned to this time frame have been grouped under the taxon 'Kebaran', rendering the term largely meaningless, while hints of the complexity of the situation have emerged in the description of some largely coeval assemblages as Late or Terminal Upper Paleolithic. This has become increasingly manifest as research has expanded out of the Mediterranean littoral zone.

On one hand there is considerable continuity in terms of the techno-typology of the lithic industries throughout this period, while on the other, there appear to be quite pronounced changes (Figure 3).

Though numerous occurrences can confidently be ascribed to the Early Epipaleolithic, particularly along the Mediterranean coast and the Jordan Valley, many of the former are mixed surface collections. Of the *in situ* sites, the majority have been subjected to limited testing only so few data are available concerning the spatial organization of such settlements.

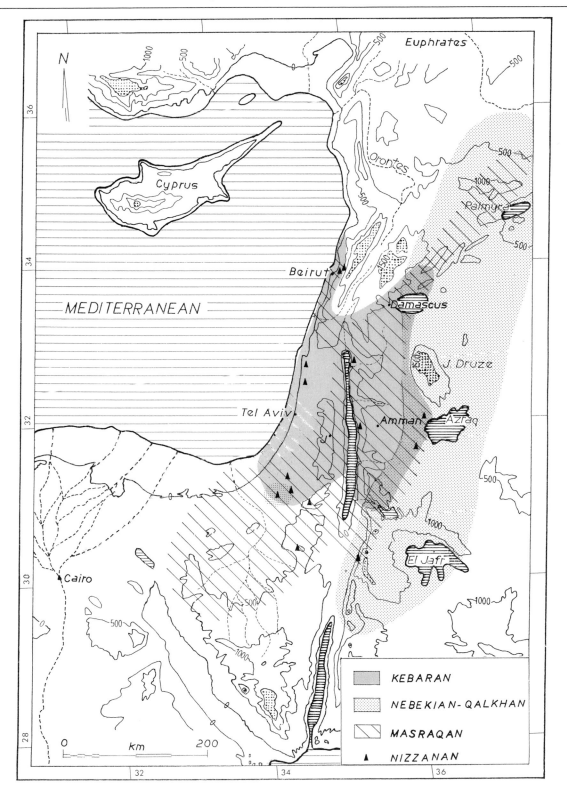

Figure 2 Distributions of Early Epipaleolithic Levantine entities, showing reconstructed topography at ca. 18,000 BP

Plate 1 Southern end of Sea of Galilee from the Golan Heights. 'Masraqan' site of Ohalo II is located on opposite shore (centre); 'Kebaran', 'Nizzanan', and 'Geometric Kebaran' occupations at Ein Gev and Haon on eastern Coastal Plain (left); the lake probably succeeded the Lisan Lake during the course of the Middle Epipaleolithic

A small number of key sites provide the chronostratigraphic framework for subdivision of the Early Epipaleolithic sequence (Table 1). These include: Ksar Aqil phases I–V (Tixier 1970; Tixier and Inizan 1981) and Jiita II (Chevaillon and Hours 1970; Hours 1976) in Lebanon; Yabrud rock-shelter III (Rust 1950; Bachdach 1982) in Syria; Wadi Jilat 6 (Garrard and Byrd 1992; Garrard et al. 1994) and Kharaneh IV (Muheisen 1990) in Eastern Jordan; Wadi Madamagh in Southern Jordan (Schyle and Uerpmann 1988); Fazael III (Bar-Yosef et al. 1974; Goring-Morris 1980) in the Jordan Valley; Nahal Oren (Bar-Yosef 1970; Noy et al. 1973) and Nahal Hadera V (Saxon et al. 1978) and Hefziba (Kaufman 1976) in the Coastal Plain.

In light of the above, it seems appropriate now to attempt to isolate and briefly define at least some of the industries constituting the early Epipaleolithic, though more detailed studies are clearly needed for others.

Masraqan

Numbers of assemblages characterized by finely retouched, elongated bladelets with little or no modification of the extremities have been recognized over the years, being variously attributed to the 'Ahmarian', 'Late Upper Paleolithic', 'Terminal Upper Paleolithic', 'Proto-Kebaran', and 'Kebaran' (Figure 4). Their geographical spread ranges from the Negev and Sinai, through the northern and (?)central Coastal Plain and the Rift Valley, to Transjordan and northeast Syria. First described from the Judean Desert occupation at Masaraq an-Na'aj (Perrot 1955), it seems apt to name this industry after that site.

Solid stratigraphic evidence is lacking, though if indeed Ksar Akil phase III and Jiita III/3–5 can be assigned to the

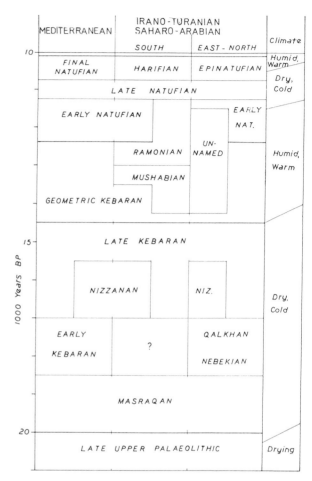

Figure 3 Scheme of cultural developments in Levant ca. 22,000–10,000 BP

Masraqan, then it predates the Lebanese early Kebaran. Elsewhere the geomorphic setting of Fazael X–XI appears to predate the early and late Kebaran at Fazael III. Further south the stratigraphic relationship between the late Upper Paleolithic of Ein Aqev and the Masraqan of Ein Aqev East remains controversial (Ferring 1977, 1988; Goring-Morris 1987; Marks 1976). Considerable numbers of radiometric dates are available, yet the precise chronological placement remains problematic, with two peaks indicated at about 20,000–18,000 BP and 16,500–15,500 BP, though the former appears to accord more comfortably with the meagre stratigraphic correlations (see Table 1 and Figure 1).

Elongated, narrow single platform cores for the production of bladelets are common, sometimes with removal surfaces at either end of the core. The removal surfaces commonly display evidence of intensive preparatory abrasion, resulting in carination. Bladelet

Table 1 Stratigraphic correlation of Epipaleolithic sites in the southern Levant

	Jilat 6	Kharaneh 4	Yabrud	Ksar Akil	Jiita	Hayonim Cave/Ter	Nahal Oren	Hadera V	Fazael	Hamifgash	Mushabi XIV	Nahal Neqarot	Umm-Tlel 2	Khiam	Wad Madamagh
Natufian	—	—	III/1	—	—	B	5	+	—	—	—	+	—	6–7	—
Ramonian	—	—	—	—	—	—	—	—	—	VII	—	+	—	—	—
Mushabian	—	—	—	—	—	—	—	—	—	—	1	—	—	—	—
Geometric Kebaran	—	C/D	III/3	—	—	Ter D	—	—	IIIC	I	2	+	3	8–9	—
'Late Kebaran'	—	B	III/4?	I(1)	—	Ca	—	1–3	IIIA/D	—	—	—	—	—	—
Nizzanan	Upper	A	—	I(3)	II/1–2 II/3–5	Cb	7–8?	4–6	—	IV	—	—	—	—	—
'Early Kebaran'	—	—	—	II	III/1–2 III/3–5?	Cc	9	—	IIIB	—	—	—	—	—	—
Qalkhan	Middle	—	III4–5	—	—	—	—	—	—	—	—	—	—	—	—
Nebekian	Lower	—	III6–7	—	—	—	—	—	—	—	—	?	—	—	A1–2
Masraqan	—	—	—	III	III/3–5?	—	—	—	(X–XI)	—	—	—	—	—	—
'Late UP'	—	—	III/8 II/1?	—	—	—	62–3?	—	—	—	—	—	5	—	A3–E
Atlitian	—	—	III/9 II/2	IV	—	—	B7?	—	(IX)	—	—	—	—	10	—
Levant Aurig C	—	—	II/3–4	V–VI (VII)	—	D	—	—	—	—	—	—	—	?	?

NOTES:
1. Ksar Akil phases after Tixier.

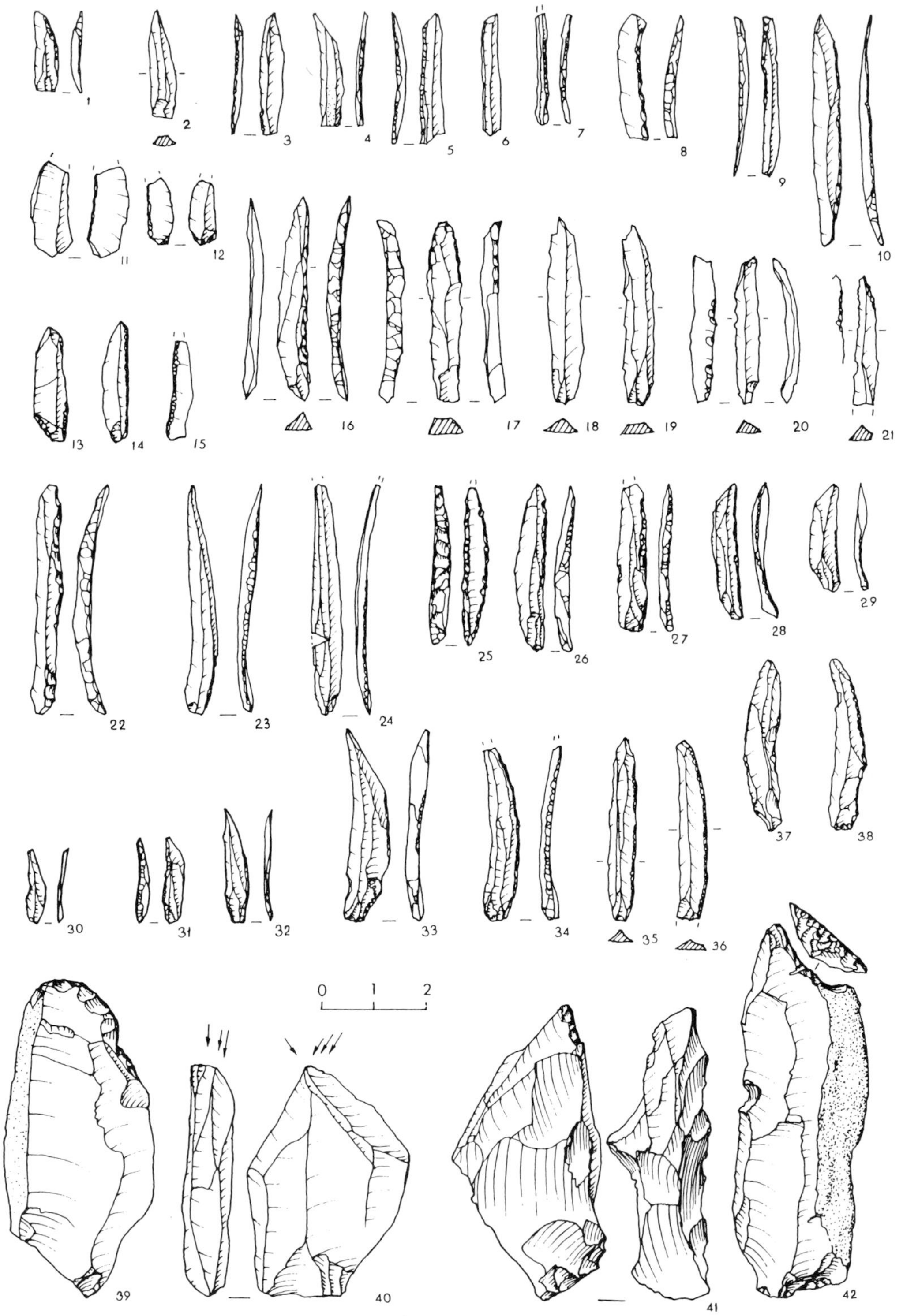

Figure 4 Tools of Early Epipaleolithic 'Masraqan' industry: 1–12, Fazael X; 13–15, 40, Wadi Hasa 784x; 16–21, 41, Ohalo II; 22–24 Azariq XIII; 25–29, 42, Ein Aqev East; 30–34, 39, Shunera XVI; 35–38, Lagama X

Plate 2 *Fond de cabane* (Locus 1) at 'Masraqan' site of Ohalo II at southern end of Sea of Galilee. Note that the structure is D-shaped, seemingly with entrance facing the shore, and large workslab on right (scale 20 cm) (courtesy D. Nadel)

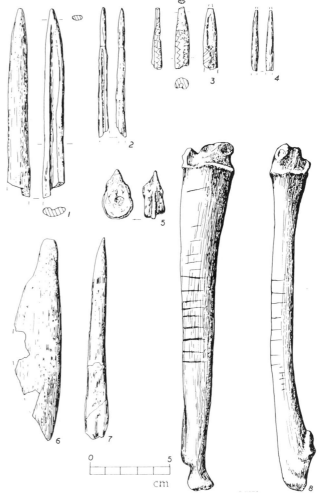

Figure 5 Bone tools from Early and Middle Epipaleolithic entities: 1, Urkan e-Rubb II; 2–3, 5, Fazael X; 4, Jiita II; 6–7, Mushabi XIV/1; 8, Kharaneh IV/D

blanks tend to be narrow, elongated and thin, with incurvate but not twisted profiles. Retouch varies from nibbled (Ouchtata) through semi-abrupt to abrupt, often along the length of single blanks, frequently petering out before the tip. Distal and proximal ends are commonly unmodified. Unsurprisingly, the microburin technique is absent. The likely function of such microliths remains enigmatic, since many do not appear robust enough for use as projectile points.

There would also appear to be a quite separate core technology for the production of larger blade blanks. Scrapers are quite common, being large and simple. Of note is the presence of concave scrapers/truncations on blades. Burins include both truncation and dihedral varieties, and among the latter polyhedral varieties are notable, sometimes verging on lateral carinated scrapers.

Data concerning internal spatial arrangements are available from several sites in the Negev, where occupations range from small temporary encampments with a single hearth and associated artifact scatters like Azariq XIII, through more complex sites such as Shunera XVI, Lagama X(?) and Ein Aqev East, which are larger and feature several hearths each with their own artifact scatter, sometimes of similar items and sometimes differentiated. Hearths rarely contain or are delimited by stones. Sites vary considerably in size from *ca.* 25 m^2 through 250 m^2. Further north, in the Rift Valley, in addition to Fazael X–XI and Wadi Jiftlik, details of the excellently preserved site of Ohalo II adjacent to the present Sea of Galilee are becoming available (Nadel 1991, Kislev et al. 1992; and see Window and Plates 1 and 2). Ohalo II provides a frustratingly rare glimpse of the impressive range of vegetal resources exploited for both dietary and other purposes.

Rare groundstone tools are documented, e.g. Fazael X,

though the present sample is too restricted to provide a reliable indicator as to variability. Similarly a few simple bone points and awls have also been recovered (Figure 5).

In some sites marine mollusks are quite profuse, indicating fairly widespread procurement/exchange networks. Shells are almost exclusively of Mediterranean derivation, with tiny sliced beads of narrow, costate *Dentalium*, as well as *Mitrella* and *Columbella*.

The Nebekian

This term was first used by Rust (1950) based on the assemblages he recovered from Yabrud III/6–7. The term largely fell out of use (though see Besancon et al. 1975–7), but has again found favour with some researchers following recent research in Jordan at Jilat 6 lower, Uwanid 14 lower and Uwanid 18 upper (Garrard et al. 1994). This research provides the stratigraphic position of the entity, which may be more or less coeval with at least part of the Masraqan industry. It has been suggested that other sites further south in Jordan may also be related to the Nebekian, such as Wadi Madamagh levels A1–A2, Tor Hamar C and J431. The geographical distribution of the Nebekian thus appears to be restricted to the area east of the Rift Valley. Though the few dates available are widely spread, on the basis of stratigraphic and other criteria, a range of *ca.* 20,000–18,000 BP seems a reasonable preliminary estimate.

Though most assemblages have at best been only cursorily described to date, the characteristic features of the lithic industry seem to include frequently high percentages of finely-made, elongated, narrow and symmetrically curved, pointed, arch-backed pieces, sometimes tending to oblique truncations. They are often fabricated using the microburin technique – the earliest habitual use documented in the Near East. Retouch tends to be abrupt and hence invasive relative to the blank.

Notable among the non-microlithic tools are truncations and non-standardized retouched pieces. The presence of microgravettes at Tor Hamar C, though seemingly no triangles, may be indicative of the Nebekian as a possible precursor of the Nizzanan (see below). As such it may be at least partially coeval with what has commonly been referred to as the 'Early Kebaran'.

Unfortunately few details are available concerning intrasite spatial organization, though Yabrud III was obviously quite limited (*ca.* 50 m²), while sites in the Azraq region – even allowing for repeated reoccupation and subsequent deflation, erosion and sheetwash – were clearly of major proportions (Byrd 1990; Garrard et al. 1994). Indeed it is possible that the Azraq Basin served as a major aggregation locale, seasonal or otherwise.

Uwaynid 18 is one of the few Epipaleolithic sites in the Azraq area to display a predominance of gazelle in the fauna, in addition to equids and tortoise carapaces. Two basalt handstones and two irregular pestle fragments were recovered, also at Uwaynid 18.

Little can be said of ornamental elements due to the lack of distinction among marine mollusk assemblages between layers in multi-occupation sites, though *dentalium* beads are present at Uwaynid 18. A bone pendant at Jilat 6 (lower) is notable.

The Qalkhan

This entity was defined by Henry (1982, 1983) based on work in the Ras en-Naqb/Hisma area of southern Transjordan. It has subsequently been recognized elsewhere in Edom (Schyle and Uerpmann 1988), at Azraq (Garrard et al. 1994) and Yabrud III/5 (Rust 1950),

and possibly as far north as the el-Kowm Basin (Cauvin 1981). The only candidate for an occurrence west of the Rift, and ephemeral at that, is Nahal Lavan 1010S in the western Negev (personal observation). Thus, like the Nebekian, the known distribution of the Qalkhan appears to favor the eastern steppic regions. Stratigraphically it postdates the Nebekian and predates the Nizzanan at Jabrud III, Jilat 6 (middle) and Uwaynid 14 (Rust 1950; Garrard et al. 1994). C14 dating is, however, equivocal, though it seems likely to centre around 18,000–19,000 BP.

Few details are currently available concerning the lithic technotypological characteristics of the lithic industry, though it tends to feature large blade blanks. Typologically, the rather wide tools – often larger than the generally accepted range for microliths – include characteristic shouldered triangles made by the microburin technique – the Qalkhan point; the resulting scars are commonly unretouched. Other tools include robust la Mouillah points, double truncated bladelets and quantities of notches and denticulates.

As yet, further details concerning the Qalkhan are sparse, though a shell bead, and bone points have been reported from Jilat 6 (middle). There the faunal remains were composed mainly of equid, gazelle and tortoise.

'The Kebaran complex'

As noted in the introduction, the numerous microlithic assemblages in the Coastal Plain formed a major basis for the definition of the Terminal Pleistocene sequence in the Levant in light of their comprehensive analysis by Bar-Yosef (1970). The sequence was broadly divided into two on the basis of the frequency of geometrics, with all the non-geometric assemblages being clustered under the general taxon 'Kebaran', although evidence was presented for considerable regional and chronological diversity. However, more precise subdivision was hampered by the nature of the available evidence. Occupation sites are commonly clustered on the top of sandstone kurkar ridges, close to breaches by wadis draining westwards. Many localities were repeatedly reoccupied, sometimes over the course of several millennia. Deflation, during both the Epipaleolithic and subsequently, often mixed disparate assemblages, – a problem frequently compounded by their unsystematic collection by amateurs. Of all the Coastal Plain assemblages described by Bar-Yosef (1970), only one or two derived from systematically excavated, sealed contexts. In light of experience from semi-arid areas – the discovery and/or publication of *in situ*, stratified Early Epipaleolithic assemblages along the Lebanese Coast and in the Jordan Valley (plus other, more peripheral, regions), – it is now possible to isolate the constituent elements present in some of the Coastal Plain assemblages and remove occasional intrusive elements.

The resulting picture is one of major diversity through time and space during the early Epipaleolithic. Intensive research conducted over the past two decades in the peripheral areas to the south and east has cast doubt on the integrity of the 'Kebaran' as an entity. It has generally become synonymous for the entire Early Epipaleolithic in the southern Levant, with a diverse set of technotypological traits which could, by the same criteria, be applied to virtually the entire Epipaleolithic (e.g., presence/absence of microburin technique, specific technologies of core reduction and blank production, typological variability, etc.).

Over the years, Bar-Yosef has modified his original scheme, incorporating both the results of work by Hours (1976) in Lebanon and more recent investigations elsewhere (Bar-Yosef and Vogel 1987). This is not the appropriate forum to review matters in detail and hence the following outline is based primarily on Bar-Yosef and Hours' pioneering syntheses. These rely especially upon specific typological aspects within the microlith class (Figure 6).

1. Group A is characterized by narrow, curved micropoints. This may be subdivided into: 1. narrow micropoints with basal truncations (Kiriat Aryeh II, Kfar Darom 3, 26, Soreq 33T and Hayonim Cave Cc); and 2. broad micropoints (Kfar Darom 8; Soreq 33Q, and perhaps also Azariq VI).
2. Group B features large curved and pointed bladelets, some with basal truncations (Azariq IV, Poleg 18MII, Fazael IIIB, XII, Urkan el-Rubb II–IIa, Hefzibah south, and perhaps Soreq 33MI).
3. Group C presents a combination of micropoints and oblique truncations (Hayonim Cave Ca, Meged, Nahal Oren 9, Soreq 33M2, 33M1?, Kfar Darom 13, 28, Rakefet, Sefunim A2, Nahal Hader V/1–3, and Giveat Haesev) (Plate 3).
4. Group D has large oblique truncated backed bladelets (Kebara points) and narrow, curved backed bladelets (Ein Gev I, Ein Gev II, Haifa I, Nahal Oren 9, Umm Khalid, Nahal Hadera V/1–2, Kiriat Aryeh I, Poleg 18X, Soreq 33MI, 33M2, Kfar Darom 13, and Kharaneh IVB).

Several other variations can also be recognized as, for example assemblages with proximal Kebara points and microgravettes of Hours' Phases E and F for Lebanon (Jiita II/1, Abri Bergy IV, Dhour Chousir, Hayonim Cave Cb, Poleg 18M, and Fazael VII). Another group features micropoints and narrow trapezes (Mushabi XXI, Azariq I, VIII).

As noted by Bar-Yosef, these groupings display evidence for both temporal and spatial trends. Thus a general progression from inverse and fine retouch, through more abrupt backing techniques is apparent. Furthermore micropoint dominated assemblages tend, on stratigraphic and sparse C14 data, to precede those featuring Kebara points. The latter type also displays variability in terms of location of tips.

Spatial variability is also present, presumably representing local provinces as well as raw material availability as, for example, the proliferation of short micropoints in the southern Coastal Plain. Falita points and microgravettes are claimed to reflect an eastern province, while inverse retouch seemingly continues through most of the stratigraphic sequence in Western Galilee and the Lebanese Coast.

This extensive variability reflects the temporal and spatial trajectories of specific groups through the changing landscape over the course of at least 2000–3000 years, if not more. Groups would presumably be constantly readjusting as local conditions changed, and in response to the movements and behaviors of other groups. West of the Rift Valley and south of Lebanon, various groups appear to have shifted on a seasonal basis from the Coastal Plain (Poleg 18MII) across the Samarian Hills to the Jordan Valley in the spring (Fazael IIIB, XII, Urkan e-Rubb II) (see Lieberman 1993). Ein Gev I also displays evidence of winter occupation. Further south along the coast, territories were seemingly more circumscribed. Similarities on both sides of the Jordan Valley (Wadi Hammeh and Fazael IIIA) may indicate contacts across the Lisan as it contracted.

Kebaran sites are generally quite small, usually from *ca.* 25–100 m² and rarely exceed 250 m². Unfortunately, virtually no horizontal data are available beyond the brief descriptions of the series of superimposed flimsy *fonds de cabane* at Ein Gev I (Bar-Yosef 1970).

With the exception of the female burial under the floor, and another two at Kharaneh IV/B, few skeletal remains have been recovered, though the presence of seven seemingly cremated remains at Kebara C may provide another reason for their scarcity. Mortars, bowls, pestles and mullers are a minor but quite common component in many Kebaran occupations (Figure 7). Marine mollusks are usually present, but not particularly abundant in most sites: in addition to *dentalia*, species include *Nassa* and *Columbella rustica*. Art objects during the Early Epipaleolithic occur only sporadically on bone, as with the *'poincon a fut conique'* at Ksar Akil 8c, a similar item at Kharaneh IV/D, an engraved point at Jiita II/2, and Jilat 6 upper. The engraved pebble from Urkan e-Rubb II is unique (Hovers 1990; see opening photograph p. 142). The bone tool repertoire of the early Epipaleolithic is also quite impoverished, with occasional awls, points and spatulas.

The Nizzanan

Assemblages characterized by minute scalene and isoceles triangles made by the microburin technique and microgravettes ('spiky points') were described several decades ago from Wadi Jilat 6 (Wadi Dhobai K) and Ein Gev IV. Bar-Yosef (1970, 1981; and Bar-Yosef and Vogel

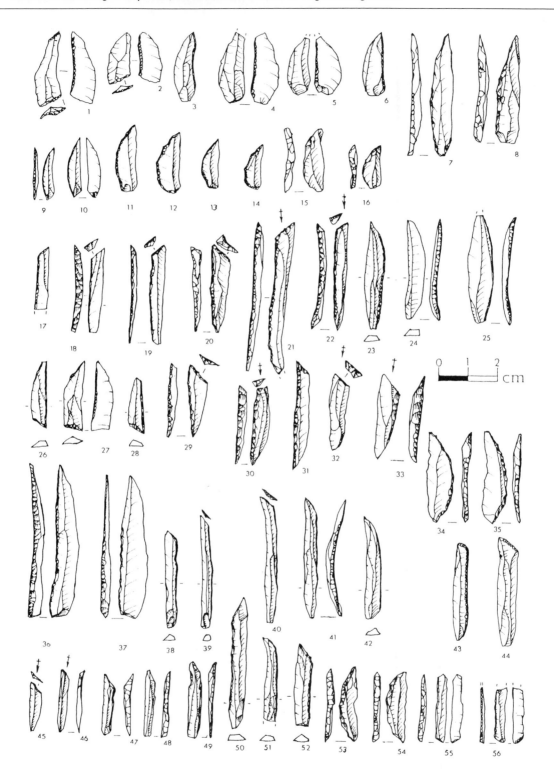

Figure 6   Microlithic forms of various Early Epipaleolithic 'Kebaran' industries: 1—2, Jiita II/2; 3—6, Kfar Darom 28; 7—8, Fazael IIIB; 9—10, Kfar Darom 26; 11—14, Kfar Darom 8; 15—16, Nahal Soreq 33Q; 17—18, 26—28, Hayonim Cb; 20—21, 29, Fazael VII; 21—22, 30—31, Jiita II superieur; 23—25, Poleg 18MII; 32—33, Givat HaEsev; 34—35, Azariq VI; 36—42, Ein Gev I; 43—44, Kharaneh IV/B; 45—49, Fazael IIIA; 50—52, Nahal Hadera V/upper; 53—56, Azariq I

Plate 3 View of Nahal Oren to the northwest across the Coastal Plain from the Carmel Hills. Site is located on opposite bank at mouth of the wadi. During the Epipaleolithic the coastline would have been located several kilometers further west

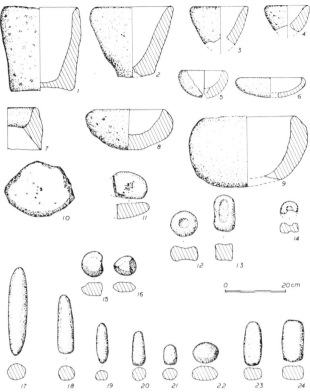

Figure 7 Grinding and pounding equipment from Early and Middle Epipaleolithic sites on basalt, phosphorite and limestone: 1, 9—10, 12, Ein Gev I; 2—4, 24, Hefzibah; 5, 11, 14, 20—23, Givat HaEsev; 6, 19, Haon; 7, Mushabi XIV/1; 8—9. Neve David; 10, Fazael VII

1987) has variously viewed them as essentially part of the Geometric Kebaran complex, either as a lateral facies or a later phase. The discovery of similar sites in the Negev and the coastal plain, and further investigations in the Azraq Basin, however, have necessitated revision, and the designation 'Nizzanan' has been advanced (Goring-Morris 1985, 1987; see also Valla 1990; Garrard and Byrd 1992). Stratigraphic considerations indicate that it predates the Geometric Kebaran (Hamifgash IV–I and Kharaneh IV phase A; phases B–D), while a considerable number of radiometric determinations cluster between 17,000–15,000 BP. As such it appears to be coeval with the later stages of the 'Kebaran'. The recent series of accelerator dates from Ksar Akil level 3 (Tixier excavations) are considered aberrant, as indeed are most of the other dates from that site.

Nizzanan sites are located east of the Jordan (Mediterranean and Irano-Turanian steppic zones), including the Rift Valley, and south of the Lisan/Dead Sea, west of the Rift, in the Negev. In the Coastal Plain Nizzanan sites can be recognized at Ksar Akil (phase III) and Nahal Oren VII, while several other occupations appear to indicate the presence of certain Nizzanan traits, e.g. Nahal Hadera V/4–6 (Saxon et al. 1978).

The lithic industry is characterized by a laminar aspect. Exhausted cores are commonly pyramidal single platform types, though opposed platform varieties occur also (Plate 4). In addition to the above-described microliths (Figure 8), it includes elegant, well-made scrapers and burins, particularly dihedral variants. Morphological considerations of the *lamelles scalenes* and the intensive use of the microburin technique provide a possible antecedent to the Middle Epipaleolithic Mushabian (see below).

Occupations vary considerably in size from the huge expanses of Wadi Jilat 6 and Kharaneh IV (20,000 m^2), through smaller camps (some still large by 'normal' standards), ephemeral locations and smaller stands. The

possibility that the two sites in the Azraq Basin represent major aggregation localities should not be dismissed lightly.

Of particular interest is the presence, albeit sometimes in small frequencies, of minute triangles in 'Kebaran' assemblages along the Mediterranean littoral from Jiita II and Ksar Akil I–II in the north through Kfar Darom 3 and Kfar Darom 28 in the south. At Nahal Hadera V/4–6 and Nahal Oren 8-7 they occur together with microgravettes and at Nahal Hadera they were made using the microburin technique. These sites could reflect sporadic incursions into the Coastal Plain from more traditional home ranges.

Nizzanan marine mollusk assemblages (of Mediterranean origin) are sometimes quite prolific, including *Anachis* and *Nassa* in addition to *Dentalium*.

Discussion

The Azraq Basin sites in the Early and Middle Epipaleolithic are presently unique and anomalous in terms of their

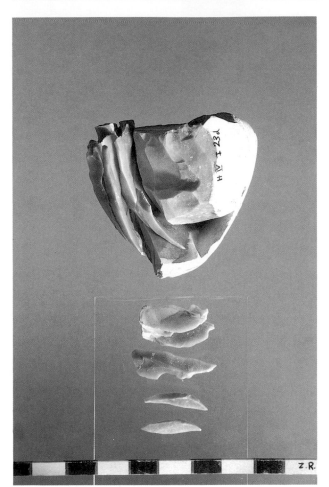

Plate 4   Core reconstruction from the 'Nizzanan' site of Hamifgash IV, Western Negev. Note cluster of microburins and *pigant triedre* (photograph: © Zev Radovan)

extent and scope of occupation. Indeed they exceed, by factors of ten or more, the largest sites known west of the Rift Valley. A likely explanation for this phenomenon is likely to be the specific, herding social behavior and migratory routes of *Gazella subguttarosa*, as opposed to other subspecies of gazelle and other medium-sized mammals. Together with the range of plant resources available in the rich lakeside environment, this may have enabled large bands to aggregate seasonally for cooperative hunts.

The Middle Epipaleolithic – *ca.* 14,500–12,250 BP

Environmental background

There is evidence that the onset of the Late Glacial was first marked in the Levant *ca.* 16,000 years ago, gradually

spreading from south to north and only affecting the Taurus and Zagros by *ca.* 12,500–10,000 BP. With the inception of climatic amelioration both the Mediterranean woodlands and, perhaps more significantly, the Irano-Turanian steppes expanded considerably in the southern and central Levant (Baruch 1994).

Conditions were wetter and warmer. Most affected would have been areas such as the Negev and Sinai (with a series of small, probably seasonal ponds and lakes where drainages had been blocked by dunefields, see Plate 5), the Hisma, and the whole eastern region from el-Jaffar, through Wadi Hasa and the Azraq Basin (also with possible evidence for local damming and higher water tables, e.g. Jilat 22 – Garrard et al. 1994), northwards by way of the Palmyra basin to the Euphrates. Concurrently sea levels began to rise, especially after 13,000 BP, causing the coastal plain to gradually shrink – by 12,000 BP (the Natufian) heights were some 70 m below present (Bard et al. 1990). At some juncture the Gulf of Eilat would have been reconnected to the Red Sea, and the Gulf of Suez would have advanced northwards separating Sinai from Africa (Figure 9).

Notwithstanding considerable research, the chronology of the end of Lake Lisan, apparently resulting from a mixture of tectonic and environmental factors, still remains to be precisely detailed, though the Geometric Kebaran site of Wadi Ahmar II near Fazael is located at -203 m below sea level (bsl), while Ohalo I is located at approximately -210 m bsl (Hovers 1989; Bar-Yosef and Nadel 1988). The Early Natufian of Salibiya XII at -218 m bsl and the Late Natufian of Salibiya I at -230 m bsl, presumably indicate the pace of retreat of Lake Lisan and the creation of the Dead Sea. Despite the likelihood of tectonic subsidence and uplift – taken together with other recent evidence, e.g. the PPNA assemblage of Gesher – the proposed reconstruction (Kouky and Smith 1986) and chronology of the post-Lisan Lake Beisan is untenable, though it is possible that both the Sea of Galilee and Lake Beisan did exist as separate water bodies during the Middle and Late Epipaleolithic.

The overall impact of these environmental changes was to make more potentially exploitable land available throughout the Levant (probably more than doubling the area), as plant and animal populations expanded out from their earlier refuges, closely followed by humans. Initially, at least, this would also have eased intergroup contacts and in many instances have reduced stress, competition and the need for delineating territorial boundaries.

Geometric Kebaran

It is perhaps within this setting that the emergence and general uniformity of the material record of the Geometric Kebaran should be viewed, extending as it does from the Euphrates right down to Southern Sinai, and from the

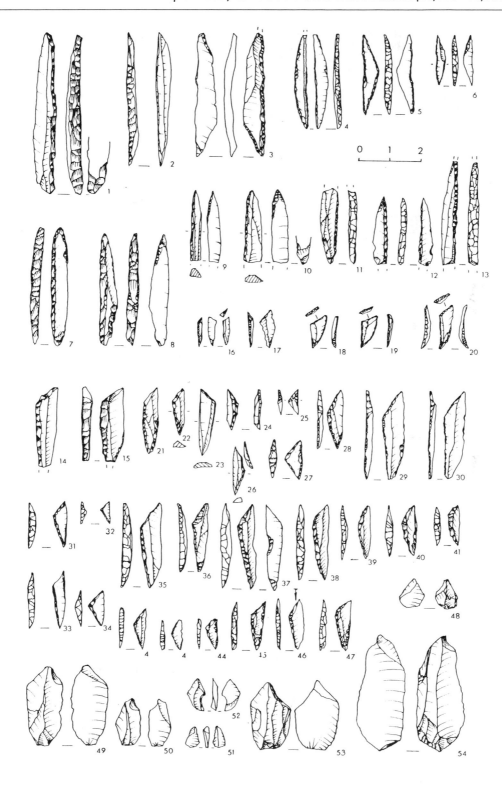

Figure 8 Microliths of Early Epipaleolithic 'Nizzanan' industry: 1, 14—15, Kharaneh IV/A; 2, 31—35, Jilat 6 upper; 3—6, 16—17, 51—52, Ksar Akil 3; 7—8, 25, 27—30, 53, Ein Gev IV; 9, 23—24, 26 Nahal Oren Pit G2/G3 and level 7; 10, 21—22, 49—50, Nahal Hadera V; 11, 37—41, 48, 54, Azariq IX; 12—13, 45—47, Hamifgash IV; 18—20, Jiita II/3; 36, 42—44, Mitzpeh Shunera III

Plate 5 View across Wadi Mushabi, Gebel Maghara in Northern Sinai, showing Middle Epipaleolithic lake sediments resulting from blockage by dunes. The stratified 'Geometric Kebaran' and 'Mushabian' site of Mushabi XIV is located at the lake edge (centre of photo) (courtesy of O. Bar-Yosef and J.L. Phillips)

Mediterranean across to the Saudi Arabian border (and perhaps beyond). Within the area as a whole several regional variants can be recognized (Figure 10).

In the Mediterranean zone the Geometric Kebaran appears to have continued contemporaneously with the changes in the south. Interestingly, Geometric Kebaran occupation of the Coastal Plain (both Israeli and Lebanese) seems to decline somewhat in comparison with the Early Epipaleolithic, both in numbers and intensity. The presence of Geometric Kebaran occupations in the Lebanese mountains and uplands of Galilee also demonstrates the 'opening up' of those areas.

Whereas the spatial arrangements of the more ephemeral occupations in the south are quite well detailed, the excavated evidence from the Mediterranean zone is extremely scanty, with limited exposures and even more limited descriptions in the literature. Flimsy constructions were seemingly fairly common features, e.g. Umm el-Tlel 2/III? and Haon II (*fonds de cabane*), Kharaneh 4 (postholes), Ein Gev III (two superimposed stone-built semi-circular structures, a stone pavement, and a 2x1 m oval stone-built installation), and possibly Neve David (though the reported architecture from the latter is almost certainly not Epipaleolithic). A number of occupation sites at the edges of the large basins in the east, as previously, appear to be much larger than those west of the Rift Valley, e.g. Umm el-Tlel 2/III (2400 m²), Nadaouiyeh 2 (2400 m²), and Kharaneh 4 (2 hectares), though subsequent deflation and slopewash may have biased the original situation and the size of occupation at any one time is still unclear.

Human remains are still notable for their rarity, though two burials with stones and grinding equipment have been recently described from Neve David (Kaufman and Ronen 1987). Again, site sizes are small (25–100 m²) west of the

Rift Valley, though much more extensive settlements are documented in the Azraq Basin (up to 6000 m²). Regional variability is evident in various aspects of the geometric microlith assemblages, whether in the appearance of large asymmetric trapezes in coastal plain sites or variations in specific retouch types and frequencies, e.g. bipolar retouch (Goring-Morris 1987).

The seasonality data from Neve David (fall/winter and ?spring) would seem to indicate a continuation of Early Epipaleolithic subsistence strategies, though more data are required (Lieberman 1993). In general (the Azraq Basin excepted), Geometric Kebaran populations seem to have exploited the landscape in small family-based, mobile groups.

A variety of grinding equipment, including stone bowls, mortars and pestles, mullers and other handstones are, again, a small but quite constant component of systematically investigated sites (see Figure 11 p. 163). A possible innovation is the presence in sites throughout the region of small limestone or sandstone disks, perhaps deriving from earlier, larger items.

Local continuity from the earlier Epipaleolithic can be recognized in several instances, as for example at Ein Gev III, while there is also local development from the Late Kebaran in the Negev and Sinai (Azariq I, Azariq VIII, and Mushabi XXI). The lithic technology of the Geometric Kebaran appears to display a shift from elongated, narrow bladelet production, through time, to an essentially blade-oriented mode which is more pronounced in the south, but for the production of microlithic rectangles and trapezes. Stylistic criteria appear to indicate two contrasting modes – on the one hand, three subregional clusters can be recognized with the central and western Negev and northern Sinai perhaps demonstrating separate provinces (based on retouch types and serration of the working edges); on the other, longer-range stylistic similarities between the western Negev dunes (Shunera I) and the central Coastal Plain of Israel (Kiriat Aryeh I and Hofith). Whether these represent two different settlement (and subsistence) systems operating in tandem, or facets of a single system, or even shifting developments within the Geometric Kebaran is still unresolved. In the east, particularly around the Azraq Basin and Wadi Hasa, there is also evidence of greater variability during the Middle Epipaleolithic, e.g., Azraq 8, 17, 22, Jilat 8, and Kharaneh IV phases C–D. These may reflect the limits of groups exploiting areas within Saudi Arabia at a time of amelioration.

In the Negev and Sinai at least the Geometric Kebaran is characterized by the noted clumping of sites of all sizes in the lowlands (100–400 m asl), corresponding almost exclusively to the extensive dunefields of northern Sinai and the western Negev. Adjacent hamadas and loess surfaces are less favored. However, a couple of larger sites are documented at higher elevations, one in the Negev and

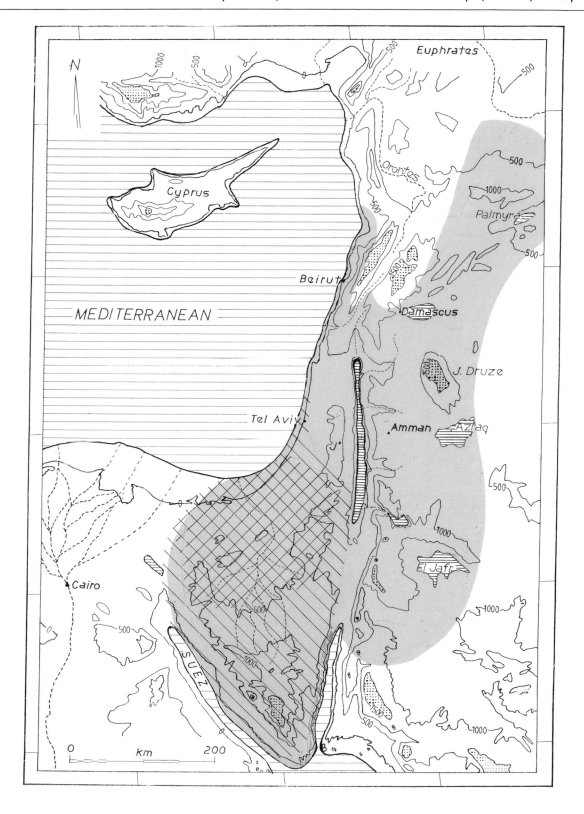

Figure 9   Distribution map of Middle Epipaleolithic Levantine entities, showing reconstructed topography of area at *ca.* 14,500 BP

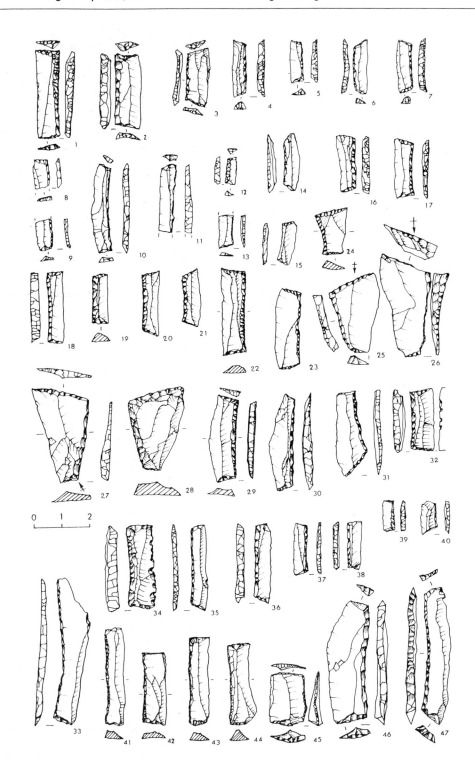

Figure 10   Microlithic tools for Middle Epipaleolithic 'Geometric Kebaran': 1–3, Abri Bergy I–II; 4–7, Hayonim Terrace E; 8–9. Ein Gev III; 10–13, Haon III; 14–15, Wadi Ahmar II; 16–17, Fazael VIII; 18–21, Gat Rimon; 22, 27–29, Shunera I; 23–26, Kiriat Aryeh I; 30–32, Azariq XVI; 33–34, Azariq XVIII; 35–36, Azariq II; 37–40, Nahal Sekher 22; 41–44, Lagama North VIII; 45–47, Nahal Lavan 105

Plate 7 The 'Geometric Kebaran' and 'Mushabian?' sites of Shunera III (right) and Shunera II in the Western Negev Dunes during excavation. Wadi es-Sid is located in the centre. Another seven Early and Middle Epipaleolithic occupations are clustered on this terrace at the edge of the dunes

Plate 6 View of shallow pit with cache of pounding stones and large cores from Qadesh Barnea 8, Northeastern Sinai (scale 20 cm) (photograph: courtesy of O. Bar-Yosef and I. Gilead)

the other in southern Sinai. The elevational data concerning the derivation of all tools in the entity display the same general pattern. Thus, there is no evidence of site size to correlate with elevation. Geometric Kebaran assemblage size is basically clinal, as has indeed been demonstrated with regard to tool-kit diversity – the larger the site, the more likely the more diverse elements of the overall Geometric Kebaran tool-kit range will be present (Goring-Morris 1985). Elongated scrapers are the only other distinctive elements in the tool-kit apart from the ubiquitous geometrics. The only features consistently documented in sites are single hearths, usually with few stones, and occasional caches of larger stone artifacts (Qadesh Barnea 8, Azariq II) (Plate 6).

There is no evidence of seasonality in the choice of site size or location. In general, Geometric Kebaran site locations are characterized by several quite specific settings, inevitably close to major water sources – perennial springs at the fringes of the highlands, principal interfluves of major drainage systems, and/or seasonal playa-type contexts caused by dunes blocking the local drainage systems (Plate 7). When coupled with the environmental information indicating more favourable conditions at this time, the notion that the Geometric Kebaran is of Mediterranean derivation is reinforced.

Little unequivocal evidence regarding animal or plant exploitation patterns during this period is available; apparently all the locally available megafauna was hunted (gazelle is the most commonly present, plus hartebeest, aurochs and onager in lowland areas away from the dunes). There was little use of marine mollusks at this time, though whether this is purely cultural or relates to rising sea levels remains to be elucidated. No information concerning the exploitation of floral resources is available. Also of some note is the apparent innovation of trapezes – rectangles hafted using limeplaster first noted at Lagama North VIII (Bar-Yosef and Goring-Morris 1977), and subsequently elsewhere.

The local demise of the Geometric Kebaran remains obscure, though there are indications that they may have been absorbed by other groups establishing themselves in the region.

The Mushabian

The Mushabian is commonly considered to have originated in North Africa, largely on the basis of habitual use of the microburin technique and general morphological similarities with some assemblages in Nubia (Phillips and Mintz 1977; Bar-Yosef and Vogel 1987). In light of more recently available evidence, however, it is at least as likely that its origins should be sought closer at hand in the east, in Transjordan (e.g., the Nizzanan, Nebekian, Galkhan), though the Mushabian *sensu stricto* has not yet been identified beyond the confines of the Negev and Sinai (Goring-Morris 1989). Whatever the case, it appears to have been more successful in its hunting and gathering adaptation to the Negev than the Geometric Kebaran, which it probably replaced and absorbed, following a short period of contemporaneity (e.g., Shluhat Qeren II, Lagama North XII, Azariq X, Mushabi XIX).

Site size, numbers of hearths and the innovation of stone-filled roasting pits, together with the intensity of occupation of some sites indicate larger agglomerations of several nuclear families – at least on occasion (Azariq XII, Mushabi V, Mushabi XIV/1, Ramat Matred II) (Goring-Morris 1990). Sites are particularly profuse in the lowland dunes, especially in northern Sinai, but also occur at higher elevations in the Negev. Microliths are profuse, and are habitually fabricated by the microburin technique into arch backed bladelets and *lamelles scalenes* (Figure 11). Other tools include scrapers, as well as numbers of more massive tools, the latter perhaps associated with plant processing. A few groundstone tools (mortar and pestle), as well as bone tools are attested (see Figures 6, 11). Marine mollusks are often quite abundant.

During the Middle Epipaleolithic other groups also emerged, as evidenced by the partially coeval Mushabian, whose geographic distribution is limited to the Negev and Sinai southwards from the Beersheva Valley. Contrary to various claims, no convincing evidence has been presented to indicate the presence of genuine Mushabian occurrences from Transjordan, while none are currently documented south of the Central Negev Highlands (though this is probably a result of research designs).

On techno-typological grounds the origins of the Mushabian are more convincingly demonstrated either locally or in Transjordan, e.g., the Nizzanan (Goring-Morris 1987, 1989), the Nebekian and Qalkhan (Garrard et al. 1994; Henry 1982), rather than the previously postulated Nile Valley and North African derivation (Phillips and Mintz 1977; Bar-Yosef 1981; Bar-Yosef and Vogel 1987). Whatever the case, a desert origin seems likely. It coalesced primarily in the Sinai and Negev lowlands, rapidly coming into contact and probable competition with local Geometric Kebaran groups, which were replaced and/or absorbed (e.g., the Qerenian, and miscellaneous assemblages such as Lagama North XII, Mushabi XIX and Azariq X).

Mushabian lithic technology is represented by rather short, stubby blade/let blanks produced from cores tending to rather globular shapes. Though single platform cores predominate, opposed platform and changed orientation forms are also common. Raw materials are almost exclusively flint and chert. On the basis of microlithic forms several facies have been defined, all characterized by the habitual use of the microburin technique. Microburins are often evenly divided between proximal and distal forms. In its most common 'classic' manifestation, sizeable arch backed to scalene bladelet forms predominate. Stylistic analysis of microliths has revealed two basic patterns – a more obvious one with probably chronological connotations, and a more subtle regional arrangement. These are accompanied by smaller quantities of splayed, backed bladelets. Some of the other facies featuring asymmetric or symmetric trapeze forms manufactured by the microburin technique and, in some instances, serration of working edges may reflect the absorption and acculturation of local Geometric Kebaran groups – the presence of two coeval socio-cultural groups exploiting the shared resources in the same area would undoubtedly have led to stresses which would have had to be resolved. An example of an apparently violent solution is found in the Nile Valley (from a later date) but other options may be envisaged (Wendorf 1968).

The Mushabian displays a broadly similar pattern to the Geometric Kebaran in terms of elevational distributions, both by assemblage numbers and total tool frequencies; most sites cluster in lowland dune locations (200–400 m asl), although a few are also documented from intermediate elevations in the highlands (600 m asl). As noted previously, however, there is a perceptible bimodality of site sizes, whether measured in terms of assemblages according to size categories, or on the basis of tools in each size category. But this does not seem to correlate particularly with elevation – the largest sites are also among the few sites in the highlands. Multiple hearths are a common feature of the largest Mushabian sites; while it is possible that such sites may be composites of several discrete occupations by the same group, their regularity in appearance and internal spatial organization makes it likely that they represent single occupational events (furthermore, no evidence for a similar pattern has been forthcoming in Geometric Kebaran contexts) (Phillips and Mintz 1977; Goring-Morris 1987). Such variation in site sizes could reflect the use of the same locality for different purposes by the same group (Binford 1980). Smaller sites usually contain a single hearth.

Lithic tool assemblages display little diversity according to either elevation, location or size. In the largest sites, though, very rare artifacts on limestone – pestles, pounders, or shallow unmodified 'bowls' (often ochre-stained) – as well as massive flint artifacts do occur. Direct evidence for faunal and floral exploitation is lacking. Bone tools are limited to a point and spatula from Mushabi XIV/1. Marine mollusks of Mediterranean derivation (*Dentalium* and *Columbella*) have commonly been recovered from larger occupations, but not in large quantities.

Proximity to water sources was clearly a major

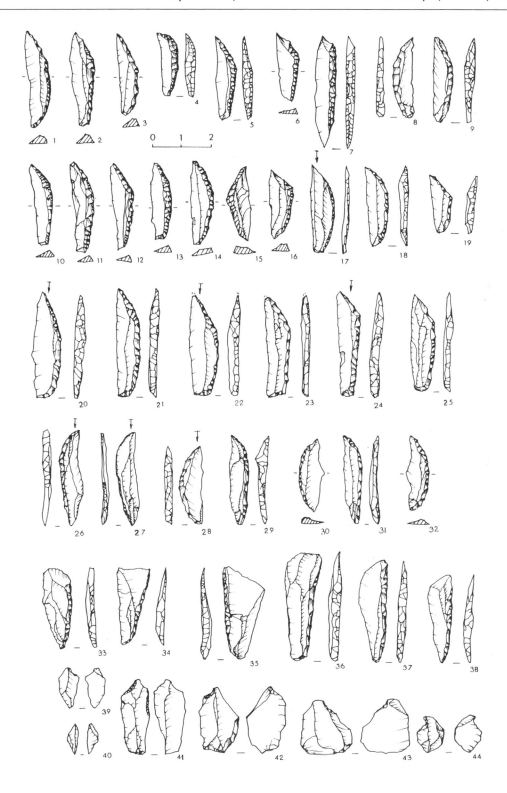

Figure 11   Microliths of the Middle Epipaleolithic 'Mushabian': 1–6, 41–42, Mushabi V; 7, 10–16 Mushabi XIV/1; 8–9, 18–19, 40, Ramat Matred II; 17, 26–29, 37–38, 43–44, Azariq XII; 20–24, 35–36, Nahal Nizzana XIV; 25, 30–32, 34, 39–40, Azariq XX

determinant of specific Mushabian site locations. However, a number of sites do appear considerably removed from possible water sources, perhaps indicating less tethering to this resource than was evident for the Geometric Kebaran. Mushabian groups often appear to have favored exposed locations or vantage points in the local topography.

The specific clustering and sizes of sites indicates a pattern of coalescence and dispersion at a subregional level, but there is no obvious evidence from the composition of tool-kits for differential exploitation of the various environmental settings.

The few systematically-investigated Mushabian sites have yielded a quantity and variability of groundstone tools similar to the Geometric Kebaran.

The Ramonian

The Ramonian has previously appeared under various headings and, like the Mushabian, is a purely Negev and Sinai manifestation (Goring-Morris 1987). There are compelling techno-typological data to suggest viewing it as deriving from the Mushabian, but various features warrant retaining its separate status. Unfortunately few C14 dates are available, though a range from *ca.* 13/13,500–12/11,500 years seems a provisional estimate for the threefold sequence. In its latest manifestation, the Terminal Ramonian, it is likely to have been contemporary with the early Natufian, and thus straddles the Middle to Late Epipaleolithic interface.

Ramonian lithic assemblages differ from the Mushabian in several significant aspects. There is a marked tendency through the sequence to use chalcedony as the preferred raw material and there may be evidence for heat treatment. Cores tend to be single platform, pyramidal varieties and blade/let blanks are frequently quite narrow and elongated. The tools are characterized by the ramon point – a commonly concave backed and obliquely truncated bladelet manufactured using the microburin technique (Figure 12). A marked preference for distal tips and microburins is present. Ramon points tend to be highly standardized. Another possible difference lies in the probable presence of a quite separate reduction sequence for larger tools, such as scrapers. These are made on thick blades, often with double patination, sometimes featuring typical 'Aurignacian' lateral retouch. Of chronological significance is the added presence in some assemblages of helwan lunates in varying quantities, together with other Early 'Natufian' features, such as spokeshave notches and denticulates (Goring-Morris 1987; Marks and Simmons 1977). These features probably indicate contemporaneity and a degree of interaction with the early Natufian of the Mediterranean zones to the north and, particularly, east.

The Ramonian settlement pattern contrasts markedly with those that preceded it. Although the majority of occurrences continue to cluster in the lowland dunes (with an emphasis on the western Negev rather than northern Sinai, in contrast to the Mushabian), for the first time significant numbers also appear at the highest elevations on loess-covered surfaces in the Irano-Turanian zone (Marks and Simmons 1977; Goring-Morris 1985). Perhaps most compelling in terms of this shift is the observation that they include many of the larger tool assemblages. A third peak can be distinguished at intermediate elevations (500–700 m asl) within the Irano-Turanian corridor; this is apparent both in terms of assemblages and tool totals. Whereas overall most Ramonian assemblages fall into the 50–250 tool category, in terms of total tools for each assemblage size category the pattern is somewhat different with a bimodal distribution – the principal peak represented by assemblages in excess of 750 tools, and the other centred on the 50–750 tool category. There appears to be a tendency for the larger assemblages to cluster in highland settings, although this is by no means exclusive. Stylistic analysis of the ramon points indicates that at least two partially overlapping provinces may be discernible.

The specific location of Ramonian sites generally indicates a pronounced disinterest in proximity to water sources – both in the highlands and at lower elevations – although Ein Qadis II is an exception. Rather, exposed locations with extensive vistas along the principal natural routes of communication are the main tethering agents; in such localities clusters of sites are found.

Unfortunately, none of the upland sites investigated to date have been *in situ*, so there is little information concerning internal spatial arrangements within such occurrences. In two instances occupations are located close to bedrock mortars (Ein Qadis II and Har Harif I); although it is tempting to assign these to the sites, hence reflecting the addition of a new processing technology, direct confirmation is lacking. In the lowlands too data are scanty; however, in the largest sites several hearths do occur at Shunera XXI, accompanied by quantities of burnt stones. Smaller sites appear to contain single hearths. Marine mollusks are not especially profuse, although a few examples of Red Sea species are documented.

The composition of Ramonian lithic assemblages display considerable variability in terms of elevational setting – highland assemblages are more diverse, with less of an emphasis on the microlithic element. This seems to reflect more than the state of preservation of assemblages, and a functional interpretation is to be preferred. In this context, it is interesting that the overlap in stylistic provinces is most pronounced in the highland area.

Thus the Ramonian represents a departure from previous patterns in that the two major phytogeographic zones (the highland Irano-Turanian and the lowland Saharo-Arabian) appear to have been exploited

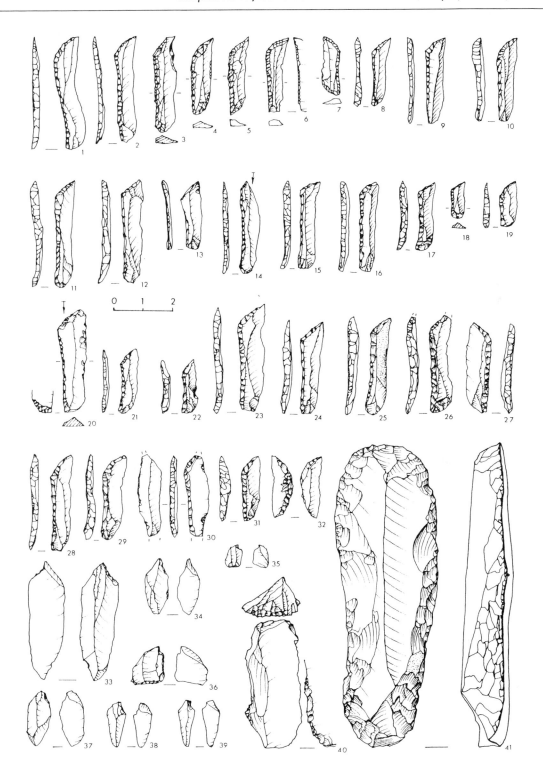

Figure 12 Tools of Middle Epipaleolithic 'Early and Middle Ramonian': 1–7, Mushabi I; 8–10, 33, Nahal Lavan 1003; 11–13, Azariq XIX; 14–19, 37–39, 41, Shunera XXI; 20–22, 36, Har Harif KV; 23–24, Nahal Nizzana XII; 25–27, 34, Har Harif II; 28–32, 35, Ein Qadis II; 40, Har Harif K6 or K7

differentially; it seems likely, though currently unproven, that this may reflect seasonal patterns of aggregation and dispersion by groups whose local ranges transected the different environmental zones.

The Late Epipaleolithic – ca. 12,250–10,000 BP

The Late Epipaleolithic is frequently considered synonymous with the Natufian Culture, which in many general treatments is often regarded as a rather monolithic entity. However, research beyond the confines of the area where it was first discovered and documented reveal that, far from being homogeneous, the Natufian should also be regarded as a complex, comprising a whole range of local adaptations and sharing a range of common traits to varying degrees through both time and space. Thus, in addition to the general sequential subdivision into Early, Late and Final phases spanning some 2500 years, it is also now possible to recognize at least five separate regional provinces or facies. Thus the more sedentary, 'classic' Core Area Natufian is located in the central Levantine Mediterranean zone with three phases and probably also several regional facies (Carmel, Jordan Valley, Galilee, Lebanese Beqaa, etc.). In the desert to the south, the Late Negev Natufian and the local Final Natufian equivalent, the Harifian, are well defined. The Terminal Ramonian is, as noted above, probably at least partially coeval with the Early Natufian of adjacent areas. In the southern Jordan corridor two Early Natufian facies can be discerned, while the Jebel Druze and adjacent Black Desert area appears to have another Natufian variant, and still further north are the Euphrates Late and Final Natufian. Outside the classic core area some are well-documented in terms of time, space and adaptational mode – such as the Negev Desert Natufian and Harifian – others, such as the Jebel Druze variant, remain poorly defined at present.

One of the most uncertain aspects of the Natufian has to do with its origins, particularly in the core area, where the early Natufian appears quite abruptly and fully fledged, with its complement of distinctive architecture, cemeteries, artistic endeavors, lithic knapping tradition and other hallmarks. Most sites are newly founded, and even where Early Natufian occupations overlie Geometric Kebaran levels (e.g. Hayonim), they are separated by a clear unconformity. Though many elements are indeed documented earlier, the scale and intensity of most facets of the Core Area Natufian material repertoire west of the Rift Valley are impressive and distinctive. However, this seemingly radical shift is perhaps more a reflection of research priorities than reality, and has to do with the relative dearth of larger scale investigations of the Middle Epipaleolithic in the region. Though extremely restricted in scope, the recent tests of both Early and Middle Epipaleolithic megasites in the Azraq Basin indicate that

the emphasis on such major contrasts may ultimately be misleading (see also Kaufman 1992).

One of the few regions to document continuity from Middle to Late Epipaleolithic is the Negev and Sinai, where the late Ramonian displays continuity into the Terminal Ramonian by the acquisition of several typically Natufian traits in the lithic repertoire, with the rest of the material culture remains, apart from Red Sea and Mediterranean mollusks, being impoverished (e.g. Mushabi IV, Shunera VII and Nahal Sekher 23, Har Harif K7). However, the Terminal Ramonian is envisaged as continuing the earlier Ramonian mode of a mobile adaptation over a large territory. Here, the question arises as to the precise nature of interaction and chronology between the Terminal Ramonian and the Early Natufian of neighbouring areas – who is influencing whom? Currently the chrono-stratigraphic framework is unable to provide an unequivocal answer. It is, however, of some interest to note the presence of isolated assemblages in the Negev, such as Azariq XV and Shunera XIII, which appear to be genuine Early Natufian campsites. On stylistic grounds these appear to represent (contemporary or later) occasional forays across the Arava by Natufian groups based east of the Arava in Moab and Edom (e.g., Tabaqa and Beidhal). Another region where some continuity may be present is southern and eastern Transjordan, though there is some uncertainty as to the integrity of some of the candidate assemblages in the south.

Discussion

The sum total of research over the past 25 years has significantly enlarged the data base for the period from 20–10,000 years ago. Although various gaps remain to be filled, the broad chronological framework is in place. Most characteristic, perhaps, is the wide range of variability at the stylistic level and the rapid pace of change (in prehistoric terms). This diversity reflects the dynamic pace of development and interaction of small hunter-gatherer bands with the landscape, readjusting their specific adaptations (within the bounds of their technological and social skills) as the physical conditions about them constantly changed.

At various times populations would have been quite isolated, at others contacts would have been eased. Territorial size, delineation and the mobility of bands would thus be likely to have depended on the specific setting, mix and distribution of resources at any given time. These are reflected in the areal spreads, depths, densities and specific contents of occupation sites, indicating the specific array of resources available. It must be emphasized that the vast majority of sites are not located in specific settings typical of the surrounding terrain, but rather in locations to maximize access to the resources to be exploited: water, plants, animals, raw materials, shelter, lines of communication, etc. Thus, localities with a wide array and dense availability of resources would have necessitated less mobility, and then over shorter distances, and could have supported larger populations (e.g., the Israeli Coastal Plain, the eastern flanks of the Rift Valley) than other more peripheral areas, where increased mobility would be advantageous and, commonly, necessary. In the latter instances, interband contacts could either be small scale (as, for example, the Geometric Kebaran in the Negev and Sinai) or could be achieved by short-term, seasonal aggregation of large groups (e.g., the Desert Natufian of the Negev, and probably on an even larger scale in the Azraq Basin earlier in the Epipaleolithic), the location being largely determined by the local, clumped availability of some specific, seasonal resource(s). Taking the Epipaleolithic as a whole it is thus likely that, as Binford was careful to stress but which is commonly overlooked, the full spectrum from forager to collector type adaptations were practised by the population occupying the Levant, even among populations sharing many common traits in terms of the material remains.

As to future fieldwork research orientations in the Levantine Epipaleolithic, given present regional political and financial realities, these will undoubtedly be largely dependent on external constraints or opportunities. Nevertheless, several avenues of research appear promising. Among these are the excavation of large horizontal exposures of sites focusing on internal spatial organization, particularly on Geometric Kebaran (and Natufian) sites. This will almost certainly be at the expense of methodical recovery techniques, given the nature of the material record, though this can be countered by well-planned sampling techniques. Otherwise, we are likely to remain bogged down in narrow test trenches, which provide virtually no data concerning spatial organization and other, non-microlithic, material remains.

Another area of study concerns the retrieval of meaningful botanical samples from occupation sites. The all too rare preservation of organic material at sites such as Ohalo and Abu Hureyra vividly illustrates the potential contribution of such assemblages to comprehending subsistence strategies and local environmental conditions. However, given the nature of sediments in the region, a combination of good fortune and judicious choice of site and retrieval techniques are required to fulfill expectations. These should supplement more, and more detailed, pollen cores throughout the region.

Ongoing attempts at conjoins from small, well-preserved occupations in the Negev are providing promising results with regard to specific lithic reduction techniques employed in particular assemblages, that appear more reliable than traditional studies of lithic technology by observation of cores and debitage alone (Marder, personal communication). Variations are already indicated between different phases of the Ramonian sequence. Furthermore these studies also provide promising data for spatial analyses within sites.

Last, but by no means least, without a rugged and detailed chronological framework, the definition of ranges of, and interactions between, the specific groups which roamed the southern Levant some 10–20,000 years ago will not be attainable.

Acknowledgments

I am grateful to Ofer Bar-Yosef for originally introducing me to the Levantine Epipaleolithic and for many conversations concerning the subject over the past two decades. I have also benefited from fruitful discussions with Anna Belfer-Cohen, Ofer Marder and Erella Hovers in recent years. Finally, I wish to thank Tom Levy for his encouragement and infinite patience, which finally brought this chapter to fruition.

OHALO II – AN EARLY EPIPALEOLITHIC LAKESHORE SETTLEMENT

The excellent preservation of organic materials at the recently investigated Masraqan site of Ohalo II on the southwest short of Lake Kineret affords a rare opportunity to reconstruct a hunter-gatherer settlement dated by a large series of C14 dates between 20–18,500 BP (Nadel 1990, 1991; Nadel and Hershkovitz 1991; Kislev et al. 1992). Located at -212 m below sea level, the occupation is located below what is considered to be the maximum extent of Lake Lisan at -180 m bsl and some 30 m lower than other Early Epipaleolithic sites in the Jordan Valley. Two explanations seem possible:

1. there was a temporary drop in the level of Lake Lisan at the time of occupation (see above); or
2. terminal or post-Lisan tectonics caused a large block upon which the site is located to subside some 20–30 m.

Given the tilted and eroded nature of the Lisan sediments upon which the site is located, and the role of tectonics in the demise of Lake Lisan, the second explanation seems more likely. Whatever the case, its preservation under the lake until exposure by a series of droughts in recent years has led to the remarkable preservation of organic remains.

The site, whose total extent was probably in the order of 1–1.5 dunams, was located close to the shoreline and comprised a series of spaced *fonds de cabane* parallel to the shore (see Figure 1.1). Three of the shelters were investigated, demonstrating that they were dug a little distance into sterile sediments and were D-shaped in plan, measuring up to 4.5 m, and with the entrance on the longer axis opening to the lake. The interior was bowl-shaped in section and 40 cm deep. It seems that the walls were constructed of brush and reeds set into the underlying Lisan sediments, and at least one shelter contained a large stone as a work surface. The three dwellings were probably not all occupied simultaneously. Small, well-defined hearths, a small circular stone-built feature, more amorphous roasting areas and garbage dumps are situated around and to the side of the shelters.

Of further note is the shallow burial of an extremely robust, mature female lying supine with fully-flexed legs, located some 5 m to the west of the nearest shelter. Less complete remains of at least two other individuals were found elsewhere on the site.

The excellent faunal and botanical preservation enables a glimpse at the wide range of dietary subsistence of hunter-gatherers at this time. Among the 40 plant species identified to date are large quantities of cereals, especially *Hordeum spontaneum* and *Aegilops geniculataperegrina*, but also *Triticum dicoccoides*, *Catabrosa aquatica* and *Avena* sp. (Kislev et al. 1992). The edible wild fruits include *Nitraria schoberi*, *Quercus* sp., and *Crataegus* sp. Based on all these remains, occupation is indicated during at least two periods: April/May and October/November. Among the faunal remains fish are prominent, as well as the more common medium-sized ungulates (gazelle, etc.). Interestingly, though distinct lithic concentrations are present, overall densities appear relatively low, leading to some doubt as to the intensity of occupation: short-term repeated visits appear the most likely interpretation.

Almost all the botanical species identified to date are Mediterranean, with the exception of *Nitraria Schoberi* which is more characteristic of the Irano-Turanian zone (Danin, personal communication), so it is likely that the lowlying reaches of the Rift Valley acted as a refuge for Mediterranean floral communities at this time.

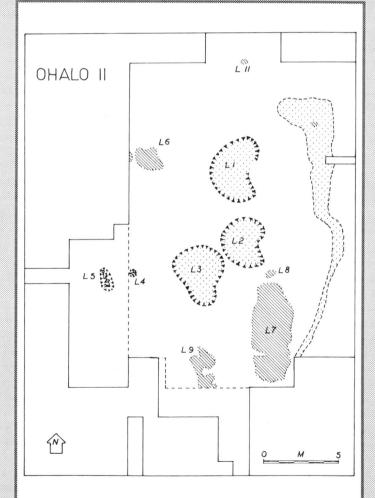

Figure 1.1 Plan of Early Epipaleolithic campsite of Ohalo II. Stippling denotes areas of high organic content; hatching represents hearths

11

THE FIRST SETTLED SOCIETIES – NATUFIAN (12,500–10,200 BP)

François Valla

Of all the prehistoric cultures in the Levant, the Natufian is often regarded as representing a particularly important episode. It is seemingly at this time, between 12,500 and 10,200 BP in radiocarbon years, that the conditions which transformed hunter-gatherer societies of the Geometric Kebaran to those of the first cultivators in the Pre-Pottery Neolithic first began to be put into place. Here, the differences between the cultural entities concerned appear more significant than anywhere else. This factor explains the deep interest with which scholars have closely studied the Natufian for over 60 years, in an effort to understand what happened during the two millennia of its existence (Figure 1).

Before we can offer an explanation of the phenomenon it is necessary to observe it, take measure of its complexity, and to describe it appropriately. Today there exists no consensus on the fundamental cultural traits of the Natufian. The debates focus on its geographical extent, whether a sedentary or mobile way of life was practised, the use of techniques such as the creation of clearings by fire, the preparation of land through cultivation, sowing, attitudes toward the gazelle (the hunting of which could be more or less controlled), and the actuality and extent of storage, not to mention the eventual hierarchization of society.

Archaeological evidence never has an unequivocal meaning, and this is more acute in prehistory than elsewhere. The view that each scholar has of the Natufian, therefore, depends upon a series of interpretations. The extreme fragility of our explanations must be stressed: with the help of hypotheses of varying boldness, all explanations try to account for situations which are themselves reconstructed from questionable opinions. In the following pages, I shall endeavor to present those main characteristics of Natufian material culture that have been recovered through excavation. Although it may be desirable to present an 'objective' account, the approach taken here leads us to enter several debates concerning the Natufian. It should thereby be possible to propose a dynamic view of the culture, without concealing the weaknesses of such a tentative approach. As in painting, all light presupposes dark corners.

The material

The industries

Identification of the Natufian rests upon its lithic industry (Figure 2). It has to be this way, since the Natufian was first recognized on the characteristics of this industry (Garrod 1932). Even today, we continue – on this basis alone – to attribute to the Natufian sphere of influence sites which lack all the other distinctive characteristics of the culture. Typically, the lithic industry makes rather eclectic use of the raw material (it can use on the same site a large variety of flints). Knapping results mainly in the production of flakes, most of them very small. There are more bladelets than blades, but usually these are relatively short. Most tools are microlithic and, among those, lunates are significant. 'Heavy duty tools' also appear. A particular type of bifacial retouch, ('the back of the implement is not blunted in the ordinary way, but is trimmed obliquely from both surfaces' (Garrod 1932: 261) termed Helwan retouch, is found frequently in the early Natufian phase, and tends to become less frequent through time, without it necessarily disappearing altogether.

These basic features are found, with some nuances, from Lebanon to the Negev, and from the middle Euphrates to southern Jordan. But envisaging the Natufian simply from the characteristics of its flint industry would be a singularly reductive approach. Such a view would fail to take into account the majority of the precise aspects of Natufian culture which form its originality and mark its most significant differences with the preceding and following cultures in the region. Next to the flint industry, the working of non-siliceous stone (basalt, limestone, etc.) and bone undergoes a relative blossoming. Previously these materials were worked only to a limited extent, but with the Natufian, their use becomes commonplace.

Mortars, pestles and grinding stones which are traditional implements although rare, now become common (Plate 2; Wright 1991). Grooved stones, absent since Aurignacian times, reappear. These are made in basalt, limestone, sandstone or steatite. Their form and

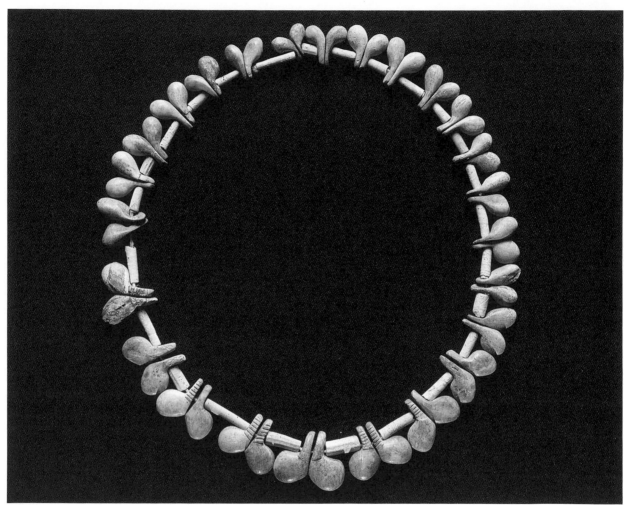

Plate 1   Reconstruction of a necklace made of bone and dentalia found in a Natufian grave at el-Wad Cave, Mt. Carmel (courtesy of the Israel Antiquity Authority and The Israel Museum, Jerusalem)

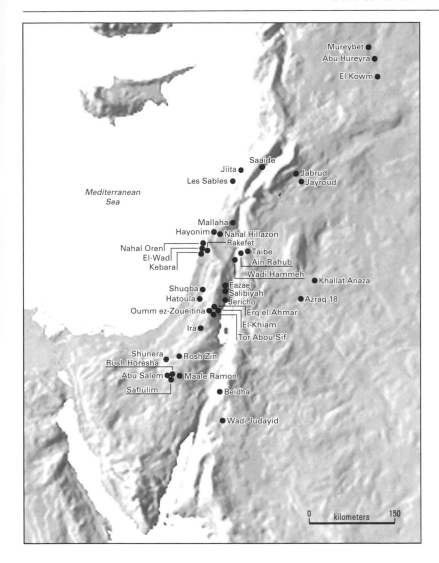

Figure 1 Map of Natufian site distribution in the Levant

dimensions vary, suggesting a variety of functions. Usually they have been interpreted as bone tool polishers or shaft-straighteners. Also known are several flat querns. More than their form, the dimensions of some vessels and pestles reveal an understanding of the raw material, a boldness of conception and a dexterity, all of which are unprecedented. Some mortars are as much as 60 cm in height. Furthermore, some of the basalt objects show fairly elaborate geometric designs.

Bone craftsmanship exhibits a growth parallel to that of stone (Campana 1989; Stordeur 1981, 1991), and there are both tools and ornamental elements (Figure 3). Traditional artifacts, mainly pointed implements made on the split long bone of a small herbivore, increase in number. New types appear, such as armatures (spearheads or arrows, some of them barbed), unknown in the Levant since the Aurignacian, and small bipoints. The most unexpected object, the 'sickle' or reaping knife,

integrates a handle and a grooved haft to facilitate the inclusion of flint armatures. Usually these tools are made either on a long bone or a rib. The most impressive are decorated with an animal representation at the extremity of the handle (Plate 3). The ornamental elements include perforated teeth (fox canines) (Belfer-Cohen 1991b: 571), the extremities of sectioned bones (gazelle phalanges, partridge tibio-tarsus) and various beads, such as the well-known 'twin-pendants' (Garrod and Bate 1937: 39) which combines two pyriform elements.

Shells were also worked for ornamentation purposes. Dentalium shells (*Dentalium* sp.), either complete or sectioned, were used to produce elongated beads (see Plate 1). Sometimes the wall of the shell was perforated. Dentalium shell beads are by far the most dominant form, followed by the less common use of *Columbella rustica*, *Nassa* sp., *Conus* sp., etc., which were sometimes worked in such a way as to allow them to be hung. Most often

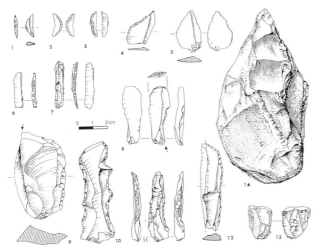

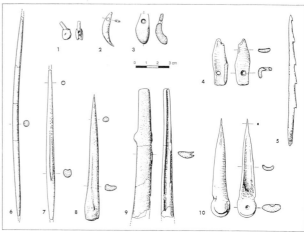

1—3: Lunates (2: with Helwan retouch), 4: Truncation, 5: Retouched flake, 6—7: Backed bladelets, 8: Burin-scraper, 9: Burin, 10: Denticulated blade, 11: Borer, 12: Sickle-blade, 13: Core, 14: Heavy duty tool (pick). (from Hayonim Terrace and Mallaha). Drawing S. Golay and D. Ladiray

Figure 2 Natufian flint industry

1—3: Bone pendants (1: Distal end of a phalange of gazelle combined with dentalium, 2: Canine tooth of a fox, 3: Imitation of a cervid canine tooth), 4: 'Retouchoir', 5—7: Projectile points, 8 and 10: Points, 9: Sickle haft. Drawing D. Ladiray

Figure 3 Natufian bone industry

this involved the perforation of the last whorl, or the abrasion of the apex. In addition to these shells, which are mainly of Mediterranean origin, some freshwater species, mainly *Theodoxus jordani*, were also put to good use.

Architecture

The newest phenomenon is undoubtedly that of the development of architecture (Perrot 1966, 1968). The existence of semi-subterranean structures is not an absolute innovation, but Natufian houses appear to be much more carefully planned than those of the preceding periods, and they required considerably more layout arrangement and installation. Moreover, they were not isolated, like the hut at Ein Gev, but were formed in small groups, which explains why we are able to refer to Natufian 'villages'. At Mallaha (Eynan) (Figure 4), the houses seem to have been aligned along the length of a slope into which they were cut. Circular or semi-circular in shape, they were delimited by a supporting wall made from carefully organized dry stones, sometimes preserved to more than a meter in height (see Plate 1.1, Window 1, p. 186). In one case, this wall was replaced by a covering of crushed limestone coated with red paint. This is one of the earliest examples of the creation of an artificial construction material. The floors were not constructed but did support installations such as hearths or arrangements of limestone slabs (Figure 5 p. 175).

Mallaha remains the most spectacular example of Natufian construction, but it is not unique in this respect.

At Hayonim, at least six 'cells', around two meters in diameter, are clustered together in the front area of the cave (Figure 6 p. 175; Bar-Yosef 1983: 14–15, 1991: 86–7). Despite their small size, most of them contained a hearth. Subsequently, more houses were built on the terrace in front of the cave (Valla et al. 1989). The two houses at Wadi Hammeh 27, on a ridge between two ravines, are rather different from those just described. They are much larger and less deeply buried. The first, ovular and with a diameter of 14 m, comprised a series of three concentric walls which defined three steps in part of the habitation. The second, adjacent to the other, was horseshoe-shaped. A small stone and clay wall along with some post-hole supports defined the limit of the habitation (Edwards 1991: 125).

In the Negev, the site of Rosh Zin contained at least four adjacent houses, basically circular, from 2.5 m to 3.5 m in diameter. Each of these houses was delimited by a dry stone wall (Henry 1976: 318). In the same region, the Harifian – the culture which corresponds to the final Natufian, but with its own particular lithic industry and, for the first time, 'proto-arrow points' – also sees the use of semi-subterranean houses. These structures are sometimes even a little more elaborate than their northern counterparts. At Ramat Harif, access to one of the houses was via a vestibule. In the main room, a raised limestone slab leaning against the wall served as a table. Elsewhere, stones with cup-marks were found on floor surfaces next to hearths (Goring-Morris 1991: 180 ff.). There is less architecture in the Euphrates Valley, but the presence of semi-subterranean structures is well attested at Abu

Plate 2 Two Natufian limestone mortars from the Hayonim Terrace (photograph: F. Valla)

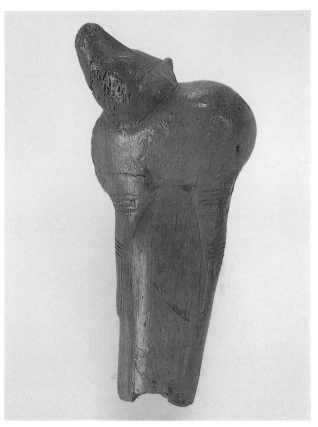

Plate 3 Young gazelle or deer representation on a probable bone sickle handle. El-Wad Cave (courtesy the Israel Antiquity Authority and The Israel Museum, Jerusalem)

Hureyra, where pits connected by passages appear to have served as dwellings (Moore 1991: 279).

Much has been said regarding Natufian pits, often interpreted as silos, which could attest to the general adoption of storage techniques. It is advisable to be cautious on this point. Mallaha, where the architecture is more developed than anywhere else, is the only site at which pits are numerous. They are of varying form and dimensions. The walls of some are coated, but the fills show that they had a variety of functions, such as graves, rubbish pits, and so on. All that can be said at the moment is that it is not out of the question that some of these pits may have served as silos. The presence of a small pit lined with limestone slabs on Hayonim Terrace could confirm this interpretation (Plate 4 p. 176). Apart from these two sites, Abu Hureyra is the only other place mentioned where structures were possibly built for storage purposes.

Food

The question of storage introduces the problem of the exploitation of plant food resources. The presence of flint blades displaying gloss on one edge led Dorothy Garrod to propose that the Natufians could have been the first farmers in the Levant (Garrod 1932: 236). Subsequently, it was suggested that rather than being farmers, they limited themselves to the systematic collection of wild cereals, which grew in dense natural 'fields' in the region. Since then, the study of carbonized plant remains has shown that all such seeds come from morphologically wild types. Nevertheless, most scholars accord with the view that the domestication of cereals came about through unconscious selection due to 'primitive' cultivation practices (Hillman and Davies 1990: 159). The remaining problem, therefore, is to know whether or not the

Natufians actually cultivated wild cereals. The main characteristic of domestic types is that they lose their ability to disperse seeds. This genetically-controlled faculty disappears through mutation. Under natural conditions, domestic-type mutants are automatically eliminated. However, in the case of harvesting by humans (if the ears are cut with sickles or if the plants are entirely uprooted), there is every chance of finding them in the crop, and if sown, then the proportion of mutants among the seeds will tend to increase from year to year. They will multiply until the farmer becomes aware of their presence and the benefits of encouraging them. Could the wild seeds of the Natufian correspond to this intermediary period, where the mutants remain as yet unnoticed in the crop? The answer partly depends on the time necessary for the mutants to become visible. Unfortunately, this time itself depends on a large number of factors which are not readily accessible, such as the stage of plant maturity when harvesting took place, the rate of sowing new areas of land, or the relative frequencies of different harvesting techniques. Some scholars think that domestication could have taken place within 20–25 years (Zohary), while

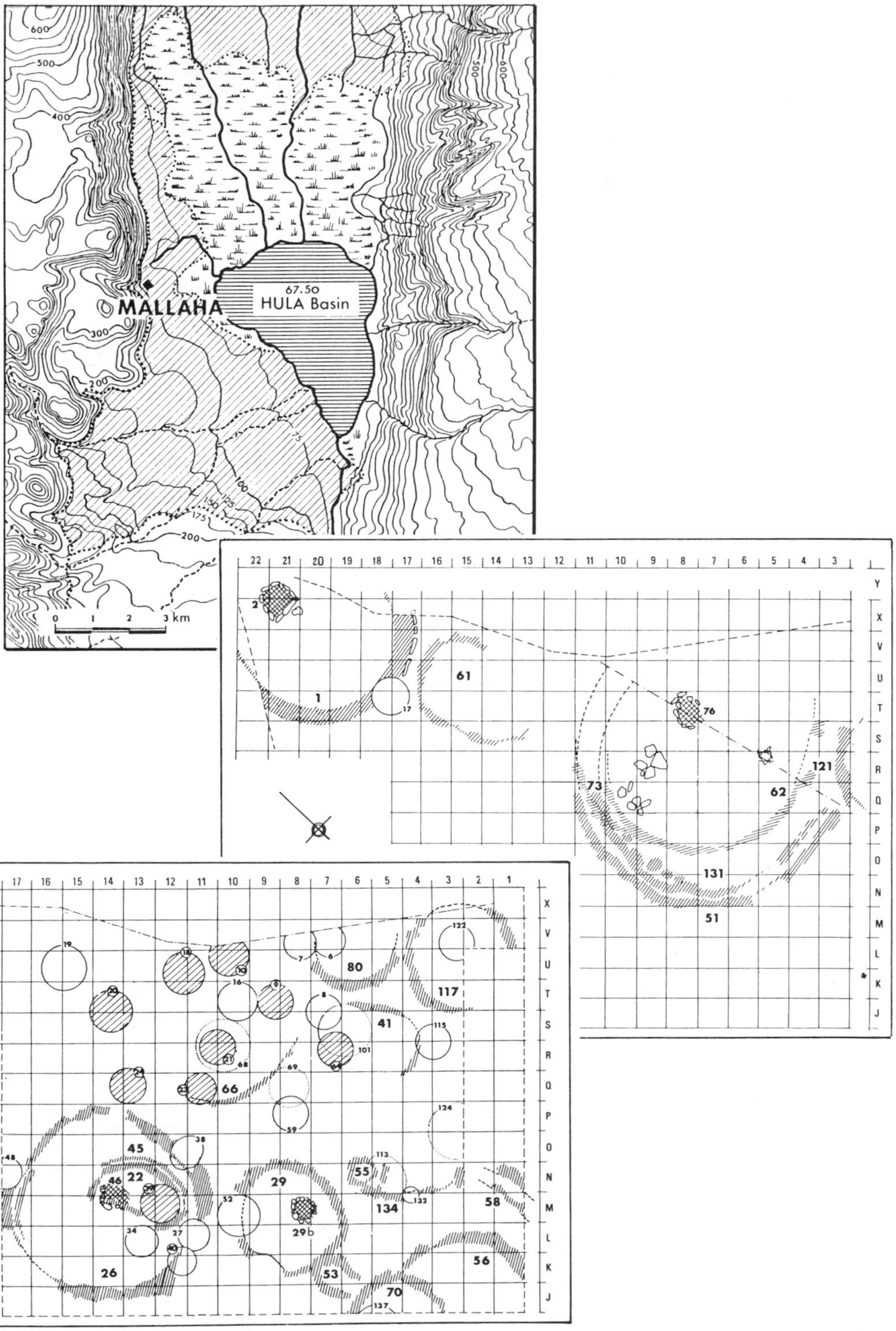

Figure 4 Detailed map of the topography near Mallaha. Maps of the Early and Late Natufian houses at the site. Hatched circles indicate grave pits

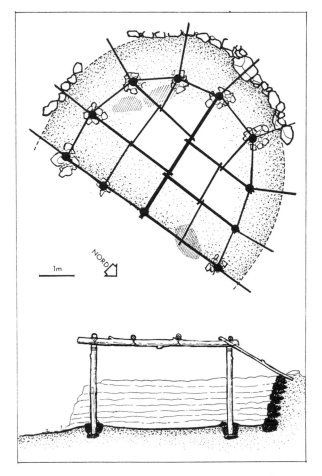

Figure 5 Plan view; reconstruction of roof from large Natufian house at Mallaha

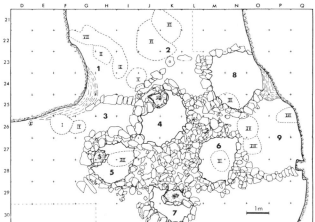

Figure 6 Plan of the Natufian structures at Hayonim Cave (Roman numerals indicate the graves; after O. Bar-Yosef 1991)

others suggest a margin of 20–200 years (Hillman and Davies 1990: 189–93) or even greater (Willcox 1991: 26). While awaiting better information, we can try to take relevant aspects of the archaeological context into account. At Abu Hureyra, the only site which provides a broad sample of plant remains, the wide variety of gathered species (around 150, and almost all edible) do seem entirely characteristic of a population of hunter-gatherers (Hillman et al. 1989: 257). The micro-traces left on the sickle blades could be another discriminative factor. The striations which accompany use-polish from the early Natufian onwards could indicate worked land and, therefore, intentional sowing. However, some scholars have stressed the fact that these striations are ambiguous, and have remarked that labor does not facilitate the growth of wild cereals. The only change apparent with the Natufian concerns gathering techniques, namely the use of sickles. This use, which could have ultimately facilitated domestication, is neither a necessary nor sufficient condition of it. At this stage, therefore, we have no

indication capable of supporting the hypothesis that the Natufians could have sown cereals and could have been the first farmers in the Levant.

In contrast to plant food remains, poorly preserved everywhere except on the Euphrates, faunal remains are abundant on Natufian sites. The Negev sites, where such remains are rare, are the exception. The structure of the 'tableau de chasse' ('the bag') displays several characteristics. Small or medium-sized herbivores dominate. These are mainly gazelle but, depending on the environment, there are also caprids (Rosh Horesha), equids (Mureybet), or cervids (Mallaha). Carnivores are rare except for the fox. Lagomorphs and rodents (hare and occasionally squirrel) were hunted. Birds became, for the first time, important game (Pichon 1984). Fish, again when the environment was suitable, reptiles (tortoise, lizard) and both land and freshwater mollusks were also exploited. In comparing the Natufian fauna with that from preceding periods (unfortunately not well known as yet), there is the impression that very old practices were maintained and even emphasized, such as the dependence for meat supplies on gazelle populations, at the same time as new practices, aimed at expanding the field of resources to include animals of small or very small size, were introduced. The large herbivores – cattle, fallow deer, red deer – seem to have been exploited only occasionally. For the first time perhaps, the impact of human action on the surrounding fauna was such as to provoke visible reactions. In the region of sedentary villages, the culling of gazelle herds (perhaps mainly males) seems to have caused a degeneration of the species resulting in the extreme variability of the size of the animals (Cope 1991). Furthermore, the modifications of the environment around the villages induced new behaviors on the part of several species. The sparrow and the mouse used the new

Plate 4 Storage pit lined with limestone slabs. Hayonim Terrace (photograph: F. Valla)

ecological niche created to develop their commensalism with humans (Tchernov 1991: 323–8). The reaction of the wolf possibly led to its domestication, attested for the first time in the Levant during the Natufian (Tchernov and Kolska-Horwitz 1991: Davis and Valla 1978).

Mortuary evidence

The Natufians often chose to bury their dead within villages. Sometimes, the graves tend to be grouped next to houses, such as those of the Early Natufian at Hayonim Cave (Belfer-Cohen 1989), and in the Late Natufian at Mallaha and Nahal Oren (Perrot et al. 1988; Noy 1989). However, in the early phases at Mallaha, the systematic superimposition of houses above burials suggests that the dead could have been, at least sometimes, buried under house floors. Many of the graves show no particular arrangement, consisting simply of a pit, refilled after the deposition of the body. There are, however, some graves which are actually constructed: i.e. the pit was partially or sometimes completely lined with stones (Hayonim, Nahal Oren) or coated (Mallaha). Occasionally, the pit was sealed with flat stones. The external marking of the grave was sometimes carried out by the placing of a stone, flat or standing. More complex examples involved the installation of stone paving (Erq el-Ahmar) (Neuville 1951: 109) or the insertion of a large breached mortar into the grave pit (Stekelis and Yisraeli 1963). But in most cases, nothing indicated the location of the grave to the living population.

As with the graves, the modes of deposition of the body are not uniform. There are individual burials in which the body seems to have been interred without any concern for its position. It may lie on its back, front or side, the limbs more or less flexed in a 'loose' position. Less frequently, the body was deliberately interred in the extended or flexed position. We do not know of any orientation principle, other than that determined by the slope of the floor into which the grave was cut (Hayonim Terrace) (Valla et al. 1991). On some occasions, a grave was cut into an earlier burial, with the disturbed bones being redeposited with the latter interment. There are also examples of graves containing several individuals, buried either together or one after the other. In such cases, the successive operations often caused disturbance which mixed up the remains of the previously deposited bodies. In El-Wad cave a grave held ten extended individuals (Garrod and Bate 1937: 14–15). A grave containing two extended individuals, accompanied by a flexed infant, was found in Hayonim Cave. Elsewhere, bodies interred in this way – sometimes a dozen together – are flexed in varying positions, some even forced flexed, knees to chin. As with the individual burials, it is likely that some of the corpses were deliberately placed in a precise position. A very different practice from those just described is also attested in the Natufian: the practice of reburial. In such cases, the skeleton only found its final resting place at least partly defleshed and often incomplete. Graves of this type are rare. Occasionally they also contain a primary burial.

In general, Natufian graves contain only skeletal remains. However, some of the dead were interred with ornamentation or wearing decorated clothing. Definite funerary materials are few, but the small amount found often appear to carry strong symbolic meaning. Sometimes stones were placed under the head of the deceased or organized to keep the body in the desired position. Other stones, sometimes quite large, were placed on the head, chest, joints, hands or feet. The use of ochre appears to have been infrequent. Manufactured objects are rare but include some cup-marked stones, and a large bone spatulate implement. Animal remains, hardly more numerous, do not represent food offerings, but are of particular interest: dogs, gazelle horn-cores, horse teeth, tortoise carapaces.

The treatment of the dead was not always limited to inhumation. Site deposits often contain human bones, like the many burnt skull fragments at Wadi Hammeh 27 (Edwards 1991: 146), which are difficult to interpret. Already in the Early Natufian a skull with atlas and axis was discovered on a floor surface near a hearth at Mallaha (Perrot 1966: 445). At the same site, a cranial cap which had been cut off, apparently deliberately, was lying on another floor. In the Early Natufian these finds are isolated. Later, towards the end of the period, the removal of the skull, with or without the mandible, almost became a custom on certain sites (Hayonim Cave, Nahal Oren), but we do not know what became of the bones which were removed. Short as it is, this survey of Natufian funerary practices reveals a complicated set of data probably not amenable to simple interpretation. Together, they display the preoccupations of a group towards a part of itself – its dead – which people do not seem to have tried to move away or keep separate from the living, even if the proximity of the dead was able to pose problems.

Art and decoration

Natufian ornamental elements attract attention due to their relative richness. Since they are often found in the 'protected' conditions of grave pits, it has been possible to carry out the reconstruction of a number of them. The most impressive combine bone and shell beads. At El-Wad, a necklace seems to have been made up of 25 'twin-pendants' separated by a similar number of lengths of dentalium shell (see Plate 1, p. 170). Some were made by simply linking together bone pendants, like a belt of perforated fox canines and a bracelet of partridge tibio-tarsus from Hayonim Cave. Others were produced from various combinations of dentalium shells and worn on the head, chest, or around the arms or legs. Examples of headdresses include one made from seven parallel rows of dentalium strung end to end, bands of dentalium assembled horizontally one below the other and falling onto the wearer's forehead, and rows of vertical dentalium falling in fringes from a circlet (Garrod and Bate 1937: plates VI and VII). These decorative elements do not appear in late Natufian graves, although the shells persist in site fills.

As with the decorative elements, art, at least that which is represented by the preserved materials, is not one of the characteristics of the prehistoric Levant prior to the Natufian. The relative frequency of artistic manifestations in this period, therefore, appears to be an innovation. These manifestations may be classified into three categories: 'single' objects (figurines, etc.), tools, and what may be considered as architectural elements. The materials used are stone, less often bone, and, exceptionally, modelled clay or eggshell (Turville-Petre 1932; Garrod and Bate 1937: 38–9; Neuville 1951: 125; Perrot 1966: 474; Henry 1976: 345; Belfer-Cohen 1991b: 570 ff.).

There is a realistic figurative art characterized by several conventions, one of the more common consisting of the gross enlargement of the subject's eyes. From there, one passes to schematic representations – sometimes difficult to interpret – and to a wide variety of designs which are more or less geometric. On some sites, excavations have recovered rather a large number of fragments displaying indecipherable incisions (Plate 5). The figurative art shows human and animal representations. The former is limited to 'single' objects; only one example displays a scene – an embracing couple in a seated position, sculpted in the round of a small block of

Plate 5 'Geometric' decoration under the rim of a basalt mortar. Mallaha (courtesy J. Perrot, CNRS)

calcite (Neuville 1951: 133 and P1 XV; Boyd and Cook 1993). Other pieces show individuals, sometimes reduced to only the head. The only clear human-animal association comes from Nahal Oren, where a long bone had a human face at one end and the head of a ruminant at the other (Noy 1991: 561). The animals represented, where they can be identified, seem to be herbivores, but there is also a 'scarab' from Mallaha. Sometimes representation is limited to the male sex. Among tools, bone sickle hafts may be carved in the shape of a herbivore (see Plate 3) and certain pestles show a phallus or an animal hoof.

The geometric motifs appear on various artifacts, the functions of which are not always discernible. Bone tools are rarely decorated. Designs may show basket or wickerwork, lines of dots, etc. Stone tools seem to be decorated more often. Designs appear on the body of vessels, pestles or, sometimes, grooved stones, and take the form of incisions, grooves, crenelated or scalloped lines, etc. The architectural elements are distinguished by their large dimensions. In this category I place a series of three engraved slabs which extend to around 1.3 m on one of the house walls at Wadi Hammeh 27. These slabs repeat, on several rows, a design of concentric lines surrounding a more or less square core. Another slab, 0.75 m long, in a secondary context at Hayonim Cave, displays a group of incisions which may represent a fish.

Population

I shall not put much emphasis on the physical aspects of the Natufian population known on the basis of around 400, often very incomplete, skeletons (Belfer-Cohen et al. 1991: 412). In general, Natufian people were dolichocephalic, although a tendency towards brachice-phaly is apparent in the population. One of the more interesting results stemming from the physical anthro-pological analysis is that there is evidence for a certain diversity between the inhabitants of different sites. Thus, the people at Mallaha and Kebara were taller than their neighbors at El-Wad, Hayonim, Nahal Oren and Shukba. Those at Hayonim and Mallaha possessed a more robust skeleton than those at Nahal Oren. These nuances are perhaps related to diet. In the same way, certain modifications come to light through time. Sexual dimorphism, measured by the difference in size between men and women, tends to diminish, which could be the result of living conditions becoming a little more difficult at the end of the period. However, broadly speaking, the Natufian skeleton shows a population free from serious diseases or deficiencies. The teeth are generally much more healthy than those of Neolithic peoples although, again, there are differences from one site to another. The people at Nahal Oren had more worn teeth than their congeners (Smith 1991). Another significant trait is that there are no signs of violence. We would, of course, like to learn more about the demographic structure of the population, but, besides the difficulties inherent in determining the age at death, especially for elderly individuals, it is well known that any archaeologically recovered population represents only a small proportion of the living population at the time.

Time and space

The foregoing analysis endeavored to put forward a global, yet static, image of the Natufian. In outlining the salient traits of the culture we were able to introduce some of its main innovations. However, this approach is somewhat limited because it does not take into account the variability of a cultural phenomenon which extends across profoundly different regions, and which occupies a period of more than 2000 years, during which neither the natural conditions nor the society itself remained unchanged. Already in the preceding pages it has proved impossible to avoid reference to regional specificities and chronological developments. It is these aspects which will now be emphasised in an attempt to place the Natufian culture in an historical perspective. Nevertheless, one should keep in mind that the seriation scheme and the correlations on which these views are based – explored elsewhere with more details (Valla 1987, Valla n.d.) – rest on interpretations, some of which are supported by solid stratigraphic data while others are just extrapolations.

Neither climate nor geography are, in themselves, sufficient to explain the solutions brought by people to the problems which confronted them. However, together they contribute to the creation of the framework within which these problems were presented and resolved. After years of trial and error, it seems that we are now beginning to understand something of the climatic fluctuations experienced during the Natufian. On average, temperatures at the end of the Pleistocene were still several degrees below those of today. But compared to the preceding periods, the Natufian was placed in a time of warming, probably accompanied in the southern Levant by an increase in rainfall. This is indicated in the variation of Oxygen 18 to Oxygen 16 in the eastern Mediterranean basin (Nesterhoff et al. 1983) and in the pollen diagrams obtained from the Hula Lake (Baruch and Bottema 1991 and Goldberg, this volume). The presence of palearctic migratory birds which no longer frequent the region confirm this reconstruction. Between 11,000 and 10,000 BP, a brief fluctuation – cold and probably dry – occurred. However, one must not overestimate the local impact of this episode: despite the dryness, the uplands of the Negev, it seems, continued to support trees. At Abu Hureyra, wild einkorn, which today has retreated 100 km to the north, and pistachios (equally dispersed) probably remained to provide for the inhabitants.

Early Natufian phase

As is often the case in prehistory, where cultural manifestations become visible only at a certain stage of maturity, the beginnings of the Natufian remain obscure. From a superficial observation one has the impression of a break in cultural tradition, accompanied by regional diversification. In Lebanon, the evidence is very limited and too elusive for us to rely on any of the proposed examples of continuity (Copeland 1991). In northern Israel the rupture is mainly expressed in the choice of inhabited places, in the extension and thickness of deposits at new sites, in new developments in the industries, etc. The break is less clear in the Negev than in the north because of the presence of lunates as early as the Final Ramonian. It is nevertheless indicated through a shift in settlement pattern: the highlands are abandoned and, contrary to that which occurs in the north, larger sites disappear while small ephemeral stations become the rule (Goring-Morris 1987: 433–6, this volume; Hall and Levy, ibid).

At this time, the most characteristic evidence of the Natufian comes from the Carmel and the Galilee areas. Sites are few and, for the most part, associated with a cave: Kebara, El-Wad, Hayonim. Wadi Hammeh 27, an open air site in the middle Jordan Valley, may also be considered as part of this group. The first occupation at Mallaha, another open air site on the bank of Lake Hula, could have taken place a little later. All of these sites are settled at low altitudes. The highest, Hayonim, is 250 m asl (Plate 6). Usually, they are found on the interface between the plain (coastal plain, Hula basin) and the mountains, sometimes in the proximity of a large spring. (Henry 1989).

The Early Natufian is not restricted to these few 'villages'. However, their extraordinary richness justifies the view that they represent the 'center' of the culture in the sense of a limited diffusion. Towards the south, the

Plate 6   General view of Hayonim Cave setting. Note the Mediterranean sea in the background (photograph: F. Valla)

coastal plain is completely empty. If sites did exist on the coast, they are now submerged and we are unaware of them. On the other hand, some sites are found in the Jordan basin both on high ground (Erq el-Ahmar: 555 m) and in the valley bottom (Fazael VI, Salibiyah XII, and perhaps Jericho, although the date of Natufian occupation there remains problematic). Further south, a highland site dating to before 12,000 BP exists on the eastern side of the Arava at Beidha (alt. 1020 m). Some other sites, at Wadi Judayid (alt. 1100 m) and on the margins of the Jordanian Desert at Tabaqa (alt. 705 m), are undoubtedly a little more recent. In contrast, the Negev sites which are smaller (often less than 80 m²) are found in lowland dunefields, to the west of the mountains that extend the Judean anti-cline.

This period lasted until around 11,250 BP. The lithic industries are characterized by the use of Helwan retouch on lunates. However, underlying their deep uniformity, which assures the cultural coherence of the Natufian, is an astonishing diversity from region to region and from one site to another. This diversity is expressed through technical choices (such as the use or refusal of a system of bladelet segmentation known as the microburin technique), through typological persistence (such as keeping relict tool types) and through stylistic preferences (as evidenced by the shape of lunates). At the regional level there is a general use of the microburin technique in the Negev as opposed to northern Israel where it is only sporadically encountered. On average, lunates are relatively longer in the south than in the north. They also tend to be more numerous than non-geometric microliths there, while the opposite is seen in the Carmel and Galilee area. At the site-to-site level, the moderate use of microburin technique at El-Wad (a unique situation in the 'center') is noticeable as is the presence of tools like Dhour Choueir bladelets at Mallaha, or the specificity of lunate shape – broader or narrower – on each of the sites

in the 'center'. Most of these choices cannot be understood in purely functional terms (despite interesting attempts by Byrd 1989b and Olszewski 1986). Some of them could be connected to the geographical origin of groups (Belfer-Cohen 1991: 182 argues that the Natufian industries are the result of a merging of older traditions). More precisely, they seem to attest to people's awareness of their social 'belonging' at a village, regional and cultural level (Valla 1984: 77 ff; 182 ff.).

These arguments may be borne out if we extend our examination to other aspects of the material assemblage. On moving away from the 'center', both stone and bone tools diminish very quickly in quantity and variety. They remain relatively abundant in the Judean desert and lower Jordan Valley and sometimes appear on the mountain sites south of the Transjordan (at Beidha and, particularly, Tabaqa, where it seems that relatively rich stone material was present). They are lacking in the Negev, but this may not be significant since bone is not preserved on the sites concerned. Even taking into account the disproportionate amount of excavation carried out in the north, this image undoubtedly reflects reality. The self esteem of individual villages in the 'center' is well attested by the choice of bone decorative elements. At Kebara, pyriform pendants largely dominate. The 'twin-pendants' are unique to El-Wad (see Plate 1). At Hayonim, fox teeth and partridge tibio-tarsus are particularly abundant, whereas sectioned gazelle phalanges seem to have been the favoured form at Mallaha and Wadi Hammeh 27. While it may be true that these differences are sometimes emphasized by the presence of one or two individuals wearing a type of bead repeated in a decorative piece, the virtual absence of, say, sectioned gazelle phalanges at Kebara and Hayonim appears highly significant in terms of the desire for group individualization.

This context helps in understanding the diversity of mortuary practices, although the time factor also has to be taken into consideration. All the villages of the 'center' area contain graves. Some burials exist in the Judean desert, and it is likely that continuing fieldwork on sites in the lower Jordan Valley will also reveal such evidence. To the east, dating from towards the end of the Early Natufian or at the beginning of the following phase, a burial has been found at Azraq 18 (Garrard 1991: 240). Further south – either because the customs were genuinely different, or there has not been enough excavation, or there is a problem of preservation - not a single human burial has been found. In an attempt to reconstruct a coherent sequence, one can suggest that the oldest burials, individual or collective, were in the extended position (Hayonim Cave, El-Wad Cave). Following this there would be some primary burials, sometimes containing disturbed, not always complete, skeletons. During this stage in the sequence the body was deposited in a more or less contracted position (El-Wad Terrace, Hayonim Cave).

Finally, people would have been buried flexed in individual graves (El-Wad, Mallaha). Decorated persons are known throughout the sequence. However, an attempted reconstruction of this type is faced with the problem of non-verifiable stratigraphic correlations. It also ignores the practice of reburial, which is present from the beginning onwards if one accepts the conclusions of the excavators. Even postulating a tendency to observe similar practices, one is forced to notice that a real uniformity was never reached.

At this stage it becomes possible to address the question of the origin of the Natufian phenomenon. In the 'center' (Carmel–Galilee), the Natufian appears to have resulted from the abandonment of alternating aggregation and dispersal periods which are characteristic of the majority of human societies and a shift towards groups coming together on a more or less permanent basis in the same place (Valla n.d.). These groups maintained, for most of the year, the intense intellectual, religious, social and sexual life, which becomes feasible in such a situation. For the essentials, they could have easily exploited traditional knowledge. The majority of the products of Natufian industry utilized old techniques, or took advantage of possibilities which were, until then, under-exploited. Similarly, neither their semi-subterranean houses nor funerary practices were without antecedents. This situation, however, could have resulted in new types of social behavior. As Mussi has remarked (1984), it may have induced a tendency to invest more time in the production of relatively durable goods. Evidence for this may be seen in architecture and in the non-siliceous stone industry. This point should not, however, be exaggerated. Plisson (personal communication) notes that flint implements continued to be exploited just as before, in that the life of tools remained extremely ephemeral. At the same time, sedentism led to a more intense exploitation of the natural resources around villages. The use of a larger variety of flint than before goes hand in hand with a reduction in the demands made of the knappers. The cutting by sickle of cereals while only near-ripe, thereby helping to reduce waste, points in the same direction, and the same can be said for the search for small game. Finally, near-sedentism could have introduced an entirely new attitude towards the surrounding world, by bringing closer together humans and dangerous animals, such as the wolf. The new way of life could, in fact, only be derived from ancestral customs. It resulted simply in the lengthening of the annual gathering periods, and of its more active life, to the detriment of the dispersal periods, during which each family was isolated from the others. Nevertheless, these periods did not completely disappear: a part of the group at least could continue to disperse themselves for several weeks during the autumn, when resources were more scarce.

Thus, the apparent dislocation between the Natufian and the preceding period does not preclude a real continuity. The attraction of the active life of annual gatherings, compared to the relatively dreary existence of dispersal periods, could have supplied the motor element of change which the warming at the end of the Pleistocene may have allowed to develop further. How would these aggregation periods have operated? We do not know. The way in which groups at the end of the Geometric Kebaran organized their territory currently eludes us, and this information could be necessary for us to respond to this question (see Goring-Morris, this volume). The few facts which show connections with previous traditions are too tenuous to offer anything better than some vague indications. At the most, one suspects that each group was limited to a few families, and that if the number of people within each group increased during the Natufian, it was only by rather modest amounts.

The way of life successfully experimented with in the Carmel and Galilee areas could have spread by diffusion. Towards the south, from where we have our best information, the Jordanian basin could have been the favored route of such a spread. However, the system could not have been transported without adaptation occurring in those environments less favorable than the forest-steppe of oak and pistachio present in the Carmel-Galilee area. A site such as Erq el-Ahmar seems to have been occupied rather briefly. Sometimes, as at Beidha, it is likely that the aggregation period did not last all year (Byrd 1989a: 85). The Negev poses a problem not yet solved. Could the occurrence of the small sites in the dunes correspond to the dispersal period of the groups which gathered on the margins of the region, as suggested by Goring-Morris? But why were the highlands abandoned when one would expect to find aggregation sites there, as is the case in the Later Natufian? Was the 'model' from the north rejected, despite the influences shown in the flint industries?

Late Natufian phase

The Late Natufian phase lasted from around 11,250 to 10,500 BP. The 'center' continued to follow the traditions it had maintained for more than a millennium. Certain sites were abandoned (Kebara, Wadi Hammeh 27). At Hayonim, the main occupation moved onto the terrace in front of the cave (see Plate 6). New settlements were established at Rakefet and, above all, at Nahal Oren – sites at low altitude. In comparison to the preceding epoch, Natufian influence seems to expand. At the foot of the western side of the Palestinian dorsal, the cave of Shukba experienced considerable occupation (Garrod and Bate 1942). In a similar position, Hatoula was perhaps inhabited on a seasonal basis (Lechevallier and Ronen 1985) despite Lieberman's suggestion of a multiseasonal occupation (Lieberman 1993). On the eastern side, high altitude sites are more numerous than before in the Judean Desert (Oumm ez-Zoueitina, el-Khiam, Tor Abou Sif) (Neuville 1951), and occupation persists in the lower Jordan Valley (Salibiyah I) (Shuldenrein and Goldberg 1981). The Negev is one of the regions where the progress of the Natufian 'model' is more clearly marked. Aggregation sites appear in the highlands at Rosh Zin, Rosh Horesha and Saflulim, although small sites continue to be found in the dunes. We know almost nothing about the mountains of southern Transjordan, where Beidha was reoccupied in an episodic fashion after a long period of abandonment. Towards the east, the sites are much more modest than those in the 'center', but the Natufian influence is clear at places such as Ain Rahub (alt. 420 m), Taibe (alt. 570 m) and in the Black Desert, Khallat Anaza (alt. 880 m), where, despite its remoteness, remains of structures were found (Betts 1991: 219). The oases of the Syrian Desert seem empty; on the other hand, the Middle Euphrates witnesses the installation of a large site at Abu Hureyra. In Lebanon the situation remains confused, but one can with certainty attribute to this period the site at Saaide II in the Beqaa (alt. 1035 m) (Schroeder 1991).

Generally, the lithic industries display a reduction in Helwan retouch and in the length of lunates; the use of the microburin technique had spread. However, behind these general shifts, the regional and local specificities of the preceding phase are maintained. It seems that Helwan retouch diminishes only very progressively on the older sites occupying the 'center'. It disappears much more quickly in the 'peripheries': central Palestine, the Negev, eastern Jordan, the Euphrates valley and probably also Lebanon. On the other hand, lunates remain rather longer in the south than those in the 'center'. They are also very large on the Euphrates. As for the microburin technique, it is sometimes in use at places in the 'center' such as El-Wad and Hayonim Terrace, in contrast to the Negev sites where its waste continues in superabundance. On the Euphrates, Abu Hureyra makes no use of it, but it is well attested at the Lebanese site of Saaide. The more subtle nuances – certain types of rare tools, the shape of lunates, etc. – which we have already seen occurring from one site to another in the Early Natufian, continue in this phase. They probably bear witness to both the permanence of local traditions on those sites where occupation goes on, and the self-esteem of each group in relation to others (Valla 1984: 130 ff, 177).

The stone and bone tool assemblages continue to demonstrate the relative richness of the 'center' in comparison to the peripheries. However, this statement should be treated with caution, especially for stone. In the 'center', one generally finds the same types of objects as in the preceding period. Perhaps there is less care taken in the production of large mortars, many of which are in limestone, as the exterior surface is often fashioned in a rather rudimentary way. However, some of these appear

to have functioned while almost entirely buried in the ground (Valla et al. 1989: 255). On the upland sites of the Negev, a particular type of artifact in the form of deep cylindrical mortars cut into the bedrock was developed. These can be numerous (e.g., 109 at Saflulim). On the Euphrates, Abu Hureyra supplies a considerable amount of original material, with flat forms (grinding dishes, querns) taking over from deep forms. The Syrian sites of Jayroud (Cauvin 1991: 226 ff.) and the Lebanese site Saaide II also appear to have been rather well supplied in terms of heavy material artifacts. In general, the bone tool assemblage tends to be rather less varied than in the early phase. In the 'center' it sometimes remains very abundant, whereas it is rare in the 'peripheries' except at Abu Hureyra.

More clearly than in the preceding phase, undoubtedly because the period is shorter, human burials display a superimposition of both regional tendencies and local customs. In the Carmel and Galilee, graves and habitations continue to be associated to some extent. On Hayonim Terrace, the graves and habitations seem to be interstratified. In Hayonim Cave, at Nahal Oren and at Mallaha they are separated. Everywhere, except at Mallaha where this is the period of multiple burials, individual graves dominate. In Hayonim Cave and Mallaha secondary inhumations are found. The custom of removing the skull, which appears in this period, is not attested at Mallaha. Only one general point can be made: the dead are no longer buried with their ornamental elements. Leaving the 'center', some burials are still found in the close 'peripheries' at Shuqba and Saaide II, but none are found in the Negev. At Abu Hureyra, dispersed human bones were recovered but there are no actual graves there.

The Late Natufian appears, therefore, to be marked by an extension of the prestige of the Carmel–Galilee 'center'. Its way of life influenced distant populations in a more evident fashion than before. The adaptations which were recognized from the preceding phase are clearer in this period. In central Palestine, Hatoula, Shukba (?), Salibiyah I, and probably also those in the Judean Desert, the sites appear to have functioned as places for seasonal gatherings. The camps which may have corresponded to dispersal periods are unknown. The picture is more complete and more coherent in the Negev. There, opposite to what we see in the 'center', the aggregation sites are all located at high altitudes. Study of the gazelle hunting season shows that these sites were frequented in autumn and winter (Lieberman 1993). For the rest of the year, it seems that groups lived in a dispersed form in the dunes and depressions. Without doubt, neither of these environments could have supported gatherings lasting all year round. The same observation holds for the Black Desert sites. On the Euphrates, on the other hand, it seems that the 'center' model could have been adopted without major transformations other than the necessary adaptations to local resources. The inhabitants of Abu Hureyra seem to have been practically sedentary. Summing up, even when the Carmel–Galilee 'center' began to give signs of impoverishment – it is at this time that the gazelle population at Hayonim degenerated because of over-exploitation – in the 'peripheries', such as the Negev and the Euphrates Valley, systems are adopted which are derived from the original model, and which went on to become capable of pursuing their own particular development during the last episode of the Natufian.

Final Natufian phase

The Final Natufian occupies, broadly, the third quarter of the eleventh millennium BP. The relative briefness of this period, which still had its own particular characteristics, may explain why some scholars prefer to include it within the Late Natufian. Its presence, however, is undoubtedly recognizable on certain 'center' sites, and is particularly evident in the Negev and on the Euphrates. Treating it as a clearly-defined phase allows us better appreciation of the range of Natufian innovations and the significance of this culture in the historical development of the Levant.

The episode is signalled by an obvious decline of the 'center' sites, where architecture is no longer in evidence (Valla 1987: 281). Hayonim is deserted, and at Mallaha the period is represented by a layer of small stones and rubble, probably displaced, but very rich in material and into which the Natufians installed some small structures such as stone basins and pits. Later, after the abandonment of the site, some (still Natufian) burials were cut into a deposit (which has since disappeared) and placed just at the summit of the rubble layer. Perhaps the ancestral way of life was best maintained in the Carmel, where Nahal Oren stands out as the main site.

Outside the Carmel and Galilee areas, the presence of the Final Natufian is seen in the Lower Jordan Valley at Fazael IV (Bar-Yosef et al. 1974), but it is above all, as previously mentioned, in the Negev and on the Euphrates that the most significant developments took place. The Harifian results from better adaptation to the desert conditions of the Negev (Scott 1977). Aggregation sites are found on the high uplands (Abu Salem alt. 970 m, Ramat Harif, Shluhat Harif) and lower down at the base of the plateau (Ma'aleh Ramon east and west), to mention only those where built structures are attested. Other sites, less substantial and lacking architecture but which also represent aggregation episodes, exist to the west on the border of the dunes (Shunera VI and IX). Finally, some sites – even more modest – are encountered everywhere right down to the north of Sinai; these could be the remains of temporary camps of isolated families (Goring-Morris 1991: 206 and this volume). By way of contrast to

this complex situation, the Euphrates only has one site, Mureybet, which was probably occupied all year round (Cauvin, 1991).

The general tendencies displayed in the lithic industries of the previous phase have a number of outcomes in the Final Natufian. Helwan retouch disappears almost everywhere. It persists only at Mallaha, which is particularly conservative in this respect. Lunates become very small, and the microburin technique is present everywhere. However, it would be wrong to suggest a standardization of industries. In the 'center', Mallaha and Nahal Oren remain very different. The former preserved Helwan retouch and broad lunates while the latter produced narrow lunates and rare microburins (Valla 1984: 171 ff.) The Negev and the Euphrates, while still part of the general trend, developed their own original traditions. The Harifian has the first arrow points, of which the most well-known is the Harif point, and thick scrapers with finely denticulated edges are unique to this assemblage. This coincides with a relative decline in the use of the microburin technique. On the Euphrates, Mureybet is known only from the excavation of small areas. In flint tool material, its main originality lies in the production of the first 'herminettes de Mureybet' (adzes) and larged tanged points which do not appear anywhere in successive periods.

The current state of the literature does not allow us to extend our analysis to other elements of Final Natufian material in any great detail. Heavy artifacts continue to be used on the Carmel and Galilee sites. At Nahal Oren, grooved stones with cylindrical bases, which are unique to this site, seem to be an innovation of this phase (Noy 1991: 557). The Negev, better known, appears very particular. Some sites (those where building activities are evidenced) yielded numerous cupstones. Bedrock mortars become less frequent. Among the artifacts unique to this region, often produced in material coming from Sinai, are bell-shaped handstones in green rock, of which we have two examples. The heavy material of Mureybet in this phase remains largely unknown. Little can be said of the Final Natufian bone industry, which probably maintained the features of the preceding phase – standardization at Mallaha, where it is still abundant; rarity in the Negev (poor preservation?) and at Mureybet (due to the relative paucity of excavation?).

Funerary customs appear to follow the same tendencies as the lithic industries. In the 'center' they are relatively standardized, but without implying a genuine homogeneity. Simple individual inhumations dominate, but multiple burials persist at Nahal Oren, as does the practice of skull removal. There is no evidence for this last custom at Mallaha, and, yet again, neither the Negev nor the Euphrates have burials.

After the apparent high point of the late Natufian, the cultural connections woven across the Levant under the influence of the Carmel–Galilee 'center' seem to slacken during the final Natufian. In the Carmel and Galilee there is even a return towards a more mobile existence. The prestigious way of life which the people there had sought to maintain tended to be abandoned. Does the reduction in the consumption of vegetal resources which may have taken place at this time (Sillen 1984; Sillen and Lee-Thorp 1991: 406) reflect a cultural choice? Or, alternatively, after almost two millennia of human exploitation, was the environment around the traditional sites exhausted? Was the social network unable to maintain the cohesion of the group for some unknown reason? Since the populations do not seem to have been subjected to strong nutritional constraints (Belfer-Cohen et al. 1991: 422), it may be necessary to envisage a combination of explanations. Whatever the case, the prestige and influence of the Carmel and the Galilee became weaker. This is evident in the Negev and on the Euphrates, where, on different lines, the societies exhibit a tendency to disassociate themselves from the practices in the 'center'. In the Negev, the Harifians seem to convert to a new system of seasonality, perhaps based on a different mode of resource exploitation. It is likely that the upland aggregation sites could have been frequented during spring and summer, but no longer in winter as was the case in the Late Natufian. Another significant shift is that most of the exotic objects, among them the decorative elements, came from the south (Red Sea, Sinai) during this period and no longer from the Mediterranean. On the Euphrates, separation from the 'center' worked in a different direction. At the time when the Carmel and Galilee were abandoning the traditional sedentary way of life, Mureybet seems to have perpetuated it. If the tendency toward sedentism has been one of the specific indicators of the Natufian, then Mureybet is, at this time, the most 'Natufian' of all the sites in the Levant. There are also, however, certain traits at Mureybet which bear witness to the spreading of influences from elsewhere. For example, unlike Abu Hureyra, Mureybet does not have dentalium; on the other hand, it has Anatolian obsidian, which arrived there in small quantities at a time when it hardly ever reached any further south.

Just like its beginnings, the end of the Natufian corresponds to a 'dislocation' in the Levantine sequence. The settlement of the country underwent a total transformation. The Carmel and Galilee seem to have become empty, with only Nahal Oren being reinhabited somewhat later. The Harifian vanished towards the end of the eleventh millennium, and the Negev lacks any evidence of occupation for a long period of time. Mureybet provides the only example of an uninterrupted human presence in the same location. In central Palestine, the brief period known as the Khiamian appears to show small, rather ephemeral, groups of hunters at sites such as Hatoula, el Khiam and Salibiyah IX. This episode is followed by the Sultanian which resumes the earlier architectural tradition, with a preference for the contemporary steppic environment of the Jordan Valley, at Jericho, Gilgal, Netiv Hagdud and Gesher, although the western side of the Judean mountains is not entirely deserted as is shown at Hatoula. It is in this type of environment, rather than in the Mediterranean zone, that the first morphologically domesticated plants appear, at Tell Aswad in Damascene. Nevertheless, in the same way that the dislocation observed at the beginning of the Natufian conceals a number of elements of continuity, the dislocation which marked its end does not prevent the further transmission of such elements (Bar-Yosef and Belfer-Cohen 1989). But this is a matter for the next chapter (see Chapter 12).

Sedentism in the Levantine sequence

It remains for us to ask ourselves what the Natufian signifies. We have said that it is situated between two points of dislocation, but we have also shown a profound continuity from the preceding period. If our analyses are reliable, then the key innovation introduced by the Natufian resides in the tendency to prolong as much as possible those periods when families grouped together, at the expense of periods of dispersal. The way of life which resulted from this has been termed, perhaps a little incorrectly, sedentary. However, it does undoubtedly appear that the practising of a less mobile way of life than before, along with the habit of returning to the same sites (where some members of the group may have stayed), is at the very heart of the majority of the changes which characterize the period.

Among the changes more visible to archaeologists are the increase in the size of sites, in the thickness of deposits and in the density of the remains which they contain. Following the ideas put forward by Binford (1968), many have regarded these phenomena as secure evidence for an increase in the size of groups compared to the preceding period and, consequently, evidence for a general increase in the population. Relative sedentism could have resulted in changes in the demographic structure, due to a reduction in the length of time between births. The increasing pressure exerted on the environment could have forced groups to divide up and to colonize land which was incapable of producing naturally the necessary staples. Agricultural practices may have been developed in these 'peripheries' where people may have tried to introduce species which did not grow there naturally, but were familiar in their region of origin. Unfortunately, the demographic expansion suggested cannot be sustained by the available evidence. The size of sites and their relative richness can be understood in terms of the way in which people frequented them – in terms of changing social practices, without having to rely on models which cannot be proven. Furthermore, the stability of traditions, which seems to be one of the characteristics of the period, does not suggest large-scale movement of the population. Finally, evidence from the 'peripheries' during the Natufian does not indicate that people there developed agricultural practices.

The general impoverishment of the culture at the end of the eleventh millennium, which occurred everywhere except in the Euphrates, along with what we observed of the 'wild' character of the plant crops, cereals, legumes and others, indicates that nowhere did the Natufians pass the stage of intensive gathering of diverse resources (of which cereals were most probably not as central as may have been thought). This point of view could become more plausible if it could be confirmed (which may be possible) that the last Natufians of the Carmel and Galilee consumed less plant food than their predecessors.

The changes evidenced by the faunal remains may also be explained by a new way of using sites. The hunting of small game could be rooted in the necessity of thoroughly exploiting the territory close to villages. In this context of limited hunting grounds, it becomes clear how the selective hunting of gazelles led to over-exploitation of the species. However, perhaps the most interesting innovations in this field result as much from the behavior of humans as from the behavior of animals, namely the invasion of commensals and the domestication of the dog. It is unclear if the domestication of the dog was so revolutionary *per se*; dogs may have existed elsewhere at the end of the paleolithic. But the way in which burials suggest domestication may have been understood at this time – opening the way for further 'humanization' of the world at the expense of nature – was in itself important for the future (see Plate 2.1, Window 2).

The development of art and decoration no longer seems unusual to this new way of living if it is indeed true that aggregation time is one of intense intellectual and religious activity. The ornamental elements which are found in Early Natufian graves have been interpreted as indicators of a hierarchical society because decorated burials seem to cross-cut age and sex differences (Wright 1978). There can be no doubt that these decorative elements had a social function, probably as a means for each group to affirm their identity. Study of the graves does suggest that certain subjects – not necessarily those individuals who are decorated – may have enjoyed particular prestige. But claiming that prestige was hereditary or that the Natufians were organized into chiefdoms (Henry 1989: 210) by imposing on the archaeological evidence an imported evolutionary model, obscures the facts instead of explaining them. With the current state of the evidence, it is difficult to properly understand Natufian social organization beyond noting the desire of each group for self-individualization, of which there are many indications. This was probably all the more necessary because, on

biological grounds, there was a constant demand for matrimonial exchange between local groups.

But art and decoration also open the way to symbolic thought. This domain is not any less problematic than that of social organization. Nevertheless, the male and female symbolic meaning of the marine shells with which the Natufian decorated themselves is universal. It is difficult to imagine that people were unaware of it. This impression is reinforced if one turns to the bone ornamental elements. The fox canines are unambiguous. Some beads appear to imitate deer canines, and these also carry male values. The 'twin-pendants' from El-Wad are probably also part of the same symbolic system, whether one wishes to see them as two stylized deer canines or, along with Marshack, as equivalent to the female figurine pendants from Dolni Vestonice. It is, maybe, not necessary to choose between the two interpretations, since the symbolic mind would be able to bring both into play. Finally, the presence of phallic representations, and that of a probable female figurine (at Hayonim Terrace), allow us to conclude that the Natufian mind uses the sexual divide to understand the world. We have already noted that towards the end of the Natufian, dentalium shells became relatively less popular – a trend which increased during the following periods. Female figurines increase in number during the Khiamian. It is appropriate to note here the beginnings of this shift, which constitutes yet another connection with the following cultures, even if for the moment one cannot refine much in this field.

Conclusion: grounds for future research

Are the Natufian the first settled societies? Probably yes. But this statement must be cautiously delimited. The Natufian does not appear as a uniform whole, either in time or space. On the contrary, we see it as a complex of regional entities, each of them maintaining their own originality, even if sharing most aspects of the same material culture. From that point of view, the main difference between sites in what is called here the 'center' (the Carmel and Galilee areas) and those in the 'peripheries', is a gradual impoverishment of sites the farther they are from the 'center'. Nevertheless, even this picture is still an oversimplification. The so-called 'peripheries' that we imagine receiving innovations from outside, do not appear to have been passive. Not being able to adopt fully the way of life of the 'center', they had to adjust the 'ideal' it may have represented for them to the limitations of the relatively poor, or at least different, environment in which they were living. Finally, when the 'center' lost its dynamism, the peripheries themselves became areas of innovation – at least in the Negev and on the Euphrates.

So, what is the Natufian culture? What is called here

'Natufian' is a 'culture' in the sense that all areas included and groups referred to are recognizable as part of it on the basis of the material elements they have in common. In other words, we do not assume among those groups a uniform way of life. Maybe this definition would not be acceptable to ethnographers. But prehistorians and ethnographers do not have at their disposal the same kind of data, and the extent to which the observations of the latter (and *a fortiori* their theoretical constructions) can be imposed on the remains of Pre-Neolithic societies has still to be demonstrated.

In this context it is relevant to evoke the controversy between those who hold that flint tools are useful cultural markers, and the supporters of the view that they reflect only specific tasks on each site. People influenced by ethnographers tend to accept this second opinion while the traditional mode of reasoning among prehistorians is based on the first . It has been argued in this paper that flint tools, at least through technology and shape, under certain conditions can be taken as cultural indicators. This is especially obvious for microliths. On-going research addressing the problem through different angles, technological study of debitage, attribute analysis and microwear analysis of tools, will help throw more light on the matter.

The ambiguous relationship between prehistory and ethnography is again illustrated in the interpretation of such cultural traits as settlement organization and funerary habits. There is no place here for a full discussion of this problem, suffice it to say that once again prehistorians are hampered by the limitations and equivocality of their data. Wright's (1978) interpretation of the graves at El-Wad may be legitimate as an exercise showing one possible avenue for further research. It is less clear if it is acceptable on methodological grounds, in that the author casts the data in a pre-existing mould without questioning whether they could fit another model. But the fragility of his conclusions become obvious if one considers both the quality of the data involved (excavated in the early 1930s) and the quantity of the material (five graves). Nothing seems to be more difficult to obtain in Pre-Neolithic prehistory than data relevant to social organization; even the ways in which past people thought, elusive as they are, may be easier to approach. What is sure, in any case, is the need for more well-excavated and reliable data as a basis for reasoning.

In short, research on the Natufian culture during the coming years has a good chance of being dominated by debates stemming from the discrepancies between the data offered by the sites (and their excavators) and the questions asked by prehistorians fascinated by the 'answers' reached by their ethnographer colleagues.

Acknowledgments

Thanks are due to O. Bar-Yosef, J. Perrot and D. Stordeur who allowed me to reproduce illustrations from their work, and to D. Ladiray and M. Barazani, from the Centre de Recherche Français de Jerusalem (CNRS) for help in completing the figures. The text was translated from French by Brian Boyd to whom I owe a special debt.

THE VILLAGE OF MALLAHA

The Natufian settled at Mallaha, near Lake Hula, at the foot of a slope into which their houses were cut. In the excavated area, the houses were aligned. They are oval or semi-circular in shape. Each one covers more or less 25 m². On the same alignment, an oval construction occupying only around 7 m² is difficult to interpret. As far as one can say there was no means of closure.

The best-known house is probably semi-circular (Plate 1.1). The interior space is broken up by two series of posts, one across the entrance, the second at around one meter in front of the wall. Life in the house seems to have been orientated around three fireplaces. The first is a large oval hearth, limited by stones laid on edge, which is located on the axis of the entrance. This hearth contains only ash and had no concentration of artifacts around it. It could have served mainly as a source of heat or to ward off insects. The second example, on the same axis, appears as a zone of ash spread around a large stone. It seems to have attracted mainly technical activities, as cores and flint tools abound in its vicinity.

The third hearth, towards the middle of the shelter, but not centered, seems to have been the real focus of domestic life. It is a double hearth, of which each of the two elements is limited by an arc of vertical stones which here and there lean against a post-hole support. The principal element of this hearth contains a number of bird-bones, probably food remains which were thrown into the fire. Nearby and in the hearth itself are some flat stones which could have served as grills or supports for whatever material was being heated at the time. Several basalt pestles were found nearby. These may have been used for grinding either food or pigments. Near this hearth, the hunters took care of their weapons, which is attested by the concentration of grooved stones and microliths, the majority of which probably served as projectile armatures. Finally, this hearth attracted objects which appear to have symbolic or ritual functions. A polished roe deer antler, sectioned at the base, was found inside the hearth. This piece could be an 'emblem' of

some kind. Two fragments of a sculpted stone — perhaps an animal representation — lay nearby, as well as a human cranial cap and an assemblage of small stones of various colours.

Although the hearths were the prime features in the organization of space, they did not attract all the activities: bone tools are dispersed throughout the house in a fairly homogeneous way. In line with the observations of physical anthropologists, who assume that people generally worked in the crouched position, there is no seat or bench in this house.

At this period, the dead were grouped in two main concentrations under the two houses which have been excavated. The dimensions of these constructions suggest that they could have accommodated a nuclear family. All this seems to point to these constructions having played the central role in the organization of space—time for their occupants.

The plan of the village was modified in the Late Natufian. The houses, semi-subterranean, remained aligned according to the topography at the foot and summit of the slope. A third range of constructions seems to have existed on the slope itself, but they remain only as very ruined traces. The houses are circular and, although they are more numerous than before, they tend to be smaller. The majority are hardly more than three meters in diameter. Their interior organization is less well-known than that of the preceding phase. They contain a hearth, either built or simply a mass of ash and small burnt stones. The largest house (28 m²) contained a large hearth bordered by stones, near to which was a big block of limestone worked to make a mortar. Against the wall, an area of hardly a meter square was marked out by upright stones, representing the first example of a fixed partition.

In this phase pits are numerous, cut into fills next to occupied houses. Two main concentrations of them have been observed. These 'pits' are of various types: some are simple basins, others are more than one meter deep; some could have been silos, but a number of them contain burials. Does the shift from large houses to smaller constructions, (perhaps for one single individual) indicate a loosening of family ties in favor of community ties? To support a hypothesis of this type, we can point to the grouping of pits and graves in communal spaces. It would appear that the symbolic representations previously attached to each house by its occupants was, at least in part, transferred to the village level.

The Final Natufian is represented by deposits rich in terms of amount and in material of all sorts, but partly displaced. Architecture does not seem to have played an important role. We know only of some stone basins and small pits. The summit of the layer is nevertheless marked by some burials, still Natufian, which seem to indicate that memory of the old village remained present in the collective memory of the group after its abandonment, and that people continued to bury their dead there, reuniting them with their ancestors (Valla 1991).

Plate 1.1   Large house from Mallaha (courtesy J. Perrot, CNRS)

THE DOMESTICATION OF THE DOG

The earliest indications for the domestication of the dog in the Levant appear in the Natufian when, for the first time, we find dogs buried with humans (Davis and Valla 1978, Valla et al. 1991: 102).

To date, this type of occurrence is known from two graves. The oldest, at Mallaha, contained an elderly individual and a puppy, which was curled up in a ball near the person's head. The deceased's left hand rested on the animal's body (Plate 2.1)

The second grave, on Hayonim Terrace, is more complex. It contains three human individuals. Of the first, mainly the skull and left arm bones remain. The head lay close to the pelvis of the second individual, a very robust male, which lay perpendicular to the first. A dog had been placed under this male, forehead to forehead with him, but the body drawn out so that one of its paws rested on the skull of the first subject. A second dog seems to have been curled up under the chest of the same male, who was also associated with two tortoise carapaces. The third individual was interred on top of the second, accompanied by one horn of a gazelle and the skull of another with its two horns. At least one stone lay on the skull of each of the humans, and the chests of the second and third subjects were crushed by large stone blocks.

Such a complex set of evidence did not occur by accident. The components collected together here are found individually elsewhere in a funerary context. Moreover, the human-dog-gazelle association was also encountered on a floor surface at Mallaha. Therefore, one can conclude with a fair degree of confidence that these components express a coherent system of thought.

The myth behind this concept has vanished but it remains possible to study the formal variations of its components, which are particularly significant as they reflect representations that were not necessarily conscious. From this point of view, the opposition between on the one hand, gazelle (always represented by a selected bone) and on the other, human and dog (sometimes represented by a selected bone, as on the floor surface at Mallaha, and at other times complete, as in the graves) cannot fail to be noticed. It signifies that, in some way, symbolic thought assimilated the dog, but not the gazelle, to humans.

This difference in treatment confirms the new closeness of humans and dogs, something that their co-presence in graves already allowed us to assume. It reveals that the Natufian saw domestication as an appealing way in which to introduce the animal into society. They thereby opened the way to the unlimited expansion of the 'humanized' world at the expense of nature.

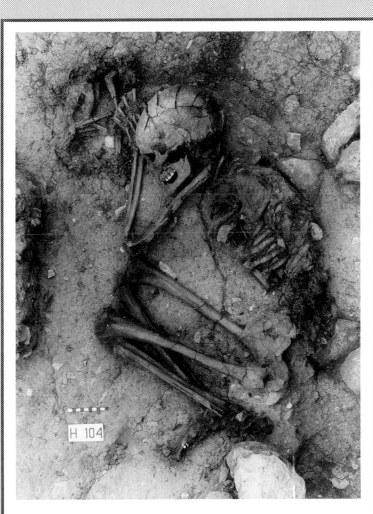

Plate 2.1   Human burial with a puppy from Mallaha (photograph: A. Dagand and F. Valla)

Part III

FARMERS, PRIESTS AND PRINCES: THE RISE OF THE FIRST COMPLEX SOCIETIES

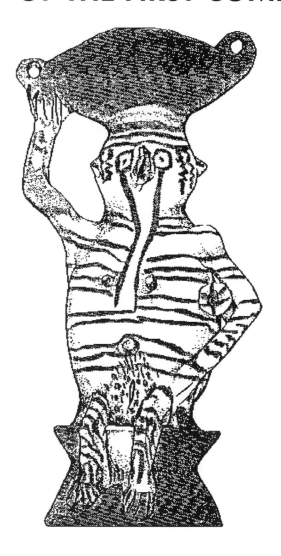

12

EARLIEST FOOD PRODUCERS – PRE POTTERY NEOLITHIC (8000–5500)

Ofer Bar-Yosef

Chronology and terminology

The establishment of cultivation and herding as the economic basis for human populations is what archaeologically separates the Early Neolithic period from the Paleolithic tradition of hunting and gathering. In addition, by the end of this period (which lasted about two and a half millennia), the emerging social complexity formed the foundations of later Near Eastern civilizations.

The various chrono-cultural terminologies used by archaeologists to describe and interpret Early Neolithic sites and sequences in the Levant are found in numerous publications (e.g., Kenyon 1957; Aurenche et al. 1981; Moore 1985; Crowfoot-Payne 1983; Bar-Yosef 1981, 1991). It should be stressed that it was during the excavations of Jericho that K. Kenyon coined the terms used for the two successive phases: Pre-Pottery Neolithic A and B (PPNA, PPNB). In addition, she described as 'Proto Neolithic' what she believed to be the earliest occupation of this mound. Detailed lithic analysis by Crowfoot-Payne (1983) made it clear that this area contained the same industry as the rest of the PPNA and that the term 'Proto Neolithic' should be abandoned.

The different schools of archaeology offered varying terms. The Lyon group suggested subdividing the period following the Natufian into Periods 1, 2 and 3. Moore (1985) preferred to name the PPNA and PPNB, Archaic Neolithic 1 and 2, while in Israel, Kenyon's terms continued to be employed. With the advent of ^{14}C dating, and currently with the ability to calibrate the dates (Stuiver and Pearson 1993), the need to determine the chronology on the basis of assemblage and architectural typology is almost obsolete. The different approaches can be summarized as two options:

1. categorizing sites as belonging to a certain time transect, or
2. defining cultural entities in space and time.

In the following pages the traditional approach of subdividing the Early Neolithic into two main time transects is kept, but social interpretation will be stressed.

The Levantine PPNA period contains two entities. The earliest is the Khiamian, originally defined by Echegaray (1966) and revised by Crowfoot-Payne (1983) with arrowheads known as El-Khiam points, sickle blades and microliths (see below). Uni-cultural sites such as Salibiya IX and, probably, Gilgal I are likely representatives of this entity (Bar-Yosef 1980, 1981; Noy 1989). In addition, Crowfoot-Payne suggested renaming the PPNA in Jericho the 'Sultanian', which is defined as an industry with 'Tahunian' tranchet axes-adzes, polished celts, sickle blades, perforators, Khiamian points, rare microliths (lunates) and Netiv Hagdud truncations.

In sum, the entire period lasted from 10,300/10,000 to 9300/9200 BP. Standard deviation and paucity of readings in the earliest sites make the beginning of this period poorly defined. The latest dates are generally based on Jericho.

The PPNB cultural sequence is divided into four sub-periods as follows: early, middle, late and final PPNB. The later phase will include what was named by G. Rollefson (1992), following his excavations at Ain Ghazal, as PPNC. The entire period covers the time span from about 9300/9200 to 5700/5500 BP. While trying to define cultural entities within the PPNB, one may suggest the name 'Tahunian' for the PPNB villages and their subsidiary sites in the main farming land. A different entity incorporates the desertic sites, such as those in Sinai where the hunting and gathering way of life continued and was replaced by pastoralism only in the following millennia.

Settlement pattern and site size

There is great diversity in site size among PPNA sites. The smallest encampments (up to 100/150 m^3), located outside the expanded Mediterranean vegetation belt of the Early Holocene (such as Abu Madi I), appear to reflect the seasonal remains of small groups of mobile hunter-gatherers (Figure 1). Small sites within the better, lusher part of the region, and closer to the farming communities,

Plate 1   Ain Ghazal human statues made from plaster (courtesy of Gary Rollefson)

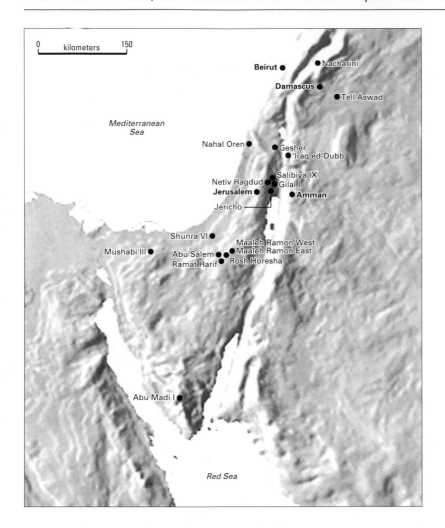

Figure 1   The distribution of Harifian sites in the Negev and northern Sinai and PPNA sites in the southern and central Levant, between Jericho in the south and Nachcharini in the north

are presumed to have been temporary campsites of hunters or task groups that gathered wild fruits and seeds. The medium-size sites (*ca.* 2000–3000 m³), as well as the larger ones (up to 2.5 hectares, such as Jericho), are often considered hamlets and villages.

PPNA village households were constructed either as one large oval room, or as a set of two adjacent rooms with small installations around them. Rounded and oval houses characterize the entire region. Typically, they are built of mud or stones, often semi-subterranean with lower courses of up to 50–70 cm below ground level. The walls, as shown in Jericho, Gilgal and Netiv Hagdud, were built of plano-convex mud bricks. Little is known about the roofs, which were probably flat. In smaller sites such as Nahal Oren, the rounded rooms were still attached to each other resembling the compound arrangement of the preceding Natufian communities. Comparison to ethnographically-observed groups suggests that increasingly open spaces between households reflect the decreasing degree of kinship relationships. Unfortunately, building activities were often accompanied by

sweeping and repeated clearing of the floors, thus eliminating in most houses the study of spatial distribution of artifacts. Only in rare cases, such as in the 'burnt house' in Netiv Hagdud or the abandoned houses in Gilgal I, do we get a glimpse of the spatial distribution of domestic artifacts such as cupholes, hearths, grinding bowls, etc. (Noy 1989; Bar-Yosef et al. 1991).

Most large sites with many structures are assumed to have been occupied all year round on the basis of the seasonal distribution of collected, harvested, gathered and hunted food resources (Bar-Yosef et al. 1991). Even if short-term mobility was practiced by these sites' inhabitants, the investment in building and storing, as demonstrated by the structures in Jericho, Netiv Hagdud and Gilgal I, indicate that these communities planned ahead for the re-use of facilities over many years. In addition it is clear that investment of time and energy for construction and maintenance also occurred at smaller sites, such as the cave of 'Iraq ed-Dubb, located in a highland of the Transjordanian plateau, where oval structures built of stones were uncovered, some 4–5

Plate 2 Oval dwellings in Netiv Hagdud, in the lower Jordan Valley (photograph: Barazani-Nir, CRFJ)

meters in diameter (Kuijt et al. 1991). Dwelling structures, therefore, are not indicative of sedentism, which can be determined solely on the basis of biological information. Hilly and upland areas could have been utilized all year round in the coastal Levant.

The best example to date for PPNA public structures is the tower in Jericho. Detailed examination of the published sections (Kenyon 1981) indicates that the only way to explain the minimal erosion of the top of the tower, and the orientation of the eroded and deposited remains (actually downward from the tower in all directions), is to assume that there was an additional brick building on top of that structure. It was suggested that a small shrine might originally have stood there (Bar-Yosef 1986). If this interpretation is correct, the nearby storage facilities (Kenyon 1981) and the adjacent open space (the so-called 'Proto-Neolithic' occupational deposits in area M) were possibly elements of a special public function, perhaps similar to the identified 'plaza' in Çayönü (Özdögan and Özdögan 1989). In addition, the walls on the western side of the mound represent a communal effort which seems to have been intended to avoid the flooding of the village (Bar-Yosef 1986).

PPNB sites are better known from various excavations, including tels such as Jericho (Figure 2). In a large number of cases PPNB sites are buried in alluvium, the result of increased aggradation during the Neolithic, and especially the Chalcolithic, period (Goldberg and Bar-Yosef 1990). Estimating site size, especially of mounds, is a highly debated issue in demographic archaeology (e.g., Kramer 1983). Ambiguities are often impossible to resolve in tels where 'circulating stratigraphy' and exact limits are hardly known. Despite these difficulties, Table 1 represents an attempt at measurement where rough estimates of site size are based on published maps or excavators' reports.

The large sites are within the 'Levantine corridor', the area covered by the Jordan Valley and its hilly margins that stretches from Edom (southern Jordan) to the Damascus basin, where freshwater lakes existed during this period. Smaller sites are located on each side of this corridor, to the west towards the Mediterranean coast, and eastwards in the Syro-Arabian steppe and desert. Site size decreases considerably within the semi-arid region and on the periphery of each major or central site.

Published archaeological evidence provides insights about the regional hierarchy among PPNB sites. Besides site size, these data include house size and contents (which are available only in rare, well-preserved cases), imported commodities (such as obsidian, marine shells, green stone, basalt mortars and pestles away from the sources), the amount of plaster used for flooring houses, presence of public structures, cultic objects, the treatment of the dead, and grave goods.

On a regional scale, the number of large settlements is small. Sites such as Ain Ghazal, Beisamoun and Basta are located far apart and match the size of Abu Hureyra, Çatal Hüyük and Asikli Hüyük (in central Anatolia). These may have served as central places in the local and regional networks of information, exchange and political competition (Rollefson 1988).

Domestic architecture in PPNB sites reflects a major change in both house plan and building techniques. Rounded structures are replaced by rectangular or squarish buildings in sites that can be interpreted as farming communities. Several sites, such as Beidha, document this gradual shift. The curvilinear dwellings continue to characterize sites in the arid zone until the second millennium BCE (e.g., Aurenche et al. 1981; Bar-Yosef 1985; Flannery 1972; Garrard et al. 1988). There are differences in the size of the structures among excavated sites, their internal subdivisions, the number of rooms and doors, types of floor, installations, etc. (Lechevallier 1977; Aurenche et al. 1981; Garfinkel 1987; Banning and Byrd 1984). Another shift among PPNB sites is the intensive use of plaster for covering the floors. While in most sites only the foundations and the lower courses of the walls are built of stones, in Basta stones make up most of the upper structure. Thus, at least in Beidha and

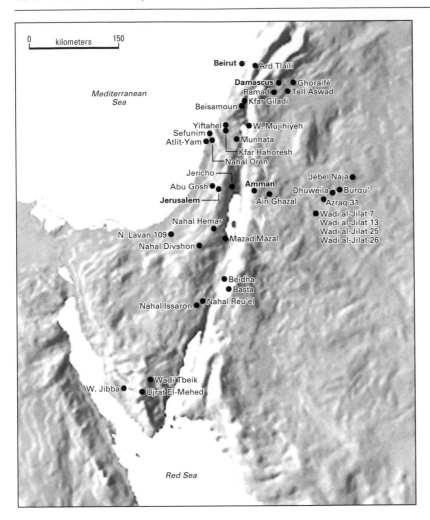

Figure 2 The distribution of the main PPNB sites in the southern Levant

Basta, there are positive indications for the presence of two-floor houses.

Public structures in PPNB sites are rare due to the small excavated surfaces. In Beidha, where a large area was exposed, a large rectangular building with plastered floors and a central basin was found to differ considerably from the other 'corridor houses'. So does the structure at the edge of the site that is interpreted as a shrine by Kirkbride (1968). The best examples in the Near East are known from Çayönü and Navali Çori. The possible presence of temples is raised by the caches of human statues uncovered at Ain Ghazal (Rollefson 1984, 1986. See Plate 1 p. 191).

Finally, a terrace wall that was intended to protect the site from erosion, with a staircase built on its outer surface, was uncovered at Beidha (Kirkbride 1966).

Innovations and technology

The PPNA lithic industry is best documented in the Jordan Valley sites (Jericho, Gilgal, Netiv Hagdud, Gesher, Salibiya IX and in the cave of Iraq ed-Dubb). Following a suggestion by Crowfoot-Payne (1983), we refer to the early phase as Khiamian, but most of the period is represented by the Sultanian (Bar-Yosef 1980, 1991; Noy 1989; Bar-Yosef et al. 1991; Nadel et al. 1990).

The Khiamian (Echegaray 1966), in my view, occupies the transition to the Sultanian villages and the sites (Salibiya IX, Gilgal I, El Khiam) that contain an industry with microliths, including lunates, Khiam points and sickle blades, but without bifacial tools (axes-adzes).

The Sultanian is characterized by single platform blades and flake cores, many of which were exhausted. Among the retouched pieces are El-Khiam points (arrowheads), sickle blades on large blades (Beit Ta'amir knives), sometimes with bifacial retouch, and a preponderance of small blades and flakes shaped into burins and perforators. Other tools include the lunates, some retouched bladelets and Netiv-Hagdud truncations. A large class of 'nibbled' tools, either finely retouched or bearing signs of utilization, are mostly blades. Tranchet axes-adzes, also known as Tahunian axes-adzes, have a working edge shaped by transverse removal. These tools

Table 1 Estimated occupied surfaces of selected Central and Southern Levantine sites (dated to or correlated with the 'PPNB'), in hectares

Ain Ghazal	12.000
Wadi Shueib	10.000
Basta	12.000
Beisamoun	10.000–12.000
Tel Aswad	5.000
Ghoraife	5.000
Ramad	2.000
Jericho	2.500
Yiftahel	1.500
Kefar Hahoresh	0.700
Nahal Oren	0.200
Semi-arid and arid	
Abu Nukheileh	0.045
Nahal Issaron	0.040
Ujrat el Mehed	0.030
Wadi Jibba I	0.015
Wadi Tbeik	0.025
Abu Madi I	0.008
Gebel Rubsha	0.003

were constantly resharpened and when abandoned had diminishing sizes. In addition, polished celts, made of either limestone or basalt, are included.

An examination of available ^{14}C dates along a geographic axis and changes in the lithic industries suggest that the PPNA period began earlier in the central Levant (between the Damascus basin and the Jordan Valley), preceding other areas. The earlier emergence of the PPNB lithic core reduction strategics, including the naviform cores, began in the northern Levant (Mureybet), and the diffusion of Helwan points was from the middle Euphrates southward (Gopher 1989; Cauvin 1987; Rollefson 1989).

The Economy: cultivation and animal domestication

Most authorities agree that the economy of the Early Neolithic communities was based on the consumption of cereals and legumes, wild seeds and fruits. Mammals, reptiles, birds and fish were obtained through hunting, trapping and fishing, while the domestication of caprovines, cattle and pigs occurred only during the ninth millennium BP uncalibrated (e.g., Flannery 1973; Clutton-Brock 1981; Davis 1991; Moore 1985; Helmer 1989; Hillman et al. 1989; Hillman and Davies 1990; Bar-Yosef and Belfer-Cohen 1989, 1991, 1992; McCorriston and Hole 1991; van Zeist 1988). Since the evidence indicates the possibilty that cereals were cultivated since the PPNA, and as this is a controversial issue, I will defer the discussion of animal bones to a later part of this section. Although a large array of seeds and fruits were exploited

during the PPNA, tubers and leaves are either poorly represented or rarely preserved. Detailed reports are available from the northern Levant, from Mureybet and Abu Hureyra, while information from the central and southern Levant is derived from Tel Aswad, Netiv Hagdud, Gilgal I, with some information from Jericho (van Zeist and Bakker-Heeres 1985, 1986; Hillman et al. 1989; Hopf 1983; Kislev 1989, 1992; Kislev in Bar-Yosef et al. 1991; Zohary and Hopf 1988; Hillman and Davies 1990, 1992; Zohary 1992; Miller 1992).

The main issue is when and where the shift from systematic gathering to cultivation took place. In the past, it was suggested that this transition happened simultaneously in different geographical locations, but recently Zohary (1989) proposed that it occurred in one small area. The best recorded pre-Neolithic floral assemblages originate in Ohalo II and the Epipaleolithic of Abu Hureyra (Kislev et al. 1992; Hillman et al. 1989; Hillman and Davies 1992). In Abu Hureyra the evidence suggests that the gathering of 150 species was done from May through July and from August to November. Given the possibility that the gathering seasons do not necessarily reflect the time of consumption, Hillman et al. (1990) argued that the site was occupied for most of the year. Importantly, there is no positive evidence that would indicate that wild Einkorn wheat or wild rye were cultivated. Field observation in the steppe region during a wet winter indicated that the distribution of 'weedy' species was not limited to cultivated fields, as was previously believed.

Unfortunately, Abu Hureyra was not occupied in the immediate PPNA period. This transition in the northern Levant is recorded in Mureybet. The stratified samples from the Late Natufian through the Early Neolithic (Mureybet phases IA, IB, II and III) enabled van Zeist and Bakker-Heeres (1986) to conclude that, besides the 60 species of wild seeds and fruits, two-seeded wild Einkorn became numerous in phase III. Size classes of lentil seeds indicate that they were also collected in the wild.

Despite the recent advances made in understanding the relationship between grain morphology and plant domestication, there is still considerable disagreement about the morphological attributes of 'domesticated species'. Hillman and Davies (1990) accept identifications based on grain morphology, size, and rare, well-preserved rachis fragments, indicating the presence of domesticated wheat and barley in Tel Aswad, Jericho, Gilgal and Netiv Hagdud. Kislev (1989, 1992), however, holds a different view. He observed that among threshed ears of wild barley, 10 per cent of the internodes still retain a fragment of the upper internode attached to the articulation scar. In a few cases, several internodes remain intact. Thus, the lower part of the ear of the wild barley manifests features which, to date, are considered characteristic of only domesticated forms. Kislev's archaeological conclusions (Kislev 1992) are that most of the barley seeds uncovered in Gilgal and Netiv Hagdud were collected in the wild stands and do not necessarily indicate intentional cultivation.

In an experiment in Jalès in June 1988, wild barley was harvested and the green ears were immediately threshed. The observations in the French field confirmed those of Kislev, which were done near Jerusalem. When the harvested barley was left to be sun-dried for 24 hours, however, only 2–3 per cent of the sample had a broken fragment of the internode still attached to the disarticulation plane. Therefore, Zohary (1992) and Hillman and Davies (1992) support the earlier contention that the carbonized grains from Netiv Hagdud, Gilgal I and Jericho indicate cultivation of two-rowed barley. In sum, the systematic cultivation of wild barley, followed by the harvesting and storage of grain as well as some human selection of seeds, led to domestication of this species (Zohary 1992).

In addition, Emmer wheat is better represented in the charred remains from Tel Aswad (van Zeist and Bakker-Heeres 1985). The plum-seeded *Triticum dicoccum* remains have been numerous since the early phase in this site, dated to 9800–9600 BP. Since the wild form is missing altogether from the early phases, it is not surprising that in a general survey of early Neolithic plant husbandry, van Zeist (1988) was willing to speculate and suggest that plant cultivation began between the Damascus basin and Jericho (van Zeist 1988: 56–8).

Several as yet unresolved questions are:

1. Was there only one locus of domestication for each species, as recently suggested by Zohary (1989), or several independent loci where various species were cultivated and exchanged?.
2. In light of the rapid morphological changes in plants recently documented by Hillman and Davies (1990, 1992), is it realistic for archaeologists to search for transitional forms?
3. What are the implications of the observable rapid change on the interpretation of archaeological remains?
4. Do shifts in the frequency of ground stone tool types reflect changes in food processing as suggested in various studies (Smith et al. 1984; Bar-Yosef and Belfer-Cohen 1989; Wright 1991)?

Whether the PPNA inhabitants of the settlement between Jericho and the Damascus basin were farmers or only intensive gatherers, they undoubtedly continued to hunt and trap (e.g., Clutton-Brock 1981; Bar-Yosef and Meadow in press). The evidence from PPNA faunal assemblages is that more caprovines and cattle were hunted in the northern Levant while gazelle dominated in the central and southern Levant, sometimes with ibex, fallow deer and wild boar. Both Jericho and Netiv Hagdud demonstrate high frequencies of foxes. Netiv Hagdud and Gilgal I resemble Jericho, but also have high frequencies of birds (which can be partially attributed to

the lack of sieving in Jericho). The site of Nahal Oren is represented, aside from the dominant gazelle, by a few bones of fallow and roe deer. At Hatoula, gazelle, hare and fox are dominant with a few bones of aurochs, wild boar, equids, hedgehogs and small carnivores. A relatively high frequency of bird bones (including aquatic species, as in Netiv Hagdud and Gilgal) and bones of marine fish complete the faunal spectrum (Davis 1989).

The overall picture (Figure 3) indicates that the main shift in animal exploitation occurred only during the PPNB when higher frequencies of caprovines (goat and sheep) meant a decrease in the frequencies of gazelle, wild boar, cattle and rare deer (e.g., Davis 1982; Helmer 1989).

Most scholars agree that there is sufficient evidence of fully-fledged farming communities existing during the PPNB along the 'Levantine Corridor' that expanded during the ninth millennium BP into Anatolia and the Zagros.

Plant remains retrieved from village sites indicate that cereals, legumes, flax and other species were cultivated. The evidence for the presence of grain in the desert sites is indirect; all desert sites contain grinding stones, sometimes in large numbers. Historical records support the contention that cereals were often grown locally, as in Biqat 'Uvda in the southern Negev, about 30 km north of Eilat. The better climatic conditions during the early to late PPNB made it possible to grow grain in oases and temporarily wet desert interior basins. The use of baskets, as indicated by the finds from Nahal Hemar, enabled people to carry grain over large distances without draft animals.

The intriguing questions are 'when', 'where' and 'why' the domestication of animals took place (e.g., Bar-Yosef and Meadow in press). Davis (1982) suggested viewing the shift in the frequencies among animal bones (NISP), as demonstrated in Figure 3, as reflecting the introduction of domesticated caprovines into the Levant. This change occurred around 9500/9000 BP, although it is not certain whether the domestication took place in the marginal belt of the coastal Levant. The beginning of the intentional tending and rearing of cattle and pigs followed at the end of the ninth and early eighth millennia BP in the northern Levant.

The current archaeo-zoological information suggests that goats and sheep were not an important component of the natural game in the central and southern Levantine sites, with the exception of *Capra aegagrus* in the mountains of Lebanon and the *Capra ibex* in south Jordan and southern Sinai. If most studies concerning hunter-gatherers are correct, they indicate that these people were familiar with the fauna of their environments, but hardly ever tried to domesticate animals. It is, therefore, suggested that goat and sheep were domesticated only when farmers moved into Anatolia and the Zagros mountains.

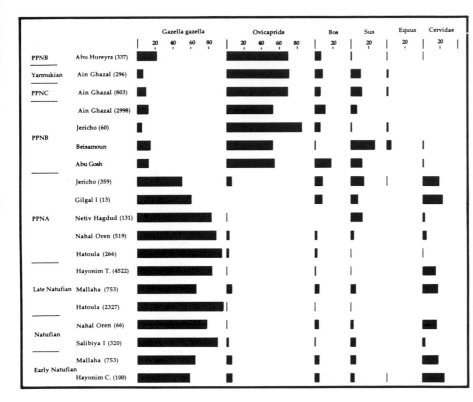

Figure 3 Frequencies of animal bones in various Natufian, PPNA, PPNB, PPNC and Yarmukian assemblages. The PPNB from Abu Hureyra was added for comparison. The number of bones in each sample is given in brackets after the site's name. The reader should note the change in the faunal spectra after the PPNA when caprovines replace, as the main group, the gazelles, thus indicating the domestication of the goats and later of sheep

Religion and ideology

Graves and burials

Burials are common in Jericho, Netiv Hagdud, 'Iraq ed-Dubb and Hatula but, surprisingly, are missing from Gilgal I, where large surfaces were excavated (Noy 1989). One possible explanation for this is that the site as a whole had an entirely different function in comparison to other PPNA sites and was used, as predicated in the case of Late Natufian sites in the Jordan Valley, only as a seasonal base.

The removal of skulls from most adult burials is a common habit while the skeletons of children remained intact. The special treatment of adult skulls is better known from the PPNB period when skulls were modelled in plaster or asphalt, and interpreted as the 'cult of the ancestors' (see below). Neither isolated Natufian nor PPNA skulls in occupational deposits exhibit a special treatment.

The main change takes place during the final PPNB when the burials are intact and no skull removal is observed (Rollefson et al. 1992). In the Sinai desert, groups of hunter-gatherers practiced secondary burials in what seem to have been storage facilities in a seasonal aggregation site (Bar-Yosef 1984, 1985). It seems that the dead were first buried at the location of death (such as in the case of Wadi Tbeik) and were later removed to the central site (Hershkovitz and Gopher 1990).

Art and/or cultic objects

The few figurines made of either limestone or clay represent the scant knowledge concerning cultic or ritual activities during the PPNA period. The female figurines are of 'seated woman' with eyes, breasts and, rarely, an incision on the head which can be interpreted as symbolizing head gear (Noy 1986). The definitely female figures mark a clear departure from the Natufian world (Cauvin 1985) where animals dominate the inventory of known objects. In addition, the use of clay is more or less new, and is well correlated with the extensive use of mudbricks that began in the PPNA and which undoubtedly reflects a change in the hierarchy of values within Neolithic society.

Small figurines are common also in the PPNB deposits. The largest collection was uncovered in Ain Ghazal (Rollefson 1983, 1986), many of which are animals, but few are human. Other human figurines are known from Munhata (Perrot 1968, 1967). These figurines could have been used in daily, domestic activities as toys or as teaching aids employed by adults to explain the secrets of nature to children. On the other hand, the figurines are also viewed as offerings or as personally-owned sacred objects. Female figurines are often referred to as 'the

Plate 4 Skulls modelled in asphalt from Nahal Hemar (photograph: Zev Radovan)

Plate 3 Two female figurines from Netiv Hagdud (photograph: Zev Radovan)

mother goddess' (e.g., Cauvin 1972, 1985). As recently suggested by Voigt (1990, 1991), clues to the use of these figurines should come from their original context, which is rarely documented or published.

A special phenomenon are the plastered and asphalt modelled skulls which have been found in Ramad, Beisamoun, Ain Ghazal, Jericho, Kefar Hahoresh and Nahal Hemar cave (Kenyon 1957; de Contenson 1981; Lechevallier 1978; Rollefson 1984; Bar-Yosef and Alon 1988; Goring-Morris 1991). Most authorities agree that they represent the 'cult of the ancestors' (Cauvin 1972, 1985; Braidwood 1975; Margalit 1983; Moore 1985; Bar-Yosef and Alon 1988; Yakar and Hershkovitz 1988). The interpretation of these finds as products within a symbolic system, aiming to strengthen the social cohesion of an extended family or group of families and their properties (whether compounds in the settlement, cultivated plots or foraging territories), seems to have been the most favorable one.

Finally, the exquisite painted plaster statues from Ain Ghazal, along with the fragmentary ones from Jericho and Nahal Hemar cave, are shaped as female busts or complete human figures of various sizes, some without clear sex signs (see Plate 1). The preservation of the collection from Ain Ghazal indicates that they must have been placed under a roof and later buried. The burial of worn-out statues of deities, seemingly produced on-site, is well known from later archaeological contexts, and hints at the presence of an organized religion with distinguished members of the community who served the cult (Hole 1983).

Social organization

The reconstruction of the social organization relies heavily on the understanding of the current social structures

among hunter-gatherers, farmers and pastoral nomads. While analogies may be carefully chosen, there is constant scrutiny to determine whether the current reconstruction stands the test of the archaeological records. The PPNA period's main change was in increased village populations (to 250–400 people), which lived all year round in the same location; this created entire biologically viable units, thus reducing trips (and the costs involved) for mate searching. This demographic change had undoubtedly other implications that are as yet not well explored.

Common attributes among PPNA sites are found in their lithic industries. Khiam points and aerodynamic arrowheads were documented from southern Sinai (Abu Madi I) to Jebel Sinjar (Qermez Dereh) in northern Iraq. These points mark the PPNA interaction sphere, and reflect the communication and exchange between hunters across the landscape. Similarly, imported obsidian pieces that reach the southern Levant from central Anatolia traveled a distance of more than 1000 km. Obsidian was apparently distributed from centers. Thus, more obsidian items were found in Jericho than in Netiv Hagdud, despite the lack of sieving. The presence of villages and smaller sites in their peripheries demonstrates that territories were delineated among farming communities. The 'outside world', from their point of view, were entities of hunter-gatherers that continued to survive in the higher mountains and the deserts.

Social change is significantly demonstrated in the shift from curvilinear to rectangular architecture. Flannery (1972) suggested that it represents the shift from nuclear family habitations to those of extended families, but a different interpretation ties the change to major shifts in wealth.

More information from PPNB is available due to a larger number of excavated sites, although the exposed areas are never more than 2000 m². Proximity between dwellings is interpreted as indicating close family relationships (e.g., Kramer 1982). In sites such as Beidha

(Kirkbride 1966) or Ain Ghazal (Rollefson et al. 1992), several extended families could have formed the village, possibly with some sort of social hierarchy created by economic wealth. The compounds of the desert groups, with a series of round structures, built simultaneously or added to one another, such as in Abu Nekheileh (Kirkbride 1978), Nahal Issaron (Goring-Morris and Gopher 1983), Wadi Tbeik and Wadi Jibba (Bar-Yosef 1984; Garrard et al. 1988; Betts 1987), may represent family compounds. In arid environments, where food and water resources are less reliable than in the Mediterranean belt, the size of these compounds was determined by the seasonal potential of a particular environment.

Faunal remains from the excavated desertic sites reflect selective hunting and trapping in what were interpreted as winter and summer camps (Tchernov and Bar-Yosef 1982; Dayan et al. 1986; Garrard et al. 1988). In southern Sinai, intensive use of grinding stones and the presence of underground silos support the proposed exploitation of seeds or grain. Unfortunately, plant remains are rare.

Territoriality among PPNB sites is more easily discerned in the deserts. For example, a regional interaction sphere is provided by the distribution of the 'burin sites' in Jordan and the Syro-Arabian desert. One may suggest that these sites are not the expressions of a particular seasonal activity, but rather the remains of a large Neolithic group that survived in the semi-steppic and desert area of the central Levant. Similarly, the sites in southern Sinai, beyond the Et-Tih escarpment, are interpreted as a regional entity.

The extent of social alliances among farming communities is unknown and is currently reconstructed on the basis of lithic typology, architectural remains and the economy, while taking into account the possible existence of seasonal camps. Within this territory there are examples of long distance exchange of Red Sea shells found at Jericho, Abu Gosh, Nahal Hemar cave, Yiftahel, Ain Ghazal, etc. (D.E. Bar-Yosef 1989), as well as of the presence of Anatolian obsidian.

A socio-economic mechanism that provided gazelle and onager tissues from the desertic groups to villagers (Bar-Yosef 1986) is probably demonstrated by the large number of game drives, nicknamed 'desert kites', that have been preserved in the Syro-Arabian desert, especially between the 'Black Desert' and Wadi Sirhan (Meshel 1974; Betts 1982, 1985). A few of these were located in the Arava valley as well as in southern Sinai. Betts (1985) proposed dating the 'Black Desert kites' to the late PPNB and early eighth millennium BP. Persian gazelle was probably the species hunted in the Syro-Arabian 'desert kites', although Mountain gazelle were present in the Sinai peninsula during the PPNB (Tchernov and Bar-Yosef 1982; Dayan et al. 1986). The proposal that game meat was exchanged by the PPNB desert groups for grain can be tested through the analysis of bone counts from village sites such as Ain Ghazal and Basta.

Plate 5 Nahal Hemar cave. Note the small opening (photograph: O. Bar-Yosef)

Within the PPNB interaction sphere (Bar-Yosef and Belfer-Cohen 1989), individual territories can be identified on the basis of material culture elements. While arrowheads, except for Jericho points, have a wide distribution, domestic objects such as the Tahunian axe/ adze or the *herminette* of Mureybet, the tanged sickle blades, the Mureybat scrapers (Cauvin and Stordeur 1978), or the stone bracelets in the central and southern Levant exhibit a clear geographic distribution among farming communities.

Inter-societal exchange systems between hunter-gatherers and farmers, and among hunter-gatherers themselves, are currently the subject of much discussion in the literature. Socio-economic stresses encourage reciprocity in exchange or warfare. Such situations either develop mutual dependence on a steady supply of food, raw materials, labor and commodities or lead to conquest. However, the evidence for extensive or intensive warfare is as yet missing from the archaeological record. Instead, the exchange of projectiles, high quality flint, obsidian and rare minerals for bead production, as well as of finished products such as body decorations and labor, was also a mechanism for the exchange of information. Material items and techniques were dispersed by the 'budding off' of new communities (the 'neolithization' of the Taurus; Cauvin 1987) and by mutual exchange between neighboring small villages, by inter-marriage, and with kin-related groups across social and geographic boundaries. The exchange networks encompassed both farmers and hunter-gatherers and were the mechanism that created the PPNB interaction sphere.

The emergence of territoriality among the farming communities seems to have been based on competition between expanding groups. Food producing techniques, such as the cultivation of fields, the intensified gathering of fruits and seeds around the village, the emergence of tended groves of fruit trees, and intensive hunting and trapping, over-exploited the home ranges of these sedentary communities. In addition, necessary adjustments of the social structure were made through 60–70 generations, and were probably a painful process. Increased personal and inter-family conflicts, as well as intensified use of public rituals, became essential. The increased cohesion of the groups was inseparable from the formation of social hierarchies (Cohen 1985).

There is a proposal to interpret the Nahal Hemar cave as a territorial 'marker' on the geographic boundary between the Negev and the Judean hills and desert (Bar-Yosef and Alon 1988). The location of such a holy place on the edge of a territory is not surprising, as both ethnographic and archaeological parallels are known. The Chalcolithic temple of Ein Gedi, for example, is like the cave, and seems to have been a marginally located cult center for a specific region. It served as a storage place for paraphernalia such as the stone masks, modeled skulls, special clothes, body decorations, and fragmented plaster statues that were employed in rituals or brought to be buried in this sacred place.

Conclusion: processes of change

The explanatory model used in this chapter takes into account the results of numerous investigations and a previously proposed models (e.g., Hole 1984; Moore 1985: Bar-Yosef and Belfer-Cohen 1989, 1991, 1992; Moore and Hillman 1992; McCorriston and Hole 1991; Bar-Yosef and Meadow in press). The main factors in this model are the climatic fluctuations of the Terminal Pleistocene, the resources in the Levant and their nature, and social considerations known from behavioral studies of hunter-gatherers and farmers.

Environmental changes resulting from abrupt climatic fluctuations are seen as triggering cultural changes that occur only after being 'filtered' through societal mechanisms devised to deal with crises. The climatic shifts began with an increase in precipitation at the end of the Late Glacial Maximum, around 14,500/14,000 BP. This was perhaps punctuated by a short dry event around 13,000/12,800. The continued increase in rainfall culminated around 11,500± and was followed by the cold and dry 'Younger Dryas' which lasted several centuries, some time between 11,000 and 10,000 B.P. (*ca.* 10,800–10,300 BP). The 'Younger Dryas' caused vegetational shifts as well as a reduction in the distribution of C3 plants such as cereals. It ceased with a rapid return to wetter conditions, although not as wet as in the previous period, around 10,000 BP.

The availability, predictability and abundance of many edible seeds, fruits and leaves, together with some mammals, formed the basis for the 'broad spectrum' (Flannery 1973) subsistence of hunter-gatherers in the Levantine Corridor since 20,000 BP. Perennial plant

resources (essentially fruits) in the Levantine region were also predictable, while acorns should be considered famine foods, not a major dietary resource (McCorriston 1994). The stationary nature of the behavior of the common local game (e.g., Mountain gazelle, roe deer, fallow deer) encouraged the establishment of a semi-sedentary settlement pattern.

The emergence of the Natufian from a population of Epipaleolithic hunter-gatherers is seen as an event which took place in a certain Levantine 'homeland' and as a point of no return (Bar-Yosef and Belfer-Cohen 1989, 1991). The rest of the Near East was continuously occupied by groups of hunter-gatherers until the socio-economic changes caused by the 'Neolithic Revolution' at the end of the 'Younger Dryas' caught up with them. The factor of 'demographic pressure' means that from *ca.* 14,500 BP, people occupied every eco-zone within the Near East; under stress conditions, territorial rearrangements and a shift in settlement patterns were necessary.

The establishment of Early Natufian base camps departed from the old seasonal settlement pattern. Permanent camp sites changed the sense of territoriality and decreased the number of options in times of stress (Tchernov 1991). These changes worked in a feedback mechanism during the ensuing millennia with the establishment of cultivating communities.

This threshold is seen as a response to the forcing effects of the 'Younger Dryas' on the Late Natufian in the Levantine Corridor. Starting intentional cultivation was the only solution for a population for which cereals became a staple food, and for which a return to a mobile hunting-gathering lifestyle was not a valid option. So far as we know from the available evidence, the Natufians were harvesting wild cereals in natural stands. Groups on the west side of the hilly area exploited the margins of the Jordan Valley on a seasonal basis. Thus, sedentary hamlets were located only on the west side, except for the Galilee. A similar pattern can be reconstructed for the Transjordanian plateau. During the 'Younger Dryas', yields of natural stands decreased and apparently motivated intentional cultivation. By establishing the Neolithic sedentary communities in the Jordan Valley, the first farmers gained the use of flat alluvial lands as fields – an area with less vegetational cover that minimized clearing efforts. The shift in settlement patterns means that the main considerations in choosing a location were primarily related to cereal cultivation and not necessarily to optimal foraging of vegetal and animal resources. Such a change led to major changes in labor and social organization, as well as to further investments in permanent dwellings and storage facilities. The pluvial conditions of the PPNA period ensured the existence of numerous small lakes and ponds, and the success of a new economy. Reasonably good conditions continued throughout most of the PPNB times, although the end of the period correlates with climatic shifts such as the retreat of the monsoonal system (COHMAP members 1988). Although the abandonment of PPNB sites was related by the excavators of Ain Ghazal to environmental deterioration caused by humans, the broad distribution of this phenomenon, which incorporates the coastal belt, goes against such a simplified explanation. Even if goat herding and the use of wood became common practices among PPNB farmers, there is no ample evidence for a region-wide impact. Climatic changes around 6000 BP (uncalibrated) were recorded over the entire Near East, as well as other places in the Mediterranean basin – in most cases away from farming communities.

The domestication of the caprovines is still a debated issue. This writer suggested that it took place in the Taurus-Zagros ranges, or their hilly flanks, during the PPNB, where both species had already been hunted extensively in the Upper Pleistocene. The initiative for a change in the pattern of exploitation, which we referred to as 'domestication', occurred as part of the domestic activity in sedentary farming communities or in the seasonal sites that belonged to farming communities with an anticipated mobility pattern. The evidence from Ganj Dareh, for example, where domesticated cereals were recovered from the earliest level (E), means that goats had already been manipulated by the occupants. The issue is whether the metrical information supports the contention that the domesticated goats appear only in the following levels (D and above, Hesse 1984). However, the possibilty of caprovine herding beginning in more than one locality, including the Levant, is still an option that needs to be tested archaeologically.

The domestication of the caprovines responds to the need for a constant supply of animal tissues (proteins, calories, fat, etc.) on a stable basis. One may speculate that the demand arose against a background of depleting game in certain areas of the Near East or, more particularly, in the central and southern Levant. This, in part, is supported by a demonstrable shift to the exploitation of smaller animals, including more hare

hunting in the lower levels at Cafer, and more water fowl trapping in PPNA Netiv Hagdud and Hatula (Helmer 1991; Davis 1989, 1991).

The earliest evidence for domesticated goats in the deserts of the Levant comes from Azraq 37 (Garrard et al. 1988), dated to the eighth millennuim BP. This supports an earlier contention that pastoralism in the Levant emerged from task groups of villagers who exploited the spring and fall pastures in the steppic-desertic belt (Bar-Yosef and Khazanov 1992; Kohler-Rollefson 1992).

The natural growth of agricultural villages and the budding-off of new communities is archaeologically visible during the ninth millennium BP, but becomes clearer by the end of the eighth millennium BP. Even with inherent uncertainties in ^{14}C dating, it seems that several sites have longer sequences than others. Chronological gaps in well-established settlements can be interpreted as resulting from 'shifting cultivation', resulting from soil exhaustion and/or salinatior The overall thickness of the deposits in the Neolithic sites and the range of the radiocarbon dates indicate that new villages were founded during the PPNB. By the final phase of this period, cattle, and later pig, were introduced as domesticated species. The existence of Near Eastern exchange networks, such as in obsidian, collected in various Anatolian sources suggests that these domesticated species were moved into the southern Levant from the north.

The establishment of farming communities, especially during the PPNB, imposed a new time schedule on females' work, possibly creating extra responsibilities for women during the sowing season, coupled with the effects of sedentism (e.g., increase in the number of children, more restricted areas of gathering wild fruits and seeds, etc.). Logistically organized long distance forays carried out by men became a necessity, thus enhancing gender differences in activities. This marked the departure from the more locally based subsistence strategies which characterized the late hunter-gatherers and the Natufian economy (Bar-Yosef and Belfer-Cohen 1989, 1991, 1992).

NAHAL HEMAR CAVE

Nahal Hemar (Heb. = bitumen) Cave is located about 250 m above sea level, near the confluence of Nahal Hemar and Nahal Dimona. The cave is a small chamber about 4 × 8 m which was formed in limestone with a small entrance. Most of the chamber area is dark. The cave was first plundered by Bedouin who were searching for scrolls, and later was hastily partially excavated. Systematic excavations in the remaining deposits were conducted in June 1983 (by the author and David Alon), when detailed stratigraphy was established from the remaining 15 per cent of the original deposits. Four major layers were identified:

- *Layer 1* (0.6−0.5 m thick) The sediment was made up of limestone rubble, coprolites, twigs, branches, organic dust, nitrate crystals and a few sherds dated to the Early Bronze I and Byzantine−Early Arabic periods. A piece of plain woven cloth derived from this layer gave the date of (OxA 1013) 660 ±200 BP calibrated as 1035−1510 AD.
- *Layer 2* (0.35−0.45 m thick) contained large quantities of limestone rubble, coprolites and a few Neolithic finds. In the northeast niche, two trodden earth floors were uncovered.
- *Layer 3* (0.60 m thick) was subdivided into two units. Both contained the same elements − limestone fragments, coprolites, twigs, branches and numerous Neolithic finds. The remains of a hearth in Layer 3A provided the following dates. (RT 650): 8100 ± 100 BP ; (Pta 3650) 8270 ± 80 BP and (BM 2298): 8250 ± 70 BP. AMS dates for knots of a net and a piece of twined napkin were (OxA 1014) 8600 ± 120, and (OxA 1015): 8500 ± 220 BP, respectively. Strings collected during the early excavations date to (BM 2300) 8690 ± 70 BP.
- *Layer 4* was of varying thickness due to the uneven cave floor. As the earliest deposit, it filled the cavities under and between the boulders, and consisted of carbonate sand, broken stalagmites, twigs, branches and a few coprolites. Two samples of linen yarn and a piece of knotted fabric provided the dates of (Pta 3625): 8850 ± 90 BP, (BM 2299): 9210 ± 300 BP and an AMS reading of (OxA 1016) 8810 ± 120 BP.

The assemblage, here treated as one entity, contains numerous uniquely preserved objects. Stems of rushes, grasses, and reeds were used in producing cordage, matting and basketry items (Plate 1.1). Fabrics were made of bast fibers, especially *Linum* sp.

Fragments of containers made of cordage and asphalt in a variety of shapes and sizes were found. Their bases were made of split reeds or coiled cordage and the body parts of spiraling coils of cordage. The whole structure was coated with a layer of asphalt on the inner, and one on the outer, surface. A small cylindrical box, 5 cm in diameter, shaped from fine 2-mm-thick spiraling cord, is one of the finest examples.

Only small fragments of mats were uncovered, made of flattened rushes or grass, fastened together with a cord in a wrapping technique.

Knotted netting is represented by numerous fragments. Two types of knots were used: a square knot and a sheet-bend knot. Most fabrics were made from fine linen yarn in single-element

techniques that are related to sewing and were done with the aid of a needle.

A conical headdress, 32 cm high and 16 cm in diameter, which consisted of 100 rhomboids alternating with open spaces in a tight, knotted looping technique, was reconstructed. Its base band was decorated with a single greenstone bead. Additional rhomboids, slightly different in yarn dimension and type of knot, were decorated with Cowrie shells.

A very well-preserved, nearly complete cloth rectangle with a compact buttonhole stitch provides an insight into how some of the smaller, poorly preserved twined fragments might have looked.

Countered weft-twining in a tight, chainlike appearance is present in about a dozen heading parts of what could belong to 'string skirts' to which the globular green-painted plaster beads, several still with the string inside them, are also attributed (Plate 1.2).

The lithic assemblage consists of numerous blades that were removed from naviform cores. Two hundred and seven blades with bilateral notches near the proximal end and a few with retouched tips were named 'Nahal Hemar knives' in order to designate their special shape, although there is no evidence that they were used as knives. Eighteen arrowheads were found: ten Byblos points, five Jericho points, and one patinated Helwan point, and a small arrowhead, probably of Pottery Neolithic or later age. Finally, 517 plain blades were collected.

Many bone tools were manufactured from the ribs and shafts of long bones of bovids. The largest group consists of flat

Plate 1.1   Nahal Hemar: a fragment of an asphalt coated basket (photograph: Zev Radovan)

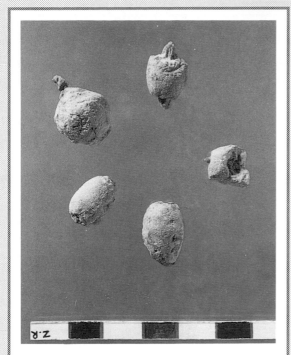

Plate 1.2 Nahal Hemar: painted green plastered pendants perhaps part of a string skirt (photograph: Zev Radovan)

They were originally painted green or red, or with both colors.

Five small figurines were found. One, made of a limestone pebble, has the form of a rodent, possibly a house mouse. The other four depict the human face. They were shaped of pieces of long bones that stressed the nose and the eyes. Asphalt, red ochre, green dioptase, and lime plaster were added to mark eyes, hair, and beard. Detailed analysis suggests that paint and asphalt were not applied at one time but on various occasions. In addition, the remains of four different plaster statues were collected. Their fragmentary remains and the many missing parts may indicate that they were brought into the cave for interment as sacred objects.

The isolated human bones in the site were skulls and neck vertebrae. Except for two fragments, all bones belonged to adults. Six of the fragmentary skulls preserved parts of asphalt coating which had been applied solely to the posterior side. The first layer of asphalt was applied directly on the dried bones with a comblike instrument, and then patted. The second phase involved the making of asphalt cords and their arrangement in a net pattern on the first layer. The forehead and the face were left untouched.

Two stone masks were uncovered in Nahal Hemar Cave. One is only a fragment of the lower part including the chin and the lower row of teeth. The second is almost complete with two rounded eye sockets, a protruding nose, an open mouth with four teeth in each row, and 18 holes perforated around the edge of the mask (Plate 1.4). Other facial characteristics are the painted stripes in red and green on a buff background, and asphalt stains, many of which still carry the residue of hair or its

spatulas (281), with either a pointed or broad rounded tip. Completing the inventory are 12 shuttles (Plate 1.3) with a small or large eye (including one decorated shuttle, four awls, seven carved and incised fragments, and one special hook that resembles a belt fastener).

A sickle was uncovered in a small niche in the northern wall near the floor. The sickle haft was made of ibex horn and three flint blades were inserted and secured in the groove with sap. The three blades show no visible gloss. A zigzag pattern was incised on the handle.

The few wooden tools were made from species common in the region from the Judean hills to the Dead Sea and the Edom-Moab area. Three objects are classified as arrowheads and six as points. The latter could also have served as projectile points. Two thick, well-rounded fragments could have been digging sticks.

Beads and pendants were made of marine shells, various stones, wood and plaster. Of the 513 marine shells, 421 originated from the Mediterranean Sea while 92 were brought from the Red Sea. Of the 29 stone beads, four are made of an unidentified black-gray material, one is carnelian, and the others are classified as greenstone (serpentine?). Several dozen lime-plaster beads were found in the cave. Most of the beads were modeled around a cord or a twig which was later pulled out, but in some beads the cord is still intact. Most of the beads were painted green, a color produced from dioptase, one of the copper minerals. They are thought to belong to a 'string skirt'. Finally, the wooden beads were shaped from a light root shaft of a monocotyledonous plant.

Plate 1.3 Nahal Hemar: bone shuttles (photograph: Zev Radovan)

imprint. The numerous asphalt stains around the mouth probably indicate the presence of a beard. The mask, the adorned skulls and the bone figurines may depict the same elderly male appearance which, as in the context of PPNB villages, is interpreted as the cult of the ancestors.

Food remains were scant and included cultivated plants such as wheat, barley and lentils, which were brought in with various species of weeds that grow in cultivated fields. Cereals were probably grown some 15 km away, while edible seeds and the fruits of Tabor oak, pistachio, coriander and colocynth were carried from the hilly areas 10 to 50 km away.

Most of the large- and medium-sized mammalian bones in the cave were introduced by hyenas. These include large cattle, caprines (ibex and goat), and gazelles. Their presence in Layer 3 may indicate that the cave became a hyena den at some time close to the end of the Neolithic occupation.

In sum, the cave of Nahal Hemar was not a domestic habitation, but was used for temporary storage of mundane items with a wealth of cultic objects such as the masks, the figurines and anthropomorphic plaster statues, and the adorned skulls. It was suggested that this place be viewed as a storage site for sacred objects that served during seasonal rituals. The location of the site on the geographic border between the Negev and the Judean Desert may indicate that it also served as a boundary marker between two populations.

Plate 1.4   Nahal Hemar: stone mask (The Israel Museum, Jerusalem)

13

EARLY POTTERY-BEARING GROUPS IN ISRAEL – THE POTTERY NEOLITHIC PERIOD

Avi Gopher

Introduction

Early Pottery-Bearing populations of the sixth and fifth millennia BC (uncalibrated C-14 years) in the Fertile Crescent area and especially in Greater Mesopotamia were the first to feature large-scale socio-political structures which influenced large tracts of land between Iran in the east and Anatolia and the Mediterranean coast in the west (e.g., LeBlanc and Watson 1973). These entities were the focal point of much research and names such as the Hassuna, Samarra, Halaf and Ubaid cultures have become household words in the investigation of processes leading to the birth of Mesopotamian urbanized civilization. This was, to an extent, the case in northern Syria and on the Syrian coast. However, in the Levant, and especially in the southern Levant, research on early pottery-bearing groups of the sixth and fifth millennia BC was neglected in favour of intensive study of the earlier periods in which the dramatic processes known as the Agricultural or Neolithic Revolution took place. Great efforts were invested in studying the Natufian culture and cultures of the Pre-Pottery Neolithic period (henceforth PPN) which resulted in a plethora of publications. Intensive research also took place, from the 1930s onwards, into cultures of the Chalcolithic period and the beginning of the Early Bronze Age (fourth millennium BC) which preceded the 'Urban Revolution' in southern parts of the Levant.

Against this background there is a conspicuous paucity both of data and interpretations of socio-economic developments in the sixth and fifth millennia BC, which preceded the incorporation of the southern Levant within the urban systems of the Early Bronze Age. The discovery of early pottery assemblages during the 1930s and 1940s in Israel at base layers of large tell sites such as Megiddo (Shipton 1939), Jericho (Garstang and Garstang 1940) and Bethshan (Fitzgerald 1934, 1935) hardly advanced the research on Pottery Neolithic (henceforth PN) cultures. The

assemblages known as Jericho IX and Jericho VIII were left isolated – curiosities of preliminary stages in research dealt with mainly in chronostratigraphic contexts. In the early 1950s, following the definition of the Yarmukian culture by Stekelis (1950/51 1972) and the Wadi Raba culture by Kaplan (1958a), the variability of the PN phenomena began to emerge. These scholars, however, turned in the late 1950s to other fields and our knowledge and understanding of PN culture has not progressed. In the 1960s Perrot led a large-scale excavation of PN layers at Munhata (e.g. Perrot 1964, 1966) and, although detailed studies of the Munhata assemblages were only published very recently (Gopher 1989a; Garfinkel 1992a), Perrot's summaries actually synthesized the whole body of available data up to the late 1960s (Perrot 1968). Wide-ranging summaries were published in the 1970s by Mellaart (1975), Moore (1978) and Redman (1978), ending that stage of research. A new wave of research in the 1980s and 1990s which includes the excavation of sixth and fifth millennia BC layers both in Jordan and in Israel is still in progress. It brings with it a growing potential for analysis and interpretation of the cultures of these periods. I should mention in this context that an up-to-date review was recently published which summarizes in detail the different aspects of sixth and fifth millennia BC cultures in the southern Levant (Gopher and Gophna 1993). Moreover, a number of doctoral dissertations analyzing and interpreting data from this period have appeared recently (Goren 1991; Garfinkel 1992b). The ideas presented here use these data to go a stage further by offering a number of interpretations of events and processes that took place in the Pottery Neolithic period.

The Pre-Pottery Neolithic background

The cultural system of the Pre-Pottery Neolithic period operated on a pan-Levantine scale from the Middle Euphrates (and maybe even further north) to the desertic

Plate 1 Neolithic pottery jar with painted and incised decoration

areas of the Southern Levant. It was described as an integral system (Gopher 1985, 1989b), an interaction sphere (Bar-Yosef and Belfer-Cohen 1989) or a *koine* (cf. Cauvin 1989). The high degree of affinity between subunits within this system was emphasized, thus describing what could fit on a schematic level the Clarkian heading of 'culture group' (Clarke 1978: 299–362). Sites of different size scales were dispersed throughout the Levant in the PPN, adapted to the different ecological zones and practising different modes of economy. These included every possible combination of hunting, gathering, fishing, agriculture of cereals and pulses, and livestock husbandry. In this framework new evidence of technological innovations appears, beginning with the Pre-Pottery Neolithic A period (PPNA) including the use of mudbrick, spinning and basketry methods, the appearance of arrowheads in lithic assemblages and so on.

An additional series of innovations and changes in architecture, lithic technology, groundstone implements and the industry of limeplaster took place in the Pre-Pottery Neolithic B (PPNB; Bar-Yosef, Chapter 12). The most conspicuous phenomenon, however, through the 2000 years of the PPNA and B, was the establishment of an economic system based on agriculture and its dispersal from the regions of its first appearance throughout the Levant (e.g., Byrd 1992). Concurrently, a demographic growth was registered – not, however, as dramatic as reconstructed by some scholars (e.g., Hershkovitz and Gopher 1990). At the same time, changes and developments occurred in the ideology of the populations, and rituals that were interpreted as ancestor worship gained credence in the PPNA and were especially prevalent in the PPNB (e.g., Kenyon 1970: Cauvin 1972; Bar-Yosef 1977). Domestic and public rituals were reconstructed (Rollefson 1983, 1986) and regional cult aggregation localities were identified through a wide variety of *objets d'art* interpreted as ritual paraphernalia (Bar-Yosef and Alon 1988: 27–8). Among the most famous manifestations of artistic-symbolic objects of the PPNB are the plastered and otherwise treated skulls, the buried caches of plaster statuary, figurines and stone masks. This continuous process of socio-economic change brought the PPNB *koine* to a climax in the seventh millennium BC. Mega sites of over a hundred dunams flourished in the different parts of the Levant.

Towards the end of the seventh millennium signs of crisis first appeared in the PPN system and it began to undergo a process of disintegration. Some scholars, adopting a deterministic view, attribute the collapse to climatic deterioration. Others claim that man's impact on the environment, together with a climatic change, brought about an over-exploitation of the area and disturbed its fragile balance. I personally would examine a stochastic attitude which views these final stages as integral parts of the PPNB ontogenetic process. In any event, it is clear from the data that towards the end of the seventh

millennium BC there was a change but it will require further research to understand the reasons for it.

Developments in the early sixth millennium BC

The recognition of the collapse of the PPN system was for many years accompanied by a reconstruction of a long settlement gap in the southern Levant or parts of this region – some claim for over a thousand years – mainly in the sixth millennium BC (e.g., deVaux 1966; Kenyon 1970; Perrot 1968). This was explained as the result of climatic deterioration, and subsequently population movements were reconstructed for desertion of the dessicated parts of the southern Levant and a move to the north into more humid regions. It was accepted by many that after this gap pottery-bearing cultures first appeared in the southern Levant.

Research in the 1980s has refined our understanding of the sequence of events in the southern Levant, and subsequently a new time unit was added following the PPNB which was termed the PPNC (Rollefson and Simmons 1986, 1988; Rollefson 1989) and covered the first half of the sixth millennium BC. This unit was first identified at 'Ain Ghazal and later a number of additional layers were dated to the same period (e.g., Atlit Yam, Galili et al. 1994). Even though data is only preliminary and PPNC cultural entities are only sporadically known, the regional diversification within it is conspicuous and, while 'Ain Ghazal is a very large site at that period, in the Damascus Basin, Israeli coastal plain and even in the Negev, a variety of different sites appear. Continuity from PPNB to PPNC can be identified in some aspects but change is observed too – in categories of material culture, in economic structure and in burial customs (Simmons et al. 1988; Rollefson et al. 1992). Against the diverse local adaptations of the first half of the sixth millennium BC, which represent the last gasps of the PPN, PN culture appeared in the southern Levant. We should remember that in northern parts of the Levant and in Mesopotamia, pottery-bearing entities of considerable size (and possibly complexity?) are already established.

Early pottery in the southern Levant

Who were the producers of early pottery in the southern Levant? This question is often raised. A number of suggestions concerning their origin were made through the years, mostly regarding them as immigrants arriving with a fully-fledged culture. I believe they were a local population that went through changes in many aspects of culture and established a new rural system. There is no clear evidence to connect these early pottery producers to any foreign populations. However, I do not claim they were isolated. It was not until the fifth millennium BC that

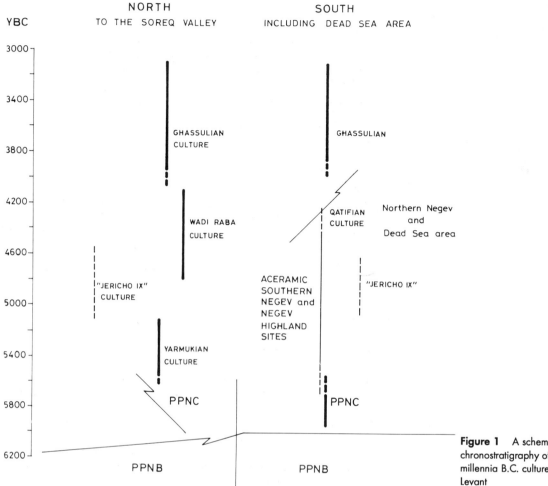

Figure 1   A scheme of the chronostratigraphy of sixth and fifth millennia B.C. cultures in the southern Levant

signs of northern influence appear in the material culture of southern Levantine entities. PN cultures and sub-cultures are defined generally following Clarke (1978: 299–302) and using Renfrew's operative definition (1972: 19) in the belief that similarity in assemblages of material culture at certain measurable levels, within a defined geographical range and a limited timespan, indicates social groupings and is sufficient for assignment to an archaeological cultural entity. I do not belittle the limitations imposed on the reconstruction of chronostrati-graphic, cultural and spatial aspects of these cultures because of a paucity of quantitative reliable data which can be systematically analyzed for measuring the level of similarity and affinity between the different assemblages.

We should remember that research methodology in earlier decades created a very partial and inadequate data base which was biased due to reasons connected to the stated research objectives, field methodology and data analysis. It is also regrettable that the data on faunal and botanical assemblages is very rare, reducing our capability

of economic reconstruction and radiometric dating. On the other hand, an important new feature is added to the record which has high analytic potential for classifying PN entities – the pottery assemblage. Despite shortcomings, and considering the growing body of data accumulating in the 1980s and 1990s, it seems that the time has come to attempt an overview of both the old and new data from the southern Levant. Even if answers to 'why' questions are not yet easily forthcoming, we need to attempt to tackle them and obtain, if not a full explanation, at least a presentation of alternative explaining events and processes of change that took place in the sixth and fifth millennia BC in the southern Levant. Even speculations based on this data are welcome. Figure 1 presents a scheme of the cultural sequence of the sixth and fifth millennia BC in the southern Levant, as reconstructed by Gopher and Gophna (1993) with minute changes. The geographical range dealt with covers mainly the Mediterranean zone of the southern Levant and the chronological span in the order of 3000 years.

Plate 2   A view of the Yarmukian layer at Munhata; a circular stone built structure (in center) (courtesy of J. Perrot)

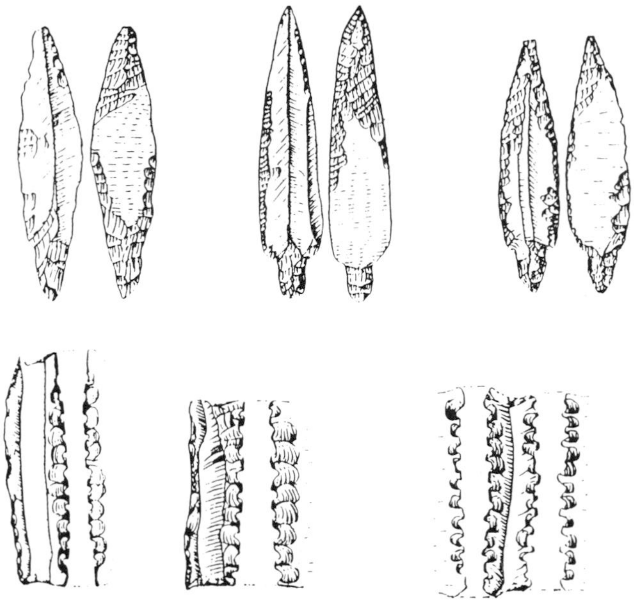

Figure 2   Yarmukian flint tools from Shaar Hagolan and Munhata (after Stekelis 1973; and Gopher 1989b) (courtesy of J. Perrot)

The Yarmukian culture

The Yarmukian culture was defined in the early 1950s following Stekelis's excavations at Shaar Hagolan (Stekelis 1950–51) and acquired recognition as a separate entity mainly by its pottery assemblage, an assemblage of stone and clay figurines and elements in the lithic assemblage (see Figure 2). The Yarmukian was paralleled to the *Neolithique Ancien* (NA) layer at Byblos and thus dated as the earliest pottery bearing entity in Israel (Stekelis 1972). A number of Yarmukian assemblages were exposed in Israel in the 1950s and 1960s of which the most conspicuous ones were from Rehov Habashan in Tel Aviv (Kaplan 1958a, 1978), Hamadiya (Kaplan 1965, 1976) and, on a large scale, Munhata (Perrot 1968). As regards stratigraphy, the Munhata excavations revealed that the Yarmukian layer lies above the PPNB layers after a gap of unknown duration and below the Wadi Raba layer. According to Perrot, it was also earlier than assemblages he assigned to the 'Munhata Phase' which in many ways resembled Garstang's Layer IX at Jericho. In the 1980s following excavations at 'Ain Ghazal (Rollefson et al. 1992), Jebel Abu Thawwab (Kafafi 1988), 'Ain Rahub (Muheisen et al. 1988) and maybe Wadi Shu'eib too (Simmons et al. 1989), the scope of the Yarmukian has extended to the Transjordanian Plateau. At 'Ain Ghazal the Yarmukian layer lies above the stratigraphic unit defined as the PPNC (e.g., Rollefson et al. 1992). In terms of relative chronology, the Yarmukian is placed post PPNC but earlier than the 'Munhata Phase' (Jericho IX) and Wadi Raba. Absolute chronology of the Yarmukian is

based on radiometric determinations from 'Ain Rahub (Muheisen et al. 1988), Munhata (Garfinkel 1992b), Nahal Qanah (Gopher et al. 1990) and Byblos (Dunand 1973), all of which fall within the second half of the sixth millennium BC. Taking into consideration PPNC (including Atlit Yam) and the Wadi Raba dates it is feasible to date the Yarmukian between 5600–5500 to around 5100–5000 BC.

Both rectangular and rounded structures have been exposed in Yarmukian sites, sometimes in the same site as in the case of Jebel Abu Thawwab (Kafafi 1985). This is the case at 'Ain Ghazal too, where rectangular and 'apsidal' structures were exposed (Rollefson et al. 1992), while at Munhata and Hamadiya only rounded structures were reported (Plate 2). One should note that rectangular structures with plastered floors in the PPNB tradition appeared at Byblos NA while at 'Ain Ghazal the Yarmukians were using late PPNB plaster floors.

Yarmukian faunal assemblages show dominance of ovicaprines, plus bovides and pigs in smaller quantities, all domesticated. This is the case at 'Ain Ghazal, Jebel Abu Thawwab, 'Ain Rahub, and most probably at Munhata too. A very small element of hunted animals persists including mainly gazelle. The question of pastoralism is naturally raised here, but no clear answers have yet been given beyond suggestions made for 'Ain Ghazal (e.g., Simmons et al. 1988: 38). Agriculture concentrated on cereals and various legumes and apparently flax too (Muheisen et al. 1988). According to data from submerged off-shore sites in the Atlit-Haifa area olives were intensively used, however, it is not clear whether they were domesticated.

In Yarmukian lithic assemblages bipolar technology of PPNB origin is still used but in decreasing frequencies and the industry is dominated by flakes. The main differences between Yarmukian and PPN flint tools lie in the sickle blade group, a number of types in the arrowhead group, bifacial knives and to an extent other bifacial tools (axes, adzes) (Figure 2). Yarmukian sickle blades stand out in their shaping and style, bearing coarse denticulation sometimes on both sides of the blade. Among the arrowheads, new shapes of Byblos and Amuq points appear and new types such as Haparsa and Herzlia points. A completely new group of tools consists of flat knives bifacially shaped and proto tabular scrapers. Seriating arrowheads and sickle blades (Gopher 1985, 1989a, 1989b) show that a sequence can be discerned within the Yarmukian in which Shaar Hagolan (and Byblos NA too) are earlier than Munhata layer 2B or Nahal Qanah.

Groundstone tools, including mainly grinding equipment and a small pounding element, were also recovered from Yarmukian sites.

Published pottery assemblages, including mainly bowls and jars, emphasized the decorated vessels to the exclusion of the major portion of the assemblage which is undecorated. The characteristic decorations consist of plain reverse bands incised with 'herringbone' motifs arranged in diagonal and horizontal configurations on red slipped backgrounds (see Plate 1). Perforated pottery disks (spindle whorls) were present in Yarmukian assemblages. Yarmukian clay and stone figurines and a number of burials will be discussed separately.

The assemblages clustered under the Yarmukian as an archaeological culture reveal conspicuous similarity in pottery and lithic assemblages and in imagery items. The economy, as far as we know it, indicates a similar range of activities and the few burials also show homogeneity. Yarmukian assemblages are dispersed in an area reaching *ca.* 10,000 km^2, and its estimated timespan is *ca.* 500 years. We still do not have sufficiently detailed data to produce a reconstruction of variability and change processes within the Yarmukian sequence but, hopefully, research in the near future will provide this.

The Lodian (Jericho IX) culture

The unit that was named Jericho IX which I call, after the 1992 excavation at Lod, the Lodian, was first identified in Garstang's excavations at Jericho (Figure 4; Garstang 1935, 1936; Garstang and Garstang 1940) and described by means of its characteristic pottery assemblage (Ben-Dor 1936) and some notes on the lithics (Crowfoot 1935, 1937). The outstanding characteristics of the pottery assemblage were its decorative qualities (painted and

Plate 3   Mudbrick–mud sunken structures from the Lodian (Jericho IX) layer at Lod

burnished geometric motifs on a plain background) and vessel shapes – and today we can recognize its technology too (Goren 1991). Similar pottery assemblages exposed in the 1950s during the renewed excavation of Jericho were assigned to the PNA according to Kenyon (1970), and Kaplan excavated an assemblage at Lod in the early 1950s (Kaplan 1977). Small pottery collections fitting the description of Jericho IX were reported, over the years, from excavations and surveys in different sites such as Megiddo (Shipton 1939), Teluliot Batashi (Kaplan 1958b), Lachish (cf. Rosen 1988–89), and possibly Tel Ali (Prausnitz 1975) and Abu Zureiq (Anati et al. 1973: 79–98) too. Recently the presence of such pottery was reported from Wadi Shu'eib (Simmons et al. 1989), the Dhra region (MacDonald 1988) and Khirbet ed-Dharih (Bossut et al. 1988). Two sites, Nizzanim (Yeivin and Olami 1979) and Givat Haparsa (Olami et al. 1977) in the southern part of the coastal plain of Israel, yielded scant pottery assemblages that were assigned to this group too.

Stratigraphically the Lodian precedes Wadi Raba assemblages – such is the case at Jericho if we consider Jericho VIII as a Wadi Raba variant, and possibly at Teluliot Batashi (Kaplan 1958b). To an extent similar stratigraphic associations can be suggested for Tel Ali, Abu Zureiq and according to the excavator at Munhata too. The absolute chronology of the Lodian has to be inferred from single dates from Nizzanim (Yeivin and Olami 1979) and Givat Haparsa (Burian and Friedman 1989), which fall in the first half of the fifth millennium BC.

Evidence for architecture in Lodian layers is scarce. At Jericho a few isolated fragmentary walls were found but the main feature was the pits, as was the case in other sites. These pits were interpreted as dwelling pits or quarries for mudbrick material (Kenyon 1957). Recently, while excavating at Lod circular sunken structures were exposed built of mudbrick and mud and a series of pits that most probably served as trash pits (Plate 3).

Lodian livestock included mainly caprovines which were dominant at Jericho (in spite of the problematic sample, Clutton-Brook 1971) and bovides and pigs (from Nizzanim). Some gazelle and fishbones were also found. In this respect the Lodian represents continuity with the Yarmukian. No botanical remains were retrieved although Hopf (1983) assumes that cereals and legumes were grown at Jericho.

In the lithic assemblage bipolar cores are completely absent, which marks the end of a tradition that started as early as the beginning of the eighth millennium BC in the northern Levant. The industry is dominated by flakes. Conspicuous within the arrowheads are the small Haparsa, Nizzanim and Herzlia points; among the sickle blades the trapezoidal-curved type is prominent, shaped in many cases by bifacial pressure flaking; bifacial knives and tabular scrapers continue to appear. Seriating arrowheads and sickle blades from sites such as Nizzanim and Givat Haparsa shows that these are later than the Yarmukian at Shaar Hagolan or Munhata, as well as those from the Jericho PNA assemblages (Gopher 1989a, 1989b). It should, however, be remembered that assigning Nizzanim and Givat Haparsa to the Lodian needs further consideration.

In the pottery assemblage, painted burnished motif decorations appear, however, we should remember that decorated pottery constitutes a small portion of the assemblage and Ben-Dor himself presented two different ceramic groups in which the majority was the coarse undecorated kind. In effect, this is also the case in the assemblage recently excavated in Lod.

Almost no *objets d'art* or figurines unique to the Lodian were found. A single figurine from Givat Haparsa (Noy 1977: 30) and a possible fragment of a clay figurine from Teluliot Batashi (Kaplan 1958a: 19) are the only known examples. Recently a number of burials were exposed at Lod enabling a first glimpse into this aspect of the Lodian culture (see below).

When attempting to define the Lodian as an archaeological culture, one confronts difficulties of data limitation. Repetitivity is discerned in material culture assemblages such as the pottery and the lithics, but in all other respects data is very scarce. The absence of Yarmukian-like figurines which were so prominent before must have meaning in this respect too. The Lodian map includes mostly small scale sites or mere find spots, however, the scale of the area covered more or less corresponds to that of the Yarmukian. The duration of this entity 'sandwiched' between the Yarmukian and Wadi Raba does not exceed a few hundred years.

The affinity level between the Yarmukian and Lodian must still be studied, but I believe that the Lodian was an independent entity which deserves recognition as part of the cultural sequence of the Pottery Neolithic period of the region even if it derives from the Yarmukian.

The Wadi Raba culture

The Wadi Raba culture was defined by Kaplan in the early 1950s following the exposure of a new characteristic pottery assemblage that he paralleled with the Amuq phase D. Stratigraphically these assemblages appeared in post-Yarmukian or post-Lodian (Jericho IX) and pre-Ghassulian layers – as was the case at Teluliot Batashi, Wadi Raba and Munhata, for example. Similar assemblages were excavated at base layers of tell sites years before the Wadi Raba culture was defined, for example, Jericho, Bethshan, and Tell Far'ah. Wadi Raba sites were excavated during the 1950s and 1960s in the Jordan Valley, the Jezreel Valley, Western Galilee and the mountains of Israel. In the 1970s and 1980s small-scale excavations, surveys and different collections in the Mediterranean zones of Israel enlarged the inventory of sites. A map of Wadi Raba sites (see Figure 7) including its different variants shows a distribution covering the area from the Soreq Vale in the south to the Huleh Valley and the northern coast of Israel. The absolute chronology of the Wadi Raba culture is based on a group of dates from Ard Tlaili in the Beqqa that is considered by Mellaart (1975: 243) to be the origin of this entity in Israel; there the sequence is dated 4900–4700 BC. A number of C14 dates from different sites in Israel enables the dating of the Wadi Raba layers mainly to the two middle quarters of the fifth millennium BC, but both extremities of this span still await more precise dating (for a list of dates see Gopher and Gophna 1993).

Rectangular architecture is prominent in Wadi Raba sites, including both single and multi-cell houses (Plate 4). Structures with trodden-earth floors are built on stone foundations while the superstructure was probably made of mudbrick and/or adobe. A small, circular mudbrick silo was recently excavated and small plaster lined basin-like installations sunken into floors were found in a number of Wadi Raba sites. No rounded dwelling structures are found in Wadi Raba sites.

The economy of the Wadi Raba population is based on livestock exploitation including goat, sheep, cattle and pigs, with emphasis on ovicaprines. Hunting was rare and this is reflected in the paucity or complete absence of arrowheads from the lithic assemblages. In summer 1992 botanic material in considerable quantity was retrieved for the first time in the Wadi Raba layer of Nahal Zehora II and it probably includes cereals and pulses.

Activities connected or associated with spinning and weaving find expression indirectly in an assemblage of spindle whorls.

The Wadi Raba lithic assemblages reflect the use of local low quality flints; most cores have one striking platform and are amorphic in shape. Flakes dominate the industry. Arrowheads are almost absent, but when they appear they include Haparsa and Nizzanim points. Burins

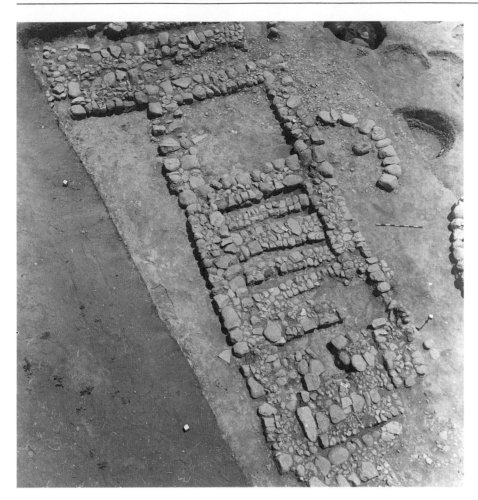

Plate 4 Wadi Raba architecture from Munhata (courtesy of J. Perrot)

seem to appear variably and chamfered pieces were recorded in one case (Gopher and Orrelle 1990). Sickle blades are rectangular in shape, truncated at both ends and backed. They are usually thick and short when compared to Yarmukian sickle blades (Gopher 1989a). Flat retouch or pressure flaking and coarse denticulation disappeared completely, as did the practice of using both sides of the sickle blade. Bifacial knives and tabular scrapers continue to appear. Groundstone tools include elongated flat or slightly concave grinding slabs and grinding stones (manos).

In the pottery, still handmade, new forms and decoration techniques appear. Most conspicuous are bowrim jars, carinated bowls, pedestal bowls, knob handles and splayed loop handles. Slip, burnish, incision, pointilee impressions, combing and applied plastic are the major elements of the decoration. A small element of painted motifs also appears. Clay spindle whorls are an ever-present element on these sites.

Objets d'art and figurines are rare in Wadi Raba layers and include clay zoomorphic figures known from a number of sites (e.g., Nahal Betzet I, Tel Tsaf, Nahal Zehora II). Relief and applied motifs and figures appear on pottery vessels including a human image on a carinated holemouth jar from Ein el Jarba (Figure 4; Kaplan 1969) and snake images. New patterns appear on pottery which may be part of the symbolic imagery including impressed crescents in linear and other configurations. The few burials from Wadi Raba sites will be dealt with below.

The term Wadi Raba includes a wider range of cultural subunits than the Yarmukian and Lodian. It also covers a wider geographical range and chronological span. The 'normative' Wadi Raba, as defined by Kaplan, constitutes a group of assemblages with repetitive pottery and lithic assemblages, and other unique finds such as sling stones, spanning some 500 years in a region similar in size to that occupied by the Yarmukian and Lodian. This system is encircled by contemporaenous units which have certain similarities to the normative Wadi Raba but vary regionally, especially in elements of their pottery assemblages.

A series of such variants was reconstructed recently on a preliminary level (Gopher and Gophna 1993, and here Figure 7), including late variants in regions south of the Soreq Valley such as the Qatifian (Gilead 1990: Goren

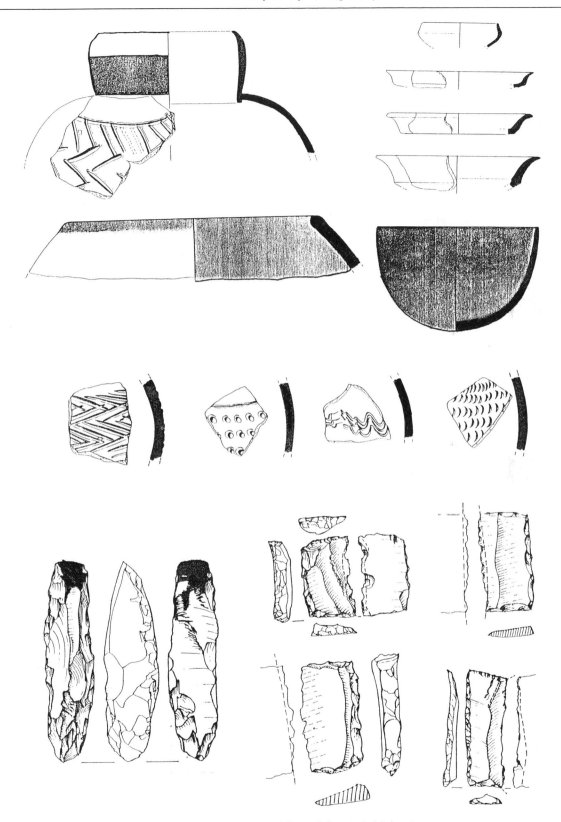

Figure 3 Pottery vessels from Ein el Jarba (after Kaplan 1969) and flint tools from Nahal Zehora I

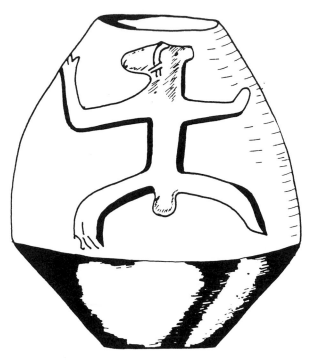

Figure 4 A relief figure on a holemouth jar from Ein el Jarba (after Kaplan 1969)

1990) which is a distinct unit both in terms of the qualities of its assemblages, and its geographical and chronological ranges. If we include all the variants within the Wadi Raba entity we may approach a span of 750 years and a geographical range covering almost every part of the Mediterranean region of the southern Levant. This means that the Wadi Raba culture is a larger-scale phenomenon than the Yarmukian and Lodian and can be viewed as a 'large culture' with regional subcultures. We must remember, however, that temporal aspects may account for parts of this variability.

Spatial aspects of Pottery Neolithic cultures

The spatial distribution of PN entities is presented in Figures 5–7, including names of all sites and find spots. The Yarmukian is distributed over diverse ecological zones on a west–east stretch of land in central Israel and Jordan from the Mediterranean coast, through the mountains, down to the Jordan Valley and up to the Transjordanian Plateau. The Soreq Valley may be viewed as the southern border, and the Jezreel and Yarmuk Valleys the border in the north. However, occurrences of Yarmukian were recorded in the Judean Desert as well as in the western Galilee (Figure 5).

Lodian sites and findspots are distributed mainly along the coastal plain and the Shephelah, in the Jordan Valley

between Lake Tiberias and the Dead Sea, and to the east and southeast of the Dead Sea. Again we observe a distribution through the longitudinal strips of Israel but in this case there are no sites in the mountainous ridge or on the Transjordanian Plateau. Thus the Lodian occupies mainly low and hilly areas and has a more southerly occurrence than the previous Yarmukian (Figure 6).

Both Yarmukian and Lodian distributions cover an area in the order of 10,000 km² and overlap considerably. This must be viewed with caution since many of the points on the maps are no more than findspots and very few are systematically excavated sites with clear stratigraphic evidence. One option for interpreting this overlap is to infer some kind of chronological relationship between the two entities. Other options include possible functional variability or different social grouping.

The distribution of the Wadi Raba sites, presented in Figure 7, shows that the 'normative' Wadi Raba appears in the northern valleys (the Beqqa and the Huleh Valley), in the central valleys of Israel (Jezreel and Bethshan) and along the coastal plain and the Shephelah down to the Soreq Valley, while the different Wadi Raba variants are dispersed in different parts of the Jordan Valley, the mountainous ridges of Israel and – if including the Qatifian – also in the northern Negev and the Dead Sea area. This distribution is wider than that of the Yarmukian or the Lodian and here too mountainous areas were a low preference option for settlement.

A significant similarity in the distribution maps of the three entities is the relatively small scale (10–15,000 km²) and the exploitation of a variety of ecological zones. This reduction of the geographical unit as compared to the PPN may be connected to the reduced role of hunting and the fact that farming enables subsistence in much smaller territories. In the case of the Yarmukian and the 'normative' Wadi Raba, dense concentrations of sites can be identified. Taking into account the possibility that this could be a false impression resulting from patchy research, I find it premature to relate these concentrations as having socio-economic structural significance in either the Yarmukian or Wadi Raba systems. Such thoughts, however, should not be ruled out.

No hierarchy can be discerned from the examination of the nature of settlements in all three entities. At the moment we cannot point to any conspicuously large-scale Yarmukian, Lodian or Wadi Raba site in Israel, even though a closer look at sites such as Tell Asawir, Ein el Jarba or the base layer of Tel Dan may change the picture. It seems at present that most of the PN sites were small in area when compared to the mega sites of the late PPNB, and even famous villages such as Byblos – mentioned in each and every discussion on the PN of the region – did not exceed one acre in the NA layer. Yarmukian and Lodian occupations such as those at Hamadiya or Lod may represent a single household only, while larger sites

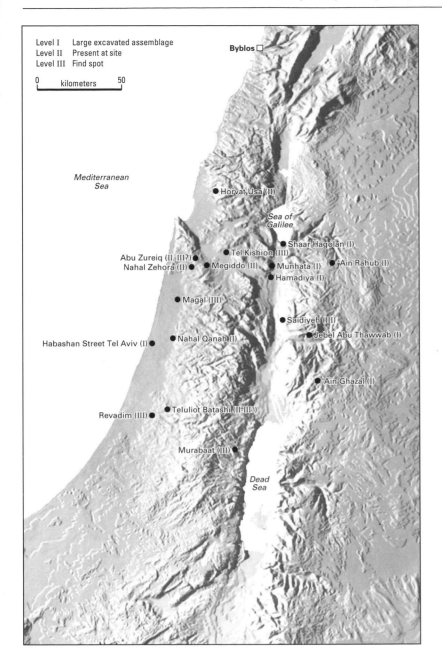

Level I   Large excavated assemblage
Level II   Present at site
Level III Find spot

0   kilometers   50

Byblos □

Mediterranean Sea

● Horvat Usa (II)

Sea of Galilee

● Shaar Hagolan (I)
● Tel Kishion (III)
Abu Zureiq (II, III?) ●
Nahal Zehora (II) ● ● Megiddo (II)   ● Munhata (I)   ● 'Ain Rahub (I)
● Hamadiya (I)

● Magal (III)

● Saidiyeh (III)
● Jebel Abu Thawwab (I)

Habashan Street Tel Aviv (I) ●   ● Nahal Qanah (I)

● 'Ain Ghazal (I)

● Teluliot Batashi (II-III?)
Revadim (III) ●

● Murabaat (III)

Dead Sea

Figure 5   Yarmukian site distribution

such as Shaar Hagolan or Jericho may represent small villages. We do not have sufficient data concerning Yarmukian or Lodian site size in Jordan, however, the Yarmukian level of 'Ain Ghazal is fairly large as may be the case for Wadi Shueib. Specific site locations such as the Yarmukian Nahal Ganah Cave should be mentioned too.

A daring interpretation made recently about settlement specialization and some kind of a center–periphery relationship in the Wadi Raba system in the Jezreel Valley (Gopher n.d.) was in the nature of a provocative speculation, since we do not yet have enough data to confirm such a model and thus to infer a reconstruction of economic organization. However, the lithic data on which it was based has good potential, as does the pottery, and further research of this kind may support such a contention.

Innovation, technology, subsistence strategies and trade

In terms of innovation expressed in the PN archaeological record, the most conspicuous phenomenon is the appearance of pottery. In my view, as crystallised in

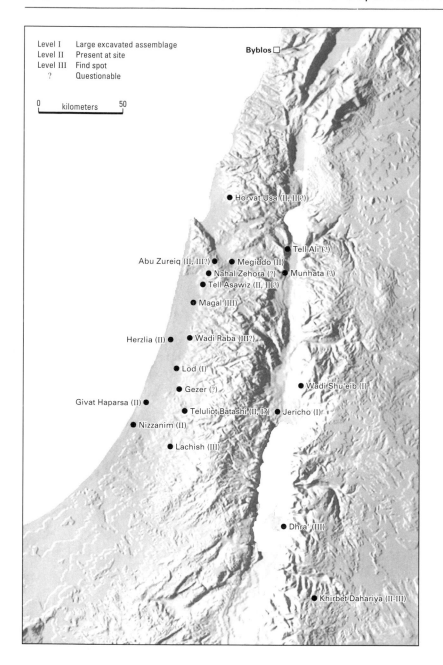

Level I   Large excavated assemblage
Level II   Present at site
Level III   Find spot
?   Questionable

0   kilometers   50

Byblos ☐

● Horvat 'Usa (II, III?)

● Tell Ali (?)
Abu Zureiq (II, III?) ●   ● Megiddo (II)
      ● Nahal Zehora (?)   ● Munhata (?)
      ● Tell 'Asawiz (II, III?)
    ● Magal (III)

Herzlia (II) ●   ● Wadi Raba (III?)

    ● Lod (I)

    ● Gezer (?)   ● Wadi Shu'eib (I)
Givat Haparsa (II) ●
     ● Teluliot Batashi (II, I?) ● Jericho (I)
● Nizzanim (II)

   ● Lachish (III)

         ● Dhra' (III)

       ● Khirbet Dahariya (II-III)

Figure 6   Lodian–Jericho IX site distribution

discussion with Y. Goren, this is not a dramatic qualitative change in terms of technology since shaping vessels in selected reworked materials was practised long before the PN. We do not view early pottery simply as a utilitarian functional innovation, but as an assemblage operating also on the social and symbolic levels (see Window 2). It is, however, clear that vessels produced from local materials in a simple and easily accessible technology with ever-increasing improvement of raw material selection and firing techniques have wide-ranging significance for Neolithic household activities.

A few changes were noted above in the lithic assemblages of the sixth and fifth millennia BC when compared to the PPN, some of which are evident already in the PPNC. This refers mainly to arrowhead frequencies which decrease conspicuously in lithic assemblages of Yarmukian and Lodian, and almost completely disappear in Wadi Raba layers – a fact which must have economic implications and correlates nicely with the composition of faunal remains found in PN sites.

The common arrowheads that do appear in the PN are considerably different in shaping and size from PPN

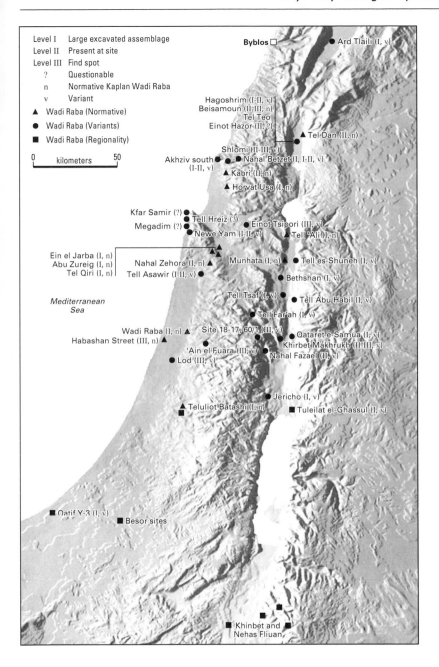

Figure 7 Wadi Raba and variant site distribution and regionality

ones. Their small size must reflect changes in bow technology or the introduction of new hunting techniques (perhaps indicating the use of poison). A sequence of changes takes place in sickle blades too. In contrast to the long, finely-denticulated PPNB reaping knives, shorter sickle blades appeared which were most probably segments of a composite sickle. In some ways this is a return to the early conception of the sickle known from the Natufian and may mark a change in harvesting techniques. This may be a result of changes in PN fields such as an increasing density of stalks per area unit, for example, or the introduction of new species. Yarmukian sickle blades, however, include an element of blades with sheen on both sides and it is thus not clear how they blend with the above suggested possible change or the notion of a composite tool – this element disappeared in the fifth millennium BC. In any event, the perception of the sickle blade and reaping changed during the PN and this must have relevance in the economic sphere. Changes also occurred in groundstone implements which find expression mostly in the disappearance of the stepped querns well known in the PPNB and the appearance of elongated grinding slabs (metate) and two-handed grinding stones (manos). Clay spindle whorls, appearing in varying quantities, may indicate a change in spinning and perhaps cloth technology techniques. Even though we have no direct evidence of textiles or looms, the increased activity inferred from the abundance of whorls may signify an exploitation of animal hair – a possibility reflected in the faunal assemblages.

Plaster lined installations, absent in Yarmukian and Lodian sites, were recently found in Wadi Raba layers. This is again a return, on a smaller scale, to an older technology – the production of limeplaster, which is a hallmark of the PPNB – a technology which combines know how and considerable energy resources.

In summary, there is evidence for change in a number of technological aspects of every day activities. In some cases known technological concepts are adjusted for new activities, for example:

1. Pottery production which plays a dual role in the social milieu and in daily subsistence functions.
2. Arrowheads, originally used for hunting, may have acquired a new role.
3. Spinning, weaving and basketry.

In other realms there is a return to old technological concepts, for example, in the use of sickle blades or in the production of limeplaster for architectural features. There seems to be no major breakthrough in any realm, but rather an establishment and consolidation – a readjustment to the new economic needs.

Considering all the above and additional data, what reconstruction can we offer of the PN economy? We have no knowledge about field location or size, or agricultural techniques such as ploughing or irrigation. I suspect that neither do we know the full range of exploited species and we should expect surprises in this sphere. For example, evidence for the use of olives is currently growing to include olive processing installations of some form, dated to the second half of the sixth millennium BC (Galilli, personal communication 1993). Faunal assemblages of the PN include animals which represent both domestic (pig) and potential herd animals (goats, sheep and cattle) whose management could include a form of movement that would naturally raise the suggestion of the practice of, at least partial, pastoral nomadism – but the data cannot yet support such a suggestion. Such forms of animal management must have wide-ranging significance for labour demands and seasonal scheduling of the community's activities as well as repercussions on settlement patterns. Any discussion on the PN economy should, however, include reference to Sherratt's suggestions on the exploitation of secondary products. It is true that no direct evidence of traction (bovid) has been found, but as regards spinning, weaving and the spectrum

of domesticated/used species of plants, we do now have some evidence in the PN for at least claiming a glimpse into the 'Revolution' as Sherratt called it (Sherratt 1981 and Levy, this volume).

Another aspect related to the economy is trade. In attempting a reconstruction of the range of trade or exchange networks of PN populations in the southern Levant we should distinguish between minute quantities of long-range imports and medium- to short-range systems of the day-to-day economy. Small quantities of obsidian from Anatolia, mainly appearing in Wadi Raba layers, are the only long-range imported items that have been identified. On another scale, different minerals were brought to PN sites from different regions of the southern Levant such as Sinai, the Negev kraters or the Funon area in Jordan. Seashells may be added here, including mostly Mediterranean species. Local, short-distance exchange-trade networks cannot be reconstructed yet, but I believe these existed and were involved mainly in food and craft items – perhaps including pottery, basketry, etc.

Belief, ideology and symbolism

An attempt to discuss the ideology and symbolic world of PN populations using the archaeological record available from this period is encouraged by the appearance of pottery that carries a wide variety of decorative elements that must have had a rich symbolic content. Analyzing pottery inventories, quantities of decorated/undecorated items or the decorative features themselves, on an intra-site or inter-site level, can contribute greatly to the understanding of PN communities in these respects. However, analyses of this type are very rare in this part of the world. The limited scope of exposures in PN sites currently prevents any attempt to identify features or specific activity areas that can be interpreted in relation to ritual or ceremonial aspects. Thus, we are left with the traditional practice of centering the discussion on imagery items – figurines and burial traditions.

Pottery Neolithic figurines

Clay and stone figurines of the Yarmukian culture include over a hundred items and clearly represent an assemblage different from that known in the PPNB. It consists of a large group of incised stone figurines and a group of anthropomorphic figures shaped in clay using an additive technology. These items appear in considerable numbers in a small number of sites (Shaar Hagolan, Munhata) but this could reflect a research bias. These figurines were usually interpreted in relation to fertility (Stekelis 1972; Yeivin and Mozel 1977). Recently it was suggested that there is an underrepresentation of organs related to fertility in these items and that these

Plate 5   A burial from the Yarmukian layer at Munhata (courtesy of J. Perrot)

are to be seen rather as objects used in religious rituals representing different deities which developed in the tradition of the artistic-symbolic array of the PPN (Garfinkel 1992b). My views on these, crystallized recently in association with E. Orrelle following an analysis of stone figurines from Munhata, are presented below in Window 1.

The assemblage of these figurines is specific to the Yarmukian and the difficulties in examining it stem, among other things, from the fact that earlier and later entities offer very little or no data of this type. This provides a clear chronological context for this assemblage, which reinforces our contention that it served a specific role in the Yarmukian society.

In the Lodian we have no comparable data but there is a certain change in pottery decoration. There is little or no use of incisions and the herringbone pattern is absent but the general patterns of Yarmukian decorations continue. In the Wadi Raba there is again change and new elements appear in pottery decoration, including new motifs. However, in imagery items we have no data on figures and the single figure from Ein el Jarba, though reflecting a change, is unique and insufficient to allow generalizations to be made.

Thus it seems that the Yarmukian inventory of figurines served a certain social need for a limited period. I would regard these items as a possible representation of social process specific to the Yarmukian. However, even within the Yarmukian system there is an impression that figurines appear differentially, for example, their relative rarity in Transjordanian sites as compared to the Middle Jordan Valley is of note. On the other hand, the fact that similar figurines appear at Byblos, NA, is very important in estimating the level of contact with Lebanese coastal populations at this stage; in addition we must note that there too these figurines are limited to the NA layer. What

exactly did these items represent? How did they operate? And why did they disappear? These questions are still open to speculation but I would be very hesitant to automatically relate them to religious activities or to some sort of fertility rituals.

Burial customs

For the first half of the sixth millennium BC, the PPNC period, two relatively large samples of graves are available – one from 'Ain Ghazal including some 27 individuals (Rollefson et al. 1992), and one from Atlit-Yam including over 30 individuals (Hershkovitz and Galili 1990; Hershkovitz and Galili personal communication). The cessation of skull removal or treatment and increasing numbers of group burials (especially at 'Ain Ghazal) are the major changes in comparison to PPNB burial customs. PN burials are few and were recently presented in a summary paper by Gopher and Orrelle (in press). To date, only three Yarmukian burials are known, all on-site, one each from Shaar Hagolan, Habashan Street and Munhata (Plate 5). All contain adults in flexed position, with skulls intact and apparently without grave offerings. The only known burials from Lodian layers are from the excavations of Lod in 1992, where three burials of adults were exposed. One was in a very bad state of preservation while the other two contained adults – in flexed positions with skulls intact and with no grave goods – interred in shallow pits dug into abandoned trash pits near to a dwelling. If we relate to Nizzanim as a site properly assigned to the Lodian entity, two additional burials can be added – one of an adult, and one of a child both buried below the floor of a hut, again with no grave goods. Thus Yarmukian and Lodian burial customs are similar in many ways.

In Wadi Raba sites, including all variants, the inventory includes the burial of three adults below a house floor at Ein el Jarba (Arensburg 1970), one adult in supine position at Nahal Betzet I (Gopher 1989a), and a child with no skull in a flexed position with a large stone placed in the position of the head in Nahal Zehora II. A new phenomenon in the spectrum of burial customs appearing in the Wadi Raba culture is the use of jars for the burial of babies and fetuses. This phenomenon is known from Tel Teo and Tel Dan in the Huleh Valley (Eisenberg 1987; Gopher and Greenberg 1987), Nahal Zehora II (Plate 6) in the Jezreel Valley area and from Qatif Y-3 in the Gaza coast area (Epstein 1984). At Byblos too, jar burial of the young is practised from the period of NA (Dunand 1973).

What can we learn from the few burials in PN sites discussed above?

- All PPNC and PN graves are on-site, as was the case in the PPN, thus the beginning of separate offsite graveyards is not observed at this period and has to be related, most

Plate 6   A jar burial of a fetus from Nahal Zehora II, Wadi Rabah phase

probably, to the following Chalcolithic period in which these graveyards are common (see Levy, Chapter 14).

- The custom of separating skulls and treating them ceased. If indeed it was related to ancestor worship, as suggested by a few scholars (c.f. Arensburg and Hershkovitz 1988), this apparently was no longer relevant to population of the PPNC and the PN. This strengthens our contention that changes took place in society during these periods.
- PN burials all contain one individual and are mostly primary.
- Grave goods are rarely found in PN burials but at Byblos there may have been cases in which such offerings were found (de Contenson 1992).
- There is a change in attitude towards baby and fetus burial in the Wadi Raba culture (which may have started earlier) and they are buried in pottery jars.

If indeed early pottery had social and symbolic significance, the use of jars for burial of infants indicates that a change in their place in society has occurred. Perhaps the social status and place of both adults and children are now dictated by affinity lines, and initiation is not a prerequisite as was probably the case in the PPN. There may be signs of some special customs relating to children's burials in the PPNB (Rollefson 1986; Rollefson et al. 1992) but, the use of pottery containers for burial – a custom which gained popularity in the Chalcolithic period with the appearance of ossuaries, some of them house shaped – may be an early manifestation relating women, pottery, houses and death in symbolic association.

Social organization

Considering the size of reconstructed territories for the Yarmukian and Lodian, I believe that these communities operated on a face-to-face level. I do not believe that splitting these entities or viewing them as parts of a larger-scale social organization is justified in the light of available data. The Wadi Raba culture is not essentially different

even though it is a somewhat larger system than the Yarmukian and Lodian, and perhaps more complex.

We do not yet have data on the structure of the family in PN communities (was polygyny practised?) since household analysis is in its infancy. In the PPNB, different researchers already suggest, the operative economic unit was the family or extended family, and thus economic and political maneuvring took place at this level. What kinds of relationship were prevalent between such family units? Competitive mechanisms were suggested by Hayden for explaining socio-economic developments already in the PPN (Hayden 1990). Evidence from the Chalcolithic period also clearly indicates that these relationships were embedded and can be seen at work. Although evidence for their operation in the intervening PN has not yet crystallized, it is reasonable to assume that such elements were active there too.

Division of labor between sex and age groups has not yet been demonstrated for this period. The association of women with domestic contexts or activities carried out in the close proximity of the site can only be speculated on at the moment with our current data, although some contextual evidence of household crafts in conjunction with a possible increase in childbirth may bear this out. Such patterns were confirmed for sedentary agricultural societies (e.g., Arnold 1985). Livestock husbandry and agriculture, as we have presented above for the PN, must also have resulted in a certain level of labor division, especially relating to seasonality and labour scheduling.

We have no evidence for specialized industries beyond the household level in the early PN. Some innovative features of the Wadi Raba pottery industry, such as the firing for example, may have required cooperation between households.

Social hierarchy cannot be inferred from any set of data including burials or material culture assemblages and the architecture also shows no signs of differentiation between units – but the question remains of how many such units have yet been fully exposed.

Discussion

What then is the difference between PN and PPN societies? In terms of material culture, there is no significant breakthrough. The difference may thus be sought in the economic or social sphere – a more efficient economy, a reorganization of the different components of society or maybe in the construction of a new socio-political order? PN communities reflect an established system of agricultural villages on small territories with technological innovations adjusted to the new needs. Land use of the PN communities which gradually lost the element of hunting in their economy and concentrated on agriculture and animal husbandry is thus different to that of the PPNB. In terms of the community's internal politics and power systems, this could be an important factor. While in the PPNB long-range contacts (information networks) and control over imported goods may have been in the hands of a select group of hunters (males? – see Bar-Yosef and Belfer Cohen 1989) in the PN, this no longer operated. It was most probably replaced by a different political system based on partnerships or alliances which were aimed at controlling resources for agriculture and animal management such as land, water and pasture. Such systems based on kin groups would emphasize the role of women as a resource both in reproductive terms and politically (Gopher and Orrelle in press). If this was indeed the case, it must have had an important influence on social structuring which can be viewed as the full – even final? – departure from systems where egalitarian principles were still at work to systems tending towards complexity within a larger-scale *koine*. The marginal character of the southern Levant in this *koine* is clear but we should not assume that marginal areas are unaffected by mainstream events and developments, as the archaeological record shows. Thus small PN entities in this region absorbed current ideologies which effected change in social perceptions; they entered a new state of awareness. This could not, however, be realized as growth options, as was the case in Mesopotamia for example. The early stages of the PN in our region thus do not show a burst of innovation and growth but rather an accumulative process of steady internal change, based on a more efficient economic structure and social organization as well as a rising potential to accept change and absorb innovation (not only in material culture). In effect, this is a stage in a re-establishment of a population in a region that had suffered a crisis at the end of the seventh and beginning of the sixth millennia BC (that still featured in collective memory) and was slowly recovering towards stability throughout the sixth and fifth millennia BC.

What are the elements that combined to cause this process of change and why did it happen? In my opinion, the usual search for a climatological change is not relevant in this case. It may be applied partly to explain the diversified picture of the PPNC immediately following the disintegration of the PPNB system. We have no evidence for conspicuous changes in climate in the second half of the sixth and in the fifth millennia BC which may have brought about such change in the Mediterranean zones that were the main occupation area of the Yarmukian, Lodian and Wadi Raba cultures.

A second possible explanation is an external influence. Was it the external impetus – the shadow of the Mesopotamian-Syrian experience – that stimulated these events? I believe that in understanding systems of cultural contacts and inter-cultural influences this could have been a possible catalyst and should not be ruled out. This need not be reconstructed as wave of immigration (primary diffusion) or active political dominance by an external power, as was suggested in the past (e.g., de Vaux 1966; Perrot 1968; Kenyon 1970), but rather as the development of a general atmosphere or environment that promoted change.

A third possible way of explaining such change is, of course, through a reconstruction which lays the emphasis on internal change originating in the very structure of society but not isolated from external influences and local environmental conditions. This is, in my opinion, the most fitting explanation. An example of this is the Yarmukian, clearly a local unit, which underwent changes in a local format and represents, in my opinion, a critical stage in implementing social and ideological change of this sort. We should distinguish between structural change in society and that of material culture. The Yarmukian shows signs of 'real' change in society which might be related to events elsewhere, but in terms of material culture it represents a high degree of freedom, of local development and creativity, within which framework the earliest pottery assemblages of this region were produced, each with the unique fingerprints of its creators. Only later, in the fifth millennium BC, do diffused influences from the north acquire a somewhat stronger hold in material culture too. The peripherality of southern Levant cultures in the late sixth and in the fifth millennia BC, however, remains a major cultural characteristic both economically and politically, and this remains so for later periods. A similar pattern of retardation is apparent for the process of urbanization, in which the northern and eastern parts of the Levant precede its southern parts. Towards the end of the fourth and beginning of the third millennia BC we already see both superpowers – Mesopotamia and Egypt – involved in growth and expansion. Within this framework of rival superpower ascendancy, the southern Levant became an important region to control.

All the above may sound speculative – and in many ways it is. It is presented in a predictive spirit and is the responsibility of the author, and awaits the analysis of much data – both currently available and to be recovered in the future – for confirmation or rejection.

Acknowledgements

In this chapter I used material which I recently discussed at length with R. Gophna and I am thankful to him. My thanks also to Y. Goren, with whom I discussed pottery and pottery origins, and to E. Orrelle for her useful help in writing and editing this chapter, and for long and fruitful discussion of many aspects examined therein. Also, many thanks to J. Perrot and C. Commenge of The Centre de Recherche Français, Jerusalem, for all their help and support.

YARMUKIAN IMAGERY

A. Gopher and E. Orrelle

Stone and clay figurines were one of the important components in Stekelis's definition of the Yarmukian culture in the early 1950s. These items appeared in abundance at Shaar Hagolan and were unique to the Yarmukian. The two major groups of imagery items found are incised stones and clay figures. The stone group includes stone pebbles – showing images of women ('women pebbles') and another sub-group of pebbles with linear incisions and patterns showing, we believe, women's genitalia ('vulva pebbles'). The second group includes clay figurines of women and men, shaped around a core. Stone and clay shaped representations of phalli can be added here as another category.

Yarmukian figurines were found in the Jordan Valley, the Jezreel Valley, the Mediterranean coastal plain, the Transjordan plateau and at Byblos on the Lebanese coast. The relatively high numbers in Shaar Hagolan and Munhata (Jordan Valley) may reflect a regional research bias or the fact that only limited survey, collection and exposures at such scale or intensity were made in the few excavated Yarmukian sites apart from Shaar Hagolan and Munhata.

Yarmukian figurines were first interpreted by Stekelis in a sympathetic magic context related to fertility. Later he related these items to the Mother Goddess fertility rituals, to protection and to the cult of the dead. A later interpretation by Yeivin and Mozel was focused on a descriptive decipherment of the figurines. They saw these seated women as wearing a soutane and an elongated head mask and pointed out hairstyle details, reiterating the connection between obesity and fertility. A very recent interpretation by Garfinkel suggested that there is an underrepresentation of organs related to fertility in these items and that these are to be seen rather as objects used in religious rituals representing different deities which developed in the tradition of the artistic-symbolic array of PPN cultures.

In a larger-scale study on symbolic meanings of European figurines, Gimbutas included the Yarmukian figurines as a local Middle Eastern Neolithic manifestation of her worldwide religion of the Goddess. Recent examination by the authors of an assemblage of incised pebble figurines from Munhata in addition to a survey study of the published material from Shaar Hagolan and other sites have given rise to a new interpretation. The incised 'women pebbles' are suggested to incorporate encoded information on the different ages of women. Thus, incised women portrayed on pebbles could represent women of different age groups – the narrow elliptical pebbles showing only slits for eyes suggest young women (Figure 1.1a), and the rounder, larger oval-shaped pebbles with deep incisions indicating hips and buttocks suggest older women (Figure 1.1b). The 'vulva pebbles' are thought to portray female genitalia at different reproductive stages of development and childbearing. The lines incised on the pebbles from a

single slit incision of a young girl (Figure 1.1c) to which lines are added over her maturity and reproductive life (Figure 1.1d). The final stage, the net-patterned pebble (Figure 1.1e), may represent the climax of this process, and represent a whole history of childbearing – perhaps of an older woman who has successfully given birth to many children. Some of the pebbles bear red stains hinting perhaps at some other stage in the woman's development.

The clay figurines, apparently of seated women and perhaps men, in our view are constructed of combinations of representations of male and female genitalia and seem to be concerned with duality in the relationship between the sexes expressed by mixing symbols of both in one artifact. A figure whose costume incorporates genitalia representations of both sexes could indicate the notion of a go-between between the sexes – needed perhaps for social concerns of pollution and purity.

The collection of stone and clay phalli, naturalistic or schematic, and a small group of clay figurines of young men may have played a role in initiation rites.

Such an assemblage of previously unknown female and male imagery appearing in the Yarmukian culture must be connected with socio-economic and ideological change. One aspect of this change could be an increase in the value of the reproductive

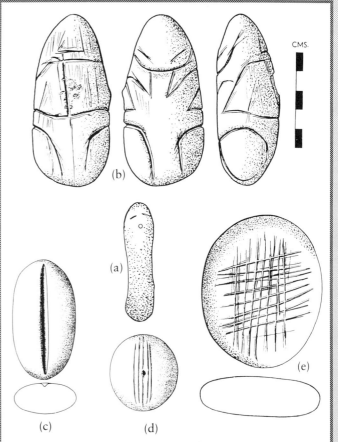

Figure 1.1 Yarmukian 'pebble' figurines from Munhata (courtesy of J. Perrot) and Shaar Hagolan (after Stekelis 1972)

resource of women in a context of resource negotiation. The women and vulva pebbles, concerned as they appear to be with the recording of reproductive stages, could be a material manifestation of social control of this resource. The exposure of eyes only of young women, and the absence of depictions of breasts which may have been covered, may be part of this phenomenon.

This suggested interpretation of Yarmukian imagery is a departure from 'fertility' or a 'sacred context' explanation. The household contexts in which these items were recovered do not support such interpretations. The figurines, however, are part of a symbolic system rooted in the new socio-economic order and male–female relationships.

Plate 1.1 A Yarmukian clay figurine from Shaar Hagolan (after Stekelis 1972)

THE BEGINNING OF POTTERY

A. Gopher and Y. Goren

The emergence of pottery production in the Near East is often associated with the Neolithic Revolution, settled life and craft specialization. It was, and still is, described as a linear development from domestic shaping of simple vessels to a full scale industry.

The technology heralding pottery production in the Levant was associated with plaster production in the Pre-Pottery Neolithic, mostly in the PPNB. This industry was engaged in producing architectural materials such as floors and 'art' objects such as sculpture, figurines, decorated skulls, beads, etc. These were, in many cases, made of mixtures of burnt lime and clay and marls. The commonly known 'white ware' (Vaisselle Blanche) of the seventh to sixth millennium BC found in the Neolithic Levant is an orientation of the lime-plaster technology towards vessel production. It was natural to suggest that the development of pottery production originated in the 'white ware' industry and this suggestion was based not only on typological considerations, but more importantly on the technological aspects. The contemporaneity of both 'white ware' technology and early pottery in the sixth millennium BC is important since some of the former type vessels were made of a mixture of burnt lime and clay or marls — thus actually being pottery objects by definition.

A thorough study on this issue by Goren which included the examination of thousands of samples from many Pre-Pottery Neolithic, Pottery Neolithic, Chalcolithic and Early Bronze Age sites in the Levant has resulted in the following general conclusions:

1. The use of burnt lime in Pre-Pottery Neolithic and the Pottery Neolithic periods was not as extensive as once thought. While there are cases in which burnt lime constitutes very high proportions of a product's mass, in many cases the raw materials were not burnt and converted into lime. Also in many cases, the mixtures included high proportions of marl, clay, ashes, vegetal matter, etc.
2. Early pottery in Israel shows a technological continuity with earlier lime-plaster and mud products.
3. A clear dichotomy exists between early undecorated and decorated pottery. The former, which is made of soils, results in a typical dark tan pottery, and the latter (bearing slip, paint, burnish, incisions or plastic elements) is usually made of highly calcareous pastes — including marl or even some burnt lime — hence inefficient functionally, but resulting in a light white-buff shade pottery easily decorated in slip and paint. (Similar results came from fifth–sixth millennia BC Mesopotamia.) In other words, a white buff-shaded vessel was desired even at the expense of practicability and decoration took precedence over other functions.

Over time, a sequence of change in raw material selection shows the gradual decrease in highly calcareous materials (which includes the cream ware of the Chalcolithic) in favor of mud-clay materials until a clearer

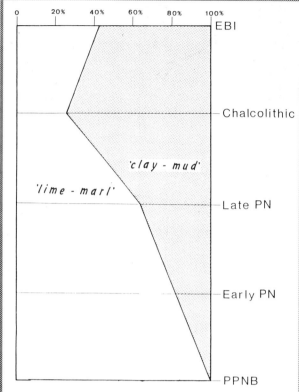

Figure 2.1 Trends of lime–marl and mud–clay production from Neolithic to Early Bronze Age

correlation between pottery form, function and raw material was achieved (see Figure 2.1). Thus, we may assume that production of early (PN) pottery was designed for its decorative aspect, which also explains the high investment per vessel in decoration, both in the Yarmukian and the Lodian (Jericho IX) assemblages. The later Wadi Raba assemblages see some change in terms of technology (the appearance of an early kiln or controlled fire) which is accompanied by a decrease in investment in the decoration of each vessel. The process continues into the Chalcolithic period which sees the cessation of decorative techniques of slip and burnish, and the standardization of painted elements which mainly consist of simple lines or bands. By the Early Bronze Age, utilitarian household vessels are mostly undecorated.

One of the most important facts that the analysis bears out is that a similar technology is used both in the manufacture of Pre-Pottery Neolithic objets d'art (beads, plastered skulls, etc.) and in the production of early pottery of the Pottery Neolithic period. The fact that the Pre-Pottery Neolithic objets d'art were active in ideological spheres and bore a high symbolic importance, in our opinion, supports the possibility that early pottery was used in a similar context.

It is thus suggested that we view early pottery not as a mere improvement in cooking and storing methods, but as a new type of objects designed to communicate symbolic and social messages by a specific decoration which required a light-colored background. Functionally-oriented selection of raw materials, to produce different vessel properties such as resistance to thermal shock, was only practised much later in the Chalcolithic and Early Bronze Period.

Thus, we see the emergence of pottery as originating from the PPNB tradition of art objects' production and 'white ware' vessels, and believe that early pottery may be viewed more in a social context than in a daily, functional context.

Plate 2.1   Yarmukian decorated pottery vessel from Nahal Qanah cave

14

CULT, METALLURGY AND RANK SOCIETIES – CHALCOLITHIC PERIOD (CA. 4500–3500 BCE)

Thomas E. Levy

Introduction

By the middle of the fifth millennium, sometime between 4500–4000 BCE, Palestine is characterized by a number of new and vibrant societies spread out over most of the geographical zones in the country (Figure 1). Unlike the previous Pottery Neolithic cultures of the Levant which are located primarily in the Mediterranean zone and in areas rich in natural springs, during the Chalcolithic period for the first time, extensive mixed farming communities expanded into the semi-arid, Irano-Turanian environmental zones. It was in these marginal semi-arid regions of the country that the foundations for the later Early Bronze Age fortified towns were laid in southern Palestine. It is suggested here that by focusing on the interrelationship between environment, population increase and changes in technology and production systems, it is possible to explain the growth of more complex societies during the Chalcolithic period.

Some of the new developments observed in the Chalcolithic period which separate it from the preceding Pottery Neolithic include a marked growth in the human population of Palestine, the establishment of public sanctuaries and burial grounds, the emergence of craft specialization and metallurgy, and the division of sites into spatial hierarchies with settlement centers which coordinated social, economic and religious activities. In earlier papers, I have suggested that these changes in southern Palestine reflect the emergence of Chiefdom organizations in the region, a term which Colin Renfrew defines as

> a society that operates on the principle of ranking, i.e., differential social status. Different lineages are graded on a scale of prestige, calculated by how closely related one is to the chief. The chiefdom generally had a permanent ritual and ceremonial center, as well as being characterized by local specialization (Renfrew and Bahn 1991: 486).

This is a particularly useful term because the numerous changes observed in Chalcolithic social and economic organization are characteristic of chiefdom organizations as studied by anthropologists (cf. Earle 1991).

The concept of Chiefdom has been criticized by scholars because of the assumed role it plays in Service's (1962) cultural evolutionary step-ladder leading from simple Bands to Tribes, Chiefdoms and finally States. Norman Yoffee (1993) has outlined some of the difficulties of the Chiefdom concept which include the different criteria used by scholars to identify their existence in the archaeological record and the problems of using a social typology based on the ethnographic present. Perhaps the biggest problem has been the assumption that Chiefdoms, as Robert Carneiro (1981) so emphatically stated, were the 'precursor of the state'. In Palestine, where state level societies may not have developed until the Late Iron Age, we did not use the Chiefdom concept as a teleological tool to explain the jump from egalitarian to state level societies. The fortified towns of EB II Palestine were never assumed to represent state level organizations. In fact, the differences between local Chalcolithic and Early Bronze Age social organization seem minimal – a relationship which needs to be systematically investigated in the future. The utility of social evolutionary typologies is that they provide archaeologists with a framework for cross-cultural comparison and a means of identifying new social organizations in the archaeological record. However, social typologies do not describe how or why significant changes in society occurred in antiquity.

Social evolution considered

Seen against the backdrop of Braudel's (1972, 1980: 25–38) notion of long-term environmental structure, developments during the Chalcolithic period in Palestine can be interpreted as flowing with general directional changes that are related to ecological, demographic, technological and economic factors. This is indeed a social evolutionary view which is anti-developmentalist and anti-

Copper standards and mace heads from the Cave of Treasure, Nahal Mishmar (photograph: © Zev Radovan)

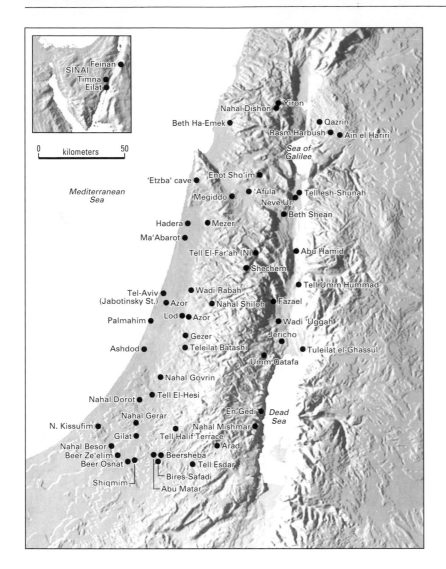

Figure 1   Chalcolithic sites in the Holy Land (source: Ben Tor 1992)

teleological. As we will see, the end of the Chalcolithic period in Palestine is characterized by a collapse in the system, rather than a developmental trend toward even more complex societies. Our model of the Chalcolithic period looks for feedback among the key variables of ecology, demography, technology, and economy, and will then isolate which factors or combinations of factors were responsible for growth and collapse. Finally, as Stephen K. Sanderson (1990: 224) points out in his critical history of *Social Evolutionism*, socio-cultural evolution occurs not only within societies, but also within whole networks or 'world systems' of societies. There comes a time in social evolution when it is impossible to understand change within a single society without rooting it in its larger 'World-Systemic' setting. Seen within this context, the mechanism of social evolution can be both 'gradualist' and 'punctionalist' and vary from one historical situation to another. With the collapse of Chalcolithic societies in

Palestine, culture change in the region becomes intimately and endlessly linked to the Near Eastern and Mediterranean World System (cf. Algaze 1993; Kohl 1987; Marfoe 1987; Moorey 1987).

The nature of societies considered

The sociologists Lenski and Lenski (1970: 6–7) define human societies as a form of organization involving sustained ties of interaction among its members, a relatively high degree of interdependence among its members, and a form of organization characterized by a high degree of autonomy. In general terms, a human society can be said to exist when a territorially bounded population maintains ties of association and interdependence and enjoys autonomy (cf. ibid.). This is a useful definition because it applies to human groups not only during the Chalcolithic period, but for the full ca. 1.0–1.5

million years of hominid occupation in the Holy Land. General similarities in assemblages of material culture can be used to identify discrete societies in the archaeological record. The five primary components of every human society are population, language, technology, social structure, and ideology. With the exception of language, for the prehistoric period (with its obvious absence of written evidence), various dimensions of all of these variables can be identified in the archaeological record. By definition then, the study of societies focuses on relatively autonomous organizations situated in different ecological settings. With Palestine's place in the Ancient Near Eastern world determined by its geographical context, to fully understand culture change in the country, the emphasis must be on investigation of the local society as seen within the context of more general center–periphery relations.

Chalcolithic societies in Palestine

Demographic trends

Most fieldworkers consider the emergence of Chalcolithic societies in Palestine as the result of a local evolutionary process connected with the growth of human population in the Late Pottery Neolithic period (Gilead and Alon 1988; Levy 1986; Hennessy 1982). The two areas where this process has been traced are along the Sinai-Negev coastal plain, where Gilead (1990) has shown the Qatifian Pottery Neolithic Culture to be a precursor to the Negev Chalcolithic societies, and the lower Jordan Valley, where Hennessy (1982) suggests the Chalcolithic type site of Tuleilat Ghassul grew out a local Late Neolithic tradition (see Gopher this volume, Chapter 13). The result of population increase at the end of the fifth millennium in Palestine was the growth of a wide range of Chalcolithic archaeological entities or 'cultures' which developed across the country, occupying a wide range of environmental zones (Figure 1). These include the Golan Heights (Epstein 1977); Hula Valley (Eisenberg 1989); the Coastal plain (Sukenik 1937; Perrot 1961), the Samarian Hills and Highlands (de Vaux and Steve 1947; Gopher and Tsuk 1991), and the Jezreel/Beth-Shean valleys (Engberg and Shipton 1934) in the north of the country. In the south of Palestine, a number of regional and subregional groups have been isolated. These include the Jordan Valley/Ammon Plateau (de Contenson 1964; Dollfus and Ibrahim, 1988; Gustavson-Gaube 1987; Ibrahim, Sauer, and Yassine 1976; Mallon et al. 1934); the Judean Desert (Bar-Adon 1980; Neuville and Mallon 1931); the Negev/Sinai Coastal Plain (MacDonald 1932; Oren and Gilead 1981); the Nahal Patish (Alon and Levy 1989); the Nahal Grar (Gilead 1989) and the Beersheva valley (Levy 1987; Perrot 1984; Commenge-Pellergrin 1987, 1990). As E. Anati (1963) first noted, most of the southern Chalcolithic 'provinces' are no greater than ca. 40 kilometers in length and represent separate societies.

Settlement pattern

The most systematic published surveys of Chalcolithic sites in the region come from the coastal plain (Gophna and Portugali 1988) and the northern Negev (Figure 2). Based on these subregions, it is possible to define the major changes in settlement pattern during the Chalcolithic. While a number of Late Neolithic entities develop into possible 'culture areas' (Gopher and Gophna, 1993; Gopher this volume, Chapter 13) and correspond to the Yarmukian, Lodian and Wadi Rabah phases, Late Neolithic sites are best described as small autonomous village sites rarely larger than 40 dunams. Surveys in the Beersheva valley show for the first time in Palestine a two-tier settlement hierarchy characterized by village centers (ca. 10 ha in area) and smaller dependent satellite sites. The largest of these centers include: Ze'elim, Shiqmim (Levy 1987), Bir es-Safadi (Perrot 1984; Eldar and Baumgarten 1985) and Nevatim (Levy and Alon 1987). In political terms, this settlement pattern represents the emergence of centers which coordinated social, economic and religious activities in the region, and indicates a much higher degree of social integration than the previous Late Neolithic pattern which was characterized by autonomous villages. A similar settlement process operated on the coastal plain (Gophna and Portugali 1988: 13) and presumably in the lower Jordan valley around Tuleilat Ghassul, the largest Chalcolithic site in Palestine (ca. +20 ha; Mallon et al. 1934).

In the last phases of development, Chalcolithic settlements in the lower Jordan Valley such as Ghassul (Mallon et al. 1934) and the Beersheva valley (Levy et al. 1991) are characterized by planned villages in two-tier settlement hierarchies along the major drainages (Figure 3). Large scale excavations in the Beersheva valley at Abu Matar, Bir es-Safadi and Shiqmim show a clear developmental settlement sequence spanning a period of approximately 700 years. The earliest settlement phases are characterized by subterranean rooms complexes, with the last occupation represented by planned open-air rectilinear villages (Plate 1 p. 232, Figure 4 p. 233). The function of these subterranean complexes has been hotly debated, with interpretations ranging from special architectural adaptations to a hot desert environment (Perrot 1984), storage facilities associated with open-air villages (Gilead 1988), and defense and storage systems established by the Chalcolithic settlers in the Beersheva valley (Levy et al. 1991) (Plate 2 p. 234). The long time span over which Chalcolithic cultures flourished in Palestine points to their stability and success as adaptive cultural systems in this part of the Near East.

Innovations and technology

Innovations in agro-technology

Growing populations in the late fifth to early fourth millennium necessitated a reorganization in technologies

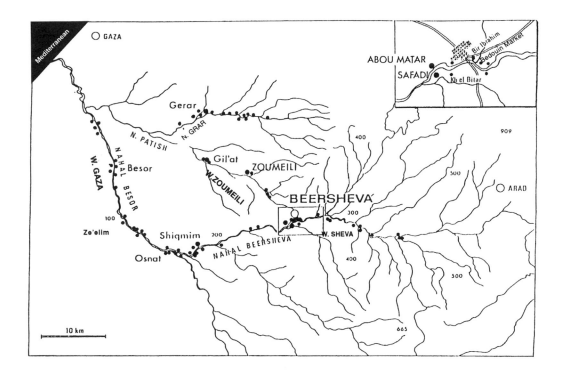

Figure 2   General settlement pattern of map of Chalcolithic sites in the northern Negev

associated with subsistence. With the expansion of Chalcolithic settlement into the major inland valleys of the northwest Negev (Levy and Alon 1987) and the arid lower Jordan valley (Mallon et al. 1934), new developments in agro-technology crystallized, some of which laid the foundations for subsistence systems in all of the following periods of human occupation in the region. In the northern Negev, the absence of widespread freshwater springs in the inland valleys led to the introduction of check dams and floodwater farming, which has been documented in the Beersheva and Patish Valleys on archaeological and botanical grounds (Levy 1981). In an innovating series of studies concerning ancient farming technologies, A. Rosen (1987, 1992) has shown a relationship between irrigation farming and silica skeleton (phytolith) formation in barley and wheat crops. Using independent botanical data, Rosen (ibid.) has examined silicified epidermal tissue from the culms of wheat and barley found on a number of Chalcolithic sites in the Beersheva valley and has demonstrated that these crops were grown under floodwater farming or simple basin irrigation.

This reconstruction of Chalcolithic agro-technology

represents an unusually elegant combination of archaeological evidence with data provided by the natural sciences to identify an important dimension of the late fifth to early fourth millennium economy. Although hoe-based cultivation was still the main means of farming – an observation based on the still widespread use of large bifacial flint tools (axes, adzes, hoes and chisels) (Figure 5 p. 235), the controlled addition of floodwater to field crops grown in the wide trough-shaped valley bottoms of the Negev produced the needed quantities of grain to support the newly emerging, large sedentary populations of the northern Negev. A similar process probably occurred at Tuleilat Ghassul and other sites in the Jordan valley which depended on diverting the freshwater springs for their crops (cf. Zori 1958). The discovery of carbonized olive (*Olea europea*) stones from Tuleilat Ghassul and the Cave of the Treasure provides some of the best indications of agricultural intensification during the Chalcolithic with the beginnings of fruit growing. Carbonized date stones (*Phoenix dactylifera l.*) were also found at these sites. Zohary and Spiegel-Roy (1975) suggested that olives from Tuleilat Ghassul were grown under irrigated conditions, similar to that of Jericho and Beth Shean today. As fruit

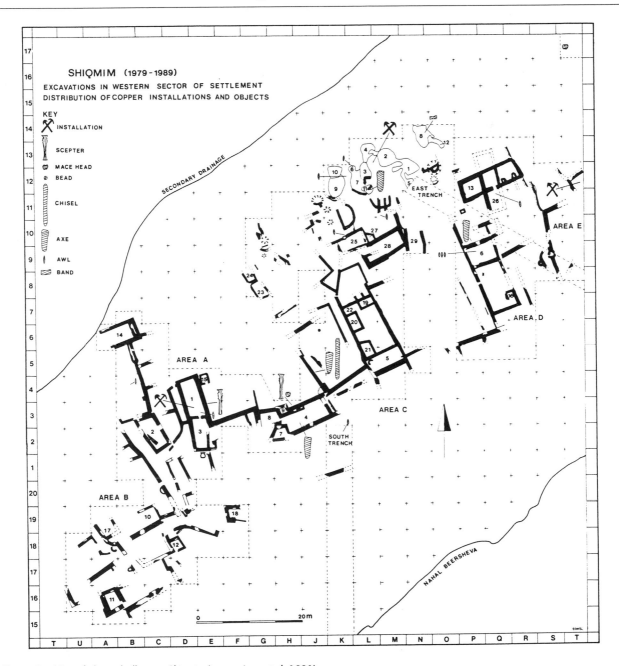

Figure 3   Map of planned village at Shiqmim (source: Levy et al. 1991)

remains are rare or totally absent from most Neolithic farming villages, they concluded that olives and dates apparently became integral elements of food production during the Chalcolithic.

Pastoralism

The largest faunal collections and most intensive archaeozoological research for this period have been carried out in the northern Negev. This biological data provides us with

a detailed picture of human/animal relations during this formative period on a scale unavailable for the previous Neolithic and later Early Bronze Age (cf. Grigson 1987; this volume, Chapter 15). The large-scale excavations in the Beersheva valley at Shiqmim (Levy et al. 1991), Bir es-Safadi (Perrot 1984), Abu Matar (Perrot 1955), Horvat Beter (Dothan 1959) and other sites provide the data necessary for characterizing herding activities at this time. If Shiqmim is taken as a representative sample for the

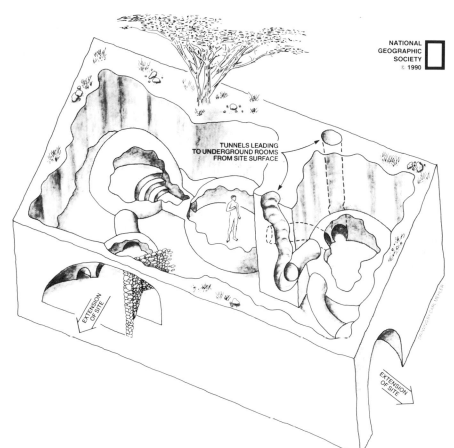

NATIONAL GEOGRAPHIC SOCIETY © 1990

TUNNELS LEADING TO UNDERGROUND ROOMS FROM SITE SURFACE

EXTENSION OF SITE

EXTENSION OF SITE

Figure 4 Schematic drawing of underground village at Shiqmim (courtesy of National Geographic Society News Service)

(Plate 4 p. 236). Other media such as *Lambis* shell from the Red Sea, Nile Valley shells and Mediterranean sea shells are common to most sites. These shells were carved into a wide range of shapes and used as pendants and bracelets. In many of the cemeteries on the coastal plain and northern Negev, shell jewelry has been found as burial offerings (cf. Levy and Alon 1982; Perrot and Ladiray 1980).

Production and metallurgy

From an *Annales* perspective, a new cycle in the organization of southern Levantine craft production is highlighted by focusing on metal. The beginnings of metallurgy in the Levant occur during this period which has produced the most spectacular early metal objects for the region, the most notable examples coming from the Cave of the Treasure in Nahal Mishmar on the western shore of the Dead Sea where more than 400 cultic/prestige and other objects were found (Bar-Adon 1980; Moorey 1988) (this chapter, opening photo). In the Beersheva valley, similarly shaped objects have also been found which were manufactured using the sophisticated 'lost wax' or *cire perdue* method, indicating an extremely sophisticated knowledge of metalworking (Levy and Shalev 1989).

Shalev and Northover (1987) have demonstrated the existence of two technologies for metal production:

1. A simple method which involved casting pure copper into an open mold to manufacture 'utilitarian' tools such as axes, adzes, and awls. This technique also utilized annealing and hammering to produce the final shape and hardness of these objects.
2. The 'lost wax' or *cire perdue* method which involves the use of arsenical copper whose casting properties, hardness and final appearance are superior to pure copper (Moorey 1985: 15).

More recently, excavations in a Chalcolithic burial cave in Nahal Qana in western Samaria (Plate 5 p. 237) have produced the earliest gold artifacts to have been found in the Levant (Gopher and Tsuk 1991). These include eight exquisite gold rings, interpreted as ingots, in which the gold would have been melted at a temperature at or below the melting point of pure gold (1064° C), a temperature well within the reach of Chalcolithic technology (Shalev and Northover 1987), and then poured into open ring-shaped molds and hammered into their final shape (Gopher et al. 1990: 440) (Plate 6 p. 238). The gold rings are outstanding because of the rarity

Plate 2 Overview of subterranean room at Shiqmim. A stone lined entrance can be seen leading to underground room 8 (photograph: © T.E. Levy)

of the material, technological advance, and implications for reconstructing Chalcolithic social organization. There are no gold sources in Palestine, so Egypt is assumed by Gopher et al. (1990) to be the origin of the raw material. As ring-shaped metal valuables are well known from late Egyptian pictographic descriptions of imperial-controlled trade in gold ingots (cf. Baines and Malek 1980; James 1985), the excavators suggest that trade in gold probably began as early as the fourth millennium BCE. As gold working requires additional metallurgical knowledge, three Chalcolithic metalworking technologies can now be identified for Chalcolithic Palestine.

The absence of known arsenical ore sources in Palestine led researchers such as Key (1980), Bar-Adon (1980), Kenyon (1985) and others to assume that these sophisticated objects could not have been produced locally but rather were made near presumed ore sources, far away from Palestine, in Anatolia or Azerbaijan. A recent archaeo-metallurgical and petrographic examination of a prestige/cultic object (a macehead) from Shiqmim shows conclusively that it was cast using a local Arava

valley glaucaunitic chalk as a core (Shalev et al. 1992). This important study shows conclusively, that contrary to diffusionist theories of an Anatolian or Azerbaijan origin, both cultic/prestige copper objects and utilitarian metal tools were produced locally in Palestine (Shalev ibid.). The precise location of the manufacture of prestige/cult metal objects still awaits identification.

The regional distribution of Chalcolithic sites with metal production debris (slags, crucibles, metal working installations) and the distribution of metal objects focus on the Beersheva valley with more limited evidence from the Wadi Feinan in Jordan's Arava valley (Hauptmann 1989; Levy and Shalev et al. 1989). Archaeo-metallurgical investigations show that the copper ores smelted in the Beersheva valley were imported from Feinan, over 100 km away. The most intriguing aspect of Chalcolithic copper exploitation at Feinan is the paucity of evidence for smelting activities (cf. Wadi Fidan 4; Hauptmann 1989: 131). While some metal working was done in the vicinity of Feinan (evidence of Chalcolithic metallurgy at Timna is inconclusive), the bulk of our evidence for actual smelting comes from the Beersheva valley (Figure 6 p. 238). This suggests that the ores were imported by the newly domesticated donkey (Davis 1976) to the Beersheva valley settlement system where they were smelted and cast under very tightly controlled circumstances and not shared with neighboring northern Negev societies.

Ideology

Durkheim (1915) wrote that religion was merely society 'stretched to the stars'. In terms of the development of religious/ideological systems, as society became more territorial religious institutions became more physically tied down to place. Michael Mann (1986: 47) has said, as society became caged, so did religion. Just as social organization becomes more complex in settled agrarian societies, so too do religious institutions grow and develop. This is best seen in Jacobsen's (1976) study of the development of Mesopotamian religion from the early fourth to third millennia BCE. In Palestine, the emergence of chiefdoms in the northern Negev and the lower Jordan valley were accompanied by two new ideological institutions: formal cemeteries and public sanctuaries.

Formal cemeteries

In the earlier prehistoric periods, the dead were usually buried within settlements, inside family houses, under floors, inside walls and in other domestic contexts (see Bar-Yosef Chapter 12, Gopher Chapter 13, both this volume). With the formation of Chalcolithic society, Palestine was dotted with formal cemeteries separated from permanent settlement sites. In the two most intensively researched areas of Chalcolithic settlement, the northern Negev and the lower Jordan Valley, the most extensive evidence for formal cemeteries has come to light. At Adeimeh, located

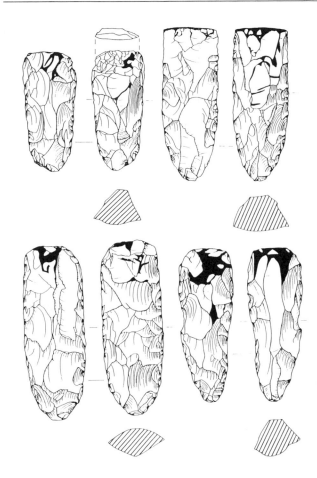

Figure 5   Bifacial flaked and polished tools from Gilat

Numerous Chalcolithic cemeteries have been found along the Israeli littoral at sites such as Azor, Ben Shemen, Bnei Braq, Hadera, Givatayim and other locales (cf. Ory 1946; Perrot 1961; Sukenik 1937), apparently without any evidence of settlement sites. The coastal cemeteries usually consist of artificial caves dug into the Kurkar ridges and are filled with ceramic ossuaries in a variety of rectangular, ovoid and cylindrical shapes. Secondary burials were commonly placed inside the ossuaries which were carefully placed in the caves. When Perrot (1955) carried out his excavations in the Beersheva Valley and found no evidence of a Chalcolithic cemetery, he suggested that the Beersheva Valley culture was primarily a pastoral society which buried its dead at these coastal cemeteries during their annual search for pasture (Perrot and Ladiray 1980). The detailed surveys by Gophna (Gophna and Portugali 1988; Gophna 1989) have produced ample evidence that settlements are indeed associated with coastal cemeteries. When this data is coupled with the new evidence for Chalcolithic cemeteries in the northern Negev, Perrot's (ibid.) pastoral model must be rejected.

The emergence of formal burial grounds has been traced cross-culturally in a number of rank societies to indicate a concern with more clearly defining territorial boundaries and a method of insuring that a corporate group has rights over the use and/or control of crucial but restricted resources. According to Lynne Goldstein (1981: 61) 'this corporate control is most likely to be attained and/or legitimized by means of lineal descent from the dead, either in terms of an actual lineage or in the form of a strong, established tradition of the critical resource passing from parent to offspring'.

Of particular interest to the study of Chalcolithic social organization is the recently discovered burial cave at Nahal Qanah in western Samaria which spans the Pottery Neolithic through Early Bronze I periods. In addition to lending support for the local transition of sixth to third millenna society in Palestine, one of the Chalcolithic graves was associated with a large quantity of gold artifacts (discussed above), which the excavators (Gopher et al. 1990) suggest as evidence of a hierarchical social organization during this period. While other Chalcolithic cemeteries, such as Shiqmim, show evidence of what Renfrew (1973) calls a group oriented chiefdom, this is the first example of an individual chiefly grave to have been found in Chalcolithic Palestine.

Public sanctuaries

Three places in Palestine were witness to the establishment of the earliest permanent public sanctuaries in the region: Tuleilat Ghassul, Ein Gedi and Gilat. Open-air sanctuaries, characterized mostly by standing stones and wall features, have been found throughout the southern Negev and Sinai (Avner 1990) but these were of a more ephemeral character. In the lower Jordan valley at Tuleilat Ghassul,

less than six kilometres southeast of Tuleilat Ghassul, an extensive Chalcolithic necropolis was found with a wide range of burial monuments including circular tumuli varying in diameter from ca. 3.80 to 7.0 m associated with rectangular cist graves (Stekelis 1935). In the northern Negev, a Chalcolithic cemetery was found near Shiqmim which extends for over a kilometer along a ridge of Eocene chalk hills which border the Beersheva valley (Plates 7a and 7b p. 239). To date, over 100 burial monuments have been excavated. Like Adeimeh, the Shiqmim cemetery has a variety of burial structures, including circular graves filled with burial offerings, cist graves and small tumuli clustered in groups on a series of seven hilltops. In a preliminary study of the burial monuments at Shiqmim, Levy and Alon (1982) were able to identify a degree of social ranking in one part of the cemetery based on energy expenditure in the building of burial monuments. More recently, Goren and Fabian (personal communication) discovered a new Chalcolithic cemetery on the Negev coastal plain near Kissufim, and Avner (1990) found a small cemetery near Eilat.

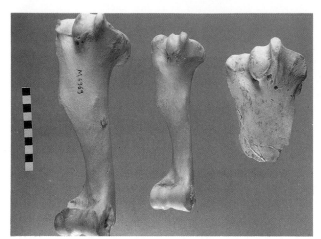

Plate 3 The proximal humerus of a horse (Shq 89 1054) from Shiqmim on the right compared with a modern donkey on the left (source: NGSBA, HUC–JIR, Jerusalem; Z. Radovan)

Hennessy has excavated several sanctuaries at the site. Although poorly published, Hennessy's (1982: 56) excavations in Area E indicate a sanctuary similar in layout to the one at Ein Gedi. Strong support for this comes from the early excavations at the site when spectacular prominent wall frescoes were found which depict ceremonial processions, mythical figures and strange animals (Cameron 1981). Resurfacing of the frescoes, with rich mineral paints, indicates that the buildings in Area E were used for a prolonged period. A series of eight superimposed wall-paintings were found in one building at the site.

Southwest of Tuleilat Ghassul, high above the western bank of the Dead Sea, an isolated sanctuary was excavated by Ussishkin (1980). The Ein Gedi sanctuary consists of four separate structures, all connected by a stone fence that encloses a roughly rectangular courtyard. These include the main gatehouse, a postern or secondary gate, a lateral chamber and the large sanctuary. The site is isolated; no settlement sites exist in the vicinity. Ussishkin (ibid.) suggests that the site was probably a central temple serving a wide region and was a focus for pilgrimage connected with the Ein Gedi springs in the wadi below.

The third Chalcolithic sanctuary is at Gilat in the northern Negev along the interface of the coastal plain and inland foothill zone. Gilat's location straddling the geographic border between these two important areas of settlement played an important role in the emergence of this site as the only northern Negev Chalcolithic sanctuary. A total of seven strata and substrata have been identified at the site and in two of these phases (Stratum IIb and IIc) architecture related to cult was identified. This includes complexes of rectilinear buildings associated with circular platforms, standing stones or *massebot*, large well-built mud brick silos, open air basins and other features.

Plate 4 Violin shaped figurine from Gilat made of chlorite–shist (source: NGSBA, HUC–JIR, Jerusalem; Z. Radovan)

Although excavations at Gilat cover a relatively small area (ca. 1200 m^2), an unusually rich assemblage of *artefacts mobilier* or small portable artifacts related to cult have been retrieved. These include over 200 fenestrated stands ('incense burners') made of non-local basalt and pottery, some 58 violin-shaped figurines, zoomorphic and anthropomorphic statuettes, stone and clay 'tokens', and other finds. A large sample of these objects was found in a single room (Room A) at the site which served as the main cult room during the Stratum IIc occupation, a kind of *Devir* or 'Holy of Holies' (Plate 8 p. 240).

A number of contextual associations of artifacts highlight Braudel's '*l'histoire evenementielle*' or events (here cult related) which took place in the Gilat sanctuary excavated by Alon and Levy. These include:

Entrance Shaft / פיר כניסה

Central Hall / האולם הגדול

Upper Chamber / החדר העליון

Copper Chamber / חדר הנחושת

Neolithic Chamber / החדר הניאוליתי

Square Chamber / החדר המרובע

Terrace Chamber / חדר הטראסות

Plate 5 Burial cave complex at Nahal Qanah (courtesy of The Israel Museum, Jerusalem)

1. the earliest dog burial in Palestine in its own individual plot associated with a grave offering;
2. a cache of four complete ostrich eggs set in a pit beneath a public courtyard;
3. a mass burial in the Stratum IIb sanctuary complex consisting of a mudbrick circular burial monument with nine complete human skeletons. Physical anthropological observations indicate that all of the individuals died at approximately the same time and were buried on a layer of hundreds of animal bones, the residue of offerings that were thrown in the grave prior to the human burials. Near the monument, a small pit was found with a complete fenestrated stand and a collection of eight bone awls surrounded by ten gazelle horns. At the time of the mass burial, these objects were intentionally burned.

These 'events' shed light on important happenings related to cult at Gilat.

Although altars, cemeteries, standing stones and other cult related phenomena have been found in other parts of the country, the artifacts associated with these features are almost all related to one archaeological entity or culture. In the Negev, for example, the Shiqmim cemetery seems to have served Shiqmim and perhaps other contemporary sites in the valley settlement system, but nothing beyond.

Gilat is unique in that material culture found in all the strata come from a wide range of Chalcolithic 'provinces' in southern Palestine. This is best illustrated by the presence of ceramics from at least nine of the eleven general petrographic groups defined by Goren (1987) for the Negev and Judean desert at the site. Additional evidence comes from the discovery of the finely carved violin-shaped figurines at Gilat, the largest number of these objects to have been found at any one site in the country (Alon and Levy 1989). These figurines are made of a wide range of non-local stone types including granite, limestone with iron oxides, chlorite, and other minerals which indicate ties with Transjordan, the Judean mountains, Sinai and other regions, and are indications of contact and exchange with many different regions in southern Palestine.

There is a marked degree of regionalism in Chalcolithic Palestine which reflects differences in community identity related to finely honed systems of adaptation to the mosaic of natural environments in the country. There may be, as Joffe (1991: 172) suggests, a common iconographic vocabulary or belief system in all the various regions. This is evidenced by the widespread distribution of violin-shaped figurines in the country, the prevalence of

Plate 6   Gold rings from Nahal Qanah, Samaria (courtesy of The Israel Museum, Jerusalem)

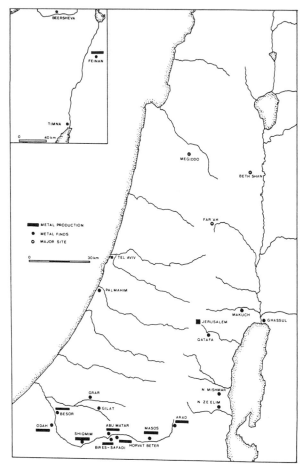

Figure 6   Distribution map of metal production sites

trapezoidal pendants in most southern Palestinian sites, the common large nose motif on statuettes and pillar figures (Epstein 1985, 1988), and the presence of standing stones in coastal plain tombs, the Negev cemeteries and throughout the desert areas (Avner 1990). These general similarities in ideological symbols cross-cut the different environmental zones in Palestine. However, according to our definition of societies given above, the regional assemblages of Chalcolithic material more importantly represent separate societies, each focused in their own territorial units.

I have suggested elsewhere (Levy 1986) that the contrast between the small scale societies of the Late Neolithic and the more complex developments of the Chalcolithic period indicates the emergence of a new social organization, the first 'chiefdoms' in Palestine. As the largest body of data for the Chalcolithic comes from the northern Negev desert, this region will provide a case study of social change in Palestine. Similar or slightly variant processes may have taken place in other regions such as the Lower Jordan valley. The following remarks

will attempt to isolate the processes responsible for social change.

Processes of change: risk management, resource competition and gift giving

Risk management

To understand the shift from Late Neolithic small scale societies to the more complex social organizations observed in the Chalcolithic period, there are three interrelated variables which worked together to promote change and insure stability. These include risk management, resource competition and gift-giving. By examining these three factors, it is possible to understand the role of craft specialization and, in particular, metalworking in strengthening elite groups within the Beersheva valley through a gift-giving system based on metal and other objects.

Risk management, or the need for social institutions

Plate 7a Aerial view of hilltop cemetery 3 at Shiqmim, northern Negev. A wide range of mortuary structures have been found in the cemetery. Pictured here are stone–lined burial circles and cist graves (courtesy of The Israel Air Force)

Plate 7b Detail of burial circle (no. 24) found in the Shiqmim cemetery 3 and pictured above. Disarticulated secondary burials were found here (source: T. Ludovise, Shiqmim expedition)

which can cope with unpredictable ecological and social situations, relates to the political economy of pre-industrial societies. Briefly, the political economy refers to the structures and rules in an economy which evolve out of the need for societies to adapt to local ecological and cultural environments (cf. Johnson and Earle 1987: 11–15). The domestic economy, on the other hand, refers to what Sahlins (1974) calls the 'Domestic Mode of Production' which is organized at the household level to meet individual family needs such as food, clothing, housing and subsistence technology. At the heart of the political economy is what Hardin (1968) calls 'the tragedy of the commons'. The archetypal case concerns the problems which arise when 'strangers' seek to exploit the same natural resources. For example, in societies where pastoralism plays an important role, if one group of herders aims at keeping pasture a viable resource by controlling their herd's grazing, another group of herders

may exploit the situation for extra grazing time for their own herd. Thus, restraint on the part of the first group of herders works to their disadvantage and greed on the part of the second group of herders only works to their temporary advantage. In the long-run, the pasture is damaged by overgrazing and all herders lose. As Johnson and Earle (ibid.) point out, the only answer is for groups to practice a code of behavior which regulates all of them and protects the common resource. I would add that one way of formalizing these behavior codes is through the evolution of regulating institutions such as cult centers, shrines, palace organizations and formal cemeteries.

In the northern Negev, the emergence of Gilat as a regional Chalcolithic cult center, along the coastal plain/ foothill interface, may relate to its function as a regulating institution which controlled and monitored pastoral activities on the rich annual pastures of this region. This is highlighted by the 'new' subsistence organization introduced with the Secondary Products Revolution in Chalcolithic societies, and the central motif of fertility and herding depicted in the anthropomorphic and zoomorphic statuettes found in the sanctuary (Alon and Levy 1989). While there is little evidence for the enclosure of agricultural land at this time, the establishment of ceremonial sites like Gilat, Ein Gedi and Tuleilat Ghassul, and formal cemeteries throughout the country indicates access to territory was controlled by the symbolism of place. Similar processes have been noted all over Europe (cf. Bradley 1991: 65). In the ethnographic record, Marx (1978) has shown how the tombs of Bedouin saints in the Sinai are established on the borders of different ecological zones to facilitate resource utilization by different social groups. The large quantities of non-local portable artifacts found in the Gilat sanctuary may reflect gifts or offerings brought to elites living at the site to secure access to grazing lands. Thus, risk management of valuable natural resources, such as grazing and farm land, may have been one factor which promoted the growth of northern Negev elites.

Resource competition

As Johnson and Earle (ibid.) point out, with population increase and intensified land use, locally rich resources such as fertile bottom land and prime pasture lands become even more precious. With intensified land use, the benefits of warfare and violent seizure of resources in a region become apparent. While mace heads, the earliest artifact clearly associated with human hand-to-hand combat begin to appear in the Late Neolithic in the Wadi Rabah phase (Stager 1992), during the Chalcolithic these objects are found in the hundreds (Sabanne – personal communication). In the northern Negev, stylistic differences in mace heads can be seen between the Patish and Beersheva valleys which probably relate to the

Plate 8   Zoomorphic statuette of the Gilat Ram, Gilat (photograph: © Zev Radovan)

different social groups which inhabited these valleys. The marked increase in mace heads found throughout the country is a clear indication of more organized inter-group conflict compared with the earlier periods. The construction of numerous 'subterranean villages' in the Beersheva valley, at sites such as Shiqmim, Abu Matar, Bir es-Safadi, Horvat Beter and other locales during the pioneer phase of settlement, may also be related to warfare. Ethnographic data from Capadoccia in Anatolia, from East Africa (Denyer 1978) and Roman Palestine (see Anderson, this volume Chapter 26) show how subterranean architectural complexes have been used as hiding devices – a defense against aggressors. The need to organize defense of key resources, such as the limited valley bottom flood plains in the Beersheva valley and the annual pasturage on the coastal plain, would also have promoted the growth of leadership in the region.

Maintaining Chalcolithic elites: gift giving

Recently, Cris Gosden (1989) drew together the role of production and debt in relation to social change in pre-industrial societies. At the heart of his study is Marcel Mauss's (1969) classic work, 'Essay on the Gift'. By examining a wide range of ethnographic and ethnohistoric sources of pre-industrial societies, Mauss concluded that

gifts were a means of setting up obligations – with the recipient under an obligation to the giver. Gift giving is organized so that the maximum number of relationships can be created and sustained by placing participants in a situation of debt. Gosden (ibid.) refers to these as 'debt-based societies'.

In debt-based societies the conditions of production are different from those where value dominates. Personal ownership of land does not exist, gardens or farmland are held in common, and clan members have rights of use, not ownership. Craft production is also not usually in private hands, but is carried out by castes or by individual households. Whereas in industrial societies commodities are freely interchanged, in debt-based societies gifts are ranked. The production of gifts for debt takes place within the relationships of the kin group and is aimed at producing items that will build lasting relationships between the transactors. For Sahlins (1974), the gift is the primitive way of achieving the peace that in civil society is obtained by the state. Seen in the context of the political economy, the relationship giver–receiver is the equivalent to that of leader–follower. As Gosden (ibid.) points out, the main factor needed to create regular flows of debt, which form the basis of social inequality, is a means of restricting access to gifts. One way of restricting access to gifts is to retain control over the means of production. The smaller the number of people who have the knowledge, skills, access to raw materials and time necessary to produce gifts, the higher the value of these items will be.

In the northern Negev, the Beersheva culture can best be described as a debt-based society where copper and other objects made of precious materials (ivory, imported stones and minerals, etc.) were used to create irregular flows of debt (Levy 1993). The distribution pattern of copper workshops which focuses on the Beersheva valley indicates a kind of monopoly over the production of copper objects that was not shared with neighboring polities. The fact that copper was smelted far away from the ore sources at Feinan and Timna indicates that metal processing and production was a highly guarded activity that was carried out primarily within the confines of the 'home territory' of the Beersheva culture. This debt-based system is in marked contrast to the industrial metalworking which took place in the following Early Bronze Age, when numerous smelting facilities are found adjacent to the ore sources at Feinan (Hauptmann 1989), hundreds of tons of slag can be attributed to the Early Bronze Age, and there was a widespread network of mines, middlemen and clients spread over the entire Negev and Sinai deserts (cf. Ilan and Sabanne 1989; Beit Arieh 1983; see Figure 6).

In this context, Chalcolithic copper objects (especially prestige/cultic items) can be seen as extremely valuable and circulated among elites as presentations. The exceptional skill and knowledge needed to mine ores, to smelt and to cast objects meant that only a small number of individuals could produce these objects. On receiving such a gift, the elites from any of the Beersheva valley settlement system were placed in a situation of social debt to the giver, presumably the paramount clan or ruler in the valley. Thus, control over metal production formed the basis of social inequality in this particular Chalcolithic society.

The collapse of Chalcolithic societies

The collapse of the Chalcolithic societies in Palestine can not be attributed to a single factor, instead it relates to a number of variables which worked together. The processes responsible for the collapse of Chalcolithic societies in Palestine are still very poorly understood and this should be an important direction for future research. The story of growth, stability and dissolution is not the same for every geographic region, or even every drainage system in Palestine. The settlement hierarchies observed in the Chalcolithic broke down all over the country and by the early EB I these societies had returned to being small autonomous village sites (Figure 7). This is seen in the north where *tell* sites such as Beth Shan XVIII–XVI (Engberg and Shipton 1934), Tell esh-Shuneh North Niveau II (de Contenson 1961), and Megiddo strata VII–V (Fitzgerald 1935) continue into the EB I and in the south a

similar process occurs at Tel Arad IV (Amiran 1978) and at Tel Halif (Site 101; Seger et al. 1990). Given the existing evidence, research in the semi-arid Irano-Turanian heartland of Chalcolithic settlement indicates a number of trends which may have precipitated collapse. Four of these possible catalysts are discussed below.

Climatic factors

The transition from the Chalcolithic to Early Bronze I (ca. 3700–3500 BCE) corresponds with the onset of more arid conditions which approximate those of today (Goldberg and Rosen 1987; A. Rosen 1989; Goldberg this volume, Chapter 4). The floret of Chalcolithic cultural growth occurred at the end of the period, probably sometime around 4000–3700 BCE in the Beersheva valley and lower Jordan valley. This was associated with the rapid build-up of rich agricultural soils and floodplains in the northern Negev, which enabled the establishment of planned villages and intensive farming in the valley bottoms (Levy et al. 1991). The onset of drier conditions may have caused changes in the discharge patterns of water in the main drainages which initiated erosional processes in the rich valley bottom soils and consequently destroyed the floodwater farming systems that supported so many northern Negev settlements. In the lower Jordan Valley, where farming seems to have depended more on the diversion of spring water and the water retentive soils around springs (cf. Raikes 1980), drier conditions may have disrupted discharge from the springs and dependent farming activities. For settlements where pig raising formed a significant proportion of husbandry practices in this semi-arid zone of ±10–15 percent (cf. Gilat, Grar, Tuleilat Ghassul, see Grigson, this volume, Chapter 15), drier conditions may have also led to the disappearance of many springs and the habitats most suited to pig raising. Taken together, these climatic changes could have disrupted the highly specialized farming methods which had crystallized during the Chalcolithic period.

Attenuation of the socio-political organization

Joffee (1991) has pointed out that the Negev Chalcolithic socio-political system – which was rich in symbols, concerned with territoriality, and engaged in the procurement of rare minerals and goods for local elites – was so tightly stretched over southern Palestine, the 'Arava and Sinai (Beit-Arieh 1983; Khalil 1987; Levy and Holl 1988; S. Rosen 1986; Rothenberg et al. 1978) that any systemic disruption in areas of resource procurement, agricultural production or the balance of political power would have disrupted the entire society. A similar process may have occurred in the lower Jordan valley and Transjordanian plateau which had extensive links with the northern Negev (cf. Gilead and Goren 1989). The inability

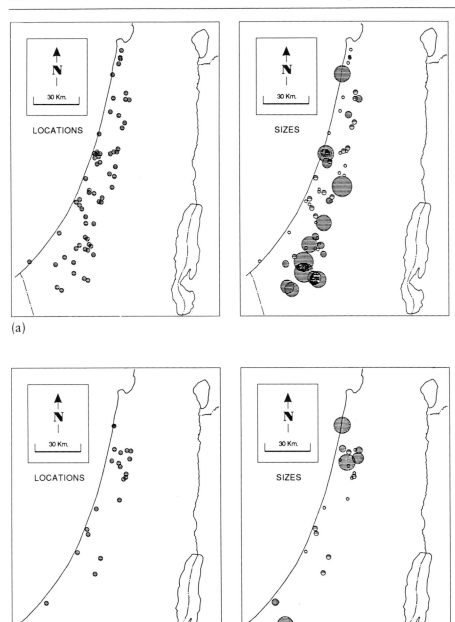

(a)

(b)

Figure 7   a) Chalcolithic settlements on the coastal plan b) Early Bronze 1A settlements on the coastal plain (source: Gophna and Portugali 1988)

to evolve alternative avenues of social power in the face of changes in the social or natural environmental framework may represent the social evolutionary dead-end which helped initiate the collapse of Chalcolithic societies in Palestine.

Commercialization

Increasing links with Egypt toward the end of the Chalcolithic and Predynastic periods also may have

initiated the erosion of the debt-based Chalcolithic social system so beautifully demonstrated in the Beersheva valley. The key to Egypt-Palestine relations during this period is the site of Maadi in the Nile Delta where subterranean rooms in the basal layers similar to those found in the Beersheva area where discovered. It is suggested by Rizkana and Seeher (1989) that these were linked to traders or other persons from the Beersheva valley. Recent radiocarbon dates from the Beersheva valley conform with dates from Maadi, supporting the contemporaneity of the cultures of these two regions at this time (Levy 1992b). Additional evidence for contacts with Palestine at Maadi include copper ores, ingots and objects (Hauptmann 1989), asphalt, presumably from the Dead Sea, and equid bones. Assuming that the site near Serabit el Khadim and the adjacent turquoise mines are Chalcolithic, Beit-Arieh (1983) has suggested that this represents entrepreneurial Canaanite mineral exploitation at this remote site for Egyptian markets, with little contact between the Chalcolithic core areas and the Sinai fringe. Joffee (1991) asks whether these contacts had a role in the breakdown of Chalcolithic patterns of authority which would have stimulated social fissioning. Seen in the context of the breakdown of Chalcolithic debt-based societies, the rise of entrepreneurs at the end of the period may indeed have whetted the appetite of growing Predynastic complex societies in the Nile valley for the mineralogical and other resources in Palestine.

Warfare

The last factor to be considered in the collapse of Chalcolithic societies relates to warfare. As shown above, the manufacture of weapons for hand-to-hand combat was developed to high degrees of craftsmanship, with the manufacture of copper mace heads using the 'lost wax' technique and hard stone (granite and hematite) mace heads which involved complicated drilling and processing methods. While it has been suggested that inter-societal conflict over resources was an important factor in the emergence of Chalcolithic elites, warfare with expeditionary Predynastic military organizations may also have contributed to the collapse of Chalcolithic societies in the northern Negev and laid the foundations for Dynasty 0 control of the Negev, with its widespread economic network which crystallized in the late EB I period. This hypothesis should be regarded as tentative, however, though the recent discovery of Predynastic Egyptian mace heads in destruction levels at the Gilat sanctuary may indicate a concerted effort by Predynastic Egyptian chieftains to eradicate the Chalcolithic symbolic and ideological system that provided the fabric which united Chalcolithic societies in southern Palestine. The thick ash layers covering the mounds at Tuleilat Ghassul were so striking that Mallon and the earliest investigators at the site mistook it for the destroyed Biblical cities of Sodom and Gomorra. Questions concerning the site formation processes and upper destruction levels at Tuleilat Ghassul still need to be addressed, however, but on developments in the Negev, the possibility that warfare was a factor in its demise cannot be discounted. The precise nature of Egypt-Palestine relations in the late to early fourth millennium still needs clarification; however, whatever its nature, this relationship marked the breakdown of debt-based social organizations in Palestine and the end of independent social evolution in the country.

Acknowledgments

My study of Chalcolithic societies in Israel has benefitted enormously through years of collaboration in the field and laboratory with David Alon, Ibrahim al-Assam, Yorke Ronan, Morag Kersel, Paul Goldberg, James Anderson, Caroline Grigson, Catherine Commenge, Patricia Smith, Yuval Goren, and others.

CRAFT SPECIALIZATION IN THE CHALCOLITHIC PERIOD

During the Chalcolithic period, craft specialization developed to a higher level than at any previous time in the history of the Levant. In addition, both long- and short-distance trade increased significantly during the Chalcolithic period. The most popular items that were traded included vessels carved out of basalt, cast copper, tabular scrapers, pottery, obsidian, sickle blades and ivory objects. The raw materials used to craft these objects came from regions scattered thoughout the Levant — from eastern Turkey in the north to Egypt in the south. By using statistical analyses, petrography and scanning electron microsopes (SEM), archaeometrists have been able to identify the intensity and nature of this ancient trade.

At sites in the Beersheva valley, some of the earliest production sites have been discovered for copper metallurgy in the Near East. The finds included tools (axes, adzes, chisels and awls; see Plate 1.1), ornaments, prestige-cult objects, ores, slags, crucibles and furnaces. Using SEM, Sariel Shalev and Peter Northover (1987) were able to match up the slags, ores and crucibles with the copper tools also found at one of the Beersheva valley sites (Shiqmim). The ores were traced to the Wadi Feinan in Jordan, south of the Dead Sea and over 100 km from the site. The results show that the raw materials used to manufacture copper tools were traded over a considerable distance. The biggest puzzle concerns why these early metal workers did not smelt the ore near the mining site at the Wadi Feinan. Why did they carry the raw ore more than 100 km away from the source area and smelt it in the Beersheva valley? One possible explanation, discussed in this chapter, concerns the nature of the control of metal production during this formative period. Metal working was probably a prized secret and not readily shared.

'Utilitarian' tools were not the only copper objects manufactured in the Chalcolithic period. In the early 1960s, Pessah Bar-Adon surveyed the Nahal Mishmar, a drainage south of Ein Gedi that empties into the Dead Sea. There, high up in a

cave that could be reached only by a rope ladder, Bar-Adon found the so-called Cave of the Treasure (1980). Hidden behind a large boulder were over 400 beautifully preserved copper mace heads, scepters, crowns and other objects — all from the Chalcolithic period. Most of these artifacts are non-utilitarian; they may have symbolized social rank and/or could have been used in cult activities. Similar objects, such as scepters and mace heads, have been found in the Beersheva valley sites. Metallurgical studies of these 'cult or prestige' objects from Shiqmim and other sites reveal that, unlike the ores, slags and ordinary tools found, these objects contain a very high arsenic content. This is a clear indication that objects such as mace heads and scepters were not manufactured on the sites in the

Plate 1.1   Cache of 'utilitarian' copper tools found at Shiqmim (photograph: © T.E. Levy)

Beersheva valley. To achieve the unusual shapes that characterize cult or prestige metal objects, the Chalcolithic craftsmen needed a copper alloy with a high arsenic content; such an alloy is more fluid than ordinary copper and, thus, is easier to cast in exotic shapes. Accordingly, we can now define two distinct metal industries during the Chalcolithic period: one for making simple, everday tools and another for cult or prestige objects, which required more complicated casting.

15

PLOUGH AND PASTURE IN THE EARLY ECONOMY OF THE SOUTHERN LEVANT

Caroline Grigson

Introduction

Most of the writings about food production in the southern Levant in the Chalcolithic and the Bronze Age periods (that is the fourth and third millennia BC and most of the second) focus on urbanism and nomadism, but do not consider the actual plant and animal remains from archaeological sites that might support the theories advanced. It is surprising that archaeologists have been so incurious about the ways in which people actually obtained their daily bread. Politics, social systems, statehood, the beginnings of urbanism, warfare, architecture and the manufacture of pottery and flint tools are all legitimate subjects for study, but none would have been possible without the provision of plant and animal food. Indeed, it is the supply of food, more than anything else, which sets the parameters within which all human societies have to operate. It must also be remembered that plants and animals are multiple resources, providing far more than merely food.

The degree of complexity which the agricultural and economic systems of the Middle East had reached by the Early Bronze Age, that is, by the third millennium BC, is apparent from the documentary evidence provided by the tablets excavated from Ebla in Syria (Pettinato 1991). Syria is not of course the area under discussion, but the information conveyed by the tablets is suggestive of the kind of question that we can at least begin to think about, though much more work will have to be done before we have satisfactory answers. By the third millennium there were complicated trading relationships between Syria and Egypt, Syria and Mesopotamia, Palestine and Egypt, which means a market economy operated. Trade in agricultural produce implies surplus production – what system allowed such a surplus to be produced? How were the goods that formed the basis of this trade transported? What happened when trading relations broke down? What effect did agriculture and husbandry have on the environment? Was the environment robust enough to buffer the ecological strains that such agriculture might lead to? How much geographical variation was there? To what extent is any variability attributable to environmental causes or to social causes?

A major problem is that we are looking for signs of *innovation*, innovation suggestive of new ways of exploiting animals and plants, yet one cannot talk about innovation unless one knows what was happening in previous times. There are about two millennia in Israel, two thousand years of the Late (or Pottery) Neolithic, from which few sites have been published in any detail. All that we do know about their subsistence base is that they seem to have been settled people with domestic animals and plants.

A multiplicity of types of evidence is relevant to the study of early farming systems, including settlement patterns and site size as well as physical artifacts such as pottery, stone tools and installations for processing olives and grapes, but the present work concentrates on the actual remains of animals and plants, which are equally artifacts – they are *what* they are and *where* they are because of past human behaviour.

Obtaining plants and animals – some theory

Before looking at the evidence for agricultural systems in the Chalcolithic and Bronze Ages, it is necessary to discuss the possible agricultural systems of the time, that is the strategies that might have been employed to maintain the supply of animals and plants, given what is known about the environment and social conditions of the time.

The cultivation of plants

The eight founder crops listed in Figure 3 were the basis for early agriculture in the Levant (Zohary 1992); by the Late Neolithic they had already been cultivated for millennia.

The founder crops can all be grown with winter rain-fed water supply in areas with more than about 350 mm of rain a year, but where there is less rain than that some

Plate 1   This clay figurine, of what seems to be a donkey carrying two pots or baskets, was found in the Late Chalcolithic level at Azor (Epstein 1985)

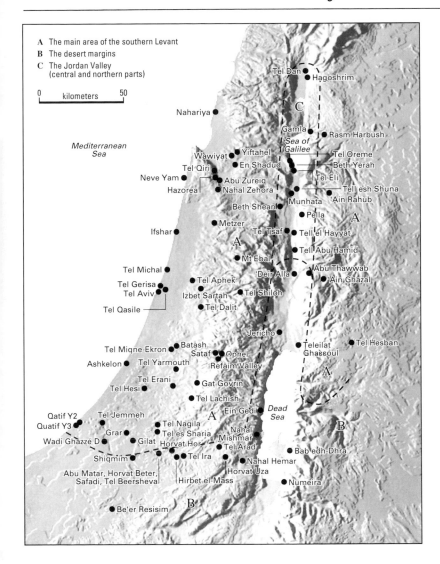

A The main area of the southern Levant
B The desert margins
C The Jordan Valley
   (central and northern parts)

Abu Matar	Qatif Y2
Abu Thawwab	Qatif Y3
Abu Zureiq	Rasm Harbush
'Ain Ghazal	Refaim Valley
'Ain Rahub	Safadi
Arad	Sataf
Ashkelon	Shiqmim
Bab edh-Dhra	Tel Aphek
Batash	Tel Arad
Be'er Resisim	Tel Aviv
Beit Shean	Tel Beersheva
Beth Yerah	Tel Dalit
Deir 'Alla	Tel Dan
Ein Gedi	Tel Eli
En Shadud	Tel Erani
Gamla	Tel es Sharia
Gat Govrin	Tel Gerisa
Gilat	Tel Hesban
Grar	Tel Hesi
Hagoshrim	Tel Ira
Hazorea	Tel Jemmeh
Hirbet el-Msas	Tel Lachish
Horvat Beter	Tel Michal
Horvat Hor	Tel Miqne-Ekron
Horvat Uza	Tel Nagila
Ifshar	Tel Oreme
Izbet Sartah	Tel Qasile
Jawa	Tel Qiri
Jericho	Tel Shiloh
Metzer	Tel Tsaf
Mt Ebal	Tel Yarmouth
Munhata	Teleilat Ghassoul
Nahal Hemar	Tell Abu Hamid
Nahal Mishmar	Tell el Hayyat
Nahal Zehora	Tell esh Shuna
Naharya	Timna
Neve Yam	Wadi Ghazzé D
Numeira	Wawiyat
Ophel	Yiftahel
Pella	

Figure 1 Map showing the location of the sites mentioned in the text, figures, tables and windows, and the main areas into which the region has been divided in the present study

of them can be grown in damp microclimates, as can be induced in some deserts by utilization of dew, or in oases, or in areas where rivers or streams bring an exotic water supply. Suitable conditions for cultivation may be artificially provided by irrigation; when utilized in the Levant this seems to have been simple control of seasonal flood water rather than elaborate, full scale irrigation by the control of river water as in Mesopotamia and Egypt.

Land can be prepared for sowing by digging, hoeing or ploughing. On hillsides, terraces may be cut to increase the area available for cultivation and to prevent erosion. Soil fertility may have been improved by the alternation of crops and by leaving land fallow on a regular basis, by manuring and by allowing animals to graze on stubble after the harvest. Seed is usually broadcast by hand, but may have been trodden into the ground by domestic sheep, goats or pigs. Threshing may be done by using cattle or donkeys to pull sledges over the harvested cereal. The

interrelationship between plants and animals in farming also includes the production of plant material as fodder for enclosed or hobbled animals. Obviously agriculture on any scale is bound to be a sedentary occupation.

Animal husbandry

The large numbers of animal remains found in archaeological sites indicate that the economy of the Levant in the Chalcolithic and Bronze ages was based on the breeding of the four ungulate species listed in Figure 4 (p. 248), and so it is to this day except in places where religious prohibitions or unsuitable environmental conditions preclude pig-keeping.

All these animals were without doubt domestic. The domestication of sheep and goats took place at least as early as the seventh millennium (Clutton-Brock 1981;

Figure 2 This nineteenth-century print of cattle threshing corn exemplifies the close relationship between animal husbandry and the cultivation of plants in the southern Levant

---

THE FOUNDER CROPS

CEREALS:
Two-row barley, *Hordeum vulgare* (also called *H. distichum*)
Emmer wheat, *Triticum turgidum*, subsp. *dicoccum*
Einkorn wheat, *Triticum monococcum*

PULSES:
Lentil, *Lens culinaris*
Pea, *Pisum sativum*
Chickpea, *Cicer arietinum*
Bitter vetch, *Vicia ervilia*

OTHERS:
Flax, *Linum usitatissimum*

Figure 3 The eight founder crops listed by Zohary (1992) which were the basis for early agriculture in the Levant

---

FOOD ANIMALS

Sheep, *Ovis aries*, 80 kg
Goats, *Capra hircus*, 80 kg
Cattle, *Bos taurus*, 625 kg
Pigs, *Sus scrofa*, 100 kg

Figure 4 The four species of domestic artiodactyls which were ubiquitous from the Late Neolithic onwards in the Middle East as sources of food, with approximate meat weights (Clark and Yi 1987)

Uerpmann 1979), that of cattle probably began in the sixth millennium and had resulted in a definite diminuation in size in the Levant by the fifth millennium (Grigson 1989). Pigs had almost certainly been domesticated by about 6,000 BC (Flannery 1983; Grigson unpublished analysis). By the Chalcolithic period all these animals had undergone a further and marked decrease in size and there is no doubt that, apart from the occasional hunted wild animal, all the remains of sheep, goats, cattle and pigs represent domestic stock. The domestic status in the fourth and third millennia of the other three important ungulates – donkeys, horses and camels – is more problematical and will be discussed separately.

As Redding (1984) has pointed out, the care and control of domestic ungulates has to be directed above all at herd security; unless enough breeding animals are kept to ensure successful reproduction, that is the replenishment of the herd over time, animal husbandry is not viable. That this requires human social organization is self-evident.

In order to survive herd animals have to feed and this must have been one of the chief preoccupations of early farmers. We can suppose that animals were fed in various ways – bringing in fodder from wild or cropped plants, feeding waste foodstuffs (this is particularly true of pigs), allowing animals to scavenge on urban rubbish, moving them around the landscape to graze on stubble fields or wherever natural pasture was most abundant, usually on a seasonal basis. Equally animals have to drink, so access to adequate water to satisfy their metabolic requirements is vital. Another aspect of survival is of course protection from predators and cattle rustlers, and it may be this which led to the enclosure of herds within village settlements, at least at night.

It is clear from these basic precepts that there is a variety of ways in which herd animals can be managed – varying from the keeping of small numbers within sedentary village communities, through small scale movements around the landscape, to large scale, nomadic movements. Each of these stages implies an increasing degree of mobility on the part of animal keepers and an increasing dislocation between animal keeping and agriculture, which is primarily a sedentary occupation. In order to ensure herd security and to maximize the food and other products obtained from animals, within the constraints of available feed, decisions have to be made regarding the control of breeding and the selective culling of males and females at particular times of the year. It is obvious that the choice of strategy is, at least in part, determined by local environmental constraints and by the uses to which animals are put.

The extent to which animals are used for the direct subsistence of the communities which own them or as segments of exchange systems with other communities, particularly urban ones, is likely to be of increasing relevance within the context of the proto-urban and early urban societies that characterize the Chalcolithic and Early Bronze Age periods. Similarly, the whole question of the ownership of animals, and the organization and control of access to them, is clearly part and parcel of the political and social organization of the time, about which, at least in preliterate societies, we have very little knowledge. Whatever the system of ownership, unless a strict balance can be maintained between what the local environment can provide and what is taken from it in the form of human and animal nutrition, the result will be environmental degradation through soil depletion, overgrazing and so on; unless corrected or adapted to, this will eventually lead to the collapse of any farming or pastoral system. This is particularly true in sensitive, marginal areas such as the desert fringes.

Agricultural systems in the past – some evidence

The cultivation of plants from the Late Neolithic to the Late Bronze Age

Most studies of the history of domestic plants in the Near East have focused on the time, place and genetics of their origin in Pre-pottery Neolithic times. There is a serious shortage of information about plants and their uses in the Late Neolithic, and thereafter the few data that exist are usually presented on a presence/absence basis of carbonized seeds and wood, with little attempt at quantification. Reviews of the Chalcolithic and Bronze Age data by Hanbury-Tenison (1986) and Liphschitz (1989) show that in addition to the eight founder crops listed in Figure 3, a large number of other species of plants were cultivated; evidence for their presence on a site-by-site basis is discussed below, the locations of the archaeological sites mentioned are shown in Figure 1.

Arable agriculture

The only data on the Late Neolithic come from two small samples. At 'Ain Rahub in the Jordan highlands Neef (in Muheisen et al. 1988) found two-row barley, emmer, a few grains of einkorn and linseeds, which were large and so considered domestic. The same cereals were the only plants identified at Late Neolithic Jericho (Hopf 1969), but in such small samples the absence of other species is not significant.

From the Chalcolithic onwards the most common cereal was two-row barley, with emmer wheat a close second. Barley is better adapted to dry conditions and is said to increase in proportion in arid areas (Zaitschek 1959; Arnon 1972).

The three subspecies of naked wheat (*Triticum aestivum*), club wheat, bread wheat and spelt, seem to have arisen later than the hulled wheats, but small quantities have been identified at several sites: Tel Tsaf, Shiqmim and Jawa in the Chalcolithic (Gophna and Kislev 1979; Kislev 1987; Willcox 1981), at Jericho in the Early and Middle Bronze Age (Hopf 1969), at Arad, Bab edh-Dhra and Numeira in the Early Bronze Age (Hopf 1978;

McCreery 1979) and at Deir 'Alla in the Jordan Valley in the Late Bronze Age (Van Zeist and Heeres 1973) – all these sites, except Tel Tsaf, are on, or close to, the desert edge. As samples are so few and so small, it is dangerous to draw inferences from the absence of any particular species, but that at Pella, farther to the north than Deir 'Alla in the Jordan Valley, seems quite large (Willcox 1992) so the absence there of naked wheat before the Iron Age may be significant. Naked wheat also seems to be absent from all other Early Bronze Age sites in the rest of the area, where conditions were moister (Liphschitz 1989). As it requires better conditions than emmer or einkorn, its presence on the desert edge suggests higher rainfall than at present or irrigation, or both (Hopf 1978). The various species of wheat have not been distinguished from each other in reports on plant remains from most other Middle and Late Bronze Age sites, but according to Helbaek (1958) naked wheat almost completely replaced emmer during the second millennium, at least at Tel Lachish.

Another cereal which appeared later than the three founder cereal crops is six-row barley *H. vulgare* subsp. *hexastichum*, and it is this species, not the two-row form, which was found at Chalcolithic Jawa (Willcox 1981); the two species have been identified together in the Early Bronze Age at Arad, Bab edh-Dhra and Numeira (Liphschitz 1989; McCreery 1979, 1980).

The four founder pulse crops (lentils, peas, chickpeas and bitter vetch) are found almost universally and must have been an important source of protein. Pulses making a minor contribution to the diet include the grass pea (*Lathyrus sativus*) and broad bean (*Vicia faba*). Hopf (1978), and also Kislev (1987), have suggested that some essential amino acids cannot be supplied in sufficient quantity by cereals alone, and would have to be obtained from either animal products or pulses ('the meat of the poor'). Thus a high proportion of pulses in the diet compared with cereals might be correlated with a low proportion of animal food and vice versa. Kislev postulated that the small quantity of legumes at Chalcolithic Shiqmim, on the desert edge, points to a greater dependence on animal products, an appropriate finding in view of the undoubted agro-pastoral nature of sites in the area at that time.

The last founder crop – flax or linseed – is rarely mentioned, but it was probably grown from the Pre-pottery Neolithic B onwards, as radio-carbon dates of about 7,000 BC have been obtained on linen yarn at Nahal Hemar in the Judaean Desert (Bar-Yosef and Alon 1988). Cultivated linseeds have been definitely identified from Chalcolithic Pella (Area XIV) (Willcox, quoted in Hanbury-Tenison 1986), and are noted from various Early Bronze Age sites (Liphschitz 1989). The large size of the linseeds retrieved from the Early Bronze Age of Bab edh-Dhra and Numeira on the eastern side of the Dead Sea (McCreery 1979, 1980) and from Deir 'Alla for levels from 1,200 BC onwards (Van Zeist and Heères 1973) was taken as evidence for irrigation, following the criteria of Helbaek (1959). It seems unlikely that linseeds were palatable, but linseed oil may have been extracted for lighting or as a solvent for resins and pigments, though the primary use of flax was probably the production of linen fibres.

Remains of vegetables and herbs are rarely retrieved, but garlic and onion were found in the Cave of the Treasure (Nahal Mishmar) in the Chalcolithic (Zaitschek 1961), onion in the Early and Middle Bronze Age at Jericho (Hopf 1969), and fenugreek (*Trigonella graecum*) at Tel Lachish (Helbaek 1958).

Horticulture

The main horticultural crops of the Chalcolithic and Early Bronze Age are listed in Figure 5; all except vines were probably domesticated during or before the Chalcolithic (Stager 1985; Zohary and Spiegel-Roy 1975).

Olive stones occur frequently from the Chalcolithic onwards, even in the Negev. Vats for the separation of olive oil, as well as olive wood, have been found in the Chalcolithic of Rasm Harbush in the Golan (Epstein 1978). The olive stones in sites in the Jordan Valley, from the Chalcolithic at Teleilat Ghassoul and from Early Bronze Age Bab edh-Dhra and Numeira, have been definitely identified as being from cultivated trees, as wild olives would not have been part of the local flora (Zohary and Spiegel-Roy 1975; Neef 1990; McCreery 1980) and the same is almost certainly true of the large numbers found in Area XIV (Chalcolithic) at Pella (Willcox 1992). The presence of olive *wood* in the Chalcolithic at Tel Tsaf, Tell Abu Hamid and Tell esh Shuna, also in the Jordan Valley but nearer to woodland where wild olives grow, suggests that in these sites too the stones were from cultivated trees (Neef 1990).

Date stones were found in the Cave of the Treasure (Nahal Mishmar) (Bar-Adon 1980, Liphschitz 1989), Teleilat Ghassul (Mallon, Koeppel and Neuville 1934: 40) in the Chalcolithic, at Bab edh-Dhra, Numeira and Jericho in the Early and Middle Bronze Age (McCreery 1979, 1980; Hopf 1969) and at Tel Gerisa, near Tel Aviv, in the Late Bronze Age (Liphschitz 1989).

Pomegranates do not occur in the wild in the Levant so the seeds found in the Chalcolithic of the Cave of the Treasure (Nahal Mishmar) and the Early Bronze Age at Arad and Jericho (Bar-Adon 1980, Hopf 1969, 1978) must be of domestic plants.

Although grape pips are reported from one Chalcolithic site (Abu Matar near Beersheva) (Negbi 1955) they seem to have been intrusive. As wild vines are not found in the Levant, any remains must be from domestic stock originally introduced from elsewhere, probably early in the Early Bronze Age (Stager 1985). Thereafter they are commonly found (Liphschitz 1989), even at Arad in the

---

FRUIT TREES

Olive, *Olea europaea*
Grape, *Vitis vinifera*
Date, *Phoenix dactylifera*
Fig, *Ficus carica*
Pomegranate, *Punica granata*

Figure 5   The main horticultural crops of the Early Bronze Age; all except vines were probably domesticated during or before the Chalcolithic

---

Negev and on the eastern side of the Dead Sea at Bab edh-Dhra and Numeira, where a hoard of 700 whole grapes was retrieved (McCreery 1979, 1980). Although they could be the remains of imported raisins, local cultivation seems more likely as grapes were, with barley, the most numerous plant remains found and vine *wood* was retrieved from Arad (Hopf 1978).

Other fruits, not necessarily cultivated, whose seeds have been retrieved include fig, peach, bullace and hawthorn (*Crataegus* sp.). Nuts, mainly almonds (*Prunus amygdalus*), pistachio (*Pistacia atlantica*), walnuts and acorns (*Quercus* sp.) were common.

All the fruit trees whose remains have been discussed are propagated not by seed but vegetatively by cloning, implying sophisticated horticultural practices, though these did not yet extend to grafting (Zohary and Spiegel-Roy 1975).

The general impression is of the consumption of a wide range of cereals, pulses, fruit and nuts, most of them cultivated, suggesting small fields, orchards and gardens, rather than large-scale monoculture.

Animal husbandry from the Pottery Neolithic to the Iron Age

What can be deduced from the study of the numerous remains of sheep, goats, pigs and cattle found in archaeological sites in the Levant? The only information that is widely available is the number of bones of each species retrieved. Horwitz and Tchernov (Tchernov and Horwitz 1990; Horwitz and Tchernov 1989b) examined the numbers of sheep and goats compared with those of cattle in a large number of archaeological sites from various periods in Israel. The sites were grouped on the basis of their geographical position according to an ingenious classification of the land of Israel into four types of area, based on modern carrying capacities. The results suggested an increasing dependence on sheep and goats from the Late Neolithic to the Iron Age, in all areas except the poorest (around Beersheva) and the richest (the Upper Jordan and the foothills). This increase seems to have begun in the Early Bronze Age.

I have used the same basic method as Tchernov and Horwitz, with a similar diachronic/geographical approach, but with the addition of data from sites on the eastern side of the Jordan Valley and from the Jordanian highlands. I have divided the geographical region into three: (a) the main area, that is the southern Levant, including the Jordan Highlands, but excluding (b) the desert margins (from Beersheva to the south and east, the southernmost part of the Jordan Valley and the Black Desert) and (c) the central and northern parts of the Jordan Valley. The data used are set out in Table 1 and the locations of the sites are shown in Figure 1.

Unlike Tchernov and Horwitz I have utilized pigs in the general assessment. As one ox is equal to many sheep and goats in terms of the food it can yield, I have translated the numbers of bones found into approximate meat weights (see Figure 4), which are the minimum figures in kilos for domestic animals given by Clark and Yi (1983). These figures are very approximate as they do not allow for sexual dimorphism, age differences, nor individual, breed and diachronic variation. However, these parameters cannot be established on the majority of archaeological material, so the figures are a useful means of establishing relative rather than absolute meat weights.

Some clear patterns of faunal change emerge when the mean percentages of meat weights of various sites within each area are compared (Figures 6a, 6b and 6c) but it must be remembered that these are only averages, there is a wide range of variation among the different sites within each group, and some groups comprise very few sites. In almost all sites, from the Late Neolithic to the Iron Age, cattle provide at least 50 per cent of the meat. The predominance of cattle is particularly marked in the Jordan Valley (Figure 6c), even at Numeira on the south-eastern side of the Dead Sea (McCreery 1980), presumably reflecting the low-lying marshy landscape.

Sheep and goats take second place to cattle in all areas of the country, though the difference is less marked on the desert edge. This is true in all periods except in the Early Bronze Age on the desert edge, where there is a marked peak in sheep and goats (Figure 6b). The peak in sheep and goats in the Early Bronze Age also occurs, though less markedly, in the main area of the country (Figure 6a). Thereafter in the main area there is a slight decline in sheep and goats but they remain more important than in the Late Neolithic and Chalcolithic. Clearly, as Tchernov and Horwitz also concluded, the Early Bronze Age was a period of marked economic change, that it was more marked on the desert edge suggests that environmental degradation may be at least one of the causes.

Pigs are scarce in the desert areas (Figure 6b) and were never of much importance elsewhere (Figures 6a and 6c); although they provided up to about 15 per cent of meat in the Late Neolithic and Chalcolithic, they declined steadily thereafter.

The difficulties of separating sheep from goat bones are well known, so most of their bones have to be put in the mixed sheep/goat category, however, on some sites, enough have been distinguished to allow a pattern to emerge (Figure 7 and Table 2). Even so the sample sizes are small and the results must be interpreted with caution. However, they seem to indicate a rise in the proportion of sheep compared with goats from the Late Neolithic, or Chalcolithic, to the Bronze Age. This suggests another possible factor in the rise of sheep/goats in the Early Bronze Age. Sheep, as Digard (1981) has pointed out, are regarded by the Bakhtiari in Iran as the rich man's animal as they require better grazing than goats. Sheep are raised largely for their secondary products which are traded with cities, allowing an accumulation of wealth. So the faunal changes in the Early Bronze Age in the Levant may reflect a shift from a subsistence to a market economy, becoming more sophisticated as a response to urbanism.

The possible causes of the changes in the mean percentages of each animal need to be discussed. Were they environmentally induced? Did changes in social systems, particularly the rise of urbanism, affect them? Do they reflect differing positions within production/ consumption systems? Are there ritualistic explanations? Were there spatial differences within sites of the fauna retrieved? Of course it is likely that different factors operated in conjunction with one another and with varying degrees of influence. Tchernov and Horwitz (1990) suggested that the increasing dependence on sheep and goats from the Late Neolithic onwards reflects environmental degradation caused by overgrazing. This may well be the case, but it does not explain the reduced numbers of sheep and goats in the Iron Age compared with the Bronze Age. It is worthwhile examining some faunas from different periods in the same site or at least in adjacent sites with these problems in mind.

The faunal spectra from Jericho (Figure 8) do not fit the general pattern for sites on the desert edge. At least the Late Neolithic sample does, but in the samples from nearby Teleilat Ghassul in the Chalcolithic (Davis 1982) and Jericho in the Early Bronze Age and even more from the Middle Bronze Age (Clutton-Brock 1979), cattle predominate in terms of meat weight, in the same way as they do further north in the Jordan Valley. Ghassul had a lush environment and an exotic water supply in the fourth millennium (Webley 1969) and Jericho was, and is, a lush oasis, so perhaps this reflects a change to more intensive utilization of the land and its water supply in the Bronze Age required by increasing urbanism, and in this respect the slight rise in the number of pigs may be relevant.

Three sites close to one another on or near the coast of the north-western Negev are of some interest (Figure 9). They are in the main geographical group adopted here. At Neolithic Qatif Y3 there are roughly equal numbers of sheep, goat, cattle and pig bones, which of course means a

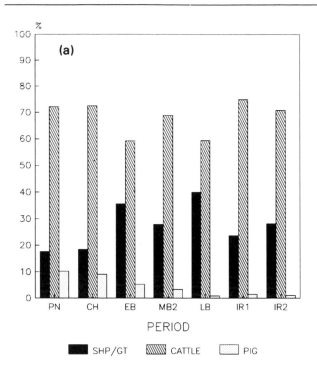

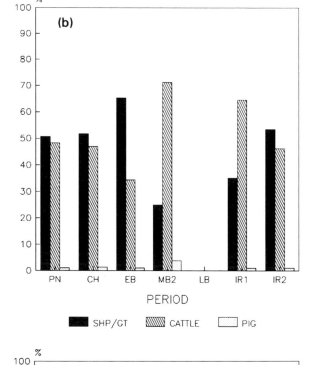

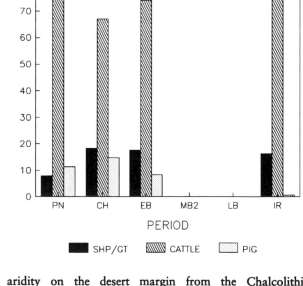

Figure 6 The relative contribution to the diet of cattle, sheep/goats and pigs found in the three areas of the southern Levant in various periods. The numbers of bones found in each site were translated into approximate meat weights and averages calculated for each period (see Table 1).

(a) the main area of the southern Levant, including the Jordan Highlands and excluding: (b) the desert margins and the southern part of the Jordan Valley and (c) the Jordan Valley (central and northern parts).

In almost all sites from the Late Neolithic to the Iron Age, cattle provide at least 50 per cent of the meat. Sheep and goats take second place to cattle in all areas of the country, though the difference is less marked on the desert edge, where there is a marked peak in sheep and goats in the Early Bronze Age (Figure 6b). The predominance of cattle is particularly marked in the Jordan Valley (Figure 6c).

Although pigs provided up to about 15 per cent of meat in the Late Neolithic and Chalcolithic in the main area and the Jordan Valley (Figures 6a and 6c), they declined steadily thereafter, and were always scarce on the desert margins (Figure 6b).

marked predominance of cattle in terms of meat weight (Grigson 1984a). The adjacent Chalcolithic site of Y2 has virtually no pigs and a corresponding increase in sheep and goats (Grigson 1984b). By the Middle Bronze Age of Tel Jemmeh, although there are some pigs, sheep and goats dominate in both numbers and meat weight (Wapnish and Hesse 1988). Perhaps these changes reflect increasing aridity on the desert margin from the Chalcolithic onwards, with the faunal spectra becoming more similar to those further east on the desert edge. Alternatively, or additionally, Tel Jemmeh may have been a redistribution centre for sheep and goats brought in by nomads from more desertic regions. However, in the Late Bronze Age there is an unexplained increase in cattle (date from Hesse

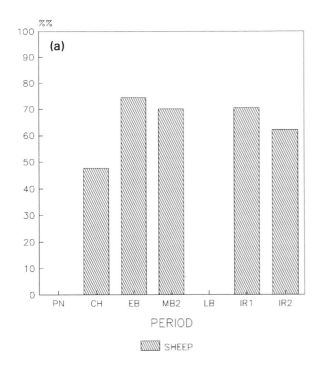

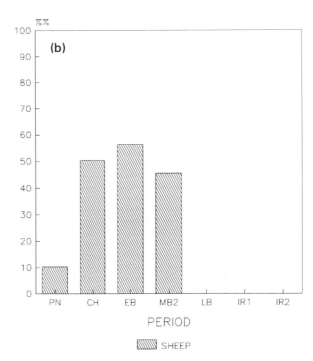

Figure 7 The mean percentages of sheep in the three areas of the southern Levant in various periods. Based on the average for each period of the numbers of bones found in each site (see Table 2).

The histograms suggest a rise in the proportion of sheep from the Late Neolithic, or Chalcolithic, to the Bronze Age, in the main area (Figure 7a) and the Jordan Valley (Figure 7c), but the sample sizes are small and the results need interpreting with caution.

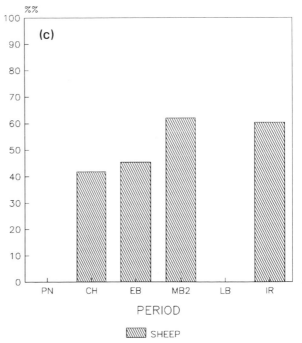

1990). An additional complication is that while Qatif is now beside the Mediterranean and was so in the Chalcolithic, in Pottery Neolithic times the coast was several kilometres to the west.

Two Early Bronze Age sites in the main area are suggestive of diachronic change with the period (Figure 10). Tel Yarmouth, in the foothills, with EBII and EBIII

levels (Davis 1988) and an EBIV site in the Refaim Valley, in the hills near Jerusalem (Horwitz 1989). There is an increase in sheep and goats over time and a corresponding decline in cattle. At first sight this could be interpreted as confirmation of Dever's (1989), Prag's (1985) and Esse's (1991) theories of a more pastoral, more nomadic economy in the EBIV, when it seems likely that the urban

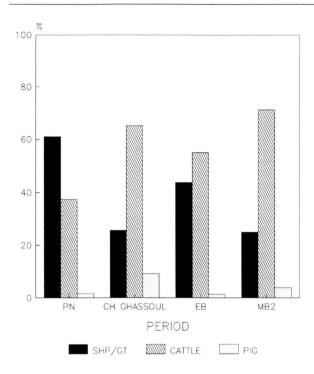

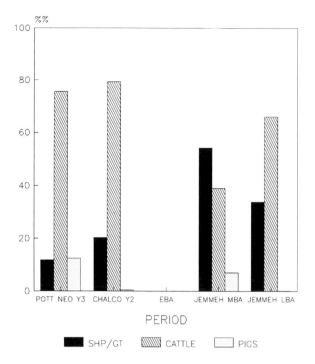

Figure 8   The faunal spectra from Jericho in the Late Neolithic, Early and Middle Bronze Ages and nearby Teleilat Ghassul in the Chalcolithic.

The Late Neolithic sample fits the general pattern for sites on the desert edge, but after that cattle predominate in terms of meat weight, as they do further north in the Jordan Valley. The slight rise in the number of pigs in the Middle Bronze Age may be related to increased urbanism.

Figure 9   Faunal spectra from three sites on or near the coast of the north-western Negev, in the main area.

In the late Neolithic at Qatif Y3 there is a marked predominance of cattle in terms of meat weight and a significant number of pigs. The adjacent Chalcolithic site of Y2 has virtually no pigs and a corresponding increase in sheep and goats. By the Middle Bronze Age of Tell Jemmeh, sheep and goats dominate in both numbers and meat weight.

societies of the Early Bronze Age were collapsing, but that does not explain the absence of pigs at Tel Yarmouth, nor the significant proportion at Refaim – pigs are *not* a component of nomadism. As Dever implies in Chapter 17 (this volume) this may indicate a change to a more *rural* rather than a *pastoral* mode of life, as is usually assumed. Prag (1974) suggested that this period, at least in the Jordan Valley, was one of sedentism, and that transhumance, if any, would have been limited in scale.

At Tel Shiloh (on the drier side of the mountains to the north of Jerusalem) faunal spectra are available from Middle Bronze, Late Bronze and Iron Age levels (Figure 11). In all these levels cattle predominate in terms of meat weight, except in the Late Bronze Age where they are overtaken by sheep and goats in a sample of quite respectable size – 2333 (Hellwing and Sadeh 1985). However the economic relevance is unclear as the LBA sample was interpreted as the remains of offerings at a cultic place made by a nomadic population (Hellwing and Sadeh 1985).

To turn to pigs. The distribution of domestic pigs was closely correlated with environmental conditions in the

Middle East in general, at least in the fifth, fourth and third millennia (Grigson unpublished), and in particular in the northern Negev in the fourth millennium (Grigson 1987; Grigson in Levy et al. 1991). Figure 12 shows that some of the Chalcolithic sites in the northern Negev, which seem to have been broadly contemporary with others and separated from them by only a few kilometres, have pigs, whereas those a short distance away in the direction of the desert do not. Almost all Chalcolithic and Bronze Age sites in the Middle East that are situated in areas which today receive more than about 350mm of rain had pigs, whereas those in drier places did not, unless the area had an exotic water supply from natural springs or from irrigation. In general pigs are scarce or absent in all the drier areas – the southern parts of the coastal plain, the foothills and the mountains, as well as the desert fringes. There seems to have been a continuous reduction in the numbers of pigs beginning in or soon after the Chalcolithic. By the Iron Age their remains are so few that they can have had no economic importance and one wonders whether they represent intrusive material, or even wild boar. Whether this is related to a cultural pig prohibition, or whether the

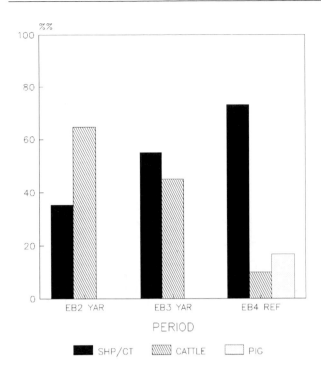

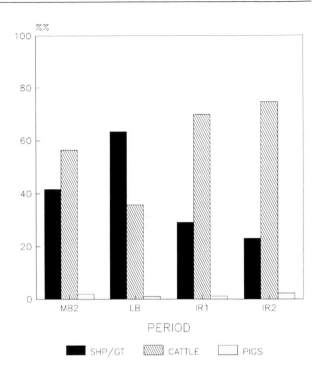

Figure 10 Faunal spectra from two Early Bronze Age sites in the main area, Tell Yarmouth (EBII and EBIII) and the Refaim Valley (Area 10 – EBIV).

The increase in sheep, goats and pigs over time and a corresponding decline in cattle may indicate a change to a more *rural* mode of life in EBIV, *not*, as frequently postulated, a more *nomadic*, existence.

Figure 11 Faunal spectra at Shiloh (Middle Bronze, Late Bronze and Iron Age I & II).

Cattle predominate in terms of meat weight, except in the Late Bronze sample where they are overtaken by sheep and goats. This has been interpreted as the remains of offerings at a cultic place made by a nomadic population.

explanation is simply environmental, that is, caused by increasing aridity, cannot be decided on the information available. However, in an important paper on the significance of the presence and absence of pigs, Hesse (1990) has shown that in general numbers of pigs declined through the Middle and Late Bronze Ages and were absent in 15 of the 18 Iron Age sites from which he had data, but the other three Iron Age I samples contain significant, but nevertheless small, proportions of pigs (Tel Miqne-Ekron in Iron Age I and II, and Ashkelon and Batash in Iron Age I). He suggests that this may be related to a restriction of the local pastoral and marketing systems by the incursions of the Sea Peoples or Philistines, that is to a system with less reliance on urban markets. However, Grigson (unpublished) suggested that on the contrary pigs, in Mesopotamia at least, might be associated with urban conditions as scavengers in city streets; this might also be the explanation for the presence of pigs in EBIII at Numeira (McCreery 1980).

Environmental change and irrigation

Floral samples are so few and often innumerate, that it is not possible to identify changes over time nor geographical

variation, except in a very limited way. A notable exception is the detailed work of McCreery (1979, 1980) at Bab edh-Dhra on the eastern side of the Dead Sea. The presence there of many cultigens that need moist conditions suggested to him that irrigation was practised there from the earliest part of the Early Bronze Age. After Early Bronze I there was an increase in the proportion of barley and fruit compared with wheat and flax, which might indicate the production of barley for animal fodder, or problems with increasing aridity or salinification, or all three.

Liphschitz (1989) has pointed out that inferences have to be made with caution because it is likely that, as well as being locally consumed, many plant foods were transported from place to place. She suggests that this is true of various fruits found in sites in the Jordan Valley where it may have been too hot and too dry for them to be grown. However, charred wood fragments of many species of fruit trees were found at Early Bronze Age Jericho, and as olive wood was found at Teleilat Ghassul, Tell esh Shuna North, Tel Abu Hamid and Tel Tsaf, which was probably obtained locally and used for firewood (Western 1971; Neef 1990; Liphschitz 1988–1989), so conditions may have been suitable for them to have been grown at

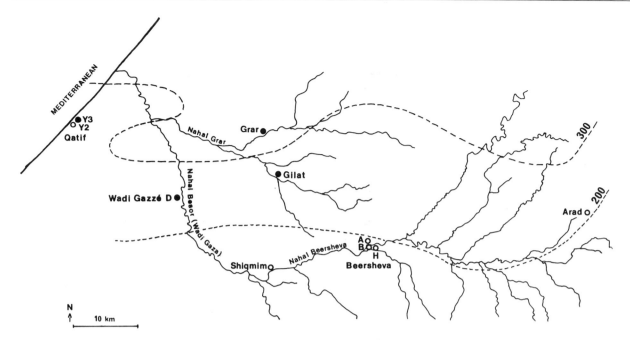

Figure 12   Domestic pigs in the Beersheva Basin. The distribution of sites with and without pigs in the Late Neolithic, Chalcolithic, and Early Bronze Age
    Black dots are sites with pigs, white dots those with none (or almost none). The dashed lines are isohyets of modern mean annual rainfall.
    As in other parts of the Middle East there seems to be a definite correlation between the presence and absence of pigs and rainfall. The presence of pigs at Gilat and Wadi Gazzé D suggests slightly moister conditions in the Chalcolithic. Their decline at Qatif from the Neolithic to the Chalcolithic (Y3 and Y2) may be due to increasing aridity. A = Abu Matar, B = Bir es-Safadi, H = Horvat Beter

that time in the Jordan Valley. There is good reason to think that the environment was considerably lusher in many parts of the Valley in Chalcolithic and Early Bronze Age times (Harlan 1982; Webley 1969) and that olives could have been grown there without irrigation (Neef 1990). It is interesting that remains of dates seem to be confined to the Jordan Valley and the coast near Tel Aviv, where one would expect that environmental conditions were optimal for growing them.

The presence of pulses, naked wheat and large linseeds at sites on the desert edge in the Chalcolithic and Early Bronze Age, and of olives and olive wood, as well as grape pips and vine charcoal at Arad, implies either a slightly moister environment than today or some form of irrigation, or both. It is unlikely that irrigation alone would have been adequate to provide suitable conditions for feeding cattle, let alone pigs, so it is reasonable to postulate that conditions were moister in the Chalcolithic and Early Bronze Age, as already shown by D.H.K. Amiran (1991) and postulated by Grigson (1987), but aridity seems to have become a problem towards the end of the Early Bronze Age, particularly on the desert margins, doubtless contributing to the collapse of urban culture in Early Bronze IV. More detailed studies on plant and animal remains might help to elucidate not only the process of this collapse but also the recovery from

it during the Middle Bronze Age. For a discussion of Chalcolithic irrigation, see Levy, Chapter 14.

The use of other animal and plant products in the Chalcolithic and Bronze Ages

Milk

There is much discussion in the literature on the use of secondary products (that is those that can be extracted without killing the animal), particularly milk, wool, hair and energy (Sherratt 1983; Levy 1992). The archaeo-zoological evidence for this relies on the establishment of ageing profiles of the various species involved (Payne 1973). Animals kept primarily for meat would be slaughtered as sub-adults, that is as soon as they reached their prime meat weight, but those kept for secondary products would be kept into old age. If the required product was milk this would involve keeping females into old age, but slaughtering most of the males when young. Of course, whatever strategy was adopted, enough breeding adults would have to be kept to maintain the herds and here too there would be an emphasis on females of reproductive age.

Only sheep and goat bones are found in large enough

numbers in Near Eastern sites for demographic analysis and this has only been done on a diachronic, *intra-site* basis on a few sites outside our area, in Turkey (Stein 1986), Iran (Davis 1984) and Syria (Grigson forthcoming). The ageing patterns from these sites suggest increasing reliance on older animals, from the Pre-pottery Neolithic B or the Late Neolithic onwards, presumably reflecting an increasing dependence on secondary products.

Some *inter-site* comparisons of ageing patterns of sheep and goats have been made in the southern Levant. For example, at Grar in the Chalcolithic the proportion of adult to juvenile mandibles and ageable teeth surviving was 76 per cent (Grigson forthcoming), a percentage similar to those in three Early Bronze Age samples aged in the same way, 78, 80 and 83 per cent (Horwitz and Tchernov 1989a), but such comparisons are likely to be biased if poor conditions of preservation favour the differential destruction of the mandibles of young animals.

Another possible line of evidence for the use of milk is the diachronic decrease in bone mass in sheep and goat metapodials (Horwitz and Tchernov 1989a; Smith and Horwitz 1991; Horwitz and Smith 1984). It was found that in goats a significant reduction in cortical thickness occurred between the Chalcolithic, the Early Bronze Age and the Middle Bronze Ages, with no change between in the Middle and Late Bronze Ages. In sheep a similar decrease occurred, but only between the Chalcolithic and Early Bronze Age (there were no LBA data for sheep). Although the samples are small, the results do suggest a decrease in bone mass over time, possibly not commencing before the end of the Chalcolithic. The bones studied were not sexed, so it is not certain that these results were confined to females – which would support the hypothesis of intensified milking; if it occurred in both sexes it might simply indicate decreasing levels of nutrition.

Grigson (1988) produced some evidence for different kill-off patterns in sheep and goats in the Chalcolithic at Safadi in the northern Negev. Figure 13 shows that while most of the male sheep and goats were killed when young, more female sheep than goats were being kept into adulthood, suggestive of a strategy for the production of wool and milk, as well as meat.

It must be remembered that a single cow would provide far more milk than a ewe or a nanny goat, and as cattle were the most important animals as providers of meat, probably the same was true of milk. However, the actual numbers of cattle bones are far fewer than those of sheep or goats, so it is not possible to produce convincing demographic profiles.

Fibres

The use of plant fibres, such as linen, and animal fibres such as wool and hair, has only been mentioned in passing and it is likely that animal sinews were also utilized.

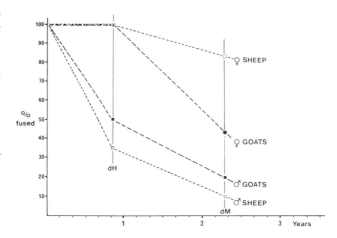

Figure 13 Ageing and sexing of sheep and goats at Safadi. Most of the male sheep and goats were killed when young, but more female sheep than goats were being kept into adulthood, suggesting a strategy for the production of milk and wool, as well as meat (Grigson 1988) (dH = distal humerus, dM = distal metapodial)

Spinning and weaving go back to at least the Pre-pottery Neolithic B, and netting and basketry even earlier, though using wild plants such as reeds. It is likely that the use of linen preceded that of wool, but more work needs doing on the associated technology so that the different artifacts, relating to fibre preparation and weaving, may be assigned to particular types of fibre. The earliest domestic sheep probably had hairy coats with only a few wool fibres and at some stage were replaced by wool sheep. When and where this happened, and when wool sheep became widespread is uncertain, but it may have been associated with the increase in sheep compared with goats during the Bronze Age which has already been mentioned.

Spindle whorls are almost ubiquitous in Neolithic, Chalcolithic and Bronze Age sites, but the earliest direct evidence for weaving are the worked wooden sticks found in the Cave of the Treasure (Nahal Mishmar) in the Chalcolithic, which are thought to be the remains of a ground loom, and the presence there of both linen and woollen fabrics (Bar-Adon 1980). However the woven linen fabrics at Nahal Hemar, which probably date from the PPNB, suggest that looms were in use well before the fourth millennium (Bar-Yosef 1985; Bar-Yosef and Alon 1988).

Leather

Animal skins must have been an important resource even before animals were domesticated and, although skins and leather rarely survive in archaeological sites, one can surmise a great many uses for them – clothes, tents, thongs, carrying bags, water transport, churning skins,

skins for fermenting wine and so on. Various types of flint scrapers are thought to have been associated with skin working and the same is probably true of bone awls. Marshall (1982) observed that bone tools thought to be burnishers for leather work were more common than thread working tools in the Pre-pottery Neolithic A at Jericho and that the situation was reversed in the PPNB. Nevertheless, the use of skins of cattle, sheep and goats, and of treated leather, must have continued to have great economic importance. The remains of cowhide sandals and a sheepskin jacket were preserved in the Chalcolithic Cave of the Treasure (Nahal Mishmar) (Bar-Adon 1980).

Transport and traction

Animal energy, as used in carrying loads and pulling vehicles or ploughs, is actually another secondary product.

Donkeys

The earliest osteological evidence for the presence of domestic donkeys in the Middle East comes from Tell Rubeidheh, in Iraq, towards the end of the fourth millennium, where Payne (1988) found equid bones with the morphological characters that distinguish domestic donkeys from wild donkeys and wild onagers. A few bones of equids of similar size have been found in almost all sites of the Chalcolithic and Early Bronze Age in the Levant (Grigson 1993a) which, together with some representations of what appear to be donkeys carrying loads (Epstein 1985; Grigson 1987), strongly suggests that domestic donkeys were present in the Levant from at least the fourth millennium and possibly one or two millennia earlier.

The fact that the bones of equids are so few in archaeological assemblages and that sometimes articulated limbs are found suggest that they did not form part of the normal diet. The obvious interpretation is that they were used for transport. According to Postgate (1986) in Mesopotamia cuneiform signs of the late fourth millennium from Uruk and Jemdet Nasr indicate domestic donkeys and Clutton-Brock (1992) has recently identified the equids pulling a four-wheeled waggon on the Standard of Ur as donkeys. In the southern Levant a number of clay figurines of what seems to be donkeys carrying loads date from the Late Chalcolithic (Epstein 1985; one example is the donkey with two pots, or baskets, from Azor (Plate 1 p. 246).

Although I have found little mention of donkeys at Ebla (Pettinato 1991), later texts contain details of highly organized donkey trains carrying goods across country and these must have been the backbone of long distance trade on land, especially through Egypt and Canaan. Sometimes these caravans were very large, like one consisting of 3,000 animals mentioned in the Mari letters. I have recently found two sizes of donkey at Timna, in an assemblage which is supposed to date from the Late Bronze/Early Iron Age transition. The bones have many lesions which may have resulted from their use as pack animals carrying copper and malachite to Egypt and the Levant (Grigson 1993b).

Cattle

It seems likely that really heavy loads were pulled by draught cattle, possibly in vehicles. In Mesopotamia, cuneiform signs of the late fourth millennium from Uruk and Jemdet Nasr indicate sledges and sledge-like vehicles with solid wheels. Queen Pu-Abi's sledge from Ur (middle of the third millennium) was buried with a pair of oxen and it seems that early solid-wheeled carts were usually pulled by oxen (Piggott 1983).

Ploughing

It is usually assumed that the change from hoe to plough agriculture which enabled intensive cultivation of heavier soils took place during the Chalcolithic, but there is very little evidence for this view. A basalt hoe from the Chalcolithic of the Golan is illustrated by Epstein (1978) and some of the large flints described as picks in the literature might have been hoes, but in general both hoes and ploughs were probably made of wood, which has rotted away. Ploughs imply the use of draught animals and are a good example of the interrelatedness of plant and animal exploitation. According to Postgate (1986), cuneiform signs indicate that domestic donkeys were frequently used for ploughing by the third millennium in Mesopotamia, and this may well have been the case in the fourth millennium too and perhaps earlier – we simply do not know, nor do we know whether the situation was the same in the Levant. However, it seems likely that cattle were used more frequently than donkeys. (See Window 3 p. 267).

Horses

There was a general supposition that domestic horses were introduced into the Levant and Egypt early in the second millennium, but Davis (1976) found horse remains at Arad in the third millennium, which he presumed to be domestic as no wild horses are known from the Holocene of the area, and recently Grigson (1993a and in Levy et al. 1991) reached the surprising conclusion, as a result of her analysis of the size of the equid bones from Chalcolithic sites in the Negev, that small domestic horses were already present in the fourth millennium. What they were used for is unknown. In the second millennium horses were used in warfare, pulling chariots with two-spoked wheels (and Late Bronze Age chariot fittings have been described from Beth Shan by James 1978), but horses are said not to have been ridden, at least in the Levant, until the first millennium BC.

Dromedaries (one-humped camels)

Zeuner's (1963) contention that domestic camels were already being utilized in urban sites in the Levant from about 1,700 to 1,500 BC was based on an article by Isserlin (1951), who pointed out that actual remains of camels had been reported in Middle Bronze Age contexts at four sites, but as Köhler (1981b) has indicated, all of these finds are, for one reason or another, dubious.

There is, however, some other evidence for the presence of camels in the Bronze Age at Arad in the northern Negev (Lernau 1978), and, although the ribs originally identified cannot now be traced, more camel remains have recently been identified from other excavations at the same site by Horwitz (pers. comm.). A few camel bones and teeth have been identified by Hakker-Orion (1984) from the Middle Bronze Age I at Be'er Resisim in the central Negev and from the Late Bronze Age at Tel Jemmeh in the north-western Negev (Wapnish 1981), and I have studied a large sample of camel bones, presumably used for transport, at Timna dating from the Late Bronze/Iron Age transition (Grigson 1993b). All these finds are peripheral to the southern Levant and probably represent animals used in the transport of goods to and from Arabia, but Kussinger (1988) has identified a camel rib from the Middle Bronze Age at Lidar Höyük in the Euphrates Valley in southern Anatolia, which is of particular interest as the site is so far to the north.

Discussion

Khazanov (1984) has emphasized that in the desert and steppe regions of Eurasia where cattle (and pigs) are characteristically involved in agriculture, the greater the number of cattle, the more important the role of agriculture in the economy. This is not necessarily the case in Sub-Saharan Africa, but here the agricultural system utilizes completely different crops.

The wide spectrum of plant species found in archaeological sites, especially those raised for fruit, as well as the presence of pigs and more particularly the high proportion of cattle, suggests that in the main area and in the Jordan Valley we are dealing with mixed farming, and McCreery (1980) has shown that this is true even on the drier eastern side of the Dead Sea. There may have been a small element of transhumance, with cattle, sheep and goats, vertically in hilly areas, particularly on the slopes of the Jordan Valley (Esse 1991), and over the landscape on the northern edges of the Negev. Even on the desert margins cattle predominate in most periods, though here mixed farming must have merged into herdsman husbandry or semi-sedentary pastoralism (Haiman 1992;

Cohen 1992), yet even in the Negev Highlands there is evidence for dry farming in the Middle Bronze Age (Rosen and Finkelstein 1992). There is no evidence that full-scale nomadic pastoralism, or even semi-nomadic pastoralism, was practised in the Levant from the Chalcolithic to the Iron Age. The conclusion that settled farming prevailed in the Levant was also reached by Khazanov (1984), who pointed out that the Bible gives chronological priority to farming, not to nomadic behaviour.

The most characteristic feature of the Early Bronze Age economy seems to have been the investment in large-scale horticultural production, implying a settled and stable mode of life (Stager 1976), as fruit trees and vines can only be reproduced by cloning (Zohary and Spiegel-Roy 1975) and do not produce fruit until many years after planting. In Stager's own words 'Permanent fields, residential stability, and general tranquillity are the prerequisites for the commercial production of horticultural crops' (Stager 1985). Indeed, it was with the adoption of horticulture in the Early Bronze Age that the Palestinian economy acquired its Mediterranean character which has endured to the present time.

Concomitant with large-scale production is long-term storage – planning ahead for years at a time, or even from generation to generation. Preservation techniques are an important aspect of storage, and one which was certainly being practised by the Chalcolithic was the extraction of oil from plants such as olives. Another, in use from at least the Early Bronze Age, is fermentation – the production of alcohol from sugar solutions by the introduction of yeasts, that is the production of wine from grape juice, from cereals and the leavening of bread from flour. A similar technique for animal products is the introduction of certain bacteria into milk, allowing it to be kept for longer periods in the form of yoghurt, as does the production of butter and cheese. Once these preservation techniques had been developed they not only allowed vegetable and animal products to be stored, they allowed them to be marketed as part of the new urban economy and to be traded over long distances.

Conclusion

Floral, faunal, artifactual and textual evidence all point to a settled agricultural life style in the Early Bronze Age, which must have had its roots in the Chalcolithic, or even the late Neolithic. Thus it is the agriculture of fellahin, not the semi-nomadic practices of the Bedouin, which is the relevant ethnographic parallel to studies of early agricultural systems in the southern Levant.

Postscript

There are many more types of evidence that are relevant to understanding the ways in which people used the natural

Table 1 Meat weights of main domestic animals found in archaeological sites in the Levant — changes over time

Site	Period	shp/gt no.	shp/gt meat%	cattle no.	cattle meat%	pig no.	pig meat%	No. of identified specimens	Reference
Main area (Area A)									
Abu Zureiq	Late Neo	20	6.9	32	86.6	15	6.5	67	Grigson nd unpublished
Ashkelon	Late Neo?	12	8.9	15	87.3	4	3.7	31	Grigson nd unpublished
Neve Yam	Late Neo	28	10.9	26	79.3	20	9.8	74	Horwitz 1988
Qatif Y3	Late Neo	138	11.8	113	75.6	117	12.5	368	Grigson 1984a
Ain Ghazal	Late Neo	209	45.4	27	45.9	32	8.7	268	Köhler-Rollefson et al. 1988
Nahal Zehora I 1990	Late Neo	31.5	13.9	20.5	70.5	28.5	15.7	80.5	Davis 1990
Nahal Zehora II 1990	Late Neo	68.5	25.2	21	60.3	31.5	14.5	121	Davis 1990
	MEAN		17.6		72.2		10.2		
Tel Aviv	Chalco	147	4.7	368	92.7	64	2.6	579	Ducos 1968
Wadi Ghaza D	Chalco	14	6.1	24	81.9	22	12.0	60	Ducos 1968
Gat Govrin	Chalco	69	9.7	76	83.6	38	6.7	183	Ducos 1968
Metzer	Chalco	103	10.8	81	66.4	174	22.8	358	Ducos 1968
Qatif Y2	Chalco	705	20.3	352	79.3	12	0.4	1069	Grigson 1984b
Grar	Chalco	717	23.1	274	69.0	194	7.8	1185	Grigson 1992a
Gilat 74–87	Chalco	539	30.4	139	61.2	119	8.4	797	Tchernov & Grigson 1990
Sataf	Chalco ?	35	41.6	5	46.5	8	11.9	48	Grigson 1992b
	MEAN		18.4		72.6		9.1		
Tel Aphek + Tel Dalit	EBI-II	?	28.3	?	70.7	?	1.0	?	Hellwing & Gophna 1984
Tel Erani	EBII	441	25.0	158	70.0	71	5.0	670	Ducos 1968
Tel Yarmouth	EBII	175	35.3	41	64.7	0	0.0	216	Davis 1988
Tel Yarmouth	EBIII	868	55.0	91	45.0	0	0.0	959	Davis 1988
Refaim Valley Area 10	EBIV	228	73.1	4	10.0	42	16.8	274	Horwitz 1989
En Shadud	EBA	28	12.7	21	74.3	23	13.0	72	Horwitz 1985
Yiftahel	EBA	59	19.3	31	79.4	3	1.2	93	Horwitz & Tchernov 1989a
	MEAN		35.5		59.2		5.3		
Tel Michal	MB IIB	49	12.0	45	85.9	7	2.1	101	Hellwing & Feig 1989
Tel Aphek + Tel Dalit	MBII	?	15.4	?	81.6	?	3.0	?	Hellwing & Gophna 1984
Ifshar	MB II	343	5.6	686	87.4	343	7.0	1372	Hesse 1990
Tel Shiloh	MBII	564	41.6	98	56.4	22	2.0	684	Hellwing & Sadeh 1985
Tel Lachish	MBII	215	46.7	30	50.9	9	2.4	254	Drori 1979
Tel Nagila	MB	302	21.2	142	77.8	12	1.1	456	Ducos 1968
Tel Miqne–Ekron	BA	370	25.9	132	72.2	21	1.8	523	Hesse 1986
Tel Jemmeh	MBA	642	54.2	59	38.9	66	7.0	767	Wapnish & Hesse 1988
	MEAN		27.8		68.9		3.3		
Tel Michal	LBA	289	12.5	258	87.4	2	0.1	549	Hellwing & Feig 1989
Tel Lachish	LBA	413	22.9	175	75.9	16	1.1	604	Drori 1979
Tel Shiloh	LBA	2152	63.4	155	35.7	26	1.0	2333	Hellwing & Sadeh 1985
Batash	LBA	217	24.4	83	73.3	17	2.3	317	Hesse 1990
Tel esh-Sharia	LBA	4134	82.2	114	17.7	4	0.1	4252	Davis 1982
Tel Jemmeh	LBA	3152	33.8	788	66.0	10	0.1	3950	Wapnish & Hesse 1988
	MEAN		39.9		59.3		0.8		
Batash	IA I	142	19.8	71	77.2	18	3.1	231	Hesse 1990
Tel Miqne–Ekron	IA I	130	11.0	129	85.1	37	3.9	296	Hesse 1986
Izbet Sartah	IAge early	635	16.5	411	83.4	5	0.2	1051	Hellwing & Adjeman 1986
Tel Michal	IA I	239	19.9	123	79.8	3	0.3	365	Hellwing & Feig 1989

continued

Table 1 *continued*

Site	Period	shp/gt		cattle		pig		No. of identified specimens	Reference
		no.	meat%	no.	meat%	no.	meat%		
Main area (Area A) *(continued)*									
Ashkelon	IA I	120	6.0	235	91.8	35	2.2	390	Hesse 1990
Tel Shiloh	IA I	1000	29.2	306	69.8	29	1.1	1335	Hellwing & Sadeh 1985
Mt Ebal	IA I	499	28.0	164	72.0	0	0.0	663	Horwitz 1986/7
Tel Hesban	IA I	460	28.2	145	69.4	31	2.4	636	Weiler 1981
Tel Hesi	IA I	77	34.2	19	65.8	0	0.0	96	Hesse 1990
Tel Qasile	IA early	212	43.2	35	55.8	4	1.0	251	Davis 1982 1985
	MEAN		23.6		75.0		1.4		
Batash	IA II	578	18.3	328	81.3	9	0.3	914	Hesse 1990
Tel Hesi	IA II	1090	33.6	272	65.6	21	0.8	1383	Hesse 1990
Ashkelon	IA II	43	3.2	164	96.0	9	0.8	216	Hesse 1990
Tel Lachish	IA II	141	11.6	137	88.4	0	0.0	278	Lernau 1975
Tel Miqne–Ekron	IA II	53	19.8	27	78.8	3	1.4	83	Hesse 1986
Tel Shiloh	IA II	99	23.1	41	74.6	8	2.3	148	Hellwing & Sadeh 1985
Ophel	IA II	437	71.8	22	28.2	0	0.0	459	Horwitz & Tchernov 1989b
Tel Hesban	IA II	1406	39.9	256	56.8	94	3.3	1756	Weiler 1981
Tel Lachish	IA II	587	31.2	166	68.8	0	0.0	753	Drori 1979
	MEAN		28.1		70.9		1.0		
Naharya	IA	691	48.7	93	51.2	1	0.1	785	Ducos 1968
Tel Qiri	IA	802	43.1	134	56.1	13	0.9	949	Davis 1987
Hazorea	IA	632	49.9	79	48.7	14	1.4	725	Davis 1982
Wawiyat	IA	302	14.7	209	79.6	93	5.7	604	Henson 1986
Desert edge (Area B)									
Abu Thawwab	Late Neo	85	40.2	16	59.2	1	0.6	102	Kafafi 1988
Jericho	Late Neo	51	61.1	4	37.4	1	1.5	56	Clutton-Brock 1979
	MEAN		50.7		48.3		1.0		
Horvat Hor	Chalco	91	56.4	9	43.6	0	0.0	100	Horwitz 1990
Jawa	Chalco	2206	56.5	217	43.5	0	0.0	2423	Köhler 1981a
Teleilat Ghassoul	Chalco	126	25.6	41	65.2	36	9.2	203	Davis 1982
Abu Matar	Chalco	153	62.0	12	38.0	0	0.0	165	Grigson nd unpublished
Horvat Beter	Chalco	156	54.0	17	46.0	0	0.0	173	Angress 1959
Safadi	Chalco	3167	56.3	314	43.6	2	0.0	3483	Grigson nd unpublished
Shiqmim 82/83	Chalco	458	50.7	57	49.3	0	0.0	515	Grigson 1987
	MEAN		51.7		47.0		1.3		
Arad 62–?	EBI	345	60.4	29	39.6	0	0.0	374	Lernau 1978
Arad 62–?	EBII	1244	60.3	105	39.7	0	0.0	1349	Lernau 1978
Arad 71–74	EBII	188	88.9	3	11.1	0	0.0	191	Davis 1976, 1982
Jericho	EBA	372	43.7	60	55.0	9	1.3	441	Clutton-Brock 1979
Bab edh-Dhra	EBI-IV	174	73.2	8	26.3	1	0.5	183	McCreery 1979; Finnegan 1979
	MEAN		65.3		34.4		0.4		
Jericho	MBA	865	24.9	317	71.3	106	3.8	1288	Clutton-Brock 1979
Tel Arad	IA I	294	36.9	64	62.7	3	0.5	361	Sade 1988
Tel Beersheva	IA I	1010	44.0	164	55.8	3	0.2	1177	Hellwing 1984
Hirbet el-Msas	IA I	278	24.6	109	75.3	1	0.1	388	Tchernov & Drori 1983
	MEAN		35.1		64.6		0.2		

continued

Table 1   *continued*

Site	Period	no.	shp/gt meat%	no.	cattle meat%	no.	pig meat%	No. of identified specimens	Reference
Desert edge (Area B) *(continued)*									
Tel Arad	IA II	2836	61.2	230	38.8	3	0.1	3069	Sade 1988
Tel Ira	IA II	480	47.2	68	52.3	4	0.5	552	Dayan 1992
Horvat Uza	IA II	4282	63.0	320	36.8	13	0.2	4615	Sade 1988
Hirbet el-Msas	IA II	163	42.7	28	57.3	0	0.0	191	Tchernov & Drori 1983
	MEAN		53.5		46.3		0.2		
Jordan Valley (Area C)									
Tel Eli	Late Neo	31	14.1	18	64.2	38	21.7	87	Jarman 1974
Tel Dan	Late Neo	10	5.5	20	86.2	12	8.3	42	Horwitz 1987
Hagoshrim	Late Neo??	29	2.8	125	95.8	11	1.3	165	Ducos 1968
Munhata II	Late Neo	21	8.7	24	77.4	27	13.9	72	Ducos 1968
	MEAN		7.8		80.9		11.3		
Tel Eli	Chalco	35	14.2	19	60.1	51	25.8	105	Jarman 1974
Tel Tsaf	Chalco	53	13.6	40	80.0	20	6.4	113	Hellwing 1988/9
Tell Abu Hamid	Chalco	270	32.4	54	50.7	113	16.9	437	Desse 1988
Munhata I	Chalco?	144	12.6	114	77.6	90	9.8	348	Ducos 1968
	MEAN		18.2		67.1		14.7		
Tel Dan	EBII+III	92	15.3	64	83.2	7	1.5	163	Wapnish & Hesse 1991
Tell el Hayyat	EBIV/MBIIA	931	14.5	588	71.4	725	14.1	2244	Metzger 1983; Falconer et al. 1984
Gamla	EBA	55	22.8	21	67.9	18	9.3	94	Horwitz & Tchernov 1989a
	MEAN		17.5		74.2		8.3		
Tel Dan	IA	258	10.1	293	89.7	4	0.2	555	Wapnish & Hesse 1991
Tel Oreme	IA II	1312	10.0	1509	89.4	66	0.6	2887	Ziegler & Boessneck 1990
Pella	IA	2497	18.4	1398	80.5	115	1.1	4010	Köhler-Rollefson 1992
Tel Dan Area B	IA	358	26.9	124	72.7	4	0.4	486	Wapnish, Hesse & Ogilivy 1977
	MEAN		16.3		83.1		0.6		

world in the past than there has been space for in the present study, but archaeobotanical and archaeozoological data are the primary sources. The retrieval of plant and animal remains requires a large investment of time and care in excavation, not least because if done properly, the pace of excavation has to be slow, and post-excavation analysis also has to be slow and painstaking, but I hope I have said enough to indicate that animal and plant remains are potential sources of a huge amount of information. The retrieval and study of animal and plant remains can help to answer some of the most important archaeological questions, particularly about the relation-ship between society, economy and environment in the distant past.

Acknowledgements

I must record my debt to Liora Kolska-Horwitz, Simon Davis and Andrew Garrard for the help they have given me with the literature; Ms Horwitz sent me photocopies of publications and translations of works unobtainable in Britain. The work would not have been possible without the excellent library of the Institute of Archaeology at University College London.

Table 2   Sheep as proportion sheep + goat — changes over time

Site	Period	Sheep	Goat	% sheep	Reference
Main area (Area A)					
Tel Aviv	Chalco	17	16	51.5	Ducos 1968
Gat Govrin	Chalco	25	44	36.2	Ducos 1968
Qatif Y2	Chalco	79	64	55.2	Grigson 1984b
Grar	Chalco	31	34	47.7	Grigson 1992a
Gilat 74–87	Chalco	45	49	47.9	Tchernov & Grigson 1990
	MEAN			47.7	
Tel Erani	EBII	142	52	73.2	Ducos 1968
Tel Yarmouth	EBII+III	69	22	75.8	Davis 1988
	MEAN			74.5	
Tel Miqne–Ekron	BA	41	27	60.3	Hesse 1986
Tel Jemmeh	MBA			80.0	Wapnish & Hesse 1988
	MEAN			70.1	
Tel Miqne–Ekron	IA I	21	3	87.3	Hesse 1986
Tel Hesban	IA I	38	29	56.7	Weiler 1981
Tel Qasile	IA early	25	12	67.6	Davis 1982 1985
	MEAN			70.6	
Tel Lachish	IA II	28	25	52.8	Lernau 1975
Tel Hesban	IA II	137	83	62.3	Weiler 1981
Tel Lachish	IA II	20	8	71.4	Drori 1979
	MEAN			62.2	
Desert edge (Area B)					
Jericho	Late Neo	3	26	10.3	Clutton–Brock 1979
Teleilat Ghassul	Chalco	30	29	50.8	Davis 1982
Safadi	Chalco	384	393	49.4	Grigson nd unpublished
	MEAN			50.4	
Arad 62–?	EBI	64	30	68.1	Lernau 1978
Arad 62–?	EBII	177	124	58.8	Lernau 1978
Arad 71–74	EBII	36.5	31.5	53.7	Davis 1976, 1982
Jericho	EBA	66	117	36.1	Clutton–Brock 1979
Bab edh-Dhra	EBI–IV			65.0	Finnegan 1979
	MEAN			56.3	
Jericho	MBA	148	177	45.5	Clutton–Brock 1979
Jordan Valley (Area C)					
Munhata I	Chalco?	60	84	41.7	Ducos 1968
Tell el Hayyat	EBIV			45.3	Metzger 1983
Tell el Hayyat	MBIIA			61.9	Metzger 1983
Tel Dar + Area B	IA	69	45	6.53	Wapnish, Hesse & Ogilivy 1977; Wapnish & Hesse 1991

PASTORAL SYSTEMS

The term *pastoralism* is widely used in contemporary archaeological literature (see, for example, the various contributions to *Pastoralism in the Levant* edited by Bar-Yosef and Khazanov (1992) with a wide variation in meaning. For some authors it is synonymous with animal keeping – that is, the keeping of all herd animals used for food, whether or not accompanied by agriculture; for others (e.g. Dever 1992) it seems to be used as a term in contradistinction to urbanism; for others it implies the movement of animals and animal keepers around the landscape, accompanying a life style largely independent of agriculture. Thus Gilead (1988) and Levy (1992) interpret the same data set (Grigson 1987; Grigson in Levy et al. 1991) from Chalcolithic sites in the northern Negev in diametrically opposite ways. Despite the fact that both acknowledge that some of the villages kept pigs and others did not, and that there was a degree of seasonal movement around the landscape, Gilead sees the local system as one of 'permanent villages of peasants practising mixed farming' which he likens to the mode of life of the 'fellahin', whereas Levy sees the same people adopting a village-based, fully transhumant system.

As the term *pastoralism* implies the use of pastures it is not synonymous with animal keeping: all animals, even sheep and goats, but certainly pigs, can be kept in sties or byres, though it is unlikely that this was done in the periods we are concerned with.

Clearly the spectrum from mixed farming to fully nomadic pastoralism is a continuous one, but within this spectrum four main stages have been recognized by Musil (1928) and Khazanov (1984), the main characteristics of each stage are shown in Figure 1.1. As Khazanov (1984) has pointed out, full nomadic pastoralism (stage 4) is practised in Arabia but not in the Levant and is not relevant here.

In the light of this classification both Gilead and Levy are surely referring to a *spectrum* of activity in which the sites with pigs represent mixed farming, probably with some movement, and grade into those without pigs in the more arid eastern part where agro-pastoralism was practised. Such gradations must surely be characteristic of marginal areas such as the northern Negev.

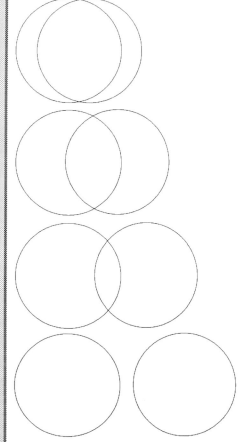

PLANT CULTIVATION · ANIMAL KEEPING · PASTORAL SYSTEM

1. Mixed farming. Plant and animal keeping completely integrated. Pigs, sheep, goats and cattle. Very limited movement of animals.

2. Agro–pastoralism, or semi-sedentary pastoralism. Plant cultivation and animal keeping less integrated. Sheep, goats and cattle, in roughly equal numbers, but not pigs. Partial seasonal transhumance.

3. Semi–nomadic pastoralism. Plant cultivation minimal, almost entirely separate from animal keeping. Sheep, goats, cattle (decreasing). Seasonal transhumance, by some of the population.

4. Nomadic pastoralism. No cultivation, but wild plant foods may be gathered. Continuous, total transhumance with sheep, goats, and camels; linked to the settled zone for access to water, pasture and the supply of plant foods (Gottwald 1980).

Figure 1.1 Pastoral systems

OIL, WINE AND MILK

The development of preservation techniques allowed the storage and trade of agricultural and animal surpluses, and one which was certainly being practised from at least the Chalcolithic was the extraction of olive oil.

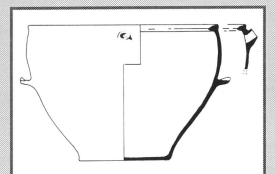

Figure 2.1 Spouted vat, thought to be for the separation of olive oil, from the Early Bronze Age at Tel Yarmouth (Esse 1991)

Plate 2.1 Spouted vat, thought to be for the separation of olive oil, from the Chalcolithic of the Golan (The Israel Museum, Jerusalem)

introduction of yeasts, that is the production of wine from grape juice, beer from cereals, and the leavening of bread from flour.

Grapes and wine
Vine pips are common in the Levant from the Early Bronze Age; as wild vines are not part of the local flora any remains must be

Olive oil

Spouted vats, thought to be for the separation of olive oil, as well as olive wood, have been found in the Chalcolithic of the Golan (Plate 2.1; Epstein 1978) and are common in the Early Bronze Age (Figure 2.1); olive stones occur on almost all sites from the Chalcolithic onwards, even in the Negev. They are thought to be from domestic trees as they are common even in sites in areas where wild olives would not have been part of the local flora. The presence of olive wood in some of these sites also suggests local cultivation. As olives are unpalatable unless pickled, and as pickling seems not to have been practised until Hellenistic or Roman times, the original use of olives must have been the extraction of oil (Neef 1990). The universal and abundant occurrences of remains of olives at Tel Lachish suggested to Helbaek (1958) that oil production was for more than home consumption in both the Early Bronze Age and the Iron Age, indeed the scale of the export of olive oil from Canaan to Egypt and other places, indicates not merely cultivation, but large-scale industrial production. An Early Bronze Age III building at Beth Yerah near the Sea of Galilee, which contained many storage jars as well as a mortar, has been identified as an olive oil factory (Figure 2.2; Esse 1991).

Fermentation

Another form of preservation, in use from at least the Early Bronze Age, is fermentation — the production of alcohol from sugar solutions by the

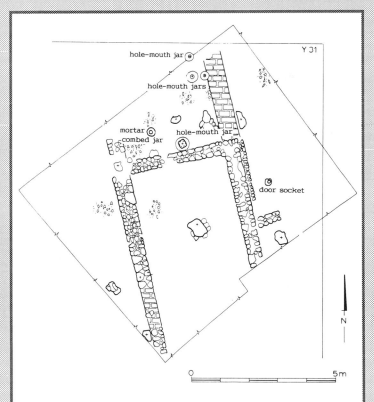

Figure 2.2 An olive oil factory from Early Bronze Age III at Beth Yarah near the Sea of Galilee, it contained many vats with spouts and storage jars, as well as a mortar for crushing the fruit (Esse 1991)

from domestic stock, introduced from elsewhere. As with olives, both vine pips and vine wood have been recovered from sites on the desert margins, suggesting local cultivation (Figure 2.3). Helbaek (1958) has pointed out that finds of grape pips may indicate the eating of grapes or raisins rather than the

products is the introduction of bacteria into milk, for the production of yoghurt, which keeps better than milk. It was probably yoghurt from which butter was churned and cheese manufactured (though it is uncertain when cheese making began). As cattle were more important than sheep or goats as providers of meat, the same was probably true of their milk.

Plate 2.2   A Ghassulian 'churn' in course of excavation at the Chalcolithic site of Gilat in the north-western Negev. Its large size, and the presence of many cattle bones, suggest that it was used for processing cows' milk

Milk could have been processed in skins before the invention of pottery, and skins are still used for this in some parts of the Middle East at the present time. Milk is poured into a skin containing enough live yoghurt to start the fermentation process that after several hours will change the milk to yoghurt. This may be used for drinking or some other form of processing, or it may be left in the skin and rocked about until the fat coagulates into butter. Modern stainless steel analogues of the same shape, suggest that the Ghassulian 'churns' from Chalcolithic sites really were used to make yoghurt and butter, and the large size of some of them suggests the use of cows' milk (Plate 2.2).

Once these preservation techniques had been developed, they not only allowed vegetable and animal products to be stored, they enabled them to be marketed as part of the new urban economy and to be traded over long distances.

manufacture of wine. However, wine was certainly being made in the Early Bronze Age as presses for crushing grapes are known in Palestine (Stager 1985). The manufacture of wine, beer and bread may have been on an industrial scale as texts also mention the export of all three from Ebla (Pettanato 1991). Biblical references to wine suggest that it was stored and fermented in 'wine skins', that is the skins of sheep, goats or cattle.

Yogurt and butter

'A land flowing with milk . . .'. The biblical reference is a reminder of the importance of milk in the Levant. However, milk quickly sours in warm climates. A similar technique to fermentation used for animal

Figure 2.3   Whole carbonized grapes from the Late Early Bronze Age of Numeira on the south east coast of the Dead Sea (McCreery 1979)

CATTLE IN THE EARLY ECONOMY OF THE SOUTHERN LEVANT

Agriculture and cattle

Analysis of the numbers of bones found in archaeological sites in the southern Levant shows that cattle almost always provided at least 50 per cent of the meat from the Late Neolithic to the Iron Age. The predominance of cattle is particularly marked in the Jordan Valley, presumably reflecting the low-lying marshy landscape. Cattle can be constituents of both farming and semi-sedentary pastoralism: their high numbers, together with the presence of pigs and indications of horticulture, suggest sedentary farming in most of the area, though this may have graded into semi-sedentary pastoralism on the desert edges.

Meat and milk

As well as providing relatively more meat, cattle would have provided much more milk than sheep or goats. The large size of some of the Ghassulian 'churns' from Chalcolithic sites suggests that they were used to process cows' milk.

Leather

Although leather rarely survives in archaeological sites one can surmise a great many uses for it – clothes, tents, thongs, carrying bags, water transport, churning skins, skins for fermenting wine and so on. The remains of cowhide sandals

Plate 3.1   Distal metapodial of an ox from the Chalcolithic of Shiqmim in the north-western Negev with lateral expansion of articular surface (Grigson 1987). Lesions like this could have been caused by carrying heavy loads or pulling ploughs or vehicles

were found in the Chalcolithic Cave of the Treasure (Nahal Mishmar) (Bar-Adon 1980).

Cattle as draught animals

The change from hoe to plough agriculture, which enabled intensive cultivation of heavier soils, probably took place during the Chalcolithic and had certainly happened by the Early Bronze Age. Ploughs imply the use of draught animals, and although donkeys could have been used, the role of cattle as draught animals, carrying loads and pulling ploughs or vehicles needs to be considered.

Cattle foot bones with lesions that could have been caused by carrying or pulling heavy loads or ploughs have been noted for several Chalcolithic sites in the Negev (Plate 3.1) and from Tel Yarmouth in the Bronze Age (Davis 1988). The figure of a bull carrying a Ghassulian churn excavated from the Sanctuary at Ein Gedi (Plate 3.2; Ussishkin 1980) indicates that the idea of cattle carrying loads was already prevalent in the fourth millennium.

The bowl containing a model of a pair of yoked oxen, which probably comes from the Early Bronze Age near Tell Farah North (Amiran, R. 1986; Horwitz and Tchernov 1988) (see Plate 3.3), is the earliest definite evidence for cattle being used for

Plate 3.2   The figure of a bull or a cow carrying a Ghassulian churn from the sanctuary at Ein Gedi (Ussishkin 1980), showing that the idea of utilizing animal energy was already current in the Chalcolithic

Plate 3.3　A bowl containing a model of a pair of yoked oxen, which probably comes from the Early Bronze Age, found near Tell Farah North (Israel Department of Antiquities and Museums) (Amiran 1986; Horwitz and Tchernov 1988). This is the earliest definite evidence for the use of cattle for draught

presence of wheeled transport in the Levant and suggests that cattle pulled them.

How were really heavy loads transported? There are records of timber, particularly cedar wood being exported from the Lebanon to Egypt by boat along the Mediterranean shore, and pine logs and trunks of plane trees went from the city of Ursu in the Ebla region to Mesopotamia, perhaps by logging down the Euphrates (Pettinato 1991). But how did these heavy loads reach the ports? How was building stone conveyed to the emerging cities? Draught cattle must be the answer.

It is probable that cattle were the backbone of the Levantine economy in the Chalcolithic and Bronze Ages, not only for the meat and milk which they provided, but as a major element in transportation and agriculture. Indeed it seems unlikely that urbanization could have happened without the heavy transport of timber and stone, not to mention trade in many other commodities, made possible by the use of cattle.

draught, though it is uncertain whether it is a plough or a vehicle that they are pulling. Ploughshares were probably made of wood which has not survived, but there are some clay models of early vehicles from Syria. One is a processional 'battle car' thought to date to the late fourth or early third millennium, and another is a covered waggon from the late third millennium (see Plate 3.4; Littauer and Crouwel 1974, 1990). According to Piggott (1983), it is likely that the early, solid-wheeled carts like these were usually pulled by oxen (Piggott 1983). Part of the late EBA Acropolis at Ebla was a stable for cattle, called the 'House of the Bulls', and another was the 'Place of the Wagons' (Pettinato 1991), which confirms the

Plate 3.4　A pottery model of a covered waggon from the late third millennium of Hammam, Syria (Littauer and Crouwel 1974). Such solid-wheeled vehicles were probably drawn by cattle (Ashmolean Museum, Oxford)

16

EARLY BRONZE AGE CANAAN: SOME SPATIAL AND DEMOGRAPHIC OBSERVATIONS

Ram Gophna

Introductory note

This chapter does not attempt to present an updated synthesis of Early Bronze Age Canaan, nor does it aim to reassess the 'hotly' debated topics pertaining to the socio-cultural developments. Several comprehensive syntheses on this period have appeared in recent years (Richard 1987; Ben-Tor 1992; Stager 1992). Rather, it presents five brief discussions on some aspects of Early Bronze Age society, as seen from the perspective of a researcher of the ancient settlement history of Canaan.

The Post-Chalcolithic resettlement process of Canaan during Early Bronze Ia (ca. 3500–3300 BCE)

Research into cultural change in Canaan during the transition from the Chalcolithic to the Early Bronze Age (ca 3500 BCE) has accelerated over the last decade. The discussions and syntheses published in recent years reflect, in their variety of topics, an intense scholarly preoccupation with this subject. Such topics include: chronological gap; overlap between the two cultures; crisis and change vs continuity; diffusion vs indigenous developments; degree of correlation between changes in the material culture and economy, and changes in social structures; etc. A characteristic feature of these recent syntheses is the meticulous comparisons between elements of the Chalcolithic material cultures and elements appearing in the archaeological record at the very beginning of the Early Bronze Age (EBIa), such as: patterns of settlement, architecture, pottery, flints, stone vessels, copper objects, cult objects, burial customs, floral and faunal remains, etc. (Amiran 1985; Hanbury-Tenison 1986; Braun 1989).

It seems to us that the settlement pattern is one of the components that can help clarify the geographical origins of the cultural change during the phase of collapse of Chalcolithic society, and the character of the transition to the EBIa.

According to the most recent radiocarbon dates from southern Canaan (i.e., from Chalcolithic sites in the Beersheva Valley, Tel 'Erani, and Taur Ikhbeineh) the very beginning of the Early Bronze Age (EBIa) may be fixed within the thirty-fifth to thirty-fourth centuries BCE (Gilead 1988; Kempinski and Gilead 1991; Oren and Yekutieli 1992). However, such high dates still need to be corroborated by future ^{14}C determinations from sites farther north.

What are the data that can be used to analyze the two settlement systems in the southern Levant (i.e., the Chalcolithic and the EBIa, respectively) and define the mechanism by which one system was replaced by another? In the map in Figure 1, which assembles most EBIa sites known from Cisjordan to date, it is possible to trace the settlement process which occurred in the EBIa. It should be noted, however, that reliable data on EBIa sites for most of the Lower Galilee and Judean hill country are still needed. Our map indicates two different kinds of sites:

1. Sites with EBIa settlement remains but no earlier Late Chalcolithic remnants: e.g., Yiftahel, Bab edh-Dhra and Site H.
2. Sites with EBIa settlement remains above earlier Late Chalcolithic remnants: e.g., Tel Teo, Meser, Palmahim and Tel Halif.

The sites of the second group are indicative of the tendency of the EBIa settlers to reoccupy sites previously preferred by the Chalcolithic or earlier groups. These places were suitable for permanent occupation, with abundant water sources and had already been cleared and prepared for agricultural cultivation in an earlier period.

The EBIa sites that were not established at earlier Chalcolithic sites attest a new settlement process apparently unconnected with the former Chalcolithic settlement system; they also indicate that the post-Ghassulian resettlement process in some areas of the southern Levant did not reach the semi-arid zone of the Beersheva–Arad Valley, sometimes defined as the 'Chalcolithic paradise' (see Levy, Chapter 14). A similar phenomenon may also be

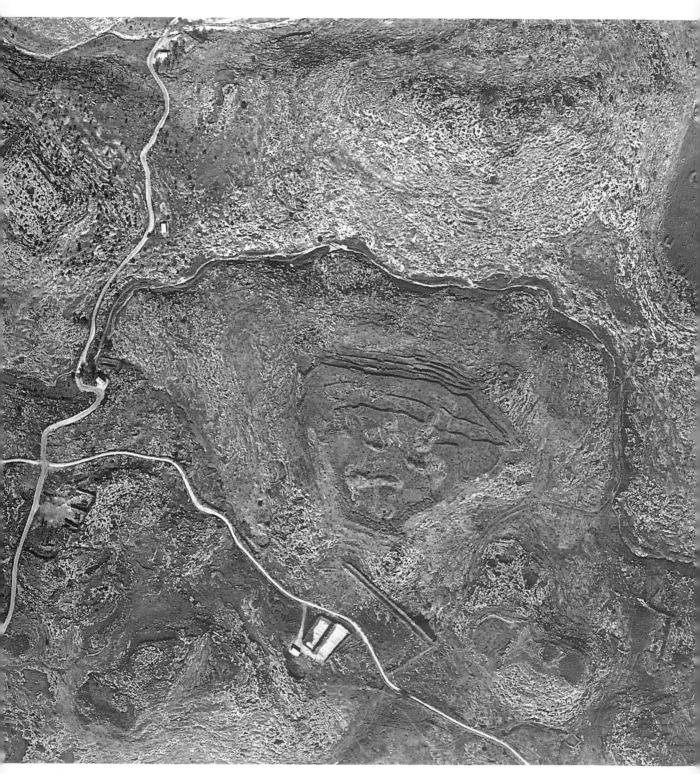

Plate 1 Tel Dalit. An EBII fortified town in the north–east Shephela (aerial view)

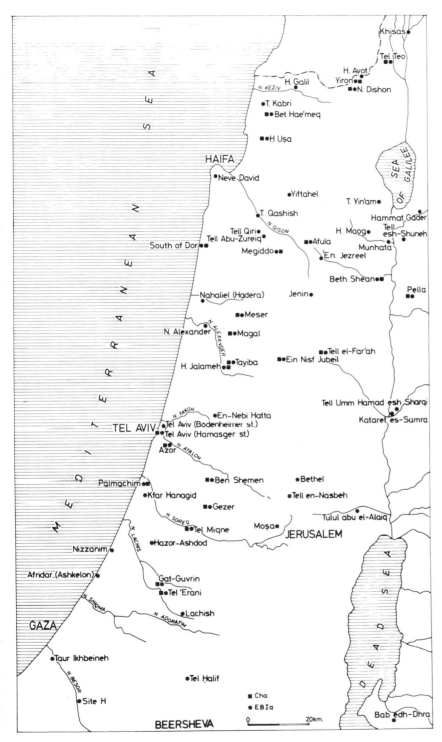

Figure 1 Distribution of EBIa sites in Canaan

observed in the western Golan Heights. All this signals the total collapse of the Chalcolithic settlement from north to south, that is in the heartland of the Mediterranean (humid) phytogeographical territory and in most of the Irano-Taurian (semi-arid) phytogeographical territory.

Currently there is no information on EBIa settlement within the arid desert regions of the Negev. It is possible to discern that prominent Chalcolithic settlements, e.g., Teleilat Ghassul and Abu Hamid, were totally deserted at the end of the Late Chalcolithic period. These sites were not reoccupied at the very beginning of the EBI period, and indeed were never reoccupied.

From the above data it may be inferred that the spatial distribution of the two settlement systems, i.e., the Chalcolithic and the EBIa, points to a chrono-stratigraphic gap between the two: a 'spatial-stratigraphic' gap (Group a) and a 'vertical-stratigraphic' gap (Group b).

This settlement gap may be used as a starting point for evaluating the new settlement process, and may also serve to fix the region where the cultural change occurred. It is archaeologically and geographically well documented that during proto-historic and early historic times Canaan (i.e., southern Levant which covers what is now Israel and Jordan) was only the southern part of a much larger cultural province, namely 'Greater Levant', which developed within the Early Mesopotamian cultural sphere. The location of Canaan at the extreme southern end of the Fertile Crescent, on the fringe of the desert, made it vulnerable to the slightest environmental or social changes, sometimes resulting in complete social disintegration and social crisis. This geographical situation must, therefore, be taken seriously into account when attempting to interpret the observed chrono-stratigraphical gap between the Chalcolithic and EB settlement systems. To what degree was this gap also a cultural gap? By all accounts, the complete disintegration of the Chalcolithic settlement system in Canaan after a long and prosperous existence entailed a severe demographic and sociocultural crisis. This may have occurred before the first new settlements of the EBIa culture began to be established in this southern area of the Levant. This hypothesis would imply that the actual process of cultural change had taken place some time previously within the area of the northern Levant (Syria-Lebanon) and subsequently reached the now utterly deserted Chalcolithic region of Canaan by diffusion. What then was the impact, if any, of the Chalcolithic population remnant on the EBIa sociocultural reshaping of Canaan (southern Levant)? Is it possible to detect and distinguish, with any degree of certainty, the traces of the old Chalcolithic traditions still inherent in some aspects of the EBIa material culture, or the apparently entirely new elements introduced from outside?

In trying to come to grips with the questions posed above it is necessary, in addition to comparing the various components of the two material cultures, to trace the dynamics implicit in the settlement process – i.e., the tempo of abandonment of Chalcolithic settlements in various areas of the country, on the one hand, and the pace of the EBIa resettlement, on the other.

Regional analysis of already published EBIa pottery assemblages from Canaan enables us to distinguish about four EBIa settlement areas (see Figure 1):

1. north-central, represented by sites such as Yiftahel and Palmahim (Braun 1989);

2. northeastern, represented by such sites as Tell Umm Hammad (Betts 1992);
3. southwestern, represented by sites such as Nizzanim, Site H and Taur Ikhbeineh (Macdonald 1932; Oren and Yekutieli 1992);
4. southeastern, represented by sites such as Bab edh-Dhra (Schaub and Rast 1989).

This regional grouping sheds light on the pace of the post-Ghassulian settlement process in Canaan, although the full decipherment of the EBIa ceramic regional distribution seems still beyond our grasp. For example, in the most recent excavations at Nizzanim and Afridar the pottery of the earliest EBIa occupation stratum indicates not only some typological continuity with the Chalcolithic (as observed long ago at several EBI sites), but also technological continuity – the old Chalcolithic technologies were integrated into the new EBIa pottery assemblages (Braun and Gophna: oral communication). Such, however, was not the case in the more northerly regions (Upper and Lower Galilee), as attested by the ceramic data reported so far from sites like Tel Teo and Yiftahel. What may be inferred from these apparently contradictory data is the possibility that in the southern Coastal Plain and in the southern Shephela the size of the surviving Chalcolithic population was far from negligible when the EBIa culture reached these regions.

In summary, any model depicting the transition from the Chalcolithic to the EB in Canaan (southern Levant) must reflect, above all, the extreme demographic decline of the Chalcolithic society following the complete disintegration of its settlement system. This is best illustrated by the archaeological chrono-stratigraphic gap both at the single-site and the spatial-regional level. The geographical location of Canaan at the southern end of the Fertile Crescent (see above) suggests a certain scenario for the Chalcolithic–Early Bronze cultural transition, namely that the new sociocultural developments took place in the more populated areas of the Levant farther north, from whence originated the groups that initiated the resettlement of deserted Canaan and reshaped its material culture (here designated EBIa). These groups may well have coalesced with some of the surviving Chalcolithic population, as implied for instance by the recent discoveries in the southwestern region where the gap between the two cultures is less pronounced. In only a short time, in this southern region at the southern tip of Canaan, there began to develop a long-distance international trade network with Late Predynastic Lower Egypt, which lasted throughout the entire EBI period (see Window 1, p. 277). This new and unprecedented development brought Canaan for the first time into direct contact with the cultural sphere of an emerging pristine civilization of the ancient Near East.

Crisis versus progress: settlement disintegration at the dawn of urbanism in Canaan

Among the main topics to which contributors to this book were requested to refer are designated 'Major Transitions' and 'Settlement Patterns'. Thus, in the following discussion I would like to dwell upon the only major internal settlement and social transition which occurred during the Early Bronze Age – a long period characterized by relatively uninterrupted cultural continuity.

It is generally accepted that the transition from EBI to EBII saw the first 'Urban Revolution' in Canaan. It was indeed a transition from a non-urban society characterized by a complex size-hierarchy of open (unwalled) settlements with dispersed buildings to an hierarchy of compact and fortified settlements, indicating an urban society. This settlement transformation is seen as the outcome of a long process of social evolution, resulting in the emergence of complex society.

A new empirical analysis of the spatial-archaeological database assembled in recent years enabled Portugali and Gophna (1993) to follow changes in the spatial organization of settlements which occurred during the late EBI, and it is now possible to suggest that the above mentioned urbanization process was not one of social progress only, but was also associated with a major socio-spatial disintegration, indicating a crisis of EBI society. This interpretation of the relevent settlement patterns (spatial data) was first suggested in Gophna's Hebrew synthesis of the Early Bronze Age, published in 1982 (Gophna 1982: 106). The new analysis of the database enables us to speculate further that this process of socio-spatial disintegration also resulted in the temporary nomadization of various EBI groups, and consequently of internal migrations and population movements within the confines of the Levant.

The study of the currently available data on the settlement patterns of EBI and EBII (for distribution of EBIb sites, see Figure 2) in Canaan reveals two main empirical socio-spatial models in the emergence of a fortified settlement system: the 'shrinking settlements' model in which the area of settlements shrank during the transition from unfortified to fortified settlements, and the 'abandoned settlements' model referring to settlements abandoned during this transition process. This second phenomenon was observed long ago by Kempinski and others (Kempinski 1978: 15–16).

A specific case study of a typical shrinking settlement can be illustrated by the following dicussion of Megiddo and the accompanying map (Figure 3). In the excavations of Tel Megiddo, the transition from the unwalled EBI to walled EBII was detected in Area BB (Strata XIX–XVIII). It can be seen that the EBI settlement (Stratum XIX) extended eastward, beyond the area of the massive EBII

city wall (Stratum XVIII). From Avner Raban's regional survey in the seventies (Mishmar Haemeq map – not yet published) we learn that this EBI settlement extended eastward, encompassing the spring of Ain el-Kubbi. The overall size of the EBI pre-urban site can be estimated as 16 hectares, while that of the walled EBII settlement as 13 hectares. The settled area thus shrank to less than ten percent of its former size.

Using the relations between settlement size and population as elaborated by Gophna and Portugali (1988), it can be seen that as a consequence of the transition from EBI to EBII, the population of Megiddo declined dramatically (about 5000 in the pre-urban EBI to 1250 in the walled, urban EBII, using the coefficients for very large EB I settlements – 80 persons per hectare – and for EB II settlements – 250 persons per hectare).

The above example of Megiddo is typical of the shrinking process which took place at other sites. It is interesting to add that it typifies not only large sites, such as Megiddo, Shimron in the Jezreel Valley, Beth Shean and Arad, but also tiny sites such as Tel Qashish (1 hectare in EBII).

Turning now to the 'abandoned settlements' model, two size-groups of abandoned sites can be identified: very small, and relatively very large EBI settlements like Akko, Tel Esor (Assawir), Lod, Palmahim and Tel Halif Terrace, which were totally abandoned in the transition to EBII.

An exceptional site in this category is Tel Shalem at the southeastern edge of the Beth Shean Valley (Eisenberg 1993). During the excavation it was found that the EBI settlement was indeed abandoned with the transition to EBII; however, toward the end of the EBI it underwent a process of shrinking and fortification generally typical of the transition from EBI to EBII.

On the basis of the above observations it is suggested that the EBI period ended with a major socio-spatial crisis – the socio-settlement system disintegrated – as is evident from the following:

1. Many large (and even small) settlements shrank, implying that these sites were abandoned and that their inhabitants became nomads/immigrants, at least temporarily.
2. Many settlements were abandoned, implying that their inhabitants became immigrants and nomads.
3. In the former cases we see, on the one hand, settlement continuity at the same sites, on the other, a break: the new EBII settlements were built practically on top of the previous EBIb settlements, thus totally demolishing their previous physical structure.

The implications of the above observations are that the EBI populations deserted their settlements and that this phenomenon characterized the entire country. This desertion of settlements implies, first and foremost, a change or a halt in the EBI way of life. It also implies a certain degree of nomadization and migration. It must be

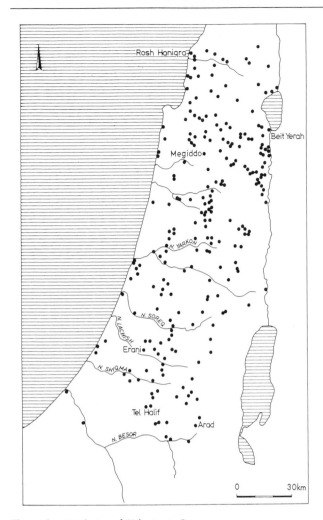

Figure 2 Distribution of EBIb sites in Canaan

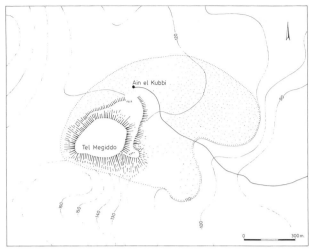

Figure 3 The site of Megiddo during EBIb: the dotted line indicates the maximum EBIb extent of the settlement

noted, however, that in our case nomadization and migration are two faces of a single phenomenon.

If the EBI ended with a socio-spatial crisis, nomadization and migration, what was the destination of these nomadic and migratory movements? Here one can offer two alternative options:

1. Inter-regional migrations, that is, from our region (southern Levant) outwards. Demographically this implies a desertion of the region under investigation: the southern Levant.
2. Intra-regional migration, that is, nomadization and migration within the region, which eventually ended in the establishment of the EBII urban culture and settlement structure in the region.

Archaeology does not provide clear evidence to decide conclusively between these two options, however, the evidence at hand tends to support the second. That is to say, the settlement crisis that ended the EBI entailed *intra-*

regional migration and nomadization, within the confines of the southern Levant. The evidence is the following: culturally, the material culture of the urban EBII is a direct continuation of that of the pre-urban EBI. Therefore, the picture is not of a new cultural group coming into the country and replacing, or assimilating with the previous EBI group, but of an internal (intra-regional) process which can be described as:

Stability (during EBI) — Instability (at the end of EBI) — Stability again (during EBII)

In other words, a stable settlement system prevails throughout most of the EBI, a socio-spatial crisis in the form of nomadization and migration marks the end of the EBI, and the system stabilizes once again with the rise of urban EBII. Note, first, that the whole sequence refers in essence to the very same socio-cultural group, and second, that it in fact describes what is conventionally called the first 'urban revolution' in Canaan.

The case study of Megiddo presents an interesting question: on one hand it is evident that EBI Megiddo was abandoned, if only for a limited period of time, since the EBII settlement was built directly on top of part of the EBI settlement. On the other hand, there still remains the following dilemma: in light of the above noted cultural continuity between the EBI and EBII, can one assume that the founders of EBII Megiddo originated from the very same group who, a short time earlier, deserted EBI Megiddo, underwent a process of nomadization in the area around the site, and eventually reconstructed EBII Megiddo? Or should we assume an alternative scenario, in which EBII Megiddo was constructed by immigrants from a distant region? Obviously we do not have information to answer such a question; however, we suggest that in light of known data on cultural territorial continuity, it is probable that the majority of the founders of EBII urban Megiddo originated from the old inhabitants of the EBI settlement. Note that a similar dilemma exists also with respect to EBI/EBII Arad and other similar sites.

To summarize, the settlement crisis at the end of the EBI period may have been associated with intra-regional migrations (i.e., within the region of Canaan) and possibly also with inter-regional migrations (from Canaan outwards). The above scenarios thus describe various aspects of the urban revolution in Canaan at the transition from EBI to EBII.

It is proposed that the key to understanding EB urbanization is the socio-spatial settlement crisis at the end of EBI. The latter, as described above, implied the disintegration of the EBI agricultural society and wide-ranging processes of nomadization and migration throughout the entire country. These processes resulted in the emergence of a 'local', relatively homogeneous, urban society. This interpretation is further supported by the finding that the rise of the EB urban system was associated with the weakening of the connections between southern Canaan and Egypt (Gophna 1987: 18–19).

These suppositions stand in contradiction to the two opposing, somewhat diffusionist, views which dominate the discussion on EB urbanization in Canaan. On the one hand, Kempinski proposed to see the urbanization at Tel 'Erani as the beginning of EB urbanization – the outcome of Egyptian influence, which at a later stage diffused northward throughout the rest of the country (Kempinski and Gilead 1991: 189). On the other hand, in the discussions of Amiran and Callaway on EB urbanism, there is an implicit view that we are dealing here with a process which originated in the north and later diffused southward to the region discussed here (Amiran 1970; Callaway 1982).

Continuity and abandonment: changes in urban settlement patterns in southern Canaan during EB II–III

In 1989 two maps were published which attempted to present the major EB II–III urban sites in Israel respectively (Amiran and Gophna 1989). These maps were based on the conventional division between two urban EB subperiods. Under scrutiny, it is now obvious that this conventional distinction is most clearly discernable in the southern part of Canaan, less in the north. On further investigation, the richer data from the south seems to enable one not only to refine the processes of settlement and abandonment of fortified towns along the EB II–III continuum, but also to speculate on shifts in their territorial and political divisions. The two maps of southern Canaan presented here (Figures 4 and 5) and the accompanying observations and comments illustrate this

possibility of refinement – even reconstruction – of some trends in the urban history of Canaan during the Early Bronze Age. One of the major questions which arises is whether the changes in the settlement history of fortified EB towns represent a country-wide process of abandonment and revival as a result of common crises, events or prosperity, or whether within this 600–800 year period of urban life each region, or even subregion, besides being affected by such common factors, underwent an individual process of changing originating from local events. If so, it will be possible, through analyses of the specific history of each urban site as manifested in its stratigraphy and regional pottery typology (Seger 1989), to refine and detail the conventional two urban subperiod divisions (EB II–III), and to build a more elaborate chronological sequence based on spatial analysis of the urban map.

As a point of departure for such an attempt in the future, two maps (Figures 4 and 5) are presented which, in comparison to those previously published, contain more recent data on sites in the southern part of Canaan.

General observations and comments

1. Examples of urban centers in the south which seem to have been relatively stable throughout most of the EB II–III continuum can be identified: Tel Erani, Yarmut, Ai, Jericho Oasis, Bab edh-Dhra. Does one or any of these represent the longest surviving fortified settlement within the framework of the urban Early Bronze Age? Is Jericho Oasis perhaps the most likely candidate?

2. A major crisis during the urban period can be distinguished in the Yarkon-Ayalon drainage basin, where the sites of Aphek, Dalit, Bareqet and Gezer were all abandoned sometime during EB II. Only the site of Gimzo seems to have been occupied during both the EB II and III (Gophna 1989). There are ceramic indications that these sites were both abandoned gradually over time, rather than instantaneously (as a result of a dramatic event), and that sometime during the EB III Gimzo was re-established, and the site of Tel Gerisa near the coast was also established. Thus, the implication is that in the Yarkon-Ayalon basin the urban system gradually deteriorated, and at a certain point in the EB II–III continuum the region was almost totally deserted. One can only speculate on the fate of the inhabitants (see below). It appears that during the first 300 years of urbanism, the Yarkon-Ayalon basin saw the existence of four fortified towns, three of them – Aphek, Gezer and Dalit – seem to have been polities, dominating a substantial agricultural territory. After an almost complete deterioration, the entire region was apparently eventually dominated by a single urban polity: Gimzo.

   A similar process occurred in the northern Negev, sometime around 2680 BCE (Amiran 1978b) when Arad was abandoned, and in the earlier part of EB III, when Tel Halif (Seger 1989) apparently replaced EB II Arad as the 'capital of the south' (Beit-Arieh 1991: 77–9).

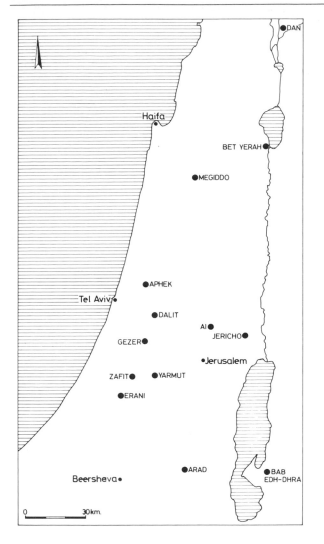

Figure 4 Major urban centers in Southern Canaan during EBII

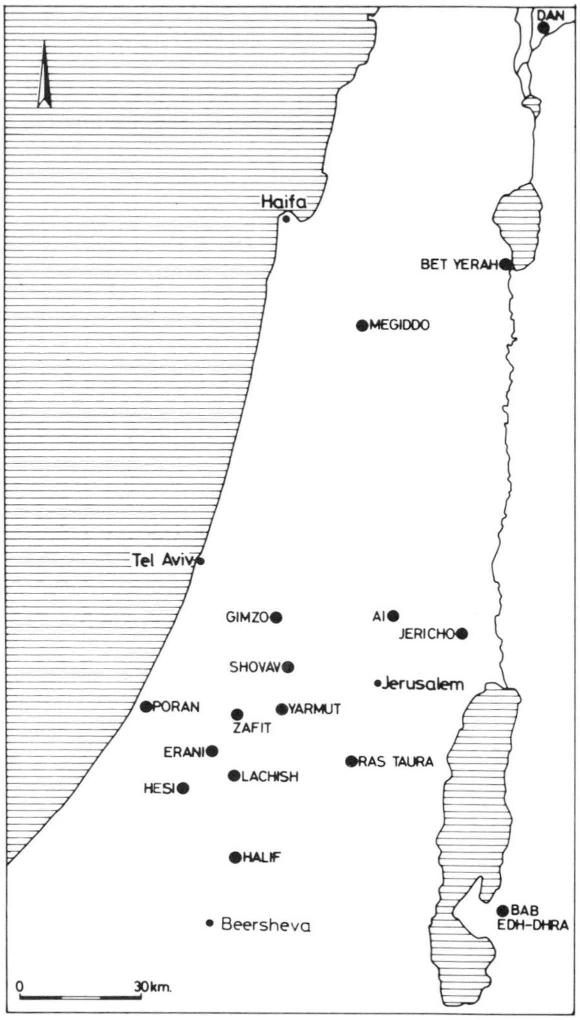

Figure 5 Major urban centers in Southern Canaan during EBIII

3. There was a renewal of settlement in the rest of the southern Coastal Plain sometime during the 'EB III', in subregions almost totally deserted during the urban transformation at the end of EB I (Gophna 1974), e.g., Tel Poran (Gophna 1992). In the case of a number of other re-established or newly-established sites, it is impossible to ascertain whether or not they were fortified, e.g., Tel Gerisa (Herzog 1993), Tel Ashkelon (Stager 1993b).

In regions other than the Yarkon-Ayalon basin and the Negev during the EB III, 13 major urban centers flourished compared to 9 in the EB II – as indicated by growth in size, population and prosperity. Their ruins often obscure the remains of earlier fortified EB II towns.

What is the demographic meaning of the phenomena listed above? The maps (Figures 4 and 5) indicate changes in population size and shifts in population concentration, as in the transition towards urbanism at the end of EB I,

when the inhabitants apparently became temporarily nomadic (see above). It is assumed that similar dynamics were also at work, perhaps intermittently, during this very long urban period. However, the calculation of the total inhabited area in southern Canaan from the two urban maps below, and the subsequent calculation of the size of population based on the principles presented in recent studies (see Window 2) indicate that the southern part of the country (south of the the Yarkon River and Wadi Far'ah) contained about one third of the total population (35,000–40,000) during the EB urban period.

The legacy of this first urban period in Canaan can still be seen in the archaeological landscape of the country (Gophna 1984). In the south this consists of the impressive ruins of major urban EB centers which were not re-fortified during the Middle Bronze Age: Bareqet, Tel Dalit, Ai, Shovav, Yarmut, Tel 'Erani, Hesi, Ras Taura and Arad.

SOUTHERN CANAAN DURING THE EBI: THE EGYPTIAN CONNECTION

In recent years it seems more and more that archaeological research of EBI in southern Israel has considerably contributed not only to the history of southern Canaan during the period of cultural change from the Chalcolithic to the EB and the very beginning of EB, but also to the history of Egypt at the end of the Predynastic and very beginning of the Dynastic period. The connections revealed also demonstrate that they were only part of the broader interconnections between Egypt and western Asia.

The accumulation of archaeological data from southern Israel pertaining to the interconnection between these two regions beginning in the 1920s and 30s (excavations at Site H and Lachish) and the dramatic eruption during the 1950s (Tel 'Erani excavations) began to accelerate in the 1960s, 70s and 80s (Arad, En Besor, Northern Sinai Survey, Tel Maahaz, Tel Halif, Taur Ikhbeineh, Nizzanim). It seems that this acceleration is still continuing (Afridar). No doubt it is possible today to view the research on the interconnections between these two regions in the EBI as a discipline in its own right.

As a result of the accumulation of data in this field in southern Israel, the geographical and chronological framework of the interconnections with Egypt in the EB must be modified. In the past, researchers used to synthesize the data from all the Levant and to place them in a wide chronological-historical perspective, namely the interconnections between Greater Canaan (Syro-Palestine) and Egypt throughout the long EB period (De Vaux 1971; Hennessy 1967; Ward 1963; Ben-Tor 1982, 1991). Today, we are witnessing the focusing of the discussion mainly on southern Canaan during the EBI — the second half of the fourth millennium BCE — the end of the Predynastic/beginning of First Dynasty — a time span of ca 300–400 years.

Moreover, if we take a retrospective look at studies which concentrated on southern Canaan and Egypt in the EBI, we would see that the excavations and impressive discoveries made at such sites as Tel 'Erani, En Besor, Maahaz, and even Arad, concentrated attention on a specific period of time at the end of EBI, when the relations between these two regions reached their climax (end of Dynasty 0, beginning of Dynasty 1 — the days of Narmer and Hor Aha). It seems that even the most recent comprehensive synthesis on these relations (Ben-Tor 1991) places little weight on the relations in the period prior to this specific formative time. Today it is clear that the evidence from the entire EBI period, not just the specific timespan of this climactic period, presents us with the challenge of crystallizing alternative models which will bring us closer to deciphering the elusive mechanisms of these relationships — an understanding of which seems increasingly beyond our grasp. One should admit that we are still handicapped by terms formulated by a growing group of researchers who are still influenced by the weight/abundance of the data relating to this formative timespan — 'invasion', 'occupation', 'trade relations', 'immigration', 'colonization', (Yeivin (1960); Amiran (1978a); Gophna (1987, 1992b); Ben-Tor (1982, 1991); Oren (1973); Stager (1993); Brandl (1992); Porat (1992) and others). In light of more recent discoveries pertaining to earlier stages of the contact between southern

Canaan and Egypt during the EBI, these above mentioned definitions seem more and more problematic and, in a way, inappropriate. We are still far from defining the minute fluctuations in the continuity, intensity and character of these unique relations throughout the long history of the EBI.

Despite this somewhat frustrating situation, it is hoped that following the new excavations carried out in southern Israel — some of which are still going on (Tel Halif, Tel 'Erani, Nizzanim, Afridar) — and a reassessment of Yeivin's excavations at Tel 'Erani on the Israeli side, coupled with new excavations at sites in the Nile Delta (Minshat Abu Omar, Tell el-Iswid (S), Tell Ibrahim Awad, to mention just a few), and the full publication of both the Maadi excavations and the new excavations at Abydos in Upper Egypt, on the Egyptian side, it is now possible to suggest new interpretations of the archaeological data — not only of their climax at the end of EBI, but also of their earlier stages.

First of all we must distinguish, geographically and chronologically, between the earlier relations of southern Canaan and the Delta settlements during the days of the Maadi-Buto culture (Naqada IIb–c) in the first part of EBI (EBIa or Early EBI), and the relations which continued with the Delta as well as Upper Egypt in the second part of EBI (EBIb or Late EBI; Naqada IIc–d/III [Dynasty 0]), until the days of Narmer and Hor-aha at the very beginning of the First Dynasty. This distinction is emphasized by the chrono-stratigraphy of certain sites in southern Canaan, some of which existed only during Early EBI (Site H and Nizzanim), and others only in the Late EBI ('En Besor,

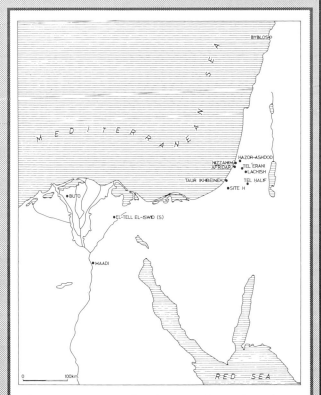

Figure 1.1 Sites in southern Canaan and Lower Egypt during EBIa

Maahaz). Alongside these sites which represent only one phase of the EBI in southern Canaan, one should mention those sites that reveal a full sequence throughout EBI — Tel 'Erani, Tel Halif, Afridar (it is worth noting that the sites surveyed in northern Sinai represent, in general, the full chronological sequence of the relations between southern Canaan and Egypt during EBI).

In light of the accumulated data from southern Canaan, a number of challenging questions can now be posed to researchers of this subject:

1. Were the relations between the Maadi-Buto culture of the Nile Delta and southern Canaan contemporary with the establishment of the first post-Ghassulian settlement system in this area, or did they only begin after some of these first EB settlements had begun to consolidate (as suggested lately by Yekutieli, pers. comm.)?
2. Is it possible to interpret the EBI finds at Maadi and the Egyptian ones in southern Canaan as an expression merely of trade relations (exports to Egypt of raw material, e.g., copper and asphalt, and finished agricultural goods, e.g., wine and oil), or do these finds indicate already some immigration of Egyptian population to the southern tip of Canaan (Site H, Taur Ikhbeineh, Lachish)?
3. During the critical period of the takeover of Lower Egypt by the bearers of the Naqada IIc–d culture, after the total

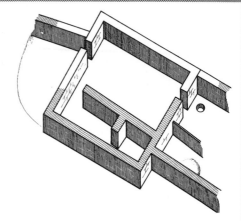

Figure 1.3 'En Besor: The Egyptian building (isometric reconstruction)

desertion of Maadi, and the disappearance of the so-called Maadi-Buto culture, did the connections with southern Canaan not break off — even for a short period of time — the trading initiative being taken over immediately by the Upper Egyptian Naqadians, who even extended it to Upper Egypt? Or, to pose the question another way, did the Naqadians manage to keep the momentum of trade relations with southern Canaan going during the takeover period? In any case, the earliest EB pottery reached Upper Egypt during Naqada IIc–d.

What was the role of the inhabitants of southern Canaan in these relations during this critical period? Does the total desertion of sites which evidenced strong Egyptian connections, e.g. Site H, indicate a certain temporary difficulty in maintaining these relations during the crucial period of time?

4. Do the new discoveries at Cemetery U at Abydos of hundreds of Canaanite wine jars hint that the organized state-sponsored trade network under Egyptian royal administration in southern Canaan, which flourished in this climactic period, had already begun in the earlier period

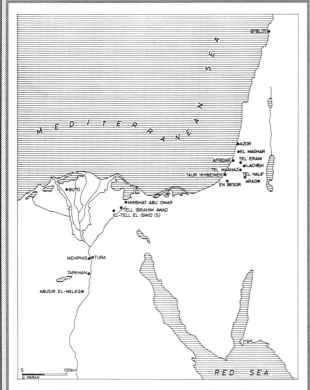

Figure 1.2 Sites in southern Canaan and Lower Egypt during EBIb

Plate 1.1 'En Besor site during excavation (looking north-east)

termed Naqada IIa2 (Kaiser terminology, or 'Dynasty 00' [van den Brink terminology], i.e., ca Middle EBIb in Canaan).

Alternatively, perhaps we must accept Hartung's interpretation (pers. comm.) that the relations during the period of usage of Cemetery U are evidence of one-sided trade — from Canaan to Egypt — initiated and directed by the inhabitants of southern Canaan only.

5. Can we delineate the geographical perimeters of the focal area in which the ethnic, cultural, economical and political interaction between Egypt and southern Canaan actually took place? The evidence seems to indicate that during the first phase of connections with Lower Egypt alone, the interaction occurred mainly in the southern tip of the settled area (Site H, Taur Ikhbeineh), but when the connections began to develop with Upper Egypt during the rest of the EBI period, the geographical area of interaction extended northwards towards the lower Soreq River drainage system (el-Maghar) and even to the Ayalon basin (Azor).

6. How can we interpret these zones in terms of the mechanism of interaction between the two countries: were they, during the entire period, trade depots ('entrepots') through which mainly raw materials and

Plate 1.2 An Egyptian cylinder seal impression

finished agricultural goods were channeled from the Coastal Plain, Shephela and highlands of Canaan? Was there really an Egyptian administrative center at Tel 'Erani at the climactic period?

The discovery of EBI settlements on the shores in the area of Ashkelon (Afridar and Tel Ashkelon) that existed throughout the EBI sequence indicate, as already pointed out by Stager (1993b), the possibility of a maritime trade route between southern Canaan and Egypt alongside the mainland route through northern Sinai. What was the impact on southern Canaan of the interaction with Egypt? It does not seem that these connections had any substantial long-term effect on the cultural development of Canaan, although it is generally assumed that these trade relations served as a catalyst affecting the social organization of the local Canaan population on the eve of urbanism. One cannot accept Kempinski's (1992) contention that this interaction with Egypt was what brought urbanism to Canaan, although one may designate Tel 'Erani as an exceptional town during this period, before the full advent of urbanism.

To sum up, the questions and statements presented above may exemplify the degree of refinement which the research on these connections between Egypt and southern Canaan during EBI has already reached. Each new excavation not only adds new information, but also raises new and perplexing questions, and researchers in this fascinating field currently await each new discovery in Egypt and in southern Canaan eagerly.

Table 1   Comparative table (revised after Amiran and Gophna, 1992).

Upper Egypt	Lower Egypt	Southern Canaan	
Period	Sites	Period	Sites
Beginning of Dynasty I	Buto str V MAO grave group 4 et-Tell el-Iswid (s) Phase B TIA phase 5	EBII	Arad Str. III
Naqada III b–c1 (Dynasty O)	Buto str. IV MAO grave group 3b et-Tell el-Iswid (s) Phase B TIA phase 6	EBIb	'En Besor str. III Arad Str. IV Malhata Maahaz Halif 101 Tel-Erani str. C Afridar
Naqada III a2 (Abydos cemetery U, Tomb J)	Buto str. III MAO grave group 3a et-Tell el-Iswid (s) Phase B TIA phase 6	EBIb	'En Besor str. IV Arad Str. IV Malhata Halif 101 Tel-Erani str. C Afridar
Naqada IIc,d	Buto str. II MAO grave groups 1–2 et-Tell el-Iswid (s) Phase A str. I–IV TIA phase 7	EBIb	Taur Ikhbeineh Lachish NW-settlement Tel-Erani str. D
Naqada IIB	Buto str. 1 Maadi	EBIa	Site H Taur Ikhbeineh Lachish NW-settlement Nizzanim Afridar
Naqada I–IIa	Maadi	Chalcolithic	

DEMOGRAPHY AND ENVIRONMENT IN THE EARLY BRONZE AGE

A considerable number of studies on the population and demography of ancient Israel have appeared in recent years, including some which deal specifically with the demography of the Chalcolithic period and Bronze Age.

The populations of the Early and Middle Bronze Ages in Palestine were first investigated in two articles by Broshi and Gophna (1984, 1986), who employed as their working hypothesis a population density coefficient for ancient settlements of ca 250 persons per hectare, based on modern ethno-archaeological data and actual archaeological evidence. An inventory of all known EB II–III and MB II sites in Israel was compiled, estimating their size, and an approximation of the population of the country for these periods was presented. According to this estimate, the population in EB II–III was about 150,000, in MB IIA 100,000, and in MB IIB 140,000. A third study by Gophna and Portugali (1988), on only one region of the country – the Coastal Plain – goes beyond these two previous discussions in several respects. First, it considers not only the total population in the various periods, but also the spatial and size distributions of the settlements and population. Second, it compares the processes of sociocultural change as reflected in changes of settlement systems from the Chalcolithic to the Middle Bronze Age. Third, the study calculates population not only by fixed density but by a variable coefficient related to settlement size and different periods. Fourth, it relates the empirical discussion on demography and settlement to various theories of sociocultural change. This study by Gophna and Portugali suggests that the first urban culture in the Early Bronze Age emerged, to a large extent, in line with a Boserupian conception that population growth initiates a sociocultural transformation. In contrast, the second urban transformation, at the beginning of the Middle Bronze Age, seems to have had a more Malthusian character, in the sense that the urban transition was followed by a further population increase. A fourth study, by Finkelstein and Gophna (1993), concentrates on the settlement, demographic and economic patterns in the highlands of Palestine in the Chalcolithic and Early Bronze Age. One of the conclusions drawn from this study is that the transition from the Chalcolithic to EB I in the highlands was characterized by a dramatic growth in the number of settlements and population. This wave of settlements in the highlands in the Early Bronze Age was the first in a series of such processes, the other two occurring in the Middle Bronze Age and Iron I.

Another study by Gophna, Liphschitz and Lev-Yadun (1986–87) utilizes some of the foregoing studies to estimate man's impact on the natural vegetation of the central Coastal Plain during the Chalcolithic and Bronze Ages. From this study it appears that human impact on the arboreal vegetation of the country during the above periods was not extensive, and therefore the severe degradation of the forest in the area took place in later periods. A further study by Liphschitz, Gophna and Lev-Yadun (1989) deals specifically with human impact on the vegetational landscape of Palestine in the EB II–III. It addresses the question of whether the Early Bronze urban culture may have caused, for the first time in the history of the country, a change in the balance of the vegetational landscape. In view of the data presented, the researchers concluded that the extent of the damage to the natural vegetation and the soils during the EB II–III could not have endangered the urban culture or caused its degeneration.

It appears that the archaeology of Israel has matured to the stage that data collected by the various excavations and surveys can be summarized and utilized reliably to draw conclusions concerning the demography of the country during the protohistoric periods of the Chalcolithic and Early Bronze, and its impact on the vegetational landscape. The figures suggested in the studies cited above cannot be considered precise; however, the relative figures are undoubtedly of greater importance than the absolute, and enable comparison of the size of the EB urban population and its impact on the environment, with that of the preceding Chalcolithic period and later Bronze Age cultures. Even if there are defects in the systems employed in these studies, these would affect only the absolute figures.

Part IV

CANAAN, ISRAEL, AND THE FORMATION OF THE BIBLICAL WORLD

17

SOCIAL STRUCTURE IN THE EARLY BRONZE IV PERIOD IN PALESTINE

William G. Dever

Introduction

The Early Bronze IV period (hereafter EB IV)[1] in Palestine, ca 2350–2000 BCE, is a non-urban interlude between the first urban horizon in the third millennium BCE, Early Bronze I–III, and an urban renaisance in the Middle Bronze Age in the second millennium BCE. During this period, most of the large *tells* were abandoned; there was a population shift to rural areas and the more marginal zones in the Jordan Valley, Transjordan, and especially the Negev; and there was a change in socio-economic strategies from intensive agriculture, industry, and trade to pastoralism and small-scale mixed agro-pastoralism. The dominant model in recent scholarship for explaining these changes has been that of 'pastoral nomadism', introduced in 1980 by this writer, but newer explanatory models are now being advanced.[2]

Long regarded as something of a 'Dark Age', EB IV was known principally from ephemeral remains on the largely-deserted major mounds, together with scattered tomb deposits, often from isolated cemeteries. In the last decade or two, however, the period has been illuminated by refined excavation strategies, extensive surveys, and more sophisticated interpretive models. Nevertheless, despite the mass of new material now at our disposal few studies have attempted to deal with social structure.[3] This deficiency has been due in part to the predilection of the older-style 'Biblical archaeology' (and even of Syro-Palestinian archaeology until recently) to focus rather narrowly on political rather than on socio-economic history.[4] Yet, as we shall argue, there are sufficient data to enable us to begin to reconstruct something of EB IV social structure in Palestine, an approach that would be more in line with current emphases in general archaeology.[5]

In the following discussion we shall understand 'society' to refer to collective, organized human relationships – in all aspects, but with particular reference to those reflections of society that leave the clearest traces in the archaeological record. Taking the systemic view of culture that I believe is necessary, these archaeological aspects of social structure can be analyzed in terms of 'subsystems', as in General Systems Theory.[6] In this case, we need to note especially:

1. economy (subsistence);
2. political structure; and
3. ideology.

Despite certain drawbacks of General Systems Theory approaches, and given the inherent limitations of the archaeological record itself (i.e., we really cannot say much about kinship patterns), I believe that such a systemic-social approach has great heuristic value.

EB IV a new look at the data — tombs and mortuary practices

A survey of the data

We may begin our analysis of social structure by looking at burials, not only because most of the data until recently have come from tombs, but also because the value of theoretical studies of social structure based on mortuary practices is widely accepted in recent archaeological literature.[7]

There is relatively abundant material from EB IV burials in Palestine. Large cemeteries have been excavated and published from such sites as Megiddo, Beth-shan, Hazorea, Dhahr Mirzbâneh/Wâdi ed-Dâliyeh, Gibeon, Jericho, Lachish, Kh. Kirmil, Jebel Qa'aqir, Tell el-'Ajjûl, Tell Umm Hammad esh-Sharqiya, and Kh. Iskander (the latter two in Transjordan). To give an idea of size, one may note that at Kh. Kirmil more than 900 EB IV shaft-tombs were found (most of them robbed); at Dhahr Mirzbâneh, near Jerusalem, some 1100 tombs were found (Finkelstein 1991). The value of what would appear to be rich data from tombs is often limited, however, by older and inadequate excavation methods, as well as by the lack of definitive publication. Thus of the cemeteries listed above, only Jericho and Jebel Qa'aqir are useful for purposes of analyzing EB IV social structure (and even Jebel Qa'aqir is published only in preliminary reports).[8]

The most appropriate question to pose of the Jericho and Jebel Qa'aqir burial data, although somewhat dichotomized, is: 'egalitarian' or 'stratified' society? Two scholars have recently approached the Jericho data (356 EB

Excavators at Jebel Qa'aqir EBIV excavation (courtesy of W.G. Dever)

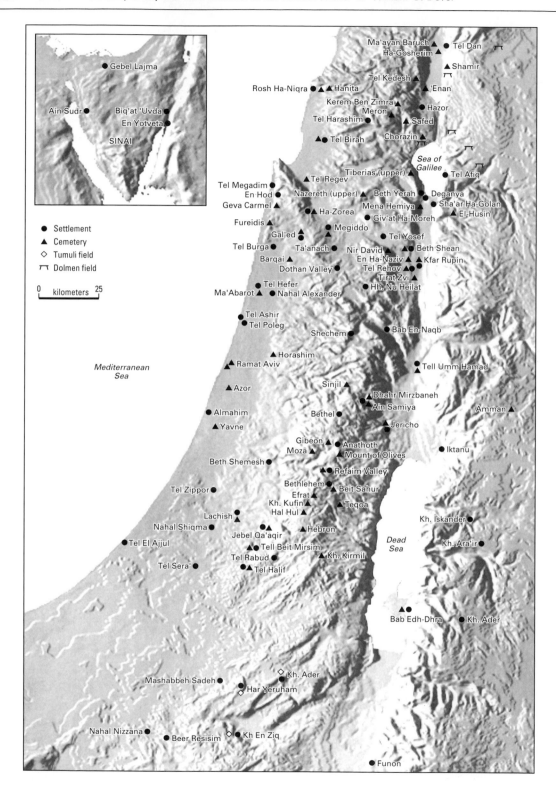

Figure 1   Principal EB IV sites and cemeteries in Palestine and the Sinai. From Ben–Tor 1993, Map 5.1

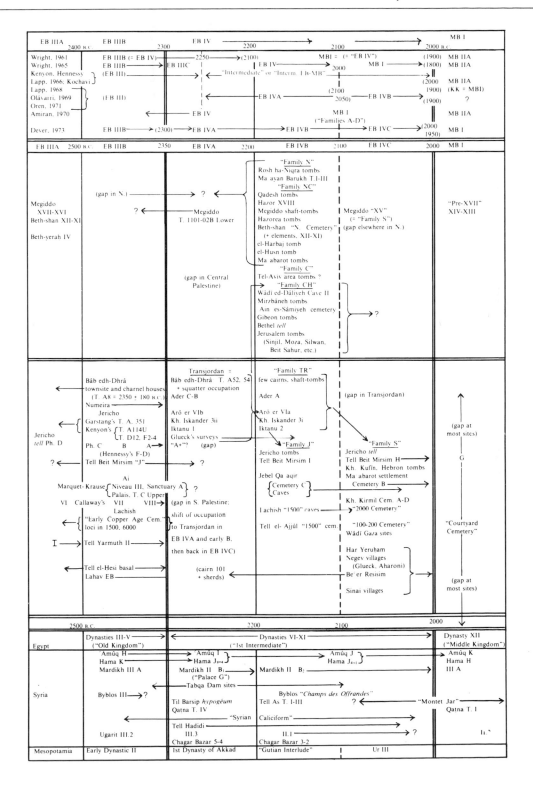

Figure 2 Table of principal related deposits from EB III to the beginning of MB I; cf. Dever 1980

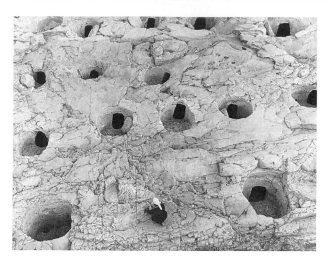

Plate 1 Cemetery B at Jebel Qaʻaqir, showing typical rockcut shaft-tombs, with stone doors moved aside. Photograph: Theodore Rosen

IV published tombs) in precisely this manner, but they have reached diametrically opposed conclusions. For Talia Shay (1983), an analysis of the various typological groups of burials (Kenyon's 'Dagger', 'Pottery', 'Outsize', etc.) produces evidence that 'would suggest that there were no great social gaps in Jericho in what must have been an egalitarian community during the Intermediate Bronze Age' (i.e., our EB IV; Shay 1983: 36). Gaetano Palumbo, on the other hand, basing himself on what I would regard as a much more comprehensive and precise analysis of the same data, concludes that 'the presence of different types of grave goods and of body treatment . . . clearly shows that this is not an egalitarian society . . . there is undoubtedly a social structure where the hierarchies are fully formed' (Palumbo 1987: 45; cf. 1991: 120–34).[9]

The writer's material from 38 very carefully dug EB IV shaft-tombs at Jebel Qaʻaqir, west of Hebron in the Shephelah (excavated in 1968–1971, but not yet fully published), is less extensive than at Jericho, but it yields a similar picture.[10] As at Jericho, there were discernible 'groups' in the vast cemetery of several hundred tombs. Cemetery B, for instance, was characterized by very well-cut shaft-tombs in the Senonian chalk along the lower terraces of the hillside. These tombs contained rather stereotypical band-combed pottery of my 'Family S' (Amiran's 'Family A'), but virtually no copper implements and no weapons whatsoever. The presence of a headless, disarticulated sheep/goat carcass in nearly every tomb may be of considerable importance (below). Cemetery C, by contrast, consisted of somewhat amorphous, rather poorly cut tombs upslope in the friable *nâri* crust (Cenomanian limestone), some of them probably artificially enlarged caves. Here the pottery was simpler (and, in my view, perhaps typologically earlier), and nearly every tomb produced excellent copper daggers and javelins. Cemeteries

E and F, some distance away, also exhibited certain peculiarities.

It would be interesting to do a statistical 'cluster-analysis' such as Palumbo (1987) did with the Jericho tombs, to see whether there are patterns that indicate the presence of elites in the Jebel Qaʻaqir burials, and whether any such patterns discerned would cut across the 'groups' of tombs that have been postulated typologically. That is, do the various cemeteries reflect the varying social structures of different ethnic groups (or perhaps even of 'tribal' configurations in EB IV, as has been suggested by several authorities)?[11]

These questions are certainly pertinent; but I doubt that we can answer them satisfactorily at the present stage of our research. At Jebel Qaʻaqir, only Cemetery B, with its 16 excavated tombs, yields sufficient data for detailed analysis. And of the relevant categories of data – 1. style of the tomb; 2. primary grave goods; 3. treatment of the deceased; and 4. associated practices that might reveal status – only the latter seems to yield specific information on social structure.

1. In Cemetery B, the rock-cut tombs are all nearly identical in size, construction, and manner of use. Even the tool-marks are the same. Some tombs have shallow body-niches or lamp-recesses, while others do not; and three tombs have enigmatic scratched panels over the entrance, or enigmatic 'miniature doorways' cut into the shaft. Otherwise there are few if any distinctions.
2. The pottery is very stereotyped and does not even vary significantly in the numbers of vessels per body in each tomb. Gloria London, who analyzed the Jebel Qaʻaqir pottery for her Arizona doctoral dissertation (London 1985), has shown that the pottery is so remarkably homogeneous, even to the details of size and decoration, that it must all have been made by the same potters – presumably made deliberately for use in tombs at the site. The fact that these potters were resident is shown by the potter's kiln discovered at the site. (That fact, in turn, must be coupled with the evidence for a group of 'professional tomb-cutters' who were probably resident year-round at the site; below.)[12] There are, however, no luxury items whatsoever alongside the pottery in the tombs, only two simple copper awls and a few beads in the entire cemetery.
3. The interments in Cemetery B are all of secondary, disarticulated bodies, often one for each tomb, but a few tombs with two burials, one with four, and one with nine.
4. Only in the custom of burying a sheep/goat carcass with some bodies, attested also at Jericho (below), do we see any evidence for differential treatment of the dead in Cemetery B at Jebel Qaʻaqir. Gloria London (1987), basing herself on Patricia Smith's (1982) preliminary report of the 46 skeletons from Cemetery B, has shown that a sizeable percentage of the remains (26 percent) are of individuals who were over 50 at the time of death. Furthermore, all but one of the burial chambers with an individual over 50 contained a sheep/goat carcass, while none of the interments of younger individuals contained such bones.

Plate 2 Interior of a shaft-tomb; note disarticulated, secondary burials, scattered tomb-offerings and tool marks on tomb wall

London thus argues that the older people of the Jebel Qa'aqir community (or at least of one 'tribal' group using the cemetery), both men and women, received preferential treatment at death, indicating that they had elite status. Such status was, however, not inherited. In this case, the slaughter of an animal that was both costly and had high symbolic value in a pastoral-nomadic society was an especially appropriate tribute to the elders. London also notes that at Jericho in the 'Outsize' tombs, on which most of the published skeletal analysis is based, 14 of 18 tombs contained sheep or goat remains, and from one tomb the remains of 10 animals were recovered (London 1987: 72, 73).

Published in 1987, and thus unavailable to London when she wrote, is Liora Horwitz' (1989b) preliminary report on the Jebel Qa'aqir animal bones from Cemetery B, which adds important information. The total of 154 bones recovered accounted for a minimum of 20 individual sheep/goat carcasses in the 16 tombs in Cemetery B. Most animals were immature (75 percent), with some (25 percent) young adults but no adults present. All the carcasses were missing the cranium and most of the bones were in partial articulation – both features indicating a deliberate sacrifice of an animal for interment with human remains. These details would seem to corroborate London's study of the elite status of at least some individuals at Jebel Qa'aqir (see also Horwitz 1989a).

Evidence of elites in EB IV tombs other than at Jericho and Jebel Qa'aqir is rare. The homogeneity of grave goods in the typical cemetery is remarkable, offerings consisting mostly of pottery from the standard local repertoire. The few exceptions, such as the squat ovid 'bottles' characteristic of tombs of the Central Hills and Jericho families, are certainly not status items, but simply vessels made deliberately, if not exclusively, for inclusion with burials.[13] There are some Syrian wheelmade 'caliciform' teapots and goblets in tombs at a few northern sites such as Qadesh and Megiddo; but these ceramic imports are probably indicative only of the trade that some migratory groups naturally carried out with Syrian urban centers, not necessarily status-symbols.[14] An occasional copper implement does turn up, mostly daggers and javelins that probably indicate only that the deceased was a male (not a 'warrior', as Kenyon thought). The *only* object that might possibly be considered an exotic, luxury item from EB IV tombs in the whole of Palestine is the North Syrian-style silver goblet in T. 204 at 'Ain es-Sâmiyeh, north of Jerusalem (Yadin 1971).

Limitations of analyses based on tombs

Despite some provocative suggestions based on the data from tombs that we have surveyed, there are limitations to this approach to social structure.

1. There are inherent problems with the raw data: tombs and their contents obviously do not give us an adequate picture of the material culture as a whole; and in any case our present sample is much too small to yield statistical reliability, even for the tombs themselves.
2. 'Models' are notoriously subject to misunderstanding and improper manipulation, and even at best they are often too theoretical to possess much real explanatory power (below).
3. Palumbo's analysis of EB IV social structure at Jericho, based on the tombs there, is the best such study to date. Nevertheless, Palumbo admits that his own conclusions are very tentative, and that in the course of his research he changed his position.
4. Finally, as Palumbo (1987: 47) also notes, there are factors *other* than social stratification that may help to explain observable variables in mortuary practice, not only from place to place but within a given cemetery. These would include the geographical location from which various groups burying their dead had come (especially in EB IV, when secondary burials were widely practiced); chronology; ethnic identity; and a host of ideological factors that may be exceedingly difficult to identify in the archaeological record.

The results of our assessment of EB IV social structure based on tombs and burial practices are, then, necessarily inconclusive. There is *some* evidence for social stratification – as one would expect in any society, since none is truly 'egalitarian' – but there are insufficient data to allow us to characterize the EB IV society as a whole.

Settlements and settlement pattern data

A survey of the data

As recently as 20 years ago, our settlement map of EB IV would have shown only a handful of sites, mostly 'squatter occupation' at sites like Megiddo, Jericho, and Bâb edh-Dhrâ'; a few occupied caves at Lachish, Tell Beit Mirsim, and Jebel Qa'aqir; an occasional village like Ikhtanu in the

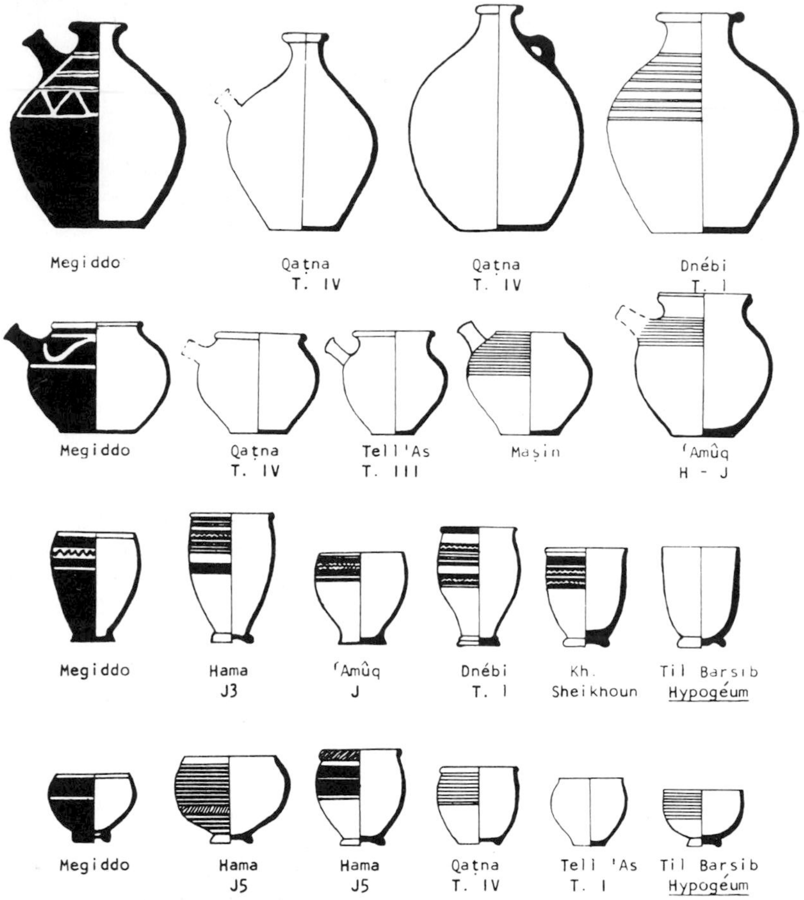

Megiddo

Qaṭna
T. IV

Qaṭna
T. IV

Dnébi
T. I

Megiddo

Qaṭna
T. IV

Tell 'As
T. III

Maṣin

'Amûq
H - J

Megiddo

Hama
J3

'Amûq
J

Dnébi
T. I

Kh.
Sheikhoun

Til Barsib
Hypogéum

Megiddo

Hama
J5

Hama
J5

Qaṭna
T. IV

Tell 'As
T. I

Til Barsib
Hypogéum

Figure 3   Comparison of Palestine and Syrian vessels of the 'Calciform' repertoir. Scale = 1:5

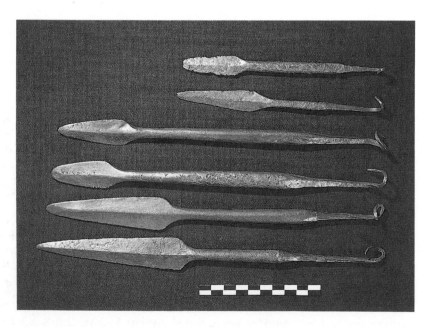

Plate 3   Copper javelins from Jebel Qa'aqir

Plate 4 Cave G26 at Jebel Qa'aqir; sleeping ledge and interior of cave behind the open-air area, hearth to left, storage bins to right (photograph: Theodore Rosen)

lower Jordan Valley or Yeruham in the northern Negev; and a few dozen sites in the Jordan Valley, the Negev, and the Sinai, known only through sporadic surface surveys of Glueck, Aharoni, Rothenberg, and Cohen. The picture had only barely begun to change in 1980, when I wrote one of the first synthetic treatments of the period (Dever 1980). Even then, the only relatively complete EB IV village-plan we had was that of Be'er Resisim (Figure 4).[15]

Today the situation has changed radically, as a result of much more focused, cooperative research strategies, which have brought to light hundreds of new pastoral-nomadic encampments, villages, and even a few supposedly 'urban' sites, in both Israel and Jordan (see Figure 1, p. 284). The latest major synthesis, that of Gaetano Palumbo (1991), lists over 1200 EB IV sites – many of the most recent having been discovered in Transjordan, as I had predicted (Dever 1971, 1973, 1980).

New socio-economic models

In 1980 it was possible to categorize most, if not all, the known EB IV settlement sites as reflecting a 'pastoral nomadic' society. We had, after all, no true towns, much less cities; very few sizeable villages, most of them not necessarily fully sedentary or sedentary year-round; scarcely a single published house of any kind, apart from huts and sleeping-shelters; no monumental architecture whatsoever. The economy appeared to be based largely on sheep and goat herding, although with some seasonal dry farming and sporadic local trade. The widespread distribution of so many small encampments and villages – many of them one-period sites – in the marginal zones indicated a non-nucleated pattern of settlement, with simple sites *not* hierarchically arranged in the typically three-tier fashion of urban cultures.[16]

Since Be'er Resisim was our only extensively excavated EB IV village in 1980, with an exposure of perhaps 80–

90 percent of the occupied areas on the site, I attempted what was at the time a pioneering study of social structure. Based on the lack of any monumental architecture or elite residences, as well as on the typical clustering of several round sleeping-shelters around a common courtyard, I concluded that 'at Be'er Resisim we are no doubt dealing with the partly-seasonal encampment of a small extended family or clan (a tribal descent group or 'section', in the ethnographic literature), subsisting largely on pastoralism' (Dever 1985b: 23). The homogeneity and physical layout of the round sleeping-shelters suggested then a largely unstratified, polygamous group of perhaps ca 80–100. Cross-cultural comparisons with similar societies in Africa, for instance, yielded good parallels for the village-plan of settlements like Be'er Resisim (Dever 1985b: 21–24).[17]

The contrast with the highly developed urban economy and society of Palestine in Early Bronze II–III (or of the subsequent Middle Bronze Age) could hardly be more striking. If one had employed specific evolutionary models like those of Fried or Service (although no one did at the time), EB IV Palestine would have been characterized as collapsing from an EB II–III 'city-state' stage, even below the Late Chalcolithic 'chiefdom' stage, reverting to a 'tribal' level approximating that of the Neolithic era two–four millennia earlier (below).

The pastoral-nomadic model that I first advanced explicitly in 1980 (but based on earlier studies; cf. Dever 1970, 1971, 1973, 1980) was designed partly to combat then-regnant theories of 'Amorite movements' or other invasion hypotheses. In the newer view, the stress was to be laid more on the role of indigenous, socio-economic factors in periods of radical cultural change such as EB IV.

Together with the pastoral-nomadic model, I suggested that the material culture of Palestine in EB IV, particularly the pottery, could best be understood in terms of several differing *regional* assemblages, or geographico-cultural 'Families'. I even attempted to arrange these families (my N, NC, CH, J, TR and S groups) into a series of overlapping chronological stages, arguing for alternating phases of sedentarization and certain movements of people from Western Palestine to Transjordan and back. The notion of sequential 'families', however, is not *essential* to the model of pastoral nomadism.[18]

The pastoral-nomadic model has fared quite well until recently, especially when one considers the virtual explosion of knowledge since 1980. Even the somewhat more speculative theory of 'regional families' has had sufficient predictive power (one of the tests of a model) that it has proven able to comprehend nearly all of the more recently discovered material. The only modification (apart from suggested chronological revisions) has been the possible addition of a new family on the Transjordanian plateau, based on new material – 'Family AZ' (for the Amman-Zerqa region).[19]

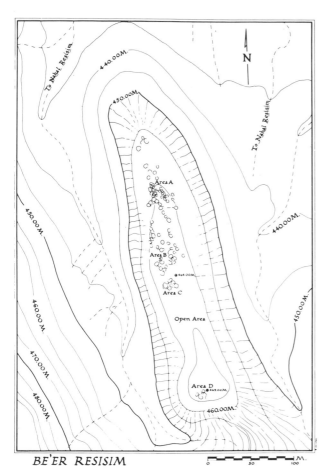

BE'ER RESISIM

Figure 4   Plan of the settlement at Be'er Resisim; cf. Cohen and Dever 1981

In the past five years or so, however, various alternatives to the pastoral-nomadic model have been put forward, often by my own students and younger colleagues, with my encouragement. Preceding these there had already been several rather idiosyncratic models. The first of these was T.L. Thompson's (1975, 1979) theory that the EB IV settlements were mostly permanent agricultural villages, following the EB II–III pattern, and specifically (in semi-arid regions) continuing EB run-off water collection and irrigation systems. Any evidence for an 'urban' EB IV culture was so slight, however, that the views of Thompson (a Biblical scholar, not an archaeologist) have never been taken seriously.[20]

Kay Prag, the excavator of the important site of Ikhtanu in the Jordan Valley, advanced (1974, 1984, 1985, 1989) a view of EB IV that originally laid a welcome emphasis on a degree of sedentism. Later, however, she reverted to notions of 'the successful infiltration of pastoralist cultivators, who did not blot out the preceding population but were absorbed by it and contributed, by a process of

nomadization, to the end of urban life' (Prag 1985: 87). Even her own site of Ikhtanu she now regards as exhibiting 'a barely sedentary economy' (Prag 1985: 82).

A final view that can be easily dismissed is that of Svend Helms (1982, 1986), who has partially excavated a cemetery and settlement at the important site of Tell Umm Hammad esh-Sharqiya (also known as Tiwal esh-Sharqi; cf. Tubb 1985), near Deir 'Allā in the Jordan Valley. Helms' view that Palestinian EB II–III 'ended in conflagration, rape, pillage in yet another invasion or incursion, this time of semi-nomadic folk' (1983: 112), a bizarre conclusion in itself, is belied by his own evidence at Umm Hammad esh-Sharqiya.

More recent alternate models are worth examining in some detail. On the basis of excavations carried out by the University of Arizona at Tell el-Ḥayyāt and Abu en-Niʿâj, near Pella in the Jordan Valley, Steven Falconer and Bonnie Magness-Gardiner (1984, 1989) have argued for models that encompass the more sedentary, agriculturally-based villages that are now coming to light in Transjordan.

At Kh. Iskander, on the Wadi Wala south of Kerak, Suzanne Richard (1987, 1990; Richard and Boraas 1988) has excavated the only true 'urban' EB IV known thus far, which even boasts a large city wall and a probable gateway. Based on Iskander, Richard contends that 'the model of pastoral nomadism (Dever 1980), which has value for regional application is obscuring our perspective on the EB IV peoples as a whole, and that new models that seek to comprehend the archaeological record as a whole are needed' (Richard and Boraas 1988: 127). She concludes that EB IV overall represents a 'loosely integrated society comprising a large pastoral element, small agricultural communities, and a few regional centers (small towns) that reflect a readaptation to a level of political autonomy probably best explained by the chiefdom model' (Service 1962); (Richard and Boraas 1988: 128). In a later work with one of her students (Richard and Long nd), Richard advances a more specific model of 'specialization-despecialization' to explain change from EB III to EB IV. This model is adopted from Bates and Lees (1977), who stress exchange between agriculturalists and pastoralists as a mechanism for maintaining 'specialization' in these two respective, complementary modes of production – the result normally being a kind of equilibrium. When conditions become unfavorable, however – as in periods of drought – 'specialization in the system at large declines, so that fewer people specialize in either mode of production, as adaptive strategies become more varied to cope with environmental change' (Bates and Lees 1977: 827–29). Richard and Long apply the model of 'despecialization' to Palestinian EB IV, arguing that this period is in continuity with the more 'specialized' EB III economy, but that it represents a shift along a continuum, i.e., toward a 'mixed-subsistence' strategy.

One current archaeological project in Jordan – the

Plate 5 Typical domestic shelter at Be'er Resisim; note intact doorway, two roof pillars, benches, hearths, etc. (photograph: Jonathan Kline)

Madeba Plains project, which has been in the field since 1968 – is deliberately testing models that seek to comprehend long-term cycles of what Oystein LaBianca (1990) calls 'intensification-abatement', i.e., constantly changing shifts between urban and nomadic, agricultural and pastoral strategies. Although this project has turned up few EB IV remains, LaBianca shows that the Transjordanian plateau from earliest to modern times reflects a basically 'mixed agro-pastoral' economy that has exhibited an almost infinite variety of permutations, as the population adapted to the endemic insecurity of this area. I would suggest that this perspective, similar to Richard and Long's 'specialization-despecialization' model, allows a truly processual approach – one that helps us to place the EB IV period within the larger settlement-history of Transjordan.

The latest, and to date the most ambitious, synthesis of the EB IV period in Palestine looks at the area as a whole. Again, its theoretical model is based largely on new data from Transjordan, some of it documenting more sedentary occupation there. Gaetano Palumbo (1991) accepts the model of pastoral-nomadism for the Negev-Central Hills complex, but rejects it for other regions, especially Transjordan. He also disavows the 'specialization-despecialization' model of Bates and Lees as adopted by Richard and Long (above). Instead, he looks to Leon Marfoe's (1979) emphasis on the *variety* of socio-economic responses that are possible for Palestine's largely rural population. Marfoe describes the Middle Eastern peasant farmer from an ethnographic perspective:

> Economically, his choices have been to diversify his subsistence base by practicing a mix of strategies; combining both agriculture and pastoralism; to shift toward one strategy or the other as necessary and to avoid investments on his own and instead to regard the urban elite as the source of credit (1979: 8).

Palumbo mentions 'ruralization' several times, but he does not develop it into a full-scale model (as I have

suggested elsewhere; Dever 1992). For Palumbo, periods of crisis, like EB IV, tend not to exclude some perennial groups within society – 'pastoral nomads, semi-nomads, peasants, villagers, and urban dwellers' – but to *heighten* their interrelationships. Thus Palestine in EB IV undergoes not 'despecialization' but rather:

> the 'ruralization' of some elements of the urban component, the dispersion of village dwellers into smaller productive units (farms or hamlets) at a domestic level of production, the adoption of a mode of production more oriented toward pastoralism [that] could have been accompanied by a corresponding sedentarization of nomadic groups which could have taken advantage of a weakened and disappearing urban power, or forced by a decrease in agricultural surplus to practice their own farming (1991: 131).

Palumbo concludes by stating that the contrast between EB II–III and EB IV is not that of the 'desert' and the 'sown', (as I once suggested, somewhat facetiously), not a contrast between nomads and sedentary peoples, but a contrast between urban and rural societies. 'EB IV marks the period when the urban society had to surrender, in favor of rural society's adaptive capabilities' (1991: 134).

In these conclusions, Palumbo is following two other members of the 'Arizona school', Steven Falconer and Alexander Joffe. Falconer's (1987) dissertation, entitled 'Heartland of Villages: Reconsidering Early Urbanism in the Southern Levant', argues that the long-term social transformations of Palestine and Transjordan have involved the superimposition of fortified towns on a more typically 'ruralized landscape' of economically diversified villages. (The contrast, of course, is between Palestine and Robert Adam's 'heartland of *cities*' in Mesopotamia.) Joffe's dissertation (1991a), entitled 'Settlement and Society in Early Bronze I and II Canaan', also characterizes Palestine's unique cultural history in terms of its distinctive geopolitical situation and ecological constraints. Because of *scalar differences* in comparison with Egypt and Mesopotamia, Palestine is 'different': its natural and cultural landscape 'preadapted' it to evolve in a minimalist fashion, based on small-scale institutions. And the recurring pattern is that of socio-economic disintegration and reintegration, as in EB IV.

However applicable the newer models above may be to Transjordan, virtually every commentator (even Palumbo) still agrees with my original insistence on the distinctiveness and significance of 'regionalism' in EB IV Palestine overall. Thus the newer models, no matter how applicable to Transjordan, may have less relevance for most parts of Western Palestine. There, the newer data on settlements (apart from the continuing documentation of cemeteries) appearing since 1980, consist largely of a few more Negev encampments like Be'er Resisim; a handful of partially sedentary sites around Jerusalem and in the north; and further survey data on areas previously known,

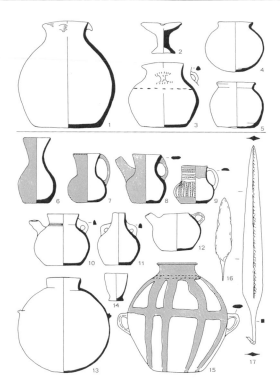

Figure 5   Diagnostic ceramic and metallic types of Families N, NC. Scale = 1.5

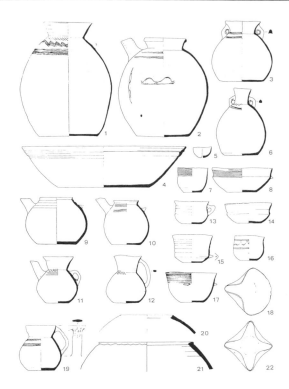

Figure 7   Diagnostic ceramic types of Family S. Scale = 1.5

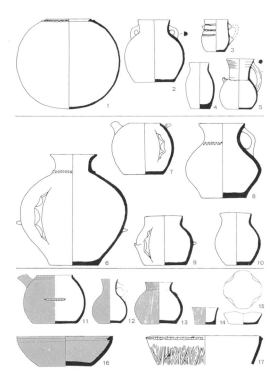

Figure 6   Diagnostic ceramic types of Families CH, J, TR. Scale = 1.5

principally the hill country north and south of Jerusalem.[21]

In the latter area, Finkelstein (1991) cites a total of some 49 EB IV settlement sites plus 42 cemeteries in the Central Hills (i.e., Samaria and Judea), based on recent surveys. That number is in contrast to 116 sites in the Early Bronze Age and 248 in the Middle Bronze Age. Furthermore, virtually all the EB IV sites are small, unwalled villages – many of them one-period sites. As Finkelstein observes quite correctly, both the EB IV settlement type and pattern of distribution mark a 'drastic change' from the urban Early and Middle Bronze Age periods (1991: 42).

> The urban centres disappeared, and the population consisted of rural groups living in small villages and a large component of pastoralists . . . Hence the various groups moved toward the middle of the agricultural/pastoral continuum . . . the IB [our EB IV] population subsisted by means of dry farming/animal husbandry, with no large-scale orchard activity (1991: 43).

As a result of these surveys, Finkelstein (1991: 44) agrees by and large with my view that the Negev EB IV sites were indeed occupied by semi-nomadic pastoralists who migrated seasonally up into the Central Hills, camped there, and buried their dead in the many large cemeteries known in that region. For the EB IV period *overall*, however, Finkelstein (1989) had already adopted a model that he termed 'multi-morphism' (as opposed to the 'dimorphism' of Rowton, myself, and others), while accepting the major tenets of Bates and Lees' 'specialization-despecialization' model. He concludes that, as a result of the socio-economic collapse at the end of EB III 'the outcome [in EB IV] was a society composed mainly of rural communities, and a much larger pastoral component' (1989: 136). Finkelstein would thus seem to agree largely with the overall view being advanced here (see further below).

The only other area of western Palestine where recent survey and excavation activities have prompted a treatment of larger EB II–EB IV settlement patterns and an attempt at a synthesis of EB IV socio-economic structure, is northern Palestine – particularly the Jezreel Valley area. For this area Douglas Esse's *Subsistence, Trade, and Social Change in Early Bronze Age Palestine* (1991) is a masterly blend of sophisticated theory and new data; of multi-disciplinary approaches; and of long-term settlement-history. Esse suggests that throughout the third millennium BCE in Palestine, including EB IV, the entire spectrum of subsistence modes was represented, from pastoral to sedentary agricultural and even fully urban. It is the diachronic analysis of settlement patterns, however, that shows how dramatically the *balance* could and did shift (Esse 1991: 173).

> The relative proportion of agricultural to pastoral sites was completely reversed between EB II–III and EB IV/MB I . . . and the pastoral end of the economy became dominant, not only in northern Palestine but also in the rest of the country. This second shift in settlement patterns was more radical than the first [i.e., from EB I to EB II] (Esse 1991: 175).[22]

Towards a sympathetic and synthetic portrait of EB IV social structure

Initial observations

An initial response to the above critiques and revisions of the pastoral-nomadic model would be to note that each of these scholars is basing him or herself primarily on their own sites and surveys. Most of these are in Jordan, where there is indeed considerable evidence of sedentism – more so than in Western Palestine (as I had predicted all along). Yet the evidence must be carefully assessed in each case, so as not to obscure what are still clearly regional assemblages with their own peculiarities, while at the same time placing these local groups in the larger cultural complex of Palestinian EB IV. Thus we must point out that Falconer and Magness-Gardiner's small site of Tell el-Ḥayyāt was undoubtedly a settled agricultural village (as is nearby Tell 'Abu en-Ni'aj); but the EB IV levels (Ph. 6) have produced no architecture whatsoever. Helms bases himself on his own extensive sedentary settlement of Umm Hammad esh-Sharqiya, yet insists on seeing the EB IV people as

'invading semi-nomads'. Richards' Kh. Iskander is admittedly large enough, sufficiently well developed, and even adequately fortified to qualify for the designation 'urban'; but thus far Iskander is *unique* and so can hardly serve as a type-site for EB IV.[23] In particular, Richards' notion of EB IV as a 'chiefdom' must be rejected (see further below).

The discovery of a very few true settlement sites in Western Palestine in recent years – like Sha'ar ha-Golan, 'Emeq Refaim, Manaḥat, Dhahr Mirzbaneh, and Efrat – does not change the overall picture of a dispersed pattern of settlement and strongly non-urban character of most of EB IV Palestine. Nor is the picture changed by the addition of survey data on several dozen EB IV sites in the West Bank, since none of these sites has yet been excavated.[24] Certainly, continued research on the hundreds of EB IV sites in the Negev has only confirmed the picture of pastoral-nomadic encampments drawn a decade ago on the basis of Be'er Resisim.[25] Where does all this leave us?

A critique of models

A fundamental point of departure must be a critique, not only of some specific models, but of models in general in archaeology.

Some specific models for EB IV

Of the specific models for EB IV summarized above, we may note here, for example, Richard's rejection of pastoral nomadism in favor of 'specialization-despecialization'. First, the model of pastoral nomadism, and the concept of a 'dimorphic society' on which it rested, was never as purely typological or as rigidly dichotomous as Richard contends – not in Rowton's usage, and certainly not in mine. In the original formulation (1980: 56–8) I had stressed:

1. nomadism as part of a socio-economic *continuum*;
2. a *mixed*, even partly sedentary, economy in EB IV that combines seasonal herding with dry farming and limited trade;
3. the necessity for having *some* fully sedentary sites to provide the 'urban' morpheme of the dimorphic society to contrast with the better-known 'village/pastoral' morpheme;
4. the probability that in time other, more sedentary, 'regional assemblages' would be found to *complement* the picture of 'Family S' in the Hebron hills and the Negev; and
5. the recognition that despite drastic changes, as for instance in settlement patterns, EB IV represents a *continuity* with EB III in many subsystems (cf. ceramic production and metallurgy).

More general models applied to Palestinian EB IV

This brings us to a critique of the broader socio-economic models sometimes applied to Palestinian EB IV, and even of the notion of 'models' generally in archaeology.

Many have noted Fried (1967) and Service's (1962, 1971, 1975) scheme of neo-evolutionary 'stages' of socio-economic and cultural development, generally arranged into 'egalitarian', 'band' and 'tribe' configurations, then more 'stratified' (or 'complex') levels of 'chiefdom' and finally of 'state' development. To be sure, bands, tribes and states are sufficiently attested in the historical and ethnographic literature that they can serve as useful categories in the analysis of archaeological data from the remote past. 'Chiefdoms', however, pose a problem. Service himself (1971) later abandoned these rather rigid categories. And in the past 20 years, as the literature on chiefdoms has proliferated, critics have raised many objections.

Renfrew (1974) developed a 'trait-list' of 20 features of chiefdoms; but Tringham (1974) has argued that most of these are unrecognizable in the archaeological record, or else apply to other aspects of social structure that are much less amenable to archaeological investigation than techno-environmental data. Peebles and Kus's 'cybernetic model' (1977) reduced the 'trait-list' to five features, all of which perhaps would be testable archaeologically; but none of the five criteria would apply to Palestinian EB IV, or would suggest that the chiefdom model is applicable there.

Carneiro's chiefdom as 'an autonomous political unit comprising a number of villages or communities under the permanent control of a paramount chief' (1981: 45) simply cannot be documented anywhere in EB IV Palestine – not even at his level of 'minimal chiefdom'. Furthermore, it is unclear to many scholars just how Carneiro's 'chiefdom' differs from a nascent 'state'. Finally, as for Carneiro's 'mechanism that brought about chiefdoms', namely war (or conscription), there is no evidence whatsoever for that at the end of Palestinian EB III and the beginning of EB IV. Of Carneiro's (1981: 53, 54) four principal features that might be diagnosable archaeologically – 1. monumental architecture; 2. ceremonial centers; 3. differentiated burials; and 4. a rank-size analysis of settlement types that would indicate some sort of subordination – the first two traits are totally absent, the third is barely present, and the fourth is thus far unmeasurable. T.K. Earle (1987, 1989) has dealt extensively with chiefdoms, especially in the New World, but cautions that models assuming 'linear causality' have been outgrown, and that simplistic syntheses are easily refuted (1989: 87). Frank Hole (1991: 323) argues that not even highly specialized Susa was stratified or centralized in the way that the chiefdom model would require. Robert Adams concludes with regard to 'chiefdoms', as applied to Ancient Near Eastern societies, that 'all this could well be an accurate description, but once again the archaeological – and somewhat too late to be directly relevant, the textual – evidence is less than conclusive' (Yoffee and Gowgill 1988: 24 and see Levy, Chapter 14, this volume).

Archaeological models generally

Of socio-cultural models generally in archaeology, we should observe the following. Models are often misunderstood; unlike theories or hypotheses, which relate in some way to the real world, models are intellectual *abstractions*, designed simply to manipulate data. Models are of limited usefulness because they are merely heuristic devices – perhaps necessary in order to organize data and facilitate analysis, but not an end in themselves. Adams (1988: 28) remarks of all theoretical hierarchical models: 'Available models tend to be essentially static. As such, they lead to a rather contrived view of change as an abrupt succession of equilibrium states.' For this reason, George Cowgill (Yoffee and Cowgill 1988: 245) remarks that often 'we have the specious clarity of the grand abstract schemes, clear because so bare of detailed and differentiated implications for different specific sets of circumstances'. Joseph Tainter goes even further: models, especially evolutionary theories, are general categories, which 'not only have little meaning, but . . . are of little utility in monitoring variation and change' (1977: 331). Tainter himself (1978; also 1988) points the way toward the assessment of social change by using a statistical and probabilistic approach to complexity in particular ancient societies.[26]

In summary

Finally, of the present debate about Palestinian EB IV specifically, it must be said that the proliferation of models is sometimes self-serving; needlessly contentious; and tends toward fragmentation, rather than increasing and integrating our empirical knowledge of the past, as models are supposed to do. A point of diminishing returns is reached with Finkelstein's 'multi-morphic' society, which seems to me not an advance, but a counsel of despair. Endlessly multiplying factors in social change, particularizing rather than generalizing, means trying to say everything and ending by being able to say nothing. As Palumbo (1987: 47) notes, even study of the social structure of contemporary nomadic peoples in terms of such categories as 'egalitarian' often results in 'mere banality'.

A trial formulation of EB IV

If no single model is adequate, we can nevertheless say something about larger patterns of social structure in Palestine in EB IV. A number of points need to be made.

1. Palestine in this period does not, as Richard thinks (above), constitute a 'chiefdom', as for instance the Late Chalcolithic period may be (Levy 1986). It lacks such essential features as 'central places'; a managed redistribution system; cult centers and elaborate ritual; and evidence of a ranked society.
2. The 'tribal' model, however, is reasonably well suited to most of Palestine in EB IV – certainly to the Negev-Central

Hills area, and probably also to the Transjordanian plateau. Evidence supporting such a 'tribal' model is well documented and would include: a dispersed pattern of non-urban settlement; a largely pastoral nomadic subsistence system and social structure (as at Be'er Resisim); and the likelihood that recognizable regional assemblages in the material culture reflect mobile, overlapping tribal groups as at Jericho, Jebel Qa'aqir, and many other sites.[27]

3. We may now turn to the rural agricultural villages that are now coming to light, which I have recently incorporated into a tentative model alongside pastoral nomadism that I simply term 'ruralism'.[28] Even though these are probably best understood as an outgrowth of 'tribal society', each village is probably still kin-based; groups of villages would then constitute a 'clan-like' conglomerate. The overall social structure, while not entirely 'egalitarian', would be classed as 'segmentary' (acephalous). I have argued elsewhere (Dever 1971, 1973, 1980) that the permanent EB IV villages that we do have are indeed relatively late in the period and represent a stage when pastoral nomads were becoming sedentary (especially in my 'Southern/Sedentary' family, but also farther north). The characterization of the agricultural villages as 'tribal' does not, however, depend upon a presumed earlier evolutionary stage of 'nomadism'.

4. Whatever model we may finally adopt for Palestinian EB IV, the overall phenomenon upon which all commentators must agree is that of 'religionalism', long recognized by most scholars.[29] No other period in the archaeological history of Palestine exhibits such strongly marked, predictable regional assemblages or 'families'. These sharp geographic distinctions surely must have socio-cultural implications.

5. Finally, the description of EB IV social structure as 'tribal' has an additional advantage. This is not a theoretical model, like 'chiefdom', but an *analogy*, based on many actual tribal societies that are known and are exceedingly well documented – historically, ethnographically and, now, archaeologically.[30]

Conclusion

Throughout this chapter, I have eschewed overly-rigid models for elucidating the social structure of EB IV Palestine. Instead, I have stressed the larger phenomenon that I think all models seek to comprehend, even my own recent 'ruralism' model; that is the shift of economic strategies and social organization along a *continuum* – an almost infinite variety of interrelated adaptive responses on a theoretical scale from 'urban' to 'nomadic'. EB IV represents a brief but dramatic shift at the end of EB III, from an urban to a rural and pastoral nomadic pattern of social organization. EB IV is thus but one episode in the long settlement-history of Palestine.[31] As Joffe (1991b: 36,37) puts it:

> The pattern of alternating phases of low-level and higher-level organization, a pattern of socio-political complexity spiralling upwards and downwards around the 'domestic

mode of production', is *the essential characteristic* of social evolution in the southern Levant. When modeling other periods, and in cross-cultural comparisons, these alternating patterns must be taken into account and individual episodes reassessed on that basis. [Emphasis the author's.]

The most fecund approach to understanding such short-term cycles of cultural complexity and change as EB IV is probably that of 'collapse', as several scholars have recently developed that notion (Yoffee and Cowgill 1988; Tainter 1988).[32] In Palestine in EB IV, the centralized political institutions that regulated the flow of goods and services in the urban EB II–III era have broken down. Socio-economic structure has collapsed down to a lower level of integration, where diversified but largely rural and pastoral nomadic strategies will enable the society to survive for more than three centuries, until the urban renaissance in Palestine begins with the Middle Bronze Age, ca 2,000 BCE. With that, the 'Dark Age' ends. Perhaps the 'darkness' was less an aspect of reality than of archaeological myopia. If so, it may be dispelled by more focused, sophisticated, and disciplined fieldwork and research in the generation to come.

Notes

1. The period under discussion is called variously 'MB I' (Albright); 'Intermediate EB MB' (or simply EM MB; Kenyon, British scholars generally, and a few Israelis); and 'EB IV' (this writer and a growing consensus). For the issues, see Dever (1973, 1980) and references there.

2. See Dever (1980); for other models, see below. Periodic overviews of the EB IV period will be found in Dever (1970, 1971, 1973, 1980, 1992b); Oren (1973); Finkelstein (1989); Palumbo (1991).

3. In Palestinian archaeology *generally* (not simply for EB IV), there has been little awareness to date of the emphasis on 'social archaeology' that emerged elsewhere in archaeology 20 years ago (see below, n. 5). See, however, Dever (1985b, 1992b); Levy (1986); Kochavi, Kasher and Bunimowitz (1988); Meyers and Meyers (1989); Esse (1991).

4. For a critique of the 'Biblical archaeology' movement, see Dever (1985a) and full references there. 'Biblical archaeology' is now *passé* as a putative *academic* discipline; it remains what it was in the beginning, either a dialogue between two professional disciplines, or else merely an amateur enterprise.

5. For an orientation to social archaeology, see especially Clark (1939); Renfrew (1974, 1984); Redman (1978; see especially the chapter 'Social Archaeology: The Future of the Past'); Watson, LeBlanc and Redman (1984; 233–75). See also n. 3 above.

6. The literature on General Systems Theory is vast, but for orientation and examples of its use in Palestinian archaeology see Dever (1989, 1992a) and references there.

7. See, for instance, Brown (1971); Tainter (1978); O'Shea (1984); and especially the review and critique in Chapman, Kinnes, Rendsberg (1981) and Dever (1987). Add now Palumbo (1991) and references there.

8. For the materials from Jericho, see Kenyon (1960, 1965); for

Jebel Qa'aqir, see Dever (1972, 1981); Gitin (1975); Smith (1982); London (1985, 1987); Horwitz (1989b). For bibliography on other and more recent cemetery sites, see for Western Palestine, Dever (1992b); Finkelstein (1991). For Transjordan, see Palumbo (1991); Palumbo and Peterman (1993) and full references there.

9. Palumbo (1991) provides the latest and most comprehensive synthesis of EB IV, but it is written largely from the perspective of Transjordan (below). Palumbo's principal contention that elite social status at Jericho is reflected in the flexed burials is an interesting suggestion, but it does not seem entirely convincing. Why *flexed* burials? What would be the connection with status? Other factors in these variables may be involved, as Palumbo (1987: 47) himself notes in other connections.

10. For references on Jebel Qa'aqir, see n. 8 above.

11. Kenyon (1960: 180–85) had already advanced the idea that her differing assemblages, or 'tomb groups', at Jericho could be correlated with basically 'tribal' entities. She did not, however, elaborate on this theory, or document it with general bibliography and ethnographic data on pastoral nomadism. For the latter, see Dever (1977, 1980); Bates and Lees (1977); Prag (1984, 1985); Castillo (1987); Finkelstein and Perevolotsky (1990), all with references to wider literature.

12. See Dever (1971: 208, 1972: 232). The evidence consists of 1. regularly spaced groups of contemporary tombs; 2. clear indications from weather of tool-marks of summer-only usage; 3. specially prepared features that are not in fact employed by those using the tombs, such as lamp and body niches.

13. These distinctive 'bottles', characteristic of tombs in my Central Hills/Jericho families, also occur sporadically in domestic contexts; see Dever 1972: 233. This simply underlines the *overlap* of tomb and domestic assemblages, as expected (*contra* the oft-repeated statements of some scholars).

14. For the view that the Palestinian painted and wheelmade 'calciform' vessels are Syrian imports, see Dever (1980: 46, 47, 50–2); and contrast Tadmor (1978: 20), who is noncommital.

15. For Be'er Resisim, see Cohen and Dever (1978; 1979; 1981); Dever (1985b).

16. For orientation to the literature on 'rank-size' hierarchies – usually three- or even four-tiered in urban societies – see Paynter (1985).

17. It would seem obvious that the architectural plan of individual units and overall village-town layout – i.e., the conception and use of *space* – could be expected to reflect social values and social structure. For the explicit rationale, however, see Chang (1968); Hodder and Orton (1976); Redman (1978); Vita-Finzi (1978); Hodder (1985: 34–54; 129–34); Trigger (1989: 279–88). Willey (1953: 1), who pioneered settlement pattern studies, says that such analyses are 'a strategic starting point for the functional interpretation of archaeological cultures . . . they reflect the environment, the level of technology on which the builders operated, and various institutions of social action and control which the culture intended.' Structuralists in recent archaeology, as expected, have made good use of this notion, following Levi-Strauss and others. Obviously, however, *much* more data will be needed than that in my (1985b) study of the architecture of one village at Be'er Resisim.

18. On the proposed chronological sequence of my 'families' see Dever (1971, 1980: 40–5); but note (1974: 46) that from the beginning I have allowed for the possibility that these regional assemblages were more *geographical* than chronological, that perhaps they all not only overlapped but were largely contemporary. Recent critics like Richard and Long (nd) and Palumbo (1991) have overlooked this point.

19. For the new 'Family AZ', see Palumbo and Peterman (1993). I am not fully convinced, however, that this 'family', which overlaps considerably with my Family TR, deserves a separate designation.

20. See Thompson (1975, 1979); but cf. the sharp critiques in Dever (1980: 56); Prag (1984); Palumbo (1991: 18).

21. Excavated EB IV sites with sufficient evidence to characterize them as 'permanently settled agricultural villages' are so few that they may be enumerated: Beth-yerah; Sha'ar ha-Golan; Tel Yosef (Murhan); Manahat; Tel Abu en-Ni'aj; Tell Umm Hammad esh-Sharqiya; Iktanu; Jericho; Kh. Iskander; Bâb edh-Dhrâ'; Wâdi ed-Daliyeh; Dhahr Mirzbâneh; 'Ein Yael/'Emeq Refaim; Ephrat; Ma'abaroti; Lachish; Tell Beit Mirsim. The above constitute less than 2 percent of the 1200 known EB IV sites. Obviously we do not include in this total EB IV sites that are known through survey, since sherd scatters may indicate only seasonal occupation, not a true 'settlement'. The most recent synthesis of Gophna (1992) places too much stress, in my opinion, on the relatively few true settlement sites; but even he admits that most of the villages to which he alludes were 'transient settlements' (Gophna 1992: 137).

22. In a recent review of Esse's book (Dever 1994) I have documented how comprehensive and balanced his treatment is.

23. Palumbo (1991: 58–61), followed by Richard and Long (nd), claims that several other EB IV sites in Jordan exhibit city walls; but since these are known only from surface survey and have not been excavated at all, the question must be left open. What is beyond debate is that *no* EB IV site in Western Palestine has a city wall. Har Yeruham and Jebel Qa'aqir have flimsy boundary walls, but these cannot possibly have served defensive purposes.

24. The bibliography on settlement sites discovered since my (1980) survey is too extensive to cite; but full references will be found in Dever (1992b); Cohen (1986); Finkelstein (1991); and especially Palumbo (1991). Cf. n. 21 above.

25. My Co-director at Be'er Resisim, Rudolph Cohen, has since then investigated many other, almost identical EB IV sites in the Negev, one at Nahal Nissana even larger than Be'er Resisim; see Cohen (1986).

26. For his own, perceptive critique of models, see Palumbo (1987: 43–4, 54–6).

27. On 'tribal' groupings and their overlap, see references in n. 11 above.

28. The model of 'ruralism', although not entirely satisfactory, is developed further in Dever (1992b).

29. For references to the significance of 'regionalism' in EB IV, see Amiran (1960); Dever (1971, 1973, 1980); Finkelstein (1991); Palumbo (1991: 129); Palumbo and Peterman (1993).

30. Recent literature on pastoral nomadism is much too vast to cite; but see, for instance, Dever (1977); Castillo (1987); Prag (1984, 1985); Levy (1983); Palumbo (1991); Finkelstein (1991); Finkelstein and Perevolotsky (1990) and references therein to the wider literature.

31. For orientation to recent studies of settlement history, see the references in n. 17 above.

32. The newer 'collapse' model has been applied fruitfully several times to Mesopotamia (e.g., Yoffee in Yoffee and Cowgill (1988: 44–68); Adams (1988); but thus far not to Palestine except for the EB III–IV period and the Late Bronze/Iron I horizon (Dever 1989, 1992a).

18

THE DAWN OF INTERNATIONALISM – THE MIDDLE BRONZE AGE

David Ilan

The polemics of nomenclature and chronology: what was and what is the Middle Bronze Age?

Of all the periods examined in the present volume, this and the preceding period have been the greatest focus of nomenclatural polemic. It is not only a question of semantics; our terminology reflects our cultural paradigm, and our interpretations and explanations of the archaeological record.

Since it was first recognized as a chrono-cultural entity by Albright (1932, 1933), the Middle Bronze Age's urban character has always been cited as its hallmark (e.g., Dever 1987; Mazar 1990: 174). This new urbanism was observed with such vivid innovations as wheel-made pottery, bronze tools and weapons, scarab seals, epigraphic evidence, massive earthen rampart fortifications, triple-entry gateways, monumental architecture, intramural burial, international trade, settlement heirarchy, and greater political and social integration and ranking (see the material culture table in Figure 2). Thus, when an excavated MB stratum is juxtaposed with a previous Intermediate Bronze Age stratum the differences appear striking.

Until a decade or so ago, this stark stratigraphic contrast led most archaeologists to posit a periodization that assumed more or less rapid cultural changes wrought by exogenous forces – most often in the form of immigrating populations, the Amorites – where each chronological phase was ushered in by a new Amorite group (e.g., Albright 1933; Kenyon 1966; Mazar 1968; Dever 1976). This paradigmatic reconstruction of culture change, though credible in some respects, is now considered by many to be a simplistic misinterpretation of the archaeological evidence, (e.g. Gerstenblith 1983: 123–6; Marfoe 1979; Tubb 1983; Ilan in press a). The forces of culture change in Canaan in the Middle Bronze Age were, as they almost always are, a complex combination of exogenous and endogenous factors, with different inputs asserting themselves to varying extents at different times and in different parts of the land. (The geographical term 'Canaan' is adopted here because it has a generic inclusive meaning and predates more politically sensitive terms such as 'Palestine', 'Israel' and 'the Holy Land'. Furthermore, religious texts from Ebla now indicate that some form of the name existed by the third millennium BC [Matthiae 1981: 187].) Certainly, individuals and groups of people with foreign origins can be detected in the archaeological record using defined criteria (see below), while certain other developments – political integration and the evolution of fortifications for example – can be attributed to more local factors such as peer-polity interaction (see Window, p. 316).

The Middle Bronze Age for the most part evinces cultural processes more evolutionary than revolutionary, and pivotal historical events are not easily discerned in the archaeological record. Thus, subdivision of the Middle Bronze Age is less a question of substance than one of convenience and, with this in mind, the straightforward tripartite nomenclature suggested by Gerstenblith (1983: 2–3) and Dever (1987: 149–50, with a summary of terminological alternatives) seems utilitarian, if somewhat artificial:

MB I (circa 2000–1800 BC)
MB II (circa 1800–1650 BC)
MB III (circa 1650–1500 BC).

All the same, our discipline is plagued by a confusion and overlapping of cultural and chronological terms. The Middle Bronze Age is a period, not a culture. Material culture features of the kind mentioned above can be singled out to distinguish its peak from the peak of the preceding Intermediate Bronze Age (IB), (so termed because it represents a significant socio-economic, and perhaps cultural, break with what preceded and what followed), but these features appeared in a non-coincidental fashion, a phenomenon schematically expressed by Figure 3 (and see below).

Does the evidence justify the notion of at least marginal contemporaneity of material culture types that characterize the Intermediate Bronze Age and the Middle Bronze Age? The Peer Polity Interaction (PPI) model adopted here suggests that processes of emulation create cultural homologies at a rate faster than can usually be detected in the archaeological record (Renfrew 1986: 7–8).

The mudbrick gate of Tel Dan (photograph: © A. Biran)

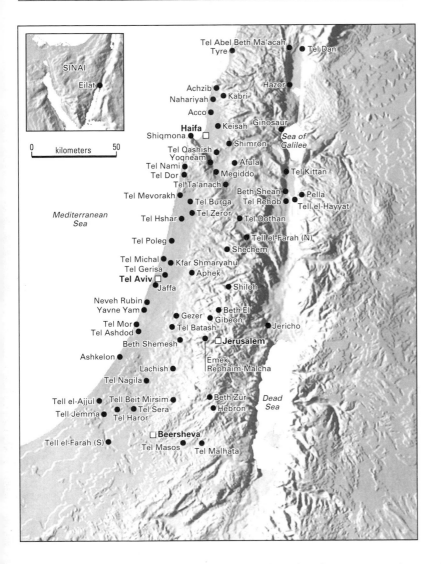

Figure 1 Map showing key MB settlement sites in Canaan

However, the PPI model operates on a regional level and leaves room for a flexible frontier; the interactions occurring outside that region, beyond the frontier, can be of another kind. The lowlands and highlands of Canaan show such a dichotomy, though both exhibit their own internal version of PPI concurrent with the contact that undoubtedly existed between them.

The above discussion brings to fore what should be a fundamental goal for the processual study of the Middle Bronze Age: the construction of a spatially sensitive absolute chronology on the basis of radiocarbon dates. It is considered axiomatic that, given the problems of standard deviation and calibration, radiocarbon dates are superfluous for Near Eastern contexts after ca 2000 BC, since relative chronology tied into Egyptian historical data can provide closer and more reliable dating. However, while largely true for the southern coastal plain of the later MB (to which time a number of Second Intermediate royal

name scarabs can be ascribed, [Weinstein 1981: 8–10]), this perception can no longer be taken for granted when:

1. the infrequency and *terminus post* nature of Egyptian or Egyptianizing finds (scarabs for example) is taken into account;
2. so many (five) alternative chronological schemes are current (Weinstein 1991: 110);
3. so many cultural facets appear to be regional and differentiated in scope (e.g., Kempinski 1983: 181–96; Ilan 1991).

Until a wide array of radiocarbon dates becomes available from successive MB stata at sites distributed over the various regions of Canaan, our thinking must display both vertical and horizontal dimensions when constructing our models of culture change. As we shall see, late Intermediate Bronze (IB) (Early Bronze IV, see Dever this volume, Chapter 17) assemblages, of the frontier regions in

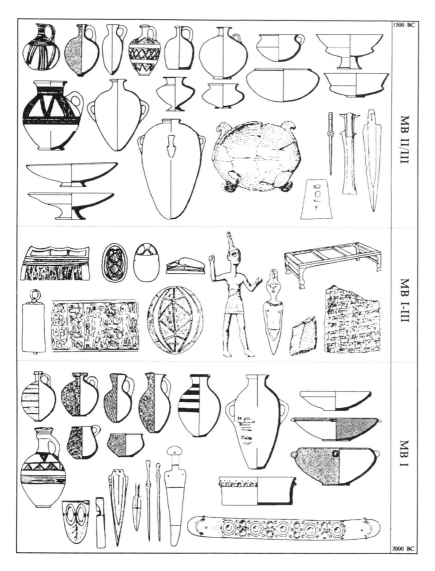

Figure 2   Material culture table

particular, are actually contemporary with those of the early MB.

Amorites and Canaanites: the question of cultural origins

In the previous section it was suggested that Middle Bronze Age culture formation was the product of both exogenous and endogenous inputs (see Figure 4). The real job is to attribute cultural features to their sources and to identify the mechanism by which these features arrived and developed.

As noted above, until the late 1970s archaeologists working in the Holy Land utilized the incursionary model with little introspection. Ever since Childean diffusionism went out of fashion with Renfrew's (e.g., 1973) refutation of its chronological underpinnings, it has become unpopular to suggest the movement of peoples as a mechanism of culture change, and most recent research is endogenously oriented in this respect (e.g., Bunimovitz 1989; Gerstenblith 1983; Marfoe 1979; Tubb 1983). But the pendulum may have swung too far towards the opposite extreme; the real issue is our ability to discern population movements in the archaeological record using explicit criteria and stated assumptions.

Several criteria, when considered together, may provide grounds for positing immigration into Canaan from or via Syria in the Middle Bronze Age; each phenomenon is observable in the latter region prior to its appearance in Canaan (Ilan in press a):

1. The construction, rapid deterioration and intentional blocking up of MB I mudbrick arched gate at Tel Dan (opening photograph, this chapter), Acco and Ashkelon.

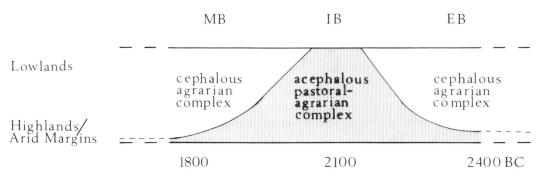

Figure 3   Schematic representation of sociocultural change from the EB to the MB (based on E. Marcus [pers. comm.] and Marfoe 1979)

These gates embody a new architectural technique maladapted to a wetter environment and quickly abandoned. Better alternative materials – lumber and stone – were readily available.

2. New mortuary practices, having precedence in neighboring areas, appearing as a supplement, not a replacement, to those traditionally in use (see below).

3. Osteological evidence showing morphometric differences beyond expected anatomical variability within one particular population (Arensberg 1973; Smith, this volume).

4. Locally made 'Monochrome Painted Cream Ware' pottery derived from a style, technique and technology with precedence in northen Syria (Ilan and Yellin, forthcoming). Its distribution is highly localized in the Tel Dan region, with just a few pieces found further south in the Jordan Valley.

Whether or not the postulated newcomers from the north can be called 'Amorites' or not is another question (on the Amorite thesis see Dever 1977 and references therein); it is notoriously difficult to correlate material culture with ethnicity, even in modern day cultures (Renfrew and Bahn 1991: 167–9, 407–9; Hodder 1982; Kramer 1977; and specifically regarding the Amorites, Gerstenblith 1983: 124). The term 'Amorite' itself was a sort of nebulous, catch-all designation that included people of different classes and from different regions, in fact probably more than one ethnic group (Kamp and Yoffee 1980). While it may not be wrong to call the group(s) that immigrated into Canaan 'Amorites', it probably does not mean much either. In any event, from personal names registered in the few texts found locally, it seems clear that at least one other major ethnic group, the Hurrians, was also present in Canaan, at least by the middle of the MB (Anbar and Na'aman 1986-1987: 10–11).

Other facets of MB material culture that show precedence in Syria and Mesopotamia indicate, at the very least, a transfer of information, if not people: e.g., lowland settlements surrounded by earthen embankments (Gophna 1984: 30–31), triple-entry gates, casemate walls and *hofhaus* domestic architecture (Kaplan 1971). The most visible artifact type – pottery – reflects an even more complex picture. Alongside the locally developed types, various other ceramic forms are present that have been accorded origins in either inland Syria or the Levantine littoral (Beck 1985). Such forms include types and techniques that show a clear EB pedigree, inferring that EB 'ceramic ideas' were retained in Syria and reintroduced into Canaan in the MB I. The underlying question is, once again, by what mechanism? The indications of population movement, together with the evidence for wide-ranging trade connections, PPI, and specialist center production, (discussed below) should lead us to the conclusion that the emulation and distribution of pottery styles, craft traditions and architectural techniques can be linked to all of these; in other words, both endogenous and exogenous factors were at work (cf. Cherry and Renfrew 1986: 152). The key to elucidating the operative patterns of exchange lies in provenience analysis using techniques such as neutron activation analysis (NAA) and petrography (e.g., Knapp 1989; Ilan and Yellin forthcoming). When a sufficient number of studies are made over a large, contiguous region, explicit patterns of interaction will emerge.

Intensification and integration: what settlement patterns tell us

The lowlands

The changing settlement patterns of the Middle Bronze Age reflect socio-political change largely brought on by endemic forces. The earliest occurrence of MB I material culture is apparently to be found in the lowlands (see Figure 1) – the coastal plain, and the Jezreel and Upper Jordan Valleys – from a non-urban but at least semi-sedentary context. Lowland sites of the early MB I, such as Ashkelon, Aphek, Tel Ifshar, Tel Nami, Tel Mevorakh, Akko, Kabri and Tel Dan, are typically founded at or near karstic springs, or in places with high groundwater, in areas rich in fertile soil for dry farming or localized, small-scale irrigation.

Why did settlement intensify from the IB to the

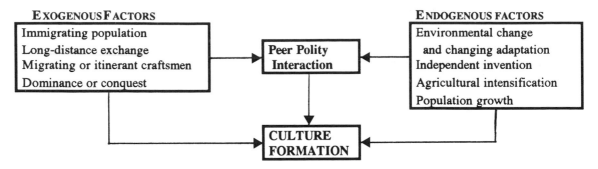

Figure 4   Some potentail inputs for Middle Bronze Age culture formation (based on Renfrew 1986)

developed MB? Marfoe's modified version of the 'frontier model', (recently utilized effectively for succeeding periods by Finkelstein (1988a) and Bunimovitz (1989), suggests 'that the periodic oscillations between phases of political growth and interludes of decline were symptoms of a process wherein the rural hinterlands of the city formed a 'reservoir' that was alternately realigned into rural communities of sedentary farmers and tribal segments of pastoral nomads' (Marfoe 1979: 9). The spring-studded lowlands are inherently preferable for dry farming and once the marginal return on cultivation and sedentary occupation of the lowlands was perceived as greater than that of the highlands, the realignment into rural/urban society began anew. Because the ineffective but resource-draining political structures of the EB were gone, there was, initially at least, little risk in the re-establishment of permanent settlement, particularly where the establishing polity laid territorial claim on the prospective plot. Almost all the earliest MB I settlements show either low-intensity IB remains or IB occupation nearby (Gophna and Portugali 1988: Figures 6–7). Other factors leading to increased sedentarization may have included exchange ties evolving out of developing overland (Gerstenblith 1983: 109–26) and maritime (Gophna 1984: 31; Marcus 1991) trade, perhaps hinted at in the Sinuhe account (e.g., Rainey 1972).

Extensive survey of the coastal plain south of Mt. Carmel (Figure 5) has revealed a number of fortified urban sites more than one hectare in size related hierarchically to smaller satellites (by a ratio of 1:3.3 for both MB I and II/III; Broshi and Gophna 1986; Gophna and Beck 1981; Gophna and Portugali 1988). Table 1 is a rank-size breakdown for the MB I and II/III respectively.

Besides testifying to central place function and hierarchical organization for both the MB I and II/III time frames, these data disclose an intricate temporal dynamic as well, evoked by the fact that only 27 out of 100 counted sites were settled in both MB I and MB II/III. The tendency to urban agglomeration from MB I to MB II/III is expressed by the lower ratio of small to large sites in the later period and by the discernment of 22 MB I sites not settled in the MB II/III. At least three major fortified

settlements were abandoned by the end of the MB I: Tel Burga, Tel Zeror, and Tel Poleg (Gophna and Portugali 1988: 17–18, 26). An increased elaboration of site ranking may be asserted in the higher proportion of mid-size settlements of between 1.1 and 4.9 ha. in the MB II/III. Such tiered settlement patterns and administrative structures have been recommended as hallmarks of the early state (e.g. Johnson 1972; Wright and Johnson 1975).

In the MB II/III 44 new settlements were established, including major fortified sites at Tels Ashdod, Nagila, Haror, Jaffa, Jemma, Mihal, Mor, Nebi Rubin, Kh. el Rujum, Farah (S.), and Sharia. All but one of these fortified sites were located south of the Yarkon River drainage, on the southern coastal plain. Gophna and Portugali (1988) have inferred that a Malthusian mechanism was at work; population rose faster than agricultural production, neccesitating the cultivation and settlement of new regions. Though not the only possible explanation for settlement expansion, this interesting idea will undoubtedly be tested and elaborated in future research.

Raban (e.g., 1985) and Marcus (1991) have observed that the coastal plain site array is oriented along the various drainages, where estuary sites provide foreland access and gateway services, and large inland sites function more as central places with hinterland access. The two complementary settlement types, and the smaller sites in between, are conceived as belonging to one polity or economic system. The concept of drainage-defined polities and an emphasis on latitudinal as opposed to longitudinal movement points up the importance of maritime interaction in culture formation and change. It is no accident that similar drainage-aligned settlement patterns have been detected by Levy (Chapter 14, this volume) in southern Canaan for the Chalcolithic (though maritime trade was less important), and by Stager (1992) for the EB.

The rank-size data, rapid urbanization, population growth, evidence for economic intensification and the large number of Hyksos royal name scarabs have suggested to some writers the administrative integrity of a united polity in the coastal plain (e.g., Bunimovitz 1989: 47–74). Maritime polities, however, can be highly integrated economically but tend to be small and jealous of their

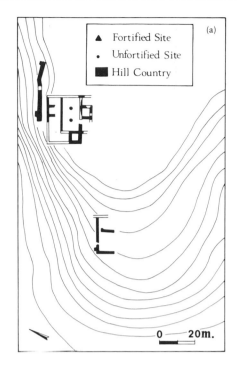

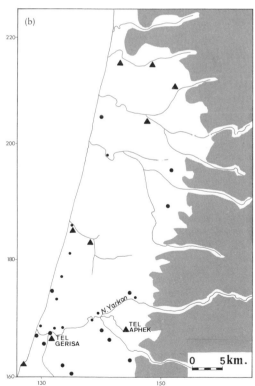

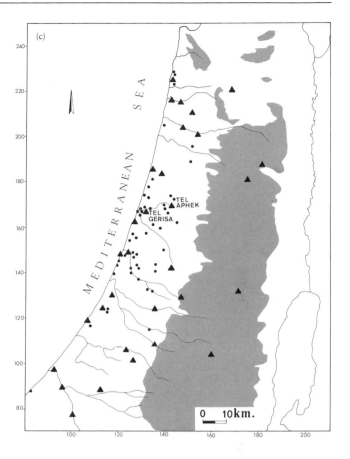

Figure 5 (a) The MB palaces at Tel Aphek, (b) MB settlements along the Yarkon River drainage, and (c) MB settlement in Canaan's southern coastal plain. Adapted from: Beck 1985: Figure 1; Gophna and Ayalon 1980: Figure 14, Gophna and Beck 1981: Figure 1

independence (e.g., Snodgrass 1986). As noted above, a certain degree of political consolidation and realignment did occur, but this docs not imply the unification of the entire littoral. The premise of administrative unity would require – in light of the royal name scarabs – that the political center be Avaris (Tell el-Dab'a in the Nile Delta), which seems a more maximalist notion than the evidence warrants.

While the above discussion on the lowland settlement pattern has dealt mostly with the coastal plain south of the Carmel range, many aspects should be applicable to other lowland regions: the explanation for the initial settlement impulses, the development of rank-size distribution, the expansion into previously unsettled or sparsely settled areas, and the importance of trade whether overland or maritime (cf. Gerstenblith 1983: 21, 125). One particular lowlands anomaly is significant; the average site area in the northern coastal plain and the Hula Valley is several times that of other lowland and highland sites (see Table 2). This is due in part to the burying of smaller sites by colluvial and alluvial deposition (cf. Gal 1991 on precisely this phenomenon in the Jezreel Valley); and less intensive surveying may also be prejudicing the results. But these caveats cannot explain all of the differences. We might conjecture that this tendency toward very large sites is an

Table 1 Rank-size heirarchy of MB settlements in the coastal plain of Israel, south of Mt. Carmel (based on Gophna and Portugali 1988: 26)

Size (ha.)	Number of MB I sites	Percentage of total		Number of MB II/III sites	Percentage of total	
0.1–0.3	33	59.0		31	42.6	
0.4–1.0	4	7.1	66.1	5	6.8	49.4
1.1–4.9	4	7.1		9	12.3	
5.0–9.9	1	1.8	8.9	4	5.5	17.8
10 or more	8	14.3		9	12.3	
unknown*	6	10.7		15	20.5	
Total	56	100.0		73	100.0	

* These are necropoli, generally without clear settlement association.

expression of a more Syrian/Mesopotamian concept of what a city should be, in keeping with a society with greater contact and more affinity to that region.

The highlands

In the highlands the settlement process shows a different tempo, though it must in some way be related to events in the lowlands. The most comprehensive work published to date comes from the central highlands, conveniently (for purposes of comparison) tangent to the southern coastal plain (e.g., Finkelstein 1988–1989; 1992; 1993; Zertal 1992). Finkelstein (1993) counts 248 settlements in the central hill country, but notes problems in isolating the MB I from the later MB (1988–1989: 140–1). Identifiable MB I sites are rare, mostly confined to intermontane valleys, and when datable can be assigned to the late MB I (e.g., Shechem, Tell el-Farah (N.), Jerusalem and Bethel; dating based on comparisons with the coastal plain ceramic repertoire). Broshi and Gophna (1986: 79–82) list 10 MB I sites, many of which (e.g. Tell Beit Mirsim, Gezer, Beth Shemesh) are better associated with the Judean Shephelah. One of four explanations may be put forward to explain the low frequency and apparently late dating of MB settlement in the central highlands:

1. the central hill country was almost completely abandoned in the early MB, perhaps with the resettlement of the lowlands;
2. the settlement regime of the IB experienced a crisis similar to that postulated by Finkelstein (this volume, Chapter 21) and Bunimovitz (this volume, Chapter 19) for the MB–LB transition – one that resulted in an earlier case of 'invisible nomads' who did, however, leave some pottery in a few reused IB tombs;
3. the existing MB pottery – usually dated to the MB II/III – is partly MB I, i.e., a regional facies that later impacts stylistically on the lowlands and continues in the highlands;
4. the material culture associated with the IB continues into the MB I, and is replaced at the same time that mass sedenterization ensues.

The abandonment scenario (1) is unlikely, and the material culture overlap (4) most likely, because demographic continuity with the IB is demonstrated by both ongoing use of IB settlements (particularly in the northern parts), and IB cemeteries such as Ein Samiyeh, Gibeon, Efrata and Khirbet Kirmil that contain MB I material (Finkelstein 1988–1989: 141). Since cemeteries are most often lineage endowed, we should understand the mixed assemblages as reflecting continuous interment by a society which eventually, or periodically, adopted elements of the lowland material culture repertoire. Figure 3 is intended to convey this construct.

By the MB II, small settlements were scattered throughout the central highlands with higher concentrations in the more amenable northern sections. A clustering of small sites occurs around Shilo and Bethel (Finkelstein 1988–1989: Figure 11). The less hospitable western hills were settled and exploited for the first time, apparently on the basis of horticultural specialization, which has been shown to engender and require greater political and social integration (e.g. Marfoe 1979: 20–30). The Malthusian principle has also been applied here, explaining the settlement impulse as being put into motion by excess population in the lowland regions (Finkelstein 1988–1989: 141; and for similar reactions to overpopulation in the Mediterannean world see Braudel 1972: 394–415). A settlement zenith was reached by the seventeenth century BC.

Sometime in the MB III, a number of sites were abandoned, while other sites, apparently central places, were heavily built up. In pointing out these massively fortified settlements' emphasis on storage facilities and cultic appurtences, and their lack of domestic architecture, Finkelstein (1993) has surmised them to be 'the strongholds of chiefs who ruled over large territories with both sedentary and pastoral groups', in which the pastoral element derived from an erstwhile sedentary population. The fact that only two polities – Shechem and Jerusalem – are ever mentioned by MB and LB Egyptian texts suggests to Finkelstein that these strongholds and their surrounding countrysides were under the aegis of large northern and southern dominions ruled by supreme chiefs at Shechem and Jerusalem respectively. An alternative interpretation of the MB III settlement pattern in the central hill country sees the local clustering around Bethel and Shechem as manifesting a more politically fragmented system with smaller polities (Bunimovitz 1989). The latter view invokes the competitive aspect of peer polity interaction – i.e., internecine conflict and its concomitant socio-economic stress – as an explanation for the system's collapse (see below).

Other highland regions are less well understood, though recent surveys of the Galilee show similar patterns and a comparable tempo at a much lower intensity (Gal 1988; and see Broshi and Gophna 1986: Tables 1–2). In the

Table 2   Summary of known Middle Bronze Age sites in Israel (after Broshi and Gophna 1986: 86)

Region		MB I			MB II/III		
		Sites	Area	Ave	Sites	Area	Ave
1	Upper Galilee	7	19.6	2.8	7	19.6	2.8
2	Lower Galilee	4	2.2	0.6	57	34.2	0.6
3	Upper Jordan Valley (Hula Valley)	7	101.1	4.4	7	101.1	14.4
4	Mid and Lower Jordan Valley (including the Beth Shean Valley)	16	13.9	0.9	34	15.8	0.5
5	Jezreel Valley	28	81.2	2.9	20	17.6	0.9
6	Samaria (including the Gilboa and Carmel)	4	10.8	2.7	105	82.6	0.8
7	Judea (including foothills)	9	31.8	3.5	33	82.6	2.5
8	Northern Coastal Plain	6	88.0	14.7	7	93.0	13.3
9	Coastal Plain (south of Carmel)	49	206.5	4.2	65	210.3	3.2
10	Arad and Beersheva Valley	—	—	—	2	3.5	1.8
Total		130	555.1	4.3	337	660.3	2.0

inland foothill zone of the northern Negev, only the Beersheva Valley was irregularly settled – and only in the later part of the MB, perhaps in connection with the east-west trade route that crossed the area (cf. Finkelstein 1988b). In the desert south of the Beersheva Valley, a few small sites yielding no datable artifacts, located in relatively amenable ecological niches, have been dated to the MB by means of radiocarbon (Avner et al. in press).

MB settlement patterns and populations: a summary

Table 2 is a summary of the MB settlement picture. The averages calculated in Table 2 should now be diminished and will require even further reduction in the future since most newly discovered sites are of the lowest rank size. In 1987, Dever (following Kotter 1986 and Mabry 1986) cited 400 known MB sites in the region covered by Table 2, while Broshi and Gophna's summary brings us closer to 500. The new data from the central highlands alone indicates 248 sites (above), suggesting a total number of MB sites at somewhere between 500 and 600. Calculating total population by multiplying total estimated settlement area by the accepted density coefficient of 250 persons per hectare, and taking undiscovered and non-representative areas into account, Broshi and Gophna (1986: 86) have arrived at figures of ca 100,000 for the MB I and ca 140,000 for the MB II/III. Using less explicit criteria, Kempinski (1992c) estimates higher figures for the later floruit: ca 120,000 in the urban centers and ca 80,000 in the rural areas, for a total of ca 200,000.

The dawn of internationalism: patterns of production, exchange and power

Middle Bronze Age Canaan evinces a picture of a society growing in population, intensifying agricultural and craft production, participating in far-flung exchange systems, and attaining over time a multi-tiered settlement hierarchy (below) expanding into new frontiers – in short, a portrayal of increasing socio-political complexity not previously seen in Canaan. Gateways were themselves centers and often of a higher order than non-gateway centers. This system was the result of a long process of political and economic rationalization that began with the first wave of sedentarism in the early MB. Villages and farmsteads always provided the bedrock for higher level socio-political structures, and it was from these that the centers emerged, elaborated and specialized over time. The spatial distribution of power in the mid MB I may have looked something like this:

1. Regional centers and gateways (on gateways and their definition, see Knapp 1989: 145, and references in n. 58).
2. Subregional centers and/or loci of specialist production or service (e.g., cult).
3. Village.
4. Farmstead.

Based on geographical location, rank-size distributions, and evidence for exchange and production (Kotter 1986; Knapp 1989), the spatial distribution and order of power at the peak of complexity in the MB II/III can be described with more detail than is usually attempted (see Figure 6):

1. First order gateway (primarily Hazor and Tell el-Dab'a).
2. Second order gateway (e.g., Ashkelon, Kabri, Pella).
3. Third order gateway (e.g., Masos, Dan, Jericho, Dor, Jaffa).
4. Regional center (e.g., Megiddo, Beth Shean, Shimron, Shechem, Gezer).
5. Subregional center and/or locus of specialist production (e.g., Tell el-Hayyat, Afula, Tel Kittan).
6. Village.
7. Farmstead or hamlet.

It is considered a truism that the largest order settlements are the most complex, dominating their surrounding countryside (e.g., Kotter 1986 and Knapp 1993 for MB

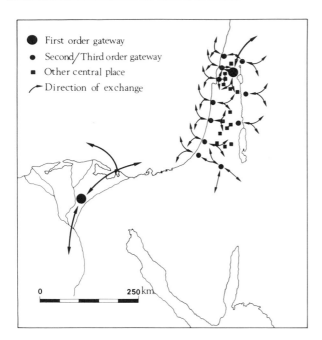

Figure 6 Map of MB central places, gateways and patterns of exchange in the eastern Mediterranean

Canaan). Marfoe's (1979) model of Bronze Age society in southern Syria in its more complex stages seems at least partly applicable for Canaan during most of the Middle Bronze Age – a polarized structure in which the social center (the elite) is focused on the palace-temple institution with a subordinate peasantry on the social periphery. Given the small size of all but the first and second tier gateways, and drawing on analogy provided by the El Amarna texts for the LB system, this elite should be seen as kin-based and as maintaining multiple roles – administrators, military commanders, traders, priests and the like. The gateway communities, however, may have been organized on somewhat different principles, with more scope for private enterprise, merchant guilds, commodity manipulation and capital lending along the lines of the Old Assyrian or Old Babylonian states (e.g., Stohl 1982). The textual evidence from Mesopotamia and Syria reveals that artisans, for example, were affiliated with controlling institutions in the urban centers, and were not freelance itinerants. Moreover, metal specialists seem to have been in short supply in the periphery during the first half of the second millennium BC (e.g., Zaccagnini 1983).

Nevertheless, certain evidence points to a more segmented system of procurement and production, and more local autonomy. The excavations at Tell el-Hayyat – located in the central Jordan Valley (Plate 1), Transjordan near the large tel of Pella – and the sanctuary at Nahariyah (Plate 2a,b), have revealed remains of both metal and ceramic industries active from the MB I through the MB III (Falconer 1987; Falconer and Magness-Gardiner 1989;

Dothan 1965). In both cases metallurgy is associated with cult structures. Tell el-Hayyat is not a higher order site where one would expect a center of production related to a scarce and costly resource. The Nahariyah sanctuary, though probably associated with a nearby urban entity, is also isolated.

The common-ware ceramic production of Tell el-Hayyat is somewhat less surprising; pottery making is/was often a less prestigious specialty associated with lower echelon social units (the family) located at the social and spatial periphery (references in Knapp 1989: 137). But in a ranked, redistributive settlement system, production tends to be rationalized over time, with the output of certain units, even lower echelon ones, achieving market dominance. Maximum efficiency is attained when that ceramic product is brought to the redistributive urban node or market – Pella in the case of Tell el-Hayyat (cf. Falconer 1987; Knapp 1989: 137, 141). The intensive production and far-flung distribution of the distinctive black punctated Tell el-Yahudiyeh Ware juglets (with a manufacturing center in Afula) is a prime example of how complex this initially localized phenomenon could become (Kaplan 1980; Zevulun 1990). It is conceivable that atelier success in the production and marketing of special pottery (or other artifact) types brought such wealth and prestige to the polity that the lower echelon's status was upgraded – by the receipt of gifts and honors to its elite, and greater economic autonomy.

The conclusion to be drawn is that the rural hinterland was more autonomous and more complex in itself than most models have recognized (cf. Falconer and Magness-Gardiner 1989; Renger 1984). The production of lower rank-size class settlements was not neccesarily confined to the domestic/subsistence mode, and a fairly high degree of agricultural surplus administration and redistributive control must be inferred. Furthermore, unlike Mesopotamia, craft specialization was not neccesarily confined to sites of the largest order. Even prestige items were both produced and consumed at the level of at least middle-tier settlements (e.g., weapons and luxury ware pottery).

Nevertheless, more expensive and elaborate goods – metal (especially tin) in particular – were acquired through the longer-range exchange ties of the larger centers (Philip 1989: 206–7). This must have been a preeminent source of power. That the largest centers had a large degree of control over the human resources of their hinterland seems clear in the quantity of labor exploited to construct their ramparts (see Window 1, p. 316).

Northern trade and the role of Hazor

Trade with Syria and regions beyond is vigorously attested to by both texts and, more obliquely, by material culture. The pertinent texts (found at Mari, on the Euphrates River, which naturally plays a central role in them), refer to

Plate 1 Tell el-Hayyat, MBI temple (courtesy of Bonnie Magness-Gardiner, photograph by J. Kline)

Hazor and Laish (Tel Dan). Tin was an important focus of commercial connections (e.g. Dossin 1970), though most of the communications allude to the movements of messengers and the role of ambassadors, without mention of commodities (e.g. Malamat 1960, 1970). Hazor is often indicated together with other kingdoms: Babylon, Eshnuna, Ekallatum, Karana, Qatna, Yamhad, Carcemish, Emar, Ugarit and Kaptara (Crete, Cyprus?). Long-term emissaries from Babylon were resident at Hazor and, in a letter from Shamshi Adad, King of Assyria, to his son Iasmah Adad, ruler of Mari, envoys from Hazor were accorded great status and appointed a special escort from Qatna. If the present excavations at Hazor should reveal an MB archive, references to a foreign traders' colony, like that at Kultepe, will not be unexpected. Material culture connections alone (pottery styles, 'International styles' of weaponry, tin, and others mentioned in the second section), point emphatically to Hazor's role as Canaan's northern gateway in a truly international system of exchange (cf. Gerstenblith 1983: 7–16).

The decline of the Assyrian trade network in the late eighteenth century BC seems to have been brought on by the consolidation of the Old Hittite state and the protectionist economic policies of Babylon (e.g., Yoffee 1981: 12, 24). While trade certainly persevered, peripheral locations such as Canaan must have felt the repercussions of the Assyrian system's demise, especially in the availability of tin and perhaps other metals. There are several indications of this.

1. The metal-containing offering deposits characteristic of the MB I (below) seem to have been curtailed in the MB II/III.
2. It seems that the relative quantity of metal in burial assemblages also diminished from the MB I to the MB II/III. At Tel Dan for example, all the weapons come from MB I or early MB II deposits while the MB II/III interments contain only stick pins (Ilan in press a).

3. A statistical analysis of MB bronzes reveals that tin content shows a constant decline after the MB I; in other words, tin was either less available or not at all, and tin bronzes were being recycled with more locally accessible copper, the result being an increasingly dilute product over time (S. Shalev personal communication).

From the late MB I at the latest, Hazor was the primary state in Canaan. In size (ca 80 ha.) and in complexity it dwarfs all other MB sites; the next largest sites in Canaan, Ashkelon (50 ha.) and Kabri (40 ha.), are roughly half its size. The nearest known sites of comparable scale lie far to the north at Qatna in Syria (though one in the Damascus basin is likely), and far to the south at Tell el-Dab'a in the Egyptian Delta. It is perhaps the only Canaanite site with a true 'acropolis' containing what appears to be a palatial structure (Yadin 1972: 124). A number of temples (or 'chapels', to borrow a term used by Woolley [1976] for a similar array of cultic structures at Ur) apparently dedicated to a variety of deities, together with examples of elite architecture, in both the upper and lower cities, indicate that this is a first order settlement site that clearly belongs to the Syrian/Mesopotamian tradition of central place urbanism (e.g., Johnson 1972). It is at a site of this order where the elite would exhibit true specialization and hierarchy; the roles of merchants, priests, administrators, scribes and the professional military would have taken on a guild-like organization with less merging of functions and more scope for private enterprise. Why did Hazor alone become such an enormous center? There are several possible explanations:

1. increased agricultural productivity, and the commeasurate surpluses, brought on by the adoption of irrigation in the Hula Valley. The dry farming potential of Hazor's catchment could in no way provide the surpluses required to explain its size (cf. Marfoe 1979: 5–12 for similar microenviroments in the Beka'a Valley of Lebanon). Greenberg (1991) ascribes the predominance of EB Tel Dan to hydraulic intensification in a similar scenario.
2. Hazor's role as a 'gateway' or emporium between north and south, east and west (cf. Knapp 1989).
3. a massive influx of new population, perhaps together with an organic command structure already in place (cf. Yadin 1972: 106). It is highly probable that more than one of these factors was operative.

Hazor demonstrates a progressively expanded area, a multiplicity of functions, increasing complexity and political ascendency. It can be suggested that by the MB III nearby Tel Dan had fallen into its orbit as part of an amplified early state module. It would also appear that, unlike the peer-polity relationship that existed between the central highlands and the southern coastal plain, Hazor maintained more control – more of a center–periphery relationship – over its surrounding highland hinterland (Finkelstein 1992: 208). Its territorial extent probably reached deep into the Galilee to the west, the Golan

Plate 2a Selected cultic offerings from the MB temple at Nahariya (photograph: The Israel Museum, Jerusalem)

Heights to the east, the Sea of Galilee to the south and the northern Hula Valley or beyond to the north.

Southern trade and Avaris

Turning south, the archaeological evidence for extensive contact with Egypt in the Twelfth Dynasty (if not earlier) is now unequivocal (Marcus 1991: 19–44; *contra* Weinstein 1975). Principally driven by trade, even the earliest relations were apparently bilateral, though by different routes; the southern Asiatics seem to have preferred, or been limited to, the overland route (as witnessed by the wall paintings in the tomb of Khnumhotep at Beni Hassan), while the northern Asiatics and the Egyptians, preferred the maritime route. Aside from Egyptian and Egyptianizing (i.e., Egyptian in style, not manufacture) artifacts (most recently and completely summarized by Marcus 1991), the settlement array of the coastal plain provides testimony for a maritime orientation as well. Commercial relations with Egypt probably began with small estuary ports provisioning ships plying the proliferate Byblos trade. One can envision central place, gateway exchange developing at these ports beyond mere provisioning, and by the Second Intermediate Period (MB III), trade with the Syrian coast had declined while that with the southern littoral was boosted. That maritime trade exchange was already highly developed and long distance in the MB I is made clear by the find at Tel Nami of *Lathyrus clumenum* (Spanish vetch), a lentil which does not grow east of Greece (Kislev et al. 1993).

Plate 2b Mould used to maufacture metal statuette on-site (photograph: The Israel Museum, Jerusalem)

Tell el-Dab'a was Hazor's functional and scalar counterpart in the south (from a southern Levantine point of view). Pottery traditions and provenience analyses, metal typology, physical anthropology and burial practices suggest that initially (in the MB I) its commercial focus was on the northern Levant – Byblos in particular. Its very establishment in the Twelfth Dynasty may perhaps be attributed to Asiatics who specialized in commerce and shipbuilding (e.g., Bietak 1991: 28–9). Metal types and pottery provenience analysis by NAA (M. Bietak, P. McGovern and L. Stager pers. comm.) indicate that by the MB II its energies were apparently transferred to the southern Levant for which it has been rightly termed the 'economic locomotive' (Philip 1989: 214). The reason for this transference in commercial focus is unclear, but it too may have been an outcome of the changing economic and political conditions in Anatolia, Syria and Mesopotamia.

These two first order gateways were nodes of a wonderfully symmetrical exchange system that also included smaller gateways tapping into other systems on frontiers to the west (the maritime zone), the south (the Negev, Sinai and Arabia), and the east (Transjordan and the Syrian desert), (Knapp 1989; and see Figure 6).

Architecture, waterworks and urban planning

Though exposure is insufficient to accurately characterize them, the earliest MB sedentary occupations apparently featured discrete domestic structures comprised of rooms of various shapes and sizes arranged with no standard formula around their courtyards (Ziffer 1990: *17–*18; Ben-Dov 1992). This pattern seems to have held throughout the MB and LB for rural architecture and is generally associated with a mixed agrarian/pastoral economy (e.g., Kramer 1982). In the developing towns, the extension of family households engendered organic growth – leading to domestic quarters that expanded both laterally, encroaching upon the remaining open spaces between domiciles, and vertically in the form of two or three story construction. At a particular level of density, structural units came to share walls to economize on space and expense. Without intervention, the culminating strategies of this process were the subdivision of larger rooms into smaller ones, and alternately, the offspring establishment of new domiciles on the settlement's periphery (see Azar et al. 1985 for ethnographic documentation). Since most towns were fortified, and those fortifications restricted settlement area over time, occupation sometimes spread to outside the fortifications (e.g., at Megiddo over the cemetery on the east slope, [Guy 1938: Plate 1]). Migration, of course, was another option, either to a major center with available property and a wider economic base such as Hazor, Ashkelon or Kabri, or to a new settlement such as those of the southern coastal plain.

Interceding central authorities could influence a different course of events. At Megiddo and Shechem, for example, we see the cancellation of domestic architecture and the superposition of well-planned elite structures, sometimes in successive versions over time (Kempinski 1992a). Furthermore, many older fortified sites show a general tendency toward an increased proportion of elite or public palace/temple architecture at the expense of domestic building from the MB I through the MB III. Another form of central authority intervention was the enclosure and fortification of an appending area designated for new settlement, clearly attested to only at Hazor. Finally, it seems that new, unattached settlements, even at some distance from their sources, were actually initiated by controlling political structures. The rectangular fortified town at Tell el-Ajjul (Figure 7) was presumably established in the late eighteenth century BC as a planned program (Kempinski 1992a: 125–6), skipping the organic early growth phases characteristic of the older towns, as evidenced by its relatively straight grid of unencumbered throughfares – almost Hippodamian in their symmetry. The rectangular shape of new and appended fortified settlements appears to be a hallmark of the MB II, e.g. Tell

el-Ajjul, Tel Batash, Yavne-Yam, Hazor, Tel Nagila and Tel Masos.

True palaces, elaborate variations of the domestic courtyard structure, appear for the first time in Canaan during this period, though their origins are clearly to be seen in the third millennium BC palaces of the north such as Eshnuna, Mari, Ebla, and Ur (Oren 1992). The earliest one recognized thus far appears to be that of Aphek (Kochavi 1989: 48–53), in the lowlands, where the processes of sedentarization, urbanization and social polarization were embryonic. Later examples are found at Aphek once again, Megiddo (Figure 8), Hazor, Shechem, Kabri, Lachish, Tell el-Ajjul and Tel Sera. Drawing on textual material from large urban centers with similar and more completely excavated palatial structures (Mari, Ebla, Ugarit, Alalakh), it seems clear that much of the palaces' roofed space was devoted to food processing, craft production, storage and administration, particularly on the ground floor (e.g., Dalley 1984: 50–77). All of this fits in with the idea that a significant portion of the economy was redistributive and organized by the palace-temple institution.

One futher innovation of the Middle Bronze Age needs mentioning in this context: hydraulic engineering, which embraces three facets – storage, drainage and irrigation. While the Early Bronze Age saw the development of runoff catchment within settlements with an emphasis on open reservoir storage (Helms 1982), the MB progressed to true closed cisterns, to clay pipes that drew rainwater down from the roofs into the cisterns (e.g., Yadin 1972: 38, 43–4, 65, 127), and to sealed, stone-built and stone-carved channels to drain off excess water – most probably to exterior reservoirs, fosses or moats (e.g., at Tel Dan, Hazor, Tell el-Ajjul, Tell Beit Mirsim, Tell el Farah (N.) and Gezer, to name a few). These exterior reservoir facilities probably made possible some limited irrigation, though not to the extent allowed by perennial water sources and good gradients at places like the Hula Valley and the Yarkon Basin.

Palatial construction, and sophisticated drainage and storage facilities belong in a class together with fortifications and gate structures in terms of labor requirements, engineering criteria and centralized planning. All intimate the mastery of the social and political elite over human resources, commodities, technology and information.

Technological revolution and the arts

The Middle Bronze Age was also marked by technological and stylistic innovations in the manufacture of mobile objects (briefly, Dever 1987: 160–2; and for a more detailed and in-depth account of the MB artifactual repertoire, see Ziffer 1990). Not surprisingly, many of

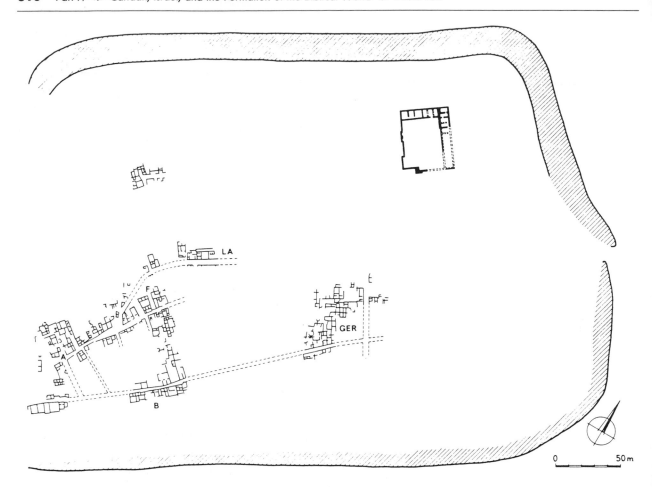

Figure 7   Site plan of Tell el-Ajjul City II (MB II—III). From Kempinski 1992a: Figure 3

these technologies and styles had precedents in Syria, Anatolia and Mesopotamia in the third millennium BC, arriving in Canaan by a variety of means (see the above section on cultural origins).

In the field of metallurgy the massive introduction of tin-bronze represented a major innovation and some of its cultural implications are discussed in other sections of this chapter. The widespread adoption of the fast wheel in the MB (though it was used for smaller vessels and larger vessel necks and rims in the later EB and IB), and proficiency in its use, resulted in more experimentation and greater variety of form. The carinated shapes that imitate metal vessels were one of the period's hallmarks (Amiran 1969: 90). Ceramics showing Anatolian and Syrian influence were not uncommon (e.g., Gerstenblith 1983: 59–87; Ilan 1991; Ilan and Yellin forthcoming) and demonstrate the international scale of information transfer, by whatever mechanism. True glass seems to have appeared in Canaan for the first time in the MB, in the form of small beads (Peltenberg 1987; Ilan et al. 1993; [the EB bead from Jericho noted by Peltenberg may not be glass]). This was most probably an offshoot

of the pyrotechnology utilized for metallurgy and frit.

Glyptics of two different media also appeared in Canaan at this stage: cylinder seals (Plate 3), the idea for which originated in the north (e.g., Collon 1987) and scarab seals (Plate 4) from Egypt (e.g., Ward 1978; Tufnell 1984; O'Connor 1985). Both types seem to have been used as marks of ownership and as protective amulets. Cylinder seals of a more schematic and less ornate variety had already been in use in Canaan throughout the EB, but in the second millennium BC the 'Syrian style' was introduced. This glyptic genre was perhaps centered at Aleppo and crystallized out of older Sumero-Akkadian styles influenced by Egyptian motifs. Almost all the cylinder seals from MB Canaan are of this class, but cylinder seals on the whole never became commonplace. It is tempting to suggest that they were reserved for a particular class, and perhaps the highest order, of the social elite. The more Egyptianizing scarab seals were fairly infrequent in the early MB and largely confined to the coastal areas, but became widespread by the MB III (Fifteenth Dynasty in Egypt). The overwhelming majority have been found in mortuary

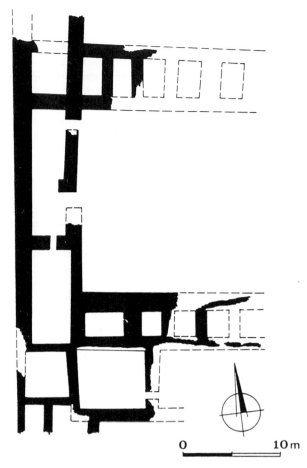

Figure 8 Palace plan from Meggido Stratum XII (MB II). From Loud 1948: Figure 415

Plate 3 A hematite cylinder seal from Tell el–Ajjul showing the weather god and his attributes (courtesy Irit Ziffer, Land of Israel Museum)

Plate 4 Scarab seals: selected MB examples from Tell el–Ajjul, Jericho and Tell Beit Mirsim (photograph: courtesy David Ilan)

contexts and should probably be associated with a regenerative amuletic symbolism (e.g., Ilan in press a).

The few cuneiform documents found at Hazor, Gezer, Hebron and Shechem show that Akkadian was the standard language of administration and commerce (e.g. Anbar and Na'aman 1986–1987). But another, simpler phonetic script began to evolve during the MB – the alphabet (Figure 9) – one of the few innovations to come out of Canaan, but one of the most significant for humanity (e.g., Naveh 1982: 23–42; Dever 1987: 169–71; Sass 1988). For the student of social and contextual archaeology it is perhaps most striking that alphabetic inscriptions occur in prosaic or more personal settings – on a dagger, a potsherd, a pithos or as graffiti – in contrast to the formal administrative and legal contexts of the Akkadian documents. The evidence is slim, but these two systems of writing may have coincided to some degree with the socio-political polarities of Canaanite society, until the tables were turned in the Iron Age and alphabetic Hebrew became the official script.

The technology and technique of warfare and the prestige of personal combat

We commonly and somewhat simplistically ask whether a society is 'warlike' or 'peaceful' and the truth is usually somewhere in between, to be elucidated in the more specific study of socio-political conflict and its archaeological manifestation. The Middle Bronze Age is considered alternately warlike (because of its tremendous fortifications [see Window, p. 316] and its plethora of weapons in tomb and cultic offerings) and peaceful (because so few destruction levels have been discerned until the end of the period). What is clear is that the Middle Bronze Age was perhaps a watershed period in terms of military tactics and weaponry; a period when several

Phon. Value	Schematic Forms	Early North-west Semitic	Early South Semitic	Early Letter Names	Meaning of Names
ʼ	ʘ ʘ	⋇(16th) ⋇(13th)	ʘ ⋉ (Jamme)	ʼalp-	ox-head
b	☐ ◻	☐(17th) ◿(13th)	⊓	bêt-	house
g	⌐	⌒(15th) ⟩(12th)	⌐ ⌐	gaml-	throw-stick
d	⇨	◁ △ (10th)	⋈ (Jamme)	digg-	fish
ḏ	= ⊏	?	H N (Jamme)	?	?
h	ψ ψ	∃(10th)	ψ	hô(?)	man calling
w	⊸ ?	Y(10th)	⊕(? used for y)	wô(waw)	mace
z	?	∓(16th) I(10th)	𝐙	zê(n-)	?
ḥ	⫟ ▯	Ⅲ(12th) ⊟(10th)	⋎	ḥê(t-)	fence (?)
ḫ	⊗ ⊗	?	⋎ (Jamme)	ḫa( )	hank of yarn
ṭ	?	⊔(16th) ⊕(10th)	⊞	ṭê(t-)	spindle ?
y	⋎ ⋎	⌐(13th) ⟩(10th)	⌐(orig w)	yad-	arm
k	⋓ ⋓	⋓(17th) ⋓(13th)	⋔ ⋔	kapp-	palm
l	⌐ ⌐ ⌐	⌐(14th) ∂(13th)	⌐ ⌐ (Jamme)	lamd-	ox-goad
m	⋀⋀ ⋏	⋀(15th) ⟨(13th)	⋈(9th) ⋈(8th)	mêm-	water
n	⌐ ⌐ ⌐	⟨(14th) ⋎(12th)	⋎ ⋎	naḥš-	snake
s	?	∓(10th)	⫴ ⫴	(samk-?)	?
ʕ	⊙ ⊙	○(12th) ○(10th)	○	ʕên-	eye
ġ	◇	⊏(15th)	⊓ ⋂(Jamme)	ġa( )	?
p	⌐ ⌐	⟩(10th)	○ ○	puʼt-(?)	corner ?
s/z	⋎ ⊤	⋎(10th)	⋈ ⋎	sa(d-)	plant
ḍ	?	?	⊟	?	?
q	⊂⊃ 8	⌒(14th) ⌒(10th)	φ φ (Jamme)	qu(p-)	?
r	⌐ ⌐	⌒(16th-14th)	⟩ ⟨	na'š-	head of man
š/t	⌐	⌐(13th) ⋎(10th)	⟩ ⟨	tann-	composite bow
s̃	⌐ ⌐	?	⋂ ⋂(Jamme)	?	?
t	+	+(16th) ✕(13th)	✕ +(Jamme)	tô(taw)	owner's mark

Figure 9 The alphabet at the mid second millenium BCE. From Albright 1966b

crucial techniques became prevalent, enhancing military effectiveness and demanding creative responses in tactics, fortification and personal protection.

The adoption of tin bronze, partially in lieu of copper, increased the longevity, sharpness and hardness of weapons, while the increased malleability of bronze facilitated the casting of more complex forms. Horses (cavalry) and the chariot introduced rapidly movable fighting platforms that could be rushed to critical locations in battle and used as shock forces against infantry. The compound and composite bows, with their bolstered power and range, made the bow a truly effective weapon in battle and seige for the first time. Battering rams were improved and became effective seige engines (Yadin 1963: 4–9; 58–75).

Most of these weapon types and techniques require highly specialized knowledge and a developed mechanism for resource procurement. Bronze, for example, required the import of tin, the nearest known possible sources being the Taurus Mountains of Anatolia (Yener and Ozbal 1987), and beyond that, in Iran and Afghanistan (e.g., Muhly and Wertime 1973). An expansive, organized exchange system with extensive channels of information must be postulated; texts, from Mari in particular, testify to the highly lucrative importing of tin from the east (Dossin 1970) and its transshipment to towns such as Laish (Tel Dan) and Hazor (Malamat

1970). It has been suggested that the manufacture and distribution of composite bows, being a complex process more effectively carried out on a mass-production basis, was the function of the palace workshop (Philip 1989: 158–61). The same might be said for chariots and other engines of war. Finally, the textual references make it clear that warfare was not unknown in the Middle Bronze Age Levant. These sources tend to emphasize 'logistics, seige techniques and equipment, patrols, blockades and so on'. (Philip 1989: 155; Yadin 1963: 69–75), all of which can be associated with social regimentation, central direction and control of productive technology.

The key to an archaeological analysis is apparently the distinction between actual warfare and personal combat (Philip 1989: 145–6). The overwhelming majority of weapons recovered in archaeological contexts come from tomb and cultic offering deposits. These are most commonly comprised of daggers, axes and spears in descending order of numerical importance, often in sets (daggers and axes are notably common, while spears are unusual and never alone). The complete absence of arrowheads or sling bolts is conspicuous, though these were known and had in fact become a major component of large-scale military confrontation. Arrows and bolts were the weapons of soldiers – low status individuals, often conscripted, who could be used for agricultural or construction work (Philip 1989: 150). But daggers, axes and spears were weapons of personal combat – they were the warrior's status symbols in what Philip has termed a traditional 'heroic' society, much as they have been in most traditional societies. Artistic depictions and texts even suggest a status hierarchy of weapon types, with axes at the top and spears at the bottom. Weapons were also a valuable gift, bestowing prestige upon both the recipient and the donor, and creating indebtedness for the recipient alone (Philip 1989: 160–1).

Stylistic change in personal weaponry should also be understood in terms of their prestige value and not always as the expression of improved functional effectiveness (Philip 1989: 155; *contra* Yadin 1963). Over time, as certain weapon styles became more and more common, their value went down. At some point, the elite-controlled centers of production would commission somewhat different forms, to reassert status distinctions and to realign alliances and indebtedness to the controlling structures.

With all the weaponry in MB assemblages, why are there so few MB destructions in layers which sometimes represent 400 years or more of occupation? Their cultic and mortuary nexus, their prominence in mythology, and the fact that so many weapons are still copper or contain too much lead, emphasize the ritualistic nature that combat may have assumed in certain contexts. Perhaps ritualistic rules of warfare precluded certain practices – the burning of settlements, for example. Moreover, the large quantity of weapons in cultic deposits, such as those at Byblos, may be related to those cult places' functions as oracles and the loci of arbitration.

Religious beliefs and the politics of cult

Defining what is cultic in an archaeological context is notoriously difficult and should require the interpreter to state his or her assumptions and methods explicitly. Though explication of this sort has not been the rule, most researchers have intuitively followed criteria similar to those proposed by Renfrew (1985: 11–26; Alon and Levy 1989). Workers in our region are also influenced by contemporary textual material relating to cult – from the archives of Mari, Meskene and Ugarit for example – and by the Bible. It would seem, however, that a holistic, interdisciplinary account of Middle Bronze Age religion and cult is still lacking.

From most indications Middle Bronze Age Canaanite religion and its cultic expression, perpetuated a well-established belief system at least as ancient as the Neolithic. As all religions are, it was concerned with the universal themes of life, death and the essence of nature, and it operated with profound effect in Canaanite society. The massive investment of wealth and energy in mortuary practices gives some impression of the magnitude and fortitude of attitudes toward and the interconnectiveness of death, ancestors, the netherworld and the regeneration of life (see Window 2, p. 318). But beyond the personal expressions of religiosity, religious beliefs and cultic activity were manipulated to regulate behavior and reinforce political structures (e.g., Alon and Levy 1989; Rappaport 1971; Geertz 1975; Johnson and Earle 1987: 264, 324).

All the archaeological manifestions of MB cultic practice

Plate 5   A jewelry group from Tell el-Ajjul (courtesy Israel Antiquities Authority)

seem to have been in place by the MB I: open-air 'altars', stelae, the symmetrical, direct-axis Syrian or 'Migdal' temples and offering deposits placed in bothroi or in or under walls (e.g., Megiddo Stratum XIII, Nahariyah, Kfar Shmariyahu, Dan and Tell el-Hayyat). These early cultic phenomena tend to be small scale with the exception of the Obelisk Temple at Byblos, which contains all the aforementioned elements but on a much larger scale (Dunand 1958: 644–54). Sequestered offering deposits are the most frequently-observed cultic activity. These deposits generally contain metal weapons, stick pins and rings (the latter too large to be finger rings, too small to be bracelets and lacking the fastening apparatus of earrings), jewelry, miniature pottery vessels and metal figurines – mostly anthropomorphic (see Plates 2a,b; Plate 5). They have been interpreted as gift offerings presented to deities by society's elite – those with access to wealth – in reciprocation for gifts divine. By so doing the elite maintained its privileged position as intermediary between deity and the lower social orders, legitimizing its dominance over those orders. As a by-product, metal supply and metal's value as a gifting commodity were regulated (Philip 1988; Ilan 1992).

The employment of stelae as a medium of cultic focusing was already of great antiquity in the Middle Bronze Age and took on a number of forms reflecting disparate cult-related purposes (Graesser 1972). It has been suggested that the famous 'high place' at Gezer (Plate 6), with its alignment of megaliths, served as a 'convenant shrine' similar to later Delphi in Greece (e.g., Dever 1987: 167); these stones certainly communicated a public message, for they were visible from many kilometers away. The rather dense array of stelae – some obelisque-shaped and others more slab-like – at Byblos has sometimes been attributed a mortuary or

Plate 6   The megalithic stelae of the Tel Gezer High Place (photograph: © HUC–JIR, Jerusalem)

memorial significance (e.g., Albright 1966), while the stelae of the open-air Megiddo Stratum XIII sanctuary are generally held to represent a straightforward, divine immanence (e.g., Loud 1948: 87–92). The salient point regarding MB stelae is that they were probably imbued with a variety of social meanings and functions, all of which came under the auspices of deity. Manipulation of cult was a primary tool of the empowered elite but to some extent also served the purposes of the disenfranchised.

As the Middle Bronze Age advanced and social complexity grew, so too did the investment in institutionalized cult in the form of large planned cultic and palatial compounds at Megiddo (see Figure 8), Hazor, Alalakh, Ebla, Tell Mumbaqat, Shechem, Tell el Ajjul, and probably Tel Dan, imposed upon more prosaic earlier remains (e.g. Matthaie 1975; Mazar 1992). By the MB III, such complexes were most often dominated by monumental 'Migdal' temples, another cultural feature with origins in Syria (e.g., Mazar 1992: 167–9), raised on a constructed platform above their surroundings so as to be conspicuous from afar – like the great ramparts, a symbol of power and a further example of the resource-consuming, competitive emulation characteristic of peer polity interaction.

Socio-political disintegration and the ascendency of Egypt: transition to the Late Bronze Age

A widespread dissatisfaction with anecdotal and monocausal explanations for the collapse of complex societies has stimulated several scholars to seek underlying structural and processual factors to account for that collapse (e.g., Renfrew 1979; Tainter 1988; Yoffee and Cowgill 1988). Central to these studies is the idea, put succinctly by Tainter (1988), that collapse can be understood as a response to declining marginal return on investment in complexity – it is essentially an economizing process. Collapse does not imply the total erasure of social and political structures, rather it connotes their fragmentation and recomposition at a lower organizational level. Concerning the Bronze Age in the southern Levant, Marfoe (1979), Bunimovitz (1989 and this volume) and Finkelstein (1993 and this volume) have all reconstructed the processes of disintegration in similar terms, and to this writer as well, they seem to carry great if not holistic explanatory potential.

Two mechanisms are most often invoked, and sometimes combined, to explain the disintegration of MB political structures; endogenous systems' collapse of the kind described above (and see also Bienkowski 1989: 176; Redford 1979; Hoffmeier 1989), and exogenous Egyptian incursions (e.g., Kenyon 1979; Dever 1990, Weinstein

1991). The hard evidence is mostly open to interpretation, and our ability to date and differentiate late MB and early LB material culture is severely limited, but it is now widely accepted that whatever the responsible agent, the process of site destruction and abandonment occurred over a fairly extended period of time – perhaps as long as 150 years (e.g., Seger 1975, Bietak 1991: 61–2). A multi-causal model is suggested here to explain socio-political disintegration in MB Canaan.

By the MB III socio-political complexity had reached a peak; integrative institutions were overextended relative to the production base and the marginal returns of complexity were declining. Resources were continuously being diverted into (a) prestige projects such as rampart, temple and palace construction, (b) an expanding non-productive elite, and (c) increasingly scarce and, therefore, costly commodities such as metal, while agricultural production at some point reached a plateau. Population was growing as well. This was a tenuous juncture; we must remember that for Mediterranean people, the uncertainty of the harvest was the rule, and drought and famine were always on the doorstep (Braudel 1972: 238–46). (A great drought in the time of Herod the Great almost cost that illustrious king his throne; he wisely imported great quantities of grain from Egypt at his own expense [Josephus, *Antiquities of the Jews* XV: 299–316]). In the Middle Bronze Age even a minor drought, undetectable in the sedimentological or palynological record, combined with a shortfall of food or seed reserves, could have brought the socio-economic periphery into the strongholds of the chiefs and kings to pillage and burn. The political contract held that the center (the urban or stronghold elite) provide protection from human enemies and risk management to counter the vicissitudes of nature, and that contract was apparently broken in many cases by the erstwhile redistributive centers (cf. the Beka'a Valley of Lebanon in the twentieth century; Marfoe 1979: 5–9).

This was also a point when many sedentary agriculturists would opt, as they had in the past and would in the future, for the alternate strategies of pastoralism and banditry (Braudel 1972: 85–101, 734–56; Marfoe 1979). These are groups that are difficult to disembed of goods and services, and who can reassert political autonomy at a lower level of organization (Yoffee 1988: 12–13).

Less important perhaps, but still a factor, is what Renfrew has called the 'confidence factor' (Cherry and Renfrew 1986: 155). Once polities begin to collapse, their limitations become apparent and their legitimacy comes into doubt. The processes of polity disintegration and reorganization in Canaan may have accelerated under similar conditions.

With the creeping failure of the social contract and the decline of agricultural production, a debilitating vicious circle relating to Egypt was set in motion. Egyptian grain, traded for Canaanite wine and oil was a sort of safety valve for times of drought and agrarian stress. The scarcity of wine and oil probably led to increased prices for the Egyptians. Correspondingly, less grain was coming into Canaan as well. In the middle was Avaris (Tell el Dab'a), trying to maintain a profitable equilibrium, but also footing the costs of its own increasing complexity. All parties were subject to economic stress and its accompanying social strains, but it was the Egyptians who went to war against the Hyksos, beseiging and destroying Avaris (Dever 1987: 172 and references there).

The fall of Avaris would have been catastrophic for southern Canaan and certainly damaging to the economy of Egypt. The destruction of this great gateway meant that there was no longer any safety valve; institutional collapse in Canaan was probably hastened. One wonders how the victorious Egyptians dealt with the absence of the erstwhile commercial agent and the shortages of highly-valued imported goods. Two alternative explanations are plausible:

1. The Canaanite polities north of Sharuhen (Tell el-Ajjul) may have transferred their allegiance to the Eighteenth Dynasty rulers (Hoffmeier 1989: 190). These polities may, by this time, have undergone 'dynastic substitution' and political reorganization following revolt.
2. The Egyptians themselves made incursions into Canaan, not solely for the purpose of vengeance and booty (Weinstein 1981), but to depose a recalcitrant (or overcharging) Canaanite elite and replace it with a more malleable partner.

In any case, there is much to read between the lines of the few inconclusive Egyptian texts that depict the ejection and pursuit of the Hyksos and the transfer of power in Egypt.

The end of the Middle Bronze Age in the northern part of the country may have occurred at a different pace and been effected by different factors. Tels Dan, Kabri, Akko, Nahariyah and Hazor, for example, were all destroyed sometime within the 1600–1480 BC horizon (Weinstein 1981: 2–5); the archaeological data precludes greater temporal precision. Most of these urban centers seem to have been resettled, perhaps immediately, but the small MB sites known from the hills of Galilee were abandoned. A social implosion sparked by drought is the preferred explanation, with the Egyptian connection playing a lesser role. Hazor in particular, continued to be of a size, and to

play a role, on a wholly different scale. The twin factors of high productivity induced by irrigation and gateway trade and by redistribution appear to have maintained its position until the thirteenth century BC.

If our criterion for periodization is socio-political change, the demise of Avaris is perhaps a justifiable benchmark for determining the end of the Middle Bronze Age. Yet the Canaanite city states did not collapse abruptly or completely, as a literal interpretation of the PPI model might predict (Cherry and Renfrew 1986: 155). Nor is there a real hiatus in material culture. Indeed, a case can be made for ending the Middle Bronze Age with the campaign of Thutmose III, when Canaan came finally and decidedly into the Egyptian orbit (e.g. Seger 1975, Bunimovitz 1989; Weinstein 1981), though apparently retaining many of its social and political structures.

The partial collapse of political structures in the late MB did not bring about the collapse of Canaanite civilization. From most indications, cultural continuity was the rule – in religious beliefs and cultic practice, in certain status categories (such as the warrior), in mortuary practices, and in material culture attributes such as architecture, pottery traditions, metal utensils and the like. The death of Canaanite civilization occurred some 1000 years later, its foundations first chipped away by the highly centralized cultic and administrative institutions of the Iron Age, with the final demise brought about by population exchanges under the Assyrians and Babylonians and the destruction of the First Temple (cf. Yoffee 1988 for a concurrent and similar process in Mesopotamia).

Acknowledgements

The author wishes to thank the editor, Tom Levy, for his invitation to participate in this volume. I am beholden to Levy, Graham Philip and Aharon Kempinski for their critical review of the manuscript for this chapter. Oral discussions with the participants of the San Diego symposium should also be credited for guidance. It is clear that we have much to debate, but the requirements of conciseness precluded more comprehensive treatments of several key issues raised by readers. In any case, responsibility for the final text is my own.

SYMBOLS OF POWER AND MODES OF DEFENSE: THE GREAT RAMPART FORTIFICATIONS

MB fortifications are the single most impressive aspect of any large, and sometimes not so large, settlement. While they show several common guiding principles – mainly centered on the integration of free-standing walls and earthen embankments – their form varies according to local topography and function (Figure 1.1). The freestanding wall was often the first defensive edifice erected, particularly in the early MB. In most cases it was comprised of a stone socle surmounted by a mudbrick superstructure. Often such walls displayed offsets and/or citadel towers which served both defensive and constructive purposes. But these walls rarely, if ever, stood alone; *terre pisée 'glaçis'* (to be distinguished from the freestanding embankments described below) were usually propped up against them from the outside (Figure 1.1a–b), and sometimes from the inside to preserve their foundations from being undermined by either rainfall or attacking sappers (Kempinski 1992b: 129). All these constructional techniques have antecedents in the Early Bronze Age (Parr 1968), though their employment in the MB was a more standard, yet more complex procedure that often resulted in a more formidable rampart than in the EB.

The real innovation is exemplified by the prodigious freestanding embankments used to create large enclosures on the level ground of the lowlands; the lower cities of Qatna, Carcemish, Ebla, Hazor (Plate 1.1 and Figure 1.1c–e), and the entire compounds of Kabri, Tel Batash, Yavne Yam, and Akko are good examples. These enclosures were not always fully occupied (e.g., Yavne Yam). The origins of this system appear to lie in Syria and Mesopotamia, in the canal and dyke building that was a ubiquitous part of irrigation agriculture (e.g., Kaplan 1975), though similar works were also characteristic of Egypt. In Mesopotamia such ramparts served a defensive purpose as well – witness the Muriq Tidnim ('keeping away Tidnum [people]') built against the Amorites by Shulgi in the Ur III period. There is some question as to whether freestanding embankments were crowned by brick walls since such walls are rarely preserved at the embankment apexes. At Carcemish (MB I/II), Mardikh (MB I/II), and Tel Nagila (MB II), however, freestanding embankments of one kind or another were surmounted by mudbrick walls (Parr 1968: 33; Wright 1985: 184), and other eroded embankment structures show layers of brick debris at or near the surface, e.g. Hazor (Yadin 1972: 54).

The third type of rampart construction (Figure 1.1f) has only recently been isolated and is only partly related to defense: it entails the structural extension and elevation of an entire settlement (Lederman 1985; Ussishkin 1989). At sites such as Jericho, Shechem, Tel Dan and Shiloh massive stone revetments were constructed, and earthen fills deposited behind and in front of them, to create wider and higher platforms for the construction of crowning walls (usually lacking but recently found in Tel Dan Area T3) or large public buildings such as the tower temple at Shechem. A site once considered a classic 'Hyksos' example of embankment fortification, Tell el-Yahudiyeh in the Egyptian delta, was convincingly placed in this category already by Wright in 1968. Constructions of this type

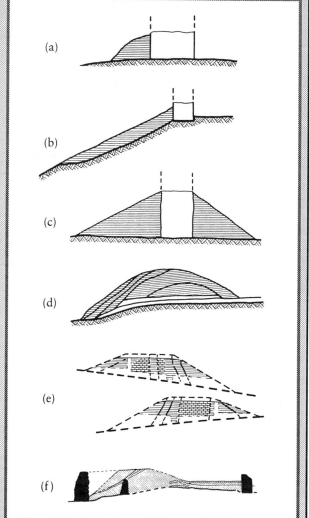

Figure 1.1 Various types of MB rampart fortification. Adapted from Kempinski 1992b and Kaplan 1975

generally imply a planned, concentrated effort and not successive increments to a fortification over time. With the exception of the Tel Dan example, dated to the MB I, these appear to be a feature of the MB III – an important observation in processual, socio-political terms.

It is usual to find a fosse at the base of all three rampart variants, which in special cases (Qatna, Kabri, Dan) may have been flooded to form a moat, if a water source was available (Kempinski 1992d).

What were these huge ramparts meant to defend against? Their very size and complexity have major socio-political implications. Traditional explanations 'explained [sloping banks of plastered earth] variously and confusedly as to facilitate archery, to incommode archery, to keep chariots in, to keep chariots away, to inhibit battering rams, to prevent the application of fire-brands etc. etc.' (Wright 1968). Some of these explanations are undoubtedly valid, especially those concerning sapping and the increased range of the composite bow (Kenyon 1966, Yadin 1963; Stager 1991: 8), though Yadin's 1955 anti-battering ram hypothesis has been invalidated by Wright (1968: n. 20). The idea that the *glaçis* was intended as consolidation and protection against both erosion and seige techniques, when tel slopes were becoming steeper, more exposed and increasingly vulnerable, has also gained wide acceptance (Parr 1968; Wright 1968).

However, a new conjecture is now gaining currency — one that emphasizes the social and political roles implied by rampart conception and construction, and one that views such tremendous undertakings as an expression of the emulation and competition characteristic of peer-polity interaction. Beyond their purely tactical function, ramparts were stategically imbued with a symbolic, propagandistic content that proclaimed the power of the polity vis-à-vis other polities, and of the ruling elites vis-à-vis the ruled (Dever 1987: 154–6; Herzog 1989; Bunimovitz 1992, and this volume, Chapter 19; Finkelstein 1992). Seen in this way, the ramparts are the pyramids or ziggurats of Canaanite civilization — a sort of conspicuous consumption of society's most precious resource: human energy.

Plate 1.1 An aerial view of Tel Hazor (Hebrew University, Institute of Archaeology Archives)

The ramparts of Hazor are comprised of more than 1,000,000 m³ of earth while smaller sites have been estimated to require less; Shiloh contained 45,000 m³ (Finkelstein 1992). Assuming that a worker can move approximately 1 m³ of earth per day (see references in Finkelstein 1992: 209), it becomes clear that hundreds of thousands — and sometimes millions — of hours were required to erect a rampart. Given both the demands and the potential surpluses of an agrarian economy, Finkelstein has adopted the estimate that 20 percent of a given population were available for construction corvée ca three months per year, inferring that in sites the size of Shiloh and Dan, with only tens or hundreds of workers available from the settlement itself, a rampart might have taken many years to construct with the attendant risk of heavy winter rainfall undoing the previous season's labors. Hence the suggestion that the ruling authority was utilizing labor from the surrounding countryside, indicating some measure of political (and economic) control over that hinterland (Finkelstein 1992).

This strategy of resource allocation to symbols of power seems to have paid off for a while. The lack of destruction layers in most MB levels, until the final collapse that is, points to this interpretation. But by the MB III, the human resources and material surpluses they consumed, added to their unfulfilled promise of protection, may have been important factors in socio-political collapse.

DEATH IN CANAAN: MORTUARY BEHAVIOR AS A REFLECTION OF SOCIETY AND IDEOLOGY

Considering the wealth of information available, mortuary remains have been perhaps the most neglected manifestation of MB society. MB burial assemblages are of particular importance because they are frequent, widely and evenly distributed, and take on variety of form and context that probably reflects a cross section of contemporary society. Of great diachronic importance is the existence of intramural tombs under successive living surfaces of settlement layers, in addition to extramural cemeteries.

Burial types   Six general tomb categories can be distinguished (Figure 2.1). Rock-carved chamber tombs, masonry chamber tombs, shaft burials (usually in combination with chamber tombs), masonry cist tombs, simple pit or cist burials, and jar burials. These can be subdivided by size and geometric form. How do we explain this variety in behavioral terms?

Social status and burial   A detailed study of the Tel Dan mortuary remains (Ilan, in press a and b) has indicated that in the context of a given intramural cemetery, the coexistence and spatial relationships of chamber, cist, shaft, pit and jar burials can best be explained by subordinate (demographic) status differentiation and kinship affiliation. Chamber tombs (masonry only) contained the skeletal material of both male and female individuals over the age of 13 years, cist tombs the remains of individuals 3–12 years, and jar burials infants under the age of 2–3 years and fetuses. This patterning is culturally suggestive; the age of 2–3 years is typically associated with a sharp downswing in mortality rates and a corresponding change in social status (e.g., Binford 1972: 233; Krahfeld-Daugherty in press; Steele in press; and references in both), while the age of 12–13 years is associated in many societies with further status enhancement and with rites of passage leading to adulthood (e.g., van Gennep 1960).

Superordinate (ascribed) status and wealth differences are not clearly attested to in the mortuary sample from Tel Dan or in other cemeteries. Ascribed status or ranking is commonly held to be indicated by widely variant assemblages within a specific

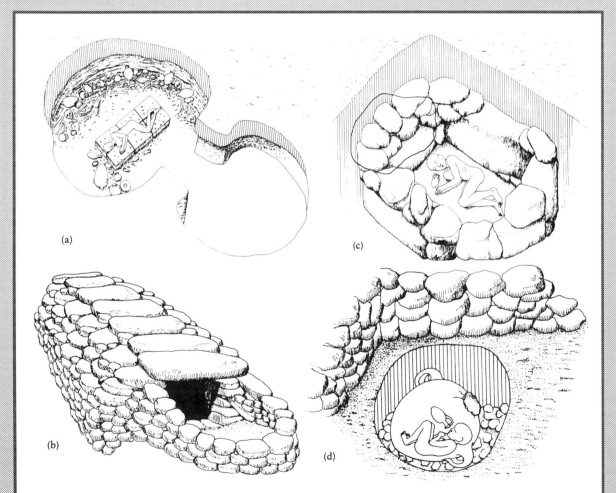

Figure 2.1   Frequent MB tomb and burial types: (a) rock–carved tomb, (b) masonry chamber tomb, (c) masonry cist tomb, (d) jar burial of an infant or fetus.

demographic category or by offering differentiation that cross-cuts demographic categories (e.g. Peebles and Kus 1977). In a hypothetical representative sample, the juvenile interments for example could be expected to show a few offering assemblages richer by several degrees than the majority of juvenile burials, and a similar pattern might be expected for other demographic categories. So-called 'rich' MB tombs are generally those with a long sequence of multiple successive burial with little evidence of plunder. The Jericho tombs are a likely candidate for an explanation of this kind. Finally, tombs always were the prime targets of plunder, especially in times of scarcity, and the symbols of prestige and wealth were probably those carried off.

One burial type that does stand out as an indicator of rank is the warrior burial, which typically is comprised of an adult male buried with weapons, a belt, and sometimes an equid. Early MB burials of this type are better known due to the period's greater propensity for single burial – for example, at Baghouz and Beth Shean (Oren 1971) – but the phenomenon continues into the MB II and MB III as well (Philip in press).

Kinship affiliation is expressed by the clustering of different demographically ordered tomb types under domestic living floors and the technique of multiple successive burial points to familial affiliation (cf. Woolley [1976: 33–5] and Salles [1987] for similar ordering at Ur and Ugarit). Early MB I cist tombs contain single burials, more in the Intermediate Bronze Age tradition, but thereafter chamber tombs and cist tombs contain multiple successive interments. Jar burials are often located next to or over cist tombs or chamber tombs.

Cosmological inferences Many patterns in MB mortuary remains are ubiquitous for all tomb types and for all age and sex categories. These can be explained as symbolic behavior motivated by concepts of rebirth, afterlife and fertility. The tomb itself can be seen as a simulation of the female reproductive organs (chamber, opening, shaft) while the usual contracted (fetal) position of the skeleton and proximity of the head to the tomb opening represents the prenatal state.

Death and rebirth were considered part of the fertility cycle observed in the natural world, and particularly in agriculture. This is evident from the Ugaritic Baal Epic (I AB: II: 30–7) and the Birth of the Gods Good and Fair (e.g., Gordon 1949: 59) where Mot, the god of death is killed by Anat in terms of the grain harvest or the pruning and binding of the grapevine. Genesis 3 can also be understood as reflecting the relationship between death and the fertility of man and nature (Ilan forthcoming).

Finally, the post-interment offerings (called *kispum* in contemporary and later texts) found frequently over or near MB tombs, serve as testimony to the continued reference of the living to the dead, perhaps providing venerated ancestors with honor and sustenance, or perhaps to placate a potential agent of social disruption (e.g.. Skiast 1980).

19

ON THE EDGE OF EMPIRES – LATE BRONZE AGE (1500–1200 BCE)

Shlomo Bunimovitz

Explaining culture change in Late Bronze Age Palestine

The archaeology of the Late Bronze Age society in Palestine is an exemplary case of feast and famine. On the one hand, rich archaeological data from numerous excavations and a relative abundance of contemporary documentary records; on the other, a conspicuous scarcity of material culture studies explicitly concerned with sociocultural processes and change (for standard archaeological overviews of the period's culture-history see, e.g., Albright 1960: 96–109; Kenyon 1979: 180–211; Leonard 1989; Mazar 1990: 232–94; for documentary-based historical reviews see, e.g., Na'aman 1982: 173–255; Redford 1992: 125–237). This 'state-of-the-art' clearly reflects the bias of social archaeology in Palestine towards the field of prehistory and the study of unstratified, non-urban societies, leaving the more complex societies of the Bronze and Iron Ages to be explored by traditional, historically-oriented archaeology. No wonder then that written evidence tends to dominate interpretations of sociocultural change in these 'documented' societies, and ideographic rather than generalizing explanations are preferred. Taking the archaeological study of the Late Bronze Age as an example, one can readily see that patterns in the material culture and their changes over time are usually explained by historical events, ignoring the fact that these patterns were created by a social system – Canaanite society – whose behavior and adaptation to a changing socio-political and ideological environment is by no means unique. However, a combination of nomothetic and ideographic elements – namely, cross-cultural perspectives and a scrutiny of the specific historical/archaeological context under consideration – seems most imperative for explaining cultural processes and change. Furthermore, since change occurs along a variety of time scales, the necessity of studying it within different time frameworks should be recognized. Thus, both long-term sociocultural patterns (mainly recognized in the material data) and short-term, particular and unexpected changes (usually documented in written sources) are legitimate subjects for enquiry. The breach between 'historical' and anthro-pological archaeology can, therefore, be bridged by a conscious dialogue between material and written evidence (Renfrew 1980; Yoffee 1982; Trigger 1984: 287–95; Adams 1984: 79–89; Bintliff 1991; Knapp 1992a, 1992c; Levy and Holl, this volume).

Using both archaeological and documentary data resources in a reciprocal examination of culture change in Palestine during the Late Bronze Age (Bunimovitz 1989; see also Knapp 1992b, 1992c), two fundamental socio-political patterns emerge:

1. Sociocultural changes at the end of the Middle Bronze Age reshaped the social landscape of Palestine and had a profound, long-term impact on Canaanite society.
2. The Late Bronze Age social fabric in Palestine was continuously changing due to dialectical relations between Canaanite society and Egyptian government.

In the following discussion the main political, social and economic changes that affected Canaanite society in Palestine during the Late Bronze Age will be concisely examined, in order to illustrate how the 'why?' questions concerning these changes can be elucidated by a close study of the above recognized patterns.

The transition from Middle to Late Bronze Age

During the Middle Bronze Age hundreds of urban and rural settlements had been established all over Palestine. This highly diversified and hierarchical pattern of settlement signifies the zenith of Bronze Age settlement processes in Palestine, and faithfully reflects socio-political and economic developments within Canaanite society during the first half of the second millennium BCE (Broshi and Gophna 1986; Gophna and Portugali 1988; Dever 1987). At the end of the seventeenth century BCE and in the course of the sixteenth century BCE, however, this pattern of settlement changed profoundly, following a long line of destructions and abandonments that laid waste many sites. According to current hypotheses these destructions should be related to the expulsion of the Hyksos from Egypt and the conquest of Canaan by the first pharaohs of

A group of anthropoid clay coffins from Deir el-Balah (photograph: The Israel Museum, Jerusalem)

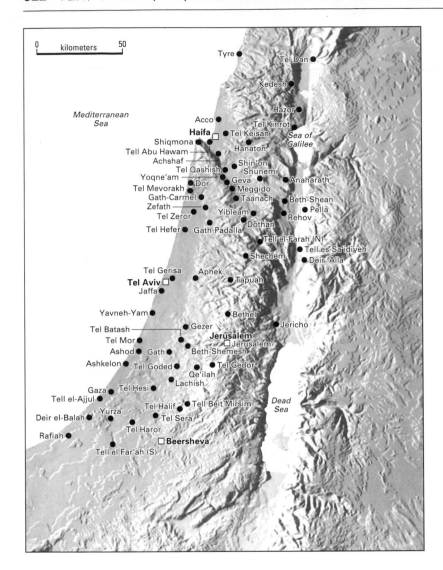

Figure 1   Settlement map of Late Bronze Age Palestine

the Eighteenth Dynasty. It has also been claimed that the geographical–chronological pattern of the destructions points to the southern and inland regions of Palestine as the principle centres of Hyksos power outside the Nile Delta (Weinstein 1981: 1–10). However, a careful examination of the transitional Middle Bronze–Late Bronze Age strata in many sites (Bunimovitz 1989: Chapter 1) reveals that destruction layers from the end of the seventeenth and the beginning of the sixteenth centuries BCE were arbitrarily related to Ahmose or his successors, thus subjugating the archaeological facts to as yet vague historical data concerning Egyptian involvement in Palestine prior to Thothmes III's early fifteenth century BCE campaigns (for the current debate about the interpretation of the Egyptian texts vis-à-vis the archaeological data see Hoffmeier 1991: Dever 1990; Weinstein 1991 and bibliography there).

In fact, the destructions present no discernible pattern and the settlement crisis at the end of the Middle Bronze

Age seems to be a continuous process, which had already begun at the end of the seventeenth century BCE and lasted to the end of the sixteenth century BCE. The early destructions, and at least some of the later ones, may therefore be related to internal instability and conflicts rather than to Egyptian military campaigns (see also Kenyon 1979: 180; Kempinski 1983: 222–3; Bienkowski 1986: 128). It should be remembered that many Middle Bronze sites were surrounded by huge earthen ramparts, sometimes crowned by walls. These were interpreted as formidable fortifications erected as defenses against a potential external threat – in anticipation of Egyptian emancipation from the Hyksos rule and concomitant assaults on the Hyksos 'backup systems' in Canaan (Dever 1985). However, as a social phenomenon (Bunimovitz 1992; Finkelstein 1992) already emerging during the Middle Bronze I (Kenyon/Dever terminology, see Window 1 p. 330), the defenses (better termed 'earth-

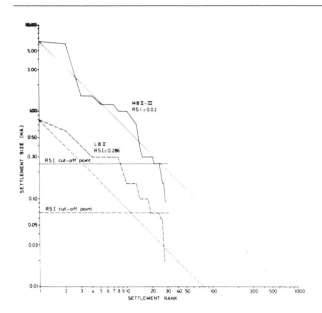

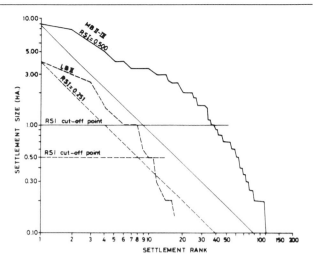

Figure 3 Middle Bronze II–III and Late Bronze II rank-size distributions of the Central Hill region

Figure 2 Middle Bronze II–III and Late Bronze rank-size distributions of the southern Coastal Plain (RSI = Rank Size Index)

works') may point to internal strife and externalisation of problems within the socio-political system. Indeed, traces of hostilities are known from a large number of sites, especially in the Central Hill region, prior to their final destruction; other signs for growing insecurity in this region during the later part of the Middle Bronze Age are also evident (Bunimovitz 1994: 181–86). Obviously, however, not all destructions were an internal Canaanite matter, and the Egyptian annihilation of Sharuhen (Tell el-'Ajjul; but see now Rainey 1993) – the main Hyksos centre in southern Palestine (Kempinski 1983: 146–8) – led to dramatic socio-political and economic changes in that region (see Ilan, this volume).

Further insight into the settlement crisis and socio-political change in Palestine at the end of the Middle Bronze/beginning of the Late Bronze Age is gained by a comparison of the politico-territorial organization in both periods. Contrary to common wisdom, according to which the politico-territorial organization in the Late Bronze Age is inferred from contemporary documents (see Alt 1925 = 1968 for a classical analysis) and projected backwards to the Middle Bronze Age, a reconstruction based on an analysis of the regional settlement systems' rank-size distributions in both periods seems preferable (presented *in extenso* in Bunimovitz 1989: Chapter 2; see also Bunimovitz 1993 for a review and critique of current methods for political reconstruction; Finkelstein 1992: 210–212 is another recent trial of Middle Bronze–Late Bronze Age politico-territorial reconstruction). This method enables the archaeologist to determine the socio-political organization in an examined region – whether centralized government or autonomous polities – by

detecting the level of integration in its settlement system (e.g., Johnson 1981; Kowalewski 1982; Paynter 1983).

In the southern Coastal Plain, the Middle Bronze II–III rank-size distribution (Figure 2) points to the existence of a large, comparatively integrated urban system – a united polity (cf. Dothan 1973: 14–17; Seger 1975: 44*–45*; Kempinski 1983: 60–4, 210–11, 222–3). This region was rapidly populated and urbanized during the Middle Bronze III (Gophna and Portugali 1988; Herzog 1989: 34–7), prospered economically, and shows the highest concentration of Hyksos royal name scarabs (Weinstein 1981: Figures 2–3) – probably an indication of administrative integration under Sharuhen. In contrast, the Late Bronze Age rank-size distribution, as well as the Amarna letters, testify to a low degree of socio-political integration – a cluster of semi-autonomous city-states. A similar situation of socio-political fragmentation prevailed also during the Late Bronze Age in the Jezreel Valley, but the rank-size distribution hints that in the Middle Bronze III the valley was more integrated, probably controlled by two main polities only: Megiddo and Shim'on (see also Finkelstein 1992: 212). In the Central Hill region the rank-size distributions (Figure 3) testify to diametrically opposite conditions, in which the settlement system was more integrated in the Late Bronze Age than in the Middle Bronze III (Bunimovitz, 1994: 187–93). Indeed, a locally-clustered pattern of Middle Bronze settlement has been identified in the central and northern parts of this region (Finkelstein 1985: 164–5; Zertal 1988: 188–90, 197), and Alt's perception of large Late Bronze Age territorial polities there (1925 = 1968) is fully supported by modern research (Na'aman 1986a, 1992).

The above observations make the great crisis at the end of the Middle Bronze Age more intelligible in terms of the socio-political structure that facilitated disintegration and collapse, disregarding its specific agents. Thus, negative interaction (i.e., competition over natural and human resources; warfare) between the peer polities that shared the Central Hill country may explain the chronic insecurity and instability in this region as well as the 'domino effect' which marked the collapse there (cf. Renfrew and Cherry 1986). Concomitantly, the disintegration of the large southern Coastal Plain polity can be reasonably explained by the destruction of its political and administrative 'capital' – Sharuhen.

Settlement patterns

It is now well established that the most powerful class of data in sociocultural explanations is settlement pattern. This may be taken as a material manifestation of the entire mode of production, and as shown above, of the social and political organization. An examination of the Late Bronze Age settlement pattern in Palestine (see Figure 1) and any changes to it is, therefore, essential for a better understanding of society in this period. However, traditional approaches to the subject were qualitative and accompanied by an implicit assumption that the Late Bronze Age settlement pattern remained stagnant for almost 400 years. Gonen's (1984) quantitative study of Late Bronze settlement data was therefore a breakthrough, but due to its limited data base and methodological drawbacks (e.g., lack of regionality, chronological ambiguity, etc.), a more detailed analysis based on a larger data base seemed imperative (Bunimovitz 1989: Chapter 3). According to data gathered from excavations and surveys all over western Palestine, the minimum number of Middle Bronze III sites is estimated at 550, presumably not all of them contemporaneous. Breaking the settlement map into subregions and examining the change in site number in each of them confirms the well known country-wide decrease in number of settlements during the Middle Bronze–Late Bronze transition, and discloses few distinct patterns of recovery during the rest of the period.

However, the full meaning of these patterns becomes clear only when one realizes the negative impact of current terminological concepts on our understanding of settlement processes in the Late Bronze Age. Thus, a perception of time as a series of discrete successive units – each possessing its unique cultural content – rather than a continuous flow (cf. Plog 1973: 189), is imposed on the material data from the end of the Late Bronze Age and creates dichotomies such as Late Bronze/Iron Age I, Canaanites/Israelites, Highlands/Lowlands. The result is an artificial splitting up of coherent and continuous cultural processes between the Late Bronze and Iron I periods (cf. Ussishkin 1985; Kempinski 1985; London 1989). In light of this insight, it is evident that many new settlements were established in most of the country's regions mainly during the thirteenth and twelfth centuries BCE. But it must be emphasized that this settlement growth was not the culmination of a 'natural', continuous recovery process spanning the fifteenth to fourteenth centuries BCE (contra Gonen 1984), but rather a unique change related to cultural processes which characterized the last phase of Egyptian dominance in Canaan (below).

Another important issue concerning settlement patterns and sociocultural change in Late Bronze Age Canaan is the relative share and importance of different sectors in the settlement hierarchy. According to recent claims the Late Bronze Age was a time of dramatic weakening of the urban fabric and a shift from urban centers to dispersed, small rural communities (Gonen 1984; London 1989). However, a close inspection of Middle Bronze III/Late Bronze settlement data, including information about rural settlements located in recent field surveys, renders a different interpretation of the evidence. Though it is true that many of the large urban centers which formed the backbone of settlement in Middle Bronze Age Canaan dramatically diminished in size, it should be emphasized that they remained urban in character.

Urbanism in the Late Bronze Age was, therefore, different in scale and appearance, and the period's settlement data obviously needs its own set of concepts and cultural criteria (other than size) for determining the function of sites. Separating the Middle Bronze III and Late Bronze settlements into 'urban' and 'rural' sectors, according to their respective sets of criteria, clearly demonstrates that despite the dramatic settlement crisis at the end of the Middle Bronze Age each sector kept its relative share within the overall number of sites and the total settled area. Obviously then, Palestine was no less urban in the Late Bronze Age than during the preceding period. However, further elaboration of these conclusions by an analysis of the regional urban/rural distributions of settlement sites brings into relief an essential social difference between the two periods. While in the Middle Bronze Age a few large urban centers dominated a wide rural hinterland, the moderate Late Bronze Age cities controlled a much diminished rural sector. Indeed, during most of this period hardly any rural settlements existed in the highlands and in few other regions of the country. Thus, contrary to current hypotheses about peasant movements and revolts during the Late Bronze Age (e.g., Mendenhall 1962; Gottwald 1979; Freedman and Graf 1983), the dichotomy epitomizing social relations in this period was not between city dwellers and peasants but between the sedentary (especially the sparse urban elite) and non-sedentary sectors of the population (below).

Politico-economic change

In a series of recent studies, the paradox of both prosperity and decline reflected in the Late Bronze Age material culture from Palestine has been addressed and debated (Bienkowski 1986: 136–55, 1989; Knapp 1989a, 1989b).

Figure 4 Late Bronze Age palaces (1–2. Megiddo), patrician houses (3–4. Tel Batash, 5. Tel Halif) and 'Governors' Residencies' (6. Beth-Shean, 7. Tell el-Farah (S), 8. Tel Aphek)

Figure 5 Late Bronze Age temples (1, 3–5. Hazor, 2. Tel Mevorakh, 6. Megiddo, 7, 8. Beth-Shean, 9. Lachish)

How can the demographic and settlement crisis, analyzed above, as well as the gradual degeneration in certain aspects of the period's material culture (Albright 1960: 101; Kenyon 1979: 199–200; Bienkowski 1986: 110–11, 150–2, 1989: 59; Knapp 1989a: 136–42) be reconciled with the remains of elaborate palaces and patrician houses (Figure 4; Oren 1992), temples (Figure 5; Mazar 1992: 169–83) and graves (Gonen 1992)? And how can one explain the rich assemblages of Cypriot and Mycenaean pottery (Plate 1; Gittlen 1981; Leonard 1981) and other important or locally-made luxury items (ivories, jewelry, faience vessels, etc.; Plate 2) unearthed in many Late Bronze governmental, religious and funerary contexts in terms of the cultural impoverishment envisaged?

Two hypotheses have been put forward in order to answer these questions. According to Bienkowski (1986: 137–56, 1989), the main causes of decline in Late Bronze Age Canaan were the diversion of resources to pay for the upkeep of the Egyptian colonial administration and the Egyptian control of trade. This decline, however, was localized due to the nature of Egyptian colonial presence: while key strategic areas under direct Egyptian control (mainly the densely populated Coastal Plain and northern valleys) flourished, the more marginal areas of Palestine and Transjordan (especially the hill regions) – not receiving any substantial benefit from agricultural surpluses and trade profits – were in economic recession.

Knapp's explanation for the Late Bronze Age material culture decline in Palestine (1989a, 1989b, 1992b, 1992c) is couched in a more holistic approach to the politico-economic structure of the country and its changes during the Middle Bronze II–Late Bronze II periods. In his opinion, the Egyptian conquest of Canaan, and especially Thothmes III's administrative and military policy, altered the politico-economic and material base of the southern Levant profoundly: the formerly independent, economically-competitive polities became imperially dominated vassal city-states. Furthermore, the Middle Bronze Age complex network of hierarchical settlements and markets, dendritic rural hinterland and presumed gateway communities (see Ilan this volume, Chapter 18) had collapsed, leaving behind a few urban centers to function as nodes on the caravan routes of a major international trade system extending from western Asia to the eastern Mediterranean. During both periods, however, power relations ensured the flow of subsistence goods and luxury items into urban centers. But whereas peripheral Middle Bronze areas had retained sufficient wealth to ensure their livelihood, the Egyptian imperial demands on Late Bronze Age polities – aimed at extracting maximum possible tribute with the minimum effort – may have exceeded the productive capacities of all but the most resilient, self-sustaining urban centers. Thus, the archaeological record reveals an apparent collapse – abandonment of villages and decline in many urban centers – as well as prosperity in other urban centers.

Plate 1 Mycenaean pottery from Tel Dan. (© Tel Dan Expedition, The Nelson Glueck School of Biblical Archaeology, Jerusalem)

Seemingly contrasting, due to their different perspectives (specific/short-term *vs.* holistic/long-term) and interpretation of Egypt's economic and imperial motives in Canaan, the above hypotheses would be better considered as complementing each other. Thus, while the economic aspects of the Egyptian occupation of Canaan and the burden imposed on the local rulers and population are still a matter of debate (Ahituv 1978; Na'aman 1981; see also Redford 1992: 209–13), Bienkowski's and Knapp's analyses reflect the complex pattern of economic decline and survival in Late Bronze Age Canaan. In this context, it seems that the costly palaces, temples and wealthy elite burials unearthed in the main urban centres should not be simplistically interpreted as symbols of localized prosperity, but as evidence for conspicuous consumption aimed to maintain power relations within an economically-impoverished and socially-unstable country (Plate 3; below).

Social organization

The most prominent features in the socio-political landscape of Palestine during the Late Bronze Age were the few urban settlements (such as Megiddo, Gezer, Lachish). Though much smaller and less impressive than the enormous Middle Bronze Age cities, contemporary texts leave no doubt that most of them were centers of petty kingdoms or city-states. Consequently, important insights concerning the material manifestation of their socio-political attributes can be gained from cross cultural research of city-states and small-scale states – a neglected field in anthropological archaeology until recently (see e.g., Griffeth and Thomas 1981; Renfrew and Wagstaff 1982).

According to the Amarna Letters, in the fourteenth century BCE Palestine seems to have been divided between 15–17 major city-states. Almost all of these central places

are identifiable, and by employing both a variety of documentary sources (the Amarna Letters; other Egyptian texts; biblical descriptions of Israelite tribal allotments) and archaeological data, their territories were ingeniously delineated by Na'aman (1986a, 1988, 1992). This reconstructed politico-territorial map brings into relief two interesting spatial qualities:

1. The average on-ground distance between each of the main city-states and its nearest peers is about 35 km.
2. The territories of these polities are roughly of the same size range, well below 1000 km^2.

These qualities, as well as the small number of main political centers, concur with the Early State Module (ESM) pattern that has been observed in many early civilizations – a cluster of 10–20 autonomous centers with a mean distance of about 40 km between them, each dominating a modular area of approximately 1500 km^2 or less (Renfrew 1975: 12–18; Figure 6). According to the politico-territorial reconstruction presented earlier, it seems that the Late Bronze Age ESMs in Palestine crystallized during the sixteenth and fifteenth centuries BCE, following the socio-political upheavals at that time (*contra* Finkelstein 1992: 212).

The limited territorial extent of the ESMs was attributed either to increasing costs of administration with increasing distance from the central place (Cherry 1978: 424–5), or to the ability of rural populations to avail themselves of center services (Johnson 1987: 115-16). In any case, a radius of about 20 km (a one day round-trip distance in the pre-automobile era) apparently formed in early complex societies the boundary both for direct administrative control of rural populations, and for the participation of such populations in the central places' economic and social activities. It seems that in Late Bronze Age Palestine, where lesser city-states and even towns could enjoy political autonomy within a distance of a few hours' ride from the major city-states (Na'aman 1986a, 1992), the reduced scale of the ESMs is a faithful reflection of the social constraints that inhibited territorial and organizational growth – demographic decline, sparseness of rural settlements and a contracted urban elite.

Indeed, population shortage seems to have troubled the Canaanite city-states during the Late Bronze Age. Since early complex societies relied on human resources as the main means of production and source of income (e.g., Claessen 1978: 549–54), the dearth of sedentary population coupled with the compulsory need to share its meagre labor resources with the Egyptian government (Na'aman 1981: 178–9), presented a serious problem for the Canaanite urban elite and generated a vicious circle. In order to maintain rule and status, great material investments were needed (for the connection between power, ideology and material culture see, e.g., Miller and Tilley 1984; Whitelam 1986; Trigger 1990) and thus the

Plate 2 An ivory plaque from the Late Bronze Age palace at Megiddo (© Israel Antiquities Authority)

burden imposed on the subjects became heavier; these subjects, in turn, reacted time and again by deserting the established social system – thereby depleting it. Under these circumstances, political and economic power meant having control of as many human resources as possible, and this seems to have been the prime motive behind the endless attempts at territorial expansion, border disputes and ad hoc coalitions which epitomized the interaction between the Canaanite city-states (cf. Marfoe 1979: 16–18).

The Shifting Frontier Model

In contrast to the maximization and stabilization strategy undertaken by the urban elite in order to survive, other sectors of Canaanite society responded more flexibly to the political and economic changes that took place in Palestine during the Late Bronze Age. Their adaptational strategy and its dialectical relations with local power and Egyptian governmental policy in Canaan can be described and explained by what I have termed 'The Shifting Frontier Model' (Bunimovitz 1989: Chapter 5, 1994: 193–202).

Following Owen Lattimore's (1940) and Robert Adams' (1974, 1978) frontier researches in China and Mesopotamia, it should be recognized that the ecological and social frontier of Palestine can oscillate within very broad limits, depending on the strength of the central ruling power. A panoramic view over the country's history reveals that in times of public security and development the frontier was pushed southward and eastward, and the lowlands enjoyed settlement stability and prosperity. However, in the absence of such conditions, they rapidly became frontier zones, populated by nomads and other non-sedentary groups (see e.g., Amiran 1953: 192–209; Amiran and Ben-Arieh 1963: 162–6; Hütteroth 1975; for an analogous situation in Syria and Jordan during the nineteenth century AD, see Lewis 1955, 1987). The collapse of the socio-political system in Palestine (especially in the Central Hill country) at the end of the Middle Bronze Age and the takeover of Canaan by the Egyptian Eighteenth Dynasty

Plate 3 A bronze plaque from Hazor depicting a Canaanite noble or king (© Hazor Expedition, Hebrew University)

brought about far reaching changes in the socio-political structure and in settlement patterns: the frontier 'came down' from the hilly regions to the Coastal Plain, the Shephela and inner valleys, and bands of 'Apiru – outcasts and various groups of nomads/pastoralists (for the derogatory meaning of this term in the Amarna Letters, see Na'aman 1986b: 275–6; Marfoe 1979: 9–10) – which descended from the hills, roamed there without interference (Na'aman 1982: 235–6; Marfoe 1979: 15). This situation

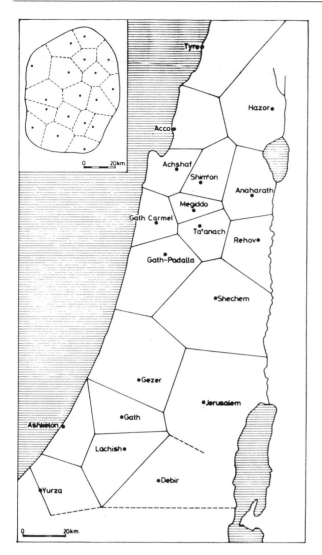

Figure 6 The spatial configuration of the Late Bronze Age city-states in Palestine compared to Renfrew's ESMs model

Figure 7 The Egyptian capture of Ashkelon by Ramesses II or Merenptah

founded settlements (e.g. 'Izbet Sartah – Finkelstein 1986; Tell Beit Mirsim B1–2 – Greenberg 1987) have usually been attributed to the Israelite Settlement.

Bridging the divide

The foregoing analysis aspired to exemplify, through the specific case study of the Late Bronze Age society, that archaeological research of 'documented' complex societies in Palestine can go beyond the limits of descriptive culture-history set by former generations of researchers. However, as already emphasized, anthropologically-oriented explanations, usually based on cross-cultural analogies or general models, should be context related. For Syro-Palestinian archaeologists, the post-processual battle-cry: 'back to historical context' actually depicts a familiar, daily reality; but unfortunately, the tyranny of the historical context in this field of study has been so powerful that broader, cross-cultural or long-term perspectives were denied. This seems to be the main reason for the provinciality of Levantine archaeology – namely, its persistent reluctance to take advantage of its tremendously rich archaeological, historical and ethnographic data in order to produce, test and improve general, worldwide archaeological models and theories. As shown above, certain anthropological conjectures concerning social processes such as socio-political disintegration of early states (Cowgill 1988), formation of secondary states via historical succession (Price 1978), continuous construction of social boundaries (Eisenstadt 1988), etc., can be examined in light of the specific socio-cultural changes taking place in Palestine during the Late Bronze

completely changed following the revolution in both the nature and extent of Egyptian involvement in Canaan during the reign of the Nineteenth and Twentieth dynasties. A close examination of historical analogies (e.g., Lewis 1955, 1987), Egyptian sources, and archaeological data suggests that, as a consequence of the vigorous measures taken by the pharaohs of these dynasties (annexation and direct rule – Figure 7; erection of a network of 'Governor's Residencies' in the main city-states – see Figure 4, Plate 4; punitive expeditions against non-sedentary groups – Plate 5; economic exploitation of the country, etc. see, e.g., Weinstein 1981: 17–23; Singer 1988 and bibliography there), public security was restored, the frontier retreated, and non-sedentary groups resettled in the lowland regions, the piedmont and the hill country. Some of these newly-

Plate 4 The 'Governor's residency' at Tel Aphek (© Tel Aphek Expedition, Tel Aviv University)

Plate 5 A victory stele of Seti I from Beth-Shean Height = 2.45 m (© Israel Antiquities Authority)

Age. It seems, therefore, that Colin Renfrew's optimistic vision (1980: 297), addressed over a decade ago to American archaeologists, carries also a message for Syro-Palestinian archaeology:

> when the interest is in general processes of change, [the Ancient World's] data are exceptionally rich. There is therefore a brilliant opportunity for anyone who can command the data and scholarship of the Great Tradition while employing the problem-orientation and research methods of current anthropological archaeology. There is no doubt in my mind that the principal development in at least the earlier part of the next century . . . will be the incorporation of some of the new strengths of anthropological archaeology into the Great Tradition, thereby bridging the Divide [between the two], to the great benefit of both sides.

WHEN DID THE LATE BRONZE AGE BEGIN? – PROBLEMS IN DEMARCATION AND TERMINOLOGY

The beginning of the Late Bronze Age was dated by Albright (1960: 84, 96–9) to *ca.* 1550 BCE on both historical and archaeological grounds – the occupation of Canaan by the Egyptian Eighteenth Dynasty and the first appearance in Palestine of Bichrome Ware. However, according to G.E. Wright (1961: 91, Charts 6, 7), the material culture typical of Late Bronze I appeared at only *ca.* 1500 BCE. More recently, J. Seger (1975: 45*) and W.G. Dever (1987: 149) claimed that the historical and archaeological demarcation line between the Middle and the Late Bronze Ages should be lowered further – to the reign of Thothmes III. Dever even suggested that both Middle Bronze IIC and Late Bronze I should be renamed 'Middle Bronze III', corresponding to a revised historical/archaeological subdivision of the Middle Bronze Period: Middle Bronze I = Early Bronze IV, Middle Bronze IIA = Middle Bronze II, Middle Bronze IIC–Late Bronze I = Middle Bronze III (1987: 149–50), in correspondence with Kenyon 1966: 53, n. 5). He further elaborated (and complicated) his terminology by suggesting a 'Transitional Middle Bronze III/Late Bronze 1A Phase', *ca.* 1550–1450 BCE (1990, especially n. 3), later redated to *ca.* 1500–1450, following the currently favored 'lower' Egyptian chronology (Dever 1992; for the recent debate concerning Syro-Palestinian Middle Bronze chronology vis-à-vis Egyptian chronology, see also Bietak 1991; Dever 1991.

Since other scholars (e.g. Tuffnell 1958: 6, 67; Kantor 1965: 23; Kempinski 1983: 223–4) prefer to begin the Late Bronze Age *ca.* 1600 BCE, more than 100 years earlier than Dever, the confusion about the Middle Bronze/Late Bronze transition seems to have reached an unprecedented peak (for comparative chronological charts see Leonard 1989: 6–7; Dever 1992: Figure 1). As a result, the validity of traditional archaeological criteria for demarcating the beginning of the Late Bronze Age (mainly pottery and patterns of settlement) is suspect and should be reconsidered.

Plate 1.2 A group of Late Bronze Age I local and Cypriot pottery from a burial near Shechem (© Israel Antiquities Authority)

Pottery As local pottery exemplifies undisturbed continuity between the Middle and Late Bronze Ages (Plate 1.1), new types of pottery (mainly imported) – 'Chocolate-on-White' (Plate 1.2) and Bichrome Wares, Gray/Black Lustrous juglets, and certain types of Cypriot pottery – serve to indicate the beginning of Late Bronze I (Plate 1.2). However, a close examination of these *fossiles directeurs* reveal that their appearance in Canaan is not accompanied by any noticeable cultural change. Moreover, it seems that the importation/local production of all 'fine' wares is another manifestation of the commercial and cultural prosperity of Palestine during the reign of the Fifteenth ('Hyksos') Dynasty (for convenient discussions concerning the above pottery types, most of which appeared *before* the end of the Middle Bronze Age, see Leonard 1989: 10–11; Oren 1969; Gittlen 1981: 49–51).

Pattern of settlement Because of the cultural continuity between the Middle and Late Bronze Ages, it has been claimed that the destructions and changes in settlement patterns – allegedly resulting from the conquest of Palestine by the Egyptian Eighteenth Dynasty – should indicate the beginning of the Late Bronze Age. However, as argued elsewhere in this chapter, this settlement crisis – whatever its causes – was a prolonged process, starting in the late seventeenth century BCE and continuing into the reign of Thothmes III. Therefore, fixing the beginning of a new period at a certain point within these time limits seems to be arbitrary.

Since neither 1600/1550 nor 1500 BCE marks an unequivocal cultural change that merits special designation from an *archaeological* point of view, a different solution to the problems of demarcation and terminology concerning the Middle and Late Bronze Ages is suggested. In accordance with current practical use of limited chronological/cultural frameworks in the study of the Iron Age in Palestine (e.g., the tenth, eighth centuries BCE, etc.), the *historically*-based terminological framework of the Late Bronze Age should be set aside. Reference to archaeological entities typical of the sixteenth and fifteenth centuries BCE etc., will thus prevent the artificial separation of cultural processes into 'periods' imposed on the material culture. To achieve this aim, the study of the Late Bronze Age material culture (including field research and publication) should be intensified.

Plate 1.1 Local Canaanite pottery from Tel Aphek (© The Israel Museum, Jerusalem)

LATE BRONZE AGE BURIAL CUSTOMS

The 'Archaeology of Death' – the study of mortuary practices of past human societies – accompanies the discipline throughout its development. In recent decades, however, an unprecedented interest in the social aspects of mortuary practices – especially in the social correlates of funerary material remains – became one of the most conspicuous research fields of social archaeology (for an overview and bibliography see, e.g., Chapman and Randsborg 1981).

In Palestine, Late Bronze Age burials were usually considered as a primary source of data for burial customs, as well as for contemporary material culture, e.g., pottery, metal artifacts, jewelry, etc. More ambitiously, a recent study (Gonen 1992) endeavored to analyze synchronic and diachronic burial patterns in Late Bronze Age Canaan in order to identify and interpret spatio-temporal cultural processes.

The burial types of Late Bronze Age Canaan fell into two main categories: indigenous and foreign. The first category, which represents the local population, is by far the dominant one – both in number and distribution. It includes cave burials for multiple interments, pit burials for individual interment (Figure 2.1), and intramural burials. The second category is comprised of various types of burials, each limited in number and geographical distribution. The introduction of foreign burial customs is believed to be only incidental, with little bearing on the major burial trends in Canaan during the Late Bronze.

According to Gonen's analysis, the indigenous burial customs of the Late Bronze Age show a clear regional differentiation: while in the mountainous regions and western foothills of the country cave burials for multiple interment were preferred, pit burials for individual interment were the most common burial type in the Coastal Plain. The inner valleys and main urban centres are characterized by a mixture of burial customs. A spatio-temporal examination of the above two major burial customs practised in Canaan during the Late Bronze Age reveals two parallel trends – the spread of pit burials along the Coastal Plain and into the inner valleys; the receding of cave burials into the hill regions.

As an explanation for these cultural processes, Gonen put forward the hypothesis that the socio-religious values in Canaan during the Late Bronze Age were affected by Egyptian cultural norms due to the long, intensive period of Egyptian rule in Canaan. She further suggested that the receptivity of the local population to the Egyptian values and norms depended on the degree of regional accessibility. Thus, the Egyptian cultural impact seems to be felt most strongly along the land communication routes between Egypt and the regions to the north and northeast of Palestine, i.e. in the lowlands which were under firm Egyptian control. Adopting essential components of the Egyptian burial customs, the lowlands population gave up the long-practised communal burials in favor of individual interment in pits.

Contemporaneously with the 'progressive' trends evidenced in the Coastal Plain and inner valleys, the mountain-dwelling people of Canaan continued to bury their dead according to the old customs of their ancestors. They did not replace cave burials for multiple interments, and no other custom penetrated the hilly regions. Due to their poor accessibility, these areas remained outside the sphere of Egyptian influence and became strongholds of traditionalism and resistance to change.

Another process noticed by Gonen is the dwindling and disappearance of intramural burials. This indigenous custom, mainly practised in the urban centers of Canaan during the Middle Bronze Age, was replaced in the Late Bronze period by formal cemeteries outside settlements.

The analysis of Late Bronze Age burial customs in Canaan raises many intriguing questions concerning culture change during this period. Since Egyptian burials in Canaan – mainly of the anthropoid coffins type (see chapter opening photograph) – are known only from Egyptian governmental centers such as Deir el-Balah, south of Gaza, and Beth-Shean (though a few more examples are known from Lachish and Pella), how they came to affect the indigenous burial customs is far from self evident. Egyptian mortuary practices and ideas, however, may have diffused into Palestine via the expelled Semites ('Hyksos') or through the Egyptian indoctrination of Canaanite princes (Redford 1992: 198). The social upheavals in Canaan at the end of the Middle Bronze Age/beginning of the Late Bronze Age most probably also affected traditional burial customs. Thus, the shift from collective family chamber tombs to individual interments seems to be a normal response to changing circumstances: destruction and abandonment of many settlements, demographic decline, social disintegration, disorder, and a growing number of uprooted and other parasocial elements within the lowlands. In such a social atmosphere, when many were dispossessed of their forefathers' tombs, people must have been less assured of their security of habitation and less inclined to cut new family tombs (cf. Mee and Cavanagh 1984: 57–61). It is of great interest, however, that the two contrasting sectors within the Late Bronze Age Canaanite society – the urban elite and the semi-nomadic pastoralists of the mountainous regions – both of which seem to be alert to their geneological succession, continued to bury their dead in communal family tombs throughout the period.

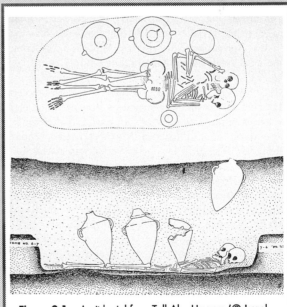

Figure 2.1 A pit burial from Tell Abu Hawam (© Israel Antiquities Authority)

20

THE IMPACT OF THE SEA PEOPLES IN CANAAN (1185–1050 BCE)

Lawrence E. Stager

Introduction

Social archaeologists have usually shunned migration (and even diffusion) as an explanation of cultural change. Partly this aversion is due to an earlier generation of archaeologists who suffered from the 'Tower of Babel' syndrome in which cultural creations were thought to emanate from a single source and spread to the rest of an uncreative world. Quite often this was accompanied by a naive belief that pots could easily be identified with people. Partly this negative attitude toward migration and diffusion springs from premises of the newer archaeology in which internal developments, more often than external ones, were assumed to explain cultural change. For this cadre of archaeologists, all archaeology (like politics) is local. They take comfort in the assumption that explanations of cultural change reside within the confines of regional research, which, in turn, justifies their ignorance of the broader field of comparative archaeology. That this assumption is equally unwarranted should become clear from the case study that follows.

The Philistines, one contingent of a larger confederation known collectively as the 'Sea Peoples' (by modern scholars), provide a classic case of mass migration from their homeland and resettlement in new parts of the coastal Mediterranean. This peopling of the eastern Mediterranean seaboard, beginning in the decade 1185–1175 BCE and continuing a generation or two later, in a zone already occupied by Canaanites (also known as Phoenicians) for a millennium or more, can be documented by a variety of written sources in Akkadian, Ugaritic, Egyptian, and Hebrew, by iconography (especially Egyptian wall reliefs), and by archaeology.

According to the eighth to seventh century BCE Biblical prophets, the Philistines came from Caphtor, the Hebrew name for Crete (Amos 9: 7 and Jer. 47: 4). That this tradition conveys a certain amount of historical memory about their Mycenaean origins, some four centuries earlier, has only recently become clearer through the comparative archaeology of the eastern Mediterranean. The Biblical and Assyrian sources indicate that the core of Philistine culture formed about five major cities – the Philistine Pentapolis – located in the coastal plain of southern Canaan (Josh. 13:

2–3; Tadmor 1966). For nearly 600 years, during most of the Iron Age, these five cities – Ashdod, Ashkelon, Ekron (Tel Miqne), Gaza, and Gath – formed the heartland of Philistia, or the biblical 'land of the Philistines'; each city and its territory being ruled by a *seren*, or 'tyrant' (if *turannos* is of pre-classical origin) (for an excellent synthesis of Philistine history and archaeology, see B. Mazar 1986; 1992).

Four of the five cities, Gath being the exception, have been convincingly identified with ancient sites. Gath is usually located at Tell es-Safi, but its proximity to Ekron makes this identification very unlikely (see below). Ashdod, Ashkelon and Ekron have been extensively excavated; Gaza, which lies under the modern city, has not. By identifying a coherent core of material culture in the heartland of Philistia and comparing that with other cultural cores of Canaan, it should be possible to differentiate this putative alien, or intrusive, culture and to establish its boundaries (for a masterful treatment of Philistine material culture, see T. Dothan 1982).

To make a persuasive archaeological case for mass migration of peoples from one homeland to another, certain criteria must be met (Adams 1968; Rouse 1958, 1965; Trigger 1968: 40–1):

1. The intrusive culture must be distinguished from contemporary indigenous (or other foreign) cultures in the new area of settlement. Massive movements of a people should produce a 'wave' of new settlements. If there is population replacement, or one group replacing another, the nature of that replacement should be clarified. For example, if the intrusive group launches an invasion, there should be synchronous discontinuities with past cultures in the zone of contention. This might appear as destruction and abandonment of some sites all together (see below, Ugarit), destruction and resettlement of some sites by the new population (Ashdod, Ashkelon, Ekron and Ibn Hani), or settlements founded *de novo* in the initial or later stages of the intrusive culture (Tell Qasile).
2. The homeland of the migrating group must be located, its material culture identified, and temporal precedence of that culture demonstrated in its place of origin.
3. The route of migration must be traced and checked for its archaeological, historical, and geographical plausibility. If

Ashdod. 'Ashdoda', enthroned mother goddess (courtesy of The Israel Museum, Jerusalem/photograph: Nahum Slapak)

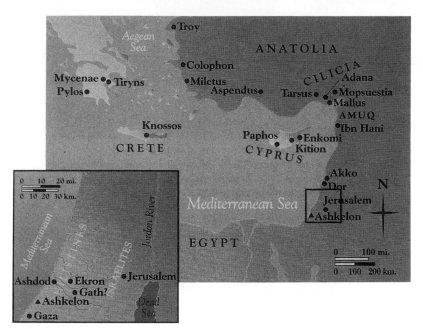

Figure 1 Map of the eastern Mediterranean (from L. E. Stager, *Ashkelon Discovered*, p. 5, Biblical Archaeology Society)

it was an overland route, spatial–temporal distribution of the material culture should indicate the path and direction of large-scale migrations. If migration was by sea, then it must be demonstrated that the immigrants had the requisite shipping technology and transport capacity for such maritime movements of peoples and belongings. The only terrestrial traces of such sea movements, if they were hostile, might be a series of coastal predations and destructions along the route and at successful beachheads.

Of the archaeological remains left by the Sea Peoples, their pottery, when properly understood, has a most expressive tale to tell about the origins of its makers, and about the events and processes by which they settled in new territories.

Pottery

Mycenaean IIIC:1b (hereafter Myc IIIC), or Sea Peoples' Monochrome (hereafter SPM) = Stage 1 of Sea Peoples' Settlement

Decorated wares are painted in a single color, usually black, with simple horizontal bands, spirals, streamers, loops, birds, and fish. Forms of this decorated pottery are mostly kraters, bell-shaped bowls (large and small), carinated bowls with strap handles, stirrup jars, and jugs with strainer spouts (Figure 3: 11–23, 25–34, 38–49). Plain wares of exotic type include a deep bowl, known as a *kalathos* in Greek (Figure 3: 20) and a one-handled cooking jug (Figure 3: 19). All of these pottery types, both plain and decorated, originated in the world of the Mycenaean Greeks (see T. and M. Dothan 1992; and T. Dothan 1994).

But, unlike the imported Myc IIIB pottery of the Late

Bronze Age, all of the Myc IIIC wares found in the Levant in the early Iron Age were made of local clays. (An exception to this may be the few possible imports of Myc IIIC pottery found at Beth Shan and at Tell Keisan.) When Myc IIIC pottery from Ashdod or Ekron in Philistia or from Kition, Enkomi, or Palaeopaphos in Cyprus was tested by neutron activation, the results were always the same: it was made from the local clays (Asaro, Perlman and Dothan 1971; Perlman, Asaro and Friedman 1971; Gunneweg et al. 1986; Asaro and Perlman 1973). That this locally manufactured pottery was not the product of a few Mycenaean potters or their workshops, brought from abroad to meet indigenous demands for Mycenaean cooking pots and coarse deep bowls as well as decorated wares, seems clear from the large quantities of decorated pottery found at coastal sites from Tarsus to Ashkelon (Stager 1985a: 62, 64, n.37). At Ibn Hani and Ekron, locally-made Mycenaean pottery constitutes at least half of the ceramic repertoire (T. Dothan 1994; J. and E. Lagarce 1981); at Ashdod, ca 30 percent (M. Dothan 1989; M. Dothan et al. 1967, 1971, 1982); whereas local Levantine ('Canaanite') pottery in the form of store jars, juglets, bowls, lamps and cooking pots makes up the remainder of the assemblage.

The appearance in quantity of Myc IIIC in Cyprus and the Levant heralds the arrival of the Sea Peoples, whose predations are recorded in the famous account of Ramesses III of 1175 BCE. It characterizes Stage 1 of the Philistine settlement in the southern coastal plain of Canaan. The notion that Myc IIIC ware does not appear until after Ramesses III (Ussishkin 1985) would mean a 30-year hiatus between destruction and resettlement in Philistia, Syria, Cyprus and elsewhere. It is inconceivable that Philistia and that stretch of the Via Maris remained unoccupied during Ramesses III's long reign (1182–1151), especially since he invested the surrounding area (see Figure 2). The sequence of cultural change is replicated at the three Pentapolis sites – Ashdod, Ashkelon, and Ekron. There new settlements characterized by Myc IIIC pottery were built upon the charred ruins of the previous Late Bronze Age II Canaanite, or Egypto-Canaanite, cities. The layout and organization of these new cities is far from clear; however, what is known about them suggests that their founders had a radically different concept of a city from that of the Canaanites. Philistine cities were also much larger than those they replaced. Later, this new urban concept and its impact on the landscape will be discussed under the rubric 'urban imposition' (see below).

Philistine Bichrome = Stage 2 of Philistine Settlement

This distinctive ware, painted with red and black decoration (Figure 3: 1–9; Plate 1), represents a regional style that developed after the Philistines had lived for a generation or two in Canaan (A. Mazar 1985; Stager 1985a, 1991; Singer 1985). To the basic Mycenaean forms already in their repertoire, they added other ones from Canaan and Cyprus (Figure 3: 1, 4–5, 8–9; see T. Dothan 1982, Ch. 3), as well as decorative motifs from Egypt (such as the floral pattern in Figure 3: 1). Bichrome technique had been known in Canaan since the Late Bronze Age I. A variant of the bichrome tradition developed in Phoenicia and in Palestine (e.g. at Ashkelon) in the Late Bronze Age II, where it was later absorbed into the Philistine repertoire.

Philistine Bichrome ware was once considered the hallmark of the first Philistines to reach the Levant, early in the reign of Ramesses III (T. Dothan 1982; Brug 1985). An earlier contingent of Sea Peoples fought with the Libyans against the Egyptian Pharaoh Merenptah (1212–1202), but the Philistines were not among them. This pre-Philistine group, or 'first wave' of Sea Peoples, supposedly brought the Myc IIIC potting traditions to the shores of Canaan, where they founded the first cities on exactly the same sites later identified with the Philistine Pentapolis (M. Dothan 1989, 1993a; T. Dothan 1989; T. and M. Dothan 1992). It seems highly unlikely that the pre-Philistine group with Monochrome pottery was displaced by the later Philistine group with Bichrome pottery at each of the Pentapolis sites.

It is obvious from the battle reliefs of Merenptah that Ashkelon, seaport of the Pentapolis, was inhabited by Canaanites, not Sea Peoples, during the reign of Merenptah (Figure 3: 57; Stager 1985a, 1991; Yurco 1986). The simplest explanation is that the confederation of Sea Peoples, including the Philistines, mentioned in texts and depicted in reliefs of Ramesses III (Figure 3: 52–5) were the bearers of Myc IIIC pottery. The first generation of Philistines to settle in Canaan made Myc IIIC pottery. The developments in style from simple Monochrome to more elaborate Bichrome represent changes in the potting tradition of the Philistines two or three generations after their arrival in southern Canaan. The eclectic style of Bichrome pottery resulted, not from a period of peregrinations about the Mediterranean during the decades between Merenptah and Ramesses III, but from a process of Philistine acculturation involving the adaptation and absorption of many traditions to be found among the various peoples living in Canaan. This acculturation process continued among the Philistines throughout their nearly 600-year history in Palestine (Stone 1993; Gitin 1992).

As one moves from core to periphery in the decades following Stage 1, the material culture of the Philistines shows evidence of spatial and temporal 'distancing' from the original templates and concepts. Failure to understand this acculturation process has led to the inclusion of questionable items in the Philistine corpus of material culture remains (for example, the anthropoid coffins), or worse, to a denial of a distinct core of Philistine cultural remains, just two or three generations after their arrival in Canaan, at the beginning of Stage 2, ca. 1150 BCE (Bunimovitz 1990).

Absolute chronology

The stratigraphically controlled ceramic sequence of Myc IIIB, followed by Myc IIIC, followed by a brief overlap of SPM and Philistine Bichrome, followed by Philistine Bichrome alone has been recapitulated at all of the Pentapolis sites which have been excavated – Ashdod, Ashkelon and Ekron. This sequence can be dated very precisely because of the synchronisms which can be established with Egypt (for absolute dates, see Wente and van Siclen 1976). However, these datable Egyptian objects must be used with discretion; usually they provide only a *terminus post* (not *ante*) *quem*.

Myc IIIB pottery was once thought to terminate with Ramesses II (1279–1212), until a sword bearing the cartouche of his son Merenptah (1212–1202) was found in the final destruction of Ugarit, where Myc IIIB was abundant and Myc IIIC did not appear. Two large Egyptian jars inscribed with the cartouches of Seti II (1199–1193) (Oren 1993c: 1390), discovered in the fortress of Haruba in northeastern Sinai, and a faience vase with the cartouche of Tewosret (1193–1185), from Deir Alla in the central Jordan Valley, were found in contexts with Myc IIIB pottery. The vase must date to ca 1186–1185, since she became pharaoh only during the last two years of her reign.

The lower date for the final appearance of Myc IIIB pottery was recently confirmed by another synchronism between Egypt and the Levant. Shortly before the final destruction of Ugarit, a Syrian named Baya or Bay, 'chief of the bodyguard of pharaoh of Egypt', sent a letter in Akkadian (RS 86.2230) to Ammurapi, the last King of

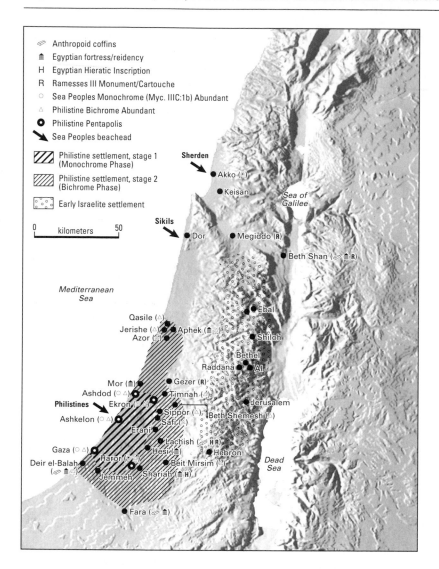

Legend:
- ⬭ Anthropoid coffins
- 🏛 Egyptian fortress/reidency
- H Egyptian Hieratic Inscription
- R Ramesses III Monument/Cartouche
- ○ Sea Peoples Monochrome (Myc. IIIC:1b) Abundant
- △ Philistine Bichrome Abundant
- ◉ Philistine Pentapolis
- ➘ Sea Peoples beachead
- ▨ Philistine settlement, stage 1 (Monochrome Phase)
- ▨ Philistine settlement, stage 2 (Bichrome Phase)
- ⬚ Early Israelite settlement

0 — kilometers — 50

Figure 2 Map of coastal Canaan, showing major Sea Peoples' enclaves (drawing by Joseph A. Greene)

Ugarit (Freu 1988; Hoffner 1992). Baya served under both Siptah (1193–1187) and Tewosret (1193–1185). His letter arrived at Ugarit while Myc IIIB pottery was still in use. Myc IIIC pottery does not appear there because the Sea Peoples did not occupy the site after they destroyed it. In fact, Ugarit lay deserted for the next seven centuries (Yon 1992). However, at nearby Ibn Hani, the Sea Peoples built over the charred remains, containing Myc IIIB ware, of the seaside palace of the Ugaritian king. More than half of the ceramic yield from their new settlement was Myc. IIIC pottery (Lagarce 1982; Lagarce and Lagarce 1981), a proportion comparable to that of Stage 1 settlements in Philistia (see below). Thus the final destruction of Ugarit, as well as many other coastal cities in the eastern Mediterranean, occurred only a decade or so before the summary of events recorded by Ramesses III (1182–1151) in his much cited 'War Against the Peoples of the Sea' (Wilson 1969a: 262):

Dateline: Year 8 under the Majesty of Ramesses III (1175 BC): '. . . The foreign countries [Sea Peoples] made a conspiracy in their islands. All at once the lands were removed and scattered in the fray. No land could stand before their arms, from Hatti, Kode [Cilicia], Carchemish, Arzawa and Alashiya [Cyprus] on, being cut off at [one time]. A camp [was set up] in one place in Amor [Amurru]. They desolated its people, and its land was like that which has never come into being. They were coming forward toward Egypt, while the flame was prepared before them. Their confederation [of Sea Peoples] was the Philistines, Tjeker [=Sikils], Shekelesh, Denye(n) and Weshesh lands united'.

The sea route of migration

The Sea Peoples established beachheads all along the shores of the eastern Mediterranean and on the coastlands of Cyprus. The route which the newcomers took to the

Plate 1 Philistine Bichrome pottery (left to right): jug with strainer spout, cylindrical bottle, stirrup jar, small bell-shaped bowl (*skyphos*), and large deep bowl (*krater*) (courtesy of The Israel Museum, Jerusalem)

Levant is clear from the synchronous destructions of Late Bronze Age coastal cities from Tarsus to Ashkelon. The same pattern of devastation can be observed for several of the coastal cities of Cyprus, which the sea raiders could have reached only by boat.

After the Sea Peoples' invasion of Cyprus, its name was changed from Alashiya to Yadanana, meaning 'Isle of the Danunians/Danaoi/Denyen' (Luckenbill 1914). The Philistines bequeathed their ethnicon to Philistia (and later to all of Palestine). The Sikils, who settled at Dor, also sailed west and gave their name to Sicily. And the Sherden, who probably established a beachhead in Akko, bequeathed their name to Sardinia (M. Dothan 1986). The renaming of whole territories after various groups of Sea Peoples provides another measure of their impact.

The sequence of beachheads followed by Stage 1 settlements is remarkably similar whether in Cyprus or the Levant. Although not all Cypriot archaeologists agree, there seems to be a series of synchronous destructions throughout coastal Cyprus, which brought several Late Bronze Age coastal cities, such as Enkomi, Hala Sultan Tekke, Kition, Maa-Palaeokastro, to a fiery end in the early twelfth century BCE (Yannai 1983; Karageorghis 1992, 1982). New cities, with Myc IIIC pottery, were built over the ruins of Late Bronze Age cities, many of which had received the last of the Greek imported pottery known as Myc IIIB. Farther inland, the Sea Peoples founded new settlements, such as Sinda and Athienou, over the ruins of Late Cypriot IIB cities.

Cypriot archaeologists invoke the Achaeans or Danaoi of Homeric epic as the agents of culture change in Cyprus (Karageorghis 1992); in the Levant, the same change is ascribed to the Sea Peoples. Both agents participated in the same 'event' recorded by Ramesses III (A. Mazar 1988) and should probably be related to the same confederacy of Sea Peoples, or Mycenaean Greeks, who invaded the coastlands and the island of Alashiya (Cyprus) ca 1185–1175.

Correspondence between the King of Cyprus and the King of Ugarit can be correlated with the archaeology of destruction to provide vivid details of the Sea Peoples' onslaught. Ugarit was the capital of a Syrian coastal kingdom under the suzerainty of the Hittites. It had over 150 villages in its hinterland. The total population of the kingdom was ca 25,000 (Yon 1992), nearly the same as that of Philistia during Stage 1. Its king also controlled a nearby port and had a seaside palace at Ibn Hani.

During the last days of Ugarit, the war correspondence between the Ugaritian king, Ammurapi, and the King of Cyprus (Alashiya) reveals, through eyewitness accounts, the desperation of the situation and the threat from the sea. The King of Alashiya writes condescendingly to Ammurapi:

> . . . What have you written to me 'enemy shipping has been sighted at sea'? Well now, even if it is true that enemy ships have been sighted, be firm. Indeed then, what of your troops, your chariots, where are they stationed? Are they stationed close at hand or are they not? Fortify your towns, bring the troops and the chariots into them, and wait for the enemy with firm feet (Sandars 1978: 142–3).

Ammurapi replies with irony and defeat:

> . . . My father, the enemy ships are already here, they have set fire to my towns and have done very great damage in the country. My father, did you not know that all my troops were stationed in the Hittite country, and that all my ships are still stationed in Lycia and have not yet returned? So that the country is abandoned to itself. . . . Consider this my father, there are seven enemy ships that have come and done very great damage (RS 20.238; Sandars 1978: 143).

An earlier text explains to whom the marauding ships belong. The Hittite Sun King writes to a veteran official of Ammurapi, while the King is still a youth, regarding the age-old practice of hostage-taking:

> From the Sun, the Great King, to the Prefect: Now, with you, the king, your master, is young. He does not know anything. I gave orders to him regarding Lanadusu, who was taken captive by the *Šikalayū*, who live on ships. Now, I have sent to you Nisahili, he is an administrative official with me, with instructions. Now, you (are to) send Lanadusu, whom the *Šikalayū* captured, here to me. I will ask him about the matter of the *Šikila* and, afterwards, he can return to Ugarit. (RS 34.129, translated by Gregory Mobley).

The Sikils, 'who live on ships', were sea raiders terrorizing the coastal waters of Ugarit before it fell to them sometime ca 1187–85. This text written by a Hittite in cuneiform Akkadian is a vivid account of Sea Peoples' activities not long before the explosions which Ramesses III recorded in his 'War Against the Peoples of the Sea', where also the Sikils (Tjeker) are mentioned as part of the Sea Peoples' confederation.

In the wall reliefs of the naval battle, the Sea Peoples' ships are depicted as oared galleys with single sails. They have finials in the shape of water birds at prow and stern (Wachsmann 1981, 1982). These depictions of Sea Peoples' ships bear a remarkable resemblance to the 'bird-boat' painted on a Late Helladic IIIC (Myc IIIC) krater from Tiryns (Figure 3: 56), and provides yet another clue to their origin in the Aegean world.

The Sikils sailed down the coast and landed at Dor, identified as a city of the Sikils in the eleventh-century Egyptian Tale of Wen-Amon (Wilson 1969b; B. Mazar 1992: 26, n. 11). There they destroyed the Late Bronze Age city of the Canaanites and built a new and much larger city on the ruins. During Stage 1 the Sikils fortified Dor with walled ramparts, including glacis construction (Stern 1992), and built a fine harbor of ashlar blocks for their ships (Raban 1987).

From their beachheads, the coastal pattern of destruction, followed in many cases by new cities with Myc IIIC pottery, reference to them as living on ships, and

Figure 3   Philistine Ceramic Horizons (1175−1050 BCE)

1−10.   Philistine Bichrome Pottery (T. Dothan 1982):
1.   Fig. 3.46; Tell Fara(S), Tomb 552. Jug with Egyptian floral motif.
2.   Fig. 3.21.2; Tell Fara(S), Tomb 859. Jug with strainer spout.
3.   Fig. 3.14; Gezer. Stirrup jar.
4.   Fig. 3.32; Tell Qasile. 'Feeding bottle'.
5.   Fig. 3.33; Tell Fara(S). Juglet with pinched body.
6.   Fig. 3.3; Ashkelon. Bell-shaped bowl, or *skyphos*.
7.   Fig. 3.7; Gezer. Krater.
8.   Fig. 3.34; Azor. Cylindrical bottle.
9.   Fig. 3.40; Beth Shemesh, Tomb 11. Horn-shaped vessel.
10.   Fig. 4.11.1; Tell 'Aitun. Female mourning figurines on Krater (reconstructed).

11−23.   Philistine Monochrome (Mycenaean IIIC). Pottery from Tel Miqne-Ekron (T. Dothan 1994: Fig. 7):
11.   Carinated bowl with strap handles.
12−14.   Bell-shaped bowls with horizontal bands.
15.   Bell-shaped bowl with concentric circles.
16.   Bell-shaped bowl with spiral and rhombus.
17.   Large bowl with bands and loops.
18.   Bell-shaped bowl with bands and streamer decoration.
19.   Cooking jug.
20.   Deep bowl, or *kalathos*.
21.   Preening water bird on krater. Transitional bichrome decoration.
22.   Preening water bird (monochrome).
23.   Fish (monochrome).
24.   T. Dothan 1982: fig. 4.11.2; Perati. *Lekane* with female mourning figurines.

25−34.   Philistine Monochrome (Mycenaean IIIC). Pottery from Ashdod Str. XIIIB (T. Dothan 1982: fig. 2.3):
25.   Bell-shaped bowl with antithetic spirals.
26.   Bell-shaped bowl with spiral.
27.   Krater with spiral; center filled with net pattern.
28.   Bell-shaped bowl with antithetic spirals.
29.   Bell-shaped bowl with horizontal bands and squiggly line below rim.
30−1.   Krater with fish.
32.   Bell-shaped bowl with antithetic spirals; center filled with net pattern.
33−4.   Elaborate loop decoration.
35.   T. Dothan 1982: fig. 4.9; Ashdod. 'Ashdoda' figurine (enthroned goddess).
36.   T. Dothan 1982: pl. 4.20; seated Mycenaean female figurine.

37.   T. Dothan 1982: pl. 4.21.2; seated Mycenaean female figurine (mother and child).

38−49.   Philistine Monochrome (Mycenaean IIIC) Pottery from Ashkelon (Grid 38 on site plan, courtesy of L.E. Stager/Leon Levy Expedition):
38−9.   Bell-shaped bowls with antithetic spirals.
40.   Bell-shaped bowl with horizontal bands.
41−3.   Carinated bowls with strap handles.
44.   Stirrup jar.
45.   Bell-shaped bowl with streamers.
46.   Jug with horizontal bands.
47.   Bell-shaped bowl.
48.   Carinated bowl with strap handles and spiral on floor.
49.   Bell-shaped bowl with horizontal bands.
50.   T. Dothan 1982: fig. 5.15; Lachish, Tomb 570 (=Str. VI). Egyptian anthropoid clay coffin with Isis and Nephthys deities and hieroglyphic funerary inscription: 'Thou givest water [a traditional mortuary offering] (of the) West [the region of the dead] to the majesty of thy [. . .]' (Gardiner in Tufnell 1958: Pl. 46).
51.   Oren 1973: Beth Shan. Egyptian anthropoid clay coffin. Fig. 53, 80; Tomb 66A.
52−3.   T. Dothan 1982: Fig. 1.5; Medinet Habu. Ox-carts carrying Sea Peoples' families, from reliefs of land battle between Ramesses III and the Sea Peoples.
54.   T. Dothan 1982: Fig. 1,6l Medinet Habu. Sea Peoples' horse and chariot, from reliefs of land battle between Ramesses III and the Sea Peoples.
55.   Adapted from Wachsmann (in press): Fig. 8.10; Medinet Habu. Sea Peoples' boats with water bird-headed prow and stern, from reliefs of the sea battle between Ramesses III and the Sea Peoples.
56.   Adapted from Wachsmann (in press): Fig. 8.32; Tiryns. Late Helladic (Mycenaean) III C krater decorated with 'bird boat'.
57.   Courtesy of Lawrence E. Stager; Karnak. Ashkelon (identified by hieroglyphic legend) besieged by Egyptians. Canaanites, inside the citadel (set on a hill, or tell), pray for mercy. Wall relief, once ascribed to Ramesses II, has recently been correctly attributed to his son Merenptah. The inscription reads: 'The vile town which his majesty overcame when it was wicked, Ashkelon. It says: 'Joyful is the one who is upon your water [i.e. loyal to you], woeful the one who trespasses your boundaries. Spare an heir that we may relate your might to any foreign lands that are unaware.' (Wilson 1969a; Yurco 1986; Stager 1985; cf. Redford 1986, 1992).

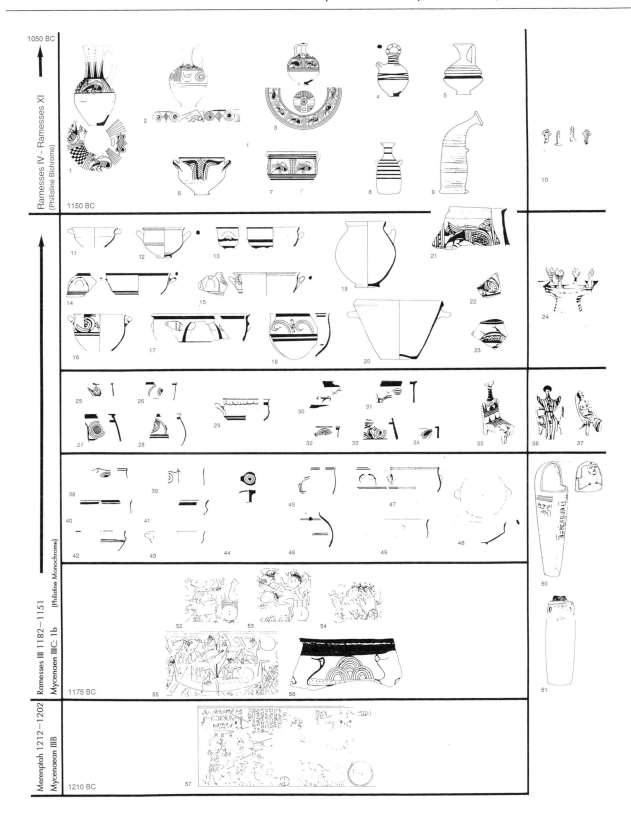

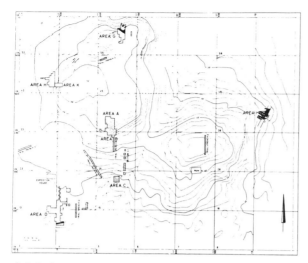

Ashdod

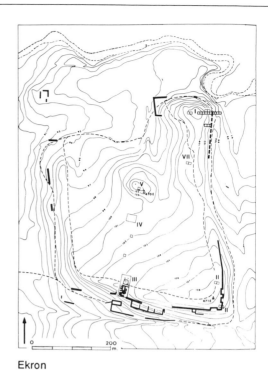

Ekron

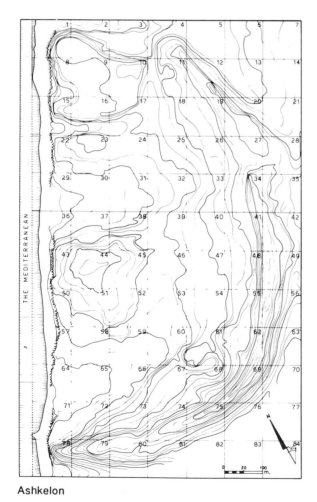

Ashkelon

Figure 4 Site plans of Ashdod, Ekron and Ashkelon

iconographic renditions of their craft leave no doubt that the Sea Peoples, including the Philistines, had the necessary maritime technology and transport capacity to effect a major migration and invasion by sea (see above, criterion 3).

Territories and boundaries

From Egyptian texts and wall reliefs of Ramesses III at Medinet Habu, the following scenario of the battle and its aftermath has achieved near canonical status. The Sea Peoples came to the Levant by land and by sea. The reliefs depict whole families trekking overland in ox-drawn carts and warriors riding in horse-drawn chariots as they engage the Egyptians in a land battle (Figure 3: 52–4), somewhere on the northern borders of Canaan or even farther north in Amurru. However, a flotilla of their ships reach the mouth of the Nile before Ramesses III defeats them at sea (Figure 3: 55). After his victory over the Sea Peoples, Ramesses III reasserts Egyptian control over much of Canaan. He recruits the defeated enemy as mercenaries for the garrisons established in Canaan and Nubia; and Egypt is once again in control of the vital military and commercial highway known as the Ways of Horus (later as the Way of the Philistines, and later still as the Via Maris) (Albright 1932b, 1975; Alt 1944; Singer 1985, 1988, 1994; T. Dothan 1982).

This scenario has been successfully challenged by Egyptologists such as Stadelmann, Helck, and Bietak (1993: 292–4). On the wall reliefs of Ramesses III there is only one departure scene prior to the land battle and then only one victory celebration following the sea battle. From this Bietak concludes that 'both encounters occurred in close proximity, one after the other, most probably near the mouth of the easternmost branch of the Nile'. Thus the Sea Peoples were threatening the Egyptians, not in distant Amurru, but at the very entrance to Egypt. If the Philistines had already established themselves in southern Canaan before the battle recorded in 1175 BCE, the chariotry and ox-carts involved in the battle for the Egyptian Delta could have been supplied from their base in southern Canaan. These terrestrial vehicles would not, then, provide evidence for a long overland trek of Sea Peoples via Anatolia into the Levant, as usually supposed. Their migration was by war- and transport ships.

Further proof for the supposed Egyptian dominance over Canaan and the subjugation of the Sea Peoples was gleaned from Papyrus Harris I, lxxvi 6–10 (Wilson 1969a: 262):

> I slew the Denyen in their islands, while the Tjeker [=Sikils] and the Philistines were made ashes. The Sherden and the Weshesh of the Sea were made nonexistent, captured all together and brought in captivity to Egypt like the sands of the shore. I settled them in strongholds, bound in my name [i.e. branded with the name of pharaoh]. Their military classes were as numerous as hundred-thousands. I assigned portions for them all with clothing and provisions from the treasuries and granaries every year.

However, it is not clear from this text that any of the Sea Peoples taken as prisoners of war were garrisoned in Egyptian fortresses in Canaan (Bietak 1993: 300).

The view that Ramesses III reasserted Egyptian hegemony over Canaan and settled Philistines as garrison troops was thought to gain archaeological support from the clay anthropoid coffins found at such Egyptian strongholds as Beth Shan, Tell Fara (S), and Lachish (Albright 1932a, 1975: 509; T. Dothan 1957, 1982; Wright 1966). At Tell Fara (S) in Cemetery 500, large bench tombs with anthropoid clay sarcophagi, Egyptian artifacts and Philistine Bichrome pottery led the excavator, Sir Flinders Petrie, to conclude that these were the sepulchres of the 'five lords [*seranim*] of the Philistines'. Others assumed Cypriot and Aegean prototypes for the bench tombs themselves (Waldbaum 1966; cf. Stiebing 1970). One of the clay coffin lids from Beth Shan bore the design of a 'feathered' headdress (Figure 3: 51), which was compared with those worn by the Philistines, Denyen, and Sikils depicted on the wall reliefs of Medinet Habu (Figure 3: 52–5; T. Dothan [1957, 1982] thought the Beth Shan coffins contained Philistines; Oren [1973], Denyen or Danunians).

The notion that Iron Age I anthropoid coffins were used to bury Sea Peoples mercenaries was dealt a decisive blow by excavations in the cemetery of Deir el-Balah, which

Plate 2 Ashdod. Clay offering stand with musicians playing out of windows in the model shrine (courtesy of The Israel Museum, Jerusalem/ photograph: David Harris)

contained dozens of these clay coffins, dating from a century or two before the Sea Peoples had arrived *en masse* in Canaan (for a different interpretation see, T. Dothan 1979: 98–104).

From the Middle Kingdom to the Roman period, anthropoid clay coffins were used to bury Egyptians, both at home and abroad. There is no reason to make the Early Iron Age I exemplar exceptions to this practice (Kuchman 1977/78). For Egyptians, burial in Egypt was the ideal. However, as the New Kingdom empire expanded and more Egyptian troops were stationed abroad, whether in Canaan or Nubia, returning every Egyptian corpse to the homeland became impracticable. Egyptians who had to forego this ideal practice could at least be buried abroad in suitable containers, such as anthropoid clay coffins.

If further evidence were needed to reclaim anthropoid clay coffins for Egyptians, it comes from an inscribed sarcophagus found in Tomb 570 at Lachish (Figure 3: 50). Beside the Egyptian deities Isis and Nephthys depicted on the coffin is an inscription which has been variously labeled Egyptian pseudo-hieroglyphs or Philistine gibberish (Wright 1966; T. Dothan 1957, 1982; Weinstein 1992). But this interpretation of the text is unwarranted. As Sir Alan Gardiner recognized in the original publication (Tufnell 1958: Pl. 46), the Lachish coffin text reads as a perfectly good Egyptian funerary inscription: 'Thou givest water [a traditional mortuary offering] (of the) West [the region of the dead] to the majesty (of) thy [. . .]' (Egyptologists Klaus Baer and Edward Wente independently translated the Lachish coffin text just as Gardiner had read it.)

Thus the most parsimonious hypothesis is to conclude that anthropoid sarcophagi found in Canaan in the Late Bronze and the Iron I periods belonged to Egyptians stationed there, and they have nothing to do with Sea Peoples and their burial customs. When properly attributed, the coffins become important artifacts in determining cultural and political boundaries between Philistia and Canaanite territory under Egyptian hegemony.

During Stage 1 the Philistines carved out a major piece of territory for themselves in southern Canaan at the expense of the Canaanites and their overlords the Egyptians. The boundaries of this territory can be roughly demarcated by plotting those settlements with large quantities (25 percent or more) of Myc IIIC pottery (for the method and a superb synthesis of the sources, see Bietak 1993). Within this rectangular coastal strip, ca 20 km wide and 50 km long, or ca 1000 km² (Figure 2; Singer 1994), the Philistines located their five major cities at key positions along the perimeter. In contrast to the Egyptians, the Philistines did not dominate their new territory by establishing military garrisons in the midst of Canaanite population centers (cf. Brug 1985). Rather, the Philistines completely destroyed the Egypto-Canaanite centers before building their new cities on the smouldering ruins of the old ones. Theirs was a wholesale takeover and occupation that must have resulted in the extirpation or displacement of many of the Late Bronze Age inhabitants there.

In the northwest corner of their new territory, the Philistines burnt to the ground the large Egyptian fortress at Tel Mor and the neighboring city of Ashdod (Str. XIV). Over the ruins of Ashdod they built a new city (Str. XIIIB) of eight ha or more (cf. M. Dothan 1989, 1993a; M. Dothan and Porath 1993, where Ashdod XIIIB is attributed to an 'early wave' of Sea Peoples, not the Philistines). Ashdod XIIIB produced large amounts of SPM (Figure 3: 25–34). To counter this new Philistine city of Ashdod, the Egyptians rebuilt, on a smaller scale, the fortress at Tel Mor, where Egyptian pottery was abundant (M. Dothan 1993b).

Inland along the northern border, some 20 km to the east, lay Ekron (Tel Miqne). There the Philistines encountered a small Canaanite city (Str. VIII, Field I) of four ha and destroyed it in an intense conflagration (Gitin and T. Dothan 1993; T. Dothan and Gitin 1994). Over its ruins and beyond, the Philistines built a city five times larger than the old Canaanite one. Their new city (Str. VII) was protected by massive mudbrick fortifications from without, and organized on a grand scale from within (see below; and Figure 4). Ekron VII yielded large quantities of SPM (Figure 3: 11–23). Northeast of Ekron stood Gezer (Dever 1993). The Canaanite city (Str. XV) was destroyed by fire at the end of the Late Bronze Age, either by the Philistines or by Merenptah. Whatever the case, Gezer (Str. XIV), with no evidence of SPM, was rebuilt during the reign of Ramesses III as an Egypto-Canaanite counterforce to Ekron. A faience vase bearing the cartouches of Ramesses III belonged originally to this city (T. Dothan 1982: 52, n.153 and 220, Fig. 2). Philistine Bichrome pottery appears later in Gezer Str. XIII–XI (Dever 1993), during Stage 2.

At Ashkelon, on the Mediterranean coast between Ashdod and Gaza, the Philistines built their seaport. Either Merenptah or, more probably, the Philistines destroyed the Late Bronze Age city there (Stager 1985a; 1993). Egyptian policy was to garrison and control, not eradicate, the Canaanite population (Figure 3: 57). During Stage 1 the new port must have extended along the coast for almost a kilometer and occupied an area of 50–60 ha. SPM was found in fills sealed by the earliest Philistine rampart on the north (Figure 4, Grid 2) and in occupational layers 900 m to the south (in Grid 50 of the Leon Levy Expedition and in Grid 57 from Phythian-Adams' trench, City VI). The arc of earthen ramparts (glacis-type construction built over the Middle Bronze Age ones; Plate 3) was fortified at the northern crest by two large mudbrick towers linked by a mudbrick curtain wall (Plate 4). This fortification system was built in early Iron Age II. Opposite Ashkelon, ca 30 km to the east, Ramesses III established another Egyptian control center at Lachish (City VI). There an Egyptian-inspired temple, hieratic bowl inscriptions recording taxes paid to the Egyptians, a large bronze gate fitting inscribed with the name of Ramesses III, and two anthropoid coffins attest to the Egyptian garrison there (Ussishkin 1985). Hardly a trace of Philistine Bichrome pottery has been found at Lachish.

The eastern boundary of Philistia during Stage 1 can be established along a 50 km line running from Ekron to Tel Haror (Tell Abu-Hureirah) in the southeast corner (Figure 2). At Haror, 20 km inland from Gaza, the Philistines devastated the Late Bronze Age city (Str. K3 and B7). Much Egyptian and some Myc IIIB pottery lay smashed in its destruction debris. As at the Pentapolis sites, a new Philistine settlement, characterized by SPM, rose above the ruins of the former Egypto-Canaanite center. In a

Plate 3 Ashkelon on the Mediterranean. Oblique aerial view, looking north. Arc of earthen ramparts enclose 60 hectare seaport in Bronze and Iron Ages (courtesy of Richard Cleave)

subsequent phase (B4–2), when both Monochrome and Bichrome pottery were in use, 25 percent of the pottery discarded in refuse pits was Philistine decorated wares (Oren 1993a). Just across the border opposite Haror was another Egyptian center at Tell esh-Shariah (Tel Sera'). There in Str. IX a large Egyptian administrative building, or governor's residency (Building 906; Oren 1984), several hieratic bowl inscriptions (Goldwasser 1984), and Egyptian pottery attest to Ramesses III's containment policy.

During Stage 2, the Egyptians abandoned Shariah and it became a Philistine city (Str. VIII). Shariah is probably to be identified with biblical Ziklag (Oren 1993b). Ziklag was subject to Achish, ruler of Gath, who gave this country town to his sometime servant David and his band of 600 men in exchange for their loyalty (1 Sam. 27–9). Achish's capital (and Goliath's home town) is usually located at Tell es-Safi (B. Mazar 1992). However, its proximity to Ekron, its distance from Ziklag, and the apparent absence of SPM (although T. Dothan will soon publish a vessel which seems to be Myc IIIC) make this identification unlikely. It seems more probable that Gath was strategically located in the southeast corner of Philistia (cf. the arguments of Wright 1966) during Stage 1, not far from its dependency Ziklag during Stage 2. If so, the most plausible candidate for Gath is Tel Haror, with both Philistine Monochrome

and Bichrome pottery. The main obstacle to this identification is the apparent small size of the Philistine settlement, a matter which the ongoing excavations there should be able to resolve.

Regardless of the identification, it seems clear that Haror was inside and Shariah was outside Philistine territory during Stage 1; but both were within the Philistine domain during Stage 2.

In the southwest corner of Philistia lay Gaza, a major outpost and caravan city of the Egyptians, which must have been taken over by the Philistines during Stage 1. Unfortunately the limited excavations that were made there have revealed little or nothing of the character of the Egyptian and Philistine cities. However, it seems unlikely that Philistia extended south of the Wadi Gaza, or Nahal Besor, during Stage 1. Probably this wadi is to be identified with the 'Brook of Egypt', which divided Canaan from Egypt (Singer 1994 and citations; cf. Josh. 13: 3). To protect his northern frontier, Ramesses III built a formidable fortress and residency at Tell Fara (S) (Oren 1984; T. Dothan 1982). This fortified center must have remained in Egyptian hands throughout much of the Ramesside era, well into Stage 2, as the sequence of tombs with anthropoid clay coffins, Egyptian artifacts, and Philistine Bichrome pottery attest.

Plate 4   Ashkelon. North slope ramparts and Philistine mudbrick towers at crest (upper right behind range rod) (courtesy of Leon Levy Expedition/photograph: Carl Andrews)

By tracing the cultural boundaries around the 1000 km² that constituted Philistia, the contrast between the territory controlled by the Philistine Pentapolis – characterized by the presence of Myc IIIC pottery and the absence of Egyptian monuments, buildings and artifacts – and that controlled by the Egyptians under Ramesses III could not be more sharply demarcated. Rather than a resurgent Egypt at the height of its imperial power, with Ramesses III dominating all of Canaan through his military might and subjugating the hapless Philistines (Singer 1994), there was a new and formidable foreign power which carved out an independent territory right up to the traditional frontier of Egypt. All that Egypt could do was to adopt a defensive posture in an attempt to contain the Philistines within a *cordon sanitaire*. This containment policy lasted until the death of Ramesses III in 1151.

Demography

Demographic changes, including population increase, help explain the expansionist policies of the Philistines a few decades after their arrival. Archaeological surveys of

Philistia have revealed few Iron Age settlements in the countryside. During Stage 1 most of the Philistines, including farmers and herders, lived in the five major cities (A. Mazar 1988: 253). Because of that demographic concentration it is possible to make a fairly reliable population estimate for the period 1175–1150 BCE. The total occupied area of the Pentapolis would be minimally ca 100 ha, which, when converted at the rate of 250 persons per ha (Stager 1985b), would indicate a total of 25,000 inhabitants. To attain this initial population so soon after arrival, boatload after boatload of Philistines, along with their families, livestock and belongings, must have arrived in southern Canaan during Stage 1. By the beginning of Stage 2, natural growth more than doubled the Philistine population and fueled their expansion in all directions (Figure 2), until by the latter half of the eleventh century BCE, they had become a menace even to the Israelites in the highlands to the east.

Economy

In their new home in southern Canaan, the Philistines had all of the natural and cultural resources to become a formidable maritime and agrarian power. They had the sea for fishing and shipping; and behind it lay a rich breadbasket as well as an oil and wine cask. They lacked a good supply of timber and had no metal resources. Early in Stage 1 they were obviously receiving both through their trading activities.

The Philistines also brought some changes to the region through their animal husbandry. In addition to their flocks of sheep and goats, by far the most common domestic livestock among the Canaanites and the Israelites, the Philistines specialized in cattle- and hog-raising (Hesse 1986). Most interesting is the sharp increase in pig production and consumption during Iron Age I in Philistia: Ashkelon (23 percent, but the sample is small), Ekron (18 percent), and Timnah (Tel Batash, 8.0 percent) (Hesse 1986 and in press). In contrast, pigs were extremely rare or completely absent in Iron Age I highland villages, usually considered to be Israelite: Ai and Raddana (absent; pers. communication Z. Lederman), Mt. Ebal (absent), Shiloh (0.1 percent) (Hellwing et al. in Finkelstein et al. 1994: 330). There can be little doubt that these differences in pig production and consumption have more to do with culture than ecology. The Mycenaeans and later Greeks had a positive attitude towards swine and a preference for pork in the diet. The Philistines brought that preference with them to Canaan in the 12th century. Probably at that time during the biblical 'Period of Judges', the pork taboo developed among the Israelites as they forged their identity partly in contrast to their Philistine neighbors. Thus during Iron Age I the pig becomes a distinctive cultural marker, just as circumcision was, between Philistine and Israelite.

Not only did the Philistines control a vital stretch of the

coastal road, once known as the Ways of Horus, but they and other Sea Peoples also soon took over the sealanes. After some stability had been achieved in the eastern Mediterranean, the Sea Peoples once again became traders rather than raiders. Shortly after landing, the Sikils built the harbor at Dor. The eleventh-century Tale of Wen-Amon makes clear that the Sea Peoples and the Phoenicians, not the Egyptians, commanded the ports and sealanes of the eastern Mediterranean at that time (Wilson 1969b: 25–9 B. Mazar 1986: 65–68). Trade with Cyprus was bustling in the eleventh century (Karageorghis 1982, 1992; Stern 1992); and presumably Ashkelon was an active seaport once again, exporting the traditional commodities of grain, wine, and oil from Philistia to other parts of the Mediterranean.

Coastal Philistia, from north of Ashdod to south of Gaza, was well suited to viticulture. Wine production reached its peak during the Byzantine era, when the wines of Ashkelon and Gaza were known throughout the world (Johnson and Stager 1994). The sandy soils and warm, sunny climate produced many good wines, from the light and palatable varieties from Ashkelon to the heavier ones from Gaza. In seventh century BCE Ashkelon, a royal winery, with pressing rooms alternating with storerooms inside a very large ashlar building, occupied the same central area where the Iron Age I public building had once stood (see below; Figure 4, Grid 38). Similar Iron II winepresses were recently excavated near Ashdod.

Throughout modern history the Philistines have been maligned as uncouth, beer-guzzling louts. One of their most common pottery vessels is the jug with strainer spout (Figure 3: 2), invariably, but unjustifiably, designated a 'beer-jug' (Albright 1961). The ecology of Philistia favors the production of grapes over barley. And, in fact, the repertoire of Philistine decorated pottery, both Myc IIIC and Bichrome, suggests that wine, not beer, was the beverage of choice. Kraters were popular among the Mycenaeans. The introduction of the krater, literally a mixing bowl, to the Levant also marked the introduction of the Greek (not Semitic) custom of mixing water with wine. The abundance of Iron Age I kraters in Philistia compared with other parts of Canaan suggests that it remained predominately a Greek drinking habit during that period. Large bell-shaped bowls for serving wine and small bell-shaped bowls or cups (Greek *skyphoi*) for drinking it were the two most popular forms of decorated Philistine pottery (Figure 3 and Plate 1). The jug with strainer spout, another popular form, completes the wine service. It served as a carafe with a built-in sieve for straining out the lees and other impurities (Eisenstein 1905). Egyptians and many others served their wine into drinking bowls or cups. According to the Talmud, linen cloth was used to strain out finer impurities. Together these vessels constituted the wine service that graced many a Philistine table and symposium (cf. Samson's wedding feast in Judg. 14: 10–20) during the twelfth and eleventh

centuries BCE. In addition, they attest to the importance of viticulture and wine production during that era.

The inner coastal zone of Philistia, with its large rolling fields and deep, fertile soils, was best suited to cereal and olive cultivation. Its oil producers supplied not only Philistia but also other parts of the Levant, and, of course, the biggest perennial consumer of all – Egypt. Ekron was the undisputed oil capital of the country, if not the world, in the seventh century BCE (Gitin 1990). The outer belt of Ekron, just inside the fortifications, was lined with more than 100 olive oil factories. The coast and interior of Philistia formed complementary zones for the production of two of the most important cash crops of the Levant: olive oil and wine.

Urban imposition

These 'sackers of cities' from the Aegean, as Homer referred to them, were also great builders of cities. In Philistia, as elsewhere, they imposed a full-blown urban tradition on the landscape, quite different from the Canaanite patterns which preceded them. It is the scope and effects of their 'urban imposition' which provides additional reasons for thinking that the Philistines were not a small military elite who garrisoned the indigenous population but, rather, a large and diverse group of settlers who transplanted many aspects of their old way of life and culture to a new locale.

The overview of the Pentapolis has shown that after the beachhead, during the first generation of new immigrants, the Philistines had successfully sited within the new territory each of their five major cities, taking maximum advantage of their military, economic, and political potential. From a closer look at the recent excavations at Ashkelon, Ashdod, and especially Ekron, it will also become clear that the Philistines brought with them templates of city planning and concepts of urban organization that the peoples of Canaan had not experienced before. In addition, the Philistines brought with them a whole range of human resources and institutions to realize such organization. Behind the archaeological residues of the Pentapolis one can detect, however faintly, the activities of a diverse community of warriors, farmers, sailors, merchants, rulers, shamans, priests, artisans and architects.

Ashkelon

Over the ruins of a much smaller Late Bronze Age city rose the Philistine metropolis, between 50–60 ha in size, with perhaps as many as 10,000–12,000 inhabitants. Internal details of the seaport's organization must await further research by the Leon Levy Expedition, for only recently have excavations reached the Iron Age in sizable exposures. However, it appears that in the center of the Philistine city (Figure 4: Ashkelon, Grid 38), there was a

Plate 5 Ashkelon. North side of south mound (Grid 38). North end of monumental Philistine building, with three pillar bases (two negatives) exposed (behind person kneeling by later well). Building dates to latter half of twelfth century BCE (courtesy of Leon Levy Expedition/photograph: James Whitred)

dramatic change in activities after the destruction which separated the Late Bronze Age from the Iron Age. Where outdoor courtyards, grain silos, bread ovens and human burials had been in the Late Bronze Age stood a major public building in the early Iron Age I. This building (Plate 5), situated in the heart of the city, was remodelled several times during its use in the Philistine Monochrome (Figure 3: 38–49) and Bichrome pottery periods. In its second phase, the building had large stone column drums, probably bearing wooden pillars, similar to palaces and temples at Ekron (Figures 5 and 6; see Plate 7), Ashdod (see below), and Tell Qasile (Str. X, Temple 131; A. Mazar 1980: Pl. 3).

Weaving industries were often associated with administrative and religious centers. At Ashkelon more than 150 cylinders of unbaked clay, slightly pinched at the waist, lay on superimposed floors of the two successive public buildings. These enigmatic installations (Plate 6) were tentatively identified with weaving industries. Some of the cylinders were still lying in place along the walls in alignments that suggested they had been dropped from vertical weaving looms. But unlike the common Levantine pyramidal loom weights with perforated tops, these unpierced cylinders might have been spools around which the thread was wound and hung from the loom. The floors on which these spoolweights were aligned had concentrations of textile fibers. Similar clay cylinders are known from the other Pentapolis sites, Ekron (T. Dothan 1994) and Ashdod (M. Dothan and Porath 1993: Fig. 24: 3–5, Pl. 39; 4, Str. XIIIa). They appear, along with Levantine loom weights, in temple precincts at Enkomi and Kition, two 'Achaean' (Sea Peoples) emporia on Cyprus. On the Mycenaean mainland, spoolweights have been recorded at Tiryns, Pylos and Mycenae (Stager 1991: 15 and 19, n.12). They are commonly found at Thera and in the Cyclades (pers. communication: Christos Doumas), and they have

appeared at the Greek ('Dark Age') site of Lefkandi (Popham and Sackett 1968).

The spoolweights, found in abundance in Stage 1 and Stage 2 contexts at Ashkelon, Ekron and Ashdod, were made from the local clays by foreign weavers, coming from the Aegean; they provide another indication of the origin of the new immigrants.

Ashdod

Urban imposition at Ashdod took dramatic form in the well-planned city of 8 ha built over the charred ruins of the earlier Egypto-Canaanite center. Just inside the demolished north gate, with a doorjamb bearing the title of a high Egyptian official – 'Fanbearer (on) the right hand of the king' – a large governmental palace completely destroyed (Figure 4: Ashdod, Area G) and over its ruins the Philistines built an artisans' quarter, including a potter's workshop, containing stacks of local Myc IIIC bowls and cups (Room 4106, Str. XIIIb; M. Dothan and Porath 1993: Fig. 14) as well as Mycenaean cooking jugs (M. Dothan and Porath 1993: fig. 15: 1,5).

In the western quarter of the city (Figure 4: Ashdod, Area H), a wide street separated two building complexes, one being a sizable public building (17 by 13 m); the other, a large hall with two stone column drums and an adjoining small apsidal shrine. Near the shrine was a female figurine built into a couch or throne (Figure 3: 35, cf. 36–7). Nicknamed 'Ashdoda' by the excavator, M. Dothan (see opening photograph), this anonymous goddess also appears at Ashkelon, Ekron and Tell Qasile, where a small fragment may indicate that she is nursing a baby, in the tradition of Mycenaean mother goddess figurines (A. Mazar 1988: 259, Fig. 2, and 260).

Ekron

The best example of urban imposition comes from another Pentapolis city, Ekron. There the ongoing Tel Miqne-Ekron Excavations have revealed for the first time the broad outlines of the use of space within a major Philistine city (T. Dothan and Gitin 1993; T. Dothan 1990, 1992, 1994).

The embers of the Late Bronze Age city were smothered under a much larger Philistine one, ca 20 ha in size, with perhaps 5000 inhabitants. Even during Stage 1 at Ekron there are signs of urban planning in which industry was located along the perimeter of the city, but still inside its strong fortification walls. The center of the site was dedicated to public buildings, such as the palace-shrine complex (Figure 4: Ekron, Field IV). The domestic quarters, although as yet only partially excavated, lie somewhere in between the outer industrial belt and the central administrative area.

In the very center of this large city stood a 'palace' with shrine rooms, or a temple. The palace-shrine (Str. VII–V)

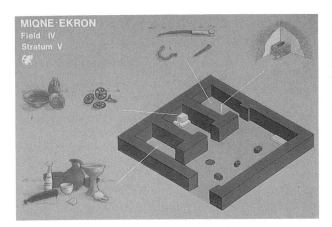

Figure 5 Ekron. Reconstruction of Stratum V public building with hearth, probably palace with shrine. Cultic objects were found in three rooms behind pillared main hall with hearth (courtesy of Trude Dothan, Tel Miqne–Ekron Excavations)

Plate 6 Ashkelon. Spoolweights, perhaps used as spools for thread and tied as weights to vertical looms. These unbaked clay cylinders are found throughout the Aegean and Cyprus, usually in association with weaving installations (courtesy of Leon Levy Expedition/Carl Andrews, photographer)

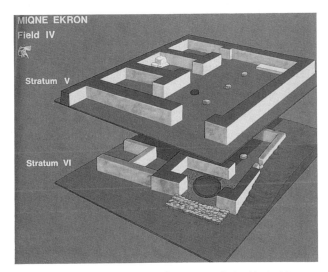

Figure 6 Ekron. Reconstruction of Strata V and VI public buildings. Note large circular hearth in main room of Stratum VI building (courtesy of Trude Dothan, Tel Miqne–Ekron Excavations)

complex went through several phases of remodeling and rebuilding during its 200-year span as the power center of Philistine Ekron (see Figures 5 and 6, Plate 7).

This mudbrick building had white plastered floors and walls. But most conspicuous was the large sunken circular hearth in the long pillared hall. This feature is not known in the Levant, but has a long history in the public and domestic architecture of the Aegean, Cypriot and Anatolian worlds.

The hearth is the central feature in Mycenaean palaces at Pylos, Mycenae and Tiryns, where they are as much as 4.00 m in diameter. There it was the focus of the civic and religious center, where these two aspects of society were often housed under the same roof. In later Greek religion,

the hearth-goddess Hestia played a prominent role in both domestic and public households.

Hearths of many shapes and sizes, square, rectangular, circular, and keyhole types, occur for the first time at Sea Peoples' centers in Cyprus during Stage 1, e.g. in large rooms at Maa and Enkomi as well as in the temple precinct at Kition (Karageorghis 1982, 1992; A. Mazar 1988; T. Dothan 1994).

By the mid-twelfth century, the Philistines had expanded north and founded Tell Qasile on virgin soil. There, in the earliest stratum, they built a large hall with an adjoining sanctuary. In the center of the hall, the focus of the precinct, was a raised keyhole-shaped hearth (A. Mazar 1988).

During Stage 2 of the public building at Ekron, three rooms opened onto the hall with hearth. The north room was for weaving, if the dozens of spoolweights are any indication; perhaps with cult personnel weaving vestments to dress the statue of the great Mycenaean mother-goddess (cf. women weaving garments for Asherah in the precincts of the Jerusalem temple [II Kings 23]).

In the middle room stood a plastered platform or an altar. Nearby lay an ivory-handle of a bimetallic knife for sacrifice identical to the complete example in the adjacent room. Bimetallic knives (iron blades with bronze rivets) are also a rarity in the Levant but more common in Aegean (and Cypriot) contexts. In the same middle room – the focus of the cult – were found three bronze wheels with eight spokes in each – once part of a mobile cult stand, again with parallels in Cyprus and in the Jerusalem temple (T. Dothan 1994). In the third room a complete bimetallic knife was lying next to another small plastered platform or altar.

At Ekron the hierarchy of space and planning, of architecture and artifact, are very much in harmony with that of the Aegean world. It represents the full expression

Plate 7 Ekron. Stratum VI public building with large circular hearth at lower left (courtesy of Tel Miqne–Ekron Excavations/photograph: Ilan Sztulman)

of urban imposition as these concepts and features were transplanted to the Semitic world.

As urbanism dissolved in Greece and Anatolia, some members of Aegean society transplanted their urban life and values to a new but similar setting, along the coast of the eastern Mediterranean and Cyprus. The 'event', sketched above as a mass migration of Sea Peoples during the decade 1185–1175 BCE and following, would appear to be an epiphenomenon: to paraphrase F. Braudel, mere 'crests of Sea Peoples' foam, which the tides of history carry on their strong backs'. However, this 'event' was much more than that. It was dialectically engaged and embedded in much longer durations, or time dimensions, which both gave rise to the event and succeeded it. Its source lies somewhere in the failure of those highly articulated, finely tuned, hierarchical polities and economies of the Aegean and Anatolia, known as the 'palace economy'. As two of the great empires of the period – the Hittites and the Ahhiyawans (Achaeans) or the Trojans and the Greeks (to use epic language) – collapsed at their palatial centers, many different kinds of centrifugal forces were released, which had a multiplier, or ripple, effect.

Within the Mycenaean and Hittite worlds there was an internal process of fragmentation and ruralization (the archaeologist's 'Dark Age') which, in turn, triggered mass migrations to the coastlands of the Levant and Cyprus. The ripple effect caused by the dislocation of large segments of the donor society and their peopling of the already crowded coastlands sent repercussions into the interior of Canaan as well.

The settlement process for highland Israel began a generation or two before the Sea Peoples arrived on the coast. It is difficult to believe that an event of such magnitude did not have the powerful effect of increasing enrollment in the highland polity of early Israel as the indigenous Canaanite population was being squeezed out

of the plains. The displacement and migration of the tribe of Dan from the coast to the north is symptomatic of the ripple effects of this event.

Summary

The settlement of the Sea Peoples along the coastlands of Cyprus and of the Levant meet the criteria for a mass migration of peoples from the Aegean to their new homelands ca. 1185–1175 BCE. The Philistines settling in southern Canaan provide a vivid case study of this process and an explanation of the cultural changes which affected the region during the 12th century BCE.

1. During Stage I of settlement, the Philistines destroyed indigenous cities and supplanted them with their own at the four corners of the territory they conquered.
2. The material culture boundaries of this territory were established by the presence of new and much larger settlements in which locally made Mycenaean pottery predominated. Along with this potting tradition there were other new elements brought or borrowed from Aegean Late Bronze Age culture: architectural traditions focussing on the hearth, craft traditions utilizing spoolweights for weaving, culinary preferences for pork, drinking preferences for wine mixed with water, and religious rituals featuring female figurines of the mother goddess type.

   Outside the heartland controlled by the Philistine Pentapolis, Late Bronze Age, Egypto-Canaanite cultural patterns persisted well into the 12th century, in settlements with predominantly Canaanite populations garrisoned by Egyptian military and administrative personnel.
3. All of the elements of the intrusive culture could be traced back to the Aegean area, where they flourished in the Late Bronze Age on the Mycenaean mainland and in Mycenaean cultural provinces. The migrating groups must have originated somewhere within these Mycenaean milieux.
4. The path of destruction along coastal Cilicia, Cyprus, Syria, and Canaan suggests that most of the new immigrants came by ship from 'their islands,' as recorded in the 8th Year Inscription of Ramesses III from Medinet Habu. There he also depicted the Sea Peoples and some of the ships they used for battle and transport. Their 'bird-boats' resembled those of the Mycenaeans.
5. During Stage 2, with the breakdown of Egyptian hegemony in Canaan, the Philistines began to expand in all directions beyond their original territory. Already by 1150 BCE their pottery and other items of their material culture show signs of acculturation even though their sense of ethnic identity remained secure for at least another half millennium.

Acknowledgments

I am grateful to Drs Charles Adelman, Trude Dothan, Seymour Gitin, Amichai Mazar and Benjamin Mazar, who gave the manuscript a critical reading and offered some valuable suggestions for improvement. However, I alone take full responsibility for any inadequacies that remain.

21

THE GREAT TRANSFORMATION: THE 'CONQUEST' OF THE HIGHLANDS FRONTIERS AND THE RISE OF THE TERRITORIAL STATES

Israel Finkelstein

Introduction

The demographic and socio-political processes that took place in the highlands of Canaan – Cis- and Transjordan alike – in the Iron Age I mark a revolutionary transformation in the history of the Southern Levant. They sealed two millennia of Bronze Age cultures, which were characterized by cyclic settlement oscillations, the rise and fall of urban societies and ups and downs in Egyptian sovereignty. These processes opened the way to the rise of the territorial-national states of the Iron Age II (ca. tenth-to-seventh centuries BCE). The unprecedented population growth which followed brought about the final reclamation of the ecological frontier-lands of the highlands (Broshi and Finkelstein 1992). The socio-political traits of the *ancien régime* would never reemerge: the destruction of the territorial-national states by the Neo-Assyrian and Neo-Babylonian campaigns in the eigth to sixth centuries BCE brought about the second great transformation in the history of the region in historical times, by clearing the way to over two millennia of Imperial domination (see Chapters 22—24, this volume).

The biblical description of the conquest of Canaan, the Israelite Settlement and the rise of the Davidic Monarchy, with its enormous impact on western civilization, has set this period in the eye of the storm of biblical and archaeological scholarship. Two main questions have dominated the research of the Iron Age I settlement transformation:

1. What was the origin of the Iron I villagers of the highlands of Cisjordan and the plateau of Transjordan – the proto-Israelites (Dever's term – 1992), proto-Amonites, proto-Moabites and proto-Edomites?
2. What was the manner of their settlement process in these regions, including the question *why* – what were the forces that stimulated the foundation of hundreds of small, isolated communities in the highlands frontier, and what were the circumstances that led these groups to establish the Iron II territorial states?

The intensive field studies in the highlands in recent years, in both excavations and survey, have refuted many of the past theories concerning these problems and have opened the way for a comprehensive understanding of the settlement history of highlands in the entire Bronze and Iron Ages.

Geographical and chronological setting

Geographically, this chapter deals with the areas that were the cradle of the rising territorial states in the early first millennium BCE. Special attention will be given to the central highlands of Israel (between the Jezreel and Beersheva Valleys, henceforth designated as the 'central hill country'). Comparisons to the Transjordanian plateau will be presented upon availability of archaeological data.

Chronologically, the core of the paper deals with the socio-economic and socio-political processes that had started at the end of the thirteenth century BCE and were concluded in the tenth century BCE. However, in order to understand proto-Israelite settlement, a much broader perspective will be employed here, with diachronic comparisons to earlier waves of settlement in the Bronze Age, and synchronic comparisons to processes that took place in the lowlands.

Sources

Reconstructions of the Iron Age I transformation have been based on data from the following four sources:

Archaeology

In recent years, both branches of modern archaeological field research have been employed in the study of the Iron Age I. Meticulous excavations were carried out in several Iron I sites (Figure 1), and published with modern methods, with special emphasis on environmental dimensions. They shed new light on the material culture and economic

Typical scene from the hill country of Southern Samaria near the village of Ras Karkar

strategies of the Iron I people. The most significant of these projects have been undertaken at Giloh, south of Jerusalem (Mazar 1981); 'Izbet Sartah in the western margin of the southwest Samaria Hills (Finkelstein 1986); Mt. Ebal near Shechem (Zertal 1986–87, without accepting his interpretation of the finds); Kh. ed-Dawwara, northeast of Jerusalem (Finkelstein 1990); and Shiloh between Jerusalem and Shechem (Finkelstein et al. 1993). Reference should also be made to the results of excavations in several important sites which have not been fully published yet – Kh. et-Tell ('Ai') and Kh. Raddana near Ramallah (Callaway 1976; and Callaway and Cooley 1971 respectively) and Sahab and Tell el-Umeiri in Jordan (Ibrahim 1978; Geraty et al. 1989 respectively; the Iron I material from the latter has not been presented yet).

The 'great leap forward' in the archaeology of the Southern Levant in recent years has been the comprehensive surveys that were carried out in the regions under discussion which enable an almost full reconstruction of their settlement patterns in antiquity. Most of the central hill country was fully examined in regional surveys in northern Samaria (Zertal 1988a), southern Samaria (Finkelstein 1988–89, 1988), the area between Jerusalem and Ramallah (Finkelstein and Magen 1993) and the Judean Hills (Ofer 1993). Intensive regional surveys have been undertaken in the Transjordanian plateau, the most significant being the ones in Gilead (Mittmann 1970), around Hesban (Ibach 1987), in the Kerak Plateau (Miller 1991) and in Wadi el-Hasa (MacDonald 1988). One should be aware that most of the surveys of the central hill country have not been fully published yet, while the dating of the material from at least some of the final reports on the surveys in Transjordan cannot be scrutinized, as pottery drawings have not been provided. Furthermore, the latter publications did not present some of the necessary data (e.g., classification of sites according to size) needed for a thorough investigation of the settlement and demographic patterns.

The Biblical text

The Biblical account of Early Israel, which dominated past archaeological research (e.g., Albright 1939; Wright 1962; Lapp 1967), has been dramatically diminished in recent years. Its relatively late date and its literary-ideological character make it irrelevant as a direct historical source (e.g., Davies 1992; Thompson 1992; Na'aman 1993; and the collection of articles in Edelman-Vikander 1991). But although it reflects the history, religious convictions and interests of people who lived centuries after the alleged events took place, some historical data may be embedded in it. In any event, the extraction of these possible historical nuclei from the biblical text is a difficult and Cisyphean task, if possible at all.

Egyptian New Kingdom sources
These are essential for the reconstruction of the political

and social background of Canaan in the Late Bronze Age (already Alt 1925; for the Amarna period, see Chaney 1983; Na'aman 1982). But direct evidence for the Late Bronze–Iron I transition-period is almost non-existent, apart from the much discussed, but vague reference to Israel in the Merneptah Stele (e.g., Stager 1985a; Ahlstrom and Edelman 1985; Yurco 1986).

Ethno-historical data
Ethno-archaeological data and ethno-historical information from recent generations shed light on the human dispersal and economic strategies in the highlands in pre-modern times. They can (and should) be employed in any attempt to reconstruct past settlement patterns (e.g., Marfoe 1979; Finkelstein 1988).

Method

Several basic paradigms run through the discussion which follows.

Environmental determinism

From the points of view of the environment and economic potential, which have a decisive affect on the development of settlement systems, the Southern Levant should be divided into three zones: lowlands, highlands and steppe-lands (Coote and Whitelam 1987). Its settlement and demographic history was shaped according to the ties between the inhabitants of these three niches. Special attention should be given to the dichotomy between the fertile, sedentary, but politically fragmented lowlands and the topographical and lithological frontier of the highlands (for the Mediterranean, see Braudel 1972: 25 ff.; for the Levant, see Marfoe 1979).

Long-term perspective

It has become conventional wisdom to view complex historical processes, such as the one discussed in this chapter, from a long-term perspective (Braudel's *la longue durée* – 1958; for the highlands of Palestine, see Alt 1925; on archaeology and long-term history see Hodder 1987; Knapp 1992). Indeed, recent studies have outlined cyclical rhythms in the occupational history of all three zones of the Southern Levant: rise and collapse of urban civilizations in the lowlands (below); settlement oscillations, and rise and collapse of desert polities in the steppelands (Finkelstein and Perevolotsky 1990); and waves of settlement with intervals of decline in the highlands. (On cyclic history in general, see Toynbee 1956; for Palestine see Mendenhall 1976; Coote and Whitelam 1987). Hence, the investigation of the processes that took place in the Iron Age I requires insights into the occupational history of a much longer period: from the inception of the first wave of settlement in the highlands in the beginning of the Early

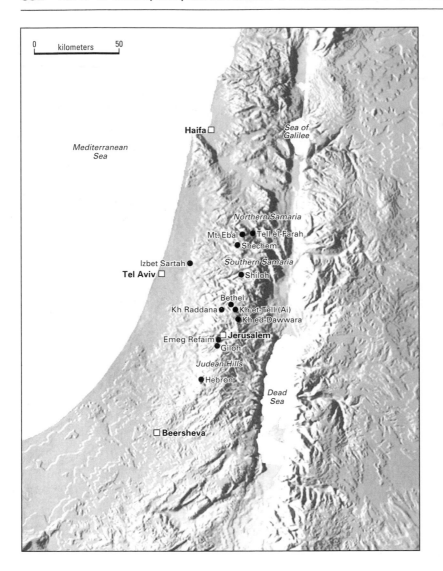

Figure 1 Main Iron Age I excavated sites in the central hill country

Bronze Age to the outcome of the Iron I transformation – that is, the rise of the territorial states of the Iron Age II.

'Pots and people'

The limitations in the use of the material culture evidence for historical research have recently been treated in a number of studies (e.g., Kamp and Yoffee 1980; Auger et al. 1987). Available data on the material remains of the Iron Age I highlands people – mainly their pottery and architecture – may shed some light on the two questions presented in the introduction, but they may, equally, be misleading (Window 3, p. 365).

Regional aspects

Regionalism played an important role in the cultural and demographic developments in the Iron Age I. These were molded by the proximity of a given area to the different urban cultures of the lowlands (or its isolation) and by its specific environmental features. One should bear in mind the different impacts of the various forces which were active at that time in the lowlands – declining Canaanite city states in the northern valleys and the Coastal Plain, remaining Egyptian strongholds in the southern Coastal Plain (in the twelfth century), and the rising Philistine pentapolis of the southern Coastal Plain and the Shephelah (Singer 1993).

The environment

Limitations to sedentary activity in the ecological frontier regions of the highlands stemmed from harsh topography (see opening photograph), difficult-to-exploit rock formations and dense cover of natural vegetation (Hopkins 1985). These obstacles drove scholars to suggest that occupation of the highlands was made possible only with the introduction of certain technological innovations – the use of iron and plastered cisterns and the terracing of hilly slopes (see Window 2, p. 364). The distance from the maritime and overland trade, the social isolation of the small communities which were separated by topographical barriers, and the constant struggle with the ecological obstacles had a decisive influence on the material culture of the highlands' communities (see Window 3, p. 365). This is reflected, for example, in the limited pottery repertoire of the highland people in all periods.

But life in the highlands had some clear advantages for the local population. The social and political isolation allowed relative freedom from the great powers which in many periods dominated the lowlands. This is demonstrated by the fact that only two highlands sites are mentioned in the Egyptian texts of the second millennium BCE, and by the independent policies conducted by the highlands polities in the Amarna Age.

Moreover, the eastern flank of the central range of the highlands of Cisjordan, and several niches in the highlands of Transjordan, were the only parts of the country which enabled their population to engage in a well-balanced, self-sufficient economy. This strategy involved all three traditional components of the Middle Eastern economy. In the case of the central hill country it meant dry farming in flat, open areas; animal husbandry in the desert fringe and summer pasture enclaves in other parts of the highlands; and horticulture in mountainous areas (Plate 1).

The proximity to steppe areas on the east and south, the availability of green pasture in the dry summer, and the fact that the highlands were not densely populated and cultivated even in periods of settlement expansion, made these regions ideal for pastoral activity. They were especially convenient for 'enclosed nomadism' (Rowton 1974), that is, migration routine between the steppe in the winter and the highlands in the summer. The eastern flank of the hilly regions was especially convenient for sedentary activity of groups which originated from a pastoral background, since they could continue to practice animal husbandry alongside dry farming. As a result of all these reasons, the highlands frontier zones were inhabited by pastoralists in all periods of the third and second millennia BCE, with changing numbers according to the fate of the sedentary communities.

When the political and socio-economic conditions permitted, the highlands communities could benefit from specializing in an horticulture-oriented economy, which included the industrialization of the orchards' products. In recent generations villages in certain parts of the central hill country, especially on the western slopes, specialized in olive orchards and oil production. They produced a large surplus of oil and exchanged it for grain (cereal growing was a wrong economic strategy in these hilly parts of the highlands). In the 1940s the central hill country, between

Plate 1 Dry farming areas in the eastern flank of the central range, southeast of Shechem (photograph: Israel Finkelstein)

the Jezreel and the Beersheva valleys, produced ca 70 percent of the total quantity of oil made in Palestine; adding the Galilee, almost all the oil of the country was made in the hilly regions; over 90 percent of the olive oil presses were located in hilly villages. The Arab Moslem population does not produce wine, and hence the area devoted to vineyards was relatively small; but according to both textual evidence (e.g., the Samaria Ostraca) and the widespread remains of wine presses (e.g., Dar 1986: 147–50) it is clear that in antiquity the hill country villagers also specialized in viniculture and that they supplied most of the wine produce of the country.

The hilly regions, never densely populated, were also receptive to population 'surplus' from the lowlands. At the same time, the special environmental conditions made them ideal for the withdrawal of marginal elements of the society. The ecological frontier zones were the last to be populated in every wave of settlement in the country and the first to suffer in times of settlement crisis.

The central hill country can be divided into two major geographical subunits:

1. Samaria – the area between Shiloh in the south and the Jezreel valley in the north. This is the most convenient part of the hill country for habitation, mainly because of the fertile intermontane valleys (Plate 2). In the area to the north of Shechem the valleys are broader, which resulted in a denser population. In the western part of the region, especially in the southwest, the terrain is rugged, rocky and less conducive for cultivation. However, terracing the slopes could made them useful for horticulture.
2. The Judean hills – the area between the village of Tayibeh in the north and the Beersheva Valley in the south. The northern part of the plateau of the central range (north of Jerusalem), and its eastern desert fringe, are relatively amenable to habitation and hence make an intermediate zone between Samaria and the Judean Hills. The area south of Jerusalem has desert fringe areas on both east and south. The central range is relatively flat and its western flank rugged and steep. Recent surveys

Plate 2 An intermontane valley in Samaria (photograph: Israel Finkelstein)

indicate that this part of the hill country was only sparsely inhabited by sedentary populations until Iron II. This was apparently due to two reasons: first, the rugged lithology made the area inhospitable for agricultural activity; and second, the extensive marginal lands on both east and south made pastoralism a better economic strategy. The recent human landscape is, therefore, the result of intensive farming in the last three millennia.

Somewhat similar geographical circumstances prevail in the Transjordanian plateau, in the sense that ecological conditions deteriorate as one goes from north (the Gilead) to south (Edom) and from the center to both east (desert) and west (rugged slopes).

The collapse of the Late Bronze culture

The collapse of the Late Bronze culture – once depicted, in correspondence with the biblical ideology, as a singular event in the history of the country – should be viewed against the background of the cyclical rise and collapse of urban cultures in the southern Levant in the third–second millennia BCE. Indeed, scholarly approaches to destruction of urban cultures have changed significantly in the last decade: theories of conquest by invading nomads (e.g., Albright 1939; Lapp 1967; Kenyon 1971: 567), or Egyptian military campaigns (e.g., Callaway 1978: 55; Dever 1987: 174–5) gave way to hypotheses on gradual socio-economic transformations.

The collapse of the urban Early Bronze, the nature of the subsequent Intermediate Bronze Age and the reurbanization in the Middle Bronze are now understood as local developments of socio-economic change from a complex urban civilization to a mixed rural-pastoral society and a shift back to an urban system (e.g., Dever 1980). The destruction of the Middle Bronze cities is also explained in local socio-political terms (Bunimovitz 1989). The final collapse of the Late Bronze culture is no doubt connected to broader events which took place in the

eastern Mediterranean in the thirteenth–early twelfth centuries BCE; but at the same time, local economic and social factors played a decisive role in this process (Bunimovitz 1989; this volume, Chapter 19).

The Iron I as a phase in long-term settlement and demographic oscillations in the highlands

Three waves of settlement and two intervals of decline

There were three waves of settlement with two intervals of decline in the central hill country in the third and second millennia BCE (Figure 2a and 2b). Settlement activity intensified from one peak period to the next. All three waves of settlement led to the rise of complex political formations, but while the first two degenerated, the third high-tide resulted in the development of full-scale statehood. These waves of settlement had much in common, especially in their demographic patterns, but also in certain aspects of their material culture.

The first wave of settlement in the highlands of western Palestine commenced in the Chalcolithic period (34 small sites with an accumulated built-up area of 14 hectares; Figure 2b) and peaked in the Early Bronze I (88 sites with an accumulated built up area of 131 hectares). In the Early Bronze II–III there was a decrease in both the number of sites and the inhabited area (66 sites and 115 hectares; for details on the Chalcolithic–Early Bronze settlement patterns, see Finkelstein and Gophna 1993). This wave of settlement was followed by a dramatic crisis in the Intermediate Bronze Age, when almost all Early Bronze sites were abandoned. There were only 49 settlement sites at that period, most of them of limited size, but 42 cemeteries not related to nearby sedentary sites have been recorded (Finkelstein 1991). The settlement crisis continued in the Middle Bronze I (Albright's MB IIA): most of the information on this period comes from reused shaft tombs in Intermediate Bronze Age cemeteries (e.g. Dever 1975).

The second wave of settlement took place in the Middle Bronze II–III (Albright's MB IIB–C). Two hundred and forty eight sites, with a total built-up area of 187 hectares have been recorded so far in the central hill country. It seems that the process started in the MB II, when scores of small sites were established in different parts of the region. In the MB III several sites developed to serve as government centers for the ruling elite and some of the small sites were abandoned. This impressive settlement system collapsed at the end of the Middle Bronze Age. The Late Bronze Age marks the second demographic crisis in the highlands of Canaan – only 29 sites were inhabited at that time; their total built-up area was only 47 hectares. Moreover, some of the remaining sites shrank in size: Late Bronze Age activity at Shiloh was limited to a cult site which was visited by people from the neighboring hill country.

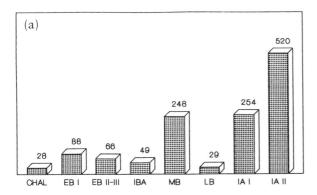
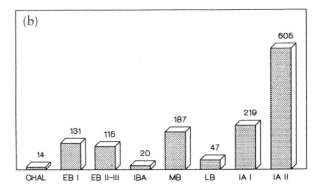

Figure 2   Settlement oscillations in the central hill country from the Chalcolithic to the Iron II periods: (a) number of sites and (b) total built-up area in hectares

The third wave of settlement began in the late-thirteenth century and peaked during the twelfth to eleventh century BCE. The comprehensive surveys have so far recorded 254 Iron Age I sites in the central hill country (Figure 3), with a total built-up area of 219 hectares (Finkelstein 1988). This settlement system expanded dramatically in the Iron Age II: the number of sites more than doubled (to 520) and the total built-up area (and thus population) almost tripled (Broshi and Finkelstein 1992).

The published data from the surveys in the Transjordanian plateau do not allow a full and detailed reconstruction of the settlement patterns throughout the ages (Finkelstein, forthcoming). But it provides enough information to trace settlement oscillations similar to those detected in the highlands of western Palestine (Figure 4).

Even in the three periods of settlement prosperity the highlands frontiers were not fully reclaimed for human cultivation, and there remained 'empty quarters' with very sparse population. In all three phases the settlement system was well-balanced, with classification of sites into several major centers, numerous small villages (see Plate 3 for an Iron I site), and scores of tiny sites, some of them apparently seasonal campsites of pastoral or transhumant groups. The population was therefore composed of both sedentary and pastoral people, which gave the highlands polities special strength (below).

There is also a surprising correspondence in the settlement locales. Many of the Iron Age I sites of the central hill country were established at sites which had been occupied already in the Early Bronze I, and especially in the Middle Bronze Age. The best evidence comes from excavated sites. Tell en-Nasbeh, Kh. Rabud and Kh. Raddana were first occupied in the Early Bronze I. Middle Bronze sherds were found in the Iron Age I sites of Tell el-Ful, Giloh and Kh. ed-Dawwara. In both cases the sites were not reoccupied until the Iron Age I. As for the results of the surveys, 116 of the 254 Iron Age I sites of the central hill country were occupied in the Middle Bronze and the overwhelming majority of them were abandoned in the Late Bronze Age.

The two periods of decline – the Intermediate Bronze and the Late Bronze Ages – also show similar features. There were only few sedentary sites, most of them relatively small, and the balance tilted toward the pastoral component of the population. Evidence for the existence of these pastoral groups includes cemeteries and open cult places not related to nearby settlement sites (for the Intermediate Bronze Age see Finkelstein 1991; for the Late Bronze Age see Finkelstein 1988: 341–5).

The usual past interpretations of such settlement oscillations, as results of migration of new groups from distant parts of the Levant or demographic expansion and withdrawal from the nearby lowlands, are not sufficient to explain the demographic history of the highlands of both Cis- and Transjordan in the Bronze and Iron Ages. First, although there are some archaeological indications for the presence of northern groups in the central hill country in both the Middle Bronze and Iron I (Finkelstein and Brandl 1985 and Kempinski 1979), the overall character of the material culture of these regions shows clear local features. Second, recent studies have shown beyond doubt that the lowlands population had never reached close to a 'carrying capacity' point, and hence there were no land-hungry demographic surpluses eager to expand into new frontiers. It is, therefore, more reasonable to explain these settlement fluctuations in terms of socio-economic change, that is, shifts toward a more sedentary or a more pastoral society, in accordance with political, economic and social transformations. Similar shifts along the sedentary-pastoral continuum, which are more typical to the marginal areas of the Middle East – highlands and steppelands alike – were recorded in recent generations in both the central hill country (Grossman 1992) and Transjordan (Lewis 1987; see also LaBianca 1990).

There are indications for the presence of significant pastoral groups in the central hill country in all periods of the third and second millennia BCE (Finkelstein 1992). Early Bronze I and Middle Bronze (mostly MB I–II) cemeteries, not related to nearby settlement sites, have been recorded in recent surveys and excavations. Small Middle

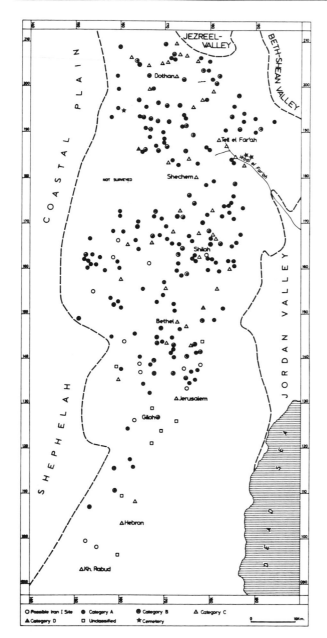

Figure 3 Settlement pattern of the Iron I in the central hill country (Category A = 0.1–0.3h; B = 0.4–1h; C = 1.1–5h; D = 5.1–10h)

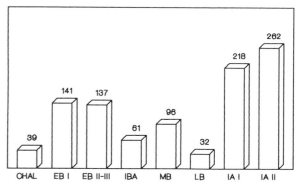

Figure 4 Settlement oscillations in the Transjordanian plateau from the Chalcolithic to the Iron II periods (number of sites)

Bronze II–III and Iron Age I sites, which revealed a handful of sherds but no architectural remains, should apparently be interpreted as seasonal sites of pastoral-nomads or transhumant groups. These sites are usually located in the desert fringe and western slopes, which are less amenable to cultivation.

The pastoral phenomenon is especially evident in times of settlement decline. Almost all Intermediate Bronze Age sites are found in the eastern flank of the central hill country – a convenient location for pastoral activity. The

exceptionally large number of Intermediate Bronze cemeteries not related to sedentary sites should also be noted.

The archaeological evidence for pastoral people dwindles in the subsequent periods of more complex political systems. All the Early Bronze I and Middle Bronze I–II cemeteries, which are not related to sedentary sites, were not reused in the Early Bronze II–III and in the Middle Bronze III. Moreover, it seems that many of the seasonal Middle Bronze II sites were abandoned in the Middle Bronze III, while the phenomenon of small seasonal sites is almost non-existent in the Iron Age II.

The shifts along the sedentary–pastoral continuum are apparently evident in the faunal material from two sites in the central hill country (Figure 5): Shiloh and Emeq Refaim. In Shiloh, the ratio of cattle bones (vs. sheep/goats) declines from 12:88 in the Middle Bronze II–III to 9:91 in the Late Bronze and then rises dramatically to 23:77 in the Iron I and to 29:71 in the Iron II (Hellwing et al. 1993). Although the Shiloh faunal assemblages may be associated with cultic activity, they must reflect the subsistence patterns of the population in each of these periods. Interestingly, the ratio of sheep/goats to cattle in the Middle Bronze II stratum at the site of Emeq Refaim near Jerusalem (78:22) is similar to that of Middle Bronze II Shiloh, while the ratio in the Intermediate Bronze Age stratum of that site (96:4 – Kolska Horwitz 1989) resembles that of Late Bronze Shiloh. These differences represent shifts between plow-agriculture communities (more cattle) and pastoral oriented groups (more sheep/goats).

The reasons behind these shifts along the sedentary–pastoral continuum will not be discussed here. Suffice it to say that, with no historical material at hand for the third millennium BCE and with very limited sources for the second millennium BCE, we have no other option but to utilize anthropological models (sometimes supported by data from recent generations), which take into consideration political difficulties, economic calamities and social disturbances (for the Early Bronze, see Dever 1989; Esse 1989; Gophna, this volume; for the Middle Bronze see

Plate 3   Iron I site in southern Samaria (photograph: Israel Finkelstein)

Bunimovitz 1989; Ilan, this volume; for the Late Bronze/Iron I transition see Finkelstein 1988).

A more sedentary north vs a more pastoral south

As noted above, there is a significant ecological difference in the central hill country between the north and south. The Samaria Hills, with vast intermontane valleys, relatively moderate topography and a comparatively fertile eastern steppe, was amenable to human activity. The Judean Hills were inhospitable for sedentary life – harsh rock formations and steppe areas on both east and south hindered agricultural activity.

The ecological disparities resulted in weighty demographic and settlement differences (Figures 6–7). Northern Samaria was more densely occupied, with larger sites and very little evidence for non-sedentary activity. The Judean Hills were sparsely inhabited by sedentary people until the Iron Age II, but the number of pastoral groups there was very significant (Ofer 1993). In southern Samaria – the area between these units – the ratio between sedentary and pastoral people was more balanced. The density of occupation in each of the three regions in the three periods of settlement prosperity was almost identical. The ecological and demographic differences between a more sedentary north and a more pastoral south also shaped the nature of the political entities that developed in them in the Middle Bronze–Late Bronze Ages and in the Iron Age II (below).

Similar traits, of a more densely occupied, sedentary north vs a sparsely settled, pastoral south, are typical of the Transjordanian plateau (Figure 8; for recent generations see Lewis 1987).

Expansion from east to west and development of specialized agriculture

All three periods of settlement prosperity in the central hill country show a gradual demographic expansion from east to west (Figure 9).

This trend is first observed in the Early Bronze I. Since the survey material does not allow a distinction between subphases of the period, one has to draw information from excavated sites. These reveal that most of the settlements which were established already in the EB IA are located in the eastern part of the central hill country (Tell el-Far'ah, Bethel, Tell en-Nasbeh), whereas nearly all the sites in the western flank of the region were founded in the EB IB (cf. Samaria, Sataf, Bidya Cave).

The only possible way (though not unequivocal) to distinguish between Early and Late Middle Bronze survey sites in the central hill country is according to typology of cooking pots. At Shiloh, handmade cooking pots with erect rim and rope decoration are dominant in Stratum VIII of the Middle Bronze II (28 percent of the cooking pots) and almost absent in the assemblage of Stratum VII of the Middle Bronze III (only 2 percent). In the latter phase they were replaced by holemouth cooking pots (39 percent). Applying this classification to the sherds collected in the 82 Middle Bronze settlement sites recorded in the Southern Samaria survey, we find that 19 of the 23 sites (83 percent) which yielded the early type of cooking pot are located in the eastern half of the region, whereas the later type is more evenly spread. An east–west expansion in the Middle Bronze is supported by another piece of evidence: all seven shaft-tomb cemeteries, which were reused in the early phase of the Middle Bronze, are found in the eastern part of the region (for excavated material, see Dever 1975).

The results of the Southern Samaria Survey show that most of the early Iron Age I sites (75 percent) are located in the eastern part of the region, that is, on the desert fringe and the eastern flank of the central range. The expansion into the ecological frontier areas of the western slopes came only in a later phase of the period, and intensified in the Iron Age II (Finkelstein 1989). An analogous process has been detected in northern Samaria (Zertal 1988a) and in the area between Ramallah and Jerusalem. In the latter, the number of sites located on the western slopes grows from 13 percent of the total in the Iron Age I to 25 percent in the Iron Age II.

The concentration of sites in the early stage of each wave of settlement in the eastern part of the hill country was dictated by ecological and socio-economic motives. In the beginning of each settlement process, when the region was sparsely inhabited and the settlers could freely choose the location of their villages, they opted for areas which were topographically moderate, ecologically convenient and agriculturally promising (the desert fringe, the intermontane valleys and flat areas in the central range). Since the volume of population was limited, there was no necessity to struggle with the ecological frontiers of the slopes. Furthermore, the eastern niches enabled their inhabitants to conduct a well-balanced economic strategy. The fact that the settlers were attracted to areas convenient for a combination of dry farming and animal husbandry

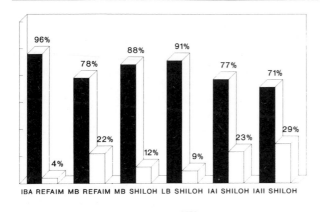

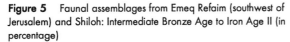

Figure 5 Faunal assemblages from Emeq Refaim (southwest of Jerusalem) and Shiloh: Intermediate Bronze Age to Iron Age II (in percentage)

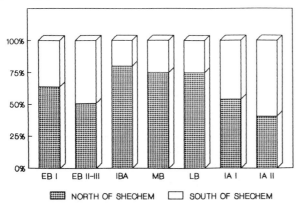

Figure 6 Early Bronze I to Iron II built–up hectares in the central hill country: north vs south (in percentage)

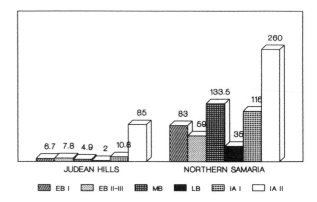

Figure 7 Early Bronze I to Iron II built–up hectares in the central hill country: Judean Hills vs northern Samaria

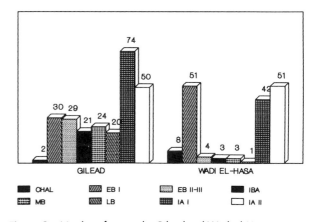

Figure 8 Number of sites in the Gilead and Wadi el-Hasa surveys, showing more continuity in the former and stronger fluctuations in the latter

may also indicate that at least some of them originated from a pastoral background.

According to this interpretation, in the early stages of each wave of settlement, when the population was still in transition from pastoral nomadism to sedentary life, it concentrated in the areas which better suited its socio-economic traditions. Hence the slope units, typical of orchard agriculture which bears fruit only after a relatively long period of cultivation, were occupied only in a later phase, when the population was fully settled, and turned to specialized economic strategies (Plate 4). The westward expansion brought about significant socio-political change (below).

Similarities in the material culture

It is quite difficult to compare the material culture of the Iron Age I to that of the preceding two periods of onset of settlement activity, especially because the few rural Early Bronze I and Middle Bronze II settlement sites which were

excavated in the central hill country yielded only fragmentary results. Nevertheless, there are clues for certain similar traits between the finds, especially concerning the Middle Bronze II and the Iron I Ages, and these are discussed below:

1. *No fortifications.* As far as we know, the Early Bronze I and the Iron Age I sites were not fortified. As for the Middle Bronze, recent research has shown that most of the stone and earth works at the periphery of the hill country sites were constructed in the Middle Bronze III (Ussishkin 1989).

2. *Architecture.* The most widespread structure in the Iron Age I hill country sites is the pillared-building. Interestingly, buildings with stone pillars have recently been uncovered in the Middle Bronze II site of Emeq Refaim. Moreover, the plan of some of them have certain features which resemble the 'four-room houses' of the Iron Age, although the pillars are situated in the spaces of the rooms rather than in the walls separating them (Eisenberg 1988/89: 89). Another typical characteristic of Iron Age I highlands and steppe architecture is the row of broadrooms surrounding a central courtyard. The plan of a section of

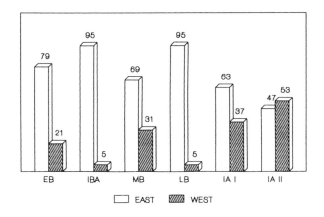

Figure 9 Early Bronze to Iron II built-up hectares in southern Samaria: east vs west

Plate 4 Olive oil installations in a site in southern Samaria (photograph: Israel Finkelstein)

the Middle Bronze II site of Manahat (Edelstein 1988/89: 122) reveals comparable elements. The differences from the Iron Age I sites – broadrooms built in a line, each open into a small courtyard, rather than broadrooms surrounding a closed, oval courtyard – do not obscure the resemblance. Both the oval and the linear layouts apparently reflect former pastoral traditions of the inhabitants (Finkelstein 1988: 238–50).

3. *Pottery*. Unfortunately, we do not yet have a full ceramic assemblage from Early Bronze I and Middle Bronze II settlement sites in the highlands. Yet, it is clear that some of the vessels have similar shapes, although they are hundreds of years apart. A good example is the marked similarity in shape, size and decoration of the neck between the typical Iron Age I collared-rim jars and some of the Middle Bronze pithoi found at Shiloh (Plate 5). The ceramic repertoire in the three periods discussed here (EB I, MB II and Iron I) was surprisingly limited, containing mainly storage jars and cooking pots. Pottery was apparently produced in local workshops. Mass production of vessels is evident only in the subsequent periods (MB III, Iron II).

4. *Mountain cult places*. Two of the three periods discussed here revealed open-air, mountain cult places. Well known Iron Age I examples are the 'Bull Site' in northern Samaria (Mazar 1982) and Mt. Ebal near Shechem (Zertal 1986–87). A similar Middle Bronze site was apparently located in the course of the Southern Samaria survey on the summit of Jebel el-Rukba, south of Shechem. Located on one of the highest peaks in Samaria and overlooking great distances, the site is composed of an isolated oval platform, 16 m×9 m in size and is made of a wall about 1 m high and a fill of small stones. It is also worth mentioning that 90 percent of the sherds collected by Zertal (1988a: 114) at the 'Bull Site' belong to his 'Einun' type, that is, should be dated to the Middle Bronze Age. Interestingly, the site of the Iron Age I raised platform at the site of Giloh also yielded some Middle Bronze sherds (Mazar 1990: 90–1).

The similarities in certain features of the material culture of the Early Bronze I, Middle Bronze II and Iron I sites in the central hill country may be explained on several grounds: the influence of the environment, the parallelism in the subsistence economy and the impact of analogous social systems. In all three periods the society was composed of isolated, small, self-sufficient communities, which had to struggle with harsh natural conditions. They were engaged in similar subsistence patterns and show only a limited degree of complex social organization. There was very little commercial activity and craft specialization.

These characteristics changed in the subsequent periods: the Early Bronze II–III, Middle Bronze III and Iron Age II people, with their sophisticated social and political organization, conducted impressive building activities and were engaged in trade, mass production and redistribution.

What has been said above clearly indicates that the material culture of the Iron Age I sites in the highlands should not be viewed in terms of ethnic perspectives (contra Dever 1993). It rather reflects the ecological background, the subsistence economy and the social frameworks of these highlands communities (Window 3, p. 365).

The rise of highlands complex societies

In all three periods under discussion, sedentary-population growth, territorial expansion, and the demand for highlands horticultural products by lowland communities led to the rise of stratified, complex societies. The distinctive ecological background of the highlands brought about the formation of large territorial polities, with some clear similarities between the three periods.

The Early Bronze Age

The dramatic increase in the number of sites and in the occupied area in the central hill country in the Early Bronze I was apparently caused by the beginning of large scale horticultural activity. The stimulant for this economic

(a)

(b)

Plate 5 Pottery assemblages from Shiloh: Middle Bronze III (left) and Iron I (right) (photograph: Yoram Weinberg)

development was the demand for Palestinian horticultural products in Egypt. The specialization in olive and vine growing, and the industrialization of the products, called for the development of advanced administration in order to manage inter- and intra-regional trade (Finkelstein and Gophna 1993; for the production of oil in the Early Bronze Age, see Stager 1985b). Large sites emerged, with massive fortifications, which could not have been constructed without control over populations of sizable areas. In the Early Bronze II–III there was a certain decrease in the central hill country in both the number of sites and the total built-up area.

It is quite clear that the site of Kh. et-Tell ('Ai) dominated the entire area of the hill country south of Shechem. This site covered 11 hectares, while the second-ranked site in the region – Ras et-Tawra, north of Hebron – reached only 6 hectares. All the rest were relatively small sites. The urban area of Kh. et-Tell covered ca 20 percent of the total built-up area in all the 35 sites south of Shechem. Ras et-Tawra could not have been a center of an independent unit in the Judean Hills, since it did not have a significant sedentary hinterland (there are only a few small sites to its south, and no sites to its north up to the area north of Jerusalem). According to this reconstruction, Kh. et-Tell controlled a far larger area than any of the lowland Early Bronze centers. It is, therefore, reasonable to assume that it ruled over a more complex political organization than a typical lowlands' city-state.

It is impossible to determine whether the area north of Shechem was controlled by one site (Tell el-Far'ah in the EBII, Dothan in the EBIII?), or by several centers. But comparing the situation in this region to that of later periods, I would argue for the first option.

The difference between the two suggested territorial

formations is that the northern one was densely populated by sedentary population, while the larger, southern one was sparsely inhabited by settled people and its population probably had a large pastoral component.

The Middle and Late Bronze Ages

The transition from the Middle Bronze II to the Middle Bronze III was apparently characterized by a similar, two-fold process: a decrease in the number of sites and the construction of highland strongholds, such as Shechem, Shiloh and Hebron. These sites served as government centers for social elites that ruled over large territories of mixed sedentary and pastoral population (Finkelstein 1993).

Two textual sources shed some light on the territorial formations in the central hill country during the early days of the Middle Bronze wave of settlement.

The Khu-Sebek stele describes a military campaign to the region in the nineteenth century BCE. The reference to the 'land' of Shechem, and the mention of Shechem as a parallel to Retenu, possibly hint that it was a center of a large territorial entity (Mazar, B. 1986: 9). Only two central hill country sites – Shechem and Jerusalem – are mentioned in the Execration Texts, apparently indicating that the entire area was divided between two large political bodies, centered in these two places. The minor highlands strongholds, such as Bethel and Hebron, were probably the seats of chiefs who were subordinates of the main centers. As mentioned above, the results of the surveys point out that both regions had a dimorphic structure, but the northern one was more sedentary and the southern one more pastoral.

The emergence of large political entities in the highlands

in the Middle Bronze was apparently also connected with an impressive population growth, an expansion into the inhospitable regions which were conducive only for horticultural activity, and the development of specialized agriculture which required balancing institutions to control the flow of commodities. Demand for these commodities in the sophisticated lowland centers must have played a role in the process.

For a better understanding of the territorial history in the Iron Age, it is also worth looking at the political organization of the central hill country in the Late Bronze Age. Despite the dramatic demographic crisis at the end of the Middle Bronze, the political division had not changed significantly. The only highland political entities mentioned in the Amarna letters are Shechem and Jerusalem. Hebron was not inhabited in the Late Bronze (Ofer 1989), which rules out the possibility that it was the seat of el-Amarna's Shuwardata. Na'aman's suggestion (1986), that Bethel and Debir were independent city-states is difficult to accept for both textual and archaeological reasons: besides the fact that they are not mentioned in the tablets, there is no archaeological evidence that they were important centers in the Late Bronze Age.

This is the first period which offers clues about the border between the two highland units. The territory of Shechem extended to the Jezreel valley in the north and to the Coastal Plain in the west. The political involvement of Shechem with Gezer (EA 253, 254) seems to indicate that it governed the plateau of Bethel. The large territories dominated by the house of Labayu explains the reference, in EA 289, to the 'Land of Shechem'. The Shechem entity included about 25 sedentary sites, most of them north of Shechem, and large areas inhabited primarily by pastoralists, mainly south of Shechem.

If we accept the identification of Bit Ninurta, which is mentioned in the archive, with Beth Horon (Kallai and Tadmor 1969), then Jerusalem dominated the plateau of Gideon. The concern of Jerusalem with the events in Keila seems to indicate that the territory of Jerusalem included the entire Judean Hills. As in the previous periods, the southern entity embraced only a very few sedentary sites, but was inhabited by a large number of pastoral groups.

Scholars have agreed that the political entities of the central hill country in the second millennium BCE ruled over larger territories and more complex social systems than the city states of the lowlands (e.g., Alt 1925; Na'aman 1982: 216). Rowton's definition of 'dimorphic chiefdoms' (1973, 1976) may fit the situation in the hill country in the Bronze Age (Finkelstein 1993). According to Rowton, a dimorphic chiefdom is a political system based on a government center in a tribal territory, and it is generally connected to areas of enclosed nomadism. The population of a dimorphic chiefdom is, therefore, composed of both sedentary and nomadic groups.

The Iron Age

The third wave of settlement in the highlands led to the emergence of the territorial-national states of the Iron Age II. This was a revolutionary development, although many of the characteristics of the Israelite and Judean monarchies have their roots in the long political history of the highlands in the third and second millennia BCE.

In the Iron Age I, as in the preceding periods, there was a clear difference in the settlement patterns of the central hill country between north and south. While the areas south of Shechem were apparently occupied mainly by local sedentarizing pastoral nomads, certain groups in northern Samaria originated from the indigenous sedentary population. Archaeologically speaking, parts of the southern hill country were now inhabited after a long occupational gap, but in northern Samaria there was a significant settlement-demographic continuity from the former period (for the reflection of this situation in the biblical material see, for instance, Noth 1960: 152–3). Furthermore, the third–second millennia phenomenon of a mostly sedentary north vs. a mostly pastoral south continued well into the first millennium BCE.

According to the biblical description, which may contain a certain core of early Iron Age reality, the central highlands were occupied by two different alignments of people – the House of Joseph in the north, and Judah and his associated elements in the south. The boundary between these groups (in this case, most probably reflecting an Iron II situation) roughly corresponded with the border of the two second millennium entities: the House of Joseph occupied the former territory of Shechem, while Judah and his fellow units occupied the one-time territory of Jerusalem (for the relations between the Late Bronze territorial division and the allotments of the Israelite tribes, see Alt 1925; Na'aman 1986).

The phenomenon of local chiefs ruling over dimorphic territories in the hill country is still evident in the early days of the Iron Age. The case of David in Hebron may be taken as an example for the southern highlands. Reviv (1966) deduced from Judges 9 that the political system in Shechem (as well as in Hebron) was different from the conventional one in the city-states of Canaan. Especially important, in his opinion, is the fact that the ruler of the town is called 'nesi ha-ares' rather than a king; the term *nasi* is possibly derived from tribal terminology. Interestingly, the layout of Shechem did not change significantly from the Middle Bronze Age through the Iron Age I. As for Jerusalem, even as the capital of the united monarchy it was no more than a typical hill country stronghold; most of its limited area was occupied by the citadel of Zion, the millo (the terracing system on the slopes?) and the temple. Jerusalem spread to become a densely populated city only in a much later phase of the Iron Age II.

At the end of the eleventh century BCE, as a result of

external pressures and internal processes, the hill country groups united to establish one highlands' state. The domestic mechanisms which brought about the rise of an advanced administration were at least partially connected to the expansion of the population into the horticulture niches of the highlands (Finkelstein 1989). But the United Monarchy was a short, singular episode in the history of the country. The traditional tensions between north and south surfaced time and again before the consolidation of the Monarchy (the struggle between Saul and David) and during its initial stages (the attempts of the north to overthrow the yoke of David). These tensions soon led to the breakdown of the United Monarchy, that is, to the reversion to the deeply rooted tradition of two hill country entities – the Judean Kingdom, centered in Jerusalem, and the Israelite Kingdom, centered around Shechem. The border between the two states followed the traditional boundary between the second millennium entities of Shechem and Jerusalem.

Alt (1966: 239–59) pointed out a major difference in the political features of the two Israelite monarchies – a unified, stable dynastic leadership in Judah vs a loosely connected, charismatic leadership of various origins in Israel (see review in Buccellati 1967). It is now clear that the roots of this contrast also lie in the political conditions of the second millennium, which in turn stemmed from the environmental differences between the two regions. The homogeneous mountain-bloc of the south had only two centers – Jerusalem and Hebron. The supremacy of Jerusalem was never threatened, probably because Hebron was too remote and isolated, and never had a sufficiently large sedentary hinterland. The northern part of the central hill country, fragmented by intermontane valleys, had several political centers which struggled for supremacy. This is manifested in the Iron Age II in the changes in the location of the capital of Israel.

Summary

The settlement processes that took place in the highlands of Canaan in the Iron Age I had much in common with two preceding waves of occupation in these areas; the first occurred in the Early Bronze and the second took place in the Middle Bronze Age. The outcome of the Iron Age I settlement activity – the emergence of the Israelite

territorial states – resembles some features of the formation of large territorial polities in the central hill country in the Middle and Late Bronze Ages, and possibly also in the Early Bronze Age. Similar long-term demographic developments can apparently be traced in the Transjordanian plateau. These analogies reinforce the hypothesis that much of the Iron Age I settlement process in both Cis- and Transjordan was part of a cyclic mechanism of alternating processes of sedentarization and nomadization of indigenous groups in response to changing political, economic and social circumstances.

But these cyclical processes were influenced by other, broader political, economic and social developments in the country. Short-term local events, foreign interventions and migrations of alien groups also played a significant role in the demographic history of the country. All of them are hardly dictated by environmental conditions and long-term processes. These non-cyclical phenomena explain the dissimilarities between the phases of the cyclic processes. The emergence of early Israel (and the other 'national' entities in the southern Levant) was, therefore, determined by a combination of long-term history and short-term circumstances, and by a balance between local developments and external influences.

The genuine exceptional event in the highlands of the southern Levant in the late-second to early-first millennium BCE was not the 'Israelite Settlement', but the emergence of the United Monarchy – the unification of the entire region and most of the lowlands under one rule. But the United Monarchy was no more than a short episode that eventually failed, and the area turned back to the traditional system of two central hill country polities. In any event, the fate of the cyclical processes of the third and second millennia BCE was sealed by the rise of the national states in the entire southern Levant. The later direct rule of foreign empires over the region tilted the historical balance from local ecological and socio-economic factors to extraneous interests, and prevented the revival of these cyclic mechanisms.

The depiction of the Israelite Settlement as a singular event in the annals of the country turned up centuries after the Iron Age I. It was influenced by the history of the Judean Monarchy in the late-Iron II, and was shaped in accordance with the ideology and interests of a fraction of the population of its capital city – Jerusalem.

THREE MODELS FOR THE EMERGENCE OF EARLY ISRAEL

The three 'classic' models for the emergence of Early Israel (for a detail discussion and a survey of literature see Weippert 1971: 5–62; Chaney 1983: 41–16; Finkelstein 1988: 295–314) differ in every aspect of the two major questions concerning the settlement and demographic processes which took place in the highlands of Canaan in the late-second millennium BCE — the origin of the inhabitants of the Iron Age I villages and the manner in which they settled down. But the advocates of all three schools, consciously or unconsciously, agreed on one point: that the 'Israelite Settlement' was a singular, epoch-making event in the history of the country.

W.F. Albright and his followers described it as a *military conquest* by the chosen people, who came from outside of the country, annihilated the *ancien régime* of Bronze Age Canaanite city-states, and settled down on the ruins of their devastated mounds (cf. Albright 1939; Wright 1962: 69–84; Lapp 1967; Yadin 1979). Recent research has ruled out this theory altogether — from both archaeological and biblical bases. Archaeologically, suffice it to say that some of the most important sites mentioned in the biblical narrative of the conquest of Canaan were not inhabited at all at the Late Bronze Age, and that recent finds have clearly demonstrated that the destruction of the Late Bronze culture was a long and gradual process, taking over a century, rather than the result of one catastrophic event. Besides, scholars have not been able to trace the origin of the Iron I population of the southern Levant outside the region.

A. Alt and his disciples portrayed the 'Israelite Settlement' as a *peaceful infiltration* from the steppe of migrating nomads. After their consolidation in the hill country, these groups engaged in bitter fights with the Canaanite city-states, and finally, following the foundation of a national state, turned to territorial expansion in the lowlands (cf. Alt 1939; Aharoni 1957; Weippert 1971). There are two drawbacks in this appealing theory; first, before the domestication of the camel as a herd animal (not earlier than the late-second millennium BCE and apparently even later), the 'inner'

deserts of the southern Levant were very sparsely settled and so these regions could not have been the source of the Iron I population. Secondly, this incoming population cannot be traced in other parts of the the ancient Near East either.

G. Mendenhall and N. Gottwald viewed the 'Israelite Settlement' in terms of a 'Marxist' *social revolution* — a classes' clash which brought down the stratified, unjust old system and opened the way to a better world with equal opportunities (Mendenhall 1962; de Geus 1976; Gottwald 1979; Chaney 1983; Lemche 1985; Ahlström 1986). However, recent surveys have revealed that the rural component of the Late Bronze society was extremely limited (Bunimovitz 1989). Moreover, there is absolutely no undisputed archaeological evidence for a *direct* shift of a significant population from the lowlands to the highlands in the Late Bronze–Iron I transition.

The available archaeological data on the Late Bronze–Iron I transition, until recent years, justified these depictions of a final destruction of an old system and the emergence of a completely new order: excavations in major mounds such as Hazor, Bethel and Lachish revealed the violent destruction of the sophisticated Late Bronze culture, followed either by remains of a poor Iron Age I village, or by an occupational gap. Furthermore, the first comprehensive surveys in the highlands disclosed a wave of Iron Age I settlements following a very sparse occupation in the Bronze Age.

Three developments in Palestinian archaeology in recent years call for a reevaluation of all three approaches. First, there has been a gradual change in the understanding of the emergence and collapse of the urban cultures of the third and second millennia BCE (e.g., Dever 1989). Second, the results of recent comprehensive surveys in the highlands, especially in the central hill country, have provided, for the first time, the necessary data for a full and comprehensive reconstruction of the settlement and demographic history of the country. Third, full coverage surveys in the marginal zones of the country, accompanied by excavations at selected sites, stimulated a new and different understanding of the history of the steppe. These aspects are the subject of discussion in this chapter.

THE ROLE OF TECHNOLOGICAL INNOVATIONS IN THE WAVE OF SETTLEMENT OF THE IRON AGE I

The obvious ecological obstacles to settlement in the highlands of the southern Levant drove scholars to suggest that the emergence of Israel in these regions in the Iron Age I was made possible due to the introduction of new technological innovations (e.g., Stager 1985c: 5–11).

Albright (1949: 113) argued that the Iron I wave of settlement in the highlands was a result of a new technology – plastering water cisterns. This idea has recently been revitalized. There are three serious flaws in this hypothesis:

1. The central hill country of Canaan was quite densely settled already in the Early Bronze Age (Finkelstein and Gophna 1993) and again in the Middle Bronze Age (Finkelstein 1991).
2. The results of recent surveys have proven beyond any doubt that the knowledge of plastering water cisterns was mastered by the Middle Bronze Age people, and most probably even earlier, in the Early Bronze Age. Scores of Early and Middle Bronze sites are located in hilly areas devoid of any permanent water sources (Finkelstein 1988–89: 136–44). The plastered water cistern was, therefore, an outcome of the penetration into these 'dry' areas, rather than the causal factor which opened the way to the expansion into these geographical niches.
3. Many of the Iron I highland sites are devoid of such water cisterns; apparently, their inhabitants brought water from distant springs and stored it in the typical, large Iron I pithoi (Zertal 1988b).

The second of these theories proposed that it was the introduction of iron tools that facilitated the human conquest of the highlands, as these tools helped the settlers to hew water cisterns and to clear the dense natural vegetation (e.g., Miller 1977: 255–7; Gottwald 1979: 655–6). However, recent research has shown that Iron was introduced into the Levant in general and the highlands in particular, at a gradual, slow pace; in addition, most metal implements found in Iron I sites in the highlands were still made of bronze (Waldbaum 1978: 24–7).

A recent popular theory proposed that the spread of settlement in the hill country in the Iron I was connected with the learned skill of terracing (e.g. de Geus 1975; Ahlström 1982; Stager 1982: 116; Callaway 1985: 33). Some scholars further argued that the sophisticated skill of building terraces (Plate 2.1)

Plate 2.1   Terraces in southern Samaria (photograph: Israel Finkelstein)

indicates that their builders came from a rural, sedentary background (de Geus 1975; Ahlström 1982; Dever 1992).

But it is now clear that the Iron I settlement process began in areas of the central hill country which do not necessitate the construction of terraces – the desert fringe, the intermontane valleys of the central range, and flat areas, such as the Bethel plateau. Moreover, Middle Bronze activity on the western slopes of the highlands – where cultivation without terracing is almost impossible – seems to indicate that terrace construction was already carried out at that time. There is good reason to believe that terracing was practiced even before, in the Early Bronze Age, with the first widespread cultivation of olives and grape vines in the hill country (Finkelstein and Gophna 1993). Terracing was, therefore, also an outcome of the demographic expansion into the rugged parts of the hill country and of the beginning of highlands horticulture, rather than an innovation which made this expansion possible. The terraces indicate that their builders practiced horticulture; they tell us nothing about the origin of these people.

MATERIAL CULTURAL AND ETHNICITY: WHO IS AN 'ISRAELITE' IN THE EARLY IRON AGE?

The question presented in the title is relevant also for the other 'national' entities that emerged in the Iron II in the southern Levant – Arameans, Amonites, Moabites and Edomites.

The crucial question regarding the material culture of the Iron I highlands sites is, whether they contain any clues to the origin of their inhabitants. This is closely related to the much discussed question of continuity or discontinuity in the material culture in the Late Bronze–Iron I transition (e.g., de Geus 1976: 167; Miller 1977: 255; Kempinski 1985; Ahlström 1986: 26–36; Dever 1993). In order to tackle this subject, one should first examine the factors which influence the making of the material culture of any

other traits of material culture, show no more than a certain influence from Iron I lowlands sites, which at that time still practiced the pottery traditions of the previous period. Signs of discontinuity reflect the fact that the highlands people lived in small, isolated, rural, almost autarkic communities. Continuity and discontinuity traits – both apparent in the pottery assemblages from the Iron I highlands sites – indicate environmental and socio-economic conditions rather than direct roots to the Late Bronze lowlands.

The same holds true for the architectural traditions of the Iron I highlands sites, especially the four-room house. This house-type gradually developed in the Iron Age I, drawing from the architectural traditions of the region in order to adapt to the hilly environment of the settlers. Other features in the architecture of the sites shed light on the socio-economic conditions of the settlers: the multitude of silos found in almost every Iron I highlands site (Plate 3.1) indicate an intensive practice of dry farming and a limited level of organization (there are no communal storage facilities). The open-court layout of some of the Iron I sites (such as 'Izbet Sartah, Giloh and Beersheva) bear evidence that their inhabitants were engaged in an animal-husbandry oriented subsistence strategy (Finkelstein 1988: 238–50).

The only clue for ethnic affiliation in the Iron I seems to be found in foodways. Pig bones are absent in the faunal assemblages of the Iron I

Plate 3.1   Silos in the Iron I site of 'Izbet Sartah (photograph: Moshe Weinberg)

group of people. Special attention should be given to the environment where people live; their socio-economic conditions; the influence of neighboring cultures; the influence of previous cultures; and in cases of migration, traditions which are brought from the country of origin. Regarding the case of the Iron Age I settlers in the highlands of Canaan, a careful analysis of these factors, combined with a meticulous examination of the geographical and quantitative distribution of the finds, lead to somewhat doubtful conclusions.

Signs of continuity of Late Bronze traditions, in pottery and

hill country sites, while they are present at that time in both the lowlands and Transjordan. Moreover, pig bones appear in significant numbers in the hill country in the Bronze Age. It seems therefore that the taboo on pigs was already practiced in the hill country in the Iron I. In any event, with the absence of reliable written documents for the Iron I, when studying the emergence of the proto-Israelites and other Iron I groups, one is left with no other alternative than to 'impose' the territorial distribution of these people in the Iron Age II, as revealed by reliable historical texts, on the settlement patterns of the Iron I.

PART V

LOCAL KINGDOMS AND WORLD EMPIRES

22

THE KINGDOMS OF ISRAEL AND JUDAH: POLITICAL AND ECONOMIC CENTRALIZATION IN THE IRON IIA–B (CA. 1000–750 BCE)

John S. Holladay, Jr

I Introduction

This study is the result of a long-standing bet with myself, stimulated by the groundbreaking studies in *Social Archaeology* (Redman 1978), that an honest and useful social history of the period of the early Hebrew monarchies could be written solely on the basis of the archaeological evidence and contemporary historical documents interpreted in the light of generally agreed archaeological, historical, economic, and anthropological methodologies and principles. These are not the methodologies or principles presently utilized in most published analytic and synthetic works of most researchers writing in the field of Syro-Palestinian 'historical' archaeology, which I read with growing feelings of frustration and annoyance, but those commonly accepted in the fields of Americanist, British, and Continental anthropologically-based archaeology, including the increasingly available and useful Russian materials. These are resources, many either made possible (e.g., data basing) or enormously enhanced (statistical modelling, manipulation, and testing) by the ready availability of the personal computer, which have been neglected far too long by the subdiscipline within which I make my living.

This is not a question, as some have suggested, between 'Biblical Archaeology' and supposedly secular 'Syro-Palestinian Archaeology', or between the 'New' and the 'Old' in archaeology, but between, as Kent Flannery argued long ago in his inimitable 'Archaeology with a Capital 'S", good and bad archaeology (1973). Archaeology based upon untestable hypotheses (Binford 1968; Watson et al. 1971), or relying upon personal reputation or expertise (Binford 1972: 48, ff.), to say nothing about sensationalism and a fixation upon 'new', 'unique', or museum quality artifacts, is bad archaeology. So is archaeological synthesis which does little more than illustrate badly-done 'biblical' 'history' with archaeological artifacts or plans.

In what follows, I have tried to develop the analysis – and some synthesis – solely on the basis of the archaeology itself, using some of the tools now commonly employed by anthropological archaeologists, and accepting as historical evidence only materials from contemporary sources. In self-defense, I must say that this is my own approach to a difficult and challenging subject, and not some simple-minded plugging-in of Syro-Palestinian data into standard-issue black boxes.

But why not use the Bible as the primary framework of the exercise? In the first place, by far the greatest part of the Old Testament was written during and after the seventh century BCE. The perspectives are, therefore, those of much later periods, and the sources employed by the anonymous writers are simply unknown to us. They may have been accurate historical documents, or they may not, and this unquestionably varies greatly throughout any one writer or editor's contribution. In the second place, even for periods closer to the seventh century, the writers' various biases and desires to make theological points render the use of a biblically-based framework questionable. Baldly put, the whole utility of archaeology as an independent materialistic perspective upon human culture is vitiated by carelessly enfolding it in a nonmaterialist matrix, even one derived from the highest ethical and moral principles. From this perspective, archaeology has much more to contribute to biblical study if it is conducted as a purely materialist pursuit in its own right than if it is somehow regarded as the 'handmaiden' to the study of the Bible.

I have made one concession to myself and the reader. In view of the familiarity of the sources, the numerous, quite unexceptional, synchronisms with externally documented foreign rulers, and the relative certainty of the dynastic succession(s), we will periodize our discussion by reference to some names and dynasties otherwise known only from the Bible. Purists may substitute the names 'Pre-Red-Burnished King Number I (and possibly II or III)' for my

Aerial view of Iron Age levels at Tel Beersheva (photograph: Zeev Herzog, Tel Aviv University)

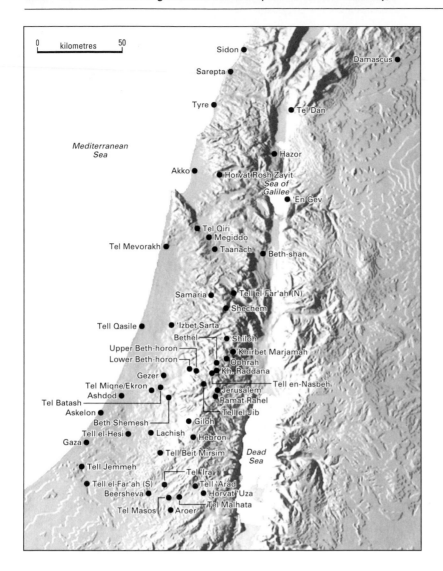

Figure 1 Selected Iron Age sites in southern Phoenicia, Israel and Judah

'David', 'Red-Burnished King' for my 'Solomon', and 'Post- Red-Burnished King I (S/N)' for the kings reigning at the point of the Sheshonq raid, or some similar system as they please. It will make absolutely no difference to the content of the study. For the uninitiated, the significance of red burnish will become clear during the course of the analysis.

Prolegomena

The early history of Israel, as archaeologically understood, has been discussed above (Chapter 21). Socially, early Israel was characterized by a dispersed network of unfortified, largely undifferentiated hamlets and villages, to date better known through archaeological survey than through published excavations. Its cultural affinities are presently discerned on the basis of several criteria. Among these is the common choice of a highland setting, land

traditionally unsettled for all but the last half-century or so of the preceding Late Bronze Age (*ca.* 1550–1200 BCE). These settlements have a distinctive and – to date – notably egalitarian architectural expression (the three- or four-roomed pillared house, new on the Palestinian scene), and commonly use small, highly utilitarian sets of shared pottery forms derivative of LB II forms, but generally distinctive *as sets* (the more isolated Galilean group differs from the Central Hill Country group) from both those of the continuing 'post-LB' urban cultures of the large valleys and lowlands and the distinctively Aegean-flavored pottery and architectural traditions of the new 'Sea Peoples' settlements along the coast. Their mixed, presumably subsistence, agrarian economy is seen by the practice of growing grain, attested by the characteristic grain-storage pits clustered around houses in the settlements, in the clearly unsuitable setting of hillside terraces in areas where bottom lands were unavailable or inadequate (Stager

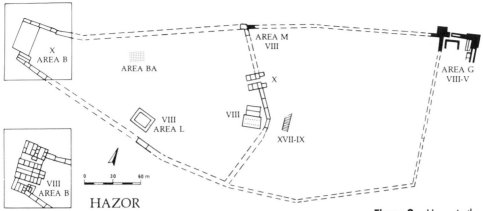

Figure 2 Hazor in the Solomonic (X) and Omri-Ahab (VIII) periods

1976a: 13a). The latter circumstance, and the apparently modest circumstances of their material culture assemblage, suggest an alienation from their lowland neighbors, particularly the Philistines (see Chapter 20, this volume; Esse 1992: 101–2). With respect to their other neighbors, the 'post-LB' lowlanders, relations seem to to be more complex (Esse 1992: 98-102), and possibly largely one-way.[1] Other than possible acts of aggression, which are notoriously hard to document archaeologically, the impact of the 'highlanders' upon the 'post-LB' lowlands can, to date, only be inferred from such equivocal trace elements as, for example, the presence in these communities of the typically highland – and Transjordanian – Collared Pithos, or 'Collar-rimmed Storejar' (Esse 1992).

Although we presently lack the resources for tight inner dating, or, aside from noting a correlation between Collared Pithoi and late imported Mycenaean and Cypriot pottery, even for determining the earliest starting dates (P. Beck and M. Kochavi 1985; discussion in Finkelstein 1988a: 315–21, 388, *passim*; M. Artzy 1990: 76; discussion in A. Mazar 1990: 90–2), the highland settlements are thought to begin only a little before *ca.* 1225 BCE (the date of the Merneptah Stele mentioning Israel) and are understood to last, in something like their pristine form, until about 1000 BCE. The latter date is fixed by a synchronism, cited by Josephus, between the fourth year of Solomon and the eleventh or twelfth year of Hiram of Tyre (*ca.* 959 BCE),[2] which in turn is reckoned backward from known synchronisms between Assyrian kings and members of the Tyrian king list as given in Josephus (Rowton 1970). By 925 BCE, the year of the well-documented Asiatic campaign of Sheshonq I,[3] we have long since been in a totally different world.

The rise of the centralized state

Like paleontologically witnessed biological evolution, archaeologically attested social evolution seems to follow

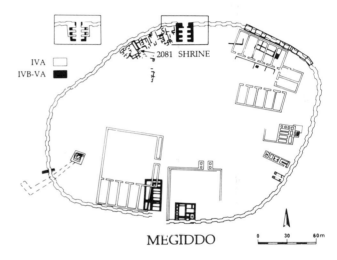

Figure 3 Megiddo in the Solomonic (VA—IVB) and Omri-Ahab (IVA) periods

a pattern of 'punctuated equilibrium' (Steven Jay Gould's term [Eldridge and Gould 1972]). Long stretches of time characterized by relative sameness or only minor change are punctuated by sudden and often violent episodes eventuating in wholesale paradigm changes, implying new levels of social organization and cultural expression. In the current instance, as far as we presently can tell, very little seems to be going on in the highland hamlets and villages (we will have more to say later) until, suddenly, somewhere around the mid-tenth century BCE, everything changed. The burnt-out ruin heaps of Hazor, Megiddo, and Gezer – respectively an early Israelite settlement, a late-blooming Canaanite city-state, and a Philistine dependency – were radically transformed into roughly comparable complex[4] fortified governmental centers (Figures 2–4), each with its own casemated wall system, six-chambered gateway (in two cases provided with an additional outer gateway), and palace complex (the palace of Hazor Strata X–IX has not

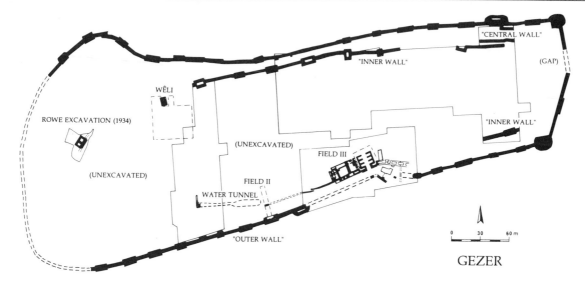

Figure 4 Solomonic Gateways and fortifications at Gezer

yet been discovered). At least one stable unit has been demonstrated for Megiddo VA/IVB (Davies 1988). Lachish was certainly occupied, but probably not yet fortified (Ussishkin 1983: 116).[5]

That the erstwhile horticulturalist, agriculturalist, and pastoralist highlanders – the early Israelites – accomplished this projection of military and political power into the former domains of the 'post-LB' cultures is abundantly clear from the material culture complex, which, however much it differs from the early restricted categories of the central highlands and the Galilee (below), clearly forms a continuum with the later material culture complex of both Israelite and Judaean sites, including the later highland sites of the ninth and eighth centuries.[6,7] That these were, above all, *political* actions designed to seize and hold the land may be seen from an analysis of the terrain dominated and the overland trade routes and access routes controlled by these new fortified governmental centers. Hazor dominates broad stretches of agricultural land in the Huleh Basin, and controls the trade routes to Syria. Megiddo dominates the Esdraelon Valley and the southern overland routes to Tyre from a position controlling the major southwest–northeast pass through the Carmel range. Gezer dominates the northern part of the Shephelah and Philistine Plain, the coastal overland transit route, and the approach to the central hill country and Jerusalem by way of Aijalon and Upper and Lower Beth Horon. Lachish dominates the southern Shephelah and Philistine Plain, the southern portions of the coastal overland transit route, and the southern approach to the central hill country and Jerusalem by way of Hebron.[8]

The uniformity exhibited by these new governmental centers and their wide-reaching political significance, seen against the backdrop of the preceeding Iron I period, *ca.* 1200–1000 BCE, and in the light of the later history of

Syria, Palestine and the Transjordan, allows for but one interpretation: in these changes we are witnessing a major instance of secondary state formation in the southern Levant. The assuredness of this inference rests upon substantial advances in archaeological theory over the past three decades. Some of the archaeologically discernible characteristics of the state (Service 1971) as developed in recent discussion (Renfrew and Bahn 1991: 154–7) are shown in Table 1.

This organizational shift, from segmented society to nation state, obviously involved significant outside assistance. None of the fortifications, palaces, or elite buildings derive from local traditions. Megiddo Palace 6000, and, to a lesser extent, 1723 are unquestionably of Syro-Hittite (and Phoenician?) origin (Figures 5, 6). The building techniques, particularly the use of ashlar masonry, point unmistakably toward heavy Phoenician involvement (Stern 1977; 1978: 71–5; Anderson 1988: 102–3, 107, 110, 119, 121, 397, 405 nn. 215–16, 406–7).

After only a short time, all of these magnificently fortified and appointed cities were destroyed and looted: Lachish, however it was constituted (see n. 5), Gezer, and Megiddo almost certainly by Sheshonq,[9] Hazor possibly around 885 BCE (Yadin et al. 1960: 37, n. 217). Sheshonq's campaign gives us our first fixed archaeological date – *ca.* 925 BCE – and archaeological benchmark (simultaneous destruction levels over most of the territory) since the departure of the Egyptians during the middle part of the twelfth century, BCE (Holladay 1990). If certain scholars are correct, it also furnishes us with our first view of the fabled riches of the Solomonic reign, which, if correctly linked to Sheshonq's campaign, far exceed anything the scholarly concensus has yet dreamt of (Millard 1988b; 1989; Kitchen 1986; 1989a,b). The possible sources of this wealth, inferrable in part on the

Table 1 Some archaeologically discernible characteristics of a state

Characteristics of a state which should be archaeologically discernible	Ca. 1000–926 BCE	Ca. 926–845 BCE [ca. 845–750 BCE]
Population generally over 20,000	28,000+ estimated for Benjamin, Ephraim, Manesseh alone (Finkelstein 1988a: 330–4)	—
Urban based hierarchical settlement pattern (cities, towns, villages, hamlets)	Yes	Yes
Often characterized by regional centers . . .	Hazor, Megiddo, Gezer, Lachish (?), Tel Masos (?)	Hazor, Megiddo, Gezer, Lachish
in addition to the primary seat of government	[Jerusalem palaces, etc., not yet archaeologically demonstrated]	Royal enclosure at Samaria
Frontier defenses	Gezer (?)	Tell el-Jib, Tell en-Nasbeh, Lachish(?)
Stratified society	Palaces, elite structures at Megiddo, Gezer; Monumental gateways at Hazor, Megiddo, Gezer	Palaces at Hazor, Megiddo, Lachish, Samaria
Headed by a king or emperor	—	References to Omri and Ahab in Kurkh Monolith, Omri in Mesha Stele
Standing army	Chariotry witnessed by stables at Megiddo, Tel Masos	Multiple stables at Megiddo, Lachish, stable at Hazor, etc.; explicit mention of chariotry in Kurkh Monolith
Centralized bureaucracy	—	Royal enclosure at Samaria
Palace distinguished from Temple	Shrines differently located than palaces at Megiddo, Lachish	Major cult site at Tell Dan
Economics based upon tribute, taxes, and tolls	Tolls [below]	Mesha Stele (tribute), [Samara Ostraca (taxes)]
with redistribution to government, army, and craft specialists	Tel Masos: store facilities (Bldg. 1065) near Stable 1039; segregated storage facilities (Bldg. 314)	Silos or granaries near stables at Megiddo, Beth Shemesh, Hazor; spatially segrgated storage facilities at Hazor (Citadel, elite houses near Citadel), [Samaria (Ostraca House)]
Generally having a writing system	(Inscribed arrowheads, Kh. Radanna Handle precede state); 'Izbet Sartah Ostracon	Gezer Calendar

basis of the impressive architectural remains, and the reasons for the Phoenician assistance, which would not have come cheap, will be sought below.

While Hazor, Megiddo, Gezer, and Lachish (Figure 7) were promptly rebuilt to new specifications, with thick, solid wall systems and, in most instances, four-chambered gateways (Gezer, Stratum IVA Megiddo), they were no longer alone, but were quickly joined by a large number of similarly fortified cities, towns and villages. Many of these newly-fortified sites were in the highlands, e.g., Tel Dan, Tell el-Far'ah (N), Shechem, probably Khirbet Marjamah (A. Mazar 1982b, 1992), Tell en-Nasbeh, and Tell el-Jib. The emergence of strongly fortified town sites (Tell en-Nasbeh, Figure 8, being an apparently undifferentiated [n. 4] farming village, on the southern side of a boundary later defining the northern limit of the distribution of Royal Stamped Jar handles – which are overwhelmingly limited to 'Judaean' sites), likely attests to the major border with a new and hostile sister kingdom (Israel). Both north and south of this line 'occupation was concentrated in [larger, fortified] . . . sites such as Bethel, Beth Horon, Ophrah and Mizpah; unfortified villages or farms, like those founded in the neighboring areas to the north and the south, did not exist here' (Finkelstein 1988a: 188). Coupled with the subsequent centralization of Israelite royal functions in the Royal Acropolis at Samaria (Figure 9),[10] this is perhaps our strongest early archaeological testimony to the Divided Monarchy, a political situation clearly referenced in numerous later historical documents.[11]

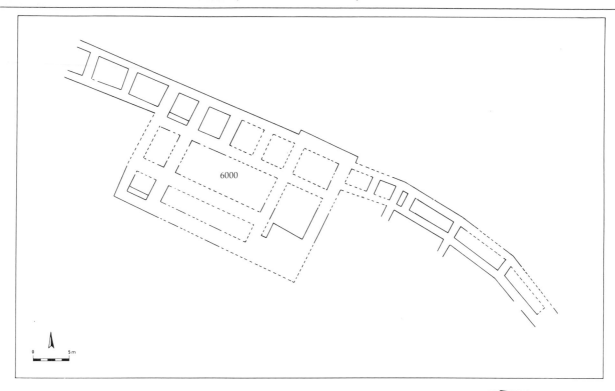

Figure 5   Megiddo Palace 6000, of the Solomonic period

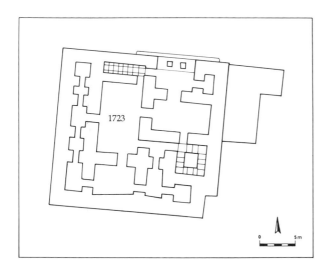

Figure 6   Megiddo Palace 1723, of the Solomonic Period

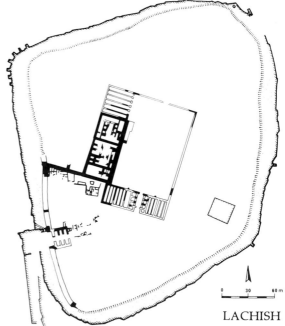

LACHISH

Figure 7   Lachish, the Palace–Fort (Phases A–C) and gateway, ca 900–700 BCE

That the economic basis for the earlier ostentatious architectural and military display (Whitelam 1986) was not destroyed by Sheshonq's raid or by the division into twin polities is abundantly clear from the archaeology of the ensuing century. During the last quarter of the tenth and the first half of the ninth centuries, both Judah and Israel witnessed unparalleled economic growth and prosperity,

evidenced in great building programs, such as the splendid royal acropolis at Samaria, the complete rebuilding to higher standards of Megiddo, Hazor, Gezer and Lachish; the impressive water-systems at Hazor, Megiddo, Gezer, Jerusalem, Beersheva and even at little el-Jib; and the

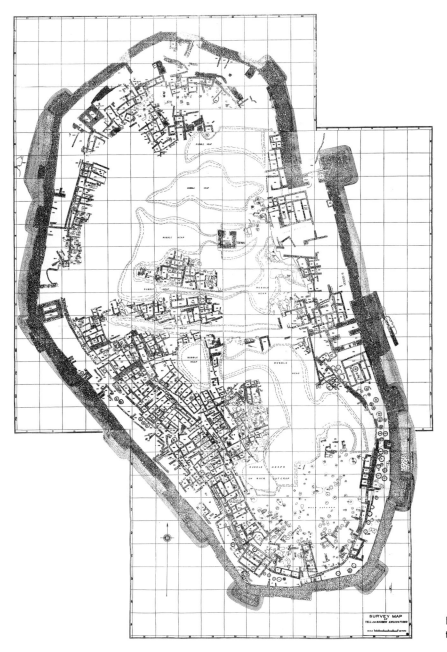

Figure 8 Tell en-Nasbeh, overall plan of the Iron II village and fortifications

massive Temple complex – yet imperfectly understood – at Tel Dan, coupled with the development of outstanding military capability, particularly in chariotry (Megiddo, Lachish, Hazor, Tell el-Hesi?, Beth Shemesh?). This military power, acting in concert with the forces of other Syro-Levantine rulers, was sufficient to blunt the westward thrust of the great Neo-Assyrian King Shalmaneser III in 853 BCE (the Kurkh Monolith, translated in Pritchard 1969b: 277–9). As with the radical political metamorphosis of the mid-tenth century, the economic mainsprings and social transformations occasioning and ensuing from

these later changes – so clearly witnessed in the archaeological record – remain to be explicated and understood. We will take up some aspects of this challenge later (Section IV). But first we must attempt to understand (Section II) the causes for the social organization shift from acephalous (lacking hereditary leadership) segmented society to centralized nation state; and the general nature of the new urban society witnessed in these Royal Cities (Section III). Finally, we will examine (Section V) the differences this change seem to have made upon the mass of the Israelite population.

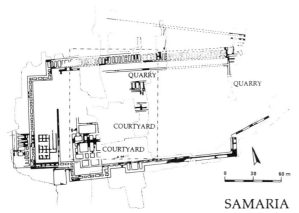

SAMARIA

Figure 9 Samaria, the royal acropolis. Ostraca House in the southwest corner

II The causes of the Israelite transformation from acephalous agriculturalism to nation-state

Human nature and particularist historical writing regularly ascribe all social change to the actions of a few key leaders: a Samuel, a Saul, a David. The longer view afforded by archaeology and cross-cultural social-economic anthropology, however, seeks to account for change on a more systematic level: by trying to understand the sorts of regular changes that occur in evolving societies that create conditions under which major paradigm shifts not only may, but normally *should*, occur (e.g., Renfrew and Bahn 1991: 406). In this instance, why does an intensive dry farming society, however socially constituted and governed, make the wrenching transition to statehood?[12]

In a recent study of the legal systems of 184 societies in Murdock and White's 'Standard Cross-Cultural Sample' (1969),[13] Katherine Newman found that class and wealth distinctions increased in societies ranked according to subsistence systems, or 'forces of production'

(1983: 121–9).[14] Some results of this analysis can be summarized as in Table 2.

For our purposes, the attractiveness of such an analysis is that it allows us to develop and test hypotheses about particular societies in which we are interested. The archaeological record can then be examined for test implications of these hypotheses, positive results tending to support the test hypothesis, negative results tending to deny the test hypothesis. Thus, in trying to understand the forces driving early Israel towards a higher form of social integration (paramount chieftainship [Saul, early David],[15] nation-state [later David, Solomon]), it is obviously important, since both hereditary paramount chieftainship and the monarchical nation-state *by definition* are class-stratified societies, to try to determine what sorts of societal ranking systems were operative in early Israel, since it is the working-out of this tendency that must be presumed to be one of the key forces driving the society towards higher levels of social organization.

More equal than others: the evolution of rich men in pre-state plow-using agricultural societies, with archaeological reference to Israel

Focusing our attention upon Newman's 'dry intensive agriculture' (Table 2), clearly the dominant subsistence mode in the Israelite Iron I, we see that 55 percent of societies practicing this mode of production are characterized by class stratification, 31 percent by wealth distinctions, and only 13.8 percent may be characterized as lacking social stratification. To the extent that they formed a separate element in early Israel, pastoralists should have had roughly a 27 percent chance of class stratification, 53 percent chance of wealth distinctions, and 20 percent chance of being an egalitarian society. Given these choices, it becomes feasible to search the archaeological record for indications of status or wealth distinctions. Given the present poor level of archaeological reporting for early

Table 2

Wealth or class distinctions	Hunting and gathering	Fishing	Pastoral	Incipient agriculture	Extensive agriculture	Dry intensive griculture	Irrigated intensive agriculture	Total
No distinctions	25	8	3	15	16	4	5	76
(percent)	89.3	44.4	20.0	68.2	34.8	13.8	19.2	41.3
Wealth distinctions	2	7	8	2	13	9	2	43
(percent)	7.1	38.9	53.3	9.1	28.3	31.0	7.7	23.4
Class stratification	1	3	4	5	17	16	19	65
(percent)	3.6	16.7	26.7	22.7	37.0	55.2	73.1	35.3
Total examples	28	18	15	22	46	29	26	184

(Source: Newman 1983: 122, Table 3.2)

Plate 1 Inscribed Judaean arrowheads attributed to the 11th century BCE: el-Khadr I (drawing) and II (photograph) (photograph: courtesy of Frank Moore Cross)

Israelite sites, this is not easy, but general tendencies are clear, and there is at least one interesting indicator.

In the first instance, the general tendency so far noted in the settlement patterns is that of essential equality in habitation type and size. Wealth, in the dispersed settlements, seems most apparent in the presence of goods stored in the Collar-rimmed Pithoi (Finkelstein 1988a: 282–3), and in grain-pits distributed in and around the separate houses (Currid and Navon 1989; Finkelstein 1988a: 264–69). Containers for luxury ointments and oils, characteristic of 'post-LB' societies, are generally lacking (Finkelstein 1988a: 177–82; Esse 1992: 95). A large amount of folding space for an essentially pastoralist element may be witnessed at Giloh (A. Mazar 1981).[16] As noted by Carol Kramer in her study of 'Aliabad', wealth distinctions (other than in storage capacity) may only poorly be reflected in domestic architecture (1979: 154; 1982: 126–36). Class distinctions, on the other hand, would more reasonably seem to be observable in the archaeological record in the form of distinctive residences, preferred location of residence within the settlement, or non-uniform distribution of elite goods – none of which have, as yet, been noted.

One possible variable with bearing on our general problem may be the highland distribution, particularly near Bethlehem, of inscribed arrowheads, similar to others from Phoenicia. Most recently, these have been interpreted as reflecting a practice of military specialist competitiveness (Cross 1992 with references; note the twofold appearance on these arrowheads, one from the Lebanese Biqa', one from el-Khadr, of the military 'patronymic' *bin-'Anāt*: Cross 1980: 7; Milik 1956: 5, n. 25; Plate 1). Uninscribed arrowheads, presumably some sort of status-marker, and possibly a precursor of the later Israelite highlands practice, are a minor component of Late Bronze II and 'post-LB'/'Late Bronze III'/Iron I tombs at Lachish, becoming much less frequent in Iron II tombs.[17]

In the later Iron I to very earliest Iron II materials, grain

pits are one of the most frequently noted architectural features (Finkelstein 1988a: 264–9; Currid and Navon 1989). While some silos were simply bell-shaped pits (personal observation at Shechem and Gezer), and not easily detected, many were either stone-cut or stone-lined cylinders. They are much less common in later Iron II contexts (Finkelstein 1988a: 266), their frequency apparently dropping precipitously around the end of the tenth century.

'Izbet Sartah Strata III–II and Tell Beit Mirsim B1–3 probably provide the best presently available Iron I to early Iron II grain pit series (Figures 10, 11). Table 3 presents a seriation of the *slip colors* for the pottery in the backfills of the Tell Beit Mirsim grain pits phased according to Raphael Greenberg's new analysis and data (1987) against the data from 'Izbet Sartah.[18] The trends through time are easily seen.

Phase B3 at Tell Beit Mirsim is said by Albright to be characterized by the disappearance of Philistine wares and the presence of burnished red slips (1932: 67–9; 1943: 8–10). As can be seen in Table 3, Greenberg's sequence unmistakably is late Late Bronze II through Philistine-influenced Iron I (the white slips – Buff, Pinkish Cream, Buff-Cream, Cream, White, etc. – are characteristically Philistine) to either Pre-Solomonic or very early Solomonic (in the Red range, only streaky unburnished slips). By the time of the Solomonic burnished Red and Dark Red slips, the massive storage of grain in pits (in at least this area) is over.[19]

Greenberg's revised plan of Tell Beit Mirsim Stratum B1–2 (1987: 56) shows one building, apparently not of the three- or four-room variety, in SE12–22–13–23. It has one internal silo and is surrounded on the east, south and west by some 18 silos of varying sizes. Fifteen other silos appear further to the east, in SE22–32–23–33, in the midst of wall fragments that do not make up into a coherent plan (1987: 57). Assuming an average capacity of one metric ton/silo, it seems clear that the SE12–22–13–33 house controlled, over a course of time, silos capable of storing something

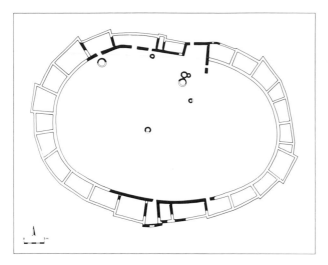

Figure 10   'Izbet Sartah, Stratum III (after Finkelstein 1986)

Figure 11   'Izbet Sartah, Stratum II (after Finkelstein 1986)

like 31 metric tons of grain (see Rosen's figures, below), and possibly, if the building fragments to the east do not add up to a house or houses (so Greenberg 1987: 57), 57 metric tons of grain – quite apart from quantities possibly stored in sacks in the house. Unfortunately, we do not know the length of time any one silo was in active service, nor, except for the relative dates of their backfilling, which ones were contemporary.

Similar problems plague our complete understanding of the early sequence at 'Izbet Sartah (Figures 10–11), which moves from early Solomonic (Stratum III, said to be long-lived, had 2.9 percent, burnished red slips, see n. 19) to a period (Stratum II) characterized by 15 percent burnished and 1 percent unburnished red slips. Taking each stratum as a unit, there were only seven grain pits in the open central courtyard of Stratum III,[20] while in Stratum II, characterized by burnished red slipped wares, there were 43 (a 614 percent increase) grain pits to the north, east and south of a large, centrally-located four-room house. Two smaller four-room houses were located to the north and east, towards the periphery of the excavated area. Nearest neighbor analysis suggests that at most ten of these silos belonged to the two smaller houses, while the spatial array of the pits (see Figure 11) suggests that all but about three probably belonged to the large house. Baruch Rosen has reasonably calculated the total average yearly holdings for Stratum II as being 53.0 metric tons of wheat, and 21.35 metric tons of barley, held in a total silo storage capacity of 150 m³ (1986: 172). By way of comparison, this is one-third the capacity of the great Storage Pit 1414 at Megiddo (below; Lamon and Shipton 1939: 66).

What can be said of the above? Minimally, we see a pattern of accumulation of agricultural surplus on considerably more than a 'subsistence' basis. We see individuals accumulating wealth, almost certainly (given the comparative ethnographic materials) on the basis of being able to coerce, without remuneration, the work of others. In early Israel, the available mechanisms for this could have included '(1) controlling the labor or products of slaves or unfree dependants [e.g., through client relationships with impoverished individuals, or polygyny – frequently practiced by intensive agriculturalists]; (2) obtaining contributions, taxes, or labor of free citizens [e.g., long-term labor in repayment of loans for social obligations such as throwing a feast, paying the brideprice; tithes for religious services – e.g., the overwhelmingly right forelimb osteological assemblage from one spatially restricted area at Tel Qiri (S. Davis 1987: 250–1)]; (3) securing rents and/or other incomes from large landholdings' (Newman 1983: 112–13).

Disproportionate wealth can be dangerous in a society operating through lower-level legal institutions such as self-redress, or advisors. Table 4 presents data from Newman's study of a selected subset of the Standard Cross-Cultural Sample (above) bearing upon legal systems (1983: 129–36; Appendix 8, 238–42). Given the present indications that ancient Israel evolved into a society with wealth, rather than class distinctions, it is immediately clear that early Israel was an odds-on candidate for operating under a system of elders' councils. In the further absence of evidence for chieftainship, this probability increases to near certainty.

'Mighty men' in an evolving pre-state society: early inscribed arrowheads and the regulation of an unequal society

Viewed diachronically, the probability is that egalitarian societies practicing an advanced mode of production are at

Table 3

Slip Color	Black %	Dk. Grey %	Dk. Brown %	Lt Brown %	Pinkish Cream %	Buff %	Cream %	White %	Buff-Cream %	Unburn. Red %	Burnished Red %
Tell Beit Mirsim											
Phase C	—	10	10	—	—	—	—	—	—	—	—
Phase B1	—	—	—	2	—	—	—	—	—	—	—
Phase B1—2	4	—	—	—	4	—	7	4	—	—	—
Phase B2	—	—	—	—	—	6	3	8	—	—	—
Phase B2b	—	—	—	—	—	—	—	—	8	8	—
'Izbet Sartah											
Stratum III	1	—	—	—	—	—	—	—	—	—	2.9
Stratum II	—	1	—	—	—	—	—	1	—	1	15
Str. II Silos	—	—	—	—	—	—	—	—	—	—	26

Table 4

Legal Systems (n=60)	Self Redress (n=12) %	Advisors (n=6) %	Mediators (n=3) %	Elders Councils (n=14) %	Restricted Councils (n=3) %	Chieftains (n=10) %	Paramount Chieftains (n=6) %	State (n=6) %	
Egalitarian	83	83	—	50	—	—	—	—	
Wealth distinctions	17	—	—	50	—	50	—	—	
Class-stratified	—	17	100	—	100	50	100	100	
Totals:	100	100	100	100	100	100	100	100	
									Totals %
Societies with wealth distinctions:									
Pastoralist societies (n=6)	17	—	—	67	—	17	—	—	100
Intensive dry Agriculturalists (n=3)	—	—	—	67	—	33	—	—	100

(Source: after Newman 1983)

relatively early stages in their social evolution. As a society evolves, structural divisions are more apt to develop, whether into wealthy/poor distinctions, or into a system of class stratification. Lacking regulatory mechanisms, the forces bringing about these distinctions will operate further to intensify the distinctions, eventually bringing about serious structural strains in the society. If that society has evolved in a class-stratified mode, the analysis indicates that chieftainship will normally replace the elders' councils, with continuing intensification leading to paramount chieftainship and eventual statehood.

In societies with wealth-related stratification, things may be more complex. As we have seen, there are some indications that a potentially destabilizing military elite was evolving in early Israel. In unfortified villages, the possibility of raids and banditry, particularly by elements suffering from repeated crop failures or enemy depredations, would have been high. This obviously threatened the wealthy, who would have seen it as inimical to the entire society. Thus, as wealthy elements leveraged their advantage over their neighbors so as to accumulate yet more wealth, a mutually advantageous alliance of rich agriculturalist and pastoralist elements with 'mighty men', i.e., leaders of warrior bands (Plate 1 p. 377), quickly leading to some form of paramount chieftainship and statist organization, would have been inevitable. The only alternative would have been the development of homeostatic devices (negative feedback) restricting the ability of individuals to accumulate wealth.[21]

III The new urban society: 'Israelite', or 'eclectic'?

Against the lines of social evolution sketched above, it is important to consider just what we see in the newly emergent 'Royal Cities'. In the first instance, as already noted, we are met with fortifications, palaces, and elite buildings wholly new both to Israel and to the 'post-LB' culture of, say, Megiddo, Gezer and Shechem. The ashlar stonework in the finest buildings and latest structures such as the outer gateway at Gezer, indicates heavy Phoenician involvement (Stern 1977; 1978: 71−5; Anderson 1988: 406−7; cf. the masonry techniques of the putatively tenth to mid-ninth century BCE Phoenician 'fort' in the Akko

Sarepta   Hazor

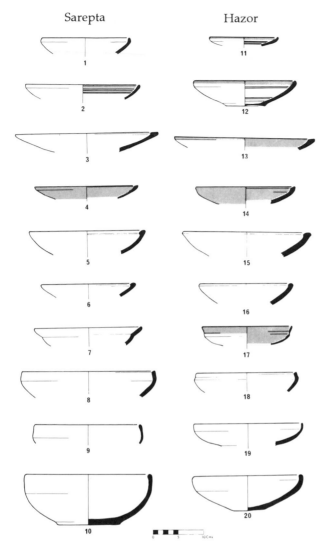

Figure 12   Side-by-side comparison of bowls excavated at Sarepta and Hazor

comparisons of early Iron II forms from Sarepta and Hazor in Figure 12 and the graph in Figure 13, showing the proportional degree of close similarity between Sarepta and Hazor through time.[22]

The Tyrian connection

While a strong case can be made for cooperation between the early monarchy and at least one Philistine port (Tell Qasile Stratum X, but probably not Ashdod, see Holladay 1990; 1993), the above materials make clear the substantive contribution of southern Phoenicia, certainly Tyre and possibly a broader group including Sarepta, to the period of state formation in early Israel. Although more research needs to be done on the subject, ashlar stonework seems to have been a Phoenician monopoly during the entire Iron Age, with major periods of Israelite or Judaean building in or with ashlar – the outer gateway at Gezer, Megiddo VA/IVB, IVA, Samaria Building Periods I–II, Hazor VIII (doorjambs and corners in Area B), Ramat Rahel VA – strongly correlated with periods of active trade and/or social interaction with Phoenicia (Shiloh 1979; Anderson 1988: 406–7; Stern 1977; 1978: 71–5; Oren 1992). Neither Cedar of Lebanon nor ashlar blocks seem to have been used in early Lachish Level IV (Ussishkin 1978: 32–3; Tufnell 1953: 101). Although careful definition of the critera for making the determinations would exceed the bounds of the present study, these periods of active contact appear to be:

1. the United Monarchy, particularly the reign of Solomon;
2. the Omride Dynasty (*ca.* 875–842 BCE);
3. the initial portion of the reign of Hezekiah (*ca.* 715–701 BCE); and
4. the last years of independent Judah, probably from the reign of Josiah (*ca.* 640–609 BCE) to 597 BCE.[23]

Quantification of the Tyrian contribution during the period of the early monarchy, whether during the period of the United Monarchy (David–Solomon, *ca.* 1000–930 BCE), or during the period of the Omride Dynasty (*ca.* 875–842 BCE) is difficult, but may be approached from a couple of directions:

1. By comparing the use of ashlar stones in the two periods. While the quantity of skilled stonecutting in both periods is impressive, the sheer volume present in Samaria Building Periods I–II and in the offsets-insets wall, Palace 338, the stables, and other buildings of the Omride portion of Megiddo VA, and to a much more limited extent in Stratum VIII at Hazor clearly outweighs that of the extant remains of the period of the United Monarchy.[24] While it is highly probable that earlier buildings furnished materials for the Omride building period at Gezer, Megiddo (Yadin 1972), and, perhaps, Hazor, the same cannot be said for Samaria, which was only a minor village or estate prior to the time of Omri (Stager 1990; Tappy 1992; below)

Plain recently published by Zvi Gal, 1992). Imported Byblian cedar, apparently a hallmark of royal construction, would have been required in quantity to accomplish the large spans required by the borrowed architectural forms (Liphschitz and Biger 1991: 172). And people living in literally outlandish Syro-Hittite *Bit Hilani* palaces, such as Megiddo Palaces 6000 and 1723, would hardly have been satisfied with local wines, clothes or furnishings. Equally surprising, though less apparent, is the character of their ordinary domestic pottery, which not only beggars the subsistence level wares of the highlands, but, in its decoration, wide range of forms and technical quality of production, would seem to have historical antecedants not obvious from the Palestinian record. Much may be owed to Phoenicia, see the side-by-side

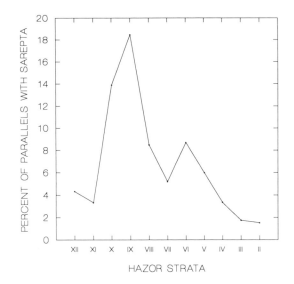

Figure 13   Hazor, percentages of published pottery in each stratum having close comparisons with the pottery of Phoenician Sarepta (Anderson 1988: 139–313)

2. By evaluating the quantity of imported Phoenician (or directly comparable pottery) at Hazor, our most closely stratified northern site (see Figure 12).[25] Basing ourselves upon Anderson's citations of close parallels between Sarepta and Hazor (1988: 139–313), we can observe (see Figure 13) a relatively low level of roughly 4 percent to 3 percent of the published pottery from the 'early Israelite settlement' Strata XII–XI looking like Phoenician imports.[26] This probably reflects localized trading patterns, e.g., local peddlers (Wood 1990: 60–77), and is not dissimilar to levels observed in the post-Israelite (i.e., the period during which control was no longer natively exercised by Samaria) Strata IV–II (respectively nearly 3.5 percent, under 2 percent, and 1.5 percent). During the United Monarchy and until *ca.* 885 BCE, Strata X–IX, parallels increase dramatically to about 14 percent and 18.5 percent of the total published pottery, sagging to about 8.5 percent for Stratum VIII, roughly coterminous with the Omride Dynasty. Parallels dropped to 5 percent under the reign of Jehu. During the ensuing Stratum VII, *ca.* 815–760 BCE, the rate was back to Omride (+8.5 percent) levels, diminishing to 6 percent during the final Stratum V period, *ca.* 760–733 BCE.

Under number 1 (above), by far the greatest degree of direct Phoenician involvement – presumably Phoenician expert stonecutters, masons, and architects – comes during the later Omride dynasty, while, judging from the relative quantities of Phoenician pottery at one representative Israelite site, the Period of the United Monarchy marked the point of greatest influence. Unquestionably both periods were heavily indebted to Phoenicia, with the span of the Omride dynasty probably getting the nod for the most extensive and most costly contribution.

New frontiers for professional service

In the rapid changeover from nondifferentiated rural settlements requiring (and offering) a small range of services to a state with large, highly differentiated central places offering a large number of services, early Israel must have found itself hard-pressed for expertise: scribal functionaries and administrators of all kinds, technical military experts (specialists in fortification technologies, stable-masters, master charioteers), skilled palace servitors, commercial agents, craftsmen, architects, builders and artisans of all sorts, etc. Life in the highlands had not trained Israelites for these tasks. Nor, for all but the most junior members of the extended family, did farming, horticulture and pastoralism diminish in importance in the new era. It must be assumed that the slack was taken up by immigrants, perhaps Phoenicians, perhaps emigrants from the Syro-Hittite city-states to the north (cf. de Vaux 1965: 1,129), and certainly absorbed members of the 'post-LB' population. A heavy Phoenician input may account for the very close similarities between most craft goods (e.g., seals, carved bone and ivory) and many of the pottery types of the later tenth–early ninth century (Megiddo VA/IVB, Hazor X–IX) and Phoenician craft products and pottery assemblages (see Figure 12). Intense scribal activity is reflected in the adaptation of tenth-century Phoenician script (e.g., the Sarcophagus of Hiram of Byblos) to the locally evolving Proto-Canaanite writing tradition (e.g., the inscribed arrowheads, see Plate 1, p. 377, the Khirbet el-Raddana handle, the Solomonic 'Izbet Sartah Ostracon). This process was certainly complete by the mid-ninth century (and probably much earlier), as the Mesha Stele, which must have been using standard Israelite lapidary script, witnesses.

Above all, however, the new opportunities for younger Israelite and 'post-LB peoples' sons must have been in one of three areas: government service, particularly in the chariotry which, for technical reasons (alongside the border and caravan-route guards), was the major full-time component of the standing army; the official cult, which now commanded vastly increased tithed resources and appears to have been centrally located in every major settlement (Stager 1985: 27–8; Ahlström 1982a: 1–9, 44–6; Holladay 1987: 268–74); and commercial enterprise. Entry into the latter on more than a purely local or regional basis, however, may have been difficult due to the longstanding business, ethnic/familial, and religious ties binding, to the north, members of the deliberately low-profile but none the less controlling Phoenician 'Trade Diaspora' together (Curtin 1984: 1–14), and, to the south, the well-entrenched Philistine-'post LB' Canaanite establishment. The joint workings of these two trading entities may probably be observed in the cultural mix witnessed in Megiddo Stratum VI. Note particularly the Philistine/Sea Peoples Helladic-style cooking pots, otherwise attested primarily at Sea Peoples' settlements

(Killebrew 1992).[27] I take the presence of ethnically distinct cooking vessels as indicating local residence of those groups. As already noted, access to ports was everything.

IV Economic factors relating to the political and economic centralization of both the United Kingdom, and the Northern Kingdom under the House of Omri

The early history of the Israelite states was punctuated by two, or possibly three, major building programs, respectively those of Solomon, the Omride dynasty, and a less-easily dated early Judaean program (e.g., Lachish, Tell en-Nasbeh, Tell el-Jib). As already noted, the significant use of Phoenician and North Syrian building plans, masonry techniques (ashlar stones, fully ashlar and pier and quoin construction), and the necessity for long spans, calling for the use of Cedar of Lebanon (a staple of royal building programs in Israel, early and late: Liphschitz and Biger 1991: 172, Table 1, note that few data are available for earlier excavations), indicates the presence of craftsmen skilled in these non-Israelite arts.[28]

Further, as we have already noted, the new urbanism and social stratification which accompanied the founding of the state required, first, a whole array of locally unavailable expertise, from scribes through military specialists to craftsmen specializing in pottery production, for its successful operation, and second, a whole range of elite goods to reward the newly ennobled and their important clients. Insofar as our evidence goes, Israel had no native access to craftsmen skilled in fine woodworking, ivory carving, metal work (e.g., lost-wax casting or the sorts of repoussé bowls made throughout the centuries by Phoenician craftsmen), the making of fine linens, lapidary work involving precious and semi-precious stones, or even craft, as opposed to domestic, pottery production (Esse 1992: 98). All the above were, however, either essential for daily living or 'essentials' for elite display – and all were available from the Phoenicians.

In materials, as well, both the United Monarchy and the Northern Kingdom under the Omrides relied, in the first instance, upon resources only obtainable through Tyrian[29] long-distance trade. As far as we know, Israel had no native access to copper,[30] tin for bronze production iron, silver, gold, ivory, or cedar – all attested in archaeological deposits of the tenth–ninth centuries.[31]

Finally, the build up of massive chariot forces, beginning with Solomon and peaking at the Battle of Qarqar, entailed enormous outlays for select horses and breeding stock, expensive equipment, elite military specialists such as stable-masters and master charioteers, and craftsmen capable of maintaining and replacing tack and equipment, to say nothing of the ongoing expense of maintaining a standing army in constant training, probably at least 10,000-strong for the chariotry alone by the Battle of Qarqar. Note that a figure of 2000 chariots as the Israelite (and Judaean, in all probability) cohort certainly meant that Israel and Judah had something in excess of 4000 stallions in training (at a possible three horses per chariot, more than 6000 stallions), quite apart from the studs, the brood mares, and the colts (Holladay 1986; 1992b). These are truly astonishing figures, fully as costly to the ancient economy as tanks and armored vehicles are to the present.

Other things came at high prices as well. In general, archaeologists dealing with early states tend to have recourse to the *corvée* as an explanation for the massive labor input required for such projects. In contrast to Egypt and Mesopotamia, however, in the yearly planting, horticulture, harvesting and pastoralist calendar required by the highly diversified Israelite subsistence regime in the highlands (Hopkins 1987: 186–8; 1985: 213–61), few long stretches of time were available, and labor taken from the village would have had a significant impact upon productivity, and indeed, upon the viability of individual communities. Particularly if payment in agricultural products were in any way required for other materials and services, heavy use of the *corvée* would have been counter-productive. In addition, in contrast to Mesopotamia and Egypt, there were no legions of temple and palace scribes, architects, etc., to organize, manage, and direct great masses of unskilled laborers. Unquestionably the *corvée* was employed, but almost certainly at a fairly moderate level for largely unskilled work such as raising glacis and fortification walls, making and laying mudbricks, etc. Possibly its burden fell more upon the lowland farmers, who had more seasonal occupations, and upon other less-enfranchised 'post-LB' elements, than upon the highland agriculturalists and pastoralists. In any case, recourse to the *corvée* cannot be made to answer, in any meaningful way, the question of massive financial outlays for expensive foreign materials, craftsmanship or the chariotry.

In exchange for the above, Israel had little to offer: primarily high-bulk, low-value agricultural goods of value for international commerce only insofar as they could be transported to seaports without incurring unsupportable transit costs: by donkey transport, roughly 35 km for wheat, less for barley and perhaps (considering the extra weight and fragility of the containers) less for wine, and perhaps twice as far for oil, which had a value roughly three times that of wheat. This makes it unlikely that Israel's contribution to the two-way trade consisted solely, or even largely, of its native commodities. Given this apparent impasse, other options must be explored. As noted in Table 1, state level economies typically derive their revenues from tribute, taxes and tolls. The latter constitute a major resource typically either ignored or undervalued in reconstructions of the ancient Israelite economy.

The South Arabian trade

General

Israel lay between the Arabian desert and the Mediterranean. She bordered on Philistia to the south and Phoenicia to the north, with smaller seaports between. Many of the most highly valued commodities of the ancient world (e.g., South Arabian and Horn of Africa incense, East Asian spices and gems, African gold, ivory, blackwood, exotic animals, animal skins and feathers) entered the Mediterranean trade via overland caravan routes snaking their way across the Arabian desert. After crossing the desert, the caravans – by the Iron Age camel caravans – (for camels in strata characterized by early burnished red slip at Izbet Sartah see Finkelstein 1986: 147) – had to negotiate passage to the Mediterranean harbors. Transit tolls unquestionably varied with the value of the cargo, but they guaranteed safe passage, not an assured matter in an unpatrolled Negev (Oates 1968). As elsewhere in early long-distance trade (the Old Assyrian overland trade with Anatolia is the best documented: see Veenhof 1972), South Arabian merchants and caravaneers practiced 'venturing' (or 'venture trading'), by which is meant that shipments were sent abroad to be sold as profitably as possible, but without previous, binding agreements which ensured the owner of the shipment a certain price for it.

The South Arabian merchants and trading houses undoubtedly could select from a number of destinations, and the final decision for any one journey must have hinged upon factors such as familiarity, convenience (including reprovisioning facilities, camping and grazing rights, and access to water), safety, transit costs, and competitive pricing at the harbor. Thus, it must have been possible, particularly in a period of Egyptian and Babylonian–Assyrian weakness, for various Levantine port cities and various polities in their respective hinterlands to 'bid' for the caravan traffic by preferential tolls (in the Old Assyrian trade tolls amounted to between 17–25 percent of the value of the cargoes, Veenhof 1972: 230–64, 305–42; Larsen 1976: 103 n.69, 245), protection, and facilities, a possibility which puts the Tyrian and Philistine relationship with Israel (or Israel and Judah) in a wholly different light. Tyre and Philistia needed Israel (or Israel and Judah) as much as the Israelites and Judahites needed them.

Space does not permit an analysis of the evidence bearing on the possible magnitude and valuation of the traffic, nor upon the lines of communication available to the South Arabian trade during the Iron II period. We can say that evidence presently at hand (see especially Van Beek 1975; and Eph'al 1982) permits the inference that as many as 3,000–5,000 camels may have been employed in the annual traffic, with an overall valuation ranging variously upwards to *ca.* $175,000,000 or $290,000,000 in 1960 US dollars.

Two major land routes serving this traffic can be traced across the territories of Judah and Israel: one entering through the Wadi Yabis-Bethshan Depression, the other through the Zered-Beersheva Depression (Baly 1974). During the Middle to Late Bronze Ages, the northern route seems to have been dominant, with a subsidiary (?) route across the northern Sinai to the Gaza region during the later Middle Bronze Age, but during the early Iron II Period the Zered–Beersheva route assumed major importance. For want of space, we will analyze only the settlement patterns of the latter, which are unusually informative.

Israelite settlement patterns in the Beersheva–Zered Depression

East of Tell el-Far'ah (South), Tell Jemmeh, and the coastal strip, there were no Late Bronze age or Iron IA settlements anywhere along the Cisjordanian portion of the Beersheva–Zered Depression. With the transition to the United Monarchy it suddenly became a different story.

Starting with the period marked by wavy-rimmed bowls – immediately before the introduction of the streaky unburnished red slip, the forerunner of the burnished red slips – we have the small circular hamlet atop Tell Esdar, 4 km south of Tel Masos. Although others may emerge, to date this is the only settlement of its period in the corridor.

Shortly afterward, settlements blossomed across the northern Negev. At Tel Malhata, a 'tenth century' walled city was destroyed [arguably by Sheshonq], and succeeded by a 'short-lived unwalled settlement'. A new city wall was built upon the remains of the earlier city wall, protecting a settlement thought to have persisted during the 'ninth–seventh centuries BCE', most of whose 'finds, however, date from the last destruction level, probably from the last years of the Judean Kingdom'. This settlement apparently featured a single stable of the sort elsewhere attributable to chariotry forces (termed a 'typical Israelite storehouse' by the excavator), which persisted through at least one major rebuilding. Among the early sixth-century finds was 'a decorated limestone incense altar' (below; Kochavi 1977).

At Tel Masos the earliest level (Stratum III) was characterized by unburnished red slip, possibly just moving into burnished red slip by the end of the phase.[32] The expanded Stratum II settlement (Figure 14) is characterized by the presence of burnished red slip.[33] It featured a strongly-built towered building (1039) with a stable featuring some standings suitable for horses, and others suitable only for donkeys.[34] Building 1065, readily accessible nearby, may have been a storeroom for the horses' grain, fodder, and bedding straw (Figure 15). Stratum II is also characterized by a building (314, Figure 16) remarkably similar in plan to the two-storied tenth-century Phoenician fort in the Plain of Akko published by Zvi Gal (1992), and not unlike the later Stratum VIII elite buildings near the Citadel at Hazor, or the much later

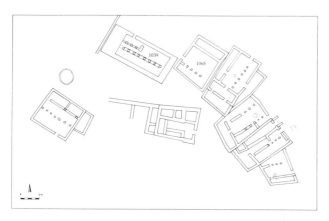

Figure 14   Tel Masos, Area A, Stratum II: Stable and stable-stores, and 'four-room' houses. The building (House 96) at lower center may be functionally related to specialized administrative store-residences, e.g. Figure 16 (after Fritz and Kempinski 1983)

'West Tower' at Tell Beit Mirsim: i.e., a large ground floor plan (in this case about 1.5 times the size of a more-or-less standard 10 × 10 m four-room house) ringed on two or three sides by store rooms (at Masos, one housed two ovens, another seems to have been a workroom). These buildings almost certainly had a midline row of wooden or stone pillars designed to support the second floor living quarters.[35] Tentatively, these plans,[36] in their later Israelite and Judaean settings, might be taken as typical quarters for mid-level officials charged with taxation and/or redistribution duties.[37] The modest size of the store facilities in all instances may give some indication of the limited scale of local redistribution. Something of the geographical and economic range of commodities handled at Tel Masos may be inferred from the pottery found in the destroyed building: hand-burnished Israelite red-slipped bowls and a krater,[38] a grain-scoop,[39] bichrome Phoenician jugs, Phoenician or Phoenician-influenced wine (?) amphorae (particularly Pl. 141: 8), a Phoenician red burnished bowl,[40] an Egyptian 'Beer Jar',[41] and decorated 'Midianite Ware' characteristic of the region of the Gulf of Aqabah (Fritz and Kempinski 1983: 40; Pls. 142: 10; 145: 1; 148: 11; 97A: 1–2), the nearest source for a number of Red Sea shells (*Tridacna, Conus, Strombus tricornis* [true Conch]) found in the same building (Reese 1983: 225). We now know, however, that this decorated 'Midianite Ware' (below) was characteristic of that area within northwestern Saudi Arabia through which ran 'the main N–S route from Arabia to Palestine and Syria, the route followed by the Mecca Pilgrims and by the Hejaz railway' (Parr 1988 and literature cited; 1992: 594). It has not only been found in quantity at the copper-production site of Timna (Rothenberg 1988: 93–6; Pls. 4, 16–18, 106; Figs. 4–13; Glass 1988), but at 'the oasis center of Tayma [Tema], on the main trade route to the S, and about a dozen sites in the

lower reaches of several wadis leading down through the Hejaz mountains to the Red Sea coast near the mouth of the Gulf of Aqaba . . . [including the site almost certainly to be identified as] Midyan [hence the original designation] . . . 'Midianite Ware'" (Parr 1992: 595). That these wares were produced in this region is indicated not only by their distribution, but also by petrographic analysis (Rothenberg and Glass 1983: 101–13; Glass 1988), and by the discovery of kilns surrounded by wasters of this pottery at the site of Qurayya (surveyed by Parr, Harding, and Dayton 1970; Parr 1988, 1992 with citations). The ware is thus more accurately known by its type-site designation: 'Qurayya Painted Ware', and its inclusion in a repertory dating to the last half of the tenth century BCE goes far to lower the terminal date for this distinctive ware (cf. Parr 1988: 75–81, who defends a date entirely within the second millennium BCE).

During the late seventh century a small fortress was built west of the earlier settlement. It was destroyed during the general destructions marking the end of the Judaean monarchy.

The initial small encampment (Stratum IX), with relatively large grain pits (?), at Tell es-Seba‘, ancient Beersheva (Herzog 1984: 8–11, Figs. 17–19) is already characterized by hand-burnished red slip, as is the next phase (Stratum VIII, Herzog 1984: 11–14, Fig. 20), which adds to a new dugout encampment a four-room house. In the ensuing Stratum VII, a series of conjoined four-roomed houses were built, perhaps encircling a large open court so as to create what the excavator calls an 'enclosed settlement', the rear rooms amounting to, in effect, a primitive casemate wall (Herzog 1984: 78).

From Stratum VII came a (miniature) tall chalk incense altar, *ca.* 12 cm wide by 24 (?) cm tall (Herzog 1984: Fig. 25:18; Pl. 13:9). Elsewhere, in roughly contemporaneous stratification, a 9-cm tall miniature limestone incense altar (Figure 17: 5) was discovered at Gezer in a mixed fill containing Stratum VIII (the Solomonic stratum) and early ninth-century (Stratum VII) materials (Dever, Lance et al. 1974: 64, pls 41:2, 75:a–b); and an altar intermediate in size between the two foregoing comes from Level B3 at Tell Beit Mirsim (Figure 17:4; Albright 1943: 28–9, which also cites another altar from Macalister's excavations at Gezer).

At Tell 'Ira a six-chambered (i.e., 'Solomonic') gateway was dated by the excavators to the seventh century, on the understanding that occupation at the site was limited to the seventh to the sixth centuries BCE. During subsequent excavations previously unnoticed evidence for a '10th–9th century' occupation was discovered (Beit Arieh 1992a: 447b; 1985a; 1985b). In the absence of contrary data (provided by the meticulous cross-checking and publication of sherds and section drawings relating to the foundation trenches and makeup fills of the gate and its associated fortifications), the rules of typological cross-dating would appear to date the gateway to the last half of the tenth

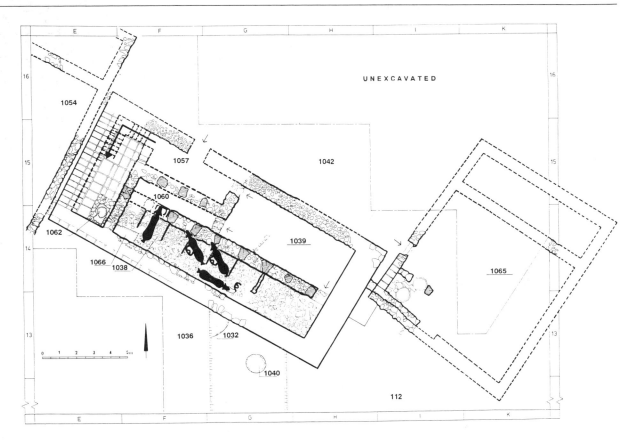

Figure 15   Tel Masos, Stratum II towered (stairway) Stable 1039 and posited service-stores Building 1065. Horse standings are reconstructed, showing one method of removing a horse from an inner standing. Note that the standings nearest the door are too small for horses, and must have been used for donkeys (after Fritz and Kempinski 1983)

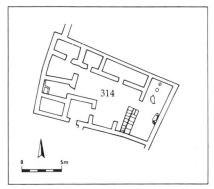

Figure 16   Tel Masos, Administrative/Stores Building 314, Stratum II, Area H

century, with possible major reuse in the later period.[42] In any case, Tell 'Ira appears to have witnessed three periods of occupation during the Iron II period, one early and two late ('early' and 'late' seventh century, respectively).

Further east, the first settlement at Tell Arad is characterized by hand-burnished red slips (M. Aharoni 1981: 181–92; Herzog et al. 1984: 2–6; Yadin 1965: 180), dating its destruction to the Sheshonq raid, in conformity

with the mention of Arad in his inscription (Mazar and Netzer 1986: 89; Kitchen 1986: 432–47).[43,44]

During the late eighth century, the central role in patrolling the desert ways fell to the military at Tel Arad and the chariot forces at Beersheva, with provisioning functions possibly being provided by Aroer and further chariot support at Tel Malhata. Of immense value in documenting the highly significant role of the southern corridor during the last half of the eighth century is Israel Eph'al's observation that 'real contact between the nomads in the border areas of Palestine and the Assyrian authorities started when Tiglath-Pileser *reached southern Philistia and Transjordan* . . . [in fragmentary annals] relating to 733 B.C., mention [is made of] "Samsi queen of the Arabs who violated the oath (sworn) by Shamash"' (1982: 83, emphasis added). Significantly, from our perspective, Eph'al ties Samsi's rebellion to that of Mitinti of Ashkelon, after 734 BCE, and before the defeat of Rezin, King of Damascus – the leader of the rebellion – in 732 BCE (1982: 84). Samsi's power, and its basis in the spice and incense trade, which at this time and through this corridor must have eventuated at the Philistine ports of Ashdod, Ashkelon, and Gaza – hence Mitinti's major role

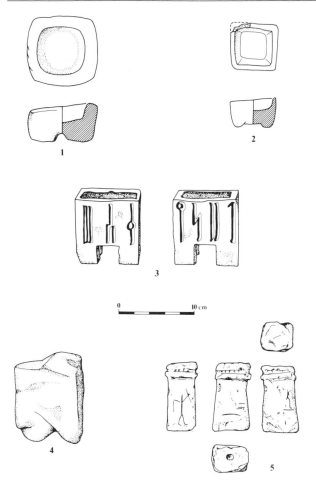

Figure 17 Miniature incense altars from Beersheva (1–2), South Arabia (3, Groom 1981: 142), Tell Beit Mirsim (4, upside down), and Gezer (5)

long ago argued, and Tel Malhata, with other late fortresses and connected settlements being established to the southeast, at Horvat ʿUza and Horvat Radum (Beit Arieh 1992b; 1992c). It is not impossible that the site of Beersheva relocated to the site of Aroer, 5 km south of Tel Masos (above), which was briefly occupied at the very end of the Judaean Monarchy; the finds included four miniature (cuboidal) limestone altars, below. There does not appear to have been any earlier Iron Age occupation (Biran 1983).

The discoveries of miniature, now cuboidal, limestone incense altars (see Figure 17:1–2) – the later analogs to the Beersheva Stratum VII, Tell Beit Mirsim, and Gezer Strata VIII/VII altars – at Beersheva, Malhata, and Aroer[45] – again witness not only to a major commodity (incense) being transported through the corridor, small quantities for local use presumably being purchased in side deals with drivers,[46] but also to substantial ongoing links with South Arabia. In later times these links are witnessed by sixth-century grafitti, incised in Old South Arabic script on local wares, at Jerusalem (Shiloh 1979: 19), and by the South Arabian seal found at Beitin.[47]

V   The impact of nationhood upon the Israelite family

The domestic economy

Here we are upon secure ground, thanks in large measure to Lawrence E. Stager and David C. Hopkins' pioneering studies (both 1985). We may take it as established that the fundamental Israelite economy was founded, early and late, upon a system of mixed peasant agriculture, involving primarily cereal crops in the basin lands and mixed agriculture, arboriculture and viticulture in the highlands, coupled with the keeping of small domestic flocks and herds, both as a matter of diversification and risk-spreading, and as a means of accumulating crop surpluses in easily sold (and readily moveable) resources (Hopkins 1985: 245–50; Holladay 1992a: 315). Pastoralist activities, both as 'enclosed nomadism' and exploiting the more marginal portions of the region, the Negev and the eastern slopes, formed the most important secondary element, but one difficult to quantify on the basis of archaeological materials (Finkelstein 1988a: 343, but see Banning 1992). In the southern Levant, even the highlands had no assured yearly rainfall, and natural disasters of all sorts were a peasant's yearly lot. Prior to the disaster-prone agricultural intensification programs of the eighth century (Chaney 1989), multi-crop risk-spreading strategies involving herds and flocks, cereal- and garden-farming, and the cultivation of vines and fruit trees ensured the survivability of the nuclear family in its localized village setting (Hopkins 1985: 250–4 takes the smallest producing unit to be the extended family; Chaney 1989: 26–7).

in the rebellion, inexplicable on the basis of his hinterland alone – is made clear in the list of booty (III R 10.2:20–21): 1000+ captives, 30,000 camels, 20,000 sheep, and 5000 [leather bags and bottles of (cf. Ephʿal 1982: 128, n. 447)] spices of all sorts (Ephʿal 1982: 85, n. 259). To this list of Samsi's wealth, gold can probably be added as well (Ephʿal 1982: 86).

With respect to the northern corridor (below), we need only note that Zabibe's tribute in 738 BCE was clearly trade-related, and was closely tied to Israel and Tyre's submission, which was necessary 'to avert a possible disruption of the Arabian trade and [for Zabibe's part] her income from it. . . . This [portion of the] trade was conducted primarily along the King's Highway, whose principal outlets were Damascus and Tyre (the western bifurcation which branched off to Tyre from the King's Highway passed through the territory of the kingdom of Israel)' (Ephʿal 1982: 83).

During the seventh century, the role played by Beersheva seems to have passed to Tel ʿIra, as Aharoni

Plate 2 Cuboidal limestone incense altars from Tell el-Maskhuta. Note the slight signs of burning. Surface finds, dated by stratified finds to the Persian occupation at the site, *ca* 525–400 BCE (courtesy of James Peacock)

The nuclear family – father, mother, children, slaves/ domestic servants – formed the basic social unit, which was upwardly organized into a segmentary society comprised of the extended family, the clan, and various tribes (Stager 1985: 17–28). Of these larger units, only the residence pattern of the extended family, or 'House of the Father', may presently be discerned (Stager 1985: 18–23; Holladay 1992a: 317), and those only in some instances, and perhaps equivocally, although in the case of small sites it is possible that the clan was coincident with the settlement. Thus, for the premonarchical period, clans and tribes may be inferred – given the normative West Asian forms of social organization – from the occupational pattern of broadly distributed hamlets and small unfortified villages across the highlands and the upper Galilee (Aharoni 1957; Finkelstein 1988a).

As we have already noted, in such a setting (pre-state intensive plow-assisted farming and horticulture, with subsidiary pastoralist pursuits), crosscultural anthropological studies suggest that the legal systems will be based upon a system of village or clan elders (Tables 2, 4), with political control characteristically passing into the hands of 'rich men' as the society evolves toward chieftainship, paramount chieftainship, and nascent statehood (above).

The Israelite house

The Israelite house serves as our single best resource for understanding the economic role of the family in Israelite society. It evolved from yet unproven prototypes (e.g., at Tel Batash/Timnah: Kelm and Mazar 1982: 9–13) sufficiently early that it appears to be the standard early highland house form (Marquet-Krause 1949: Pl. 97, Buildings 168, 184; Stager 1985: 18; Finkelstein 1988a:

250–60). It continued, with little more than refinement in the positioning of exterior doorways, in an unbroken tradition as the normative Israelite and Judaean house form, whether in its 'three-room' or 'four-room', or 'four-room with added side shed(s)' configuration (Figure 18: A, C, E; B; and D, F respectively).[48]

But how did such a plan function? We have little direct archaeological evidence,[49] but ethnographic analysis of the spatial requirements of modern Iranian peasants practicing the same modes of production and living under many of the same constraints as Iron Age Israelites indicates the absolute necessity of generous amounts of multipurpose storage space for grain, various dried and preserved foods, straw, dung, wood, etc.; stables; and one living room for each nuclear family averaging between 15 and 18 m², the lower figure being coincident with the presence of a separate kitchen area, often shared with other members of the extended family (Kramer 1979: 155 [room sizes from plans]; Watson 1979: 153–4, Table 5.2 [room sizes from plans]; Holladay 1992a: 314; Holladay in progress). Heavy goods, agricultural equipment, grain stores, dung, straw and wood are characteristically stored on the ground floor (for Iron Age Palestine, oil and wine storage must be added). Western Iranian stables are variously on the ground floor, or are semi-subterranean. Sheep and goats are often sheltered from winter storms in underground cavelike stables (not yet attested for pre-Hellenistic Palestine),[50] but are otherwise folded in the courtyard space. Like the unfortified Palestinian highland hamlets of the Iron I period, most of the Iranian villages are expansive, and space is not a problem, but where second stories do exist (particularly in older fortified villages, where they are the characteristic mode of spatial organization), living quarters and light storage (e.g., dried milk products, dried fruit, honey, cheese, etc.) are invariably on the upper story, with animals and heavy storage on the ground floor (Kramer 1979: 148; Jacobs 1979: 179–80; Watson 1979: 126, 229, 241, 292–5). To illustrate the scale of the typical household operation: by impoverished Western Iranian standards, a family of five and their animals would have required *ca.* 1800 kg of wheat and 1080 kg of barley per annum, including seed grain and reckoning a 'fairly high' 80 percent extraction rate for the flour (Watson 1979: 292–3). If stored in jars with capacity equal to that of the Judaean Royal Stamped Jar (Ussishkin 1983: 161–3), this family would have required 55 jars for wheat storage, with another 36 jars for the barley – the total of 91 jars occupying 23 m² of floor space, or 12 m² if piled two deep (Holladay 1992a: 314a). Suffice it to say that present evidence suggests that domestic grain storage was typically accomplished in ancient Israel without the extensive use of either storejars or chaff-tempered earthenware bins.[51]

When the typical three- or four-room house plan is analyzed in terms of these spatial requirements (including

Figure 18   Typical Israelite and Judaean houses and house-complexes of the Iron Age. (A) Kh. Raddana, (B) Tell el-Far'ah(N) Str. VIIb, (C) Tell en-Nasbeh (early), (D) Shechem Str. VII, (E) Beersheva Str. II, (F) Tell en-Nasbeh (6/7th century)

average minimal widths of living rooms, normal head space in living quarters, etc.), it quickly becomes apparent that such houses can function only as fully-roofed two-story structures, with the low-beamed lower story (Albright 1943: 51; Callaway 1976: 29; Fritz and Kempinski 1983: 25; Yadin et al. 1989: 183–6, 191) primarily given over to economic activities: agricultural and other storage, stables, and sufficient folding space for the overnight shelter of the family's sheep and goats (Stager 1985: 12–17; Holladay 1992a: 310–16; Netzer 1992: 199). This arrangement ensures the best possible protection for the family's wealth, concentrated in the stored grain supplies and, particularly, in the livestock. The folding space, probably the area incorrectly termed 'courtyard', was then available for work-related activities during the daytime. In western Iran, ovens could be in semi-subterranean kitchens, in communal kitchens of compounds housing extended families, or nonexistent, as at Watson's 'Hasanabad', where bread was baked over an open hearth upon a metal tray (*saj*) exactly like a Palestinian MB II–Iron II 'Baking Tray' (Watson 1979: 122–5, 162–3; Kramer 1979: 147–56).

Insofar as we define the Israelite family as that element of the population living in three- and four-room houses (which constitute by far the greatest bulk of later Iron II habitations yet published), the greatest difference between the pre-monarchical and monarchical periods seems to be that, soon after the Sheshonq raid, the bulk of the population seems to have been concentrated in or around – e.g., Megiddo (cf. n. 57, below) and Beersheva (Aharoni 1973: 1; Gophna and Yisraeli 1973) – increasingly densely-occupied fortified settlements.[52] House sizes remained within the same general range, but, except for the standard relocation of the ground-floor entrance to the mid-front wall, little else changed. Some houses had control over more courtyard space, or more storerooms, but, in general, there was probably less than a 1:3 range in available sizes and/or facilities. Since the house itself was originally designed to handle the demands of a highly individuated agriculturalist economy, this is highly significant, as we shall argue below. The only major change in this key aspect of the production system is the stripping off of the additional grain stores once accumulated in exterior grain-pits (Finkelstein 1988a: 266). *Contra* Finkelstein, however, who suggests that it was mostly taxed away, more than one mechanism may have been operative. In a distinctly mercantile milieu, surplus grain, wine, oil, dried fruits and other products probably were sold – both in bulk to professional buyers, and on a continuing private or entreprenurial basis in the local markets. As noted above, bulk shipments could have entered the international market at ports located in Philistia or anywhere along the coast. What is important to note is that, except for palace granaries (Samaria), and large grain silos and granaries located near stables (Megiddo, Hazor, Beth Shemesh),

there is a distinct shortage of mass/public grain storage in the archaeological record.[53] We will pursue this below, with a suggestion as to where these reserves were actually stored.

Evaluating the case for agricultural intensification/specialization

During the ninth and eighth centuries, the pattern of family control of agricultural surpluses evidenced by the functioning of the four-and three-room house plan obviously continued. State, cultic, and regional taxes undoubtedly had a bite, but there is no evidence in these settlements of government redistribution below the palace, military and administrative levels.[54] What has changed for Israelite agriculturalists, and those who would exploit them, are the increased opportunities and pressures generated by peace, interregional cooperation and coordination, and access to wider markets via long-distance seaborne trade and short-distance overland trade.

With the advent of the state, the powers of the elders' councils necessarily were curtailed, but almost certainly not eliminated. Acceptable forms of local government were still necessary. Land transactions, however, almost certainly could be appealed to higher authority, and the potential for alienation of lands was vastly increased. Concentration of ownership in fewer hands and increased commercial opportunities undoubtedly led to increased cash crop specialization. All of this seems eminently reasonable and fits well with contemporary eighth century literary evidence, but did it actually take place? Surprisingly, this question is fully capable of archaeological testing and some of the necessary archaeological data would seem to be to hand. It does, however, involve an approach more familiar to Americanist and British-Continental archaeology than to Syro-Palestinian archaeology.

The analysis is moderately complicated, but not difficult:

1. Since (a) olive oil was, by a good margin, the most valuable major agricultural commodity produced in the southern Levant, and (b) olive trees require specific environmental parameters for successful cultivation, factors encouraging agricultural intensification should have led to Iron II settlement patterns (our chronological and spatial grids are at present unfortunately broad) consistently biased toward olive-growing regions (termed 'horticultural' regions in Finkelstein 1988a), as opposed to regions (Finkelstein's 'topographical units') in which this was not the case. The basic assumption here is that agricultural intensification means concentration on high value products as opposed to simply bringing more land in to use.

2. Olive growing regions, as attested by Ottoman tax records and modern practices, particularly characterize the central range and western slopes of the north-central hill country, an area extensively surveyed by Israel Finkelstein and published, in preliminary form, in 1988. Finkelstein claims,

although rather *sotto voce* (1988a: 187–8, 194), that settlement patterns focusing upon suitable horticultural lands are evident in the Iron II settlement data for the territory of Ephraim, going so far as to suggest that it is likely the inhabitants were forced to barter 'oil and wine for grain and dairy products' (1988a: 194), which is probably going too far. It is obvious from the discussion, however, that no statistical tests were made of the strength of the association. In their absence, it is fully possible that much may be in the eye of the beholder, particularly the eye of a beholder cognizant of the writings of the eighth century prophets. Statistical tests do exist, however, and sufficient data for preliminary assessments are provided by data given by Finkelstein (1988a).

3. As I read Finkelstein, he assumes that optimal land use for the territory is approximated by the farming practices of the region's inhabitants in 1945 CE (1988a: 129–30). This is a useful assumption, and this is a period for which we have good census data (1988a: 130–9, especially Table 2).

Thus, if a disproportionate expansion under (1.) above fits the spatial model given by (2–3) above, the hypothesis that the Iron II expansion was governed by factors dictating intensification of high-value crops would seem to be supported, as opposed to the null hypothesis that Iron II expansion in these regions was occasioned purely by chance or by other, unconsidered, factors.

This null hypothesis may be tested most directly by means of a regression analysis (Shennan 1988: 114–33; Wilkinson 1990a: 115–28, 147–89; Wilkinson 1990b: 198–230) testing the relationship of the number of new or expanded Iron II sites to the relative proportions of horticultural lands (as indicated by landuse patterns in the 1945 census, Finkelstein 1988a: 1931–32, Table 2) in the respective topographical units. The graphic representation of this analysis may be seen in Figure 19, the curving line at top center being the upper 95 percent confidence line (Wilkinson 1990b: 301). It will instantly be noted that the 'least squares' regression line does not 'fit' the data well, an indication that the one predictor (presence of horticultural lands) apparently does not form the only determining influence. Initially, analysis of this regression yields a correlation coefficient (r, cf. Shennan 1988: 126–31) of .145, and a squared correlation coefficient, or *coefficient of determination* of only .021 (or 2 percent), which is to say that, in the model analyzed (horticultural area in average dunams per person = constant * numbers of new sites and Iron I sites expanding in II), only 2 percent of the variation seems to be accounted for by the relative availability of horticultural lands within the different topographical units. Finally, the results of a two-tailed t test (Blalock 1979: 188–93) tell us that results like this could occur purely by chance 78.4 times out of 100. These findings would appear to invalidate Finkelstein's informal assessment of the trends (above), but inspection of Figure 19 suggests that the two main outliers, SCR and NCR, the Southern Central Range and the Northern Central Range, should be reconsidered

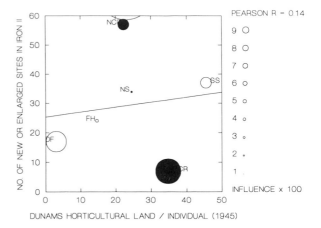

Figure 19   Ephraim: Scatterplot of new and enlarged Iron II sites vs. dunams of horticultural land per individual (1945 census), all regions, with regression line and upper limit (curved line, top center) of the 95 percent confidence band. The size of the plot symbols indicates how much the correlation coefficient would change if that point were eliminated, negative influences being indicated by the filled circles, positive influences by the open circles. In this example, the Southern Central Range (large filled circle lower right), and the North Central Range (top center) are jointly exercising a large negative influence on Pearson's r. In such a situation, the data for the major outliers (SCR, NCR) should be reassessed (see text). *Given this set of data*, the very low value of Pearson's r, which ranges in scale from +1 for perfect positive correlation to −1 for perfect negative correlation, makes it clear that the availability of horticultural land played only the most marginal of roles in determining Iron II site selection (cf. Figure 20)

for inclusion in the model. As we have already noted, the Southern Central Range is clearly impacted by being 'a sensitive border area . . . Unfortified villages or farms, like those . . . [elsewhere] did not exist here' (Finkelstein 1988a: 188). In other words, the demography of this topographical unit is dictated by political/military considerations, and not by landuse considerations. Similarly, the Northern Central Range, which is 'oversubscribed' in terms of numbers of new and expanded sites (57 in all), may be heavily influenced by being on a main highway, and site location may be dictated by considerations other than the simple availability of desirable agricultural lands.

Eliminating these two topographical units weakens the analysis by leaving only four cases (topographic units), but the new regression line fits the remaining data points much more comfortably (Figure 20, Table 5), yielding a vastly improved r of .936 and a coefficient of determination (r^2) of .876 or 88 percent. This is strong confirmation of Finkelstein's intuitive reading of the significance of the survey data. The results of a two-tailed t-test allow the rejection of the null hypothesis (that site placement was not conditioned by the availability of horticultural lands) at the .064 level – not quite the statistician's preferred .05, but close enough.

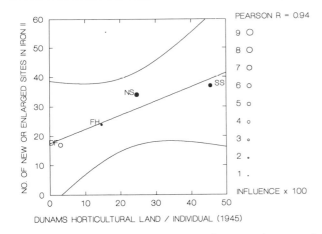

Figure 20 As Figure 19, eliminating the Southern Central Range and the Northern Central Range from the analysis (see text). Note the much narrower 95 percent confidence line, the small influence symbols, and the high value for Pearson's r, supporting the hypothesis that, for these topographic units, the availability of horticultural land seems to be the key determinant for Iron II site selection

VI Israelite agrarian society: socio-economic organization under the state

The contribution of the Israelite family

The preceding sketch is essential for understanding not only the evolutionary/processual dynamics of the Israelite and Judaean nation-state at the beginning of the tenth century BCE (below), but also for understanding its workings throughout the 400-odd years of its independent existence. The highlands of Israel and Judah were a complicated mosaic of small, varied ecological niches, each capable of various modes of agricultural (virtually all dry farming) and pastoral exploitation, but, except for a few 'garden spots', none sufficiently extensive to allow for the sorts of massed labor forces of centralized control which have been predicated for the functioning of Mesopotamian irrigated agriculture, or for the largely temple- or palace-dominated basin agriculture of ancient Egypt (see Finkelstein, this volume). In Israel, with some exceptions, e.g., the possible royal vineyards represented by the inscriptions on the Royal Stamped Jar handles, and possible land-seizures by the highly placed, everything seems to have been up to the individual family production

unit, whether working its allotted share of the extended family's holdings, its own freehold, or land rented from a rich neighbor or absentee landlord. For the eighth century BCE − except for the foregoing not under investigation here − it should not pass notice that agricultural intensification efforts could as easily be focused upon tenants or even freeholders dependent upon market forces for the sale of their produce as upon a paid labor force.[55]

Residence patterns, land alienation and agricultural intensification

In the system described above, once the potentials of the highland 'frontier' (Stager 1985: 3−10) were completely realized, alienation of land and exploitation of the weak represented a new 'frontier of opportunity', limited only by the legal system (below) and the force of custom, backed by divine sanction. While certainly attested in the prophetic literature, sociologically explicable and ethnographically documentable, nothing in the archaeological record clearly points either to a dramatic degradation of the living standards of most of those elements of Israelite society who lived in the large villages, towns and cities which have, to date, been excavated;[56] or to a concomitant rise in the living standards of a few 'great houses', a very few late outsized 'four-room houses' at Tell en-Nasbeh notwithstanding (e.g., Figure 18:F).[57]

But perhaps a *dramatic* degradation was not involved. Owing to a longstanding practice of concentration on large, multicomponent *tells*, we presently have relatively little information on the archaeology of non-urban intrasite settlement patterns of small agriculturalist sites during the period of the early state(s). Two different sites, however, located in quite different parts of the region, seem to point in an interesting direction. As we have seen, 'Izbet Sartah located in the rolling foothills, the Shephelah, of the Judaean mountains, seems briefly to have been a hamlet specializing in grain cultivation, balanced by risk-spreading investment in domestic herds and flocks (Hellwing and Adjeman 1986; Rosen 1986). It would appear to have been paralleled by a number of similarly sited Iron II settlements all along the western flank of the Shephelah (Ledermann 1990). This would appear to have been 'new land' for Israelite exploitation, made possible by the expansionistic establishment of the nation-state, and the 'estate' may have been a land grant to a palace retainer. As already noted,

Table 5

Dep. Var. [see note]	N: 4	Multiple R: .936	Squared multiple R: .876			
Adjusted squared multiple R: .814		Standard error of estimate: 3.969				
Variable	Coefficient	Std error	Std coef	Tolerance	T	P (2 tail)
Constant	17.525	3.421	0.000		5.122	0.036
Avghort	0.478	0.127	0.936	.100E+01	3.758	0.064

Note: The dependent variable was the number of new sites in Iron II *plus* the number of Iron I sites that expanded in Iron II.

'Izbet Sartah Stratum 2 was dominated by one large house surrounded by grain-pits, interpreted as indicating a major wealth distinction in the local setting (Figure 11, above). Pre-Omride Samaria, on the other hand, seems to have specialized in olive oil and wine production, witnessed primarily by rock-cut bell-shaped pits and olive- and wine-presses on the crest of the hill (Stager 1990: 94, Fig. 1, cf. Figure 21 here, modified). These economic pursuits were undoubtedly balanced by domestic flocks and herds and, presumably, by exchanging some surpluses with neighboring bottom-land hamlets specializing in grain production. According to 1 Kings 16: 23–24 (here we break our general rule against using biblical data), this land was purchased by Omri from an individual named Shemer, after whom Omri named the new capitol. This detail is important only in that it suggests that one individual owned this valuable parcel, which suggests a wealth distinction, under the monarchy, similar to that previously observed at 'Izbet Sartah. Superimposing the excavated portion of the expansive 'Izbet Sartah settlement pattern, typical of an unwalled village, upon Stager's plan of the rock-cuttings at Samaria (Figure 21) allows us to visualize something of the general appearance of this 'estate' (Stager's term), which, given all the data presently at our disposal, probably looked far more like a rural hamlet dominated by one household (whether the owner's or his agent's, e.g., Watson 1979: 152, Fig. 5.29, is immaterial) than like any later Persian, Hellenistic, or Roman estate.

The point to be stressed here, and in other analyses of Israelite social structure under the monarchy, is that, as far as present evidence goes – and there is a lot of evidence – the pattern of residence in four- and three-roomed houses clearly designed to house livestock, process crops and store agricultural produce on a family-by-family basis (as opposed to redistributive mechanisms involving communal store facilities) is, as was noted above, unvarying from Early Israel down through the late eighth-century highland and Shephelah materials (little has been published from the lowlands) typified by the Lachish Level III material culture complex: e.g., from Khirbet Raddana through Khirbet ed-Dawwar (Finkelstein 1988a) and 'Izbet Sartah, on down through Tell Beit Mirsim 2A, Beersheva Stratum II, most of Tell en-Nasbeh, Strata VIIb–d at Tell el-Far'ah (N),[58] and much of Beth Shemesh – all extensively excavated (Albright 1932, 1943; Aharoni 1973; McCowan 1947; Chambon 1984; Grant and Wright 1939 with references). As far as we presently know, similar residence patterns continued, though less well documented in terms of excavated remains, on down to the final destruction of the Judaean state in 586–582 BCE (e.g., Tufnell 1953; N. Lapp 1981). During this entire span of time we know nothing about one- or two-room hovels, or worker barracks or the like, and we do know enough to render the likelihood of discovering large numbers of the latter highly improbable.

In short, on good present evidence, it is clear that Israel

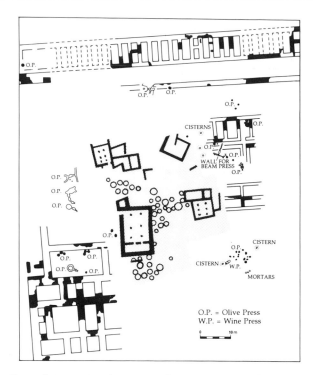

Figure 21 Pre-Omride Samaria (after Stager 1990), with the excavated portions of 'Izbet Sartah, Stratum II (shaded) superimposed

and Judah remained peasant economies (which characteristically display wealth distinctions) throughout their independent existences, with independent household control of agricultural surpluses (after taxes, tithes, and possible rents or share-cropping costs) and – except for rulers' palaces and associated elite structures in the cities, and outsized houses with specialized storage facilities (the 'West Tower' at Tell Beit Mirsim; Building 314 in Tel Masos Stratum II) in the large villages – a remarkably limited range of household sizes, each organized around the economically all-important first-floor stables, folding space and store facilities. Aside from palaces and clearly governmental residences (by the late Judaean period, these are witnessed even on the largely undifferentiated village level, e.g., the late 'West Tower' built over the remains of the casemate wall at Tell Beit Mirsim), no residence from Iron II Palestine outstrips the average 'four-room house' by much more than a factor of two, or three at the outside. As witnessed by the more completely excavated sites, eighth-century Tell Beit Mirsim being one of the best examples, some people do have somewhat larger houses, with adjoining courtyards and extra storerooms (or casemates); and some have smaller houses, squashed in between larger neighbors. But in many cases, it would appear that the space for the smaller house comes at the expense of the courtyard or other space of an adjacent larger house. The simplest and most probable explanation in those instances lies in the concept of the '*bet 'ab*', or patrimonial estate:

i.e., a residence created for a son or younger brother on family land still standing free in the midst of the increasingly densely packed fortified village, where land must have been at a premium.

Conclusion: redistribution and the storage of commodities

What all the above boils down to is that, contrary to the operative assumption governing most recent studies, Israel was emphatically not a 'redistributive economy'. Certainly there was both private and governmental exploitation. Certainly there was taxation. Certainly the palace, the standing army, and the cultus had their own dependency networks, presumably based upon localized patterns of taxation, purchase, and tithing (since agricultural commodities could not economically be forwarded over long distances). But the notion of 'ration bowls' for the general populace, as this has been forwarded in misguided explanation of the 'Beveled Rim Bowl' phenomenon in early Mesopotamian civilization,[59] would be ludicrous in the decentralized settlements sprawled across the broken highlands and dissected slopes of the Judaean and Israelite heartland, whether early or late. This deductive inference is strongly supported by consideration of the fact that the basic architectural unit initially devised (or adapted) for the highly successful, highly individualistic, agro-economic exploitation of the highland frontier – which obviously was no redistributive economy – was (a) the basic nuclear family's standard residence, functioning, as Frank Lloyd Wright put it, as 'a machine for living', to which we could add, 'and for successfully exploiting a difficult and unforgiving environment, and for successfully curating the fruits of that exploitation for the well-being of that particular family' (Stager 1985: 17b; Holladay 1992a: 310–12, 316); and (b), as we have already noted, that same plan, with no substantive alteration, persisted as the standard rural and dominant urban residence for the entire period of the Hebrew monarchies. In ancient Israel, debts, rents, tithes, and taxes exempted, the harvests of field, vine, orchard, flocks and herds were gathered into the individual *houses,* there to remain until sold, eaten, planted, stolen, or otherwise disposed of either by the smallest social unit in the society, or in concert with the larger *'bet 'ab'* to which it belonged. In economic and logistical terms, these were the 'Storehouses of Israel'. At considerably more than 15 m³ per household, the designed storage capacity of a mere village of 100 houses would amount to more than 1500 m³, or 3.75 times as much as the estimated capacity of the Area G Silo at Hazor (n. 54 above), and 3.33 times as much as Storage Pit 1414 at Megiddo (Lamon and Shipton 1939: 66–7), the two largest store facilities yet demonstrated for ancient Israel.[60,61]

Only in the drastically reduced populations of the exilic, Persian, and Hellenistic periods, with their drastically

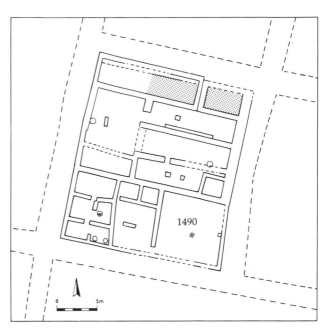

Figure 22 A non-Israelite (Babylonian?) 'insula'-style housing block from Megiddo Stratum III

altered housing arrangements, e.g., the agricultural estate utilizing the ruins of the Assyrian palace-fort at Hazor (Yadin et al. 1958: Pl. 177), is it possible to witness the rise of the sorts of agricultural estates which seemingly persist into Hellenistic and Roman Palestine.[62,63] The latter point is perhaps made most strongly by comparison of a major housing block at Tell el-Far'ah (N) (see Figure 18:B) with one of the completely non-Palestinian insulae (translocated Babylonians?) of the succeeding settlement of Stratum III Megiddo (Figure 22). From the former, paralleled by the typical private houses of every Judaean and Israelite site yet excavated (Shiloh 1970, 1987; Braemer 1982), it is easy to infer the nuclear family as the basic economic module of the society, and agrarian activity as the dominant element of the economy (Stager 1985; Netzer 1992; Holladay 1992a). On the other hand, it is extremely hard to fathom either the basic social module (some variant of the extended family plus retainers?), or, indeed, the nature of the local economy at Assyrian Megiddo without invoking models from text-rich Late Bronze Age Nuzi or Isin-Larsa and Old Babylonian Nippur (to see how far this approach may take one, cf. Stone 1987).

Notes

1. Esse's argument rests, in part, on the widely-shared assumption that these 'large pithoi . . . were too awkward to transport' (Finkelstein 1988a: 285). In the light of the disconfirmation of this working hypothesis by the results from neutron activation analyses (NAA) of Collared-rim Pithoi from Tel Dan (Yellin and Gunneweg 1989, noted by Esse 1992: 96, n. 73), Esse suggests

that 'it seems unlikely that these vessels were transported far from their centers of production' (1992: 96). With respect to filled jars, this still seems reasonable: Esse's observation that 'the weight of a nearly complete jar in the Oriental Institute Museum from Megiddo . . . was over 32 kilograms' (1992: 96, n. 72) is pretty compelling, unless we postulate either oxcart or camel transport, when we realize that the much smaller Royal Stamped Handle storejars of the later Iron II period contained roughly 45 kg of liquid (Ussishkin 1983: 161–3). On the other hand, two well-made large storage pithoi would have made a good donkey load, even for an ordinary village donkey, and probably would have made a good trading item for an itinerant peddler, who need not even have been an 'early Israelite'. It seems to me that this is not an unreasonable reading of the Tel Dan NAA results. For a variety of reports on the carrying capacities of donkeys (see Ogunremi 1982 and Veenhof 1972). At this stage of our knowledge, NAA analysis of a major sampling of the Megiddo Collar-rim Pithoi would make a world of difference in our ability to formulate more robust hypotheses.

2. The tenth century BCE is one of the 'Dark Ages' in Near Eastern history. Neither David nor Solomon, nor any of their immediate successors is known from contemporary documents. The honor of first mention falls to Ahab, the seventh king of Israel, mentioned (after 853 BCE) by Shalmaneser III of Assyria, who later, on the Black Obelisk, mistakenly cites Ahab's father, Omri, as dynastic forbear to Jehu. About 830 BCE, Mesha, king of Moab cites 'Omri, King of Israel . . . [and] his son' as occupying powers during the past 'forty years' (Pritchard 1969b: 279a; 281a; 320).

3. This is simply a damaged, and probably incomplete, list of places conquered; see Kitchen 1986: 432–47. Sheshonq I was the first king of the 22nd Egyptian Dynasty (*ca.* 945–924 BCE). A fragment of his large victory stele was found – not in context – in the destroyed Israelite Royal City of Megiddo Stratum VA/IVB.

4. As they are used in this chapter, the terms 'complex', 'partially differentiated', and 'undifferentiated' or 'largely undifferentiated' have to do with the degree of architectural diversity apparent in the plans of a particular settlement site, or an individual stratum at such a site. In general, we may assume that the greater the variety of architectural expression, e.g., palaces, sanctuaries, store facilities, stables, complex enigmatic structures, simple enigmatic structures, private houses, small industrial installations, etc., the larger the range of services offered by that particular site; i.e., the greater the probability that we have identified some sort of 'central place', or governmental center (e.g., Jerusalem, Megiddo, Hazor). There may be a good deal of variety in the functions of various of these complex sites: e.g., the site of Samaria [a royal acropolis] vs Megiddo IVA [a giant and itself complex 'chariot city'?] vs Hazor [a major provincial center, but perhaps also a major defense point and a node on a major overland trading route]. At the opposite extreme, where the entire site consists of little more than a series of domestic structures, with perhaps a headman's or local governor's house and a few industrial installations (e.g., olive presses, store pits), we may infer a dependent village (Tell Beit Mirsim, Tell en-Nasbeh, Tel Qiri), or, at an even lower level of differentiation, a hamlet (Khirbet Radanna). In between, and, in ideal Christallerian space evenly arrayed in hexagonal fashion around each central place, we would expect the 'partially differentiated' 'Town' site (Beth Shemesh, Beersheva, Ta'anach), offering a limited range of services, but ultimately dependent upon either a central place or a major government center (Christaller 1933: 66, Figure 1; 71, Figure 2; cf. Baskin 1957. For

archaeological applications see Flannery 1976: 161–80, with citations; Earle 1976).

5. A dating of the six-chambered gateway at Lachish, and especially the Palace-fort, with its stables and chalk-plastered courtyard (Ussishkin 1983: 147–54), to the period after Sheshonq, perhaps even within the second quarter of the ninth century, would put the multiple stables at Lachish more on a par with the situation in Megiddo (below). This interpretation is supported by a number of factors, not the least being that a general destruction, which overwhelmed the small one-room shrine (below), occurred at Lachish at the same general time (i.e., an early burnished red slip phase) as it did at the other Royal Cities, yet the Palace Fort and its courtyard, complete with stables, does not seem to have been the setting for that destruction. The recent discovery of a six-chambered gateway at Tell 'Ira, attributed by the excavators to the eighth century, but more plausibly to be attributed to the tenth-century materials later discovered at the site, with later reuse, raises the possibility of still other provincial centers of this formative era, probably less impressive than the three (four?) already mentioned, but impressive nevertheless, waiting to be discovered (Beit Arieh 1985a; 1985b; 1992a: 447b; below).

6. On this ground and others developed above I must reject the nihilistic views of Paul Jacobs (1992) in favor of a strongly nuanced/corrected version of Israel Finkelstein's basic analysis of the *highland* settlement patterns. I cannot, however, accept Finkelstein's 'nomadic sedentarization' hypothesis, for which I see little or no archaeological evidence, certainly nothing to compare with our evidence for similar phenonena in the EB I and particularly in the MB I/EB IV periods (cf. especially now Banning and Köhler-Rollefson 1992; Rosen 1992). Some version of the Mendenhall-Chaney-Frick-Gottwald hypothesis presently seems the best answer to the question of the primary 'donor society', though other options may be on the horizon.

7. For a comparison of the eighth and ninth century pottery of Shechem, Tell el-Far'ah (N), and Samaria with Hazor, see Holladay 1966.

8. The three royal cities by no means exhaust the list of excavated townsites occupied in the tenth century. A. Mazar (1990) lists: Dan Stratum IV, Tel Kinrot/Tell el-'Oreme Stratum IV, Taanach Period II, Yoqneam Stratum 11, Tel Amal, Tell Abu Hawam Stratum III, Shiqmona, Tel Mevorakh Stratum VII, Tell el-Far'ah (N) Stratum VIIb, Tell el-Hama (in the Jordan Valley south of Beth Shan), Tell el-Mazar in Transjordan near the junction of the Jabbok and the Jordan, Tell Qaisle Stratum IX–VIII [*contra,* cf. Holladay 1990, who argues for Strata XI–X being pre-Sheshonq and the stratum destroyed by Sheshonq, respectively; in this perspective, Stratum IX would commence in the tenth century], Beth Shemesh Stratum IIa, Tel Batash Stratum IV, Tell Beit Mirsim Stratum B3, Lachish Stratum V, Arad Stratum XII, and Tel Beersheva Strata VII–VI (*contra,* p. 44 below, where Stratum IX may already be post-Sheshonq). Cf. Holladay 1976, Chart 3, which specifies Stratum III at Tell 'Amal, suggests a division in the Tell el-Far'ah (N) 'Niv. III' materials, adds Beth Shan Lower Level V, early elements of Samaria (below), Shechem Stratum XI(?), elements of Tell Jemmeh, tombs, implying settlement, from Tell en-Nasbeh, and in which B. Maisler's Tell Qasile IX,1 (1951) should now be corrected to A. Mazar's Strata XI–X (1985).

9. Of these three sites, Sheshonq's lengthy, but poorly preserved, campaign list mentions only Megiddo by name (Kitchen 1986: 432–47). For strong archaeological warrants for the simultaneity of major destructions at Ashdod, Tell Qasile, Gezer, Megiddo, Ta'anach, and Beth Shan, see Holladay 1990.

10. Without the support of the biblical text, de Vaux's presumptive unfinished Palace of Omri (Building 411) at Tell el-Far'ah (N) would hardly have been identified as the seat of the centralized government of a significant Levantine nation state (de Vaux 1955: 582–83, Pl. VII; Chambon 1984: 38–9, Pl. 18). The question is probably moot, however. See Holladay 1966: 114–16 for the suggestion, accepted without attribution by McClellan 1987, that these remains are foundations related to the Str. VIId Palace 148 (Chambon 1984: 44–7) destroyed by the Neo-Assyrians *ca.* 725–22 BCE).

11. E.g., the Kurkh Monolith of Shalmanezer III (858–824 BCE), the Mesha Stele (*ca.* 830 BCE), the Stone Slab from Calah of Adad-Nirari III (810–783), the annals of Tiglath-Pileser III (744–727 BCE), Sargon II (721–705 BCE), Sennacherib (704–681 BCE), etc. (Pritchard 1969b: 278–9; 281; 282–4; 284–7; 287–8).

12. Explanation of social transformations in complex societies is one of the most challenging areas of social anthropology and social archaeology. Simplistic evolutionary or monocausal explanations are looked on with disfavour (Renfrew and Bahn 1991: 405–34; 421). Given present space limitations, it is not possible to develop and document a truly multivariate explanation. It is possible, however, to postulate certain alternate paths of social evolution based upon cross-cultural analysis, examine the archaeological record with respect to these variables, and then to attempt some sort of hypothetical explanation variously drawing upon the resources of Marxist, processualist, and post-processualist archaeology. The following analysis utilizes a Marxist analysis of pre-industrial social systems to derive a set of alternative social structures appropriate to the early Israelite Highland societies (intensive agriculturalist, pastoralist). It then analyzes the archaeological record for material correlates of these alternative structures (elite structures vs signs of differential wealth accumulation), noting in passing signs of the development of specialization in the military arts. Finally, it puts the 'explanation' of the transformation from segmentary agriculturalist society to nation-state in the form of an historical narrative, while acknowledging (here) the stronger explanatory force – and greater opportunities for testing – of a systems/cybernetics [positive feedback] approach to modeling the transformation. Cf. particularly the concise and extremely lucid 'history of modern archaeological theory' in Renfrew and Bahn 1991: 405–34.

13. This number represents cases from the *Ethnographic Atlas* (Murdock 1967) judged 'superior' with respect to observations concerning legal systems.

14. Recognition of this non-hereditary form of social stratification (wealth distinctions) nuances to a considerable degree the early stages of societal evolution discussed in Frick's *The Formation of the State in Ancient Israel* (1985), which should be consulted as the most painstaking review of this process presently available. It should further be noted that recent developments, particularly the lowering of the dates for Tel Masos, have invalidated or heavily compromised his use of some of the archaeological materials.

15. Convincing archaeological data for this transitional stage have not yet been demonstrated. Note that burnished red slips characterize the fortress at Tell el-Ful, formerly ascribed to Saul.

16. The differently sized 'fortresses' in the Negev Highlands, which most likely are pastoralist encampments (Finkelstein 1988a: 241–2) are typically characterized by the presence of burnished red slips, and date, as R. Cohen has long argued, to the last half of the tenth century.

17. Note that the el-Khadr (5 km west of Bethlehem) hoard, found in a field in 1953 and broken up and distributed among a number of dealers, as of a publication date of 1980, contained at least 26 arrowheads, of which five (19%) were inscribed (Cross 1980: 4).

18. For all but the Stratum III burnished red-slipped materials at 'Izbet Sartah, which are based upon the total sherdage, these percentages are based on vessels illustrated in the figures (Finkelstein 1986). For clarity of analysis, the 'Izbet Sartah Stratum II silo fills are tabulated separately from the general Stratum II materials.

19. The chronological significance of red slips in early Israel has long been recognized (Albright 1932: 63–73; 1943: 5–10), though variously interpreted with reference to absolute chronology. For preliminary studies involving quantified observations of colored slips and other surface colors of pottery, taken together with various modes of burnish, through stratigraphic sequences, see Holladay 1990; 1993. For Albright's statement on the chronological value of 'creamy wash', as he termed it, see Albright 1932: 62.

20. Reconstructed by Finkelstein as a 'Southern Fortress'-style enclosure, but by Zvi Lederman as a typical highlands hamlet (1990).

21. It will not pass unnoticed that this is precisely the role of the eighth-century prophets, something that Morris Silver misses in his adherence to the 'oughtness' of supply-side economics (1983) – i.e., Silver would have allied himself unhesitatingly with the cause of the wealthy. Whether the prophets are 'radical' in the original sense of attempting to perpetuate and intensify (patently unsuccessful) regulatory mechanisms of the pre-state society, or whether they are 'radical innovators' is an interesting subject for further study. In either case, as Silver has argued, successful application of negative feedback with respect to wealth accumulation would probably have had disastrous effects upon key mechanisms of the state, leading, if successful, to societal 'collapse' and reintegration/reformation of the society at a lower level of social organization – something that indeed happened during the period of the Babylonian Exile, and again during the long period of the Diaspora.

22. This observation seems to be more certain for Hazor and Megiddo than for smaller sites in their vicinity. Cf., in particular, the quantified observations of Melvin Hunt with respect to the Yokneam Regional Project and Tell Qiri. At Tell Qiri, out of some 7000 sherds saved during the main season of excavations, 344 cooking pot rims, 376 storejar rims, 336 bowl rims, and 262 krater rims were type-sorted and systematically analyzed in terms of their stratigraphic occurrence in the Area D sequence. Figures are not given for jugs and 'secondary forms' such as chalices, baking trays, Collared-rim Pithoi, other pithoi, Philistine Ware, Bichrome Ware, 'Samaria Ware', Cypro-Phoenician Ware, Phoenician Ware, Assyrian/Assyrianizing Ware, and other imported wares; or 'minor types' such as juglets, lamps, 'Cups-and-Saucers', flasks, goblets, pyxides, amphoriskoi, incense burners, tall stands, etc. Out of, presumably, the entire corpus of rims saved from the site (quantities for two minor seasons are not documented), Hunt gives no count for the 'not frequent' Philistine pottery (his Fig. 42 illustrates 7), but there were 8 Bichrome Ware rims, 9 'Samarian Ware' rims (probably Phoenician products, so Anderson 1988: 355), 18 Cypro-Phoenician 'Black-on-Red' rims, and 2 Phoenician rims ('dull reddish fabric and black-painted decoration' only) (1987: 200–3).

23. Cedar of Lebanon was identified in the remains of Stratum II Buildings 314 (Room 343) and 480 (Rooms 483, 487) at Tel

Masos (Liphschitz and Waisel in Fritz and Kempinski 1983: 210, 212); in the construction of Temple 131 in Tell Qasile Stratum X (Liphschitz and Waisel in A. Mazar 1985: 139); in the building of Beersheva III–II (Liphschitz and Waisel 1973: Table 1, 104–5). A piece of cedar came from Locus 4286 of the Level III drainage channel in Area G at Lachish (Ussishkin 1983: 167). Liphschitz and Waisel 1974–81, *Dendroarchaeological Investigations Tel Lachish*, Mimeographed reports nos. 20, 41, 46, 58, 75, 103, Tel Aviv University, were not available to me.

24. Quantification of these elements at Megiddo is one of the design objectives of the proposed new excavations at Megiddo (private communication, B. Halpern).

25. While pottery and goods shipped in pottery containers obviously were not the major commodities supplied by Tyre/Phoenicia to Israel, this pottery index nevertheless should serve as something of a barometer to give some rough measure of the strength of the trading relationship.

26. Although Anderson stress differences in relative frequencies of various types (based upon reported examples at Tyre) between the Tyrian and Sareptan (where Anderson has access to more complete data) assemblages, it seems reasonably clear that there is no major difference in the two assemblages which would invalidate the hypothesis that most of the Sareptan parallels with Israelite sites could, in point of fact, be either Tyrian or Sareptan, both, or even more characteristically 'Phoenician' in a broader sense (Anderson 1988: 395–421, more exactly, pp. 144–231). In the case of a few forms, it is possible that the equation could be made more exactly, but this is impossible to establish on the basis of data presently available.

27. E.g., Loud 1948: 75:18 (VIB); 77:5–6 (VIA); 84:1–2 ('VI').

28. Cf. the eleventh century quest of Wen-Amun for timber, including seven expertly dressed structural members sent as samples (II. 35–40), for the Barque of Amun (Pritchard 1969b: 25–9).

29. Given that Phoenicia is clearly involved, Tyre, archaeologically known in any modern sense only through Patricia Bikai's excavations (1978), is the most likely trading partner. This emerges purely from consideration of its proximity to Israelite territory, although it is completely at one with traditions concerning David, Solomon and the Omrides. Without functioning seaports of her own, Israel would have been dependent upon a third party – Tyre or Philistia – for access to trade with either Sarepta or any Phoenician entity further to the north.

30. The Timna mines were not worked during the period of the United Monarchy (Rothenberg 1988: 3–18). The Feinan sources, however, may well have contributed via the Beersheva-Zered Depression trade corridor, as Knauf has recently argued (1988: 112, n. 509).

31. For evidence for an iron industry in the northern Transjordan, in the territory traditionally assigned to Gilead, see Coughenour 1976: 71–8; 1989: 61–4.

32. Fritz and Kempinski 1983: Plates 131:11,16; 132:12 [burnished]; 133:12.

33. E.g., Fritz and Kempinski 1983: Plates 135:1,2,11 [all unburnished]; 136:1,10,116 [all burnished], 4, 11 [unburnished]; 137:8 [burnished]; 142: 1,2,7 [burnished], 8 [burnished]; 144:3,4 [burnished], 5 [unburnished], etc.

34. Herzog (1992: 225) independently classes this building with the tripartite pillared buildings. He, however, considers all buildings of this type, including the paved, pillared side aisles of private houses, to be either storehouses or work/store rooms (idem). The mangers are only for the convenience of pack animals bringing goods to the stores (1992: 227). I must admit that the workability, and indeed, the economics of this reconstruction completely elude me.

35. Note that the location of the outer doorway is restored. An alternative reconstruction might place the doorway in the eastern wall. The midline row of pillars is present at Hazor (e.g., Building 3067), although thought by the excavators to be a later addition to each plan, and a line of flagstone bases for wooden pillars, similar to the flagstones in Building 314, seems to be present in the 'West Tower' at Tell Beit Mirsim. The excavators of Tel Masos suggest the plan harks back to Late Bronze age antecedents and is, in fact, a typical 'Canaanite' house (Fritz and Kempinski 1983: 42–3). If so, it is out of its milieu by something like 250 years. The similarity in plan to a tenth-century Phoenician 'fort' has already been noted above. Coupled with the strong presence of Phoenician pottery in Building 314, the indications are that we may have either an entreprenurial activity modelled on Phoenician prototypes and in commercial contact with Phoenicia, or even an actual Phoenician presence at Tel Masos. The presence of a second story in this building is supported by the fact that at least eight vessels were reconstructed from sherds variously distributed through two to three of four different rooms in the western end of the house (1983: 40, n. 6, to which compare Gal 1992: 173b).

36. We must also note the close analogies with portions of the Ostraca House at Samaria (Yadin 1972: 171 n. 8), and Buildings 1482 and 10 (?) at Megiddo.

37. Presumably records were kept in situations of this sort, but the buildings' primary function can hardly be assumed to be 'scribal activity'. Herzog's suggestion (1992) that all buildings of this general plan are 'scribes' chambers' [full stop] stands the matter entirely on its head. This 'identification', unfortunately, amounts to a parade example of the ascription of function on the basis of personal expertise and a handful of inappropriate literary citations. The sole evidentiary warrants forwarded are the buildings' 'location, . . . symmetrical plan and the difference between them and typical Iron Age dwellings', coupled with the fact that 'scores of administrative documents were found in the building consequently dubbed the 'Ostraca House' (neither Kaufman 1982 or his dissertation are cited, cf. n. 54 below). Herzog continues: 'This find is sufficient evidence that the building was used by official scribes *and should be identified with the biblical "scribes' chamber'* (Jeremiah 36: 10, 12, 20, 21)' (1992: 229, emphasis added). Following this logic, an even better case could be made for the 'rooms' of the typical Iron II gateways, which are symmetrical, do not look like houses, and have 'administrative documents', cf. the find-spot of the Lachish Letters and compare the physical location described in Jeremiah 36: 10. For, on the other hand, a wholly convincing analysis yielding evidence for a particular type of scribal work-station in association with Egyptian store-rooms (granaries), cf. Kemp 1986. To my knowledge, nothing like the Egyptian work-station exists in either Israel or Judah, which seems on the archaeological evidence to have had a markedly different economy than Pharaonic Egypt. See *The Israelite House*, below.

38. Fritz and Kempinski 1983: Pls. 142:1–2; 147:3.

39. Fritz and Kempinski 1983: Pl. 141:1.

40. Fritz and Kempinski 1983: *Text*: 81–8. Bichrome Jugs: Pls. 144:11; 145:1; 146:1; 149:5. Cf. Bikai 1978: Pls. 25:9-15; 31:15; 33:22, 25. Amphorae: 141:8, cf. Bikai 1978: Pl. 35:13; 143:10, 148:7–9, cf. Bikai 1978: Pls. 24:2, 4; 26:13, 15, 17, 18, 21; 29:13, 14; 35:11, 13. Phoenician red burnished bowl Pl. 144: 3, cf. Bikai 1978: XXXIII:10 (so also V. Fritz, *Text*: 82, with other

parallels noted from Tell Abu Hawam Stratum IV, Beth Shan Lower Level V, and Tell Qasile Stratum XI). Parallels noted are from Tyre Stratum XIII–I to Stratum X–I.

41. Fritz and Kempinski 1983: Pl. 151:7, called a 'Flower pot', or (Tafel 95:B) 'Ägyptischer "Blumentopf"'. Cf. James 1966: 28; Figs. 49: 6; 51: 6; 54: 1.

42. It is hard to explain the building of a battleship in an era of guided missile cruisers and frigates.

43. The pottery presently attributed to the first fortress phase (Stratum XI, Herzog et al. 1984: 6–8) is clearly much later (in agreement with A. Mazar in Mazar and Netzer 1986: 89–90. Cf. also Zimhoni 1985: 85–6; Ussishkin 1988: 150–1 for the essential contemporaneity of Strata X–VIII.

44. In the main, the difference between the above sketch and Finkelstein's more extensive article (1988b) on the same topic, which reached far different historical conclusions concerning the settlement history of this trade route, may be summed up in six words: *red slips and burnished red slips*. Prior to the new quantified stratigraphic data introduced in Holladay 1990, almost any date between the twelfth and mid-tenth centuries could be, and was, proposed for the introduction of this distinctive surface treatment by the various excavators involved (cf., in Holladay 1990, Table 2 and Figs. 16A and 16B with Fig. 18), to say nothing about the various interpreters. A date within the reign of Solomon for the introduction of burnished red slips is now assured, with the introduction of unburnished streaky red slips coming only slightly earlier.

45. See Stern 1973:52. These altars derive from South Arabian prototypes (G. Ryckmans 1935: Pls III–IV; Caton-Thomson 1944: 49–50, 61–2, Pls XVI–XVII; Groom 1981: 142; J. Ryckmans 1992: 173a, 174b), where they were also used in domestic settings (J. Ryckmans 1992: 173b). See Fig. 17:3 here. These altars, at the present time mostly from the Hellenistic period, typically are found – as a cultural effect of the incense trade – along routes followed by that trade and in north-western Arabia, as witnessed in nearly every volume of *Atlal* (in both clay and stone). Compare, for example, the clay cuboidal altars in Babylonia (refs. in Stern 1973) and the Persian period altars from Tell el-Maskhuta (see Plate 2). The two Beersheva altars came from House 430, which also numbered the head of a pillar-based figurine and a model couch among its finds. In other words, these two altars were associated with materials characteristic of what I have called the 'nonconformist' element in Israelite Iron II religion (1987; below). Several pillar-based figurines were found at Aroer, but connections, if any, with the cuboidal altars also found there are, as yet, unpublished. Two other miniature altars were found, with pillar-based figurines, in a 'nonconformist' corporate worship setting in a grotto outside Jerusalem, Kenyon's 'Cave 1'. See Holland 1977: 154, Fig. 9: 21–22; Holladay 1987.

46. For textual explication of this practice, cf. Veenhof 1972: 26: 'The freighters [long term contracted employees] – . . .earned their wages by carrying on some private trade, with funds put at their disposal interest free . . . [They] could ship their private small quantities of merchandise in a top-pack [where the 'loose tin', used to defray tolls and subsistence costs *en route*, was also kept]. For archaeological attestation in the southern Levant during the late second millennium BCE, cf. Bergoffen 1991: 71–3.

47. Ingeniously termed a forgery by Yadin (1969; rebuttals by Van Beek and Jamme, and Kelso [both 1970]), but, in the light of other contacts with South Arabia, no longer so easily dismissed.

48. Whether the 'Four-room House' was exclusively or even primarily 'Israelite' is not material to the discussion. Early

examples at Tell Qasile Stratum X and Tell esh-Shari'a fall into the period characterized by burnished red slip, and thus may easily be the houses of resident 'Israelites', e.g., traders or functionaries. Note that the house form has not yet been identified at the Iron II Philistine site of Tel Miqne/Ekron. On the other hand, the form has recently been identified in at least three separate Iron II settings in Moab (oral communication, B. Routledge).

49. For an artifactually-based analysis of spatial use in Middle and Late Bronze Age houses in Palestine, see Daviau 1993.

50. E.B. Banning suggests that some of the subterranean structures of the Chalcolithic Period in the Negev may have served for animal shelters (personal communication).

51. This exercise does, however, put Gal's figure of 300 storejars, distributed over two phases of the small Phoenician fortress at Hurbat Rosh Zayit (Gal 1992; above) into more realistic perspective. Note that, of these 300, some apparently once held olive oil and some had burnt residues suggestive of wine storage, leaving only a reduced number holding carbonized grain.

52. The central hill country north of Tell en-Nasbeh may constitute an exception to this generalizing statement.

53. The prime candidate for a public storage complex during the period of the Monarchy is that in Area G at Hazor (A. Mazar 1990: 412). Detailed analysis suggests, however, that these facilities probably served yet unexcavated stables, relocated in Stratum VI to a position near the new city gateway.

54. Governmental store facilities suited to the segregated storage of grain, wine, oil, and other commodities are documented by discarded dockets, apparently not in primary context (Kaufman 1982: 231–3; 1992), at the 'Ostraca House' at Samaria, the long rooms probably serving for grain storage.

55. This effort, abundantly documented in the contemporary writings of the eighth-century prophets, is the subject of a current study by Marvin Chaney (in progress).

56. It must be admitted that our present knowledge of the late seventh and early sixth centuries (i.e., stratigraphy equiavalent to Lachish Level II) is less than ideal.

57. We must be sensitive to the possibilities inherent in suggestions like those of Ahlstrom or London (1982b; 1992) to the effect that the bulk of the Israelite and Judaean population might not have lived on the fortified *tells* (by which I take London to include fortified villages such as Tell Beit Mirsim and Tell en-Nasbeh). Such settlements seem to be present on the lower terraces at Megiddo (Yadin 1974), which otherwise, prior to the Neo-Assyrian occupation, is severely lacking in housing space on the *tell*, and must be posited for Samaria, where nonroyal domestic quarters have to date eluded investigators. Recent surveys, however, do not seem to have documented the dense pattern of dispersed occupational remains required by these models, nor have extensive excavations in 'large villages' like Tell Beit Mirsim or Tell en-Nasbeh shown the range of coexisting house sizes predicted by London (1992: 77).

58. Except for Houses 362, 366, 366, and associated loci, which seem to date to the first half of the ninth century BCE, nullifying de Vaux's socio-economic interpretation that this was a 'poor quarter' separated by a heavy wall from a much richer quarter. See Holladay 1966 (120–1), followed without attribution by McClellan 1987 (similarly unattributed is McClellan's treatment of the 'Unfinished Building', considered by de Vaux to be Omri's unfinished palace: cf. Holladay 1966: 114–16).

59. Nissen 1973; Johnson 1973. Based upon her analysis of the distribution of beveled rim bowls at Tal-e Malyan, Ilene Nicholas 1987 has proposed that they functioned as 'presentation bowls'

for payment of taxes owed to the government. More satisfying, however, is the explanation offered by Schmidt (1982), Millard (1988a) and M. Chazan and M. Lehner (1990), that these bowls, and some of their more restricted successors, served as Bread Molds, exactly analogously to pictorially-documented Egyptian Bread Molds of the third and second millennia. With respect to redistribution, note that rations of bread and beer characterized both Egyptian and Greater Mesopotamian societies. In our limited excavations at the small site of Tell el-Maskhuta we discovered, in various parts of the Saite and Hellenistic levels, three 'industrial' bakeries, one with 12 ovens simultaneously functioning, attached – in two cases (and almost certainly the third as well) to granaries – obviously for the provisioning of large work-forces (and their dependants). Nothing like this is known for Palestine.

60. Against the attribution of this facility to the notably non-Israelite site plan of Stratum III, note the very close resemblence to the great silo in Area W 31 at Beth Shemesh (Grant and Wright 1939:70), also sited near a stable complex.

61. By way of reference, at 450 m^3 capacity, Storage Pit 1414 could have contained 450 * 770 kg/m^3 [for wheat] = 346.5 metric tons of wheat. At a 15 percent milling, storage loss, and wastage rate, probably minimal for any public activity at this scale, this would be enough to sustain 1178 people for one year ((346.5 * 0.85) /

.25 metric tons/individual/year = 1178), or 4712 people for three months, assuming that wheat contributed more than 85 percent of their caloric intake (conveniently, B. Rosen 1986: 172–3). From a military viewpoint, however, it would not have been required that the authorities annually put by this much wheat against possible siege conditions. Assuming the completion of the barley harvest and the safe delivery of the annual levies/contracts for the provisioning of the chariot horses in the southern stables prior to an invasion (reasonable, since the enemy had to bring in his harvest as well), the stored barley (450 m^3 * 610 kg/m^3 [for barley] = 274.5 metric tons), with a nutritional value only 65 percent that of wheat, would have constituted an adequate grain reserve for all but a protracted siege, sufficing for some 2427 people for three months (0.65 nutritional value *(274.5 metric tons * 0.85 wastage factor) / .250 metric tons wheat equivalent/individual/0.25 yr) (cf. Rosen 1986: 172–3).

62. It is not impossible that Khirbet Abu Tabaq, in the Judaean Buqe'ah (Stager 1976b) is an early forerunner of these later estates.

63. The preceding comments apply to Israel and Judah as a whole, but may not apply to the functioning of the vastly expanded city of Jerusalem during the late eighth to early sixth centuries, about which we presently know very little.

23

THE KINGDOMS OF AMMON, MOAB AND EDOM: THE ARCHAEOLOGY OF SOCIETY IN LATE BRONZE/IRON AGE TRANSJORDAN (CA. 1400–500 BCE)

Øystein S. LaBianca and Randall W. Younker

Introduction

In this chapter our task is to elucidate the nature of society in central and southern Transjordan during the Late Bronze and Iron Ages (*ca.* 1400–500 BCE). More specifically, our assignment is to offer an anthropological perspective on the nature of the Kingdoms of Ammon, Moab and Edom. According to various ancient texts, including the Old Testament, the Ammonites once ruled the region surrounding Jordan's present-day capital city, Amman; the Moabites controlled the highland plateau east of the Dead Sea; and the Edomites made their home in the territory which extends eastward and westward from Wadi Arabah.

As the theme of this volume is the archaeology of society in the Holy Land, and one of its goals is to formulate proposals which may serve to stimulate new lines of inquiry in the 1990s and beyond, we shall not be held back by the inadequacies of much of the archaeological information currently to hand from our area – inadequate in terms of what it can tell us about society in Late Bronze and Iron Age Transjordan. We offer this chapter in the belief that explicitly-formulated proposals based on the limited data we already do have, will spark efforts by ourselves and others to devise new and even better ways to proceed with the process of empirical validation in the future.

To indicate where our discussion is headed, we provide here a summary statement of our main proposal: that the political entities which came into prominence in Iron Age Transjordan – namely those of the Ammonites, Moabites and Edomites – were not true nation-states, but rather, are better described as 'tribal kingdoms'. These kingdoms came into existence in a cascading fashion – first Ammon, then Moab and, last of all, Edom. Their emergence is attributable to the operation of several synergistically-related factors. To begin with, there was the expansion of plow agriculture by indigenous tribes in these Transjordanian highlands – a development stimulated in part by

the collapse of the Late Bronze Age city-state system. To counter mounting threats – especially from the Israelites – to their increasingly sedentary way of life, these tribes were forced to form more permanent cooperating polities than was possible by means of their traditional tribal coalitions. The solution was to establish 'tribal kingdoms' – polities which gave greater permanence to the cooperative networks customarily forged by tribal peoples to counter external threats to their homeland territories.

Before delving into the details of this proposal, however, we would like to comment briefly on previous work concerned with the question of the origins and nature of these three kingdoms.

Past proposals regarding the origin of the people of Iron Age Transjordan

As is well known, all of us who work in Transjordan owe a great debt to the pioneering research of Nelson Glueck (1934, 1935, 1939). On the basis of surface surveys he conducted in central and southern Transjordan in the 1930s, he came to the conclusion that – since there was very little evidence for *settled* occupation in Transjordan between *ca.* 1900 and 1300 BCE – the kingdoms of Ammon, Moab and Edom must have emerged rather suddenly towards the end of the Late Bronze Age. He claimed, in fact, that he could define the territories of their respective kingdoms from a string of border forts which he believed had already been built to protect their boundaries by the end of the thirteenth century BCE.

Glueck's conclusions were generally accepted by the scholars of his day, and were thus instrumental in shaping the direction of future research. Naturally, one of the first questions these findings prompted scholars to ask was: If there were no Ammonites, Moabites and Edomites in Transjordan prior to *ca.* 1300 BCE, where did they come from and what caused them to settle in Transjordan at this particular time?

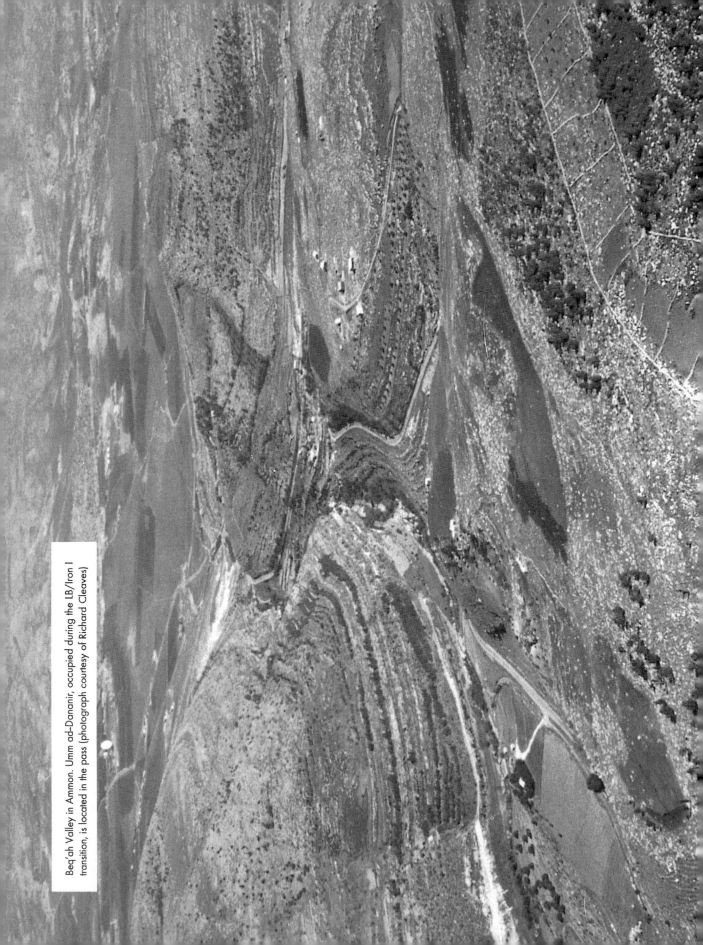

Beqʿah Valley in Ammon. Umm ad-Dananir, occupied during the LB/Iron I transition, is located in the pass (photograph courtesy of Richard Cleaves)

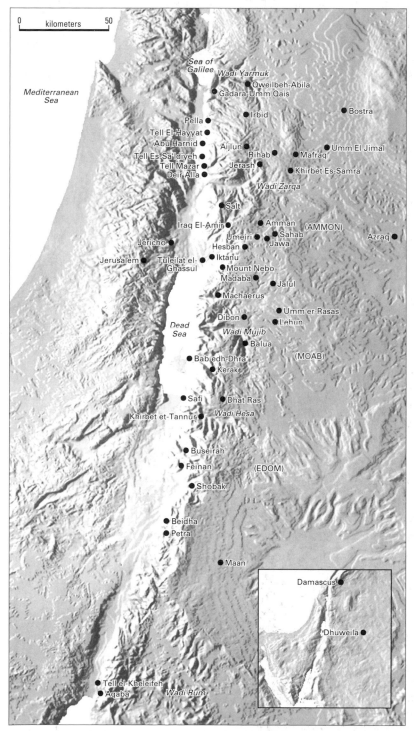

Figure 1 Map of key archaeological sites in Jordan (drawing by Laura M. Bredall, courtesy of the Horn Archaeology Museum)

Probably influenced by the then popular 'wave' hypothesis that suggested that cultural changes were the result of periodic migrations or invasions (cf. Luke 1965), Glueck, himself, suggested that the 'sparse' Late Bronze II occupation 'gave way early in that period to new waves of semi-Bedouins who became known as Edomites, Moabites, Ammonites, and Amorites' (Glueck 1971: 153). Glueck's lead was generally followed, with variations, by others including Alt (1940: 215), Noth (1960: 154) and Landes (1956: 31–5).

A challenge to this 'wave hypothesis' was Mendenhall's new theory that a 'peasants' revolt' in Palestine – which he believed was caused by widespread socio-economic collapse towards the end of the Late Bronze Age (Mendenhall 1973: 167, 168; 1983: 94–100) – led to people fleeing across the river to Transjordan and settling down there. Mendenhall believed that these refugees, along with others from Anatolia and southern Syria, became the founders of the kingdoms of Ammon, Edom and Moab. A slightly revised version of this view has recently been presented by Gottwald. His theory puts even greater emphasis on the role of upheavals in the collapsing urban centers of Late Bronze Age Palestine in causing people to migrate to the highlands on both sides of the Jordan river (Gottwald 1979: 429, 433).

Mention must also be made of recent proposals by McGovern with regard to Ammon (1981, 1986, 1987); Miller, Worschech and Knauf with reference to Moab (Miller 1992a, 1992b; Worschech 1990; Knauf 1992); and Bartlett and Knauf in the case of Edom (Bartlett 1989; Knauf 1992). To begin with, McGovern follows the lead of Mendenhall and Gottwald in attributing the origin of the highland monarchies of Iron Age Israel and Jordan to the collapse of the Late Bronze Age city-state system. McGovern's (1986) unique contribution is in positing the existence of a Late Bronze Age city-state system in the Amman area of Transjordan.

Miller, who has recently concluded a major archaeological survey in the Moab region, seems to depart altogether from proposals based on migration or urban collapse. In his view the origins of the Moabites are to be sought in the preexisting population of the highland plateau of Transjordan (Miller 1992a). Bartlett follows a similar line of argument for the origin of the Edomites (1989: 64, 65).

Worschech and Knauf, on the other hand, seem to be continuing the German tradition of Alt by maintaining a migration hypothesis in explaining the origins of the Moabites and Edomites, respectively. Worschech argues that the land of Moab was occupied by sedentary Emites and nomadic Shasu towards the end of the Late Bronze Age. Another nomadic group, the Shatu, infiltrated the region during the LB/Iron transition, merged with the nomadic Shasu and then displaced the sedentary Emites (Worschech 1990).

Knauf basically reverses the Old Testament account by suggesting that the Edomites were indigenous nomads who were later joined by migrating Horite tribes who had fled agricultural lands in Canaan after the collapse of the Late Bronze Age Canaanite city-state system (Knauf 1992: 49). We would refer to Bienkowski's recently published collection of essays by leading scholars on Moab and Edom for an excellent overview of the current state of research on Moab and Edom (Bienkowski 1992a).

The food systems as a barometer of local level social organization

Conspicuously absent from all the scholarly proposals we have mentioned thus far is any attempt to examine the available data from the perspective of anthropological/sociological models, to determine what the data can tell us about the nature of local level social organization among the Late Bronze and Iron Age societies of Transjordan. An excellent barometer of such local level social organization is, in our opinion, the local food system. This is because any people living in marginal environments, such as Transjordan, necessarily focus a considerable amount of time and attention on securing their subsistence base. This preoccupation with subsistence is, in turn, reflected in the institutions of that society which are structured in large part to facilitate the procurement of food by men, women and children.

Fortunately, not only are many aspects of these institutions, themselves, reflected in the archaeological record (Hopkins 1985: 251–61; Stager 1985), the activities they foster, in terms of obtaining subsistence security, also leave discernible traces and are, therefore, particularly amenable to archaeological reconstruction (LaBianca 1990, 1991). To the extent that these activities involved changes in patterns of land ownership, labor requirements, security arrangements, residential patterns, land use, and diet, they provide a window onto changes over time and space in local level social organization.

Pivotal to understanding the dynamic aspects of food systems' variability are the concepts of intensification and abatement. As we have explained elsewhere (LaBianca 1990, 1991), these concepts give an idea of the direction of variability in terms of the extent to which a given region is managed or exploited. Generally, as a region's food system intensifies, its inhabitants tend to become increasingly land-tied, due to increased investment in plow agriculture. Consequently, their residential patterns tend to become more sedentary. Intensification, therefore, is normally accompanied by sedentarization.

Abatement is said to occur when a given region's inhabitants diminish their reliance on plow agriculture in favor of livestock production within a given territory or home range. This generally involves adoption of more mobile residential patterns, or nomadization, whereby people, for the sake of their increased investment in range-tied pastoralism, turn to seasonal migration between watering places, ploughlands and pasturelands within a given home range.

Regional differences in availability of water

Rainfall data published for Jordan clearly show that the certainty of reliable and adequate rainfall for agriculture decreases as one moves from north to south (Howayej 1973; Shehadeh 1985). In the vicinity of Amman, for example, the

Plate 1 Rabbath–Amman (Citadel Hill) of Ammon, looking north. Ammon's abundant rainfall seems to have contributed to relatively early and dense settlement in this region in contrast to that of Moab and Edom to the south (photograph courtesy of Richard Cleaves)

long-term rainfall average is 500 mm annually, compared with 300-350 mm in Moab and 100-200 mm in Edom. In dry years, a minimum of 200 mm can be counted on in Ammon, whereas in Moab nor Edom dry years may result in significantly less rainfall. Commensurate with these data is the fact that there are between 10 and 15 days per year when rainfall exceeds 10 mm in Ammon, compared with only five to ten such days in Moab and Edom.

More important than the annual averages, of course, is the variability of seasonal rainfall; even if a given region gets plenty of annual rainfall, if it falls at the wrong time of the year it does no good (cf. Hopkins 1985; 84–90). The coefficient of seasonal rainfall variation ranges from an average of 36 percent in the northern and central regions of Jordan to 55 percent in the mountains of Kerak and Shoubak. Further south the percentage is even higher (Shehadeh 1985: 31). Other data may be brought to bear, but clearly, people in the south could not count on rainfall as a reliable source of water as their neighbors in the north could.

Regional differences in settlement and land use

Because of these differences in availability of water, and because of related differences in availability of cultivatable soils, wild plants and animals, and pasturage conditions, the ways in which these three homelands historically have been exploited by humans have differed significantly as well.

An idea of the historical differences between these three regions when it comes to their land use potential can be inferred from the modern patterns recorded in the Agricultural Atlas for Jordan (Howayej 1973). The picture provided of the land of Ammon, for example, is that of a region well suited to intensive cultivation of fruit trees and cereals, while offering excellent pasturage for cattle, sheep and goats.

The land of Moab also offers excellent conditions for production of cereals and pasture animals, and, in the Kerak region, fruit trees are readily produced. In contrast

to Ammon and Moab, the land of Edom is primarily suited to pasturing animals and limited production, especially in the Buseirah region, of cereals, olives and grapes.

Regional differences in relation to environmental risks

It is important to note at this point that the word 'suitable' is a relative term, since, given the necessary technological inputs and political and economic conditions, most of the various crops produced in Ammon, and the crop yields attained there, could well be duplicated in certain regions in Moab and Edom.

To begin with, the crucial environmental difference is the quantity of rain available in dry years. Given that 200 mm annual rainfall is considered to be a standard prerequisite for low-input rainfed production of cereals, fruits and vegetables in Jordan, only the land of Ammon offers farmers a dependable supply of rainfall. In other words, in Ammon a minimum of 200 mm can be counted on even in dry years. As noted earlier, this does not hold true for Moab and Edom, where minimum rainfall is less and, therefore, a sequence of three or four dry years can have more devastating consequences for farmers.

The consequence of this situation is that to become permanently attached to cultivatable plots of land in order to produce food has always been most risky in Edom, less so in Moab, and least so in Ammon. To understand how people have dealt with such risks in the past, it is necessary to probe deeper into the role of tribalism, on the one hand, and the state, on the other, in structuring options and influencing people's responses at the grass-roots level to changing political and economic influences (cf. Hopkins 1985: 258–60).

Tribalism, sedentarization and nomadization

Pivotal to understanding the dynamics of tribalism in Transjordan are the processes of sedentarization and nomadization mentioned earlier. This is because there appears to be a direct correlation between fluctuations in food system intensity levels, sedentarization, nomadization, local-level political organization (specifically tribalism) and the larger world system (especially as seen in externally imposed supra-tribal polities).

An integral factor in understanding this relationship is, in turn, the age-old notion of 'tribalism' – by which we simply mean strong in-group loyalty based on variously fluid notions of common unilineal descent. As we have examined the oscillations over time in patterns of land use and settlement in central Transjordan, we have come to see tribalism as being the enabling socio-cultural mechanism that has made it possible for small groups of kin to adapt to a succession of variously effective supra-tribal polities.

For example, over the past three millennia, the

indigenous population of Transjordan has had to adapt to a wide range of different types of supra-tribal polities. These included the indigenous Iron Age Kingdoms of Ammon, Moab, and Edom and the late first millennium BC Kingdom of Nabatea. These polities were followed by a succession of externally-imposed government bureaucracies, beginning with the Persian provincial administration about 2500 years ago and ending with the Late Ottoman administration in the early twentieth century. Thus, for more than two and a half millennia, Transjordan was 'ruled' – with extremely varying degrees of effectiveness – from Persia, Rome, Constantinople, Damascus, Cairo, Baghdad and Istanbul (LaBianca 1990).

Against the backdrop of these transient and mostly externally imposed supra-tribal polities, tribalism has provided a highly resilient and flexible system of local-level political organization by means of which small groups of kin have been able to cope with political and economic uncertainties in an already hazardous natural environment. Based as it is on the principle of unilineal descent, tribalism has provided a system of local-level political organization that has enabled both cultivators and herders to acquire, maintain and defend such ploughlands, pasturelands, habitation sites and water sources as they have needed to maintain their way of life. One way to conceptualize the notion of 'tribe', therefore, is to think of it as a 'unit of subsistence' (Marx 1973).

It is possible, in fact, to posit the existence of an axis along which local-level political organization shifted in the past. At one end of this axis is a comparatively rigid system of unilineal descent which typically accompanied increased investment in crops; at the other end is a comparatively loose system of unilineal descent which typically accompanied increased investment in pasture animals.

The reason why sedentarization normally leads to development of more rigid lineage, is that as kin-groups begin to expend labor on clearing, terracing, ploughing, planting, watering and guarding particular plots of ploughland, their sense of ownership and investment – along with feelings of in-group loyalty and obligation – are heightened. Such sentiments make it harder for 'outsiders' to be incorporated – hence the tendency towards more rigid lineages as people become more settled and land-tied.

The reason why nomadization normally leads to development of looser, more flexible, lineages is that as kin-groups become more dependent on access to widely-dispersed rangeland pastures, cooperative alignments which enable them to reach beyond the social and territorial boundaries of smaller blood-related kin groups offer distinct advantages. By means, therefore, of such processes as 'telescoping', 'fusioning' and 'grafting', pastoral nomads continually generate loose and flexible networks of cooperation and alignments, through which they maintain control over widespread rangeland pastures, watering places, camping sites, storage depots and burial

grounds (see Peters 1970 for a good discussion of these processes). Hence the tendency toward more loose and flexible lineages as people become more mobile and range-tied. (cf. Marx 1967: 190, 1973; Lancaster 1981; 35, 151; Hiatt 1984; Eickelman 1989: 89).

Most tribes in Jordan are made up of a combination of variously land-tied and range-tied households and kin groups (e.g. Glubb 1938; Hiatt 1984; Van Der Kooij and Ibrahim 1989; LaBianca 1990; cf. Barth 1961). This is because, at any given point in time, a certain amount of sedentarization and nomadization is continually occurring among individual households, depending on personal circumstances and shifts in economic and ecological conditions within the tribe's homeland. Thus, some households may be in the process of becoming more land-tied and settled, others may be in the process of becoming more range-tied and mobile.

The greater flexibility of predominantly nomadic tribes – such as Jordan's 'bedouin' tribes – has traditionally made it easier for them to form larger corporate groups than has been the case among predominantly settled tribes (cf. Barth 1961, 1973). This fact, in turn, has given them a political advantage vis-à-vis more land-tied tribes living in hamlets, villages and towns within their territories. In the past, therefore, such settled tribes have frequently been politically enmeshed in various ways under the more inclusive organizational structures of the more nomadic tribes. In the Hesban region, for example, the Beni Sakhr and the Adwan – the politically dominant tribes in this region during the nineteenth century (CE) – were both predominantly nomadic tribes. Within the traditional rangeland of each existed several smaller, more land-tied tribes, whose relationship to these dominant tribes was that of clients or slaves (LaBianca 1990: 51–106).

The extent to which a particular tribe includes both land-tied and range-tied households appears to vary over time. For example, when political and economic circumstances make land-tied production of crops more attractive, the center of gravity – in terms of the tribe's social organization – is likely to shift in the direction of clans and lineages bonded by means of more or less rigid lines of descent. However, when circumstances make range-tied production of pasture animals more attractive, the organizational center of gravity is likely to shift in the direction of hierarchically organized groups of kin and non-kin, more or less loosely bonded together via lineal descent through a claimed common ancestor.

A consequence of the co-occurrence of the processes of sedentarization and nomadization among Jordan's tribal people is that residential patterns representing different segments along the sedentism-nomadism continuum have coexisted in varying proportions in time and space. At any given point, nomadic, seminomadic, semisedentary, or sedentary groups have lived together in varying ratios (see Gubser 1984: 24–25 for a succinct description of each of these terms); what has changed over time and space is the extent to which each has been represented proportionally.

The role of supra-tribal polities

While there can be little doubt about the fact that tribalism has always played an important role at the local level of Jordanian society – up to and including the present (cf. Gubser 1984; Shami 1984) – what has been its role in facilitating the emergence of various supra-tribal polities in Jordan's past? How, in turn, has the emergence of such polities impacted on tribalism at the grass-roots level? A consideration of these two questions is relevant here.

The birth of the modern nation-state of Jordan provides a clue, of sorts, to the role of tribalism in the formation of indigenous kingdoms. In Jordan, as in other countries of the modern Middle East, there are many reminders of the continuing importance of the tribal order. This can be seen, for example, in the fact that tribal law exists side-by-side with civil law and Islamic law. Furthermore, as is well known, King Hussein of Jordan has depended on Transjordan's indigenous tribes and their descendants for his most loyal support since the earliest days of his administration (Glubb 1938). Thus, although an important role was initially played by the British in the establishment of the present-day monarchy, its remarkable persistence and continued popularity is, to a significant degree, attributable to the fact that Jordan's tribal elite coalesced around their new king – seeing his role as that of a sort of 'sheikh of sheikhs'.

This ability to coalesce – to unite together into one body – is something which Transjordan's tribes have done for centuries in response to a variety of external threats. What the monarchy did, however, was to give a greater degree of permanence to the common goal of unity for the sake of mutual defense and prosperity. Before the monarchy, alliances among different tribes tended to be impermanent and ever-shifting in response to circumstances; the establishment of the monarchy provided a supra-tribal rallying point for demonstrating unity in the face of western colonial ambition and the threat it presented to the way of life of Jordan's indigenous peoples (Glubb 1938; cf. Bates and Rassam 1983: 259, 261).

With the coalescence of tribes around a supra-tribal leader – as in the case of the present-day Hashemite monarchy – centrifugal forces typically come into play which tend to weaken, to some extent, the political power of the traditional tribal order and its elite. This is especially true in the case of predominantly land-tied tribes. This process of depoliticization was partly a result of the introduction of government representatives and bureaucrats, who gradually became more powerful than traditional tribal leaders, especially in the more settled areas. The modern government of Jordan, to use a contemporary example, has established a large array of ministries, each with its special mandate – defense, agriculture, education, health, forestry, or tourism and antiquities. These ministries have assumed responsibility for setting priorities and instituting changes in how things are done. Ironically, a priority with many of them is to encourage the settlement of nomadic and seminomadic households and tribes. Other priorities might include land registration; the establishment of a standing army; the construction of large-scale water collection and storage facilities; road building; enhancement of commerce and exchange; and similar undertakings for the sake of the common good.

A consequence of changes in the extent to which Transjordan has come under the control of supra-tribal powers is that the influence of the tribal order over organization of production in the region has waxed and waned. Thus, during periods of increasing centralized control of production, urban-controlled bureaucracies have arisen to compete with preexisting tribally-based systems of control. When these bureaucratic systems have run out of steam, the tribally based systems have reemerged to take full control again. Consequently, tribalism has coexisted with a succession of competing systems of supra-tribal organization throughout most of Transjordan's history (cf. Bates and Rassam 1983: 258).

The spread of supra-tribal systems of organization in Transjordan has historically followed a particular pattern. More often than not, they have progressed from the north to the south and from the west to the east. Thus, in the twentieth century, the northern part of the country was settled before the central part, and the central part before the southern part.

Tribalism – more than an evolutionary stage

In the Middle Eastern context, the concept of 'tribe' is far broader than is implied by those who would see it as a level of social organization somewhere between a 'band' and a 'chiefdom' (Service 1962; Frick 1985; Renfrew and Bahn 1991: 156). As Khuri (1980: 12) has noted, tribalism is 'not a single phenomenon, an undifferentiated whole, a peripheral social system or simply a stage in the evolution of human civilization'. It is rather, as Bates and Rassam (1983: 258) explain, 'a persistent social and political force bringing together people for many different purposes, and doing so in the context of many different, competing, or alternative principles of alignment'. In fact, they continue, 'what most distinguishes the Middle East politically is the persistence of tribalism coexisting with the state'.

It is the unique challenge which marginal environments throughout much of the Middle East present their local inhabitants that has assured a continuing and unique role for tribalism in this part of the world. By marginal, we refer to a unique set of complex environmental conditions that bestow unpredictable, alternating periods of feast and famine in a complex, variegated pattern across the landscape. In such environments, the way to endure is to join risk-reducing networks of people that not only enable individuals and families to survive (Hopkins 1985: 251–61), but, in some cases, to even accumulate a surplus.

Predictions regarding Ammon, Moab and Edom

The foregoing discussion provides a basis for seven hypotheses regarding the development of society in Ammon, Moab, and Edom during the Iron Age:

1. The ancestral roots of the people of Ammon, Moab and Edom are to be found among peoples who lived in their homelands prior to their sojourn into the light of recorded history.
2. Ammon would have reached a higher level of settlement density, food system intensity, and supra-tribal organization than Moab, and that Moab exceeded Edom in this regard.
3. Land-tied tribalism would have emerged most fully in Ammon, less so in Moab, and least of all in Edom.
4. As a correlate of the third prediction, range-tied tribalism persisted to the greatest extent in Edom, less so in Moab, and least of all in Ammon.
5. The ideological template of the kingdoms which arose in Iron Age Transjordan was rooted in the network-generating tribalism of the population that brought them into existence.
6. The tribal kingdoms which came into existence in Iron Age Transjordan were not true nation-states as commonly defined by anthropologists.
7. Finally, we would predict that the factors which contributed to the rise of these tribal kingdoms were synergistic in nature in that they included a combination of cooperating external and internal stimuli and developments.

Society and societal changes in Iron Age Transjordan

We turn next to an examination of the archaeological evidence from Iron Age Transjordan to see which, if any, of the above listed hypotheses find support in the available data.

Origins

With regard to the ancestral roots of the people of Ammon, Moab and Edom, there are no compelling archaeological reasons for supposing that the Iron Age inhabitants of these homelands originated outside them. To begin with, studies of the material culture from Tell el-Umeiri – an Ammonite site excavated by the Madaba Plains Project under the direction of Larry Herr – point to a process of continuous development between the Late Bronze Age and the Iron Age (Herr 1992). Similar conclusions have been reached by Wimmer (1987a, 1987b) at Tell Safut and McGovern at Umm ad-Dananir (1986, 1987).

The situation in Moab is similar. Miller (1992a: 889), for example, states explicitly with regard to Moab that there is no evidence for a cultural break between the Late Bronze Age and the Iron Age. While some excavations in Moab such as Dibon (Winnett and Reed 1964; Tushingham 1972), Balua (Worschech 1986 et al.), have so far failed to turn up evidence for occupation during the crucial LB/Iron I transitional period, others, such as Lehun (Homès Fredericq 1992), Jalul (Younker et al. 1993: 216) and Hesban (Sauer, personal communication) have (Plate 2).

As for Edom, it must be admitted that at present the evidence for LB/Iron I occupation is quite sparse (MacDonald 1992a, b). Nevertheless, we agree with Bartlett's assessment that '[i]n the absence of any clear evidence that Edom was resettled by the invasion of foreign groups with new distinctive ways of life, it is easier to believe that the indigenous, if limited, population expanded with improving economic circumstances' (Bartlett 1989: 65). (We might add that while some specialists of the region doubt the evidence for Iron I sedentary occupation in Edom (e.g., Hart 1992; Bienkowski 1992b), others are not so sure (e.g., Sauer 1985, 1986; Finkelstein 1992a, 1992b; Herr, personal communication). Hopefully, future analysis and publication will resolve this dispute.)

The one dissenting voice to the story told by these other investigators is that of Knauf, who has most recently argued that Iron Age sedentary occupation in Edom was precipitated by a migration of Canaanite agricultural newcomers (whom Knauf would equate with the Horite tribes of Gen. 36) (1992: 49). But even he acknowledges the contribution of the preexisting population in the region to the mixture of people who eventually became known as Edomites (ibid.).

Here we do not necessarily disagree with Knauf (although his specific identity for these people may be debated), for although the majority of the ancestors of the Iron Age Ammonites, Moabites and Edomites apparently came from among populations which had existed in their respective homelands previously, this does not rule out the role of a certain amount of migration. It is, in fact, very likely that these homelands became the end-destination for many individuals and groups of kin displaced by the upheavals of the Late Bronze Age. However, in our opinion, there are no compelling reasons to argue that these refugees supplanted the indigenous tribes as the new masters of Iron Age Transjordan.

Ammon most densely settled, Edom least

Most scholars working in Transjordan seem to agree that the density of the sites decreases as one moves southward (e.g., Weippert 1979: 26). It would be reassuring if this perception could be confirmed by a comparative analysis of site densities of the Ammon, Moab and Edom regions which have been derived from recent surveys. However, because not all survey methods are uniform and the dating

Plate 2   Lehun of Moab and the Wadi Mujib looking north. Recent excavations there indicate occupation during the LB/Iron transition period (photograph courtesy of Richard Cleaves)

Plate 3   Buseirah in Edom, looking northwest. The excavators of Buseirah, Tawilan and Umm el-Biyara believe that occupation at these settlements began in Iron II, although some scholars believe some Iron I pottery was found as well. Certainly, sedentary occupation appears later in Edom than in Moab and Ammon (photograph courtesy of Richard Cleaves)

of surface sherds is difficult, any such analysis would at present yield uncertain results (Miller 1992b: 80).

However, if one limits the comparison to fortified settlements, a distinctive pattern emerges (Dearman 1992: 72–3). Ammon appears to have a number of fairly substantial walled settlements with occupational histories that continue from the Late Bronze Age into the Iron Age. These include Umm ad-Dananir (McGovern 1986), Tell Safut (Ma'ayeh 1960: 115; Wimmer 1987a, 1987b), Rabbath-Amman (Ward 1966: 9–15; Bennett 1979: 159; Dornemann 1983: 105–21), Tell el-'Umeiri (Geraty et al. 1986, 1990a,b; Herr et al. 1990; Younker et al. 1990), possibly Tell Jawa (Younker et al. 1990) and Tell Sahab (Ibrahim 1987: 77). The significance of walled settlements lies in the fact that they reflect a more sedentary occupation with more permanent ties to their surrounding ploughland.

When one moves into Moab there are *no* clear LB walled settlements whose occupational history continued into the Iron Age (Dearman 1992: 72). A possible exception may be Jalul, located in the northern half of the Madaba plateau, well north of the Wadi Mujib, where environmental conditions were more conducive to intensive agriculture. Indeed Jalul is closer to the Ammon sites listed above than it is to the Moabite sites south of the Wadi Mujib.

The paucity of walled settlements in the heart of Moab, south of the Wadi Mujib on the Kerak plateau, is confirmed by the scarcity of classical *tell* sites in Moab – since it is the presence of walled settlements which provide the physical structure upon which the *tell* will form (Dearman 1992: 73). This is not to say there were no sedentary villages in Moab at this time. Surveys clearly show that there were (Miller 1991). However, there is no evidence of interest in protecting long-term agricultural investments such as LB/Iron I fortified settlements in Ammon imply. In our opinion, Dearman correctly interprets the lack of continually occupied walled settlements in LB and Iron I Moab as reflective of a population whose economy was largely based on range-tied pastoralism.

Finally, in Edom not only are there no clear LB walled settlements that continue into the Iron Age, there are virtually no LB settlements at all. The only exceptions are six sites in the northernmost area of Edom (MacDonald 1992b). The scarcity of settlements, however, does not necessarily mean a lack of inhabitants. More likely, it reflects a shift along the subsistence continuum to a very high degree of pastoral nomadism (LaBianca 1990). Evidence that people did inhabit this region during the Late Bronze Age is provided by contemporary Egyptian literary sources (Kitchen 1992).

Land-tied tribalism most prevalent in Ammon

Given, as we have seen, that Ammon seems to have been both most densely settled and most intensively cultivated, it is reasonable to infer that here, to a greater degree than in Moab or Edom, the ranks of land-tied cultivators swelled the most. This is not to say, however, that range-tied pastoralists were completely displaced in Ammon – they most surely were not. They continued, no doubt, to coexist and accommodate themselves to the ascent of land-tied tribalism and the new, supra-tribal polity which came to be known as the Kingdom of Ammon.

The description we have proposed for the relations between land-tied cultivators and range-tied pastoralists in Ammon during Iron II applies pretty well to Moab also. Using slightly different language, Miller has described it well:

> There will have been a few modest cities, each with its king who also controlled some of the surrounding countryside. However tribal elders also will have played a role in the political structure, especially among the villages scattered throughout the land. Also from time to time there will have arisen local chieftains who carved out local kingdoms (Miller 1992a: 890).

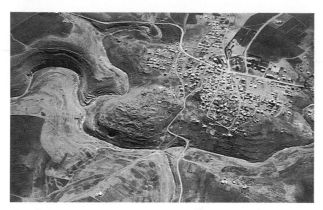

Plate 4 Dibon of Moab, looking east (photograph courtesy of Richard Cleaves)

In our opinion, it is also not impossible that during times of severe economic, political, and other challenges, the inherent fluidity which tribal people have in forming networks and cooperative alignments could result in over-arching regional alliances that would encompass the entire territory of Moab periodically and – on even rarer occasions – include neighboring tribal kingdoms such as Ammon and Edom. Such an example may be found in 2 Chr. 20 where the Ammonites, Moabites and Edomites form a common alliance against the Judahite King, Jehoshaphat.

Range-tied tribalism most prevalent in Edom

As we have seen, Edom also experienced a certain amount of sedentarization of its inhabitants, especially during Iron II. Particularly in the best agricultural areas, communities of tribal settlers came into existence. We know this, for example, from the results of excavations at sites such as Umm el-Biyara, Buseirah (Plate 3) and Tawilan (cf. Bienkowski 1992b). The fact that the land of Edom was a much riskier place for people to settle down and live, however, assured that bedouin tribes would continue to be both proportionately better represented and more influential ideologically in Edom.

Practically speaking, what this meant was that the 'safety net' of cooperative alignments and personal connections – which for generations had enabled the bedouin inhabitants of the high-risk Edomite homeland to survive – persisted and prevailed. To a much greater extent than in Moab and Ammon, therefore, the lives of the tribal settlers who succeeded in establishing themselves in Edom were enmeshed in the politics and economics of the bedouin. For this reason Knauf's characterization of Edomite society as 'never more than . . . a "tribal state", i.e. a state where a thin veneer of central administration hardly disguised the structure of a society that basically functioned on a level not penetrated by the state' (Knauf 1992: 52) is, in our opinion, essentially accurate.

Interestingly, the greater emphasis on network generating range-tied tribalism in the environmentally more severe territory of Edom may receive support from the 'Edomite king list' in Gen. 36. Scholars have long noted that none of the kings in this list was the son of his predecessor, and that each king is attributed to a different city. Moreover, these kings are introduced as 'the kings who reigned *in* Edom, not Kings *of* Edom' (Weippert 1982: 155). Regardless of when one would date this text (e.g., Weippert 1982: 155; Knauf 1992: 52), it accurately reflects the proliferation of tribes and tribal chieftains which is typical of an ecologically hazardous region such as Edom.

The ideological roots of Transjordan's tribal kingdoms

We believe that the ideological roots of the kingdoms which arose in Iron Age Transjordan are to be found primarily within the experience and knowledge of the populations who brought them into existence. In other words, we would argue that the kingdoms which arose in Ammon, Moab and Edom came into existence through the same process of expansion of social networking that in the past had brought tribes and tribal federations into variously transient alignments. Their emergence thus represented a coalescence of land-tied cultivators and range-tied pastoralists for the purpose of collectively defending – now on a more permanent basis – their common home territories.

Although it is true that an ancient Near Eastern 'king' (*milk, malik, malk, sharru*) could include the head of an empire, state or tribe (Knauf 1992: 49), there is evidence that the individuals who appropriated the title generally laid claim to power and influence that surpassed that of mere local bedouin sheikhs or village headmen. To see more precisely what the nature of this difference in power was, we shall take a closer look at the ninth century BCE polity of Mesha of Moab.

According to the Mesha Inscription (see Window 2, Figure 2.1 p. 414), Mesha identified himself as *Dayboni*, that is, a Dibonite. His people were called Dibonites and his place of residence was the city of Dibon (Plate 4). However, he clearly claimed authority beyond the boundaries of his home city and people, for he was not merely the ruler of Dibon or the Dibonites; rather, he was the 'king of Moab'. During times of external threat he could call upon 'men from Moab', that is, individuals beyond his kin circle of 'obedient' or 'loyal' Dibonites. His ability to call up the 'men from Moab' clearly elevated him beyond the level of a local Dibonite sheikh or chief. Even Mesha's enemies, the Israelites, who knew Mesha primarily as a 'cattle magnate' (*noged*, 2 Kgs. 3: 4), also recognized him as 'king of Moab' (ibid.).

It is important to note, however, that none of these activities or achievements (including his claim to have built water systems and roads) demands a social organization at the level of the state as defined by anthropologists (see below). Besides the absence of characteristics typical of state level organization (see Renfrew and Bahn 1991: 156–7 and below), Mesha does not appear to have had jurisdiction over all land that was traditionally considered to be the land of Moab. While part of the reason for this was that aliens clearly occupied some of this land, there is, nevertheless, little evidence that Mesha was active in Moabite land south of Wadi Mujib. Indeed, Miller argues convincingly that only certain areas north of the Wadi Mujib were definitely under Mesha's control. Both Mesha's military campaigns and 'public works' projects are concentrated almost exclusively in this northern region, in and around Dibon and the lands immediately adjacent to it. While it has been suggested that the individual commemorated on the Kerak Inscription, '[k]mshyt, the king of Moab', was Mesha's father and, thus, a pan-Moab dynastic kingdom must have existed, Miller is correct in asserting that there is, in fact, no definite evidence that this individual is the father of Mesha. If [k]mshyt of the Kerak Inscription is not Mesha's father, this inscription could, ironically, actually be used as evidence of a non-Dibonite, Moabite tribal king over the Kerak Plateau. If so, that would mean there could have been several 'Moabite' tribes within Moab. As Miller points out, all we know for sure 'is that a ruler who claimed the title "king of Moab" left an inscription at Kerak' (1992b: 87). In short, everything we currently know about Moab at this time is consistent with the presence of a tribal society.

The nature of Transjordan's tribal kingdoms

In further support of our claim that the kingdoms which arose in Ammon, Moab and Edom are best understood as 'tribal kingdoms' rather than 'states' we will note the absence of a number of essential features which typify true 'states' as commonly defined by anthropologists. True states are generally understood to be the most complex level of social organization; the role of kinship relations in such a society is diminished, religious and political authority are typically separate, the ruler usually maintains a standing army and a significant amount of the population is settled in urban centers which function within a pronounced settlement hierarchy (cf. Renfrew and Bahn 1991: 156, 157). Such complex societies are characterized by a significant amount of ethnic plurality and social differentiation (Kamp and Yoffee 1980: 87).

To illustrate briefly what state-level social complexity might look like 'on the ground' in Syro-Palestine one might examine western Palestine during the Late Bronze Age (but see Falconer 1987). Even a cursory view of the archaeological remains of Late Bronze Age western Palestine shows a considerable variation in size, function and ethnic inhabitation of the numerous settlements there.

Some sites such as Megiddo and Hazor appear to be major centers which exhibit fairly sophisticated city planning with special areas set apart for administrative complexes, temples, etc. The fact that the palace is separated from the city's temples suggests the presence of competing centers of authority within the same society.

Other settlements such as Aphek, which appear to be 'residencies' for Egyptian governors, testify to additional layers of influence and authority within Canaanite society at large. Isolated temple sites such as Mevorakh and Lachish, reflect a variety of religious practices and beliefs. Other settlements appear to be nothing more than simple agricultural villages which supported the larger centers. Still others, such as Tel Masos, appear to be trading centers with a diverse ethnic composition. This rather complex and sophisticated view of western Palestine's Late Bronze Age society is reflected in Egyptian texts such as the Amarna Tablets.

However, this picture of western Palestine stands in contrast to that of the Transjordanian plateau during the Late Bronze Age. In addition to the fact that technical studies on the ceramics at Deir Alla suggest that Transjordan (at least in the north) appears to have developed a unique pottery tradition distinct from that of Cisjordan (Franken 1969; Franken and Power 1971), the variety and complexity reflected in Cisjordan's settlements is lacking to the east. While a great deal of attention has been given to the discovery of LB sites in Transjordan, so far none display the size or complexity of, say, Megiddo or Hazor. In fact, the only significant LB sites are limited to Amman (although little is really yet known about the LB occupation), Safut, Sahab, Umeiri, Jalul, and possibly Jawa (south), mostly in the north of Transjordan.

So far, little monumental architecture has been recovered – no palaces, or 'governor's residences', and the only possible temple that has been reported is the enigmatic Amman Airport Structure, an isolated building whose precise origin and function is still a matter of debate (see Wright 1966; Campbell and Wright 1969; Hennessy 1966; Finkelstein 1988: 343; especially intriguing is Finkelstein's resurrection of an idea originally put forward by Campbell and Wright, that this structure served tribal pastoralists). Finally, none of these sites in Transjordan are comparable to the larger sites west of the Jordan river, and were probably self-sufficient in terms of subsistence (see above). The presence of exotic wares – such as Mycenaean and Cypriot pottery which appear in both western Palestine and Transjordan and undoubtedly arrived via trade – does not necessitate the presence of an urban or state society.

However, what about the Iron Age, especially the Iron II period, for which archaeological evidence clearly shows a peak in sedentarization (including urbanization) and intensive agriculture? The impressive material remains from this period, especially monumental remains such as

Figure 2 Statue of Ammonite King (Iron IIB). More statuary appears in Iron Age Ammon than in any other of the Transjordanian kingdoms (drawing by Laura M. Bredall after the Museum of Tourism and Antiquities, Jordan, courtesy of the Horn Archaeology Museum). Height = .48 meters

Figure 3 Statue of Crowned Figure (Ammonite) (Iron IIB). Numerous busts of 'crowned' figures, similar to the head of this statue, have been found in the Amman region. They have generally been interpreted as busts of Ammonite kings, although some scholars have suggested they represent deities (drawing by Laura M. Bredall after the Museum of Tourism and Antiquities, Jordan, courtesy of the Horn Archaeology Museum). Height = .25 meters

the Ammonite statuary (Figures 2 and 3), the Balu'a Stele (Figure 4), the Mesha Stele (see Window 2, Figure 2.1), and the 'Warrior Stele' (Figure 5) suggest to many the presence of fully-fledged, albeit minor or secondary, states.

Certainly, by the time of the Assyrian period (Iron IIB) it appears that supra-tribal polities had fully developed in each of the Transjordanian tribal territories – that is, within each territory leaders had emerged who were able to build networks that ultimately coalesced all of the related tribes within the traditional territory. Formerly intrusive tribes, such as the Israelites, had by this time either been physically ejected or fully absorbed.

Synergism of contributing factors

It remains to account for the reasons why these tribal kingdoms came into existence in the first place. We would highlight three causal factors.

First, the changes in rural highland regions of Palestine occasioned by the collapse of the Late Bronze Age city-state system (Coote and Whitlam 1987; Dever 1992) would have disrupted the economic networks which the Transjordanian tribes were tied into. While in many ways these tribes were self-sufficient, the presence of items such as cylinder seals from North Syria, Mycenaean pottery, and faience amulets and scarabs from Egypt

suggest that they supplemented their wants and needs through a variety of trade networks (e.g., Deir Alla and the Amman Airport Structure). Undoubtedly, the disruption of these external contacts served as a catalyst for local farmers, craftsmen, etc. to fill the vacuum with locally-produced goods and products. Thus, the development was set in motion which led gradually to the intensification of plow agriculture during the Iron Age.

Second, the collapse of the lowland cities in adjacent regions such as western Palestine would have produced a number of refugees. Some of these refugees, who are likely to have included traders, craftsmen and farmers, were probably assimilated into the indigenous population of Iron I Transjordan – adding, as it were, a leaven to the mix. Their modifying effect resulted in the opening up of these highlands to wider trade networks and the creation of a market for the exchange of textiles and agricultural products. This situation no doubt increased the momentum of the move towards intensified sedentary agriculture.

Third, the arrival around 1200 BCE of the Philistines in Palestine escalated the threat to the region's land-tied settlers. This threat was first felt by the Israelites who, sometime toward the end of the eleventh century BCE, eventually responded to it by appointing a king and

Figure 4 Balu'a stele from Moab (thirteenth–twelfth century BCE) (drawing by Laura M. Bredall after the Museum of Tourism and Antiquities, Jordan, courtesy of the Horn Archaeology Museum). Height = 1.7 meters

creating a standing army. The Israelites, in turn, soon embarked on their own conquests, including invasion of the lands of Ammon and Moab. This situation is what seems to have precipitated the formation of supra-tribal polities in Ammon and Moab.

The collapse of the Iron Age kingdoms of Transjordan

As Sauer has noted, most scholars, following Josephus (*Antiquities* 10.9.7), assume that Ammon, Moab and Edom were destroyed by the Neo-Babylonians shortly after the destruction of Jerusalem *ca.* 586 BCE (e.g., Landes 1961; cf. Sauer 1986: 18). However, closer analysis of literary sources, as well as new archaeological evidence, suggests these kingdoms actually continued well into the Hellenistic period (Sauer 1986: 18). For example, the Madaba Plains Project Survey (see Window 1 pp. 412–13) has located numerous 'farmstead' sites that appear to have been occupied into the Persian and Hellenistic periods.

This has been confirmed by excavations at one of these sites, Rujm Selim (Geraty et al. 1988). Moreover, the recent discovery of several seal inscriptions at Tell el-Umeiri suggest that Ammon was organized as a Persian province, similar to that of Judah to the west (Herr 1992).

By the Roman and Byzantine periods, however, the Transjordanian kingdoms do seem to have disappeared from historical accounts. This is not to say that these people completely disappeared. However, it would appear that the tribal polities were completely subsumed by the rise of the Roman Empire. As new tribal configurations emerged to confront the new challenges, the ancient identities of Ammon, Moab and Edom were lost.

Figure 5 The Rujm al-'Abd ('Shihan Warrior') stele from Moab (thirteenth–twelfth century BCE). Thought to represent a warrior god. The occurrence of monumental reliefs and inscriptions such as the Rujm al-'Abd stele, the Balu'a stele and the Mesha Inscription appear to reflect the growing power of Transjordan's tribal kingdoms during the Iron Age (drawing by Laura M. Bredall after Réunion des musées nationaux, Paris, courtesy of the Horn Archaeology Museum.

Conclusion

Because of Transjordan's inland location, the environmental hazards of it being a desert frontier, and its position astride a corridor linking three continents – Europe, Asia and Africa – tribalism has not only survived, but thrived there. Over successive centuries, it has coexisted with supra-tribal polities of various kinds. At times, Transjordanian tribalism has spawned some of these polities – as appears to have been the case with the Kingdoms of Ammon, Moab and Edom. At other times, it has been suppressed under the weight of externally imposed bureaucracies, as in Roman times.

Because, however, it is a force that is rooted in the age-old loyalties of family and kin, it has not gone away, instead, it has persisted through the centuries and millennia in Transjordan and throughout much of the rest of the Middle East. It thus represents a powerful example of what Braudel (1972) has called the *longue-durée* – a deep historical undercurrent which has enabled and facilitated the response of Transjordan's population to ecological, political, and economic uncertainties and changes since the dawn of history.

THE STORY OF THE MADABA PLAINS PROJECT

How a team of archaeologists decide where to dig and what to look for when they dig are questions many people often ask. How, for example, did the Madaba Plains Project — with its excavations at Tell Hesban, Tell el-Umeiri, Tell Jawa, Tell Jalul and several other sites in central Transjordan — end up studying the way of life of the Ammonites?

The Madaba Plains Project began with the Heshbon Expedition, an excavation organized by Professor Siegfried S. Horn of Andrews University and Professor Roger S. Boraas of Upsala College. Its original aims were twofold: First, from the perspective of Horn (its director) and his financial backers, to excavate Tell Hesban to see if it was the Heshbon frequently mentioned in Old Testament accounts in connection with the Israelite conquest of Palestine. Second, from the perspective of Boraas, its chief archaeologist, to dig the *tell* as carefully as possible to attain for central Transjordan a solid stratigraphic and ceramic baseline.

These dual aims were at times difficult to harmonize because they called for almost opposing approaches in terms of excavation strategy. Whereas the quest for biblical Heshbon called for rapid removal of layers above the Iron Age, the quest for a multi-period stratigraphic baseline for central Transjordan called for the meticulous peeling away of layers, one by one. These conflicting aims resulted in numerous strategy discussions, both inside and outside the trenches throughout the first three seasons (1968, 1971, 1973).

By the end of the third season, however, when it had become apparent that there was not much to be found at Tell Hesban that

had direct bearing on the Israelite conquest question, the second aim emerged as the excavation's primary one. When, in 1974, Professor Lawrence T. Geraty, Horn's successor at Andrews, took over as director (1974, 1976), he continued to make systematic excavation of the site — as well as scientific recovery of geological samples, animal bones, and carbonized seeds — a top priority. He also lent full support to ethno-archaeological research in the village of Hesban.

In the meantime, however, a search had been launched for other possible sites that might someday be excavated and may turn up information relevant to the conquest question. This hope, along with a desire to trace the remains of the Roman road leading to and from Tell Hesban, led to the start-up in 1973 of the Hesban Regional Survey (1973, 1974, 1976). This survey, which concentrated on the region within ten kilometers of Tell Hesban, ended up locating 148 archaeological sites — representing the entire span of history in the region.

As a consequence of the multiple lines of research begun by the Heshbon Expedition — stratigraphic excavations, collection of scientific samples of all kinds, regional survey — a dilemma emerged as plans for final synthesis and publication were being made. This dilemma was how to fit all of these different lines of scientific information together, in a systematic way. It was as a solution to this dilemma that the food systems perspective was proposed.

More than anything else, the food system perspective came to serve as an heuristic device for fitting together the data. It is founded on the assumption that all of the things people think and do in their daily quest for food — how they go about producing,

Plate 1.1   Tell el-Umeiri in Ammon, looking south. The Madaba Plains (and the border with Moab) lay beyond the tree-lined ridge behind the *tell* (photograph by Madaba Plains Project)

processing, storing, distributing, preparing, consuming, and wasting food — are part of a complex unity of purposive, patterned (institutionalized) and interdependent activities.

The advantages of this perspective were that, first, it heightened awareness of the fact that almost all of the data collected in the course of excavation and survey at Hesban and in the vicinity — remains of buildings and walls, broken pieces of pottery, fragments of animal bones, stone tools of various kinds — represented, in one way or another, a daily life activity related to either producing, storing or preparing food. Second, it focused attention on the interconnection between what was happening on the *tell* and what was going on in the surrounding environment.

Third, it provided a research question relevant to all periods — namely, how, in the broadest sense, did people go about providing the food and the security they needed to produce, store and distribute it? And fourth, it provided a sound basis for studying the present as a means to spark insights for use in interpreting the fragmentary archaeological record of the past.

One of the most important outcomes resulting from using this perspective to interpret the data from Hesban and its vicinity was that it brought into focus the dynamic coexistence of both nomadic and sedentary modes of existence in the project area. By focusing research on the quest for food in the broader sense, not just on agriculture — which Westerners tend to associate with settled life — this perspective opened a window on the dynamic shifts over time in the intensity with which people in this region exploited their land and animals to produce food. Out of this insight evolved research on food system intensification and abatement, and the related processes of sedentarization and nomadization.

A major reason for the decision to continue to do fieldwork in the Madaba Plains region in the 1980s and 1990s was to be able to investigate these processes. Another reason was the presence of several sites in the region which had what Tell Hesban did not have — well-stratified layers from the Iron and Bronze ages. The best two candidates were Tell el-Umeiri and Tell Jalul. Excavations at the former were begun in 1984 and at the latter in 1992. In addition, an intensive 'food system survey' in the region surrounding Tell el-Umeiri has been completed.

To return to the original question of how we ended up studying the Ammonites, the answer is that in starting work at Tell el-Umeiri, which happens to be located in the part of Jordan which according to Old Testament accounts is where they lived, we have encountered them. In particular, we identified them through their seal impressions, of which we have found over a dozen containing their script and iconography. This is a happy discovery, for it allows us to study them as a particular example, along with others from other periods, of a people who entered the light of recorded history, then disappeared. In this chapter we attempt to understand their sojourn, along with that of the Moabites and the Edomites, in terms of our sedentarization-nomadization model.

The sponsors of the excavations at Tell el-Umeiri and Tell Jalul are Andrews University in consortium with Atlantic Union College, Canadian Union College, and Walla Walla College.

ANCIENT AND MODERN TRIBALISM IN TRANSJORDAN

Mohammed Jamrah has provided an ethnographic report for the Deir Alla Project in Jordan which describes the people who inhabited this region during the last century (Van Der kooij and Ibrahim 1989: 12, 13). Many aspects of their lifestyle provide a possible model for understanding the ways of life of the ancient Ammonites, Moabites and Edomites.

According to the informant, Abu Shihab, the nineteenth century (CE) inhabitants around Deir Alla were tribally organized as the el-Fa'ur tribe. Of interest is the fact that this tribe maintained a mixed residence mode which facilitated their pursuit of a mixed subsistence strategy. For a good portion of the year most of the tribe were tent-dwelling pastoralists who seasonally moved with their herds (sheep, goat, cattle and camel) to new grazing grounds. Nevertheless, they did maintain a few houses (huts) which they lived in for part of the year and built barns and

Figure 2.1 Mesha Inscription (Moabite Stone) — (Iron II, ninth century BCE) (drawing by Laura M. Bredall after Drinkard, courtesy of the Horn Archaeology Museum). Height = 1.15 meters

The Mesha Inscription

(translation by Jackson 1989)

1. I am Mesha` son of Kemosh[yat], king of Moab, the
2. Daibonite, My father ruled over Moab thirty years, and I ruled
3. after my father. I made this high place for Kemosh in Qarhoh. BM [
4. S` because he delivered me from all the kings, and because he let me
5. prevail over all my enemies, Omri
6. was king of Israel, and he oppressed Moab for many days because Kemosh was angry with his country
7. But I prevailed over him and over his house, and Israel utterly perished forever. Now Omri had taken possession of a[ll the lan]d
8. of Mehadaba. He lived in it during his days and half of the days of his son(s) — forty years; but
9. Kemosh returned it in my days. I built Ba`lma`on and made the reservoir in it; and I buil[t]
10. Qiryaten. Now the Gadites had lived in the land of `Atarot forever, and the king of
11. Israel had rebuilt `Atarot for himself. But I fought against the city and took it, and I killed the entire population of
12. the city — a satiation for Kemosh and for Moab. I brought back from there the altar hearth of its DWD and
13. [d]ragged it before Kemosh in Qiryat. I settled in it the Sharonites and the
14. Maharatites. Now Kemosh said to me, 'Go seize Nebo from Israel.' So i
15. went at night and fought against it from the break of dawn until noon. I
16. seized it and killed everyone of [it] — seven thousand native men, foreign men, native women, for[eign]
17. women, and concubines — for I devoted it to `Ashtar-Kemosh. I took from there th[e ves]-
18. sels of Yahweh and dragged them before Kemosh. Now the king of Israel had built
19. Yahas, and he occupied it while he was fighting against me. But Kemosh drove him out from before me.
20. I took from Moab two hundred men, its entire unit. I took it up against Yahas and captured it
21. to annex (it) to Daibon. I built Qarhoh: the walls of the parks and the walls of
22. the acropolis. I rebuilt its gates, and I rebuilt its towers. I
23. built the palace and made the retaining walls of the reservoi[r for the spr]ing insi[de]
24. the city. Now there was no cistern inside the city — in Qarhoh — so I said to all the people, 'Make your
25. selves each a cistern in his house.' I dug the ditches for Qarhoh with Israelite cap-
26. tives. I built `Aro`er and made the highway at the Arnon, [and]
27. rebuilt Bet Bamot because it had been torn down. I built Beser — because [it] was in ruins —
28. with fifty Daibonites, for all Daibon was obedient. I rule[d]
29. over] hundreds in the cities which I had annexed to the country. I built
30. [Mehada]ba, Bet Diblatēn, and Bet Ba`lma`on, and I took up there the [
31.]S'N of the land. And Hawronēn lived in it B[ ] WQ[ ] 'Š[
32. And] Kemosh said to me, 'Go down, fight against Hawronēn.' So I went down[
33. and] Kemosh [retur]ned it in my days, and `L{`[ ]DH from there `Š
34.]ŠT ŠDQ.
    and I[

silos (above and below ground) to store agricultural surplus. They also built a dam and water canals to bring water from the River Zerqa, some 3 km to the east, to Deir Alla to irrigate crops. Their crops included wheat, barley, sesame and doura. The land-owning sheikh hired non-kin migrant workers to help with the crops. Part of the harvest was traded for fruit and other goods from towns on the plateau.

An additional point of interest is the fact that the el-Fa'ur migration pattern was restricted to a 7 km circle around Deir Alla. In other words this tribe had a restricted territory within which they migrated. The territory, however, included lands next to the river, in the Zor, as well as lands in the foothills. The winters were spent in the Zor, while the hot summers were spent in the foothills above the Wadi Rajib. This restricted vertical migration pattern, combined with the practice of sedentary agriculture, corresponds on a small scale to what Johnson has described as 'constricted-oscillatory nomadism' a variant of 'vertical nomadism', (Johnson 1969: 170–3).

Many of the characteristics of the el-Fa'ur tribe appear similar to those reflected in archaeological and inscriptional records of the ancient peoples of this region. For example, in the case of the Moabites the biblical record describes 'king' Mesha as a 'raiser of sheep' (2 Kgs 3: 4), suggesting that pastoralism provided the foundation of the Moabite economy. There was a clear recognition of the existence of Moabite territory (e.g., Num. 21: 13–15 and 2 Kgs 3: 21, although the precise boundaries of the territory were in constant dispute – e.g. Num. 21: 26–30), and that this territory included lands both on the plateau and down in the valley (Num. 22: 1), reflective of constricted-oscillatory,

vertical nomadism. At the same time, it is clear that the Moabites inhabited a number of important sedentary centers such as Dibon (Mesha Inscription [MI] line 2 – see Jackson 1989 for translation) and Kir Hareseth (2 Kgs 3: 25). Mesha, himself, claimed that he directed the building of a number of projects including water reservoirs, cisterns and roads (MI lines 23–5), activities not unlike that of the sheikh of the small el-Fa'ur tribe.

While Mesha's inscription does not describe agricultural activity, the plains of Moab are well known for their wheat, especially the Madaba Plains region. An Ammonite site, Minnith, on the northern portion of this plain, was in fact explicitly noted for its wheat (Ezek. 27: 17). Undoubtedly, grain crops were important in Moab as well. Regardless of the nature of his projects, Mesha appears to have relied on captured slaves for labor, such as the Israelites (MI line 25) rather than hired migrant workers.

As for Moab's actual social organization, there is little direct inscriptional evidence. However, the fact that their cousins to the west, the Israelites, were tribal (see Stager 1985) would suggest that Moab was too. Also, the fact that in the Mesha inscription Mesha refers to himself, as both a 'Dibonite' and a king of Moab (MI lines 2, 20, 28) suggests that the Moabites were subdivided into local tribal elements analogous to the way the el-Fa'ur tribe is apparently an element of the larger Adwan tribe (Peake 1958: 170). Thus, many factors suggest that the lifestyles of the ancient Transjordanians were not too different from the tribal peoples who have inhabited Jordan during the last few centuries up to the present.

24

SOCIAL STRUCTURE IN PALESTINE IN THE IRON II PERIOD ON THE EVE OF DESTRUCTION

William G. Dever

Introduction

A fundamental issue of this chapter is scope. The Iron II period in Palestine is generally considered to cover the period *ca.* 920–586 BCE, i.e., the era of the Divided Monarchy of Israel and Judah – the principal and best documented ancient national polities in the region. Other less well known Iron II entities in Palestine, however, would include southern Phoenicia and Philistia along the Mediterranean coast; and the regional states of Ammon, Moab and Edom in Transjordan (see this volume, Chapters 20 and 23).

The usual chronological schemes are based, not surprisingly, on historical events in Israel and Judah that are documented (to some degree) in literary texts in the Hebrew Bible and in Egyptian, Neo-Assyrian, and Neo-Babylonian inscriptions. The terminology and chronology of most Israeli archaeologists begin Iron II with the tenth century BCE., i.e., they include the United Monarchy (Aharoni and Amiran 1958; *EAEHL*; 1975–1978; Mazar, 1990: 295, 296; Barkay 1992: 305); and this indeed makes archaeological sense. American usage, following Albright and others, divides Iron I and II at *ca.* 920 BCE, with the death of Solomon and the breakup of the United Kingdom, a more 'historical' (and, of course, biblical) notion. Despite some misgivings, the latter scheme is adopted here.

A second issue concerns the basic category of 'social structure' that is to be discussed here. Standard works on ancient Palestine or Israel in the biblical period, based largely on literary data, have rarely dealt with social structure. Refreshing exceptions would be J. Pedersen's pioneering *Israel. Its Life and Culture* (1926–1940); and R. de Vaux's monumental *Ancient Israel: Its Life and Institutions* (1961). In addition, the more recent trend towards the adoption of socio-anthropological models in biblical studies has produced a number of non-traditional, seminal works, some of which at least make an effort to employ archaeological data.[1] In archaeological studies *per se*, we are fortunate that there have appeared recently several authoritative treatments of the archaeology of Palestine, including Transjordan.[2] Yet, however adequate these may be as introductions to the basic data, none makes any attempt to organize the data in terms of social structure, even though there are many suggestive possibilities. This is a serious deficiency in Syro-Palestinian and biblical archaeology, when one considers that the general field of archaeology has been moving toward social archaeology for 20 years or more. The orientation, however, reflects the typical bias toward 'political history', one that this volume is deliberately designed to counter.[3]

In the following discussion we shall usually treat the Iron II period as a whole, despite typical divisions into such phases as Iron IIA, (*ca.* 920–722 BCE) and Iron IIB (*ca.* 722–586 BCE), which are well enough documented to be legitimate and useful for certain purposes. Our decision is based on the fact that the Iron I period is regarded by all authorities as one of gradual change, of striking continuity, and of overall homogeneity (except for a few north-south distinctions). Moreover, the phenomenon that we are seeking to comprehend – social structure – is so fundamental to the 'Israelite' culture that now dominates western Palestine in this period that it is better viewed synchronically (i.e., functionally) than diachronically. As for the more peripheral areas noted above, a 'lumping' rather than 'splitting' approach is necessary, since we do not yet have detailed, chronologically-fixed sequences of material culture remains.

One unique aspect of the Iron II period that must be addressed is the availability – for the first time in the long historical-cultural sequence of Palestine – of fairly comprehensive, contemporary literary records (i.e., of pertinent *textual* data, both biblical and extra-biblical).[4] This may be, however, a mixed blessing. Certainly a former generation of 'Biblical archaeologists' were distracted from proper archaeological objectives by a theological agenda drawn largely from problems in the interpretation of biblical texts. Even though this form of naive positivism has been largely outgrown in Syro-

Israelite City Wall in the Jewish Quarter (photograph by Werner Braun) (courtesy of Hillel Geva and Israel Exploration Society)

Palestinian archaeology, we have not solved the problem of correlating texts and artifacts in writing any sort of history of ancient Israel and Palestine, including the desired 'social history' yet to be written (below). We shall, however, use the biblical and other texts wherever they can be harmonized with artifactual remains, even though we regard them in this context as secondary, rather than primary, data.[5]

Finally, it must be cautioned that in this initial attempt to discern Iron Age social structure *archaeologically*, we can rarely be more than suggestive; the data as excavated and published were not designed originally to address the issue focused upon here, and they can be redirected only to a limited extent. Adequate data on social structure in ancient Palestine will emerge only from the newer research designs that are gradually coming into vogue in Syro-Palestinian archaeology.

The evidence from centralization and nationalization

It should be self-evident that the study of social institutions cannot be separated from that of political organization and economic structure, since these are all subsystems of a larger, organic whole.

The basic political organization of Palestine (and even of Syria) in the Iron II period is that of regional or 'peripheral' states, most of them emerging for the first time in the history of the southern Levant.[6] While small-scale compared to Egypt and Mesopotamia, they nevertheless constituted 'nations', i.e., conglomerates that represented distinct ethnic entities – usually competing with one another – with centralized administrative systems. For ancient Israel, the archaeological evidence for the rise of statehood is clearest in the trends towards urbanization, centralization, and ethnic consciousness, as reflected in material culture. All these have far-reaching implications for social structure.

Urbanization

Urbanization has been notoriously ill-defined in Near Eastern archaeology generally, but a few recent discussions have begun to adopt more deliberate and sophisticated models from other disciplines. The most promising approach utilizes a modified 'Central Place Theory' – especially in the analysis of site size, character, and location in terms of a 'rank-size hierarchy'.[7] The typical configuration that is thought to define 'urbanism' is a settlement pattern that exhibits a 'three-tier hierarchy'. In this pattern there are a few very large 'central places' that function as administrative and economic centers; a much larger number of middle-sized towns ('nodes' in the network) that are relatively evenly distributed across the landscape, and exchange goods and services both with each other and with

the 'central places'; and, finally, a still larger number of small villages, hamlets and farmsteads in rural areas.[8]

The point is that in a truly urban society, even though the bulk of the population will live in middle- and lower-tier sites, administrative control of the society will be centralized in the hands of a few elites in the major centers. These sites are, by definition, 'cities', even if those in Iron Age Palestine are small by comparison with the much larger urban conglomerates in Egypt, Syria, or Mesopotamia (Figure 1). It is the intrinsic *scalar difference* of the southern Levant, due to the unique physical environment and geo-political situation of the region, that defines and shapes *all* political, economic and social institutions.[9]

Steven Falconer (1987), a student of mine, has developed a formula that calculated population size in relation to the local carrying capacity of the immediate outlying region, and that also measures the threshold at which a given site will outgrow its ability to feed itself. At that point, it must subjugate and organize the more distant hinterland, and thus by definition it becomes a 'city', i.e., an administrative center. In Mesopotamia, Falconer's test-case, the urban threshold is *ca.* 85 acres – or, using typical formulae for demographic estimates of 100 per acre, a site with a population of some 8000–9000.[10] For Palestine, however, the scalar differences noted above would, in my opinion, reduce the 'urban threshold' to some 20 acres and 2000 people. By this criterion, some six sites known thus far in Iron II Palestine (five of them in Israel-Judah, one in Philistia) would qualify as cities (Jerusalem, Dan, Hazor, Gezer, Lachish and Ekron). While a full-scale 'rank-size' analysis of all sites has never been done, this number is probably sufficient, relative to the total, to characterize Palestine in this period as urban – indeed very highly urbanized in comparison to the Bronze Age, and especially so when compared with the Iron I or pre-Monarchic era.[11] We shall turn below to the precise social implications of this phenomenon of relatively rapid urbanization in Iron II.

Centralization

Political and administrative centralization are the inevitable results of urban development, which concentrates population, resources and power in a relatively few cities. These cities come to dominate the society and economy even in the countryside – in fact, especially in the surrounding countrysides, which become tributary to the urban centers. The social consequence is, of course, stratification – or differential access to goods and services.

We need not dwell on the archaeological evidence for centralization in Iron II Palestine, since the urban trends documented above entailed precisely that (see Holladay this volume, Chapter 22). In particular, there emerged early in the Divided Monarchy two true national capitals. Jerusalem, continuing from the tenth century BCE, in

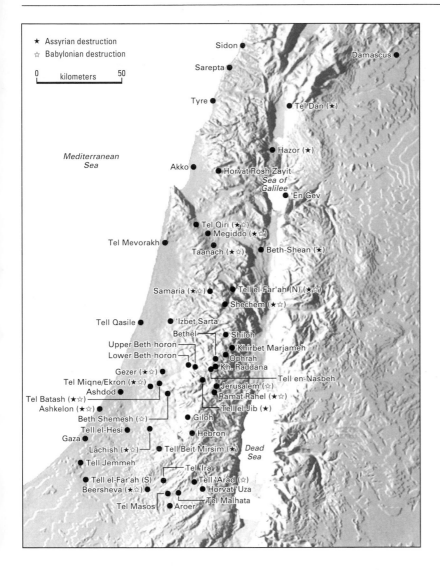

★ Assyrian destruction
☆ Babylonian destruction

0   kilometers   50

Sidon

Damascus

Sarepta

Tyre

Tel Dan (★)

Mediterranean Sea

Hazor (★)

Akko

Horvat Rosh Zayit

Sea of Galilee

'En Gev

Tel Qiri (★☆)

Megiddo (★☆)

Tel Mevorakh

Taanach (★☆)

Beth-Shean (★)

Samaria (★☆)

Tell el-Far'ah (N) (★☆)

Shechem (★☆)

Tell Qasile

'Izbet Sarta

Bethel

Shiloh

Upper Beth-horon

Khirbet Marjameh

Lower Beth-horon

Ophrah

Kh. Raddana

Gezer (★☆)

Tell en-Nasbeh

Tel Miqne/Ekron (★☆)

Ashdod

Jerusalem (☆)

Ramat Rahel (★☆)

Tel Batash (★☆)

Tell el-Jib (★)

Ashkelon (★☆)

Beth Shemesh (☆)

Giloh

Tell el-Hesi

Hebron

Gaza

Lachish (★☆)

Tell Beit Mirsim (★) *Dead Sea*

Tell Jemmeh

Tell Ira

Tell el-Far'ah (S)

Tell Arad (☆)

Beersheva (★☆)

Horvat 'Uza

Tel Masos

Aroer

Tel Malhata

Figure 1 Map of selected Iron Age II sites in Southern Phoenicia, Israel and Judah: # = Assyrian destruction; * = Babylonian destruction

Judah; and first Dan, then Samaria in Israel. Jerusalem is less well known archaeologically than Dan and Samaria; but all three have produced evidence of a monumentally fortified lower city, a separate and well defended acropolis-citadel, a sacred precinct, and (in the case of Samaria) an impressive palatial complex (Plate 1).[12]

In addition to these national capitals, we now have several Iron II sites that are certainly regional administrative centers, such as Hazor, Megiddo, Gezer, Lachish, and Beersheva (Figure 2 p. 421). These sites tend to exhibit such features as a highly centralized, planned layout; impressive city walls and multiple entryway gates; a palace-administrative complex near the city gate and/or elsewhere; monumental, well-engineered water systems to defend against siege warfare; large colonnaded buildings that are best understood as government storehouses; and other distinctive features that set these sites apart from ordinary cities, even those of the same size.[13]

In both national capitals and regional centers we see clear evidence of the centralization of political, economic and, in some cases (the capitals), religious institutions and functions. The result was a transformation of Israelite society. This had begun already in the United Monarchy, of course; but it crystallized early in the Divided Monarchy and only intensified after that.

This transformation under the onslaught of urbanization and nationalization resulted in an Israelite and Judean society that, above all, must have been highly stratified. This basic, cumulative change, occurring throughout the Monarchy, had a number of interrelated effects. One result was a society and economy that gradually became more diverse, more specialized, and finally more segregated. With increasing competition between various elements of society, economic inequalities resulted and tended to become endemic. Centrifugal forces developed that had to be counterbalanced by attempts at

Plate 1   Ahab's palace at Samaria (courtesy W.G. Dever)

greater centralized control, which necessitated coercion and finally usurpation by the authorities. Bureaucratic bungling and political corruption only made matters worse, and the end result was the collapse of the system. By the time of the Assyrian conquest in the late eighth century BCE in the north and the Babylonian campaigns in the early sixth century BCE in the south, both Israel and Judah were severely weakened by the social problems that we have described (see Figure 1). This scenario might appear

overly speculative; but in addition to the archaeological evidence, which in itself is admittedly inconclusive, there is considerable evidence from biblical texts that can be used in conjunction with archaeological finds to illuminate social structure (see details below and Window 1 p. 431).

Ethnic consciousness

Ethnic consciousness, which is an essential concomitant of national identity and statehood, is often thought to be difficult or even impossible to trace in the archaeological record, but that is not necessarily the case.[14] Artifacts may be considered properly the 'material correlates of behavior', that is, they reflect patterns of both individual and social behavior, as well as the thought and intent that behavior expresses. In that sense, archaeological remains are indeed an index not merely to material culture, but to culture, indeed to a *particular* culture. And when there emerge consistent, distinctive regional patterns – i.e., archaeological 'assemblages' – we can compare and contrast these with other such assemblages in order to isolate what may be called an archaeological culture (such as ''Ubaid'). Finally, if we happen to possess literary texts that are sufficiently detailed and can be closely correlated with such an archaeological culture and its development

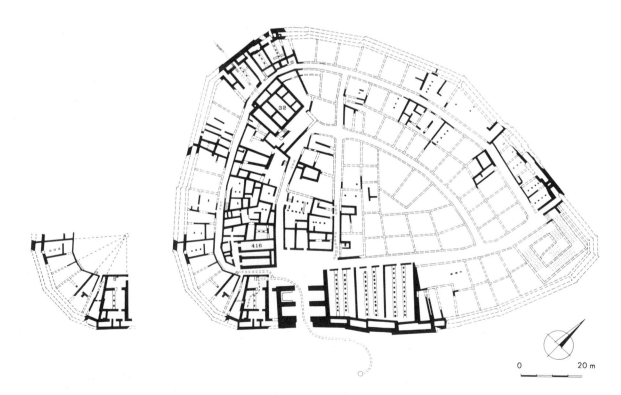

Figure 2   Tel Beersheva Stratum II. Source: *Tel Aviv 2* (1975: 148, Figure 1)

Figure 3 Palmette capitals, reconstructed gate at Hazor (ninth century BCE). Source: Kempinski and Reich 1992: 213, Figure 10

over time, then we may be able legitimately to attach a specific ethnic label ('Sumerian').

In the case of ancient Israel, we do have the label 'Israel' in both biblical and non-biblical texts from at least the ninth century BCE onwards (and even earlier, in the Merneptah stele). As for a distinctive 'Israelite' material culture assemblage, that emerged by the tenth century BCE, if not earlier.[15] Diagnostic Iron II traits of the ninth to early sixth centuries BCE would include an homogeneous ceramic repertoire with numerous distinctive forms and characteristic red slip and burnish; defenses that feature stereotyped multiple entryway gates and both casemate and solid walls; monumental buildings with ashlar masonry and palmette capitals (Figure 3); standardized four-room courtyard houses; bench-style rock-cut tombs; many unique small finds, such as seals, bullae, Asherah (or 'Astarte') figurines; and ostraca and other inscribed material that in language, orthography and script can be characterized only as Hebrew – closely related if not identical to the oldest stratum of the Hebrew Bible.[16]

Some of these traits are borrowed, especially from Phoenicia. The precise development and combination of features, however, is found nowhere else except throughout western Palestine, excluding portions of the Coastal Plain – precisely the area assumed by the biblical texts to be the heartland of the states of Israel and Judah. As archaeological knowledge progresses, we are able to speak more confidently of other such Iron II cultures and peoples of Palestine – Phoenician, Neo-Philistine, Ammonite, Moabite and Edomite – but in every case the 'Israelite' culture can be distinguished rather easily from these. The only question remaining is how far back into

Iron I we can project the origins of this culture, in a 'Proto-Israelite' complex of the twelfth–eleventh century BCE.[17]

Here we do not need to elaborate on the Iron II Israelite material culture, but only to point out the fact that 'Israelite' ethnic consciousness and ideology – a fundamental concept of society – is reflected faithfully in the rich archaeological remains that we now have. While the biblical texts often comment on that society only obliquely (below), the archaeological data are increasingly able to shed light directly on it. And, with newer research designs oriented more toward social archaeology, the explanatory potential of archaeology can only increase.

The evidence from tombs and burial customs

In most branches of archaeology it has been assumed that mortuary practices often contain clues to social customs, especially social differentiation.[18] A full-scale treatment of Israelite and Judean burial customs, long a desideratum, has now appeared in E. Bloch-Smith's *Judahite Burial Practices and Beliefs about the Dead* (1992). Bloch-Smith's exhaustive analysis of the material is more concerned with ideology than with social structure, but the data she collects (much of it long known) can easily be utilized for our purposes.[19]

Commoners were presumably buried individually in simple pit-graves, which survive so infrequently that they are scarcely attested in the archaeological record. What do survive are much more monumental tombs, many of which presumably represent elites. This is indicated both by the very small percentage of the projected Iron II population reflected in such burials, and also by many distinctive, often unique, features of the burials.

1. The tombs themselves are larger, more elaborate, 'architectural' in style, usually with a central arcosolium, several chambers and well-cut doorways. The tombs may be rock-cut, but occasionally they are above-ground monuments with elaborate facades, some of them still visible today.
2. These tombs have special features not found elsewhere, such as waist-high benches around the walls; carved head and foot niches for the body; and repositories for earlier burials. These features point to preferential treatment of the dead.
3. In several instances, these tombs have Hebrew inscriptions with rather standardized warning and blessing formulae, reflecting not only literacy but well known Phoenician customs.
4. The large number of successive burials, the long use of the repositories, the number of tomb offerings, the chronological range of the pottery, and the names in some of the inscriptions all suggest that these tombs are those of noble families, used over several generations. Bloch-Smith is no doubt correct in suggesting that the ideology behind the collective burials of these elite families

was based upon the concern not only to ensure the continuity of the living with the dead, but also to preserve the common *naḥalā*, or patrimony, of the ancestral family (the *bet 'āb*), which in ancient Israelite society included not only inherited wealth, but status deriving from what was deemed a 'proper' genealogy.

5. Finally, the graves themselves reflect wealth and status, including as they do jewelry, costly metals, numerous items of personal adornment, imported Cypriot and Egyptian pottery and objects, juglets for unguents, scarabs and seals, model furniture, terra-cotta figurines, and other luxury items.[20]

A number of such rock-cut tombs are found throughout the country, but especially in eighth–seventh century BCE Judah. Some seem to be isolated, such as the one at Beit Lei; but others occur grouped in local cemeteries, such as the cemetery at Kh. el-Qôm (Figure 4, Plate 2), west of Hebron. The most elaborate tombs of all are, not unexpectedly, in and around Jerusalem – especially the monumental tomb in the garden of the École Biblique; the Ketef Hinnom tomb, with its silver amulet inscribed with priestly blessing formulae from Numbers; and the several elaborate above-ground tombs in the village of Silwan, east of the Temple Mount. Among the latter is a robbed tomb still visible in the Silwan cliffside, with an eighth-century BCE Hebrew inscription that has been partially restored to read 'Belonging to [Shebna]yahu, who is "over the house"' i.e., the Royal Steward.[21] This may indeed be the tomb of the very Shebna mentioned in Isa. 22: 15, 16, who was 'over the house' (Figure 5). Interestingly, the prophet Isaiah rebuked this Shebna, presumably for his ostentatious plans for his burial:

> What have you to do here and whom have you here, that you have hewn here a tomb for yourself, you who hew a tomb on the height, and carve a habitation for yourself in the rock?

The evidence from material culture generally

We have already surveyed several aspects of the archaeological remains, noting their significance for social structure, but we now turn to look at some of these and other categories of material culture in more detail. We shall select, in particular, those imports or luxury items that denote wealth and status. Two main categories are pertinent: architecture and art.

Architecture

The architecture of the Iron II period develops directly out of that of Iron I. In defensive architecture, casemate walls generally are replaced by solid masonry offsets-insets walls; and four-entryway city gates yield to three- and then to two-entryway gates (Figure 6). More and

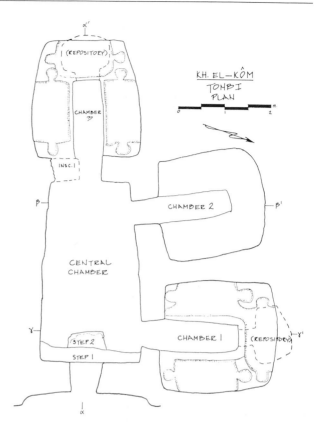

Figure 4   Kh. el-Qôm, Tomb 1 (eighth century BCE); courtesy W.G. Dever

Plate 2   Kh. el-Qôm, Tomb 1. Inscription #1 removed at left (courtesy of W.G. Dever)

more evidence is also turning up of massive Iron Age embankments, probably a defense against battering rams. Some sites have both an upper and a lower city wall, with an embankment between. Among typical heavily fortified Iron II sites, we could list Tel Dan, Hazor, Megiddo, Yoqneam, Samaria, Shechem, Tell en-Nasbeh, Jerusalem, Beth-Shemesh, Tel Batash, Gezer, Lachish, Tell

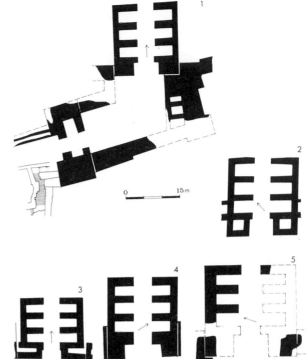

Figure 5 Tomb of (Shebna) the royal steward: facade and inscription (eighth century BCE). Source: Ben-Tor 1992: 371, Figure 9.49

Beit Mirsim, Tel Halif/Lahav, Arad, Beersheva, and some of the Negev fortresses.[22]

The significant point is that such massive defensive architecture reveals not only sophisticated centralized planning and well-engineered construction, but also the borrowing and skillful adaptation of military strategies that go back to a long Bronze Age tradition that extends from Anatolia across Syria to Northern Mesopotamia.[23] In particular, the ashlar or drafted masonry that is used in the finest city gates of the tenth/ninth centuries BCE is of Phoenician origin (as suggested already by such biblical texts as I Kings 5: 17, 18; 6: 7; 7: 9–11), probably first brought from the Aegean world by 'Sea Peoples' settling the Levantine coast in the twelfth century BCE.[24]

No 'free enterprise' system could have introduced and perfected such massive, integrated defenses: they are products of a hierarchical, state-sponsored economy and society. The same thing can be said of the ninth to eighth-century water systems, also defensive works, at Hazor, Megiddo, Gibeon, Gezer (?), Jerusalem, Beersheva, and other sites.[25]

Domestic architecture in Iron II also follows in the Iron I tradition. It is characterized chiefly by the further development of the ubiquitous four-room or courtyard house, which provided a module of considerable flexibility (Figure 7, Plate 3). Most of these houses are rather ordinary; but some are so spacious and well laid out that they could be regarded as villas, no doubt of the upper classes (Figure 8).[26]

In addition to these relatively isolated patrician dwellings, there are large multi-roomed residencies, mostly at district administrative centers, that can properly be called palaces, indeed in some cases citadels. These would include Hazor, Megiddo, Jezreel, Samaria, Tell en-Nasbeh, Gezer, Jerusalem (?), Ramat Raḥel, Lachish, and

Figure 6 Ninth century BCE city gates: 1 Megiddo; 2 Hazor; 3 Gezer; 4 Ashdod; 5 Lachish. Source: Kempinski and Reich 1992: 198, Figure 9

Tell Beit Mirsim (Figure 9a–c). Again, costly ashlar masonry characterizes the finest of the structures, particularly at ninth century BCE Samaria, the northern capital (see Plate 1).[27] Such luxurious palaces and their imported furnishings (below) can only have been the residences of ruling elites.

Art

Conventional wisdom has held that ancient Israel and Judah did not possess any real artistic tradition, supposedly because of the Second Commandment's prohibition against most of the forms of figural representation that were favored in Ancient Near Eastern art and iconography. The only exceptions of the Iron II period were thought to be the ninth–eighth century BCE carved ivory inlays, and the seventh–sixth century BCE stamp seals – both of which were regarded as of Phoenician inspiration, if not manufacture. Several recent studies, however, have questioned this assumption, particularly several publications of the 'Freibourg school' of Othmar Keel and his colleagues. Notable among these studies are Keel and Christoph Uehlinger, *Göttinnen, Götter, and Gottessymbole. Neue Erkentnisse zur Religionsgeschichte Kanaans und Israels aufgrund bislang unerschlossener ikonographischer Quelle* (1992); and Silvia Schroer, *In Israel gab es Bilder.*

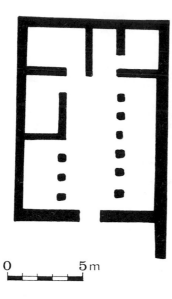

Figure 7   Dwelling, Tell en–Nasbeh, house M.379 *ca.* eighth century BCE). Source: Kempinski and Reich 1992: Figure 51

Plate 3   Iron II houses at Gezer, Field VII (courtesy of J.D. Seger)

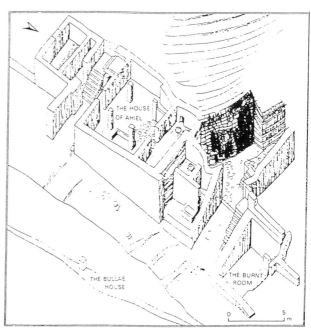

Figure 8   Private dwellings on the eastern slope of the City of David (Iron II). Source: Ben–Tor 1992: Figure 9:44

Nachrechten von darstellender Kunst im Alten Testament (1987).

These and previous studies have isolated the ivories as a distinctively Israelite art-form, even though it may be derivative. The prototypes are to be found in Phoenician or North Syrian 'schools' of ivory-carving; but it is reasonable to suppose that these Phoenician-style ivories were also made locally. The skills required are similar to, and no more difficult than, those employed in making engraved seals, and these certainly are of local manufacture (below; Figure 10).[28]

By far the largest corpus of these ivory inlays, used for decorating wooden furnishings of all sorts, was found, not unexpectedly, in the ruins of the Israelite palace at Samaria. Although the several hundred fragments and whole pieces recovered from the Assyrian destruction of Building Period VI date to 722/721 BCE, many of the ivories are most likely heirlooms that go back to the ninth century BCE. These well known Samaria ivories constitute an especially eloquent witness to social stratification in ancient Israel: first, they are relatively rare in any context, i.e., true luxury items; second, they were found not only at the capital, but in the ruins of the royal palace; and third, they provide clear evidence of both a sophisticated taste for 'exotic' furnishings of foreign derivation, and the means for acquiring such costly items. Finally, we have contemporary biblical texts that no doubt refer precisely to these ivories at Samaria – couched in the form of a social protest against the conspicuous consumption of the upper classes. Ahab, the original architect of the palace in the ninth century

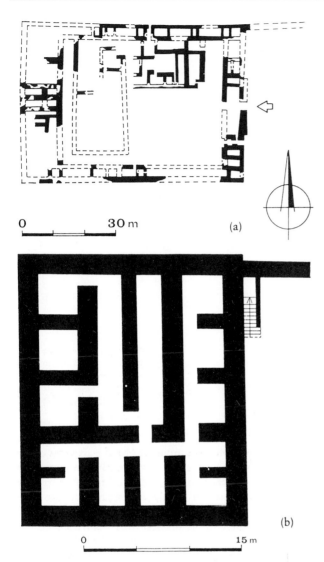

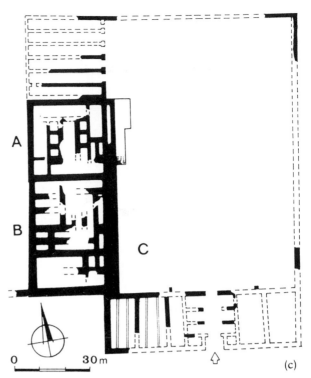

Figure 9 (a) Ramat Rahel, palace (source: *Ramat Rahel* II, Figure 6); (b) Hazor, Area B, the 'citadel' (source: *Hazor* II, Pl. CCV); (c) Lachish, palace (source: *Tel Aviv* 10, 1983: 148, Figure 23)

BCE, is said by the editors of Kings to have built an 'ivory house' (I Kings 22: 39). In the eighth century BCE, the prophet Amos enters a populist protest: 'Woe unto those who lie upon beds of ivory' (Amos 6: 4). He predicts furthermore that Yahweh will 'smite the winter palace with the summer palace; and the houses of ivory shall perish' (Amos 3: 15).

A second category of Israelite art consists of engraved seals and seal impressions from the ninth–sixth centuries BCE (Figure 11). Seals are common enough – several thousand are known – that many ordinary citizens must have possessed them, no doubt using them, as they were intended, for signet rings. This would be true for the plainer varieties of non-precious stones, especially the simple, undecorated examples from the seventh to sixth centuries BCE, which have only personal names. On the other hand, a number of these seals have ornate designs, are exquisitely carved in precious stones, and are even

bound in gold rings. In addition, the inscriptions include such titles as 'priest', 'servant of the king', and 'prince', among others.[29] And, of course, the Royal Stamped Jarhandles of the late eighth century BCE are stamped with seals reading '*le-melekh*', 'royal', and clearly indicate crown supervision of many aspects of production and distribution of goods – no doubt under high-ranking government officials.[30] Finally, the widespread ownership and use of seals – which are designed primarily for sealing rolled papyrus documents – indicates widespread literacy (below). This would apply to some extent even to women, whose names are increasingly attested in the seals that have come to light.

In addition to luxury goods like ivories and seals, both of foreign derivation, there are other exotic items in the Iron II repertoire, some of them imported. These would include many of the items enumerated among the contents of the elite tombs discussed above, some of which are imports from Egypt and Cyprus and must have been quite costly.

The evidence of literacy

A generation ago we possessed so few written remains from ancient Israel, apart from the Hebrew Bible, that

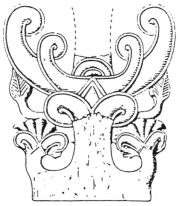

Figure 10 Carved ivory inlays from Ahab's palace at Samaria, in Phoenician style (ninth to eighth century BCE). From J.W. Crowfoot, J.M. Crowfoot 1938, Plates 5, 6, 17, 22

Israelite society appeared to have been largely illiterate. Today the picture is a very different one. We still have very few royal or monumental inscriptions, but hundreds of ostraca; innumerable inscribed pottery and stone vessels, ivories, weights, seals; and several tomb inscriptions have now been found.[31] Among the epigraphic finds are a number of abecedaries, including some from rather remote sites, indicating perhaps the existence of scribal and other schools (Lemaire 1981), where people learned to write. All this evidence has suggested to most scholars that literacy was almost universal in ancient Israel.

That may be true, but one can easily argue that while most people could read and write in an elementary fashion, i.e., were 'functionally literate', relatively few – probably only the well-educated upper class – were truly literate. This is suggested by the fact that a number of inscriptions – like most of those in the Judean tombs, and a number of the cultic graffiti at Kuntillet 'Ajrûd in the eastern Sinai (Figure 12) – are not easily read in the light of biblical Hebrew, and may not be fully intelligible at all (Figure 13).[32] Is the problem our mistaken assumption that the Hebrew Bible, with its Persian-Hellenistic final redaction and medieval pointed vowels, is the proper standard for literary Hebrew of the Iron Age? Or is it possible that most of the non-biblical inscriptions, representing ordinary folk and vernacular Hebrew, are only partially literate? The

second is surely the case supported by the growing corpus of graffiti that we have. It may thus be suggested that sermons such as those of the eighth century BCE prophet Isaiah – if they are not simply later literary compositions and were never read by an earlier public – would have been unintelligible to the masses. If that is true, then such literature – and indeed much of the Hebrew Bible in the form in which we now have the consonantal text – must have circulated, and been edited and preserved, only among the intelligentsia. The Hebrew Bible, in its external form as well as in its ideology, would then presuppose a minority, elite class.[33]

Another aspect of the epigraphic material at our disposal deserves comment. One of the earliest corpora of Hebrew ostraca was that brought to light from Samaria (Figure 14).[34] It consisted of several dozen documents dated to the eighth century BCE, most of them receipts for taxes, apparently paid in kind (i.e., oil and grain) into government warehouses. It is significant that the names of only a few individuals occur on these documents, occurring repeatedly in connection with transactions involving quite large amounts of commodities. It would appear that these individuals were owners of large estates in the Samaria district. Such amassing of wealth in real estate, no doubt at the expense of 'the poor of the land', gives point to the frequent protests of prophets such as Isaiah. He complains

Figure 11 A selection of Israelite and Judean seals (eighth to seventh century BCE). Source: Dever 1990, Figure 59

about those who buy up land, 'who add house to house and join field to field till there is no room left' (Isa. 5: 8). And Micah condemns unscrupulous landlords who 'if they covet fields they seize them; if houses, they take them' (Mic. 2: 2).

In numerous other poignant passages, the eighth to seventh century BCE prophets of Israel and Judah excoriate the ruling class for their rapacious business practices, their luxurious lifestyles, their arrogant manners and dress, their disenfranchisement of the poor and of the Israelite commoners. This prophetic protest – rooted in a sense of justice, mercy, and honorable conduct – is an eloquent commentary on the social stratification that existed in Iron Age Israel (King 1988).

The evidence of the biblical texts

There are innumerable references in passing in the Hebrew Bible to social stratification. Despite the general difficulties noted above in using the texts of the Hebrew Bible as sources for history-writing, these references may be considered prima-facie evidence of actual socio-economic conditions in the Monarchy. This is precisely because they

are the sort of artless details, handed down in annalistic sources, that would have escaped the heavy editorial hand of the final redactors of the Priestly and Deuteronomistic schools in the Exilic and post-Exilic periods, preoccupied as they were with theocratic history. It is as though the biblical writers and editors have inadvertently preserved for us authentic glimpses of everyday life, and thus of the larger social structure in which they themselves had little direct interest.[35]

If one 'reads between the lines' in the Hebrew Bible, there are indications of many social classes:[36]

1. Royalty, including kings, queens, princes and princesses, queen-mothers and concubines.
2. Courtly circles, including viziers, commanders of the army and the guard, ministers, ambassadors and emissaries, scribes, secretaries, heralds, guards and other functionaries.
3. The military, including officers of many ranks, cadets or career professionals, regular enlistees and conscripts, mercenaries, various specialists like runners and charioteers, and even sailors.
4. An aristocracy consisting of noble families, often attached to the court, landed gentry, and even entre-

Figure 12 Inscription and scene from a large storejar at Kuntillet 'Ajrûd in the eastern Sinai. Source: Meshel 1979

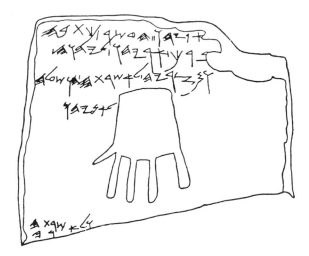

Figure 13 Inscription III from Kh. el-Qôm (eighth century BCE). From A. Lemaire 1977, Figure 1

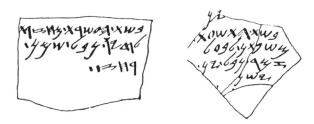

Figure 14 Two ostraca from Samaria. Source: Naveh 1982: 72, Figure 65

Plate 4 Monumental building project: the water tunnel at Gibeon (courtesy of W.G. Dever)

preneurs who had become wealthy and may have achieved elite status through contributions of goods or services to the crown.

5. A professional class, including physicians, judges and local court officials, as well as lower-echelon administrators like census-takers, tax collectors, chiefs of the *corvée*, municipal counsellors, prefects, judges and local court officials, district governors, and other functionaries.

6. A religious establishment, including high priests, ordinary priests, temple 'door-keepers' or supervisors, treasurers, scribes, musicians of various kinds, dancers, keepers of vestments, those 'dedicated' to temple service, interpreters of the Law, prophets (according to some scholars), and perhaps even male and female prostitutes; and, in 'popular cults', especially in the countryside, local clergy, non-establishment prophets, and diviners and magicians of various sorts.

7. A mercantile class, including purveyors of all sorts of commodities, suppliers of services, middlemen, traders, importers, lenders, financiers, bail officers, real-estate speculators, and entrepreneurs of all kinds.

8. A class of artisans and craftsmen, including masons, builders (Plate 4), woodworkers, metalsmiths, jewelers, ivory and seal carvers, potters, weavers, and others.

9. Common laborers, including miners, millers, bakers, barbers, launderers, charcoal-burners, domestics, and day laborers of many kinds.

10. An agricultural class including large-scale estate-owners, small freeholders, family farmers, agricultural workers, peasant farmers (the biblical *'am ha-'āretz* or 'poor of the land').

11. The lowest classes, including resident aliens (*gêrîm*), indentured servants and slaves – often attached to agricultural lands – and, of course, widows, orphans, the handicapped, the chronically ill, beggars and other destitute or outcast persons.

It should be pointed out that, of the dozens of vocations and social classes listed above, there is some degree of archaeological documentation for the vast majority. The evidence is too extensive to cite here; but the existence of such external corroboration should give us confidence in the ability of the biblical writers and editors to write descriptive and narrative history, when they chose to do so.

Conclusion

As we noted at the outset, the extensive archaeological data for the Iron II period in Palestine have rarely been utilized to comment on the social structure of ancient Israel. Biblical scholars have been equally derelict, and only recently have they begun to move away from narrow theological questions of the Bible as *Heilsgeschichte* to a 'secular history' of ancient Israel that addresses broader issues of society and the social context of the events of biblical history. Even this rather modest effort is hampered by the fact that biblical scholars have come to regard most biblical texts in their present form as stemming from the world of post-Exilic Judaism. They are thus too late and too tendentious to be used as reliable sources for the history of the Monarchy.[37] In our view, that is too extreme. The proper, critical use of biblical texts, in conjunction with modern archaeological data, can yield a satisfactory socio-economic history, as well as a political and ideological history of ancient Israel.

Notes

1. For orientation to recent literature of this genre, see Gottwald 1985: 26–31 and references there. Gottwald's own pioneering work on the origins of Israel in Early Iron I (1979) did attempt to use the archaeological data then available. Since 1985, other socio-anthropological works of biblical scholars on the Iron I period would be Frick 1985 and Flanagan 1988, but both are deficient archaeologically; for a critique, see Dever 1994a. More congenial to archaeologists is the settlement-history approach of Coote and Whitelam 1987. On the sad state of the supposed 'dialogue' between Syro-Palestinian archaeologists and biblical historians of ancient Israel, see Dever 1994b and references there.

2. For general works, see Weippert 1988; Mazar 1990; Ben-Tor 1992. On Transjordan, add Dornemann 1983; Sawyer and Clines 1983; Bartlett 1989; Bienkowski 1992. In this discussion,

we shall confine ourselves primarily to western Palestine (i.e., Israel) in the Iron Age. Wherever possible, we shall refer to the general works listed here, in the interest of simplifying documentation; full references will be found there.

3. On the belated impact of social archaeology on the disciplines involved in the discussion here, see my remarks in Chapter 17 of this volume; and on the history of 'biblical' and Syro-Palestinian archaeology generally, see Dever 1985 and references there.

4. Two qualifications are necessary. First, there are, of course, textual data available for the Bronze Age; but the sources, while relevant, are all extra-Palestinian. Second, in stating that the ninth century and later biblical texts are the 'earliest' chronologically, we do not discount the possibility that some texts incorporated into the literary tradition as we have it stem from the tenth century BCE, or even earlier. See further n. 32 below.

5. For full discussion, see Dever 1985; 1991a; and especially 1994b.

6. See further Frick 1985; Coote and Whitelam 1987; Flanagan 1988; and the critique of all three in Dever 1994a.

7. For orientation to 'rank-size' models, see Paynter 1983.

8. For a detailed application of this model to the rise of urbanism in the Middle Bronze Age, see Dever 1994c. Fritz (1990) sees Iron Age urbanism in Israel principally as the revival of the typical Palestinian Middle–Late Bronze Age pattern, as I do in Dever 1994a. Cf. n. 9 below.

9. On the all-important scalar differences in the rise of complexity in the southern Levant, especially Palestine, see Joffe 1993.

10. The figure of 100 persons per acre is considerably lower than the figure of *ca.* 160–200 per acre used in Shiloh 1980: 29, and it agrees rather with Stager 1985: 18–23.

11. The data for this conclusion, albeit tentative, are drawn from Shiloh 1980: 31. Note that I have taken only Shiloh's size estimates, not his population figures; cf. n. 10 above. Shiloh does not deal explicitly with 'rank-sized' hierarchies, only with rather rough statistics. Note that Frick 1985, Coote and Whitelam 1987 and Flannagan 1988, inexplicably, all discuss the rise of the Israelite state but not the development of urbanism. The only detailed treatment of this topic is Fritz 1990; although cf. Herzog 1992: 263–5, on urban planning.

12. On Samaria, see the summaries of Weippert 1988: *passim*; Mazar 1990: 406–10; and Barkay 1992: 319–23. Add now Tappy 1992.

13. On these administrative centers, see Weippert 1988: *passim*; Mazar 1990: 411–15; 427–35; 441, 442; Herzog 1992: 223–30; 250–61.

14. On the vexed question of ethnicity in the archaeological record, with reference to early Iron I, see Dever 1993 and references there.

15. See further Mazar 1990: 463–530; on the tenth century BCE as the formative period, cf. Dever 1993.

16. See n. 15 above. On the tombs, add Bloch-Smith 1992; on seals, Mazar 1990: 514–20; Keel and Uehlinger 1992; Hestrin and Dayagi 1979; Avigad 1986; and on the epigraphic evidence, Naveh 1982. See Biran and Naveh 1993 for the recently discovered 'Tel Dan Stele Inscription' and the mention of the 'House of David' and cover photograph of this volume.

17. For basic resources on Israel's neighbors, see the references in n. 2 above and Chapter 23 in this volume. For the term 'Proto-Israelite' and the question of Israel's earliest origins, cf. Finkelstein 1988; Dever 1991b; 1993. The literature on 'Israelite origins' is now proliferating beyond our ability to cite it here.

18. For orientation to the literature on mortuary practice, see n. 7 in Chapter 17, this volume.

19. See my forthcoming review in the *Israel Exploration Journal* (1994).
20. For details, see Bloch-Smith 1992: 65–108.
21. Avigad 1953.
22. Mazar 1990: 465–71.
23. Cf. Fritz 1990; for the Middle Bronze Age defenses, see Dever 1987; 153–7. Further on Iron II defenses, see Mazar 1990: 465–71; Barkay 1992: 307–8; 329–32; 338–46; Herzog 1992: 265–74.
24. On this masonry, see Shiloh 1979, who thinks it originally Israelite; the notion that ashlar masonry is, however, of Phoenician origin is now common (cf. Mazar 1990: 474). Few have pursued it back to its likely origins in the Aegean world. It is common in Cyprus in connection with the appearance of 'Sea Peoples' there, as at Kalavassos and elsewhere. See Chapter 20, this volume, for a discussion of the Sea Peoples.
25. Mazar 1990: 478–85; Barkay 1992: 332–4; Shiloh 1979.
26. Mazar 1990: 437; 485–9; Barkay 1992: 332; cf. also Shiloh 1979; Netzer 1992: 193–201.
27. Mazar 1990: 406; 437; Barkay 1992: 310–14; Reich 1992: 202–11; on the masonry, see Shiloh 1979.
28. On the ivories, see Winter 1981; Barnett 1982. Most scholars assume that the ivories are imports from Phoenicia or Syria (as Mazar 1990: 505). But a few late eighth-century examples found at Arslan Tash and Nimrud, the latter no doubt booty taken from Palestine, have Phoenician or Hebrew letters inscribed on the back; see Barkay 1992: 320–3; Mazar 1990: 503–5.

29. On these seals, see references in n. 16 above.
30. On the Royal Stamped Jarhandles, see the excellent discussion of Na'aman 1986 and references there.
31. On the epigraphic evidence, see references in n. 16 above; cf. Mazar 1990; 514–20; Barkay 1992: 349–51.
32. See further Davies 1992: 102–9; Thompson 1992: 336–9. I do not agree, however, with Davies' and Thompson's view that 'biblical Hebrew' is a *Bildungssprache* (i.e., an artificially-constructed *literary* language of the Persian-Hellenistic period). For bibliography on the Kh. el-Qôm and Kuntillet 'Ajrûd inscriptions, see Ackerman 1993: 391–94.
33. See further Davies 1992: 113–33; and cf. Thompson 1992: 412–23. Both are wrong, however, in seeing an elite or scribal class emerging only in the Persian period.
34. Mazar 1990: 409, 410; cf. King 1988: 139–49.
35. For an orientation to the growth of the literary tradition in the Hebrew Bible, and the related issue of the historicity of the texts, see nn. 5, 6, 32 above.
36. The following discussion is much too detailed to be documented with references to the biblical texts; but details will be found throughout de Vaux's unique, magisterial work (1961) on the social institutions of ancient Israel.
37. Thus Davies 1992; Thompson 1992; cf. my critique in Dever 1994b. Much better balanced as a 'history of ancient Palestine', using both biblical texts and archaeological data, is Ahlström 1993. See, however, my forthcoming work (in collaboration with Susan Ackerman), *A Social History of Iron Age Palestine and Biblical Israel.*

CONQUESTS, DESTRUCTIONS AND THE ARCHAEOLOGICAL RECORD

Near Eastern historical archaeologists have traditionally sought to explain cultural change by invoking notions of 'invasions', particularly when written records imply catastrophic events accompanying large-scale military campaigns or movements of peoples. Such models inevitably stress abrupt and sweeping change at the expense of cultural continuity. Examples of oversimplistic reconstructions based on invasion hypotheses might include the end of the Early Bronze Age in Palestine ('Amorites'); the end of the Late Bronze Age ('Israelites'); the end of the Bronze Age throughout the Levant and in Cyprus ('Sea Peoples', and others); and even in Greece (the 'Dorian Invasion'). These models rarely do justice to the complexity of the archaeological record as it becomes increasingly clear, and they generally possess little explanatory power.

Recently more sophisticated 'collapse' models have been advanced, often employing General Systems Theory to analyze the multiple factors that may 'trigger' the entropy of social systems in a similar way to biological systems. Seminal treatments, with many cross-cultural examples, have recently been published by Tainter (1988) and Yoffee and Cowgill (1988). Here the emphasis is upon indigenous, systemic change; on techno-ecological factors; on socio-economic rather than 'political' history – in short, on the *continuities*, rather than on the *discontinuities*. This current trend in anthropology was already anticipated by Braudel and the *annales* school of historians, who spoke eloquently of *la longue durée* (see Levy, Introduction; Levy and Holl, Chapter 6 this volume). On the surface of history – 'the froth on the crest of the waves' – are superficial accounts of public events and the deeds of great men. But underneath the waves are great, slow swells – the deep undercurrents of events – in large part anonymous and often environmentally determined, measured only in millennia. Neither of these newer approaches to the understanding of the past, however, has had much measurable impact on Near Eastern or Syro-Palestinian archaeology (Dever 1985; 1988). There is, however, some introductory literature with reference to these branches of archaeology, such as A.B. Knapp's *Archaeology, Annales, and Ethnohistory* (1992). The present volume will go a long way towards incorporating the *longue durée* perspective into Syro-Palestinian archaeology.

Two examples of the 'punctuated equilibriums' that Palestinian and biblical archaeologists must seek to explain are the destructions of northern Israel by the Neo-Assyrian empire in 735–722 BCE and the similar destruction of the southern kingdom of Judah by the Neo-Babylonian empire between 597–586 BCE. Standard histories of ancient Israel written by biblical scholars take as data the relatively brief references in 2 Kings (chapters 17, 24, 25), together with the rather fuller descriptions in cuneiform records from Assyria and Babylonia. The textual descriptions of the siege and destruction of the capitals of Samaria and Jerusalem, and the references to other towns and cities that were captured in the Assyrian and Babylonian invasions, are borne out in archaeological excavations, which have turned up rather dramatic evidence of destruction at a number of sites (see Figure 1 and opening photograph, this chapter). For instance, Shechem and Samaria (the capital) show a wholesale destruction in nearly all the excavated areas; and other major sites and district administrative centers, like Hazor and Megiddo, are severely disrupted then undergo a radical transformation into Assyrian-style citadels. The most poignant example of Assyrian destruction is that of Lachish III in the south, attributed with certainty to the well-known Judean campaign of Sennacherib in 701 BCE. Here we have not only the

biblical texts (2 Kings 18, 19), the accounts in the Assyrian annals, and the monumental pictorial reliefs found in a display room of Sennacherib's palace at Ninevah (Plate 1.1), but also extensive excavations of Lachish by British and Israeli archaeologists. For the Babylonian conquest, the archaeological evidence in Jerusalem is especially telling – heaps of destruction debris on the eastern slopes below the Temple Mount, still visible on the surface of the ground today.

The overwhelming picture produced by both the textual and the archaeological evidence is that devastating invasions of Palestine did take place in the late eighth century BCE and again in the early sixth century BCE. In this instance the identity of the agents of destruction is clear, thanks to literary texts that specify the Assyrians and Babylonians. Thus, while 'invasion hypotheses' in general are suspect as explanations of socio-economic and cultural change in Palestinian archaeology, here we have the exceptional *historical* circumstances where 'collapse' models, however productive for other archaeological eras, must yield to other more relevant models, such as 'catastrophe' (using Colin Renfrew's (1979) 'anastrophe-catastrophe' scheme, as opposed to the more typical 'rise-collapse' paradigm).

Nevertheless, the notion of 'collapse' may still be applicable in this instance, but having influence after the destruction we have noted – i.e., as the *effect*, rather than the cause, of the changes in question. Thus, northern sites did continue to be occupied after the late eighth century BCE disruptions, but at a much lower level of political organization and socio-economic integration or perhaps witnessing the reduction of Israel from an independent state to an Assyrian province. Archaeological surveys in Judah have shown that while major cities may have been destroyed by the Babylonian invasion, dozens of smaller towns and perhaps hundreds of villages in the rural hinterland continued throughout the sixth century BCE and into the Persian period, with little interruption in occupation and only the usual, predictable changes in material culture. These sites would illustrate Simon's principle of 'near decomposability' (1965). Thus, in the post-destruction debris and remnants of the partial collapse of society in Israel and Judah, the seeds of a new order were sown – one that would emerge in the Persian and Hellenistic–Roman eras. In time, one would see the reemergence of Jewish political independence, at least briefly, in the Hasmonean Kingdom of Judah and again, much later, in the twentieth century.

Plate 1.1   The siege of Lachish: detail from the Lachish relief found at the palace of Sennacherib at Ninevah

25

BETWEEN PERSIA AND GREECE: TRADE, ADMINISTRATION AND WARFARE IN THE PERSIAN AND HELLENISTIC PERIODS (539−63 BCE)

Ephraim Stern

Introduction: the administrative organization of Palestine within the Persian and Hellenistic Empires

During the Persian period Palestine was included in the territory of the satrapy of Abar Nahara (Ezra 4: 10,11), a term derived from the Assyrian administration (*ebir-Nari*), established in the days of Esarhaddon or even much earlier (compare I Kings 4: 24). Pseudo-Scylax refers to the area as Coele-Syria, which is a translation of the Aramaic term *kol-Swryya'*, an early name for the interior of Syria. At that time the country was already divided into designated political units.

M. Avi-Yonah (Avi-Yonah, 1966: Ch. 1) suggested that Palestine was divided into three types of political entities:

1. National 'states', that is, units whose borders coincide with the various ethnic elements dwelling in the country, such as Judah and Samaria, Megiddo, Ashdod, and the Edomite province around Hebron as well as Ammon and Moab.
2. The Phoenician commercial cities along the coast.
3. The tribal system of the Arabs. Avi-Yonah was of the opinion that Akko and Gaza were ruled directly by the Persians.

While the existence of National States (*Medinoth*), headed by governors ('Pahat'), is certain, from both written as well as archaeological sources (Figure 1), it appears that the Arab settlement was basically tribal, while that of the Phoenicians was urban. Nevertheless it is difficult, from the standpoint of the Persian satrapal organization, to accept Avi-Yonah's proposal that 'free Phoenician cities' existed in Palestine, which were under self rule. The king of Sidon, for example, was himself known to be governed directly by a resident Persian satrap (Diodorus, XVI.41:5 – his palace was excavated and was found to be built in a pure Archemenid style [Clermont-Ganneau 1921, Contenau 1923]) who had his own Persian garrison troops. If the king of Sidon was under direct Persian control, the concept

that the coastal cities in Palestine enjoyed political independence under the supervision of the king becomes doubtful. However, it does seem that these cities did possess commercial freedom. Moreover, in another contemporary source – that of Eshmunazar II, king of Sidon – in the late sixth or early fifth century BCE, the region indicated coincides perfectly with the boundaries of the Assyrian-Persian province of Dor (Cooke 1903: 30–40).

The same seems to have been the case in the southern region of Palestine – the area linked in the Bible with the name 'Geshem the Arabian' (see also Rabinowitz 1956). In recent excavations a number of military fortresses have been unearthed, for example, at Tell Jemmeh, Tell el-Fara (south), Beersheva, Arad, Kadesh-Barnea, and Tell el-Kheleifeh. Ostraca found at some of these sites indicate the presence of garrison troops. Two ostraca from Arad even designate the unit by name, 'degel' (standard), which is the name of a Persian military unit also mentioned in the Elephantine papyri (Cowley 1923; Porten 1968: 28–35; Naveh 1981: 158). In the opinion of the author, this entire area was under the direct rule of a Persian governor.

In summary, Palestine in the Persian period was apparently organized into a number of provinces or states (*medinoth*). Each unit was ruled by a dynasty of governors ('Pahat'), generally of a local family: Jews in Judah, Samaritans in Samaria (Gropp 1986), and Arabs in the south. These governors had small courts, imitating those of the satraps, and they stood at the head of small administrative organizations. They were probably in charge of small military garrisons and were allowed to keep official stamps of the 'state' in their possession. They also seem to have been permitted to strike the small silver coins, which are now known as 'Palestinian' coins (Hill 1914; Kindler 1963; Meshorer 1982; Mildenberg 1988; Meshorer and Qedar 1991). Thus far, the inscriptions of four of the provinces are clearly legible: Samaria, Judah, Ashdod and Gaza.

A Cypriot limestone head of the goddess Tiche from the Persian Period at Tel Dor (courtesy of E. Stern; photograph: © Zev Radovan)

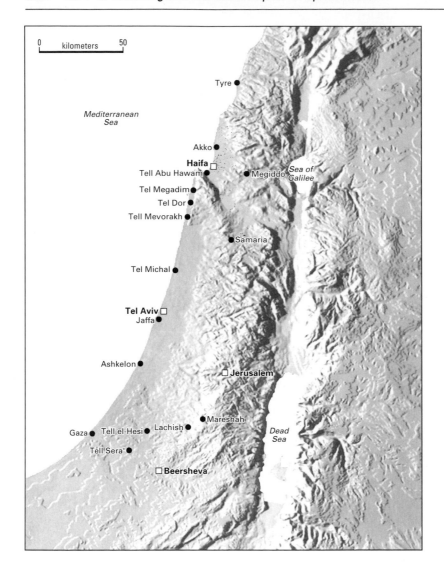

Figure 1   Map of major excavated sites from the Persian and Hellenistic periods mentioned in the text

Alexander the Great did not have time to introduce basic changes in this local organization and neither did his direct heirs. Only during the Ptolemaic rule of the country – especially at the time of their greatest king Ptolemais II Philadelphos (285–246 BCE) – was a new administrative organization introduced. According to the Zenon Papyri from the year 259 BCE the country had been divided anew: the larger unit called Hyparchia and the smaller Toparchia, the Hyparchia replacing the previous 'state'. Some of the older states survived: others, such as the kingdoms of Tyre and Sidon, ceased to exist (Avi-Yonah 1966: Ch. 1).

The trade between Palestine and Greece

During the Iron Age, Palestine was relatively isolated and the archaeological evidence for imports from the west is scarce indeed (see Holladay, this volume). Only by the end of this period, mainly from the Babylonian Age onwards,

was the situation radically changed. The evidence for a rapid growth in international commerce is abundant. We shall start our discussion with the revolutionary transitions which occurred in the traditional means of payment – moving from weights to coins, and a similar transfer from the local or Persian-Phoenician standard to the Greek one. In the following we shall discuss the archaeological evidence for the trade with Greece.

The weights

The use of the unit of silver by weight in financial transactions was the only one used during the Iron Age and earlier, and was still common in Palestine and neighboring countries throughout the sixth to the fourth centuries BCE, alongside the use of coins (Stern 1982: 215–17). The types of weights which are supposed to have existed, on the basis of literary sources and archaeological finds, are:

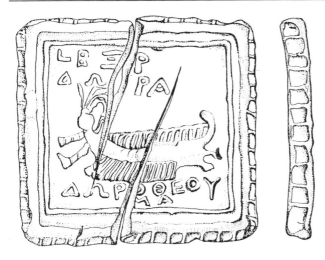

Figure 2 A lead weight inscribed with the name of the city of Dor and depicting its emblem, Hellenistic Period

Plate 1 (a) An Athenian silver tetradrachma of the fifth century BCE; two silver coins of (b) Ptolemaios 1 (300 BCE) and (c) Ptolemaios 2 (267 BCE) (courtesy of E. Stern; photograph by Zev Radovan)

1. the royal Persian standard;
2. the local Palestinian standard, which preserved the Hebrew names of Israelite times;
3. the Egyptian standard;
4. the Phoenician-Punic standard; and
5. the Greek standard.

The Greek standard became during the Persian period and mainly later – in the Hellenistic period – dominant in the country. The Greek weights of these periods found here were made of lead, shaped as rectangular disks on which are depicted some numbers and the names of the officials responsible for their accuracy (Stern, 1992a: 133–4, Fig. 181).

The coins

Our best evidence for the rapid growth of international commerce in the period is the introduction of coins.

The use of coins in Palestine began in the first half of the sixth century BCE (Meshorer 1961; Wright 1965: 168–9, Fig. 95; Barkay 1986: 34). Only a very few coins are extant from this early period and from the first half of the fifth century BCE; thus we may assume that the use of coins was common only from the end of the fifth century and mainly during the fourth century BCE (see Plate 1a). The coins in use in this period were all minted in three principal standards: the Persian, the Phoenician and the Attic.

An examination of the Greek coin types of the Persian period discovered in excavations reveals that most come from Athens and a few from Kos, Thasos and Aegae. But a comparison with the finds in neighboring lands shows that these hoards of Greek coins were composed of thousands of coins from all the known mints in the Greek world (Noe 1937). Of the Phoenician coins found in Palestine, only several hundred are recorded, almost all of them from Tyre and Sidon; very few are from Aradus and almost none from Byblos (Kindler 1967).

During the late Persian period, coins now called 'Philisto-Arabian' were also in use in Palestine, and these should be regarded as local coinage (Hill 1914: 83–9; Kindler 1963; Lambert 1932). What is unique in these coins is the abundance of types; there are very few examples of duplicates. We suggest that the privilege of minting these coins had been granted by the Persian authorities to the officials appointed over the various satrapal treasuries in Palestine, for local business use. The minting was done by treasury officials, each using the device of his own seal. As for date, it is agreed that they begin at the end of the fifth century and that the bulk are from the fourth century BCE.

A special branch of the local 'Philisto-Arabian' family consists of those coins bearing the names of the provinces of Judea, Samaria, Ashdod and Gaza (Rahamani 1971; Meshorer 1961; 1982: 13–34; Barag 1986; Mildenberg 1988; Meshorer-Qedar 1991). It seems that, like the others in this group, these were also minted by the royal officials in charge of the treasury who were permitted to coin small silver denominations for day-to-day business needs within the province.

The other types of coin in use in Palestine were those common in the Persian period in neighboring lands to the north, south and east of Palestine. These can be grouped as follows:

1. Persian coins of large denomination from the central imperial mint – *darics* and *sigloi*, which were common throughout the empire (Pope 1938; Zayadin 1967–8);
2. Cypriot coins, many of which have been found in Syria and Egypt, but have not yet come to light in Palestine;
3. Egyptian coins, struck in Egypt during the brief period of independence (400–344 BCE) (Stern 1982: 228, Fig. 378).

Plate 2   Attic (right) and 'West Slope' kraters from Tel Dor (courtesy of E. Stern; photograph by Zev Radovan)

It should also be noted that the privilege of minting in gold was held by the Persian imperial mint alone. In this manner the Persian authorities could control the economy of the areas under their rule. It also seems that the privilege of minting granted to various cities and vassal states was closely controlled and inspected – both in respect of the amounts minted and the standard used (see Plate 1a,b).

During the Hellenistic period the use of coins was expanded and they became the main means for trade transactions. In addition to the coins of the country's rulers, the Ptolemaics and the Seleucians, many city coins had been struck, belonging to the autonomic polis which had been granted the privilege of minting their own coins. A typical Hellenistic hoard would consist of Ptolemaic and Seleucid coins, the coins of the cities (such as Akko, Dor, Jaffa, Ashkelon, Gaza, etc.), city coins of the major commercial cities in neighboring countries (e.g., Alexandria in Egypt and Antiochia in Syria), and coins of the small kingdoms, such as that of the Hashmonaeans.

Pottery imports

Another way to examine the expansion of the international trade is by analyzing the spread of imported Greek clay vases in Palestine. The earliest Greek vases found in Palestine are of the late Protogeometric type, dating to the end of the eighth century BCE (Ben-Tor and Portugali 1987: 110, Pl. 50; Stern 1992a: 56, Fig. 65). Later Greek vessels came from different regions. In the Babylonian Age and the early Persian period most of them came from Corinth, which then held the mastery of the seas. These vessels were still rare in Palestine and only a few have been found. Only from the sixth century BCE onwards did imports from the eastern Greek islands increase – from Rhodes, Kos, Knidos, Chios, Samos, Lesbos, etc., as well as from the Greek settlements along the northeastern Mediterranean coast, such as Al-Mina. These East-Greek vases included bowls with painted bands and horizontal handles, jugs with black-painted decoration or geometric

designs on the upper part, and vessels in the Wild Goat style. During the sixth century BCE, especially towards its close, Greek vessels from Athens began to arrive. Though imported initially in small numbers, they quickly became an integral part of vessels used in the country (Plate 2).

The first Athenian vessels to arrive were painted in black on a red background ('black-figured'); later the colors were reversed, with the figures being painted in red on a black background ('red-figured'); and, finally, the plain black-glazed types arrived (Stern 1982: 136–41; cf. also Herzog 1988: 145–52; Bennett and Blakely 1989: 69–137).

The changes in the source of the imported Greek ware and the absolute dominance of the Attic pottery throughout the Persian period in Palestine is also conclusively proven by the finds in neighboring lands, and in fact all around the Mediterranean area, including its islands (cf. Gjerstad 1948: 279–80).

The influx of Greek goods to the eastern coast of the Mediterranean brought with it a Greek colonization on the coasts of Phoenicia and Palestine. Clear evidence for this process has been recovered at Al-Mina, Tel-Sukas, Tabat el Hammam and elsewhere along the Phoenician coast (cf. Braidwood 1940: 198; Wooley 1953: 127–88; Boardman 1964: 70–9; Parrot 1969: 435–50; Riis 1970, 1979; Ploug 1973; Niemeyer 1982: 237–55).

Evidence for the settlement of Greek merchants has also been discovered in Israel. We shall mention here several examples. At Tel Akko a rich assemblage of Attic-Greek pottery was discovered in buildings in the western part of the mound, and, on the basis of this find, the excavator, M. Dothan, stated: 'The finds in area F attest that the northwest section of the mound contained in the Persian period a rich merchants' quarter, mostly Greeks, who inhabited the finest section of the town' (Dothan 1979: 151; Tcherikover 1963: 31 n. 5).

From the excavations at Jaffa, a large warehouse of the Persian period that has close affinities with the plan of the warehouses at Al Mina was published in the 1980s. A sizeable amount of pottery was found on the floor of one of the rooms. All the vessels were of a single type and all bore similar red-figured decoration. The excavator compared this find with the form of commerce practiced at Al Mina. Like that northern Phoenician port city, it is very likely that a group of Greek merchants resided in Jaffa during this period and engaged in the wholesale trade of the products of Athenian potteries (Ritter-Kaplan 1982).

In the same manner Athenian pottery was also apparently brought to Tell Jemmeh. According to one account, the discoveries there included: 'About a dozen of the Red-figured cups [which] were evidently painted by the Pithos Painter; although not found on the same site, they may have been purchased at the same time in Athens and carried over on the same vessel to the Eastern Mediterranean coast, whence they were distributed to several merchants.' (Clairmont 1956–58: 120; cf. also

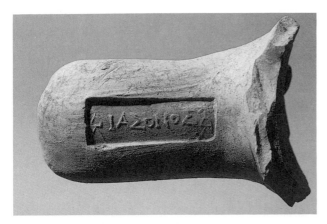

Plate 3   Stamped Greek jar handle, Hellenistic Period (courtesy of E. Stern; photograph by Zev Radovan)

Crowfoot et al. 1957: 212–13). But the best examples of the phenomenon of Greek settlers are perhaps the finds from Tel Dor, Mesad Hashavyahu and Migdol (Stern 1989a; Naveh 1962; Oren 1984).

The general impression received from the Greek settlement of the seventh–fourth centuries BCE in Phoenicia and apparently also in Israel, is of Phoenician cities containing a strong Greek element. The Greek population in these cities did not constitute a majority of the inhabitants – as in the Greek colonies in the western Mediterranean (except perhaps at Tell Sukas for a brief period) (Riis 1970, 1979; Niemeyer 1982: 237–55) – rather, they reflected the quality of *Enoikismos* – a settlement of Greeks among Phoenicians, or the more or less peaceful coexistence of a foreign Greek element in an already populated city. No matter which of these alternatives is applicable, it now seems that there is a more solid archaeological basis for the statement W.F. Albright made many years ago: 'In the sixth century BCE numerous Greek trading posts were established on the coasts of Egypt, Palestine, and Syria' (Albright 1960: 124).

During the Hellenistic period when the entire country had been conquered by the Greeks and became almost completely Hellenized, new groups of imported vases reached the country from all around the Mediterranean – even from North Africa, Spain and Italy. Among the new imported groups one should mention such wares as the 'west slope', the 'Megarian' and the 'Terra Sigilata' vases and the many new types of lamps (Stern 1992a: 117–26, Figs 155–67) found side by side with the decorated Greek wares.

Undecorated everyday ware from Greece also began to appear in Palestine during the Persian-Hellenistic periods. These included heavy bowls, cooking pots, etc., and prominent among them are the wine amphorae from the eastern Greek islands. It seems that even though Palestine produced large quantities of excellent wine, considerable amounts of wine still had to be imported from abroad,

undoubtedly intended for consumption by the increasing numbers of Greeks who had settled in Palestine.

The importing of Greek wine gradually increased in volume until it became a veritable flood in the fourth and third centuries BCE. The wine was brought from all the Greek islands, each of them producing its own jar-type. Most jars had stamped handles, designating the producers and the official in whose days the wine had been produced (Plate 3). Most jars came from the east Greek Islands such as Rhodes, Knidos, Samos, Kos, etc. (cf. for example Ariel 1990; Stern 1992a: 92–3; 124).

From the above discussion it should be concluded that in the Babylonian-Persian periods, and even before, Greek trade and its material culture became prominent in Palestine, bringing with it Greek settlers, soldiers and traders. Thus 200 years before its actual conquest by Alexander's armies the country was already Hellenized (Stern 1989a).

The material culture of the Persian-Hellenistic Age: the transition into the Greek world

City planning

The review of the results of the surveys and excavations in settlements of the Persian period throughout Palestine reveals that each area presents a different picture of urban life. We lack a full account of the cities in the mountain region. The coastal plain, on the other hand (and perhaps Galilee as well), were very densely populated in this period, and without doubt, were the scene of active urban life. It is sufficient in this matter to recall Herodotus' description of Gaza: 'it is not inferior to Sardis' (III,5). Indeed, an examination of the building remains in this area reveals several examples of well-planned settlements.

Careful study of the plans of cities outside Palestine shows that most were built according to a Hippodamic plan (a type of town plan named after Hippodamus of Miletus in Asia Minor, who lived in the fifth century BCE and was the first to write about the 'correct' principles of town planning). This plan type divides the residential areas into symmetrical blocks, separated by streets which cross each other at right angles.

It is important to note that this plan assigned different functions to different parts of the town: residential, public, cultic, for sport, etc. The clearest example of a classical Hippodamic plan can be seen at Olynthus in Greece (Stern 1990: 78–9).

In Palestine, along the coastal region there are some examples of well-planned towns. A certain amount of planning could be observed in the latest city at Tell Abu-Hawam. The front of a building was uncovered facing a main road which ran roughly parallel to the longitudinal axis of the city. At Shiqmona, a residential quarter

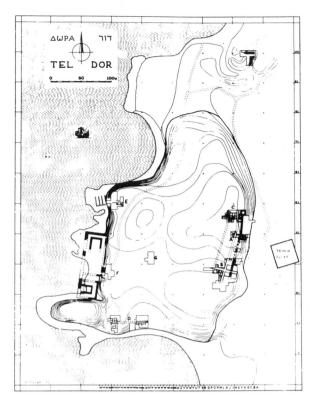

Figure 3   General plan of the excavations at Tel Dor, Hellenistic Period

Plate 4   Tel Dor, air view from the west (courtesy of E. Stern; photograph by Zev Radovan)

consisting of two streets set at right angles to one another contained houses built with a great degree of symmetry. A similar discovery was made in the excavations at neighboring Tel Megadim, where a built-up quarter was found to be intersected by a broad straight thoroughfare. The large blocks of buildings on either side of the road were separated by lanes which crossed the main road at right angles. The houses themselves are divided into a number of smaller units of similar plan (cf. Stern 1982: 47–9; Hamilton 1934; Finkielsztein 1987; Elgavish 1968: Pl LXIX; cf. also Herzog 1988: 88–114; Bennett and Blakely 1989: 1–67).

The large-scale recent excavations at Dor have uncovered another coastal town. Here it became apparent that all the strata and remains from the Persian and Hellenistic periods were laid out according to the Hippodamic plan (Figure 3, Plate 4). It is possible to say that the residential quarter at Dor is the finest and best-preserved example of Hippodamic planning yet found in Palestine (Stern 1985: 171–3; idem 1992a: 77–81). In fact, the closest parallel to the plan of Dor in the Persian period is that of Olynthus in Greece, mentioned above – even a superficial glance at the two town plans shows this very clearly.

The picture emerging from the investigations in Dor is that a long row of stores and workshops stood along the entire length of the inner face of the city-wall (Figure 4).

The doors of the shops opened onto a ruler-straight street, running parallel to the wall from north to south. On the opposite side of the street, whose width is about 2 m, we found the fine facade of a long, narrow residential block of buildings. The eastern doors of each unit of houses open onto the street, opposite the row of shops. The building is about 20 m wide. Its western side, which faces another street, parallel to that on its east, was also uncovered. This elongated block of buildings, preserved to a height of over 2 m and traced for a length of dozens of meters, was probably crossed by passages leading from one street to the other, but these seem to fall outside the areas excavated so far. Another, identical building or block of houses existed to the west of this second street. The block was divided by partition walls – lengthwise as well as widthwise – into smaller units or 'apartments', whose doors opened onto the closest street. It is reasonable to assume that what we have discovered is the ground floor, and that above it was another story. In one or two places we found traces of basements. It seems also that the easternmost street, between the residences and the stores, was originally roofed to provide shelter for pedestrians.

The structure described above was in use, according to the finds, throughout the Persian and Hellenistic periods. It seems not to have been violently destroyed, at least not until the days of Alexander Jannaeus, but was rebuilt from time to time. With each reconstruction the floor was raised, resulting in as many as two Persian and three Hellenistic floor levels; the openings were blocked and the walls rebuilt on a higher level. In this way, from one phase to the next, the inner divisions of the building and the function of its rooms varied; for example, in one stage, two plastered storage pools for water were added. However, none of the alterations changed the external walls. Many coins were found on the different floors, as well as stamped handles from Greek wine amphorae, especially from Rhodes and Knidos (see above), yielding reliable dates for the different stages.

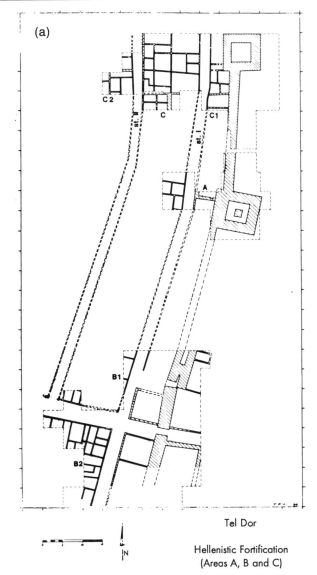

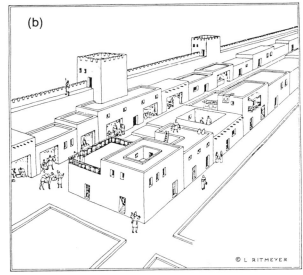

Figure 4 Plan (a) and reconstruction (b) of buildings in Areas A, B and C 'the residential quarter' at Tel Dor, Hellenistic Period

wave of building within these towns, most of which were certainly built according to the Hippodamic rules. Our problem is that even from this later period we possess only a few examples. Dor serves here also here as the best preserved remains (Stern 1992a: 108–14) of the Hellenistic town planning; the others are to be found at Marissa (Horowitz 1980; Kloner 1991). In the town plan at Dor, one can see the new fortification system (see below) as well as the careful division of the city quarters by function – into residential and public. Both at Dor and Marissa the new division of the city into an inner city surrounded by a wall and an outer one has been uncovered. Smaller Hellenistic towns such as Tel Anafa, Shiqmona, and Tel Michal also reveal elements of similar planning (Elgavish 1974; Herzog 1988: 165–76).

Fortifications – town planning and ethnicity: the 'oriental' to Hellenistic transformation at Tel Dor

Defensive walls assigned by their excavators to the Persian and Hellenistic periods have also been uncovered at a few sites, such as Akko, Tell Abu-Hawam, Gil'am, Tel Megadim, Tel Mevorakh, Jaffa, and Tell el-Hesi. All of these towns are on the coast and in the Shephelah. Remains of other walls have been cleared at Samaria, Jerusalem, Tell en-Nasbeh, Marissa and Lachish, and also recently at Heshbon in Transjordan (cf. Stern 1982: 50–3; Dothan 1976; Horowitz 1980; Kloner 1991).

By far the most important and best preserved fortifications of these periods also have been uncovered at Tel Dor (Stern 1988). They also represent a good source for a renewed study of the process of Hellenization which took place in Palestine in the fourth–third centuries BCE.

The outer walls of the building were constructed in the usual style of the period, mostly of well-hewn hard sandstone ashlars laid in 'headers'. The inner walls and divisions, however, were built in the typical Phoenician style of ashlar piers with a fill of rubble (cf. Sharon 1987).

The surprising fact about these plans is that, while the town plan of Olynthus seems to have been designed in the fourth century BCE, i.e. after the time of Hippodamus and the publication of his writings, that of Dor was probably laid out in its earliest form in the late sixth century BCE – *before* Hippodamus. Thus, Dor may have served as one of the examples from which Hippodamus developed his theories.

The new Hellenistic reorganizations of the Palestinian cities as Greek Polis were done by the great Ptolemaic king Ptolemy II Philadelphus (285–246 BCE), and caused a new

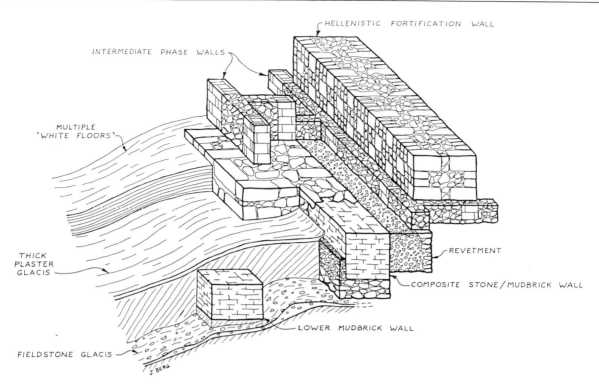

Figure 5 Section across fortifications during the Persian–Hellenistic Periods, Dor Area C

For most of the Persian period Dor's fortifications remained the same as in the preceding period, i.e. the last city wall built in the Iron Age which was actually the 'Assyrian' wall, with insets and offsets and a two-chambered gate. We can say that this wall protected the city for its entire period as a provincial capital – at first provincial capital of an Assyrian, then a Babylonian, and finally a Persian province. This massive and sophisticated fortification system was destroyed by the Persians when they suppressed the great Phoenician revolt against Persian rule in the mid-fourth century BCE. Judging from the archaeological evidence revealed in the excavations, a new fortification system was built at Dor very soon afterwards – still in the fourth century BCE.

The outer line of the city wall was built almost directly above the line of the earlier offset-inset wall, though this time it ran in a straight line, apart from a few small projections. This line was formed of buildings constructed close together in the space between the city wall and the inner street. Their outer (eastern) walls, over a meter thick, formed the outer defensive line.

The interesting feature of this fortification system is its method of construction (see Figure 5): it is quite clear that the Phoenician tradition of building was still used here in the mid-fourth century BCE. The outer wall and all the inner dividing walls were built in the style characteristic of this tradition: ashlar piers built in 'header and stretcher' fashion, i.e. with one stone laid lengthwise and two

widthwise across the pier, with fieldstone fill in between them. As far as we know, all the city walls of coastal Palestine and Phoenicia were built in this way from the tenth-ninth centuries BCE, at Megiddo and Tyre, down to the third century BCE, at Dor and Jaffa (cf. Stern 1992b; Sharon 1987).

Some parts of this Phoenician wall have been preserved to a height of over two meters and are among the most impressive of their kind yet found in Palestine. In the third century BCE, when this last 'Phoenician' wall of the fourth century together with its adjacent buildings was apparently still standing, the city received a new fortification system. The wall was built in a totally Greek style, previously encountered only rarely at sites in Palestine – in particular Samaria, Akko and Marissa, which had become Greek settlements at the very beginning of the Macedonian conquest (cf. Crowfoot 1940: pls 24–25; Dothan 1976; Kloner 1991).

This new wall was built of large, thick rectangular blocks of sandstone (about one meter long), most of them laid in headers facing the outside. It was a massive construction, about two meters thick, and was built of stone to its full height. Its foundations cut through all the preceding walls on its eastern side. Square towers, set about 30 m apart and built in the same style, projected beyond the wall. So far, two of these towers have been uncovered. The interior of the northern tower was not well preserved, but its outer contours are quite clear. The

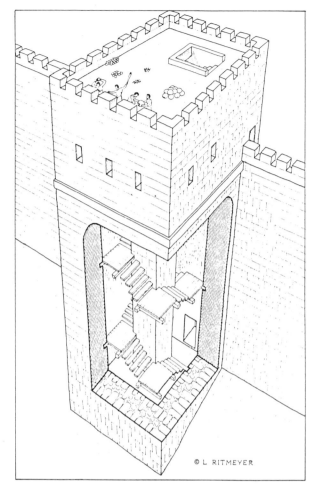

Figure 6 Reconstruction of the tower in Area A at Tel Dor. Note central staircase (courtesy of E. Stern)

foundations of the southern tower have survived in their entirety. It is one of the most outstanding remnants of fortifications from the beginning of the Hellenistic period. The stones of this tower are also about 1 m long and 0.5 m wide, and all of them were laid in headers facing the exterior. The relative flexibility of sandstone and its ability to receive blows without breaking enabled them to withstand the advanced siege machines of the period. In several spots, this wall has survived to a height of more than 3 m. Also preserved was the central pillar of the southern tower. It apparently supported a wooden spiral staircase which encircled it and led to the roof (Figure 6). This seems to be the earliest example of a tower of this type uncovered in Palestine (cf. Yadin 1977: 165–8; Magen 1984; Patrich 1986).

In our opinion, it can be concluded that this new wall, with its distinctive style and towers and its impressive innovations, represents an unmistakably Greek fortification. According to the stratigraphic evidence, the wall was not erected at the very start of the Hellenistic period since it

lay over a level dating from the beginning of the period, which contained, *inter alia*, a coin of Ptolemy II Philadelphus (285–246 BCE). It was, therefore, probably built in the last years of the reign of this king, or shortly afterwards, for by 219 BCE it was already in existence.

In any event, the change at Dor from fortifications built in Phoenician style to those in Greek style represents the final stage in the transformation of the city from a largely 'oriental' city to a Hellenistic one – a process which had started much earlier.

Similarly, with this change of walls, the gates of these towns were also changed, turning them from the two-room gates of the eastern tradition such as those from Megiddo and Dor (Stern 1990) to pure Greek-style gates (Sharon 1991). These changes were certainly due to the introduction of the new Greek siege weapons such as the balista (Schatzman 1991).

Cult and cult objects

General

The study of the local cults also testifies to the many changes that had occurred during these periods, i.e. the transformation from the older Israelite-Phoenician into the newer Greek. It was a gradual transition which lasted hundreds of years, beginning with the acceptance of Greek-styled figurines and ending with the complete victory of the Hellenic cult over the local, during the late Hellenistic Age (with the exception of the Jewish and Samaritan belief systems).

The temples

Only two temples have been uncovered in Palestine from this period which, by chance, represent the two main temple plans of the time:

1. The long building composed of three successive areas, in which the ritual was conducted mainly in the holy-of-holies.
2. The broad type of building of one or more chambers. Here the ritual usually took place in an enclosed court in front of the temple building.

An examination of these plans and of the remains of the architectural ornaments discovered in the temples in Phoenicia and Cyprus, in our opinion, revealed that both plans are of Phoenician origin. This conclusion also agrees with the cult objects found in the temples (Stern 1982: 61–7).

A third temple has been uncovered recently in lower Galilee (Frankel 1990), in which some unique Phoenician stone and bronze figurines were found, including a Phoenician dedication to the Goddess Astarte. The temples of the Hellenistic Age are following indeed the concepts of Greek architecture.

(a)   (b)

Plate 5 Heads of two clay figurines: one depicts a god's head in Egyptian style (a), and the other in a Greek style (b) (courtesy of E. Stern; photograph by Zev Radovan)

Cult objects

The cult objects of the Persian period that have been discovered primarily comprise large numbers of stone statuettes as well as clay and bronze figurines. Most of the stone statuettes originated in Cyprus and belong to the style known as 'sub-archaic Cypro-Greek 1–2', and date from 500 to 380 BCE (see opening photograph, this Chapter). A separate group are the statuettes of Egyptian origin, which could be ascribed only on general lines to the fifth-fourth centuries BCE.

The terra cotta figurines constitute a heterogeneous group, which exhibits stylistic influences from Phoenicia, Persia, Egypt, Cyprus, Rhodes and Greece. However, like most of the finds from the Persian period, these figurines can also be divided on general lines into two types: the earlier eastern and the later western. The figurines of the first group were widespread in Phoenicia and Palestine, and to a certain extent also in Cyprus. Isolated examples in eastern style are also known in Mesopotamia and Egypt, but none has been uncovered in the Aegean Islands or in Greece proper. The figurines of the western group, in addition to Palestine, Phoenicia and Cyprus, are also found in Rhodes, western Anatolia, Greece and, also in smaller numbers, in the western Mediterranean.

The two groups are clearly differentiated as to style. The eastern group is marked by numerous stylistic influences,

Canaanite, Egyptian and Mesopotamian-Persian, which were merged in the finest artistic tradition of the Phoenicians (see Plates 5a,b). The western group, on the other hand, is more uniform in style and the origin of each type can be more readily distinguished.

The bronze figurines found to date, on the other hand, are all either in local Phoenician or Egyptian style. Greek bronze figurines are still not earlier than the Hellenistic age (Iliffe 1935; Frankel 1990).

From the point of view of form, we may say that the common Iron Age figurines were still in use at the beginning of the Persian period. These include the 'Pillar' Astarte type and certain types of horses and riders. Later – perhaps by the end of the sixth to the beginning of the fifth century – statuettes and molds for casting figurines in Cypriot or east-Greek style, which were far superior in terms both of workmanship and artistic quality, began to be imported. These became the dominant types in Palestine and Phoenicia throughout the Persian period. Only at the beginning of the Hellenistic period were they replaced by figurines in Attic style, which became models for the local (Phoenician) craftsmen who began to produce new types, copying the innovative Greek technique of hollow and molded figurines (Plate 6). This also led to an all-round improvement in the skills of local artists. In these figurines can be observed older motifs in a changed form (fertility

Figure 7   Drawing of a stamp depicting the Persian king fighting two monsters (source: Tel Dor, courtesy of E. Stern)

Plate 6   Clay figure of the child–god Horus, Persian Period (courtesy of E. Stern; photograph by Zev Radovan)

goddesses, etc.), together with contemporary influences which are expressed mainly in minor details of dress, jewelry, etc. (Stern 1982: 158–82, idem 1992a: 81–91, 126–30).

The Glyptic art

Another perspective from which one can observe the gradual change of the Phoenician material culture from its older eastern tradition to that of the Greeks, is through the study of the Glyptic art. We have already partly discussed it when dealing with the motifs on the coins during the Persian and Hellenistic ages (see above). From the same periods we also possess some assemblages of seals and bullae (Figures 7, 8).

The study of the finds shows that the Assyrian occupation of Palestine opened a new chapter in its Glyptic art: suddenly the Mesopotamian Glyptic penetrated the country and shortly afterward local people – from all the country's various nations – started to imitate the Assyrian motifs. The continuous occupation of the country by the two additional Mesopotamian empires – Babylon and Persia – had deepened and established the penetration of the new motifs, and in this matter we should regard the three periods as one cultural unit.

Figure 8   Drawing of a stamp depicting the same motif as in Figure 7, but in Greek style, Persian period. (Source: Tel Dor, courtesy of E. Stern)

The imported seals, and later the imitated ones, were absorbed into the local repertoire all over the country. Besides accurate imitations of the Mesopotamian ones, some were made which were 'customized', according to the special taste of each of the local nations. The changes took place mainly in the 'cultic' motifs and less among the official ones.

At the end of the period, i.e., in the fourth century BCE, these stamps were mass-produced from cheap materials – glass or faience – and also stamped on Phoenician and Palestinian coins. At this stage some Greek and Egyptian elements were added to the old Assyrian and Persian ones in accordance with the mixed cult common in Palestine during the period (Stern 1982: 196–200, idem, 1993b; see Figures 7 and 8).

This tendency continued into the Hellenistic period. It is since the fourth century BCE onwards that the newly introduced Greek motifs gradually replaced the older eastern-Mesopotamian and local ones.

At the close of the Persian age, even though seal impressions in the Phoenicio-Persian local style are still uncovered, more and more seals in the Athenian-Greek style begin to appear. We have already indicated this phenomenon in relation to the Samaritan coins (Meshorer and Qedar 1991); now we may add the depictions on some dozens of Samaritan bullae which were also recently published (Cross 1974: 28–9; Leith 1990; Stern 1993a, 1993b). On these bullae, beside the local Babylonian, Assyrian and Egyptian motifs, more and more Greek ones appear by the fourth century BCE. These include cult scenes presenting Zeus, Hermes, Herakles, Athena, etc., and scenes of everyday life. During the Hellenistic age the Greek influence became dominant, adding many additional Greek scenes as well as the portraits of the new country's rulers – from Alexander the Great through the Ptolemaic kings to the Seleucians.

Summary

The most recent archaeological research has been of great value for the understanding of the transition of the material culture of Palestine from its age-old eastern tradition into the new western-Greek concept, during the Persian and Hellenistic ages.

We have seen that the coastal cities of Palestine already had a Phoenicio-Greek population in the pre-Alexandrine period and that this population as a whole encouraged rapid Hellenization during the late fifth–fourth centuries BCE, *before* the Greek conquest.

The study of the material culture of Palestine at this early stage reveals that the country was already divided into two regions at the beginning of the Persian period: on the one hand the mountainous area of Judaea and Transjordan (and to a lesser extent also Samaria), and on the other, Galilee and the coastal area. The border between these two cultural areas is at times very sharp – almost like a border dividing two countries. Without an understanding of this division of Palestine it is almost impossible to understand the material development of the culture of the period.

An analysis of the culture of these two regions demonstrates that the mountain culture remained basically 'eastern' in character. It was made up of local cultures which continued the Israelite tradition and eastern influences (Assyrian, Babylonian, Persian and Egyptian). In the coastal culture, on the other hand, which was basically 'western' in nature, eastern Greek, Cypriot and Athenian elements can be observed. It is, therefore, probable that the Greek material culture considerably preceded the Macedonian conquest. At the same time there is no doubt that this was exclusively an external conquest, that is to say, Greek cultural products were used without acquiring the significance they had in their native land; they were adapted to local traditions and customs. It appears that the main bearers of this new culture in Palestine were the Phoenicians and, only in the Hellenistic period, the Greek soldiers and settlers.

By the third century BCE the entire country had become completely Hellenized. The most important contribution to this final step had been made by Ptolemy II Philadelphus, in whose days many new towns had been built or rebuilt – both on the coast and in the country's interior – in the Greek polis concept. Also the entire local administration and the internal division had been changed into the Greek-Hellenistic one, modeled first on the Egyptian-Ptolemaic system.

WARFARE

The warfare in the Persian and Hellenistic periods had two aspects: first, the fortification of the settlements, city walls, towers, gates, etc. (see main text). In these the process of transition from the older eastern tradition to the new Greek one can be observed. In the second aspect — the armies and their weapons — a similar transition can also be observed. During this period of time the inferior traditional eastern armies were slowly giving way to the new Hellenistic-Greek military and logistic systems. All this actually happened long before the physical Greek takeover in the time of Alexander the Great.

We possess clear archaeological evidence from Mesad Hashavyahu, located in Judaean territory on the Philistine coast, that Greek mercenaries had already served in the armies of the last Judaean kings (Naveh 1962; cf. Oren 1984). Units of Greek mercenaries, of all sorts and types, both small and large, took an active role in the country's wars during the Persian period. These mercenaries left large numbers of actual remains, including weapons — daggers, arrow heads, lance heads — armour-scales and even metal headgear (Stern 1982: 154–7). Greek warriors are depicted on stamps and impressions found in local sites; for example, a clay bulla from Dor, belonging perhaps to a Greek officer and depicting a phalanx of Greek hoplites (Stern 1992a: 97, fig. 129; see Figure 1.1). It also seems that in this early period the Greeks had already introduced the new siege weapons such as the catapult and the balista (see Plate 1.1). At Tel Dor we found many balista stones, some of which belonged to this period (Shatzman 1991; Sharon 1991). In addition, evidence from Paphos, Cyprus,

Figure 1.1 Drawing of a Persian Period bulla depicting a Greek 'Phalanx'. (Source: Tel Dor, courtesy of E. Stern)

strengthened the hypothesis that by 490 BCE the Persians had used them there (Iliffe-Mitford 1953). In any case, they were certainly already in Palestine at the beginning of the Hellenistic Age (Dothan 1976)

From this period onwards we have rich evidence concerning every aspect of the activity of the Greek and Hellenistic armies in the country, which completely replaced the older eastern ones. This evidence comes from the historical records as well as from many sculptures, reliefs and inscriptions detailing the morphology of the army and its equipment (which was many times left on the battlefields and subsequently found in the excavations). Such are the recent discoveries in Dor and in the Jerusalem citadel, attributed to the siege of Antiochus VII Sidetes against Tryphon and John Hyrcanus in 133/2 BCE (Gera 1985; Sivan and Solar 1984) and from Akko (Dothan 1976).

Plate 1.1 Catapult stones of the Persian and Hellenistic Periods from Tel Dor (courtesy of E. Stern; photograph by Zev Radovan)

26

THE IMPACT OF ROME ON THE PERIPHERY: THE CASE OF PALESTINA – ROMAN PERIOD (63 BCE–324 CE)

James D. Anderson

The sudden political transformation of Judaea in 63 BCE from nominal independence under the last of the Hasmonean priest-kings to the status of a Roman vassal province has left no sure indication in the archaeological record. It is rather in the gradual signs of ever-greater integration in the Roman world system during the reign of the client king, Herod the Great (37–4 BCE), that a decided change at last becomes visible in the material culture of the country. From the excavations of that king's new port city of Caesarea and his opulent palace villas at Jericho, Masada and Herodion, and from the aristocratic residences excavated in the Jewish Quarter of Jerusalem, the extent of stylistic and technical borrowing from Roman culture, at least in the realm of architecture and decorative arts, becomes increasingly obvious.

The archaeological investigation of the larger economic, social and ecological issues of Roman rule in Judaea (later, Palestine), however, remain in their initial stages. Detailed archaeological studies of the nature of agricultural production, of the economic relationship between rural areas and the cities, and the connection between ethnic or religious identifications and other elements of material life are only now being addressed. The extent of political integration has long been clear as Palestine was incorporated into an imperial mosaic that stretched over an area from Scotland to the north, Portugal to the west, Aswan to the south, and Palmyra to the east (see Figure 2). Throughout the centuries covered by this chapter, the people of the Holy Land were exposed to the socio-political process of 'Romanization', which has clear manifestations in the archaeological record.

This chapter will describe three main periods of material life in Judaea and Palestine through a correlation of the archaeological data with the main literary sources. It should also be noted that although the population of the country comprised pagan Greeks, Jews, Samaritans and, from the first century CE, Christians, the following chapter will focus primarily on the material culture of the Greeks and the Jews.

Historical background

Second Temple Period: 63 BCE to 70 CE

In an effort to split what the Hasmonaeans had united, Pompeius removed Jewish control from the Greek cities of the sea-coast, Transjordan (known as the League of the Decapolis) and the interior, so that Judaea now included Judaea proper, Samareitis, Galilee, Peraea and Idumaea. In 57–55 BCE Gabinius reconstituted the Greek cities of the coast and Transjordan, and Julius Caesar later restored to Judaea her port of Jaffa and remitted tribute in the Sabbatical Year.

After the Parthian invasion of Judaea in 40 BCE, Herod 'the Great', with Roman support, reclaimed Jerusalem in 37 BCE and thereafter ruled Judaea as 'client king' of Rome. As a result of his capable services as king, as well as his diplomatic prowess and dexterity, (Josephus *Bellum Judaicum* (*BJ*) 1 12.4.242; *Antiquities* (*Ant*) 14.11.2.274), Herod received from Augustus several Greek cities and territories across the Jordan (Jones 1938). Herod's reign is marked by a feverish building program, including the reconstruction of the Second Temple in Jerusalem. The remains of his building program, which strongly reflect Hellenistic and Roman architectural influences, are found in almost every city across Palestina. Although the son of an Idumaean Jew, Herod was generally considered by Jews as a tyrant, and his reign as well as that of his son, Herod Archelaus, was marked by frequent Jewish insurrections.

Upon his death in 4 BCE, Herod's kingdom was divided among his sons and daughter Salome. However, at the request of the Jews, Augustus replaced Archelaus in 6 CE with a Roman equestrian *praefectus* (later *procurator*), who thereafter ruled Archelaus' former territories of Judaea, Idumaea, Samaria, Caesarea and Sebaste (*Ant* 17.13.2–344; *BJ* 2.7.3–111). This was at once followed by a property census and direct taxation – a point marking the beginning of continuous Jewish revolutionary ferment. Herod's kingdom was united under his grandson M. Julius Agrippa, who received Philip's territory (Batanaea,

Aerial view of Masada (photograph by Werner Braun)

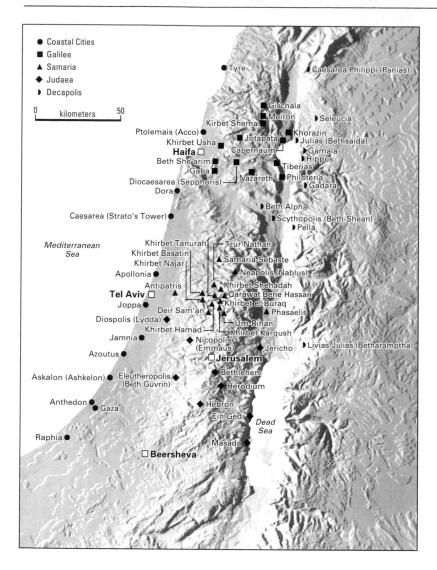

Figure 1 Principal sites from the Roman period

Trachonitis, Aurantis, Gaulanitis, Paneas, Ulatha) in 38 CE, Herod Antipas' (Galilee and Peraea) in 39 CE, and what had been Archelaus' in 41 CE (*Ant* 19.9.1–356; 18.7.2–252; *BJ* 2.9.6–183). With his sudden demise in 44 CE, all of Agrippa's territories were transferred to a Roman *praefectus* residing in Caesaraea (*Ant* 19.9.1–356; *BJ* 2.11.6–220): the Herodian period had thus come to an end.

The First Revolt of 66 CE resulted from various events and circumstances occurring over a long period of time, including chronic procuratorial incompetence and insensitivity, Jewish religious susceptibilities, class tensions and friction between Jews and pagans in mixed cities (Levine 1975a: 29). Jerusalem, as well as the Second Temple was destroyed in 70 CE, becoming thereafter the base of *Legio X Fretensis* (*BJ* 7.1.3–17). Herod's palace, Masada, defended throughout the revolt by Jewish Zealots, fell in 74 CE (see Window 1, pp. 466–7).

Post-First Revolt Period: 70 CE to 132 CE

Judaea was then made a praetorian province administered by a senatorial legate, with the new capital Caesarea eclipsing Jerusalem's political supremacy (Levine 1975a: 32). As for the Jews, in addition to the destruction of the Temple and worship therein, evidence suggests a period of ruinous agrarian conditions created by oppressive taxes and conversion of large tracts to imperial land. In 105–6 CE Trajan consolidated control of the Red Sea–Mediterranean overland trade with the creation of *Provincia Arabia* from what had been Nabataea. *Provincia Arabia* now comprised the Negev and Transjordan as far north as Bostra.

In *ca.* 132 CE the Jews, under the leadership of Simeon Bar-Kosiba, known as Bar Kochba, and Aquiva ben Joseph, rebelled against Rome in the 'Second Revolt'. In addition to the oppressive agrarian situation, ancient

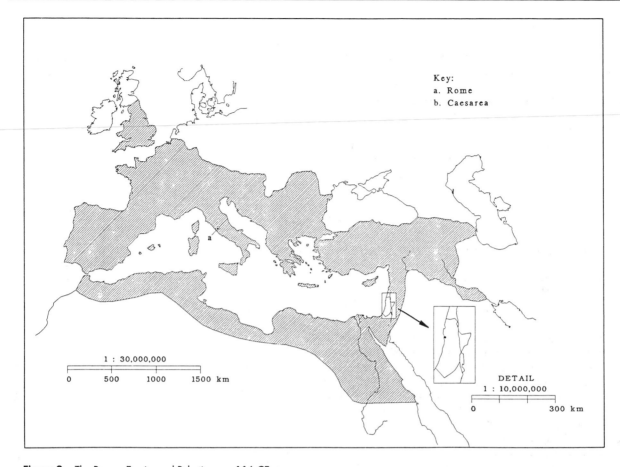

Key:
a. Rome
b. Caesarea

1 : 30,000,000

0   500   1000   1500 km

DETAIL
1 : 10,000,000

0   300 km

Figure 2   The Roman Empire and Palestina, ca. 116 CE

sources cite the reasons precipitating the Revolt as Hadrian's plan to convert Jerusalem to a Roman – and pagan – colony (Dio Works LXIX 12–14), and a prohibition on circumcision (Eusebius *Historia Ecclesiastica* IV 6). Excavation has proven that the revolt was finally suppressed in the Judaean desert (Bar-Adon in Kochavi 1972: 25), and the sources suggest that the revolt was centered in Judaea. That it did not spread into Galilee is supported by numismatic evidence (Applebaum 1976: 23; Meyers et al. 1976: 169) as well as a lack of evidence for site destruction (see Goodman 1983: 137).

Post-Second Revolt Period: 132 CE to 325 CE

The Second Revolt resulted in the annihilation of two-thirds of the Jewish population of Judaea (Applebaum 1989: 157), a restriction against Jews entering Jerusalem on pain of death (Eusebius *HE* IV.6.3), and a mass emigration of Jews from Judaea to the coastal cities and Galilee, which became henceforth the center of Jewish learning and autonomous institutions. The province, now officially named Palestina (a revival of the term used by Herodotus: 1.105), seems to have taken on a new importance in the

Empire after the Second Revolt. Indeed, it was made consular (Isaac and Roll 1979: 54–66), another legion was added, high profile legates were appointed (Smallwood 1981: 546), and large military forces were stationed in Jerusalem and Legio (see Window 2, p. 468).

From the Severan period (*ca.* 193–235 CE), not only was the process of urbanization renewed (Jones 1931: 82–5), but many of the emperors developed favorable relations with the Jews – notably scholars representing the Jewish leadership. For example, Severus allowed Jews to become decurions and so participate in municipal affairs (*Digest* 50.2.3.3), and Caracalla fostered a close relationship with R Judah I (Levine 1975a: 65). As a result, Palestina became more peaceful, Jews and pagans developed closer ties, and the nation prospered economically. However, it appears that by the second half of the third century CE Palestina was suffering the consequences of Empire-wide political and economic crises. Indeed, Talmudic references attest to villagers afraid to remain in their fields, to the erection of fortifications and the crowding of the population into defended settlements (Sperber 1978: 51–5). In addition, during the years 260–266 CE Palestina fell under the domination of Palmyra.

With the reign of Diocletian the provinces of the empire, including Palestina, entered a radical period of transition. After the harsh experience of third century CE power politics, the power of individual provincial governors was diluted by the division of large geopolitical units. Diocletian transferred *Legio X Fretensis* from Aelia to Aila (Aqaba) to face the new pressure of the Arab tribes (295 CE) and in so doing moved the Negev (including Petra) from Arabia to Palestina, and Trachonitis and Batanaea to Arabia. Of the Herodian lands beyond the Jordan, only the Golan remained in Palestina. In addition, bureaucracies were centralized, inflated, and divided between the military and state. The period of this survey concludes with the defeat of Licinius in 324 CE by Constantine, who thereafter added the eastern provinces to his realm.

Settlement patterns

Cities

Rome had much impact on the urbanization of Palestina. Fully-evolved Roman provincial cities differed from Hellenistic city-states in that the former were not only forbidden to wage war or make alliances with each other, but were required to carry out the wishes of the provincial governor. In addition, the governments were essentially aristocratic rather than democratic. Although normally permitting the retention of much of the original form of government (for Bashan, Edessa, and Gerasa, see Goodman 1983: 252), the Roman provincial governors preferred to deal with the Greek form of oligarchic *boule* rather than the popular assembly. In addition, the Romans insisted that council candidates must own land and, once elected, retain their seats for life. Thus, much of the responsibility of government, especially that of a financial nature, within these cities and their requisite territories was left to the local aristocratic class. Once the aristocratic and landed council had become the governing body of the city the popular assembly declined in importance and eventually ceased to meet.

Ancient sources suggest that Rome endeavored to devolve powers of government in conquered areas from centralized administrations to a number of autonomous cities through a process of municipal foundation or restoration. A result of such devolution was that the Roman government gained considerable leverage, as the cities now depended upon Roman support to maintain their prestige. Indeed, the governor could promote or relegate the status of any city (such as Antioch in 196 CE), alter its spheres of influence, or endorse or revoke its right to mint coins.

City foundations
According to Josephus, city foundations began under Gabinius, proconsul of Syria in 57–55 BCE (*Ant*

14.5.3.88; *BJ* 1.8.4.166). However, with the exception of houses and a wall built under Gabinius recovered at Sebaste (Crowfoot et al. 1957: 5), not a single excavated site has produced evidence for building activities during this period (Isaac 1990: 339). Then again, numismatic evidence attests to some inhabitants calling themselves 'Gabinians' (Isaac 1990: 340; Schürer 1979: (2) 162 for Samarians). In total, the negative evidence suggests that at most Pompeius and Gabinius *restored* rather than founded new cities.

Archaeology has confirmed many of the literary references to the foundation of cities by Herod and his sons. Excavations (Crowfoot et al. 1966: 31–3) at Sebaste attest to Herod's construction of a temple in an enclosed precinct, and much of Caesarea and its harbour constructed by him at the site of Strato's Tower has been excavated (Raban 1985; Levine and Netzer 1986). Excavations have been carried out at Herod Antipas' Sepphoris (Waterman et al. 1937), Livias-Julias (Waterhouse and Ibach 1975: 227), and Tiberias (see Avi-Yonah and Stern 1975–8 (4) 1171–7). Philip is recorded as having established Caesarea Philippi (Paneas) as his capital (*Ant* 18.2.1.28; *BJ* 2.9.1.168), while Agrippa II further enlarged the temple at Caesarea (*Ant* 20.9.4.211) and granted city status to the village of Bethsaida, north of lake Tiberias, renaming it Julias (*Ant* 18.2.1.28; *BJ* 2.9.1.168; Schürer 1979: 2171ff.). However, despite their many foundations, the Herodian period represents an hiatus in the civic devolution process: indeed, the cities were most likely governed more directly and severely by the Herodians than by the Romans (see Schürer 1979: (2) 97). Herod seems to have centralized his power and administration after Ptolemaic models (*contra* Goodman 1983: 135), with *toparchies* divided into villages, headed by a village clerk appointed by the crown.

Roman colonies (see Window 2) were founded from the Flavian period. However, apart from Hadrian's revival of Jerusalem as Aelia Capitolina, the policy of urbanization was not carried out again until the Severan period (the end of the second–early third centuries CE). Diospolis (Lydda), Eleutheropolis (Beth Gabra) and Nicopolis (Emmaus) were granted municipal status (which in turn diminished the large territory of Aelia), while the southern coastal towns of Jamnia, Ashkelon, Azotus and Gaza developed separate port communities which finally attained independent city rank (Applebaum 1967: 11, 14).

Spheres of influence
It has been argued traditionally that a normal city served as a market for the surrounding country and as a distributive center for such few imported or locally-manufactured articles as the neighboring peasantry required (Jones 1974: 30). However, apart from collectors selected and sent to the villages by the city council to exact imperial taxes, levy recruits for the imperial army, and requisition supplies and

transport, the villages seem to have been left to themselves (Jones 1974: 31). Indeed, a recent study of rabbinical texts (Goodman 1983: 130) suggests that, in the Galilee, tax collection was the city's only important function and that the provision of security, a market for goods, or a coinage to facilitate exchange had little effect on the villages.

Attempts to calculate the size of such city territories include a survey of the locations of milestones found inscribed with a particular city's name (Avi-Yonah 1977: 127–9). However, the accuracy of this system is questionable, as such stones were more likely to have been intended to serve as a benefit to long-distance travel than to demarcate territorial boundaries (Goodman 1983: 130). Alternatively, comparative models from across the Empire have been used to define the extent of city territories in Palestina (Hopkins 1980). Accordingly, major cities have been found to include in their territories minor urban centers, which served a number of towns usually located on the periphery of the territory, which in turn served villages. From the period after the First Revolt, five lesser cities were situated at a 50 km radius from Caesarea, the provincial capital; six lesser cities within a 40km radius from Scythopolis, the chief city of the Decapolis; and three lesser cities at radii of both 51 km and 32 km from Jerusalem. Evidence from 134 Roman period settlements in the Golan suggest a similar scheme (Urman 1985), with 5 cities with areas of over 120 dunams, 40 towns of 40–120 dunams, 28 large villages of 20–40 dunams, and 28 agricultural settlements of less than 20 dunams in area.

Population

For the most part, those Greek cities revived under Gabinius retained their pagan majority throughout the Roman period, most likely because early emperors favored Greek or mixed cities (Applebaum 1989: 159). Literary evidence suggests that Jewish populations in mixed cities were the recipients of very harsh treatment during the wars and insurrections of the Roman period. Indeed, at Caesarea, although a Jewish community is known before 70 CE, there is no record of one existing until the third century, at which point pagans, Jews, Christians and Samaritans were about equally represented (Levine 1975a: 34). As for Jewish cities, those founded by Herod's sons could not maintain their purely Jewish populations. After the Second Revolt, the literature is very succinct in its description of Hadrian expelling Jews from Aelia Capitolina (previously Jerusalem) and replacing them with foreign, pagan colonists. Hadrian also may have expelled the Jewish population from the cities of Sepphoris and Tiberias, which had been Jewish during the First Revolt (*BJ* 2.599; Rajak 1973: 346). That the ruling Jewish aristocracies were disenfranchised at this time is suggested by the early third century CE rescript of the emperors Severus and Caracalla that Jews might serve on municipal councils (*Digest* 5.2.3.3), as well as by an attempt to build

a temple in honor of Hadrian in Tiberias (Avi-Yonah 1976: 46). Indeed, pagan types such as the Capitoline Triad (Jones 1937: 279) and Victory (Smallwood 1981: 243) appear on the coinage of Sepphoris and Tiberias, respectively, after the Bar Kochba revolt. Alternatively, the use of such symbolism, which was similar to types favored by neighboring cities (Hill 1914: 1–10), may have been due to the unwillingness of Jewish leaders to offend the Roman authorities after the Second Revolt (Goodman 1983: 129). Even if such a policy *was* pursued by Hadrian, by the fourth century Tiberias and Diocaesarea were so completely controlled by the Jews that no pagan, Samaritan, or Christian was allowed entry (Eusebius *Martyrs of Palestine* 29).

Villages

Effects of the *Pax Romana*: population increases

A major development during the Roman period was an overall rise of the rural population across Palestina (excluding Judaea), despite wars and insurrections. In the mountainous area of upper Galilee archaeological survey has shown 19 Early Iron Age sites and 32 of the Roman–Byzantine periods (Meyers et al. 1974). In western Galilee, 53 Roman–Byzantine sites compared with 36 Hellenistic have been observed (Avi-Yonah 1976: 19), and in the northern Jordan Valley 12 Early Iron Age sites have been found compared to 36 Roman–Byzantine (Avi-Yonah 1976: 19). In the Golan, 75 settlements have been identified for the Hellenistic period, against 182 for the Roman period (Urman 1985: 104).

Village siting

Villages of the first century CE, such as Gamala, Jotapata, Gischala (Goodman 1983: 29) and Nazareth (Bagatti 1969), are situated on top of steep hills in the interests of defense. However, ceramic and Talmudic evidence suggests that the favored sites for settlements, such as at Meiron, Khirbet Shema, Usha and Beth Shearim, were constructed from the second century CE on the lower slopes of hills adjacent to level ground (Goodman 1983: 194). Even some long-established sites, such as Jotapata and Sepphoris (Meyers et al. 1978), had second century settlements below their citadels. Such a change resulted from the expansion of population and settlement after 135 CE, as well as from the change in political atmosphere after the Second Revolt. The increase in numbers of villages meant that they were now sited much more closely together than previously, especially in Upper Galilee (Avi-Yonah 1976: 17). For example, Khorazin is only two kilometers from Capernaum, and Hammat Tiberias less than one kilometer from Roman Tiberias.

In contrast, excavations in the Golan (Urman, 1985: 83–4) have revealed that most Roman and Byzantine period settlements were constructed on hills or spurs (123 of 211). However, most of these settlements have been recovered near springs, and it seems proximity to a water source outweighed considerations of security or access to trade routes. In addition, the siting of these agricultural settlements on hills would have preserved the better lands in the valleys below for agriculture.

Village planning

Aerial photographs attest to second century CE Galilean villages having well-planned central areas with public buildings, the most important of which was the synagogue (discussed below). Although varying in size and style, the houses were commonly small and even one-roomed, and were clustered around courtyards and down alleyways leading off the main streets (Yeivin 1971: vii–viii, xi; Mazar et al. 1973–4: (1) 16). Industrial quarters, including oil presses at Khorazin and Beth Shearim, and workshops at Meiron (Meyers et al. 1974: 80; Avi Yonah and Stern 1975–8: (1) 299), are generally found adjacent to the main residential areas, and sometimes outside the village.

Aerial photographs also indicate the various shapes of ten villages constructed in the Golan and Galilee from the second century CE as round, bow-shaped, square, rectangular, or gamma-shaped (Yeivin 1971: vii). Shapes of these and earlier settlements are apt to follow the topography: Khorazin is rectangular with a long main street running along a slight ridge (Yeivin 1971: iv); Kfar Einan, like Meiron, is split into terraces running down the slope of the hill (Yeivin 1971: x; Meyers et al. 1974: 12); only Kh. Usha is found with a network grid in a square shape on its plateau (Yeivin 1971: x). However, those of the third to fourth century CE settlements in the Golan are fixed and generally ignore the local topography (Goodman 1983: 30). As for the size of these villages, modern estimates vary, at least partly on account of the lack of a rigid convention in antiquity. On the basis of aerial photographs of ten sites, 1–10 ha in size has been argued (Yeivin 1971: v), while the excavators of Kh. Shema and Meiron estimate *ca.* 30 hectares (Meyers et al. 1974, 22; 1981: 76–7).

Not only were second century CE villages constructed on sites much more difficult to defend, research has yet to uncover evidence for walls protecting these villages. Although Josephus (*BJ* 2.573) writes that some of the villages were fortified during the First Revolt, apart from Beth Shearim (Mazar et al. 1973–4), none of the excavated sites of the second century CE or later in Galilee have produced a village wall (Goodman 1983: 30).

Village class systems

Ancient literature (especially Josephus *Vita*: 79 and St Mark 6: 21) attests to a clear-cut aristocracy in first century CE Galilean villages, where leading men won political influence through their wealth as landowners, moneylenders, or market speculators. However, excavation

of second century CE Galilean sites argues generally against a large gap between different social strata, especially compared to other areas of the empire (Duncan Jones 1974: 17–32). Specifically, the rarity of homogeneous housing styles (Yeivin 1971: xi–xii) suggests against rented housing in favor of individual ownership by most villagers, although a few villages may have been wholly-owned by large landowners (Goodman 1983: 34, 60, 120).

Effects of political upheaval

Evidence from across Palestina suggests that the two great Jewish revolts had a major impact on village life. In western Samaria, village life at Um-Rihan seems to have ended about this time (Applebaum 1986), and the lapse of the field tower pattern (discussed below) in the second century CE seems to have been a consequence of the same upheaval, which put an end to occupation at the Jewish townlets of Hirbet Najar, Um-Rihan, and Hirbet Karqush (Dar 1986: 42–51). These may have belonged to the 13 Jewish villages in Samaria which were 'submerged', according to talmudic sources, after the war (see Applebaum 1986: 265 for references). As for the Second Revolt, the increase in settlements of Galilee and the Lower Golan (Urman 1985) is likely due to Judaean emigration.

Confiscations

Before 70 CE, the royal Jewish house owned private estates throughout Palestina in areas of great fertility (*AJ* 14.207). With the procuratorship, it is likely that such land became imperial domain (Applebaum 1967: 283), and Talmudic evidence, together with Bar Kochba's correspondence found in the Judaean Wilderness (Yadin 1963), suggests that after the First Revolt large tracts of land were converted to *praedia Caesaris* (Applebaum 1976: 9). Some of this land can be located in Judaea, Jericho and Peraea, and probably Ein Gedi (Avi Yonah 1977: 12). By the second century CE much land may have become *territoria* or *prata* for specific legions or auxiliary units stationed throughout the country, such as the valley of Jezreel for the legion at Legio (Avi Yonah 1977: 141). However, by the Severan period, it appears that R Judah I received the lease of extensive areas of state land in Galilee, the Golan and Bashan, suggesting that at least some Jews were made *conductores* of imperial lands (Applebaum 1989: 149).

Farmsteads

The classical Roman villa constructed in rural areas across the empire, and which comprised an isolated farm equipped with amenities such as baths and mosaics (Rivet 1969), is not found in Roman period Palestina (Applebaum 1989: 125). Indeed, the bigger town houses excavated in Galilee are only of moderate size (Safrai and Stern 1974–6: (2) 643). This absence of villas is best explained by the

Plate 1 One of many field towers grouped around the fortress at Qarawat Bene Hassan, western Samaria (photograph by Dar, 1986)

political, social and economic instability of Palestina which did not foster such development (Dar 1986: 249). Rather than villas, the mainstay of farming across Palestina seems to have been the small, private holding. The size of these holdings is suggested by a survey of western Samaria where small farms of 2.5 hectares were recorded (Safrai and Stern 1974–6: (2) 657).

Field systems

It seems that a change in field patterns occurred in western Samaria, at least, as a result of the Second Revolt (Applebaum 1986: 262). Ceramic evidence suggests that a system of cultivation by smallholders based around massive stone field towers (see Plate 1) did not survive beyond the second century CE, and that such holdings gave way to larger estates controlled by fewer people (Dar 1986: 109). These towers, 45 of which have been excavated out of 1200 identified throughout Samaria, are square, oblong or circular in form and were constructed for the most part in the third century BCE (Dar 1986: 109).

Josephus attests to large estates, or *latifundia*, existing across first century CE Golan (*Vita* 33, 47, 58) and Judaea (*Vita* 4.22). That some of these estates were transformed in the Roman period to smaller centrally-managed farmsteads may be in evidence at Hirbet Shehadah in western Samaria (Dar 1986: 18–21). Forty-four field towers suggest cultivation by smallholders or tenants in the pre-Roman period, after which the towers were abandoned, and the settlement became centered on a strongly-fortified acropolis. A concentration of threshing floors and livestock enclosures connected by a paved roadway suggests (Dar 1986: 20) that the agricultural areas were cultivated under supervision. It may be that the entire area passed into the ownership of one estate which cultivated these lands through tenants who dwelt on the fringes of the farmstead (Applebaum 1977). A possible explanation (Dar 1986) for the centralization of management might be that

the farm belonged to the Roman government and was operated by government officials (*conductores*).

Fortifications

Despite the absence of Roman forts in the countryside (see Window 2), evidence has been found in western Samaria for rural settlement influenced by the army. The fortified farmhouse (Figure 3) at Hirbet Tanurah (Dar 1986: 225–9), guarding the Qana gorge and the roads in the hills of western Samaria, contained four gates, a surrounding defensive wall, an administrative command post, storeroom areas and barracks. The first fortification (the central fortlet) may have been built between Revolts. The second phase, perhaps from the Second Revolt, had room in its barracks for 40 men. In the third to fourth centuries CE the site was converted from a fortified enclosure to a fortified farmstead which produced oil, wine, olives and cereals. In addition, local defense arrangements were made in villages and townlets of western Samaria, such as fortified towers which, attached to houses, converted the fronts of settlements into defensive walls. Good examples of such are found at the villages of Hirbet Najar and Um-Rihan (Dar 1986: 47–51).

Caves

As a result of insurrection and war, many caves were inhabited in Palestina. Most have been found in the western and south-western foothills of Judaea, and a number recently have been identified in Lower Galilee (Isaac and Oppenheimer 1985). Most of these are adjacent to villages and were clearly made by the local village population (Isaac 1990: 85).

Some caves have been dated archaeologically to the Second Revolt, and indeed they adhere very closely to the description given by Dio Works (69.12.1.3) of Bar Kochba's hideouts. In the *Cave of the Letters*, on the northern bank of Nahal Hever in the Judaean Desert, 15 letters were found from Bar Kochba to the commanders of En-Gedi as well as an archive of 35 documents from the period 132 CE (Yadin 1963). The letters were recovered in a cache which also included 19 metal vessels, glass plates, keys, clothing, sandals, mats, wool, and a hunting net. The cave had been inhabited by Jonathan b Bayan, one of Bar Kochba's commanders, and his family.

In general, the caves of the Bar Kochba period are entered through openings masked by cisterns or other innocent-looking cavities in the rock; the caves themselves are linked by horizontal passages and vertical shafts connecting different levels, and many contain ventilation-shafts, water tanks, storerooms, and niches for lamps (Isaac 1990: 85). As it is more likely that the caves near the settlement at Qumran were used for storage purposes rather than for habitation, the Qumran settlement will be discussed separately.

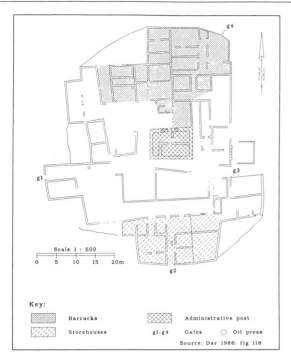

Figure 3   Hirbet Tanurah, western Samaria — a fortified enclosure and farmstead

Religious settlements: Qumran

The Roman impact upon Palestina was felt at its most oppressive with the wholesale destruction of what seems to have been a religious settlement near the Wadi Qumran. Excavations in the years 1949 and 1953–6 have revealed a Hellenistic-Roman occupation stretching *ca.* 6 km along the west shore of the Dead Sea. At the hub of this settlement and below the caves within which the Dead Sea Scrolls were discovered, a main building complex with secondary buildings has been excavated. The settlers lived in caves (IV–X), tents, and solid constructions across an area radiating from the main building complex, shared a common irrigation system, and depended upon common stores of food and water supplied by the installations at the main building complex (de Vaux 1961).

The occupation phases of the Roman period in the main building complex, assessed through numismatic evidence and radiocarbon dating, include Occupation II, represented by a large community sometime after Occupation IIb had been destroyed (possibly by a large earthquake *ca.* 31 BCE [*BJ* I.370–2; *Ant* 15.121–47]). Occupation II ended in a stratum dated to the First Revolt of 66–73 CE, which was characterized by demolished walls, a layer of black ash across the site, and a quantity of arrowheads. Occupation III saw habitation by a Roman garrison for some 20 years to *ca.* 90 CE, and Occupation IV contained Jewish rebels during the Bar Kochba Revolt *ca.* 132–135 CE (de Vaux 1961).

That the 37.5 square meter building complex of Occupation II was the headquarters of an Essene religious community that authored the Dead Sea Scrolls is suggested by the following. First, Pliny the Elder (*NH* 5.73) describes the Essenes as living on the western shores of the Dead Sea: '[and] below them the town of Ein Gedi once stood' – in this case, 'below' would have been to the south. Second, in the floor of one of the many rooms of the building complex of Occupation II a jar was recovered of the same type as those in which the scrolls in Cave 1 had been placed, and along with it was a coin bearing a date equivalent to 10 CE. Altogether, the chronology of the site agrees very well with that established for the manuscripts. Third, a long central chamber in the southwest part of the building has been identified as a scriptorium, as it contained a narrow plaster table and bench built into the wall, three shorter tables, and two inkpots, one of which contained traces of dried ink.

The character of the building complex also suggests the headquarters of a large, well-organized, communal, and virtually self-sufficient community (see de Vaux 1961 for a full description). The complex includes an assembly hall, large cisterns fed by aqueducts, basalt flour mills, storage bins, bakery ovens, a laundry, a stable, smelting furnaces and workshops with metal implements. One of the smaller rooms contained over 1080 ceramic cooking ware and table ware vessels, made by an on-site kiln and levigating pit. Finally, a cemetery east of the complex, dated by pottery (in the fill) to the same period as the community occupation of the complex, contained about 1200 graves, laid out in parallel rows lying north and south, each completely devoid of coffins or funerary offerings.

Therefore, it seems that during the First Revolt, the community was prevented by the Roman army from carrying away their manuscripts, and so abandoned them in at least 11 caves in the nearby cliffs. Most notable are the contents of Cave I, which include the seven manuscripts of the original shepherd find, including the Isaiah scroll and a lesser copy, a commentary on Habakkuk, the Rule of the Community, a collection of thanksgiving psalms, the Order of the War Between the Children of Light and the Children of Darkness, and A Genesis Apocryphon (Cross 1956a: 121–5). Cave IV produced the library of the Essene community, which includes a cross section of the literature of sectarian Judaism at the end of the pre-Christian era (Cross 1956b: 9–13), and Cave XI includes among others the Book of Psalms and a copy of Leviticus.

Technological innovations

Architecture

The Roman presence affected architecture across Palestina in many ways. First, the Roman impact held in place and

Plate 2   Roman period bridge, Scythopolis (Beth Shean) (photograph by T.A. Whetstone)

Plate 3   Roman period theater, Caesarea, facing east (photograph by T.A. Whetstone)

fostered the Hellenistic styles of architecture which had proliferated throughout the eastern Mediterranean before the Roman conquest. Hellenistic structures, such as hippodromes, which included courses for chariot racing and theaters for spectators, have been excavated 600 m south of Jericho (Netzer 1981), east of the harbour at Caesarea (Bull 1982: 32), Scythopolis (Foerster 1993). Herod's stadium in the northeastern part of Sebaste has been recovered, and that at Tiberias had already fallen into disuse by the third century CE (Applebaum 1989: 160). As mentioned, Herod constructed Greek temples to Augustus at Sebaste and Caesarea Philippi in addition to the one at Caesarea (*BJ* 1.21.1–7.402–14).

Second, Roman building technology such as domes, arches and vaults, bridges (see Plate 2) and staircases were incorporated into and used to build various structures throughout the nation. Elements such as these are found most notably in the reconstruction of the Second Temple in Jerusalem (below), and Herodian palaces of Herodium (Netzer 1981), Jericho (Pritchard et al. 1958) and Masada (see Window 1) as well as in the restoration of the great *temenos* at Mamre near Hebron (Mader 1957). Third, Roman imperial architectural models were used from the Herodian period. Indeed, all of the theaters in Palestina, with the exception possibly of Dora, are of the Roman rather than Hellenistic type (Applebaum 1989: 160). Caesarea boasted an Herodian theater (Plate 3) in the southern part of the town (Frova 1993), and others were built at Gerasa by the Flavians, and at Neapolis and Scythopolis by the Severans (Applebaum 1961). Amphitheaters of Severan date have been recovered at Scythopolis and Eleutheropolis (Applebaum 1989: 160).

Third, Roman architectural innovations were used throughout Palestina, such as common Roman baths in Herodian palaces and houses (Gichon 1978). Each bath complex consisted of a *caldarium* (hot room), *tepidarium* (tepid room), *frigidarium* (cold room), an *apodyterium* (entrance and disrobing room), and a furnace located most

often in the courtyard (Hachlili 1988: 57). Antoninus Pius built a bath-house in Caesarea (Levine 1975b), and Talmudic texts attest to the proliferation of baths and their use by Jews. The baths were known by their Hebrew term, but the name of the bath-master was *basileus*, indicating their Greek origin (Schürer 1979: (2) 55). Although not yet recovered in an archaeological context, Talmudic evidence suggests that most settlements in the Galilee possessed a bath of some kind, and that they adopted almost every aspect of Greek bathing (Goodman 1983: 83).

At least four Second Temple period aqueducts fed water to Jerusalem from sources south of Jerusalem at the Wadi Arrub, Biyar, and Solomon's Pools (Mazar 1975). Two adjacent aqueducts 21 km long and serving Caesarea from a spring in the Carmel mountains (see Plate 4) were probably built under Herod (the easternmost) and Hadrian (Levine 1975b). Herod also built an aqueduct to serve the north wing, the pool complex, the gardens and other structures in Lower Herodium (Netzer 1981: 53). Pools, *triclinia*, peristyle courts and gardens were constructed across Palestina following Roman Imperial models.

Finally, the Roman 'umbrella' allowed the client king Herod to carry out unhindered his building projects across Palestina – especially in Jerusalem, where the monumental splendor of the Second Temple period, beginning with the spread of Hellenistic architecture under the Hasmonaeans, reached a peak. His major project was the reconstruction of the Second Temple, the only remains of which are the Antonia fortress (Benoit 1976: 87–9) on the saddle connecting the eastern hill with the northern ridge, and the expansion of the Temple Mount to double its previous size by means of huge retaining walls, measuring 485 m west, 280 m south, 470 m east, and 315 m north (Avigad 1976b: 14). Herod also built a new administrative and defensive center by constructing a royal palace at the northwestern corner of the Upper City (Bahat and Broshi 1976: 55), where he erected three towers to protect the palace as well as the weakest flank of the city. Today, only the base of the largest of the three towers, Phasael, is extant (Amiran and Eitan 1976: 52–4).

Plate 4   High aqueduct at Caesarea, facing north (photograph by T.A. Whetstone)

Plate 5   Western wall, Jerusalem (photograph by T.A. Whetstone)

Roads

One of the greatest impacts of the Roman presence in Palestina was the attention the authorities paid to the road network (Figure 4). The Roman army organized the system in Palestina, as it had across every province of the empire,

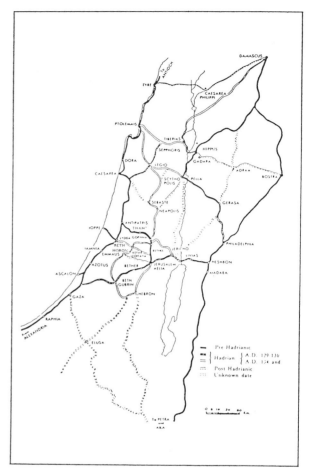

Figure 4   A road map of Roman Palestina (source: Avi-Yonah 1977: 187)

so that it could maintain itself in conquered territory and ensure its authority over the population. That the army was to be the primary user of the roads is attested by the use of Latin on the many milestones recovered across Palestina: Latin was the predominant language of the army, but was used only by a small minority of the civilian population (Isaac 1990: 306). During the Roman period the road system was organized by improving existing roads and constructing entirely new routes.

The majority of the known Roman roads of Palestina follow the more ancient routes (Applebaum 1967: 20). Archaeological survey in western Samaria (Roll and Ayalon 1983; Dar 1986: 250) attests to a pre-Roman road network integrated into the Roman road complex (Figure 5). The improvement of the trunk-route along the coastal road, based largely on the *Via Maritima* connecting Egypt with Damascus via the Plain of Esdraelon, was begun in Nero's time, and completed under pressure of the First Revolt. This revolt also resulted in the connection of Caesarea with Jerusalem via Antipatris (Applebaum 1967:

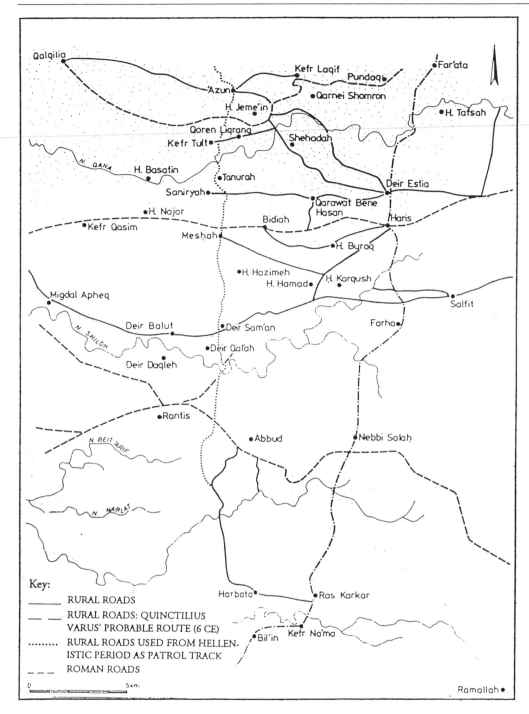

Key:

——————— RURAL ROADS

— · — RURAL ROADS: QUINCTILIUS
VARUS' PROBABLE ROUTE (6 CE)

············ RURAL ROADS USED FROM HELLEN-
ISTIC PERIOD AS PATROL TRACK

— — — ROMAN ROADS

0   5 km

Figure 5 Hirbet
Tanurah and nearby sites
in western Samaria
(source: Dar 1986: fig.
135)

20). Trajan (106–14 CE) constructed the Judaean ridge-way linking Beersheva, Jerusalem and Sebaste, and the 'King's Highway' between the Red Sea and Damascus along the fringe of the Arabian Desert which laid the basis of the *Limes Arabiae* (see Isaac 1990: 165). These routes were improved with continuous metalling, bridge-building, milestones and road-stations (Isaac and Roll 1982; Roll and Ayalon 1983: 113–34).

New roads were constructed especially in difficult terrain, such as that from Antipatris to Caesarea (Dar and Applebaum 1973, 91–9) and Legio to Scythopolis (Isaac 1990: 109). Hadrian's visit in 129 CE produced the routes Gerasa–Philadelphia, Heshbon–Jericho–Jerusalem and Jerusalem–Gaza, and the Second Revolt the roads encircling Bethar. In the north, Ptolemais, Sepphoris and Tiberias were also then linked by road, as well as Caesarea,

Plate 6 Olive Press (Type 7) at Hirbet Najar, western Samaria (photograph by Dar, 1986). This facility expanded during the Roman to Byzantine periods from a small nucleus to a large complex serving 80 to 90 families

Legio and Sepphoris. Other less important roads were added under M. Aurelius, Commodus and Severus, and repairs were intensive in the second, third and fourth centuries CE, more especially in connection with the Parthian campaigns (Applebaum 1967: 20).

Presses

The pressing of the residues with the help of a roller for the making of wine was common in the Greek and Roman world (Columella *De re Rustica* 12: 26, 28). Although the 'screw'-type press was used in Palestina between the Hellenistic and Byzantine periods (Ahlström 1978: 19–49), those from the Roman period were often constructed and used on much grander scales than previously.

With the advent of the large estates in western Samaria, olive oil production was concentrated in large presses (Dar 1986: 152, Type 3–5) which replaced the small vineyard presses of independent farmers. For example, Press 26 at Hirbet el-Buraq and 274 at Tzur Nathan, both close to their respective settlements, indicate far greater production than presses of earlier contexts (Dar 1986: Types 1–2), and that at Hirbet Najar (Dar 1986: 180, Type 7) expanded during the Roman to Byzantine periods from a small nucleus to a large complex serving a settlement of 80 to 90 families (Plate 6).

In contrast, many olive oil presses have been found in single settlements dating from the mid-second century CE across the Golan (Urman 1985: 158). It is uncertain whether these presses, which proliferate across the Golan throughout the Roman period, were public or private property. However, they indicate cultivation of olives on a scale large enough to have allowed considerable export of olive oil (Urman 1985: 161).

Trade

The long periods of peace, as well as the construction of the road system under Roman rule, would have facilitated trade into, within and from Palestina. Although theoretically 'military' road systems, provincial networks across the Empire were nevertheless used widely by the general population. In addition, the construction of fleets under Pompeius and the creation by Augustus of the Imperial navy, manned by freeborn provincials and based in the east at Alexandria and Seleucia in Syria, resulted in the virtual elimination of piracy in the eastern Mediterranean for certain periods. The maritime cities of Palestina thrived on inter-provincial sea-borne trade created by this maritime *pax Romana*. Such trade included exportation of agricultural produce as well as industrial products (Avi-Yonah 1977; see Schürer 1979: (2) 68 for full references). Much literature attests to ships putting into Caesarea (see Levine 1975a: 42), and the rabbis instituted various laws on behalf of merchants and transporters to encourage the flow of overseas imports inland from the coastal cities (*J Bava Mezia* 5.8.10c). The commerce emanating to and from Caesarea is reflected in the coinage found there: examples include coins minted at Dora, Aelia, Antipatris, Ashkelon, Gaza, Raphia, Neapolis, Gaba, Sebaste, Scythopolis, Ptolemais, Gadara, Tyre, Tiberias and Sepphoris (Levine 1975a: 54).

Overland trade from the regions east of Palestina would have been facilitated by the improvement of the Transjordan road system under Trajan and other Antonine emperors following the annexation of Roman Arabia (Kraeling 1938). Whereas the bulk of this trade formerly came through the Red Sea and Alexandria (see Casson 1959), alternative overland routes proved more desirable. The most lucrative trade routes in the Empire passed through the Roman East and by way of the caravan cities of Palmyra, Petra, Gerasa and Bostra, they reached Syria, Palestina and the Mediterranean ports (Heichelheim 1938: 198–9).

Coinage

Another impact of Roman rule was the imposition of Roman currency denominations. Although not permitted to mint silver coins, the Herodians struck copper and occasionally bronze coins (Figure 7: m) corresponding to the Roman *as*, *semis*, and *quadrans*. This system continued under the governors, with gold (*aurei*) and silver (*denarii*; Figure 7: n) minted abroad (Schürer 1979: (2) 63). By the first century CE the quantities of such Roman imperial coinage superseded the Greek and Hebrew coinage in circulation (Schürer 1979: (2) 64).

In addition to coins of imperial mintage, the Roman government granted to certain cities in Palestina the right to mint their own coins. Such mintage not only bolstered a

Plate 7   Herodian mosaic floor (photograph by T.A. Whetstone)

city's prestige but was profitable, as minted coins were sold at a higher rate than the raw material (Abbott and Johnson 1926: 80). The proliferation of such city mints reflects the economic prosperity and the growth of urbanization throughout Palestina – and the East in general – in the second century CE (Kadman 1961: 37–8; Levine 1975a: 176). Indeed, the coins most likely to be found on excavation or as scattered finds are ordinary bronze city coins and bronze weights (*perutot*) (Ben-David 1971: 123). Not only did this period see increased mint activity in terms of numbers of local mints, but, unlike imperial coins which underwent a long period of continual silver debasement, city coinages maintained their metallic value and, from the Severan period, increased it by issuing larger coins (Levine 1975a: 50).

Such proliferation of city mints also meant that individual cities could not monopolize the currency (Goodman 1983: 133). Indeed, the contents of the hoards found in Galilee suggest that even villages in the immediate vicinity of Sepphoris and Tiberias (such as Migdal) did not rely on the coinage of those cities, but preferred the products of the mints of Tyre and elsewhere (Goodman 1983: 133; Meshoyer 1976: 54–71). Evidence from hoards also suggests that silver coins, especially those from Tyre (Schürer 1979: (2) 66), became relatively scarce in the second century CE (Ben-David 1971: 120).

Nothing in the contemporary literature suggests a barter economy (Goodman 1983: 57), and the ubiquity of city coins attests to the high degree of monetarization within the rural economy of Palestina, especially when compared to the much lesser degree of monetarization argued for rural Italy and the northern provinces (Crawford 1970: 43–5). The necessity to pay Roman taxes in coin most likely played the largest part in monetarization. Such taxes included the *census* (first imposed in 6 CE; *AJ* 18.3–4); the *tributum soli* (land tax in kind); *tributum capitis* (perhaps one percent of capital: Appian, *Syr*, 50); a special Jew's tax of two drachmas, payable from 70 CE (Smallwood 1981:

375–8); customs duties (*AJ* 14.250); possibly a tax on each village market (Harper 1928: 155); the exaction by Roman courts of fines agreed on by the parties in civil cases, as well as the confiscation of goods in criminal cases (Goodman 1983: 146); and the two military taxes of *annona* (an ad hoc exaction of supplies) and *angareia* (enforced loan of transport or physical labor).

Religion

The Roman presence in Palestina had its greatest and most enduring effects in the realm of religion. Judaism was to change radically throughout the three major periods, and although pagan religions were nurtured, by the end of this survey they were superseded by Christianity – the new state religion.

Judaism

The Second Temple period

From Herod's rise to power until the outbreak of the First Revolt there arose in Judaea groups unwilling to accept the Roman 'order', and religious ferment steadily increased. The resistance of the Jewish Zealots was inspired primarily by religious commitment (*Ant* 17.10.5.18; *BJ* 2.4.1.56; 8.1.117–18), and significant resistance existed even within mainstream Judaism. Indeed, in an attempt to shield itself against a Hellenistic culture fully supported by the Romans, the enforcement of the Torah injunctions within the Jewish community was stricter than at any other time in Jewish history (Avigad 1976a: 178).

The prohibition against the use of images is seen most strikingly in Second Temple period Jewish decorative art. Despite the fact that motifs and ornamental devices were borrowed from the general stream of eastern Mediterranean Roman art, neither figurative nor symbolic motifs were depicted. The strength of the Torah injunctions and resistance to Rome is thus reflected in the fact that all Jews of this period, including the Hellenized Herod and his family, were reluctant to decorate any public building or tomb with religious or iconic symbols – particularly human or animal.

Burial customs in the Second Temple period

As shown by the excavations of two cemeteries in Jerusalem (Avigad 1950–51; Rahmani 1981) and in Jericho (Hachlili 1980; Hachlili and Killebrew 1983), burial customs in Second Temple period Judaea adhered to two very different techniques. The earlier involved primary burial of one individual in a wooden coffin (Hachlili 1980), and the latter involved secondary burial of the bones placed either in individual ossuaries (or sometimes sarcophagi), or in communal *loculi* or pit burials (Geva 1993; Hachlili and Killebrew 1983: 123–4). The importance of this change cannot be overstated: indeed, burial practices are usually among the most conservative customs in a society (Hachlili 1988: 101). This change likely resulted from a reaction to events of the mid-first century CE: Jews may have blamed their loss of independence and state on their sinful behavior, and re-burying the bones, after the flesh had decayed, in ossuaries may have become a way to expiate sins (Hachlili 1988: 101). By the same token, only floral and geometric designs were used on the decorated ossuaries and sarcophagi, as well as tomb facades of this period.

The Post–Second Revolt period

Various events acting together created a transition in Judaism which became fully manifest by the third century CE. The destruction of the temple in Jerusalem in 70 CE and the consequent end of Temple worship created the development of the synagogue as the center of Jewish life. The upheavals attendant upon the Bar Kochba war and other events, such as the power struggle between Severus and Niger in 193–4 CE (see Levine 1975: 192 for references), spurred the emigration of Jews from Judaea north (Mazar et al. 1973–4: 16), especially to the cities, the Galilee, and the Lower Golan (Urman 1985: 183). The emigration of rabbis, especially to Galilee, fueled the development of rabbinic Judaism (below). Further, the rapprochement which developed between the Jews and Romans under the Severi (193–235 CE), who supported attempts to systemize local ethnic law (Levine 1975a: 66), provided a favorable atmosphere for the compilation and promulgation of the Mishna of R Judah I. The Roman authorities now enforced the decisions of a Jewish court (Levine 1975a: 66), rabbis were given authority to adjudicate in cases of capital punishment (Origen *Letters* 4.392 from Levine 1975a: 194), and the right of the fourth century CE Patriarchs to collect taxes, exercise judicial power and supervise communal administration may have been originally extended by the Severi to R. Judah I (Levine 1975a: 66, 194 for references).

As for the growth of rabbinic Judaism, among the emigres from Judaea were members of the rabbinical schools which, having grown steadily in influence among the Galileans, and with the new rapprochement, became a secular power by the mid-third century CE. The gradual acquisition of power by the rabbis, together with the influence of the prosperous Galilean population upon them, resulted in a modification of the ideals of the *tannaim*. The rabbis became more lenient, and the complexion of Judaism changed (Goodman 1983: 180). One result was that Jews within Galilee achieved an independent confidence and relaxed their hostility to external trends (Urbach 1959). At the same time, the influence of surrounding cultures, from which certain pagan and mythological motifs were taken, became much stronger (Hachlili 1988: 286). However, the line was drawn at actual worship of images, especially those of the emperor (see Schürer 1979: (2) 59).

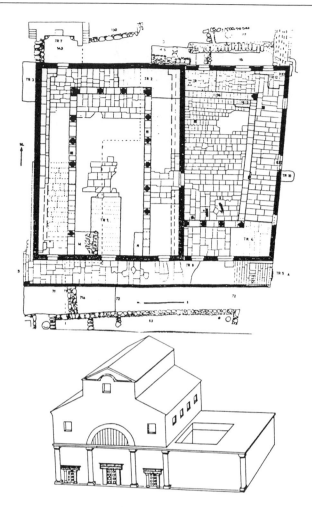

Figure 6 Capernaum Synagogue plan and reconstruction (source: Hachlili 1988: 174, fig. 24a; 162, fig 10b)

The Post–Second Revolt period — synagogues

Such a change in attitude is reflected in the many synagogues constructed across Galilee from the second century CE, in terms of architecture, motifs, and their place in village life. Their plans, uniform over three centuries (Hachlili 1988: 198; Figure 6), were basically basilical, massively-built, and included rich monumental carving inside and out, as well as an elaborate facade containing the Torah shrine on its narrow end facing Jerusalem. The latter consisted of an *aedicula*, niche, or apse, and contained the Ark of the Scrolls, all of which symbolized the sanctity of the place and acted as a reminder of the temple (Hachlili 1988: 197, 228). Similar to pagan architects of the surrounding rural area, Galilean Jewish architects used the same amalgam of motifs with the same mixture of influences (Avi-Yonah 1961: 32; Foerster 1972), and planned their synagogues in prominent locations in the villages (Goodman 1983: 70). Indeed, so similar were the synagogues to pagan temples that the

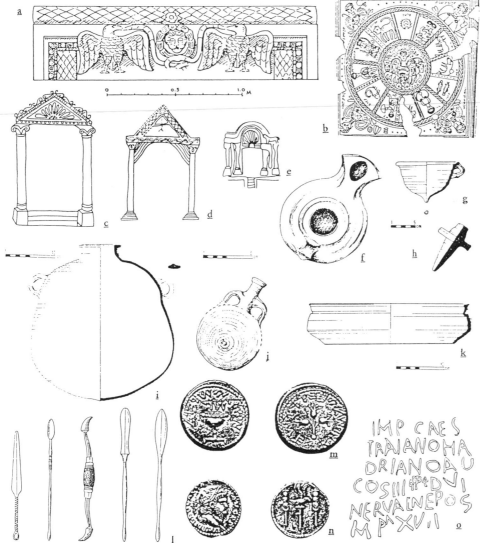

a. Lintel with eagles: Hachlili 1988: 208 fig. 46.a.

b. Jewish Zodiac mosaic, Beth 'Alpha synagogue: Hachlili 1988: 304 fig. 40.a.

c–e. Torah shrine depictions at synagogues of Beth Shearim, Beth She'an, and Hammat Tiberias: Hachlili 1988: 186 fig. 30.

f–k. Ceramics from Herodium, Second Temple Period: Netzer 1981.

f. Oil Lamp: p. 124, pl 8.1.

g. Funnel: p. 124 pl 8.8.

h. Stopper : p. 124 pl 8.9.

i. Storage jar: p. 114 pl 2.2.

j. Flask: p. 7 pl 4.12.

k. Cooking pot: p. 119 pl 5.21.

l. Typical surgical instruments used throughout the Roman Empire: Paoli 1958: 214.

m. Jewish shekel circulated in Palestina during the 3rd year of the First Revolt: Mildenberg 1990: 71.

n. *Denarius* from the reign of Nero (68 CE) circulated in 1st century CE Palestina: Mildenberg 1990: 71.

o. Latin Milestone Inscription from the Neapolis–Lydda road, Hadrianic period: Roll and Ayalon 1986: 120.

Figure 7 Artifacts and motifs of Roman Palestina

Talmud (b *Shab*. 72b) warned Jews not to bow down toward synagogues in case they made a mistake and worshipped a pagan god (Goodman 1983: 87). Differences include architectural detail, especially in the facades and portals (Hachlili 1988: 229; see Figure 7c,d,e), and size. With the destruction of the Temple, the village synagogue had become the venue for ritual practices and held an entire congregation; in contrast, pagan temples had only to accommodate priests and so were much smaller than contemporary synagogues.

The striking feature of all these buildings is the use of sculptured or mosaic ornamentation representing humans and living creatures, in contradiction to the Second Commandment, and in stark contrast to the attitudes of religious leaders in the first century CE to pagan idolatry (Avi-Yonah 1961: ch.1; Schürer 1979: (2) 81–3, 59).

Although the architectural relief in the synagogues may have been too high up on the buildings and out of the way to embody deep religious significance (Bickerman 1967: 131–61), nevertheless such change in Galilean Jewish art after the Second Revolt was dramatic and rapid. The carvings include various pagan symbols drawn from Nabataean, Roman-Syrian, and Parthian influences (Hachlili 1988: 200). The extant human figures are without exception from pagan mythology, as are most likely the Victories, cupids, lions, griffins, capricorns, eagles, vine motifs, wreaths, shells, and rosettes (see Goodenough 1965: (12) 43; Figure 7: a,b).

Galilean society in the second century CE was moving toward, if it had not already attained,[1] a system centered around a public synagogue that would dominate the surroundings (Sukenik 1934: 27). Although the exact functions of the first century CE synagogues identified at Masada (Yadin 1965: 1981), Herodium (Foerster 1981), Migdal (Saltz 1977: 3), and Gamala (Shanks 1979: 76) are as yet uncertain, the building of a synagogue was presumably not considered essential for a community while the Temple stood (Goodman 1983: 86). However, by the third century CE, the Galilean synagogue, as shown by ample inscriptions and literary references, was an educational center, law-court, and center of communal administration, recreation and industry, and some were associated with baths and hostels (Applebaum 1967: 21).

Burial customs in the Post-Second Revolt period

In addition to synagogues, the Jewish burials from the second century CE went through radical changes in architecture and motifs, incorporating much from paganism, such as vines, grapes, cups, rosettes and 'round objects', columns approached by steps, flowers resembling tulips, trees, wreaths, zigzags, and *burcania*. Excellent examples of second to fourth century CE burials are found at the necropolis of Beth Shearim in western Galilee. These tombs were rock-cut with 3 m ceilings, and include a descending corridor (one of which is 30 m long) branching into halls with individual chambers three stories high. That these tombs belonged to Jews, and most likely very loyal Jews, is attested to by the numerous menorahs depicted on the walls, as well as the *lulab, ethrog, shofar,* Jewish wine jar, and roll-case (Avigud and Mazar 1993). At the same time, the tombs contain numerous pagan motifs. Deserving specific mention is a facade in relief in Room VII within Hall A of Catacomb number 4, and a mausoleum adjacent to Catacomb 11.

The facade is 0.82 m high and consists of a portico with four columns, each with base and capital, and a high arch joining the central two columns, representing an Holy Ark (Mazar et al. 1973–4: 176). A closed double door occupies the center of the ark, which is reached by a flight of five narrow steps. Above the entrance is a conch; between the two columns on the right a vase with (most likely) a *lulab*; and standing on the columns to the right and facing the conch a lion. It is argued (Mazar et al. 1973–4: 177) that this holy ark recalls Torah shrines built into the Jerusalem-facing walls in the nearby Galilean synagogues, and so followed accepted convention. Alternatively, it is argued (Goodenough 1965: (1) 93) that this relief contains much mystical symbolism.

The mausoleum included an animal frieze over the arch, with bulls, sheep, perhaps a lion, and a marble inscription in Greek on a sarcophagus, now in fragments (Goodenough 1965: (1) 101; Schwabe and Lifshitz 1974). The inscription, dating to the first half of the third century CE, records a certain Justus, the Leontide, on his way to Hades, and fragments of the sarcophagus depict pagan motifs such as a *leda* and a battle between Greeks and Amazons. Again, the arches of the mausoleum, their

borders, and the artistic style of construction recalls the architecture of contemporary Galilean synagogues (Mazar et al. 1973–4).

Coinage in the Post-Second Revolt period

Before 70 CE, the Herodians minted coins with pagan motifs, apparently to please the Romans, and the procurators employed designs to placate the Jews. Indeed, the imperial family was identified with regnal years and Greek legends rather than images, and motifs were used which were common on contemporary Jewish ossuaries (above) such as three lilacaeous flowers together and three stalks of grain, grapes, grapevines, and cups (Goodenough 1965: (12) 27). When the Jews minted their own coins in the First Revolt, such symbols continued, with the addition of the *lulab, ethrog,* wine and objects used in synagogue (or household) worship (Goodenough 1965: (3) figs 685–91). However, between the revolts only pagan symbols were depicted on coins (Goodenough 1965: (3) figs 692–99). With the Second Revolt, coins were once again struck with Jewish symbols including the same three flowers or fruit, or stalks of grain, wine symbols, the lyre, the *ethrog, lulab,* star, and a peculiar temple facade with an ark (Goodenough 1965: (10) 84). Therefore, it seems that the Messianic Jews who led the two revolts struck, with the first opportunity, symbols of Judaism to the complete exclusion of pagan influences.

Symbols in general in the Post-Second Revolt period

Symbols borrowed from paganism and used in Jewish synagogues, tombs and coinage include representations of Victory, the bull's head, lion, tree, including its branches and fruit, crown, rosettes, wheels, and 'round objects', birds, sheep, hare, shell, cornucopia, centaur, eagle and ship (Goodenough 1965: (1) 213, 132–9; (12) 142–51). At the same time there arose the use of purely Jewish symbols. Indeed, the menorah became a prominent symbol only after the destruction of the Temple, when the need for concrete images was most strongly felt (Hachlili 1988: 255). In addition, the menorah is often flanked in synagogues and funerary art by the *shofar, lulab, ethrog* and incense shovel. Together with the Ark of the Scrolls and the conch, these motifs developed during the third century CE as a unified design of Jewish symbols recalling the Temple and ceremonial ritual (Hachlili 1988: 185).

Paganism

For the most part cities in Palestina with Gentile majorities (especially Philistine and Phoenician) retained the essence of their indigenous cults throughout the Roman period, but they were to a significant extent transformed by Greek elements (see Schürer 1979: (2) 29 for references). Such was the case in Ashkelon, where worship was directed to

Astarte, as well as to the Semitic Atargatis or Derceto, represented as a mermaid (Diodorus 2.2.4; 2 Macc. 12: 26). The coins of Ashkelon also depict a god named Phanebal, possibly identified with Apollo (British Museum Collection *Palestine* lix–lxi). These gods are mixed with Greek deities, Heracles, Poseidon and the Dioscuri (xlviii–lxiv). Excavations at Gerasa have revealed Hellenized local cults alongside Sarapis and Isis, as well as emperor worship elsewhere (Kraeling 1938: 56; Rostovtzeff 1935: 26). At Scythopolis, figurines and statuettes found in tombs indicate private allegiances (Avi-Yonah and Stern 1975–8: (1) 221), and together with the excavated temples revealing magnificent public cults, form an amalgam of Greek-Egyptian, Roman, and Semitic cults (Goodman 1983: 47).

Elsewhere, numismatic evidence suggests that during the Roman period purely Greek or Roman cults often entirely supplanted indigenous cults (Schürer 1979: (2) 29). Coins of Raphia depict Apollo and Artemis in Greek form (BMC *Palestine* lxxxi–ii), and the tutelary goddess of the city of Anthedon is presented as Astarte (xlv–vii). In Gaza, coinage depicts Roman and Greek deities with the exception of the Semitic Marnas, the principal deity of the city, although he too was Hellenized (see Schürer 1979 (2) 30–1 for references). The pantheon of Greek and Roman gods common throughout the Roman world is represented on second- and third-century CE coins of Caesarea (Kadman 1957: 56ff.; Levine 1975a: 42). The coins of this colony also include representations of Tysche-Astarte, sometimes in a triad with Dionysus, Demeter and Sarapis (Kadman 1957). Such colonial coinage is also present at Ptolemais from the end of the second century CE (Kadman 1961).

Imperial cult

As with most other Hellenized cities of the eastern Roman Empire, those of Palestina adopted the Imperial cult during the reign of Augustus. As such a cult was similar to the Hellenistic concept of monarchy, the pagan population, especially in the cities, hastened to embrace the emperor as a god (Jones 1974: 101). Augustus encouraged imperial cult worship (Tacitus *Annals* 1.10), with the provision that Rome should be associated with himself as the object of cult (Suetonius *Div Aug* 52). By so doing, the cult became a useful means of focusing the loyalty of the provincials to the head of the Empire. According to Josephus, Herod founded temples to Caesar in many cities, including Caesarea Philippi (*Ant* 15.363), Caesarea (*BJ* 1.21.4.407; *Ant* 15.9.5.328) and Sebaste, which was later established by Severus and Caracalla as a center for the imperial cult (Smallwood 1981: 490). The temple at Caesarea, located on a hill facing the entrance to the harbour, contained two large statues – one of Augustus (modeled after Olympian Zeus); one of Rome (after Hera of Argos).

The imperial cult was celebrated in various cities during periodic festival games: by the second and third centuries CE, no provincial town of any significance was without them, and many possessed elaborate amphitheaters and/or theaters (Schürer 1979: (2) 45; Avi-Yonah and Stern 1975–8). The games were held quadrennially in the emperor's honor and connected with his worship from the time of Augustus (Suetonius *Div Aug* 59). Herod introduced games into Caesarea (*Ant* 17.10.2.255; *BJ* 2.3.1.44) and built a theater and amphitheater in Jerusalem (*Ant* 15.8.1.268) as well as Jericho (*Ant* 17.6.3.161; *BJ* 1.33.8.666; see Kelso and Baramki 1955 for excavations). Tiberias may even have had a stadium (*BJ* 2.21.6.618; *Vita* 17.92, 64.331).

Social structures

Cities

Ancient literature suggests that although Rome endeavored to return to the cities the autonomy with which they could govern themselves, the result was that they became less willing to do so, and more reliant on the central government in Caesarea. The council, now permanent and based on property qualification, had become an imposition by the second century CE, so that public elections of both magistrates and councillors gradually ceased. Indeed, elected magistrates and councillors were expected to pay for their election through civic contributions which, by the second century, increased in cost so dramatically that only the wealthiest citizens could hold office (Jones 1974: 14). With the exorbitant cost of election, the offices became honorable obligations rather than a means to improve one's social and political standing (Jones 1974: 14). As a result, men of ambition qualified to take office ceased running for election and even began evading the obligation, so that it fell to the council to persuade or to press its members to stand for the higher offices, and propose their sons or other qualified persons for the junior offices. Membership became increasingly more hereditary so that by the time of Diocletian, sons of decurions were automatically enrolled on attaining their majority, and service on the council thus became the hereditary obligation of the class known as *curiales* (Jones 1974: 15).

Although the cities were originally left to control their finances, by the second century CE – or perhaps from the reign of Vespasian (69–79 CE) (Magie 1950: 556–7), imperial commissioners, or *curatores,* began to be appointed occasionally to supervise the financial affairs of individual or groups of eastern cities (Pliny *Letters* 10.8.1). By the end of the third century CE the office of *curator* had become a normal institution in most cities (Jones 1974: 9). The jurisdiction of the city courts also steadily waned during the Roman period (Jones 1974: 20). By the end of the same period the jurisdiction of the provincial governor had absorbed all – even the most petty – litigation within the cities. At times the cities themselves encouraged the trends toward governmental control by soliciting aid in settling certain claims (Pliny *Letters* 10.10).

However, despite the political demise of the city, the spirit of civic patriotism survived. Although forbidden to wage war, the cities continued to compete with each other. As a result of such rivalry, municipal contests fostered the study of grammar, rhetoric, music and drama; the profusion of gymnasia and public games fostered athletics; and impressive building programs allowed the continued development of civic architecture which included temples, triumphal arches, theaters, odea, stadia, nymphaea, baths, colonnaded streets, markets, and statues (Jones 1974: 96; see sites in Stern 1993).

Villages

In addition to major changes in the settlement patterns across rural Palestina (discussed above), it also seems that Roman rule had an impact upon social structures and organization. It has been argued (Dar 1986: 86) that in Second Temple period western Samaria the courtyard house was dominated by a large yard surrounded by residential and agricultural buildings for the extended family. However, confiscation of lands across Palestina forced many farmers into tenancy. Evidence in the Roman and Byzantine periods for such a change is the decrease in size of the courtyard house and the proliferation of small dwellings within what had been the common yard (Dar 1986: 86). It is possible that the farming unit began to reorganize around the nuclear rather than extended family. Such nuclearization created an increase of craftsmen and non-agricultural occupations within a settlement (Dar 1986: 86).

Brigandage

The wars and insurrections, as well as Roman taxation, confiscations and religious insensitivity, all led to endemic banditry in most areas and periods of Roman Palestina. In 23 BC, Augustus gave Trachonitis, Batanaea and Aurantis to Herod, whose task was to suppress robber bands (*Ant* 15.10.1.343–8; *BJ* 1.20 4.398–400). Josephus ascribes the increase in banditry in the first century CE to governmental maladministration (Isaac 1990: 82). During the reign of Caligula, it appears that banditry was the result of poverty and oppressive taxation. Indeed, in 39–40 CE Jewish leaders asked the governor of Syria to point out to Caligula 'that, since the land was unsown, there would be a harvest of banditry because the requirements of tribute could not be met' (Isaac 1990: 82 for reference). In later periods, banditry is described in Talmudic sources as a direct cause of instability. R. Aha wrote (*Leviticus Rabbah* 9.8) that bands of *listim* appear when the empire takes over the government. Even though no major wars occurred in Palestina after Bar Kochba, again Talmudic sources attest to endemic banditry (Isaac 1990: 87).

Conclusion

The Roman period in Palestina involved the imposition of imperial government upon an area which had hitherto been ruled by dynasts. Throughout the period, the population both resisted and developed under the umbrella of the *pax Romana*.

After the brief period of the Herodian centralization of the administration, the Roman government endeavored to devolve power to the municipal level. Although the cities were stripped of their political autonomy insofar as they could wage war, make alliances with other cities, or elect democratic governments to rule over them, they were nevertheless permitted to govern themselves in the financial, legislative and jurisdictional spheres – and the cities in fact managed to maintain and even foster some of the key elements of Hellenism. However, the city-state died as a political entity: most major decisions concerning the cities were eventually made by the Roman governor, and the cities were relegated to the status of municipalities.

The settlement pattern across the countryside reflects both the periods of peace and strife during the Roman period. By the second century CE, villages in Galilee were being constructed with little regard for defense. At the same time, the numbers of villages greatly increased as a result of the mass emigrations from war-torn Judaea following the Second Revolt. In western Samaria, settlement patterns may reflect the confiscations known to have occurred during the Roman period after insurrection or war. Other settlements reflect a movement away from farms based upon an extended family toward large farms with central olive and wine presses (built on much larger scales than previously) worked by nuclear families. Still other evidence suggests the working of large farms by one landowner, possibly a representative of the Roman government. Finally, some farmsteads were developed into virtual fortresses, again reflecting unsettled periods under Roman rule.

The disposition of the Roman army would have had a large impact upon the population of Palestina. Those soldiers billeted in the cities became brutal and corrupt, and were despised by all accounts. Those in the countryside controlled roads and nodal points in the communication system, while veteran colonies represented loyal elements in otherwise hostile areas.

The organization of the road system, the medium by which the Roman army controlled conquered areas across the Empire, would have had great impact on communications, transport and trade into, within, and from Palestina. Traditional routes were improved with metalling, bridges, milestones, and road-houses, and other routes were constructed through difficult areas. In addition, trade would have been stimulated by the long periods of peace enjoyed not only across Palestina, but also throughout the desert regions to the east, the provinces of Syria to the north and Egypt to the south, and over the eastern Mediterranean Sea.

The greatest impact of Roman rule in Palestina was felt in the realm of religion. Judaism underwent dynamic changes under Roman rule. Zealots resisted strenuously any ruler other than a representative of the Hebrew God, and the two great revolts were fueled largely by their inspiration. During the Second Temple period, Palestina was a Jewish state with a central Temple in Jerusalem. The ruling classes, although Hellenized, retained parts of their faith and laws. Jewish art, which withstood foreign influences by evolving strictly aniconic features, reflects Judaism's struggle against paganism and idolatry.

However, the destruction of the Temple, the emigration of Judaeans into Galilee, the compatibility which arose between the Roman rulers and Jewish population after Bar Kochba, and the decline of paganism together gave rise to a new, more 'relaxed' rabbinic Judaism. The new atmosphere allowed the use of images borrowed from paganism. Such images were incorporated into 'Galilean'-type synagogues, which were now constructed in the villages, and came to represent the centers of Jewish religious, national, and social life. These synagogues included a Torah shrine on the Jerusalem-oriented wall, and in many ways resembled local and pagan traditions of temple construction. Funerary art and architecture were also influenced by the above forces. Indeed, pagan images were found in tombs, which had ceased to include the sarcophagus and ossuary.

At the same time, paganism was fostered, and became highly political with the advent of the Imperial Cult. The Hellenistic deities were adopted most often as a supplement to the pantheon of local gods and goddesses, some of Semitic origin, others Egyptian or Babylonian. However, despite the investment in the pagan cults by both the Gentile population and government of Palestina, this survey represents the swan song of Roman period paganism. Under Constantine, the traditional as well as the new gods were swept away by the new state religion – Christianity.

For the Gentile population, the *pax Romana* allowed long periods of development. However, Gentiles remained culturally Semitic and Greek, and were 'Romanized' only in terms of political organization and material life (Applebaum 1989: 165). For example, Greek and Aramaic remained the languages of the people at large, almost without exception (Levick 1967; Levine 1975a: 71), while most surviving Latin inscriptions are connected with the army, or local or imperial officials. The Jewish population too was influenced only superficially by Roman culture, managing to retain their essential cultural integrity; following the Second Revolt, they flourished under the *pax Romana*. However, the great achievement of Judaism throughout the period of Roman Palestina was that it survived the social upheavals brought about by the brutal suppression of two major revolts.

Note

1. Although the facade type corresponds best to second and third century CE styles elsewhere in the empire, 'early style' relief in any particular area cannot be assumed to indicate second or third century synagogues, as conservative communities might have continued building religious edifices in an earlier style many centuries after new ideas had appeared elsewhere (Goodman 1983: 85). Indeed, excavation of sealed materials under the floors of stylistically early synagogues has revealed late third century material at Meiron (Meyers et al. 1974: 84), and 5th century material at Capernaum.

Acknowledgments

I wish to thank T.A. Whetstone and Dr Shimon Dar for permission to use their photographs, R. Harrower and K. Errington for their contributions towards the line drawings, and Dr E.G. Wilson, D. Ulveland, and J. White for reading the manuscript. I would like also to thank the anonymous reviewers for their critical comments.

MASADA

The fortress of Masada is the site of one of the most dramatic episodes in the history of Judaism, and has come to symbolize Jewish resistance against Roman rule. During the period 36–30 BCE, Herod the Great constructed numerous facilities on top of a large (600 m north–south by 300 m east–west), rhomboid-shaped, dolomite plateau, on the eastern edge of the Judaean desert, about 25 km south of En-Gedi and overlooking the Dead Sea 400 m below (Plate 1.1 and see opening photograph, this chapter). The facilities included a casemate wall around the top, defense towers, storehouses, large cisterns, barracks, arsenals and palaces (see Figure 1.1). Throughout the first century CE Jewish religious ferment increased as a result mainly of procuratorial maladministration and insensitivity, resulting in the First Revolt in 66 CE (see text). After Jerusalem was taken by Titus in 70 CE, Masada became the last stronghold in the rebellion.

According to Josephus (*BJ* 7.8.6), whose writings represent the only historical mention of Masada, a group of Jewish Zealots captured the Roman garrison at Masada at the beginning of the First Revolt and held it to the very end. After the fall of Jerusalem they were joined by some survivors, and used Masada as a base for continued raiding. In 72 CE the Roman governor, Flavius Silva, marched to Masada with the Tenth Legion, its auxiliary troops and thousands of prisoners of war carrying water, timber and provisions. Silva laid siege to the fortress by constructing eight camps and a circumvallation around the base of the plateau, as well as a ramp of beaten earth and large stones scaling the plateau's west aspect. The Romans then rolled a siege tower up the ramp to provide covering fire for the battering ram, which, in 74 CE, eventually succeeded in breaching the wall. Once their fate was decided, the Zealots, numbering 960 men, women and children, all under the command of Eleazar ben Yair, chose 'neither to serve the Romans nor any other save God' (*BJ* 7.8.6.323) and took their lives before the Romans entered the breach. Afterwards, a Roman garrison inhabited Camp F, as well as the plateau itself from 73–111 CE. During the fifth and sixth centuries a group of monks constructed a small church, refectory and kitchen, and dwelt in caves and small stone cells across the summit.

Fortress First identified as Masada in the modern period by E. Robinson and E. Smith in 1838, who viewed it by telescope from En-Gedi, the fortress has since been thoroughly excavated (Yadin 1965). Its wall was constructed from local dolomite as a casemate, or in two rows with the area in the middle divided into chambers with partitioning walls. It encircles all of the summit apart from the northern tip over a length of 1280 m, and includes four gates, 30 towers and 70 rooms. The gates consist of a room with an outer and inner entrance and benches along the walls, while the towers are small casemates built according to the topography at unequal distances. Excavation has shown that many more rooms had been added to the casemate with the construction of additional partitions, and that cupboards and ovens had been constructed within the rooms. Together with the recovery of coins dating to the First Revolt, it has been suggested (Yadin 1965: 144–5) that these rooms housed the rebels and their families during the revolt.

Mikve Within the southern section of the casemate wall was found a complex of baths consisting of three adjacent pools of differing sizes. Steps descended to the bottom of the two larger baths, and water flowed between the three by a connecting hole.

Plate 1.1 Herod's palace, Masada (photograph by T.A. Whetstone)

A plastered water conduit fed the largest, most likely with collected rainwater (Yadin 1965: 166). A second and identical complex was recovered in the northeast corner of the administration building west of the storehouses. That these are Jewish ritual baths, or *mikve*, is suggested by their being built secondarily into existing structures, and because they were constructed according to ritual regulations of Jewish law (Yadin 1965: 167). Their secondary construction also indicates that they belong to the period of the First Revolt.

Synagogue Adjoining the northwest section of the wall is a structure measuring 12×15 m. It was originally a triclinia and later converted first to what seems to be a synagogue, and later a reception and ceremonial hall. That it was converted to a synagogue (Yadin 1965, 1981) is based on the building's orientation towards Jerusalem, the recovery of a column base beneath a floor, which produced an ostracon with the inscription 'priestly tithe' as well as an intrusive pit, possibly a *geniza*, containing scrolls. In addition, a cell was added, and an interior wall was torn down and replaced by two pillars to make room for more people. Furthermore, the oblong walls and stepped benches erected along all four walls of the hall facing the center are features similar to those in other synagogues dating from the same period across Judaea (see Hachlili 1988: 84 for references). That the synagogue was constructed by the Zealots is suggested by the recovery of First Revolt coins on the floor, the secondary use of masonry — including portions of column drums and capitals perhaps from the lower or upper palaces — for the construction of benches along the walls, and evidence for the burning of articles of furniture (Yadin 1965).

Storerooms Large rectangular buildings in the northeast section of the plateau and belonging to two groups are thought to be storerooms. The larger group, lying to the south, was separated by an east–west road with the smaller group lying just east of the bath-house. The entrance to the storehouses, as well as to the bath-house and northern palace villa was possible only through a gate next to an administration building at the western corner of the stores compound. The storeroom walls comprise a double row of dolomite slabs, and the floors were found covered with a thick layer of ashes, charred beams, and sherds of various storage vessels. Although the types of vessels were Herodian in style, they were inscribed in ink and charcoal with Hebrew names, thought to belong to the Zealots (Yadin 1965: 96). Indeed, coins were recovered dating to the second and third years of the First Revolt.

Garrison building   South of the storerooms is a large square building which housed the administrators in Herodian Masada and most likely the leaders of the Revolt (Yadin 1965: 108). Indeed, two hoards of coins were recovered, the first consisting of 38 unused silver shekels and half-shekels struck in the fourth year of the Revolt, the second consisting of six shekels and six half-shekels in a bronze box. It is argued (Yadin 1965: 108) that these coins were hidden under the floor to prevent their recovery by the Roman soldiers.

Large bath-house   West of the storerooms and south of the northern palace (below) is situated the large bath-house. The floors of the *tepidarium* and courtyard were paved with *opus sectile* and mosaics, respectively. The *caldarium*, most likely domed, was heated by a hypocaust and contained two niches. One niche was round and contained a huge tub; the other was rectangular and contained a basin (Yadin 1965: 75−88).

Northern palace villa   Consisting of three terraces, one above the other, built on the northern edge of the plateau, the northern palace villa was intended mostly for leisure (Yadin 1965: 47). The upper terrace contains the entrance on its east side, rooms along the sides of an open court, living quarters and a semi-circular balcony (porch) which probably had two rows of columns. About 20 m below the upper terrace and connected to it by a staircase is the middle terrace, consisting of a circular pavilion or *tholus* with two rows of columns, the foundation of which includes stones packed between two concentric walls. East of this is a large hall decorated with a colonnade, a 'false facade', fresco imitating marble, and a staircase leading to the lower terrace about 15 m below. The lower terrace includes a bath-house on the east, and a 17.6 m square building constructed on a raised area of supporting walls. The porticoed central area consists of a double colonnade of sandstone half-columns with colored Corinthian capitals. The lower parts of the portico walls are decorated with fresco imitating marble. Behind the portico is a 'false facade' wall, with half-columns attached to the rock and fresco panels between them. On the whole, this palace adheres to a typical Roman-style luxury dwelling (Netzer 1981: 110). Throughout the environs there was much ash and coins dating from the First Revolt, and recovered in the small bath-house were remains, most probably of some of the Zealot defenders: a warrior with scaled armor, arrows, prayer shawl and ostracon with Hebrew letters; a young woman with plaited hair, and a child.

Western palace   The western palace, covering 4000 m² , is the largest of the palaces. Two Ionic columns mark the opening of a central court flanked by the royal apartments. South of the court is a hall with three entrances leading to a throne room, while north of the court is the bath-house, ritual bath and other installations, all paved with mosaics. This wing probably had several stories, and is similar in plan to the two in Hasmonaean

palaces at Jericho. On the basis of this, it has been suggested (Netzer 1982: 23, 25) that the Masada palaces had already been built by the Hasmonaeans, and were only expanded and improved by Herod. However, it is also argued (Hachlili 1988: 45) that Herod, when building the Masada palaces, utilized a plan which had also been used earlier by the Hasmonaeans. Another court contained workshops and dwelling rooms on its north aspect. Several long storerooms occupy the southwestern part of the palace, with those abutting the south wall of the royal apartment wing belonging to the second stage of the palace buildings. The administrative wing consists of three blocks of buildings, the northernmost of which housed the palace officials.

Other palaces   Palaces XI, XII and XIII, constructed close to the western palace, have a central court and a hall with two columns, leading into another corner hall which was probably a reception room. Palaces VII and VIII are near to the storeroom, and have the same general plan as the other palaces. Building VII has a storeroom attached to it which probably contained valuable commodities. Building IX probably served as a barracks for the guard. It has a central court surrounded by rooms divided into small units, each of which has two small rooms and a court. Three units lie on three sides of the building, and the east side contains two large halls and the main entrance.

Key:

a-c: Herod's palace villa
a. Lower terrace with wall paintings and double colonnade
b. Middle terrace with circular pavilion and colonnade
c. Upper terrace; living quarters with semi-circular porch
d. Large bath-house
e. Store rooms
f. Water gate
g. Spot where the 'lots' were found
h. Administrative building
i. Synagogue
j. Casemate containing the first scrolls
k. Snake-path gate
l. Casemate containing scroll of the Ecclesiasticus
m. Room containing large hoard of silver shekels
n. Apartment building
o. Small Byzantine structure
p. Byzantine church
q. Herod's Western Palace
r. Throne room
s. West gate
t. Small palaces
u. Swimming pool
v. Zealot's living quarters
w. Byzantine structure with mosaic workshop
x. Small palace converted into Zealot's quarters
y. The mikve
z. Southern water gate
aa. Huge underground cistern
bb. Southern bastion

SCALE   1:4000
0   50   100   150m

Figure 1.1   The palace of Masada (source: Yadin 1965)

THE IMPACT OF THE ROMAN ARMY IN PALESTINA

One of the greatest impacts upon Palestina in the Roman period was the disposition of the army, which, compared to most other provinces, was very large (Smallwood 1981: 481). The permanent garrison before 67 CE consisted of 3–4000 men (Isaac 1990: 105), while a diploma of 86 CE (*Corpus Inscriptiorum Latinasum* 16.33) indicates six units, or 5000 auxiliaries in Judaea after the First Revolt. As the number of auxiliaries equaled that of the legionaries (Tacitus *Ann* 4.5.6), the total number of troops would have been 10,000. Under Hadrian, the legionary force was doubled to 10,000 (Isaac and Roll 1979: 54–66), and evidence suggests (Isaac, 1990: 106) an increase of auxiliaries to 8500, totaling 18,500. A diploma of 186 CE lists two alae and seven cohorts, two of them milliary (Roxan 1985: 69), or 5500 auxiliaries, totaling some 15,500 (Isaac 1990: 106).

Cities and colonies   Soldiers of the Roman army were permanently billeted in the cities of Emmaus, Nicopolis, Hebron, Neapolis, Sebaste, and Eleutheropolis (Beth Gabra) (Isaac 1990: 115–16). Much reference is made in the Talmud to the maltreatment of urbanites by Roman soldiers billeted in cities, as well as the consequent riots and massacres (see Isaac 1990: 116–18, 309). Indeed, Tacitus (*Ann* 13.35) writes that such troops became slack and undisciplined.

According to Josephus, Herod settled 6000 veterans and civilians drawn from the surrounding area on confiscated land at Sebaste (*Ant* 15.7.3; *BJ* 1.20.3.396), a colony of veteran cavalry-men at Gaba (*BJ* 3.3.1.36; *Ant* 15.8.5.294), and at Heshbon a military colony (*Ant* 15.8.5.294). After the First Revolt, Vespasian may have settled thousands of veterans (Levine 1975a: 36) at Caesarea – now proclaimed a colony (Pliny *NH* 5.14.69) – and extended an exemption, first from the poll-tax (*Dig* 50.15.8.7) and later, under Titus, the land-tax (*Dig* 50.15.1.6). Vespasian also gave the fertile land around Emmaus to 800 of his veterans (*BJ* 7.6.6.216–17). After (or perhaps precipitating) the Second Revolt, Hadrian established the colony of Aelia Capitolina and, on the basis of inscriptions and colonial coinage with *vexilla* and the emblems of the legions, settled it with veterans of *Legio X Fretensis* also stationed at the legionary base in Jerusalem (Isaac 1990: 324, 349). However, apart from these, the colonies of Palestina were granted their titles without the settlement of veterans and consequent confiscation of estates. For example, coinage attests to the extension of the name 'Flavia' to both Joppe and Neapolis, although nothing suggests the planting of settlers in these towns.

These colonies would have provided a focus of loyalty and stability in hostile and strategically important areas. Indeed, Herod's settlers would have kept him informed of dangerous activity among potentially rebellious Jews living nearby (Isaac 1990: 397). It is argued (Levine 1975a: 36) that the settling of veterans in Caesarea may have been an attempt to rid the capital of 'anti-Roman' sentiment, and to provide *Lebensraum* for certain classes of Roman citizens. In addition, once auxiliaries recruited from the local Greek cities of Judaea (e.g. Caesarea, Sebaste, Ashkelon: *Ant* 19.9.2.365) had served their requisite periods of service, they would have returned home as emissaries of Roman culture and methods (Applebaum 1989: 162). Inscriptions attest to veterans and their descendants living for generations on what had been confiscated lands in well-organized and fiscally responsible communities (Isaac 1990: 332, 420). Veterans will often have sent their sons to the army, and descendants of veterans can be traced as representatives of the provincial upper class for centuries after the original foundation.

Countryside   Archaeological survey in western Samaria attests to substantial changes taking place during the Roman period in the overall defensive arrangements (Dar 1986: 224). Most of the forts of the previous periods were completely abandoned, and if they were reoccupied in the Roman period, it was for brief periods. Indeed, it seems that the Roman army, if not billeted in cities, was stationed at large bases rather than in small forts across the countryside. Material remains of Roman forts in Galilee are negligible (Goodman 1983: 142): indeed, only one tile of *Legio VI Ferrata* attests to the presence of a Roman soldier in the second and third centuries CE in Upper Galilee (Applebaum 1976: 31). Therefore, it must be assumed that most troops who entered Galilee were stationed in nearby Legio which belonged to the VI *Ferrata* (Applebaum 1976: 52, 1967: 19). However, evidence attests to the proliferation of *burgi*, or road stations which held *stationarii* who served as road police and suppressed banditry. Archaeological evidence for such *burgi* of perhaps the Hadrianic period exists between Sepphoris and Tiberias (1976: 19).

Desert   In those areas of Palestina where the settled regions met the desert, the Roman army would have had to deal with nomadic pastoralism and transhumance. However, it seems unlikely that the army was involved in continual and intensive pressure from nomadic raids from without (Banning 1986: 25-50). Indeed, permanent structures or a system of defense is not certain before the fourth century CE, and not a single ancient source mentions serious difficulties caused by nomadic tribes before the Byzantine period (Gichon 1980: 843–64; Isaac 1990: 72). In addition, pre-Islamic nomads did not engage in siege warfare (Isaac 1990: 236) and were ineffective against towns or in set battles (Ammianus 25.6.8; Procopius *Bell* 19.12), so that nomadic raiding would have entailed merely the burning or trampling of crops, destroying palm groves, fruit trees, and water systems, as well as filling wells. In the face of this threat the army most likely provided no more than police action in the desert to maintain security at an acceptable level until the fourth century.

One exception may be the fighting between the Safaitic tribes and the Romans in the first three centuries CE, as attested by graffiti in the Sinai, Negev and desert regions of Transjordan (see Isaac 1990 for references). However, it is uncertain whether the texts refer to large-scale fighting or merely periodic low-intensity raiding of Roman positions.

The last quarter of the third century CE and the beginning of the fourth century marked the establishment of various permanent structures along the so-called *Limes Palestinae* (Avi-Yonah 1958; for an Herodian date, see Applebaum 1989: 132–3). An expansion of the Roman presence in the Negev is attested by the *Notitia* and the Be'ersheba *Edict*, which indicate the extent of military occupation across the steppe and desert, even if individual sites cannot always be identified with certainty (see Isaac 1990: 213 for references).

As for the impact of the army upon the more sedentary populations of the desert or pre-desert, a papyrus from the Judaean desert suggests that a close commercial relationship existed between the civilians and soldiers garrisoned in a fort in En Gedi (Avigad et al. 1962: 259). Indeed, evidence dating from 124 CE and probably 171 CE has been recovered for soldiers granting loans to locals (Goodman 1983).

PART VI

THE RISE OF CHRISTIANITY AND ISLAM IN THE HOLY LAND

27

CHURCH, STATE AND THE TRANSFORMATION OF PALESTINE – THE BYZANTINE PERIOD (324–640 CE)

Joseph Patrich

In terms of material culture, the chronological limits of our period are marked by non-catastrophic historical events. Nevertheless, regarding the archaeology of Palestine, the Byzantine period thus defined is rightly regarded as a distinct period. The main transformation that Roman Palestine underwent, starting in 324 CE, when Palestine fell under the aegis of a philo-Christian emperor, was the christianization of the country – the change from *Provincia Palaestina* to *Terra Sancta*. This transformation gradually affected all facets of social life. Earlier, for some 200 years, *Provincia Palaestina* had been a remote province, with no special significance, on the eastern border of the Roman Empire. But in 324 CE, when Constantine the Great became sole Emperor of a christianizing Roman Empire, a new era began in the life of this province. From then on it officially became the Holy Land, whose holy places deserved a special attention on behalf of the central government – the land of religious aspirations for multitudes of believers who flocked in from the entire Christian world (Hunt 1982). This era came to an end in 640 CE, with the final conquest of Palestine by the Muslim Arabs. But even this conquest cannot be considered as a sharp turning point in all domains of material culture.

Unlike the much earlier periods, the one under discussion abounds in literary sources and inscriptions that should be taken into account when we try to interpret the mute archaeological data.

The landscape of the country underwent a transformation due to its christianization. This was achieved by establishing a network of holy places and embellishing them with churches and memorials. Enormous funds were invested in this in Palestine – by emperors, wealthy believers and local ecclesiastics – to take care of the spiritual as well as the corporal needs of the pilgrims, monks and local citizens. The Byzantine period was a period of economic prosperity in Palestine (Avi-Yonah 1958). The christianization of the country was also achieved by a great increase in Christian population and settlements, both in areas previously inhabited by the Jews, like the Judean Hills, and in desert regions, such as the Negev, which had been only sparsely inhabited previously.

Before proceeding, a few remarks are required regarding the geographical borders and administrative government of the Province. Until ca. 300 CE the Negev did not constitute a part of the Province of Palestine. It was a part of *Provincia Arabia*, which also comprised the main part of Transjordan. Only later, within the framework of the reforms of Diocletian, were the Negev, Southern Transjordan and Sinai detached from that province and attached to *Provincia Palaestina*. During the fourth century several reforms in the provincial administration took place and, by 409 CE, we have instead of a single large province, three smaller ones: *Palaestina Prima*, with Caesarea as its capital; *Palaestina Secunda* in the north, with Scythopolis as its capital; and *Palaestina Tertia* in the South, with Petra as its capital.

Each province was governed by a civil governor, while one military commander was responsible for all three provinces; he was *Dux Palaestinae*, residing in Caesarea. The Byzantine provincial government, like the imperial one, was very bureaucratic and centralized. Under the governor, there were various provincial offices and there was also a separate municipal administration in each major city. Administratively, each province was divided into many units, each comprising a city and its territory, but there were rural administrative units as well, centered on large villages and estates. The Church administration was organized in a similar manner, with a bishop (*episcopos*) at the head of each unit, and a *metropolites* (the bishop of the civil capitals – Caesarea, Scythopolis and Petra) at the top of the ecclesiastical hierarchy. But Jerusalem – now Aelia, or Hierosolymma – claimed supremacy. The struggle came to an end in 451 CE, when Jerusalem was recognized by the entire Christian world as the fifth Patriarchate, next to Rome, Alexandria, Antioch and Constantinople, and Caesarea became subordinate to it.

Next, some ethnic considerations should be discussed. During the Byzantine period the Christians became a

Plate 1 Caesarea. A hoard of gold coins (*solidi*) found at a spacious dwelling (photograph by Aaron M. Levin; courtesy of the Combined Caesarea Expedition)

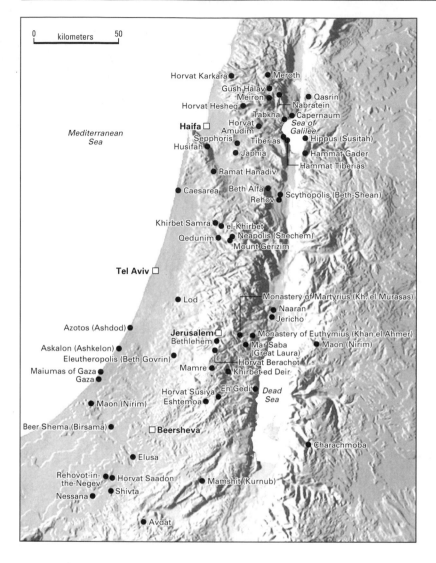

Figure 1 Byzantine Palestine. Map of principal archaeological sites

majority in the country. They grew in number mainly at the expense of the Gentiles, but the process of christianization of the pagans was gradual, enforced by law, the missionary zeal of the monks, and sometimes even by use of the army. The number of Christians was also augmented by immigration and settlement of pilgrims, monks and Arab tribes in a province that underwent economical and cultural prosperity. A cosmopolitan society was thus attained, mainly in Jerusalem and in the monasteries, introducing cultural influences from all over the Christian world. The dominant language was Greek, but Palestinian Syriac prevailed, mainly among the indigenous, rural population. Christians inhabited the previous pagan regions in the coastal plain, central Judea (from where the Jews had already been expelled by Hadrian) and the Negev (a former Nabatean territory).

But Christians were not the only element in the society. Jews lived in large rural areas in lower and upper Galilee,

and in the Golan – within the confines of *Palaestina Secunda*. In the Galilean cities of Tiberias and Sepphoris the Jews constituted a majority, and Caesarea was another center of cultural Rabbinic activity. Synagogue remains were found in many of the coastal cities, as well as in southern Judea, in the Valley of Jericho and En Gedi, and in Transjordan (Gerasa). The Samaritans flourished in their rural land, with Mount Gerizim, overlooking Neapolis, as their religious center. They were influential both in Scythopolis and Caesarea. Arabs – nomads or semi-settled – were present in the semi-arid grazing lands. Some were christianized, while others adhered to their pagan customs (Nevo 1991). Efforts were made to christianize all these ethnic groups and to convert the country into an entirely Christian land, but these efforts failed.

Byzantine Palestine experienced a tremendous growth of population, reaching levels never seen before (Tsafrir 1993b). Avi-Yonah gave a figure of 2.5 million inhabitants, while Broshi (1980), offering convincing arguments, estimates their number as 1 million at most. Both maximalists and minimalists agree that at that time there was a peak in the population of ancient Palestine; regions that had been sparsely populated became densely populated. The towns and farms of the Negev (see Window 2 p. 487) are the most outstanding example of this process. In the northern regions, the villages of the Golan were resettled after a period of desertion that had lasted more than 250 years – since their destruction in the first Jewish revolt against Rome (66–70 CE). Throughout Palestine wherever archaeological surveys were conducted, they consistently yielded the largest number of settlements and installations for the Byzantine period. This expansion is attested in the urban centers as well. Caesarea, Scythopolis and Jerusalem – the provincial and religious capitals of the country – during the Byzantine period reached their largest dimensions as Roman cities.

Some scholars have suggested that this florescence should be associated with some global climatic changes. Namely, that due to global processes, the Byzantine period was rainier and colder than the earlier, Roman period and the later, Arab period. The evidence for this is far from decisive. Moreover, from the literary sources we hear about periods of drought (the longest lasting five years, between 516–521 CE). If a climatic change did occur, it was on a minor scale – perhaps increasing the average yearly precipitation by not more than 50 mm and increasing only slightly the number of rainy days per annum. In any case, the prosperity and density of the Negev settlements should be attributed primarily to state encouragement and human labor, rather than to major climatic factors (Rubin 1989).

Before proceeding to talk about settlement patterns and aspects of architecture, several historical events that bear upon the archaeology should be mentioned. Until the Persian conquest of 614 CE, that lasted fourteen years, and the final conquest by the Arabs (633–41/2 CE), the Byzantine period was relatively peaceful, with no foreign forces crossing the country and causing damage on their way. This tranquility was interrupted by the following events: several local revolts of the Jews (351–3 CE) and the Samaritans (484, 495, 529, 556 CE), that were violently suppressed; local incursions of Saracens; a heavy plague in the winter of 541/2 CE; and two major earthquakes (in 363 and 551 CE; Russell 1985). The reign of Julian the Apostate (361–3 E), who caused disorder by trying to revive paganism and rebuild the Jewish temple in Jerusalem, was a short episode. Other sources of unrest, sometimes resulting in violence, were associated with Christian theological disputes in which the Palestinian church and monks were intensively involved.

The archaeological remains represent a large variety of settlement patterns: large cities (*metropoleis*), cities (*poleis*), towns (*polichnai*), large villages (*komai megistai*) and villages (*komai/ktemata*), farmsteads, military posts, monasteries, isolated holy sites enshrined by a church, annexed by an hostel or a monastery, road inns (*mansiones*), and road posts for changing of horses (*mutationes/allagai*). There was also a pastoral activity. The *Onomastikon* of Eusebius gives the names of many settlements and sites, classifying them according to their size and function (Thomsen 1903). A graphical representation reflecting internal hierarchy of settlements is to be found in the Madaba mosaic map (Avi-Yonah 1954).

Secular architecture

As in the Roman period and earlier, the city was the principal social organization within each province, demonstrating the main achievement in the domain of secular architecture. Two competing tendencies can be found in urban planning and architecture: continuity of the Roman tradition versus an introduction of non-classical trends.

After the reforms of Diocletian and Constantine, characterized by a tendency towards centralization and bureaucracy, the involvement of the imperial authorities – and later, of the Church – in city life increased, and the autonomy of the cities was further decreased. The *boulé* (or *curia*, in the Latin) almost disappeared as a central institution, and the *bouleutai* (*curiales*), as a social hereditary class, lost their previous prestige and wealth, and decreased in number. People tried to escape the burden of *curiales*, on whom various liturgies, including tax collection for the central government, were imposed. Instead new classes took the lead, constituting the group of *proteuontes/ principales* (the leaders of the city) – the landlords (*ktetores/possessores*), who possessed large estates; the dignitaries (*honorati*), generally imperial officials or ex-officials, who got an imperial honorary title; the bishop and the church leaders. These classes were thus in charge of the election of the city officials (*magistrates*). These executive officials, nominated in the past by the *boulé* from among its members, were replaced by non-*bouleutes* officers, whose nomination had to be approved by the central government. The authority of the civic organs in terms of taxation, jurisdiction and even their involvement in building projects decreased in comparison with that of the central government, or the bishop. Nevertheless, the cities remained political, social and religious centers: the upper classes resided there; in terms of provincial administration, the city still retained its authority over its *territorium* with regard to taxation and civil jurisdiction; and similarly, the bishop of each city had an ecclesiastical jurisdiction over his see – consecrating the priests, deacons and other clerics in the villages, and being in charge of all religious affairs therein. Actually, the bishop, more than any other citizen, was the most prominent individual in the

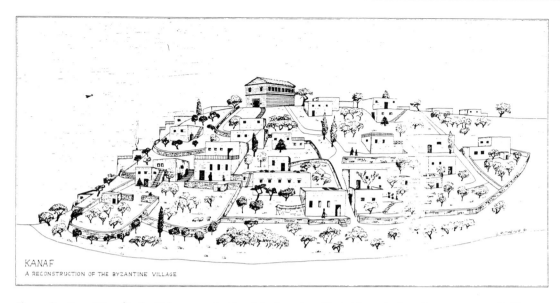

Figure 2   Horvat Kanaf in the Golan, reconstruction of the Byzantine villagte (drawn by Leen Ritmeyer; courtesy Z. Maoz, Israel Authority of Antiquities)

society and in the civic government. He also took part in public building projects – not solely ecclesiastical ones – and in the election of the civic administration. The bishop and the imperial *honorati* were patrons of urbanism, initiating the construction of public buildings (Jones 1964: 737–63; Claude 1969: 107ff.; Dan 1984: 51–117).

The *poleis* of Byzantine Palestine were the ones established as such in the Hellenistic and Roman periods. No new *poleis* were established during the Byzantine period, and only a few villages of the past were raised to a civic status, by becoming regional administrative centers. Greco-Roman architecture prevailed, but modifications and adaptations were enforced by the changing social attitudes and by the new religion. In terms of street engineering, order of magnitude, and quality of workmanship on decorative details such as capitals, there is a clear decline in comparison with those of the second century. A utilitarian, 'spontaneous' approach to urban planning, following the natural contours of topography, is more and more evident – mainly in the new suburbs, remote from the civic center, and in the smaller towns and villages (Figure 2). But the formal Roman orthogonal approach continued to prevail as well. All these processes can be demonstrated by the finds in Jerusalem/Aelia (Tsafrir 1978, 1984; Vincent and Abel 1914–26; Avigad 1983; Ben Dov 1985), Caesarea (Frova 1966; Holum et al. 1988; Holum 1982; Varɪn 1932; Levine 1975: 40–5), and Beth Shean/Scythopolis (Tsafrir and Foerster 1987–92; Mazor and Bar-Nathan 1987–92) – the religious center and the two provincial capitals of *Palaestina Prima* and *Palaestina Secunda*.

The cities were surrounded by walls and had civil public buildings. In terms of urban planning, the Roman standards

still prevailed, expressed in broad colonnaded, or arcaded streets (appearing graphically in the depiction of all the cities – Jerusalem, Neapolis, Diospolis, Charachmoba, Eleutheropolis, Azotos on the Sea, Askalon, Gaza and Pelousion – on the Madaba Mosaic Map, where the walls and other public buildings, not only churches, are depicted as well). The two colonnaded streets of Jerusalem were extended southward under Justinian. In Caesarea, located in the coastal plain, the city plan retained its Roman, orthogonal layout, with paved colonnaded streets, equipped with sidewalks paved with mosaic floors, dividing the city into square *insulae* of about 90 × 80 m. A cardo found to the south of the Crusaders' city, has its level 1.5 m higher than the earlier Roman pavement. One east–west street at least was first paved at that time. In Scythopolis, topographical restrictions prevented a strict orthogonal plan in the entire area (Figure 3). The city center was renovated after the severe damage caused by the 363 CE earthquake. The renovation is attributed by inscriptions to Governor Flavius Tavius Ablabius (ca 375 CE), and other governors or dignitaries (*honorati*) of the city. 'Palladius Street' – a colonnaded street (*stoa* in one of the inscriptions) – was built later in the fourth century (Plate 2), and 'the Byzantine Shops Street' (or 'Silvanus Street') – an arcaded street (*basilica* in an inscription) – was built in the early sixth century. The main streets were 12–25 m wide (cf. Broshi 1977), including the sidewalks, that in many instances were paved by mosaics and opus sectile floors, rather than by regular flagstones. In Sepphoris the Roman streets continued to be used and mosaic floors were laid in the sidewalks of the cardo by a local bishop.

Roman standards were also evidenced in the supplying of water by elaborate aqueducts and nymphea, and in the

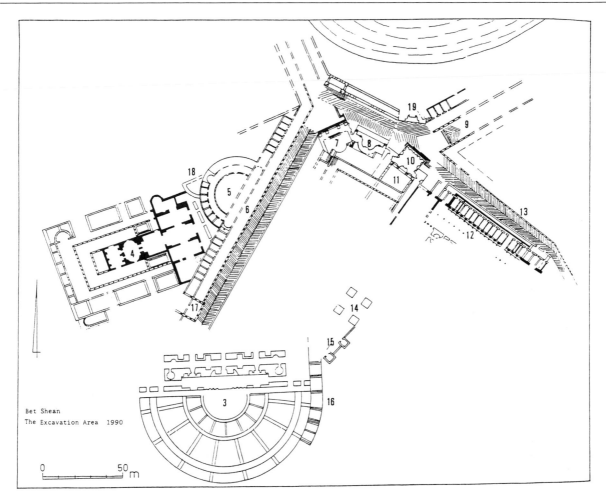

Figure 3   Beth Shean (Scythopolis). Plan of the excavated area at the urban center. 3. Roman Theater; 4. Byzantine Bath; 5. Byzantine semi-circular piazza; 6. Colonnaded street with shops ('Palladius Street') from the early Byzantine period; 7. Roman Temple; 8. Nymphaeum; 9. Roman colonnaded street; 10. 'Central Monument' (Roman); 11. Roman civil basilica; 12. Roman stoa and a reflection pool to its front; 13. Byzantine street with shops on its southern side built on top of the Roman reflection pool; 14. Massive pillars of the frigidarium of a large Byzantine Bath; 15. Public fountain (Byzantine); 16. Graded street along the outer wall of the theater; 17. Byzantine Propylon (decorated Gate) at the entrance to Bath no. 4. 18. Odeon/Bouleterion (Roman); 19. Roman Monument (courtesy the expeditions to Beth Shean)

construction and maintenance of improved sewage systems under the paved streets. In Jerusalem the ancient lower level aqueduct, leading from Solomon Pools in the Hebron Hills, was maintained with care (Abel 1926), as were many ancient pools. In Caesarea the water supply was augmented by the construction of the 'Lower Level Aqueduct'; a 1.8 m wide tunnel, built on the ground, with a vaulted roof, that could conduct 2500 m³ of water per hour – six times as much as the earlier, arcaded aqueducts (Peleg 1989). In Scythopolis the nympheum was renovated in *ca.* 400 by the provincial governor. It went out of use in the sixth century.

But city life was now a mixture of the Roman traditions of the past and new Christian concepts. The most important change that occurred in its landscape during the Byzantine period was the gradual disappearance of the pagan temples, that were either demolished or just deserted, and the prevalence of churches, whose numbers in each city exceeded the numbers of temples previously found there. In Caesarea a vast octagonal building, uncovered in recent years – perhaps the Martyrium of St. Procopius known from literary sources – took the place of the former Herodian temple dedicated to Augustus and Rome. This is the only Byzantine church excavated so far in Caesarea. The literary sources mention nine other churches and *martyria* in the city or in its immediate vicinity, none of which have been uncovered. In Scythopolis, the single church so far uncovered in the city center is of a circular plan, and is located on the top of the Tell. It was erected in the fifth century near the destroyed Roman Temple of Zeus Akraios. In Jerusalem, 25 churches in all were counted in the *Corpus* of Ovadiah 1970, and 6

Plate 2 Beth Shean (Scythopolis). 'Palladius Street', looking south (photograph Gabi Laron, courtesy of the archaeological expeditions to Beth Shean)

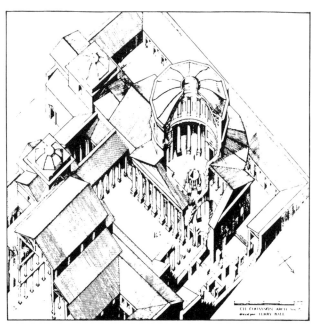

Figure 4 The church of the Holy Sepulcher, Jerusalem. Reconstruction of the fourth-century Rotunda (Coüasnon) 1974, Pl XVII)

more in the *Supplements* of Ovadiah and de Silva 1982–84. The most important churches were the *memoria*, erected over holy sites, the most celebrated of which were the Golgotha and the Holy Sepulcher (Figure 4). The structures erected there by Constantine (Coüasnon 1974; Corbo 1981), in the center of the city next to the *Cardo Maximus* and the Roman forum, included a basilical cathedral, known as Constantine's Martyrium, the Anastasis, concentric in shape; a baptistery (Warton 1992), and an episcopal palace. This complex constituted the religious and administrative center of the city. Many other churches were liturgical stations for solemn processions, headed by the archbishop, that made their way in the Christian feasts between the various holy sites. Such were the Church of Holy Zion, the Church of St. Mary at the Sheep Pool (*Probatica*), and the Church of Siloam, inside the city walls, and St. Stephen's Church, Gethsemane, Eleona, and the round Church of Ascension, outside the walls. Important monasteries were erected inside and outside the walls, and on the Mount of Olives.

The theaters and the amphitheaters were gradually abandoned. In Scythopolis the theater continued to be used until the end of the fifth century CE, though the amphitheater went out of use in the fourth century, and a new quarter was built in the fifth century along its northern wall. In Caesarea the theater had already gone out of use by the fourth century (Frova 1966: 57–159, 165–86), as was probably the fate of the amphitheater. The outer *cavea* walls of the Roman theater were integrated in the eastern flank of the inner fortress or *kastron*, with its semicircular towers, that was erected in the sixth century near the governor's sea palace (Frova 1966: 159–64). The hippodrome retained its popularity until the sixth century (Humphrey 1974). The chariot race was a popular entertainment, and the circus factions – the 'Greens' and the 'Blues' – also carried political, social and religious connotations (Dan 1984: 209–21).

In Scythopolis a public bath (*thermae/demosion*) was constructed at the beginning of the fifth century, preserving the best Roman standards. Another one is presently being exposed there. It is the largest of its kind uncovered so far (1993) in Israel. Another vast bath house is being exposed in Caesarea, several were excavated in Jerusalem, and one in Ashkelon. The Roman healing *thermae* of Hammat Gader were intensively reconstructed by the Empress Eudocia, and later by Anastasius (Green and Tsafrir 1982; Di Segni and Hirschfeld 1986).

The odeon of Scythopolis, that may have served in the past as an assembly hall for the city council, fell into disuse, perhaps with the disappearance of this institution –

Plate 3 Beth Shean (Scythopolis). The 'Sigma' structure – a semi-circular, colonnaded plaza (photograph by Gabi Laron, courtesy of the archaeological expeditions to Beth Shean)

Plate 4 Sepphoris. Mosiac floor from a Byzantine public building (photograph by Gabi Laron, courtesy of Ehud Netzer and Zeev Weiss)

the *boulé* (Kennedy 1985; Dan 1984: 51–67). New institutions of public welfare, such as hospitals, poor-houses and soup-kitchens, monasteries and the palace of the bishop, were added to the urban landscape. The architects were skillful enough to introduce new types of civic buildings, such as the 'Sigma' (Plate 3) – a semicircular colonnaded plaza with shops and taverns on its circumference – at Scythopolis, and the large public building uncovered recently in Sepphoris, comprising a basilical hall and an inner courtyard surrounded by rooms, including a reception hall or a triclinium. The entire building was embellished by magnificent mosaic floors (Plate 4), the one in the triclinium depicting scenes of celebration of the Nile's flood in Alexandria.

The Persian conquest was a trigger that intensified the processes of urban decline that had begun earlier – in the late sixth century – and continued later under the Muslim regime (Tsafrir 1984: 317–31; Tsafrir and Foerster 1992; Kennedy 1985; Holum et al. 1988: 93–6; 1989). The expansion of private businesses into public thoroughfares and plazas was no longer considered to be a major offense.

Religious architecture

The house of prayer, in the spirit of the Jewish synagogue, became for all – Christian, Jews and Samaritans the main edifice of religious architecture. The pagan temples, housing the statues of gods and emperors, gradually disappeared. Among the Christians – mainly of Gentile origin – the veneration of idols was substituted by the veneration of icons, holy places and relics. An altar stood at the focal point of each church, and the ritual reached its culmination in an act of sacrifice. In the synagogues, on the other hand, it was the prayer and the reading in the Scriptures that constituted the ritual.

Churches

The principal means of christianizing the landscape of the country, influencing thus the conversion of its inhabitants, was by establishing a network of Holy Places and embellishing them with spectacular memorial churches. This was the policy of both emperors and bishops. A biblical, Christian geography was thus constituted, attracting multitudes of monks and pilgrims to admire these holy sites. Parish churches were erected in cities, towns and villages – to serve as houses of prayer and to fulfill other religious and social functions.

To date, about 300 churches are known in Israel, but their number was much larger, since every Christian village and monastery possessed at least one church, and there were several in each town or city. The first effort to produce a synthetized study of the churches of Palestine, by Crowfoot (1941), was augmented and elaborated by the *Corpus* of Ovadiah (1970) – also, in turn, updated by Ovadiah and de Silva (1981–4). Other important contributions are those of Bagatti (1971) and Tsafrir (1984: 223–64). More recent finds are presented in Bottini et al. (1990) and in Tsafrir (1993a).

Constantine and his mother Helena were the first to erect churches in Palestine. Earlier Christians did not have a prayer house with distinctive architectural features; their place of assembly was a *domus ecclesia* – a domestic building that was adjusted to serve this purpose. The erection of churches was a major domain of imperial enterprise. Four churches were erected by Constantine: the Church of the Holy Sepulcher in Jerusalem, the Church of Nativity in Bethlehem, the Church of Abraham's Oak at Mamre, and the Eleona Church on the Mount of Olives.

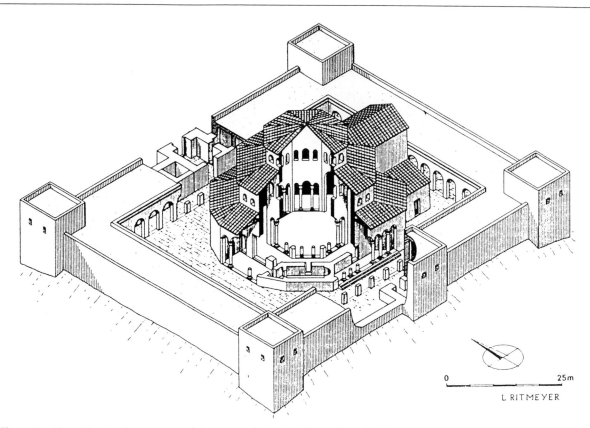

Figure 5   Mount Gerizim. Reconstruction of the octagonal church and the enclosure built by the emperor Zeno (484 CE) (drawn by Leen Ritmeyer, courtesy Y. Magen)

The first three were built on the sites of pagan shrines, thereby destroying them. Such was also the case with two other imperial churches: the first church of Gaza (407), and the church on the top of Mount Gerizim (484), the second being preceded by a Samaritan sacred place (see Figure 5). Other Emperors and Empresses that were engaged in ecclesiastical building in Palestine (Armstrong 1967) include Eudoxia (Gaza), Eudocia (St. Stephen in Jerusalem and other churches), Zenon (Mt. Gerizim), Anastasius (St. John near the Jordan) and Justinian (the Nativity Church, the Nea in Jerusalem, the church of the holy bush at Sinai). But most churches were erected by wealthy patrons, both male and female, bishops and other members of the clergy, members of the congregation itself and leading townsmen and monks, as we can learn from the dedicatory inscriptions (Meimaris 1986).

Architecturally, the local churches can be divided into four distinct types, according to their plan: basilicas (155 altogether in the Supplemented *Corpus* of Ovadiah and de Silva), chapels (93 altogether), churches of central plans (either circular, or octagonal), and churches of a cruciform plan. All these types (except the cruciform) were derived, with adaptations, from Roman prototypes – Roman civil basilica or palace basilica, Roman funerary architecture, or palatial reception halls. Only the cruciform type is a

Byzantine innovation, first introduced by Constantine in his Church of the Apostles in Constantinople, where he was interred. Transept basilicas, like the trefoil Justinianean Church of the Nativity in Bethlehem, or the Church of Loaves and Fishes at Tabkha, are variants of this type.

The orientation of the apse toward the east became a convention in Palestine since the foundations of Constantine. It appears that the earlier practice was to direct the facade, rather than the apse, to the east. This was the case with the 'House of St. Peter' in Capernaum, and with the pre-Constantinian Cathedral of Paulinus bishop of Tyre, described in detail by Eusebius. Such was also the orientation of almost all of the Constantinian foundations in Rome, and it prevailed in the West until 420 CE (Landsberger 1957: 193–203; Wilkinson 1984). The Constantinian basilica of the Holy Sepulcher compound is in accord with this early tradition, although the common explanation in this case is that the presence of the Sepulcher itself – to the west of the basilica – was the factor that determined its orientation. A similar dichotomy is to be found in the orientation of the Jewish and the Samaritan synagogues, as we shall see later.

In many instances a chapel was appended to the south or to the north of the basilica. It has been suggested that this chapel was the place where the deacon received the

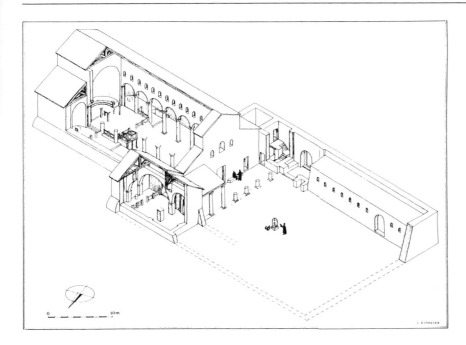

Figure 6 Rehovot-in-the-Negev. An isometric reconstruction of the northern church. The basilical church is annexed by a chapel on the north, and a stairs-tower on the south. An atrium extends to the west of the basilica (Tsafrir et al. 1988, fig. 10)

offerings of the faithful and wrote them down, and where the sacred elements were prepared, to be brought from there in a solemn procession to the main altar (Crowfoot 1941: 55, 57; Krautheimer 1975: 99).

The cult of relics of martyrs and saints was another rite that took place in the church besides the daily prayers and the celebration of the Eucharist. Relics were generally held in a special stone or marble container, shaped like a tiny *sarcophagus* – a *reliquiarium*. Generally, the relics were placed under the main altar, but more than one saint could have been venerated in a single church and then one or both of the lateral rooms or apses, flanking the central apse, could have been used for this purpose. This is indicated by such finds as those discovered in Mamshit eastern church and in other churches of the Negev, and in Horvat Hesheq in Upper Galilee (Negev 1974, 1989; Aviam 1990). In the lateral spaces the *reliquiarium* was put under an altar or in an elevated niche. In major sites of pilgrimage, and if the resources permitted, an underground crypt was constructed under the bema, with two staircases leading down from the aisles. Such was the case in the rural church at Horvat Berachot to the north of Hebron (Tsafrir and Hirschfeld 1979) and in the Northern Church at Rehovot-in-the Negev (Tsafrir et al. 1988; Figure 7).

The baptismal rite was another function associated with the church. In a recent study (Ben Pechat 1989), 53 baptismal installations found in 42 sites were explored. The baptisteries were always attached as a chapel or a room annexed to the body of the church. They were simple in shape, not independent buildings of octagonal or cruciform plan, and sophisticated architecture. The font was generally located near the eastern end of the baptistery. It may be either masonry built, or monolithic, either partially sunk into the floor, or standing on it. Nine basic types were defined, according to the shape of the font's interior rim: rectangular, hexagonal, semicircular, cruciform, mushroom-like, trefoil, circular, oval and quatrefoil. The most prominent types are the quatrefoil (21 fonts), mostly monolithic, with four variants, and the cruciform (10 fonts), mostly masonry built, with three variants.

Jewish Synagogues

The synagogue was the central institution in each Jewish village or town. To date, more than 100 synagogues have been explored. The Jewish synagogues were influenced by the contemporary sacral architecture – pagan in the Late Roman period and Christian in the Byzantine period. The Jews insisted on meeting the standards of the Gentiles, so that the Jewish house of worship would not be less attractive than theirs. On the other hand, the very adoption of the Roman civil basilica as a genre appropriate to serve as a prayer house was first adopted by the Jews, and only later by the Christians. Liturgical demands was another factor that dictated the shape of the Jewish synagogue and the introduction of changes in its layout. The most important liturgical prescription was that the direction of prayer should be toward Jerusalem (Palestinian Talmud, *Berakhot* 4.5, 8bc).

In terms of their plan, Jewish synagogues demonstrate greater variety than the Christian churches. It seems that there was no central authority to impose a single specific plan everywhere. Regionality, conservatism, and inventiveness in accord with the liturgical restrictions were factors that determined the actual layout. The traditional classification of ancient synagogues is according to three types:

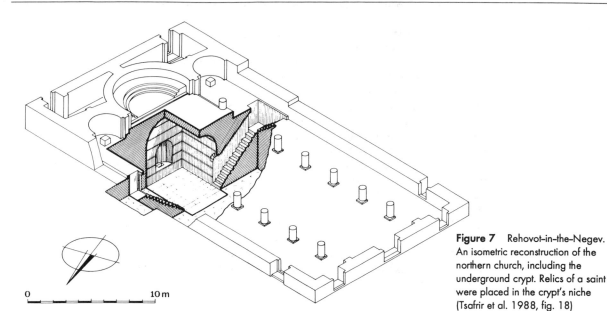

Figure 7 Rehovot-in-the-Negev. An isometric reconstruction of the northern church, including the underground crypt. Relics of a saint were placed in the crypt's niche (Tsafrir et al. 1988, fig. 18)

'early' or 'Galilean', 'transitional' – dated to the fourth– fifth centuries; and 'late' – dated to the fifth–seventh centuries (Avi-Yonah 1981: 271–81). The two later types fall within the Byzantine period.

Excavations at the Galilean Synagogues of Meiron, Gush Halav, Horvat Amudim and Nabratein indicated that they are indeed the earliest type, but their date falls in the late third century, not in the second and early third, as had been assumed. (The Capernaum synagogue, the most elaborate in this group, was dated by its excavators to the late fourth–mid-fifth century. This date is debated by other scholars, though this is not the place to elaborate on this issue.) The sense of regional conservatism in this exclusively Jewish, rural region, is best expressed in the ashlar built synagogue of Meroth, erected in the late fourth–early fifth century and still preserving the features of the earlier Galilean synagogues: external decorations cut in relief and entrances in the south. These entrances were blocked only in the early seventh century, when new entrances were pierced in the northern wall. Yet there was neither an apse, nor any recess throughout its existence, just an inward protruding bema on which the Ark was standing.

The Golan synagogues (25 altogether, four of which have been excavated; see Figure 8) reveal a Galilean (as well as southern Syrian) influence, although being erected in the fifth and sixth centuries – contemporary with the basilical, 'late' synagogues (Maoz 1981). Like the Galilean synagogues, their plan is basilical without an apse, they are ashlar built – at least in their facade – and decorated in stone cut reliefs, mainly on the door frames. Also like the Galilean type, the facade is generally directed to Jerusalem in the south. But there are instances where both the entrance and the direction of prayer were to the west, in accordance with the Transjordanian synagogue of Gerasa.

Only in Qasrin – from its first phase in the late fourth–fifth century – was the entrance in the north (Maoz and Killebrew 1988). In none of the Golan synagogues was there any recess in the wall to place the Ark in; rather, it was placed on a raised platform or dais, projecting into the nave. Yet, several characteristics are typical to the Golan, differentiating this group from the Galilean synagogues: all have just a single door; only two rows of columns, none of which is heart shaped; and, with one exception, the columns stand on the floor rather than on pedestals.

The transitional features in the 'transitional' type are manifested in attempts to move the entrance to a wall perpendicular or opposite to the direction of Jerusalem, and to find a better architectural solution for the housing of the Torah Shrine or Ark, more elaborate than an aedicule flanking the main entrance. Rather than standing on a simple dais, the Ark was placed inside a special recess, or a niche – mainly rectangular – constructed in the side directed toward Jerusalem (Hachlili 1988). A mosaic floor, appearing already in the Galilean type-building at Horvat Amudim, dated to *ca.* 300 CE, is prevalent among the synagogues of this group, which include 'Severus' Synagogue' at Hammat Tiberias, and the synagogues at Husifah, Japhia and En Gedi. A distinct subtype in this group is the broadhouse, having no columns on the inside, and being entered from the east. To this subgroup belong the late-fourth to early-fifth century synagogues of Eshthemoa and Horvat Susiya in southern Judea, but other types existed there as well, so that the broadhouse cannot be considered as the exclusive Judean type.

The 'late' type synagogue resembles the Christian basilica in its plan, decorations and furnishing (Tsafrir 1987). The apse – where the Torah Shrine is located, standing on a raised bema, surrounded by a chancel screen

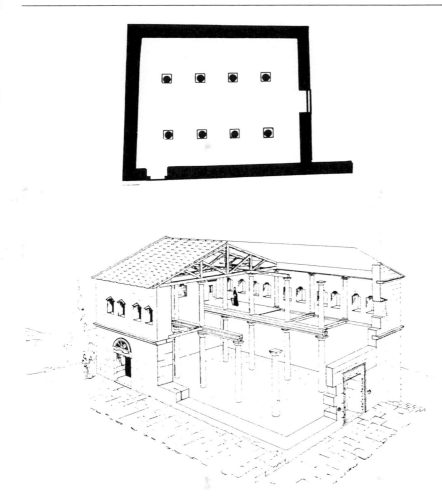

Figure 8 The synagogue of Horvat Kanaf in the Golan, plan and reconstruction (drawn by Leen Ritmeyer; courtesy Z. Maoz, Israel Authority of Antiquities)

– is aligned toward Jerusalem, while the entrance is in the opposite wall. The decorations are internal, consisting mainly of magnificent mosaic floors. To this group belong the synagogues of Beth Alfa, Jericho, Naaran, Nirim, and Maiumas of Gaza (for a summary of the finds in each synagogue and an extensive bibliography, see Hüttenmeister and Reeg 1977; Chiat 1982).

In several cases, like in Qasrin and Meroth, a Torah school – *Beth Midrash* – was annexed to the synagogue.

Samaritan synagogues

Excavated sites number about seven (Magen 1992). Others are known from the literary sources (compiled by Reeg; see Hüttenmeister and Reeg 1977, Vol. II and Safrai 1986: 157–86). Samaritan synagogues are aligned with their facade or their rear wall toward Mount Gerizim. The recently excavated fourth–fifth century synagogues of el-Khirbe and Khirbet Samra, show a unique plan, never encountered before. They are rectangular halls, entered through a single door and roofed by a vault. The longitudinal walls are therefore *ca.* twice as thick as the

short ones. Stone benches are built along the walls. It appears that the Samaritan synagogues underwent later a development similar to the Jewish synagogues in terms of the final prevalence of the Christian basilical type, and the introduction of an apse for the placement of the Ark. The sixth century synagogue of Beth Shean is basilical in plan, with two colonnades and an apse which is facing away from Mount Gerizim. The plan of the Zur Nathan (and Ramat Aviv?) synagogues was similar, except that a small apse in the rear wall faced eastward – towards Mount Gerizim.

Burial practices

As in earlier periods, burial in underground, rock-cut tombs was still common. There were also subterrenean public burial halls (*Polyandria*). The burial places were shaped like shelves or troughs, arranged along three walls of the chamber, sometimes in arched niches (*arcosolia*). Large cemeteries of tombs dug in the ground were found in the Negev towns – those around Rehovot were thoroughly surveyed. In such cemeteries there is no indication that the place allotted for burial was determined by family relationship. This reality seemingly reflects a society of new settlers, without deep family roots at a particular site.

Interment within or in proximity to a church, like in the case of the northern church of Rehovot-in-the-Negev, was another factor that dictated the location of the burial place. Interment in a church was considered a great privilege, reserved for pious members of the congregation – and for the wealthy ones. In many churches tombs were cut under the floor, and marked with a burial inscription. Burial in monumental mausolea, or large, decorated sarcophagi were not as popular as before. *Coemeteria* (roofed burial halls), like the Constantinian ones at Rome, were not found in Israel.

Aspects of artistic creativity

In architectural decoration there is a clear shift from the extrovertial to the internal. Wall and floor mosaics were the main medium of artistic expression. Wall mosaics are known mainly from the literary sources, especially from the descriptions of two churches at Gaza by the local, sixth-century rhetor Choricius. The apse mosaics in the Justinianean church at St. Catherine Monastery at Sinai represent the metropolitan art of Constantinople. Two frescoes preserved therein depict Abraham sacrificing Isaac, and the sacrifice of Jeptah (Forsyth and Weitzmann 1970), but there are other more fragmentary finds, both from churches, synagogues and tombs (Tsafrir 1984: 435–41). The principal studies of the mosaic floors are those of Avi-Yonah (1975; 1981: 283–382, first published in 1932–5), Kitzinger (1965), and Ovadiah and Ovadiah (1987). The wall and floor mosaics take the place of the former decorated entablature and stone reliefs. This process is evident in churches, synagogues, and in the urban landscape. Churches and synagogues were similarly decorated, sometimes by the very same school of artists (Ovadiah and Ovadiah 1987: 154–5), but symbols of religious significance made the difference. The polichrome compositions were figurative, floral or geometric (see Plate 5). The layout of the various compositions is generally simple, consisting of separate panels or 'carpets', each depicting a single composition.

The biblical injunction against graven images, that prevailed in Judaism during the early Roman period, had already faded by the second and third centuries. Jewish art abounds with figurative representations, since the ancient fear of idolatry no longer dominated. Biblical figurative scenes include the binding of Isaac (Beth Alfa), Daniel in the lion's den (Naaran, Horvat Susiya), Noah's Ark (Gerasa), and King David as Orpheus (Maiumas of Gaza). The zodiac wheel with Helios in the center – a purely pagan motif – was depicted in Hammat Tiberias, Beth Alfa, Naaran, Husifah and presumably also at Horvat Susiya synagogues. Its exact meaning and significance

Plate 5 Beth Loya. Geometric patterns and a Greek inscription in the mosaic floor of the chapel flanking the church from the north (photograph by Avraham Hay)

among the Jews, whether magical, astrological or cosmic/astronomical, is not yet clear. This motif was not found in any church and, generally, Christian mosaic pavements lack any pagan motifs – even the representation of the human figure is uncommon (Ovadiah and Ovadiah 1987: 162–5). Figures are represented as two dimensional, without ground line or background – seeming to float in space. The story of Jonah was depicted in a church at Beth Govrin, and the Multiplication of the Loaves and Fishes was laid down at Tabkha. No additional scenes from the Old or New Testaments are known on mosaic pavements; rather they were depicted on wall mosaics which have since perished (except in Sinai).

The Torah Ark, flanked by two *menorot* is a common Jewish motif, as seen at Beth Alfa, Naaran, Hammat Tiberias and Horvat Susiya. The two motifs may also appear separately, and in Samaritan synagogues (Magen 1992). Most interesting are mosaic floors containing only literary inscriptions, like the one in Rehov synagogue in the Beth Shean valley, depicting a Rabbinic *halakhic* text, or those at En Gedi synagogue, the content of which seemingly represents the zodiac wheel, mentioning the

Plate 6 Beer Shema (Birsama, northern Negev). Mosaic floor of the church (photograph by Nahshon Sneh, courtesy Y. Lander and D. Gazith, Israel Authority of Antiquities)

names of all the symbols. Scriptural quotations are common on pavements of churches.

A popular composition, in synagogues and churches alike, consists of an intertwining vine-trellis emerging from an amphora, forming medallions in which various birds, animals, vignettes, or vessels are depicted. An almost intact mosaic floor of this kind (Plate 6) was uncovered recently in a church at Beer Shema/Birsama (Kh. el Far). It was suggested (Avi-Yonah 1981: 389–95), that these floors were laid by a Gazaean school of mosaic artists, but its distribution reaches the regions of Beth Govrin (Eleutheropolis) and Jerusalem. 'Peopled' scrolls of acanthus leaves were popular as border strips.

Opus sectile floors, of geometric design, are less common. They appear in public buildings and on sidewalks, as well as churches. Other decorations included carved capitals, and reliefs on lintels, chancel screen panels and screen posts. They were made of local limestone, or of imported marble, mainly grey Proconnesian. The cross was the most prominent Christian symbol since the second half of the fourth century. Its depiction on mosaic floors is quite rare, though not unknown. An edict of Theodosius II of 427 CE prohibited the inclusion of Christian symbols in the floor. Nevertheless, this cannot be considered as a universal *terminus ante quem* for mosaic floors displaying crosses.

The ultimate victory in the Byzantine period of the oriental approach to the representational arts was brilliantly demonstrated by Avi-Yonah (1981: 1–118, first published in 1942–50; 1961) in the case of Palestine. This approach always existed as a sub-classical trend, side by side with the main stream of the Greco-Roman art. This oriental triumph is evident in Byzantine art everywhere – not only in provincial and popular art, but in official imperial art as well. The art is conceptual, rather than illusionistic. Its characteristic features are frontality, stylization, ignoring of proportions and *horror vacui*. The

same is true in all domains of artistic creativity – both monumental and minor, and in all media, such as carved ivory or bone, woodcuts, textiles, metal work, numismatics, etc.

The manufacture of Christian souvenirs for pilgrims was an important source of income in the various *Loca Sancta*. Of a special artistic significance are the lead ampules, depicting in low relief various christological scenes (Grabar 1958). It was suggested that these ampules, produced in Jerusalem, were miniature representations of scenes depicted in the apse mosaics of the principal churches of the Holy Land. Some of the icons preserved in St. Catherine Monastery in Sinai are pre-seventh century (Weitzmann 1976).

Agricultural installations

More than in terms of technology, agriculture reached its peak during the Byzantine period in terms of exploitation of all tillable lands. Larger areas of the hilly regions of Judea, Samaria, and Galilee were covered by terraces. The most significant plants were cereals, lentils, olives for oil and mainly grapes for wine. Mills, operated by water power, are preserved near the dam where the lower aqueduct to Caesarea starts. The water, conducted by a channel, exerted power on the mill by falling down through a chimney. This was an innovation of the Byzantine period. The oil presses were of two major types: the older type, known already in the Hellenistic period, where one end of the press-beam was laid in a deep recess inside the wall, and heavy stone, each weighing less than 100 kg, were attached to the other end; and a newer type, where the pressing power was obtained by means of a stationary wooden screw anchored to a heavy monolith, several tons in weight (Figure 9). Nice examples of both types were excavated in Qedumim (Samaria) and in Karkara (Upper Galilee) (Frankel 1992).

A well-preserved farmstead was excavated in Horvat Aqav (Mansur el-Aqab) at Ramat Hanadiv (Plates 7 and 8), near Caesarea (Hirschfeld and Birger 1991). The Byzantine estate, designed as a rural villa (*villa rustica*), was an approximately square building (22 × 24 m), with a central courtyard flanked on three wings by a storeroom, two stables and a wine-cellar, all roofed by barrel vaults. The living quarters were on the second floor. At a distance of some 50 m to the southwest was a screw-operated winepress.

The transition to mass production is best revealed in the agricultural estate excavated recently to the north of Ashkelon, in an area covered by post-Byzantine dunes (like many other areas in the northwestern Negev and the coastal plain). The buildings uncovered consist of several large oil and wine-presses, two-story warehouses of a basilical plan for the storing of the products, kilns for the production of the jars – the so-called 'Gaza and Ashkelon

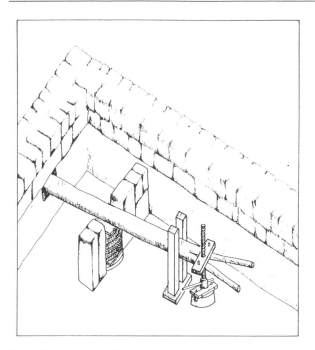

Figure 9   Beth Loya. Oil-press

Plate 8   Pottery vessels from Ramat Hanadiv (photograph by Zev Radovan, courtesy Y. Hirschfeld)

jars' (Mayerson 1992), in which the oil and wine were exported, and ponds for the artificial breeding of fish. A private, but large, bath-house was another component of this estate. A survey conducted along the coastal plain from Ashdod to Gaza, and even farther to the southwest, revealed a large number of such estates with similar installations. The agricultural regime of the Negev is to be viewed in this larger context.

In the windows which follow, the social dimensions of the towns and farms of the Negev are presented. In addition a new perspective on the emergence of monasteries and their impact on the social landscape of the Holy Land is discussed.

Plate 7   Ramat Hanadiv. The Byzantine farmstead after the reconstruction (photograph by Zev Radovan, courtesy Y. Hirschfeld)

THE TOWNS AND FARMS OF THE NEGEV

The settlements of the central Negev reached their zenith in the Byzantine period, after moderate beginnings under the Nabatean monarchy and under the Roman rule of *Provincia Arabia*. The security conditions were improved by the reforms of Diocletian, which brought about the transfer of the Tenth Legion from Aelia to Aila, and the formation of the *Limes Palaestinae*, consisting of a network of military posts garrisoned by *limitanei*. These military posts, located along the main routes to Aila in the Arava and along the *Via Traiana Nova* — routes of military significance — secured the borders of the Empire as well as the Red Sea commerce with India. A third longitudinal route connected Aila to Gaza, through Nessana and Elusa. Within the framework of this reform, that was carried on later by Constantine, fortresses were also erected on the *acropoleis* of Nessana and Avdat, and Mamshit (Kurnub) was surrounded by a wall. The loyalty of the Arab Saracens was guaranteed by yearly allotments. The Church worked hand in hand with the provincial government of *Palaestina Tertia*, as is evident from the proximity of the fortresses and the churches at Avdat and Nessana. In the fifth and sixth centuries soldier settlers were given plots of land to cultivate and tax reductions, besides their regular payments (Jones 1964: 649–54; 660–1; Negev 1990).

The settlement process by which these desert regions were integrated within the *oicumene* was marked by a combination of an agricultural military-settlement of foreign elements — loyal to the Romans — and of provincial officials, on the one hand; and by the christianization of the indigenous population, of Nabatean and Arab origin, on the other hand. Six towns are regularly mentioned by scholars in this group (the numbers in brackets give the estimated population — 30,000 altogether for the entire Negev according to Broshi 1980): Elusa (10,000), Nessana (4,000), Shivta (2,000), Rehovot-in-the-Negev (4,000), Avdat (3,000), and Mamshit (1,500). (Rubin [1990: 62] prefers a figure of 80,000 for the population of the Negev, already suggested by Avi-Yonah.) Of these six towns, only Elusa, 350 dunams in area, was a seat of a bishop, and had other municipal organs and institutions, such as a head of a police, a theater (the pavement in front of which underwent reconstruction in 454/5 CE), and an academy of rhetoric. The others range in area between 35–130 dunams, and should be considered as small towns or villages. Nessana is accordingly defined in the papyri retrieved therein as a village in the region of Elusa. Horvat Saadon should also be added to this group.

The settlement patterns also included a vast agricultural hinterland, consisting of farmsteads (some of them fortified), field towers, villages, guard towers and a large variety of installations such as fields, dams, wells, water reservoirs and cisterns, and wine and oil-presses (Rubin 1990). The same was true all over the country.

Among the towns, Shivta is one of the best surveyed and explored. The town plan demonstrates a spontaneous development from the center — where two open pools are located — outward, along the paths that led to the fields. These paths became streets. The town plan of Rehovot (Plate 1.2) and of Horvat Saadon demonstrate more regular-orthogonal features. Shivta, Rehovot and Elusa were not surrounded by a wall, but the outer houses were built adjacent to each other, the street entrances were narrowed and their number reduced. Shivta streets, spanning like radians of different length, are not straight, and are not uniform in width. Several wider sections in the town center, and near the northern church, form open plazas.

The most prominent public buildings in Shivta were the churches, three in number, of tri-apsidal plan.

Multiplicity of churches is typical to other towns as well. The largest church was uncovered in Elusa, with dimensions of ca. 40 × 17 m and a vast atrium in front. Unlike the other Negev churches, the columns and capitals of which were made of local limestone, in case of the Cathedral of Elusa they were made of grey Proconnesian marble. All churches had gabled tile roofs, supported by a construction of wood, and were the tallest edifices in each town. On the chronology and development of the Negev churches see: Negev 1989.

In Rehovot, 130 dunams in area, two churches out of the four were excavated. The central one, on a raised area in the town center, was mono-apsidal. It seems that it was preceded by a Nabatean temple on the same spot, similar to the case of the northern church at Avdat. The second excavated church in Rehovot is the northern one (Tsafrir et al. 1988). Another public structure in Rehovot which has been partially excavated, already constructed by the earlier Nabatean-Roman period, is a caravanseray (khan), comprising four rows of rooms surrounding a central courtyard. One wing held a stable.

The architecture reflects a sense of regionality. The floors were generally of stone or marble slabs. Mosaics were found only in the two churches at Mamshit — the most northern town — and in the complex of the northern church at Shivta. Fragmentary frescoes were retrieved in a side room of the northern church at Rehovot. In the most lavish churches the walls were faced with marble slabs. The reliefs on the limestone screen posts and panels were done in the *kerbschnitt* technique, depicting floral motifs and endless patterns composed of lathe-made intersecting circles. Pseudo-Corinthian capitals, covered by a single or a double story of stylized acanthus leaves, are the result of early, Nabatean influence and the evolution of the Byzantine impost capitals, of a

Plate 1.1 Agricultural system consisting of fields and irrigation channels in the Negev

trapezoidal cross-section. Numerous Greek inscriptions were found in the churches.

The layout of the private houses, excavated in all of the towns, and the building techniques they display, preserve the best tradition of the Nabatean dwelling houses as revealed at Mamshit. They consist of several rooms surrounding an inner courtyard with a water cistern underneath. Instead of the elaborate stairs-tower that leads to the second floor, we find a simpler staircase, built adjacent to an outer wall. The walls are thick, built of two faces of partially-dressed stone. The roofing system of each room, like in the preceding Nabatean and Roman periods, is supported by several transversal arches, with stone beams spanning the interval between adjacent arches. In northern regions, wooden beams were used for this purpose; only in the basalt regions in the Golan (and Southern Syria), did similar stone roofing prevail (Hirschfeld 1987).

Plate 1.2   Rehovot-in-the-Negev. Aerial photograph

A popular public institution was the bath-house, in the Roman tradition. One was excavated in Avdat; another in Mamshit, built in the Roman period, and a third in Rehovot. Deep wells supplied the water to the Avdat and Rehovot baths.

The fields were located around the towns, along main wadis and secondary rivulets. Kedar (1967) estimated as 40,000 dunams the tillable area of the towns of the central Negev. Two main types of fields were defined. The first, in main tributaries, consists of dams several hundreds of meters long, slowing the stream flow, and channels diverting the water to the cultivated plots that are located on old terraces of the wadis, where a deep layer of soil was accumulated. The fields in the secondary tributaries were irrigated by an elaborate system of channels, that drained the runoff of rain water from the spurs on both sides of the rivulet, and conducted it to the fields that were artificially built-up by a series of terrace walls constructed across the stream bed. A thick layer of soil was thus accumulated on each terrace, that was irrigated by a pair of channels. The water flow could be controlled by means of sluice-gates. Each terrace was flooded, and excess water could flow moderately from one terrace to another. Both types of fields were fenced by a wall in order to prevent herds and beasts from causing damage to the fruits and crops (Mayerson 1960).

The wine-grapes for export were the most important crop. Ten elaborate wine presses have been explored in the towns of the Negev (Mazor 1981). They are well built and paved by flagstones. The collecting vats are circular in shape, with a stone revetment and a thick layer of plaster. In the center of the treading floor there is a stationary screw device for pressing grape pulp, with an underground pipe leading the grape juice into a settling basin and then into the gathering vat. There are also other presses, rock-cut and of a simpler shape. This wine, if good enough, may have been exported through Gaza, the wine of which was renowned in the Roman world (*Expositio Totius Mundi*, ed. Rouge, p. 162; Mayerson 1985). There were also fields of wheat and barley, gardens with a sort of lentils called *arkos*, dates, figs, and olives for oil. Another source of income was escorting and guiding caravans of pilgrims on their way to Mount Sinai (Rubin 1990). Stables for the raising and tending of horses, already constructed in Mamshit already in the Late Nabatean Period, were found also in Byzantine Shivta and Rehovot.

Plate 1.3   Beth Loya. Wine-press. The circular stone in the treading floor was used for anchoring the wooden screw of the press; the juice flowed to the square settling basin and hence to the circular collecting basin (photograph by Avraham Hay)

Encampments of a pastoral society, of Arabian stock, were found on the outskirts of the towns and villages, and even in Makhtesh Ramon — farther away from the agricultural belt that surrounded them (Rosen 1987). Nevo (1991) found in the area of Sede Boqer pre-Islamic Arab inscriptions, open shrines, houses and runoff farms and other structures, which he attributed to pagan, Arab herders that lived in this region, neighboring the Christian population.

MONASTERIES

The monastic movement started spontaneously in the early fourth century. At the beginning of the fifth century it was integrated within the ecclesiastical establishment. The monks were the soldiers in the service of the Church. In many cases they were the ones to dictate religious policy to the patriarch. Unlike in Egypt and Syria, Palestinian monasticism was not an indigenous movement, but mainly a Greek-speaking one, with a cosmopolitan flavor. Monks had a tremendous influence on the Christian congregations. Their leaders were perceived and venerated as Holy Men, possessing supernatural powers, and often functioned as representatives and patrons of the population of the country. Members of communal monasteries took part in social activities, for the welfare of the old and the poor (Chitty 1966; Vailhé 1899–1900).

Institutionally and architecturally the monasteries can be divided into two main types – the laura and the coenobium. The different way of life in each of them dictated the different physical structure of the two types. The laura was a community of anchorites, being therefore restricted only to remote or desert zones. During the week, each monk lived in solitude in his cell, and only at weekends would they all assemble together for communal prayer and a communal meal. In a coenobium, on the other hand, the monks would live and work together, and meet daily with each other in the church and in the dining room.

The most comprehensive archaeological and historical study refers to monasticism in the Judean desert (Hirschfeld 1992; Patrich 1994). The ruins of some sixty monasteries and monastic installations were explored in this area, some – Kh. el Murasas, Kh. el Kiliya, Khan el Ahmar and Kh. ed Deir (Plate 2.1) – being entirely excavated (Magen and Talgam 1990; Magen 1993: 170–96; Magen 1990; Meimaris 1989; Hirschfeld and Birger 1986). All others were surveyed comprehensively. Five monasteries on the fringes of the desert, adjacent to Bethlehem, were excavated by Corbo (1955).

Architecturally, the coenobium was an enclosed monastery, with all its components confined within its walls. The Monastery of Martyrius (Kh. el Murasas) is the best representative of this type (Figure 2.1). The laura, by contrast, was composed of dispersed cells, connected to each other and to the communal buildings by a network of paths that converted the scattered elements into an integral architectural entity. The Great Laura of Saint Sabas (Mar Saba), was the most elaborate example of this type (Patrich 1994). The communal buildings in a coenobium consisted of one or more churches, a refectory, kitchen and bakery, storerooms, stables, and sometimes a hostel for the lodging of pilgrims and guests. There might also be a hospital or cells furnished with stone beds for the care of the sick, and even a bath house, like in the Monastery of Martyrius. Rain water was collected by means of a most efficient and well-cared for system of plastered channels and gutters into large water cisterns constructed under the courtyard. Special reservoirs were constructed for the irrigation of the garden of the monastery. Open spaces and passages were paved by flagstones. In some instances, the large halls – the monastic chapel, refectory, and the rooms adjoining them – were paved with colorful mosaic floors of various patterns. There were also burial chapels and cemeteries, in which the monks were interred according to their monastery hierarchy: abbots apart, priests and deacons in another group, and unordained monks in a third. The tomb of the founding father was sometimes marked by a special building, or he was buried in the cave in which he had spent his life. The tomb could become a focal point for the veneration of monks and pilgrims.

Almost all of the communal buildings found in a coenobium

Plate 2.1 Khirbet ed–Deir in the Judean Desert. Aerial view of the cliff coenobium (courtesy Y. Hirschfeld)

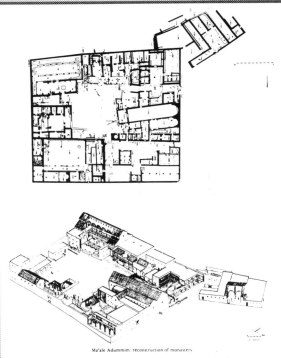

Ma'ale Adummim: reconstruction of monastery

Figure 2.1 The Monastery of Martyrius at Maale Adummim. Ground plan and reconstruction (drawn by Leen Ritmeyer, courtesy Y. Magen)

were also present in the core of a laura, except that the latter had no walls or gates. Typologically, both kinds of monasteries could be constructed either on a plain or moderately hilly area, or upon steep cliffs (Hirschfeld 1992; Patrich 1994).

The laura hermitages were of various types. The simplest cells had a single room and a courtyard, while the complex ones consisted of several rooms, including a private chapel or a prayer niche. All cells had one or several water cisterns. In coenobia, generally each monk lived separately, but a cell might have been shared by two or three monks or there might have been larger dormitories, in accordance with the regulations for monks legislated by Justinian.

28

ISLAM AND THE SOCIO-CULTURAL TRANSITION OF PALESTINE – EARLY ISLAMIC PERIOD (638–1099 CE)

Donald Whitcomb

Major transitions

The study of cultural processes which characterize the Holy Land during the 450 years or so covered in this chapter is best divided into three 150-year periods. These should be seen as archaeological periods, not political periods per se, though political/dynastic events have influenced the periodization. As more archaeological evidence becomes available and, more importantly, as more sophisticated interpretation of existing data becomes possible, more precise phasing should become prevalent.

This whole period is often reduced to tales of violence and destruction; Gil relates the almost obligatory story of suffering populations, destruction of villages, and, most particularly, 'the destruction of the synagogues and churches of the Byzantine era, remnants of which have been unearthed in our own time and are still being discovered' (Gil 1992, 61). This sad picture has become a modern literary topos, but it ill-fits the archaeological data. The psychological background to this interpretative mode has been explored by Silberman under the wonderful rubric of 'thundering hoards' (n.d.). Archaeological evidence is now beginning to rectify historians' generalizing assumptions, and the prevalent impression that the Abbasids tended to neglect Palestine in favor of their eastern provinces is being recognized as correct only in terms of political patronage (Whitcomb 1990a). Very recent studies of Caesarea (Holum 1992) and the Tyropoean valley (Magness 1992) are reexamining old interpretations of archaeological data; the research of Schick (n.d.) on the 'fate' of churches adds even more careful documentation, both archaeological and literary, revising such earlier assumptions (n.d.) (see Figure 1).

More convincing are natural disasters as cataclysmic events, 'the earthquakes of 551, 633, and 659 . . . bracket the Persian invasion of 614 and the Islamic assaults . . . between 629 and 640.' If the damage from these earthquakes is interpreted as the result of invasion, then 'given the geographic extent and general depositional magnitude . . . both the Persian army and the forces of Islam invaded . . . with bulldozers and cranes.' (Russell 1985, 51). On the other hand, the close temporal proximity of the earthquake of 748 CE and the Abbasid revolution provides a remarkably convenient fixed point for change in period designation. It is less clear that this should mark sudden cultural change.

In contrast to the dramatic impact of natural disaster, and possibly violent conquest and immigration, there is the enervating process of repeated military movements, internal revolt, and political instability producing chronic anarchy and cultural decline. Passage of armies and the fortunes of political entities need not have a lasting cultural effect until a cumulative pattern is generated; but from the tenth century on, Palestine became a zone of conflict of increasing intensity. The cautionary point is that earthquakes and conquests do not necessarily make useful cultural periodizations. Even more to the point, the prevalent use of dynastic history (labelling periods Tulunid, Ikhshidid, Fatimid, Seljuq, Jarrahid, etc.) introduces potential distortions into archaeological evidence. It is crucial that a neutral archaeological peroidization, such as used for earlier periods (EB or such), be used in conjunction with generalizing dynastic names (Whitcomb 1990a).

Settlement patterns

Provincial organization changed from Roman provinciae to two provinces, the junds of al-Urdunn and Filastīn. Walmsley (1987) has argued that the administrative reorganization of Palestine into these *ajnād* must date from 'Umar's rule, from as early as 639 CE. The jund of al-Urdunn ranges from the coast, through Galilee, to the northern portion of the Jordan valley and Transjordan, the former Palestina Secunda. Filastīn is the Byzantine Palestina Prima, still including the southern Jordan valley and Transjordan. The region south of the Dead Sea, Palestina Tertia, was generally considered part of Filastīn,

The Dome of the Rock (photograph: © Garo)

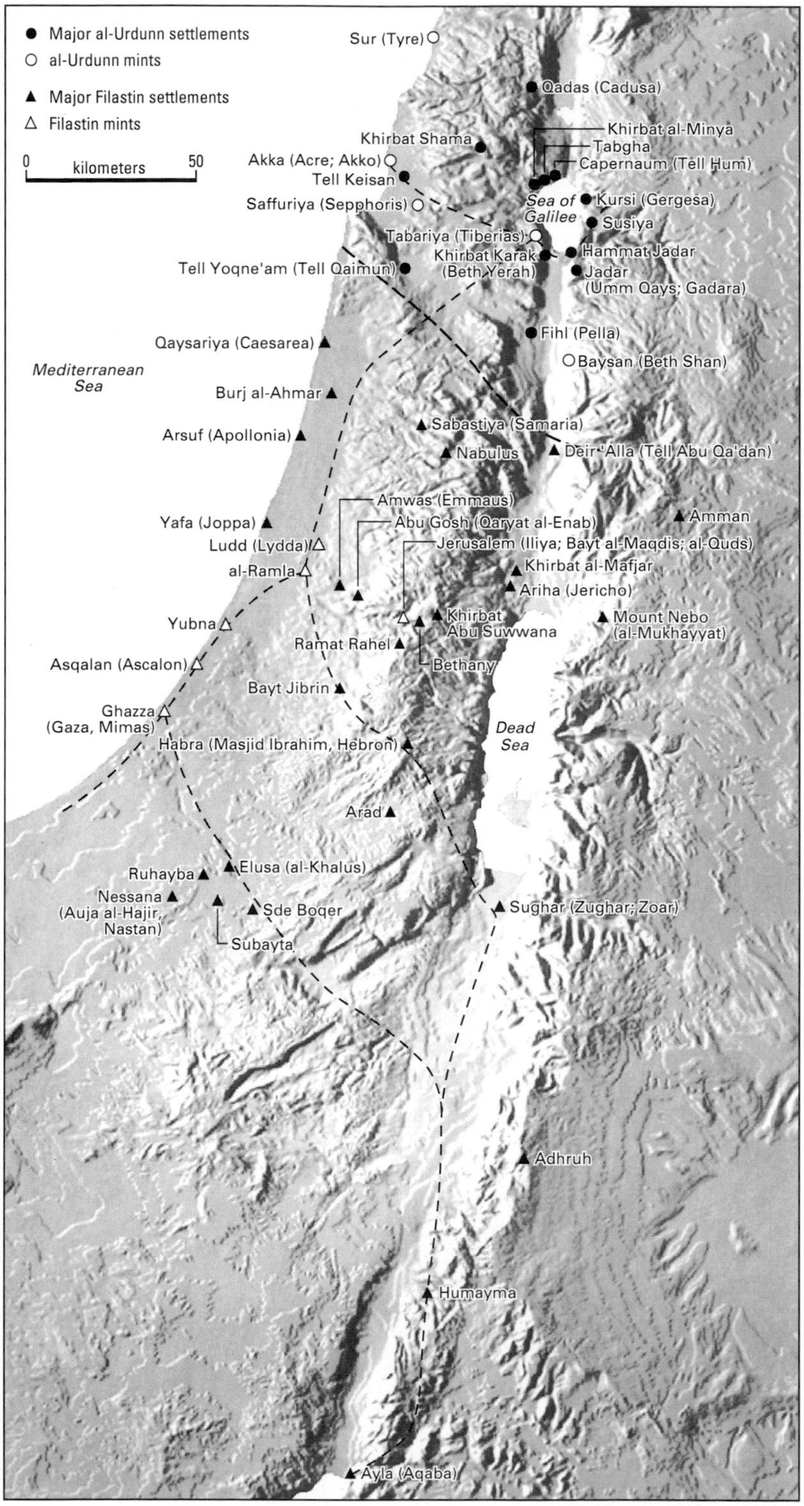

Figure 1 Map of al-Urdunn and Filastin

Figure 2   Reconstruction of Khirbat al-Mafjar (after Hamilton 1988, Fig. 27)

though the province of al-Sharat, centered on Ṣughar (Zughar or Zo'ara) and ranging from Ayla to eastern Jordan, was later created in this region (see Figure 1).

The presence of tribal groups in Palestine before the conquest was reinforced by immigration; new settlement was confined by policy to towns, either as occupation of abandoned properties or, more likely, a system of *amsār*, new urban foundations placed next to older cities (early Islamic Capharnum is one clear example, Tzaferis 1989; Ayla is another, see below). An interrelated aspect of settlement was the intense interest in developing agricultural estates, the *diyā' al-khilāfa*; this acquisition of lands by tribal aristocracy continued well into the Abbasid period and is estimated to have accounted for as much as one third of the total revenue of Palestine (Khalidi 1984: 185).

The so-called desert castles, of which Khirbat al-Mafjar and Khirbat al-Minya are two excavated examples, may be representatives of such estates, as Sauvaget originally suggested (1939). These structures are composed of many elements: baths, reception halls, lodgings (see Figure 2). While they usually have strong walls with gates and towers on the periphery, there is no specific evidence of a militaristic function (Urice 1987). One might suggest that the walls and formal, peripheral elements functioned rather as definitional elements for an urban entity, rather like the towered walls used as the symbol for cities on early maps. These isolated structures, most commonly found in eastern Syria and Jordan, are known as *qusūr* (sing. *qusr*; Conrad 1981) and, like this term, are the subject of cycles of

functional interpretation. One aspect should be emphasized, that these 'chateaux' are unlikely to have been loci of innovation but rather reflections of architectural developments within (or adjacent to) cities (contra Helms 1990). Thus, Khirbat al-Mafjar (Hamilton 1959) was just outside of Arīḥā (Jericho) and Khirbat al-Minya (Grabar et al. 1960) was ancillary to Ṭabarīya. The 'chateaux' were perhaps more typical of contemporary urban contexts than generally recognized, though we know little of the latter since they have not benefited from abandonment and preservation.

Ṭabarīya, the former city of Tiberias, became capital of the *jund* of al-Urdunn. The summary of archaeological research by Harrison details expansion in the Umayyad period north and south of the Classical town (1992). The excavation of Oren in the southern portion, Ḥammām Ṭabarīya, offers a tantalizing glance at planned urban settlement including a large structure with workshops; the suggestion of pottery glazing has made the lack of a detailed report lamentable (Oren 1971). Umayyad ceramics from Ḥammām Ṭabarīya (Stacey 1988–9) seem to rest on virgin soil. Harrison has shown the northern expansion, beneath the modern city, is an early Islamic foundation and makes a strong case for this being another *misr*. This settlement, 'while perhaps initially created for military reasons, soon developed into a vital urban center . . .' (Harrison 1992: 51); it became the administrative center for the province of al-Urdunn. Most excavators agree to continuities in this settlement into the eleventh century.

The city of al-Ramla was founded by Sulaymān ibn

'Abd al-Malik before 717 CE. While this settlement is often cited as an exceptional Islamic urban foundation, the proximity of Ludd (Lydda) suggests another example of the *misr* phenomenon (the placement of a new Islamic urban center next to an older city). The story of a palace built by 'Abd al-Malik suggests the expansion of a 'desert castle'. In this case, al-Ramla was intended as the capital of the *jund* of Filasṭīn, an administrative center on a crossroads from the coast (Jaffa) to Jerusalem and Jericho, and from Egypt to Nābulus, Ṭabarīya and Damascus.

By the tenth century al-Ramla (see Rosen-Ayalon, this volume) contained numerous public buildings (caravanserais, baths, mosques), wide avenues, large markets, residences of dressed stone and fired brick, all within an area of a square mile (*ca.* 2 × 2 km). The gates of Ramla, (Figure 3) as listed by Muqaddasī (165), may reflect an underlying order revealing both the urban configuration of the late tenth century an the original Umayyad city plan. The Umayyad gates appear to reflect principal toponyms in four directions: Bayt Maqdis (Jerusalem) in the southeast, Ludd (the pre-Islamic antecedent) in the northeast, Yafa (the port of Jaffa) in the northwest, and Miṣr (Egypt) in southwest. This arrangement of gates strongly indicates that the original plan was an orthogonal rectangle or square with axial streets meeting in the center (Sourdel 1981, 390; similar townplans are found at Anjar and Aqaba, see below).

Other gates are named for a particular quarter (*darb*), suggesting that by the tenth century urban sprawl encapsulated some of the earlier gates. Again, direction of toponyms allows a relative location of these gates: Masjid Annabah (the present village of Annabah) in the southeast, Bil'ah (Balah, associated with Abu Gosh) in the east, and Dājūn (the village of Bayt Dajan) in the northwest. The remaining gate, Bi'r'Askar, may be located approximately to the south; this follows from the order of Muqaddasī's list. The gates (numbered 1 to 8) begin in the south and move counter-clockwise around the city of Miṣr (7) in the southwest. Dājūn (8) appears to have been added as an afterthought. This system parallels precisely the Muqaddasī's list of gates in early Islamic Shiraz (Whitcomb 1985: 227).

The implication of this expansion of the city principally to the southeast is that the newer parts of the city, as indeed the modern town, should lie in that direction. Conversely, the ruins of the Umayyad foundation should lie to the northwest, as is generally recognized (e.g., SWP map XIII). The spatial implication for the organization of the Umayyad city is that the mosque, confidently identified with the present White Mosque (see Plate 1, Chapter 30) must have been in the southern quadrant and not the center (as suggested by Sourdel 1981). As Sauvaget has clearly shown, earlier plans can often be deduced by archaeologists from the later palimpsest by using good city plans (1934, 1941).

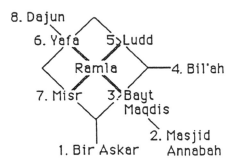

Figure 3   The gates of al-Ramla, according to Muqaddasī

Excavations at al-Ramla have been remarkably vague in site location; the clearest is the map published by Rosen-Ayalon. This shows her excavations in 1965 at Shikun Giora, where there was a pottery workshop on the 'south-western margin of the city' datable to the eighth and beginning of the ninth centuries (Rosen-Ayalon and Eitan 1969). Southeast of this area is the White Mosque, presumably the congregational mosque of the town; excavations by Kaplan in 1949 and 1956 indicated an original Umayyad construction (Kaplan 1959). Finally, a remarkable series of eighth-century mosaics was excavated by M. Brosch in 1973 to the southeast of this mosque; though thought to belong to a private residence (Rosen-Ayalon 1976), this might be associable with the *Dār al-Imāra* or other official building. Ramla continued as an important walled city under the Fatimids and provides an example of tribal organization in a city when the Jarrāḥids administered through a *hilla* (Khalidi 1984: 185).

The early Islamic concept of settlement patterns in southern Bilād al-Shām, i.e. Greater Syria, is revealed on tenth-century maps (Miller 1986, Bologna 3; see Figure 4). From the Egyptian border, a string of ports lies along the Mediterranean coast, most often listed were 'Asqalān, Yāfā, Qaysarīya, 'Akkā, and Ṣūr (this line of fortifications was sometimes referred to as the *ribāṭāt*). The river Jordan and a 'mountain' range present an eastern limit, with only Alya, Ma'an, and smaller unnamed towns visible. The main road linked Gaza with the provincial capitals of al-Ramla and Ṭabarīya before extending north to Damascus. The mapmakers' interest was confined to this triangle in which two lakes, those of Ṭabarīya (the Sea of Galilee) and Zo'ara (the Dead Sea), appear with a few towns; Baysān, Nābulus, Rīḥā, Bayt al-Maqdis (or al-Quds, Jerusalem), Masjid Ibrāhīm (Hebron) and Zo'ara (Ṣughar) are most often named.

Such maps only imperfectly reflect the urban hierarchy of southern Bilād al-Shām. The capitals of the two provinces are naturally emphasized; by contrast, Jerusalem and other cities of religious importance are left undistinguished. The remaining towns may have some significance as district centers, though the nature of medieval map making (and copying) makes inclusion/absence of dubious value. Some implications of provincial structure may be inferred from mint locations. Coinage was initially limited to copper *fulūs* from disparate mints (at least 14) (see Plate 1). In the Abbasid period, coin production was limited to only four mints (al-Ramla, Ghazza, Ṭabarīya, Ṣūr), the provincial capitals and their principal ports respectively. This pattern continued under the Tulunids and Fatimids, but with precious metals (Qedar 1980).

The primacy of the trunk road from Egypt via Gaza, al-Ramla and Ṭabarīya and then on the Damascus has obscured the road system of the two provinces. This seems to have been a reorganization of the Byzantine system, with more attention to the south resulting from the new importance of Hijaz. Connections to Damascus and the new provincial capitals were solidified as the *barīd* system (post-roads), probably under 'Abd al-Malik, as witnessed by milestones on main routes (those between Damascus and Jerusalem studied by Sharon 1966). The role of ports seems to have been largely negative (aside from 'Akkā and Ṣur as arsenals for naval operations) until the Tulunid and Fatimid periods, when the coastal cities provided maritime links with Egypt.

Settlement patterns in the eleventh century seem to have changed to a remarkable degree. Administrative control from Egypt may have resulted in the reorganization of the region first under the Ikhshidids (Walmsley 1987) and more dramatically under the Fatimids (as reflected in the geographers, particularly Muqaddasī). A result of the potent colonization may have been a drain of resources into the center, Cairo (e.g., numerous craftsmen; Goitein 1967: 51), combined with the chronic insecurity of the period. One effect of this drain was the decline of major cities, such as those discussed above. Pringle has melded the evidence of the Burj al-Ahmar and occupation in the Sharon Plain into a comprehensive picture of changes, many antecedent to the advent of Crusader occupation (Pringle 1986: 7–12). Although much more detailed study is needed, there is a temptation to see this abatement in urbanism as a cyclical phenomenon similar to that of the sixth century (Kennedy 1985).

Innovations and technology

During the early Islamic period, ceramics become a locus of intense change, technological improvements, and aesthetic attentions. These features have drawn special interest from art historians and unfortunately have been defined in terms of the early excavations at Fustat in Egypt and Samarra in Iraq (in the 1920s). 'The coming of the Arabs not only introduced glazed pottery into Palestine but saw a great improvement in the unglazed ware as well' (Baramki 1969:

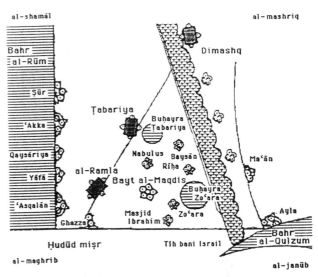

Figure 4 Map of Palestine, after tenth-century maps

213). The latter is a corpus of fine cream wares (often called Mafjar wares); but Baramki's interpretation of the stratigraphic evidence was too imprecise to be of chronological value (Whitcomb 1988a). The presence of decorative glazing on ceramics is a pervasive marker for Islamic archaeology. As admirable as stylistic studies may be, they have misled generations of field archaeologists and distorted historical evidence. Presence or absence of glazed ware has often determined an Islamic occupation. Similarly, the site of Ṣughar was claimed to have 40 per cent glazed sherds (in reality, 40 per cent of the collection made by surveyors was glazed; Whitcomb 1992: 116; see Figure 5).

Misinterpretation of ceramic evidence, whether from inaccuracies of early excavations or from erroneous historical assumptions, have produced tautological fallacies and as a result mistrust of archaeology by historians. For instance, it is becoming evident that much which archaeologists have labelled 'Byzantine' has a high probability of being early Islamic, Umayyad and often Abbasid. The dramatic peak of population and prosperity attributed to the Byzantine period is an archaeological fabrication – the result of ignorance and inattention.

Ceramics of the earliest Islamic period were obviously stylistically related to the latest Byzantine; associational finds such as the kilns at Aqaba (see Plate 2) will begin to define this relationship more closely (Melkawi 1992). The same problem is being dissected with great care by Walmsley, using the results of the Pella excavations (1988; n.d.). The most important ceramic types for the period 660–900 CE at Pella may be outlined as follows:

1. The continuities of metallic wares [Walmsley's types W.11–14] are most characteristic. These are also present at Mafjar (Whitcomb 1988a: 56). Type W.10 is identical to

Plate 1 Abbasid coins from Capernaum (photograph courtesy John F. Wilson)

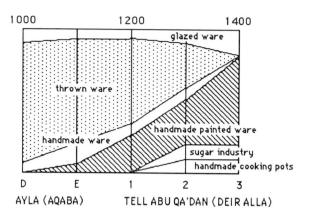

Figure 5 Distribution of ceramic types (after Franken and Kalsbeek 1975, Fig. 77)

the 'fine Byzantine ware' described by Gichon (1974) but continues into the Abbasid period and may be more at home in this later period.

2. There is an appearance of cream wares [W.7]. The forms are distinctive from the slightly later Mahesh wares (Whitcomb 1989c), though some of these differences may be regional.

3. Red-painted wares appear after *ca.* 700 CE, making this readily identifiable type diagnostic of late Umayyad and early Abbasid [W.8].

4. The Abbasid period shows the introduction of glazed wares, fine cream wares, and imitations of steatite vessels [W.15–19]. These cream wares are the classic definition of 'Mafjar wares', though potentially confused with [W.7] and Mahesh wares. The earliest glazed ceramics relate closely to Coptic glaze wares found at Aqaba (Whitcomb 1989b).

Progress in identification of Umayyad and early Abbasid diagnostics illustrates the potential utility of archaeological evidence in analysis of increasingly sophisticated historical questions.

Unfortunately the late Abbasid and Fatimid periods continue to be a wasteland where the term 'Arab' ceramics remains the descriptive norm. The excavations at Qaryat al-'Enab, Abu Gosh (de Vaux and Stave 1950), contemporary with the work at Khirbat Mafjar have pointed the way to Abbasid glazed and unglazed wares, primarily through a corpus of splash decorated wares. The glazed wares from Capernaum begin with splash wares in stratum IV (Berman 1989: 124); these wares become dominant in the following stratum with the addition of incised wares (one should note that these strata must be raised one period, thus IV = 750–850 CE, III = 850–950 CE). The absence of eleventh- twelfth-century 'Crusader' wares makes this corpus particularly valuable. For unglazed wares, one may note the detailed presentation in the Khirbat al-Karak report (Delougaz and Haines 1960). The site of Ayla, though located in the remote south, has a large corpus of ceramics spanning these periods, including Egyptian and Samarran imports (the glazed wares have recently been studied; Whitcomb n.d.).

The latest period considered here reveals major changes in the ceramic inventory. Just as settlement changes seem to anticipate 'Crusader' patterns, many later ceramic features have their beginnings in the Fatimid period. In other words, the preoccupation by archaeologists with an Ayyubid-Mamluk complex has effectively masked a more complex historical change, rather like the Byzantine/early Islamic transition. For instance, while many sites have lustre wares and other types from Fatimid Egypt, this period witnessed the introduction of handmade wares ('Tupper ware', Whitcomb 1988b; Baramki 1969: 216) and the beginnings of Islamic geometric painted wares.

The handmade geometric painted wares vividly recall the allied craft of basketry (and perhaps textile) decoration. Likewise, imitations of steatite vessels of the ninth century reinforce the probable date of importation of this Arabian artifact. Finally the very existence of the glazed ceramic industry must relate to the manufacture of glass in this region (Hasson 1979). This interrelatedness of production complexes (and not simply decorative styles) is clearly reflected in excavation and survey data and presents a strong argument for such archaeological research. The textile industry was the mainspring of medieval economies and, other than mention of a few products of Ṭabarīya and al-Ramla, these manufactures were apparently minor in Palestine (Serjeant 1972: 118–19). This lack suggests a corresponding predominance of agriculture in the local economy, including production of dyes.

There appears to have been a considerable net population increase on the back of a 'medieval green revolution' (Ashtor 1976: 90–2; Watson 1983). This may be foreseen in the agricultural estates developed in Filasṭīn and the Negev during the early Islamic period (see Figure 6). Rice, indigo, and linen and later sugar cane were cultivated at Baysan and other locations in the Ghors (see detailed description in Whitcomb 1992 for the southern Ghor). The hinterland of Qaysariya, to take one example, was constantly praised for its fertility and abundant

Plate 2 The early Islamic kilns at Aqaba (photograph by Donald Whitcomb)

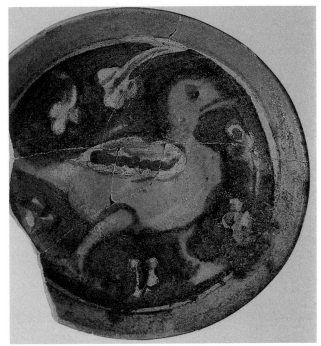

Plate 3 A bowl of Coptic glazed ware from Caesarea (after Holum 1988, Fig. 157)

agricultural production (by contrast, an absence of descriptions of its harbor is taken as indication of radical decline [Sharon 1976: 84]). Likewise, al-Ramla was described as being in a fertile agricultural region. Indeed, Ibn Ḥauqal describes Filasṭīn as 'the most fertile province in the *iqlīm* [of al-Sham]' (171); he and other geographers provide copious details of this productivity. Muqaddasī notes that a sizable part of the fruit crop was exported to Egypt and other areas (172).

The new Muslim foundations, the *amsār*, may represent a significant innovation in which urbanization was used for administrative, social and ideological purposes. Such enclaves or cantonments may have been a causal factor in the success of Islamic culture in the early years. These cities are archaeological artifacts reflecting a structural innovation (details of which present an area of archaeological research, see discussion below). A definition used here is that '. . . the city is not merely an aggregation of population of critical size and density but also an organizing principle, an agent of regional integration . . . a creator of effective space' (Wheatley 1983: 7–8). Thus cities are nodes of interaction networks characterized by the institutional exchange of both information (encompassing administrative and ritual functions) and material

goods (primary economic functions). These administrative, ceremonial and economic functions have archaeological manifestations in architectural features indicating urban sites. Thus the presence of a *Dār al-Imāra*, congregational mosque, and suq necessarily indicate urban functions relating the particular settlement to a regional system.

In the absence of any direct evidence for the configuration of an Arab military camp in the early Islamic or immediately pre-Islamic periods, the *amsār* have been traditionally characterized as primitive military camps, as 'mass encampments, tent or makeshift settlements . . . of bedouin migrants'. (Lapidus 1973: 24). On the contrary, recent studies of early Islamic sites have shown a set of characteristics consistent with orthogonally-planned cities.

The current excavations at Aqaba have shown that the early Islamic city of Ayla was founded as a *misr*, within the caliphate of 'Uthmān ibn 'Affān, about 650 (Whitcomb 1989a: 167–75). As is characteristic of other *amsār*, the new city was placed adjacent to an earlier Byzantine town, in this case pre-Islamic Ailana (Meloy 1991). Early Islamic Ayla, as revealed in the excavations (1986–1992), had an orthogonal plan with four gates connected by axial streets within towered walls (see Figure 7 p. 498). An initial impression is that it appears to be a Byzantine legionary camp; detailed study shows the plan to be intermediate between typical Byzantine form and that of various early Islamic sties (Whitcomb 1990b).

In external configuration, Ayla finds its closest parallel with the Large Enclosure at Qaṣr al-Ḥayr al-Sharqī. The

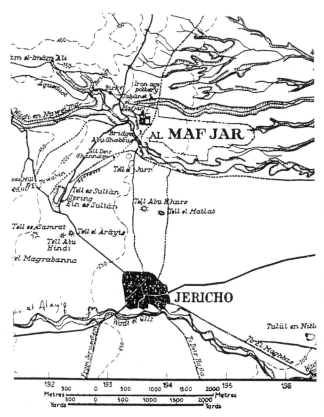

Figure 6   Map of the enclosure at Khirbat al–Mafjar, a possible agricultural estate (after Hamilton 1959, Fig. 1)

best known of the *amsār*, Baṣra, Kūfa and Fusṭāṭ, may be posited to have had orthogonal central elements (the Ahl al-Rāya in Fusṭāṭ, for example). Each urban center apparently had axial streets, residential areas (*qatā'i'*), and a relatively open institutional center (containing the mosque and *Dār al-Imāra*). The plan of Ayla, and perhaps those of the desert castles, may represent models of the urban core (orthogonal central elements) around which the larger city developed.

The extensive implantation of *amsār* and the possible expansion of Arabian (non-Classically derived) urban forms are important areas for future research. This initial phase of Islamic urban planning should not be confused with the reorganization of numerous cities following the 748 CE earthquake. Rather than the disorganization and cultural regression often posited for that time, archaeologically one finds increasing examples of highly structured, reorganized Abbasid cities, as seen in sites such as Baysan (Tell el-Husn; Zayadeh 1991), Tell Yoqne'am (Ben-Tor and Rosenthal 1978; Ben-Tor et al. 1979), Arsūf (Roll and Ayalon 1987), and Ayla (Whitcomb 1989c). For example, the Abbasid stratum at Tall Qaimun (Tell Yoqne'am) is described as 'an unfortified . . . centrally planned, urban settlement. [This is] . . . evident in the organized road system, the terraced and symmetrically planned buildings, and the uniform and distinctive construction methods used' (Ben-Tor et al. 1979: 72–3).

Religion and ideology

As suggested above, even settlement patterns may reflect an ideological purpose. The Islamic conquest introduced a new factor into the confessional social organization of this region. The bitter history of Jewish and Christian populations now had a third religious force to consider. As mentioned above, the old myths of fire and rampage, death or conversion may be dismissed with the careful research of Schick (n.d.) and others.

Southern Bilād al-Shām was referred to as a Holy Land (*ard al-muqaddas*) by Muqaddasī, who gives a detailed listing of the holy places and monuments. While the importance of the Muslim pilgrimage far exceeded pilgrimage in older religions, the example may have promoted an increase in pilgrimage to Jerusalem. An expansion of visitation to other holy places, such as those described by Muqaddasī, to virtually the entire population and extra-regional travelers was an important aspect of economy and the arts. These places, as 'common goals for the followers of the three religions' (Goitein 1967: 56), became renowned as elements in an ideological hierarchy upon which the identity and prosperity of Palestine depended.

Given the limited nature of archaeological investigation specific to the early Islamic period and the difficulty in

latter complex is described by Grabar as 'a planned urban entity – essential units of a medieval Islamic city: mosque, suq, bath and residential quarters', and indeed, he identifies this site as the '*madīna*' mentioned in a lost inscription (Grabar et al. 1978: 79–80). The enclosure had four gates, though two were sealed shut quite early, rather like the Hijaz gate at Ayla. The six *bayts* of this structure seem a rather limited residential area for a city, unless this complex was to house representatives of six groups (tribes or clans?). This idea of a residence of representatives may tie in to the *madīna* as a place of authority – the fundamental sense of the word (Meloy, pers. com). Another analogy for Ayla is the larger *misr* of 'Anjar, twice the size of Ayla, with axial streets and four gates.

Amsār such as Ayla, 'Anjar, and Qaṣr al-Ḥayr al-Sharqī were settlements of a type intermediate between the theoretical camp and the metropolis; as structures comprising residential, religious and political functions, they may properly be designated as urban centers. The examples of Ramla and Ṭabarīya, while not proven to have been orthogonal in design, add another dimension to the *amsār*. These cities reflect the transformation of the term to describe capital cities (an extreme usage is found in Muqaddasī's system of urban hierarchy). The largest and

identifying early mosques architecturally, it is not surprising that mosques and Muslim shrines are rarely mentioned in the literature; there has been no attempt at codification of such monuments since the early work of Mayer (Mayer et al. 1950; and the excavations of most of those monuments are later in date). There are now many more synagogues and churches excavated which give varying stories of continued use, abandonment, and redefinition (e.g., Khirbat al-Karak). The exception to this general lack of early Muslim monuments is in Jerusalem where the Aqṣā mosque and Dome of the Rock on the Ḥaram and the churches in the town below punctuated the urban scene.

Social organization

Treaties with cities, beginning with Ayla and the 'Jewish towns' of the south (Magma, Jarba, Adhruh; Gil 1992: 30), the covenant of Jābiya, and Umar's attitude toward Jerusalem give some evidence of initial conditions in Palestine at the time of the Islamic conquest. Much of this discussion revolves around the relationship of the Muslims, particularly the immigrant Arabic speaking population, and the confessional groups already established in the Holy Land. Patterns of tolerance and identity, of dominance and cooperation, may find expression in urban organization and, more particularly, in a new process of urbanization. This was the process of the *amsār*, already mentioned in other contexts.

The phenomenon of the *amsār* may be seen as a new phase in the urbanization or, more precisely, the urban process in the history of the Middle East. Wheatley has proposed that this developmental process is of two types: urban imposition or urban generation (Wheatley 1983: 5). 'Urban imposition . . . is virtually inseparable from the expansion of empire and is usually accompanied by the establishment of an administrative organization designed to sustain the value system of the colonial power'. The position adopted here is that the *amsār* represent a program of urban imposition, and implies that early Islamic culture intentionally reconstituted the social organization of the conquered lands. This view presupposes the existence of institutional components of fully urbanized society in pre-Islamic western Arabia.

An urban style of life is more recognizable in the classically-derived towns of north Syria than the settlements of western, and more particularly southwestern, Arabia. The question is whether an urban ideology as part of Islamic culture was part of the legacy of pre-Islamic Arabia or was formalized in the aftermath of the conquests. Delineation of archaeological features which may indicate an Arabian urban type is only beginning with new excavations (such as those at Rababdha, al-Mabiyat and Najrān). Some preliminary observations may be seen at the site of Umm al-Jimāl. The plan of this city, dating to

the sixth and seventh centuries, does not derive from its classical antecedents. In the words of its excavator, 'The striking feature of the town plan is its disorder and lack of preconceived design . . . Umm al-Jimal . . . represents the indigenous way of life . . .' (De Vries 1982: 20). The standing ruins of more than 150 buildings (within *ca.* 800 m × 500 m) are grouped into three irregular clusters; Knauf has pointed to Arabic features of the domestic architecture (Knauf 1984: 579) and a broader case might be made for a cluster system as typically Arabian (Whitcomb n.d.a.); see Plate 4.

Mez has defined one of the urban traditions contributing to the early Islam city as 'the [south] Arabian city such as Ṣan'ā', to which type Mekka and Fusṭāṭ belonged' (1937: 412). Amplification of this urban system will depend on study of the sociocultural background. Dostal has proposed two urban types based on social organization (1984: 188–9). The first is called the Ṣan'ā'-formation, developed from a market center and inhabited by groups of the same tribe with social differentiation based on his 'farmer-craftsman' technological specializations. The second urban type is the Tarīm-formation, in which quarter organization reflects the social structure of a multi-tribal settlement. This latter ethnographic type might have approximated the social organization, and hence the physical structure, of the *amsār*.

Cities of the early Islamic period may be seen as a 'generational process' in which cultural traits of the fully urbanized milieu of the Middle East were integrated into a distinctive Islamic urbanism. In other words, one might see the *amsār* as an imposed form while the internal structure of these new settlements, both social and physical, involved component traits adopted from existing cities. The orthogonal urban core may be viewed as a mechanism for facilitating this interaction in conjunction with the tradition of the Arabian city, as yet to be fully defined.

Many diagnostics for later Ayyubid-Mamluk times seem to begin during the late Abbasid or Fatimid period. Evidence of the Cairo geniza, the great corpus of documentation on the Jewish community in the Fatimid and Ayyubid periods, testifies to the tremendous amount of travel and trade in this time. Indeed, the travels of Nasr-i Khusrow provide abundant descriptions toward the end of this period. All of this suggests that archaeological evidence must be viewed ever more cautiously, examining potential interregional influences. The evidence of the geniza documents provides an abundant resource for archaeologists, particularly items of daily life (Goitein 1983). One especially relevant aspect is description of cities and their architectural elements; the subject of intra-urban ruins is a cautionary tale for any stratigrapher (Goitein 1983: 21–6). Specific data on socio-economic factors such as rental systems and repair costs add dimensions to continuity and shifting of

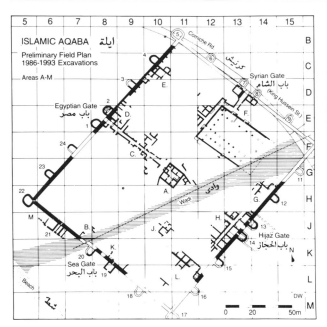

Figure 7   Plan of excavations of Ayla, early Islamic Aqaba

Plate 4   Sixth- to seventh-century ruins at Umm al-Jimal (photograph by Donald Whitcomb)

settlement (urban occupation at Aqaba seems to have relocated almost every 450 years).

The later tenth century witnessed the rise of tribal groups to political power (e.g. the Banū Jarrāḥ), who periodically controlled al-Ramla and other cities. As with the preconceptions surrounding the bedouin (Arabs) of the conquest period, this tribal element is assumed to involve destruction and social disruption of a different sort from that inflicted by massive state armies. Evidence of a notable decline in manufactures and settlement seems clear in spite of still clouded chronological control of artifacts. One should guard, however, against applying a simple cyclical model to the complex period.

Conclusions: processes of change

The Islamic Conquest has been given the form of a 'Great Divide', an end to antiquity and archaeological research. There is ample precedent for ending an archaeology of the Holy Land with the Islamic Conquest. Perhaps the volume of most enduring popularity is that of Kenyon (19XX). In a volume of some 400 pages, her enthusiasm suddenly runs out with the Byzantines (who are allotted two pages). The real curiosity is the half-page devoted to the Crusades, with not a word about the archaeology preceding or following this brief interlude. This is more than Eurocentricism and has its roots in two parallel phenomena: the attitude that

medieval periods are more properly the realm of history and not archaeology, and that somehow archaeological research suddenly ceases in 636 CE (to be fair, others place the cut off earlier; my own institution may be accused of using an operative date of 331 BCE to end archaeological concerns). The present volume, which spans the Early Paleolithic to the British conquest of Palestine, represents a challenge to the Eurocentricity of earlier scholars.

The initial Islamic period, which may be called Early Islamic 1 [638–750 CE], represents a transition from late Byzantine culture through the formative processes of Islamic culture. Thus the predominant continuities are punctuated with Umayyad artifacts which may seem derivative or innovative, depending on one's perspective and view to subsequent development.

The Abbasid period (the Early Islamic 2 period [750–900 CE] began with dramatic political and natural events. The poor historical visibility is slowly being clarified through archaeological evidence, revealing an acceleration of cultural development of a sophisticated Islamic civilization.

The third period may be seen as an Egyptian period, during which the long arm of Cairo made its influence predominant in social and political spheres. In many areas, the period signifies the beginning of developments which would reach fruition during the subsequent Crusader and Mamluk periods. For this reason, the transitional nature of the period yields the title of Middle Islamic 1 period [900–1099 CE]. More importantly, the eleventh century seems to have witnessed remarkable changes in settlement patterns, particularly in the decline of major cities. This unsettled situation seems to have been antecedant to the Crusades.

MEANING OF THE DOME OF THE ROCK

The Dome of the Rock (Qubbat al-Ṣakhra) is a building set on a rectangular raised platform in the middle of the al-Ḥaram al-Sharīf of Jerusalem (known in the early Islamic period as Īliyā', from Aelia); the structure is octagonal in plan and entered by four doors (each facing a cardinal direction). A date is inscribed on the bottom of the dome, 691–692 (during the reign of 'Abd al-Malik; his name later erased by the Abbasid, al-Manṣūr; this is usually thought to be a completion date but may now be more plausibly argued to be a beginning date (Blair 1992). Both plan and decoration scheme are commonly accepted as Umayyad, in spite of numerous repairs and restorations.

This was a shrine built over exposed rock, around which was a double ambulatory. The shrine was linked with the Isrā' and Mi'rāj, the night journey and ascension of the Prophet, but these seem to be late traditions (perhaps not fully established until Mamluk times). An earlier explanation (according to Ya'qūbī; 897) was that this was built by 'Abd al-Malik to divert pilgrimage away from Mecca during the conflict with Ibn Zubayr. This thesis was followed by Goldziher and Creswell (and more recently by Elad 1992) but is rejected by Goitein and Grabar and most commentators. Grabar posits that the inscriptions on the inner drum reflect contemporary Christian-Muslim dialogue. Muqaddasī, writing in the tenth century, suggested an expression of the sanctity of the Ḥaram in architectural terms to rival the Christian churches and shrines, expecially the Holy Sepulcher. Quoting his uncle, he viewed the building of the Qubbat al-Ṣakhra as a response to the cultural needs of the second generation of Muslims, as an irrefutable statement of the greatness and preeminence of Islam (159; Wheatley n.d.: n. 172).

Grabar has recently reiterated his ideas on aesthetic and political meaning of the Dome of the Rock (Grabar 1990). He continues with an important suggestion, that the Dome of the Rock was planned by Mu'āwiya, well before Abd al-Malik (cf. Goitein 1980: 325). He suggests that this building was part of a larger urban plan including the rebuilding of the south and southwestern walls of the Ḥaram (with the adjacent, newly-discovered buildings) and the cutting of possibly the entire northern third of the Ḥaram. Rosen-Ayalon has made a strong case for both the Golden gate (see Plate 1.1) and the Double gate as belonging to the Umayyad period (1989). The Aqṣā mosque has also been attributed to Mu'āwiya (Goitein 1982: 176). Magness has reexamined the ceramic criteria for a number of localities within the walls of Jerusalem and redated many of these strata to the Umayyad period (Magness 1991). This accords with the portion of an Umayyad towered structure in the citadel of Jerusalem (Geva 1983: 69–71).

The structures excavated south and southwest of the Ḥaram (excavated 1968–77) have been accepted as parts of an Umayyad complex. Interest has focused on building II, south of the Aqṣā mosque, which has been tentatively identified as the *Dār al-Imāra* (Rosen-Ayalon 1989: 9). These remains, and the other nearby buildings are long, narrow rooms ranged around a large courtyard. These belonged to the ground floor (Ben-Dov 1971: 37), and were probably storerooms; the configuration of these supportive walls allows reconstruction of a building not unlike a typical 'desert castle' (ibid.). This structure had been known from de Vaux's excavations, where it was thought to have been a Byzantine hospital; this was presumably an error in ceramic interpretation – a continuing problem given the paucity of published data. It is Rosen-Ayalon's dramatic demonstration – of

the axial relationship of the Dome of the Rock, the Aqṣā mosque, the double gate, the street beside the Dar al-Imāra – that this entire complex is one plan. Goitein recognizes in this complex the creation of a new city as the regional administrative center (1980: 326).

Ben-Dov noted that the street system implied an extension of the 'early Arab' settlement throughout the lower city (1971: 39). In fact, the street excavated in the Tyropoean valley, where Magness has recently shown the fallacy of the supposed Sasanian destruction (1992), seems likely to have been part of an Islamic city plan. This massive destruction and period of abandonment may follow the 551 CE earthquake or possibly the 660 CE cataclysm. In either case, the stage was set for an Umayyad foundation, in fact a *miṣr*, with the Dome shrine marking the center as a reinterpretation of the classical tetrapylon. The orientations of streets and, more importantly, their later chronology must be more complex than that ably demonstrated by Wilkinson (1975).

One may thus posit that the axis of the buildings on the Ḥaram and its continuity as a street to the south is only one element in a larger plan. That plan is an orthogonal layout of a new city, situated on the abandoned eastern portion of the city. An attribution to the time of Mu'āwiya's rule (from 640 CE onward) is readily acceptable given 'Uthmān's interest in the creation of *amṣār*. The Dome of the Rock, whatever its ideological meaning, was a focal point and possibly functioned as a tetrapylon marking the crossing of the axes of the Islamic city (as also found at Anjar and Ayla; Whitcomb 1990b: 158). This approach sees the context of this shrine as part of concepts of urbanism in early Islamic times. Other contexts are also being studied: the social context of Mu'āwiya and tribal or dynastic structures in early Islam (Grabar 1990: 156–7), the ideological context of 'Abd al-Malik and apocalyptic ideas of that time (Rosen-Ayalon 1989; van Ess 1992; Hauting n.d.). Understanding the Holy City is a challenge on which new excavations and reexamination of earlier archaeological assumptions are having an important impact.

Plate 1.1 Jerusalem Golden Gate (Israel Antiquities Authority)

REVISIONISM IN THE NEGEV

Discussion of the Negev in pre-Islamic times seems to revolve around the 'Saracens and Romans', the problems of Roman-Byzantine borderlands and pastoral societies. Archaeological evidence of Arab population, in the sense of pastoral nomads, has been advanced by Rosen (1987, 1992) and Banning (1986). The latter sparked a brief debate turning on perceptions by historians and anthropologists of nomads on civilized frontiers (Parker 1987). These positions were neatly defined by Mayerson as micro and macro views (1989), though he accepts dual ethnic division based on exclusive economic patterns. The fallacy of such a bipolar society was acknowledged without a full recognition of the complexities of urban society in the Negev. By concentrating attention on 'Arab tribes' and 'Saracens' much of the interaction within cities by these ethnic groups was ignored. Mayerson has noted that '. . . as population swelled, there was a concomitant increase in the migration of tribes to the frontiers of the eastern provinces, where there were opportunities for brigandage or [profit by providing a variety of services]' (Mayerson 1989: 73).

Negevite cities, often founded under the Nabataeans, became Arabian cities with a complex range of tribal interactions, a kaleidoscope of changing relations only rarely recorded or subject to archaeological hypothesis. The fragility of understanding by historians and archaeologists is exemplified in the evidence of the Nessana. The papyri show clear continuation of administration and relationship with 'Arab' populations well into the early Islamic period; no corresponding artifactual evidence has been adduced for this or other cities in the Negev. Confrontational attitude is an invariable explanation for cessation of these cities. Thus A. Negev describes the end of Kurnub (Mampsis) as the result of 'one of the earlier Arab attacks that preceded the conquest of A.D. 636. If this is so the Arab conquest of the Negev must have been a gradual process, with Mampsis the first town to suffer, followed by Oboda, while the western cities still continued to exist for some time under Arab rule.' (1986: 227). This gradualism is also reflected in Rosen's assessment that 'The early Arab period seems to show infiltration and absorption of nomadic groups, apparently Moslems, who seem to have co-opted the Byzantine rule at some point' (1992: 160). These archaeologists clearly reflect a new interpretation of the Muslim conquest, one which finds its most explicit proponent in the work of Y. Nevo. His interpretation of the settlement at Sde Boqer in the central Negev, itself typical of rural desertic communities over a wide area, is remarkable and has been accepted or unchallenged by many archaeologists and historians. An outline of this remarkable argument must be quoted:

> At Sde Boqer the pagans began cult activities about the time of Hiššām's reign (105–25.724–43), while the end of the sanctuary can be dated by coins to al-Mahdi's reign (158–69.775–85) or the early years of Hārūn (170–94/786–809) (Nevo and Koren 1990: 26).

> . . . what appears to have been refuse from cult ceremonies [consisting] of ash . . . and a large quantity of broken pieces of glass, pottery and stone vessels, . . . either offerings or perhaps ritual vessels rendered taboo by

their use in ceremonies . . . [Seashells, metal, marble, and gemstones] apparently were brought to the site . . . to serve as offerings (idem: 31–2).

> . . . the Sde Boqer sanctuary . . . now may be considered typical of the many cult sites of the central Negev. . . . pagan belief continued, and in the early eighth century . . ., it reasserted its existence with the construction of many cult centers . . . . [This] sudden revival under Hiššām suggests active government encouragement' (idem: 33, 43).

This analysis represents a misinterpretation of archaeological evidence on a scale not witnessed in the Holy Land for almost 100 years. One is returned to the view of ruins seen through cultic glasses. Further, Nevo uses this interpretation of evidence – never systematically presented – to dramatically rewrite history. (Nevo's volume, *Pagans and Herders*, 1991, repeats and only partially expands this evidence.)

The archaeology of cult has a long history under the guise of 'archaeology and the Bible' (clearly summarized in Dever 1987, 1990). Alon and Levy, also working in the Negev, have concluded that 'in Palestine, traditional studies of . . . cult have approached the subject in a non-systematic fashion that relies heavily on untested assumptions' (1989: 171). While Alon and Levy's study does not include the Islamic period, they carefully examine earlier

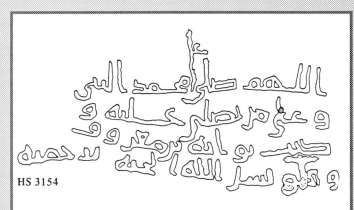

HS 3154

Figure 2.1   Seventh–Eighth Century AD Arabic inscription found at Sde Boqer (source: Y.D. Nevo 1985 *Sde Boqer and the Central Negev, 7th–8th Century AD*. Jerusalem, Israel Publication Services)

cult practices and offer a system of evidential tests to address the problem of archaeological recognition of cult (1989: 172ff.).

Nevo's interpretation of the archaeology of Sde Boqer is part of an ideological program (outlined in Koren and Nevo 1991). This is a self-styled 'revisionist' approach which seeks to challenge the traditional historiography of Islam. The authors claim to be part of a wider historiographical movement and seek to strengthen their arguments by enlisting archaeological (including epigraphic and numismatic) evidence. They feel confident in asserting that

> [Archaeologists working in Jordan and Arabia] have found Hellenistic, Nabatean, Roman, and early Byzantine remains, but no signs of local Arab cultures from the sixth and early seventh centuries . . . . Furthermore, the

archaeological work has revealed no trace of Jewish settlement at Medina, Xaybar or Wādī al-Qurrà. Both these points contrast directly with the Muslim literary sources' descriptions of the demographic composition of the pre-Islamic Ḥijāz. This is of course an *argumentum e silentio* . . . (Koren and Nevo 1991: 102).

Not only is it an argument from silence, but the type of evidence which is 'missing' has never been sought. The argument has a further weakness, it is grounded on a tautological fallacy in which an admittedly difficult type of identification is replaced by self-fulfilling interpretive agendas.

A broader pattern of interpretation of history through archaeological evidence (and its lack) may be seen in the history of Biblical archaeology. In his treatment of 'archaeology and Israelite settlement', Dever presents the analytic sequence of dominance of the conquest model (Albright et al.), then the Peaceful Infiltration model (Alt, Noth), and then the Peasants' revolt model (Mendenhall, Gottwald) (Dever 1990: 39–84). Curiously, the collapse of the destruction model for the Islamic conquest has led to questions about the reality of this conquest in general. Just as the violence under Joshua is seen by many as problematic, some would now question the reliability of later and often confused accounts of seventh-century events. The various interpretations of Israelite settlement mentioned above are limited by the problem of ethnic identification in material culture; for many, 'Israelite' becomes synonymous with early Iron culture in Palestine (Dever 1990). Likewise pre-Islamic Christian Arab culture, whatever its material manifestation, is replaced by early Islamic

culture gradually; non-recognition of ethnic identity is not the same as non-existence of the ethnic group.

The revisionism in its most seductive form is to be found in the studies of Sharon, an epigraphic associate of the Sde Boqer project. He argues for (at least) three independent amirates in competition with one another, an absence of a unifying religious concept — Islam — before the caliphate of Abd al-Malik, and thus an extensive rewriting of history in the Abbasid period. As with Nevo's position, the power of negative evidence is usually adduced. More importantly, there seems to be an underlying negative assessment of the character of a polity arising out of Arabia — in short, ascription of negative characteristics to Arab tribal social organization.

Nevo and his associates see the evidence from the Negev as crucial to an undermining of 'traditional' history of the Islamic conquest and to understanding 'true' characteristics of the development of early Islamic culture. Whether historians will find merit in their assertions or not, the approach gives a new immediacy and centrality to archaeological evidence not generally acknowledged. While utilization of archaeological evidence should find a crucial role — particularly in the absence of contemporary documentary evidence — the palpable distortions introduced in this initial interpretation of Negvite data threaten to discredit the value of study of material culture. The archaeological corpora have increased dramatically over the past decade and demand more sophisticated interpretation for the study of early Islamic culture.

29

SETTLEMENT AND SOCIETY FORMATION IN CRUSADER PALESTINE

Ronnie Ellenblum

The 200-year long Frankish rule in Palestine can be divided into two subperiods: the first, beginning with the occupation of the country by the participants of the first Crusade [*ca.* 1099 CE) which ended with the battle of Hattin (July 1187). The second period began after the third Crusade and ended with the fall of Acre in 1291. Between these two periods, the kingdom borders, social characteristics, settlement patterns, strategic concepts, government, economy and other aspects were altered considerably.

In conformity with the character of this book, this chapter will confine itself to dealing with the process of settlement of the Franks in the Latin Kingdom of Jerusalem, and ignore the parallel processes that took place in other Frankish centers in the Levant.

Studies of the Frankish settlement published over the last 40 years have paid little attention to the differences between the two periods of Frankish rule. In many of them it was assumed that Frankish rural settlement in the Levant was very limited. The Franks, it was argued, confined themselves almost exclusively to the large cities and fortresses, did not settle in rural areas and did not engage in agricultural activities.[1] '. . . [T]he Crusaders' society', wrote Joshua Prawer, 'was predominantly, almost exclusively, an urban society.'[2] The Frankish urban society is contrasted with the rural one, which consisted of Muslim farmers, who had no social or cultural relations with the ruling Franks.

This cultural and geographical segregation is explained by a series of 'conceptions' which crystallize into a frequently cited and very influential paradigmatic framework. R.C. Smail who was, together with Prawer, the first to draw this dichotomous picture, used the term 'conception' in order to describe his own basic assumptions. In the famous *Crusading Warfare 1097–1193*, Smail contrasted his new interpretation of Frankish society with the previous interpretation which had prevailed until the end of the 1940s:

The student is left to choose between two sharply differing conceptions of the nature of Franco-Syrian society. On the one hand are the scholars who have regarded the orientalizing of Frankish manners in Syria, and the instances which appear in the sources of friendly relations between Franks and Muslims, as the evidence of the creation of a Franco-Syrian nation and civilization; on the other hand are those who have assigned greater importance to other aspects of social organization in the Latin states, and to the instances of hostile relations between Franks and Muslims. They consider that the Franks remained a ruling class, separated from their Syrian subjects by language and religion, with force as the ultimate sanction of their dominion.[3]

Smail and Prawer created a framework of interrelated assumptions – each emerging from a previous one and sustaining all the others. The external and internal dangers are perceived as being the all-important element. It is assumed that the Franks were exposed to perpetual attacks which threatened their very existence; that they could not find peace even in the heart of their own Kingdom since the decisive majority of the country's inhabitants were Muslims who preferred to collaborate with the 'Muslim Enemy'.[4]

The local Christians also preferred, according to this theoretical framework, to collaborate with the Muslims with whom they shared a common language and culture.[5] The precarious existence of the Frankish states was aggravated still further by the fact that the demographic ratio clearly favoured the Muslim inhabitants of the country.[6] The Franks, the theory goes on to say, could therefore find their security only in the fortified cities and castles, and hence their abstention from building unfortified villages and rural estates. They profited from the very existence of cities in the Levant since cities like Antioch, Tripoli, Acre and Jerusalem had no equivalent in contemporary Europe.[7]

These assumptions, which have influenced scholarly thinking over the last 40 years, sound convincing and reasonable but leave several historical points unanswered. The basic assumption – that the Franks never really settled in the rural areas – is based, *argumentum e silentio*, on the scarcity of documents which mention explicitly such settlement; and since no comprehensive survey of Frankish rural settlements had then been made, the assumption was

St. Anne's church built at the time of the Crusades (photograph: © Garo)

never strengthened by archaeological evidence. However, the pioneering archaeological fieldwork carried out by Clermont-Ganneau, Rey, Conder, Kitchener, Abel, Bagatti, Benvenisti and Pringle has provided proof for the existence of many Frankish rural sites.[8] The accumulated number of these archaeological findings far exceeds the modest estimates of the protagonists of the above hypothesis.

The actual extent and frequency of Muslim raids on the Latin Kingdom do not justify a Frankish reluctance to settle in rural areas.[9] I believe that Conder's 100-year-old description of the state of security in the Frankish Kingdom is still of value:

> . . . the Latins in Syria enjoyed, for nearly a century, an amount of peace and prosperity greater than that of most European lands during the same period, and that often for many years they were untroubled by war, while for the first sixty years their contests were all on the boundaries of the kingdom.[10]

It is risky to search for analogies in the northern Frankish entities. The Turkish tribes who time and again menaced the very existence of Edessa, Antioch and Ma'arsh hardly threatened the Kingdom of Jerusalem. This Kingdom enjoyed, throughout a substantial part of the twelfth century, a military supremacy over its enemies, and there were very few attacks which reached one of its centers.

The second assumption, alleging internal insecurity caused by the subject peoples, is actually composed of two interrelated assumptions. In the first it is assumed, to quote Prawers' own words, that 'The countryside [of the Latin Kingdom of Jerusalem] was settled in an overwhelming majority by Muslims,' and that the local population was almost totally Islamized.[11] It should be remembered, however, that the history of the Islamization of the Levantine world is still poorly understood and that many scholars are of the opinion that a major phase of Islamization took place after the expulsion of the Franks from the Holy Land.[12] It is not possible to assume safely, without additional research, that the process of Islamization of Palestine had already attained its final phase in the twelfth century and, therefore, that the majority of the population by that time was already Muslim.[13] The second reason for this supposed internal insecurity is the assumption that the local Christians, who were totally Arabized and who were connected to the Muslims by history, language and habits, increased the Franks' military problems. This assumption is based mainly on several instances where local Christians betrayed their coreligionists and cooperated with the Muslims and on the fact that the Latin authorities confiscated property and seized ecclesiastical positions traditionally held by the Greek clergy.[14] However, even if it were reasonable to accept that the majority of the local Christians were totally Arabized by the twelfth century, it would still be difficult to accept that cultural or linguistic connections were the

causes for such so-called 'acts of treason'. It should be remembered that both Frankish and Arabic chroniclers usually defined the adversaries of the Franks as 'Turks', not as 'Arabs' or 'Saracens'. There were no historical or cultural connections between Oriental Christians who spoke Arabic and Syriac and the semi-nomadic Turks. The Franks and the different Christian communities formed a social system too complex to be described by simplistic terms such as 'collaboration' or 'treason'; so-called 'acts of treason' also existed among the ranks of the Franks, the Muslims and the Turkish tribes.[15] In short, the relationship between the Franks and the local Christians merits thorough research.

The last two main 'conceptions' of the present paradigm surpass the scope of the present study, but they deserve at least a brief observation. Prawer assumed that 'The creation of the Crusaders' city-settlement and city population was conditioned and defined by the intrusion of a mainly agricultural and village-dwelling society into a country where the city had been for centuries an established and central institution'.[16] However, it is very difficult to establish what was a city in Crusader Palestine and it is even more difficult to define 'urban society' at that time. The concepts of city and fortress, used by many scholars, cover a whole spectrum of settlement types. No doubt that Acre, Antioch, Tripolis and Jerusalem were cities in the twelfth century, even though practically nothing is known about their urban structure. But can the other 'cities' of the Latin Kingdom be defined? Was Nablus a city of a village? What about Nazareth, Beissan, Jinnin, Gaza, Darom, Athlith and the other major Frankish settlements?

Even the very important argument that the number of Franks in the Levant was comparatively very small cannot be based on credible demographic studies since we do not have any reliable data to count on. The number estimated by Prawer, Benvenisti and Russel, as being* more than 100,000 cannot be considered a small or marginal part of the total population of 400,000 to 500,000.[17]

In any case, all these conceptions are interrelated and are based on a very limited number of documents. The scarcity of written sources has already led to the creation of two opposing paradigms, each of which was supported by the most prominent scholars of each relevant period – one propounded the integration of the Franks into eastern society and the other their total segregation. A field survey, however, could at least verify or refute the assumption dealing with the settlement of the Franks exclusively in cities and fortresses – an assumption which is a cornerstone of this whole paradigmatic system. For this reason, a documentary and archaeological survey of Frankish settlements in Palestine was conducted (by the author) during the years 1985–88 and 1989–91. The combined number of Frankish rural sites discovered in this survey, plus the sites known from earlier surveys, surpassed

200 (see Figure 1). It is not possible, within the limits of this chapter, to discuss all of these sites. Therefore, this study will confine itself to some common types.

Rural burgi

Many of the Frankish castra in fact consisted of the castles themselves and the rural burgi attached to them. The rural burgi were inhabited by Frankish settlers who worked the fields. The process of the creation of such rural burgi must be compared to the process of transferral to collective, fortified settlements which was widespread in Europe from the tenth century on. It is now commonly accepted that the intensive process of fortification which accompanied the settlement in the tenth to twelfth centuries was not a result of any external or internal threat. An appreciable number of new fortresses were erected as kernels for new rural settlements, and many others were built near temporary markets and regional economic centers. Toubert, in his study of Latium, called the process 'incastellamento', and this expression, widely accepted since then, is applicable also in the Levant.[18]

Sufficient proof for the existence of rural burgi can be found in many of the Frankish castles, for example Castellum Regis [Mi'ilya],[19] Caimont, Ibelin, Saint Gille [Sinjil], Bayt Jubrin and many others. Frankish villages existed also in places such as Shfar'am, Kafar Kana, Safad 'Adi, Tira, Mimas, Al Bassa, Qalansaua, Ascar and many others.

Maisons fortes

Such edifices were built usually in remote places, away from the main roads and in sites which do not possess any strategical value. However, as Pringle already mentioned, it is very difficult to distinguish between Frankish 'maisons fortes' and Frankish small castles since the architectural ground plans of these two types of buildings bear a resemblance.[20] Nevertheless, our definition of a Frankish construction as a private agricultural domain is not based solely on the architecture of the main building but on the agricultural context. The construction of many of these places was associated with a complete reorganization of fields, with the establishment of irrigation systems and with the creation of new networks of paths which connected the main buildings with the fields. In many cases, all these components correspond to one general plan and it is possible to assume that the 'maisons fortes' and their dependencies were conceived as a whole. The context, in conjunction with the architectural details of the main building, enabled the classification of this Frankish rural estate as such.[21]

There is nothing surprising about the existence of such rural estates or manor houses in the Frankish East. 'Maisons fortes' existed in all parts of contemporary

Plate 1 The Frankish village of Mi'ilyā, general view (photograph: D. Tal; courtesy of R. Ellenblum)

Europe and there is no reason why the Franks who settled the Latin Kingdom should have abandoned this very common form of habitation and of rural management.[22] The novelty lies more probably in the fact that the Franks succeeded, in a relatively short time, in mastering technologies of irrigation with which they were not well acquainted in their countries of origin. Sophisticated water installations, like the channel networks running along the terraces and the implements used for regulating and distributing water to the fields, may testify to help being given to the Franks by the local villagers.

In some cases it was possible to identify the owners of a certain maison forte. This happened, for example, in the case of a farmhouse owned by Johannes Gothman. This Frankish knight witnessed many charters, the first of which was issued in 1104, and he was still alive in 1164.[23] According to William of Tyre, Gothman participated in the Frankish raid on the Hauran in 1147. When it became evident that the raid was a failure, it was suggested that the King should take flight on Gothman's horse which was considered the fastest of the Kingdom's horses.[24] His daughter was married to Hugo of Caesarea, one of the most important knights of the realm.[25] Johannes Gothman was taken prisoner in 1157 and his wife had to sell his property to the Chapter of the Holy Sepulcher, in order to raise the money that was needed to release him from captivity.[26] The documents which are concerned with the sale contain the names of the four villages which belonged to this property, the first of which is the village of Bethaatap, undoubtedly the Arab village of Bayt 'Itab, 15 kilometers to the west of Jerusalem. A very impressive Frankish 'maison forte' is still to be seen in the ancient core of Bayt 'Itab and it is very probable that it was used by Johannes Gothman as a residence when he stayed in his domain.[27]

A similar example is that of the property of the family of Francoloco, or Franclue. Franclue's property was sold in 1179 to the Church of Mount Zion.[28] Here, too, the list of

Plate 2 The Frankish Manor-House of Kh. al-Lanza (photograph: R. Rubin; courtesy of R. Ellenblum)

the villages which were owned by the Francolocos, enables the location of the family's 'maison forte'. The list consists of 10 villages, all situated in the same region northeast of Jerusalem. The first village on the list is Gebea, undoubtedly the village of Jaba. The 'maison forte' is still to be seen in the ancient core of this village.[29]

Settlement patterns

The Frankish achievements in the rural development of the Latin Kingdom of Jerusalem, were far more significant than it is customary to assume. The map of Frankish rural settlement includes over 200 sites, more than half of which are mentioned in the written sources. The Franks interconnected many of the sites by a network of roads; they constructed bridges and renovated ancient aqueducts. They created a parochial system which was capable of collecting tithes in kind; their fields were measured and were redistributed among petty landlords; they marked their parcels of land with stones and crosses, and built watermills and windmills. They mastered the complicated traditional techniques of irrigation and even succeeded in the husbandry of animals such as camels and black goats – animals which were, of course, unknown in contemporary Europe. The assumption according to which the Franks were only interested in their share of the crops and did not settle in the countryside, is not based on the documentary or archaeological sources, and it is in no way accurate.

In the course of fieldwork, it became evident that the aforementioned sites were not uniformly distributed. The Franks settled only in some of the regions while they refrained from settling in others. In the western part of the Galilee, for example, there is a comparatively large number of Frankish rural sites, whereas in the eastern part of the same region, east of the imaginary line joining the villages of Fassuta and Tarshiha, there is not a single Frankish rural site. A similarly uneven distribution characterizes the Frankish settlement north of Jerusalem. South of an imaginary line, drawn between the villages of 'Abud and Sinjil, there is an area of dense Frankish settlement, whereas to the north of it there are no such settlements at all. Both of these lines – the eastern border of Frankish settlement in the Galilee and the northern border of Frankish settlement in Samaria – were not established during the twelfth or thirteenth centuries; they were both important cultural frontiers back in the sixth century, when the country was under Christian-Byzantine rule.

An attempt to reconstruct the spatial distribution of the various religious edifices which existed in Palestine on the eve of the Arab conquest was made, in order to point out that these borderlines date back to the Byzantine period. Figure 2 shows the spatial distribution of Jewish synagogues and Christian churches while Figure 3 shows the locations of Samaritan villages. It is evident that in the last centuries of the Byzantine regime the country was divided between various religious groups, each dominating its own region. The different communities did not intermingle, at least not in the rural areas. The same line that divided fifth-century Central Samaria into a Samaritan region in the north and a Christian region in the south, and the same border which divided sixth-century Galilee into a Jewish region in the east and a Christian region in the west, still existed in the twelfth century – as the ultimate border of Frankish rural settlement.

The very existence and the continuity of such borders, both in the Galilee and in Samaria, cannot be interpreted on a deterministic basis since there are no significant economic, geological or climatological differences between these regions. A detailed study of the ruins and villages inside the regions as well as along their borders, might explain their nature as cultural borderlines. One might find it hard to believe that the sixth century's cultural frontiers outlived the Early Muslim Period and still existed in the twelfth century – many years after the disappearance of the Samaritans, who were the cause for the creation of one border, and the weakening of the Jewish communities who had created the other. But, on the other hand, it is difficult to accept the continuity of the cultural borderlines as a mere geographical and historical coincidence.

The continuity may well have resulted from the success of the local Christians in maintaining, throughout the Early Muslim Period, their dominance in these two regions, whereas the formerly Jewish and Samaritan areas underwent a total or partial Islamization. Thus the region once inhabited by the Samaritans, by the twelfth century was inhabited by Muslims only. Similarly, the region once inhabited by the Jews underwent a partial process of Islamization ad by the twelfth century was inhabited by a mixed community of Muslims and Jews. This conclusion is based primarily on the study of medieval Latin and Arabic documents which refer to local inhabitants in both regions, but it is also strengthened by the results of archaeological surveys.

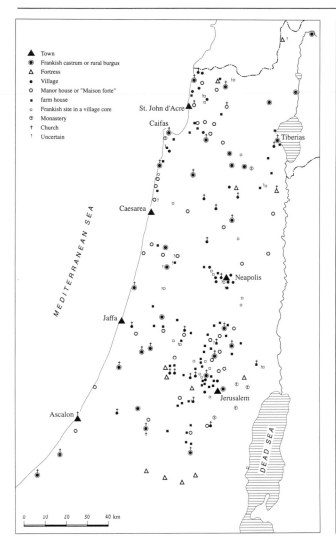

Figure 1 Frankish sites in Palestine

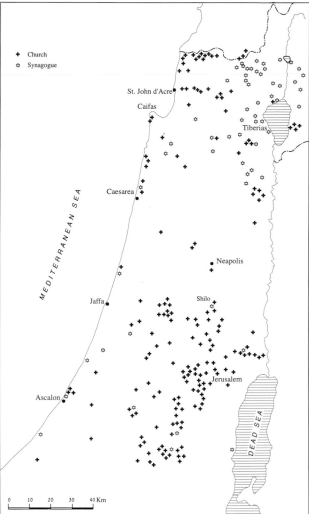

Figure 2 Byzantine churches and synagogues in Palestine. Sources: The northern part is based on information given by Mr Mordechai Aviam of the Israel Antiquities Authority. The southern part, based mainly on A. Ovadya, *Byzantine Church*

The villages which were situated to the south of the Samarian cultural border are mentioned in Frankish documents as being inhabited by 'Syrians' who were native Orthodox Christians who used Syriac for their rituals and Arabic for their daily life. The documents enumerate the names of many villagers, and names such as Cosmas, Georgius, Samuel, Nicolas, Hanna, Elias, Salomon and Butrus, appear again and again in many of them.[30] Other villages, which are not mentioned in Frankish documents, were certainly inhabited by local Christians in the Mamluk and Ottoman periods. The villages of Taiyba, 'Abud, Jifna, Bir Zayt, 'Ain 'Arik and Ramallah were dominated by the Christian population until the beginning of the twentieth century.[31] The only village in this region which apparently was not inhabited by local Christians in the twelfth century is the village of Bayt Surik and there, too, there is no mention of any typical Muslim name such as Muhamad or 'Ali, Husein or Hasan.[32] It should be noted that impressive

remains of Frankish buildings were discovered in almost all of these Christian villages.

There is no evidence, neither historical nor archaeological, of the existence of medieval Christian communities to the north of the borderline up to Nablus. On the other hand, there definitely is evidence of Muslim inhabitants there. A twelfth-century religious mutiny of Muslim farmers against their Frankish landlord, seated at Mirabel, resulted in the immigration of a few hundred Muslims from Central Samaria to Damascus. One of their descendants, Diya' al-Din who was born in 1173 and died in 1245, recalled these events and gave a detailed description of his parents' native villages, all of which were located north of the cultural border.[33] Moreover, Diya' al-Din refers to the existence of six rural mosques in these

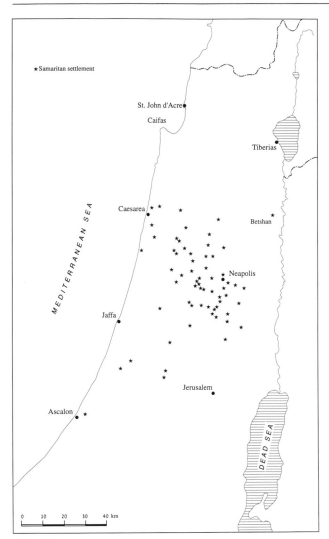

Figure 3   Samaritan sites of the Byzantine period in Palestine

villages and a dedication inscription of a seventh, which was built five years after the battle of Hattin, was discovered in this Muslim, formerly Samaritan region (by the author). The process of Islamization was more accelerated in the formerly Samaritan regions of Samaria and it was much slower in the southern Christian ones.

The general picture of the Galilee in the same period is very similar: the process of Islamization of the eastern Jewish parts had started already by the Early Muslim Period, and many villages were deserted even though the Jewish communities were less antagonistic towards the Muslims. There were no mixed communities in the beginning, but, as Elhanan Reiner of Tel Aviv University informs us in his doctoral dissertation, a new Jewish-Muslim culture which was based, in the first place, on mutual veneration of the same Saints' tombs, existed already by the twelfth century.[34] On the other hand, the main phase of Islamization of the Christian region took

place only in the Mamluk period, after the expulsion of the Franks from Palestine.

In any case, during the Frankish period there were still enclaves in which the Christians formed a substantial minority, or even a majority, of the local population. The Franks, so it seems, preferred to settle in such regions and refrained from moving into the Muslim ones. This observation may well be as valid for the subregions of Palestine as it is for the northern regions of Syria, such as Antioch, Edessa, Ma'arash, Cilicia and so forth. Wherever they settled in the Levant, the Franks sought the neighborhood of the local Christians and stayed away from centers of Muslim population. This is true not only in the wider geographical sense, but also as regards the small villages themselves. There is even documentary and archaeological proof of the existence of mixed communities of Franks and Oriental Christians in the same village, and the parish churches of St. George near Tiberias,[35] Tayiba, 'Abud, 'Amwas in Samaria and Bayt Jibrin in Judea were probably attended both by Syrians and by Franks.[36] In some of these places the Crusaders rebuilt the existing churches in a Frankish Romanesque style.

Conclusion

Three main conclusions derive from this study.

The first is that Frankish rural settlement was quite intensive and that the number of rural sites which can still be traced and identified surpass the previous modest estimates.

The second claim is that in certain regions of the country the local Christian population constituted the larger part of the population.

The third and final conclusion claimed is that the Franks settled only in the regions which were inhabited by local Christians and sometimes even in the Christian villages themselves.

These conclusions bring us back to the former French model which explained the relation between the Franks and the local population and which was rejected by Smail and Prawer at the beginning of the 1950s. The protagonists of this model claimed that the Crusades created an integrated society which consisted of the Franks and their subjects. The Franks, they argued, were deeply influenced by the oriental habits and were responsible for the unprecedented atmosphere of law, order, and tolerance which prevailed in Palestine during the twelfth and the thirteenth centuries.[37] Rey, Dodu, Madelaine and even Grousset, idealized this allegedly friendly relationship and did not make any distinction between local Christians and Muslims. This idealization of the intercultural relationship, which Smail did not hesitate to label 'French propaganda,'[38] facilitated the creation of the existing model, which, in its turn, told a completely different story of social, political and geographical segregation.

A possible synthesis suggests the existence of a mixed society which consisted of local Christians and Franks, and which had common interests and common establishments. No doubt that Franks occupied the higher ranks of the seigneorial and ecclesiastical hierarchies, and that they had a proper judiciary, but they settled and lived only in the neighborhood of the local Christians.

It would not be right to describe the relationship between the Franks and the local Christians as idyllic – which is what the French model attempted to do. The relations were more complex; motivated more by need than by will, they certainly had their ups and downs. The Franks, being an immigrant society, needed the help of the locals, whereas the latter regarded the former as a last barrier in the face of the Turkish conquest – a conquest which eventually brought about the final destruction of many of the Christian congregations.

Hans Mayer has already noted that the Latin chroniclers ignored the existence of the Muslim subjects: 'If I am not mistaken,' he wrote, 'the Muslim inhabitants of the Latin Kingdom hardly ever appear in the Latin chronicles.'[39] Mayer was not mistaken and the approach which is suggested here, of a multi-leveled Franco-Oriental–Christian society, may well explain the absence of the Muslim subjects from the Frankish collective mental map. The Franks referred only to those of their subjects with whom they had social and geographical connections.[40]

Notes

1. Cahen, Cl. 'Notes sur l'histoire des croisades et de l'Orient latin', II: 'Le régime rural syrien au temps de la domination franque', *Bulletin de la Faculté des lettres de Strasbourg* 29 (1950–51), 286; Smail, R.C., *Crusading Warfare (1097–1193). A Contribution to Medieval Military History*, Cambridge, 1956, pp. 57–63 [hereafter cited as Smail, Crusading Warfare]; Prawer, J. 'Colonization Activities in the Latin Kingdom', *Crusader Institutions* Oxford, 1980, pp. 102–42; [Hereafter cited as Prawer, Colonization]; Richard, J. La feodalite dans l'Orient latin et le mouvement communal: un etat des questions', *Structures feodales et feodalisme dans l'Occident mediterraneen (X–XIII siecles)*, Rome, 1980, p. 665; Hamilton, B. The Church, *The Latin Church in the Crusader States, The Secular Church* London, 1980, p. 90; Pringle, D. *The Red Tower (al-Burj) al-Ahmar): Settlement in the Plain of Sharon at the Time of the Crusaders and Mamluks*, London, 1986, p. 12 [Hereafter cited as: Pringle, D. 1986]; Pringle, D. 'Crusader Castles: The First Generation', *Fortress*, I, (1989), pp. 18–19 [Hereafter cited as: Pringle, D. 1989]; Benvenisti, M. *The Crusaders in the Holy Land*, Jerusalem, 1970 [Hereafter cited as Benvenisti 1970], p. 219 and p. 233: distinguished between Frankish villages, the number of which being very small, less than ten and manor houses which were quite numerous. Cf. Benvenisti, M. 'Bovaria-babriyya: A Frankish Residue on the Map of Palestine', in B.Z. Kedar, H.E. Mayer and R.C. Smail (eds), *Outremer, Studies in*

the history of the Crusading Kingdom of Jerusalem, presented to Joshua Prawer*. Jerusalem, 1982, p. 130–52 [Hereafter cited as Outremer].
2. Prawer, J. Colonization, p. 102–3.
3. Smail, R.C. Crusading Warfare, p. 40. Cf. Ibid., pp. 62–63.
4. 'The countryside was settled in an overwhelming majority by Muslims, but with a fair sprinkling of Oriental Christians of different denominations . . .' Prawer, J. 'Serfs, Slaves, and Bedouins', *Crusader Institutions*, Oxford, 1980 [Hereafter cited as Prawer, Serfs], p. 201; 'Not only was the threat of invasion almost continuous, but many of the subject peoples never fully consented to Latin rule, and on important occasions were to show themselves either doubtfully loyal or actively hostile.' Smail, R.C. Crusading Warfare, p. 204.
5. 'All Syrian Christians, . . . had lived for centuries under the generally tolerant Muslim rule . . . . Between them and their Latin overlords there was the bond of a common faith, but they were tied also to the Muslims by history, language, and habits . . . . It would therefore appear that the native Christians provided no firm basis for Latin rule, and that they increased rather than alleviated the Franks' military problems.' Smail, R.C. Crusading Warfare, p. 52.
6. Prawer, J. *Histoire du royaume latin de Jerusalem*, 2 vols, Paris, 1969–1971; 2nd edn, Paris, 1975, vol I, p. 570–1; Prawer, J. Colonization, p. 117; Russel, J.C. 'The Population of the Crusader States', K.M. Setton (General Editor), *A History of the Crusades*. 5 vols, Wisconsin University Press, 1955–1985, vol. 5; N.P. Zacour and H.W. Hazard (eds), *The Impact of the Crusades on the Near East*, Wisconsin University Press, 1985, pp. 295–314; Benvenisti, M. 1970, pp. 26–8.
7. Prawer, J. Colonization, pp. 102–3; Prawer, J. 'Crusader Cities', in H.A. Miskimin et al. (eds), *The Medieval City*, New Haven and London, 1977, pp. 179–99; Benvenisti, M. 1970, pp. 25–6.
8. Abel, F.M. 'Les deux "Mahoruerie" el-Bireh, El Quobeibeh', *Revue Biblique* 25 (1926), 272–83; Idem, 'Yazour et Beit Dedjan ou le Chastel des Plains et le Chastel de Maen', *Revue Biblique* 36 (1928), 83–9; Bagatti, B. 'Gifna. Villaggio cristiano di Guidea', *La Terra Santa*, 47 (1971), 247–56; Idem, I monumenti di Emmaus el-Qubeibeh e dei dintorni, Jerusalem 1947, 'Il Christianesimo ad Eleuteropoli (Beit Gobrin), *Liber Anus* 22 (1972), 109–29; Idem, *Antichi villaggi cristiani dl Samaria*, Jerusalem, 1979; Benvenisti, M. 1970, 1982; Clermont-Ganneau Ch. *Recueil d'archelogie orientale*, 8 vols, Paris, 1888–1924 (Hereafter cited as RAO), vol. I (1888), pp. 308–11, 334–6, 336–7, 351–92; RAO, II (1898), pp. 91–2, 95–7; RAO, III (1900), pp. 141–2; RAO, V (1903), pp. 70–9; Conder, C.R. 'Medieval Topography of Palestine', C.W. Wilson (ed.), *Survey of Western Palestine Special Papers on Topography, Archaeology, Manners and Customs etc.* London (1881), pp. 274–80; Frankel, R. Topographical Notes on the Territory of Acre in the Crusader Period', *Israel Exploration Journal* 38 (1988), 249–72; Pringle, D. Two Medieval Villages North of Jerusalem: Archaeological Investigation in al-Jib and ar-Ram', *Levant* 15 (1983), 141–77; Idem, 'Magna Mahumeria (al-Bira): The Archaeology of a Frankish New Town in Palestine', Edbury, P.W. (ed.), *Crusade and Settlement*, London (1985), pp. 147–68; Idem, 1986; Idem, 1989; Rey, E.G. *Recherches geographiques et historiques sur la domination des Latins en Orient*. Paris, 1877; Idem. *Les colonies franques de Syrie aux XIIe et XIIIe siecies*, Paris, 1883.
9. There is no record of Muslim attacks on the coastal plain north of the river Yarkon until the time of Salah al-Din. The mountain area of Jerusalem was raided only twice. For the raid of 1124 see:

H. Hagenmeyer (ed.), *Fulcheri Carnotensis Historia Hierosoly-mitana (1095–1127)*, Heidelberg, 1913 [Hereafter cited as Fulcher of Chartres], pp. 731–2. According to William of Tyre the Ascalonites dared to attack Jerusalem only when they discovered that the entire army was occupied with the siege on Tyre. The inhabitants who remained in the city sufficed to hold back the onslaught: *Willelmi Tyrensis Archiepiscopi Chronicon* (ed.) R.B.C. Huygens, *Corpus Christianorum Continuatio Mediaevalis*, 63–63a, Turnhout, 1986, 13, 8, p. 595; cf. Prawer, J. 'Ascalon and the Ascalon Strip in Crusader Politics', *Eretz-Israel* 4 (1956), 231–51 [in Hebrew]. For the unsuccessful raid of 1152 see: William of Tyre, 20, 17, pp. 787–9. Cf. Grousset, Grousset, R, 'Sur un passage obscur de Guillaume de Tyr', *Les Melanges syriens, offerts a M.R. Dussaud*, Paris, 1939, 637–9; Robricht, R., *Geschichte des Konigsreichs Jerusalem (1100–1291)*, Innsbruck, 1898, p. 271. The region of Nablus was raided three times in the same period. For the raid of 1113 see: Ibn al-Qalanisi, (ed.) RHC.HOr. p. 186; *An Arab-Syrian Gentleman and Warrior in the Period of the Crusades. Memoirs of Usamah Ibn-Munqidh*, (trans. P.K. Hitti), New York, pp. 138–40; Fulcher of Chartres, pp. 572–3; William of Tyre, 11, 19, pp. 523–5; Albert of Aachen, XII, 9–10, pp. 694–5. For the raid of 1137: see Kedar, B.Z., 'The Frankish Period' in A.D. Crown (ed.), *The Samaritans*, Tubingen, 1989, pp. 91–2. The Galilee was raided only once between 1121 and 1169. For the raid of 1121 see: William of Tyre, 12, 16, pp. 565–6; Ibn al-Qalanisi (ed.) RHC, pp. 86–7; Fulcher of Chartres, pp. 643–4. For the raid of 1134 see: Ibn al Qalanisi (ed.) RHC, pp. 216–18; Ibn al-Athir (ed.) RHC, pp. 392–7. For the raid of 1169 see: J. Delaville Le Roulx (ed.), *Cartulaire general de l'Ordre des Hospitaliers de Saint-Jean de Jerusalem, 1100–1310*. 4 vols, Paris, 1894–1906 [Hereafter cited as Hospital), vol. 1, 1894, no. 404, pp. 279–80, 1169.

10. Conder, C.R. *The Latin Kingdom of Jerusalem, 1099 to 1291 A.D.*, London, 1897, p. 161.

11. Prawer, J., Serfs, p. 201.

12. Cahen, Cl. 'An Introduction to the First Crusade', *Past and Present* 6 (1954), 6–7; Hitti, P.K. 'The Impact of the Crusades on Eastern Christianity', in S.H. Hanna (ed.), *Medieval and Middle Eastern Studies in Honor of Aziz Suryal Atiya*, Leiden, 1972, p. 212; Gil, M. *A History of Palestine, 634–1099*, Cambridge, 1992, pp. 140–3. Cf. Sivan, E. 'Note sur la situation des chretiens a l'epoque ayyubide', *Revue de l'histoire des religions* 172 (1967), 117: 'De l'avis general des specialistes, le changement decisif dans la position des minoritis confession-nelles dans le Proche-Orient islamique au Moyen Age doit etre rattache a l'invasion mongole de 1258–1260.'

13. For the actual state of the research cf. Morony M.G. 'The Age of Conversions: A Reassessment' in M. Gervers and R.J. Bikhazi (eds.), Conversion, pp. 135–50.

14. Smail, R.C. Crusading Warfare, pp. 48–52.

15. For Jocelin's collaboration with the Turks against Bohemond: see William of Tyre, 13, 22, pp. 614–15. For the intentions of Alice [the daughter of Baldwin the second] to place Antioch under Zanki's rule: see William of Tyre, 13, 27, pp. 623–4. For Hugo's collaboration with the Ascalonites against Fulco of Anjou: see William of Tyre, 14, 16, p. 653. For the presumed reasons for the failure of the second crusade: see William of Tyre, 17, 5, p. 766. For the betrayal of the defenders of Cavea de Tyrun, and for the hanging of the commander, who was the only one who had not defected to the Turkish camp: see William of Tyre, 19, 11, pp. 878–9. For the hanging of 12 of the Templars of the cave castle: see William of Tyre, 19, 11, p. 879. For the betrayal of the commander of Baniyas, together with a canon named Roger: see William of Tyre, 19, 10, p. 877. For the suspects of treason during the Frankish and Greek siege on Damietta: see William of Tyre, 20, 15, p. 930. For the fear that Bohemond would collaborate with the Turks because of the interdict afflicted on him for marrying a second wife: see William of Tyre, 22, 6, p. 1012–13. For acts of treason during the surrender of the cave castle in the Gilead: see William of Tyre, 22 16 (15), pp. 1028–9. For a messanger to the Turks, who was formerly suspected to be their collaborator [*qui suspectus habebatur quod alia vice in legatione simili contra Christi populum malicioise fuisset versatus*] but was sent to them again because of his mastering of the [Turkish?] language: see William of Tyre, 16, 12, pp. 731–2. For acts of 'treason' which were directed against the Turks; a Turkish 'Satrap' of Armenian origin from Tantass, who proposed to deliver to the Franks both Bosra and Zarhad: see William of Tyre, 16, 8, p. 724. For a Turkish soldier who asked the Franks to take Bosra, thus rescuing the Frankish army: see William of Tyre, 12, 16, p. 732. These few examples were taken from one source only – William of Tyre. It would be impossible, within the limits of this paper, to cite all the incidents concerning treason of Franks, Turks, Saracens and local Christians. A paper referring to such acts is now under preparation.

16. Prawer, J. Colonization, p. 102.

17. Prawer, J. History, vol I, pp. 568–76; Benvenisti, M. 1970, pp. 26–8; Russel, J.C. Population.

18. The pioneer research of P. Toubert on medieval Latium opened the way to new conceptions concerning Mediterranean settlement during the same period. See: Toubert, P. *Les structures de Latium medieval. Le Latium meridional et Sabine du IXe siecle a la fin du XIIe siecle*, Roma, 1973, Ch. 4, L''incastellamento' Rythme et formes d'une croissance, pp. 303–447. Cf. Bourin-Derruau, Monique, *Bas Languedoc, Villages medievaux en Bas Languedoc. Genes d'une sociabilite: X–XIV siecle*, 2 vols, Paris, 1987; Bonnassie, P. *La Catalogne du milieu du Xe a la fin du XIe siecle. Croissance et mutations d'une societe*, 2 vols, Toulouse, 1975; Idem, 'From the Rhone to Galicia: origins and modalities of the feudal order', in Idem, *From Slavery to Feudalism in South-Western Europe*, Cambridge, Paris, 1991, 104–31.

19. See: Ellenblum, R., 'Colonization Activities in the Frankish East: The Example of Castellum Regis [Mi'ilya]', *English Historical Review*, forthcoming.

20. Pringle, D. 1989, p. 20.

21. See. Ellenblum, R., Rubin, R. and Solar, G. 'Kh. al-Lawza, a Frankish Farm House in the Judean Hills in Central Palestine', *Levant*, forthcoming.

22. For various 'maisons fortes' in medieval Europe see: Michel Bur (ed.), *La maison forte au Moyen age, actes de la Table ronde de Nancy-Pont-a-Mousson, des 31 mai-3 juin 1984*, Paris, 1986.

23. Rohricht considered the various instances of 'Gothman' mentioned in the documents as relating to one person, but there exists a possibility of there being two different people. In the earlier documents 'Gothman' appears with no mentioning of his first name, whereas in the later documents, dating from the year 1125 onwards, the first name Johannes is always associated with the name Gothman. The relatively long period of time [*ca.* 10 years] that elapsed between the two groups of documents, as well as Johannes Gothman's participation in battle in the year 1157, support this assumption. If this were the same man, then Gothman should have been about 70 years old when taken prisoner.

24. '... *equum domini Iohannis Goman, qui omnes alios eiusdem exercitus equos celeritate et laboris paciencia longe superare dicebatur.*' William of Tyre, 16, 10, p. 729, 1. 52–3.

25. Rohricht, Regesta, no. 368, 1161.

26. '*Captus est inter ceteros ... Johannes Gomannus.*' William of Tyre, 18, 14, p. 831, 1. 16; Genevieve Bresc-Bautier (ed.) *Le Cartulaire du chapitre du Saint-Sepulchre de Jerusalem*, Paris, 1984 [Hereafter cited as Holy Sepulcher], no. 87, 21.11.1161, p. 200; ibidem, no. 88, 3.12.1161, pp. 201–2.

27. See: Clermont-Ganneau, Ch. *Archaeological Researches in Palestine during the Years 1873–1874*, Paris, 1899, II, p. 217; Bagatti, B. *Antichi villaggi cristiani di Samaria*, Jerusalem, 1979, p. 128; Rohricht, R. Studien zur mittelalterlichen Geographie und Topographie Syriens, ZDPV 10 (1887), 202; Robinson E. and Smith, E. *Biblical Researches in Palestine*, Boston, 1841, p. 594; *Survey of Western Palestine*, vol. III, p. 83.

28. Rohrict, Regesta, no. 576, 1179.

29. For the plan of the place see, M. Kochavi (ed.) *Judaea, Samaria and the Golan: Archaeological Survey 1967–68*, Jerusalem, 1972 [Archaeological Survey of Israel, I. In Hebrew.], no. 125, p. 183. For a Frankish 'maison forte' in one of the villages which belonged to this fief see: Bagatti, 1979, Plate no. 1, Fig. 3.

30. Caiandia: Holy Sepulchre, No. 69, p. 166, 1151; ibidem, No. 43, pp. 120–1, 25.7.1150; ibidem, No., 36, pp. 103–104, 1152. Ar-Ram [Ramathes, cf. Pringle, 1983, pp. 160–3] Holy Sepulchre, No. 43, pp. 120–1, 25.7.1150; ibidem, No., 36, pp. 103–104, 'Adasa [Bethelegel, cf. Clermont-Ganneau, RAO, II, p. 92] Holy Sepulchre, No. 43, pp. 120–1, 25.7.1150; Holy Sepulchre, No. 131, p. 258, circa 1161. Turcho: Holy Sepulchre, No. 156, p. 306, 14.3.1171; cf. Prawer, J. Crusader Institutions, p. 302 and p. 331. Caphaer: Hospital, No. 487, p. 336, 29.11.1175. Belveer: Hospital, No. 450, pp. 311–12 [Rohricht, Regesta, No. 501]. See also: Hospital, No. 150, pp. 121–2, 1143; *Archives de l'Orient latin* [Hereafter cited as AOL], IIB No. 7, p. 128, 1150; AOL, IIB, No. 8, p. 129, 1150; Hospital, No. 554, p. 376, 1179; AOL, IIB, I, p. 123, 1130–1145; AOL, IIB, No. X, p. 130, 1151.

31. Villages with a significant Christian population in the sixteenth century [according to Hutteroth W.D. and Abdulfattah, K. *Historical Geography of Palestine, Transjordan and Southern Syria in the Late 16th Century*, Erlangen, 1977.]: 'Ain 'Arikh [42%]; 'Abud [55%]; Ramalla [89%]; Jifna [according to Toledano 100%]; Tayba [35%]; Baytaniya, Ramun, 'Ain Samia, Bayt Rima. Villages with a significant Christian population at the beginning of the twentieth century [according to the 1922 census]: Tayba [100%] (cf. Anthymus, 'Description of the Boundaries of the Apostolic See of the Patriarch of Jerusalem, in 1838', in G. Williams, *The Holy City*, London, 1849, pp. 490–5; Bir Zayt [87%]; 'Ain 'Arikh [56%]; 'Abud [54%]; 'Ain Karim [28%]; Ramalla [96%]. There is a possibility that the Ottoman figures of Christians in some of the villages are diminuated. See Lewis, B. 'Studies in the Ottoman Archives – I', *BSOAS* 16 (1954), 479: 'A curious feature is the absence of any reference to Christians in a number of places known in later times as Christian centres – such as Jafna, Rafidiya, Zababida, Kafr Yasif, Mi'iliya, 'Ailabun, Bir'im, Ma'lul, Bir Zait, Ramallah, etc.'

32. Holy Sepulchre, No. 36, pp. 103–104, 1152. For Muslim names cf. Bulliet, Conversion, pp. 64–79.

33. Diya' al-Din, *Sabab hijrat al Maqadisa ila Dimashq*, in Ibn Tulun, Shams al-Din Muhammad Ibn 'Ali, *al-Qala'id al jawharlyya fi ta'rikh al Salihilyya*, (ed.) M.A. Duhman, 2 vols., Damascus, 1980, vol. 1, p. 68. For a partial English translation see: Drory, J., 'Hanbalis of the Nablus Region in the Eleventh and Twelfth Centuries', *Asian and African Studies* 22 (1988), 93–112. For a translation into Hebrew of unknown passages of this author see: Talmon-Heller, D. *The Shaikh and the Community, Jerusalem*. Unpublished M.A. thesis, 1990 [in Hebrew], pp. 27–63.

34. Reiner, E. Jewish Immigration and Pilgrimage to Palestine [1099–1517]. Doctoral dissertation, The Hebrew University of Jerusalem, 1988 [in Hebrew], pp. 252–3.

35. For the church of St George see: Hamilton, B. The Church, p. 87; 100; Cf. Delaborde, H.F. (ed.), *Chartes de la Terre Sainte provenant de l'abbaye de Notre-Dame de Josaphat*, Paris, 1880 [Hereafter cited as Delaborde], no. 14, p. 40, 1126; Kohler, C. (ed.), 'Chartes de l'abbaye de Notre-Dame de la valle de Josaphat en Terre Sainte (1108–1291). Analyse et extraits', *Revue de l'Orient latin* 7 (1889), 108–222. Kohler, no. 2, pp. 113–14, 1109; Delaborde, no. 40, pp. 87–8, 1178.

36. In all these locations were found churches which existed before the Frankish period and were renovated by the Franks: For the Church in Taiyba see: Schneider, A.M., et-Taijibe, 'Die Kirche von et-Taijibe', *Oriens Christianus* 28 (1931), 15–22. For the Frankish Castle there see: Kedar, B.Z., 'Ein Hilferuf aus Jerusalem vom September 1187, 'Dtsch, Arch. 38 (1982), 112–22; Benvenisti, M. 1983, no. 21, pp. 147–51. For the Church in 'Abud see: Pringle, D. 'Church Building in Palestine Before the Crusades', J. Folda (ed.), *Crusader Art in the Twelfth Century, BAR, International Series*, 152 (1982), p. 31; Milik, J.T. 'Inscription aramsenne christo-palestinienne de 'Abud', *Liber Annus* 10 (1959–60), pp. 197–204; Bar-Asher, *Palestinian Syriac, its Sources, its Traditions and Selected Grammatical Problems* Doctoral dissertation [in Hebrew], Jerusalem 1976, p. 123. For the church on 'Amwas see: Vincent, L.H. and Abel, F.M. *Emmaus, sa basilique et son histoire*. Paris, 1932; SWP, Judea, p. 63. For the Church in Bayt-Jubrin see: SWP, Judea, p. 276.

37. Rey, E.G. *Essai sur la domination française en Syrie durant le moyen âge*, Paris, 1866, pp. 17–19; Idem, *Les colonies franques de Syrie aux XIIe et XIIIe siècles*, Paris, 1883, pp. 4–14; Dodu, G. *Le Royaume latin de Jerusalem. Conference donnee le 20 novembre 1913 a l'Universite Nouvelle de Bruxelles*, Paris, 1914, pp. 42–75; Madelin, L. 'La Syrie franque', *Revue des deux mondes*, 6eme serie, 38 (1917), 314–58; Idem, *L'Expansion francaise; de la Syrie au Rhin*, Paris, 1918, pp. 258–314; Duncalf, F. 'Some Influences of Oriental Environment in the Kingdom of Jerusalem', *Annual Report of the American Historical Association for the Year 1914*, Washington, 1916, 135–45; Grousset, R. *Historie des croisades et du royaume franc de Jerusalem*, 3 vols., Paris 1934–36, vol. I, p. 287, 314; vol.II, pp. 141, 225, 264, 518, 615, 754–5; vol. III, Intro. pp. xiv–xv; and pp. 57–9, 61–2.

38. Smail, R.C. Crusading Warfare, pp. 41–42.

39. Mayer, H.E. 'Latins, Muslims and Greeks in the Latin Kingdom of Jerusalem', *History*, 63 (1978) p. 175.

40. The author is grateful to the editor, Thomas Levy, for his patience during the preparation of this chapter.

30

BETWEEN CAIRO AND DAMASCUS: RURAL LIFE AND URBAN ECONOMICS IN THE HOLY LAND DURING THE AYYUBID, MAMLUK AND OTTOMAN PERIODS

Myriam Rosen-Ayalon

Major developments

For the sake of convenience, the lengthy period in the history of the Holy Land which is the chronological framework of this chapter will be treated as three, very distinct, subdivisions. This, however, calls for a brief survey of more than seven centuries of history in Palestine.

Not only do the Ayyubid, Mamluk and Ottoman periods differ in length of time, they vary considerably in their relative importance when observed from sociocultural or artistic-archaeological viewpoints. Thus, the short Ayyubid period (1187–1250 CE) is marked by rather dynamic, multi-faceted developments, especially when compared to what emerged from the more placid, lengthy period of uninterrupted Ottoman rule (1517–1917 CE). Between them is the Mamluk era (1250–1517 CE), probably the core of the period under discussion. It will undoubtedly reflect, in many respects, the crystallization of most of the patterns which would endure long after it drew to a close.

The subdivision into three periods clearly coincides with quite distinct layers of material evidence that relate well to their respective identities and conveniently bear the names of dynasties. In all three cases, one can point to this distinctiveness in a meaningful manner, though there is, occasionally, some confusion as to the material remains, mainly with regard to the identification of Crusader, Ayyubid and Mamluk pottery (Ben-Tor et al. 1978: 66). On the whole, however, each of the three periods – Ayyubid, Mamluk and Ottoman – implies a distinct entity.

Each period, irrespective of the different length of its time-span, is extremely important in its own right. The influence of these periods, however, was unevenly felt throughout Palestine, so that while there will obviously be a repeated discussion of developments in such a focal center as Jerusalem, other locations throughout the country gain our attention at one point and are neglected at others. The Ayyubid period marks a turning point in the history of Palestine: the defeat of the Crusaders signalled the immanent re-establishment of Muslim rule over Palestine; the Mamluk period was one in which this rule was stabilized; and the Ottoman Turks brought the Holy Land into the modern orbit. We cannot point to important archaeological excavations or dramatic discoveries for these periods, with one exception which will be discussed below. However, there is substantial information available from the surviving memorials.

Ayyubid rule over most of the Holy Land began in 1187 CE, the year in which Saladin (Ṣalāḥ al-Dīn) achieved his great victory over the Crusaders at the Horns of Hattin near the Sea of Galilee. The most significant result of this development was the transfer of Jerusalem from Christian to Muslim domination.

The Mamluk period, on the whole, reflects a period of relative quiet. The Mamluk rulers of Palestine were not to be disturbed by many developments from outside its borders. Except for two brief incursions by the Mongols, in 1260 and in 1299–1300 CE, diversified activities could develop quietly in Palestine throughout the entire Mamluk period.

The title chosen for this chapter, 'Between Damascus and Cairo', is indicative of the status of Palestine throughout the period, in which it was not an independent entity. During the early Muslim period in Palestine, much of the political and cultural activity in that country was influenced primarily by Damascus. In the ninth century, this orientation shifted towards Cairo, when the Egyptian Tulunids annexed Palestine. This state of affairs, wherein the Holy Land was part of the Egyptian sphere of influence, would prevail for centuries, despite the turnover of Muslim ruling dynasties (Ikhshidis, Fāṭimids and Seljuks) and regardless of the interregnum represented by the Crusader Kingdom. Egypt's significant influence would prevail in the Holy Land throughout the Ayyubid and Mamluk periods.

The Ottoman mosque in Acre (photograph by Zev Radovan)

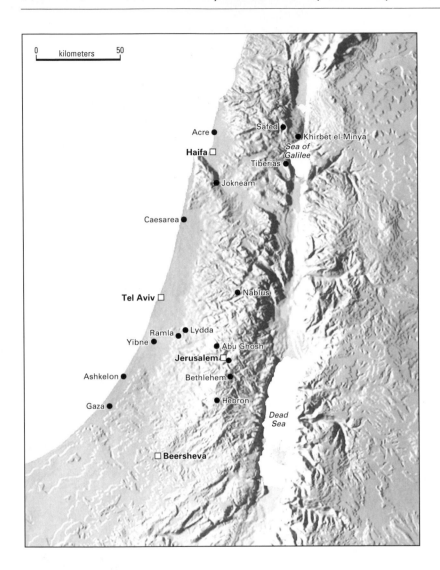

Figure 1 Map of the sites referred to from the Ayyubid, Mamluk and Ottoman periods

The Ottoman period presents a rather different picture. Since Istanbul was the seat of government of the Ottoman dynasty, this major center of the Sultanate would naturally influence much of what occurred in Palestine.

Settlement patterns

This chapter begins with the emergence – more correctly, the re-emergence – of Islam in the Holy Land. Between 1099 and 1187 CE, Palestine was under Crusader domination. After the massacre that accompanied the Crusader conquest of Jerusalem in July 1099 CE, whatever Muslim communities survived in that city or elsewhere throughout the country lived under Christian rule. It took them some time to recover and reorganize (see Figure 1 for a map of major sites mentioned in the text).

The rural population in the villages was less affected by these developments, for agriculture continued to provide its needs (Jacoby 1982: 205). Thus, the Crusader period was merely an episode in the life of much of the hinterland, which quickly returned to normal conditions with the end of Christian domination. Actually, the beginning of Ayyubid rule does not coincide with the complete disappearance of the Crusaders, who retained control over various areas of Palestine, while the city of Acre remained their stronghold until the fall of the last remnants of the Crusader Kingdom in 1291 CE. The existence of such Christian enclaves had a dual implication. On the one hand, there existed a certain state of coexistence of two political powers, which at times fought each other and at other times observed a truce of sorts. On the other hand, the enclaves signalled the inevitable decline of the Christian presence in the Holy Land, gradually yielding to the Muslim forces (see Chapter 29, this volume).

The retaking of Jerusalem by the Muslims in 1187 CE

had various implications for that city, first and foremost in relation to its residents. Immediately, the overwhelming majority of Jerusalem's population was Muslim. The Jews were able to re-establish a community, which gradually increased in numbers over the years (Prawer 1991: 203). Christians were not completely barred from the city, even being able to renew their pilgrimages to the holy sites, though under very strict military control. After 1187 CE, the sources even mention a hostel, called the asnerie (donkey's stable), which served Christian pilgrims (Schein 1985: 83).

It was under Ayyubid rule that the most important and dramatic transformation occurred in the settlement pattern of Palestine. Ṣalāḥ al-Dīn initiated a hitherto unknown strategy, continued by his successors: destruction of the coastal area and desolation of many of its cities. This policy, which differed from 'scorched earth' tactics, was intended to prevent possible attacks from the sea and resulted from the fear of an eventual return of the Crusaders. Thus, most of the existing coastal cities, from Tyre in the north to Gaza in the south, were literally destroyed (Ayalon 1967). Obviously, the objective was to prevent any possible landing from the sea. To that end, material of every sort was dumped into the water, obstructing access to the ports. The port of Caesarea is still blocked by debris to the preset day. Ascalon was the first city to suffer this fate, the order for its destruction being given by Ṣalāḥ al-Dīn himself. The remains of its walls are scattered not far from where they originally stood. These walls, which – according to all existing evidence – were constructed by the Fāṭimids, had continued to serve the Crusaders, but fell victim to the Ayyubid policy of destruction (Mujīr al-Dīn 1866: 422).

This fate did not befall the coastal cities alone. The walls, gates and fortifications of Jerusalem were dismantled – and this shortly after they had been built. All historical sources record this policy, which, in a quite extraordinary manner, was recently corroborated by archaeological evidence. The most striking confirmation is undoubtedly the discovery made by M. Broshi (1976: 78), who excavated a portion of the southern wall of Jerusalem. There he unearthed the foundation inscription of one of the gates constructed by al-Malik al-Muʿaẓẓam ʿĪsā, which he himself had ordered to be destroyed shortly after it had been completed.

So thorough and systematic was the destruction carried out by the Ayyubids – and continued by their Mamluk successors, especially by Baybars at the beginning of that dynasty's rule – that the entire coastal area remained barren and sparsely populated for centuries. This state of affairs prevailed throughout the Mamluk period and well into that of their Ottoman successors. Acre, for example, slowly became once more a vital city only towards the second half of the eighteenth century, particularly under the rule of Djazzar Pasha ('Akka, *EI²*).

Plate 1 The Ayyubid mosque of Ramla (photograph by Gaby Laron)

Undoubtedly, the desolation that was the lot of the coastal areas had implications for the entire country. Life in the Holy Land, as a rule, moved at a slow pace. Obviously, most of the activity was concentrated in small inland towns such as Safed, Tiberias, Nablus, Hebron and Ramla. Jerusalem, it seems, underwent a process of development on a larger scale, but – as we shall see below – this was not necessarily a result of natural urban dynamics (see 'Religion and Ideology' below).

Towards the end of the nineteenth century, the final stage of Ottoman rule in Palestine, some revival of urban life can be discerned along the country's coastline. One case in point is Jaffa (Joppa), which became the major port of entry for pilgrims. Their numbers grew constantly, reflecting both a growing interest in the shrines, saints and memorial holy sites of the three faiths in the Holy Land, as well as technological improvements and modernization of the means of transportation (see Kark, this volume for a discussion of the development of the country's infra-structure in the nineteenth century CE).

Not much material evidence has survived from the Ayyubid period. In Ramla, we can view the remains of the ruined Umayyad 'White Mosque' (see Plate 1) and particularly the two rows of pillars parallel to the qibla wall, which – it is fairly certain – date from the Ayyubids (Mujīr al-Dīn 1866: 416). The spring of the pointed arches, and the mouldings which frame them, seem to confirm a post-Crusader (i.e. Ayyubid) stage of construction. In all probability, this construction represented restoration work on the mosque, which must have suffered damage by earthquake during the Fāṭimid period. It stands to reason that under the Crusaders the mosque remained in its partly damaged condition and that Ṣalāḥ al-Dīn undertook its restoration after he captured the city.

Ever since it was founded by Caliph Suleiman early in the eighth century, Ramla had been designated as the administrative center of Palestine. Though predominant in the religious sphere, Jerusalem played a secondary administrative role – a status which was to continue throughout the three dynasties which form the chrono-logical framework of this chapter. Yet, the largest concentration of remnants from the Ayyubid period is undoubtedly to be found in Jerusalem. Though they do not belong to large ensembles, they are quite significant. Such is the case, for example, with the miḥrāb of the Aqṣā mosque and its most important glass mosaic inscription dated A.H. 588 (1187 CE) (Van Berchem 1927: 403).

The Ayyubid period in Jerusalem was marked by both secular and religious architecture (to be discussed below), as well as military and utilitarian construction. Several surviving inscriptions, some of them dated, provide us with evidence of this varied activity. An appreciable number of them refer to the fortification of the city, which must have been a very ambitious project. It is a well-known fact that Ṣalāḥ al-Dīn was instrumental in initiating the restoration of the city walls and was personally involved in its implementation. Apparently a long-term project, we have evidence that it was even continued by his nephew, al-Malik al-Muʿaẓẓam ʿĪsā. Inscriptions survive which testify to the building of a gate, a moat and a tower. It is likely that they were also responsible for the construction of another tower, for which no inscription has been found (Avigad 1983: 251–4), as well as several wall sections which can be identified as Ayyubid. The tragedy of this ambitious undertaking, however, is that the very people who built these fortifications were also those who tore them down (see above). The material culture of the Ayyubid period will be discussed below.

The major centers reflecting Mamluk involvement in construction are unevenly scattered throughout the country, and offer equally uneven evidence of that period. Nevertheless, one who travelled the road from Damascus to Cairo would meet them along the route: Safed in the North; Ramla, Yibne, Jerusalem and Hebron in the central regions; and Gaza in the South. Lydda, with its bridge, was undoubtedly the axis connecting Syria and Egypt.

Safed, the northernmost city of the Holy Land and the one closest to Syria, was a stronghold. Much of the urban life of the entire region was concentrated within its precincts. Its citadel (Qalaʿ) dominated the area, and its governor was directly responsible to the Sultan (al-Qalqashandi 1919: vol. 4). Some of Safed's cultivated areas sprawled towards Tiberias; Jennin, Acre, Nazareth and Tyre were among the urban centers which were administrative satellites of Safed. Little has survived from those medieval days to illustrate the beautiful past. The most significant works of architecture in the area are an emir's tomb and a mosque (Mayer et al. 1950: 41–8).

During the early Mamluk period, Sultan Baybars had given the order to rebuild the city that was to become the northern administrative capital of Palestine. Various secular public buildings – such as a hospital and bath-houses – were erected, but nothing survives of them today. Among the remains of Mamluk Safed are interesting examples of the 'ablaq' style (bichrome architectural decoration) with the local variant of inlaid block basalt stone, instead of the plain black stone encountered elsewhere.

A number of caravansaries (khans) dotted the country, conveniently distributed along the main north–south and east–west roads, allowing pilgrims and merchants to rest overnight. They were also intended to ensure the operation of postal services (barid), already introduced into Palestine by the Umayyads (Sauvaget 1941; Barid, EI^2).

Emmaus – Abū Ghōsh was one of these khans on the road to Jerusalem. When excavated, both architecture and pottery revealed an important Mamluk stratum (thirteenth–fourteenth centuries) on top of an earlier ʿAbbāsid stage, which preceded the Crusader conquest. The layout of the khan very closely follows the ʿAbbāsid plan – a traditional caravansary with rooms laid out around an open-air courtyard. The rooms seem to have been two stories high, with the lower one providing storage space for merchandise and shelter for the animals, while the upper floor was reserved for the travelers (De Vaux and Stève 1950: 105).

The city of Ramla has apparently decreased in size considerably since it served as the prosperous capital of Palestine prior to the Crusader conquest. Much of it was destroyed by an earthquake in the eleventh century (Nāṣir-i Khusraw 1881: 19), including the walls which had surrounded the city (Mujīr al-Dīn 1866: 416).

Here too, the most tangible evidence of involvement by the rulers in construction and architectural initiative in Ramla relates to its main mosque. It had twice been restored by the Mamluks. Two inscriptions bear witness to their efforts, both of them located on the minaret (the tower from which the faithful are called to prayer) to the north of the main building. The sources also attribute the restoration of a dome over the prayer hall to Baybars during the second half of the thirteenth century. This must have been rebuilt over the covered area of the mosque, which itself was renewed a century earlier during the Ayyubid period (see above) and continued to be in use.

The other Mamluk contribution to this Umayyad monument was the rebuilding of the minaret and its restoration by Nāṣir Muḥammad b. Kalaun in the first half of the fourteenth century (see Plate 2). The excavations conducted by Kaplan (1957: 96) seem to confirm that throughout the Middle Ages, this mosque maintained its original plan and general layout, despite undergoing restoration three times – once by the Ayyubids and twice by the Mamluks.

It is interesting to note that the minaret of the 'White Mosque' – the only remnant of this compound and the single surviving monument from Mamluk Ramla – is an excellent example of Mamluk architecture, incorporating many of its characteristics such as the ablaq, inserted columns as tie-beam supports, and a sunken entrance in

Plate 2   The Ramla minaret (Mamluk) (photograph by Gaby Laron)

Plate 3   The Mamluk bridge at Lydda (photograph by Gaby Laron)

the facade with a prominent porch. At the same time, it integrated several Crusader elements, such as the typical trilobe arch, some of the mouldings and – of course – the military character of this minaret, which combined religious with military functions.

Obviously, Ramla's city plan has changed over the centuries. As noted above, the city decreased in size. However, while some of its older sections, mainly in the south and south-west, were abandoned, the city developed towards the north and east. The clearest evidence of this process has been presented by the excavations and trial digs conducted in the city. These disclosed a concentration of strata containing later medieval pottery in the center of the city and towards its northern area, whereas those in the south and south-west yielded only artifacts dating from the eighth and ninth centuries (Rosen-Ayalon and Eitan 1969: 4).

The central region of the country could well be claimed to have been the focal point of all traffic in and through the Holy Land. Commercial, religious, military and secular transportation moving back and forth between Damascus and Cairo, as well as local travel along the north–south

axis, were channeled along one main central highway. This state of affairs is best illustrated by the extraordinary bridge, dating from Mamluk times, giving access to Lydda and known as Jisr Gindas (Creswell 1959: 150). It is amazing that a seven-centuries-old bridge not only remains intact, but is still in use.

Built in 1273 by Baybars, as its inscription informs us, this bridge reminds us of a contemporary and very similar – although much longer – one constructed by that very ruler in the vicinity of Cairo. Here is an example of utilitarian Mamluk architecture which, in addition to excellent technology, has features so very characteristic of that period (Plate 3). As already noted in the case of its contemporary Ramla minaret, the Lydda bridge offers such details such as inlaid columns which provide support for the tie-beams. Framed inscriptions are found on both faces of the bridge. However, the most impressive element is provided by two decorative reliefs on either side of each of the inscriptions. The reliefs display two panthers – Baybar's emblem – facing each other across the inscription, with a small quadruped at their feet.

Late in the nineteenth century, noted French archaeologist Clermont-Ganneau suggested that the bridge's three arches were in secondary use, having been transferred to their present site from a nearby Crusader church (Clermont-Ganneau 1888: 276). He based his strongest argumentation on the crowning stone of the pointed arch, considered to be unique to Crusader architecture, as opposed to what scholars held to be Islamic style – construction of the pointed arch by the use of two stones meeting at the apex, with the joint in between them. This argument, however, is not conclusive, for there are several examples of Mamluk architecture which combine both principles in the same building.

In the south, Gaza served as Palestine's second capital during the Mamluk period, together with Safed in the north. There are hardly any Mamluk remains in Gaza; the most significant landmark in the south is probably in Khan Yunis.

There can be no doubt as to the predominant role of Jerusalem during the Mamluk period. For nearly three centuries, life developed harmoniously in that city, which became an urban center of varied activity. Surprisingly enough, one of the most important factors that seems to have contributed to its development was a negative one. Ayalon has shown that, during the Mamluk period, Jerusalem became a city of exile to which were banished undesirable commanders (Ayalon 1972: 25). Thus, the city profited from much of their personal involvement in its affairs. It was transformed into an organized medieval city, provided with all the necessary installations, services and public buildings. In a way, it was at this time that the character of Jerusalem was shaped. Even today, the 'Old City' – Jerusalem within the walls – reflects the stamp it acquired during the period of Mamluk domination.

Most of the urban fabric of Jerusalem within the walls dates back to the late Middle Ages, whose numerous surviving monuments bear witness to the glory of this medieval city (Burgoyne 1987: 77). Apparently, Jerusalem was not enclosed by walls or, at most, only sectors of the previous walls and gates (destroyed by the Ayyubids) remained, providing a convenient frame around the peaceful city. Discussion of developments in Jerusalem at this time would best be divided into two sections: the evolving character of Ḥaram al-Sharīf (the Islamic name for the Temple Mount) on the one hand, and the rest of the city, on the other.

Obviously, much of the Mamluk contribution to the development of the Temple Mount centered around religious initiatives, which will be discussed below. However, even on this holy site, several more secular, utilitarian structures were erected. One outstanding example is the water fountain, built towards the end of the fifteenth century by al-Malek al-Ashraf Qāyet Bēy (Van Berchem 1927: 159; Plate 4).

As for the rest of the city, the rich variety of types of buildings and compounds that owe their existence to the Mamluk rulers of Jerusalem may even today illustrate daily life in the thirteenth and fourteenth centuries. The construction of several markets (suq, plural aswaq) is indicative of the city's expanding commercial activity. Some of this construction expanded earlier installations, those along the north–south main artery of the city which had developed out of the Roman and Byzantine Cardo (Elad 1982, 1991). Other markets were a true creation of the Mamluk period. The most outstanding example is the *suq el-Qattanin*, with its magnificent portal opening on the Ḥaram al-Sharīf (Plate 5). This market, dating from the first half of the fourteenth century, is so well preserved that it presents the most typical, classical formula in architectural terms of the Near Eastern covered suq. In fact, most covered marketplaces imitated this style for several centuries, as was the case with the nineteenth-century 'White Market' in Acre, that followed this same plan exactly.

Plate 4   The Sabil (water fountain) of Qāyet Bēy in Jerusalem (Mamluk) (photograph by Zev Radovan)

Mamluk construction in the rest of the city included utilitarian structures such as caravansaries like Khan al-Sultan (Burgoyne 1987: 479; Plate 6), or another major contribution to the daily life of Jerusalem's residents and urban activity, the important water installation that was introduced, restored, developed and used for a variety of functional buildings. This enterprise was initiated by Emir Tankiz, ruler of Syria and Palestine, on behalf of the Mamluk Sultan al-Nāṣir Muḥammad b. Kalaun, during the first half of the fourteenth century. It was a 'modern' water supply system that ran along Jerusalem's main axis, from Solomon's Pool to the Temple Mount. It made possible the construction of public baths (*hammams*), water fountains and reservoirs, while the crowning achievement was the beautiful water basin ('al-Kas') before al-Aqṣā mosque.

Obviously, it would be difficult to emulate the rapid and intensive developments that turned Jerusalem into an elaborate, well-established urban center under the Mamluks. It is hardly surprising, therefore, that under the Ottomans the city took on a somewhat stagnant

Plate 5 The gate of the Cotton market in Jerusalem (Mamluk) (photograph by Gaby Laron)

Plate 6 Khan al-Sultan in Jerusalem (Mamluk) (photograph courtesy of M. Rosen-Ayalon)

Plate 7 Ottoman walls of Jerusalem (photograph courtesy of M. Rosen-Ayalon)

character. Commerce and the economy were well organized (Cohen 1989: 8), but the four centuries of Ottoman rule were rather an uneventful period in the history of Jerusalem.

The Holy Land was very much dependent upon inspiration coming from Istanbul (Constantinople), the capital of the Ottoman Empire. Its rulers did not contribute greatly to the development of Jerusalem, which was not much more than a provincial town. Whatever imprint they did leave on the city dates almost exclusively from the early Ottoman period and is mostly to the credit of Sultan Suleiman the Magnificent (1494–1566 CE). His two most significant contributions to the urban fabric of Jerusalem were the reconstruction of the city's walls and gates (Van Berchem 1922: 431; Plate 7) and the erection of a series of public water fountains (*sabīls*) (Rosen-Ayalon 1985: 589).

The massive military architectural project – hardly intended against a potential foe – replaced the deteriorating walls which had been largely torn down by the Ayyubids. In all probability, the major aim was to

enclose the city within protective walls which could withstand any possible threat from the various nomads and bedouin tribes who roamed the region. More than anything else, however, the walls gave to Jerusalem the defined character of a well-organized urban center. In the best Ottoman tradition, the city's administration kept records which provide an immense mine of information on the population of Jerusalem and its character during that period (Lewis 1953; Cohen and Simon-Pikali 1993: 1–4).

Several other cities developed independently of each other without gaining primacy: Tabaryya (Tiberias), Nablus, and al-Khalil or Masjid Ibrahim (Hebron), whose repute often vied with that of Jerusalem (al-Quds). The northern city of Acre was an exception to this rule.

Several factors contributed to Acre's exceptional status. Politically, it was an enclave – semi-autonomous, if not completely independent of the center of empire and its administration. This began when a local chieftain, Dahr al-'Umar, established himself as an independent ruler in the

Plate 9   Ottoman khan in Acre (photograph courtesy of M. Rosen–Ayalon)

Plate 8   The Ottoman mosque in Acre (photograph courtesy of M. Rosen–Ayalon)

city. His self-declared sovereignty was expanded and interpreted on an even broader scale by his successor, Jazzar Pacha.

Acre was also an exception in that it was the first of the major sites along the Mediterranean coast that renewed its function as a port city since the destruction wreaked upon them by the Ayyubids and Mamluks. Within a very short period of time, Acre bloomed into a city possessing several mosques (Plate 8 and chapter opening photograph), caravansaries (Plate 9), baths and markets. It also boasted fortified walls and an aqueduct to ensure its water supply (Makhouly and Johns 1946: 93). The villages further inland developed most of what was to become the basis of Palestine's agricultural economy (Layish 1975: 527).

Innovations and technology

Though the entire period of their rule in Palestine lasted for less than a century, the Ayyubids can be credited with the introduction of some important and original innovations whose impact would be felt not only in the Holy Land but throughout the entire Muslim world.

In all probability, their most striking innovation was the adoption of the cursive Arabic script (naskhī), which was to spread throughout the world of Islam, having implications to this very day. Thus it quickly replaced the earlier hieratic kufi script to a great extent. In fact, the impetus of the naskhī script was such that one finds several types of paleography with distinct particularities dating from the Ayyubid period itself (Sourdel, Khatt, *EI²*).

In the realm of material culture, the archaeological evidence points to an overwhelming impact on the production of pottery throughout the country. The ceramic finds in all the excavated sites dating from the Ayyubid period tend to be similar, and apparently no distinct types have been produced with regional particularities. Such homogeneous manufacture highlights the problem repeatedly encountered by archaeologists – they are often unable to distinguish between various groups of ceramics unearthed in their excavations because they are so very similar to one another in style.

The difficulty lies in identifying the passage from Crusader pottery to that of the Ayyubids. Some of the families of glazed pottery do not allow for a clear-cut distinction – a distinction made more difficult by the political history of Palestine at this time. While the Crusaders still held Acre, the Ayyubids – and even the

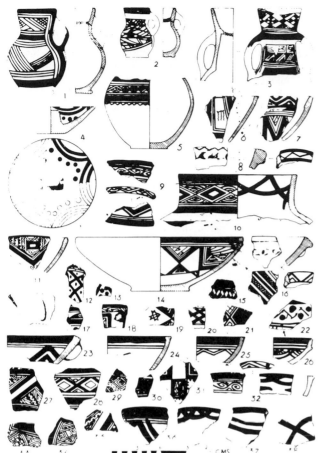

Figure 3 Mamluk unglazed painted ceramics (after Vincent and Stève)

Mamluks after them – controlled other parts of the country. A similar problem exists with regard to clear differentiation between Ayyubid pottery and that of the Mamluk period. Such difficulties were encountered not only in major centers, such as Jerusalem (Ben-Dov, 1982: 325), but also in smaller localities (Ben-Tor et al. 1978: 66).

In broad terms, the ceramic finds from this period can be divided into two main categories: light buff, unglazed pottery and glazed pottery. Each of these groups can be further subdivided, but only some of the most prominent of them will be discussed here.

The unglazed variety have a more 'greenish' tinge and are somewhat harder than the softer and lighter – in both weight and color – unglazed ware of the early Muslim period in Palestine. The difference in shape between the two periods is very conveniently illustrated in the finds at Abū Ghōsh, where the Mamluk stratum offers a whole typological range that can be compared with that of the earlier 'Abbāsid period (De Vaux and Stève 1950: P1.G; Figure 3).

The unglazed pottery of this period includes a very unique type, with painted decoration. After having created some of the most sophisticated ceramics, the Mamluk period potter quite unexpectedly produced handmade pottery (i.e. without using the wheel). At times, the artisan's fingerprints, or the imprint of the cloth he held during the production process, are still visible. The motifs are overwhelmingly geometric and monochrome, painted in red, brown or dark purple over a pinkish slip. Many such vessels have been found in various parts of Israel, but also outside the country in areas bordering on Palestine, in contemporaneous strata (Riis and Poulsen 1957: 270).

Most of the glazed pottery production of this period can be classified into six prominent types:

1. Monochrome glazed ceramics, primarily either in yellow of green, which are found in most of the medieval sites.
2. Bichrome painted ware, usually in black and green or yellow and brown, under colorless transparent glaze. This type, too, is quite common throughout the Mamluk period (De Vaux and Stève 1950: P1. 18; 2).
3. Polychrome painting on buff ware, under transparent glaze (Avigad 1983: 259).
4. A development of earlier Iranian-Mesopotamian 'sgraffiti' ware, though somewhat different, and, of course, with typological alterations (De Vaux and Stève 1950: P1. 18; 2).
5. Polychrome glazed decoration with moulded ornament, usually an inscription, is also very frequently found in Mamluk sites (Ben-Dov 1982: 365).
6. 'Blue and White' decoration, under transparent glaze, prominent throughout the Mamluk period in Syria (Riis and Poulsen 1957: 202).

The Mamluk period is also notable for the increasing use of ceramics in architectural decoration, as a result of the growing taste for ceramics in general and probably also due to external, perhaps Seljuk, influences (Rosen-Ayalon, forthcoming). Having begun as pieces of inlay, this trend would reach its height in the Ottoman period in the form of large panels of painted glazed tiles. A very good example is the facade of the Dome of the Rock restored during the reign of Suleiman the Magnificent, in the first half of the sixteenth century, emulating the fashion then prevailing in Istanbul, the capital of the Ottoman Empire (Van Berchem 1927: 335).

Classification of Ottoman period pottery, colorful and striking as it is with its rich repertoire of painted motifs under glazes, has not received much attention, and its stratigraphy is hardly known. Being relatively recent, these layers have been practically ignored. Unglazed pottery is almost unclassified, with the exception of some contributions from underwater archaeology, which recovered a quantity of unglazed vessels, though they have not really been sorted (for a recent study of this problem, see Cohen-Finkelstein 1991). The glazed Ottoman pottery found in

Palestine, with its overwhelmingly floral designs, fits into the Syrian pottery families. In all probability, most of it was imported.

A unique regional type of ceramic ware was developed in the late Ottoman period in northern Palestine (Haaretz Museum 1983: 7). We refer to unglazed pottery, decorated with red or brown painting, which seems to reincarnate the Mamluk handmade, painted, unglazed ware described above, although this pottery was turned on the wheel.

Another important innovation of the Mamluk period is the production of glass. This seems to have been a significant industry in Jerusalem (Hasson 1983: 109), with various finds providing evidence of local production of the famous 'marvered' glass or 'trailed glass' (basically an inlay of threads of white glass into darker glass). A few centuries later, in the Ottoman period, Hebron would develop its own glass industry, producing primarily colored monochrome, exclusively blown glass (Lehrer 1969: 5).

Other small industries developed, identified with a region or a particular city. These were very often family-controlled industries, especially from the eighteenth century onwards. Such was the case, for example, with the soap industry in Nablus, or the production of tourist souvenirs from mother-of-pearl and carved olive wood, which is so closely identified with Bethlehem.

Religion and ideology

A recent study has shown that the literary genre known as 'Praises of Jerusalem' (Faḍāil Bayt al-maqdis) may have begun at quite an early date (Elad 1991: 41). However, most of the known texts of this form of religious literature date from the eleventh century (Hasson 1987). The appearance on the scene of the Crusaders contributed to the flourishing of Faḍāil literature. Though it related to several cities, the major share of the praises fell to Jerusalem (Sivan 1971).

An innovation of great importance dating from the Ayyubid period is the introduction of the madrasa. The founding of such institutions, which were basically theological schools, was encouraged by the Ayyubids as part of their campaign to use every means at their disposal against their dual enemies: the Crusaders from without and the Fāṭimid Shi'ite Muslims from within. The madrasa was intended by the Ayyubids to consolidate Sunni Islam. In a quite significant political act, initiated by none other than Ṣalāḥ al-Dīn, one of the first such institutions in the Holy Land was established on the site of the former Crusader church in Jerusalem, the beautiful Church of St. Anne (see p. 503). The inscription commemorating that act is dated A.H. 588 (1192 CE) and bears the name Ṣalāḥiyya, obviously after Ṣalāḥ al-Dīn himself. This newly-founded madrasa would be granted a donation, to be administered as a waqfiyya (religious endowment), in order to cover all its financial needs.

Even though Jerusalem was not the administrative capital of Palestine, it became the religious focal point of the entire country. The establishment of madrasas, begun by the Ayyubids, reached an extraordinary scale under the Mamluks, who built dozens of them in Jerusalem alone – mainly concentrated in the Muslim quarter and in the immediate vicinity of the Ḥaram al-Sharīf (Burgoyne 1987: 35). The stated objective of the profusion of religious structures erected during this period was, of course, to perpetuate theological learning. However, they also had a secondary purpose: to provide 'insurance' for the numerous Mamluks in Jerusalem and their descendants through the ample donations that provided for the existence of these institutions.

In addition to 'madrasas, a great number of other religiously-oriented structures were erected. One case is the rebuilding of the Tomb of the Patriarchs at Hebron (Vincent et al. 1923: 68), while other types of institutions include hostels for religious sects and tombs constructed over the graves of Muslim saints. Though primarily in Jerusalem, these were also built in many other parts of the country, Haram Sidni 'Ali, on the coast, being one of them (Mayer et al. 1950: 36).

Several of the Christian religious monuments were converted into Muslim religious buildings. We have already referred to the Church of St. Anne in Jerusalem. Another example is the Crusader church in Ramla, which became that city's Great Mosque in what was to become the central area of Ramla after its south-western areas, the urban center during the Umayyad period, had been gradually abandoned (see above: 'Settlement patterns').

One of the most remarkable facts emerging from the period discussed in this chapter is that the Mamluks created a distinct style which distinguished their period of rule in Palestine from all others. These unique characteristics are discernible in every item that survives from the Mamluk era, whether it be a monument with elaborate architectural decoration or the single details found in the pottery, glassware, metalwork or coins of that period.

Social organization

Palestine was part of the vast Mamluk kingdom that stretched from Egypt to Syria. The earlier administrative system, with a Dar al-Imara (governor's house) as a major center in the cities, had become obsolete. Control of the country and its administration were now organized along a more general pattern: the Mamluk sultan ruled from Cairo, appointing an emir to administer Syria and Palestine in his stead.

The heritage of the early Muslim period in the Holy Land gradually became a thing of the past during the later

Middle Ages and the Ottoman period. The country underwent a slow process of acculturation of the asmar (military outposts that developed into provincial capitals). The country, for the most part, was sparsely populated, characterized by cities bearing a medieval stamp in which trade and small industry prevailed, with some exceptional cases of religiously-oriented activity.

The hinterland was dotted with typical agricultural villages (Cohen-Finkelstein 1991). The major crops raised were the traditional ones: wheat, olives, sugarcane, dates, figs, rice, pomegranates, flax, grapes and even bananas, to mention only the best-known products. Historical sources have repeatedly praised the quality of agricultural produce and the great fertility of the country.

The Geniza documents, discovered in the old synagogue of Fūsṭāṭ (ancient Cairo), illuminate much of the nature of the commercial activity conducted by the Jews of Palestine and their relations with other communities of Jews abroad, especially during the twelfth and thirteenth centuries. This is, indeed, an extraordinary source through which one can trace family connections, trade between Egypt and Palestine, and the various products that were particularly in demand (Goitein 1967–88). Although these fragments deal primarily with the Jewish community, they nevertheless shed much light on commercial activity in medieval Palestine.

Under the Ottomans, the Holy Land seems to have been relegated to the status of a minor province. Though relatively not too distant from the center of the Ottoman Empire, then a world power, Palestine did not greatly interest the rulers in Constantinople (Istanbul).

Recent surveys provide us with ample evidence relating to the rural settlements of Palestine in the later Middle Ages. They particularly point to the existence of a number of small agricultural villages. Only future excavation of those sites will enable us to interpret the information that could be supplied by the shards collected, illustrating these historical periods.

During the Ottoman period, especially in its later stages, more active and dynamic Christian and Jewish communities developed in the Holy Land. Churches and synagogues were once more established in the country's cities. Several synagogues in Safed, Tiberias, Hebron and Jerusalem date from as early as the sixteenth century, while, somewhat later, churches were built in Lydda, Jerusalem and Bethlehem. International developments, which led to the system of 'capitulations' in the nineteenth century, also provided special status and improved conditions for the Christian Church in the Holy Land, which enjoyed the protection of the European powers. Following the Tanzimat – the reforms and modernization of the Ottoman Empire – Palestine increasingly opened up to the West, especially to European influences (Lewis 1988).

Conclusion: processes of change

The later Islamic period in Palestine brings us up to modern times, to the most recent archaeological strata. Since it is also the youngest of the archaeological disciplines, much still remains to be accomplished – both in laying the foundations and in the study of the wide range of subject matter – compared to earlier periods. The samples provided by the surveys of various archaeological teams, taken together, will provide us with a better understanding of the complete picture. One fact is obvious – no new cities were founded during the lengthy period we have been discussing and the rural population continued to be unevenly dispersed throughout the country.

The Ayyubid period, which marked the return of Muslim control of Palestine, was characterized by several ups and downs. There were some foreign intrusions, such as the decade of renewed Crusader rule in Jerusalem (1229–1239) and the brief invasion by the Khorazmians in 1243–1244 CE. But, on the whole, it was an extraordinarily dynamic period which paved the way for the very productive Mamluk one that followed. Despite the return of Islam, some Crusader influences were incorporated into the material culture of the country. Above all, the Ayyubid period contributed some important innovations to most fields of cultural activity.

During the almost three centuries of Mamluk rule, Palestine acquired the solid foundations for much of what it became in later eras. This holds true for the urban fabric of the respective cities – their administration, layout and style of architecture – and also for various aspects of the material culture of the country. In this latter respect, all the material evidence surviving from this era is extraordinarily similar to what one finds in both Mamluk Cairo and Damascus.

The direct line between the earlier and later periods also holds true for the distinctive patterns of urban and rural life in Palestine – much of what was prevalent in the nineteenth century was formulated in the later Middle Ages. No major catastrophes introduced meaningful changes into the medieval patterns, whose foundations were laid during the period of Mamluk rule.

Only towards the final phases of Ottoman rule in Palestine would major changes be introduced, as a result of modernization and industrialization. Innovations and transformations, the introduction of printing and modern means of transportation and manufacturing, followed one another at an accelerated pace, moving the Holy Land into a new, modern period in its history.

31

THE INTRODUCTION OF MODERN TECHNOLOGY INTO THE HOLY LAND (1800–1914 CE)

Ruth Kark

I Theoretical and comparative background

This chapter is part of a study on the historical geography of Palestine in the nineteenth century, the last century of Ottoman rule in the region. Research on technological innovation and the introduction of modern technologies into the Holy Land, in historical and prehistoric periods, can gain much from an integrative, multivariate approach to political, economic, demographic, social, cultural, geographic, and environmental factors and processes. It pertains to the international, imperial Ottoman, and local arenas and benefits from the recent, more general and theoretical literature dealing with technological change, innovation diffusion, and development. However, notwithstanding certain unique phenomena in different historical periods, we must keep in mind the limited scale of our topic in a country as small as Palestine. As this historical geographic study of modern (nineteenth century) technology concerns material culture and its effect on social change, this approach is most appropriate for investigating the later archaeological record in the Holy Land.

As is to be expected, the approach of scholars in this field has been largely determined by the disciplines in which they are engaged. Many archeologists have regarded human progress primarily in technological terms ('How did they make and use tools?'). This reflects the nineteenth-century division of human history into 'ages', or 'ages of tools', when most technology was based on the direct physical application of human energy. Thus we have the Stone Age, the Bronze Age, the Iron Age. Modern archeological research tends more and more to regard technology as one component within a broader social context – an approach adopted in this volume by Thomas Levy (Renfrew and Bahn 1991: 150–1, 271; Greene 1986: 9–16; Levy 1994).

Historians have tried to answer the question of how technological innovation occurred in the ancient and modern world, why it developed as it did, whether it was culture-dependent, and why and how a given society assimilated those new technologies that it accepted. Graubard (1980: v–vi) insists that technology be thought of as a system whose social, cultural, intellectual, managerial, and political components are integral to it. Landes (1969, 1980), writing on the Industrial Revolution in Britain and its wider historical implications, sees industrialization as part of the modernization process. He suggests that the material advances induced a large complex of economic, social, political, and cultural changes that reciprocally influenced the pace and course of technological development (Landes 1969: 5). Adas (1989) and Headrick (1988) weigh the contribution of modern Western technology against indigenous powers in non-Western peoples or Third World countries in the nineteenth and twentieth centuries.

Economists tend to regard technological change, inventions and innovations in their economic contexts, asserting their impact on economic well-being, growth, and progress in general. They stress the relationship between changes in the technology entailed by the production process, and growth in the economy as a whole (Gomulka 1990; Maddison 1991; Mokyr 1990, 1992).

Sociologists, anthropologists and geographers have developed models and conducted empirical studies concerning processes of technological diffusion. The sociological approach focuses on the diffusion of an innovation within social groups and the interrelation of this process with the social structure (Katz et al. 1963: 240). Rogers and Shoemaker presented information-based diffusion theory (Rogers and Shoemaker 1971; Rogers 1983). However, Fischer complains of the decline and the 'sorry state' of the sociology of technology. He deplores the relative paucity of studies dealing with the social consequences of technology, when much has been written on the influence of society on technology – how academic settings, business interests, cultural perspectives, values, etc., shape the creation and use of technologies (Fischer

Wagner's factory in Jaffa (source: Australian War Memorial [AWM] 1917/18: B3172)

1985: 284–5). The anthropologist Kroeber (1930: 139) defines the diffusion process as the spreading of elements or systems of culture by contagion: an invention or new institution adopted in one place is espoused in adjacent and neighboring areas until it reaches every part of the world.

Geographers examined diffusion in its spatial context and the processes that altered spatial form (Fischer and Carroll 1986: 5–6). They focus on ecological variables and identify spatial contiguity and location within the urban hierarchy as two macroscopic determinants of innovation diffusion (Hägerstrand 1967; Pedersen 1970; Pred 1973, 1990). Blaut criticized the narrow view of the formal Hägerstrand theory (the communication of information about an innovation) and its unsuitability for understanding diffusion or non-diffusion in the non-Western or the ancient world. He called for more stress on the understanding of cultural process and its effects on diffusion in a cultural area, and recommends more exchange between the formal theory and the traditional approach of cultural geographers such as Kniffen (Blaut 1977: 343–9). Brown (1981: 197–280) adds the development perspective – the role of infrastructural conditions and marketing organizations in shaping the diffusion of innovations in Third World settings, and the interrelationships between development processes and diffusion. This brings us to a discussion of the Middle East, on the eve of its entry into the Western world economic system – its level of technology and innovation diffusion into it.

II Technological growth and decline in the Middle East before and during the nineteenth century

Ever since prehistory, certain periods in the Middle East have seen impressive technological progress (see Chapters 7–21, this volume; Avitsur 1986: 7–8). In a lecture on 'Discoveries and Inventions' in 1860 (before his nomination for the presidency), Abraham Lincoln mentioned one example of a brilliant invention that was not fully exploited:

> The advantageous use of *Steam-power* is, unquestionably a modern discovery. And yet, as much as two thousand years ago the power of steam was not only observed, but an ingenious toy was actually made and put in motion by it, at Alexandria in Egypt. What appears strange is, that neither the inventor of the toy, nor any one else, for so long a time afterwards, should perceive that steam would move *useful* machinery as well as a toy. (Lincoln 1915)

Technological advance and decline in the Middle East should be seen in the context of the cycles of growth and decay throughout its long history. The last of these cycles shows a slow and prolonged decline from about the twelfth until the nineteenth century CE, followed by sharp recovery and steady growth to this day (Issawi 1966: 3–

13). After the rise of Islam in the Near East, and between the eighth and the twelfth centuries, Muslim society was more sophisticated and better educated than that of Western Europe. The culture and technology of Islam was a synthesis of Hellenistic and Roman elements, with ideas from Central Asia, India, Africa, and even China. The ability of Islamic society to preserve, adapt and develop techniques borrowed from others is a lasting testimony to their creativity (Mokyr 1990: 22–34). Al-Hassan and Hill (1986) have shown the wealth and ingenuity of Islamic technology and its contribution to science in the realms of power technology, metallurgy, textile production, mechanical engineering, and agriculture. Progress in these fields was expressed mainly in the cultivation of high-value crops, irrigation, and hydraulics (Wittfogel, 1957).

However, by about 1200 CE, the economies of Western Europe had absorbed most of what Islam and the Orient had to offer. From then on they pulled ahead under their own impetus. Brilliant innovations in the West, between 1200 and 1500 prepared the way for Europe's technological leadership (Mokyr 1992: 39–45). The Renaissance (1500–1750) and the Industrial Revolution (1750–1830) followed, leading to mercantilism, colonialism and capitalist imperialism, which contributed to the economic development of Europe, but may have caused the retardation of the rest of the world (Landes 1969: 34–9).

The causes for economic and technological decline, and the ensuing social and cultural retrogression of the Arab Middle East have still to be determined. Among some of the factors are severe deficiencies in three major resources: forests, minerals and rivers (Issawi 1966: 3–13); religious outlooks that obstructed the introduction of outside knowledge (Landes 1969: 28–31); and the devastation caused by the Mongol invasions, as well as the lack of law and order and of personal security and property rights (Mokyr 1992: 176–89; Landes 1969: 34–9). Historians of the development of the Middle East since 1800 adopted a series of criteria for examining the determinants of its economic and social change (Issawi 1966, 1982, 1988; Owen 1981). Some of these criteria are the establishment of a centralized regime; increase in population; the expansion and improvement of agricultural production; growth of trade and entry into international commerce and finance; the creation of export-import economies; 'deindustrialization' – the destruction of local crafts and industries by powerful competition from machine-made goods; growth in income; and development of infrastructures – transport, communication, and health.

There is some debate about the role played by the industrialized nations in the Middle East in relation to local governments and indigenous populations. It entails different definitions and assessments of concepts concerning dichotomies or agents – backward–advanced; traditional–modern; internal–external (indigenous–foreign); and core–periphery (mainly in its geographic expression in coast and inland) – and their usefulness or aptness as frameworks for analysis (Cuno 1980: 245–75; Owen 1984: 475–87).

The introduction of modern technology into the Ottoman Middle East in the nineteenth century was closely connected with, and found its expression in, almost all of the above trends. Davison (1990: 133–65), for example, cites the very rapid adoption (i.e. it was already in use during the Crimean War of 1853–1856) by the Ottoman Government and Army of the telegraph (invented in 1833, with the first commercial line opened between Washington and Baltimore in 1844). Although they were motivated mainly by considerations of political and military control, the telegraph also had significant administrative and social impact. Cuno (1980: 245–75) and Richards (1981: 45–67) discuss the work of 'dependencia' theorists, growth and technical change, and the larger role that should be attributed to indigenous forces in reappraising socio-economic and technological change in Egypt between 1800 and 1914.

Gottheil (1980: 1–35) tries to understand why the Middle East including Palestine, despite the increasing introduction of new technologies in the nineteenth century (steam navigation in the 1830s, telegraph in 1861, carriage roads in 1868, railroads in 1892), by 1914: 'remained much the less developed region it had been half a century earlier, having produced little in the way of infrastructure formations that are associated with self-generating technological change.' A detailed study of this process in Palestine must be seen against the same background and conceptual frameworks.

III The introduction of modern technology into the Holy Land– Palestine 1800–1914

Background and the state of research and sources

Only recently has a beginning been made in evaluating the impressive technological achievements in ancient Palestine. This relates mainly to cultivation methods, exploitation of water resources and water power, irrigation methods, mining of copper, production of dyes from plants and animals, and the development of the first engine – the water wheel (Avitsur 1986: 7–8). At the beginning of the nineteenth century, Palestine was a peripheral area of the Ottoman Empire with a population of only 250,000 and a very low level of agricultural and industrial production. In some branches the technological level was even lower than at the end of the Second Temple period and later. To give just one example, wheeled carriages disappeared from the country at the end of Byzantine rule in the seventh century CE and only reappeared briefly at the time of the Crusades. Wheeled vehicles were finally reintroduced by settlers from

the West in the 1860s (Avitsur 1989: 16–17; Kark 1990b: 57–76).

There is little systematic research dealing with the topic of this chapter, and there is room for more theoretical sophistication and more detailed empirical study. In reviewing what does exist, we must single out the pioneering studies, over the past fifty years, by Shmuel Avitsur, a geographer with an engineering and technical background. His work, which laid the foundation for subsequent investigation, focused on the collection of technological remains of former recent material cultures along with studies of written sources; it is summed up in an atlas (1976), several books and numerous articles (detailed to 1977 in Avitsur 1977a: 210–23). More recently, other geographers, archeologists, historians, sociologists and botanists have followed with analytical and comparative studies. Most of them – Ran Aaronsohn (1990, 1993); Yossi Ben-Artzi (1988); Nili Lipschitz, Simcha Lev-Yadun and Gideon Biger (1988); Ruth Kark (1986, 1990a, 1990b); Shaul Katz (1982, 1986); Derek Penslar (1991); Naftali Thalmann (1991) – concentrated on the European influence through Christian American and German, and Jewish settlers in Palestine in the period 1831–1914, dealing with modern technological ideology and practice, mainly in the fields of settlement planning, construction, and agriculture. Joseph Glass and Ruth Kark (1991) studied the theme of entrepreneurship and local entrepreneurs in Palestine, and their role in the economy, society, and settlement within the Middle East context. Kark also wrote on the development of infrastructure and the reintroduction of wheeled vehicles into Ottoman Palestine, using present-day geographical methodology to discuss transport (roads, railways, ports), and applying models based on Turkey, West Africa, and a model of transport expansion in underdeveloped countries (Kark 1990a: 57–76). In the future, a study of the contribution of the local Arab population to this process will be initiated.

Notwithstanding the variety of material available for the study of nineteenth-century Palestine, there are serious limitations in locating sources concerning technological change and innovation diffusion. Most of the material is descriptive and hard to quantify or map. Nevertheless there are still many sources to be tapped in Ottoman, consular and local archives, such as in the archives of European countries, the United States National Archives, the Israel State Archive, and the Central Zionist Archive in Jerusalem. Other possible sources are Arab, German, and Hebrew newspapers published in Palestine, and surveys of surviving specimens of machinery, buildings, and installations. Two examples of good sources for the study of technological diffusion are the local Hebrew periodical press in Jerusalem and correspondence kept in the United States National Archives. The former, summed up in a map by Mendel (1984), shows the source of innovations as reflected in advertisements in the years 1885 to 1900

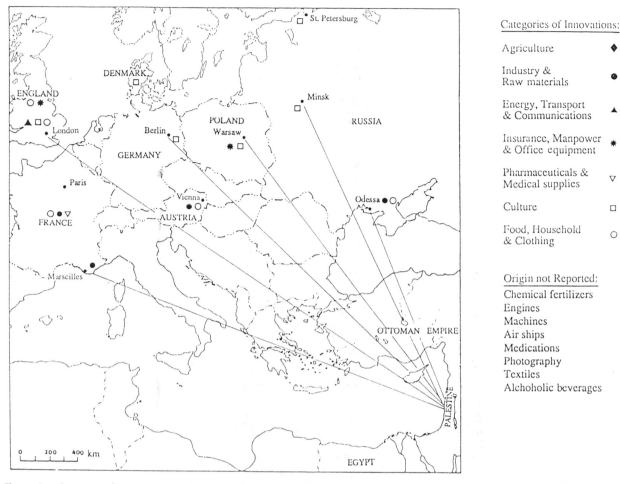

Figure 1 The source of innovations as reflected in advertisements in Hebrew newspapers in Jerusalem, 1885–1900 (after Mendel 1984)

(Figures 1 and 2). The latter, based on Kark (1994) and detailed below (see Window 2 p. 540; Figures 2.1 and 2.2), presents United States marketing inquiries in Palestine in 1908–1914.

Change in the nineteenth century

From the mid-nineteenth century Palestine became an important core for the introduction into the Ottoman Empire of modern innovations and technologies which came at an increased pace from Europe and America. This process continues to the present: Israel is today the most advanced, innovative and technological center in the Middle East. The determinants of this change, and its impact on the dichotomy or continuum between tradition and modernity and on development, should be viewed in a broad political, economic, social, cultural and geographic context.

This may be presented in a schematic diagram demonstrating the interaction between political transformation, economic and technological change, demographic, social and cultural developments, and environmental, physical and spatial change. Although one-dimensional it should be viewed as a dynamic process, reflecting a hierarchical system in three different contexts – all relevant to Palestine (Figure 3). The international context entails the changes in the political structure of the great powers, increased Western influence in the Ottoman Empire – also as affected by the Industrial Revolution in Europe and developments in the European economy in the nineteenth century (trade and international capital market and technological advances that greatly improved both marine and overland communications, and enabled the opening of the Suez Canal). The second context is that of the Ottoman Empire. Strengthening links of the Empire with the West and substantial changes in the nature of Ottoman administration brought about by reforms within the Empire benefited foreign trade, communications, urbanization, and structural social change. The third context comprises the region of Palestine. Although not a unified administrative unit in the nineteenth century, it had its own unique character. The special attraction of the Holy Land and

Figure 2 Advertisement of Stein's factory in Jaffa (source: *Hashkafa* 13 March 1903: 178)

Jerusalem, and growing European and American political and religious interests, influenced many spheres of life in the local arena.

The introduction of modern technology into Palestine after hundreds of years of stagnation started only in the second third of the nineteenth century. The motivating forces were both internal and external. Among them were imperialist political and economic endeavors of the Western powers in seeking mineral deposits, agricultural products or potential markets. The Ottoman Government was concerned with political and military control. Philanthropic and religious bodies were driven by belief-systems or social and national aspirations. Foreign and local entrepreneurial companies and individuals were intent mainly on profit and status.

The agents and opponents of technological change

In his study on technology transfer in the age of imperialism in 1856–1940, Headrick (1988: 10–13) identifies four basic categories: geographic relocation of technology by Western experts; by non-Western experts; cultural diffusion of technology by Western experts; and by non-Western experts.

In Palestine these categories are only partially relevant due to the difference in scale; nor was it a case of classic imperialism. Apart from the 'external' introduction of technological change from Europe and America, there were 'internal' introducers, i.e., select semi-local or local groups which served as agents of change. First among the external introducers were philanthropists (Sir Moses Montefiore,

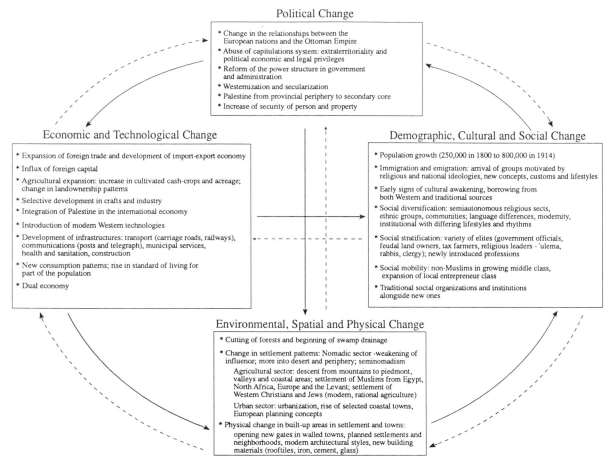

Figure 3   The interrelations between elements of change in Palestine, 1908–1914

the Alliance Israélite, Baron Edmond de Rothschild), foreign consuls and Protestant missionaries. Later, important agents of technological transfer were Christian American and German settlers who came to the Holy Land in the 1850s and 1860s, and Muslim Circassians and Bosnians who immigrated to Palestine in the 1860s and 1870s from the Balkans and the Caucasus with Ottoman encouragement. From 1882 on, the dominant factor was the influx of Jews from Europe influenced by the 'settlement engineers' and policies of Jewish institutions and leaders, including the Zionist movement from the 1890s on. They applied to Palestine concepts and models of French, German, and Eastern European nineteenth-century technology and settlement (Kark 1984: 183–96; Penslar 1991; Window 1 p. 538; Figure 1.1). Among the Jewish immigrants to Palestine were some who engaged in occupations and professions new to the country (Table 1). Here must be mentioned a class of semi-local and local entrepreneurs – Muslims (effendis and the local Arab elite), Christians (including Christian Arabs), and Sephardi and other Jews originating from the Middle East and North Africa – that served from the

beginning of the nineteenth century as mediators between the West and Palestine.

These local and foreign classes, numbering on the eve of World War I about one-fifth of the country's population, were the ones who not only introduced but enjoyed most of the modern technologies, thus creating a dual society and economy. Some opposition to change came from the Muslim Arab majority of the country: cutting telegraph wires and poles (in 1865), damaging carriages, and the like (Shva and Ben-Amotz 1973: 181). Some of this opposition was motivated by xenophobia, or, as in some Western countries (e.g., Stein 1991: 10) and in tropical Africa and India, Western technology was seen as a threat to the prevailing culture and traditional employment patterns (Headrick 1988: 12).

When the British consul in Jerusalem, James Finn, spoke in 1856 to an Arab effendi in Jaffa about the necessity of building jetties along the Mediterranean coast, and the need to open an additional gate in the city wall, the improvement of roads and the introduction of coach transportation, he received the following answer: '"But," said the effendi (not a Turk but one of the Arab city

Table 1 Professions and occupations of Jewish immigrants to Palestine 1905–1907

Professions and occupations	Jerusalem 1906–1907	Jaffa 1905–1907	Total	Total family members
Medical doctors		3	3	10
Dentists		2	2	9
Midwives	3	2	5	10
Pharmacists and assistants	1	4	5	10
Engineers, architects, chemists, agronomists	2	4	6	15
Teachers, governesses, calligrapher	16	18	34	67
Teachers of music, poetry, art		7	7	16
Bookkeepers and correspondents	7	10	17	32
Photographers and signpainters	3	4	7	11
Commercial representatives and middlemen	3	7	10	26
Traders, shopkeepers, peddlers, makers of paper bags	2	36	38	157
Typesetters and bookbinders	3	2	5	18
Carpenters, framers, mattress makers	2	2	24	83
Locksmiths, blacksmiths, boiler makers, galvanizers, jewelers	6	18	24	48
Watchmakers and parasol makers	7	4	11	26
Tailors, seamstresses, hatmakers, embroiderers	34	21	55	89
Pressers, dyers		7	7	21
Weaver	1		1	2
Shoemakers, leather workers, stocking knitters	17	21	38	93
Barbers, wig makers		6	6	10
Barrel maker		1	1	8
Housepainters and whitewashers	4		4	4
Stonemasons and fence makers	15		15	16
Bakers and assistants	1	5	6	14
Pastrycooks and macaroni makers		2	2	7
Butchers		2	2	12
Petty manufactures (locks, skins, seltzer water)		3	3	14
Innkeepers, coffeehouse owners and assistants	4	4	8	48
School administrators, school janitors, letter carriers		3	3	14
Mill owners	2		2	7
Laborers	8	5	13	18
Students				14
No permanent work		18	18	76
Total of persons supported by working Jewish immigrants				1,005

notables), "we don't do this on principle. When I have money to spare I lay it out on a house, a slave, a diamond, a fine mare or a wife; but I do not make a road up to that object in order to invite strangers to come that way..." (Finn 1878 Vol. I: 191). Western prejudice attributed this attitude to Muslim nature:

> No artificial fertilizers are used. Modern machinery and implements are little known. The cheap labor in Anatolia often makes their use uneconomical. It is hard to change the customs of Oriental peoples: this statement is particularly true of the Moslems, since they are not mechanically inclined and soon abandon any mechanical contrivance when it gets out of order. (Nickoley 1924: 281)

This seemed true also to British military intelligence in Palestine in World War I: 'The Arab *fellah* is still contented to follow the method of the Bible.' (Great Britain 1917:

64). The United States consul in Jerusalem, Thomas R. Wallace, in a report to the State Department in 1910, gives a more balanced explanation for the meager sales of modern American farm implements in Palestine, but agrees that the existing tools and implements used by the local Arab farmer classes 'are but little different from those used by the patriarchs'. Among the reasons for this he adduces the stony conditions of the land, the unsuitability of machinery for some types of soil, lack of proper instruction, want of care and indifference as to the implements used, the cheapness of labor, cultivation in small patches, the communal system of farming, and the poverty of the farmers. He went on to say that even the Jewish and German farmers, who are far in advance of the natives in methods of cultivation, use out-of-date farm implements (Wallace 1910c: 370–5).

However, in time, the local Arabs also began to appreciate the modernization of infrastructure in the

Plate 1 Soldering-iron heated on a 'Primus' kerosene burner placed inside a petroleum tin for protection against the wind (photograph Kark 1977)

Plate 2 New breach in the Jerusalem city wall to accommodate a roadway just south of the Jaffa Gate and the Ottoman clock-tower at the beginning of the twentieth century (source: Jerusalem Municipal Archives [JMA])

spheres of transportation, communication and health. They imitated and assimilated agricultural innovations and machinery, adopted new building materials and styles, and became accustomed to new consumption goods. One example is kerosene introduced into Palestine in 1865 for home consumption, primarily for lighting. Strange as it may seem today, kerosene was first imported from America and marketed in five-gallon tins, which came packaged in wooden crates, two tins to a crate. A wide variety of uses were found by the local population for the empty crates and tins, as Selah Merrill, the US consul in Jerusalem reported in 1885:

> One who has not lived here can hardly realize to what extent the petroleum boxes are used not only by the people in the towns but by the Arabs in the desert. They are strong, light and convenient size, and are used everywhere and for *hundreds of purposes*. As the name of the oil company is proudly printed upon the boxes, the universal distribution of these becomes a capital advertising medium; but unfortunately the people cannot read English. It would be a good idea for the oil companies to print their names *in Arabic* at least on one end of the boxes. (Merrill 1885; Plate 1)

The Ottoman Government and the local Turkish authorities evinced a selective attitude to the introduction of technological innovations into Palestine by both their own initiative and that of others. Their main direct contribution was the construction of urban and interurban infrastructure – roads, railways, postal and telegraph services, streets, parks, water fountains, clocktowers, hospitals, schools, urban water supply and rural irrigation systems (Plate 2). At the beginning of the twentieth century they built new towns (Beersheva, Beit Shean) and planned modern agricultural and drainage projects and the introduction of electricity, telephones, automobiles and tramways. In 1913 they also took measures to promote industrial enterprises, but due to the outbreak of World War I, none of these advances materialized (Kark 1986, 1990a, 1990b; Ruppin 1918: 51–4).

Sometimes the manufacturers in Europe thought that Palestine was not ready for innovation. In July 1908, Ekrem Bey, the Ottoman governor of the Jerusalem special province, approached the British consul for information about his project to utilize motor cars for the transport of grain in the southern districts of the province, and motors for pumping water. The consul supplied him with catalogs of British firms and the pasha's choice fell on a steam car, but 'the manufacturers came to the conclusion that the country was not adapted to the employment of their cars (owing to the advance of roads and the sandy nature of the soil) and preferred not to quote a price.' (Blech 1908: 167–70). It seems that Ekrem Bey was inspired by an American tourist from Boston, Charles J. Glidden, who at the beginning of 1908 was the first to bring an automobile into the country. After covering about 750 miles on Palestine roads, he suggested that cars having high road clearance held the promise of a lucrative export trade (Kark, 1994:

Plate 3 Jewish almshouses and the modern windmill erected by Moses Montefiore in Jerusalem (source: Manning 1874: 115)

Plate 4 The irrigated gardens at Artas south of Bethlehem, the first modern European agricultural experiment in Palestine (photograph Kark 1980)

278). The first airplane arrived at the end of 1913, but it was just a curiosity.

Spheres of technological diffusion

The main spheres into which modern technology was introduced into Palestine during the period 1800–1914 were agriculture, crafts, manufacture and industry, infrastructure (transport and road services, communications, energy, finance, education, health and welfare), construction and private consumption. Important criteria for examining technological development in its cultural and economic context are the processes of transformation in the energy-base of the country (Avitsur 1972, 1974, 1989). Avitsur identified four stages. Two parallel ones for the period 1800–1860 were characterized by technological advance and the beginnings of mechanization based on the improvement of biological (human and animal), water and wind power. The third stage, from 1860 on, was marked by the introduction and use of steam power to operate machines in industry, agriculture and transportation. The fourth stage began in 1897 with the importation of internal combustion engines running on kerosene.

Agriculture

The agricultural sector took prime place in technological experimentation and progress. This included new agricultural tools and machinery and different cultivation methods and crops. From 1831 and until the organized settlement of the German Templars in 1868, there had been only a few pioneering and short-lived beginnings – the introduction of wind-powered flour mills (by Ibrahim Pasha the Egyptian governor of Syria and Palestine and the Armenian monastery in the 1830s, and by Sir Moses Montefiore in the 1850s) (Plate 3), and the installation in Jerusalem, Jaffa, Haifa and Nablus of European mechanized oil-presses and hydraulic cotton balers, and water pumps from England. These improvements were introduced chiefly by Protestant missionaries, who strove to bring the native Arab Christians and Muslims, and the local Jews, 'nearer heaven'. The British consul James Finn, and his wife Elizabeth Anne were very much involved in such activities (Finn 1878).

Two groups of American settlers in Artas (Plate 4) and Jaffa – the former led by Clorinda S. Minor in 1851–1855, and the latter by George W.J. Adams in 1866–1867 – had advanced ideas about farming methods and introducing modern machinery in order to achieve agricultural progress and economic success in the Holy Land. Minor's small group sent or brought from Philadelphia seeds, agricultural tools, farm implements and fixtures (plows, mechanical tools, a flour-mill and medicines). The Adams group placed special emphasis on bringing with them – apart from prefabricated wooden houses from Maine – machines, tools, seeds and animals that could further modern farming methods: Johnson's 'patent shifting mold-board and gang plow', Smith's 'double-back action drill', and a wonderful combined self-adjusting reaping, threshing, sacking, grinding and bolting machine. Despite their shortlived existence in the country, these pioneering groups were to have a lasting influence in these realms (Kark 1990c: 76–89).

In the 1860s and 1870s a few Muslim Circassians and Bosnians, coming from Russia and Bosnia introduced advanced agricultural methods (the use of the scythes for mowing), and skills in animal husbandry (Ruppin 1918: 33). But the main innovators in agriculture from the late 1860s on were, undoubtedly the pietist German Templars who came from Germany, Russia and the United States. They also inspired the Jewish agricultural school Miqve Yisrael, founded in 1870 by the French philanthropic Alliance Israélite Universelle, and the first Jewish agricultural settlements established from 1878 on. As Thalmann (1991: 158–71) has shown, the Templar settlement was accompanied by a process of diffusion of modern agricultural innovations from Germany in particular, and from Europe and America. In agrotechnology, it included tools and modern machinery: light and heavy steel plows from Ulm; plows operated by horse gear (*manège*) – 'Göpelpflug' – and later by steam locomobiles, some of which were not always suitable for local conditions; scythes, harvesting machines, drills and mowing machines. A ribbed stone threshing roller was imported from Russia to replace the local threshing sleds. These machines were either imported from Europe and the US, and sold in Jaffa and Haifa (see advertisement for McCormick machines, Figure 4), or assembled, adapted and, toward the end of the period, manufactured in Palestine.

The Templars instituted rational, intensive farming using irrigation and fertilizers (unknown to Arab *fellahin*), and regular crop rotation, including green fodder such as clover, which enabled feeding cattle in barns and stimulated the development of dairy farming. They planted vineyards for wine production, and also introduced improved strains of animals and plants, and methods of disease and pest control.

The agricultural school at Miqve Yisrael concentrated on orchards, dairy farming and European vegetable gardening using modern machinery. It experimented with different crops (avocado, eucalyptus trees, grapefruit) and developed an advanced agricultural industry (wine, dairy, vegetable and fruit processing) (Avitsur 1984: 235–46). Besides providing an agricultural education, the school aimed to introduce modern technology into Palestine by means of trained technicians (Penslar 1991: 15–25). However, the early Jewish *moshavot* could not afford modern technology and adopted inexpensive, simple tools. They engaged in traditional agricultural dry-farming practices – mainly of grain crops. When Baron Rothschild of Paris became involved in the Jewish settlements in the 1880s, he tried by means of his administrators and experts to inculcate contemporary technical, social and cultural French concepts for the creation of an ideal Jewish farmer community in the *moshavot*. This was done through heavy capital investment in advanced technological know-how (systematic fertilization, spraying against pests and diseases, thinning of orchards, and improvement of harvesting methods) and modern European machinery (pumps, mechanized plows, reapers, threshers, steam engines), in order to develop intensive commercial agriculture based on monoculture of wine-grapes (Aaronsohn 1993: 1–14). By the 1890s and the beginning of the twentieth century, the Jewish agricultural sector tended towards diversification and modern mixed farming – the introduction of new species and expansion of citrus groves, almond, olive and mulberry plantations, and dairy and poultry farms. Modern machines and packing machinery were imported from the US and Europe.

Plate 5 Mansion on the Zarghania estate in the northern Sharon Plain – one of many built in the 1870s by absentee landlords on their estates (photograph Kark 1985)

From the little we know about Arab agrotechnology it seems that it remained mostly traditional, with no intensification or development of an agricultural infrastructure. However, there was an expansion of cultivated areas and extensive planting of citrus and olive groves in selected areas (Schölch 1981: 47). It was chiefly the Arab entrepreneurial absentee landlord class that adopted some innovations in the cultivation of their newly-acquired estates from the 1870s on (Plate 5).

Waterworks

The opening of the Suez Canal in 1869 greatly stimulated international shipping in the eastern Mediterranean. One of the effects this had on Palestine was increased demand for Jaffa oranges in Europe, which was the prime moving force behind the 'water revolution' which permitted intensive agriculture, and the expansion of citrus groves and irrigated gardens. The area of citrus groves grew from a few hundred dunams (1 dunam = 1,000 square meters, or ca a quarter of an acre) at the beginning of the nineteenth century, to 30,000 dunams in 1914 – in the Jerusalem province alone. With European equipment it was now possible to drill down to a depth of 100 m and to pump the water up through pipes, instead of digging 10–12 m wells. The traditional noria water-raising wheel operated by draft animals which could provide about 5 cubic meters of water an hour was improved from the mid-nineteenth century. From 1897, larger buckets and iron gears were operated by oil engines (3–5 hp) to raise 16–24 cubic meters of water an hour. Later, vertical force pumps of two or three cylinders operated by oil engines or suction coal-gas motors (7–15 hp) were able to raise 25–60 cubic meters per hour. From a detailed report in 1908, it seems that 50 percent of the oil suction engines in the vicinity of Jaffa came from one firm (Hornsby) in England, 45 percent from one German firm (probably Deutz) and 5 percent from other firms, mostly English. The norias cost $140–$200

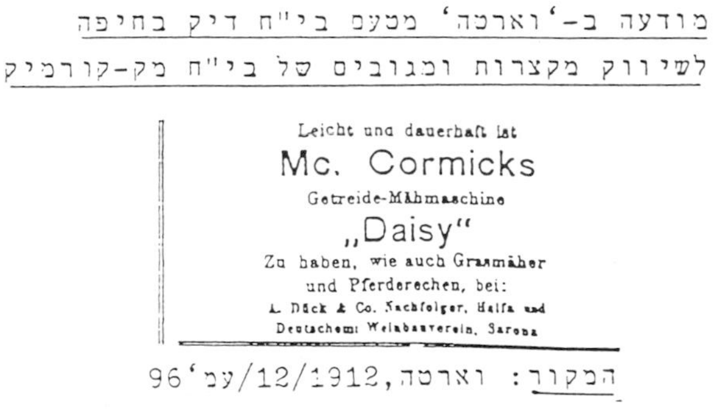

מודעה ב-'ווארטה' מטעם בי"ח דיק בחיפה
לשיווק מקצרות ומגובים של בי"ח מק-קורמיק

Leicht und dauerhaft ist

Mc. Cormicks

Getreide-Mähmaschine

„Daisy"

Zu haben, wie auch Grasmäher
und Pferderechen, bei:
L. Dück & Co. Nachfolger, Haifa und
Deutschem Weinbauverein, Sarona

המקור: ווארטה ,1912/12/ עמ' 96

Figure 4 An advertisement for McCormick reapers, rakes, mowers and harvesters in *Die Warte des Tempels*, the newspaper of the German Templars (source: *Warte* 1912. 12: 96)

and the pumps $500–$1,065. Two local firms in Jaffa (the Jewish Leon Stein Co. and the German Wagner Brothers) handled all the business, stocked spare parts, and assured customer confidence (Avitsur 1977b: 113–20; Wallace 1908: 69–73). These factories, which opened in Jaffa in 1888 and 1890 respectively, imported, assembled, adapted and developed irrigation facilities, and played a central role in the diffusion of these innovations not only in Palestine but also in Lebanon, Syria, Transjordan and Egypt (Kark 1990c: 258; Thalmann 1991: 169–70; Figure 4). In 1910 there were in Palestine over 500 oil engines employed in pumping water for irrigation (Great Britain 1917: 63–4). The Jewish and German settlers were the first to introduce large-scale improvements in irrigation infrastructure. According to Ruppin, the diffusion of this technology was relatively rapid: 'lately the natives have followed the example of the Palestinian [Jewish] colonies and have used suction pumps and kerosene coal-gas motors' (Ruppin 1918: 25–6). This was accompanied by the use of iron pipes and improved cement-lined irrigation channels.

Industry

Industry did not play a very important role in the economic life of Palestine before 1914. Only 10–15 percent of the population in the Levant lived from industries and trades – mostly home manufactures. In all of Syria, Lebanon and Palestine there were not more than 100 industrial enterprises with more than 50 workers in a single factory, and hardly a dozen employing more than 100 (Ruppin 1918: 46).

The information we have regarding growth and technological change in Palestine is erratic and fragmentary. From the sources available, which may be biased, it seems that the pioneers in this sphere were again the German urban settlers, British and French Jewish philanthropists, and indigenous and immigrant Jews. Most capitalists and entrepreneurs among the local Arabs and the long-established minority groups preferred to invest in other sectors of the economy, mainly due to their

lack of technological experience and their reluctance to become involved in risk-taking (Gross 1977: 53–7). The few industrial establishments equipped with modern machinery were agriculture-related. According to Ruppin's economic survey of Syria, including the Lebanon and Palestine (Ruppin 1918: 46–54),

> Only a few mills, machine factories and silk spinning establishments may be considered factories in the technical sense. Many of the chief industries are in the hands of Europeans, especially machine factories and mechanical workshops (Germans, Jews), silk spinning establishments (French), and mills (Germans and Levantines). The trades and the peculiarly Syrian industries are almost exclusively in the hands of natives.

In the production of olive oil and soap, both for local use and export, iron screw-presses began to replace the traditional wooden presses, and later, hydraulic presses came into use. In the Jerusalem and Jaffa areas hydraulic presses were introduced in two Jewish factories for producing sesame oil. Milling for local consumption was one of the more progressive industries. In the middle of the nineteenth century windmills were built in several towns, such as in Jerusalem (by Montefiore, Armenians, Greeks; see Plate 3) to be replaced by treadmills and steam engines (in 1869, by Z. Lewin) and, from the turn of the century, by coal-gas motors (Avitsur 1976: ix–xvi). Modern wine cellars for export were established first by the German Templars and then, in 1890 and 1892, by Baron Rothschild in two Jewish *moshavot* – Rishon le-Zion and Zikhron Ya'aqov. These wineries were equipped with the best and most modern technical means of the time (steam engines of 80 and 200 hp, internal combustion engines, electricity, telephone) and employed experts brought over from Europe. These two wine cellars, which are still operating today, were the largest and most advanced industrial plants, not only in Palestine, but in the whole eastern Mediterranean region (Aaronsohn 1993: 7–9). A large up-to-date glass factory was built in 1890 by Baron Rothschild in Tantura, south of Haifa, where bottles were to be produced for the wineries (Ruppin 1918: 52).

European styles of architecture, and new building materials and technologies were introduced in parts of the old cities and in their new European sections, and also in the new Jewish and German agricultural colonies. They revolutionized the building industry in a virtually tree-less country. It began with the importation of lumber from Europe and Asia Minor for doors, windows, door and window frames, and came to include rooftiles from Marseilles (Plate 6), iron in all forms and dimensions, tempered steel girders and rails, pipes and metal of all types, German and British tin plate, glass, Portland cement, and assorted building fixtures and materials (Glass and Kark 1991: 153, 161). The import of cement, from 1890, and European machines permitted local manufacture of

Plate 6 Marseilles rooftile commonly used in the towns and in the German and Jewish settlements (source: YIBZ)

Plate 7 The Jerusalem railway station at the end of the nineteenth century (source: Shiloni Collection)

floortiles, sewer components, water conduits, railings, cornices, stairs, and building blocks (Wallace 1910a: 54–63). This industry in Jaffa, Haifa, Tiberias and Jerusalem was mostly in Jewish and German hands. Before the War broke out, a silicate brick factory was being set up in Jaffa (Ruppin 1918: 49).

The traditionally important textile and dyeing industries, mainly located in the southern part of the country (Majdal, Gaza), remained relatively backward in scope and technology, but even they adopted and used cotton yarn imported from Manchester for weaving (Gross 1977: 53–7; Ruppin 1918: 46–7). Baron Rothschild opened a silk processing plant in Rosh Pinna which was in operation in 1895–1905 (Glass 1991: 83–94).

Apart from the industrial branches enumerated above, many small and experimental factories were started from the 1880s onwards – most of them by European residents, again Germans and Jews in particular. Some of these were quite successful (modern printing presses, macaroni, ice, soda water, furniture) while others (weaving, matches, rooftiles, bricks) failed.

Transport, communications, personal consumption

During the nineteenth century, modern transport technologies and infrastructure were introduced into Palestine – steamships (from the 1830s), wheelbarrows (1840s), animal-drawn wheeled vehicles (1860s), and trains (1892) (Plate 7). In the years immediately preceding World War I a few automobiles had also made their appearance, and plans were afoot to develop motor- and electrically-powered transport. The network of roads and railways was extended, travel time was shortened, and the level of service improved. This entailed sizable financial investments which, however, cannot be estimated with any precision. After a trial period, the railways and roads proved to be quite profitable enterprises, and provided

employment not only to those directly connected with them but also to many others in ancillary and technical services (Kark 1990a: 57–76).

A new postal system in Turkey in 1834, and permits obtained by Austria and France to provide postal services in the principal cities of Turkey's Asiatic provinces in 1837, together with the developments in transport much improved the mails in Palestine from the 1840s on. The Ottoman Government operated international and local post offices in almost every large city in Palestine (Acre, Haifa, Safed, Tiberias, Nablus, Jerusalem, Jaffa, Gaza). Foreign post offices were opened in the large cities by the European nations: Austria and France in 1852, Russia in 1856, Germany in 1898, and Italy in 1908. They provided more reliable service and facilitated family and social contacts and transfers of money from Europe to the local Jewish community in the Holy Land. In 1865 the country was connected to the new Ottoman telegraph network. By 1914 regular telegraph service was available between Palestine and the neighboring countries, as well as with Europe and America. An efficient postal and telegraph system had a positive direct bearing on economic and commercial life (Kark 1990c: 217–20).

Baron Rothschild was one of the first to introduce, in 1896/7, electricity, for lighting, and a telephone into Palestine. In 1910 there was also a private telephone line in Jerusalem and four electric plants – in two hotels, a French convent and a German sanatorium. The American consul believed that many more telephones would have been installed, had they not been prohibited by the government which intended to install a telephone system in all the cities of Turkey (Wallace 1910b: 236–8). On the eve of World War I, plans (including one by the Anglo-Palestine Bank) were made to produce electricity for lighting and power, and telephone networks, but they began to materialize only in the 1920s (Plate 8).

Select sections of the population of the country

Plate 8 The Anglo–Palestine Bank in the Old City of Jerusalem before 1914 (source: JMA: 10519)

experienced changes in their lifestyle, tastes, and consumption habits. A few random examples illustrate these innovations: European clothing fashions and furniture, sewing machines (1880s), typewriters (1890s), magic-lantern projectors (1890s), phonographs (1897). In June 1900 the first cinematograph film was projected in Jerusalem and in 1908 the first movie house opened in the Holy City. New, diversified and improved food products became available: fine white flour, potatoes, tomatoes, oats, coffee. Many clocks and clock-towers were added to public buildings, symbolizing the changing times (see Plate 2; Eliav 1978: 247–8). Architecture and construction were among the most conspicuous spheres to be influenced by new concepts of physical planning and by new technologies, mostly imported. New neighborhoods and suburbs, and modern and better buildings were constructed in the towns and some rural settlements, changing the built-up landscape of the country.

Conclusion

On the eve of World War I and the end of Ottoman rule in Palestine, the country had not yet joined the industrial revolution. About 80 percent of its population remained rural and pre-industrial with traditional social and economic structures. We accept, at least at the present stage of research, that Gottheil's model (1980: 1–35, and see below) for the Fertile Crescent is relevant to that majority sector of the population in Palestine in 1914, and even in 1921, after the War (Metzer 1982: 1–23).

However, several new studies on nineteenth-century Palestine (Glass and Kark 1991, Gross 1977; Schölch 1981; Shamir 1986) indicate that from the 1830s on, the country had already begun on its path toward development, growth and modernization. Figure 3, prepared by the author, sums up in a simplified manner

some interrelationships of these elements of change. This trend was motivated by forces operating at the international, imperial Ottoman and local levels. It was led by the advanced minority sector of the population which was also the main one to enjoy its fruits. These were the people who effected the technological transfer described in this chapter. Due to the cultural and religious uniqueness of Palestine in the nineteenth century, and the weight of non-economic factors, the geographic relocation of technology discussed by Headrick (1988: 3–17) was followed by its cultural diffusion in select groups. The relocation and diffusion of Western innovations reflected these culture groups, and their beliefs and ideologies – Christian missionaries and settlers from America and Germany; Jewish philanthropists and settlers from Europe; local and foreign capitalist entrepreneurs. This sector in itself was very heterogeneous, and each cultural group was spatially segregated in its separate agricultural settlements or urban neighborhoods.

The main spheres of technological change, and some of its impacts have been mentioned above. It is difficult to evaluate the effect of the town people involved in local industries, trades and crafts, on the indigenous rural population. The trend to an export-import economy that characterized Palestine toward the end of the nineteenth century did not lead to the destruction of local trades and industries (if we may call them industries), as is commonly described in the literature on nineteenth-century Palestine and Syria. The findings of our study do not bear this out. Indeed, apart from a few select branches, the trend seems to have had rather the opposite effect. In the coastal towns there was a considerable expansion of handicrafts in the second half of the nineteenth century, despite the imports of cotton products and wool cloth. The importation of European products, such as motors and machinery, contributed to the development of new branches in handicrafts and industry (Kark 1990b: 83).

It was under the British Mandate, in the period 1921–1936, that the traditional Arab sector experienced fast and wide-ranging growth in output and productivity generated by technological progress (Metzer 1982: 1–23). It took fifty more years for the Bedouin tribe of Arab esh-Shibly, which led a nomadic existence in Galilee until about forty years ago and is now permanently settled at Mount Tabor, to install personal computers in the local kindergarten and have their children busily working on them. Another example which helps to illustrate the diffusion of modern technologies in the region is drip irrigation: Israeli drip irrigation systems are now common in the West Bank and have contributed to the striking agricultural settlement development in the Kingdom of Jordan. As seen in this chapter, the control, manipulation, and acceptance or rejection of technological change has played a key role in shaping different societies in Palestine and the eastern Mediterranean.

STAGES IN THE PROCESS OF SPATIAL CHANGE IN PALESTINE 1800–1914

From the point of view of settlement, the generalized process of spatial change in nineteenth-century Palestine can be divided into three subperiods as illustrated in Figure 1.1. When studying this period one must keep in mind the basic physical structure of the country comprising four longitudinal subregions paralleling the Mediterranean coastline: the coastal plains; the hills regions (the Negev in the south, Judea and Samaria in the central part, and the Galilee in the north — rising to about 700 m elevation on average); the Jordan Valley (including the Dead Sea and the Sea of Galilee — part of the Great Rift Valley); and the mountains of Transjordan in the east (see Chapters 3 and 4, this volume).

During the first three decades of the nineteenth century, the settlement situation in Palestine was characterized by a process of decline and stagnation, which had affected the entire Ottoman Empire since the seventeenth century (see Figure 1.1, Section 1). The total population of the country did not exceed 250,000. The settled rural population was mainly confined to the mountainous areas of Judea-Samaria and the Galilee and was too small to cultivate all the available land. Bedouin tribes controlled most of the plains, valleys and arid areas, including the coastal plains, the Jordan Valley and the Negev in the south. Thus only a small part of the country was cultivated. At the beginning of the nineteenth century the towns of Palestine were at best large villages, each occupying a small area and having a limited economic base and a small population of up to 10,000.

The Ottoman Government and its officials were not strong enough to impose security and order in either the mountainous rural areas or marginal regions of the desert in the east and south. The former were ruled by independent local chieftains, fighting each other for supremacy, and the latter were controlled by Bedouin tribes. The endemic internal warfare between the local chiefs and periodic raids by the nomadic tribes harmed the economy, and sometimes caused the destruction or total desertion of villages and even of entire regions.

Such conditions presented great difficulties in the registration of land, which in turn precluded the obtaining of secure titles. Although it was possible at that time to settle in the unpopulated areas (which were nominally state lands) and cultivate them, there was no security of title or ownership. The expansion of settled areas in Palestine began only in the second third of the nineteenth century. In this second subperiod (1831–1881), new patterns were beginning to emerge (see Figure 1.1, Section 2) characterized by:

1. The expansion of the rural population from the small core area to peripheral regions where settlement had not been possible until then.
2. The penetration of settlers and entrepreneurs from outside Palestine, both to peripheral regions and areas close to the towns and to the towns themselves. This group included Muslims and native Christians from Syria and Lebanon, Egypt, North Africa; non-Arab Muslims from Turkey and other parts of the Ottoman Empire — mainly Bosnians, Circassians; agents of the Sultan's private investments; and representatives of Christian Churches and religious orders, along with private Christians and Jews who came independently — mostly from Europe, although there were also some from America.
3. The partial retreat of the Bedouins, which paralleled these processes of settlement, was connected with the changes in the Ottoman regime beginning in the nineteenth century.

James Finn, the British consul in Jerusalem in 1851, gives us an interesting if somewhat biased description of the state of the country, attesting to the progress taking place in Palestine. He speaks of 'the extension of agriculture, . . . the rebuilding of villages from utter heaps of desolation, and the improvement of others which have not ceased to be inhabited.' He also noticed that 'the sudden rise of the little town of Chiffa [Haifa, R.K.] is very remarkable.' Other towns, and especially Jerusalem and Jaffa, were also beginning to develop rapidly at this time.

The end of the nineteenth and the beginning of the twentieth century were a time of marked increase in the development of the country (see Figure 1.1, Section 3). The population grew, and the settled rural area expanded along with a major increase in the agricultural output.

There was a movement of the rural population from the hill areas to settling in the plains, valleys and on the fringes of the desert. It became a common practice to establish new villages on old ruins. Yet, despite these developments, of the total area of western Palestine (26.3 million square kilometers), only ten percent was under cultivation in 1895.

At the same time, urban entrepreneurs (absentee landlords known as 'effendis') originating from Palestine and Syria, Lebanon and adjacent regions, were concentrating huge tracts of land in their hands. These holdings sometimes amounted to hundreds of thousands of dunams (1 acre = 4.047 dunams). An outstanding example of this type of entrepreneur is Sursuk, a Greek from Beirut, who acquired approximately 250,000 dunams in Palestine. By the end of the Ottoman period, 144 big landowners controlled 3.1 million dunams. While their main motive was economic, the effendis also settled tenants on their land and sometimes tried to reclaim or develop waste tracts.

Ownership and control by effendis of areas which were not settled previously made possible the purchase and settlement of part of this land by Jewish immigrants from Europe. The Jewish settlement effort succeeded despite attempts of the Ottoman regime to prevent it. Besides the Jews and Christians, other small ethnic and religious groups settled in Palestine at the end of the nineteenth century. The Bahais, for example, fled from Persia and settled in the Haifa-Acre area and in the Jordan Valley.

The Ottoman Government and Sultan were involved in an effort to bring large deserted tracts of land under state control. The Sultan demonstrated his intention to develop the state lands by building roads and other public works, founding new towns in his holdings (such as Beit Shean and Beersheva), and by subduing the Bedouin tribes, or trying to settle them. In order to generate income, part of the state land was sold to effendis, officials or foreign settlers.

Compared to the rural areas, the towns developed at a faster pace. The urban population increased from an estimated 18 percent of the total in 1800, to 27 percent in 1882, and to 38 percent in 1907. This population growth correlated with the expansion of the built-up area — some of it in modern neighborhoods and new suburbs — and the development of the urban economy.

(Based on Kark 1984: 183–96.)

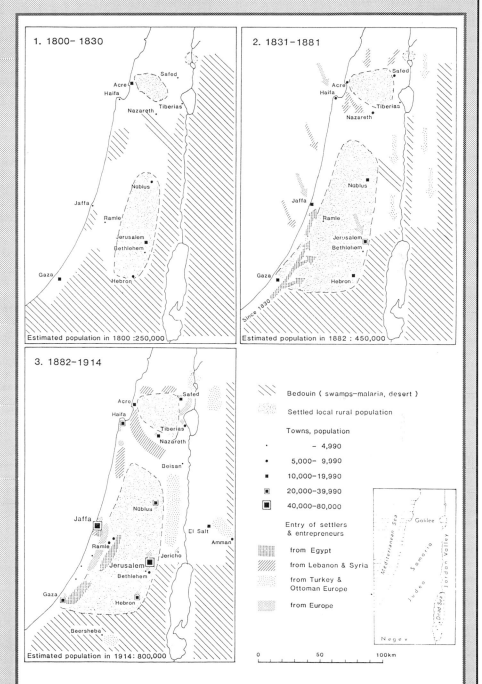

Figure 1.1   The process of spatial change in Palestine, 1800–1914 (source: Kark 1984)

INTERNATIONAL MARKETING INQUIRIES IN PALESTINE 1908–1914

Although it was but a small corner of the Ottoman Empire, Palestine was a potentially important market in the region because of its growing European population. The consuls of the European powers and of the United States in Jerusalem, and the consular agents in Haifa — and especially in Jaffa, which was becoming an important port city of the eastern Mediterranean — made efforts to foster their nations' economic interests by collecting information and reporting to their governments on commercial activities. But there were also direct contacts between companies, commercial houses, and industrial establishments and their respective consular representatives in Palestine for names and referrals to reliable local businessmen who may qualify as commercial agents, and who could be entrusted to accept consignments of goods and merchandise on credit.

During the second half of the nineteenth century, the American consuls in Jerusalem and Beirut usually restricted themselves to reporting to the Department of State and to other governmental departments. A change came about in 1909–1914 as a result of a real turn of interest in the American Government and business community regarding the Ottoman Empire, including Palestine, as a potential market for its products. It was probably no coincidence that it occurred with the inception of 'dollar diplomacy' during the Taft administration. This appears from a detailed analysis of a large amount of relevant material in the archives of the United States consulate in Jerusalem and in the Haifa and Jaffa consular agencies. In these repositories are found hundreds of letters from American firms (see Figure 2.1), including catalogs, descriptions, and price lists of various products manufactured or handled by them; questions regarding local market conditions, supply and demand, and marketing possibilities in different fields; as well as queries about local businessmen and commercial houses that could represent American firms, and about their reputations and the scope of their activities.

This archival material is important not only for a better understanding of the frameworks for developing foreign trade in the American economy, and of the functions and contribution of the consuls to this end, but also for illustrating the penetration and diffusion of new products and technologies to underdeveloped parts of the world, and how it influenced changes in economic activity of these regions. From over 200 letters in the archives of the Jaffa consular agency for the years 1909–1914, and over 150 such requests in the Jerusalem consular archives for 1908–1914, a picture emerges regarding the types of products and the places from which marketing outlets were sought. The main categories were:

- agriculture (farm machinery, engines, pumps, as well as agricultural produce and animals, and/or means for processing and marketing, such as mill machinery, packing paper and boxes for citrus fruits, incubators, etc.);

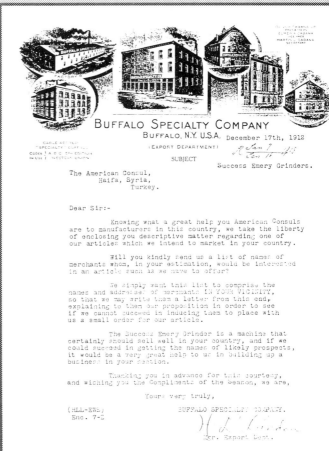

Figure 2.1 A marketing inquiry in 1913 from Buffalo to the American consul in Haifa for the sale of Success Emery Grinders (source: USNA RG84 C38/5991)

- industry (machinery and tools);
- raw materials, minerals, and construction (lead, cement, coal, steel);
- energy, transport, and communications (petroleum, electrical equipment, locomotives, electric vehicles, bicycles, boats, telegraph lines, wireless equipment);
- insurance and manpower services;
- pharmaceutical and medical services;
- music, entertainment and culture (musical instruments, moving pictures, books);
- office equipment (writing supplies, typewriters);

- food products (canned preserves, powdered foods);
- household (furniture, ice boxes, cutlery);
- footwear, clothing, and personal equipment (wigs, razors, watches);
- miscellaneous.

The letters came from different states and cities in and outside the United States and from Europe and the Middle East (Figure 2.2).

(Based on Kark 1994)

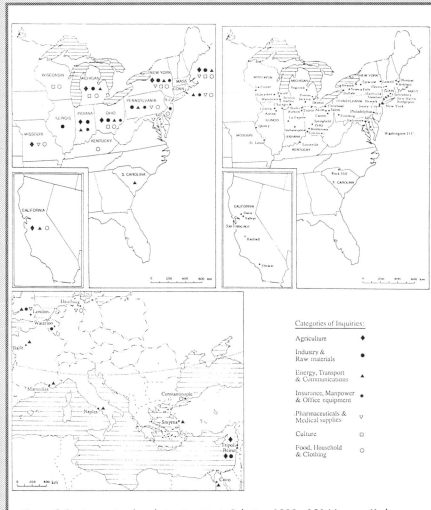

Figure 2.2 International marketing inquiries in Palestine, 1908–1914 (source: Kark, *American Consuls*: 315–6)

32

CONCLUSION: A MASS IN CELEBRATION OF THE CONFERENCE

Norman Yoffee

I hope that it will not be taken as merely irreverent if I present this discussion of the conference[1] in the form of a Mass. In the *Kyrie* I ask mercy on the humble supplicant/discussant; the *Gloria* gives thanks to the sainted patron of this conference, Fernand Braudel and to the nineteen symposiasts who graciously sent their papers to me in time for me to compose this commentary: thanks for your faxes, fed-exes, and uploaded e-mailed files. In the *Credo* I affirm my commitment to the Comparative Method and to the principle of conjoining of archaeology and history that is exemplified so well in so many of the papers. My most critical comments are only that there may be more and perhaps some different sorts of comparisons, and that disciplinary boundaries need to be further broken down. The *Sanctus* is dedicated to our paragon of archaeological hosts, Tom Levy: the idea and execution of the conference have been splendid and could only be done by one connected intimately with powers higher than those to which I have access – specifically, Richard E. Friedman and the collected notables in the UCSD chancellery and deanery and Mr. C. Paul Johnson. The *Benedictus* naturally sings a Hosanna to the progress made in the last days.

Kyrie

According to Sir Isaiah Berlin there is an excellent Hebrew prayer to be uttered when seeing a monster: 'Blessed be the Lord our God who introducest variety amongst Thy creatures'. This prayer of mercy is certainly appropriate for a discussant who is beset by the 'monstrous' task of assimilating information from year dot to 1917 in the bit of earth called in the papers variously The Holy Land, Palestine, Jordan, Syro-Palestine, the southern Levant, Canaan, and sometimes even (ancient) Israel and all possible hyphenated versions of the above. This confusion doubtless reflects the parlous state of political affairs in the region today. All of the 'geographic' terms seem fine for some periods and all are horribly and anachronistically wrong for others; I have no intention of sorting them out except for the term 'Holy Land': this designation can only further ghettoize the study of Region X from its place in Departments of Religion, Anthropology, or even Near

Eastern Studies (that is, Western Asian studies, of course. In the old film, *The Mole People*, celluloid Sumerians regarded *their* 'Holy Land' as Tibet! – which is an eminently reasonable 'Holy Land', if not for the Sumerians).

I was quite surprised when Tom asked me to be discussant of this symposium but I recognized the organizer's syndrome: find an outsider to keep the insiders honest; that is, it is hoped that the presence of an outsider will make the insiders speak to an audience larger than the initiated brethren and sistren. Outsiders are also thought to be able to identify area or disciplinary biases that are less visible to insiders. Sometimes the procedure works well and the discussion stirs up useful commentary. The trade-off can be, however, that the discussant is so distant from the action that he/she never quite gets the point and writes something hopelessly mired in his/her own area's problems and intellectual boundaries. I ask your assembled mercy for the exceeding modest comments I have and for the disproportionately long time it will take to make them.

Finally in this *Kyrie*, I ask Tom Levy's specific forgiveness, since I do not intend to do the one thing he has specifically charged me to do, that is to 'synthesize' the papers; and I also cannot accept his description (in the circulars preceding the conference and in his generous introduction of me) of the task, or of myself certainly, as 'Herculean'. No one can, or should, try to synthesize these papers: the attempt would be hubristic and the result would only trivialize the hard-won insights that have been presented. Although I shall say something about the ultra-*longue-durée*, as I am required to do, it will not be a synthesis. I also eschew the description of the task of commenting on the papers as 'Herculean', because that term might evoke the image of one of Hercules' labors, namely cleaning out the Augean Stables – and I do not regard the symposiasts as dropping anything so fragrant in La Jolla that it needs discussing away. Lord have mercy upon me.

Gloria

We are gathered to pay homage to the spectre of Braudel which looms over this conference. According to Levy and

Jebel Mussa and St. Catherine's in the central Sinai (photograph: Werner Braun)

Holl, the *Annales* perspective of the 'long duration' represents a 'new approach to the past' because it is through the fundamental conditions imposed by geology, geography, and climate that events and structures are given meaning. Taking a long look at a region's prehistory and history is also supported because it demands genuine interdisciplinary research. Interdisciplinary does not mean simply that an archaeologist should employ a botanist to appraise pollen or send a charcoal sample to a physicist for radiocarbon dating. Rather, one must use all possible resources – as the remarkable trinity of Goldberg, Smith, and Grigson have demonstrated – from as many disciplines as are pertinent in order to understand the historical nature of social relations. Social organization and change are dependent – the trendy word is 'contingent' – on a past that 'agents' reproduced, reacted against, and otherwise used to mold the present; and, of course, the past was and is itself continuously shaped and interpreted by human actors in the historical present. In the recent history of archaeology, of course, this is a modernist, almost post-modernist view, and it is to be contrasted explicitly with the so-called 'New Archaeology'. That archaeological school, founded in the heady days of the 1960s, in which positivism, functionalism, ecological adaptationism, systems theory, and unilinear evolutionsim flourished, is now regarded as an intellectual embarrassment in the history of the archaeology. We have absorbed certain of New (or processual) Archaeology's contributions – mainly the attention to research design and quantitative methods – and have jettisoned most of the rest, especially the misguided rejection of historical method. In this context, espousal of the *longue durée* is certainly praiseworthy and perhaps even a 'new approach'.

The *Annales* perspective and its interdisciplinary emphasis also holds that disciplinary territorialism cannot be allowed to control the process of analysis. Since we cannot assume that technical analyses represent unassailable truth, especially when they defy archae-ological and historical logic, scientists must be integrated within the interpretive processes of archaeology and history. Archaeology, thus, is not merely a technique of how to get things from the ground and it is no more free from intellectual bias, as Silberman has shown, than textual analysis. Indeed, the fun of archaeology is that it is a quintessentially integrative endeavor, as much concerned with *mentalités* as it is with pots. From my outsider's purview, it has always seemed odd that those self-styled 'Syro-Palestinian' archaeologists who condemn the term 'Biblical Archaeology' most vociferously are just the ones who know how to employ the complicated layers of the Biblical text to best effect! – none better than Bill Dever, the *Biblical Archaeology Review*'s Prince of Darkness. Indeed, in modern anthropological archaeology, the growth fields are ideology and historical archaeology and these are the fields in which Region X archaeologists

are spectacularly well placed to make contributions. That ideology is not necessarily limited to historical periods is shown in Gopher's suggestion that actors in the PNA were consciously recovering from the crisis at the end of the seventh millennium BCE. But I suppose that one person's 'Biblical Archaeology' may be hopelessly retrogressive (say, in ASOR meetings) while another's 'Biblical Archaeology' is moving into the vanguard of latest archaeological research (for example, at the SAA or AAA, or in this volume with Bunimovitz's and Stager's chapters).

In the required perspective of the *longue durée*, it seems to me that there are three themes that can be identified as underlying social organization and change in ancient Palestine/Israel: diversity, scale, and foreign impact (aka exogenous change, diffusion). All three can be sub-stantively separated although they cannot be sealed in analytical tunnels. Since it is not my task to repeat to you what the papers have already made clear, I shall be brief in this *Gloria* about diversity, while adding a few comments on foreign impact. I will reserve comments on scale for the *Credo*.

As nearly as I can tell, almost every paper I read refers to the diversity of the region. I do not believe this is due to a desire to read modern concerns with multiculturalism into the past; rather, it reflects something – dare I say? – Braudellian. Danin and Goldberg discuss the region's 'high geographic richness and diversity', its extremes of zonation in a relatively small area, its 'high numbers of plant species'; Gilead notes 'impressive techno-typological variety' among simple Upper Paleolithic foragers; Goring-Morris claims to identify niches and specific groups of people in the Epipaleolithic and Valla did so easily for the Natufian; Levy talks of 'regionalism' and the classically structural contradiction between the production of elite goods for interregional exchange and the local regulation of common resources and the management of risk; Finkelstein pluralizes dimorphism (rightly, in my estimation); many see the region as a land of villages (I'll return to that topic in the *Credo*); Ilan and Finkelstein, with fabulously rich data, isolate different behaviors in lowlands, highlands, steppelands, the social isolation of small communities, the marginality of much of the land; Holladay cites 'broken highland and dissected slopes'; Anderson delineates the amalgamation of various motifs of differing religious orientations on tombs; Whitcomb stresses 'zones of conflict of increasing intensity'. Social groups/orientations include the following: Neanderthals and Sapiens (perhaps these are biological orientations), Canaanites, Israelites, Romans, Arameans, Amonites, Moabites, Edomites, Phoenicians, Sea Peoples, Philistines, Greeks, Persians, Franks, Assyrians, Byzantines, Arabs, Ottomans – and this is only a partial list.

Some of the folk listed above, of course, must be booked under foreign impact, as well as under diversity. The most serious and consistent of the peoples that impacted the region, at least in the early historic periods, were the Egyptians – the King Kong of foreign influences on ancient Palestine/Israel/the Levant. While no one in this conference dealt thoroughly with the theme of Egytian impact, it seems that many considered Egypt to have been a 'constraint on growth' of stratification and the state in ancient Israel/Palestine in the early historical period.

Let me close the *Gloria* with this hymn of praise to Braudel: the slow rhythms of the 'histoire de la longue durée' in Palestine/Ancient Israel enfold diverse, competing social corporations and political and economic strategies, played out in a forbidding or at least formidable environment. Themes of small-group inclusiveness, uneasy alliances, and the conscious definition and exclusion of others tend to prevent regional integration – even given the small distances of the region.

Credo

Since I believe in the Comparative Method, I intend to do some comparing. Not all comparisons, however, are created equal. Thus, while it is refreshing that many of the 'new approaches to the archaeology of the Holy Land' (ed. note: this was the original title of the symposium) explicitly recognize sacred principles of comparison, the employment of certain anthropologically archaeological concepts and terms requires controls. My brief comments (*obiter dicta* rather than extended analyses) on some of the concepts/terms raised in the papers – ruralization, peer-polity interaction, chiefdoms, city-states, and complexity – underscore the difficulties of using these terms. Indeed, in the most recent literature, there has been a severe reaction to the use of 'types' and 'categories' (see Paynter 1989, Bawden 1989) since these 'types' have tended to become 'essences', used by archaeologists as the end of analysis, rather than a step in doing research. Furthermore, anthropology must not be regarded as some mine from which ethnographic analogies can be uncritically chipped out by archaeologists and 'operationalized' to explain the past (see Yoffee and Sherratt 1993). In fact, archaeology is held to deal with the sorts of problems and kinds of societies for which no ethnographic analogy may be appropriate. Many of the ideas in the conference's papers are especially interesting precisely because they are built from specific archaeological and historical analysis, and do not rely on over-generalized and essentialized categories. I single out some of these ideas and return to the point in my concluding *Benedictus*.

If archaeology is not a subset of sociocultural anthropology, but an equivalent anthropological subfield, I think a brief history of comparative methodology in archaeological and social evolutionary theory is warranted: In the 1960s, as many sociocultural anthropologists were abandoning the comparative method (which in the 1990s

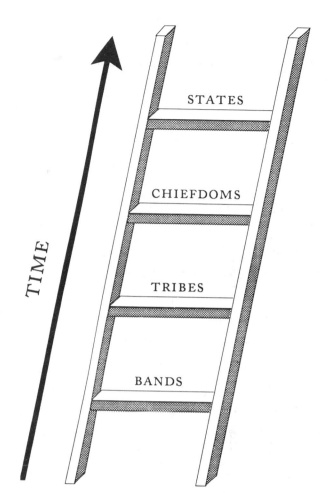

Figure 1 Evolutionary step-ladder

stands in little favor in Anthropology Departments, with the exceptions of the cultural ecologists and the HRAF-faithful), archaeologists, flushed with the fervor of 'New Archaeology', embraced the return to social evolutionary theory and a dogmatic belief in comparison, especially as taught by Leslie White at the University of Michigan. Briefly, the methodological notion, as enshrined in Sahlins' 1960 text, was that 'any representative of a given cultural stage is inherently as good as any other, whether the representative be contemporaneous and ethnographic or only archaeological.' Thus, the stage of 'chiefdom', as known from countless ethnographic descriptions, was supposed to precede the stage of the state (see Figure 1, drawn from Yoffee 1993a). When investigating the rise of the state, therefore, archaeologists could turn to a favorite account of the chiefdom (of course, there are lots of kinds of chiefdoms) and correlate (ideally) one or more central features with excavated material. In a process called 'inference', the archaeologist could then extrapolate the

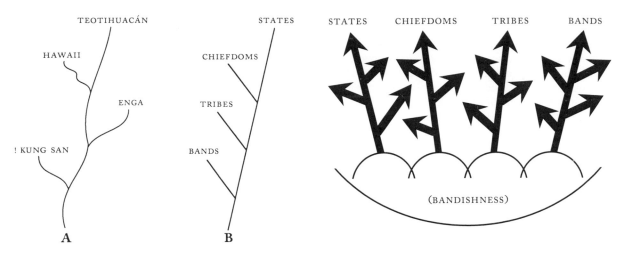

Figure 2   Our contemporary ancestors   **Figure 3**   Possible evolutionary trajectories

rest of the postulated characteristics of the state and so bring the not directly observable dimensions of ancient reality into view (Figure 2).

In recent years this use of the comparative method has been refuted. While all the arguments need not be rehearsed here, it may be important to note that they entail a complete reevaluation of the use of the comparative method in anthropological archaeology. If, as the argument goes (see Yoffee 1993a), there are various evolutionary trajectories, not simply a single step-ladder leading to the state on which all societies can be ranked (Figure 3), then no formative stage of a state-level society can be modelled according to any whole ethnographic example. Chiefdoms, for example, which assuredly do exist and are extremely variable, may not precede the state at all, but rather may be part of an alternate evolutionary trajectory to it. In 'new social evolutionary theory', the basis for cross-cultural analysis consists (in part) in comparing – and contrasting – trajectories of social change, not the projection into the archaeological record of ethnographic analogies jerked out of time, place and historical sequence.

Tom Levy's chapter, which uses the term chiefdom, I believe deserves wide distribution among archaeology's many chiefdom afficionados. Levy explicitly argues that Chalcolithic chiefdoms do *not* fall into an evolutionary stage that precedes states. This argument is similar to David Anderson's (1990) on the Mississippian of the American Southeast, in which a cycle (also discussed by Israel Finkelstein) of chiefdoms is delineated; I reckon that this cycle may hold for the Puebloan American Southwest as well. The point is that elaborated chiefdoms usually cycle back to less elaborated chiefdoms; this may be the syndrome of non-linear social change Gophna has discussed in his chapter. If this estimation of the Ancient Israel/Palestine situation is correct, and it has also been

argued in University of Arizona dissertations by Alexander Joffe (1993) and Steven Falconer (1987) for the MB and EB respectively, the archaeological world is going to have to pay increasing attention to evidence such as that presented by Tom Levy.

From this brief discussion of chiefdoms, it can be seen that in recontextualizing some categories which have been elevated to intellectual fetishes in social evolutionary theory, new insights can emerge. Certainly, we do not move forward by labelling Region X a 'chiefdom' at some point in time; rather, we need to characterize specific modes of production, orders of stratification, and ideological structures. I am not arguing against *any* use of categories and typologies; rather, having got a category, we must immediately unpack it, trace the variability within it, and proceed to more and better investigations. Simple declarations that x-residues fit an abstract, ideal type and thus can earn a typological name should not be considered a model of advanced thinking by Region X archaeologists newly ticketed on the good ship Anthropology.

Unpacking is also just what is needed in considering the terms 'city', 'city-state', and 'urbanism' which are used in many of the chapters dealing with early historical periods of ancient Israel/Palestine. Now, in a worldwide, comparative perspective it should be noted that all the earliest states (Mesopotamia, Indus Valley, China, Andes, Maya, Teotihuacan: the exception is Egypt, which is a regional state) are not states at all, they are city-states (although being city-states is not the only thing that can be said about them). In early Mesopotamia, for example, city-states are all autonomous, independent of larger regional authority (which occasionally does form, after which it collapses), they depend on a productive, adjacent hinterland, and they exist within a larger ideological boundary that can be called a 'civilization'. This 'civilization' is what makes Mesopotamia 'Mesopotamia' (or the Maya 'Maya'); that is, the Mesopotamian city-states may be considered part of 'Mesopotamia', not because there is any political boundary of Mesopotamia but because the concept of Mesopotamian civilization is culturally demarcated. Furthermore, in these Mesopotamian city-states, there are no totalitarian Asiatic Modes of Production, oriental despotisms, monolithic controllers of production, temple-states, or all-knowing, all-seeing bureaucratic apparatuses of any kind. There are rather various kinds of elites and social orientations; while craftsmen work for great estates, independent entrepreneurs contract with those same organizations (van de Mieroop 1992; Charpin 1982; Stol 1982; Yoffee 1993b). Social groups and their leaders struggle for dominion or independence within the city-states and the city-states with each other.

Two other terms that must be unpacked are 'collapse' and 'ruralism' (or 'ruralization'). Although archaeologists who study the evolution of early states have explained regions and regional hierarchies in terms of urban places, they have seldom meditated that cities are not simply superimpositions on a traditional and stable countryside. To be sure, comments have been made about change in rural communities but, it seems to me, these comments have been based largely on modern ethnographic analogies, usually drawn from fields such as development economics, and have not been rooted in empirical investigations on the nature of social organization and the reasons for change in the rural communities of the ancient states themselves.

In the earliest states (and especially in Mesopotamia, due to the pioneering settlement pattern research of Adams), it can be shown that rural communities are *made* rural; they are not relicts of past communities, 'building blocks' that are parts of a simpler state of nature, as it were, upon which cities, states, or city-states are erected. 'Ruralization' (a term I think I coined in an SAA symposium in 1986, and which has been discussed in ancient Israel/Palestine by Falconer and Joffe) is the evil twin of 'urbanization' – since the countryside is restructured through its relation to cities – and one cannot consider the two independently. In Palestine/Ancient Israel, the argument can be made (and has been made by Falconer and Joffe) that cities are 'collapses' from the rural normalcy in the region. That is, if collapse is not an end of anything and in fact usually leads to reformulation (see Yoffee and Cowgill 1988), it is cities in Palestine/Ancient Israel that are atypical and thus represent 'collapses' from the normal village-level organization of social and political life. 'Ruralization' in Mesopotamia is thus a different process than the one resulting in villages in Palestine/Ancient Israel; in fact, in urbanization there is the formal counterpart of ruralization in Mesopotamia. If Adams can dub Mesopotamia the

'Heartland of Cities' (Adams 1981), Falconer is justified in calling ancient Israel/Palestine the 'Heartland of Villages' (Falconer 1987).

I close this *Credo* with some really big and inspirational thoughts on the term 'complexity': *all* human social and cultural systems are complex – from hunter-gatherers, who have the most complex array of kinship categories and ceremonial life, to states that are riven in complex economic and political ways. It seems to me that 'complexity inflation' in archaeology (as in 'complex hunter-gatherers' or 'complex chiefdoms' or in this conference Gilead's reference to 'complex Neanderthals') has resulted from a confusion in which the complexities of recovery and analysis in modern scientific archaeology have become a shorthand for the complexity of social organization that is being studied. Naturally, we need to understand what kind of complexity – complex subsistence rounds, complex genealogical patterns, or complex, stratified societies – we might be dealing with; but let us eschew the inevitably value-laden oppositions of 'simple' vs 'complex' when dealing with different kinds of human complexity. Similarly, in considering 'peer-polity interaction', which was developed by Renfrew and Cherry (1986) for the polities of Greece and the Aegean, we can see that some 'peers' in some systems were not evolving at the same pace and in the same direction as others. Nowhere is this clearer than ancient Western Asia in which ancient Israel/Palestine is certainly not a 'peer' of its neighbors. I suspect that LaBianca's attempt to portray an alternate kind of complexity and a different set of peers to understand his data in Jordan may turn out in the end quite useful.

Sanctus

As can be seen from the above liturgical sections, I have composed a Mass of Celebration not a Requiem Mass: there is no *Lacrimosa* – weeping over the state of archaeology in Ancient Palestine/Israel here, no *Confutatis* – intention to confound the assembled experts, who have have had to endure these remarks which they may rightly consider do less than justice to their papers, and, most of all, there is no *Dies Irae*: my view is just the opposite.

If these papers show that Palestine/Ancient Israel is not an early state like Mesopotamia (or other early states), and I have argued consequently that categories like chiefdom, city-state and ruralism must be unpacked and historicized, disembedded from their associations with a now discredited old social evolutionary theory, the study of Palestine/Ancient Israel seems to me more relevant to mainstream academic enterprises, especially Anthropology, History, and Near Eastern Studies, than ever before.

Exactly as Shlomo Bunimovitz said at the conference, there is little theory that is appropriate for the analysis of small-states, village-based states, secondary states, or the constraints on growth of states and city-states. If comparison with the earliest states is to be guarded against, and for the most part resisted, one must insist that comparison also entails an appreciation of contrast and it is the specification of contrast that is that rarest of avises in social evolutionary theory. The future is bright for those archaeologists of Palestine/Ancient Israel who have the courage to halt being theory-consumers and to start becoming theory-providers.

I realize that I have said little about some periods and this is not only because I didn't get some papers in time to think about them or even because I'm utterly unqualified to appraise them: the clarity and skill of Whitcomb, Rosen-Ayalon, and Kark do not need my impertinences. But in my last nod to Braudel and his disciple Levy, I do wish to resume one point with which Silberman began the conference: if we are to take seriously the long perspective of history, we ancient folk need to look seriously at the excellent scholarship on Ottoman and Byzantine periods. By way of reference, one can observe in Adams' *Heartland of Cities* most clearly what is the shape and scale of ancient Mesopotamia by seeing just how different was a really centralized administration in the same area in Abbasid and Umayyad times, and especially how such centralization affected the environment in ways unthinkable to rulers in the more ancient past.

Benedictus

I do not think I need to remind you that one of the most traditional questions asked in God's Own Country is 'Why are things different there than in other countries?' The answer may be that while ancient Israel, Palestine, the Levant, Canaan, or whatever the region is called is different from the earliest states, and especially different from its neighbors Egypt and Mesopotamia, it is not necessarily different from all other societies. By using the impressive array of survey data, vast and continuing excavation projects, and unparalleled historical sources that have been assembled by talented, open-minded scholars (and especially now by younger scholars who are no longer compelled to fight the battles for and against 'Biblical Archaeology' that have always seemed so bizarre to outsiders), new approaches to the past will continue to flourish – in the Region we can't quite name, but which we love nonetheless, or which we would love, if it only could get its act together. *Hosanna in excelsis.*

Note

1. This chapter is a slightly revised version of my dsicussion presented in San Diego and I maintain much of the style of the oral presentation. It is based on reading of the papers sent to me and my notes on papers presented at the conference but which I did not receive. Note that the original title of the conference was 'Archaeology of the Holy Land: New Approaches to the Past'.

BIBLIOGRAPHY

Preface

Bennett, J.W. 1976. *The Ecological Transition: Cultural Anthropology and Human Adaptation.* New York: Pergamon.

Butzer, K. 1982. *Archaeology as Human Ecology: Method and Theory for a Contextual Approach.* London: Cambridge University Press.

Braudel, F. 1972. *The Mediterranean and the Mediterranean World in the Age of Phillip II* (revised edition, trans: S. Reynolds). London: Collins.

Clarke, D.L. 1978. *Analytical Archaeology* (Second Edition). London: Methuen & Co.

Dever, W.G. 1993. Biblical Archaeology: Death and Rebirth. In *Biblical Archaeology Today, 1990* (eds A. Biran and J. Aviram). Jerusalem: Israel Exploration Society, pp. 706–22.

Hodder, I. 1987. The Contextual Analysis of Symbolic Meanings. In *The Archaeology of Contextual Meanings* (ed. I. Hodder). Cambridge: Cambridge University Press, pp. 1–10.

Hodder, I. and Orton, C. 1976. *Spatial Analysis in Archaeology.* Cambridge: Cambridge University Press.

Holl, A. and Levy, T.E. 1993. *Spatial Boundaries and Social Dynamics – Case Studies from Food-Producing Societies.* Ann Arbor: International Monographs in Prehistory.

Johnson, A.W. and Earle, T. 1987. *The Evolution of Human Societies – From Foraging Group to Agrarian State.* Stanford: Stanford University Press.

Levy, T.E. 1993. Interdisciplinary Archaeological Research in Israel. In *Biblical Archaeology Today, 1990* (eds A. Biran and J. Aviram). Jerusalem: Israel Exploration Society, pp. 465–81.

Mazar, A. 1990. *Archaeology of the Land of the Bible, 10,000–586 BCE.* New York: Doubleday.

Stager, L.E. 1992. The Periodization of Palestine from Neolithic through Early Bronze Times. In *Chronologies in Old World Archaeology,* Third Edition (ed. R.W. Ehrich). Chicago: University of Chicago Press, pp. 22–41, 17–60.

Stern, E. (ed.) 1994. *The New Encyclopedia of Archaeological excavations in the Holy Land.* New York: Doubleday.

Stuiver, M. and Braziunas, T.F. 1993. Modeling Atmospheric 14C Influences and 14C Ages of Marine Samples to 10,000 BC. *Radiocarbon.* 35, 1: 137–89.

Tchernov, E. 1981. The biostratigraphy of the Levant. In *Préhistoire du Levant. Chronologie et Organisation de l'Espace depuis les Origines jusqu'au VIe Millénaire* (eds J. Cauvin and P. Sanalaville). Paris: Editions du C.N.R.S., pp. 67–97.

Tchernov, E. (ed.) 1986. *The Lower Pleistocene Mammals of 'Ubeidiya (Jordan Valley).* Mémoires et Travaux du Centre de Recherche Français de Jérusalem 5. Paris: Association Paléorient.

Chapter 1

Asher, R. 1961. Analogy in archaeological interpretation. *Southwestern Journal of Anthropology* 17: 317–25.

Barker, G. 1991. Two Italys, one valley: an Annaliste perspective. In *The Annales School and Archaeology* (ed. J. Bintliff). London: Leicester University Press, pp. 34–56. .

Binford, L. 1986. In pursuit of the future. In *American Archaeology Past and Future* (eds D. Meltzer, D. Fowler and J. Sabloff). Washington: Smithsonian Institution Press, pp. 459–79.

Bintliff, J. (ed.) 1991. *The Annales School and Archaeology.* London: Leicester University Press.

Birnbaum, N. 1978. The Annales School and Social Theory. *Review* 1: 225–35.

Bloch, M. 1939/40. *La Societe Feodale.* Coll. L'Evolution de l'Humanite. Paris: A. Michel.

Bloch, M. 1949. *Apologie Pour l'Histoire ou le Metier d'Historien.* Paris: A. Colin.

Bloch, M. 1966. *French Rural History: An Essay on its Original Characteristics.* London: Routledge.

Braudel, F. 1972. *The Mediterranean and the Mediterranean World in the Age of Phillip II* (revised edition, trans: S. Reynolds). London: Collins.

Bulliet, R.W. 1992a. Pottery Styles and Social Status in Medieval Khurasan. In *Archaeology, Annales, and Ethnohistory* (ed. A.B. Knapp). Cambridge: Cambridge University Press, pp. 75–82.

Bulliet, R.W. 1992b. Annales and Archaeology. In *Archaeology, Annales, and Ethnohistory* (ed. A.B. Knapp). Cambridge: Cambridge University Press, pp. 131–4.

Champion, T.C. (ed.) 1989. *Centre and Periphery – Comparative Studies in Archaeology.* London: Unwin Hyman.

Chartier, R. (trans. L.G. Cochrane) 1988. *Cultural History: Between Practices and Representations.* Oxford: Polity Press.

Cherry, J.F. 1987. Power in Space: Archaeological and Geographical Studies of the State. In *Landscape and Culture: Geographical and Archaeological Perspectives* (ed. J.M. Wagstaff). London: Blackwell, pp. 146–72.

Clark, S. 1985. The Annales historians. In *The Return of Grand Theory in the Social Sciences* (ed. Q. Skinner). Cambridge: Cambridge University Press, pp. 177–98.

Clarke, D.L. 1968. *Analytical Archaeology.* London: Methuen.

Dever, W.G. (ed.) 1986. *Gezer IV: The 1969–71 Seasons in Field VI, the 'Acropolis'.* Jerusalem: Annual of the Nelson Glueck School of Biblical Archaeology.

Dever, W.G. 1987. The Contribution of Archaeology to the Study of Canaanite and Early Israelite Religion. In *Ancient Israelite Religion: Essays in Honor of Frank Moore Cross* (eds P. Miller, P. Hanson, and S. McBride). Philadelphia: Fortress Press, pp. 209–47.

Dever, W.G. 1990. *Recent Archaeological Discoveries and Biblical Research.* Seattle: University of Washington Press.

Dever, W.G. 1992. Syro-Palestinian and Biblical Archaeology. In *The Anchor Bible Dictionary, Volume 1* (ed. D.N. Freedman). New York: Doubleday, pp. 354–67.

Duke, P. 1992. Braudel and North American Archaeology: an example from the Northern Plains. In *Archaeology, Annales, and Ethnohistory* (ed. A.B. Knapp). Cambridge: Cambridge University Press, pp. 99–111.

Eisenstadt, S.N. 1988. Beyond Collapse. In *The Collapse of Ancient States and Civilizations* (eds N. Yoffee and G.L. Cowgill). Tucson: University of Arizona Press, pp. 236–43.

Febvre, L. 1920. *La Terre et L'evolution Humaine.* Paris: Renaissance du Livre.

Febvre, L. 1949 (1973). A new kind of history, reprinted in *A New Kind of History* (ed. P. Burke). London: Routledge and Kegan Paul, pp. 27–43.

Finkelstein, I. 1986. *Izbet Sartah – An Early Iron Age Site near Rosh Ha'ayin, Israel.* Oxford: BAR International Series 299.

Fletcher, L. 1992. Time perspectivism, Annales, and the Potential of Archaeology. In *Archaeology, Annales, and Ethnohistory* (ed. A.B. Knapp). Cambridge: Cambridge University Press, pp. 35–49.

Forster, R. and Ranum, O. 1975. *Biology of Man in History: Selections from the Annales: Economies, Societies, Civilisations.* Baltimore: Johns Hopkins University Press.

Fried, M. 1967. *The Evolution of Political Society.* New York: Random House.

Gitin, S. 1990. *Gezer III.* Jerusalem: Annual of the Nelson Glueck School of Biblical Archaeology.

Goldberg, P. 1988. The Archaeologist as Viewed by the Geologist. *Biblical Archaeologist* 51: 197–202.

Hexter, J.H. 1972. 'Fernand Braudel and the Monde Braudellien . . .' *Journal of Modern History* 44: 480–539.

Hodder, I. 1986. *Reading the Past.* Cambridge: Cambridge University Press.

Hufton, O. 1986. Fernand Braudel. *Past and Present* 112: 208–13.

Johnson, A.W. and Earle, T. 1987. *The Evolution of Human Societies – From Foraging Group to Agrarian State.* Stanford: Stanford University Press.

Jones, R. 1991. Archaeology, the longue duree and the limits of the Roman Empire. In *The Annales School and Archaeology* (ed. J. Bintliff). London: Leicester University Press, pp. 93–107.

Knapp, A.B. (ed.) 1992a. *Archaeology, Annales, and Ethnohistory.* Cambridge: Cambridge University Press.

Knapp, A.B. 1992b. Independence and Imperialism: Politico-Economic Structures in the Bronze Age Levant. In *Archaeology, Annales, and Ethnohistory* (ed. A.B. Knapp). Cambridge: Cambridge University Press, pp. 83–98.

Knapp, A.B. 1993 *Society and Polity at Bronze Age Pella – An Annales Perspective.* Sheffield: Sheffield Academic Press.

La Bianca, O. 1990. *Sedentarization and Nomadization: Food System Cycles at Hesban and Vicinity in Transjordan.* Hesban 1. Berrien Springs, MI: Institute of Archaeology, Andrews University.

Le Goff, J. and Nora, P. 1985. *Constructing the Past.* Cambridge: Cambridge University Press.

Le Roy Ladurie, E. 1974. *The Peasants of Languedoc.* Urbana: University of Illinois Press.

Levy, T.E. (ed.) 1987. *Shiqmim I. Studies Concerning Chalcolithic Societies in the Northern Negev Desert, Israel (1982–1984).* Oxford: BAR International Series 356.

Lombard, M. 1971. *Monnaie et histoire d'Alexandre a Mahomet* (= *Etudes d'economie medievale*, volume 1). Civilisations et societes 26. Paris: Mouton.

Lombard, M. 1974. *Les Metaux dans l'ancien monde du Ve au XIe siecle* (= *Etudes d'economie medievale*, volume 2). Civilisations et societes 38. Paris: Mouton.

Lombard, M. 1978. *Les Textiles dans le monde musulman du VIIe au XIIe siecle* (= *Etudes d'economie medievale*, volume 3). Civilsations et societes 61. Paris: Mouton.

Mazar, A. 1990. *Archaeology of the Land of the Bible, 10,000–586 B.C.E.* New York: Doubleday.

Moreland, J.F. 1992. Restoring the Dialectic: Settlement Patterns and Documents in Medieval Central Italy. In *Archaeology, Annales, and Ethnohistory* (ed. A.B. Knapp). Cambridge: Cambridge University Press, pp. 112–29.

Rowlands, M., Larsen, M. and Kristiansen, K. (eds) 1987. *Centre and Periphery in the Ancient World.* Cambridge: Cambridge University Press.

Schneider, J. 1977. Was There a Pre-Capitalist World System? *Peasant Studies* 6: 20–9.

Service, E. 1962. *Primitive Social Organization.* New York: Random House.

Sherratt, A. 1992. What Can Archaeologists Learn from Annalistes? In *Archaeology, Annales, and Ethnohistory* (ed. A.B. Knapp). Cambridge: Cambridge University Press, pp. 135–42.

Smith, M.E. 1992a. Braudel's Temporal Rhythms and Chronology Theory in Archaeology. In *Archaeology, Annales, and Ethnohistory* (ed. A.B. Knapp). Cambridge: Cambridge University Press, pp. 23–34.

Smith, M.E. 1992b. Rhythms of Change in Postclassic Central Mexico: Archaeology, Ethnohistory, and the Braudelian Model. In *Archaeology, Annales, and Ethnohistory* (ed. A.B. Knapp). Cambridge: Cambridge University Press, pp. 51–74.

Snodgrass, A. 1991. Structural History and Classical Archaeology. In *The Annales School and Archaeology* (ed. J. Bintliff). London: Leicester University Press, pp. 57–72.

Stager, L.E. 1985a. The First fruits of Civilization. In *Palestine in the Bronze and Iron Ages (Papers in Honour of Olga Tufnell)* (ed. J.N. Tubb). London: Institute of Archaeology, pp. 172–88.　•

Stager, L.E. 1985b. Merenptah, Israel and the Sea Peoples: New Light on an Old Relief. *Eretz Israel* 18: 56*–64*.

Stager, L.E. 1987. Archaeology, Ecology, and Social History: Background Themes to the Song of Deborah. *Supplements to Vetus Testamentum* 40: 221–34).

Stager, L.E. and Walker, A.M. 1989. *American Expedition to Idalion, Cyprus 1973–1980.* Chicago: Oriental Institute Communications No. 2.

Stoianovich, T. 1976. *French Historical Method: The Annales Paradigm.* Ithaca, NY: Cornell University Press.

Stone, L. 1985. A Life of Learning. *American Council of Learned Societies Newsletter* 36: 3–22.

Toynbee, A. 1954. *A Study of History, vol. 8.* Oxford: Oxford University Press.

Vallat, J.P. 1991. The Place and Role of the Annales School in an Approach to the Roman Rural Economy. In *The Annales School and Archaeology* (ed. J. Bintliff). London: Leicester University Press, pp. 73–92.

Yoffee, N. 1992. Too Many Chiefs? (or, Safe Texts for the 90s). In *Archaeological Theory – Who Sets the Agenda?* (eds N. Yoffee and A. Sherratt). Cambridge: Cambridge University Press, pp. 60–78.

Chapter 2

Aharoni, Y. 1967. *The Land of the Bible.* London: Burns & Oates.

Albright, W.F. 1932. *The Archaeology of Palestine and the Bible.* New York: Fleming H. Revell Co.

Albright, W.F. 1940. *From the Stone Age to Christianity: Monotheism and the Historical Process.* Baltimore: Johns Hopkins University Press.

Albright, W.F. 1949. *The Archaeology of Palestine.* Harmondsworth: Pelican Books.

Albright, W.F. 1964. *History, Archaeology, and Christian Humanism.* New York: McGraw-Hill.

Anderson, B. 1983. *Imagined Communities.* London: Verso.

Ben-Arieh, Y. 1979. *The Rediscovery of the Holy Land in the Nineteenth Century.* Jerusalem: The Magnes Press.

Besant, W. 1895. *Thirty Years' Work in the Holy Land of the Palestine Exploration Fund – A Record and Summary.* London: Palestine Exploration Fund.

Bliss, F.J. 1907. *The Development of Palestine Exploration.* New York: Scribner.

Brawer, A.J. 1965. From the Early Days of the Israel Exploration Society. In *Western Galilee and the Coast of Galilee* (ed. J. Aviram). Jerusalem: Israel Exploration Society, pp. 228–36.

Broshi, M. 1987. Religion, Ideology, and Politics and Their Impact on Palestinian Archaeology. *Israel Museum Journal.* 7: 17–32.

Brown, P. 1981. *The Cult of the Saints.* Chicago: The University of Chicago Press.

Canaan, T. 1922. *Studies in Palestinian Customs and Folklore.* Jerusalem: Palestine Oriental Society.

Clarke, E.D. 1817. *Travels in Various Countries of Europe, Asia, and Africa.* London: Cadell and Davies.

Cohn, N. 1970. *The Pursuit of the Millennium.* Oxford: Oxford University Press.

Dever, W.G. 1973. Two Approaches to Archaeological method – the Architectural and the Stratigraphic. *Eretz-Israel.* 11: 1–8.

Dever, W.G. 1980. Biblical Theology and Biblical Archaeology: An Appreciation of G. Ernest Wright. *Harvard Theological Review.* 73: 1–15.

Dever, W.G. 1985. Syro-Palestinian and Biblical Archaeology. In *The Hebrew Bible and Its Modern Interpreters.* (eds D.A. Knight and G.M. Tucker). Philadelphia: Fortress Press.

Dothan, T. and Dothan, M. 1992. *People of the Sea.* New York: MacMillan.

Duri, A.A. 1990. Jerusalem in the Early Islamic period. In *Jerusalem, A History* (ed. K.J. Asali). New York: Olive Branch Press. 105–29.

Ettema, M.J. 1987. History Museums and the Culture of Materialism. In *Past Meets Present* (ed. J. Blatti). Washington: Smithsonian Institute Press, pp. 62–85.

Foucault, M. 1973. *The Order of Things: An Archaeology of the Human Sciences.* New York: Vintage Books.

Fowler, D.D. 1987. Uses of the Past: Archaeology in the Service of the State. *American Antiquity.* 52: 229–48.

Geary P.J. 1990. *Furta Sacra: Thefts of Relics in the Central Middle Ages.* Princeton: Princeton University Press.

Gitin, S. 1985. Stratigraphy and Its Application to Chronology and Terminology. In *Biblical Archaeology Today* (eds A. Biran et al.). Jerusalem: Israel Exploration Society, pp. 99–107.

Glock, A.E. 1983. The Use of Ethnography in Archaeological Research Design. In *The Quest for the Kingdom of God: Studies in Honor of George E. Mendenhall* (eds H.B. Huffman, F.A. Spina and A.R.W. Green). Winona Lake, IN: Eisenbrauns, pp. 171–9.

Glock, A.E. 1985. Tradition and Change in Two Archaeologies. *American Antiquity.* 50: 464–77.

Glock, A.E. 1987. Prolegomena to Archaeological Theory. *Birzeit Research Review.* 4: 4–39.

Government of Palestine. 1929. Provisional Schedule of Historic Sites and Monuments. *Official Gazette.* June 15, 1929.

Grabois, A. 1982. Christian pilgrims in the Thirteenth Century and the Latin Kingdom of Jerusalem: Burchard of Mount Sion. In *Outremer: Studies in the History of the Crusading Kingdom of Jerusalem* (eds B.Z. Kedar, H.E. Mayer and R.C. Smail). Jerusalem: Yad Izhak Ben-Zvi, pp. 285–96.

Greenblatt, S. 1991. *Marvelous Possessions: The Wonder of the New World.* Chicago: University of Chicago Press.

Hadidi, A. 1982. *Studies in the History and Archaeology of Jordan Vol. I.* Amman: Department of Antiquities.

Hadidi, A. 1985. *Studies in the History and Archaeology of Jordan Vol. II.* Amman: Department of Antiquities.

Halevi, N. 1983. The Political Economy of Absorptive Capacity: Growth and Cycles in Jewish Palestine under the British Mandate. *Middle Eastern Studies.* 19: 456–69.

Hareouveni, E. 1979. *The Settlements of Israel and Their Archaeological Sites.* Ramat-Gan, Israel: Massada. (In Hebrew.)

Harvey, D. 1990. *The Condition of Postmodernity.* Oxford: Basil Blackwell.

Herold, J. Christopher 1962. *Bonaparte in Egypt.* New York: Harper & Row.

Hodder, I. 1982. *The Present Past.* New York: Pica Press.

Hopwood, Derek. 1969. *The Russian Presence in Syria and Palestine, 1843–1914.* Oxford: Oxford University Press.

Hunt, E.D. 1984. *Holy Land Pilgrimage in the Later Roman Empire AD 312–460.* Oxford: Clarendon Press.

Jacoby, D. 1986. The Franciscans, the Jews, and the Issue of Mount Zion in the Fifteenth Century. *Cathedra.* 39: 51–70. (In Hebrew.)

Kempinski, A. 1989. *Megiddo: A City-state and Royal Centre in Northern Israel.* Munich: Verlag C.H. Beck.

King, P.J. 1983. *American Archaeology in the Mideast.* Philadelphia: American Schools of Oriental Research.

Lach, D. 1977. *Asia in the Making of Europe. Volume II: A Century of Wonder. Book Three: The Scholarly Disciplines.* Chicago: University of Chicago Press.

Larkin, J. 1988. *The Reshaping of Everyday Life 1790–1840.* New York: Harper and Row.

Larsen, M.T. 1989. Orientalism and Near Eastern Archaeology. In *Domination and Resistance* (eds D. Miller, M. Rowlands and C. Tilley). London: Unwin Hyman. 229–39.

Leone, M.P., Potter, P.B. and Shakel, P. 1987. Toward a Critical Archaeology. *Current Anthropology.* 28: 283–302.

Le Strange, G. 1890. *Palestine Under the Moslems.* London: Palestine Exploration Fund.

Lowance, M.I. 1980. *The Language of Canaan: Metaphor and Symbol in New England from the Puritans to the Transcendentalists.* Cambridge, MA: Harvard University Press.

Macalister, R.A.S. 1912. *A History of Civilization in Palestine.* Cambridge: Cambridge University Press.

Macalister, R.A.S. 1925. *A Century of Excavation in Palestine.* London: The Religious Tract Society.

Marlowe, J. 1971. *Perfidious Albion: The Origins of the Anglo-French Rivalry in the Levant.* London: Elek Books.

Mazar, B. 1975. *The Mountain of the Lord.* Garden City, NY: Doubleday.

Miller, D. 1980. Archaeology and Development. *Current Anthropology.* 21: 709–26.

Moorey, P.R.S. 1991. *A Century of Biblical Archaeology.* Louisville: Westminster/John Knox Press.

Patterson, T.C. 1986. Some Postwar theoretical trends in U.S. Archaeology. *Culture.* 6: 43–54.

Patterson, T.C. 1987. Development, Ecology, and Marginal Utility in Anthropology. *Dialectical Anthropology.* 12: 15–31.

Petrie, W.M.F. 1912. *The Revolutions of Civilization.* New York: Harper & Brothers.

Poliakov, L. 1971. *The Aryan Myth: A History of Racist and Nationalist Ideas in Europe.* New York: Basic Books.

Ra'anan, U. 1976. *The Frontiers of a Nation.* Westport, CT: Hyperion Press.

Robinson, E. 1841. *Biblical Researches in Palestine, Mount Sinai, and Arabia Petraea.* Boston: Crocker & Brewster.

Rodinson, M. 1987. *Europe and the Mystique of Islam.* Seattle: University of Washington Press.

Running, L.G. and Freedman, D.N. 1975. *William Foxwell Albright, A Twentieth Century Genius.* New York: Two Continents Publishing Group.

Said, E. 1978. *Orientalism.* New York: Pantheon Books.

Schick, R. 1988. Christian life in Palestine During the Early Islamic Period. *Biblical Archaeologist.* 51: 219–21, 233–7.

Sellin, E. 1905. *Der Ertrag des Ausgrabungen im Orient fur die Erkenntnis der Entwicklung der Religion Israels.* Leipzig: A. Deichert.

Shavit, Y. 1987. 'Truth Shall Spring Out of the Earth': The Development of Jewish Popular Interest in Archaeology in Eretz-Israel. *Cathedra.* 44: 27–54.

Silberman, N.A. 1982. *Digging for God and Country.* New York: Knopf.

Silberman, N.A. 1984. Restoring the Reputation of Lady Hester Stanhope. *Biblical Archaeology Review.* 10: 68ff.

Silberman, N.A. 1989. *Between Past and Present.* New York: Henry Holt.

Silberman, N.A. 1990. The Politics of the Past: Archaeology and Nationalism in the Eastern Mediterranean. *Mediterranean Quarterly.* 1: 99–110.

Silberman, N.A. 1991. Desolation and Restoration: The Impact of a Biblical Concept on Near Eastern Archaeology. *Biblical Archaeologist.* 54: 76–86.

Silberman, N.A. 1993. Petrie and the Founding Fathers. In *Biblical Archaeology Today, 1990* (eds Avraham Biran and Joseph Aviram). Jerusalem: Israel Exploration Society.

Simon, R. 1980. The Struggle for Christian Holy Places in Eretz-Israel in the Ottoman Period, 1516–1853. *Cathedra.* 17: 107–26. (In Hebrew.)

Stocking, G.W. 1987. *Victorian Anthropology.* New York: Free Press.

Tibawi, A.L. 1961. *British Interests in Palestine, 1800–1901.* Oxford: Oxford University Press.

Tibawi, A.L. 1966. *American Interests in Syria, 1800–1901.* Oxford: Oxford University Press.

Tilley, C. 1989. Archaeology as socio-political action in the present. In *Critical Traditions in Contemporary Archaeology* (eds V. Pinsky and A. Wylie). Cambridge: Cambridge University Press, pp. 104–16.

Trigger, B. 1984. Alternative Archaeologies: Nationalist, Colonialist, Imperialist. *Man.* 19: 355–70.

Van Keuren, D.K. 1984. Museums and Ideology: Augustus Pitt-Rivers, Anthropological Museums, and Social Change in Later Victorian Britain. *Victorian Studies.* 28: 171–89.

Vilnay, Z. 1973–8. *The Legends of Eretz-Israel.* Philadelphia: Jewish Publication Society of America.

Wallach, J.L. (ed.). 1975. *Germany and the Middle East, 1835–1939.* Tel Aviv: University of Tel Aviv.

Warren, C. 1876. *Underground Jerusalem.* London: R. Bentley.

Wilken, R.L. 1992. *A Land Called Holy: Palestine in Christian History and Thought.* New Haven: Yale University Press.

Wolff, S. 1991. Archaeology in Israel. *American Journal of Archaeology.* 95: 489–538.

Wright, G.E. 1962. *Biblical Archaeology.* Philapdelphia: The Westminster Press.

Yadin, Y. 1972. *Hazor.* London: The British Academy.

Chapter 3

Aloni, R. and Orshan, G. 1972. Vegetation map of the Lower Galilee. *Israel Journal of Botany* 21: 209–77.

Dan, J. and Raz, Z. 1970. *Soil association map of Israel* (1 : 250,000). Bet Dagan: The Volcani Institute.

Dan, J., Yaalon, D.H., Koyumadjisky, H. and Raz, Z. 1975. *The Soil association map of Israel.* (1 : 500,000). Pamphlet No. 147, Bet Dagan: The Volcani Institute.

Danin, A. 1972. Mediterranean elements in rocks of the Negev and Sinai deserts. *Notes of the Royal Botanic Garden Edinburgh* 31: 437–40.

Danin, A. 1978. Plant species diversity and ecological districts of the Sinai desert. *Vegetatio* 36: 83–93.

Danin, A. 1981. The impact of geomorphologic and climatic conditions on the vegetation of the salt marshes along the Mediterranean coast of Israel and Sinai. *Anales Jardin Botanico Madrid* 37: 269–75.

Danin, A. 1983. *Desert Vegetation of Israel and Sinai*. Jerusalem: Cana.

Danin, A. 1988. Flora and vegetation of Israel. In *The Zoogeography of Israel* (eds Y. Yom-Tov and E. Tchernov). Dordrecht: Dr. Junk, pp. 129–57.

Danin, A. 1989. Nests of harvester ants – a primary habitat of a few synanthropic plants in Israel. In *Environmental Quality and Ecosystem Stability* (eds E. Spanier, Y. Steinberger and M. Luria) V-B. Jerusalem: ISEEQS Publication, pp. 449–57.

Danin, A. 1991a. Synanthropic flora of Israel. *Flora et Vegetatio Mundi* 9: 95–103.

Danin, A. 1991b. Roadside vegetation in Israel. In *Urban Ecology* (eds M.A. Oztuerk, U. Erdem and G. Goerk). Izmir: International Urban Ecology Symposium, pp. 392–402.

Danin, A. 1992. Check-list of the vascular plants collected during Iter Mediterraneum II. *Bocconea* 3: 43–216.

Danin, A., Bar-Or, Y., Dor, I. and Yisraeli, T. 1989. The role of cyanobacteria in stabilization of sand dunes in southern Israel. *Ecologia Mediterranea* 15(1/2): 55–64.

Danin, A. and Orshan, G. 1970. Distribution of indigenous trees in the northern and central Negev Highlands. *LaYaaran* 20: 115–20.

Danin, A. and Orshan, G. 1990. The distribution of Raunkiaer's life forms in Israel as related to environment. *Journal of Vegetation Science* 1: 41–8.

Danin, A. and Plitmann, U. 1986. Revision of the plant geographical territories of Israel and Sinai. *Plant Evolution and Systematics* 150: 43–53.

Danin, A. and Yaalon, D.H. 1982. Silt plus clay sedimentation and decalcification during plant succession in sands of the Mediterranean coastal area of Israel. *Israel Journal of Earth-Sciences* 31: 101–9.

Danin, A. and Yom-Tov, Y. 1990. Nests of harvesting ants as primary habitats of *Silybum marianum* L. *Plant Evolution and Systematics* 169: 209–17.

Eig, A. 1931–32. Les elements et les groupes phytogeographiques auxiliaires dans la flore Palestinienne. 2 parts. *Fedde's Repertorum Species Novarum Regni Vegetabilis Beihafte* 63(1): 1–201; (2): 1–120.

Eig, A. 1938. On the phytogeographical subdivision of Palestine. *Palestine Journal of Botany (Jerusalem)* 1: 4–12.

Evenari, M., Shanan, L. and Tadmor, N.H. 1971. *The Negev. The Challenge of a Desert*. Cambridge, Massachusetts: Harvard University Press.

Feinbrun-Dothan, N. 1978. *Flora Palaestina* part iii. Jerusalem: The Israel Academy of Sciences and Humanities.

Feinbrun-Dothan, N. 1986. Ibid, part iv.

Feinbrun-Dothan, N. and Danin, A. 1991. *Analytical Flora of Eretz Israel*. Jerusalem: Cana (in Hebrew).

Halevy, G. 1971. Studies in *Acacia albida* Del. in Israel. *LaYaaran* 21: 52–63.

Halevy, G. and Orshan, G. 1972. Ecological studies on *Acacia* species in the Negev and Sinai. I. Distribution of *Acacia raddiana, A. tortilis* and *A. gerrarddii* ssp. *negevensis* as related to environmental factors. *Israel Journal of Botany* 22: 120–38.

Johnson, M.P. and Raven, P.H. 1970. Natural regulation of plant species diversity. *Evolutionary Biology* 4: 127–62.

Keshet, M., Danin, A. and Orshan, G. 1990. Distribution of ecomorphological types along environmental gradients in Israel: 1. Renewal bud location and leaf attributes. *Ecologia Mediterranea* 16: 151–61.

Kislev, M.E., Nadel, D. and Carmi, I. 1992. Epipalaeolithic (19,000 BP) cereal and fruit diet at Ohalo II, Sea of Galilee, Israel. *Review of Palaeobotany and Palynology* 73: 161–6.

Kutiel, P., Danin, A. and Orshan, G. 1979/80. Vegetation of the sandy soils near Caesarea, Israel. I. Plant succession. *Israel Journal of Botany* 28: 20–35.

Lipkin, Y. 1971. Vegetation of the Southern Negev. Ph.D. thesis. Department of Botany, The Hebrew University, Jerusalem (in Hebrew).

Monod, T. 1954. Modes contracte et diffus dans la vegetation saharienne. In *Biology of Deserts* (ed. J.L.E. Cloudsley-Thompson). London: Institute of Biology. pp. 35–44.

Noy-Meir, I. and Seligman, N.G. 1979. Management of semi-arid ecosystems in Israel. In *Management of Semi-Desert Ecosystems* (ed. B.H. Walker). Amsterdam: Elsevier, pp. 113–60.

Rabinovitch (vin), A. 1979. Influence of parent rock on soil properties and composition of vegetation in the Galilee. Ph.D. Thesis. The Hebrew University, Jerusalem (in Hebrew).

Rudich, D. and Danin, A. 1978. The vegetation of Hazeva area, Israel. *Israel Journal of Botany* 27: 160–76.

Yaalon, D.H. 1963. On the origin and accumulation of salts in groundwater and soils of Israel. *Bulletin of the Research Council of Israel* 11c: 105–31.

Zohary, D. and Spigel-Roy, P. 1975. Beginnings of fruit growing in the old world. *Science* 187: 319–27.

Zohary, M. 1962. *Plant Life of Palestine (Israel and Jordan)*. New York: Ronald Press.

Zohary, M. 1966. *Flora Palaestina* part i. Jerusalem: The Israel Academy of Sciences and Humanities.

Zohary, M. 1972. Ibid. part ii.

Zohary, M. 1973. *Geobotanical Foundations of the Middle East*. 2 vols. Stuttgart: Fischer.

Zohary, M. 1983. Man and vegetation in the Middle East. In *Man's Impact on Vegetation*. (eds W. Holzner, M.J.A. Werger and I. Ikusima). The Hague: Dr Junk, pp. 287–95.

Chapter 4

Atlas of Israel. 1970. *Atlas of Israel*. Jerusalem: Survey of Israel, Ministry of Labor, Amsterdam: Elsevier.

Baruch, U. 1986. The late Holocene vegetational history of Lake Kinneret (Sea of Galilee), Israel. *Paléorient*. 12: 37–48.

Baruch, U. and Bottema, S. 1991. Palynological evidence for climatic fluctuations in the Southern Levant ca. 15,000 to 8000 yrs ago. In *The Natufian Culture in the Levant* (eds O. Bar-Yosef and F. Valla). Ann Arbor: International Monographs in Prehistory, pp. 11–20.

Bar-Yosef, O. 1970. The Epi-Palaeolithic Cultures of Palestine. Doctoral dissertation, Institute of Archaeology, Hebrew University, Jerusalem.

Bar-Yosef, O. 1981. The Epi-Palaeolithic complexes in the Southern Levant. In *Prehistoire du Levant* (eds J. Cauvin and P. Sanlaville). Paris: CNRS, pp. 389–408.

Bar-Yosef, O. 1987. Prehistory of the Jordan Rift. *Israel Journal of Earth-Sciences*. 36: 107–19.

Bar-Yosef, O. 1989a. The excavations at 'Ubeidiya in retrospect: An eclectic view. *British Archaeological Reports*, International Series. 497: 101–11.

Bar-Yosef, O. 1989b. Geochronology of the Levantine Middle Palaeolithic. In *The Human Revolution* (eds P. Mellars and C. Stringer). Edinburgh: Edinburgh University Press, pp. 589–610.

Bar-Yosef, O., Gopher, A., Tchernov, E. and Kislev, M.E. 1991. Netiv Hagdud: An Early Neolithic village site in the Jordan Valley. *Journal of Field Archaeology*. 18: 416–24.

Bar-Yosef, O. and Goren-Inbar, N. 1993. *The Lithic Assemblages of 'Ubeidiya: A Lower Palaeolithic Site in the Jordan Valley*. Qedem, no. 34. Jerusalem: Institute of Archaeology, Hebrew University of Jerusalem.

Bar-Yosef, O. and Tchernov, E. 1972. *On the Palaeoecological History of the Site of 'Ubeidiya*. Jerusalem: Israel Academy of Sciences and Humanities.

Bar-Yosef, O., Goldberg, P., and Leveson, T. 1974. Late Quaternary stratigraphy and prehistory of Wadi Fazael, Jordan Valley: a preliminary report. *Paléorient*. 2: 415–28.

Bar-Yosef, O., Vandermeersch, B., Arensburg, B., Belfer-Cohen, A., Goldberg, P., Laville, H., Meignen, L., Rak, Y., Speth, J.D., Tchernov, E., Tiller, A.-M., and Weiner, S. 1992. The Excavation in Kebara Cave, Mt. Carmel. *Current Anthropology*. 33(5): 497–550.

Begin, Z.B., Ehrlich, A. and Nathan, Y. 1974. Lake Lisan: The Pleistocene precursor of the Dead Sea. *Bulletin of the Geological Survey of Israel*. No. 63.

Begin, Z.B., Ehrlich, A. and Nathan, Y. 1980. Stratigraphy and facies distribution in the Lisan Formation: New evidence from the area south of the Dead Sea, Israel. *Israel Journal of Earth-Sciences*. 29: 182–9.

Begin, Z.B., Broecker, W., Buchbinder, B., Druckman, Y., Kaufman, A. Magaritz, M. and Neev, D. 1985. Dead Sea and Lake Lisan Levels in the Last 30,000 years: a Preliminary Report. *Internal Report, Geological Survey of Israel*. 29/85: 1–8.

Bruins, H..J. and Yaalon, D.H. 1979. Stratigraphy of the Netivot section in the desert loess of the Negev (Israel). *Acta Geological Academiae Scientiarum Hungaricae*. 22: 161–9.

Bull, P.A. and Goldberg. P. 1985. Scanning electron microscope analysis of sediments from Tabun Cave, Mount Carmel, Israel. *Journal of Archaeological Science*. 12: 177–85.

Courty, M.A., Goldberg, P. and Macphail, R.I. 1989. *Soils and Micromorphology in Archaeology*. Cambridge: Cambridge University Press.

Dan, J. 1988. The soils of the land of Israel. In *The Zoogeography of Israel* (eds Y. Yom-Tov and E. Tchernov). Dordrecht: Junk, pp. 95–128.

Dan, J., Yaalon, D.H., and Koyumdjisky, H. 1968. Catenary soil relationships in Israel, 1. The Netanya Catena on coastal dunes of the Sharon. *Geoderma*. 2: 95–120.

Farrand, W.R. 1979. Chronology and palaeoenvironments of Levantine prehistoric sites as seen from sediment studies. *Journal of Archaeological Science*. 6: 369–92.

Farrand, W.R. and Ronen, A. 1974. Observations on the kurkar-hamra succession on the Carmel Coastal Plain. *Tel-Aviv*. 1: 45–54.

Ganor, E. 1975. *Atmospheric Dust in Israel: Sedimentological and Meteorological Analysis of Dust Deposition*. Doctoral Dissertation. Jerusalem: Hebrew University of Jerusalem (in Hebrew).

Garfinkel, Y. 1987. Yiftahel: A Neolithic village from the seventh millennium B.C. in Lower Galilee, Israel. *Journal of Field Archaeology*. 14: 199–212.

Garrod, D.A.E. and Bate, D.M. 1937. *The Stone Age of Mount Carmel*, Vol. I. Oxford: Clarendon Press.

Ginzbourg, D. and Yaalon, D.H. 1963. Petrography and origin of the loess in the Be'ersheva basin. *Israel Journal of Earth-Sciences*. 12: 68–70.

Goldberg, P. 1973. Sedimentology, Stratigraphy and Paleoclimatology of et-Tabun Cave, Mount Carmel, Israel. Doctoral dissertation. Department of Geological Sciences, University of Michigan, Ann Arbor.

Goldberg, P. 1977. Late Quaternary stratigraphy of Gebel Maghara. In *Prehistoric Investigations in Gebel Maghara, Northern Sinai* (eds O. Bar-Yosef and J.L. Phillips). Qedem, no. 7. Jerusalem: Institute of Archaeology, Hebrew University, pp. 25–51.

Goldberg, P. 1978. Granulometrie des sediments de la grotte de Taboun, Mont Carmel, Israël. *Geologie Mediterraneenne*. 5: 371–83.

Goldberg, P. 1986. Late Quaternary environmental history of the Southern Levant. *Geoarchaeology*. 1: 225–44.

Goldberg, P. 1987. Geology and stratigraphy of Shiqmim. In *Shiqmim I Prehistoric Investigations of Early Farming Societies of the Northern Negev, Israel* (ed. T.E. Levy). British Archaeological Reports, International Series, No. 356, pp. 35–43.

Goldberg, P. 1990. Paleoclimates as reflected in sediments from Levantine cave sites? Abstracts, Society for American Archaeology, Annual Meeting, Las Vegas.

Goldberg, P. in press. Interpreting late Quaternary continental sequences in Israel. In *Late Quaternary Chronology and Paleoclimates of the eastern Mediterranean* (eds O. Bar-Yosef and R.S. Kra). Cambridge: Radiocarbon/Peabody Museum, Harvard University.

Goldberg, P. and Bar-Yosef, O. 1982. Environmental and archaeological evidence for climatic change in the Southern Levant and adjacent areas. In *Palaeoclimates, Palaeoenvironments and Human Communities in the Eastern Mediterranean Region in Later Prehistory* (eds J.L. Bintliff and W. van Zeist). British Archaeological Reports, International Series, No. 133. pp. 399–414.

Goldberg, P. and Bar-Yosef, O. 1990. The effect of man on geomorphological processes based on evidence from the Levant and adjacent areas. In *Man's Role in the Shaping of the Eastern Mediterranean Landscape* (eds S. Bottema, G. Entjes-Nieborg and W. van Zeist), Balkema, Rotterdam, pp. 71–86.

Goldberg, P. and Bar-Yosef, O. in press. *Sedimentary environments of prehistoric sites in Israel and the southern Levant*. Lubbock Lake Symposium. Lubbock: Texas Tech. Press.

Goldberg, P. and Laville, H. 1988. Le contexte stratigraphique des occupations paléolithiques de la grotte de Kébara (Israël). *Paléorient*. 14: 117–22.

Goldberg, P. and Nathan, Y. 1975. The phosphate mineralogy of et-Tabun cave, Mount Carmel, Israel. *Mineralogical Magazine*. 40: 253–8.

Goodfriend, G.A. 1990. Rainfall in the Negev Desert during the Middle Holocene, based on ^{13}C of organic matter in land snail shells. *Quaternary Research*. 34: 186–97.

Goodfriend, G.A. and Magaritz, M. 1988. Palaeosols and late Pleistocene rainfall fluctuations in the Negev Desert. *Nature*. 332: 144–6.

Goren-Inbar, N. 1990. The Acheulian site of Gesher Benot Ya'akov – an Asian or an African entity? The Evolution and dispersal of modern humans in Asia, University of Tokyo Symposium Abstracts, Nov. 1990, p. 14.

Goren-Inbar, N. and Belitzky, S. 1989. Structural position of the Pleistocene Gesher Benot Ya'akov site in the Dead Sea Rift zone. *Quaternary Research*. 31: 371–6.

Goren-Inbar, N., Belitzky, S., Goren, Y., Rabinovich, R. and Saragusti, I. 1992. Gesher Benot Ya'akov – the "Bar": An Acheulian Assemblage. *Geoarchaeology*. 7: 27–40.

Goring-Morris, A.N. 1987. *At the Edge, Terminal Pleistocene Hunter-Gatherers in the Negev and Sinai*. British Archaeological Reports, International Series, No. 361.

Goring-Morris, N. and Goldberg, P. 1990. Late Quaternary dune incursions in the Southern Levant: Archaeology, chronology and palaeoenvironments. *Quaternary International*. 5: 115–37.

Grün, R., Stringer, C.B. and Schwarcz, H.P. 1991. ESR dating of teeth from Garrod's Tabun Cave collection. *Journal of Human Evolution*. 20: 231–48.

Gvirtzman, G., Schachnai, E., Bakler, N. and Ilani, S. 1983/1984. The stratigraphy of the Kurkar Group (Quaternary) of the Coastal Plain of Israel. *Geological Survey of Israel, Current Research*. 70–82.

Haas, G. 1970. *Metridiochoerus evronensis* N. SP. A new Middle Pleistocene Phacochoerid from Israel. *Israel Journal of Zoology*. 19: 179–81.

Horowitz, A. 1979. *The Quaternary of Israel*. New York: Academic Press.

Horowitz, A. 1988. The Quaternary environments and paleogeography in Israel. In *The Zoogeography of Israel* (eds Y. Tom-Tov and E. Tchernov). Dordrecht: Junk, pp. 35–57.

Horowitz, A. and Sneh, A. 1984. Flow regimes in Late Quaternary wadis in the northwestern Negev. Abstracts, Israel Geological Society, Annual Meeting, p. 48.

Hovers, E. 1989. Settlement and subsistence patterns in the Lower Jordan Valley from Epipalaeolithic to Neolithic times. In *People and Culture in Change* (ed. Israel Hershkovitz), British Archaeological Reports International Series. 508: 37–51.

Hovers, E. and Bar-Yosef, O. 1987. Prehistoric survey of eastern Samaria: a preliminary report. *Israel Exploration Journal*. 37: 77–87.

Issar, A. 1968 Geology of the central coastal plain of Israel. *Israel Journal of Earth Sciences*. 17: 16–29.

Issar, A.S. and Bruins, H.J. 1983. Special climatological conditions in the deserts of Sinai and the Negev during the latest Pleistocene. *Palaeogeography, Palaeoclimatology, Palaeoecology*. 43: 63–72.

Issar, A. and Kafri, U. 1972 Neogene and Pleistocene geology of the Western Galilee Coastal Plain. *Geological Survey of Israel Bulletin*, 53: 1–13.

Jelinek, A.J. 1982. The Tabun Cave and Palaeolithic Man in the Levant. *Science*. 216: 1369–75.

Jelinek, A.J., Farrand, W.R., Haas, G., Horowitz, A., and Goldberg, P. 1973 New excavations at the Tabun Cave, Mount Carmel, Israel, 1967–1972: a preliminary report. *Paléorient*. 1: 151–83.

Karmeli, A., Yaalon, D.H., and Ravina, I. 1968. Dune sand and soil strata in Quaternary sedimentary cycles of the Sharon coastal plain. *Israel Journal of Earth-Sciences*. 17: 45–53.

Katz, A., Kolodny, Y. and Nissenbaum, Y. 1977. The geochemical evolution of the Pleistocene Lake Lisan-Dead Sea system. *Geochimica et Cosmochimica Acta*. 41: 1609–26.

Kaufman, A. 1971. U-series dating of Dead Sea Basin carbonates. *Geochimica et Cosmochimica Acta*. 35: 1269–81.

Kaufman, A., Yechieli, Y. and Gardosh, M. 1992. Reevaluation of the lake-sediment chronology in the Dead Sea Basin, Israel, based on new 230Th/U dates. *Quaternary Research*. 38: 292–304.

Laville, H. and Goldberg, P. 1989. The collapse of the Mousterian sedimentary regime and the beginning of the Upper Palaeolithic at

Kebara Cave, Mount Carmel. In *Investigations in South Levantine Prehistory* (eds O. Bar-Yosef and B. Vandermeersch). British Archaeological Reports, International Series No. 497, pp. 75–95.

Leroi-Gourhan, Arl. and Darmon F. 1987. Analyses palynolgiques de sites archeologiques du Plistocene final dans la vallee du Jourdain. *Israel Journal of Earth-Sciences.* 36: 65–72.

Levy, T. E. 1986. The Chalcolithic Period. *Biblical Archaeologist.* 49: 82–108.

Magaritz, M. 1986. Environmental changes recorded in the Upper Pleistocene along the desert boundary, southern Israel. *Palaeogeography, Palaeoclimatology, Palaeoecology.* 53: 213–29.

Marks, A.E. (ed.). 1976. *Prehistory and Paleoenvironments in the Central Negev, Israel*, Vol. I. Dallas: Southern Methodist University Press.

Marks, A.E. (ed.). 1983. *Prehistory and Paleoenvironments in the Central Negev, Israel*, Vol. III. Dallas: Southern Methodist University Press.

Meignen, L., Bar-Yosef, O. and Goldberg, P. 1989. Les structures de combustion mousteriennes de la grotte de Kébara (Mont Carmel, Israel). *Memoires du Musee de Prehistoire d'Ile de France.* 2: 141–6.

Neev, D., Bakler N. and Emery, K.O. 1987. *Mediterranean Coasts of Israel and Sinai.* New York: Taylor and Francis.

Noy, T., Schuldenrein J. and Tchernov, E. 1980. Gilgal, a Pre-Pottery Neolithic A site in the Lower Jordan Valley. *Israel Exploration Society.* 30: 63–82.

Orni, E. and Efrat, E. 1971. *The Geography of Israel.* Jerusalem: Keter.

Picard, L. 1965. The geological evolution of the Quaternary in the Central Northern Jordan Graben. *Geological Society of America Special Paper*, 84: 337–66.

Picard, L. and Baida, U. 1966. *Geological report on the Lower Pleistocene deposits of the 'Ubeidiya excavations.* Jerusalem: Israel Academy of Sciences and Humanities.

Ronen, A. 1977. Mousterian sites in red loam in the Coastal Plain of Mount Carmel. Eretz-Israel. *Israel Exploration Society.* 13: 183*–190*.

Ronen, A. and Amiel, A. 1974 The Evron quarry: A contribution to the Quaternary stratigraphy of the coastal plain of Israel. *Paléorient.* 2: 167–73.

Ronen, A. and Kaufman, D. 1976. Epi-Palaeolithic sites near Nahal Hadera, Central Coastal Plain of Israel. *Tel-Aviv.* 3: 16–30.

Ronen, A., Kaufman, D., Gophna, R., Bakler, N., Smith, P. and Amiel, A. 1975. The Epi-Palaeolithic site of Hefziba, Central Coastal Plain of Israel. *Quartär.* 26: 53–72.

Rosen, A. 1986a. Alluvial stratigraphy of the Shephela and its paleoclimatic implications. *Geological Survey of Israel, Jerusalem, Report* GSI/25/86.

Rosen, A. 1986b. Environmental change and settlement at Tel Lachish, Israel. *BASOR.* 266: 45–58.

Sandler, A., Goldberg, P. and Gilbert, D. 1988. Nahal Heimar Cave: Geological observations on the sediments. *Atiqot.* 18: 64–7.

Saxon, E., Martin, G. and Bar-Yosef, O. 1978. Excavations at Nahal Hadera V, Coastal Plain, Israel. *Paléorient.* 4: 253–65.

Schattner, I. 1973. *Physiography of Israel.* Israel Pocket Library, Geography. Jerusalem: Keter, pp. 24–93.

Schuldenrein, J. and Goldberg, P. 1981. Late Quaternary paleoenvironments and prehistoric site distribution in the Lower Jordan Valley: a preliminary report. *Paléorient.* 7: 57–72.

Schwarcz, H.P., Blackwell, B., Goldberg, P. and Marks A.E. 1979. Uranium series dating of travertine from archaeological sites, Nahal Zin, Israel. *Nature.* 277: 558–60.

Sneh, A. 1983. Redeposited loess from the Quaternary Besor Basin, Israel. *Israel Journal of Earth-Sciences.* 32: 63–9.

Stekelis, M. 1960. The Palaeolithic deposits of Jisr Banat Yaqub. *Bulletin of the Research Council of Israel*, Section G, 9G: 61–90.

Stringer, C.B., Grün, R., Schwarcz, H.P., and Goldberg, P. 1989. ESR dates for the hominid burial site of Es Skhul in Israel. *Nature*, 338: 756–8.

Tchernov, E. 1975. *The Early Pleistocene Molluscs of Erq-el-Ahmar.* Jerusalem: Israel Academy of Science and Humanities, pp. 1–36.

Tchernov, E. 1987. The age of the 'Ubeidiya Formation, an Early Pleistocene hominid site in the Jordan Valley, Israel. *Israel Journal of Earth-Sciences.* 36: 3–30.

Valladas, H. Joron, J.L., Valladas, G., Arensburg, B., Bar-Yosef, O., Belfer-Cohen, A., Goldberg, P., Laville, H., Meignen, L., Rak, Y., Tchernov, E., Tillier, A.M. and Vandermeersch, B. 1987.

Thermoluminescence dates for the Neanderthal burial site at Kebara in Israel. *Nature.* 330: 159–60.

Valladas, H., Reyss, J.L., Joron, J.L.G., Valladas, G., Bar-Yosef, O. and Vandermeersch, B. 1988. Thermoluminescence dating of Mousterian 'Proto-Cro-Magnon' remains from Israel and the origin of modern man. *Nature.* 331: 614–16.

Vogel, J.C. and Waterbolk, H.T. 1972. Groningen radiocarbon dates X. *Radiocarbon.* 14: 6–11.

Weiner, S., Goldberg, P. and Bar-Yosef, P. 1993. Bone preservation in Kebara Cave, Israel, using on-site Fourier transform infrared spectrometry. *Journal of Archaeological Science*: 613–27.

Weiner, S. and Goldberg, P. 1990. On-site Fourier Transform Infrared Spectrometry at an archaeological excavation. *Spectroscopy.* 5: 47–50.

Yaalon, D.H. 1967. Factors affecting the lithification of eolianiate and interpretation of its environmental significance in the coastal plain of Israel. *Journal of Sedimentary Petrology.* 37: 1189–99.

Yaalon, D.H. and Dan, J. 1967. Factors controlling soil formation and distribution in the Mediterranean coastal plain of Israel during the Quaternary. *Quaternary Soils*, 7th INQUA Congress Proceedings 1965, 9: 321–38.

Yaalon, D.H. and Ganor, E.. 1973. The influence of dust on soil during the Quaternary. *Soil Science.* 116: 146–55.

Yair, A. and Enzel, Y. 1987. The relationship between annual rainfall and sediment yield in arid and semi-arid areas. The case of the northern Negev. *CATENA SUPPLEMENT.* 10: 121–35.

Chapter 5

Anati, E. and Haas, N. 1967. A Paleolithic site with Pithicanthropian remains in the plain of Esdraelon, near Kibbutz Hazorea. *Israel Exploration Journal* 17: 114–18.

Arensburg B. 1973. The people in the land of Israel from the Epipaleolithic to present times. Doctoral Dissertation. Department of Anatomy and Anthropology, University of Tel Aviv, Tel Aviv. pp. 10–40, 62–74.

Arensburg, B. 1977. New Upper Paleolithic human remains from Israel. In *Eretz-Israel* vol. 13 (eds B. Arensburg and O. Bar-Yosef). Jerusalem: Israel Exploration Society, pp. 208–15.

Arensburg, B. 1991. The vertebral column, thoracic cage and hyoid bone. In *Le Squelette Mousterien de Kebara 2* (eds O. Bar-Yosef and B. Vandermeersch). Cahiers de Paleoanthropologie. Paris: Editions du Centre National de La Recherche Scientifique.

Arensburg, B. and Bar-Yosef, O. 1973. Human remains from Ein Gev I, Jordan Valley, Israel. *Paleorient* 1: 201–6.

Arensburg, B. and Hershkovitz, I. 1988. Neolithic Human Remains. In *Nahal Hemar Cave* (eds O. Bar-Yosef and D. Alon). Jerusalem: Atiqot (English Series), vol. XVIII, pp. 50–62.

Arensburg B. and Rak, Y. 1985. Jewish Skeletal Remains from the Period of the Kings of Judea. *Palestine Exploration Quarterly* 117: 30–4.

Arensburg, B., Smith, P. and Yakar, R. 1978. The human remains from Abu Gosh. In *Abou Gosh et Beisamoun* (ed. M. Lechevallier). Paris: Memoires et Travaux du Centre de Recherches Prehistoriques Francais de Jerusalem No. 2, pp. 95–105.

Arensburg, B., Goldstein, M., Nathan, H. and Ray, Y. 1981. Skeletal remains of Jews from Hellenistic, Roman and Byzantine periods in Israel. I: Metric Analysis. *Bulletin et Memoires de la Societe d'Anthropologie, Paris* 7: 175–86.

Arensburg, B., Bar-Yosef, O., Belfer-Cohen, A. and Rak, Y. 1990. Mousterian and Aurignacian human remains from Hayonim Cave, Israel. *Paleorient* 16: 107–9.

Bar-Yosef, O. 1980. The Prehistory of the Levant. *Annual Review of Anthropology* 9: 101–33.

Bar-Yosef, O. 1992. The role of Western Asia in modern human origins. *Philosphical Transactions of the Royal Society of London, series B*: 183–200.

Bar-Yosef, O. and Valla, F. (eds) 1991. *The Natufian Culture in the Levant.* Ann Arbor: International Monographs in Prehistory.

Bar-Yosef, O. and Vandermeersch, B. (eds) 1991. *Le Squelette Mousterien de Kebara 2.* Cahiers de Paleoanthropologie. Paris: Editions du Centre National de La Recherche Scientifique.

Belfer-Cohen, A. 1991. The Natufian in the Levant. *Annual Review of Anthropology* 20: 167–86.

Belfer-Cohen, A., Arensburg, B., Bar-Yosef, O. and Gopher, A. 1990. Human remains from Netiv Hagdud-a PPNA site in the Jordan Valley. *Mitekufat Haeven* 23: 79–85.

Belfer-Cohen, A., Schepartz, L.A. and Arensburg, B. 1991. New biological data for the Natufian populations in Israel. In *The Natufian Culture in the Levant* (eds O. Bar-Yosef and F. Valla) Ann Arbor: International Monographs in Prehistory, pp. 411–24.

Ben-Itzak, S., Smith, P. and Bloom, R.A. 1988. Radiographic study of the humerus in Neanderthals and Homo sapiens sapiens. *American Journal of Physical Anthropology* 77: 231–42.

Brown, M.B and Forsythe A.B. 1974a. The small sample behaviour of some statistics which test the equality of several means. *Technometrics* 16: 129–32.

Brown, M.B and Forsythe A.B. 1974b. Robust test for the equality of variances. *Journal of the American Statistical Association* 69: 364–7.

Corrucini, R.S. 1992. Metrical reconsiderations of the Skhul IV and IX and border Cave I crania in the context of modern human origins. *American Journal of Physical Anthropology* 87: 433–46.

Crognier, E. and Dupouy-Madre, M. 1974. Les Natoufiens du Nahal Oren. *Paleorient* 2: 103–21.

Ferembach, D. 1961a. Squelettes du Natoufien d'Israel, etude anthropologique. *L'Anthropologie* 65: 46–66.

Ferembach, D. 1961b. Les restes humains de Gat. In *Preliminary Excavations at Tel Gat* (ed. S. Yeivin). Jerusalem: Sivan Press, pp. 12–20.

Ferembach, D. 1977. Les Natoufiens de Palestine. In *Eretz-Israel* vol 13 (eds B. Arensburg and O. Bar-Yosef). Jerusalem: Israel Exploration Foundation, pp. 241–52.

Ferembach, D. 1978. Les cranes surmodeles. In *Abou Gosh et Beisamoun* (ed. M. Lechevallier). Paris: Memoires et Travaux du Centre de Recherches Prehistoriques Francais de Jerusalem No. 2, pp. 179–81.

Frayer D.W. 1984. Biological and Cultural Change in the European Late Pleistocene and Early Holocene. In *The Origins of Modern Humans* (eds F.H. Smith and F. Spencer). New York: Alan R. Liss, Inc., pp. 211–50.

Garrod, D.A.E. and Bate, D.M. 1937. *The Stone Age of Mount Carmel* Volume I. Oxford: Clarendon Press.

Geraads, D. and Tchernov, E. 1983. Femurs humains du Pleistocene moyen de Gesher Benot Ya'acov (Israel). *L'Anthropologie* 87: 138–41.

Giles, M. 1958. The human remains: the crania. In *Lachish IV the Bronze Age*. Volume I. (ed. O. Tufnell) Oxford: Oxford University Press, pp. 318–33.

Grün, R. and Stringer, C.B. 1991. Electron spin resonance dating and the evolution of modern humans. *Archaeometry* 33: 153–9.

Grün, R., Stringer, C.B. and Schwarz, H.P. 1991. ESR dating of teeth from Garrod's Tabun Cave collection. *Journal of Human Evolution* 20: 231–48.

Haas, N and Nathan, H. 1973. An attempt at a Social interpretation of the significance of the Chalcolithic burials from Nahal Mishmar. In *Essays in Honour of Professor Shemuel Yeivin*. Tel Aviv: Institute of Archaeology. 143–53.

Hershkovitz, I., Arensburg, B. and Nadel, D. 1992. Ohalo II – the Natufian's bridge to the past. Proceedings of the Third International Congress on Human Paleontology in *Mitekufat Haeven Supplement* 1: 57.

Hershkovitz, I. and Gopher, A. 1988. Human Burials from Horvat Galil: A Prepottery Neolithic Site in the Upper Galilee, Israel. *Paleorient*, 14: 119–25.

Hershkovitz, I., Garfinkel, Y. and Arensburg, B. 1986. Neolithic skeletal remains at Yiftahel, Area C. *Paleorient* 12: 73–81.

Hershkovitz, I., Arensburg, B. and Nadel, D. 1992. Ohalo II. The Natufians bridge to the past (Abstract). *Mitekufat Haeven Supplement*. 1: 57.

Hrdlicka, A. 1938. Skeletal remains. In *Megiddo tombs* (eds P.L.O Guy and R.M. Engberg) Chicago: Oriental Institute Publication 38, pp. 192–208.

Kafafi, Z., Rollefson, G.O. and Simmons, A.H. 1990. The 1989 season at Ain Ghazal. Preliminary report. *Annals of the Department of Antiquities of Jordan* XXXIV: 11–23.

Kaufman, D. 1989. Observations of the Geometric Kebaran: A view from Newe David. In *Investigations in South Levantine Prehistory* (eds O.

Bar-Yosef and B. Vandermeersch). Oxford: BAR International Series 497, pp. 275–86.

Keita, S.O.Y. 1988. An analysis of crania from Tell-Duweir using multiple discriminant functions. *American Journal of Physical Anthropology* 75: 375–90.

Keith, A. 1927. A Report on the Galilee Skull. In *Research in Prehistoric Galilee (1925–1926)* (ed. F. Turville-Petrie). Jerusalem: British School of Archaeology, pp. 53–106.

Keith, A. 1934. The late Paleolithic inhabitants of Palestine. *Proceedings of the 1st International Conference of Prehistory and Protohistoric Sciences*. London, pp. 46–7.

Krogman, W.M. 1974. Cranial Material. In *Discoveries in the Wadi ed-Daliyeh* (eds P.W. Lapp and N.L. Lapp). Annual of the American School of Oriental Research. XLI: 89–96.

Krogman, W.M. 1989. Representative Early Bronze crania from Bab edh-Dhra. In *Expedition to the Dead Sea Plain, Jordan (1965–1967). Bab edh-Dhra: excavations in the cemetery* (eds P.W. Lapp, R.T. Schaub and W.E. Rast). pp. 507–20.

Kurth, G. and Rohrer-Ertl, O. 1981. On the anthropology of the Mesolithic to Chalcolithic human remains from the Tell es-Sultan in Jericho Jordan. In *Excavations at Jericho*. vol III (ed. K.M. Kenyon). Jerusalem: British School of Archaeology, pp. 407–99.

Lacombe J. P. 1980. Les ossements humain de Ben Shemen. In *Tombes et Ossuaires de la region cotiere Palestiniene au ive millenaire avant l'ere chretiennne* (eds J. Perrot and D. Ladiray). Paris: Association Paleorient, pp. 80–92.

McCown, T.D. 1939. The Natufian Crania from Mount Carmel. Doctoral dissertation. University of California, Berkeley.

McCown, T.D. and Keith, A. 1939. The fossil human remains from the Levalloiso-Mousterian. In *The Stone Age of Mount Carmel*. Vol. II. Oxford: Clarendon Press.

Miller, R.G. 1981. *Simultaneous Statistical Inference*, New York: Springer-Verlag.

Molleson, T.I. and Jones, K. 1991. Dental evidence for dietary change at Abu Hureyra. *Journal of Archaeological Science* 18: 525–39.

Molleson, T.I. and Oakley, K.P. 1966. Relative antiquity of he Ubeidiya hominid. *Nature* 209: 1268.

Nadel, D. and Hershkovitz, I. 1991. New subsistence data and human remains from the earliest Levantine Epipaleolithic *Current Anthropology* 32: 631–35.

Ozbek M. 1974. Etude de la deformation cranienne artificielle chez les Chalcolithiques de Byblo. *Bulletin et Memoirs de la Societe d'Anthropologie de Paris*. XIII: 455–81.

Rak Y. 1991. The Pelvis. In *Le Squelette Mousterien de Kebara 2* (eds O. Bar-Yosef and B. Vandermeersch). Cahiers de Paleoanthropologie. Paris: Editions du Centre National de La Recherche Scientifique.

Rak, Y., Kimbel, W. and Hovers, E. 1992. Neanderthal autopomorphies new finds Amud 1992. Paper presented at The Third International Congress of Human Paleontology, Jerusalem 1992.

Risdon, D.L. 1939. A study of the cranial and other human remains from Palestine excavated at Tell-Duweir (Lachish) by the Wellcome-Marston Archaeological Research Expedition. *Biometrika* 31: 99–166.

Rollefson, G.O. and Simmons, A.H. 1985. The early Neolithic village of Ain Ghazal, Jordan: Preliminary report on the 1983 season. *BASOR Supplement* 23: 35–52.

Rollefson, G.O., Simmons, A.H., Donaldson, M.L., Gillespie, W., Kafafi, Z., Kohler-Rollefson, I., McAdam, E., Rolston, S.L. and Tubb, M.K. 1985. Excavation at the Pre-Pottery Neolithic B village of Ain Ghazal (Jordan), 1983. *Mitteilungen der Deutschen Orient Gesellschaft* 117: 69–116.

Ronen, A., Kaufman, D., Gophna, R., Backler, N., Smith, P. and Amiel, A. 1975. The epipaleolithic site Hefziba, central coastal plain of Israel. *Quarter* 26: 53–72.

Schulz, M. 1987. Human skeletal remains. In Report on the first two seasons of excavations at Basta (1986–1987) (eds H.J. Nissen, M. Muheisen and H.G. Gebel). *Annals of the Department of Antiquities of Jordan* XXXI: 96–7.

Schulz, M. and Scherer, A. 1991. Human skeletal remains. In Report on the excavations at Basta 1988. (eds H.J. Nissen, M. Muheisen and H.G. Gebel). *Annals of the Department of Antiquities of Jordan* XXXV: 18–19.

Schwarcz, H.P., Grün, R., Vandermeersch, B., Bar-Yosef, O., Valladas, H. and Tchernov, E. 1988. ESR dates for the hominid burial site of Qafzeh in Israel. *Journal of Human Evolution* 17: 733–7.

Schwarcz, H.P., Buhay, W.M., Grün, R., Valladas, H., Tchernov, E., Bar-Yosef, O. and Vandermeersch, B. 1989. ESR dating of the Neanderthal site, Kebara Cave, Israel. *Journal of Archaeological Science* 16: 653–9.

Smith, P. 1979. Regional diversity in Epipaleolithic populations. *International Journal of Skeletal Research* 6: 243–50.

Smith, P. 1988. Evolutionary trends in Pre-agricultural communities. *Rivista di Antropologia (Roma) supp.* LXVI: 281–94.

Smith, P. 1989a. Dental Ontogeny in Fossil Hominids. In *Hominidae. Proceedings of the 2nd International Congress of Human Paleontology* (ed. G. Giacobini). Milan: Jaca Books, pp. 347–50.

Smith, P. 1989b. Paleonutrition and subsistence patterns in the Natufians. (ed. I. Hershkovitz). *People and Culture in Change. Proceedings of the Second Symposium on Upper Palaeolithic, Mesolithic and Neolithic Populations of Europe and the Mediterranean Basin.* BAR International Series 508 (i), Oxford: 375–84, 1989.

Smith, P. 1989c. The skeletal biology and paleopathology of Early Bronze Age populations in the Levant. In *L'Urbanisation de la Palestine a l'Age du Bronze Ancien* (ed. P. de Miroschedji). Oxford: BAR International Series 527 (ii), 297–313.

Smith, P. 1991. The dental evidence for nutritional status in the Natufians. In *The Natufian Culture in the Levant* (eds O. Bar-Yosef and F. Valla). Ann Arbor: International Monographs in Prehistory No. 1, pp. 425–32.

Smith, P. and Arensburg, B. 1977. A Mousterian skeleton from Kebara Cave. In *Eretz-Israel.* Vol. 13 (eds B. Arensburg and O. Bar-Yosef). Jerusalem: Israel Exploration Society, pp. 164–76.

Smith, P. and Tillier, A.M. 1989. Additional infant remains from the Mousterian Strata, Kebara Cave (Israel). In *Investigations in South Levantine Prehistory* (eds O. Bar-Yosef and B. Vandermeersch). Oxford: BAR International Series 497, pp. 323–35.

Smith, P., Bar-Yosef, O. and Sillen, A. 1984. Archaeological and skeletal evidence for dietary change during the late Pleistocene/early Holocene in the Levant. In *Paleopathology at the Origins of Agriculture* (eds M.N. Cohen and G.J. Armelagos). New York: Academic Press, pp. 101–30.

Smith, P., Mazar, E., Sabari, P., Selah, M. and Ganshrow, R. 1993. Achziv Phoenicians. *National Geographic Research and Exploration* 9: 54–69.

Soliveres, O. 1978. Les restes post-cephalique. In *Abou Gosh et Beisamoun* (ed. M. Lechevallier). Paris: Memoires et Travaux du Centre de Recherches Prehistoriques Francais de Jerusalem No. 2, pp. 181–91.

Soliveres, O. 1988. Les Hommes de Mallaha (Eynan) Israel. Part II *Etude Anthropologique.* Paris: Memoires et Travaux du Centre de Recherches Prehistoriques Francais de Jerusalem No. 7.

Stringer, C., Hublin, J.J. and Vandermeersch, B. 1984. The origin of anatomically modern humans in western Europe. In *The Origins of Modern Humans* (eds F.H. Smith and F. Spencer). New York: Alan R. Liss, Inc., pp. 51–135.

Strouhal, E. 1973. Five plastered skulls from Pre-pottery Neolithic B Jericho. Anthropological Study. *Paleorient* 1: 231–47.

Suzuki, H. and Takai, F. 1970. *The Amud Man and His Cave Site.* Tokyo: The University of Tokyo.

Tobias, P.V. 1966. Fossil hominid remains from Ubeidiya, Israel. *Nature* 211: 130–3.

Tillier, A.M. 1989. Les enfants proto-Magnons de Qafzeh (Israel) mise au point. In *Investigations in South Levantine Prehistory* (eds O. Bar-Yosef and B. Vandermeersch). Oxford: BAR International Series 497, pp. 343–8.

Tillier, A.M. 1992. The origins of modern humans in Southwest Asia: Ontogenetic aspects. In *The Evolution and Dispersal of Modern Humans in Asia* (eds T. Akazawa, K. Aoki and T. Kimura). Tokyo: Hokusen-Sha, pp. 29–38.

Trinkhaus, E. 1983. *The Shanidar Neandertals.* New York: Academic Press.

Trinkhaus, E. 1992. Morphological contrasts between the Near Eastern Qafzeh-Skhul and Late Archaic human samples: Grounds for a behavioural difference? In *The Evolution and Dispersal of Modern Humans in Asia* (eds T. Akazawa, K. Aoki and T. Kimura). Tokyo: Hokusen-Sha, pp. 277–94.

Valla, F.R. 1987. Chronologie absolue et chronologies relatives dans le Natoufien. In *Chronologie du Proche Orient* (eds O. Aurenche, J. Evin and F. Hours). Oxford; BAR International Series 379: 267–94.

Valladas, H., Joron, J.L., Valladas, G., Arensburg, B., Bar-Yosef, O., Belfer-Cohen, A., Goldberg, P., Laville, H., Meignen, L., Rak, Y., Tchernov, E., Tillier, A.M. and Vandermeersch, B. 1987. Thermoluminescence dates for the Neanderthal burial site at Kebara in Israel. *Nature* 330: 159–60.

Vallois, H.V. 1936. Les ossements Natoufiens d'Erq el-Ahmar (Palestine). *L'Anthropologie* 46: 529–39.

Vandermeersch, B. 1981a. Les premiers *Homo sapiens* au Proche Orient. In *Les Processus de l'Hominisation* (ed. D. Ferembach). Paris: CNRS, pp. 97–103.

Vandermeersch, B. 1981b. *Les Hommes Fossiles de Qafzeh (Israel).* Paris: Cahiers de Paleontologie Editions du CNRS.

Vandermeersch, B. 1992. The Near Eastern hominids and the origins of modern humans in Eurasia. In *The Evolution and Dispersal of Modern Humans in Asia* (eds T. Akazawa, K. Aoki and T. Kimura). Tokyo: Hokusen-Sha, pp. 29–38.

Zilberman, U., Skinner, M. and Smith, P. 1992. Tooth components of mandibular deciduous molars of Homo sapiens sapiens and Homo sapiens neanderthalensis: a radiographic study. *American Journal of Physical Anthropology* 87: 255–62.

Chapter 6

Bailey, R.C. 1991. *The Behavioral Ecology of Efe Pygmy Men in the Ituri Forest, Zaire.* Ann Arbor: Anthropological Papers, Museum of Anthropology No. 86.

Bar-Yosef, O. 1980. Prehistory of the Levant. *Annual Review of Anthropology.* 6: 101–33.

Bar-Yosef, O. and Mazar, A. 1982. Israeli Archaeology. *World Archaeology.* 13: 310–25.

Bar-Yosef, O. and Valla, F. (eds) 1991. *The Natufian Culture in the Levant.* Ann Arbor: International Monographs in Prehistory.

Bar-Yosef, O. and Vandermeersch, B. (eds) 1989. *Investigations in South Levant Prehistory – Prehistoire du Sud Levant.* Oxford: British Archaeological Reports.

Binford, L.R. 1980. Willow smoke and dog's tails: hunter-gatherer settlement systems and archaeological site formation. *American Antiquity.* 45: 1–17.

Binford, L.R. 1982. The archaeology of place. *Journal of Anthropological Archaeology.* 1: 5–31.

Close, A.E., Wendorf, F. and Schild, R. 1979. *The Afian: A Study of Stylistic Variation in a Nilotic Industry.* Dallas: Southern Methodist University Press.

Daniel, G. 1981. Introduction: the necessity for an historical approach to archaeology. In *Towards a History of Archaeology* (ed. G. Daniel). London: Thames and Hudson, pp. 9–13.

Dever, W.G. 1992. Syro-Palestinian and Biblical Archeology, In *The Anchor Bible Dictionary* (ed. D.N. Freedman). New York: Doubleday pp. 354–67I.

Edelman, G.M. 1992. *Biologie de le Conscience.* Paris: Editions Odile Jacob.

Eder, J. F. 1984. The impact of subsistence on mobility and settlement pattern in a tropical forest foraging economy: some implications for archaeology. *American Anthropologist* 86: 837–53.

Goring-Morris, A.N. 1987. *At the Edge: Terminal Pleistocene Hunter-Gatherers in the Negev and Sinai.* Oxford: British Archaeological Reports.

Goring-Morris, A.N. 1988. Reply to reviews of 'At the Edge'. *Mitekufat Haeven* 21: 79–86.

Gould, S.J. 1991. *La Vie est belle: Les Surprises de l'Evolution.* Paris, Editions du Seuil.

Hall, M. 1984a. The burden of tribalism: the social context of Southern Africa Iron Age studies. *American Antiquity.* 49: 455–67.

Hall, M. 1984b. Pots and politics: ceramic interpretations in Southern Africa. *World Archaeology.* 15: 262–73.

Halstead, P. and O'Shea, J. 1989. Introduction: cultural response to risk and uncertainty. In *Bad Year Economics: Cultural Responses to Risk and Uncertainty.* (eds P. Halstead and J. O'Shea). Cambridge: Cambridge University Press, pp. 1–7.

Henry, D.O. 1988. Review of *At the Edge* by A.N. Goring-Morris. *Mitekufat Haeven* 21: 53–9.

Holl, A. 1989. Social issues in Saharan prehistory. *Journal of Anthropological Archaeology.* 8: 313–54.

Holl, A. 1990. West African archaeology: colonialism and nationalism. In *A History of African Archaeology* (ed. P. Robertshaw). London: James Currey Ltd., pp. 296–308.

Hull, D.L. 1988. *Science as a Process: An Evolutionary Account of the Social and Conceptual Development of Science.* Chicago: University of Chicago Press.

Isaac, G. 1989. Aspects of human evolution. In *The Archaeology of Human Origins: Papers by Glynn Isaac.* (ed. B. Isaac). Cambridge: Cambridge University Press, pp. 96–119.

Kaufman, D. 1986. A reconsideration of adaptive change in the Levantine Epipaleolithic. In *The End of the Paleolithic in the Old World* (ed. L.G. Straus). Oxford: British Archaeological Reports; pp. 117–28.

Kaufman, D. 1988. Lithic assemblages and settlement patterns of the Late Upper Paleolithic of Israel. *Mitekufat Haeven* 21: 7–19.

Kuhn, T.S. 1970. *The Structure of Scientific Revolutions.* Chicago: University of Chicago Press.

Kuhn, T.S. 1990. *La Tension Essentielle: Tradition et Changement dans les Sciences.* Paris: Gallimard.

Leroi-Gourhan, A. 1971. *L'Homme et la Matiere.* Paris: Albin Michel.

Levy, T.E. (ed.) 1987. *Shiqmim I. Studies Concerning Chalcolithic Societies in the Northern Negev Desert, Israel (1982–1984).* Oxford: BAR International Series 357.

Marks, A.E. 1976–1977. *Prehistory and Paleoenvironments in the Central Negev, Israel. Vol. I: The Avdat/Aqev Area; Vol. II: The Avdat/Aqev Area Part 2 and Har Area.* Dallas, Southern Methodist University Press.

Marks, A.E. 1983. The Middle to Upper Paleolithic transition in the Levant. In *Advances in World Archaeology.* Vol. 2 (eds F. Wendorf and A.E. Close). London: Academic Press, pp. 51–98.

Marks, A.E. 1988. At the Edge or over it? A critique of Goring-Morris' construct for Upper Paleolithic development. *Mitekufat Haeven* 21: 59–67.

Mayr, E. 1982. *The Growth of Biological Thought: Diversity, Evolution and Inheritance.* Cambridge: Harvard University Press.

Mitchell, P. J. 1988. *The Early Microlithic Assemblages of Southern Africa.* Oxford: British Archaeological Reports.

Moorey 1992. *A Century of Biblical Archaeology.* Cambridge: Westminster/John Knox.

Nicolis, G. 1989. Physics of far-from-equilibrium systems and self-organization. In *The New Physics* (ed. P. Davies). Cambridge: Cambridge University Press, pp. 316–47.

Ohel, M.Y. 1986. *The Acheulean of the Yiron Plateau, Israel.* Oxford: British Archaeological Reports.

Ohel, M.Y. 1990. *Lithic Analysis of Acheulean Assemblages from the Avivim Sites.* Oxford: British Archaeological Reports.

Olami, Y. 1984. *Prehistoric Carmel.* Jerusalem: Israel Exploration Society.

Phillips, J. L. 1987. Sinai during the Paleolithic: the early periods. In *Prehistory of Arid North Africa* (ed. A.E. Close). Dallas: Southern Methodist University Press, pp. 105–22.

Popper, K. 1991. *La Connaissance Objective.* Paris: Editions Aubier.

Prigogine, I. 1988. Origins of complexity. In *Origins* (ed. A.C. Fabian). Cambridge: Cambridge University Press.

Prigogine, I. and Stengers, I. 1984. *Order out of Chaos.* New York: Bantam Books.

Renfrew, C.A. 1984. *Approaches to Social Archaeology.* Edinburgh: Edinburgh University Press.

Ronen, A. 1984. *Sefunim Prehistoric Sites, Mount Carmel, Israel.* Oxford: British Archaeological Reports.

Shott, M. 1986. Technological organization and settlement mobility: an ethnographic examination. *Journal of Anthropological Research.* 42: 15–51.

Smith, A.B. 1992. *Pastoralism in Africa: Origins and Development Ecology.* London: C. Hurst.

Speth, J.D. 1988. Lithic analysis and the reconstruction of prehistoric forain economies: comments on 'At the Edge: Terminal Pleistocene

Hunter-Gatherers in the Negev and Sinai' by A.N. Goring-Morris. *Mitekufat Haeven* 21: 68–78.

Torrence, R. 1983. Time budgeting and hunter-gatherer technology. In *Hunter-Gatherer Economy in Prehistory: A European Perspective* (ed. G. Bailey). Cambridge: Cambridge University Press, pp. 11–22.

Torrence, R. 1986. *Production and Exchange of Stone Tools.* Cambridge: Cambridge University Press.

Trigger, B. 1984. Alternative archaeologies: Nationalist, Colonialist, Imperialist. *Man* (NS) 19: 355–70.

Trigger, B. 1990. The History of African Archaeology in world Perspective. In *A History of African Archaeology* (ed. P. Robertshaw). London: J. Currey Ltd., pp. 309–19.

Valla, F.R. 1988. At the Edge – Commentaire. *Mitekufat Haeven* 21: 50–3.

Vita-Finzi, C. and Higgs, E. S. 1970. Prehistoric economy in the Mount Carmel Area of Palestine: site catchment analysis. *Proceedings of the Prehistoric Society.* 36: 1–37.

Wendorf, F. and Schild, R. 1992. The Middle Paleolithic in Northern Africa: A Status Report. In *New Light on the Northeast African Past* (eds F. Klees and R. Kuper). Köln: Heinrich Barth Institut, pp. 39–78.

Wilk, R. 1985. The ancient Maya and the political present. *Journal of Anthropological Research.* 41: 307–26.

Wobst, M. 1983. Paleolithic archaeology: some problems with form, space and time. In *Hunter-Gatherer Economy in Prehistory: A European Perspective* (ed. G. Bailey). Cambridge: Cambridge University Press, pp. 220–5.

Chapter 7

Arensburg, B. and Bar-Yosef, O. 1967. Yacimiento paleolitico en el valle de Refaim, Jerusalem, Israel. *Ampurias.* 29: 117–33.

Bar-Yosef, O. 1975. Archaeological occurrences in the Middle Pleistocene of Israel. In *After the Australopithecines: Stratigraphy, Ecology and Culture Change in the Middle Pleistocene* (eds K.W. Butzer and G.L. Isaac). Chicago: Aldine, pp. 571–604.

Bar-Yosef, O. and Goren, N. 1980. Afterthoughts following prehistoric surveys in the Levant. *Israel Exploration Journal.* 30: 1–16.

Bar-Yosef, O. and Goren-Inbar, N. 1993. *The lithic assemblages of the site of 'Ubeidiya, Jordan Valley.* Jerusalem: Qedem 34.

Bar-Yosef, O. and Tchernov, E. 1972. *On the paleo-ecological history of the site of 'Ubeidiya.* Jerusalem: The Israel Academy of Sciences and Humanities.

Bar-Yosef, O., Vandermeersch, B., Arensburg, B., Belfer-Choen, A., Goldberg, P., Laville, H., Meignen, L., Rak, Y., Speth, J.D., Tchernov, E., Tullier, A.-M. and Weiner, S. 1992. The excavations in Kebara Cave, Mt. Carmel. *Current Anthropology.* 33 (5): 497–550.

Belitzky, S., Goren-Inbar, N. and Werker, E. 1991. A Middle Pleistocene wooden plank with man-made polish. *Journal of Human Evolution.* 20: 349–59.

Besançon, J., Copeland, L., Hours, F., Muhesen, S. and Sanlaville, P. 1981. Le Paleolithique d'el Kowm. Rapport preliminaire. *Paleorient.* 7 (1): 33–55.

Blanckenhorn, M. 1914. *Surien, Arabien und Mesopotamien.* Heidelberg: Hand. Region. Geol.

Bordes, F. 1955. Le Paleolithique inferieur et moyen de Jabroud (Syrie) et la question du Pre-aurignacien. *L'Anthropologie.* 59: 486–507.

Bordes, F. 1977. Que sont le Pre-Aurignacien et le labroudien? In *Moshe Stekelis Memorial Book* (eds B. Arensburg and O. Bar-Yosef). Jerusalem: The Israel Exploration Society, pp. *49–55*.

Clark, J.D. 1975. Comparison of the Late Acheulian industries of Africa and the Middle East. In *After the Australopithecines: Stratigraphy, Ecology and Culture Change in the Middle Pleistocene* (eds K.W. Butzer and G.L. Isaac). The Hague: Mouton, pp. 605–59.

Copeland, L. 1983. The stone industries. In *Adlun in the stone age – the excavations of D.A.E. Garrod in the Lebanon 1958–1963* (ed D.A. Roe). Oxford: BAR International Series, 159.

Copeland, L. and Hours, F. 1978. La sequence acheuleen du Nahr el Kebir, region septentrionale du littoral syrien. *Paleorient.* 4: 5–31.

Copeland, L. and Hours, F. 1981. La fin de l'Acheuleen et l'avenement du Paleolithique moyen syrien. In *Prehistoire du Levant. Chronologie et organisation de l'espace depuis les origines jusqu'au 6° millenaire* (eds J. Cauvin and P. Sanlaville). Paris: CNRS, pp. 225–38.

Dauvois, M. 1981. De la simultaneite des concepts Kombewa et Lavallois dans l'Acheuleen du Maghreb et du Sahara Nord-Occidental. In *Recherche sur les Grandes Civilizations, Synthese no. 6 Prehistoire Africaine. Melange Offerts au Doyen Lionel Balout* (eds C. Raubet, H.-J. Hugot and G. Sauville). Paris: ADPF, pp. 313–21.

Debard, E., Bar-Yosef, O., Chech, M., Eisenmann, V., Faure, M., Guérin, C., Libermann, D. and Tchernov, E. 1989. Nouvelle mission archaeologique et paleontologique d'Oubeidiyeh (Israël): premiers resultats. *Paleorient.* 15 (1): 231–7.

Eisenmann, V., Ballesio, R., Beden, M., Faure, M., Geraads, D., Guerin, C. and Heintz, E. 1983. Nouvelle interpretation biochronologique des grands mammiferes d'Ubeidiya, Israel. *Geobios.* 16 (5): 629–33.

Feraud, G., D.Y., C.M. Hall, Goren, N. and H.P. Schwartz. 1983. 40 Ar/39Ar age limit for an Acheulian site in Israel (sample site: Berekhat Ram). *Nature.* 304 (5923): 263–5.

Garrod, D.A.E. 1956. Acheuleo-Jabroudien et 'Pre-Aurignacien' de la Grotte du Taboun (Mont Carmel); etude stratigraphique et chronologique. *Quaternaria.* 3: 39–59.

Garrod, D.A.E. and Bate, D.M. 1937. *The stone age of Mount Carmel.* Oxford: Oxford University Press.

Garrod, D.A.E. and Kirkbride, D. 1961. Excavations at Abri Zumoffen, a Paleolithic rock-shelter near Adlun, in Southern Lebanon. *Bulletin du Musée de Beyrouth.* 16: 7–45.

Geraads, D. and Tchernov, E. 1983. Femurs Humains du Pleistocene Moyen de Gesher Benot Ya'aqov (Israel). *L'Anthropologie.* 87 (1): 138–41.

Gilead, D. 1968. Gesher Benot Ya'aqov. *Hadashot Archeologiot.* 27: 34–5.

Gilead, D. 1970a. Handaxe industries in Israel and the Near East. *World Archaeology.* 2: 1–11.

Gilead, D. 1970b. *Early paleolithic cultures in Israel and the Near East.* Ph. D thesis, Hebrew University, Jerusalem.

Gilead, D. 1973. Cleavers in the early Palaeolithic industries in Israel. *Paleorient.* 1: 73–86.

Gilead, D. 1975. Lower and Middle Paleolithic settlement patterns in the Levant. In *Problems in prehistory: North Africa and the Levant* (eds F. Wendorf and A.E. Marks). Dallas: Southern Methodist University, pp. 273–82.

Gilead, I. 1993. *The assemblage of layer I–15: The lithic assemblages of the site of 'Ubeidiya, Jordan Valley.* Jerusalem: Qedem 34, pp. 95–120.

Gisis, I. and Bar-Yosef, O. 1974. New excavations at Zuttiyeh cave, wadi Amud, Israel. *Paleorient.* 2: 175–80.

Goren, N. 1981a. *The Lithic Assemblages of the Site of 'Ubeidiya, Jordan Valley.* Ph.D. thesis, Hebrew University, Jerusalem.

Goren, N. 1981b. The Lower Palaeolithic in Israel and adjacent countries. In *Préhistoire du Levant* (eds P. Sanlaville and J. Cauvin). Lyon: CNRS, Colloque 598, pp. 193–205.

Goren-Inbar, N. 1985. The lithic assemblages of Berekhat Ram Acheulian site, Golan Heights. *Paleorient.* 11 (1): 7–28.

Goren-Inbar, N. 1986. A figurine from the Acheulian site of Berekhat Ram. *Mitekufat Haeven.* 19: 7–12.

Goren-Inbar, N. 1988. The Lower Palaeolithic–synthesis. *Paleorient.* 13 (2): 109–11.

Goren-Inbar, N. 1992. The Acheulian site of Gesher Benot Ya'aqov – an Asian or an African entity? In *The evolution and dispersal of modern humans in Asia* (eds T. Akazawa, K. Aoki and T. Kimura). Tokyo: Hokusen-sha, pp. 67–82.

Goren-Inbar, N. and Belitzky, S. 1989. Structural Position of the Pleistocene Gesher Benot Ya'aqov Site in the Dead Sea Rift Zone. *Quaternary Research.* 31: 371–6.

Goren-Inbar, N., Belitzky, S., Verosub, K., Werker, E., Kislev, M., Rosenfeld, A., Heimann, A. and Carmi, I. 1992a. New discoveries at the Middle pleistocene Gesher Benot Ya'aqov Acheulian site. *Quaternary Research.* 38: 117–28.

Goren-Inbar, N., Belitzky, S., Goren, Y., Rabinovitch, R., and Saragusti, I. 1992b. Gesher Benot Ya'aqov – the 'bar': an Acheulian assemblage. *Geoarchaeology.* 7 (1): 27–40.

Goren-Inbar, N. and I. Sargusti. In prep. An Acheulian biface assemblage from the site of Gesher Benot Ya'aqov, Israel: indications of African affinities.

Grün, R. and Stringer, C.B. 1991. Electron Spin Resonance dating and the evolution of modern humans. *Archaeometry.* 33 (2): 153–99.

Grün, R., Shackleton, N.J. and Deacon, H.J. 1990. Electron-spin-resonance dating of tooth enamel from Klasies River Mouth Cave. *Current Anthropology.* 31 (4): 427–32.

Grün, R., Stringer, C.B. and Schwarcz, H.P. 1991. ¯SR dating of teeth from Garrod's Tabun cave collection. *Journal of Human Evolution.* 20: 231–48.

Hennig, G.J. and Hours, F. 1982. Dates pour le passage entre l'Acheuleen et le Paleolitique moyen a El-Kowm (Syrie). *Paleorient.* 8: 81–4.

Horowitz, A. 1979. *The Quaternary of Israel.* New York: Academic Press.

Hours, F. 1975. The Lower Paleolithic of Lebanon and Syria. In *Problems in prehistory: North Africa and the Levant* (eds F. Wendorf and A.E. Marks). Dallas: Southern Methodist University, pp. 249–71.

Hours, F. 1979. La fin de l'Acheuleen en Syrie du Nord, note préliminaire. *Paleorient.* 5: 9–16.

Hours, F. 1981. Le Paléolithique inférieur de la Syrie et du Liban. In *Préhistoire du Levant* (eds J. Cauvin and P. Sanlaville). Paris: CNRS, pp. 165–84.

Hours, F., Copeland, L. and Aurenche, O. 1973. Les industries paleolithiques du Proche Orient: essai de correlations. *L'Anthropologie.* 77 (3–4; 5–6): 229–80; 437–96.

Howell, F.C. 1959. Upper Pleistocene stratigraphy and Early Man in the Levant. *Proceedings of the American Philosophical Society.* 103 (1): 1–65.

Isaac, G.L. 1972. Chronology and the tempo of cultural change during the Pleistocene. In *Calibration of hominid evolution* (eds W.W. Bishop and J. Miller). Edinburgh: Scottish Academic Press, pp. 381–430.

Isaac, G.L. 1977. *Olorgesailie Archaeological Studies of a Middle Pleistocene Lake Basin in Kenya.* Chicago: The University of Chicago Press.

Jelinek, A.J. 1975. A preliminary report on some Lower and Middle Paleolithic industries from the Tabun Cave, Mount Carmel (Israel). In *Problems in prehistory: North Africa and the Levant* (eds F. Wendorf and A.E. Marks). Dallas: Southern Methodist University, pp. 297–315.

Jelinek, A.J. 1981. The Middle Paleolithic of the Southern Levant from the perspective of the Tabun Cave. In *Prehistoire du Levant* (eds J. Cauvin and P. Sanlaville). Paris: CNRS, pp. 265–80.

Jelinek, A.J. 1982. The Middle Paleolithic in the southern Levant with comments on the appearance of modern *Homo sapiens*. In *The transition from the Lower to the Middle Paleolithic and the origin of Modern Man* (ed. A. Ronen). Oxford: BAR International Series, 151, pp. 57–104.

Jelinek, A.J. 1990. The Amudian in the context of the Mugharan tradition at the Tabun Cave (Mount Carmel), Israel. In *The emergence of modern humans. An archaeological perspective* (ed. P. Mellars). New York: Cornell University Press, pp. 81–90.

Jelinek, A.J., Farrand, W., Haas, G., Horowitz, A. and Goldberg, P. 1973. New excavations at the Tabun Cave, Mt Carmel, Israel, 1967–1972; a preliminary report. *Paleorient.* 1 (2): 151–83.

Keith, A. 1927. A report on the Galilee skull. In *Researches in prehistoric Galilee: 1925–1926* (ed. F. Turville-Petre). London: British School of Archaeology in Jerusalem, pp. 53–106.

Kirkbride, D., Saint-Mathurin, S. d. and Copeland, L. 1983. Results, tentative interpretations and suggested chronology. In *Adlun in the stone age – the excavations of D.A.E. Garrod in the Lebanon 1958–1963* (ed. D.A.Roe). Oxford: BAR International Series, 159, pp. 415–31.

Klein, R. 1989 *The human career, human biological and cultural origins.* Chicago: The University of Chicago Press.

Leakey, M.D. 1971. *Olduvai Gorge. Excavations in BEds I and II, 1960–1963.* Cambridge: Cambridge University Press.

Leakey, M.D. 1975. Cultural patterns in the Olduvai sequence. In *After the Australopithecines: stratigraphy, ecology and culture change in the Middle Pleistocene* (eds K.W. Butzer and G.L. Isaac). The Hague: Mouton, pp. 477–93.

Mercier, N. 1992. *Apport des methodes radionucleaires de datation a l'etude du peuplement de l'Europe et du Proche-Orient au cours du Pleistocene superieur.* Ph.D. thesis, L'Universite de Bordeaux I.

Mor, D. 1986. *The volcanism of the Golan Heights.* Jerusalem: Geological Survey of Israel.

Moshkovitz, S. and Magaritz, M. 1987. Stratigraphy and isotope records of Middle and Late Pleistocene mollusks from a corehole in the Hula

Basin, northern Jordan Valley, Israel. *Quaternary Research*. 28: 226–37.

Neuville, R. 1951. *Le Paleolithique et Mesolithique du desert de Judee*. Paris: Archives de L'Inst. de Paleont. Humaine.

Olami, Y. and Gilead, D. 1979. Handaxe industries in the region of the Nahal Daliya and Nahal Menashe. *Mitekufat Haeven*. 16: 40–67.

Picard, L. and Baida, U. 1966a. *Geological report on the Lower Pleistocene of the Ubeidiya excavations*. Jerusalem: The Israel Academy of Sciences and Humanities.

Picard, L. and Baida, U. 1966b. Stratigraphic position of the 'Ubeidiya Formation. *Proceedings of the Israel Academy of Science and Humanities*. 4: 1–16.

Porat, N. and Schwarcz, H.P. 1991. Use of signal subtraction methods in ESR dating of burned flint. *Nuclear Tracks and Radiation Measurements*. 18 (1/2): 203–12.

Rust, A. 1950. *Die Höhlenfunde von Jabrud (Syrien)*. Neumünster: Wachholtz.

Schroeder, B.H. 1969. *The lithic industries from Jerf Ajla and their bearing on the problem of a Middle to Upper Palaeolithic transition*. Ph.D. thesis, University of Columbia.

Schulman, N. 1962. *The geology of the Central Jordan Valley*. Ph.D. thesis, Hebrew University, Jerusalem.

Schwarcz, H.P., Goldberg, P.D. and Blackwell, B. 1980. Uranium Series Dating of archaeological sites in Israel. *Israel Journal of Earth-Sciences*. 29: 157–65.

Stekelis, M. 1960. The paleol:thic deposits of Jisr Banat Yaqub. *The Bulletin of the Research Council of Israel*. G9: 61–87.

Stekelis, M. 1966. *Archaeological excavations at Ubeidiya, 1960–1963*. Jerusalem: The Israel Academy of Sciences and Humanities.

Stekelis, M., Bar-Yosef, O. and Schick, T. 1969. *Archaeological excavations at Ubeidiya, 1964–1966*. Jerusalem: The Israel Academy of Sciences and Humanities.

Stekelis, M., Picard, L. and Bate, D.M.A. 1937. Jisr Banat Ya'qub. *Quarterly of the Department of Antiquities in Palestine*. 6: 214–15.

Stekelis, M., Picard, L. and Bate, D.M.A. 1938. Jisr Banat Ya'qub. *Quarterly of the Department of Antiquities in Palestine*. 7: 45.

Tchernov, E. 1973. *On the Pleistocene molluscs of the Jordan Valley*. Jerusalem: The Israel Academy of Sciences and Humanities.

Tchernov, E. 1975. *The Early Pleistocene molluscs of Erq el-Ahnar*. Jerusalem: The Israel Academy of Sciences and Humanities.

Tchernov, E. 1986. *Les Mammiferes du Pleistocene Inferieur de la Vallee du Jordain a Oubeidiyeh*. Paris: Association Paleorient.

Tchernov, E. 1988. The biogeographical history of the southern Levant. In *The zoogeography of Israel* (eds Y. Yom-Tov and E. Tchernov. Dordrecht: W. Junk Publishers.

Tobias, P. 1966. *A member of the genus homo from Ubeidiya*. Jerusalem: Israel Academy of Sciences and Humanities.

Trinkaus, E. 1991. Les hommes fossiles de la grotte de Shanidar, Irak: evolution et continuite parmi les hommes archaique tradifs du Proch-Orient. *L'Anthropologie*. 95 (2/3): 535–72.

Turville-Petre, F. 1927. Researches in prehistoric Galilee (1925–1926) and a report on Galilee skull. *British School of Archaeology in Jerusalem Bulletin*. 14: 119 pp.

Vandermeersch, B. 1982. The first *Homo sapiens sapiens* in the Near East. In *The transition from Lower to Middle Palaeolithic and the Origin of Modern Man* (ed. A. Ronen). Oxford: BAR International Series, 151, pp. 297–9.

Weiner, S., Goldberg, P. and Bar-Yosef, O. 1993. Bone preservation in Kebara Cave, Israel using on-site Fourier transform infrared spectrometry. *Journal of Archaeological Science*. 20: pp. 613–27.

Chapter 8

Akazawa, T. 1987. The Ecology of the Middle Paleolithic Occupation at Douara Cave. *Bulletin of the University Museum, University of Tokyo*. 29: 155–66.

Arensburg, B., Schepartz, L.A., Tillier, A.M. Vandermeersch B. and Rak, Y. 1990. A Reappraisal of the Anatomical Basis for Speech in Middle Palaeolithic Hominds. *American Journal of Physical Anthropology* 83: 137–46.

Arensburg, B., Tillier, A.M., Vandermeersch, B., Duday, H., Schepartz, L.A. and Rak, Y. 1989. A Middle Paleolithic Human Hyoid Bone. *Nature* 338: 758–60.

Bar-Yosef, O, 1989a. Upper Pleistocene Cultural Stratigraphy in Southwest Asia. In *Patterns and Processes in Later Pleistocene Human Emergence* (ed. E. Trinkaus). Cambridge: Cambridge University Press, pp. 154–79.

Bar-Yosef, O. 1989b. Geochronology of the Levantine Middle Paleolithic. In *The Human Revolution: Behavioural and Biological Perspectives on the Origins of Modern Humans* (eds P. Mellars and C. Stringer). Edinburgh: Edinburgh University Press, pp. 589–610.

Bar-Yosef, O. 1992a. The Role of Western Asia in Modern Human Origins. *Philosophical Transactions of the Royal Society, B (London)*. 337: 193–200.

Bar-Yosef, O. 1992b. Middle Paleolithic Human Adaptations in the Mediterranean Levant. In *The Evolution and Dispersal of Modern Humans in Asia* (eds T. Akazawa, K. Aoki and T. Kimura). Tokyo: Hokusen Sha, pp. 189–216.

Bar-Yosef, O, and Meigen, L. 1992. Insights into Levantine Middle palaeolithic Cultural Variability. In *The Middle Paleolithic: Adaptation, Behavior and Variability* (eds H. Dibble and P. Mellars). Philadelphia: The University Museum, University of Pennsylvania Press, pp. 163–82.

Bar-Yosef, O. and Vandermeersch, B. 1991. *Le squellete mousterien de Kebara 2*. Paris: Editions du CNRS.

Bar-Yosef, O., Laville, H., Meignen, L., Tillier, A.M., Vandermeersch, B., Arensburg, B., Belfer-Cohen, A., Goldberg, P., Rak, Y. and Tchernov, E. 1988. La sepulture neanderthalienne de Kebara (unite XII). In *L'Homme de Neanderthal* (ed. M. Otte). Liège: ERAUL, pp. 17–24.

Bar-Yosef, O., Vandermeersch, B., Arensburg, B., Belfer-Cohen, A., Goldberg, P., Laville, H., Meignen, L., Rak, Y., Speth, J.D., Tchernov, E., Tillier, A.-M. and Weiner, S. 1992. The Excavations in Kebara Cave, Mt. Carmel. *Current Anthropology*. 33: 497–550.

Belfer-Cohen, A. and Hovers, E. 1992. In the Eye of the Beholder: Mousterian and Natufian Burials in the Levant. *Current Anthropology*. 33: 463–71.

Binford, L.R. 1980. Willow Smoke and Dogs' Tails: Hunter-Gatherer Settlement Systems and Archaeological Site Formation. *American Antiquity*. 45: 4–20.

Binford, S.R. 1968. Early Upper Pleistocene Adaptations in the Levant. *American Anthropologist*. 70: 707–17.

Boëda E. 1988. Le Concept Levallois et l'Evaluation de son Champ d'Application. In *L'Homme de Neandertal: La Technologie*, (ed. M. Otte). Liège: ERAUL, pp. 13–26.

Bouchud, J. 1974. Etude preliminaire de la faune provenant de la grotte du Djebel Qafzeh, pres Nazareth, Israel. *Paléorient*. 2: 87–102.

Boutié, P. 1989. Etude Technologique de l'industrie Mousterienne de la Grotte de Qafzeh, pres de Nazareth, Israel. In *Investigations in South Levantine Prehistory: Prehistoire du Sud-Levant* (eds O. Bar-Yosef and B. Vandermeersch). Oxford: BAR International Series 497, pp. 213.

Clark, G.A. and Lindly, J.M. 1989. The case for continuity: Observations on the biocultural transition in Europe and Western Asia. In *The Human Revolution: Behavioural and Biological Perspectives in the Origins of Modern Humans* (eds P. Mellars and C. Stringer). Edinburgh: University of Edinburgh Press, pp. 626–76.

Clark, J.D. 1992. African and Asian Perspectives on the Origins of Modern Humans. *Philosophical Transactions of the Royal Society, B, London*, 337: 201–15.

Copeland, L. 1975. The Middle and Upper Palaeolithic of Lebanon and Syria in the light of recent research. In *Problems in Prehistory: North Africa and the Levant* (eds F. Wendorf and A.E. Marks). Dallas: SMU Press, pp. 317–50.

Davis, S.M.J., Rabinovich, R. and Goren-lnbar, N. 1988. Population Increase in Western Asia: The Animal Remains from Biq'at Quneitra. *Paléorient*. 14/1: 95–106.

Dibble, H.L. 1987. The interpretation of Middle Paleolithic scraper morphology. *American Antiquity*. 52: 109–17.

Farrand, W.R. 1979. Chronology and Paleoenvironment of Levantine Prehistoric Sites as Seen from Sediment Studies. *Journal of Archaeological Science*. 6: 369–92.

Farrand, W.R. 1982. Environmental conditions during the Lower/Middle Palaeolithic transition in the Near East and the Balkans. In *The Transition from Lower to Middle Palaeolithic and the Origin of Modern Man* (ed. A. Ronan). Oxford: BAR International Series: 151. pp. 105–12.

Fleisch, S.J. 1970. Les Habitats du Paleolithique moyen a Naame, (Liban). *Bulletin du Musee Beyrouth*. 23: 25–98.

Garrod, D.A.E. and Bate, D.M. 1937. *The Stone Age of Mount Carmel*. Oxford: Clarendon Press.

Geneste, J.M., Boëda, E. and Meignen, L. 1990. Identification des chaines operatoire lithique du Pleolithique ancien et moyen. *Paleo*. 2: 43–80.

Gilead, I. 1988. Le site Mousterien de Fara II (Neguev septentrional, Israel) et le remontage de son industrie. *Anthropologie*. 92: 797–808.

Gilead, I. 1991. The Upper Paleolithic in the Levant. *Journal of World Prehistory*. 5: 105–54.

Gilead, I. and Grigson, C. 1984. Farah II: A Middle Palaeolithic open air site in the northern Negev, Israel. *Proceedings of the Prehistoric Society*. 50: 71–97.

Goldberg, P. 1986. Late Quarternary environmental history of the Southern Levant. *Geoarchaeology*. 1: 225–44.

Goldberg, P. and Laville, H. 1991. Etude geologique des depots de la grotte de Kebara (Mont Carmel): campagne 1982–1984. In *Le Squelette Mousterien de Kebara* (eds O. Bar-Yosef and B. Vandermeersch). Paris: Editions du CNRS, pp. 29–42.

Goren-Inbar, N. 1990. *Quneitra: A Mousterian Site on the Golan Heights*. Jerusalem: QEDEM, Monographs of the Institute of Archaeology, Hebrew University.

Grün, R. and Stringer, C.B. 1991. Electron spin resonance dating and the evolution of modern humans. *Archaeometry*. 33: 153–99.

Harrold, F.B. 1989. Mousterian, Chatelperronian and Early Aurignacian in Western Europe: Continuity or Discontinuity? In *The Human Revolution: Behavioural and Biological Perspectives on the Origins of Modern Humans* (eds P. Mellars and C. Stringer). Edinburgh: Edinburgh University Press, pp. 677–713.

Henry, D.O. 1986. The prehistory and palaeoenvironments of Jordan: An overview. *Paleorient*. 12: 5–26.

Horowitz, A. 1979. *The Quaternary of Israel*. New York: Academic Press.

Hovers, E., Rak, Y. and Kimbel, W.H. 1991. Amud Cave – 1991 Season. *Journal of the Israel Prehistoric Society*. 24: 152–7.

Jelinek, A.J. 1981. The Middle Palaeolithic in the Southern Levant from the Perspective of the Tabun Cave. In *Préhistoire du Levant*, edited by J. Cauvin and P. Sanlaville, pp. 265–80. Paris: Editions CNRS.

Jelinek, A.J. 1982a. The Middle Palaeolithic in the southern Levant with comments on the appearance of modern *Homo sapiens*. In *The Transition from Lower to Middle Paleolithic and the Origin of Modern Man: International Symposium to Commemorate the 50th Anniversary of Excavations in the Mount Carmel Caves by D.A.E. Garrod* (ed. A. Ronen). Oxford: BAR International Series 151, pp. 57–104.

Jelinek, A.J. 1982b. The Tabun Cave and Paleolithic Man in the Levant. *Science*. 216: 1369–75.

Jelinek, A.J. 1990. The Amudian in the context of the Mugharan Tradition at the Tabun Cave (Mount Carmel), Israel. In *The Emergence of Modern Humans* (ed. P. Mellars). Edinburgh: Edinburgh University Press, pp. 81–90.

Lieberman, D.E. and Meadow, R.H. 1992. The Biology of Cementum Increments (with an Archaeological Application). *Mammal Review*. 22(2): 1–21.

Marks, A. 1981. The Middle Paleolithic of the Negev. In *Préhistoire du Levant* (eds J. Cauvin and P. Sanlaville). Paris: Centre National de la Recherche Scientifique, pp. 287–98.

Marks, A.E. 1990. The Middle and Upper Palaeolithic of the Near East and the Nile Valley: the Problem of Cultural Transformations. In *The Emergence of Modern Humans* (ed. P. Mellars). Edinburgh: Edinburgh University Press, pp. 56–80.

Marks, A. and Kaufman, D. 1983. Boker Tachtit: the Artifacts. In *Prehistory and Paleoenvironments in the Central Negev, Israel* (ed. A. Marks). Dallas: Southern Methodist University, pp. 69–126.

Marks, A. and Volkman, P. 1986. The Mousterian of Ksar Akil. *Paléorient*. 12: 5–20.

Meignen, L. and Bar-Yosef, O., 1991. Les outillage lithiques moustériens de Kébara.,In *Le Squelette mousterienne de Kebara 2. Mt. Carmel. Israël* (eds O. Bar-Yosef and B. Vandermeersch). Paris: Editions CNRS, pp. 49–76.

Mercier, N. and Valladas, H. in press. Thermoluminescence Dates for the Paleolithic Levant. In *Late Quaternary Chronology and Paleoclimates of the Eastern Mediterranean* (eds O. Bar-Yosef and R.S. Kra). Tucson: Radiocarbon and the Peabody Museum.

Munday, F. 1979. Levantine Mousterian technological variability: a perspective from the Negev. *Paléorient*. 5: 87–104.

Neuville, R. 1951. *Le Paléolithique et le Mésolithique de Désert de Judée*. Paris: Masson et Cie, Editeurs.

Ohnuma, K. 1988. *Ksar Akil, Lebanon: A Technological Study of the Earlier Upper Palaeolithic Levels at Ksar Akil: Vol. III: Levels XXV–XIV*. Oxford: BAR International Series 426.

Ohnuma, K. and Bergman, C.A. 1990. A Technological Analysis of the Upper Palaeolithic Levels (XXV–VI) of Ksar Akil, Lebanon. In *The Emergence of Modern Humans* (ed. P. Mellars). Edinburgh: Edinburgh University Press, pp. 91–138.

Otte, M. and Keeley, L.H. 1990. The Impact of Regionalism on Palaeolithic Studies. *Current Anthropology*. 31: 577–82.

Roe, D. 1983. *Adlun in the Stone Age*. Oxford: BAR International Series: 159.

Ronen, A. 1974. *Tirat-Carmel: A Mousterian Open-Air Site in Israel*. Tel Aviv: Institute of Archaeology, Tel Aviv University.

Ronen, A. 1979. Paleolithic Industries. In *The Quaternary of Israel* (ed. A Horowitz). New York: Academic Press, pp. 296–307.

Ronen, A. 1984. *Sefunim prehistoric sites, Mount Carmel, Israel*. Oxford: BAR International Series: 230.

Sanlaville, P. 1981. Stratigraphie et chronologies du Quaternaire marin du Levant. In *Prehistoire de Levant* (eds J. Cauvin and P. Sanlaville). Paris: Editions du CNRS, pp. 21–32.

Schick, T. and Stekelis, M., 1977. Mousterian Assemblages in Kebara Cave, Mount Carmel. *Eretz Israel* 13 (M. Stekelis Memorial Volume), 97–150.

Schwarcz, H.P., Goldberg, P.D. and Blackwell, B. 1980. Uranium Series Dating of Archaeological Sites in Israel. *Israel Journal of Earth-Sciences*. 29: 157-165.

Schwarcz, H.P., Grün, R., Vandermeersch, B., Bar-Yosef, O., Valladas, H. and Tchernov, E. 1988. ESR dates for the hominid burial site of Qafzeh in Israel. *Journal of Human Evolution*. 17: 733–7.

Schwarcz, H.P., Buhay, W.M., Grün, R., Valladas; H., Tchernov, E., Bar-Yosef, O. and Vandermeersch, B. 1989. ESR dating of the Neanderthal site, Kebara Cave, Israel. *Journal of Archaeological Science*. 16: 653–9.

Shea, J.J. 1988. Spear Points from the Middle Paleolithic of the Levant. *Journal of Field Archaeology*. 15: 441–50.

Shea, J. 1989. A functional Study of the Lithic Industries Associated with Hominid Fossils in the Kebara and Qafzeh Caves, Israel. In *The Human Revolution* (eds P. Mellars and C. Stringer). Edinburgh: Edinburgh University Press, pp. 611–25.

Stevens, D.S. and Hietala, H.J. 1977. Spatial Analysis: Multiple Procedures in Pattern Recognition. *American Antiquity*. 42: 539–59.

Stiner, M.C. 1991. Food procurement and transport by humans and non-human predators. *Journal of Archaeological Science*. 18: 455–82.

Stringer, C.B. 1992. Reconstructing recent human evolution. *Phil. Trans. R. Soc. Lond*. B: 217–24.

Suzuki, H. and Takai, F. 1970. *The Amud Man and His Cave Site*. Tokyo: Academic Press of Japan.

Tchernov, E. 1981. The biostratigraphic of the Levant. In *Prehistoire du Levant. Chronologie et Organisation de L'Espace depuis les Origines jusqu'a Vle Millenaire* (eds J. Cauvin and P. Sanlaville). Paris: Editions du CNRS, pp. 67–97.

Tchernov, E. 1988. Biochronology of the Middle Paleolithic and dispersal events of hominids in the Levant. In *L'Homme de Neandertal* (ed. M. Otte). Liège: Etudes et Recherches Archeologiques de l'Universite de Liège 34, pp. 153–68.

Tillier, A.M., Arensburg, B., Rak, Y. and Vandermeersch, B. 1988. Les sepultures neanderthaliennes du Proch Orient: etat de la question. *Paléorient*. 2: 130–6.

Tillier, A.M. 1992. The origins of modern humans in southwest Asia: Ontogenetic aspects. In *The Evolution and Dispersal of Modern Humans in Asia* (eds T. Akazawa, K. Aoki and T. Kimura). Tokyo: Hokusen-Sha, pp. 15–28.

Trinkaus, E. 1984. Western Asia. In *The Origins of Modern Humans: A World Survey of the Fossil Evidence of Modern Humans* (eds F.H. Smith and F. Spencer). New York: Alan R. Liss, Inc., pp. 251–93.

Trinkaus, E. 1989. The Upper Pleistocene transition. In *The Emergence of Modern Humans* (ed. E. Trinkaus). Cambridge: Cambridge University Press, pp. 42–66.

Trinkaus, E. 1992. Morphological contrasts between the Near Eastern Qafzeh-Skhul and Late Archaic human samples: Grounds for a behavioral difference? In *The Evolution and Dispersal of Modern Humans in Asia* (eds T. Akazawa, K. Aoki and T. Kimura). Tokyo: Hokusen-Sha, pp. 277–94.

Valladas, H., Joron, J.L., Valladas, G., Arensburg, B., Bar-Yosef, O., Belfer-Cohen, A., Goldberg, P., Laville, H., Meignen, L., Rak, Y., Tchernov, E., Tillier, A.M. and Vandermeersch, B. 1987. Thermoluminscence dates for the Neanderthal burial site at Kebara in Israel. *Nature*. 330: 159–60.

Valladas, H., Reyss, J.L., Joron, J.L., Valladas, G., Bar-Yosef, O. and Vandermeersch, B. 1988. Thermoluminescence dating of Mousterian 'Proto-Cro-Magnon' remains from Israel and the origin of modern man. *Nature*. 331: 614–15.

Vandermeersch, B. 1981. Les hommes fossiles de Qafzeh (Israel). Editions CNRS: Paris.

Vandermeersch, B. 1989. The evolution of modern humans: recent evidence from southwest Asia. In *The Human Revolution* (eds P. Mellars and C. Stringer). Edinburgh: Edinburgh University Press. pp. 155–64.

Vandermeersch, B. 1992. The Near Eastern Hominids and the origins of Modern Humans in Eurasia. In *The Evolution and Dispersal of Modern Humans in Asia* (eds T. Akazawa, K. Aoki and T. Kimura). Tokyo: Hokusen-Sha, pp. 29–38.

Wreschner, E. 1967. Excavation, finds and summary. *Quaternaria* 9, 69–89.

Wolpoff, M.H. 1989. Multiregional evolution: The fossil alternative to Eden. In *The Human Revolution: Behavioural and Biological Perspectives in The Origins of Modern Humans* (eds P. Mellars and C. Stringer). Edinburgh: Edinburgh University Press, pp. 62–108.

Ziaei, M., Schwarcz, H.P. Hall, C.M. and Grün, R., 1990. Radiometric dating of the Mousterian site at Quneitra. In *Quneitra: a Mousterian Site on the Golan Heights* (ed. N. Goren-Inbar). QEDEM, Monographs of the Institute of Archaeology 31, Jerusalem: Hebrew University. pp. 232–35.

Chapter 9

Arensburg, B. 1977. New Upper Palaeolithic human remains from Israel. *Eretz Israel*. 13: 208*–15*.

Avnimelech, M. 1937. Sur les mollusques trouvees dans les couches prehistorique et protohistorique de Palestine. *Journal of the Palestinian Oriental Society* 17: 81–92.

Bankroft, H. 1937. Report on the charcoal fragments. In *The Stone Age of Mount Carmel, Vol. 1* (D.A.E. Garrod and D.M.A. Bate). Oxford: Clarendon Press, p. 129.

Bar-Yosef, O. 1983. The Natufian of the Southern Levant. In *The Hilly Flanks and Beyond* (eds T.C. Young, P.E.L. Smith and P. Mortensen). Studies in Ancient Oriental Civilization, No. 36. Chicago: University of Chicago Press, pp. 11–42.

Bar-Yosef, O. and Belfer, A. 1977. The Lagaman industry. In *Prehistoric Investigations in Gebel Maghara, Northern Sinai* (O. Bar-Yosef and J.L. Phillips). Qedem 7. Jerusalem: The Hebrew University, pp. 42–88.

Bar-Yosef, O. and Belfer-Cohen, A. 1989. The origins of sedentism and farming communities in the Levant. *Journal of World Prehistory*. 3: 447–98.

Bar-Yosef, O. and Vandermeersch, B. 1972. The stratigraphical and cultural problems of the passage from Middle to Upper Palaeolithic in the Palestine caves. In *The Origins of Homo Sapiens* (ed. F. Bordes). Paris: UNESCO, pp. 221–6.

Bar-Yosef, O., Vandermeersch, B., Arensburg, B., Belfer-Cohen, A., Goldgerg, P., Laville, H., Meignen, L., Rak, Y., Speth, J.D., Tchernov, E., Tillier, A-M. and Weiner, S. 1992. New excavations in Kebara cave, Mt. Carmel. *Current Anthropology*. 33: 497–550.

Bate, D.M.A. 1937. Part II: Palaeontology: The fossil fauna of the Wady El-Mughara caves. In *The Stone Age of Mount Carmel, Vol. 1* (D.A.E. Garrod and D.M.A. Bate). Oxford: Clarendon Press, pp. 135–247.

Begin, Z.B., Nathan, Y. and Ehrlich, A. 1980. Stratigraphy and facies distribution in the Lisan formation: new evidence from the south of the Dead Sea. *Israel Journal of Earth Sciences*. 29: 182–9.

Belfer-Cohen, A. 1988. The appearance of symbolic expression in the Upper Pleistocene of the Levant as compared to western Europe. In *L'Homme de Neandertal, Vol. 5* (ed. M. Otte). Liège: ERAUL, pp. 25–9.

Belfer-Cohen, A. and Bar-Yosef, O. 1981. The Aurignacian at Hayonim cave. *Paléorient*. 7: 19–42.

Bottema, S. and Van Zeist, W. 1981. Palynological evidence for the climatic history of the Near East 50,000–6,000. In *Préhistoire du Levant* (eds J. Cauvin and P. Sanlaville). Paris: CNRS, pp. 111–32.

Danin, A. 1983. *Desert Vegetation of Israel and Sinai*. Jerusalem: Cana Publishing House.

Demars, P.-Y. and Hublin J.-J. 1988. La transition Neandertaliens/ hommes de type moderne en Europe occidentale: aspects paleontologiques et culturelles. In *L'Homme de Néandertal, Vol. 7* (ed. M. Otte). Liège: ERAUL, 23–37.

Ferring, C.R. 1976. Sde Divshon: an Upper Palaeolithic site in the Divshon plain. In *Prehistory and Palaeoenvironments in the Central Negev, Israel, Vol. I* (ed. A.E. Marks). Dallas: SMU Press, pp. 199–226.

Ferring, C.R. 1977. The Late Upper Palaeolithic site of Ein Aqev East. In *Prehistory and Palaeoenvironments in the Central Negev, Israel, Vol. II* (ed. A.E. Marks). Dallas: SMU, pp. 81–111.

Garrard, A.N. and Gebel, G-H. (eds) (1988) *The Prehistory of Jordan: the State of Research in 1986*. BAR International Series 396. Oxford: BAR.

Garrod, D.A.E. 1951. A transitional industry from the base of the Upper Palaeolithic in Palestine. *Journal of the Royal Anthropological Institute*. 80: 121–30.

Garrod, D. 1957. Notes sur le Paleolithique Superieur du Moyen Orient. *Bulletin de la Societe Prehistorique Française*. 55: 439–45.

Garrod, D.A.E. and Bate, D.M.A. 1937. *The Stone Age of Mount Carmel Vol. 1*. Oxford: Clarendon Press.

Gat, J.R. 1981. Paleo-climate conditions in the Levant as revealed by the isotopic composition of paleowaters. *Israel Meteorological Research Papers*. 3: 13–28.

Gilead, I. 1981. Upper Palaeolithic tool assemblages from the Negev and Sinai. In *Prehistoire du Levant* (eds J. Cauvin and P. Sanlaville). Paris: CNRS, pp. 331–42.

Gilead, I. 1983. Upper Palaeolithic occurrences in Sinai and the transition to the Epi-Palaeolithic in the Southern Levant. *Paléorient*. 9: 39–53.

Gilead, I. 1984. Palaeolithic sites in northeastern Sinai. *Paléorient*. 10: 135–42.

Gilead, I. 1988. The Upper Palaeolithic to Epi-Palaeolithic transition in the Levant. *Paléorient*. 14: 177–82.

Gilead, I. 1989. The Upper Palaeolithic in the southern Levant: periodization and terminology. In *Investigations in South Levantine Prehistory* (eds O. Bar-Yosef and B. Vandermeersch). BAR International series 497. Oxford: BAR, pp. 231–54.

Gilead, I. 1991. The Upper Paleolithic period in the Levant. *Journal of World Prehistory*. 5: 105–54.

Gilead, I. 1993. Upper Paleolothic sites in the Ramat Matred area. *Palestine Exploration Quarterly*. 125: 19–42.

Gilead, I., and Bar-Yosef, O. 1993. Early Upper Paleolithic sites in the Kadesh Barnea area, northeastern Sinai. *Journal of Field Archaeology*. 20: 265–80.

Gladfelter, B.G. 1990. The geomorphic setting of Upper Paleolithic sites in Wadi el Sheikh, southern Sinai. *Geoarchaeology*. 5: 99–119.

Goldberg, P. 1986. Late Quaternary environmental history of the southern Levant. *Geoarchaeology*. 1: 225–44.

Goodfriend, G.A. and Magaritz, M. 1988. Palaeosols and late Pleistocene rainfalls fluctuations in the Negev Desert. *Nature*. 332: 144–6.

Goring-Morris, A.N. 1980a. Upper Palaeolithic sites from Wadi Fazael, Lower Jordan Valley. *Paléorient*. 6: 173–91.

Goring-Morris, A.N. 1980b. Late Quaternary in Wadi Fazael, Lower Jordan Valley. M.A. thesis. Institute of Archaeology, The Hebrew University, Jerusalem.

Goring-Morris, A.N. 1986. Sociocultural aspects of marine mollusks use in the Terminal Pleistocene in the Negev and Sinai regions of the Southern Levant. In *Proceedings of the 1986 Shell Bead Conference. Selected Papers* (ed. C.F. Hays III), Research Records No. 20. New York: Rochester Museum and Science Centre, pp. 175–88.

Goring-Morris, A.N. 1987. *At the Edge: Terminal Pleistocene Hunters-Gatherers in the Negev and Sinai*. BAR International Series 361. Oxford: BAR.

Goring-Morris, A.N. 1988. Trends in the spatial organization of Terminal Pleistocene hunters-gatherers occupations as viewed from the Negev and Sinai. *Paléorient*. 14: 231–44.

Horowitz, A. 1979. *The Quaternary of Israel*. New York: Academic Press.

Hovers, E. 1990. Art in the Levantine Epi-Palaeolithic: an engraved pebble from a Kebaran site in the Lower Jordan Valley. *Current Anthropology*. 31: 317–22.

Inizan, M.-L. and Gaillard, J.M. 1978. Coquillages de Ksar-'Aqil: elements de Parure? *Paléorient*. 4: 295–306.

Issar, A. and Gilead, I. 1986. Pleistocene climates and hydrology of the Negev (Israel) and Sinai (Egypt) deserts. In *Impact of Climatic Variation on East Saharan Groundwaters – Modelling of Large Scale Flow Regimes* (ed. U. Thorweihe) Berliner Geowissenschaftliche Abhandlungen A/72. Berlin: Verlag von Dietrich Reimer.

Jones, M., Marks, A.E. and Kaufman, D. 1983. Boker: The artifacts. In *Prehistory and Palaeoenvironments in the Central Negev, Israel, Vol. III* (ed. A.E. Marks). Dallas: SMU, pp. 283–329.

Kaufman, D. and Ronen, A. 1987. La sepulture Kebarienne Geometrique de Neve-David Haifa, Israel. *L'Anthropologie*. 91: 335–41.

Keeley, L.H. 1980. *Experimental Determination of Stone Tool Uses, a Microware Analysis*, Chicago and London: University of Chicago Press.

Kozlowski, J.K. 1988. L'apparition du Paleolithique Supérieur. In *L'Homme de Neandertal, Vol. 8* (ed. M. Otte). Liège: ERAUL, pp. 11–21.

Lee, R.B. 1968. What hunters do for living, or, how to make out on scarce resources. In *Man the Hunter* (eds. R.B. Lee and I. DeVore). Chicago: Adline Publishing Company, pp. 30–48.

Lévêque, F. 1988. L'homme de Saint-Césaire: sa place dans le Castelperronien de Poitou-Charantes. In *L'Homme de Neandertal, Vol. 8* (ed. M. Otte). Liège: ERAUL, pp. 99–108.

Liphschitz, N. and Waisel, Y. 1977. Dendrochronological investigations in Israel: Central Negev – Nahal Zin. In *Prehistory and Palaeoenvironments in the Central Negev, Israel, Vol. II* (ed. A.E. Marks). Dallas: SMU, pp. 355–6.

Marks, A.E. 1976. Ein Aqev: A late Levantine Upper Paleolithic site in the Nahal Aqev. In *Prehistory and Palaeoenvironments in the Central Negev, Israel, Vol. I* (ed. A.E. Marks). Dallas: SMU, pp. 227–91.

Marks, A.E. 1977. Introduction: a preliminary overview of the central Negev prehistory. In *Prehistory and Palaeoenvironments in the Central Negev, Israel, Vol. II* (ed. A.E. Marks). Dallas: SMU, pp. 3–34.

Marks, A.E. 1981. The Upper Palaeolithic in the Negev. In *Prehistoire du Levant* (eds. J. Cauvin and P. Sanlaville). Paris: CNRS, pp. 343–52.

Marks, A.E. 1983a. The sites of Boker and Boker Tachtit: a brief introduction. In *Prehistory and Palaeoenvironments in the Central Negev, Israel, Vol. III* (ed. A.E. Marks). Dallas: SMU, pp. 15–37.

Marks, A.E. 1983b. The Middle to Upper Palaeolithic transition in the Levant. In *Advances in World Archaeology, Vol. II* (eds. F. Wendorf and A.E. Close). New York: Academic Press, pp. 51–97.

Marks, A.E. and Freidel, D.A. 1977. Prehistoric Settlement Patterns in the Avdat/Aqev Area. In *Prehistory and Palaeoenvironments in the Central Negev, Israel, Vol. II* (ed. A.E. Marks). Dallas: SMU, pp. 131–58.

Naveh, Z. 1984. The vegetation of the Carmel and Nahal Sefunim and the evolution of the cultural landscape. In *Sefunim Prehistoric Sites Mount Carmel, Israel* (A. Ronen). BAR International Series 230. Oxford: BAR, pp. 23–63.

Neuville, R. 1934. Le prehistorique de Palestine. *Revue Biblique*. 43: 237–59.

Neuville, R. 1951. *Le Paleolithique et le Mesolithique du Desert de Judee*. Paris: Archives de l'Institut de Paleontologie Humaine.

Olami, Y. 1984. *Prehistoric Carmel*. Jerusalem and Haifa: Israel Exploration Society and M. Stekelis Museum of Prehistory.

Perrot, J. 1951. La terrace d'El-Khiam . In *Le Paleolithique et le Mesolithique du Desert de Judee* (R. Neuville). Paris: Archives de l'Institut de Paleontologie Humaine, pp. 134–78.

Phillips, J.L. 1988. The Upper Paleolithic of the Wadi Feiran, southern Sinai. *Paléorient*. 14: 183–200.

Ronen, A. 1975. The Palaeolithic archaeology and chronology of Israel. In *Problems in Prehistory: North Africa and the Levant* (eds F. Wendorf and A.E. Marks). Dallas: SMU Press, pp. 229–48.

Ronen, A. 1984. *Sefunim Prehistoric Sites Mount Carmel, Israel*. BAR International Series 230. Oxford: BAR.

Ronen, A. and Vandermeersch, B. 1972. The Upper Palaeolithic sequence in the cave of Qafza (Israel). *Quaternaria*. 16: 189–202.

Tchernov, E. 1976. Some late Quaternary faunal remains from the Avdat Aqev area. In *Prehistory and Palaeoenvironments in the Central Negev, Israel, Vol. I* (ed. A.E. Marks). Dallas: SMU Press, pp. 69–73.

Tchernov, E. 1984. The fauna of Sefunim cave, Mt. Carmel. In *Sefunim Prehistoric Sites Mount Carmel, Israel, Vol. 2* (A. Ronen). BAR International Series 230, Oxford: BAR, pp. 401–19.

Van Andel, T.H. 1989. Late Quaternary sea-level changes and archaeology. *Antiquity*. 63: 733–45.

Wreschner, E.E. 1980. Red ochre and human evolution: a case for discussion. *Current Anthropology*. 21: 631–44.

Chapter 10

Aurenche, O., Cauvin, J., Cauvin, M-C., Copeland, L., Hours, F., and Sanlaville, P. 1981. Chronologie et Organization de l'Espace dans le Proche Orient de 12,000 a 5,600 avant J.C. In *Prehistoire de Levant* (eds J. Cauvin et P. Sanlaville). Paris: CNRS, pp. 571–601.

Bachdach, J. 1982. Das Jungpalaolithikum von Jabrud in Syrien. Unpublished doctoral thesis, University of Koln.

Bard, E., Hamelin, B., Fairbanks, R.G. and Zindler, A. 1990. Calibration of the 14C Timescale Over the Past 30,000 Years Using Mass Spectrometric U-Th Ages from Barbados Corals. *Nature*. 345: 405–10.

Baruch, U. 1994. The Late Quaternary Pollen Record of the Near East. In *Late Quaternary Chronology and Palaeoclimates of the Eastern Mediterranean* (eds O. Bar-Yosef and R. Kra). Supplement to *Radiocarbon*.

Baruch, U., and Bottema, S. 1991. Palynological Evidence for Climatic Changes in the Levant ca. 17,000–9,000 B.P. In *The Natufian Culture in the Levant* (eds O. Bar-Yosef and F.R. Valla). Ann Arbor, International Monographs in Prehistory, Archaeological Series 1: 11–21.

Bar-Yosef, O. 1970. The Epi-paleolithic Cultures of Palestine. Unpublished doctoral thesis, Hebrew University of Jerusalem.

Bar-Yosef, O. 1975. Les Gisements 'Kebarien Geometrique A' d'Haon, Vallee du Jourdain, Israel. *Bulletin de la Societe Prehistorique Francaise*. 72: 10–14.

Bar-Yosef, O. 1981. The Epi-paleolithic Complexes in the Southern Levant. In *Prehistoire du Levant: Chronologie et l'Organisation de l'espace depuis les origines jusqu'au VIe millenaire* (eds J. Cauvin and P. Sanlaville). Colloques Internationaux du CNRS No. 598. Lyon: Maison de L'Orient, pp. 389–408.

Bar-Yosef, O. nd. The Mediterranean Levantine Epi-paleolithic as the Background to the 'Neolithic Revolution'. In *The Origins of Agriculture and Technology: West or East Asia?* (eds P. Sorensen and P. Mortensen). Aarhus.

Bar-Yosef, O. 1987. Pleistocene Connexions Between Africa and Southwest Asia: An Archaeological Perspective. *The African Archaeological Review*. 5: 29–38.

Bar-Yosef, O. 1987. Late Pleistocene Adaptations in the Levant. In *The Pleistocene Old World: Regional Perspectives* (ed. O. Sofer). New York: Plenum Press, pp. 219–36.

Bar-Yosef, O. and Belfer-Cohen, A. 1991. The Origins of Sedentism and Farming Communities in the Levant. *Journal of World Prehistory*. 3/4: 447–98.

Bar-Yosef, O. and Goring-Morris, A.N. 1977. Geometric Kebaran A Occurrences. In *Prehistoric Investigations in Gebel Maghara, Northern Sinai* (eds O. Bar-Yosef and J.L. Phillips). Qedem 7. Jerusalem: Monographs of the Institute of Archaeology, Hebrew University. pp. 115–148.

Bar-Yosef, O. and Nadel, D. 1988. Ohalo – A Prehistoric Site in the Sea of Galilee. *Mitekufat Haeven*. 21: 87–94.

Bar-Yosef, O. and Phillips, J.L. 1977. *Prehistoric Investigations in Gebel Maghara, Northern Sinai*. Qedem 7. Jerusalem: Monographs of the Institute of Archaeology, Hebrew University.

Bar-Yosef, O. and Vogel, J. 1987. Relative and Absolute Chronology of the Epi-paleolithic in the Southern Levant. In *Chronologies in the Near East* (eds O. Aurenche, J. Evin and F. Hours). Oxford, BAR International Series 379: pp. 220–45.

Bar-Yosef, O., Goldberg, P. and Leveson, T. 1974. Late Quaternary Stratigraphy and Prehistory of Wadi Fazael, Jordan Valley – A Preliminary Report. *Paleorient.* 2: 415–28.

Begin, Z.B., Broeker, W., Buchbinder, B., Drukman, Y., Kaufman, A., Magaritz, M. and Neev, D. 1985. Dead Sea and Lake Lisan Levels in the Last 30,000 Years. Jerusalem.

Belfer-Cohen, A. 1989. The Natufian Issue: A Suggestion. In *Investigations in South Levantine Prehistory* (eds B. Vandermeersch and O. Bar-Yosef). Oxford: BAR International Series 497: 297–307.

Belfer-Cohen, A., Gilead, I., Goring-Morris, N., and Rosen, S. 1991. An Epipaleolithic Rockshelter at Nahal Negarot in the Central Negev. *Journal of the Israel Prehistoric Society – Mitekufat Haeven.* 24: 164–168.

Besancon, J., Copeland, L. and Hours, F. 1975-7. Tableaux de Prehistoire Libanaise. *Paleorient.* 3: 5–45.

Binford, L.R. 1980. Willow Smoke and Dogs' Tails: Hunter-Gatherer Settlement Systems and Archaeological Site Formation. *American Antiquity.* 45: 4–20.

Binford, L.R. and Binford, S. 1966. A Preliminary Analysis of Functional Variability in the Mousterian of Levallois Facies. *American Anthropologist.* 68: 238–95.

Bottema, S. 1987. Chronology and Climatic Phases in the Near East from 16,000 to 10,000 B.P. In *Chronologies in the Near East. Relative Chronologies and Absolute Chronology 16,000–4,000 B.P.* (eds O. Aurenche, J. Evin and F. Hours). Oxford: BAR International Series 379: 295–310.

Bottema, S. and Van. Zeist, W. 1981. Palynological Evidence for the Climatic History of the Near East, 50,000 – 6000 B.P. In *Prehistoire du Levant: Chronologie et l'Organisation de l'espace depuis les origines jusqu'au VIe millenaire* (eds J. Cauvin and P. Sanlaville). Lyon: Colloques Internationaux du CNRS No. 598. Maison de L'Orient, pp. 411–15.

Butler, B.H., Tchernov, E., Hietala, H. and Davis, S. 1977. Faunal Exploitation During the Late Epipaleolithic in the Har Harif. In *Prehistory and Paleoenvironments in the Central Negev, Israel. Volume II. The Avdat/Aqev Area, Part 2, and the Har Harif* (ed. A.E. Marks). Dallas: SMU Press, pp. 327–46.

Byrd, B.F. 1990. Late Pleistocene Assemblage Diversity in the Azraq Basin. *Paleorient.* 14/2: 257–65.

Byrd, B.F. and Rollefson, G.O. 1984. Natufian Occupation in the Wadi El Hasa, Southern Jordan. *Annual of the Department of Antiquities of Jordan.* 28: 143–50.

Cauvin, M.-C. 1981. L'Epipalaeolithique de Syrie d'apres les Premieres Recherches dans le Cuvette D'El Kowm (1978–1979). *Prehistoire du Levant* (eds J. Cauvin and P. Sanlaville). Lyon: Colloque International de CNRS No. 598, 1980. pp. 375–88.

Cauvin, M.-C. and Coqueugniot, E. 1990. L'Oasis d'El Kowm et le Kebarien Geometrique. *Prehistoire du Levant. Processus des Changements Culturels, Paleorient.* 14/2: 270–82.

Chavaillon, J., and Hours, F. 1970. Jiita II (Dahr el Mghara). Campagne 1971, Rapport Preliminaire. *Bulletin du Musee de Beyrouth.* 23: 215–31.

Childe, G.V. 1952. *New Light on the Most Ancient East.* New York: Praeger.

Clark, G.A., Lindly, J., Donaldson, M., Garrard, A., Coinman, N., Schuldenrein, J., Fisj, S. and Olszewski, D. 1988. Excavations at the Middle, Upper, and Epipaleolithic Sites in the Wadi Hasa, West-Central Jordan. In *The Prehistory of Jordan. The State of Research in 1986* (eds A.N. Garrard and H.G. Gebel). Oxford, BAR International Series 396 (i): pp. 209–85.

Close, A. 1978. The Identification of Style in Lithic Artifacts. *World Archaeology.* 10: 223–37.

COHMAP members. 1988. Climatic Changes of the Last 18,000 Years: Observations and Model Simulations. *Science.* 241: 1043–52.

Coinman, N., Clark, G.A. and Lindley, J. 1986. Prehistoric Hunter-Gatherer Settlement in the Wadi Hasa, West-Central Jordan. In *The End of the Paleolithic in the Old World* (ed. L.G. Strauss). Oxford: BAR International Series 284: 129–70.

Copeland, L. 1982. The Ksar Aqil Scraper: A Late Upper Paleolithic Tool Type of the Levant. *Archeologie au Levant, Recueil R. Saideh.* Lyon, Collection de la Maison de L'Orient Mediterraneene, Serie Archeologique 9: 57–67.

Copeland, L. and Hours, F. 1977. Engraved and Plain Bone Tools from Jiita (Lebanon) and their Early Kebaran Context. *Proceedings of the Prehistoric Society.* 43: 295–301.

Danin, A. 1983. *Desert Vegetation of Israel and Sinai.* Jerusalem: Cana.

Davis, S.J.M., Goring-Morris, A.M. and Gopher, A. 1982. Sheep Bones from the Negev Epipaleolithic. *Paleorient.* 8: 87–93.

Davis, S.J.M. 1989. Hatoula 1980–86. Why Did Prehistoric People Domesticate Food Animals? In *Investigations in South Levantine Prehistory* (eds O. Bar-Yosef and B. Vandermeersch). Oxford: BAR International Series 497: pp. 43–60.

Druckman, Y., Magaritz, M. and Sneh, A. 1987. The Shrinking of Lake Lisan, As Reflected by the Diagenesis of its Marginal Oolithic Deposits. *Israel Journal of Earth Science.* 36: 101–6.

Edwards, P.C. 1987. Late Pleistocene Occupation in Wadi al-Hammeh, Jordan Valley. Unpublished doctoral thesis, University of Sydney.

Edwards, P.C., Bourke, S.J., Colledge, S.M., Head, J. and Macumber, P.G. 1988. Late Pleistocene Prehistory in the Wadi el-Hammeh, Jordan Valley. In *The Prehistory of Jordan. The State of Research in 1986* (eds A.N. Garrard and H.G. Gebel). Oxford BAR International Series 396 (ii): pp. 525–565.

Ferring, C.R. 1977. The Late Upper Paleolithic Site of Ein Aqev East. In *Prehistory and Paleoenvironments in the Central Negev, Israel. Volume II. The Avdat/Aqev Area, Part 2 and the Har Harif* (ed. A.E. Marks). Dallas: SMU Press. pp. 81–118.

Ferring, C.R. 1980. *Technological Variability and Change in the Late Paleolithic of the Negev.* Unpublished doctoral thesis, Dallas: SMU, Ann Arbor, University Microfilms International.

Ferring, C.R. 1988. Technological Change in the Upper Paleolithic of the Negev. In *Upper Pleistocene Prehistory of Western Eurasia* (eds H. Dibble and A. Montet-White). Philadelphia: University Museum, pp. 333–48.

Garrod, D.A.E. 1932. A New Mesolithic Industry: The Natufian of Palestine. *Journal of the Royal Anthropological Institute.* 62: 257–69.

Garrard, A.N. and Byrd, B. 1992. New Dimensions to the Epipalaeolithic of the Wadi Jilat in Central Jordan. *Paleorient.* 18/1: 47–62.

Garrard, A., Byrd, B., Harvey, P. and Hivernel, F. 1985. Prehistoric Environment and Settlement in the Azraq Basin. A Report on the 1982 Survey Season. *Levant.* 17: 1–28.

Garrard, A.N., Baird, D., and B. Byrd. 1994. The Chronological Basis and Significance of the Late Palaeolithic and Neolithic Sequence in the Azraq Basin, Jordan. In *Late Quaternary Chronology and Paleoclimates of the Eastern Mediterranean* (eds. O. Bar-Yosef and R. Kra). Supplement to *Radiocarbon.*

Gilead, I. 1981. Upper Palaeolithic Tool Assemblages from the Negev and Sinai. In *Prehistoire du Levant. Chronologie et l'organisation de l'espace depuis les origines jusqu'au VIe millenaire* (eds J. Cauvin and P. Sanlaville). Lyon: Colloques Internationaux du CNRS No. 598. Maison de L'Orient, pp. 331–42.

Gilead, I. 1989. The Upper Paleolithic in the Southern Levant: Periodization and Terminology. In *Investigations in South Levantine Prehistory* (eds B. Vandermeersch and O. Bar-Yosef). Oxford: BAR International Series 497: 231–54.

Goldberg, P. 1981. Late Quaternary Stratigraphy of Israel: an Eclectic View. In *Prehistoire du Levant: Chronologie et L'organisation de l'espace depuis les origines jusqu'au VIe millenaire* (eds J. Cauvin and P. Sanlaville). Colloques Internationaux du CNRS. No. 598. Lyon: Maison de L'Orient, 55–66.

Goldberg, P. and Bar-Yosef, O. 1982. Environmental and Archaeological Evidence for Climatic Change in the Southern Levant. In *Palaeoclimates, Palaeo-environments and Human Communities in the Eastern Mediterranean Region in Later Prehistory* (eds J.L. Bintliff and W. Van Zeist). Oxford: BAR International Series 133: 399–414.

Goring-Morris, A.N. 1980. Late Quaternary Sites in Wadi Fazael, Lower Jordan Valley. Unpublished M.A. thesis, Hebrew University of Jerusalem.

Goring-Morris, A.N. 1985. Terminal Pleistocene Hunter/Gatherers in the Negev and Sinai. Unpublished doctoral thesis, Hebrew University of Jerusalem.

Goring-Morris, A.N. 1987. *At the Edge: Terminal Pleistocene Hunter-Gatherers in the Negev and Sinai.* Oxford: BAR International Series 361.

Goring-Morris, A.N. 1989. Developments in Terminal Pleistocene Hunter-Gatherer Socio-Cultural Systems: A Perspective from the

Negev and Sinai Deserts. In *People and Culture in Change* (ed. I. Hershkovitz). Oxford: BAR International Series 508 (i): pp. 7–28.

Goring-Morris, A.N. 1990. Socio-cultural Aspects of Marine Mollusc Use in the Terminal Pleistocene of the Negev and Sinai Regions of the Southern Levant. In *Proceedings of the 1986 Shell Bead Conference. Selected Papers* (ed. C. Hayes III). New York: Rochester Museum and Science Center, Research Records No. 20: 175–88.

Goring-Morris, A.N. 1991. The Harifian of the Southern Levant. In *The Natufian Culture in the Levant* (eds O. Bar-Yosef and F.R. Valla). Ann Arbor: International Monographs in Prehistory, Archaeological Series 1: 173–234.

Goring-Morris, A.N. 1993. Negev: The Prehistoric Periods. *New Encyclopedia of Archaeological Excavations in the Holy Land*. New York: Doubleday. pp. 1119–123.

Goring-Morris, A.N. and Goldberg, P. 1991. Late Quaternary Dune Incursions in the Southern Levant: Archaeology, Chronology and Palaeoenvironments. *Quaternary International*. 5: 115–37.

Henry, D.O. 1973. The Natufian of Palestine: its Material Culture and Ecology. Unpublished doctoral thesis, Dallas: Southern Methodist University.

Henry, D.O. 1977. An examination of the Artifactual Variability in the Natufian of Palestine. *Eretz Israel*. 13: 229–39.

Henry, D.O. 1981. An Analysis of Settlement Patterns and Adaptive Strategies of the Natufian. In *Prehistoire du Levant: Chronologie et l'organisation de l'espace depuis les origines jusqu'au VIe millenaire* (eds J. Cauvin and P. Sanlaville). Colloques Internationaux du CRNS No. 598. Lyon: Maison de L'Orient, pp. 421–32.

Henry, D.O. 1982. The Prehistory of Southern Jordan and Relationships with the Levant. *Journal of Field Archaeology*. 9: 417–44.

Henry, D.O. 1983. Adaptive Evolution Within the Epipaleolithic of the Near East. In *Advances in World Archaeology Volume 2* (eds F. Wendorf and A. Close). New York: Academic Press, pp. 99–160.

Henry, D.O. 1989. *From Foraging to Agriculture. The Levant at the End of the Ice Age*. Philadelphia: University of Pennsylvania Press.

Henry, D.O. and Garrard, A.N. 1988. Tor Hamar: An Epipaleolithic Rockshelter in Southern Jordan. *Palestine Exploration Quarterly*. 120: 1–24.

Henry, D.O., Leroi-Gourhan, A., and Davis, S.J. 1981. The Excavation of Hayonim Terrace: An Examination of Terminal Pleistocene Climatic and Adaptive Changes. *Journal of Archaeological Science*. 8: 33–58.

Henry, D.O., Hassan, F.A., Henry, K.C. and Jones, M. 1983. An Investigation of the Prehistory of Southern Jordan. *Palestine Exploration Quarterly* 115: 1–24.

Hillman, G.C. 1989a. Late Paleolithic Plant Foods from Wadi Kubbaniya in Upper Egypt: Dietary Diversity, Infant Weaning, and Seasonality in a Riverine Environment. In *Foraging and Farming* (eds D.R. Harris and G.C. Hillman). London: Unwin Hyman, pp. 207–39.

Hillman, G.C. 1989b. Plant Food Economy During the Epipalaeolithic Period of Tell Abu Hureya, Syria: Dietary Diversity, Seasonality and Modes of Exploitation. In *Foraging and Farming* (eds D.R. Harris and G.C. Hillman). London: Unwin Hyman, pp. 240–68.

Hours, F. 1973. Le Kebarien au Liban: Reflexions à Partir des Fouilles de Jiita en 1972. *Paleorient*. 2: 185–200.

Hours, F. 1976. L'Epipaleoithique au Liban. Resultats acquis en 1975. Preprint from *XIème Congrès de L'Union Internationale des Sciences Préhistoriques et Protohistoriques*. Nice, pp. 106–31.

Hovers, A. 1989. Settlement and Subsistence Patterns in the Lower Jordan Valley from Epi-Palaeolithic to Neolithic Times. In *Investigations in South Levantine Prehistory* (eds B. Vandermeersch and O. Bar-Yosef). Oxford: BAR International Series 497: 37–42.

Hovers, A. 1990. Art in the Levantine Epipalaeolithic: An Engraved Pebble from a Kebaran Site in the Lower Jordan Valley. *Current Anthropology*. 31/3: 317–22.

Hovers, E. and Bar-Yosef, O. 1987. A Prehistoric Survey of Eastern Samaria: Preliminary Report. *Israel Exploration Journal*. 37: 77–87.

Hovers, E. and Marder, O. 1991. Typo-chronology and Absolute Dating of the Kebaran Complex: Implications from the Second Season of Excavations at Urkan E-Rubb IIa. *Journal of the Israel Prehistoric Society – Mitekufat Haeven*. 24: 34–58.

Hovers, E., Kolska Horwitz, L., Bar-Yosef, D.E. and Cope-Miyashiro, C. 1988. The Site of Urkan E-Rubb IIa; A Case Study of Subsistence and Mobility Patterns in the Kebaran Period in the Lower Jordan Valley.

Journal of the Israel Prehistoric Society – Mitekufat Haeven. 21: 20*–48*.

Inizan, M.L. and Gaillard, J.M. 1978. Coquillages de Ksar-'Aqil: Elements de Parure? *Paleorient*. 4: 295–306.

Kaufman, D. 1976. Typological and Technological Analysis of Two Epipaleolithic Assemblages from the Coastal Plain of Israel. Unpublished M.A. Theses, Tel Aviv University.

Kaufman, D. 1987. Interassemblage Variability of Metric Attributes from Lithic Assemblages of the Late Upper Paleolithic of Israel. *Journal of the Israel Prehistoric Society – Mitekufat Haeven*. 20: 37*–49*.

Kaufman, D. 1988. Lithic Assemblages and Settlement Patterns of the Late Upper Paleolithic in Israel. *Journal of the Israel Prehistoric Society – Mitekufat Haeven*. 21: 7–19.

Kaufman, D. 1989. Observations on the Geometric Kebaran: A View from Neve David. In *Investigations in South Levantine Prehistory* (eds B. Vandermeersch and O. Bar-Yosef). Oxford: BAR International Series 497, 275–86.

Kaufman, D. 1992. Hunter-Gatherers of the Levantine Epipalaeolithic: The Socioecological Origins of Sedentism. *Journal of Mediterranean Archaeology*. 5/2: 165–201.

Kaufman, D. and Ronen, A. 1987. La Sepulture Kebarienne Geometrique de Neve-David, Haifa: Israel. *L'Anthropologie*. 91/1: 335–42.

Kislev, M.E., Nadel, D. and Carmi, I. 1992. Epipalaeolithic (19,000 BP) Cereal and Fruit Diet at Ohalo II, Sea of Galilee, Israel. *Review of Palaeobotany and Palynology*. 73: 161–6.

Kouky, F.L. and Smith, R.H. 1986. Lake Beisan and the Prehistoric Settlement of the Northern Jordan Valley. *Paleorient*. 12/2: 27–36.

Kraybil, N. 1976. Pre-agricultural Tools for the Preparation of Foods in the Old World. In *Origins of Agriculture* (ed. C.A. Reed). The Hague: Mouton, pp. 485–521.

Kukan, G.J. 1978. A Technological and Stylistic Study of Microliths from Certain Levantine Epipaleolithic Assemblages. Unpublished Doctoral Thesis, University of Toronto.

Legge, A.J. and Rowley-Conwy, P.A. 1987. Gazelle Killing in Stone Age Syria. *Scientific American*. 257/2: 76–83.

Lieberman, D.E. 1991. Seasonality and Gazelle Hunting at Hayonim Cave: New Evidence for 'Sedentism' During the Natufian. *Paleorient*. 17/1: 47–57.

Lieberman, D.E. 1993. Mobility and Strain: The Biology of Cementosis and Its Application to the Evolution of Hunter-Gatherer Seasonal Mobility during the Late Quaternary in the Southern Levant. Unpublished Doctoral Thesis, Harvard University.

Liphschitz, N. 1986. The Vegetational Landscape and Macroclimate of Israel during Prehistoric and Proto-historic Periods. *Mitekufat Haeven*. 19: 80*–85*.

Liphschitz, N. and Waisel, Y. 1977. Appendix: Dendroarchaeological Investigations in Israel: Central Negev–Nahal Zin. In *Prehistory and Paleoenvironments in the Central Negev, Israel. Volume II. The Advat/Aqev Area, Part 2 and the Har Harif* (ed. A.E. Marks). Dallas: SMU Press pp. 355–56.

Lotter, A.S. 1991. Absolute Dating of the Late Glacial Period in Switzerland Using Annually Laminated Sediments. *Quaternary Research*. 35: 321–30.

Luz, B. 1982. Palaeoclimatic Interpretation of the Last 20,000 yr Record of Deep-Sea Cores around the Middle East. In *Palaeo-climates, Palaeo-environments and Human Communities in the Eastern Mediterranean Region in Later Prehistory* (eds J.L. Bintliff and W. Van Zeist). Oxford: BAR International Series 133: 41–61.

Macumber, P.G. and Head, M.J. 1991. Implications of the Wadi al-Hammeh Sequence for the Terminal Drying of Lake Lisan, Jordan. *Palaeogeography, Palaeoclimatology, Palaeoecology*. 84: 163–73.

Marks, A.E. 1976. *Prehistory and Palaeoenvironments in the Central Negev, Israel. Volume I. The Advat Aqev Area, Part 1*. Dallas: SMU Press.

Marks, A.E. 1977. *Prehistory and Paleoenvironments in the Central Negev, Israel. Volume II. The Avdat/Aqev Area, Part 2 and the Har Harif*. Dallas: SMU Press.

Marks, A.E. 1981. The Upper Paleolithic of the Negev. In *Prehistoire du Levant: Chronologie et l'Organisation de l'espace depuis les origines jusque'au VIe millenaire* (eds J. Cauvin and P. Sanlaville). Colloques Internationaux du CNRS. No. 598. Lyon: Maison de L'Orient, pp. 343–52.

Marks, A.E. and Friedel, D.A. 1977. Prehistoric Settlement Patterns in the Avdat/Aqev Area. In *Prehistory and Paleoenvironments in the Central Negev, Israel. Volume II. The Avdat/Aqev Area, Part 2, and the Har Harif* (ed. A.E. Marks). Dallas: SMU Press, pp. 131–58.

Marks, A.E. and Larson, P.A. 1977. Test Excavations at the Natufian Site of Rosh Horesha. In *Prehistory and Paleoenvironments in the Central Negev, Israel. Volume II. The Avdat/Aqev Area, Part 2, and the Har Harif* (ed. A.E. Marks). Dallas: SMU Press, pp. 191–232.

Marks, A.E. and Simmons, A.H. 1977. The Negev Kebaran of the Har Harif. In *Prehistory and Paleoenvironments in the Central Negev, Israel. Volume II. The Avdat/Aqev Area, Part 2, and the Har Harif* (ed. A.E. Marks). Dallas: SMU Press, pp. 233–70.

Mazel, A. and Parkinson, J. 1981. Stone Tools and Resources: A Case Study from Southern Africa. *World Archaeology*. 13: 16–30.

Mellars, P. and Tixier, J. 1989. Radiometric-accelerator Dating of Ksar Aqil (Lebanon) and the Chronology of the Upper Paleolithic Sequence in the Middle East. *Antiquity*. 63: 761–8.

Mienis, H.K. 1977. Marine Molluscs from the Epipaleolithic and Harifian of the Har Harif, Central Negev (Israel). In *Prehistory and Paleoenvironments in the Central Negev, Israel. Volume II. The Avdat/Aqev Area, Part 2, and the Har Harif* (ed. A.E. Marks). Dallas: SMU Press, pp. 347–54.

Molist, M. and Cauvin, M-C. 1990. Une Nouvelle Sequence Stratifee pour La prehistoire en Syrie Semi-desertique. *Paleorient*. 16/2: 55–63.

Moore, A.M.T. 1985. The Development of Neolithic Societies in the Near East. In *Advances in World Archaeology* (eds F. Wendorf and A.E. Close). New York: Academic Press. 4: 1–69.

Muheisen, M. 1988. The Epipalaeolithic Phases of Kharaneh IV. In *The Prehistory of Jordan. The State of Research in 1986* (eds A.N. Garrard and H.G. Gebel). Oxford: BAR International Series 396 (i): pp. 353–67.

Muheisen, M. 1990. Le Gisement de Kharaneh IV, Note Sommaire de la Phase D. *Prehistoire du Levant. Processus des Changements Culturels, Paleorient*. 14/2: 265–9.

Nadel, D. 1990. Ohalo II – A Preliminary Report. *Journal of the Israel Prehistoric Society – Mitekufat Haeven*. 23: 48*–59*.

Nadel, D. 1991. Ohalo II – The Third Season. *Journal of the Israel Prehistoric Society – Mitekufat Haeven*. 24: 158–63.

Nadel, D. and Hershkovitz, I. 1991. New Subsistence data and Human Remains from the Earliest Epipalaeolithic in Israel. *Current Anthropology*. 32/5: 631–5.

Neev, D. and Emery, K.O. 1967. The Dead Sea: Depositional Processes and Environments of Evaporites. *Israel Geological Survey Bulletin*. 41.

Neev, D. and Hall, J.K. 1977. Climatic Fluctuations during the Holocene as reflected by the Dead Sea levels. In *Desertic Terminal Lakes* (ed. D. Greer). Logan: Utah State University, pp. 53–60.

Neuville, R. 1934. Le Prehistorique de Palestine. *Revue Biblique*. 43: 237–59.

Newcomer, M.H. 1974. Study and Replication of Bone Tools from Ksar Akil (Lebanon). *World Archaeology*. 6/2: 138–53.

Newcomer, M.H. and Watson, J. 1984. Bone Artifacts from Ksar 'Aqil (Lebanon). *Paleorient*. 10/1: 143–7.

Noy, T., Legge, A.J. and Higgs, E.S. 1973. Recent Excavations at Nahal Oren, Israel. *Proceedings of the Prehistoric Society*. 39: 75–99.

Noy, T., Schuldenrein, J. and Tchernov, E. 1980. Gilgal, a Pre-pottery Neolithic A Site in the Lower Jordan Valley. *Israel Exploration Journal*. 30: 63–82.

Olszewski, D.I., Clark, G.A. and Fish, S. 1990. WHS 784X (Yutil al-Hasa): A Late Ahmarian Site in the Wadi Hasa, West-central Jordan. *Proceedings of the Prehistoric Society*. 56: 33–49.

Perrot, J. 1955. Le Paleolithique Superieur d'El-Quseir et de Masaraq an Na'aj (Palestine). *Bulletin de la Societe Prehistorique Francaise*. 52/8: 493–506.

Perrot, J. 1968. La Prehistoire Palestinienne. *Supplement au Dictionaire de la Bible*. Volume 8. Paris: Letouzey et Ane, pp. 286–446.

Phillips, J.L. and Mintz, E. 1977. The Mushabian. In *Prehistoric Investigations In Gebel Maghara, Northern Sinai* (eds O. Bar-Yosef and J.L. Phillips). Qedem 7. Monographs of the Institute of Archaeology, Hebrew University of Jerusalem: pp. 149–83.

Potts, T.F., Colledge, S.M. and Edwards, P.C. 1985. Preliminary Report on a Sixth Season of Excavation by the University of Sydney at Pella in Jordan (1983/4). *Annual of the Department of Antiquities of Jordan*. 29: 181–206.

Reese, D.S. 1991. Marine Shells in the Levant: Upper Paleolithic, Epipaleolithic, and Neolithic. In *The Natufian Culture in the Levant* (eds O. Bar-Yosef and F.R. Valla). International Monographs in Prehistory, Archaeological Series 1. pp. 613–28.

Rolston, S.L. 1982. Two Prehistoric Burials from Qasr Kharaneh. *Annual of the Department of Antiquities of Jordan*. 26: 221–9.

Rosen, S.A. 1987. Demographic Trends in the Negev Highlands: Preliminary Results from the Emergency Survey. *BASOR*. 266: 45–58.

Rossignol-Strick, M., Nesteroff, W., Olive, P. and Vergnaud-Grazzini, C. 1982. After the Deluge: Mediterranean Stagnation and Sapropel Formation. *Nature*. 295: 105–10.

Rust, A. 1950. *Die Hohlenfunde von Jabrud (Syrien)*. Neumunster: Karl Wachholtz.

Saxon, E.C., Martin, G. and Bar-Yosef, O. 1978. Nahal Hadera V: An Open Air Site on the Israeli Littoral. *Paleorient*. 4: 253–66.

Schyle, D. and Uerpmann, H-P. 1988. Palaeolithic Sites in the Petra Area. In *The Prehistory of Jordan. The State of Research in 1986* (eds A.N. Garrard and H.G. Gebel). Oxford: BAR International Series 396 (i): pp. 39–65.

Simmons, A.H. and Ilany, G. 1975–77. What Mean these Bones? – Behavioral Implications of Gazelles' Remains from Archaeological Sites. *Paleorient*. 3: 269–74.

Testart, A. 1982. The Significance of Food Storage among Hunter-gatherers: Residence Patterns, Population Densities, and Social Inequalities. *Current Anthropology*. 23/5: 523–37.

Tixier, J. 1963. *Typologie de l'Epipaleolithique du Maghreb*. Paris: CRAPE.

Tixier, J. 1970. L'Abri Sous Roche de Ksar Aqil: La Campagne de Fouilles 1969. *Bulletin de la Musee de Beyrouth*. 33: 173–91.

Tixier, J. 1974. Poincon Decore de Paleolithique Superieur a Ksar Aqil (Liban). *Paleorient*. 2: 187–93.

Tixier, J. and Inizan, M.L. 1981. Ksar Aqil: Stratigraphie et Ensembles Lithiques dans le Paleolithique Superieur: Fouilles 1971–1975. In *Prehistoire du Levant* (eds J. Cauvin and P. Sanlaville). Paris: Editions CNRS, pp. 353–67.

Valla, F.R. 1990. En Guise de Synthese: Quelques Questions Posees par L'Epipaleolithique Levantin. *Prehistoire du Levant. Processus des Changements Culturels, Paleorient*. 14/2: 316–320.

Valla, F.R., Gilead, I. and Bar-Yosef, O. 1979. Prospection Prehistorique dans le Neguev Septentrional. *Paleorient*. 5: 221–31.

Van Zeist, W. and Bottema, S. 1982. Vegetational History of the Eastern Mediterranean and the Near East during the last 20,000 years. In *Palaeo-climates, Palaeo-environments and Human Communities in the Eastern Mediterranean Region in Later Prehistory* (eds J.L. Bintliff and W. Van Zeist). Oxford: BAR International Series 133, pp. 277–321.

Wendorf, F. 1968. Site 117: A Nubian Final Paleolithic Graveyard Near Gebel Jebel Sahaba, Sudan. In *The Prehistory of Nubia, Volume 2* (ed. F. Wendorf). Dallas: Fort Burgwin Research Center and Southern Methodist University Press.

Wiessner, P. 1983. Style and Social Information in Kalahari San Projective Points. *American Antiquity*. 48: 253–76.

Wiessner, P. 1984. Reconsidering the Behavioral Basis for Style: A Case Study among the Kalahari San. *Journal of Anthropological Archaeology*. 3: 190–234.

Wobst, H.M. 1974. Boundary Conditions for Palaeolithic Social Systems: a Simulation Approach. *American Antiquity*. 39: 147–78.

Wobst, H.M. 1976. Locational Relationships in Palaeolithic Society. *Journal of Human Evolution*. 5: 49–58.

Wright, K. 1991. The origins and development of groundstone tool assemblages in Late Pleistocene Southwest Asia. *Paleorient*. 17/1: 19–45.

Yechieli, Y., Magaritz, M., Levy, Y., Weber, U., Kafri, U., Woelfli, W. and Bonani, G. 1993. Late Quaternary Geological History of the Dead Sea Area, Israel. *Quaternary Research*. 39: 59–67.

Yellen, J.E. 1976. Long Term Hunter-gatherer Adaptation to Desert Environments: A Biogeographical Perspective. *World Archaeology*. 8/3: 262–74.

Chapter 11

Baruch, U. and Bottema, S. 1991. Palynological evidence for climatic changes in the Levant *ca.* 17,000–9,000 BP. In *The Natufian Culture in the Levant* (eds O. Bar-Yosef and F.R. Valla). Archaeological series 1. Ann Arbor: International Monographs in Prehistory, pp. 11–20.

Bar-Yosef, O. 1983. The Natufian in the southern Levant. In *The Hilly flanks and beyond* (eds T. Young, P.H. Smith and P. Mortensen). SAOC 36. Chicago: The University of Chicago Press, pp. 11–42.

Bar-Yosef, O. 1991. The archaeology of the Natufian Layer at Hayonim Cave. In *The Natufian Culture in the Levant* (eds O. Bar-Yosef and F.R. Valla). Archaeological Series 1. Ann Arbor: International Monographs in Prehistory, pp. 81–92.

Bar-Yosef, O. and Belfer-Cohen, A. 1989. The Origins of Sedentism and farming Communities in the Southern Levant. *Journal of World Prehistory* 3 (5): 447–89.

Bar-Yosef, O., Goldberg, P. and Leveson, T. 1974. Late Quaternary and Stratigraphy in Wadi Fazael, Jordan Valley: a preliminary report. *Paleorient* 2 (2): 415–27.

Belfer-Cohen, A. 1989. The Natufian Graveyard in Hayonim Cave. In *Prehistoire du Levant, processus des changements culturels* (eds O. Aurenche, M.C. Cauvin and P. Sanlaville). Paris: Editions du CNRS, pp. 297–308.

Belfer-Cohen, A. 1991a. The Natufian in the Levant. *Annual Review of Anthropology* 20: 167–86.

Belfer-Cohen, A. 1991b. Art items from layer B, Hayonim Cave: A case study of art in a Natufian context. In *The Natufian Culture in the Levant* (eds O. Bar-Yosef and F.R. Valla). Archaeological series 1. Ann Arbor: International Monographs in Prehistory, pp. 569–88.

Belfer-Cohen, A., Schepartz, L.A. and Arensburg, B. 1991. New biological data for the Natufian population in Israel. In *The Natufian Culture in the Levant* (eds O. Bar-Yosef and F.R. Valla). Archaeological series 1. Ann Arbor: International Monographs in Prehistory, pp. 411–24.

Betts, A. 1991. The Late Epipaleolithic in the Black Desert, Eastern Jordan. In *The Natufian Culture in the Levant* (eds O. Bar-Yosef and F.R. Valla). Archaeological Series 1. Ann Arbor: International Monographs in Prehistory, pp. 217–34.

Binford, L.R. 1968. Post-Pleistocene adaptations. In *New Perspectives in Archaeology* (eds L.R. Binford and S.R. Binford). Chicago: Aldine, pp. 313–41.

Boyd, B. and Cook, J. 1993. A Reconsideration of the 'Ain Sakhri' Figurine. *Proceedings of the Prehistoric Society* 59: 399–405.

Byrd, B.F. 1989a. *The Natufian encampment at Beidha: Late Pleistocene adaptations in the southern Levant* Aarhus: Denmark. Jutland Archaeological Society Publications Vol. 23.

Byrd, B.F. 1989b. The Natufian: Settlement variability and economic adaptations in the Levant at the end of the Pleistocene. *Journal of World Prehistory.* 3: 159–97.

Campana, D.V. 1989. *Natufian and Protoneolithic Bone Tools.* Oxford: BAR International Series 494.

Cauvin, M.C. 1991. Du Natufien au Levant Nord? Jayroud et Mureybet, Syrie. In *The Natufian Culture in the Levant* (eds O. Bar-Yosef and F.R. Valla). Archaeological Series 1. Ann Arbor: International Monographs in Prehistory, pp. 295–314.

Cope, C. 1991. Gazelle hunting strategies in the Natufian. In *The Natufian Culture in the Levant* (eds O. Bar-Yosef and F.R. Valla). Archaeological Series 1. Ann Arbor: International Monographs in Prehistory, pp. 341–58.

Copeland, L. 1991. Natufian sites in Lebanon. In *The Natufian Culture in the Levant* (eds O. Bar-Yosef and F.R. Valla). Archaeological Series 1. Ann Arbor: International Monographs in Prehistory, pp. 27–42.

Davis, S.J.M. and Valla, F.R. 1978. Evidence for the domestication of the dog 12,000 years ago in the Natufian of Israel. *Nature.* 276: 608–10.

Edwards, P. 1991. Wadi Hammeh 27: an early Natufian site at Pella, Jordan. In *The Natufian Culture in the Levant* (eds O. Bar-Yosef and F.R. Valla). Archaeological Series 1. Ann Arbor: International Monographs in Prehistory, pp. 123–48.

Garrard, A.N. 1991. Natufian settlement in the Azraq basin, eastern Jordan. In *The Natufian Culture in the Levant* (eds O. Bar-Yosef and F.R. Valla). Archaeological Series 1. Ann Arbor: International Monographs in Prehistory, pp. 235–44.

Garrod, D.A.E. 1932. A New Mesolithic Industry: The Natufian of Palestine. *Journal of the Royal Anthropological Institute.* 62: 257–66.

Garrod, D.A.E. and Bate, D.M.A. 1937. *The Stone Age of Mount Carmel.* Oxford: The Clarendon Press.

Garrod, D.A.E. and Bate, D.M.A. 1942. Excavations at the Cave of Shoukbah, Palestine, 1928. *Proceedings of the Prehistoric Society.* 8: 1–20.

Goring-Morris, A.N. 1987. *At the Edge: Terminal Pleistocene Hunter-Gatherers in the Negev and Sinai.* Oxford: BAR International Series 361.

Goring-Morris, A.N. 1991. The Harifian of the southern Levant. In *The Natufian Culture in the Levant* (eds O. Bar-Yosef and F.R. Valla). Archaeological Series 1. Ann Arbor: International Monographs in Prehistory, pp. 173–216.

Henry, D.O. 1976. Rosh Zin: A Natufian settlement near Ein Avdat. In *Prehistory and Palaeoenvironments in the Central Negev I: the Avdat-Aqev area part 1* (ed. A.E. Marks). Dallas: Southern Methodist University Press, pp. 311–47.

Henry, D.O. 1989. *From foraging to agriculture: the Levant at the end of the Ice Age.* Philadelphia: University of Pennsylvania Press.

Hillman, G.C. and Davies, M.S. 1990. Measured Domestication Rates in Wild Wheats and Barley Under Primitive Cultivation, and their archaeological implications. *Journal of World Prehistory.* 4: 157–222.

Hillman, G.C., Colledge, S.M. and Harris, D.R. 1989. Plant-food economy during the Epipaleolithic at Tell Abu Hureyra, Syria, dietary diversity, seasonality and modes of exploitation. In *Foraging and Farming: the evolution of Plant Exploitation* (eds D.R. Harris and G.C. Hillman). London: Unwin Hyman, pp. 240–68.

Lechevallier, M. and Ronen, A. 1985. *Le site Natoufien–Khiamien de Hatoula, pres de Latroun, Israel. Fouilles 1980–1982.* Jerusalem: Cahier du Centre de Recherche Français de Jerusalem 1.

Lieberman, D.E. 1993. The Rise and Fall of Seasonal Mobility among Hunter-Gatherers. The Case of the Southern Levant. *Current Anthropology.* 34, 5: 599–631.

Moore, A.M.T. 1991. Abu Hureyra I and the antecedents of agriculture on the Middle Euphrates. In *The Natufian Culture in the Levant* (eds O. Bar-Yosef and F.R. Valla). Archaeological Series 1. Ann Arbor: International Monographs in Prehistory, pp. 277–94.

Mussi, M. 1984. Un modele des debuts de l'agriculture au Proche-Orient. In *Origin and Early Development of Food-Producing Cultures in North-Eastern Africa* (eds L. Krzyzaniak and M. Kobusiewicz). Poznan, pp. 73–9.

Nesteroff, D., Vergnaud Grazzini, C., Olive, P., Rivaut-Znaidi, J., Rossignol-Strick, M. 1983. Evolution climatique de la Mediterranee orientale au cours de la derniere glaciation. In *Paleoclimatic Research and Models* (ed. A. Ghazzi). Dordrecht: D. Reidel Publishing Company, pp. 81–94.

Neuville, R. 1951. *Le Paleolithique et le Mesolithique du Desert de Judee.* Archives de l'Institut de Paleontologie Humaine. Memoire 24. Paris: Masson.

Noy, T. 1989. Some aspects of Natufian mortuary behaviour at Nahal Oren. In *People and Culture in Change* (ed. I. Hershkovitz). Oxford: BAR International Series 508, pp. 53–7.

Noy, T. 1991. Art and decoration of the Natufian at Nahal Oren. In *The Natufian Culture in the Levant* (eds O. Bar-Yosef and F.R. Valla). Archaeological Series 1. Ann Arbor: International Monographs in Prehistory, pp. 557–68.

Olszeswki, D.I. 1986. *The North Syrian Epipaleolithic. The earliest occupation at Tell Abu Hureyra in the context of the Levantine Late Epipaleolithic.* Oxford: BAR International Series 309.

Perrot, J. 1966. Le gisement natoufien de Mallaha (Eynan), Israel. *L'Anthropologie.* 70 (5–6): 437–83.

Perrot, J. 1968. La préhistoire palestinienne. *Supplement au Dictionnaire de la Bible VIII.* Col. 286–446.

Perrot, J., Ladiray, D., et Solivers-Massel, O. 1988. *Les Hommes de Mallaha (Eynan). Israel.* Memoires et travaux du Centre de Recherche Français de Jerusalem 7. Paris: Association Paleorient.

Pichon, J. 1984. L'avifaune natoufienne du Levant. These de Doctorat. University de Paris VI. Paris.

Schroeder, B. 1991. Natufian in the central Beqaa valley, Lebanon. In *The Natufian Culture in the Levant* (eds O. Bar-Yosef and F.R. Valla). Archaeological Series 1. Ann Arbor: International Monographs in Prehistory, pp. 43–80.

Schuldenrein, J. and Goldberg, P. 1981. Late quaternary palaeoenvironments and prehistoric site distributions in the Lower Jordan Valley: a preliminary report. *Paleorient*. 7 (1): 57–71.

Scott, T.R. 1977. The Harifian of the central Negev. In *Prehistory and palaeoenvironments in the central Negev II: the Avdat/Aqev area, part 2 and the Har Harif* (ed. A.E. Marks). Dallas: Southern Methodist University Press, pp. 271–322.

Sillen, A. 1984. Dietary change in the Epi-Paleolithic and Neolithic of the Levant: The Sr/Ca evidence. *Paleorient*. 10 (1): 149–55.

Sillen, A. and Lee-Thorp, J.A. 1991. Dietary Change in the Late Natufian. In *The Natufian Culture in the Levant* (eds O. Bar-Yosef and F.R. Valla). Archaeological series 1. Ann Arbor: International Monographs in Prehistory, pp. 399–410.

Smith, P. 1991. The dental evidence for nutritional status in the Natufians. In *The Natufian Culture in the Levant* (eds O. Bar-Yosef and F.R. Valla). Archaeological series 1. Ann Arbor: International Monographs in Prehistory, pp. 425–32.

Stekelis, M. and Yisraeli, T. 1963. Excavations at Nahal Oren. *Israel Exploration Journal*. 13: 1–12.

Stordeur, D. 1981. La contribution de l'Industrie de l'os a la delimitation des aires culturelles: l'example du Natoufien. In *Prehistoire du Levant* (eds J. Cauvin and P. Sanlaville). Paris: CRNS, pp. 433–7.

Stordeur, D. 1991. Le Natoufien et son evolution a travers les artefacts en os. In *The Natufian Culture in the Levant* (eds O. Bar-Yosef and F.R. Valla). Archaeological series 1. Ann Arbor: International Monographs in Prehistory, pp. 467–82.

Tchernov, E. 1991. Biological evidence for human sedentism in southwest Asia during the Natufian. In *The Natufian Culture in the Levant* (eds O. Bar-Yosef and F.R. Valla). Archaeological series 1. Ann Arbor: International Monographs in Prehistory, pp. 315–40.

Tchernov, E. and Kolska-Horwitz, L. 1991. Body Size Diminution under Domestication: Unconscious selection in Primeval Domesticates. *Journal of Anthropological Archaeology*. 10: 54–75.

Turville-Petre, F. (1932). Excavations at the Mugharet el-Kebarah. *Journal of the Royal Anthropological Institute*. 62: 271–6.

Valla, F.R. 1984. *Les industries de silex de Mallaha (Eynan) et du Natoufien dans le Levant*. Memoires et travaux du Centre de Recherche Français de Jerusalem 3. Paris: Association Paleorient.

Valla, F.R. 1987. Chronologie relative et chronologie absolue dans le Natoufien. In *Chronologies in the Near East* (eds O. Aurenche, J. Evin and F. Hours). Oxford: BAR International Series 379, pp. 267–94.

Valla, F.R. 1991. Les Natoufiens de Mallaha et l'espace. In *The Natufian Culture in the Levant* (eds O. Bar-Yosef and F.R. Valla). Archaeological Series 1. Ann Arbor: International Monographs in Prehistory, pp. 111–22.

Valla, F.R. (n.d.) Natufian seasonality: a guess. Paper read at the Annual Meeting of the Society for American Archaeology, 1992.

Valla, F.R., Plisson, H., Buxo, I. and Capdevila, R. 1989. Notes preliminaires sur les fouilles en cours sur la terrasse d'Hayonim. *Paleorient*. 15 (1): 245–57.

Valla, F.R., Le Mort, F., Plisson, H. 1991. Les fouilles en cours sur la terrasse d'Hayonim. In *The Natufian Culture in the Levant* (eds O. Bar-Yosef and F.R. Valla). Archaeological Series 1. Ann Arbor: International Monographs in Prehistory, pp. 95–110.

Willcox, G. 1991. La culture inventee, la domestication inconsciente: le debut de l'agriculture au Proche Orient. In *Rites et rythmes agraires* (ed. M.C. Cauvin). TMO 20. Paris: De Boccard, pp. 9–29.

Wright, G.A. 1978. Social differenciation in the Early Natufian. In *Social Archaeology, beyond subsistence and dating* (eds C. Redman, M. Berman, E. Curtin, W. Langhorne Jr, N. Versaggi and J. Wanser). London: Academic Press, pp. 201–33.

Wright, K. 1991. The origin and development of ground stone assemblages in Late Pleistocene Southwest Asia. *Paleorient*. 17 (1): 19–46.

Chapter 12

Aurenche, O., Cauvin, J., Cauvin, M.-C., Copeland, L., Hours, F. and Sanlaville, P. 1981. Chronologie et Organisation de l'Espace dans le Proche Orient de 12,000 à 5,600 AV. J.C. (14,000 à 7,600 BP). In *Préhistoire du Levant* (eds J. Cauvin and P. Sanlaville). Paris: CNRS, pp. 571–8.

Banning, E.B. and Byrd, B.F. 1984. The Architecture of PPNB 'Ain Ghazal, Jordan *Bulletin of the American School of Oriental Research* 225: 15–20.

Bar-Yosef, D.E. 1989. Late Paleolithic and Neolithic Marine Shells in the Southern Levant as Cultural Markers. Shell Bead Conference, Rochester, New York: Rochester Museum and Science Center.

Bar-Yosef, O. 1980. A figurine from a Khiamian site in the lower Jordan Valley *Paléorient* 6: 193–200.

Bar-Yosef, O. 1981. The 'Pre-Pottery Neolithic' period in the southern Levant. In *Préhistoire du Levant* (eds J. Cauvin and P. Sanlaville). Paris: Editions CNRS, pp. 551–70.

Bar-Yosef, O. 1984. Seasonality among Neolithic hunter-gatherers in southern Sinai. In *Animals and Archaeology, 3: Early Herders and Their Flocks* (eds J. Clutton-Brock and C. Grigson). Oxford: BAR International Series 202, pp. 145–60.

Bar-Yosef, O. 1985. The Stone Age of the Sinai Penninsula. In *Studi di Paleontologia in Onore i Salvatore M. Puglisi* (eds M. Liverani, A. Palmieri and P. Peroni). Rome: Universita di Rome 'La Sapienza', pp. 107–22.

Bar-Yosef, O. 1986. The Walls of Jericho: An Alternative Interpretation *Current Anthropology* 27: 157–62.

Bar-Yosef, O. 1991. The Early Neolithic of the Levant: Recent Advances *The Review of Archaeology* 12(2): 1–18.

Bar-Yosef, O. and Alon, D. 1988. Excavations in the Nahal Hemar Cave *Atiqot* 18: 1–30.

Bar-Yosef, O. and Belfer-Cohen, A. 1989. The PPNB Interaction Sphere. In *People and Cultures in Change* (ed. I. Hershkovitz). Oxford: BAR International Series 508, pp. 59–72.

Bar-Yosef, O. and Belfer-Cohen, A. 1991. From Sedentary Hunter-Gatherers to Territorial Farmers in the Levant. In *Between Bands and States* (ed. S.A. Gregg). Carbondale: Center for Archaeological Investigations, pp. 181–202.

Bar-Yosef, O. and Belfer-Cohen, A. 1992. From Foraging to Farming in the Mediterranean Levant. In *Transitions to Agriculture in Prehistory* (eds A.B. Gebauer and T.D. Price). Madison: Prehistory Press, pp. 21–48.

Bar-Yosef, O. and Schick, T. 1989. Early Neolithic organic remains from Nahal Hemar Cave. *National Geographic Research*. 5(2): 176–90.

Bar-Yosef, O., Gopher, A., Tchernov, E. and Kislev, M.E. 1991. Netiv Hagdud – An Early Neolithic Village Site in the Jordan Valley. *Journal of Field Archaeology* 18: 405–24.

Bar-Yosef, O. and Khazanov, A. (eds) 1992. *Pastoralism in the Levant: Archaeological Materials in Anthropological Perspectives*. Monographs in World Archaeology, 10. Madison: Prehistory Press.

Bar-Yosef, O. and Meadow, R.H. in press. The Origins of Agriculture in the Near East. In T.D. Price and G. Gebauer (eds). Santa Fe: School of American Research.

Betts, A. 1982. Prehistoric Sites at Qa'a Mejalla, Eastern Jordan. *Levant* XIV: 1–34.

Betts, A. 1985. Black Desert Survey, Jordan: Third Preliminary Report. *Levant* XVII: 29–52.

Betts, A. 1987. 1986 excavations at Dhuweila, eastern Jordan: a preliminary report. *Annual of the Department of Antiquities of Jordan* XXXI: 121–8.

Braidwood, R.J. 1975. *Prehistoric Men*. Glenview, Illinois: Scott, Freeman and Co.

Cauvin, J.C. 1972. *Les Religions Néolithiques de Syro-Palestine*. Paris: Maisonneuve.

Cauvin, J. 1985. La Question du 'Matriarcat Préhistorique' et le Rôle de la Femme dans la Préhistoire. In *La Femme dans le Monde Mediterranéen* (ed. A.M. Vérilhac). Lyon: Travaux de la Maison de l'Orient, pp. 7–18.

Cauvin, J. 1987. Chronologie Relative et Absolue dans le Neolithique du Levant Nord et d'Anatolie Entre 10,000–8,000 BP. In *Chronologies in the Near East* (eds O. Aurence, F. Evin and F. Hours). Oxford: Bar International Series, pp. 325–42.

Cauvin, M.-C. and Stordeur, D. 1978. *Les Outillages Lithiques et Osseux de Mureybet, Syrie*. Paris: CNRS.

Clutton-Brock, J. 1981. *Domesticated Animals from Early Times*. Austin: University of Texas.

Cohen, M.N. and Brown, J.A. eds 1985. Prehistoric Hunter-Gatherers: The Meaning of Social Complexity. In *Prehistoric Hunter-Gatherers:*

The Emergence of Social Complexity. New York: Academic Press, pp. 99–119.

COHMAP. 1988. Climatic Changes of the Last 18,000 years: Observations and Model Simulations. *Science* 241: 1043–52.

Crowfoot-Payne, J. 1983. The flint industries of Jericho. In *Excavations at Jericho* (eds K.M. Kenyon and T.A. Holland). London: The British School of Archaeology in Jerusalem, pp. 622–759.

Davis, S.J.M. 1982. Climatic change and the advent of domestication or ruminant artiodactyls in the late Pleistocene-Holocene period in the Israel region. *Paléorient* 8: 5–16.

Davis, S.J.M. 1989. Hatoula 1980–1986: Why Did Prehistoric People Domesticate Food Animals? In *Investigations in South Levantine Prehistory* (eds O. Bar-Yosef and B. Vandermeersch). Oxford: BAR International Series 497, pp. 43–59.

Davis, S.J.M. 1991. When and why did prehistoric people domesticate animals? Some new evidence from Israel and Cyprus. In *The Natufian Culture in the Levant* (eds O. Bar-Yosef and F.R. Valla). Ann Arbor: International Monographs in Prehistory, pp. 381–90.

Dayan, T., Tchernov, E., Bar-Yosef, O. and Yom-Tov, Y. 1986. Animal exploitation in Ujrat el Mehed, a Neolithic site in southern Sinai. *Paléorient* 12: 105–16.

de Contenson, H. 1981. L'Art du Neolithique Preceramique en Syrie-Palestine. *Bollettino del Centro Camuno di Studi Preistorici* XVIII: 53–65.

Echegaray, G. J. 1966. *Excavation en la Terraza de El-Khain (Jordania)*. Madrid: Consejo Superior de Investigciones Cientificas.

Flannery, K.V. 1972. The origins of the village as a settlement type in Mesoamerica and the Near East: A comparative study. In *Man, Settlement and Urbanism* (eds P.J. Ucko, R. Trigham and G.W. Dimbleby). London: Duckworth, pp. 23–53.

Flannery, K.V. 1973. The origins of agriculture, *Annual Review of Anthropology* 2: 271–310

Garfinkel, Y. 1987. Burnt Lime Products and Social Implications in the Pre-Pottery Neolithic B Villages of the Near East. *Paléorient* 13(1): 69–76.

Garrard, A.N., Betts, A., Byrd, B. and Hunt, C. 1988. Summary of Palaeoenvironmmental and Prehistoric Investigations in the Azraq Basin. In *The Prehistory of Jordan* (eds A.N. Garrard and H.G. Gebel). Oxford: Oxford University press, pp. 311–37.

Goldberg, P. and Bar-Yosef, O. 1990. The effect of man on geomorphological processes based upon evidence from the Levant and adjacent areas. In *Man's Role in Shaping the Eastern Mediterranean Landscape* (eds S. Bottema, G. Entjies-Nieborg and W. Van Zeist). Rotterdam: Balkema, pp. 71–86.

Gopher, A. 1989. Neolithic Arrowheads in the Levant: Results and Implications of a Seriation Analysis. *Paléorient* 15: 57–64.

Goring-Morris, A.N. and Gopher, A. 1983. Nahal Issaron: A Neolithic Settlement in the Southern Negev. *Israel Exploration Journal* 33: 149–62.

Goring-Morris, N. 1991. A PPNB settlement at Kfar Hahoresh in Lower Galilee: a preliminary report of the 1991 season. *Mitekufat Haeven* 24: 77–101.

Helmer, D. 1989. Le developement de la domestication au Proche-Orient de 9500 à 7500 B.P.: Les Nouvelles donnees d'El Kowm et de Ras Shamra. *Paléorient* 15/1: 111–21.

Helmer, D. 1991. Les changements des strategies de chasse dans le neolithique preceramique de Cafer Hoyuk est (Turquie). *Cahiers de l'Euphrate* 5–6: 131–7.

Hershkovitz, I. and Gopher, A. 1990. Paleodemography, Burial Customs, and Food-Producing Economy at the Beginning of the Holocene: A Perspective from the Southern Levant. *Mitekufat Haeven, Journal of the Israel Prehistoric Society* 23: 9–48.

Hesse, B. 1984. These are our goats: the origins of herding in West Central Iran. In *Animal and Archaeology: 3. Early Herders and Their Flocks* (eds J. Clutton-Brock and C. Grigson). Oxford: BAR International Series 202, pp. 243–64.

Hillman, G.C. and Davies, M.S. 1990. Measured Domestication rates in Wild Wheats and Barley Under Primitive Cultivation. *Journal of World Prehistory* 4(2): 157–222.

Hillman, G.C. and Davies, M.S. 1992. Domestication Rate in Wild Wheats and Barley Under Primitive Cultivation: Preliminary Results and the Archaeological Implications of Field Measurements of

Selection Coefficient. In P.C. Anderson (ed.): *Prehistoire de l'Agriculture*. Paris: Editions du CNRS, pp. 119–58.

Hillman, G.C., Colledge, S. and Harris, D. R. 1989. Plant food economy during the Epi-Palaeolithic period at Tell Abu Hureyra, Syria: Dietary diversity, seasonality and modes of exploitation. In *Foraging and Farming: The Evolution of Plant Exploitation* (eds G.C. Hillman and D.R. Harris). London: Hyman Unwin, pp. 240–66.

Hole, F. 1983. Symbols of Religion and Social Organization at Susa. In *Prehistoric Archeology Along the Zagros Flanks* (eds L. Braidwood, J.R. Braidwood, B. Howe, C.A. Reed and P.J. Watson). Chicago: Oriental Institute, The University of Chicago, pp. 315–31.

Hole, F. 1984. A Reassessment of the Neolithic Revolution. *Paléorient* 10(2): 49–60.

Hopf, M. 1983. *Jericho plant remains*. London: The British School of Archaeology in Jerusalem.

Kenyon, K. 1957. *Digging Up Jericho*. London: Benn.

Kenyon, K. 1981. *Excavations at Jericho*. London: British School of Archaeology in Jerusalem.

Kirkbride, D. 1966. Five seasons at the prepottery neolithic village of Beidha in Jordan. *Palestine Exploration Quarterly* 98: 5–61.

Kirkbride, D. 1968. Beida 1967: An Interim Report. *Palestine Exploration Quarterly* 100: 90–6.

Kirkbride, D. 1978. The Neolithic in Wadi Rumm: Ain Abu Nekheileh. In *Archaeology in the Levant* (eds P.R.S. Moorey and P.J. Parr). Warminster: pp. 1–10.

Kislev, M.E. 1989. Pre-Domesticated Cereals in the Pre-Pottery Neolithic A Period. In *People and Culture Change* (ed. I. Hershkovitz). Oxford: BAR International Series 508 (i), pp. 147–52.

Kislev, M.E. 1992. Agriculture in the Near East in the 7th Millennium bc. In *Prehistoire de L'Agriculture, Nouvelles Approches Experimentale et Ethnographiques* (ed. P.C. Anderson). Paris: CNRS, pp. 87–93.

Kislev, M.E., Nadel, D. and Carmi, I. 1992. Epi-Palaeolithic (19,000 BP) Cereal and Fruit Diet at Ohalo II, Sea of Galilee, Israel *Review of Palaeobotany and Palynology* 71: 161–6.

Köhler-Rollefson, I. 1992. A model for the development of nomadic pastoralism in the Transjordanian Plateau. In *Pastoralism in the Levant: Archaeological Materials in Anthropological Perspectives*. Monographs in World Archaeology, Madison: Prehistory Press, pp. 11–18.

Kramer, C. 1982. *Village Ethnoarchaeology*. New York: Academic Press.

Kramer, C. 1983. *Spatial organization in contemporary southwest Asian villages*. Chicago: OIC, Studies in Ancient Civilization No. 36.

Kuijt, I., Mabry, J. and Palumbo, G. 1991. Early Neolithic Use of Upland Areas of Wadi El-Yabis: Preliminary Evidence from the Excavations of 'Iraq Ed-Dubb, Jordan. *Paléorient* 17(1): 99–108.

Lechevallier, M. 1977. Les débuts de l'architecture domestique en Palestine. *Eretz-Israel* 13 (Moshe Stekelis Memorial Volume): 253–9.

Lechevallier, M. 1978. *Abou Ghosh et Beisamoun, deux gisements du VIIe millenaire avant l'ere chretienne en Israel*. Paris: Paleorient.

Margalit, B. 1983. The 'Neolithic Connexion' of the Ugarit poet of Aqht. *Paléorient* 9: 93–8.

McCorriston, J. and Hole, F. 1991. The Ecology of Seasonal Stress and the Origins of Agriculture in the Near East. *American Anthropologist* 93: 46–94.

McCorriston, J. 1994. Acorn eating and agricultural origins: California ethnographies and the formal use of analogy. *Antiquity* 68(258): 97–107.

Meshel, Z. 1974. New data about the 'desert kites'. *Tel Aviv* 1: 129–43.

Miller, N.F. 1992. The Origins of Plant Cultivation in the Near East. In *The Origins of Agriculture* (eds C.W. Cowan and P.J. Watson). Washington: Smithsonian Institution Press, pp. 39–58.

Moore, A. 1985. The Development in Neolithic Societies in the Near East. In *Advances in World Archaeology* (eds F. Wendorf and A.E. Close). New York: Academic Press, pp. 1–69.

Moore, A.M.T. and Hillman, G.C. 1992. The Pleistocene to Holocene Transition and Human Economy in Southwest Asia: The Impact of the Younger Dryas. *American Antiquity* 57: 482–94.

Nadel, D. 1990. The Khiamian as a Case of Sultanian Intersite Variability. *Mitekufat Haeven, Journal of the Israel Prehistoric Society* 23: 86–99.

Noy, T. 1986. Seated Clay Figurines from the Neolithic Period, Israel. In *Archaeology and Fertility Cult in the Ancient Mediterranean* (ed. A. Bonanno). The University of Malta, pp. 63–351.

Noy, T. 1989. Gilgal 1. A Pre-Pottery Neolithic site in Northern Iraq. *Paléorient* 15/1: 11–18.

Özdögan, M. and Özdögan, A. 1989. Çayönü, a Conspectus of Recent Work. *Paléorient* 15: 65–74.

Perrot, M.J. 1967. Munhata. *Bible et Terre Sainte* 93: 4–16.

Perrot, J. 1968. La Préhistoire palestinienne. In *Supplement au Dictionnaire de la Bible 8* (ed. Paris: Letouzey and Ané, pp. cols. 286–446.

Rollefson, G.O. 1983. Ritual and Ceremony at Neolithic Ain Ghazal (Jordan). *Paléorient* 9: 29–38.

Rollefson, G.O. 1984. 'Ain Ghazal: An Early Neolithic Community in Highland Jordan, Near Amman. *Bulletin of the American Schools of Oriental Research* 255: 3–14.

Rollefson, G. 1986. Neolithic Ain Ghazal (Jordan): Ritual and Ceremony II. *Paléorient* 12: 45–52.

Rollefson, G.O. 1988. Local and External Relations in the Levantine PPN Period: 'Ain Ghazal (Jordan) as a Regional Centre. In *Studies in the History and Archaeology of Jordan III* (ed. A. Hadidi). pp. 29–32.

Rollefson, G.O. 1989. The Late Aceramic Neolithic of the Levant: A Synthesis. *Paléorient* 15: 168–73.

Rollefson, G.O., Simmons, A. H. and Kafafi, Z. 1992. Neolithic Cultures at 'Ain Ghazal, Jordan. *Journal of Field Archaeology* 19: 443–70.

Smith, P., Bar-Yosef, O. and Sillen, A. 1984. Archaeological and skeletal evidence for dietary change during the Late Pleistocene–early Holocene in Levant. In *Paleopathology and the Origins of Agriculture* (eds M.N. Cohen and G. Armelagos). New York: Academic Press, pp. 101–36.

Stuiver, M. and Pearson, G. 1993. High-Precision Bidecadal Calibration of the Radiocarbon Time Scale, AD 1950–500 BC and 2500–6000 BC. *Radiocarbon* 35/1: 1–23.

Tchernov, E. 1991. Biological Evidence for Human Sedentism in Southwest Asia during the Natufian. In *The Natufian Culture in the Levant* (eds O. Bar-Yosef and F.R. Valla). Ann Arbor: International Monographs in Prehistory, pp. 315–40.

Tchernov, E. and Bar-Yosef, O. 1982. Animal exploitation in the PrePottery Neolithic B period at Wadi Tbeik, southern Sinai. *Paléorient* 8: 17–37.

van Zeist, W. 1988. Some aspects of Early Neolithic plant husbandry in the Near East. *Anatolica* 15: 49–68.

van Zeist, W. and Bakker-Herres, J.A.H. 1985. Archaeobotanical studies in the Levant: Neolithic sites in the Damascus Basin, Aswad, Ghoraife, Ramad. *Prehistoria (1982)* 24: 165–256.

van Zeist, W. and Bakker-Herres, J.A.H. 1986. Archaeobotanical Studies in the Levant. III. Late Paleolithic Mureybet. *Palaeohistoria* 26: 171–99.

Voigt, M.M. 1990. Reconstructing Neolithic societies and economies in the Middle East: An esssay. *Archaeomaterials* 4: 1–14.

Voigt, M.M. 1991. The Goddess from Anatolia: An Archaeological Perspective. *Oriental Rug Review* 11: 32–9.

Wright, K. 1991. The Origins and Development of Ground Stone Assemblages in Late Pleistocene Southwest Asia. *Paléorient* 17: 19–45.

Yakar, R. and Hershkovitz, I. 1988. The modelled skulls of Nahal Hemar. *Atiqot* 18: 59–63.

Zohary, D. 1989. Domestication of the Southwest Asian crop assemblage of cereals, pulses and flax: the evidence from the living plants. In *Foraging and Farming: The Evolution of Plant domestication* (eds D.R. Harris and G. Hillman). London: Unwin and Hyman, pp. 359–73.

Zohary, D. 1992. Domestication of the Neolithic Near East crop assemblage. In *Prehistoire de l' Agriculture* (ed. P.C. Anderson). Paris: CNRS, pp. 81–6.

Zohary, D. and Hopf, M. 1988. *Domestication of Plants in the Old World*. Oxford: Oxford University Press.

Chapter 13

Anati, E., Avnimelech, M., Haas, N. and Meyerhof, E. 1973. *Hazorea I*. Archivi, vol. 5. Edizioni del Centro, Capo di Ponte.

Arensburg, B. 1970. The Human Remains from 'Ein El-Jarba, *Bulletin of the American Schools for Oriental Research* 197: 49–52.

Arensburg B. and Hershkovitz, I. 1988. Neolithic human remains. In *Nahal Hemar Cave* (eds O. Bar-Yosef and D. Alon). Jerusalem: Atiqot, English Series Vol. XVIII, pp. 50–8.

Arnold, D.E. 1985. *Ceramic Theory and Cultural Process*. Cambridge: Cambridge University Press.

Bar-Yosef, O. 1977. The Neolithic Cultures in Eretz-Israel. *Quadmoniot*. 10: 38–59 (in Hebrew).

Bar-Yosef, O. and Alon, D. 1988. Excavations in the Nahal Hemar cave. *Atiquot*. 18: 1–30.

Bar-Yosef, O. and Belfer-Cohen, A. 1989. The Levantine 'PPNB' Interaction Sphere. In *People and Culture in Change* (ed. I. Hershkovitz). Oxford: BAR International Series 508, pp. 59–72.

Ben-Dor, E. 1936. Pottery of the Middle and Late Neolithic Periods. *Liverpool Annals of Archaeology and Anthropology*. XXIII: 77–90.

Bossut, P., Kafafi, Z. and Dollfus, G. 1988. Khirbet ed-Dharih (Survey Site 49/WHS 524), Un Nouveau Gisement Neolithique avec Ceramique du Sud-Jordanien. *Paleorient*. 14/1: 127–31.

Burian, F. and Friedman, E. 1989. A Note concerning the C14 dating of Givat Haparsa and Nahal Lavan 109, and the use of ancient ostrich eggshells for bead production. *Mitekufat Haeven*. 22: 93–4.

Byrd, B.F. 1992. The dispersal of food production across the Levant. In *Transitions to Agriculture in Prehistory* (eds A.G. Gebauer and T. Douglas Price). Madison: Prehistory Press, pp. 49–61.

Cauvin, J. 1972. *Religion Neolithique de Syrie-Palestine*. Paris: Documents Librairie d'Amerique et d'Orient, J. Maisonneuve.

Cauvin, J. 1989. La Neolithisation du Levant, huit ans apres. *Paleorient* 15 (1): 174–78.

Clarke, D.L. 1978. *Analytical Archaeology*. New York: Columbia.

Clutton-Brock, J. 1971. The Primary Food Animals of the Jericho Tel from the Proto-Neolithic to the Byzantine Period. *Levant*. III: 41–55.

Crowfoot, J. 1935. Notes on the flint implements of Jericho 1935. *Liverpool Annals of Archaeology and Anthropology*. 22: 174–84.

Crowfoot, J. 1937. Notes on the flint implements of Jericho 1936. *Liverpool Annals of Archaeology and Anthropology*. 24: 35–51.

de Contenson, H. 1992. Les Coutumes funeraires dans le Neolithique syrien. *Bulletin de la Societe Prehistorique Francaise*. 89/6: 184–91.

de Vaux, R. 1966. Palestine during the Neolithic and Chalcolithic Periods. In *Cambridge Ancient History* Vol. I, (eds I.E.S. Edwards, C.J.Gadd, N.G.L. Hammond). Cambridge: Cambridge University Press, pp. 498–520.

Dunand, M. 1973. *Fouilles de Byblos V*. Paris: Maisonneuve.

Eizenberg, E. 1987. Excavations at Tel Teo. *Israel Exploration Journal*. 37: 173–5.

Epstein, C. 1984. A Pottery Neolithic Site Near Tel Qatif. *Israel Exploration Journal*.. 34: 209–19.

Fitzgerald, G.M. 1934. Excavations at Beth Shan in 1933. *Palestine Exploration Fund Quarterly Statement*. LXVI: 123–34.

Fitzgerald, G.M. 1935. The Earliest Pottery of Beth Shan. *The Museum Journal*. XXIV: 5–22.

Galili, E., Weinstein-Evron, M. and Zohari, D. 1989. The appearance of Olives in submerged Neolithic sites along the Carmel Coast. *Mitekufat Haeven*. 22: 95–7.

Galili, E., Hershkovitz, I., Gopher, A., Weinstein-Evron, M., Lernau, O., Kislev, M., Horwitz, L. 1994. Atlit-Yam: A Prehistoric Site on the Sea Floor off the Israeli Coast. *Journal of Field Archaeology*. 20 (2): 133–57.

Garfinkel, Y. 1992a. *The pottery Assemblages of the Sha'ar Hagolan and Rabah stages of Munhata (Israel)*. Les cahiers du centre de recherche francais de Jerusalem. Vol. 6. Paris: Association Paleorient.

Garfinkel. Y. 1992b. The Material Culture in the Central Jordan Valley in the Pottery Neolithic and Early Chalcolithic Periods. Unpublished doctoral thesis, Hebrew University, Jerusalem (in Hebrew with English summary).

Garstang, J. 1935. Jericho: city and necropolis (fifth report). *Liverpool Annals of Archaeology and Anthropology*. 22: 143–84.

Garstang, J. 1936. Jericho: City and Necropolis. *Liverpool Annals of Archaeology and Anthropology*. 23: 67–100.

Garstang, J. and Garstang, J.B.E. 1940. *The Story of Jericho*. London: Marshall, Morgan and Scott.

Gilead, I. 1990. The Neolithic-Chalcolithic Transition and the Qatifian of the Northern Negev and Sinai. *Levant*. XXII: 47–63.

Gopher, A. 1985. Flint Industries of the Neolithic Period in Israel. Unpublished doctoral dissertation, Hebrew University, Jerusalem.

Gopher, A. 1989a. Horvat Galil and Nahal Betzet I: Two Neolithic Sites in the Upper Galilee. *Mitekufat Haeven.* 22: 82–92.

Gopher, A. 1989b. *The Flint Assemblages of Munhata – Final Report.* Les Cahiers Du Centre de Recherches Francais de Jerusalem, Vol. 4. Paris: Association Paleorient.

Gopher, A. 1989c. Neolithic Arrowheads of the Levant: Results and implications of a seriation analysis. *Paleorient.* 15/1: 43–56.

Gopher, A. n.d. Implications of the analysis of lithic aspects of the Wadi Raba culture in the Nahal Zehora sites (Israel) of the fifth millennium BC. Lecture delivered at the UISPP conference, Bratislava, September 1–7, 1991.

Gopher, A. and Gophna, R. 1993. The cultures of the Eighth and Seventh Millennia B.P. in the Southern Levant – A Review for the 1990s. *Journal of World Prehistory.* 7 (3): 297–353.

Gopher, A. and Greenberg, R. 1987. Pottery Neolithic Levels at Tel Dan. *Mitekufat Haeven.* 20: 91*–113*.

Gopher, A. and Orrelle, E. 1990. The Flint Industry of Nahal Zehora I, a Wadi Raba site in The Menashe Hills. *Bulletin of the American Schools of Oriental Research.* 276: 67–76.

Gopher, A. and Orrelle, E. in press. New data on burials from the Pottery Neolithic Period (6th–5th millennia B.C.) in Israel in *The Archaeology of Death in the Ancient Near East* (eds A. Green and S. Campbell).

Gopher, A. and Orrelle, E. in press. Material imagery of the Yarmukian, a Neolithic Culture of the sixth millennium B.C. the Southern Levant. *Rock Art Research.*

Gopher, A., Tsuk, Z., Shalev, S. and Gophna, R. 1990. Earliest Gold Artifacts discovered in the Southern Levant. *Current Anthropology.* 31 (4): 436–43.

Goren, Y. 1990. The 'Qatifian Culture' in Southern Israel and Transjordan: Additional Aspects for its definition. *Mitekufat Haeven.* 23: 100–12.

Goren, Y. 1991. The beginnings of pottery production in Israel: technology and typology of proto-historic ceramic assemblages in Eretz-Israel (6th–4th mill. BC). Unpublished doctoral thesis, Hebrew University, Jerusalem (in Hebrew).

Hayden, B. 1990. Nimrods, Piscators, Pluckers and Planters: The Emergence of Food Production. *Journal of Anthropological Archaeology.* 9: 31–69.

Hershkovitz, I. and Galili, E. 1990. 8000 year-old human remains on the sea floor near Atlit, Israel. *Journal of Human Evolution.* 5 (4): 319–58.

Hershkovitz, I. and Gopher, A. 1990. Paleodemography, Burial Customs, and Food-Producing Economy at the Beginning of the Holocene: A Perspective from the Southern Levant. *Mitekufat Haeven.* 23: 9–47.

Hopf, M. 1983. Jericho plant remains. In *Excavations at Jericho* (eds K.M. Kenyon and T.A. Holland). London: British School of Archaeology in Jerusalem c/o The British Academy. Volume V, App. B, pp. 576–621.

Kafafi, Z. 1985. Late Neolithic architecture from Jebel Abu Thawwab, Jordan. *Paleorient.* 11/1: 125–8.

Kafafi, Z. 1988. Jebel Abu Thawwab: A Pottery Neolithic Village in North Jordan. In *The Prehistory of Jordan* (eds A.N. Garrard and H.G. Gebel). Oxford: BAR International Series 396. pp. 451–71.

Kaplan, J. 1958a. The Neolithic and Chalcolithic Settlement in Tel Aviv and Neighbourhood. Unpublished doctoral thesis, The Hebrew University. Jerusalem (in Hebrew).

Kaplan, J. 1958b. Excavations at Teluliot Batashi, Nahal Soreq. *Eretz Israel.* 5: 9–24.

Kaplan, J. 1965. Hamadiya. *Revue Biblique.* 72: 543–4.

Kaplan, J. 1969. 'Ein el Jarba. *Bulletin of the American Schools of Oriental Research.* 194: 2–39.

Kaplan, J. 1976. Hamadiha. *Encyclopedia of Archaeological Excavations in the Holy Land.* Jerusalem: The Israel Exploration Society and Massada Press, Vol. II, pp. 468–9.

Kaplan, J. 1977. Neolithic and Chalcolithic Remains at Lod. *Eretz Israel.* 13: 57–75 (in Hebrew, with English Summary).

Kaplan, J. 1978. Habashan Street. *Encyclopedia of Archaeological Excavations in the Holy Land.* Jerusalem: Massada Press, Vol. IV, pp. 1159–61.

Kenyon, K.M. 1957. *Digging Up Jericho.* London: Benn.

Kenyon, K.M. 1970. *Archaeology in the Holy Land* (3rd Edn). New York: Praeger.

LeBlanc, S.A. and Watson, P.J. 1973. A comparative statistical analysis of painted pottery from seven Halafian sites. *Paleorient.* 1: 117–33.

MacDonald, B. 1988. *The Wadi el Hasq Archaeological Survey 1979–1983, West Central Jordan.* Ontario: Laurier University Press.

Mellaart, J. 1975. *The Neolithic of the Near East.* London: Thames and Hudson.

Moore, A.M.T. 1978. The Neolithic of the Levant. Unpublished doctoral dissertation. Oxford University.

Muheisen, M., Gebel, H.G., Hannss, C. and Neef, R. 1988. 'Ain Rahub, a new Final Natufian and Yarmukian site near Irbid. In *The Prehistory of Jordan* (eds A.N. Garrard and H.G. Gebel). Oxford: BAR International Series No. 396 (ii), pp. 472–502.

Noy, T. 1977. Neolithic Sites in the Western Coastal Plain. *Eretz Israel.* 13: 18–33 (in Hebrew).

Olami, Y., Burian, F. and Friedman, E. 1977. Givat Haparsa – A Neolithic site in the coastal region. *Eretz Israel.* 8: 34–47 (in Hebrew with English summary).

Perrot, J. 1964. Les deux premieres campagnes de fouilles a Munhata (1962–63), premieres resultats. *Syria.* 41: 323–45.

Perrot, J. 1966. La troisieme campagne de fouilles a Munhata (1964). *Syria.* 43: 49–63.

Perrot, J. 1968. La prehistoire Palestinienne. *Supplement au Dictionnaire de la bible.* Paris: Letouzeh and Ane, No. 8: 286–446.

Prausnitz, M.W. 1975. 'Ali, Tell. *Encyclopedia of Archaeological Excavations in the Holy Land.* Jerusalem: Israel Exploration Society and Massada Press, Vol. I, pp. 61–4.

Redman, C. 1978. *The Rise of Civilization.* San Francisco: Freeman.

Renfrew, C. 1972. *The Emergence of Civilization.* London: Methuen and Co. Ltd.

Rollefson, G. 1983. Ritual and Ceremony at Neolithic 'Ain Ghazal (Jordan). *Paleorient.* 9 (2): 29–38.

Rollefson, G. 1986. Ritual and Ceremony at Neolithic 'Ain Ghazal II. *Paleorient.* 12: 45–52.

Rollefson, G.O. 1989. The Late Aceramic Neolithic of the Levant: A synthesis. *Paleorient.* 15/1: 168–73.

Rollefson, G.O. and Simmons, A. 1986. The Neolithic Village of 'Ain Ghazal, Jordan: Preliminary Report on the 1984 Season. *Bulletin of the American Schools of Oriental Research Supplement.* 24: 145–64.

Rollefson, G.O. and Simmons, A. 1988. The Neolithic Village of 'Ain Ghazal. Jordan: Preliminary Report on the 1985 Season. *Bulletin of the American Schools of Oriental Research Supplement.* 25: 93–106.

Rollefson, G.O., Simmons, A.H. and Kafafi, Z. 1992. Neolithic Cultures at 'Ain Ghazal, Jordan. *Journal of Field Archaeology.* 19: 443–71.

Rosen, S.A. 1988–89. Pottery Neolithic Flint Artifacts from Tell Lachish. *Tel Aviv.* 15–16: 193–6.

Sherratt, A. 1981. Plough and Pasturalism: aspects of the secondary products revolution. In *Pattern of the Past* (eds I. Hodder, G. Isaac and N. Hammond). Cambridge: Cambridge University Press.

Shipton, G.M. 1939. *Notes on the Megiddo Pottery of Strata VI–XX.* The Oriental Institute of the University of Chicago. Studies in Ancient oriental civilizations No. 17. Chicago: The University of Chicago Press.

Simmons, A., Kohler-Rollefson, K., Rollefson, G.O., Mandel, R.D. and Kafafi, Z. 1988. 'Ain Ghazal: A Major Neolithic Settlement in Central Jordan. *Science.* 240: 35–9.

Simmons, A.H., Kafafi, Z., Rollefson, G.O. and Moyer, K. 1989. Test Excavations at Wadi Shu'eib, a Major Neolithic Settlement in Central Jordan. *Annals of the Department of Antiquities of Jordan.* XXXIII: 27–42.

Stekelis, M. 1950–51. A new Neolithic industry: the Yarmukian of Palestine. *Israel Exploration Journal.* 1: 1–19.

Stekelis, M. 1972. *The Yarmukian Culture of the Neolithic Period.* Jerusalem: Magnes Press.

Yeivin, E. and Mozel, I. 1977. A Fossil Directeur Figurine of the Pottery Neolithic A. *Tel Aviv.* 4: 194–200.

Yeivin, E. and Olami, Y. 1979. Nizzanim – A Neolithic site in Nahal Evtah: excavations of 1968–1970. *Tel Aviv.* 6: 99–135.

Chapter 14

Algaze, G. 1993. *The Uruk World System: The Dynamics of Expansion of Early Mesopotamian Civilization.* Chicago: The University of Chicago Press.

Alon, D. and Levy, T. E. 1989. The Archaeology of Cult and the Chalcolithic Sanctuary at Gilat. *Journal of Mediterranean Archaeology* 2: 163–221.

Amiran, R. 1978. *Early Arad: The Chalcolithic Settlement and Early Bronze City I. First-Five Seasons of Excavations 1962–1966.* Jerusalem: Israel Exploration Society.

Anati, E. 1963. *Palestine Before the Hebrews.* New York: Doubleday.

Avner, U. 1990. Ancient agricultural settlement and religion in the Uvda valley in southern Israel. *Biblical Archaeologist.* 53: 125–41.

Baines, J. and Malek, J. 1980. *Atlas of Ancient Egypt.* Oxford: Phaidon.

Bar-Adon, P. 1980. *The Cave of the Treasure.* Jerusalem: Israel Exploration Society.

Beit-Arieh, I. 1980. A Chalcolithic site near Serabit el-Khadim. *Tel Aviv.* 7: 45–64.

Beit-Arieh, I. 1983. Central southern Sinai in the Early Bronze Age II and its relationship with Palestine. *Levant.* 15: 39–48.

Bökönyi, S. 1985. The animal remains of Maadi, Egypt: a preliminary report. In *Studi Di Palentologia in Onore Di Salvatore* (eds M. Liverani, A. Palmieri and R. Peroni). Rome: University of Rome, pp. 495–99.

Bradley, R. 1991. The pattern of change in British prehistory. In *Chiefdoms: Power, Economy, and Ideology* (ed. T. Earle). Cambridge: Cambridge University Press, pp. 44–70.

Braudel, F. 1972. *The Mediterranean and the Mediterranean World in the Age of Phillip II* (revised edition, trans: S. Reynolds). London: Collins.

Braudel, F. 1980. *On History.* Chicago: The University of Chicago Press.

Cameron, D.O. 1981. *The Ghassulian Wall Paintings.* London: Kenyon-Deane.

Caneva, I., Frangipane, M. and Palimieri, A. 1987. Predynastic Egypt: new data from Maadi. *African Archaeological Review.* 5: 105–114.

Carneiro, R.L. 1981. The chiefdom as precursor of the state. In *The Transition to Statehood in the New World* (eds G. Jones and R. Kautz). Cambridge: Cambridge University Press, pp. 37–79.

Commenge-Pellerin, C. 1987. *La Potterie D'Abou Matar Et De L'Ouadi Zoumeili (Beersheva) au IVe Millenaire Avant l'ere Chretienne.* Paris: Association Paleorient.

Commenge-Pellerin, C. 1990. *La Potterie de Safadi (Beersheba) au IVe Millenaire avant l'ere Chretienne.* Paris: Association Paleorient.

Contenson, H. de 1961. Remarques sur le Chalcolithique recent de Tell Esh Shuna. *Revue Biblique.* 68: 546–56.

Contenson, H. de 1964. The 1953 Survey in the Yarmuk and Jordan Valleys. *Annual of the Department of Antiquities of Jordan* 8–9: 30–46.

Davis, S. J. 1976. Mammal Bones from the Early Bronze Age City of Arad, N. Negev, Israel. Some Implications Concerning Human Exploitation. *Journal of Archaeological Science* 3: 153–64.

Denyer, S. 1978. *African Traditional Architecture: An Historical and Geographical Perspective.* London: Heinemann.

Dollfus, G. and Ibrahim, M. 1988. *Abu Hamid – Village du 4e Millenaire de la Vallee du Jourdain.* Amman: CNRS.

Dothan, M. 1959. Excavations at Horvat Beter (Beersheba). *Atiqot.* 2: 1–42 (English Series).

Durkheim, E. 1915 (1965). *The Elementary Forms of the Religious Life.* New York: The Free Press.

Earle, T. (ed.) 1991. *Chiefdoms: Power, Economy, and Ideology.* Cambridge: Cambridge University Press.

Eisenberg, E. 1989. The Chalcolithic and Early Bronze I Occupations at Tell Teo. In *L'urbanisation de la Palestine a l'age du Bronze ancien* (ed. P. de Miroschedji). Oxford: BAR International Series 527, pp. 29–40.

Eldar, I. and Baumgarten, Y. 1985. Neve Noy: A Chalcolithic site of the Beersheva culture. *Biblical Archaeologist.* 48: 134–9.

Engberg, R.M. and Shipton, G.M. 1934. *Notes on the Chalcolithic and Early Bronze Age Pottery of Megiddo.* Studies in Ancient Oriental Civilization, No. 10. Chicago: University of Chicago Press.

Epstein, C. 1977. The Chalcolithic Culture of the Golan. *Biblical Archaeologist* 40: 57–62.

Epstein, C. 1985. Laden animal figurines from the Chalcolithic period in Palestine. *Bulletin of the American Schools of Oriental Research.* 258: 53–62.

Epstein, C. 1988. Basalt pillar figures from the Golan and Huleh region. *Israel Exploration Journal.* 38: 205–23.

Fitzgerald, G. M. 1935. The earliest pottery of Beth-Shan. *The Museum Journal.* 24: 5–22.

Gilead, I. 1988. The Chalcolithic Period in the Levant. *Journal of World Prehistory.* 2: 397–443.

Gilead, I. 1989. Grar: A Chalcolithic Site in the Northern Negev, Israel. *Journal of Field Archaeology.* 16: 377–94.

Gilead, I. 1990. The Neolithic-Chalcolithic Transition and the Qatifian of the Northern Negev and Sinai. *Levant.* 22: 47–63.

Gilead, I. and Alon, D. 1988. Excavations of Protohistoric sites in the Nahal Besor and the Late Neolithic of the Northern Negev. Mitekufat Haeven (*Journal of the Israel Prehistoric Society*). 21: 109–30.

Gilead, I. and Goren, Y. 1989. Petrographic analysis of fourth millennium B.C. pottery and stone vessels from the northern Negev, Israel. *Bulletin of the American Schools of Oriental Research.* 275: 5–14.

Goldberg, P. and Rosen, A. 1987. Early Holocene paleoenvironments of Israel. In *Shiqmim I,* (ed. T.E. Levy). Oxford: BAR International Series 356, pp. 23–34.

Goldstein, L.G. 1981. One-dimensional archaeology and multidimensional people: Spatial organization and mortuary analysis. In *The Archaeology of Death* (eds R. Chapman, I. Kinnes and K. Randsborg). Cambridge: Cambridge University Press, pp. 53–69.

Gopher, A. and Gophna, R. 1993. The Pottery Neolithic Period in the Southern Levant – A Review. *Journal of World Prehistory.* 7: 297–353.

Gopher, A. and Tsuk, T. 1991. *Ancient Gold – Rare Finds from the Nahal Qanah Cave.* Jerusalem: Israel Museum.

Gopher, A., Tsuk, T., Shalev, S. and Gophna, R. 1990. Earliest Gold Artifacts in the Levant. *Current Anthropology.* 31: 436–43.

Gophna, R. 1989. From village to town in the Lod Valley: A Case Study. In *L'urbanisation de la Palestine a l'age du Bronze Ancien* (ed. P. de Miroschedji). Oxford: BAR International 527, pp. 97–107.

Gophna, R. and Portugali, Y. 1988. Settlement and demographic processes in Israel's coastal plain from the Chalcolithic to the Middle Bronze Age. *Bulletin of the American Schools of Oriental Research.* 269: 11–36.

Goren, Y. 1987. The Petrography of Ceramic Assemblages from the Chalcolithic Period of Southern Eretz Israel. Unpublished Masters Thesis, The Hebrew University of Jerusalem.

Goren, Y. and Gilead, I. 1986. Quaternary environments and man at Nahal Sekher, northern Negev. *Mitekufat Haeven.* 19: 66*–79*.

Gosden, C. 1989. Debt, production and prehistory. *Journal of Anthropological Archaeology.* 8: 355–87.

Grigson, C. 1987. Shiqmim: Pastoralism and other aspects of animal management in the Chalcolithic of the Northern Negev. In *Shiqmim I* (ed. T.E. Levy). Oxford: BAR International Series 356, pp. 219–41.

Grigson, C. 1993. The earliest domestic horses in the Levant – New finds from the 4th millennium of the Negev. *Journal of Archaeological Science.* 20: 645–55.

Gustavson-Gaube, C. 1987. Tell esh-Shuna North: 1984 and 1985. In *Studies in the History and Archaeology of Jordan III* (ed. A. Hadidi). Amman: Department of Antiquities, pp. 237–40.

Hardin, G. 1968. The tragedy of the commons. *Science.* 162: 1243–8.

Hauptmann, A. 1989. The earliest periods of copper metallurgy in Feinan, Jordan. In *Old World Archaeometallurgy* (eds A. Hauptmann, E. Pernicka and G.A. Wagner). Bochum: Selbstverlag des Deutschen Bergbau-Museums, pp. 119–35.

Hennessy, J. B. 1982. Teleilat Ghassul: It's Place in the Archaeology of Jordan. In *Studies in the History and Archaeology of Jordan* (ed. A. Hadidi). Amman: Department of Antiquities, pp. 55–88.

Ibrahim, M., Sauer, J. and Yassine, K. 1976. The East Jordan Valley Survey, 1975. *Bulletin of the American Schools of Oriental Research,* 222: 41–66.

Ilan, O. and Sabanne, M. 1989. Metallurgy, Trade and the Urbanization of Southern Canaan in the Chalcolithic and Early Bronze Age. In *L'urbanisation de la Palestine a l'age du Bronze Ancien* (ed. P. de Miroschedji). Oxford: BAR International 527, pp. 139–62.

Jacobson, T. 1976. *Treasure of the Darkness.* New Haven, London: Yale University Press.

James, T.G.H. 1985. *Egyptian Painting and Drawing in the British Museum.* London: British Museum Publications.

Joffee, A. 1990. Settlement and Society in Early Bronze I and II Canaan. Unpublished Ph.D. thesis, Department of Near Eastern Studies, University of Arizona, Tucson.

Joffee, A. 1991. Early Bronze I and the Evolution of Social Complexity in Canaan. *Journal of Mediterranean Archaeology.* 4: 3–58.

Johnson, A. W. and Earle, T. 1987. *The Evolution of Human Societies – From Foraging Group to Agrarian State.* Stanford: Stanford University Press.

Kenyon, K. 1985. *Archaeology in the Holy Land* (4th edn). London: Routledge and Kegan Paul.

Key, C.A. 1980. The trace-element composition of the copper and copper alloy artifacts of the Nahal Mishmar hoard. In *The Cave of the Treasure* (ed. P. Bar-Adon). Jerusalem: Israel Exploration Society, pp. 238–43.

Khalil, L. 1987. Preliminary report on the 1985 season of excavations at el-Maqass-'Aqaba. *Annual of the Department of Antiquities of Jordan.* 31: 481–3.

Kohl, P. 1987. The Ancient Economy, transferable technologies and the Bronze Age World-System: A View from the Northeastern Frontier of the Ancient Near East. In *Centre and Periphery in the Ancient World* (eds M. Rowlands, M. Larsen and K. Kristiansen). Cambridge: Cambridge University Press, pp. 13–24.

Lenski, G., and Lenski, J. 1970. *Human Societies – An Introduction to Macrosociology.* New York: McGraw-Hill Book Company.

Levy, T.E. 1981. Chalcolithic Settlement and Subsistence in the Northern Negev Desert, Israel. Unpublished Ph.D. thesis, University of Sheffield, U.K.

Levy, T.E. 1983. The Emergence of Specialized Pastoralism in the Southern Levant. *World Archaeology.* 15: 15–36.

Levy, T.E. 1986. Archaeological sources for the study of Palestine: The Chalcolithic period. *Biblical Archaeologist.* 49: 82–108.

Levy, T.E. (ed.) 1987. *Shiqmim I: Studies Concerning Chalcolithic Societies in the Northern Negev Desert, Israel.* Oxford: BAR International Series 356.

Levy, T.E. 1992a. Transhumance, Subsistence, and Social Evolution. In *Pastoralism in the Levant – Archaeological Materials in Anthropological Perspectives* (eds O. Bar-Yosef and A. Khazanov). Madison: Prehistory Press, pp. 65–82.

Levy, T.E. 1992b. Radiocarbon Dating of the Beersheva culture and Predynastic Egypt. In *The Nile Delta in Transition – 4th–3rd Millennium B.C.* (ed. Edwin C.M. van den Brink). Jerusalem: Israel Exploration Society, pp. 345–56.

Levy, T.E. 1993. Production, Space and Social Change in Protohistoric Palestine. In *Spatial Boundaries and Social Dynamics* (eds A. Holl and T.E. Levy). Ann Arbor: International Monographs in Prehistory, pp. 63–81.

Levy, T.E. and Alon, D. 1982. The Chalcolithic mortuary sites near Mezad Aluf, northern Negev desert: a preliminary study. *Bulletin of the American Schools of Oriental Research.* 248: 37–59.

Levy, T.E. and Alon, D. 1987. Settlement patterns along the Nahal Beersheva – Lower Nile) Besor: Models of Subsistence in the Northern Negev. In *Shiqmim I* (ed. T.E. Levy). Oxford, BAR International Series 356, pp. 45–138.

Levy, T.E. and Alon, D. 1992. A Corpus of Ivories from Shiqmim. *Eretz Israel.* 23: 65–71 (Hebrew).

Levy, T.E. and Holl, A. 1988. Les societes chalcolithiques de la Palestine et l'emergence des chefferies. *Archives Europeens de la Sociologie.* 29: 283–316.

Levy, T.E. and Shalev, S. 1989. Prehistoric Metalworking in the Southern Levant: Archaeometallurgical and Social Perspectives. *World Archaeology.* 20: 353–72.

Levy, T.E., Alon, D., Grigson, C., Holl, A., Goldberg, P., Rowan, Y. and Smith, P. 1991. Subterranean settlement in the Negev desert, ca. 4500–3700 B.C. *Research & Exploration.* 7: 394–413.

MacDonald, B. 1988. *The Wadi el-Hasa Archaeological Survey, 1979–1983, West Central Jordan.* Waterloo, Ontario: Wilfrid Laurier University Press.

MacDonald, E. 1932. Prehistoric Fara. *Beth Pelet II.* London: British School of Archaeology in Egypt.

Mallon, A., Koeppel, R. and Neuville, R. 1934. *Tuleilat Ghassul I: Compte Rendu Des Fouilles de L'Institute Biblique Pontifical 1929–1932.* Rome: Pontifical Biblical Institute.

Mann, M. 1986. *The Sources of Social Power, Volume 1: A History of Power from the Beginning to A.D. 1760.* Cambridge: Cambridge University Press.

Marfoe, L. 1987. Cedar Forest to Silver Mountain: Social Change and the Development of Long-Distance Trade in Early Near Eastern Societies. In *Centre and Periphery in the Ancient World* (eds M. Rowlands, M. Larsen and K. Kristiansen). Cambridge: Cambridge University Press, pp. 25–35.

Marx, E. 1978. The ecology and politics of nomadic pastoralists in the Middle East. In *The Nomadic Alternative* (ed. W. Weissleder). The Hague-Paris: Mouton Publishers, pp. 41–74.

Mauss, M. 1969. *The Gift.* London: Routledge and Kegan Paul.

Moorey, P.R.S. 1985. *Materials and Manufacture in Ancient Mesopotamia: The Evidence of Archaeology and Art.* Oxford: British Archaeological Reports International Series 237.

Moorey, P.R.S. 1987. On Tracking Cultural Transfers in Prehistory: The Case of Egypt and Lower Mesopotamia in the Fourth Millennium BC. In *Centre and Periphery in the Ancient World* (eds M. Rowlands, M. Larsen and K. Kristiansen). Cambridge: Cambridge University Press.

Moorey, P.R.S. 1988. The Chalcolithic hoard from Nahal Mishmar, Israel, in context. *World Archaeology.* 20: 171–89.

Neuville, R. and Mallon, A. 1931. Les debuts de l'age des metaux dans les grottes du desert de Judee. *Syria.* 12: 24–47.

Oren, E. and Gilead, I. 1981. Chalcolithic sites in north-eastern Sinai. *Tel Aviv.* 8: 25–44.

Ory, J. 1946. A Chalcolithic necropolis at Bnei Berak. *Quarterly of the Department of Antiquities of Palestine.* 12: 43–57.

Perrot, J. 1955. The excavations at Tell Abu Matar, near Beersheba. *Israel Exploration Journal.* 5: 17–40, 73–84, 167–89.

Perrot, J. 1959. Statuettes en ivoire et autres objets en ivoire et en provenent des gisements prehistoriques de la region de Beersheba. *Syria.* 36: 8–19.

Perrot, J. 1961. Une tombe a ossuaries du IVe millenaire a Azor pres de Tel Aviv. *Atiqot.* 3: 1–83 (English Series).

Perrot, J. 1984. Structures d'habitat, mode de vie et environment, les villages souterrains des pasteurs de Beersheva, dans le sud d'Israel au IVe millenaire avant l'ere chretienne. *Paleorient.* 10: 75–96.

Perrot, J. and Ladiray, D. 1980. *Tombes A Ossuaries de la Region Cotiere Palestinenne Au IVe Millenaire L'ere Chretienne.* Paris: Association Paleorient.

Raikes, T. 1980. Note on some Neolithic and later sites in the Wadi Araba and the Dead Sea valley. *Levant.* 12: 40–60.

Renfrew, C. 1973. Monuments, Mobilization, and Social Organization in Neolithic Wessex. In *The Explanation of Culture Change: Models in Prehistory* (ed. C. Renfrew). London: Duckworth, pp. 539–58.

Renfrew, C. and Bahn, P. 1991. *Archaeology – Theories, Methods, and Practice.* London: Thames and Hudson.

Rizkana, I. and Seeher, J. 1989. *Maadi III: The Non-Lithic Small Finds and the Structural Remains of the Predynastic Settlement.* Mainz: von Zabern.

Rosen, A.M. 1987. Phytolith Studies at Shiqmim. In *Shiqmim I* (ed. T.E. Levy). Oxford: BAR International Reports 356, pp. 243–9.

Rosen, A.M. 1989. Environmental change at the end of Early Bronze Age Palestine. In *L'urbanisation de la Palestine a l'age du Bronze Ancien* (ed. P. de Miroschedji). Oxford: BAR International 527, pp. 246–56.

Rosen, A.M. 1992. Phytoliths as Indicators of Ancient Irrigation Farming. In *Prehistoire De L'Agriculture: Nouvelles Approches Experimentales et Ethnographiques* (ed. CNRS). Monographie du CRA no. 6. Paris: CNRS, pp. 281–7.

Rosen, S.A. 1986. The analysis of trade and craft specialization in the Chalcolithic period: comparisons from different realms of material culture. *Michmanim.* 3: 21–32.

Rosen, S.A. 1987. The Potential of Lithic Analysis in the Chalcolithic of the Northern Negev. In *Shiqmim I* (ed. T.E. Levy). Oxford: BAR International Series 356, pp. 295–312.

Rothenberg, B., Tylecote, R.F. and Boydell, P.J. 1978. *Chalcolithic Copper Smelting. Archaeometallurgy One.* London: Institute of Archeo-Metallurgical Studies.

Sahlins, M. 1974. *Stone Age Economics.* London: Tavistock.

Sanderson, S.K. 1990. *Social Evolutionism – A Critical History.* Oxford: Basil Blackwell.

Seger, J.D., Baum, B., Borowski, O., Cole, D.P., Forshey, H., Futato, E., Jacobs, P.F., Laustrup, M., O'Conner-Seger, P. and Zeder, M. 1990.

The Bronze Age Settlements at Tell Halif: Phase II excavations. *BASOR Supplement*. 26: 1–32.

Service, E.R. 1962. *Primitive Social Organization: An Evolutionary Perspective*. New York: Random House.

Shalev, S. and Northover, J.P. 1987. The Chalcolithic metal and metal working from Shiqmim. In *Shiqmim I* (ed. T.E. Levy). Oxford: BAR International Series 356, pp. 357–71.

Shalev, S., Goren, Y., Levy, T.E. and Northover, P.J. 1992. A Chalcolithic Mace Head from the Negev. Technological Aspects and Cultural Implications. *Archaeometry*. 34: 63–71.

Sherratt, A. G. 1981. Plough and pastoralism: Aspects of the secondary products revolution. In *Patterns of the Past: Studies in Honour of David Clarke* (eds I. Hodder, G. Isaac and N. Hammond). Cambridge: Cambridge University Press, pp. 261–305.

Stager, L.E. 1992. The Periodization of Palestine from Neolithic through Early Bronze Times. In *Chronologies in Old World Archeology* (ed. R.W. Ehrich). Chicago: University of Chicago Press.

Stekelis, M. 1935. *Les Monuments Megalithiques de Palestine*. Archives de l'Institut de Paleontologie Humaine, Memoire 15. Paris: Masson et Cie.

Sukenik, E.L. 1937. A Chalcolithic necropolis at Hadera. *Journal of the Palestine Oriental Society*. 21: 1–79.

Ussishkin, D. 1980. The Ghassulian shrine at Ein Gedi. *Tel Aviv*. 7: 1–44.

Vaux, R. de and Steve, A.M. 1947. La premiere campagne de fouilles a Tell el-Far'ah, pres Naplouse. *Revue Biblique*. 54: 394–433, 573–89.

Yoffee, N. 1993. Too Many Chiefs? (or, Safe Texts for the 90s). In *Archaeological Theory – Who Sets the Agenda?* (eds N. Yoffee and A. Sherratt). Cambridge: Cambridge University Press, pp. 60–78.

Zohary, D. and Spiegel-Roy, P. 1975. Beginnings of Fruit Growing in the Old World. *Science*. 187: 319–27.

Zori, N. 1958. Neolithic and Chalcolithic Site in the Valley of Beth Shan. *Palestine Exploration Quarterly*. 90: 44–51.

Chapter 15

Amiran, D.H.K. 1991. The climate of the ancient Near East: the early third millennium BC in the northern Negev of Israel. *Erkunde*. 45 (3): 133–67.

Amiran, R. 1986. Some cult-and-art objects. In *Insight through Images. Studies in Honour of Edith Porada* (eds M. Kelly-Buccellati, P. Matthiae and M. van Loon). Malibu: Undina Publications, pp. 7–13.

Angress, S. 1959. Mammal remains from Horvat Beter (Beersheba). *Atiqot*. 2: 53–71.

Arnon, I. 1972. *Crop Production in Dry Regions*. London: Leonard Hill.

Bar-Adon, P. 1980. *The Cave of the Treasure. The Finds from the Caves in the Nahal Mishmar*. Jerusalem: Israel Exploration Society.

Bar-Yosef, O. 1985. *A Cave in the Desert: Nahal Hemar Cave 9000-year-old-finds*. Jerusalem: The Israel Museum.

Bar-Yosef, O. and Alon, D. 1988. Nahal Hemar Cave. *Atiqot*. 18.

Bar-Yosef, O. and Khazanov, A. 1992. *Pastoralism in the Levant, Archaeological Materials in Anthropological Perspectives*. Monographs in World Archaeology 10. Madison, Wis.: Prehistory Press.

Clark, G. and Yi, S. 1983. Niche-width variation in Cantabrian archaeofaunas: a diachronic study. In *Animals and Archaeology: 1. Hunters and their Prey* (ed. J. Clutton-Brock and C. Grigson). Oxford: British Archaeological Reports, International Series 163: 183–208.

Clutton-Brock, J. 1979. The mammalian remains from the Jericho Tell. *Proceedings of the Prehistoric Society*. 45: 135–57.

Clutton-Brock, J. 1981. *Domesticated Animals from Early Times*. London: Heinemann and British Museum Natural History.

Clutton-Brock, J. 1992. *Horse Power*. London: Natural History Museum Publications.

Cohen, R. 1992. The nomadic or semi-nomadic Middle Bronze Age I settlements in the Central Negev. In *Pastoralism in the Levant, Archaeological Materials in Anthropological Perspectives* (eds O. Bar-Yosef and A. Khasanov). Monographs in World Archaeology 10. Madison, Wis.: Prehistory Press, pp. 105–32.

Davis, S.J.M. 1976. Mammal bones from the Early Bronze Age City of Arad, northern Negev, Israel: some implications concerning human exploitation. *Journal of Archaeological Science*. 3: 153–64.

Davis, S.J.M. 1982. Climatic change and the advent of domestication: the succession of ruminant artiodactyls in the Late Pleistocene-Holocene in the Israel region. *Paleorient*. 8: 5–15.

Davis, S.J.M. 1984. The advent of milk and wool production in western Iran: some speculations. In *Animals and Archaeology: 3. Early Herders and their Flocks* (eds J. Clutton-Brock and C. Grigson). Oxford: British Archaeological Reports, International Series 202, pp. 265–78.

Davis, S.J.M. 1985. The large mammal bones. In *Excavations at Tel Qasile. Part 2* (ed. A. Mazar). *Qedem* 20, pp. 112–17.

Davis, S.J.M. 1987. The faunal remains from Tel Qiri. In *Tell Qiri. A Village in the Jezreel Valley* (eds A. Ben Tor and Y. Portugali). *Qedem* 24, pp. 249–51.

Davis, S.J.M. 1988. The mammal bones Tel Yarmouth. In *Yarmouth 1, Rapport sur les trois premieres campagnes de fouilles a Tel Yarmouth Israel), 1980–1982* (ed. P. Miroschedji). Paris: Editions Recherche sur les Civilisations, pp. 143–9.

Davis, S.J.M. 1990 (unpublished). The animal remains from two fifth millennium BC sites in the Menashe Hills, Israel; 1990 excavations.

Dayan, T. 1992 (unpublished). Animal exploitation at Tel Ira.

Desse, J. 1988. The animal bone remains. In G. Dollfuss, Z. Kafifi, J. Rewerski, N. Vaillant, E. Cogneughiot, J. Desse and R. Neef. Abu Hamid, an early fourth millennium site in the Jordan Valley. In *The Prehistory of Jordan. The State of Research in 1986* (eds A. Garrard and H. Gebel). Oxford: British Archaeological Reports, International Series 396, pp. 595–7.

Dever, W.G. 1989. The collapse of the urban early Bronze Age in Palestine – towards a systemic analysis. In *L'Urbanisation de la Palestine a l'Age du Bronze Ancien* (ed. P. Micoschedji). Oxford: British Archaeological Reports, International Series, 527 (ii), pp. 225–46.

Dever, W.G. 1992. Pastoralism and the end of the Urban Early Bronze Age in Palestine. In *Pastoralism in the Levant, Archaeological Materials in Anthropological Perspectives* (eds O. Bar-Yosef and A. Khazanov). Monographs in World Archaeology 10. Madison, Wis.: Prehistory Press, pp. 83–92.

Digard, J.-P. 1981. *Techniques des Nomades Baxtyari d'Iran*. Cambridge: Cambridge University Press.

Drori, I. 1979. Tel Lachish: Subsistence and Natural Environment. Unpublished M.A. thesis. Dept. of Archaeology and Ancient Near Eastern Studies, Tel Aviv University. (In Hebrew.)

Ducos, P. 1968. *L'Origine des Animaux Domestiques en Palestine*. Bordeaux: Publications de Préhistoire de l'Université de Bordeaux 6.

Epstein, C. 1978. A new aspect of Chalcolithic culture. *Bulletin of the American Schools of Oriental Research*. 229: 27–45.

Epstein, C. 1985. Laden animal figurines from the Chalcolithic period in Palestine. *Bulletin of the American Schools of Oriental Research*. 258: 53–62.

Esse, D.L. 1991. *Subsistence, Trade and Social Change in Early Bronze Age Palestine*. Oriental Institute Chicago: Studies in Oriental Civilization 50.

Falconer, S.E., Magness-Gardiner, B. and Metzger, M.C. 1984. Preliminary report on the first season of the Tell el-Hayyat Project. *Bulletin of the American Schools of Oriental Research*. 255: 49–74.

Finnegan, M. 1979. Faunal remains from Bab edh-Dhra and Numeira. In W.E. Rast and R.T. Schaub. The southeastern Dead Sea Plain Expedition: An interim report of the 1977 season. *Annual of the American Schools of Oriental Research*. 46: 177–80.

Flannery, K.V. 1983. Early pig domestication in the fertile crescent: a retrospective look. In *The Hilly Flanks. Essays on the Prehistory of Southwestern Asia* (ed. L.S. Braidwood). University of Chicago, Studies in Oriental Civilisation 36, pp. 163–87.

Gilead, I. 1988. The Chalcolithic period in the Levant. *Journal of World Prehistory*. 2: 397–443.

Gophna, R. and Kislev, M. 1979. Tel Saf 1977–8. *Revue Biblique*. 86: 112–14.

Gottwald, N.K. 1980. *The Tribes of Yahweh*. London: SCM Press.

Grigson, C. 1984a (unpublished). Preliminary report on the mammal bones from Neolithic Qatif, site Y3, on the Sinai coastal plain, excavations of 1979, 1980 and 1983.

Grigson, C. 1984b (unpublished). Preliminary report on the mammal bones from Chalcolithic Qatif, site Y2 (including Ya), on the Sinai coastal plain, excavations of 1979, 1980 and 1983.

Grigson, C. 1987. Shiqmim: pastoralism and other aspects of animal management in the Chalcolithic of the Northern Negev. In *Shiqmim I* (ed. T.E. Levy). Oxford: British Archaeological Reports, International Series 356, pp. 219–41 and 535–46.

Grigson, C. 1988. Different herding strategies for sheep and goats in the Chalcolithic of Beersheva. *Archaeozoologia.* 1 (2): 115–25.

Grigson, C. 1989. Size and sex – morphometric evidence for the domestication of cattle in the Middle East. In *The Beginnings of Agriculture* (eds A. Milles and D. Williams). Oxford: British Archaeological Reports, International Series 496, pp. 77–109.

Grigson, C. 1992a (in press). Cattle keepers of the northern Negev: animal remains from the Chalcolithic of Grar. In *Grar, a Chalocolithic Site in the Northern Negev* (ed. I. Gilead). Beersheva: Ben Gurion University Press.

Grigson, C. 1992b (in press). The animal remains from Sataf, with notes on the human bones. In: Gibson, S. Sataf. *Levant.*

Grigson, C. 1993a. The earliest domestic horses in the Levant? – New finds from the fourth millennium of the Negev. *Journal of Archaeological Science.* 20: 645–55.

Grigson, C. 1993b (in press). The camels and donkeys from Timna site 30 (ed. B. Rothenberg).

Grigson, C. (forthcoming). Animal husbandry in the Late Neolithic and Chalcolithic at Arjoune – the secondary products revolution revisited. in *Arjoune: Chalcolithic Sites beside the Orontes* (ed. P.J. Parr).

Grigson, C. (unpublished). Culture, ecology and pigs.

Haiman, M. 1992. Sedentism and pastoralism in the Negev Highlands in the Early Bronze Age: results of the western Negev Highlands emergency survey. In *Pastoralism in the Levant, Archaeological Materials in Anthropological Perspectives* (eds O. Bar-Yosef and A. Khazanov). Monographs in World Archaeology 10. Madison, Wis.: Prehistory Press, pp. 93–104.

Hakker-Orion, D. 1984. The role of the camel in Israel's early history. In *Animals and Archaeology 3. Early Herders and their Flocks* (eds J. Clutton-Brock and C. Grigson). Oxford: BAR International Series 202, pp. 207–12.

Hanbury-Tenison, J.W. 1986. *The Late Chalcolithic to Early Bronze Age Transition in Palestine and Transjordan.* Oxford: British Archaeological Reports. International Series, 311.

Harlan, J.R. 1982. The garden of the Lord: a plausible reconstruction of natural resources of southern Jordan in Early Bronze Age. *Paleorient.* 8 (1): 71–8.

Helbaek, H. 1958. Plant economy ancient Lachish. In *Lachish IV. The Bronze Age* (ed. O. Tufnell). London: Oxford University Press, pp. 309–17.

Helbaek, H. 1959. Notes on the evolution and history of *Linum. Kuml.* 1959: 103–29.

Hellwing, S. 1984. Human exploitation of animal resources in the early Iron Age at Tel Beersheva. In *Beersheva II: The Early Iron Age Settlement* (ed. Z. Herzog). Tel Aviv: Institute of Archaeology and Ramot Publishing Co., pp. 105–15.

Hellwing, S. 1988–1989. Animal bones from Tel Tsaf. *Tel Aviv.* 15–16: 47–51.

Hellwing, S. and Adjeman, Y. 1986. Animal bones. In *Izbet Sartah, an early Iron Age site near Rosh, Ha'ayin, Israel* (ed. I. Finkelstein). Oxford: British Archaeological Reports, International Series, 299, pp. 141–52.

Hellwing, S. and Feig, N. 1989. Animal bones. In *Excavations at Tel Michal, Israel* (eds Z. Herzog, G. Rapp and O. Negbi). Tel Aviv: Tel Aviv University; Sonia and Marco Nadler Institute of Archaeology, pp. 236–47.

Hellwing, S. and Gophna, R. 1984. The animal remains from the Early and Middle Bronze Ages at Tel Aphek and Tel Dalit: a comparative study. *Tel Aviv.* 11: 48–59.

Hellwing, S. and Sadeh, M. 1985. Animal remains: preliminary report. Tel Shiloh. *Tel Aviv.* 12: 177–80.

Henson, B. 1986 (unpublished). In Hesse 1990.

Hesse, B. 1986. Animal use at Tel Miqne-Ekron in the Bronze Age and Iron Age. *Bulletin of the American Schools of Oriental Research.* 264: 17–27.

Hesse, B. 1990. Pig lovers and pig haters: patterns of Palestinian pork production. *Journal of Ethnobiology.* 10 (2): 195–225.

Hopf, M. 1969. Plant remains and early farming in Jericho. In *The Domestication and Exploitation of Plants and Animals* (eds P. Ucko and G.W. Dimbleby). London: Duckworth, pp. 355–9.

Hopf, M. 1978. Plant remains, strata V–I. In *Early Arad* (ed. R. Amiran). Jerusalem: Israel Exploration Society, pp. 64–82.

Horwitz, L.K. 1985. The En Shadud faunal remains. In *En Shadud. Salvage Excavations at a Farming Community in the Jezreel Valley, Israel* (ed. E. Braun). Oxford: British Archaeological Reports, International Series, 249, pp. 168–77.

Horwitz, L.K. 1986–1987. Faunal remains from the Early Iron Age site on Mount Ebal. *Tel Aviv.* 13–14: 173–89.

Horwitz, L.K. 1987. Animal remains from the Pottery Neolithic levels at Tel Dan. *Mitekufat Haeven, Journal of the Israel Prehistoric Society.* 20: 114–18.

Horwitz, L.K. 1988. Bone remains from Neve Yam. A pottery neolithic site off the Carmel coast. *Mitekufat Haeven, Journal of the Israel Prehistoric Society.* 21: 99–108.

Horwitz, L.K. 1989. Sedentism in Early Bronze IV: a faunal perspective. *Bulletin of the American Schools of Oriental Research.* 275: 16–25.

Horwitz, L.K. 1990. Animal bones from the site of Horvat Hor: a Chalcolithic cave-dwelling. *Mitekufat Haeven, Journal of the Israel Prehistoric Society.* 23: 153–61.

Horwitz, L.K. and Smith, P. 1984. Radiographic evidence for changing patterns of animal exploitation in the southern Levant. *Journal of Archaeological Science.* 11: 467–75.

Horwitz, L.K. and Tchernov, E. 1988. The relationship between man and beast in the Early Bronze Age. *Qadmoniot.* 21 (1/2): 2–5. (In Hebrew.)

Horwitz, L.K. and Tchernov. E. 1989a. Animal exploitation in the Early Bronze Age of the southern Levant: an overview. In *L'Urbanisation de la Palestine a l'Age du Bronze Ancien* (ed. P. Micoschedji). Oxford: British Archaeological Reports, International Series. 527 (ii), pp. 279–96.

Horwitz, L.K. and Tchernov, E. 1989b. Subsistence patterns in ancient Jerusalem: a study of animal remains. *Qedem.* 29: 144-54.

Isserlin, B.S.J. 1951. On some possible early occurrences of the camel in Palestine. *Palestine Exploration Quarterly.* 1950–51: 50–3.

James, F. 1978. Chariot fittings from Late Bronze Age Beth Shan. In *Archaeology in the Levant* (eds R. Moorey and P.J. Parr). Warminster: Aris and Phillips, pp. 102–15.

Jarman, M.R. 1974. The fauna and economy of Tel Eli. *Mitekufat Haeven, Journal of the Israel Prehistoric Society.* 12: 50–70.

Kafafi, Z.A. 1988. Jebel Abu Thawwab: a pottery Neolithic village in North Jordan. In *The Prehistory of Jordan. The State of Research in 1986* (eds A. Garrard and H. Gebel). Oxford: British Archaeological Reports, International Series 396, pp. 451–71.

Khazanov, A. 1984. *Nomads and the Outside World.* Cambridge: Cambridge University Press.

Kislev, M. 1987. Chalcolithic plant husbandry and ancient vegetation at Shiqmim. In *Shiqmin I* (ed. T.E. Levy). Oxford: British Archaeological Reports, International Series 356, pp. 251–79.

Köhler, I. 1981a. Animal remains. In *Jawa. Lost City of the Black Desert* (ed. S.W. Helms). London: Methuen, pp. 249–52.

Köhler, I. 1981b. Zur Domestikation des Kamels. Inaugural Dissertation. Tierarztliche Hochschule, Hannover.

Köhler-Rollefson, I. 1992. Animal remains of the Iron Age. In *Pella in Jordan 2* (eds A.W. McNicholl, P.C. Edwards, J. Hanbury-Tenison, J.B. Hennessy, T.F. Potts, R.H. Smith, A. Walmsley and P. Watson). Mediterranean Archaeology Supplement 2, pp. 243–51.

Köhler-Rollefson, I., Gillespie, W. and Metzger, M. 1988. The fauna from Neolithic Ain Ghazal. In *The Prehistory of Jordan. The State of Research in 1986* (eds A. Garrard and H. Gebel). Oxford: British Archaeological Reports, International Series 396, pp. 423–30.

Kussinger, S. 1988. Tierknochenfunde vom Lidar Höyük im Südostanatolien Grabungen 1979–86. Inaugural Dissertation. Ludwig-Maximilians Universität, Munich.

Lernau, H. 1975. Animal remains. In *Investigations at Lachish. The Sanctuary and the Residency, Lachlish V* (ed. Y. Aharoni). Tel Aviv: Gateway Publishers, pp. 88–103.

Lernau, H. 1978. Faunal remains, strata III–I. In *Early Arad* (ed. R. Amiran). Jerusalem: Israel Exploration Society, pp. 83–113.

Levy, T.E. 1992. Transhumance, subsistence and social evolution. In *Pastoralism in the Levant, Archaeological Materials in Anthro-*

pological Perspectives (eds O. Bar-Yosef and A. Khazanov). Monographs in World Archaeology 10. Madison, Wis.: Prehistory Press, pp. 65–82.

Levy, T.E., Alon, D., Grigson, C., Holl, A., Goldberg, P., Rowan, Y. and Smith, P. 1991. Subterranean Negev settlement. *National Geographic Research*. November 1991: 394–413.

Liphschitz, L. 1988–1989. Analysis of the botanical remains from Tel Tsaf. *Tel Aviv*. 15–16: 47–51.

Liphschitz, N. 1989. Plant economy and diet in the Early Bronze Age in Israel: a summary of present research. In *L'Urbanisation de la Palestine a l'Age du Bronze Ancien* (ed. P. Miroschedji). Oxford: British Archaeological Reports, International Series, 527 (ii). pp. 269–77.

Littauer, M. and Crouwel, J.H. 1974. A terracotta model as evidence for vehicles with tilts in the ancient Near East. *Proceedings of the Prehistoric Society*. 40: 20–36.

Littauer, M. and Crouwel, J.H. 1990. A terracotta wagon model from Syria in Oxford. *Levant*. 22: 160–2.

Mallon, A., Koeppel, S. and Neuville, R. 1934. *Teleilat Ghassul, 1*. Rome: Pontifical Institute.

Marshall, D.N. 1982. Jericho bone tools and objects. In *Excavations at Jericho. IV*. (eds K.M. Kenyon and T.A. Holland). London: British School of Archaeology, pp. 570–622.

McCreery, D.W. 1979. Flotation of the Bab edh-Dhra and Numeira plant remains. In W.E. Rast and R.T. Schaub. The southeastern Dead Sea Plain expedition: an interim report of the 1977 season. *Annual of the American Schools of Oriental Research*. 46: 165–70.

McCreery, D.W. 1980. *The nature and cultural implications of Early Bronze Age agriculture in the southern Ghor of Jordan*. Ann Arbor: University Microfilms.

Metzger, M. 1983. Faunal remains at Tell el-Hayyat. *Annual of the Department of Antiquities of Jordan*. 27: 98–9.

Muheisen, M., Gebel, H.-G., Hauss, C. and Neef, R. 1988. Excavations at 'Ain Rahub, a final Natufian and Yarmoukian site near Irbid 1985. In *The Prehistory of Jordan. The State of Research in 1986* (eds A. Garrard and H. Gebel). Oxford: British Archaeological Reports, International Series 396, pp. 473–502.

Musil, A. 1928. *The Manners and Customs of the Rwala Bedouins*. American Geographical Society. Oriental Explorations and Studies 6.

Neef, R. 1988. The botanical remains. In G. Dollfuss et al. Abu Hamid, an early fourth millennium site in the Jordan Valley. In *The Prehistory of Jordan. The State of Research in 1986* (eds A. Garrard and H. Gebel). Oxford: British Archaeological Reports, International Series 396, pp. 597–8.

Neef, R. 1990. Introduction, development and environmental implications of olive culture. In *Man's Role in the Shaping of the Eastern Mediterranean Landscape* (eds S. Bottema, G. Entjes-Nieborg and W. Van Zeist). Rotterdam: Balkema, pp. 295–306.

Negbi, M. 1955. The botanical finds at Tell Abu Matar, near Beersheba. *Israel Exploration Journal*. 5: 257–8.

Payne, S. 1973. Kill-off patterns in sheep and goats: the mandibles from Asvan Kale. *Anatolian Studies*. 23: 281–303.

Payne, S. 1988. Animal bones from Tell Rubeidheh. In *Tell Rubeidheh, an Uruk village in the Jebel Hamrin* (ed. R.G. Killick). Iraq Archaeological Reports 2. Warminster: Aris and Phillips, pp. 98–135.

Pettinato, G. 1991. *Ebla: a New Look at History*. Baltimore and London: Johns Hopkins University Press.

Piggott, S. 1983. *The Earliest Wheeled Transport from the Atlantic Coast to the Caspian Sea*. London: Thames and Hudson.

Postgate, J.N. 1986. The equids of Sumer, again. In *Equids in the Ancient World* (eds R.H. Meadow and H.-P. Uerpmann). Beihefte zum Tübinger Atlas des Vorderen Orients (Reihe A Naturwissenschaften), 19/1. Wiesbaden: Reichert, pp. 194–206.

Prag, K. 1974. The intermediate Early Bronze-Middle Bronze Age: an interpretation of the evidence from Transjordan, Syria and Lebanon. *Levant*. 6: 69–116.

Prag, K. 1985. Ancient and modern pastoral migration in the Levant. *Levant*. 17: 81–8.

Redding, R.W. 1984. Theoretical determinants of a herder's decisions: modelling variation in the sheep/goat ratio. In *Animals and Archaeology: 3. Early Herders and their Flocks* (eds J. Clutton-Brock and C. Grigson). Oxford: British Archaeological Reports, International Series 202, pp. 233–41.

Rosen, B. and Finkelstein, I. 1992. Subsistence patterns, carrying capacity and settlement oscillations in the Negev Highlands. *Palestine Exploration Quarterly*. Jan–June 1992: 42–58.

Sade, M. 1988. Domestic Mammals in Iron Age Economy of the Northern Negev. Unpublished M.A. thesis. Dept. of Archaeology and Ancient Near Eastern Cultures. Tel Aviv University. (In Hebrew.)

Sherratt, A.G. 1983. The secondary exploitation of animals in the Old World. *World Archaeology*. 15: 90–103.

Smith, P. and Horwitz, L.K. 1991. A study in diachronic change in bone mass of sheep and goats Jericho Tell-Es Sultan. *Archaeozoologia*. 4(1): 29–38.

Stager, L.E. 1976. Agriculture. In *The Interpreters' Dictionary of the Bible. Supplementary Volume*. Nashville: Abingdon, pp. 11–13.

Stager, L.E. 1985. The first fruits of civilization. In *Palestine in the Bronze and Iron Age* (ed. J.N. Tubb). Institute of Archaeology Occasional Paper 11, pp. 172–88.

Stein, G.J. 1986. Village level pastoral production: faunal remains from Gritille Höyük, southeast Turkey. *Masca Journal*. 4: 2–11.

Tchernov, E. and Drori, I. 1983. Economic patterns and environmental conditions at Hirbet el-Masas during the Early Iron Age. In *Ergebnisse der Ausgrabungen auf der Hirbet el-Masas Tel Masos. Teil 1* (eds V. Fritz and A. Kempinski). Wiesbaden: Otto Harrassowitz, pp. 213–20.

Tchernov, E. and Grigson, C. 1990 (unpublished). Preliminary report on the vertebrate remains from Chalcolithic Gilat. Seasons 1974–1987.

Tchernov, E. and Horwitz, L.K. 1990. Herd management in the past and its impact on the landscape of the southern Levant. In *Man's Role in the Shaping of the Eastern Mediterranean Landscape* (eds S. Bottema, G. Entjes-Nieborg and W. Van Zeist). Rotterdam: Balkema, pp. 207–16.

Uerpmann, H.-P. 1979. *Probleme der Neolithisierung des Mittelmeeraums*. Wiesbaden: Reichert.

Ussishkin, E. 1980. The Ghassulian shrine at Ein Gedi. *Tel Aviv*. 7: 1–44.

Van Zeist, W. and Heeres, J.A.H. 1973. Paleobotanical studies of Deir 'Alla, Jordan. *Paleorient*. 1: 21–38.

Wapnish, P. 1981. Camel caravans and camel pastoralists at Tell Jemmeh. *Journal of the Ancient Near Eastern Society of Columbia University*. 13: 101–21.

Wapnish, P. and Hesse, B. 1988. Urbanization and the organization of animal production at Tell Jemmeh in the Middle Bronze Age Levant. *Journal of Near Eastern Studies*. 47: 81–94.

Wapnish, P. and Hesse, B. 1991. Faunal remains from Tel Dan: perspectives on animal production at a village, urban and ritual center. *Archaeozoologia*. 4 (2): 9–86.

Wapnish, P., Hesse, B. and Ogilvy, A. 1977. The 1974 collection of faunal remains from Tel Dan. *Bulletin of the American Schools of Oriental Research*. 227: 35–62.

Webley, D. 1969. A note on the ecology of Teleilat Ghassoul. *Levant*. 1: 22–3.

Weiler, D. 1981. Saugetierknochenfunde vom Tell Hesban in Jordanien. Dissertation. Institut für Palaeoanatomie, Domestikationsforschung und Geschichte der Tiermedizin der Universität München.

Western, A.C. 1971. The ecological interpretation of ancient charcoals from Jericho. *Levant*. 3: 31–40.

Willcox, G.H. 1981. Plant remains. In *Jawa. Lost City of the Black Desert* (ed. S.W. Helms). London: Methuen, pp. 247–8.

Willcox, G.H. 1992. Archaeobotanical investigations at Pella 1983. In *Pella in Jordan 2* (eds A.W. McNicholl et al.). Mediterranean Archaeology Supplement 2, pp. 253–6.

Zaitschek, D.V. 1959. Remains of cultivated plants from Horvat Beter Beersheva. *Israel Exploration Journal*. 2: 48–52.

Zaitschek, D.V. 1961. Remains of cultivated plants from the cave of Nahal Mishmar. *Israel Exploration Journal*. 11: 70–1.

Zeuner, F.E. 1963. *A History of Domesticated Animals*. London: Hutchinson.

Ziegler, R. and Boessneck, J. 1990. Tierreste der Eisenzeit II. In *Kinneret. Ergebnisse der Ausgrabungen am See Gennesaret 1982–1985* (ed. V. Fritz). Wiesbaden: Otto Harrassowitz, pp. 133–229.

Zohary, D. 1992. Domestication of the Neolithic Near Eastern crop assemblage. In *Préhistoire de l'Agriculture, Nouvelles Approches Experimentales et Ethnographiques* (ed. C. Anderson). Monograph du CRA, 6. Paris: CNRS, pp. 81–6.

Zohary, D. and Spiegel-Roy, P. 1975. The beginnings of fruit growing in the Old World. *Science.* 187: 319–27.

Chapter 16

Amiran, R. 1970 The Beginning of Urbanization in Canaan. In *Near Eastern Archaeology in The Twentieth Century: Essays in Honor of Nelson Glueck* (ed. J.A. Saunders). Garden City, New York: Doubleday, pp. 83–100.

Amiran, R. 1978a. *Early Arad. The Chalcolithic Settlement and Early Bronze City: First–Fifth Seasons of Excavations 1962–1966.* Jerusalem: Israel Exploration Society.

Amiran, R. 1978b. The Date of the End of the EBII City of Arad. A Complementary Note to Early Arad I. *Israel Exploration Journal.* 28: 182–4.

Amiran, R. 1985. The Transition from the Chalcolithic to the Early Bronze Age. In *Biblical Archaeology Today.* Proceedings of the International Congress on Biblical Archaeology, Jerusalem, April 1984, pp. 108–12.

Amiran, R. and Gophna, R. 1989. Urban Canaan in the Early Bronze II and III Periods – Emergence and Structure. In *L'Urbanisation de la Palestine a l'Age du Bronze Ancien* (ed. P. de Miroschedji). Oxford: BAR International Series 527: (i), pp. 109–16.

Amiran, R. and Gophna, R. 1992. The correlation between lower Egypt and Southern Canaan during the EB I period. In *The Nile Delta in transition: 4th–3rd millenium BC* (ed. E.C.M. Van den Brink, pp. 357–60.

Beit-Arieth, I. 1991. An Early Bronze Age III Stratum at Tel Ira in the Northern Negev. *Eretz Israel.* 21 (Ruth Amiran Volume): 66–79 (Hebrew).

Ben-Tor, A. 1982. The relations between Egypt and the land of Canaan during the 3rd millenium BC. *Journal of Jewish Studies,* 33: 3–18.

Ben-Tor, A. 1991. New light on the relations between Egypt and Southern Palestine during the Early Bronze Age. *BASOR.* 281: 3–10.

Ben-Tor, A. 1992. The Early Bronze Age. In *The Archaeology of Ancient Israel* (ed. Ben-Tor). New Haven and London: Yale University Press, pp. 81–125.

Betts, A.V.G. 1992. *Evacations at Tell Um Hammad 1982–1984, The Early Assemblages (EBI–II),* Edinburgh: Edinburgh University Press.

Brandl, B. 1992. Evidence for Egyptian colonisation in the Southern Coastal Plain and lowlands of Canaan during the EB I period. In *The Nile Delta in Transition: 4th–3rd millenium BC* (ed. E.C.M. Van den Brink). Tel Aviv: Van den Brink, pp. 441–77.

Braun, E. 1989. The Transition from the Chalcolithic to the Early Bronze Age I in Northern Israel and Transjordan: Is there a Missing Link? In *L'Urbanisation de la Palestine a l'Age du Bronze Ancien, Bilan et Perspectives des Recherches Actuelle* (ed. P. de Miroschedji). Oxford: BAR International Series 527(i): pp. 7–27.

Broshi, M. and Gophna, R. 1984. The Settlements of Palestine During the Early Bronze Age II–III. *Bulletin of the American Schools of Oriental Research.* 253: 41–53.

Broshi, M. and Gophna, R. 1986. Middle Bronze Age II Palestine: Its Settlements and Population. *BASOR.* 261: 73–90.

Callaway, J.A. 1982. A Review of Arad I, Review Article. *BASOR.* 247: 71–7.

Eisenberg, E. 1993. 1988–1989, Tel Shalem. *Excavations and Surveys in Israel.* 7–8: 165–6.

Finkelstein, I. and Gophna, R. 1993. Settlement, Demographic and Economic Patterns in the Highlands of Palestine in the Chalcolithic and Early Bronze Periods. *BASOR.* 289: 1–22.

Gilead, I. 1988. The Chalcolithic Period in the Levant. *Journal of World Prehistory.* 2(4): 397–443.

Gophna, R. 1974. The Settlement of the Coastal Plain of Eretz-Israel During the Early Bronze Age. Unpublished doctoral thesis. Dept. of Archaeology and Ancient Near Eastern Culture. Tel Aviv University (Hebrew).

Gophna, R. 1982. The Early Bronze Age. In *The History of Eretz-Israel I, The Early Periods* (ed. I. Ephal). Jerusalem: Keter, pp. 13–21.

Gophna, R. 1984. The Settlement Landscape of Palestine in the Early Bronze Age II–III and Middle Bronze Age II. *Israel Exploration Journal.* 34: 24–31.

Gophna, R. 1987. Egyptian trading posts in Southern Canaan at the dawn of the archaic period. In *Egypt, Israel, Sinai Archaeological and Historical Relationships in the Biblical Period* (ed. A.F. Rainey). Tel Aviv: Tel Aviv University, pp. 13–21.

Gophna, R. 1989. From Village to Town in the Lod Valley: A Case Study. In *L'Urbanisation de la Palestine a l'Age du Bronze Ancien* (ed. P. de Miroschedji). Oxford: BAR International Series 527(i), pp. 109–16.

Gophna, R. 1992a. Early Bronze Age Fortification Wall and Middle Bronze Age Rampart. *Tel Aviv.* 19: 267–73.

Gophna, R. 1992b. The contacts between 'En Besor oasis Southern Canaan and Egypt during the late predynastic and the threshold of the first dynasty: a further assessment. In *The Nile Delta in Transition: 4th–3rd millenium BC* (ed. E.C.M. Van den Brink, pp. 385–94.

Gophna, R. and Portugali, J. 1988. Settlement and Demographic Processes in Israel's Coastal Plain from the Chalcolithic to the Middle Bronze Age. *BASOR.* 289: 11–28.

Gophna, R., Liphschitz, N. and Lev-Yadun, S. 1986–1987. Man's Impact on the Natural Vegetation of the Central Coastal Plain of Israel During the Chalcolithic Period and the Bronze Age. *Tel Aviv:* 13–14: 71–84.

Hanbury-Tenison, J.W. 1986. *The Late Chalcolithic to Early Bronze I Transition in Palestine and Transjordan.* Oxford: BAR International Series 311.

Hennessey, J.R. 1967. *The Foreign Relations of Palestine During the Early Bronze Age.* London: Bernard Quaritch.

Herzog, Z. 1993. Tel Gerisa. In *The New Encyclopedia of Archaeological Excavations in the Holy Land* (ed. E. Stern). Jerusalem: Israel Exploration Society, pp. 359–63.

Kantor, H.J. 1965. The relative chronology of Egypt and its foriegn correlations before the Late Bronze Age. In *Relative Chronologies in Old World Archaeology* (2nd edn) (ed. R.W. Ehrich). Chicago: University of Chicago Press.

Kempinski, A. 1978. *The Rise of an Urban Culture: the Urbanization of Palestine in the Early Bronze Age 3000–2150 BC.* Jerusalem: Israel Ethnographic Society.

Kempinski, A. 1992. Reflections on the role of the Egyptians in the Shephelah of Palestine in the light of recent soundings at Tel Erani. In *The Nile Delta in Transition: 4th–3rd millenium BC* (ed. E.C.M. Van den Brink, pp. 419–25.

Kempinski, A. and Gilead, I. 1991. New Excavations at Tel Erani: A Preliminary Report of 1985–1988 Seasons. *Tel Aviv.* 18: 164–91.

Liphschitz, N., Gophna, R. and Lev-Yadun, S. 1989. Man's Impact on the Vegetational Landscape of Israel in the Early Bronze Age II–III. In *L'Urbanisation de la Palestine a l'Age du Bronze Ancien, Bilan et Perspectives des Recherches Actuelle.* Actes du Colloque d'Emmaus (20–24 Octobre 1986) (ed. P. de Miroschedji). Oxford: BAR International Series 527: 263–8.

Macdonald, E. 1932. *Beth Pelet II: Prehistoric Fara.* London: The British School of Archaeology in Egypt.

Oren, E.D. 1973. The Overland Route Between Egypt and Canaan in the Early Bronze Age (preliminary report). *Israel Exploration Journal* 23: 198–205.

Oren, E.D. and Yekutieli, Y. 1992. Taur Ikhbeineh: Earliest Evidence for Egyptian Interconnections. In *The Nile Delta in transition: 4th–3rd Millenium B.C.* (ed. E.C.M. Van den Brink). Tel Aviv: Van den Brink, pp. 361–84.

Porat, N. 1992. An Egyptian Colony in Southern Palestine During the Late Predynastic/Early Dynastic Period in *The Nile Delta in Transition: 4th–3rd Millennium B.C.* (ed. E.C.M. Van den Brink). Tel Aviv: Van den Brink, pp. 433–440.

Portugali, J. and Gophna, R. (in press). Crisis, Progress and Urbanisation. The Transition from Early Bronze I to Early Bronze II in Palestine. *Tel Aviv* 20.

Richard, S. 1987. The Early Bronze Age. The Rise and Collapse of Urbanism. *Biblical Archaeologist.* 50: 22–43.

Schaub, R.T. and Rast, W.E. 1989. *Bab edh-Dhra. Excavations in the Cemetery Directed by Paul W. Lapp (1965–1967).* Winona Lake: Eisenbrauns.

Seger, J.D. 1989. Some Provisional Correlations in EBIII Stratigraphy in Southern Palestine. In *L'Urbanisation de la Palestine a l'Age du Bronze Ancien* (ed. P. de Miroschedji). Oxford: BAR International Series 527: pp. 117–35.

Stager, L.E. 1993. The periodisation of Palestine from the Neolithic through Early Bronze times. In *Relative Chronologies in Old World Archaeology* (3rd edn) (ed. R.W. Ehrich). Chicago and London: University of Chicago Press.

Stager, L.E. 1993b. Ashkelon. In *The New Encyclopedia of Archaeological Excavations in the Holy Land* (ed. E. Stern). Jerusalem: Israel Exploration Society, p. 101.

Vaux, R. de Palestine in the Early Bronze Age in *The Cambridge Ancient History I, part II 3rd edition*. Cambridge: Cambridge University Press, pp. 208–37.

Ward, W.A. 1963. Egypt and the East Mediterranean from Predynastic times to the end of the Old Kingdom. *Journal of the Economic and Social History of the Orient*. 6: 1–57.

Weinstein, J.M. 1984. The Significance of Tel Erani for Egyptian-Palestinian Relations at the Beginning of the Bronze Age. *Bulletin of the American Schools of Oriental Research* 256: 61–9.

Yeivin, S. 1960. Early Contacts Between Canaan and Egypt. *Israel Exploration Journal* 10: 193–203.

Chapter 17

Adams, R. McC. 1988. Contexts of Civilizational Collapse. In *The Collapse of Ancient States and Civilizations* (eds N. Yoffee and G.L. Cowgill). Tucson: University of Arizona Press, pp. 20–43.

Amiran, R. 1960. Pottery of the Middle Bronze Age I in Palestine. *Israel Exploration Journal*. 10: 204–25.

Bates, D.G. and Lees, S.H. 1977. The Role of Exchange in Production Specialization. *American Anthropologist*. 79: 824–41.

Ben-Tor, A. (ed.) 1993. *The Archaeology of Ancient Israel*. New Haven: Yale University Press.

Brown, J.A. (ed.) 1971. *Approaches to the Social Dimensions of Mortuary Practices*. Washington: Society for American Archaeology.

Castillo, J.S. (ed.) 1987. *Nomads and Sedentary Peoples*. Mexico City: El Colegio de Mexico.

Chang, K.C. (ed.) 1968. *Settlement Archaeology*. Palo Alto: National Press Books.

Carneiro, R.L. 1987. The Chiefdom: Precursor of the State. In *The Transition to Statehood in the New World* (eds G.D. Jones and R.R. Kurtz). Cambridge: Cambridge University Press, pp. 37–79.

Chapman, R., Kinnes, I. and Randsborg, K. (eds) 1981. *The Archaeology of Death*. Cambridge: Cambridge University Press.

Clark, J.G.D. 1939. *Archaeology and Society*. London: Methuen.

Cohen, R. 1986. The Settlement of the Central Negev in the Light of Archaeological and Literary Sources During 4th–1st Millennia B.C.E. Unpublished doctoral dissertation, Institute of Archaeology, The Hebrew University of Jerusalem (Hebrew).

Cohen, R. and Dever, W.G. 1978. Preliminary Report of the Pilot Season of the 'Central Negev Highlands' Project. *Bulletin of the American Schools of Oriental Research*. 232: 29–45.

Cohen, R. and Dever, W.G. 1979. Preliminary Report of the Second Season of the 'Central Negev Highlands' Project. *Bulletin of the American Schools of Oriental Research*. 236: 41–60.

Cohen, R. and Dever, W.G. 1981. Preliminary Report of the Third and Final Season of the 'Central Negev Highlands' Project. *Bulletin of the American Schools of Oriental Research*. 243: 57–77.

Dever, W.G. 1970. The 'Middle Bronze I Period' in Syria-Palestine. In *Near Eastern Archaeology in the Twentieth Century* (ed. J.A. Sanders). Garden City: Doubleday, pp. 132–63.

Dever, W.G. 1971. The Peoples of Palestine in the Middle Bronze I Period. *Harvard Theological Review*. 64: 197–226.

Dever, W.G. 1972. A Middle Bronze I Site in the West Bank of Jordan. *Archaeology*. 25: 231–3.

Dever, W.G. 1973. The EB IV–MB I Horizon in Transjordan and Southern Palestine. *Bulletin of the American Schools of Oriental Research*. 210: 37–63.

Dever, W.G. 1974. The Middle Bronze Occupation and Pottery of 'Arâq en-Na'asâneh (Cave II). In *Discoveries in the Wâdi ed-Dâliyeh* (eds P.W. and N.L. Lapp). Cambridge, MA: American Schools of Oriental Research, pp. 33–48.

Dever, W.G. 1977. Palestine in the Second Millennium B.C.E.: The Archaeological Picture. In *Israelite and Judean History* (eds H.J. Hayes and J.M. Miller). Philadelphia: Westminster Press, pp. 70–120.

Dever, W.G. 1980. New Vistas on the EB IV ('MB I') Horizon in Syria-Palestine. *Bulletin of the American Schools of Oriental Research*. 232: 35–64.

Dever, W.G. 1981. Cave G26 at Jebel Qa'aqir: A Domestic Assemblage of Middle Bronze I. *Eretz-Israel*. 15: 22*–32*.

Dever, W.G. 1985a. Syro-Palestinian and Biblical Archaeology. In *The Hebrew Bible and Its Modern Interpreters* (eds. D.A. Knight and G.M. Tucker). Philadelphia: Fortress Press, pp. 31–74.

Dever, W.G. 1985b. Village Planning at Be'er Resisim and Socio-Economic Structure in Early Bronze Age IV Palestine. *Eretz-Israel*. 18: 18*–28*.

Dever, W.G. 1987. Funerary Practices in EB IV (MB I) Palestine: a Study in Cultural Discontinuity. In *Love and Death in the Ancient Near East: Essays in Honor of Marvin H. Pope* (eds J.H. Marks and R.M. Good). Guilford, CN: Four Quarters Publishing Company, pp. 9–19.

Dever, W.G. 1989. The Collapse of the Urban Early Bronze Age in Palestine. In *L'urbanisation de la Palestine à l'âge du Bronze ancien. Bilan et perspectives des recherches actuelles* (ed. P. de Miroschedji). Oxford: BAR International Series, 527, pp. 225–46.

Dever, W.G. 1992a. The Late Bronze-Early Iron I Horizon in Syria-Palestine: Egyptians, Canaanites, and 'Sea Peoples'. In *The Crisis Years: The Twelfth Century B.C. From Beyond the Danube to the Tigris* (eds M. Joukowsky and W.A. Ward). Dubuque: Kendall/Hunt Publishing Company, pp. 99–110.

Dever, W.G. 1992b. Pastoralism and the End of the Urban Early Bronze Age in Palestine. In *Pastoralism in the Levant. Archaeological Materials in Anthropological Perspective* (ed. O. Bar-Yosef and A. Khazanov). Madison: Prehistory Press, pp. 83–91.

Dever, W.G. 1994. Review of D.L. Esse, *Subsistence, Trade, and Social Change in Early Bronze Age Palestine*. Chicago: The Oriental Institute, 1991. *Journal of the American Oriental Society*. Forthcoming.

Earle, T.K. 1987. Chiefdoms in Archaeological and Ethnohistorical Perspective. *Annual Review of Anthropology*. 16: 279–308.

Earle, T.K. 1989. The Evolution of Chiefdoms. *Current Anthropology*. 30: 84–8.

Esse, D.L. 1991. *Subsistence, Trade, and Social Change in Early Bronze Age Palestine*. Chicago: The Oriental Institute, University of Chicago.

Falconer, S.E. 1987. *Heartland of Villages: Reconsidering Early Urbanism in the Southern Levant*. Unpublished doctoral dissertation, Department of Near Eastern Studies, University of Arizona.

Falconer, S.E. and Magness-Gardiner, B. 1984. Preliminary Report of the First Season of the Tell el-Hayyat Project. *Bulletin of the American Schools of Oriental Research*. 255: 49–74.

Falconer, S.E. and Magness-Gardiner, B. 1989. Bronze Age Village Life in the Jordan Valley: Archaeological Investigations at Tell el-Hayyât and Tell Abu en-Ni'âj. *National Geographic Research*. 5: 335–47.

Finkelstein, I. 1989. Further Observations on the Socio-demographic Structure of the Intermediate Bronze Age. *Levant*. 21: 129–40.

Finkelstein, I. 1991. The Central Hill Country in the Intermediate Bronze Age. *Israel Exploration Journal*. 41: 19–45.

Finkelstein, I. and Perevolotsky, A. 1990. Processes of Sedentarization and Nomadization in the History of Sinai and the Negev. *Bulletin of the American Schools of Oriental Research*. 279: 67–88.

Fried, M.H. 1967. *The Evolution of Political Society. An Essay in Political Anthropology*. New York: Random House.

Gitin, S. 1975. Middle Bronze Age I 'Domestic Pottery' at Jebel Qa'aqir: a Ceramic Inventory of Cave G23. *Eretz-Israel*. 12: 46*–62*.

Gophna, R. 1992. The Intermediate Bronze Age. In *The Archaeology of Ancient Israel* (ed. A. Ben-Tor). New Haven: Yale University, pp. 126–58.

Helms, S.W. 1982. Paleo-Bedouin and Transhumant Urbanism. In *Studies in the History and Archaeology of Jordan*, Vol. I. (ed. A. Hadidi). Oxford: Oxford University Press, pp. 97–113.

Helms, S.W. 1983. The EB IV (EB-MB) Cemetery at Tiwal esh-Sharqi in the Jordan Valley, 1983. *Annual of the Department of Antiquities in Jordan XXVII*: 55–85.

Helms, S.W. 1986. Excavations at Tell Um Hammad, 1984. *Levant*. XVIII: 25–49.

Hodder, I. 1985. *Reading the Past. Current Approaches to Interpretation in Archaeology*. Cambridge: Cambridge University Press.

Hodder, I. and Orton, C. 1976. *Spatial Analysis in Archaeology*. Cambridge: Cambridge University Press.

Hole, F. 1991. Symbols of Religion and Social Organization at Susa. In *The Hilly Flanks. Essays on the Prehistory of Southwestern Asia* (eds T.C. Young, P.E.L. Smith and P. Mortenson). Chicago: The Oriental Institute, University of Chicago, pp. 315–31.

Horwitz, L.K. 1989a. Diachronic Changes in Rural Husbandry practices in Bronze Age Settlements from the Refaim Valley, Israel. *Palestine Exploration Quarterly*. 121: 44–54.

Horwitz, L.K. 1989b. Sedentism in the Early Bronze IV: A Faunal Perspective. *Bulletin of the American Schools of Oriental Research*. 275: 15–25.

Joffe, A.H. 1991a. Settlement and Society in Early Bronze I and II Canaan. Unpublished doctoral dissertation, Department of Near Eastern Studies, University of Arizona.

Joffe, A.H. 1991b. Early Bronze I and the Evolution of Social Complexity in the Southern Levant. *Journal of Mediterranean Archaeology*. 4: 3–58.

Kenyon, K.M. 1960. *Excavations at Jericho I. The Tombs Excavated in 1952–1954*. London: British School of Archaeology in Jerusalem.

Kenyon, K.M. 1965. *Excavations at Jericho II. The Tombs Excavated in 1955–1958*. London: British School of Archaeology in Jerusalem.

Kochavi, M., Kasher, A. and Bunimowitz, W. (eds) 1988. *Settlement, Population, and Economy in Ancient Palestine*. Ramat Aviv: Tel Aviv University. (Hebrew).

LaBianca, O.S. 1992. *Hesban I. Sedentarization and Nomadization: Food System Cycles at Hesban and Vicinity in Transjordan*. Berrien Springs, MI: Andrews University.

Levy, T.E. 1983. The Emergence of Specialized Pastoralism in the Southern Levant. *World Archaeology*. 15: 15–36.

Levy, T.E. 1986. The Chalcolithic Period in Palestine. *Biblical Archaeologist*. 49: 83–108.

London, G.A. 1985. Decoding Designs: The Late Third Millennium B.C. Pottery from Jebel Qaʻaqir. Unpublished doctoral dissertation, University of Arizona.

London, G.A. 1987. Homage to the Elders. *Biblical Archaeology*. 50: 70–4.

Marfoe, L. 1979. The Integrative Transformation: Patterns of Sociopolitical Organization Southern Syria. *Bulletin of the American Schools of Oriental Research*. 234: 1–42.

Meyers, C. and Meyers, E.M. 1989. Expanding the Frontiers of Biblical Archaeology. *Eretz-Israel*. 20: 140*–7*.

Oren, E.D. 1973. The Early Bronze IV Period in Northern Palestine and its Cultural and Chronological Setting. *Bulletin of the American Schools of Oriental Research*. 210: 20–37.

O'Shea, J.M. 1984. *Mortuary Variability: An Archaeological Investigation*. New York: Academic Press.

Palumbo, G. 1987. 'Egalitarian' or 'Stratified' Society? Some Notes on Mortuary Practices and Social Structure at Jericho in EB IV. *Bulletin of the American Schools of Oriental Research*. 267: 43–59.

Palumbo, G. 1991. *The Early Bronze Age IV in the Southern Levant. Settlement Patterns, Economy, and Material Culture of a 'Dark Age'*. Rome: University of Rome.

Palumbo, G. and Peterman, G. 1993. Early Bronze Age IV Ceramic Regionalism in Central Jordan. *Bulletin of the American Schools of Oriental Research*. 289: 23–32.

Paynter, R.W. 1985. Expanding the Scope of Settlement Analysis. In *Archaeological Hammers and Theories* (eds. J.A. Moore and A.S. Keene). New York: Academic Press, pp. 233–75.

Peebles, C.S. and Kus, S.M. 1977. Some Archaeological Correlates of Ranked Societies. *American Antiquity*. 42: 421–48.

Prag, K. 1974. The Intermediate Early Bronze-Middle Bronze Age: An Interpretation of the Evidence from Transjordan, Syria and Lebanon. *Levant*. VI: 69–116.

Prag, K. 1984. Continuity and Migration in the South Levant in the Late Third Millennium; A Review of T.L. Thompson's and Some Other Ideas. *Palestine Exploration Quarterly*. 116: 58–68.

Prag, K. 1985. Ancient and Modern Pastoral Migration in the Levant. *Levant*. XVII: 81–8.

Prag, K. 1989. Preliminary Report on the Excavations at Tell Iktanu, Jordan, 1987. *Levant*. XXI: 33–45.

Redman, C.L. (ed.) 1978. *Social Archaeology. Beyond Subsistence and Dating*. New York: Academic Press.

Renfrew, A.C. 1974. Beyond a Subsistence Economy: The Evolution of Social Organization in Prehistoric Europe. In *Reconstructing Complex Societies* (ed. C. Moore). Cambridge, MA: American Schools of Oriental Research, pp. 69–88.

Renfrew, A.C. 1984. *Approaches to Social Archaeology*. Cambridge, MA: Harvard University Press.

Richard, S. 1987. The Early Bronze Age in Palestine: The Rise and Collapse of Urbanism. *Biblical Archaeologist*. 50: 22–43.

Richard, S. 1990. The 1987 Expedition to Khirbet Iskander and its Vicinity: Fourth Preliminary Report. In *Supplements to the Bulletin of the American Schools of Oriental Research*. 26 (ed. W.E. Rast). Baltimore: American Schools of Oriental Research, pp. 33–58.

Richard, S. and Boraas, R.S. 1988. The Early Bronze IV Fortified Site of Khirbet Iskander, Jordan: Third Preliminary Report, 1984 Season. In *Supplements to the Bulletin of the American Schools of Oriental Research*. 25 (ed. W.E. Rast). Baltimore: American Schools of Oriental Research, pp. 107–30.

Richard, S. and Long, J.C. nd. Specialization-Despecialization: A Model to Explain Culture Change and Continuity at the End of the Early Bronze Age, ca 2350–2000 BC. Unpublished manuscript.

Service, E.R. 1962. *Primitive Social Organization: an Evolutionary Perspective*. New York: Random House.

Service, E.R. 1971. *Primitive Social Organization: an Evolutionary Perspective*, 2nd edition. New York: Random House.

Service, E.R. 1975. *Origins of the State and Civilization: The Process of Cultural Evolution*. New York: W.W. Norton.

Shay, T. 1983. Burial Customs at Jericho in the Intermediate Bronze Age: A Componential Analysis. *Tel Aviv*. 10: 26–37.

Smith, P. 1982. The Physical Characteristics and Biological Affinities of the MB I Skeletal Remains from Jebel Qaʻaqir. *Bulletin of the American Schools of Oriental Research*. 245: 65–73.

Tadmor, M. 1978. A Cult Cave of the Middle Bronze I near Qadesh. *Israel Exploration Journal*. 28: 1–30.

Tainter, J.A. 1977. Modeling Change in Prehistoric Social Systems. In *For Theory Building in Archaeology* (ed. L.R. Binford). New York: Academic Press, pp. 327–51.

Tainter, J.A. 1978. Mortuary Practices and the Study of Prehistoric Social Systems. In *Advances in Archaeological Method and Theory*, Vol. I (ed. M.B. Schiffer). New York: Academic Press, pp. 105–41.

Tainter, J.A. 1988. *The Collapse of Complex Societies*. Cambridge: Cambridge University Press.

Thompson, T.L. 1975. *The Settlement of Sinai and the Negev in the Bronze Age*. Wiesbaden: Ludwig Reichert.

Thompson, T.L. 1979. *The Settlement of Palestine in the Bronze Age*. Wiesbaden: Ludwig Reichert.

Trigger, B.G. 1989. *A History of Archaeological Thought*. Cambridge: Cambridge University Press.

Tringham, R. 1974. Comments on Professor Renfrew's Paper. In *Reconstructing Complex Societies* (ed. C. Moore). Cambridge, MA: American Schools of Oriental Research, pp. 88–90.

Tubb, J.A. 1985. Excavations in the Early Bronze Age Cemetery of Tiwal esh-Sharqi: a Preliminary Report. *Annual of the Department of Antiquities in Jordan*. 29: 115–30.

Vita-Finzi, C. 1978. *Archaeological Sites in Their Setting*. London: Thames and Hudson.

Watson, P.J., LeBlanc, S.A. and Redman, C.L. 1984. *Archaeological Explanation: the Scientific Method of Archaeology*. New York: Columbia University Press.

Willey, G.R. 1953. *Prehistoric Settlement Patterns in the Virú Valley, Peru*. Washington: Bureau of American Ethnology.

Yadin, Y. 1971. A Note on the Scenes Depicted on the ʻAin-Samiya Cup. *Israel Exploration Journal*. 21: 82–5.

Yoffee, N. and Cowgill, G.L. (eds.) 1988. *The Collapse of Ancient States and Civilizations*. Tucson: University of Arizona Press.

Chapter 18

Albright, W.F. 1932. *The Excavation of Tell Beit Mirsim in Palestine* I: *The Pottery of the First Three Campaigns*. AASOR 12. New Haven: Yale University Press.

Albright, W.F. 1933. *The Excavation of Tell Beit Mirsim IA: The Bronze Age Pottery of the Fourth Campaign*. AASOR 13. New Haven: Yale University Press.

Albright, W.F. 1966a. Remarks on the chronology of the EBIV – MBIIA in Phoenicia and Syria-Palestine. *BASOR*. 184: 26–35.

Albright, W.F. 1966b. *The Proto-Sinaitic Inscriptions and their Decipherment.* Havard Theological Studies 22. Cambridge MA: Harvard University Press.

Alon, D. and Levy, T.E. 1989. The Archaeology of Cult and the Chalcolithic Sanctuary at Gilat. *Journal of Mediterranean Archaeology* 2: 163–221.

Amiran, R. 1969. *Ancient Pottery of the Holy Land: from its beginnings in the Neolithic Period to the Iron Age.* Ramat Gan, Israel: Massada.

Anbar, M. and Na'aman, N. 1986–1987. An account tablet of sheep from ancient Hebron. *Tel Aviv* 13–14: 3–12.

Arensberg, B. 1973. The People in the Land of Israel from the Epipaleolithic to Present Times. Unpublished doctoral dissertation. Tel Aviv University.

Avner, U., Carmi, I. and Segal, D. In press. Settlement in the southern Negev from the Neolithic Period to the Bronze Age in light of radiocarbon dating. In *Late Quaternary Chronology and Paleoclimates of the Eastern Mediterranean* (eds R. Kra and O. Bar-Yosef).

Azar, Gh., Chimienti, G. Haddad, H. and Seeden, H. 1985. Busra: housing in transition. *Berytus.* 33: 103–42.

Beck, P. 1985. The Middle Bronze Age IIA pottery from Aphek, 1972–1984: first summary. *Tel Aviv.* 12: 181–203.

Ben-Dov, M. 1992. Middle and Late Bronze Age dwellings. In *The Architecture of Ancient Israel* (eds A. Kempinski and R. Reich). Jerusalem: Israel Exploration Society, pp. 99–104.

Bienkowski, P. 1989. The division of the MB IIB-C in Palestine. *Levant.* 21: 169–79.

Bietak, M. 1986. *Avaris and Piramesse: Archaeological Exploration in the Eastern Nile Delta.* Revised reprint from the Proceedings of the British Academy 65 (1979): 225–96.

Bietak, M. 1991. Egypt and Canaan in the Middle Bronze Age. *BASOR.* 281: 27–72.

Binford, L. 1972. Mortuary practices: their study and their potential. In *An Archaeological Perspective.* New York: Seminar Press, pp. 208–43.

Braudel, F. 1972. *The Mediterranean and the Mediterranean World in the Age of Philip II.* New York: Harper and Row.

Broshi, M. and Gophna, R. 1986. Middle Bronze Age II Palestine, its settlement and population. *BASOR.* 261: 73–90.

Bunimovitz, S. 1989. The Land of Israel in the Late Bronze Age: A Case Study of Socio-Cultural Change in a Complex Society. Unpublished doctoral thesis. Tel Aviv University (Hebrew with English summary).

Bunimovitz, S. 1992. The Middle Bronze Age fortifications in Palestine as a social phenomenon. *Tel Aviv.* 19: 221–34.

Cherry, J. and Renfrew, C. 1986. Epilogue and prospect. In *Peer-Polity Interaction and Sociopolitical Change* (eds C. Renfrew and J.F. Cherry). Cambridge. Cambridge University Press, pp. 149–58.

Collon, D. 1987. *First Impressions.* London: British Museum Publications.

Dalley, S. 1984. *Mari and Karana: two Old Babylonian cities.* London: Longman.

Dever, W.G. 1976. The beginning of the Middle Bronze Age in Syria-Palestine. In *Magnalia Dei: The Mighty Acts of God, Essays on the Bible and Archaeology in Memory of G. Ernest Wright* (eds F.M. Cross, W.E. Lemke and P.D. Miller). Garden City, New York: Doubleday, pp. 3–38.

Dever, W.G. 1977. Palestine in the Second Millennium BCE: the archaeological picture. In *Israelite and Judean History* (eds J.M. Miller and J.H. Hayes). Philadelphia: Westminster Press, pp. 70–120.

Dever, W.G. 1987. The Middle Bronze Age: The zenith of the urban Canaanite era. *Biblical Archaeologist.* 50: 148–77.

Dever, W. G. 1990. 'Hyksos', Egyptian destructions, and the end of the Palestinian Middle Bronze Age. *Levant.* 22: 75–81.

Dossin, G. 1970. La route de l'etain en Mesopotamie au temps de Zimri-Lim. *Revue d'assyriologie et et d'archeologie orientale.* 64: 97–106.

Dothan, M. 1965. The cult at Nahariya and Canaanite high places. In *Western Galilee and the Coast of Galilee: the Nineteenth Archaeological Convention, October 1963.* Jerusalem: Israel Exploration Society, pp. 63–75 (Hebrew).

Dunand, M. 1958. *Fouilles de Byblos, 1933–1938.* Tome II. Texte. Etudes et Documents d'Archeologie, Tome III. Paris: Librarie d'amerique et l'Orient Adrien Maisonneuve.

Falconer, S. 1987. Village pottery production and exchange: a Jordan Valley perspective. In *Studies in the History and Archaeology of Jordan III* (ed. A. Hadidi). London: Routledge and Kegan Paul, pp. 251–59.

Falconer, S. and Magness-Gardiner, B. 1989. Bronze Age village life in the Jordan Valley: archaeological investigations at Tell el-Hayyat and Tell Abu en-Ni'aj. *National Geographic Research.* 5: 335–47.

Finkelstein, I. 1988a. *The Archaeology of the Israelite Settlement.* Jerusalem: Israel Exploration Society.

Finkelstein, I. 1988b. Arabian trade and socio-political conditions in the Negev in the twelfth–eleventh centuries B.C.E. *JNES.* 47: 241–52.

Finkelstein, I. 1988–1989. The Land of Ephraim Survey 1980–1987: Preliminary Report. *Tel Aviv.* 15–16: 117–83.

Finkelstein, I. 1992. The Middle Bronze Age 'fortifications': a reflection of social organization and political formation. *Tel Aviv.* 19: 201–20.

Finkelstein, I. 1993. The socio-political organization of the central hill country in the second millennium BCE. In *Biblical Archaeology Today II: The Proceedings of the Second International Congress of Biblical Archaeology, Pre-Congress Symposium: Population, Production and Power, Jerusalem, June 1990* (eds A. Biran and J. Aviram). Jerusalem: Israel Exploration Society, pp. 119–31.

Gal, Z. 1988. The Late Bronze Age in Galilee: a reassessment. *BASOR.* 272: 79–84.

Gal, Z. 1991. A Note on the Settlement Pattern of the MB II Jezreel and Beth Shan Valleys. *BASOR.* 284: 29–32.

Geertz, C. 1975. Religion as a cultural system. In *The Interpretation of Cultures* (ed. C. Geertz). London: Hutchinson.

Gerstenblith, P. 1983. *The Levant at the Beginning of the Middle Bronze Age.* ASOR Dissertation Series No. 5. Winona Lake, Indiana: Eisenbrauns.

Gophna, R. 1984. The settlement landscape of Palestine in the Early Bronze Age II–III and Middle Bronze Age II. *IEJ.* 34: 20–31.

Gophna, R. and Ayalon, E. 1980. Survey of the central Coastal Plain, 1978–1979: settlement pattern of the Middle Bronze Age IIa. *Tel Aviv.* 7: 147–51.

Gophna, R. and Beck, P. 1981. The rural aspect of the settlement pattern of the southern coastal plain in the Middle Bronze Age II. *Tel Aviv.* 8: 45–80.

Gophna, R. and Portugali, Y. 1988. Settlement and demographic processes in Israel's coastal plain from the Chalcolithic to the Middle Bronze Age. *BASOR.* 269: 11–28.

Gordon, C.H. 1949. *Ugaritic Literature.* Rome: Pontificum Institutum Biblicum.

Graesser, C. 1972. Standing stones in ancient Palestine. *BASOR.* 35: 34–63.

Greenberg, R. 1991. The Settlement of the Hula Valley in the urban phase of the Early Bronze Age. *Eretz Israel.* 21: 127±31 (Hebrew).

Guy, P.L.O. 1938. *Megiddo Tombs.* Oriental Institute Papers 33. Chicago: University of Chicago Press.

Helms, S.W. 1982. Paleo-Bedouin and transmigrant urbanism. In *Studies in the History and Archaeology of Jordan* (ed. A. Hadidi). Amman: Department of Antiquities of Jordan.

Herzog, A. 1989. Middle and Late Bronze Age settlements (Strata XVII–XV) In *Excavations and Tel Michal, Israel* (eds Z. Herzog, G. Rapp Jr. and O. Negbi). Minneapolis: University of Minnesota Press, pp. 29–42.

Hodder, I. 1982. *Symbols in Action.* Cambridge: Cambridge University Press.

Hoffmeier, J.K. 1989. Reconsidering Egypt's part in the termination of the Middle Bronze Age in Palestine. *Levant.* 21: 181–93.

Ilan, D. 1991. 'Stepped-rim' juglets from Tel Dan and the 'MB I–II (MB IIA–B) Transitional Period'. *IEJ.* 41: 229–38.

Ilan, D. 1992. A Middle Bronze Age Offering Deposit from Tel Dan and the Politics of Cultic Gifting. *Tel Aviv.* 19: 247–66.

Ilan, D. forthcoming. Culture transfer in the Middle Bronze Age Levant: some archaeological criteria for determining emigration. In *Material Culture and Ethnicity* (ed. M. Kochavi).

Ilan, D. In press a. The Middle Bronze Age tombs. In *Dan I* (eds A. Biran, D. Ilan and R. Greenberg). The Annual of the Nelson Glueck School of Biblical Archaeology, Hebrew Union College. Jerusalem.

Ilan, D. In press b. Mortuary practices at Tel Dan in the Middle Bronze Age: a reflection of Canaanite society and ideology. In *The*

Archaeology of Death in the Ancient Near East (eds A. Green and S. Campbell).

Ilan, D. and Yellin J. forthcoming. The Middle Bronze Age painted pottery of Tel Dan.

Ilan, D., Vandiver, P. and Spaer, M. 1993. An early glass bead from Tel Dan. *IEJ.* 43: 230–34.

Johnson, A.W. and Earle, T. 1987. *The Evolution of Human Societies.* Stanford, CA: Stanford University Press.

Johnson, G.A. 1972. A test of the utility of Central Place Theory in archaeology. In *Man, Settlement and Urbanism* (eds P.J. Ucko, R. Tringham and G.W. Dimbleby). London: Duckworth, pp. 769–85.

Kamp, K.A. and Yoffee, N. 1980. Ethnicity in ancient western Asia during the early second millennium B.C.: archaeological assesments and ethnoarchaeological prospectives. *BASOR.* 237: 85–104.

Kaplan, J. 1971. Mesopotamian elements in the Middle Bronze II culture of Palestine. *Journal of Near Eastern Studies,* 30: 293–307.

Kaplan, J. 1975. Further aspects of the Middle Bronze Age II fortifications in Palestine. *ZDPV.* 91: 1–17.

Kaplan, M. 1980. *The Origin and Distrubution of Tell el-Yehudiyeh Ware* (Studies in Mediterranean Archaeology 42). Goteborg: Paul Astrom's Forlaag.

Kempinski, A. 1983. *Syrien und Palastina (Kanaan) in der letzten Phase der Mittelbronze II-B-Zeit (1650-1570 v. Chr.) AAT 4.* Wiesbaden: Harrassowitz.

Kempinski, A. 1992a. Urbanization and town plans in the Middle Bronze Age II. In *The Architecture of Ancient Israel* (eds A. Kempinski and R. Reich). Jerusalem: Israel Exploration Society, pp. 121–6.

Kempinski, A. 1992b. Middle and Late Bronze Age fortifications. In *The Architecture of Ancient Israel* (eds A. Kempinski and R. Reich). Jerusalem: Israel Exploration Society, pp. 127–42.

Kempinski, A. 1992c. The Middle Bronze Age. In *The Archaeology of Ancient Israel* (ed. A. Ben-Tor). New Haven: Yale University Press and The Open University, pp. 159–210.

Kempinski, A. 1992d. Dan and Kabri – a note of the planning of two cities. *Eretz Israel.* 23: 76–81.

Kenyon, K.M. 1966. *Amorites and Canaanites.* London: Oxford University Press.

Kenyon, K.M. 1979. *Archaeology in the Holy Land* (4th revised edition). London: Ernest Benn Ltd.

Kislev, M., Artzy, M. and Marcus, E. 1993. Import of an Aegean food plant to a Middle Bronze IIA coastal site in Israel. *Levant.* 25: 145–54.

Kochavi, M. 1989. *Aphek-Antipatris. Five thousand years of history.* Tel Aviv: Hakibbutz hameuchad (Hebrew).

Kotter, W. 1986. Spatial Aspects of the Urban Development of Palestine During the Middle Bronze Age. Unpublished doctoral dissertation. University of Arizona.

Knapp, A.B. 1989. Complexity and collapse in the north Jordan Valley: archaeometry and society in the Middle–Late Bronze Ages. *IEJ.* 39: 129–48.

Knapp, A.B. 1993. *Society and Polity in Bronze Age Pella, An Annales Perspective.* JOST/ASOR Monograph Series 6. Sheffield: Sheffield Academic Press.

Krafeld-Daugherty, M. In press. Observations on children's burial customs. In *The Archaeology of Death in the Ancient Near East* (eds A. Green and S. Campbell).

Kramer, C. 1977. Pots and people. In *Mountains and Lowlands: Essays in the Archaeology of Greater Mesopotamia* (eds L.D. Levine and T.C. Young Jr.). Bibliotheca Mesopotamica 6. Malibu, CA: Undena, pp. 99–112.

Kramer, C. 1982. *Village Ethnoarchaeology: Rural Iran in Archaeological Perspective.* New York: Academic Press.

Lederman, Z. 1985. The Middle Bronze Age IIC defence system. In *Excavations in Shiloh 1981–1984: preliminary report* (ed. I. Finkelstein). *Tel Aviv.* 12: 140–6.

Loud, G. 1948. *Megiddo II: Seasons of 1935–39.* Text and Plates. Oriental Institute Papers 62. Chicago: University of Chicago Press.

Mabry, J. 1986. *The Canaanite Countryside.* Unpublished doctoral dissertation. University of Arizona.

Malamat, A. 1960. Hazor, 'the head of all those kingdoms'. *Journal of Biblical Literature.* 79: 12–19.

Malamat, A. 1970. Northern Canaan and the Mari texts. In *Near Eastern Archaeology in the Twentieth Century. Essays in Honor of*

Nelson Glueck (ed. J.A. Sanders). Garden City, New Jersey: Doubleday, pp. 164–77.

Marcus, E. 1991. Tel Nami: A Study of a Middle Bronze Age IIA Period Coastal Settlement. Unpublished M.A. thesis, University of Haifa.

Marfoe, L. 1979. The Integrative Transformation: patterns of sociopolitical organization in Southern Syria. *BASOR.* 234: 1–42.

Matthiae, P. 1975. Unite et development du temple dans le Syrien du Bronze Moyen. In *Le temple, et le culte, compte rendu de la vingtieme rencontre assyriologique internationale.* Nederlands Historisch-Archaeologisch Instituut te Istambul, pp. 43–72.

Matthiae, P. 1981. *Ebla: An Empire Rediscovered.* New York. Doubleday.

Mazar, A. 1990. *Archaeology of the Land of the Bible.* New York: Anchor Bible Reference Library. Doubleday.

Mazar, A. 1992. Temples of the Middle and Late Bronze Age and the Iron Age. In *The Architecture of Ancient Israel* (eds A. Kempinski and R. Reich). Jerusalem: Israel Exploration Society, pp. 161–87.

Mazar, B. 1968. The Middle Bronze Age in Palestine. *IEJ.* 18: 65–97.

Muhly, J.D. and Wertime, T.A. 1973. Evidence for the sources and use of tin during the Bronze Age of the Near East: a reply to J.E. Dayton. *World Archaeology.* 5: 111–22.

Naveh, Y. 1982. *Early History of the Alphabet.* Jerusalem: Magness Press.

O'Connor, D. 1985. The chronology of scarabs of the Middle Kingdom and the Second Intermediate Period. *The Journal of the Society for the Study of Egyptian Antiquities.* 15: 1–41.

Oren, E. 1971. A Middle Bronze Age I warrior tomb at Beth-Shan. *ZDPV.* 87: 106–39.

Oren, E. 1992. Palaces and patrician houses in the Middle and Late Bronze Ages. In *The Architecture of Ancient Israel* (eds A. Kempinski and R. Reich). Jerusalem: Israel Exploration Society, pp. 105–20.

Parr, P. 1968. The origin of the rampart fortifications of Middle Bronze Age Palestine and Syria. *ZDPV.* 84: 18–45.

Peebles, C.M. and Kus, S.M. 1977. Some archaeological correlates of ranked societies. *American Antiquity.* 42: 421–48.

Peltenberg, E.J. 1987. Early faience: recent studies, origins and relations with glass. In *Early Vitreous Materials* (eds M. Bimson and I.C. Freestone). Occasional Paper No. 56. London: British Museum, pp. 5–29.

Philip, G. 1988. Hoards of the Early and Middle Bronze Ages in the Levant. *World Archaeology.* 20: 190–208.

Philip, G. 1989. *Metal Weapons of the Early and Middle Bronze Ages in Syria-Palestine.* Oxford: BAR International Series 526.

Philip, G. In press. Bronze Age warrior burials. In *The Archaeology of Death in the Ancient Near East* (eds A. Green and S. Campbell).

Raban, A. 1985. The ancient harbours of Israel in biblical times. In *Harbour Archaeology: Proceedings of the First International Workshop on Ancient Mediterranean Harbours, Caesarea Maritima 24–28.6.83* (ed. A. Raban). Oxford: BAR International Series 257, pp. 11–44.

Rainey, A.F. 1972. The world of Sinuhe. *Israel Oriental Studies.* 2: 369–408.

Rappaport, R. 1971. Nature, culture and ecological anthropology. In *Man, Culture and Society* (ed. L. Shapiro). New York: Oxford University Press, pp. 237–67.

Redford, D.B. 1979. A gate inscription from Karnak and Egyptian involvement in western Asia during the early Eighteenth Dynasty. *Journal of the American Oriental Society.* 99: 270–87.

Renfrew, C. 1973. *Before Civilization: The Radiocarbon Revolution and Prehistoric Europe.* London: Cape.

Renfrew, C. 1979. Systems collapse as social transformation: catastrophe and anastrophe in early state societies. In *Transformations: Mathematical Approaches to Culture Change* (eds C. Renfrew and K.L. Cooke). New York: Academic Press, pp. 481–506.

Renfrew, C. 1985. *The Archaeology of Cult.* London: Thames and Hudson.

Renfrew, C. 1986. Introduction: Peer-Polity Interaction and Socio-political Change. In *Peer-Polity Interaction and Sociopolitical Change* (eds C. Renfrew and J.F. Cherry). Cambridge: Cambridge University Press, pp. 1–18.

Renfrew, C. and Bahn, P. 1991. *Archaeology: Theories, Methods and Practice.* London: Thames and Hudson.

Renger, J. 1984. Patterns of non-institutional trade and non-commercial exchange in ancient Mesopotamia at the beginning of the second millennium B.C. In *Circulation of Goods in Non-Palatial Contexts in the Ancient Near East* (ed. A. Archi). Rome: Incumabula Graeca 82: 31–123.

Salles, J-F. 1987. Deux nouvelles tombes de Ras-Shamra. In *Ras-Shamra Ougarit III: Le centre de la ville, 38e-44e campagnes (1978-1984)* (ed. M. Yon). Paris: Editions Recherche sur les civilisations, 587–95.

Sass, B. 1988. *The Genesis of the Alphabet and its Development in the Second Millennium BC.* Wiesbaden: Harrasowitz.

Seger, J.D. 1975. The MB II fortifications at Shechem and Gezer – a Hyksos retrospective. *Eretz-Israel.* 12: 34–45.

Skiast, A. 1980. The ancestor cult and succession in Mesopotamia. In *Death in Mesopotamia: XXVI*[e] *Rencontre assyriologique internationale* (ed. B. Alster). Copenhagen: Akademisk Forlag, pp. 123–8.

Snodgrass, A. 1986. Interaction by design: the Greek city-state. In *Peer-Polity Interaction and Sociopolitical Change* (eds C. Renfrew and J.F. Cherry). Cambridge: Cambridge University Press, pp. 47–58.

Stager, L.E. 1991. *Ashkelon Discovered.* Washington: Biblical Archaeological Society.

Stager, L.E. 1992. The Periodization of Palestine from the Neolithic through Early Bronze Timnes. In *Chronologies in Old World Archaeology* 3rd ed. (ed. R.W. Ehrich). Chicago: University of Chicago Press, pp. 22–41, 46–60.

Steele, L. in press. Differential burial practices in Cyprus at the beginning of the Iron Age. In *The Archaeology of Death in the Ancient Near East* (eds A. Green and S. Campbell). Oxford: Oxbow.

Stohl, M. 1982. State and private business in the Land of Larsa. *Journal of Cuneiform Studies.* 34: 127–252.

Tainter, J.A. 1988. *The Collapse of Complex Societies.* Cambridge: Cambridge University Press.

Tubb, J.N. 1983. The MBIIa period in Palestine: its relationship with Syria and its origin. *Levant.* 15: 49–62.

Tufnell, O. 1984. *Studies on Scarab Seals II. Scarab Seals and Their Contribtion to History in the Early Second Millennium B.C.* Warminster: Aris and Phillips.

Ussishkin, D. 1989. Notes on the fortifications of the Middle Bronze Age II Period at Jericho and Shechem. *BASOR.* 276: 29–53.

van Gennep, A. 1960 (originally published 1909, translated by M.B. Vizedom and G.L. Caffee). *The Rites of Passage.* Chicago: University of Chicago Press.

Ward, W. 1978. *Studies on Scarab Seals I. Pre-12th Dynasty Scarab Seals.* Warminster: Aris and Phillips.

Weinstein, J.M. 1975. Egyptian relations with Palestine in the Middle Kingdom. *BASOR.* 217: 1–16.

Weinstein, J. 1981. The Egyptian Empire in Palestine: A Reassesment. *BASOR.* 241: 1–28.

Weinstein, J. 1991. Egypt and the Middle Bronze IIC/Late Bronze IA transition in Palestine. *Levant.* 23: 105–15.

Woolley, C.L. 1976. *Ur Excavations.* Volume VII: *The Old Babylonian Period.* London: The British Museum and the University of Pennsylvania Museum.

Wright, G.R.H. 1968. Tell el-Yehudiyah and the glacis. *ZDPV.* 84: 1–17.

Wright, G.R.H. 1985. *Ancient Building in South Syria and Palestine.* Vol. 1 – text, Vol. 2 – plates. Leiden-Koln: E.J. Brill.

Wright, H.T. and Johnson, G.A. 1975. Population, exchange and early state formation in southwestern Iran. *American Anthropologist.* 77: 269–89.

Yadin, Y. 1955. Hyksos fortifications and the battering ram. *BASOR.* 137: 23–32.

Yadin, Y. 1963. *The Art of Warfare in Biblical Lands in the Light of Archaeological Discovery.* London: International Publishing Co.

Yadin, Y. 1972. *Hazor: The Schweich Lectures of the British Academy 1970.* London: Oxford University Press.

Yener, A.K. and Ozbal, H. 1987. Tin in the Turkish Taurus Mountains: the Bolkardag mining district. *Antiquity.* 61: 220–26.

Yoffee, N. 1981. Explaining trade in ancient western Asia. *Monographs on the Ancient Near East* 2, fasicle 2. Malibu: Undena.

Yoffee, N. 1988. Orienting collapse. In *The Collapse of Ancient States and Civilizations* (eds N. Yoffee and G.L. Cowgill). Tucson, AR: University of Arizona Press, pp. 1–19.

Yoffee, N. and Cowgill, G.L. 1988. *The Collapse of Ancient States and Civilizations.* Tucson, AR: University of Arizona Press.

Zaccagnini, C. 1983. Patterns of Mobility among Ancient Near Eastern Craftsmen. *JNES.* 42: 245–64.

Zertal, A. 1992. *The Shechem Syncline.* Tel Aviv: Ministry of Defense Publications (Hebrew with English summary).

Zevulun, U. 1990. Tell el-Yahudiyah juglets from a potter's refuse pit at Afula. *Eretz-Israel.* 21: 174–90.

Ziffer, I. 1990. *'At that time the Canaanites were in the Land': daily life in Canaan in the Middle Bronze Age 2, 2000-1550 B.C.E.* Tel Aviv: Eretz Israel Museum.

Chapter 19

Adams, R. McC. 1974. The Mesopotamian Landscape: A View from the Frontier. In *Reconstructing Complex Societies* (ed. C.B. Moore). Cambridge, Mass.: BASOR Supplement No. 20, pp. 69–95.

Adams, R. McC. 1978. Strategies of Maximization, Stability, and Resilience in Mesopotamian Society, Settlement, and Agriculture. *Proceedings of the American Philosophical Society.* 122: 329–35.

Adams, R. McC. 1984. Mesopotamian Social Evolution: Old Outlooks, New Goals. In *On the Evolution of Complex Societies. Essays in Honor of Harry Hoijer 1982* (ed. T. Earle). Malibu: Undena Publications, pp. 79–129.

Ahituv, S. 1978. Economic Factors in the Egyptian Conquest of Canaan. *IEJ.* 28: 93–105.

Albright, W.F. 1960. *The Archaeology of Palestine.* Harmondsworth: Penguin Books.

Alt, A. 1968. The Settlement of the Israelite in Palestine. *Essays on Old Testament History and Religion.* Garden City, NY: Doubleday, pp. 172–221.

Amiran, D. 1953. The Pattern of Settlement in Palestine. *IEJ.* 3: 65–78; 192–209; 250–60.

Amiran, D. and Ben-Arieh, Y. 1963. Sedentarization of Beduin in Israel. *IEJ.* 13: 16–181.

Bintliff, J. 1991. *The Annales School and Archaeology.* New York: New York University Press.

Broshi, M. and Gophna, R. 1986. Middle Bronze Age II Palestine: Its Settlement and Population. *BASOR.* 261: 73–90.

Bienkowski, P. 1986. *Jericho in the Late Bronze Age.* Warminster: Aris & Phillips.

Bienkowski, P. 1989. Prosperity and Decline in LBA Canaan: A Reply to Leibowitz and Knapp. *BASOR.* 275: 59–61.

Bietak, M. 1991. Egypt and Canaan during the Middle Bronze Age. *BASOR.* 281: 27–72.

Bunimovitz, S. 1989. The Land of Israel in the Late Bronze Age: A Case Study of Socio-Cultural Change in a Complex Society. Doctoral dissertation. Department of Archaeology and Near Eastern Cultures, Tel Aviv University. Tel Aviv.

Bunimovitz, S. 1992. The Middle Bronze Age Fortifications in Palestine as a Social Phenomenon. *Tel Aviv.* 19: 221–34.

Bunimovitz, S. 1993. The Changing Shape of Power in Bronze Age Canaan. In *Biblical Archaeology Today 1990. Proceedings of the International Congress on Biblical Archaeology. Supplement: Pre-Congress Symposium.* Jerusalem: Israel Exploration Society, pp. 142–49.

Bunimovitz, S. 1994. Socio-Political Transformations in the Central Hill Country in the Late Bronze–Iron I Transition. In *From Nomadism to Monarchy. Archaeological and Historical Aspects of Early Israel* (eds N. Na'aman and I. Finkelstein). Jerusalem: Yad Izahk Ben-Zvi, pp. 179–202.

Chapman, R. and Randsborg, K. (eds) 1981. *The Archaeology of Death.* Cambridge: Cambridge University Press.

Cherry, J.F. 1978. Generalisation and the Archaeology of the State. In *Social Organisation and Settlement.* BAR Supplementary Series 47 (eds D.R. Green, C.C. Haselgrove and M. Spriggs). Oxford: British Archaeological Reports, pp. 411–37.

Claessen, H.J.M. 1978. The Early State: A Structural Approach. In *The Early State* (eds H.J.M. Claessen and P. Skalnik). The Hague: Mouton Publishers, pp. 533–95.

Cowgill, G.L. 1988. Onward and Upward with Collapse. In *The Collapse of Ancient States and Civilizations* (eds N. Yoffee and G.L. Cowgill).Tucson: University of Arizona Press, pp. 244–76.

Dever, W.G. 1985. Relations Between Syria-Palestine and Egypt in the 'Hyksos' Period. In *Palestine in the Bronze and Iron Ages. Papers in*

Honour of Olga Tufnell (ed. J.N. Tubb). London: Institute of Archaeology, University of London, pp. 69–87.

Dever, W.G. 1987. The Middle Bronze Age. *BA.* 50: 149–77.

Dever, W.G. 1990. 'Hyksos', Egyptian Destructions, and the End of the Palestinian Middle Bronze Age. *Levant.* 22: 75–81.

Dever, W.G. 1991. Tell el-Dab'a and Levantine Middle Bronze Age Chronology: A Rejoinder to Manfred Bietak. *BASOR.* 281: 73–9.

Dever, W.G. 1992. The Chronology of Syria-Palestine in the Second Millenium B.C.E.: A Review of Current Issues. *BASOR.* 288: 1–25.

Dothan, M. 1973. The Foundation of Tel Mor and of Ashdod. *IEJ.* 23: 1–17.

Eisenstadt, S.N. 1988. Beyond Collapse. In *The Collapse of Ancient States and Civilizations* (eds N. Yoffee and G.L. Cowgill). Tucson: University of Arizona Press, pp. 236–43.

Finkelstein, I. (ed.) 1985. Excavations at Shiloh 1981–1984: Preliminary Report. *Tel Aviv.* 12: 123–80.

Finkelstein, I. 1986. *'Izbet Sartah. An Early Iron Age Site near Rosh Ha'ayin, Israel.* BAR Supplementary Series 299. Oxford: British Archaeological Reports.

Finkelstein, I. 1992. Middle Bronze Age 'Fortifications': A Reflection of Social Organization and Political Formations. *Tel Aviv.* 19: 201–20.

Freedman, D.N. and Graf, D.F. (eds) 1983. *Palestine in Transition.* Sheffield: Almond Press.

Gittlen, B.M. 1981. The Cultural and Chronological Implications of the Cypro-Palestinian Trade during the Late Bronze Age. *BASOR.* 241: 49–59.

Gonen, R. 1984. Urban Canaan in the Late Bronze Period. *BASOR.* 253: 61–73.

Gonen, R. 1992. *Burial Patterns and Cultural Diversity in Late Bronze Age Canaan.* Winona Lake, Indiana: Eisenbrauns.

Gophna, R. and Portugali, J. 1988. Settlement and Demographic Processes in Israel's Coastal Plain from the Chalcolithic to the Middle Bronze Age. *BASOR.* 269: 11–28.

Gottwald, N.K. 1979. *The Tribes of Yahweh.* Maryknoll, NY: Orbis.

Greenberg, R. 1987. New Light on the Early Iron Age at Tell Beit Mirsim. *BASOR.* 265: 55–80.

Griffeth, R. and Thomas, C.G. (eds) 1981. *The City-State in Five Cultures.* Santa Barbara: ABC-Clio.

Herzog, Z. 1989. Middle and Late Bronze Age Settlements (Strata XVII–XV). In *Excavations at Tel Michal, Israel* (eds Z. Herzog, G. Rapp, Jr and O. Negbi). Minneapolis: University of Minnesota and Sonia and Marco Nadler Institute of Archaeology, pp. 29–42.

Hoffmeier, J.K. 1991. James Weinstein's 'Egypt and the Middle Bronze IIC/Late Bronze IA Transition': A Rejoinder. *Levant.* 23: 117–24.

Hütteroth, W. 1975. The Pattern of Settlement in Palestine in the Sixteenth Century. In *Studies on Palestine during the Ottoman Period* (ed. M. Ma'oz). Jerusalem: Magnes Press pp. 3–10.

Johnson, G.A. 1981. Monitoring Complex System Integration and Boundary Phenomena with Settlement Size Data. In *Archaeological Approaches to Complexity* (ed. S.E. van der Leeuw). Amsterdam: Universiteit van Amsterdam, pp. 144–87.

Johnson, G.A. 1987. The Changing Organization of Uruk Administration on the Susiana Plain. In *The Archaeology of Western Iran* (ed. F. Hole). Washington D.C.: Smithsonian Institution Press, pp. 107–39.

Kantor, H.J. 1965. The Relative Chronology of Egypt and Its Foreign Correlations before the Late Bronze Age. In *Chronologies in Old World Archaeology* (ed. R.W. Ehrich). Chicago: University of Chicago Press, pp. 1–46.

Kempinski, A. 1983. *Syrien und Palästina (Kanaan) in der letzten Phase der Mittelbronze IIB–Zeit (1650–1570 v. Chr).* Wiesbaden: Otto Harrassowitz.

Kempinski, A. 1985. The Overlap of Cultures at the End of the Late Bronze Age and the Beginning of the Iron Age. *Eretz-Israel.* 18: 399–407. (Hebrew with English summary).

Kenyon, K.M. 1966. *Amorites and Canaanites.* London: Oxford University Press.

Kenyon, K.M. 1979. *Archaeology in the Holy Land* (4th edn). London: Ernest Benn.

Knapp, A.B. 1989a. Complexity and Collapse in the North Jordan Valley: Archaeometry and Society in the Middle–Late Bronze Ages. *IEJ.* 39: 129–48.

Knapp, A.B. 1989b. Response: Independence, Imperialism, and the Egyptian Factor. *BASOR.* 275: 64–7.

Knapp, A.B. (ed.) 1992a. *Archaeology, Annales, and Ethnohistory.* Cambridge: Cambridge University Press.

Knapp, A.B. 1992b. Independence and Imperialism: Politico-Economic Structures in the Bronze Age Levant. In *Archaeology, Annales, and Ethnohistory* (ed. A.B. Knapp). Cambridge: Cambridge University Press, pp. 83–98.

Knapp, A.B. 1992c. *Society and Polity at Bronze Age Pella: An Annales Perspective.* Sheffield: Sheffield Academic Press.

Kowalewski, S.A. 1982. The Evolution of Primate Regional Systems. *Comparative Urban Research.* 9: 60–78.

Lattimore, O. 1940. *Inner Asian Frontiers of China.* London: Oxford University Press.

Leonard, A. Jr 1981. Consideration of Morphological Variation in the Mycenaean Pottery from the Southeastern Mediterranean. *BASOR.* 241: 87–101.

Leonard, A. Jr 1989. The Late Bronze Age. *BA.* 52: 4–39.

Lewis, N.N. 1955. The Frontier of Settlement in Syria 1800–1950. *International Affairs.* 31: 48–60.

Lewis, N.N. 1987. *Nomads and Settlers in Syria and Jordan 1800–1980.* Cambridge: Cambridge University Press.

London, G. 1989. A Comparison of Two Contemporaneous Lifestyles of the Late Second Millenium B.C. *BASOR.* 273: 37–55.

Marfoe, L. 1979. The Integrative Transformation: Patterns of Sociopolitical Organization in Southern Syria. *BASOR.* 234: 1–42.

Mazar, A. 1990. *Archaeology of the Land of the Bible.* New York: Doubleday.

Mazar, A. 1992. Temples of the Middle and Late Bronze Ages and the Iron Age. In *The Architecture of Ancient Israel* (eds A. Kempinski and R. Reich). Jerusalem: Israel Exploration Society, pp. 161–87.

Mee. C.B. and Cavanagh, W.G. 1984. Mycenaean Tombs as Evidence for Social and Political Organization. *Oxford Journal of Archaeology.* 3: 45–64.

Mendenhall, G.E. 1962. The Hebrew Conquest of Palestine. *BA.* 25: 66–87.

Miller, D. and Tilley, C. (eds) 1984. *Ideology, Power and Prehistory.* Cambridge: Cambridge University Press.

Na'aman, N. 1981. Economic Aspects of the Egyptian Occupation of Canaan. *IEJ.* 31: 172–85.

Na'aman, N. 1982. Eretz-Israel in the Canaanite Period. The Middle Bronze Age and the Late Bronze Age (*ca.* 2000–1200 B.C.E.). In *The History of Eretz-Israel I* (ed. I. Eph'al). Jerusalem: Keter, pp. 129–256 (Hebrew).

Na'aman, N. 1986a. The Territorial Organization of the Canaanite City-States in the Late Bronze Age and the Inheritance of the Tribes of Israel. *Tarbuth.* 55: 463–88 (Hebrew).

Na'aman, N. 1986b. Habiru and Hebrews: The Transfer of a Social Term to the Literary Sphere. *JNES.* 45: 271–88.

Na'aman, N. 1988. Historical-Geographical Aspects of the Amarna Tablets. *Proceedings of the Ninth World Congress of Jewish Studies. Panel Sessions Bible Studies and Ancient Near East.* Jerusalem: Magnes Press, pp. 17–26.

Na'aman, N. 1992. Canaanite Jerusalem and its Central Hill Country Neighbours in the Second Millenium BCE, *UF.* 24: 275–91.

Oren, E.D. 1969. Cypriot Imports in the Palestinian Late Bronze I Context. *Opuscula Atheniensia.* 9: 127–50.

Oren, E.D. 1992. Palaces and Patrician Houses in the Middle and Late Bronze Ages. In *The Architecture of Ancient Israel* (eds A. Kempinski and R. Reich). Jerusalem: Israel Exploration Society, pp. 105–20.

Paynter, R.W. 1983. Expanding the Scope of Settlement Analysis. In *Archaeological Hammers and Theories* (eds J.A. Moore and A.S. Keene). New York: Academic Press, pp. 233–75.

Plog, F.T. 1973. Diachronic Anthropology. In *Research and Theory in Current Archaeology* (ed. C.L. Redman). New York: Wiley-Interscience, pp. 181–98.

Price, B.J. 1978. Secondary State Formation: An Explanatory model. In *Origins of the State* (eds R. Cohen and E. Service). Philadelphia: Institute for the Study of Human Issues, pp. 161–86.

Rainey, A.F. 1993. Sharhan/Sharuhen – The Problem of Identification. *Eretz-Israel* 24: 178–87.

Redford, D.B. 1992. *Egypt, Canaan, and Israel in Ancient Times.* Princeton: Princeton University Press.

Renfrew, C. 1975. Trade as Action at a Distance: Questions of Integration and Communication. In *Ancient Civilization and Trade* (eds J. Sabloff and C.C. Lamberg-Karlovski). Albuquerque: University of New Mexico Press, pp. 3–59.

Renfrew, C. 1980. The Great Tradition versus the Great Divide: Archaeology as Anthropology: *AJA*. 84: 287–98.

Renfrew, C. and Cherry, J.F. (eds) 1986. *Peer Polity Interaction and Socio-Political Change*. Cambridge: Cambridge University Press, pp. 149–58.

Renfrew, C. and Wagstaff, M. 1982. *An Island Polity. The Archaeology of Exploitation in Melos*. Cambridge: Cambridge University Press.

Seger, J.D. 1975. The MB II Fortifications at Shechem and Gezer. A Hyksos Retrospective. *Eretz-Israel*. 12: 34*–45*.

Singer, I. 1988. Merneptah's Campaign to Canaan and the Egyptian Occupation of the Southern Coastal Plain of Palestine in the Ramesside Period. *BASOR*. 269: 1–10.

Trigger, B. 1984. Archaeology at the Crossroads: What's New? *Annual Review of Anthropology*. 13: 275–300.

Trigger, B. 1990. Monumental Architecture: A Thermodynamic Explanation of Symbolic Behaviour. *World Archaeology*. 22: 119–31.

Tufnell, O. 1958. *Lachish IV. The Bronze Age*. London: Oxford University Press.

Ussishkin, D. 1985. Levels VII and VI at Tel Lachish and the End of the Late Bronze age in Canaan. In *Palestine in the Bronze and Iron Ages. Papers in Honour of Olga Tufnell* (ed. J.N. Tubb). London: Institute of Archaeology, University of London, pp. 213–30.

Weinstein, J.M. 1981. The Egyptian Empire in Palestine: A Reassessment. *BASOR*. 241: 1–28.

Weinstein, J.M. 1991. Egypt and the Middle Bronze IIC/Late Bronze IA Transition in Palestine. *Levant*. 23: 105–15.

Whitelam, K.W. 1986. The Symbols of Power: Aspects of Royal Propaganda in the United Monarchy. *BA*. 49: 166–73.

Wright, G.E. 1961. The Archaeology of Palestine. In *The Bible and the Near East. Essays in Honor of William Foxwell Albright* (ed. G.E. Wright). Garden City, NY: Doubleday, pp. 73–112.

Yoffee, N. 1982. Social History and Historical Method in the Late Old Babylonian Period. *JAOS*. 102: 347–53.

Zertal, A. 1988. The Israelite Settlement in the Hill-Country of Manasseh. Doctoral dissertation. Department of Archaeology and Near Eastern Cultures, Tel Aviv University. Haifa (Hebrew).

Chapter 20

Adams, W.Y. 1968. Invasion, Diffusion, Evolution. *Antiquity*. 42: 194–215.

Albright, W.F. 1932a. An Anthropoid Clay Coffin from Sahab in Transjordan. *American Journal of Archaeology*. 36: 295–306.

Albright, W.F. 1932b. The Excavation of Tell Beit Mirsim, I: The Pottery of the First Three Campaigns. *Annual of the American Schools of Oriental Research*. 12. New Haven: ASOR.

Albright, W.F. 1961. *The Archaeology of Palestine*. Harmondsworth: Penguin.

Albright, W.F. 1975. Syria, the Philistines, and Phoenicia. *The Cambridge Ancient History*, 3rd edn. (eds J.E.S. Edwards et al.), vol. 2, pt. 2. Cambridge: Cambridge University Press, pp. 507–36.

Alt, A. 1944. Ägyptsche Tempel in Palästina und die Landnahme der Philister. *Zeitschrift des Deutschen Palästina Vereins*. 67: 1–20. (Reprinted in *Kleine Schriften zur Geschichte des Volkes Israel I* [Munchen, 1953], pp. 216–30.)

Asaro, P., Perlman, I. and Dothan, M. 1971. An Introductory Study of Mycenaean IIIC:1 Ware from Tel Ashdod. *Archaeometry*. 13: 169–75.

Asaro, P. and Perlman, I. 1973. Provenience Studies of Mycenaean Pottery Employing Neutron Activation Analysis. In *The Mycenaeans in the Eastern Mediterranean, Acts of International Archaeological Symposium*. Nicosia, Cyprus: Department of Antiquities, pp. 213–24.

Bietak, M. 1993. The Sea Peoples and the End of the Egyptian Administration in Canaan. In *Biblical Archaeology Today, 1990*. (Proceedings of the Second International Congress on Biblical Archaeology, eds A. Biran and J. Aviram) pp. 292–306.

Brug, J.E. 1985. *A Literary and Archaeological Study of the Philistines*. London: BAR International Series 265.

Bunimovitz, S. 1990. Problems in the 'Ethnic' Identification of the Philistine Material Culture. *Tel Aviv*. 17: 210–22.

Dever, W.D. 1993. Gezer. In *New Encyclopedia of Archaeological Excavations in the Holy Land* (ed. E. Stern), vol. 2. Jerusalem: Israel Exploration Society, pp. 496–506.

Dothan, M. 1986. Šardina at Akko? In *Studies in Sardinian Archaeology: Sardinia in the Mediterranean*, vol. 2 (ed. M. Balmuth). Ann Arbor: University of Michigan Press, pp. 105–15.

Dothan, M. 1989. Archaeological Evidence for Movements of the Early 'Sea Peoples' in Canaan. In *Recent Excavations in Israel: Studies in Iron Age Archaeology* (eds Seymour Gitin and William G. Dever). American Schools of Oriental Research Annual, Vol. 49. Winona Lake, IN: Eisenbrauns, pp. 59–70.

Dothan, M. 1993a. Ashdod. In *The New Encyclopedia of Archaeological Excavations in the Holy Land*, vol. I. pp. 93–102.

Dothan, M. 1993b. Mor, Tel. In *The New Encyclopedia of Archaeological Excavations in the Holy Land*, vol. 3, Jerusalem: Israel Exploration Society, pp. 1073–4.

Dothan, M. et al. 1967. *Ashdod I: The First Season of Excavations, 1962*. Jerusalem: *'Atiqot*. 7 (English Series). Jerusalem: Department of Antiquities.

Dothan, M. 1971. *Ashdod II-III: The Second and Third Seasons of Excavation. 'Atiqot*. 9–10 (English Series). Jerusalem: Department of Antiquities.

Dothan, M. 1982. *Ashdod IV: Excavation of Area M. 'Atiqot*. 15 (English Series). Jerusalem: Department of Antiquities.

Dothan, M. and Porath, Y. 1993. *Ashdod V: Excavation of Area G. 'Atiqot*. 23 (English Series). Jerusalem: Israel Antiquities Authority.

Dothan, T. 1957. Archaeological Reflections on the Philistine Problem. *Antiquity and Survival*. 2: 151–64.

Dothan, T. 1979 *Excavations at the Cemetery of Deir al-Balah. Qedem* 10. Monographs of the Institute of Archaeology, The Hebrew University of Jerusalem.

Dothan, T. 1982. *The Philistines and Their Material Culture*. New Haven: Yale University Press.

Dothan, T. 1989. The Arrival of the Sea Peoples: Cultural Diversity in Early Iron Age Canaan. *Recent Excavations in Israel: Studies in Iron Age Archaeology. ASOR*, 49: 1–14.

Dothan, T. 1990. Ekron of the Philistines, Part I: Where They Came From, How They Settled Down and the Place They Worshipped In. *Biblical Archaeology Review*. 16(1): 26–36.

Dothan, T. 1992. Social Dislocation and Cultural Change in the 12th Century B.C.E. *The Crisis Years: The 12th Century B.C.: From Beyond the Danube to the Tigris* (eds W.A. Ward and M.W. Joukowsky). Dubuque, IA: Kendall/Hunt Publishing.

Dothan, T. 1994. Tel Miqne-Ekron: The Aegean Affinities of the Sea Peoples (Philistines) Settlement in Canaan in Iron Age I. In *Recent Excavations in Israel: A View to the West* (ed. S. Gitin), ch. 3. Archaeological Institute of America, Conference and Colloquium Series, No. 1. Boston: AIA.

Dothan, T. and Dothan, M. 1992. *People of the Sea: The Search for the Philistines*. New York: Macmillian.

Dothan, T. and Gitin, S. 1993. Miqne, Tel Ekron. In *The New Encyclopedia of Archaeological Excavations in the Holy Land*, vol. 3, pp. 1051–1059.

Dothan, T. and Gitin, S. 1994. Tell Miqne-Ekron: The Rise and Fall of a Philistine City. *Qadmoniot* (in Hebrew).

Eisenstein, J.D. Wine. In *The Jewish Encyclopedia*. vol. 12, pp. 532–35. New York: Funk and Wagnalls.

Finkelstein, I., Bunimovitz, S. and Lederman, Z. 1994. *Shiloh: The Archaeology of a Biblical Site*. Tel Aviv Monograph.

Freu, J. 1988. La tablette RS 86.2230 et la phase finale du royaume d'Ugarit. *Syria*. 65: 395–8.

Gitin, S. 1990. Ekron of the Philistines, Part II: Olive Oil Suppliers to the World. *Biblical Archaeology Review*. 16(2): 32–42, 59.

Gitin, S. 1992. Last Days of the Philistines. *Archaeology* May/June: 26–31.

Gitin, S. and Dothan, T. 1987. The Rise and Fall of Ekron of the Philistines: Recent Excavations at an Urban Border Site. *Biblical Archaeologist*. 50: 197–222.

Gitin, S. and Dothan, T. 1993. Tel Miqne-Ekron. *ASOR Newsletter*. 43/3: 5.

Goldwasser, O. 1984. Hieratic Inscriptions from Tel Sera' in Southern Canaan. *Tel Aviv*. 11: 77–93.

Gunneweg, Jan, et al. 1986. On the Origin of Pottery from Tel Miqne-Ekron. *Bulletin of the American Schools of Oriental Research*. 264: 3–16.

Hesse, B. 1986. Animal Use at Tel Miqne-Ekron in the Bronze Age and Iron Age. *Bulletin of the American Schools of Oriental Research*. 264: 17–28.

Hesse, B. in press. The Animal Economy of Iron Age Ashkelon: The 1985 Collection. In *Ashkelon 1* (ed. L.E. Stager). Harvard Semitic Museum Archaeology and Cultural History. Cambridge, MA: Harvard University.

Hoffner, H.A., Jr. 1992. The Last Days of Khattusha. *The Crisis Years: the 12th Century B.C.: From Beyond the Tigris to the Danube* (eds W.A. Ward and M.W. Joukowsky). Dubuque, IA: Kendall/Hunt Publishing, pp. 46–52.

Johnson, B.L. and Stager, L.E. 1994. Ashkelon: Wine Emporium of the Holy Land. In *Recent Excavations in Israel: A View to the West* (ed. S. Gitin), ch. 6. Archaeological Institute of America, Conference and Colloquium Series, No. 1. Boston: AIA.

Karageorghis, V. 1982. Excavations at Maa-Palaeokastro. In *Annual Report of the Department of Antiquities for the Year 1981*. Nicosia, pp. 27–9.

Karageorghis, V. 1992. The Crisis Years: Cyprus. *The Crisis Years: The 12th Century B.C.: From Beyond the Danube to the Tigris* (eds W.A. Ward and M. Joukowsky). Dubuque, IA: Kendall/Hunt Publishing, pp. 79–86.

Kuchman, Liza 1977/78. Egyptian Clay Anthropoid Coffins. *Serapis*. 4: 11–22.

Lagarce, J. 1982. Ras Ibn Hani au Bronze Recent Problemes et Perspectives. In *La Syrie au Bronze Recent*. Paris: Editions Recherche sur les Civilisations, Vol. 15, pp. 31–6.

Lagarce, J. and Lagarce, E. 1981. The Intrusion of the Sea Peoples and Their Acculturation: A Parallel between Palestinian and Ibn Hani Data. Paper given at the First International Symposium on Palestine Antiquities held in Aleppo, Syria, 1981 (unpublished).

Luckenbill, D.D. 1914. Jadanan and Javan (Danaans and Ionians). *Zeitschrift für Assyriologie*, pp. 92–9.

Mazar, A. 1980. *Excavations at Tell Qasile I. The Philistine Sanctuary, Architecture and Cult Objects. Qedem* 12. Monographs of the Institute of Archaeology, The Hebrew University of Jerusalem.

Mazar, A. 1985. The Emergence of the Philistine Material Culture. *Israel Exploration Journal*. 35: 95–107.

Mazar, A. 1988. Some Aspects of the 'Sea Peoples' Settlement. In *Society and Economy in the Eastern Mediterranean* (eds M. Heltzer and E. Lipinski). Orientalia Lovaniensia Analecta 23. Leuven: Peeters, pp. 251–60.

Mazar, B. 1986. The Philistines and the Rise of Israel and Tyre. In *The Early Biblical Period: Historical Studies* (eds S. Ahituv and B.A. Levine). Jerusalem: Israel Exploration Society, pp. 63–82.

Mazar, B. 1992. The Philistines. In *Biblical Israel: State and People* (ed. S. Ahituv). Jerusalem: Magness Press, pp. 22–46.

Oren, E.D. 1973. *The Northern Cemetery at Beth Shan*. Leiden: E.J. Brill.

Oren, E.D. 1984. 'Governor's Residencies' in Canaan under the New Kingdom: A Case Study in Egyptian Administration. *Journal of the Society for the Study of Egyptian Antiquities*. 14: 37–56.

Oren, E.D. 1993a. Haror, Tel. In *New Encyclopedia of Archaeological Excavations in the Holy Land*, vol. 2, pp. 580–4.

Oren, E.D. 1993b. Sera', Tel. In *New Encyclopedia of Archaeological Excavations in the Holy Land*, vol. 4, pp. 1329–35.

Oren, E.D. 1993c. Sinai. In *New Encyclopedia of Excavations in the Holy Land*, vol. 4, pp. 1384–96.

Perlman, I., Asaro, P. and Friedman, J.D. 1971. Provenience Studies of Tel Ashdod Pottery Employing Neutron Activation Analysis. In *Ashdod II–III*, pp. 215–19.

Popham, M.R. and Sackett, L.H. 1968. *Excavations at Lefkandi, Euboea 1964–66*. Athens: Thames and Hudson.

Raban, A. 1987. The Harbor of the Sea Peoples at Dor. *Biblical Archaeologist*. 50(2): 118–26.

Redford, D.B. 1986. The Ashkelon Relief at Karnak and the Israel Stela. *Israel Exploration Journal*. 36: 188–200.

Redford, D.B. 1992. *Egypt, Canaan, and Israel in Ancient Times*. Princeton: Princeton University Press.

Rouse, I. 1958. The Inference of Migrations from Anthropological Evidence. In *Migrations in New World Culture History* (ed. Raymond H. Thompson). University of Arizona Social Science Bulletin No. 27: 63–68, Tucson: Arizona.

Rouse, I. 1965. The Place of 'Peoples' in Prehistoric Research. *The Journal of the Royal Anthropological Institute of Great Britain and Ireland*. 95: 1–15.

Sanders, N.K. 1978. *The Sea Peoples*. London: Thames and Hudson.

Singer, I. 1985. The Beginning of Philistine Settlement in Canaan and the Northern Boundary of Philistia. *Tel Aviv*. 12: 109–22.

Singer, I. 1988. Mereneptah's Campaign to Canaan and the Egyptian Occupation of the Southern Coastal Plain of Palestine in the Ramesside Period. *Bulletin of the American Schools of Oriental Research*. 269: 1–10.

Singer, I. 1994. Egyptians, Canaanites, and Philistines in the Period of the Emergence of Israel. In *From Nomadism to Monarchy* (eds I. Finkelstein and N. Na'aman). Jerusalem: Israel Exploration Society, pp. 232–38.

Stager, L.E. 1985a. Merenptah, Israel and Sea Peoples: New Light on an Old Relief. *Eretz-Israel*. 18 (Avigad Volume): 56–65.

Stager, L.E. 1985b. The Archaeology of the Family in Ancient Israel. *Bulletin of the American Schools of Oriental Research*. 260: 1–35.

Stager, L.E. 1991. When Canaanites and Philistines Ruled Ashkelon. In *Ashkelon Discovered*. Washington DC: Biblical Archaeology Society, pp. 2–19.

Stager, L.E. 1993. Ashkelon. In *The New Encyclopedia of Archaeological Excavations in the Holy Land*, vol. 1 (ed. E. Stern). Jerusalem: Israel Exploration Society, pp. 103–12.

Stern, E. 1992. The Many Masters of Dor. *Biblical Archaeology Review*. 19(1): 22–31, 76–8.

Stiebing, W.H., Jr. 1970. Another Look at the Origins of the Philistine Tombs at Tell el-Far'ah (S). *American Journal of Archaeology*. 74(2): 139–44.

Stone, B. 1993. *The Philistines and Acculturation*. B.A. Thesis. Harvard University.

Tadmor, H. 1966. Philistia Under Assyrian Rule. *Biblical Archaeologist*. 29: 86–102.

Trigger, B.G. 1968. *Beyond History: The Methods of Prehistory*. New York: Holt, Rinehart and Winston.

Tufnell, O. 1958. *Lachish IV (Tell ed-Duweir): The Bronze Age*. London: Oxford University Press.

Ussishkin, D. 1985. Levels VII and VI at Tel Lachish and the End of the Late Bronze Age in Canaan. In *Palestine in the Bronze and Iron Ages (Papers in Honour of Olga Tufnell)* (ed. J.N. Tubb). London: Institute of Archaeology, University of London, pp. 213–30.

Wachsmann, S. 1981. The Ships of the Sea Peoples. *International Journal of Nautical Archaeology*. 10: 187–220.

Wachsmann, S. 1982. The Ships of the Sea Peoples. Additional Notes. *International Journal of Nautical Archaeology*. 11: 297–304.

Wachsmann, S. in press. *Seagoing Ships and Seamanship in the Bronze Age Levant*.

Waldbaum, J. 1966. Philistine Tombs at Tell Fara and their Aegean Prototypes. *American Journal of Archaeology*. 70: 331–40.

Weinstein, J. 1992. The Collapse of the Egyptian Empire in the Southern Levant. In *The Crisis Years: The 12th Century B.C., From Beyond the Danube to the Tigris* (eds W.A. Ward and M. Joukowsky). Dubuque, IA: Kendall/Hunt Publishing.

Wente, E.F. and van Siclen III, C.C. 1976. A Chronology of the New Kingdom. (*Studies in Honor of George Hughes*). *Studies in Ancient Oriental Civilization*, Vol. 39. Oriental Institute: Chicago.

Wilson, J.A. 1969a. Egyptian Historical Texts. In *Ancient Near Eastern Texts Related to the Old Testament*, 3rd edn (ed. James B. Pritchard). Princeton, NJ: Princeton University Press, pp. 227–64.

Wilson, J.A. 1969b. The Journey of Wen-Amon to Phoenicia. ANET. 25–9.

Wright, G.E. 1946. The Literary and Historical Problem of Joshua 10 and Judges 1. *Journal of Near Eastern Studies*. 5: 105–14.

Wright, G.E. 1962. *Biblical Archaeology* (revised edn). Philadelphia: Westminster Press.

Wright, G.E. 1966. Fresh Evidence for the Philistine Story. *Biblical Archaeologist*. 29: 70–86.

Yannai, A. 1983. *Studies on Trade Between the Levant and the Aegean in the 14th to 12th Centuries B.C.* Ph.D. dissertation, Linacre College.

Yon, Marguerite 1992. The End of the Kingdom of Ugarit. In *The Crisis Years: The Twelfth Century B.C., From Beyond the Danube to the*

Tigris (eds W.A. Ward and M. Joukowsky). Dubuque, IA: Kendall/Hunt Publishing, pp. 111–22.

Yurco, F. 1986. Merenptah's Canaanite Campaign. *Journal of the American Research Center in Egypt.* 23: 189–215.

Chapter 21

Aharoni, Y. 1957. *The Settlement of the Israelite Tribes in Upper Galilee.* Jerusalem: Magnes (Hebrew).

Ahlström, G.W. 1982. Where did the Israelites Live. *JNES.* 41: 133–8.

Ahlström, G.W. 1986. *Who were the Israelites?* Winona Lake: Eisenbrauns.

Ahlström, G.W. and Edelman, D. 1985. Merneptah's Israel. *JNES.* 44: 59–61.

Albright, W.F. 1939. The Israelite Conquest of Canaan in the Light of Archaeology. *BASOR.* 74: 11–23.

Albright, W.F. 1949. *The Archaeology of Palestine.* Harmondsworth: Penguin.

Alt, A. 1925. Die Landnahme der Israeliten in Palästina. *Reformationsprogramm der Universitat Leipzig.* Leipzig: Universität Leipzig.

Alt, A. 1939. Erwägungen über die Landnahme der Israeliten im Palästina. *PJb.* 35: 8–63.

Alt, A. 1966. *Essays on Old Testament History and Religion.* Oxford: Basil Blackwell.

Auger, R., Glass, M.F., MacEachern, S. and McCartney, P.H. (eds) 1987. *Ethnicity and Culture.* (Proceedings of the Eighteenth Annual Conference of the The Archaeological Association of the University of Calgary). Calgary: University of Calgary.

Braudel, F. 1958. La longue durée. *Annales Economies Societes Civilisations.* 13: 725–53.

Braudel, F. 1972. *The Mediterranean and the Mediterranean World in the Age of Philip II.* New York: Harper and Row.

Broshi, M. and Finkelstein, I. 1992. The Population of Palestine in Iron Age II. *BASOR.* 287: 47–60.

Buccellati, G. 1967. *Cities and Nations of Ancient Syria* (Studi semitici 26). Rome: Instituto di Studi de Vicini Oriente.

Bunimovitz, S. 1989. The Land of Israel in the Late Bronze Age: A Case Study of Socio-Cultural Change in Complex Society. Unpublished doctoral thesis. Institute of Archaeology. Tel Aviv University (Hebrew).

Callaway, J.A. 1976. Excavating Ai (et-Tell): 1964–1972. *BA.* 39: 18–30.

Callaway, J.A. 1978. New Perspectives on Early Bronze III in Canaan. In *Archaeology in the Levant* (eds R. Moorey and P. Parr). Warminster: Aris and Phillips, 46–58.

Callaway, J.A. 1985. A New Perspective on the Hill Country Settlement of Canaan in Iron Age I. In *Palestine in the Bronze and Iron Ages. Papers in Honour of Olga Tufnell* (ed. J.N. Tubb). London: Institute of Archaeology, pp. 31–49.

Callaway, J.A. and Cooley, R.E. 1971. A Salvage Excavation at Raddana, in Bireh. *BASOR.* 201: 9–19.

Chaney, M.L. 1983. Ancient Palestinian Peasant Movements and the Formation of Premonarchic Israel. In *Palestine in Transition* (eds D.N. Freedman and D.F. Graf). Sheffield: Almond, pp. 39–90.

Coote, R.B. and Whitelam, K.W. 1987. *The Emergence of Early Israel in Historical Perspective.* Sheffield: Almond.

Dar, S. 1986. *Landscape and Pattern: An Archaeological Survey of Samaria 800 B.C.E.–636 C.E.* (BAR International Series 308). Oxford: BAR International Series.

Davies, P.R. 1992. *In Search of 'Ancient Israel'* (Journal for the Study of the Old Testament Supplement Series 148). Sheffield: JSOT Press.

Dever, W.G. 1975. Middle Bronze IIA Cemeteries at 'Ain es-Samiyeh and Sinjil. *BASOR.* 217: 23–36.

Dever, W.G. 1980. New Vistas on the EB IV ('MB I') Horizon in Syria-Palestine. *BASOR.* 237: 35–64.

Dever, W.G. 1987. The Middle Bronze Age: The Zenith of the Urban Canaanite Era. *BA.* 50: 148–77.

Dever, W.G. 1989. The Collapse of the Urban Early Bronze Age in Palestine – Towards a Systemic Analysis. In *L'urbanisation de la Palestine a' l'age du Bronze ancien* (ed. P. de Miroschedji). (BAR International Series 527). Oxford: pp. 225–46.

Dever, W.G. 1992. How to Tell a Canaanite from an Israelite. In *The Rise of Ancient Israel* (eds H. Shanks, W.G. Dever, B. Halpern and P.K. McCarter). Washington, DC: Biblical Archaeology Society, pp. 26–56.

Dever, W.G. 1993. Cultural Continuity, Ethnicity in the Archaeological Record, and the Question of Israelite Origin. *Eretz-Israel.* 24: 22–33.

Edelman-Vikander, D. (ed.) 1991. *The Fabric of History: Text, Artifacts and Israel's Past* (Journal for the Study of the Old Testament Supplement Series 127). Sheffield: JSOT Press.

Edelstein, G. 1988/89. Manahat – 1987/1988. *Excavations and Surveys in Israel.* 7–8: 117–23.

Eisenberg, E. 1988/89. Nahal Refa'im. *Excavations and Surveys in Israel.* 7–8: 84–9.

Esse, D. 1989. Secondary State Formation and Collapse in Early Bronze Age Palestine. In *L'Urbanisation de la Palestine a' l'age du Bronze ancien* (ed. P. de Miroschedji) (BAR International Series 527). Oxford: pp. 81–96.

Finkelstein, I. 1986. *'Izbet Sartah: An Early Iron Age Site near Rosh Ha'ayin, Israel* (BAR International Series 299). Oxford.

Finkelstein, I. 1988. *The Archaeology of the Israelite Settlement.* Jerusalem: Israel Exploration Society.

Finkelstein, I. 1988–89. The Land of Ephraim Survey 1980–1987: Preliminary Report. *Tel Aviv.* 15–16: 117–83.

Finkelstein, I. 1989. The Emergence of the Monarchy in Israel: The Environmental and Socio-Economic Aspects. *JSOT.* 44: 43–74.

Finkelstein, I. 1990. Excavations at Kh. ed-Dawwara: An Iron Age Site Northeast of Jerusalem. *Tel Aviv.* 17: 163–208.

Finkelstein, I. 1991. The Central Hill Country in the Intermediate Bronze Age. *IEJ.* 41: 19–45.

Finkelstein, I. 1992. Pastoralism in the Highlands of Canaan in the Third and Second Millennia B.C.E. In *Pastoralism in the Levant: Archaeological Materials in Anthropological Perspective* (eds O. Bar Yosef and A. Khazanov). Madison: Prehistory Press, pp. 133–42.

Finkelstein, I. 1993. The Sociopolitical Organization of the Central Hill Country in the Second Millennium BCE. In *Biblical Archaeology Today, 1993, Proceedings of the Second International Congress on Biblical Archaeology: Pre Congress Symposium Supplement* (eds A. Biran and J. Aviram). Jerusalem: Israel Exploration Society: pp. 98–118.

Finkelstein, I. forthcoming. From Sherds to History: The Settlement History of the Jordanian Plateau According to Recent Survey Publications. *IEJ.*

Finkelstein, I., Bunimovitz, S. and Lederman, S. 1993. *Shiloh: The Archaeology of a Biblical Site.* Tel Aviv: Institute of Archaeology.

Finkelstein, I. and Brandl, B. 1985. A Group of Metal Objects from Shiloh. *The Israel Museum Journal.* 4: 17–26.

Finkelstein, I. and Gophna, R. 1993. Settlement, Demographic and Economic Patterns in the Highlands of Palestine in the Chalcolithic and Early Bronze Periods and the Beginning of Urbanism. *BASOR.* 289: 1–22.

Finkelstein, I. and Magen, Y. (eds) 1993. *Archaeological Survey in the Hill Country of Benjamin.* Jerusalem: Antiquities Authority.

Finkelstein, I. and Perevolotsky, A. 1990. Processes of Sedentarization and Nomadization in the History of Sinai and the Negev. *BASOR.* 279: 67–88.

Geraty, L.T., Herr, L.G., LaBianca, O.S. and Younker, R.W. (eds) 1989. *Madaba Plains Project: The 1984 Season at Tell el-'Umeiri and Vicinity and Subsequent Studies 1.* Berrien Springs: Andrews University Press.

de Geus, C.H.J. 1975. The Importance of Archaeological Research into the Palestinian Agricultural Terraces, with an Excursus of the Hebrew Word gbi. *PEQ.* 107: 65–74.

de Geus, C.H.J. 1976. *The Tribes of Israel.* Amsterdam: Van Gorcum.

Gottwald, N.K. 1979. *The Tribes of Yahweh.* New York: SCM Press.

Grossman, D. 1992. *Rural Process-Pattern Relationships: Nomadization, Sedentarization, and Settlement Fixation.* New York: Praeger.

Hellwing, S., Sadeh, M. and Kishon, V. 1993. Faunal Remains. In *Shiloh: The Archaeology of a Biblical Site,* ed. I. Finkelstein. Tel Aviv: Tel Aviv University Institute of Archaeology: 309–52.

Hodder, I. 1987. The Contribution of the Long Term. In *Archaeology as Long-Term History* (ed. I. Hodder). Cambridge: Cambridge University Press, pp. 1–8.

Hopkins, D.C. 1985. *The Highlands of Canaan.* Sheffield: JSOT Press.

Ibach, R.D. 1987. *Archaeological Survey of the Hesban Region* (Hesban 5). Berrien Springs: Andrews University Press.

Ibrahim, M. 1978. The Collared-rim Jar of the Early Iron Age. In *Archaeology in the Levant* (eds R. Moorey and P. Parr). Warminster: Aris and Phillips, pp. 116–26.

Kallai, Z. and Tadmor, H. 1969. Bit Ninurta = Beth Horon – On the History of the Kingdom of Jerusalem in the Amarna Period. *Eretz-Israel*. 9: 138–47 (Hebrew).

Kamp, K.A. and Yoffee, N. 1980. Ethnicity in Ancient Western Asia During the Early Second Millennium B.C.: Archaeological Assessments and Ethnoarchaeological Prospectives. *BASOR*. 237: 85–104.

Kempinski, A. 1979. Hittites in the Bible – What does Archaeology Say? *BAR*. 5(4): 20–46.

Kempinski, A. 1985. The Overlap of Cultures at the End of the Late Bronze Age and the Beginning of the Iron Age. *Eretz-Israel*. 18: 399–407 (Hebrew).

Kenyon, K.M. 1971. Syria and Palestine c. 2160–1780 B.C.: The Archaeological Sites. *CAH*. I/2: 567–94.

Knapp, B. (ed.) 1992. *Archaeology, Annales and Ethnohistory*. Cambridge: Cambridge University Press.

Kolska Horwitz, L. 1989. Diachronic Changes in Rural Husbandry Practices in Bronze Age Settlements from the Refaim Valley, Israel. *PEQ*. 121: 44–54.

LaBianca, O. 1990. *Sedentarization and Nomadization: Food System Cycles at Hesban and Vicinity in Transjordan* (Hesban 1). Berrien Springs: Andrews University Press.

Lapp, P.W. 1967. The Conquest of Palestine in the Light of Archaeology. *Concordia Theological Monthly*. 38: 283–300.

Lemche, N.P. 1985. *Early Israel*. Leiden: E.J. Brill.

Lewis, N.N. 1987. *Nomads and Settlers in Syria and Jordan, 1800–1980*. Cambridge: Cambridge University Press.

MacDonald, B. 1988. *The Wadi el Hasa Archaeological Survey 1979–1983, West-Central Jordan*. Waterloo: Wilfrid Laurier University Press.

Marfoe, L. 1979. The Integrative Transformation: Patterns of Socio-Political Organization in Southern Syria. *BASOR*. 234: 1–42.

Mazar, A. 1981. Giloh: An Early Israelite Settlement Site near Jerusalem. *IEJ*. 31: 1–36.

Mazar, A. 1982. The 'Bull Site' – An Iron Age I Open Cult Place. *BASOR*. 247: 27–42.

Mazar, A. 1990. Iron Age I and II Towers at Giloh and the Israelite Settlement. *IEJ*. 40: 77–101.

Mazar, B. 1986. *The Early Biblical Period*. Jerusalem: Israel Exploration Society.

Mendenhall, G.E. 1962. The Hebrew Conquest of Palestine. *BA*. 25: 66–87.

Mendenhall, G.E. 1976. *The Tenth Generation*. Baltimore: The Johns Hopkins University Press.

Miller, J.M. 1977. The Israelite Occupation of Canaan. In *Israelite and Judean History* (eds J.H. Hayes and J.M. Miller). London: SCM Press, pp. 213–84.

Miller, J.M. (ed.) 1991. *Archaeological Survey of the Kerak Plateau*. Atlanta: Scholars Press.

Mittmann, S. 1970. *Beiträge zur Siedlungs und Territorialgeschichte des nördlichen Ostjordanlandes*. Wiesbaden: Otto Harrassowitz.

Na'aman, N. 1982. Eretz Israel in the Canaanite Period: The Middle and Late Bronze Ages. In *The History of Eretz Israel* Vol. 1. (ed. I. Ephal). Jerusalem: Keter, pp. 129–256 (Hebrew).

Na'aman, N. 1986. The Canaanite City-States in the Late Bronze Age and the Inheritances of the Israelite Tribes. *Tarbiz*. 55: 463–88 (Hebrew).

Na'aman, N. 1994. The 'Conquest of Canaan' in the Book of Joshua and in History. In *From Nomadism to Monarchy: Archaeological and Historical Aspects of Early Israel* (eds I. Finkelstein and N. Na'aman). Jerusalem: Israel Exploration Society, pp. 218–31.

Noth, M. 1960. *The History of Israel*. London: Adam and Charles Black.

Ofer, A. 1989. Excavations at Biblical Hebron. *Qadmoniot*. 87–8: 88–95 (Hebrew).

Ofer, A. 1994. 'All the Hill Country of Judah': From a Settlement Fringe to a Prosperous Monarchy. In *From Nomadism to Monarchy: Archaeological and Historical Aspects of Early Israel* (eds. I.

Finkelstein and N. Na'aman). Jerusalem: Israel Exploration Society, 92–121.

Reviv, H. 1966. The Government of Shechem in the El-Amarna Period and in the Days of Abimelech. *IEJ*. 16: 252–7.

Rowton, M.B. 1973. Urban Autonomy in a Nomadic Environment. *JNES*. 32: 201–15.

Rowton, M.B. 1974. Enclosed Nomadism. *JESHO*. 17: 1–30.

Rowton, M.B. 1976. Dimorphic Structure and the Tribal Elite. In *Al-Bahit: Festschrift Joseph Henniger* (Studia Instituti Anthropos 28). St Augustin bei Bonn: 219–57.

Singer, I. 1993. Egyptians, Canaanites, and Philistines in the Period of the Emergence of Israel. In *From Nomadism to Monarchy: Archaeological and Historical Aspects of Early Israel* (eds. I. Finkelstein and N. Na'aman). Jerusalem: Israel Exploration Society: 282–338.

Stager, L.E. 1982. The Archaeology of the East Slope of Jerusalem and the Terraces of the Kidron. *JNES*. 41: 111–21.

Stager, L.E. 1985a. Merenptah, Israel and Sea Peoples: New Light on an Old Relief. *Eretz-Israel*. 18: 56*–64*.

Stager, L.E. 1985b. The Firstfruits of Civilization. In *Palestine in the Bronze and Iron Ages, Papers in Honour of Olga Tufnell* (ed. J.N. Tubb). London: Institute of Archaeology, pp. 172–88.

Stager, L.E. 1985c. The Archaeology of the Family in Ancient Israel. *BASOR*. 260: 1–35.

Thompson, T.L. 1992. *Early History of the Israelite People*. Leiden: E.J. Brill.

Toynbee, A.J. 1956. *A Study on History* Vol. IV. London: Oxford University Press.

Ussishkin, D. 1989. Notes on the Fortifications of the Middle Bronze II Period at Jericho and Shechem. *BASOR*. 276: 29–53.

Waldbaum, J.C. 1978. *From Bronze to Iron* (Studies in Mediterranean Archaeology 54). Goteborg: P. Astroms.

Weippert, M. 1971. *The Settlement of the Israelite Tribes in Palestine*. London: SCM Press.

Wright, G.E. 1962. *Biblical Archaeology*. London: Duckworth.

Yadin, Y. 1979. The Transition from a Semi-Nomadic to a Sedentary Society in the Twelfth Century BCE. In *Symposia Celebrating the Seventy-Fifth Anniversary of the Foundation of the American Schools of Oriental Research (1900–1975)* (ed. F.M. Cross). Cambridge: American Schools of Oriental Research, 57–68.

Yurco, F.J. 1986. Merenptah's Canaanite Campaign. *JARCE*. 23: 189–215.

Zertal, A. 1986–87. An Early Iron Age Cultic Site on Mount Ebal: Excavation Seasons 1982–1987. *Tel Aviv*. 13–14: 105–65.

Zertal, A. 1988a. *The Israelite Settlement in the Hill Country of Manasseh*. Haifa: Haifa University (Hebrew).

Zertal, A. 1988b. The Water Factor during the Israelite Settlement Process in Canaan. In *Society and Economy in the Eastern Mediterranean (c. 1500–1000 B.C.)* (eds M. Heltzer and E. Lipinski). Leuven: Uitgeverig Peeters, 341–52.

Chapter 22

Aharoni, M. 1981. The Pottery of Strata 12–11 of the Iron Age Citadel at Arad. *Eretz Israel* 15: 181–204 (Hebrew), 82*.

Aharoni, Y. 1957. The Settlement of the Israelite Tribes in Upper Galilee. Unpublished doctoral dissertation. Jerusalem: Hebrew University (Hebrew)

Aharoni, Y. 1973. *Beer-sheba I: Excavations at Tel Beer-sheba, 1969–1971 Seasons* (ed. Yohanan Aharoni). Tel Aviv: Tel Aviv University, Institute of Archaeology.

Aharoni, Y. 1975. *Investigations at Lachish: The Sanctuary and the Residency.* (*Lachish V*). Tel Aviv: Gateway Publications.

Aharoni, Y. 1979. *The Land of the Bible: A Historical Geography*. Second revised edition. Philadelphia: Westminster.

Ahlström, G.W. 1982a. *Royal Administration and National Religion in Ancient Palestine*. Leiden: E.J. Brill.

Ahlström, G.W. 1982b. Where did the Israelites Live? *Journal of Near Eastern Studies* 41: 133–38.

Albright, W.F. 1932. *The Excavation of Tell Beit Mirsim. Vol. I: The Pottery of the First Three Campaigns. Annual of the American Schools of Oriental Research*. Vol. 12, for 1930–31. New Haven: American Schools of Oriental Research.

Albright, W.F. 1943. *The Excavation of Tell Beit Mirsim. Vol. III: The Iron Age. Annual of the American Schools of Oriental Research.* Vols. 21–2, for 1941–43. New Haven: American Schools of Oriental Research.

Anderson, W.P. 1988. *Sarepta I: The Late Bronze and Iron Age Strata of Area II,Y. The University Museum of the University of Pennsylvania Excavations at Sarafand, Lebanon. Publications de l'Université Libanaise, Section des Études Archéologiques* 2. Beirut: Department des Publications de l'Universite Libanaise.

Artzy, M. 1990. Notes and News: Nami Land and Sea Project, 1985–1988. *Israel Exploration Journal.* 40: 73–6.

Baly, D. 1974. *The Geography of the Bible.* New and revised edition. Guildford and London: Lutterworth.

Banning, E.B. and Köhler-Rollefson, I. 1992. Ethnographic Lessons for the Pastoral Past: Camp Locations and Material Remains near Beidha, Southern Jordan. In *Pastoralism in the Levant, Archaeological Materials in Anthropological Perspective. Monographs in World Archaeology* 10. (eds O. Bar-Yosef and A. Khazonov). Madison WI: Prehistory Press, pp. 181–204.

Baskin, C.W. 1957. *A Critic and Translation of Walter Christaller's Die zentralen Orte in Süddeutschland.* Ann Arbor MI: University Microfilms.

Beck, P. and Kochavi, M. 1985. A Dated Assemblage of the Late 13th Century BCE from the Egyptian Residency at Aphek. *Tel Aviv.* 12: 29–42.

Beit Arieh, I. 1985a. Tel 'Ira – A Fortified City of the Kingdom of Judah. *Qadmoniyot.* 18/1–2: 17–25 (Hebrew).

Beit Arieh, I. 1985b. Tell 'Ira – 1984. *Excavations and Surveys in Israel.* 4: 51.

Beit Arieh, I. 1992a. 'Ira, Tel. *Anchor Bible Dictionary*, vol. 3: 446–8. New York: Doubleday.

Beit Arieh, I. 1992b. 'Uza, Horvat. *Anchor Bible Dictionary*, vol. 3: 771–5. New York: Doubleday.

Beit Arieh, I. 1992c. Horvat Radum. *Eretz Israel.* 23 (the Biran Volume): 106–12 (Hebrew), 150*.

Bergoffen, C.J. 1991. Overland Trade in Northern Sinai: The Evidence of the Late Cypriot Pottery. *Bulletin of the American Schools of Oriental Research.* 284: 59–76.

Bikai, P.M. 1978. *The Pottery of Tyre.* Warminster: Aris & Phillips.

Binford, L. 1968. Archaeological Perspectives. In *New Perspectives in Archaeology* (eds S.R. Binford and L.R. Binford). Chicago: Aldine, pp. 5–32.

Binford, L. 1972. Smudge Pits and Hide Smoking: The Use of Analogy in Archaeological Reasoning. *American Antiquity.* 32: 1, 1–12. Republished in L.R. Binford, *An Archaeological Perspective* (ed. L.R. Binford). New York: Seminar Press, pp. 33–51.

Biran, A. 1983. And David Sent Spoils to the Elders in Aroer. *Biblical Archaeology Review.* 9: 28–37.

Blalock, H.M. 1979. *Social Statistics*, 2nd ed., revised. New York: McGraw-Hill.

Braemer, F. 1982. *L'architecture domestique du Levant à l'àge du fer: protohistoire du Levant. Éditions recherche sur les civilisations, cahier no.* 8. Paris: Éditions Recherche sur les civilisations.

Callaway, J.A. 1976. Excavating Ai (et-Tell): 1964–1972. *Biblical Archaeologist.* 39: 18–30.

Caton-Thomson, G. 1944. *The Tombs and Moon Temple of Hureidha (Hadhramaut).* London: University Press for the Society of Antiquaries.

Chambon, A. 1984. *Tell el-Farah 1: l'àge du Fer.* Paris: Éditions Recherche sur les Civilisations.

Chaney, M. 1989. Bitter Bounty: The Dynamics of Political Economy Critiqued by the Eighth-Century Prophets. In *Reformed Faith and Economics* (ed. R.L. Stivers). Lanham MD: University Press of America, pp. 15–30.

Chazan, M. and Lehner, M. 1990. An Ancient Analogy: Pot Baked Bread in Ancient Egypt and Mesopotamia. *Paléorient.* 16/2: 21–35.

Christaller, W. 1933. *Die Zentralen Orte in Süddeutschland; eine ökonomisch-geographische Untersuchung über die Gesetzmüsigkeit der Verbreitung und Entwicklung der Siedlungen mit stüdtischen Funktionen.* Jena: G. Fischer.

Coughenour, R.A. 1976. Preliminary Report on the Exploration and Excavation of Mugharat el Wardeh and Abu Thawab. *Annual of the Department of Antiquities of Jordan.* 21: 71–8, 186–9.

Coughenour, R.A. 1989. A Search for Mahanaim. *Bulletin of the American Schools of Oriental Research.* 273: 57–66.

Cross, F.M. 1980. Newly Found Inscriptions in Old Canaanite and Early Phoenician Scripts. *Bulletin of the American Schools of Oriental Research.* 238: 1–20.

Cross, F.M. 1992. An Inscribed Arrowhead of the Eleventh Century BCE in the Bible Lands Museum in Jerusalem. *Eretz Israel.* 23 (the Biran Volume): 21*–26*.

Curtin, P.D. 1984. *Cross-cultural Trade in World History.* Cambridge: Cambridge University Press.

Currid, J.D. and Navon, A. 1989. Iron Age Pits and the Lahav (Tel Halif) Grain Storage Project. *Bulletin of the American Schools of Oriental Research.* 273: 67–78.

Daviau, P.P.M. 1993. *Houses and Their Furnishings in Bronze Age Palestine. Domestic Activity and Artefact Distribution in the Middle and Late Bronze Ages. JSOT/ASOR Monograph Series* 8. Sheffield: JSOT Press.

Davies, G.I. 1988. Solomonic Stables at Megiddo After All? *Palestine Exploration Quarterly.* 120: 130–41.

Davis, S. 1987. The Faunal Remains from Tell Qiri. In *Tell Qiri: A Village in the Jezreel Valley, Report of the Archaeological Excavations 1975–77. Qedem* 24 (eds A. Ben-Tor, Y. Portugali et al.). Jerusalem: Institute of Archaeology, Hebrew University, pp. 249–51.

Dever, W.G. 1984. Asherah, Consort of Yahweh? New Evidence from Kuntillet 'Ajrud. *Bulletin of the American Schools of Oriental Research.* 255: 55–80.

Dever, W.G. 1987. The Contribution of Archaeology to the Study of Canaanite and Early Israelite Religion. In *Ancient Israelite Religion: Essays in Honor of Frank Moore Cross* (eds P.D. Miller, P.D. Hanson and S.D. McBride). Philadelphia: Fortress, pp. 209–47.

Dever, W.G., Lance, H.D., Ballard, R.G., Cole, D.P. and Seger, J.D. 1974. *Gezer II: Report of the 1967–70 Seasons in Fields I and II. Annual of the Hebrew Union College/Nelson Glueck School of Biblical Archaeology*, 2. Jerusalem: Hebrew Union College.

Earle, T.K. 1976. A Nearest-Neighbor Analysis of Two Formative Settlement Systems. In *The Early Mesoamerican Village* (ed. K.V. Flannery). New York: Academic, pp. 196–223.

Eldridge, N. and Gould, S.J. 1972. Punctuated Equilibria: An Alternative to Phyletic Gradualism. In *Models in Paleobiology* (ed. Thomas J.M. Schopf). San Francisco: Freeman, Cooper, pp. 82–115.

Eph'al, I. 1982. *The Ancient Arabs: Nomads on the Borders of the Fertile Crescent. 9th–5th Centuries B.C.* Jerusalem and Leiden: Hebrew University and E.J. Brill.

Eph'al, I. and Naveh, J. 1993. The Jar of the Gate. *Bulletin of the American Schools of Oriental Research.* 289: 59–65.

Esse, D.L. 1992. The Collared Pithos at Megiddo: Ceramic Distribution and Ethnicity. *Journal of Near Eastern Studies.* 51: 81–103.

Finkelstein, I. (ed.) 1986. *'Izbet Sartah: An Early Iron Age Site near Rosh Ha'ayin, Israel. BAR International Series* 299. Oxford: British Archaeological Reports.

Finkelstein, I. 1988a. *The Archaeology of the Israelite Settlement.* Jerusalem: Israel Exploration Society.

Finkelstein, I. 1988b. Arabian Trade and Socio-Political Conditions in the Negev in the Twelfth–Eleventh Centuries B.C.E. *Journal of Near Eastern Studies.* 47: 241–52.

Finkelstien, I. (ed.) 1988c. New and Notes: Kh. ed-Dawwar, 1985–1986. *Israel Exploration Journal.* 38: 79–80.

Flannery, K.V. 1973. Archeology with a Capital 'S'. In *Research and Theory in Current Archeology* (ed. C. Redman). New York: Wiley, pp. 47–58.

Flannery, K.V. 1976. *The Early Mesoamerican Village.* New York: Academic.

Frick, F.S. 1985. *The Formation of the State in Ancient Israel.* In *The Social World of Biblical Antiquity Series.* No. 4. Sheffield: JSOT Press.

Fritz, V. and Kempinski, A. 1983. *Ergebnisse der Ausgrabungen auf der Hirbet el-Masas (Tel Masos) 1972–1975.* Text and Plates. Wiesbaden: Harrassowitz.

Gal, Z. 1992. Hurvat Rosh Zayit and the Early Phoenician Pottery. *Levant.* 24: 173–86.

Gibson, McGuire, 1977. Summation. In *Seals and Sealings in the Ancient Near East. Bibliotheca Mesopotamica* 6 (eds M. Gibson and R.D. Biggs). Malibu: Undena, pp. 147–53.

Gitin, S. 1992. New Incense Altars from Ekron: Context, Typology and Function. *Eretz Israel.* 23: 43*–49*.

Glass, J. 1988. Petrographic Investigations of the Pottery. In *Researches in the Arabah 1959–1984, with Contributions by H.G. Bachmann, et al.* (ed. B. Rothenberg). London: Institute for Archaeo-Metallurgical Studies, pp. 96–113.

Gophna, R. and Yisraeli, Y. 1973. Soundings at Beer Sheva (Bir es-Seba'). In *Beer-sheba I: Excavations at Tel Beer-sheba, 1969–1971 Seasons* (ed. Y. Aharoni). Tel Aviv: Tel Aviv University, Institute of Archaeology, pp. 115–18.

Grant, E. and Wright, G.E. 1939. *Ain Shems Excavations, Part V.* Haverford PA: Haverford College.

Greenberg, R. 1987. New Light on the Early Iron Age at Tell Beit Mirsim. *Bulletin of the American Schools of Oriental Research.* 265: 55–80.

Groom, N. 1981. *Frankincense and Myrrh: A Study of the Arabian Incense Trade. Arab Background Series.* Harlow: Longman.

Hellwing, S. and Adjeman, Y. 1986. Animal Bones. In *'Izbet Sartah: An Early Iron Age Site near Rosh Hacayin, Israel. BAR International Series 299* (ed. I. Finkelstein). Oxford: British Archaeological Reports, pp. 141–52.

Herzog, Z. 1984. *Beer-sheba II: The Early Iron Age Settlements.* Tel Aviv: Tel Aviv University.

Herzog, Z. 1992. Administrative Structures in the Iron Age. In *The Architecture of Ancient Israel from the Prehistoric to the Persian Periods* (eds A. Kempinski and R. Reich). Jerusalem: Israel Exploration Society, pp. 223–30.

Herzog, Z., Aharoni, M., Rainey, A. F. and Moshkovitz, S. 1984. The Israelite Fortress at Arad. *Bulletin of the American Schools of Oriental Research.* 254: 1–34.

Holladay, J.S. Jr. 1966. The Pottery of Northern Palestine in the Ninth and Eighth Centuries B.C. Unpublished doctoral Dissertation, The Faculty of Harvard Divinity School, Harvard University.

Holladay, J.S. Jr. 1976. Of Sherds and Strata: Contributions toward an Understanding of the Archaeology of the Divided Monarchy. In *Magnalia Dei: The Mighty Acts of God. Essays on the Bible and Archaeology in Memory of G. Ernest Wright* (eds F.M. Cross, W.E. Lemke and P.D. Miller, Jr). Garden City NY: Doubleday, pp. 253–93.

Holladay, J.S. Jr. 1986. The Stables of Ancient Israel: Functional Determinants of Stable Construction and the Interpretation of Pillared Building Remains of the Palestinian Iron Age. In *The Archaeology of Jordan and Other Studies: Presented to Siegfried H. Horn* (eds Lawrence T. Geraty and L.G. Herr). Berrien Springs, MI: Andrews University, pp. 103–65.

Holladay, J.S. Jr. 1987. Religion in Israel and Judah Under the Monarchy: An Explicitly Archaeological Approach. In *Ancient Israelite Religion: Essays in Honor of Frank Moore Cross* (eds P.D. Miller, P.D. Hanson and S.D. McBride). Philadelphia: Fortress, pp. 249–99.

Holladay, J.S. Jr. 1990. Red Slip, Burnish, and the Solomonic Gateway at Gezer. *Bulletin of the American Schools of Oriental Research.* 277/78: 23–70.

Holladay, J.S. Jr. 1992a. House, Israelite. *Anchor Bible Dictionary,* vol. 3: 308–18. New York: Doubleday.

Holladay, J.S. Jr. 1992b. Stable, Stables. *Anchor Bible Dictionary,* vol. 6: 178–83. New York: Doubleday.

Holladay, J.S. Jr. 1993. The Use of Pottery and Other Diagnostic Criteria, from the Solomonic Era to the Divided Kingdom. *Proceedings of the Second International Congress of Biblical Archaeology, Jerusalem, 1990,* Jerusalem: Israel Exploration Society. 86–101

Holland, T.A. 1977. A Study of Palestinian Iron Age Baked Clay Figurines, with Special Reference to Jerusalem: Cave 1. *Levant.* 9: 121–55.

Hopkins, D.C. 1985. *The Highlands of Canaan: Agricultural Life in the Early Iron Age. Social World of Biblical Antiquity Series 3.* Sheffield, England/Decatur GA: Almond Press.

Hopkins, D.C. 1987. Life on the Land: The Subsistence Struggles of Early Israel. *Biblical Archaeologist.* 50: 178–91.

Hunt, M. 1987. Part Two: The Iron Age, Chapter VII. The Pottery. In *Tell Qiri: A Village in the Jezreel Valley, Report of the Archaeological Excavations 1975-77. Qedem 24* (eds A. Ben-Tor, Y. Portugali, M. Avissar, U. Baruch and M. Hunt). Jerusalem: Institute of Archaeology, Hebrew University, pp. 139-223.

Jacobs, L. 1979. Tell-i Nun: Archaeological Implications of a Village in Transition. In *Ethnoarchaeology: Implications of Ethnography for Archaeology* (ed. C. Kramer). New York: Columbia University, pp. 175–91.

Jacobs, P. 1992. Review of William G. Dever, *Recent Archaeological Discoveries and Biblical Research* (Seattle/London: University of Washington, 1990). *Catholic Biblical Quarterly.* 54: 744–5.

James, F.W. 1966. *The Iron Age at Beth Shan: A Study of Levels VI–IV. Museum Monographs.* Philadelphia: University Museum, University of Pennsylvania.

Johnson, G.A. 1973. Local Exchange and Early State Development in Southwestern Iran. *Anthropological Papers.* 57,1. Ann Arbor, MI: University of Michigan Museum of Anthropology.

Kaufman, I.T. 1982. The Samaria Ostraca: An Early Witness to Hebrew Writing. *Biblical Archaeologist.* 45: 229–39.

Kaufman, I.T. 1992. Samaria (Ostraca). *The Anchor Bible Dictionary:* Vol. 5: 921–6. New York: Doubleday.

Kelm, G.L. and Mazar, A. 1982. Three Seasons of Excavations at Tel Batash – Biblical Timnah. *Bulletin of the American Schools of Oriental Research.* 248: 1–36.

Kelso, J.L. 1970. A Reply to Yadin's Article on the Finding of the Bethel Seal. *Bulletin of the American Schools of Oriental Research.* 199: 65.

Kemp, B. 1986. Large Middle Kingdom Granary Buildings (and the Archaeology of Administration). *Zeitschrift fur Ägyptische Sprache.* 113: 120–36.

Killebrew, A. 1992. Paper read at the annual meeting of the American Schools of Oriental Research at San Francisco, November 1992.

Kitchen, K.A. 1986. *The Third Intermediate Period in Egypt (1100–650 B.C.)* (Second Edition with Supplement). Warminster: Aris and Phillips.

Kitchen, K.A. 1989a. Where did King Solomon's Gold Go? *Biblical Archaeology Review.* 15/3: 32–3.

Kitchen, K.A. 1989b. Shishak's Military Campaign in Israel Confirmed. *Biblical Archaeology Review.* 15/3: 32–3.

Knauf, E.A. 1988. *Midian: Untersuchungen zur Geschichte Palästinas und Nordarabiens am Ende des 2. Jahrtausends v. Chr. Abhandlungen des Deutschen Palästinavereins.* Wiesbaden: Harrassowitz.

Kochavi, M. 1977. Tel Malhata. In *Encyclopedia of Archaeological Excavations in the Holy Land* (eds Michael Avi-Yonah and Ephriam Stern). Jerusalem: Israel Exploration Society and Massada Press, pp. 771–5.

Kramer, C. 1979. An Archaeological View of a Contemporary Kurdish Village: Domestic Architecture, Household Size, and Wealth. In *Ethnoarchaeology: Implications of Ethnography for Archaeology* (ed. C. Kramer). New York: Columbia University, pp. 139–63.

Kramer, C. 1982. *Village Ethnoarchaeology: Rural Iran in Archaeological Perspective.* New York: Academic Press.

Lamon, R.S. and Shipton, G.M. 1939. *Megiddo I. Oriental Institute Publications* 42. Chicago: University of Chicago.

Lapp, N. (ed.) 1981. *The Third Campaign at Tell el-Ful: The Excavations of 1964. Annual of the American Schools of Oriental Research.* 45.

Ledermann, Z. 1990. Nomads They Never Were: A Re-evaluation of Izbet Sarta. *American Academy of Religion/Society of Biblical Literature, Abstracts.* 1990: 238.

Liphschitz, N. and Biger, G. 1991. Cedar of Lebanon (*Cedrus libani*) in Israel during Antiquity. *Israel Exploration Journal.* 41: 167–75.

Liphschitz, N. and Waisel, Y. 1973. Analysis of the Botanical Material of the 1969–1970 seasons and the Climatic History of the Beer-Sheba Region. In *Beer-sheba I: Excavations at Tel Beer-sheba, 1969–1971 Seasons* (ed. Y. Aharoni). Tel Aviv: Tel Aviv University, Institute of Archaeology, pp. 97–105.

Liphschitz, N. and Waisel, Y. 1983. Analysis of the Botanical Material. In *Ergebnisse der Ausgrabungen auf der Hirbet el-Msas (Tel Masos) 1972–1975. Abhandlungen des Deutschen Palästinavereins* (eds V. Fritz and A. Kempinski). Text and Plates. Wiesbaden: Harrassowitz.

Liphschitz, N. and Waisel, Y. 1985. Analysis of Wood Remains from Tell Qasile. In *Excavations at Tell Qasile. Part Two, The Philistine Sanctuary: Various Finds, The Pottery, Conclusions, Appendixes. Qedem 20* (ed. A. Mazar). Jerusalem: Institute of Archaeology, Hebrew University, p. 139.

London, G. 1992. Tells: City Center or Home? *Eretz Israel* (the Biran Volume) 23: pp. 71*–9*.

Loud, G. 1948. *Megiddo II. Oriental Institute Publications*. 62. Chicago: University of Chicago.

Marquet-Krause, J. 1949. *Les fouilles de 'Ay (et-Tell), 1933–1935: Entreprises par le Baron Edmond de Rothschild . . . La risurrection d'un grande cite biblique. Bibliotheque archiologique et historique, t.* 45. Paris: Geuthner.

Maisler, B. (Mazar) 1951. The Excavations at Tell Qasile, Preliminary Report. *Israel Exploration Journal*. 1: 61–76, 125–40, 194–218.

Mazar, A. 1980. *Excavations at Tell Qasile. Part One, The Philistine Sanctuary: Architecture and Cult Objects. Qedem* 12. Jerusalem: Institute of Archaeology, Hebrew University.

Mazar, A. 1981. Giloh: An Early Israelite Settlement Site Near Jerusalem. *Israel Exploration Journal*. 31: 1–36.

Mazar, A. 1982a. The 'Bull Site' – An Iron Age I Open Cultic Place. *Bulletin of the American Schools of Oriental Research*. 247: 27–42.

Mazar, A. 1982b. Three Israelite Sites in the Hills of Judah and Ephraim. *Biblical Archaeologist*. 45: 167–78.

Mazar, A. 1985. *Excavations at Tell Qasile. Part Two, The Philistine Sanctuary: Various Finds, The Pottery, Conclusions, Appendixes. Qedem* 20. Jerusalem: Institute of Archaeology, Hebrew University.

Mazar, A. 1990. *Archaeology of the Land of the Bible, 10,000–586 B.C.E.. Anchor Bible Reference Library*. New York: Doubleday.

Mazar, A. and Netzer, E. 1986. On the Israelite Fortress at Arad. *Bulletin of the American Schools of Oriental Research*. 263: 87–91.

McClellan, T.L. 1987. Review of Alain Chambon's *Tell el-Far'ah I: L'âge du fer. Bulletin of the American Schools of Oriental Research*. 267: 84–6.

McCowan, C.C. 1947. *Tell en-Nasbeh I, Archaeological and Historical Results*. Berkeley and New Haven: The Palestine Institute of Pacific School of Religion and The American Schools of Oriental Research.

Milik, J.T. 1956. An Unpublished Arrow-head with Phoenician Inscription of the 11th–10th Century B.C. *Bulletin of the American Schools of Oriental Research*. 143: 3–6.

Millard, A.R. 1988a. The Bevel Rim Bowls: Their Purpose and Significance. *Iraq*. 50: 49–57.

Millard, A.R. 1988b. King Solomon's Gold. Biblical Records in the Light of Antiquity. *Bulletin of the Society for Mesopotamian Studies*. 15: 5–11.

Millard, A.R. 1989. Does the Bible Exaggerate King Solomon's Golden Wealth? *Biblical Archaeology Review*. 15/3: 20–9, 31, 34.

Miller, J.M. and Hayes, J.H. 1986. *A History of Ancient Israel and Judah*. Philadelphia: Westminster.

Murdock, G.P. 1967. *Ethnographic Atlas*: a summary. *Ethnology*. 6: 109–236.

Murdock, G.P. and White, D. 1969. Standard Cross-Cultural Sample. *Ethnology*. 8(4).

Netzer, E. 1992. Domestic Architecture in the Iron Age. In *The Architecture of Ancient Israel from the Prehistoric to the Persian Periods* (eds A. Kempinski and R. Reich). Jerusalem: Israel Exploration Society, pp. 193–201.

Newman, K.S. 1983. *Law and Economic Organization: A Comparative Study of Preindustrial Societies*. Cambridge: Cambridge University Press.

Nicholas, I.M. 1987. The Function of Bevelled-Rim Bowls: A Case Study at the TUV Mound, Tal-e Malyan, Iran. *Paleorient*. 13/2: 61–72.

Nissen, H.J. 1973. Grabung in der Quadraten K/L XII in Uruk-Warka. *Baghdader Mitteilungen*. 5: 137.

Oates, D. 1968. *Studies in the Ancient History of Northern Iraq*. London: Oxford University Press for the British Academy.

Ogunremi, G.O.O. 1982. *Counting the Camels: The Economics of Transportation in Pre-Industrial Nigeria*. New York and Lagos: NOK Publishers (Nigeria).

Oren, E.D. 1992. Ashlar Masonry in the Western Negev in the Iron Age. *Eretz Israel*. 23 (the Biran Volume): 94–105, 149*–50*.

Parr, P.J. 1988. Pottery of the Late Second Millennium B.C. from North West Arabia and its Historical Implications. In *Araby the blest: Studies in Arabian Archaeology* (ed. D.T. Potts). Copenhagen: Carsten Niebuhr Institute of Ancient Near Eastern Studies, University of Copenhagen, Museum Tusculanum Press, pp. 73–89.

Parr, P.J. 1992. Qurayya. *The Anchor Bible Dictionary*: Vol. 5: 594–96. New York: Doubleday.

Parr, P.J., Harding, G.L. and Dayton, J.E. 1970. Preliminary Survey in N.W. Arabia, 1968. *Bulletin of the Institute of Archaeology, University of London*. 8–9: 219–41.

Pritchard, J.B. 1943. *Palestinian Figurines in Relation to Certain Goddesses Known Through Literature*. American Oriental Society Monograph 24. New Haven: American Oriental Society.

Pritchard, J.B. (ed.) 1969a. *The Ancient Near East in Pictures Relating to the Old Testament*, Second Edition with Supplement. Princeton: Princeton University Press.

Pritchard, J.B. (ed.) 1969b. *Ancient Near Eastern Texts Relating to the Old Testament*, Third Edition with Supplement. Princeton: Princeton University Press.

Redman, C.L. (ed.) 1978. *Social Archaeology: Beyond Subsistence and Dating*. New York: Academic Press.

Reese, D.S. 1983. Marine Shells. In *Ergebnisse der Ausgrabungen auf der Hirbet el-Msas (Tel Masos) 1972–1975. Abhandlungen des Deutschen Palästinavereins* (eds V. Fritz and A. Kempinski). Text and Plates. Wiesbaden: Harrassowitz, pp. 224–6.

Renfrew, C. and Bahn, P. 1991. *Archaeology: Theories, Methods, and Practice*. New York: Thames and Hudson.

Rosen, B. 1986. Subsistence Economy of Stratum II. In *'Izbet Sartah: An Early Iron Age Site near Rosh Ha'ayin, Israel. BAR International Series* 299 (ed. I. Finkelstein). Oxford: British Archaeological Reports, pp. 156–85.

Rosen, S.A. 1992. Nomads in Archaeology: A Response to Finkelstein and Perevoltsky. *Bulletin of the American Schools of Oriental Research*. 287: 75–88.

Rothenberg, B. 1988. *Researches in the Arabah 1959–1984, with Contributions by H.G. Bachmann, et al.* London: Institute for Archaeo-Metallurgical Studies.

Rothenberg, B. and Glass, J. 1983. The Midianite Pottery. In *Midian, Moab, and Edom: The History and Archaeology of Late Bronze and Iron Age Jordan and North-west Arabia* (eds J.F.A. Sawyer and D.J.A. Clines). Sheffield: JSOT Press, pp. 65–124.

Rowton, M.B. 1970. Chronology: II. Ancient Western Asia. In *Cambridge Ancient History, Third edition, Vol. I: 1. Prolegomena and Prehistory* (eds I.E.S. Edwards, C.J. Gadd and N.G.L. Hammond). Cambridge: Cambridge University Press, pp. 193–239.

Ryckmans, G. 1935. Inscriptions Sud-Arabes. Troisième série. *Le Muséon*. 48: 163–87.

Ryckmans, J. 1992. South Arabia, Religion of. *Anchor Bible Dictionary*, vol. 6: 171–6. New York: Doubleday.

Schmidt, K. 1982. Zur Verwendung der Mesopotamischen 'Glockentöpf'. *Archäologisches Korrespondenzblatt*. 12: 317–19.

Service, E.R. 1971. *Primitive Social Organization. An Evolutionary Perspective*. (Second edition). New York: Random House.

Shennan, S. 1988. *Quantifying Archaeology*. Edinburgh and San Diego: Edinburgh University and Academic Press.

Shiloh, Y. 1970. The Four-Room House – Its Situation and Function in the Israelite City. *Israel Exploration Journal*. 20: 180–90.

Shiloh, Y. 1979. *The Proto-Aeolic Capital and Israelite Ashlar Masonry. Qedem* 11. Jerusalem: Israel Exploration Society.

Shiloh, Y. 1987. The Casemate Wall, the Four Room House, and Early Planning in the Israelite City. *Bulletin of the American Schools of Oriental Research*. 268: 3–15.

Silver, M. 1983. *Prophets and Markets: The Political Economy of Ancient Israel*. Hingham MA: Kluwer-Nijhoff Publications.

Stager, L.E. 1976a. Agriculture. In *Interpreter's Dictionary of the Bible. Supplementary Volume*. Nashville: Abingdon, pp. 11–13.

Stager, L.E. 1976b. Farming in the Judean Desert during the Iron Age. *Bulletin of the American Schools of Oriental Research*. 221: 145–58.

Stager, L.E. 1985. The Archaeology of the Family in Ancient Israel. *Bulletin of the American Schools of Oriental Research*. 260: 1–35.

Stager, L.E. 1990. Shemer's Estate. *Bulletin of the American Schools of Oriental Research*. 277/78: 93–107.

Stern, E. 1973. Limestone Incense Altars. In *Beer-Sheba I: Excavations at Tel Beer-Sheba, 1969–1971 Seasons* Ed. Y. Aharoni). Tel Aviv: Tel Aviv University, Institute of Archaeology, pp. 52–3.

Stern, E. 1977. The Excavations at Tell Mevorakh and the late Phoenician Elements in the Architecture of Palestine. *Bulletin of the American Schools of Oriental Research*. 225: 17–27.

Stern, E. 1978. *Excavations at Tel Mevorakh (1973–76) Part One: From the Iron Age to the Roman Period. Qedem* 9. Jerusalem: Institute of Archaeology, Hebrew University.

Stone, E.C. 1987. *Nippur Neighborhoods. Studies in Oriental Civilization.* 44. Chicago: Oriental Institute of the University of Chicago.

Taylor, J.G. 1988. The Two Earliest Known Representations of Yahweh. In *Ascribe to the Lord: Biblical and other Studies in Memory of Peter C. Craigie. Journal for the Study of the Old Testament Supplement Series* 67 (eds L. Eslinger and G. Taylor). Sheffield: JSOT Press, pp. 557–66.

Tappy, R.L. 1992. *The Archaeology of Israelite Samaria. Volume 1.* Atlanta: Scholars Press.

Tufnell, O. 1953. *Lachish III: The Iron Age.* Oxford: Oxford University Press.

Ussishkin, D. 1978. Ecavations of Tel Lachish – 1973–1977, Preliminary Report. *Tel Aviv.* 5: 1–97.

Ussishkin, D. 1982. *The Conquest of Lachish by Sennacherib.* Tel Aviv: Tel Aviv University, The Institute of Archaeology.

Ussishkin, D. 1983. Excavations at Tel Lachish 1978–1983: Second Preliminary Report. *Tel Aviv.* 10: 97–185.

Ussishkin, D. 1988. The Date of the Judaean Shrine at Arad. *Israel Exploration Journal.* 38: 142–57.

Van Beek, G.W. and Jamme, A. 1970. The Authenticity of the Bethel Stamp Seal. *Bulletin of the American Schools of Oriental Research.* 199: 59–65.

de Vaux, Père R. 1955. Les fouilles de Tell el-Fâr'ah près Naplouse – Cinquième Campagne. *Revue Biblique.* 62: 541–89.

de Vaux, Père R. 1965. *Ancient Israel. Volume 1: Social Institutions. Volume 2: Religious Institutions.* New York: McGraw-Hill.

Veenhof, K.R. 1972. *Aspects of Old Assyrian Trade and its Terminology. Studia et Documenta ad Iura Orientis Antiqui Pertinentia.* 10. Leiden: E.J. Brill.

Watson, P.J. 1979. *Archaeological Ethnography in Western Iran. Viking Fund Publications in Anthropology.* 57. Tucson: Wenner-Gren Foundation for Anthropological Research Inc. and University of Arizona Press.

Watson, P.J., LeBlanc, S.A. and Redman, C.L. 1971. *Explanation in Archeology: An Explicitly Scientific Approach.* New York: Columbia University Press.

Whitelam, K.W. 1986. The Symbols of Power: Aspects of Royal Propaganda in the United Monarchy. *Biblical Archaeologist.* 49: 166–73.

Wilkinson, L. 1990a. *SYSTAT: The System for Statistics.* Evanston IL: SYSTAT, Inc.

Wilkinson, L. 1990b. *SYGRAPH: The System for Graphics.* Evanston IL: SYSTAT, Inc.

Wood, B.G. 1990. *The Sociology of Pottery in Ancient Palestine. The Ceramic Industry and the Diffusion of Ceramic Style in the Bronze and Iron Ages. Journal for the Study of the Old Testament Supplement Series* 103; *Journal for the study of the Old Testament/American Schools of Oriental Research Monographs* 4. Sheffield: Sheffield Academic Press.

Yadin, Y. 1965. Note on the Stratigraphy of Arad. *Israel Exploration Journal.* 15: 180.

Yadin, Y. 1969. An Inscribed South-Arabian Clay Stamp from Bethel? *Bulletin of the American Schools of Oriental Research.* 196: 37–45.

Yadin, Y. 1972. *Hazor, The head of all those Kingdoms, Joshua 11: 10. With a Chapter on Israelite Megiddo. Schweich Lectures of the British Academy* 1970. London: British Academy (Oxford University Press).

Yadin, Y. 1974. Notes and News: Megiddo. *Israel Exploration Journal.* 24: 275–6.

Yadin, Y., Aharoni, Y., Armiran, R., Dothan, T., Danayevsky, I. and Perrot, J. 1958. *Hazor I: An Account of the First Season of Excavations, 1955.* Jerusalem: Magnes.

Yadin, Y., Aharoni, Y., Armiran, R., Dothan, T., Danayevsky, I. and Perrot, J. 1960. *Hazor II: An Account of the Second Season of Exvacations, 1956.* Jerusalem: Magnes.

Yadin, Y., Aharoni, Y., Amiran, R., Ben-Tor, A., Dothan, M., Dothan, T., Dunayevsky, I., Geva, S. and Stern, E. 1989. *Hazor III-IV, Text* (ed. A. Ben-Tor and S. Geva). Jerusalem: Israel Exploration Society and The Hebrew University.

Yellin, J. and Grunneweg, J. 1989. Instrumental Neutron Activation Analysis and the Origin of Iron Age I Collared-rim Jars and Pithoi from Tell Dan. In *Recent Excavations in Israel: Studies in Iron Age Archaeology* (eds S. Gitin and W.G. Dever). Annual of the American School of Oriental Research 49. Winona Lake, IN: Eisenbrauns, pp. 125–41.

Zevit, Z. 1984. The Khirbet el-Qom Inscription Mentioning a Goddess. *Bulletin of the American Schools of Oriental Research.* 255: 39–47.

Zimhoni, O. 1985. The Iron Age Pottery of Tel 'Eton and its Relation to the Lachish, Tell Beit Mirsim and Arad Assemblages. *Tel Aviv.* 12: 63–90.

Chapter 23

Abujaber, R.S. 1989. *Pioneers Over Jordan: The Frontier of Settlement in Transjordan, 1850–1914.* London: I.B. Tauris and Co. Ltd.

Adams, R.McC. 1965. *Land Behind Baghdad: A History of Settlement on the Diyala Plains.* Chicago: The University of Chicago Press.

Adams, R.McC. 1974. The Mesopotamian Social Landscape: A View from the Frontier. In *Reconstructing Complex Societies* (ed. C.B. Moore). Supplement to the Bulletin of the American Schools of Oriental Research No. 20, pp. 1–20.

Adams, R.McC. 1978. Strategies of Maximization, Stability, and Resilience in Mesopotamian Society, Settlement and Agriculture. *Proceedings of the American Philosophical Society.* 22: 329–35.

Adams, R.McC. 1981. *Heartland of Cities.* Chicago: the University of Chicago Press.

Allison, N.E. 1977. A Case of Honor: Arab Christians in a Jordanian Town. Unpublished doctoral dissertation. Department of Anthropology, University of Georgia.

Alt, A. 1940. Emiter und Moabiter. *Palästina Jahrbuch.* 36: 29–43. Reprinted in A. Alt, *Kleine Schriften zur Geschichte des Volkes Israel I.* Munich: C.H. Beck, pp. 203–15.

Alt, A. 1967. The Settlement of the Israelites in Palestine. In *Essays on Old Testament History and Religion.* Reprint. Garden City, NY: Doubleday.

Antoun, R.T. 1972. *Arab Village: A Social Structural Study of a Transjordanian Peasant Community.* Bloomington: Indiana University Press.

Antoun, R.T. 1979. *Low-Key Politics: Local-Level Leadership and Change in the Middle East.* Albany, NY: State University of New York Press.

Asad, T. 1973. The Bedouin as a Military Force: Notes on Some Aspects of Power Relations Between Nomads and Sedentaries in Historical Perspective. In *The Desert and the Sown: Nomads in the Wider Society* (ed. C. Nelson). Berkeley, CA: University of California Institute of International Studies, pp. 61–73.

Awad, M. 1970. Living Conditions of Nomadic, Semi-Nomadic and Settled Tribal Groups. In *Readings in Arab Middle Eastern Societies and Cultures* (eds A.B. Lutfiyya and C.W. Churchill). The Hague, Netherlands: Mouton and Co., pp. 133–48.

Barth, F. 1961. *Nomads of South Persia.* Boston: Little, Brown, and Co.

Barth, F. 1973. A General Perspective on Nomad-Sedentary in the Middle East. In *Desert and the Sown: Nomads in the Wider Society* (ed. C. Nelson). Berkeley, CA: University of California Institute of International Studies, pp. 11–21.

Bartlett, J.R. 1989. *Edom and the Edomites.* Sheffield: Journal for the Study of the Old Testament Press.

Bartlett, J.R. 1992a. Edom. In *The Anchor Bible Dictionary, Vol II* (ed. D.N. Freedman). New York: Doubleday, pp. 287–95.

Bartlett, J.R. 1992b. Biblical Sources for the Early Iron Age in Edom. In *Early Edom and Moab: The Beginning of the Iron Age in Southern Jordan* (ed. P. Bienkowski). Sheffield: J.R. Collis, pp. 13–20.

Bates, D. and Rassam, A. 1983. *Peoples and Cultures of the Middle East.* Englewood Cliffs, NJ: Prentice-Hall.

Bennett, C. 1979. Excavations at the Citadel (al-Qal'ah), Amman, Jordan. *Annual of the Department of Antiquities of Jordan.* 23: 151–9; 161–70.

Bennett, C. 1982. Neo-Assyrian Influence in Transjordan. In *Studies in the History and Archaeology of Jordan I* (ed. A. Hadidi). Amman: Department of Antiquities, pp. 181–7.

Bienkowski, P. 1992a. The Beginning of the Iron Age in Southern Jordan: A Framework. In *Early Edom and Moab: The Beginning of the Iron*

Age in Southern Jordan (ed. P. Bienkowski). Sheffield: J.R. Collis, pp. 1–12.

Bienkowski, P. 1992b. The Date of Sedentary Occupation in Edom: Evidence from Umm el-Biyara, Tawilan and Buseirah. In *Early Edom and Moab: The Beginning of the Iron Age in Southern Jordan* (ed. P. Bienkowski). Sheffield: J.R. Collis, pp. 99–112.

Boling, R.G. 1988. *The Early Biblical Community in Transjordan*. Decatur, GA: Almond.

Bowersock, G.W. 1983. *Roman Arabia*. Cambridge: Harvard University Press.

Braudel, F. 1972. *The Mediterranean and the Mediterranean World in the Reign of Philip II*. Collins: London.

Brown, R. 1991. Ceramics from the Kerak Plateau. *Archaeological Survey of the Kerak Plateau* (ed. J.M. Miller). Atlanta: Scholars Press, pp. 169–280.

Campbell, E.F. and Wright, G.E. 1969. Tribal League Shrines in Amman and Shechem. *Biblical Archaeologist*. 32: 104–16.

Cohen, R. and Schlegel, A. 1968. The Tribe as a socio-political Unit: a Cross-cultural Examination. In *Essays on the Problem of Tribe* (ed. J. Helm). Seattle: University of Washington, pp. 120–49.

Cole, D.P. 1973. The Enmeshment of Nomads in Saudi Arabian Society: The Case of Al Murrah. In *The Desert and the Sown: Nomads in the Wider Society* (ed. C. Nelson). Berkeley, CA: University of California Institute of International Studies, pp. 113–28.

Coote, R. and Whitelam, K. 1987. *The Emergence of Early Israel in Historical Perspective*. Sheffield: Almond Press.

Crone, P. 1980. *Slaves on Horses: The Evolution of the Islamic Polity*. Cambridge: Cambridge University Press.

Dearman, A. 1992. Settlement Patterns and the Beginning of the Iron Age in Moab. In *Early Edom and Moab: The Beginning of the Iron Age in Southern Jordan* (ed. P. Bienkowski). Sheffield: J.R. Collis, pp. 65–76.

Dever, W.G. 1992. The Late Bronze–Early Iron I Horizon in Syria-Palestine: Egyptians, Canaanites, 'Sea Peoples', and Proto-Israelites. In *The Crisis Years: The 12th Century B.C. (From Beyond the Danube to the Tigris)* (eds W.A. Ward and M.S. Joukowsky). Dubuque, Iowa: Kendall/Hunt Pub., pp. 99–110.

Donner, F. 1981. *The Early Islamic Conquests*. Princeton: Princeton University Press.

Dornemann, R.H. 1982. The Beginning of the Iron Age in Transjordan. In *Studies in the History and Archaeology of Jordan*. Vol. 1 (ed. A. Hadidi). Amman: Department of Antiquities of Jordan, pp. 135–40.

Dornemann, R.H. 1983. *The Archaeology of the Transjordan*. Milwaukee, WI: Milwaukee Public Museum.

Dostal, W. 1985. *Eqalitat und Klassengesellshafr in Sudarabien: Anthropologische Untersuchungen zur sozialen Evolution*. Vienna.

Eickelman, D.F. 1989. *The Middle East: An Anthropological Approach* (2nd edn). Englewood Cliffs, NJ: Prentice-Hall.

Falconer, Steve. 1987. Heartland of Villages: Reconsidering Early Urbanism in the Southern Levant. Unpublished doctoral dissertation, University of Arizona.

Finkelstein, I. 1988. *The Archaeology of the Israelite Settlement*. Israel Exploration Society: Jerusalem.

Finkelstein, I. 1992a. Edom in the Iron I. *Levant*. 24: 159–66.

Finkelstein, I. 1992b. Stratigraphy, Pottery and Parallels: A Reply to Bienkowski. *Levant*. 24: 171–2.

Finkelstein, I. and Perevolotsky, A. 1990. Processes of Sedentarization and Nomadization in the History of Sinai and the Negev. *Bulletin of the American Schools of Oriental Research*. 279: 67–88.

Franken, H.J. 1969. *Excavations at Deir Alla, a Stratigraphical and Analytical Study of the Early Iron Age Pottery*. Leiden: E.J. Brill.

Franken, H.J. and Ibrahim, M.M. 1977–78. Two Seasons of Excavations at Deir 'Alla, 1976–1978. *Annual of the Department of Antiquities of Jordan*. 22: 57–79.

Franken, H.J. and Power, W.J.A. 1971. Glueck's *Explorations in Eastern Palestine* in the Light of Recent Evidence. *Vetus Testamentum*. 21: 119.

Frick, F.S. 1985. *The Formation of the State in Ancient Israel*. Decatur, GA: Almond.

Fried, M. 1967. *The Evolution of Political Society*. New York: Random House.

Fried, M. 1975. *The Notion of Tribe*. Menlo Park: Cummings.

Geraty, L.T. and LaBianca, Ø.S. 1985. The Local Environment and Human Food Procuring Strategies in Jordan: The Case of Tell Hesban

and Its Surrounding Region. In *Studies in the History and Archaeology of Jordan II* (ed. A. Hadidi). Amman: Department of Antiquities, pp. 323–30.

Geraty, L.T. and Willis, L. 1986. Archaeological Research in Transjordan. In *The Archaeology of Jordan and Other Studies* (eds Lawrence T. Geraty and Larry G. Herr). Berrien Springs, MI: Andrews University Press, pp. 3–72.

Geraty, L.T., Herr, L.G., LaBianca, Ø.S. and Younker, R.W. 1986. Madaba Plains Project: A Preliminary Report of the 1984 Season at Tell el-'Umeiri and Vicinity. In *Bulletin of the American Schools of Oriental Research*, Supplement 24: 117–24.

Geraty, L.T., Herr, L.G. and LaBianca, Ø.S. 1988. The Madaba Plains Project: A Preliminary Report of the 1987 Season at Tell el-'Umeiri and Vicinity. *Andrews University Seminary Studies*.

Geraty, L.T. 1990a. Madaba Plains Project: A Preliminary Report of the 1987 Season at Tell El-'Umeiri and Vicinity. *Bulletin of the American Schools of Oriental Research*, Supplement 26: 59–88.

Geraty, L.T. 1990b. A Preliminary Report of the 1987 Season at Tell el-'Umeiri and Vicinity. *Annual of the Department of Antiquities of Jordan XXXIII*: 145–76.

Gerstenblith, P. 1977. The Levant in the Middle Bronze I and its Connections with Mesopotamia and Anatolia: A Study in Trade and Settlement Patterns. Unpublished doctoral dissertation, Department of Near Eastern Languages and Cultures, Harvard University.

Glubb, J.B. 1938. The Economic Situation of the Trans-Jordan Tribes. *Journal of the Royal Central Asian Society*. 25: 448–59.

Glueck, N. 1934. Explorations in Eastern Palestine I. *Annual of the American Schools of Oriental Research*. 14.

Glueck, N. 1935. Explorations in Eastern Palestine II. *Annual of the American Schools of Oriental Research*. 15.

Glueck, N. 1937. Explorations in the Land of Ammon. *Bulletin of the American Schools of Oriental Research*. 68: 13–21.

Glueck, N. 1939. Explorations in Eastern Palestine III. *Annual of the American Schools of Oriental Research*. 18–19.

Glueck, N. 1971. *The Other Side of the Jordan*. Cambridge, MA: The American Schools of Oriental Research.

Gottwald, N.K. 1979. *The Tribes of Yahweh. A Sociology of the Religion of Liberated Israel 1250–1050 B.C.E.* Maryknoll, NY: Orbis.

Gubser, P. 1984. *Jordan: Crossroads of Middle Eastern Events*. Boulder, CO: Westview Press.

Gulick, J. 1971. The Arab Levant. In *The Central Middle East* (ed. L. Sweet). New Haven: HRAF Press, pp. 79–171.

Hart, S. 1992. Iron Age Settlement in the Land of Edom. In *Early Edom and Moab: The Beginning of the Iron Age in Southern Jordan* (ed. P. Bienkowski). Sheffield: J.R. Collis, pp. 93–8.

Hennessy, J. 1966. Excavation of a Late Bronze Age Temple at Amman. *Palestine Exploration Quarterly*. 98: 155–62.

Herr, L.G. 1976. The Amman Airport Excavations 1976. *Annual of the Department of Antiquities of Jordan*. 21: 109–11.

Herr, L.G. 1992. Shifts in Settlement Patterns of Late Bronze and Iron Age Ammon. In *Studies in the History and Archaeology of Jordan IV* (eds M. Zaghloul et al.). Amman: Department of Antiquities of Jordan, pp. 175–7.

Herr, L.G., Geraty, L.T., LaBianca, Ø.S. and Younker, R.W. 1990. The Madaba Plains Project: Three Seasons of Excavation at Tell el-'Umeiri and Vicinity, Jordan. *Echoes do Monde Classique/Classical Views*. 34 n.s. 9: 129–43.

Hiatt, J.M. 1984. Between Desert and Town: A Case Study of Encapsulation and Sedentarization Among Jordanian Bedouin. Unpublished doctoral dissertation. Department of Anthropology, University of Pennsylvania.

Hole, F. 1978. Pastoral nomadism in Western Iran. In *Explorations in Ethnoarchaeology* (ed. R.A. Gould). Albuquerque NM: University of New Mexico, pp. 127–67.

Homes-Fredericq, D. 1992. Late Bronze and Iron Age Evidence from Lehun in Moab. In *Early Edom and Moab: The Beginning of the Iron Age in Southern Jordan* (ed. P. Bienkowski). Sheffield: J.R. Collis, pp. 187–202.

Hopkins, D. 1985. *The Highlands of Canaan: Agricultural Life in the Early Iron Age*. Series: Social World of Biblical Antiquity 3. Decatur, GA: Almond.

Howayej, B. Abu 1973. *Agricultural Atlas of Jordan*. Amman, Jordan: Ministry of Agriculture, Hashemite Kingdom of Jordan.

Hutteroth, W. 1975. The Pattern of Settlement in Palestine in the Sixteenth Century. In *Studies on Palestine during the Ottoman Period* (ed. M. Ma'oz). Jerusalem: Magnes Press, pp. 2–22.

Ibach, R. 1978. An Intensive Surface Survey at Jalul. *Andrews University Seminary Studies.* 16: 215–22.

Ibach, R. 1987. *Hesban 5: The Regional Survey.* Berrien Springs, MI: Institute of Archaeology, Andrews University.

Ibrahim, M. 1972. Archaeological Excavations at Sahab, 1972. *Annual of the Department of Antiquities of Jordan.* 17: 23–36.

Ibrahim, M. 1974. Second Season of Excavation at Sahab, 1973. *Annual of the Department of Antiquities of Jordan.* 19: 55–61; 187–98.

Ibrahim, M. 1975. Third Season of Excavation at Sahab, 1975. *Annual of the Department of Antiquities of Jordan.* 20: 69–82; 169–78.

Ibrahim, M. 1987. Sahab and its Foreign Relations. In *Studies in the History and Archaeology of Jordan III.* Amman: Department of Antiquities, pp. 73–81.

Jackson, K.P. 1989. The Language of the Mesha' Inscription. In *Studies in the Mesha Inscription and Moab* (ed. A. Dearman). Atlanta, Georgia: Scholars Press, pp. 96–130.

Johnson, D.L. 1969. *The Nature of Nomadism.* The University of Chicago: Department of Geography Research Paper No. 118.

Johnson, D.L. 1973. *Jabal al-Akhdar, Cyrenaica: An Historical Geography of Settlement and Livelihood.* University of Chicago: Department of Geography Research Paper No. 148.

Kamp, K. and Yoffee, N. 1980. Ethnicity in Ancient Western Asia During the Early Second Millennium B.C.: Archaeological Assessments and Ethnoarchaeological Prospectives. *Bulletin of the American Schools of Oriental Research.* 237: 85–104.

Khuri, F. 1980. *Tribe and State in Bahrain.* Publications of the Center for Middle Eastern Studies, No. 14, Chicago, Ill: University of Chicago Press.

Kitchen, K.A. 1992. The Egyptian Evidence on Ancient Jordan. In *Early Edom and Moab: The Beginning of the Iron Age in Southern Jordan* (ed. P. Bienkowski). Sheffield: J.R. Collis, pp. 21–34.

Kletter, R. 1991. The Rujm el-Malfuf Buildings and the Assyrian Vassal State of Ammon. *Bulletin of the American Schools of Oriental Research.* 284: 33–50.

Knauf, E.A. 1984. Abel Keramim. *Zeitschrift des Deutschen Palastina-Vereins.* 100: 119–21.

Knauf, E.A. 1988. *Midian: Untersuchungen zur Geschischte Palastinas und Nordarabiens am ende des 2. Jahrtausends v. Chr.* Wiesbaden: Harrassowitz.

Knauf, E.A. 1992. The Cultural Impact of Secondary State Formation: The Cases of the Edomites and Moabites. In *Early Edom and Moab: The Beginning of the Iron Age in Southern Jordan* (ed. P. Bienkowski). Sheffield: J.R. Collis, pp. 47–54.

Kohler-Rollefson, I. 1987. Ethnoarchaeological Research into the Origins of Pastoralism. *Annual of the Department of Antiquities of Jordan.* 31: 535–9.

Koucky, A. 1987. Survey of the Limes Zone. In *The Roman Frontier in Central Jordan Vol. 1* (ed. S.T. Parker). BAR International Series 340, pp. 41–106.

Kupper, J.R. 1959. La Rôle des nomades dans l'histoire de la mésopotamie ancienne. *Journal of the Economic and Social History of the Orient.* 2: 113–27.

LaBianca, Ø.S. 1976. Tell Hesban 1974: The Village of Hesban, An Ethnographic Preliminary Report. *Andrews University Seminary Studies.* 11: 133–44.

LaBianca, Ø.S. 1989. Intensification of the Food System in Central Transjordan During the Ammonite Period. *Andrews University Seminary Studies.* 27: 169–78.

LaBianca, Ø.S. 1990. *Hesban 1: Sedentarization and Nomadization.* Berrien Springs, MI: Andrews University Press.

LaBianca, Ø.S. 1991. Food Systems Research: An Overview and a Case Study from Madaba Plains, Jordan. *Food and Foodways.* 4(3+4): 221–35.

Lancaster, W. 1981. *Changing Cultures: The Rwala Bedouin Today.* New York: Cambridge University Press.

Landes, G.M. 1956. A History of the Ammonites. Baltimore, MD: Unpublished doctoral dissertation, Johns Hopkins University.

Landes, G.M. 1961. The Material Civilization of the Ammonites. *Biblical Archaeologist.* 24/3: 66–86.

Leonard, A. Jr. 1979. Kataret Es-Samra: A Late Bronze Age Cemetery in Transjordan? *Bulletin of the American Schools of Oriental Research.* 234: 53–65.

Leonard, A. Jr. 1981. Kataret es-Samra: A Late Bronze Age Cemetery in Transjordan. *Annual of the Department of Antiquities in Jordan.* 25: 179–95.

Linder, M. 1992. Edom Outside the Famous Excavations: Evidence from Surveys in the Greater Petra Area. In *Early Edom and Moab: The Beginning of the Iron Age in Southern Jordan* (ed. P. Bienkowski). Sheffield: J.R. Collis, pp. 143–66.

Luke, J.T. 1965. Pastoralism and Politics in the Mari Period: A Reexamination of the Character and Political Significance of the Major West Semitic Tribal Groups on the Middle Euphrates, *ca.* 1828–1758 B.C. Unpublished doctoral dissertation, University of Michigan.

Lyall, M.D. 1969. The Bedouin of Southeast Jordan. Unpublished doctoral dissertation. University of New York.

Ma'ayeh, F.S. 1960. Recent Archaeological Discoveries in Jordan. *Annual of the Department of Antiquities of Jordan.* 4–5: 114–16.

MacDonald, B. 1988. *The Wadi el Hasa Archaeological Survey 1979–1983, West-Central Jordan.* Waterloo, Ontario: Wilfrid Laurier University Press.

MacDonald, B. 1992a. Archaeology of Edom. In *The Anchor Bible Dictionary, Vol II* (ed. D.N. Freedman). New York: Doubleday, pp. 295–301.

MacDonald, B. 1992b. Evidence from the Wadi el-Hasa and Southern Ghor and North-east Arabah Archaeological Surveys. In *Early Edom and Moab: The Beginning of the Iron Age in Southern Jordan* (ed. P. Bienkowski). Sheffield: J.R. Collis, pp. 113–42.

McGovern, P. 1980. Explorations in the Umm ad-Dananir Region of the Baq'ah Valley. *Annual of the Department of Antiquities of Jordan.* 24: 55–67.

McGovern, P. 1981. The Beq'ah Valley Project. *Annual of the Department of Antiquities of Jordan.* 25: 356–7.

McGovern, P. 1986. *The Late Bronze Age and Early Iron Ages of Central Transjordan: The Beq'ah Valley Project, 1977–1981.* University of Pennsylvania: The University Museum.

McGovern, P. 1987. Central Transjordan in the Late Bronze and Early Iron Ages: An alternate Hypothesis of Socio-Economic Transformation and Collapse. In *Studies in the History and Archaeology of Jordan III* (ed. A. Hadidi). Amman, Jordan: Department of Antiquities of Jordan, pp. 267–73.

Marx, E. 1967. *Bedouin of the Negev.* Manchester: Manchester University Press.

Marx, E. 1973. The Tribe as a Unit of Subsistence: Nomadic Pastoralism in the Middle East. *American Anthropologist.* 79: 343–65.

Mattingley, G.L. 1983. The Exodus-Conquest and the Archaeology of Transjordan: New Light on an Old Problem. *Grace Theological Journal.* 4: 245–62.

Mattingley, G.L. 1992. The Culture-Historical Approach and Moabite Origins. In *Early Edom and Moab: The Beginning of the Iron Age in Southern Jordan* (ed. P. Bienkowski). Sheffield: J.R. Collis, pp. 55–64.

Mendenhall, G. 1962. The Hebrew Conquest of Palestine. *Biblical Archaeologist.* 25: 66–87.

Mendenhall, G. 1973. *The Tenth Generation: The Origins of Biblical Tradition.* Baltimore: Johns Hopkins.

Mendenhall, G. 1983. Ancient Israel's Hyphenated History. In *Palestine In Transition* (eds D.N. Freedman and D.F. Graf). Sheffield: Almond Press, pp. 95–103.

Millard, A. 1992. Assyrian Involvement in Edom. In *Early Edom and Moab: The Beginning of the Iron Age in Southern Jordan* (ed. P. Bienkowski). Sheffield: J.R. Collis, pp. 35–40.

Miller, J.M. 1979. Archaeological Survey of Central Moab: 1978. *Bulletin of the American Schools of Oriental Research.* 234: 43–52.

Miller, J.M. (ed.) 1991. *Archaeological Survey of the Kerak Plateau.* Atlanta, GA: American Schools of Oriental Research/Scholars Press.

Miller, J.M. 1992a. Moab. In *The Anchor Bible Dictionary, Vol IV* (ed. D.N. Freedman). New York: Doubleday, pp. 882–93.

Miller, J.M. 1992b. Early Monarchy in Moab? In *Early Edom and Moab: The Beginning of the Iron Age in Southern Jordan* (ed. P. Bienkowski). Sheffield: J.R. Collis, pp. 77–92.

Mittmann, S. 1970. *Betrage zur Siedlungs- und Territorialgeschichte des nordlischen Ostjordanlandes.* Wiesbaden: Otto Harrassowitz.

Noth, M. 1935. Die israelitischen Siedlungsgebiete im Ostjordenland. *Zeitschrift des Deutschen Palastina-Vereins.* 58: 230–55.

Noth, M. 1941. Die israelitischen Siedlungsgebiete im Ostjordenland. *Palastinajahrbuch des Deutschen Evangelischen Instituts fur Altertumswissenschafr des Heiligen Landes zu Jerusalem.* 37: 66.

Noth, M. 1960. *The History of Israel.* Second edn (Tr. P.R. Ackroyd). New York: Harper and Row.

Oakeshott, M.F. 1983. The Edomite Pottery. In *Midian, Moab, and Edom: The History and Archaeology of Late Bronze and Iron Age Jordan and North-West Arabia* (eds J.F.A. Sawyer and D.J.A. Clines). Sheffield: JSOT Press, pp. 53–63.

Oded, B. 1970. Observation on Methods of Assyrian Rule in Transjordania after the Palestinian Campaign of Tiglath-Pileser III. *Journal of Near Eastern Studies.* 29: 177–86.

Oded, B. 1979. Neighbors on the East. In *The Age of the Monarchies: Political History* (ed. A. Malamat). Jerusalem: Masada Press Ltd. pp. 247–75; 358–63.

Parker,. S.T. 1986. *Romans and Saracens: A History of the Arabian Frontier.* ASOR Dissertation Series No. 6. Winona Lake, IN: ASOR.

Peake, F.G. 1958. *History and Tribes of Jordan.* Coral Gables, FL: University of Miami Press.

Peters, E. 1970. The Proliferation of Segments in the Lineage of the Bedouin of Cyrenaica [Libya]. In *Peoples and Cultures of the Middle East. Volume 1: Depth and Diversity* (ed. L.E. Sweet). Garden City, New York: The Natural History Press, pp. 361–98.

Posener, G. 1940. *Princes et Pays d'Asie et de Nubie.* Brussels.

Prag, K. 1985. Ancient and Modern Pastoral Migration in the Levant. *Levant.* 17: 81–8.

Prag, K. 1987. Decorative Architecture in Ammon, Moab, and Judah. *Levant.* 19: 121–7.

Pritchard, J.B. 1985. *Tell Es-Sa'idiyeh: Excavations on the Tell, 1964–1966.* Philadelphia, Penn: University of Pennsylvania.

Redford, D.B. 1982. A Bronze Age Itinerary in Transjordan (Nos. 89–101 of Thutmose III's List of Asiatic Toponyms). *Journal for the Society of Egyptian Archaeology.* 12/2: 55–74.

Reifenberg, A. 1955. *The Struggle Between the Desert and the Sown.* Jerusalem: Government Press.

Renfrew, C. and Bahn, P. 1991. *Archaeology: Theories, Methods and Practice.* New York, NY: Thames and Hudson.

Rostovtzeff, M. 1928. Syria and the East. In *The Cambridge Ancient History: Volume VII, The Hellenistic Monarchies and the Rise of Rome* (eds S.A. Cook, F.E. Adcock and M.P. Charlesworth). Cambridge, University Press, pp. 155–96.

Rostovtzeff, M. 1932. *Caravan Cities.* Oxford: Clarendon Press.

Rowton, M.B. 1973a. Urban Autonomy in the Nomadic Environment. *Journal of Near Eastern Studies.* 32: 201–15.

Rowton, M.B. 1973b. Autonomy and Nomadism in Western Asia. *Orientalia.* 42: 247–58.

Rowton, M.B. 1974. Enclosed Nomadism. *Journal of the Economic and Social History of the Orient.* 17: 1–30.

Rowton, M.B. 1976a. Dimorphic Structure and the Problem of the 'Apiru-'Ibrim. *Journal of Near Eastern Studies.* 35: 13–20.

Rowton, M.B. 1976b. Dimorphic Structure and Topology. *Oreins Antiquis* 15: 17–31.

Rowton, M.B. 1976c. Dimorphic Structure and the Tribal Elite. *Studia Instituti Anthropos.* 28: 219–57.

Rowton, M.B. 1977. Dimorphic Structure and the Parasocial Element. *Journal of Near Eastern Studies.* 36: 181–98.

Russel, M.B. 1989. Hesban during the Arab Period: A.D. 635 to the Present. In *Historical Foundations. Hesban 3* (eds L.T. Geraty and L.G. Running). Berrien Springs, MI: Andrews University Press, pp. 25–35.

Sahlins, M. 1968. *Tribesmen.* Englewood Cliffs, NJ: Prentice-Hall.

Salibi, K.S. 1977. *Syria Under Islam: Empire on Trial 634–1097.* Delmar, NY: Caravan Books.

Sauer, J.A. 1982. Prospects for Archaeology in Jordan and Syria. *Biblical Archaeology.* 45/2: 73–84.

Sauer, J.A. 1985. Ammon, Moab, and Edom. In *Biblical Archaeology Today: Proceedings of the International Congress on Biblical Archaeology, Jerusalem, April 1984.* Jerusalem: Israel Exploration Society, 206–14.

Sauer, J.A. 1986. Transjordan in the Bronze and Iron Ages: A Critique of Glueck's Synthesis. *Bulletin of the American Schools of Oriental Research.* 263: 1–26.

Service, E. 1962. *Primitive Social Organization.* New York: Random House.

Service, E. 1975. *Origins of the State and Civilization: The Process of Cultural Evolution.* New York: W.W. Norton and Company.

Shahid, I. 1984a. *Rome and the Arabs: A Prolegomenon to the Study of Byzantium and the Arabs.* Washington, DC: Dumbarton Oaks.

Shahid, I. 1984b. *Byzantium and the Arabs in the Fourth Century.* Washington, DC: Dumbarton Oaks.

Shami, S.K. 1984. Ethnicity and Leadership: The Circassians in Jordan. Unpublished doctoral dissertation. Department of Anthropology, University of California, Berkeley.

Shehadeh, N. 1985. The Climate of Jordan in the Past and Present. In *Studies in the History and Archaeology of Jordan II.* Amman, Jordan: Department of Antiquities of Jordan, pp. 25–37.

Stager, L.E. 1985. The Archaeology of the Family in Ancient Israel. *Bulletin of the American Schools of Oriental Research.* 260: 1–35.

Swidler, W.W. 1973. Adaptive Processes Regulating Nomad-Sedentary Interaction in the Middle East. In *The Desert and the Sown: Nomads in the Wider Society* (ed. C. Nelson). Berkeley, CA: University of California Institute of International Studies, pp. 23–41.

Thompson, H.O. 1972. The 1972 Excavation of Khirbet el-Hajjar. *Annual of the Department of Antiquities of Jordan.* 17: 47–72.

Thompson, H.O. 1977. The Ammonite Remains at Khirber al-Hajjar. *Bulletin of the American Schools of Oriental Research.* 227: 27–34.

Thompson, H.O. 1989. *Archaeology in Jordan.* American University Studies: Series 9, History, Volume 55. New York: Peter Lang.

Tushingham, A.D. 1972. The Excavations at Dibon (Dhibân) in Moab: The Third Campaign 1952–53. *Annual of the American Schools of Oriental Research.* 40.

Van Der Kooij, G. and Ibrahim, M. 1989. *Picking Up the Threads. . .A Continuing Review of Excavations at Deir Alla, Jordan.* Leiden: University of Leiden.

Van Zyl, A.H. 1960. *The Moabites.* Pretoria Oriental Series, Vol. 3 (ed. A. van Selms). Leiden: E.J. Brill.

Wahlin, L. 1992. *Back to Settled Life? An Historical Geographical Study of Changing Living Conditions in the 'Allan Area of Jordan, 1867–1980.* Stockholm, Sweden: Stockholm University.

Ward, W.A. 1966. Scarabs, Seals and Cylinders from Two Tombs at Amman. *Annual of the Department of Antiquities of Jordan.* XI: 5–18.

Weippert, M. 1971. Edom: Studien und Materialien zur Geschichte der Edomiter auf Grund schriftlicher und archaologisher Quellen. Unpublished dissertation and Habilitationsschrift, University of Tubingen.

Weippert, M. 1979. The Israelite 'Conquest' and the Evidence from Transjordan. In *Symposia* (ed. F.M. Cross). Cambridge, MA: American Schools of Oriental Research, pp. 15–34.

Weippert, M. 1982. Remarks on the History of Settlement in Southern Jordan during the Early Iron Age. In *Studies in the History and Archaeology of Jordan I* (ed. A. Hadidi). Amman: Department of Antiquities of Jordan, pp. 153–62.

Weippert, M. 1987. The Relations of the States East of Jordan. In *Studies in the History and Archaeology of Jordan III* (ed. B A. Hadidi). Amman: Department of Antiquities, pp. 97–105.

Wimmer, D. 1987a. The Excavations at Tell Safut. In *Studies in the History and Archaeology of Jordan III* (ed. A. Hadidi). Amman, Jordan: Department of Antiquities of Jordan, pp. 279–82.

Wimmer, D. 1987b. Tell Safut Excavations, 1982–1985 Preliminary Report. *Annual of the Department of Antiquities of Jordan.* 31: 159–74.

Winnett, F.V. and Reed, W.L. 1964. The Excavations at Dibon (Dhibân) in Moab. *Annual of the American Schools of Oriental Research.* 36–37.

Worschech, U.F. 1984. Archäologischer Survey der nördlichen Ard el-Kerak 1984. *Liber Annuus.* 34: 445–7.

Worschech, U.F. 1985a. *Northwest Ard el Kerak 1983 and 1984: A Preliminary Report.* Munich: Manfred Görg.

Worschech, U.F. 1985b. Preliminary Report on the Third Survey Season in the Northwest Ard el-Kerak. *Annual of the Department of Antiquities of Jordan.* 29: 161–73.

Worschech, U.F. 1985c. Die Sehburgen am Wadi Ibn Hammad: Eine Studie zu einer Gruppe von Bauten im antiken Moab. *Biblishe Notizen*. 28: 66–88.

Worschech, U.F. 1990. *Die Beziehungen Moabs zu Israel und Ägypten in der Eisenzeit: Seidlungsarchäologische und siedlungshistorische Untersuchungen im Kernland Moabs (Ard el-Kerak)*. Wiesbaden: Harrassowitz.

Worschech, U.F., Rosenthal, U. and Zayadine, F. 1986. The Fourth Survey Season in the Northwest Ard el-Kerak, and Soundings at Balu' 1986. *Annual of the Department of Antiquities of Jordan*. 30: 285–309.

Wright, G.H.R. 1966. The Bronze Age Temple at Amman. Zeitschrift fur die altestimentliche Wissenshaft 78: 350–57.

Yadin, Y. 1979. The Transition from a Semi-nomadic to a Sedentary Society in the Twelfth Century B.C.E. In *Symposia Celebrating the Seventy-fifth Anniversary of the Founding of the American Schools of Oriental Research* (ed. F.M. Cross). Cambridge, MA: American Schools of Oriental Research, pp. 57–68.

Yassine, K. 1988. *The Archaeology of Jordan: Essays and Reports*. Amman, Jordan: Dept of Archaeology, University of Jordan.

Younker, R.W. 1985. Israel, Judah, and Ammon and the Motifs on the Baalis Seal from Tell el-'Umeiri. *Biblical Archaeologist*. 48/3: 173–80.

Younker, R.W. 1990a. Present and Past Plant Communities of the Tell el-'Umeiri Region. In *Madaba Plains Project 1: The 1984 Season at Tell el-'Umeiri and Vicinity and Subsequent Studies* (eds L.T. Geraty, L.G. Herr, Ø.S. LaBianca and R.W. Younker). Berrien Springs, MI: Andrews University, pp. 32–40.

Younker, R.W. 1990b. Towers in the Region Surrounding Tell Umeiri. In *Madaba Plains Project 1: The 1984 Season at Tell el-'Umeiri and vicinity and Subsequent Studies* (eds L.T. Geraty, L.G. Herr, Ø.S. LaBianca and R.W. Younker). Berrien Springs, MI: Andrews University, pp. 195–8.

Younker, R.W. 1993. The Ammonites. In *Peoples of the Old Testament*. Grand Rapids, MI: Baker Books.

Younker, R.W. 1994. Ammonites. In *Peoples of the Old Testament World* (eds A.J. Hoerth, G.L. Mattingly and E.M. Yamauchi). Grand Rapids, MI: Baker Books, pp. 293–316.

Younker, R.W., Geraty, L.T., Herr, L.G. and LaBianca, Ø.S. 1990. A Preliminary Report of the 1989 Season of the Madaba Plains Project: The Regional Survey and Excavations at Al Dreijat, Tell Jawa, and Tell el-'Umeiri. *Andrews University Seminary Studies*. 28/1: 5–52.

Younker, R.W., Geraty, L.T., Herr, L.G. and LaBianca, Ø.S. 1993. The Joint Madaba Plains Project: A Preliminary Report of the 1992 Season, including the Regional Survey and Excavations at Tell Jalul and Tell el'Umeiri (June 16–July 31, 1992). *Andrews University Seminary Studies*. 31/3: 205–38.

Ziadeh, N.A. 1953. *Urban Life in Syria under the Early Mamluks*. Beirut: American University of Beirut. Oriental Series.

Chapter 24

Ackerman, S. 1993. The Queen Mother and the Cult in Ancient Israel. *Journal of Biblical Literature* 112/3: 384–401.

Aharoni, Y. and Amiran, R. 1958. A New Scheme for the Sub-Division of the Iron Age in Palestine. *Israel Exploration Journal*. 8: 171–84.

Ahlström, G.W. 1993. *The History of Palestine from the Paleolithic Period to Alexander's Conquest*. Sheffield: Journal of the Study of the Old Testament (JSOT) Press.

Avigad, N. 1953. The Epigraph of a Royal Steward from Siloam Village. *Israel Exploration Journal*. 3: 137–52.

Avigad, N. 1986. *Hebrew Bullae from the Time of Jeremiah*. Jerusalem: Israel Exploration Society.

Barkay, G. 1992. The Iron Age II–III. In *The Archaeology of Ancient Israel* (ed. A. Ben-Tor). New Haven: Yale University Press, pp. 302–73.

Barnett, R.D. 1982. *Ancient Ivories in the Middle East*. Qedem 14. Jerusalem: The Hebrew University of Jerusalem.

Bartlett, J.R. 1989. *Edom and the Edomites*. Sheffield: Journal of the Study of the Old Testament (JSOT) Press.

Ben-Tor, A. (ed.) 1992. *The Archaeology of Ancient Israel*. New Haven: Yale University Press.

Bienkowski, P. (ed.) 1992. *Early Edom and Moab. The Beginning of the Iron Age in Southern Jordan*. Sheffield: Sheffield University Press.

Biran, A. and Naveh, J. 1993. An Aramaic Stele Fragment from Tel Dan. *Israel Exploration Journal*. 43: 81–98.

Bloch-Smith, E. 1992. *Judahite Burial Practices and Beliefs about the Dead*. Sheffield: Journal of the Study of the Old Testament (JSOT) Press.

Coote, R.B. and Whitelam, J.W. 1987. *The Emergence of Early Israel in Historical Perspective*. Sheffield: Almond Press.

Crowfoot, J.W. and Crowfoot, J.M. 1938. *Early Ivories from Samaria*. London: Palestine Exploration Fund.

Davies, P.R. 1992. *In Search of 'Ancient Israel'*. Sheffield: Journal of the Study of the Old Testament (JSOT) Press.

Dever, W.G. 1969/1970. Iron Age Epigraphic Material from the Area of Khirbet el-Kom. *Hebrew Union College Annual*. 40–41: 139–204.

Dever, W.G. 1985. Syro-Palestinian and Biblical Archaeology. In *The Hebrew Bible and Its Modern Interpreters* (eds D.A. Knight and G.M. Tucker). Chico, CA: Scholars Press, pp. 31–74.

Dever, W.G. 1987. The Middle Bronze Age: Zenith of the Urban Canaanite Era. *Biblical Archaeologist*. 50: 148–77.

Dever, W.G. 1988. Impact of the 'New Archaeology'. In *Benchmarks in Time and Culture. An Introduction to Palestinian Archaeology* (eds J.F. Drinkard, G.L. Mattingly and J.M. Miller). Atlanta: Scholars Press, pp. 337–52.

Dever, W.G. 1991a. Archaeology, Material Culture and the Early Monarchical Period in Israel. In *The Fabric of History, Text, Artifact and Israel's Past* (ed. D.V. Edelman). Sheffield: Journal of the Study of the Old Testament (JSOT) Press, pp. 103–15.

Dever, W.G. 1991b. Archaeological Data on the Israelite Settlement: A Review of Two Recent Works. *Bulletin of the American Schools of Oriental Research*. 284: 77–90.

Dever, W.G. 1993. Cultural Continuity, Ethnicity in the Archaeological Record, and the Question of Israelite Origins. *Eretz-Israel*. 24 (the Avraham Malamat volume): 22–33.

Dever, W.G. 1994a. From Tribe to Nation: State Formation Processes in Ancient Israel. *Nuove fondazioni nel Vicino Oriente antico: realita ed ideologia* (ed. S. Mazzoni). Pisa: University of Pisa.

Dever, W.G. 1994b. Archaeology and the Current Crisis in Israelite Historiography. *Eretz-Israel*. 25 (the Yosef Aviram volume)

Dever, W.G. 1994c. Settlement Patterns and Chronology in Middle Bronze Age Palestine. *Middle Bronze Age and Hyksos Culture: Cultural Interconnections in the Ancient Near East* (ed. E. Oren).

Dever, W.G. 1994d. Review of E. Bloch-Smith, *Judahite Burial Practices and Beliefs about the Dead* (Sheffield: Journal of the Study of the Old Testament (JSOT) Press. 1992). Jerusalem: Israel Exploration Society.

Dornemann, R.H. 1983. *The Archaeology of the Transjordan in the Bronze and Iron Ages*. Milwaukee: Milwaukee Public Museum.

EAEHL Avi-Yonah, M. and Stern, E. (eds). *Encyclopedia of Archaeological Excavations in the Holy Land*, Vols. I-IV. Jerusalem: Israel Exploration Society/Massada Press, 1975–79.

Falconer, S.E. 1987. *Heartland of Villages: Reconsidering Early Urbanism in the Southern Levant*. Unpublished doctoral dissertation, Department of Near Eastern Studies, University of Arizona.

Finkelstein, I. 1988. *The Archaeology of the Israelite Settlement*. Jerusalem: Israel Exploration Society.

Flanagan, J.W. 1988. *David's Social Drama. A Hologram of Israel's Early Iron Age*. Sheffield: Almond Press.

Frick, F.S. 1985. *The Formation of the State in Ancient Israel*. Sheffield: Almond Press.

Fritz, V. 1990. *Die Stadt in Alten Israel*. Munich: Beck.

Gottwald, N.K. 1979. *The Tribes of Yahweh: A Sociology of the Religion of Liberated Israel 1250–1050 B.C.E.* Maryknoll: Orbis.

Gottwald, N.K. 1985. *The Hebrew Bible. A Socio-literary Introduction*. Philadelphia: Fortress.

Herzog, Z. 1992. Administrative Structures in the Iron Age; Settlement and Fortification Planning. In *The Architecture of Ancient Israel from the Prehistoric to the Persian Periods* (eds A. Kempinski and R. Reich). Jerusalem: Israel Exploration Society, pp. 223–30; 231–74.

Hestrin, R. and Dayagi, M. 1979. *Ancient Seals: First Temple Period. From the Collection of the Israel Museum*. Jerusalem: The Israel Museum.

Joffe, A.H. 1993. *Settlement and Society in the Early Bronze I and II Southern Levant. Complementary and Contradiction in a Small-scale Complex Society*. Sheffield: Sheffield Academic Press.

Keel, O. and Uehlinger, C. 1992. *Gottinnen, Gotter und Gottessymbole. Neue Erkenntnisse zur Religionsgeschichte Kanaans und Israels aufgrund unerschlossener ikonigraphischer Quellen*. Freiburg: Herder.

Kempinski, A. and Reich, R. (eds) 1992. *The Architecture of Ancient Israel from the Prehistoric to the Persian Periods*. Jerusalem: Israel Exploration Society.

King, P.J. 1988. *Amos, Hosea, Micah – An Archaeological Commentary*. Philadelphia: Westminster Press.

Knapp, A.B. 1992. *Archaeology, Annales, and Ethnohistory*. Cambridge: Cambridge University Press.

Lemaire, A. 1977. Les inscriptions de Khirbet el Qôm et l'Ashérad de Yhwh. *Revue Biblique*. 89: 597–608.

Lemaire, A. 1981. *Les ecoles et la formation de la Bible dans l'ancien Israël*. Göttingen: Vandenhoeck and Ruprecht.

Mazar, A. 1990. *Archaeology of the Land of the Bible 10,000–586 B.C.E.* New York: Doubleday.

Meshel, Z. 1979. Did Yahweh Have a Consort? The New Religious Inscriptions from Sinai. *Biblical Archaeology Review*. 5/2: 24–35.

Na'aman, N. 1986. Hezekiah's Fortified Cities and the LMLK Stamps. *Bulletin of the American Schools of Oriental Research*. 261: 5–21.

Naveh, J. 1982. *The Early History of the Alphabet*. Jerusalem: Magness Press.

Netzer, E. 1992. Domestic Architecture in the Iron Age. In *The Architecture of Ancient Israel from the Prehistoric to the Persian Periods* (eds A. Kempinski and R. Reich). Jerusalem: Israel Exploration Society, pp. 193–201.

Paynter, R.W. 1983. Expanding the Scope of Settlement Analysis. In *Archaeological Hammers and Theories* (eds J.A. Moore and A.S. Keene). New York: Academic Press, pp. 233–75.

Pedersen, J. 1926–1940. *Israel. Its Life and Culture* I–IV. London: Oxford University Press.

Reich, R. 1992. Palaces and Residencies in the Iron Age. In *The Architecture of Ancient Israel from the Prehistoric to the Persian Periods* (eds A. Kempinski and R. Reich). Jerusalem: Israel Exploration Society, pp. 202–22.

Renfrew, C. 1979. Systems Collapse as Social Transformation: Catastrophe and Anastrophe in Early State Societies. In *Transformations: Mathematical Approaches to Cultural Change* (eds C. Renfrew and K.L. Cooke). New York: Academic Press, pp. 481–506.

Sawyer, J.F.A. and Clines, D.J.A. (eds) 1983. *Midian, Moab and Edom: The History and Archaeology of Late Bronze and Iron Age Jordan and North-West Arabia*. Sheffield: Almond Press.

Schroer, S. 1987. *In Israel Gab es Bilder. Nachrechten von darstellender kunst im Alten Testament*. Freiburg: Universitatsverlag.

Shiloh, Y. 1979. *The Proto-Aeolic Capital and Israelite Ashlar Masonry*. Qedem 11. Jerusalem: The Hebrew University of Jerusalem.

Shiloh, Y. 1980. The Population of Iron Age Palestine in the Light of a Sample Analysis of Urban Plans, Areas, and Population Density. *Bulletin of the American Schools of Oriental Research*. 239: 25–35.

Simon, H.A. 1965. The Architecture of Complexity. *Yearbook of the Society for General Systems Research*. 10: 13–76.

Stager, L.E. 1985. The Archaeology of the Family in Ancient Israel. *Bulletin of the American Schools of Oriental Research*. 260: 1–35.

Tainter, J.A. 1988. *The Collapse of Complex Societies*. Cambridge: Cambridge University Press.

Tappy, R.E. 1992. *The Archaeology of Israelite Samaria*. Harvard Semitic Studies 24. Atlanta: Scholars Press.

Thompson, T.L. 1992. *Early History of the Israelite People from the Written and Archaeological Sources*. Leiden: Brill.

de Vaux, R. 1961. *Ancient Israel: Its Life and Institutions*. New York: McGraw-Hill.

Weippert, H. 1988. *Palästina in vorhellenistischer Zeit*. Munich: C.H. Beck.

Winter, I. 1981. Is There a South Syrian Style of Ivory Carving in the Early First Millennium B.C.? *Iraq*. 43: 101–30.

Yoffee, N. and Cowgill, G.L. (eds) 1988. *The Collapse of Ancient States and Civilizations*. Tucson: University of Arizona.

Chapter 25

Albright, W.F. 1960. *The Archaeology of Palestine*. Harmondsworth: Pelican.

Ariel, D.T. 1990. Imported Stamped Amphora Handles. In Excavations at the City of David, Vol II; *Qedem* 30. Jerusalem.

Avi-Yonah, M. 1966. *The Holy Land from the Persian to the Arab Conquest*. Michigan: Baker Book House.

Barag, D. 1986. A Silver Coin of Yohanan the High Priest and the Coinage of Judaea in the Fourth Century BC. *Israel Numismatic Journal*. 9: 4–21.

Barkay, G. 1986. *Ketef Hinnom, A Treasure Facing Jerusalem Walls*, Jerusalem: The Israel Museum.

Bennet, W.J. and Blakely, J.A. 1989. *Tell el Hesi, The Persian Period*. (St. V) Winona Lake, Indiana: Eisenbrauns.

Ben-Tor, A. and Portugali, Y. 1987. Tel Qiri, A Village in the Jezreel Valley. *Qedem*. 24.

Boardman, J. 1964. *The Greeks Overseas*. Harmondsworth: Penguin.

Braidwood, R.J. 1940. Report on two Sondages on the Coast of Syria. *Syria*. 21: 198.

Clairmont, C. 1956–58. Greek Pottery from the Near East. *Berytus*. 11: 85–139; 12: 1–34.

Clermont-Ganneau, C.H. 1921. Le Paradeisos Royal Archémenide de Sidon. *RB*. 30: 106–9.

Contenau, G. 1923. Sculptures provenant de la Ville. *Syria*. 4: 276–8.

Cooke, G.A. 1903. *Northern Semitic Inscriptions*. Oxford: Clarendon Press.

Cowley, A. 1923. *Aramaic Papyri of the Fifth Century BC*. Oxford: Clarendon Press.

Cross, F.M. 1974. Discoveries in the Wadi ed Daliyeh. *AASOR*. 41: 17–29.

Crowfoot, G.W., Crowfoot, G.M. and Kenyon, K.M. 1957. *Samaria Sebaste III: The Objects*. London: Palestine Exploration Fund.

Crowfoot, G.W. 1940. *The Buildings of Samaria*. London: Palestine Exploration Fund.

Dothan, M. 1976. The Fortifications of Ptolemais. *Qadmoniot*. 34–5: 71–4 (Hebrew).

Dothan, M. 1979. An Attic Red-Figured Bell Krater from Tell 'Akko. *IEJ*. 29: 148–51.

Elgavish, J. 1968. *Archaeological Excavations at Shikmona Field Report No. 1: The Levels of the Persian Period, Seasons 1963–1965*. (Hebrew) Haifa: Haifa City Museum of Ancient Art.

Elgavish, J. 1974. *Archaeological Excavations at Shikmona The Level of the Hellenistic Period*. (Hebrew). Haifa: Haifa City Museum of Ancient Art.

Finkielsztein, G. 1987. *Les Niveaux I et II de Tell Abu Hawam: Les Periods Perse et Hellenistique*, unpublished doctoral thesis.

Frankel, R. 1990. Mount Mizpeh Hayamim, 1988–89. *Hadashot Archaeologiot*. 85: 13–15 (Hebrew).

Gera, D. 1985. Tryphon's Sling Bullet from Dor. *IEJ*. 35: 153–63.

Gjerstad, E. 1948. *The Swedish Cyprus Expedition*. Vol. IV: 2. Stockholm: Berlingska Boktryckerlet.

Gropp, D.M. 1986. *The Samaria Papyri from Wadi ed-Daliyeh*. Cambridge, unpublished doctoral thesis. Mass.

Hamilton, R.W. 1934. Excavations at Tell Abu Hawam. *QDAP*. 4: 1–69.

Herzog, Z., Rapp, G. and Negbi, O. (eds) 1988. *Excavations at Tel Michal, Israel*. Minneapolis: University of Minnesota Press.

Hill, G.F. 1914. *A Catalogue of Greek Coins of Palestine*. London: British Museum.

Horowitz, G. 1980. Town Planning of Hellenistic Marisa: A Reappraisal of the Excavations after Eighty Years. *PEQ*. 112: 93–111.

Iliffe, J.H. 1935. A Hoard of Bronzes from Ashkelon, c. Fourth Century BC. *QDAP*. 5: 61–8.

Iliffe-Mitford, J.H. 1953. *Illustrated London News*. pp. 613–16.

Kloner, A. 1991. Maresha. *Qadmoniot*. 24: 70–85 (Hebrew).

Kindler, A. 1963. The Greco-Phoenician Coins struck in Palestine in the time of the Persian Empire. *INJ*. 1: 2–6; 25–7.

Kindler, A. 1967. The Mint of Tyre: The Major Source of Silver Coins in Ancient Palestine. *Eretz-Israel*. 8: 318–24.

Lambert, C. 1932. The Egypto-Arabian, Phoenician and other Coins of the Fourth Century BC Found in Palestine. *QDAP*. 2: 1–10.

Leith, M.J.W. 1990. *Greek and Persian Images in Pre-Alexandrian Samaria: The Wadi ed-Daliyeh Seal Impressions* (unpublished doctoral thesis). Ann Arbor.

Magen, Y. 1984. Beit ha-Mesibah in the Temple Scroll and in the Mishna. *Eretz Israel.* 17: 226–35 (Hebrew).

Meshorer, Y. 1961. An Attic Archaic Coin from Jerusalem. *Atiqat.* 3: 185.

Meshorer, Y. 1966. A New Type of YHD Coin. *IEJ.* 16: 217–19.

Meshorer, Y. 1982. *Ancient Jewish Coinage.* Vol. I, Persian Period through Hasmonaeans. New York: Amphora Books.

Meshorer, Y. and Qedar, Sh. 1991. *The Coinage of Samaria in the Fourth Century B.C..* Jerusalem: Numismatic Fine Arts International.

Mildenberg, L. 1988. YAHUD, Munzen. In *Handbuch der Archaeologie: Palastina in vor Hellenistichen Zeit* (ed. H. Weipert). Munchen: pp. 721–8.

Naveh, J. 1962. The Excavations at Mesad Hashavyahu – Preliminary Report. *IEJ.* 12: 89–113.

Naveh, J. 1981. The Aramaic Ostraca from Tel Arad. In *Arad Inscriptions* (ed. Y. Aharoni). Jerusalem: Israel Exploration Society.

Niemeyer, H.G. 1982. *Phonizier im Westen. Die Beitrage des Internationalen Symposiums uber 'Die phonizische Expansion im Westlichen Mittelmeeraum'.* Madrider Beitrage, Band 8, Mainz am Rhein: Deutsches Archäologisches Institut, Madrid.

Noe, S.P. 1937. A Bibliography of Greek Coin Hoards. *NNM.* 78.

Oren, E. 1984. Migdol: A New Fortress on the edge of the Eastern Nile Delta. *BASOR.* 256: 7–44.

Parrot, A. 1969. *Urgaritica VI.* Mission de Ras Shamra, XVII. Paris: P. Geuthner.

Patrich, J. 1986. The Mesibah of the Temple according to the Tractate Middot. *IEJ.* 36: 215–33.

Ploug, G. 1973. *Sukas II: The Aegean, Corinthian and Eastern Greek Pottery and Terracottas.* Copenhagen: Munksgaard.

Pope, A.O. (ed.) 1938. *A Survey of Persian Art.* Oxford: Oxford University Press.

Porten, B. 1968. *Archives from Elephantine.* Berkeley and Los Angeles: University of California Press.

Rahmani, L.Y. 1971. Silver Coins of the Fourth Century B.C. from Tel Gamma. *IEJ.* 21: 158–60.

Rabinowitz, I. 1956. Aramaic Inscriptions of the fifth Century B.C.E. From a North-Arab Shrine in Egypt. *JNES.* 15: 1–9.

Riis, P.J. 1970. *Sukas I: The North-East Sanctuary and the First Settling of Greeks in Syria and Palestine.* Copenhagen: Munksgaard.

Riis, P.J. 1979. *Sukas V: The Graeco-Phoenician Cemetery and Sanctuary at the South Harbour.* Copenhagen: Munksgaard.

Ritter-Kaplan, H. 1982. The Ties Between Sidonian Jaffa and Greece in the Light of Excavations. *Qadmoniot.* 15: 64–8. (Hebrew).

Shatzman, I. 1991. Balista Stones from Tel Dor and the Artillery of the Greco-Roman World. *Qadmoniot.* 24: 94–104 (Hebrew).

Sharon, I. 1987. Phoenician and Greek Ashlar Construction Techniques at Tel Dor, Israel. *BASOR.* 267: 24–42.

Sharon, I. 1991. The Fortifications of Dor and the Transition from the Israeli-Syrian concept of Defense to the Greek Concept. *Qadmoniot.* 24: 105–13 (Hebrew).

Sivan, R. and Solar, G. 1984. Discoveries in the Jerusalem Citadel 1980–1984. *Qadmoniot.* 17: 114–15 (Hebrew).

Stern, E. 1982. *The Material Culture of the Land of the Bible in the Persian Period.* Warminster: Aris and Phillips.

Stern, E. 1985. The Excavations at Tel Dor. In *The Land of Israel: Crossroad of Civilizations* (ed. E. Lipinski). Leuven: Peeters, pp. 169–91.

Stern, E. 1988. The Walls of Dor. *IEJ.* 38: 6–14.

Stern, E. 1989a. The Beginning of the Greek Settlement in Palestine. In *Recent Excavations in Israel: Studies in Iron Age Archaeology* (eds S. Gitlin and W.G. Dever). *AASOR.* 49: 107–24.

Stern, E. 1989b. What happened to the Cult Figurine? *BAR.* XV: 22–54.

Stern, E. 1990. Hazor, Dor and Megiddo in the time of Ahab and Under Assyrian Rule. *IEJ.* 40: 12–30.

Stern, E. 1992a. *Dor, the Ruler of the Seas.* (Hebrew). Jerusalem: Israel Exploration Society.

Stern, E. 1992b. Phoenician Architectural Elements During the Iron Age and the Persian Period. In *The Architecture of Ancient Israel* (eds A. Kempinski and R. Reich). Jerusalem: Israel Exploration Society, pp. 302–4.

Stern, E. 1993a. A Hoard of Persian Period Bullae from the Vicinity of Samaria. *Michmanim.* (Hebrew). 6: 7–30.

Stern, E. 1993b. Notes on the Development of Stamp Glyptic Art in Palestine during the Assyrian, Babylonian and Persian Periods. In *Studies in the Archaeology and History of Ancient Israel in Honour of Moshe Dothan.* Haifa. (Hebrew). 11–22.

Tcherikover, V.A. 1963. *Hellenistic Civilization and the Jews.* (Hebrew). Tel Aviv: Devir.

Wooley, C.L. 1953. *A Forgotten Kingdom.* Harmondsworth: Pelican.

Wright, G. Ernest 1965. *Shechem, the Biography of a Biblical City.* New York: McGraw Hill.

Yadin, Y. 1977. *The Temple Scroll.* Jerusalem: Israel Exploration Society.

Zayadin, F. 1967. Samaria-Sebaste Clearance and Excavations. *ADAJ.* 12–13: 77–80.

Chapter 26

Abbott, F.F. and Johnson, A.C. 1926. *Municipal Administration in the Roman Empire.* Princeton.

Ahlström, G.W. 1978. Wine Presses and Cupmarks of the Jenin/Megiddo Survey. *BASOR.* 231: 19–49.

Amiran, R. and Eitan, A. 1976. Excavations in the Jerusalem Citadel. In *Jerusalem Revealed: Archaeology in the Holy City 1968–1974* (ed. Y. Yadin). New Haven: Yale University Press, pp. 52–4.

Applebaum, S. 1961. The Roman Theatre at Beth She'an. *Yediot.* 25: 147ff.

Applebaum, S. 1967. Israel and Her Vicinity in the Roman and Byzantine Periods: Notes offered to Delegates. In *The Seventh International Congress of Roman Frontier Studies*, Tel Aviv.

Applebaum, S. 1976. *Prolegomena to the Study of the Second Jewish Revolt (AD 132–135).* BAR Supplementary Series 7, Oxford.

Applebaum, S. 1977. Judaea as a Roman Province. *ANRW.* 2.8: 355–96.

Applebaum, S. 1986. The Settlement Pattern of Western Samaria from Hellenistic to Byzantine Times: A Historical Commentary. In *Landscape and Pattern: An archaeological survey of Samaria 800 BCE–636 CE.* (ed. S. Dar). Oxford: Vol. 1, pp. 255–69.

Applebaum, S. 1989. Judaea in Hellenistic and Roman Times. In Neusner. Volume 40.

Avigad, N. 1950–1. The Rock-carved Facades of the Jerusalem Necropolis. *IEJ.* 1: pp. 96–109.

Avigad, N. 1976a. *Beth She'arim: Report on the Excavations During 1953–1958. Volume III: Catacombs 12–23.* Rutgers University.

Avigad, N. 1976b. The architecture of Jerusalem in the Second Temple Period. In *Jerusalem Revealed: Archaeology in the Holy City 1968–1974* (ed. Y. Yadin). New Haven: Yale University Press, pp. 14ff.

Avigad, N. and Mazar, B. 1993. Beth She'arim. In *The New Encyclopedia of Archaeological Excavations in the Holy Land*, vol. 1 (ed. E. Stern). Jerusalem: Israel Exploration Society, pp. 236–48.

Avigad, N. 1962. The Expedition to the Judaean Desert, 1961. *IEJ.* 12: 167–262.

Avi-Yonah, M. 1958. The date of the Limes Palestinae. *Eretz Israel.* 5: 135–7.

Avi-Yonah, M. 1961. *Oriental Art in Roman Palestine.* Rome.

Avi-Yonah, M. 1976. *The Jews of Palestine: A Political History from the Bar Kokhba War to the Arab Conquest.* Oxford.

Avi-Yonah, M. 1977. *The Holy Land: From the Persian to the Arab conquest (536 BC–AD 640).* Michigan.

Avi-Yonah, M. and Stern, E. (eds) 1975–8. *Encyclopedia of Archaeological Excavations in the Holy Land.* 4 vols, London and Oxford: Massada Press, Jerusalem.

Bagatti, B. 1969. *Excavations in Nazareth: From the Beginning until the XII Century* (translated by E. Hoade). Jerusalem.

Bahat, D. and Broshi, M. 1976. Excavations in the Armenian Garden. In *Jerusalem Revealed: Archaeology in the Holy City 1968–1974* (ed. Y. Yadin). New Haven: Yale University Press, pp. 55–6.

Banning, E.B. 1986. Peasants, Pastoralists and *Pax Romana*: Mutualism in the Southern Highlands of Jordan. *BASOR.* 265: 52–4.

Ben-David, A. 1971. Jewish Roman Bronze and Copper Coins: Their Reciprocal Relations in Mishnah and Talmud from Herod the Great to Trojan's Hadrian. *PEQ.* pp. 109–29.

Benoit, P. 1976. The Archaeological Reconstruction of the Antonia Fortress. In *Jerusalem Revealed: Archaeology in the Holy City 1968–1974* (ed. Y. Yadin). New Haven: Yale University Press, pp. 87–9.

Bickerman, E. 1967. Sur la Theologie de l'Art Figuratif a Propos de l'Ouvrage de E R Goodenough. *Syria*. 44: 131–61.

Casson, L. 1959. *The Ancient Mariners*. New York.

Cross, F.M. 1956a. Qumran Cave I. *JBL*. 75: 121–5.

Cross, F.M. 1956b. A Report on the Biblical Fragments of Cave Four in Wadi Qumran. *BASOR*. 141: 9–13.

Crowfoot, J., Crowfoot, G.M. and Kenyon, K. 1957. *The Objects from Samaria*. London: Palestine Exploration Fund.

Crowfoot, J.W., Kenyon, K. and Sukenik, E.L. 1966. *The Buildings at Samaria*. London: Palestine Exploration Fund.

Dar, S. 1986. *Landscape and Pattern: An archaeological survey of Samaria 800 BCE–636 CE*. BAR International Series 308, 2 vols. Oxford.

Dar, S. and Applebaum, S. 1973. The Roman Road from Antipatris to Caesarea. *PEQ*. 105: 91–9.

de Vaux, R. 1961. *L'archeologie et les Manuscrits de la Mer Morte*. London.

Duncan-Jones, R. 1974. *The Economy of the Roman Empire: Quantitative Studies*. Cambridge: Cambridge University Press.

Foerster, G. 1972. Ancient Synagogues in Eretz-Israel, *Qadmoniot*. 5: 38–42.

Foerster, G. 1993. Beth-Shean. In *The New Encyclopedia of Archaeological Excavations in the Holy Land*, vol. 1 (ed. E. Stern). Jerusalem: Israel Exploration Society, pp. 223–35.

Frova, A. 1993. Caesarea. In *The New Encyclopedia of Archaeological Excavations in the Holy Land*, vol. 1 (ed. E. Stern). Jerusalem: Israel Exploration Society, pp. 273–74.

Geva, H. 1993. Jerusalem. In *The New Encyclopedia of Archaeological Excavations in the Holy Land*, vol. 2 (ed. E. Stern). Jerusalem: Israel Exploration Society, pp. 745–49, 753–56.

Gichon, M. 1978. Roman Bath-houses in Eretz Israel. *Qadmoniot*. 11: 37–53 (Hebrew).

Gichon, M. 1980. Research on the *Limes Palestinae*: a Stocktaking. *Roman Frontier Studies 1979*, pp. 843–64.

Goodenough, E.R. 1965. *Jewish Symbols in the Greco-Roman Period*. 13 vols. New York and Toronto.

Goodman, M. 1983. *State and Society in Roman Galilee, AD 132–212*. New Jersey.

Hachlili, R. 1980. A Second Temple Period Necropolis in Jericho. *BA* 43: 235–40.

Hachlili, R. 1988. *Ancient Jewish Art and Archaeology in the Land of Israel*. New York: EJ Brill.

Hachlili, R. and Killebrew, A. 1983. Jewish Funerary Customs during the Second Temple Period in Light of the Excavations at the Jericho Necropolis. *PEQ*. 115: 109–39.

Harper, G.M. 1928. Village Administration in the Roman Province of Syria. *YCS*. 1: 102–68.

Heichelheim, F. 1938. An Economic Survey of Ancient Rome, volume four (ed. T. Frank). Baltimore: T. Frank.

Hill, C.F. 1914. Catalogue of the Greek coins of Palestine. *Catalogue of the Greek coins in the British Museum*. London: The British Museum. pp. 1–10.

Hopkins, I.W.J. 1980. The City Region in Roman Palestine. *PEQ*. 112: 19–32.

Isaac, B. 1990. *The Limits of Empire: The Roman Army in the East*. Oxford.

Isaac, B. and Oppenheimer, A. 1985. The Revolt of Bar Kokhba, Scholarship and Ideology. *JJS*. 36: 33–60.

Isaac, B. and Roll, I. 1979. Judaea in the Early Years of Hadrian's Reign. *Latomus*. 38: 54–66.

Isaac, B. and Roll, I. 1982. *Roman Roads in Judaea, i, The Legio-Scythopolis Road*. BAR International Series 141, Oxford.

Jones, A.H.M. 1931. The Urbanization of Palestine. *JRS*. 21.

Jones, A.H.M. 1937. *The Cities of the Eastern Roman Provinces*. Oxford.

Jones, A.H.M. 1938. *The Herods of Judaea*. Oxford: Oxford University Press.

Jones, A.H.M. 1974. *The Cities of the Roman Empire*. (ed. P.A. Brunt). New Jersey.

Kadman, L. 1957. *The Coins of Caesarea Maritima: Corpus Nummorum Palestinensium* II.

Kadman, L. 1961. *The Coins of Akko Ptolemais: Corpus Nummorum Palestinensium*. Series 1, vol. IV.

Kasher, A., Rappaport, U. and Fuks, G. (eds) 1990. *Greece and Rome in Eretz Israel: Collected Essays*. Jerusalem: Israel Exploration Society.

Kelso, J.L. and Baramki, D.C. 1955. Excavations at New Testament Jericho and Khirbet en-Nitla. *Ann Am Sch Or Res*, pp. 29–30ff.

Kloner, A. 1993. Beth Guvrin. In *The New Encyclopedia of Archaeological Excavations in the Holy Land*, vol. 1 (ed. E. Stern). Jerusalem: Israel Exploration Society, pp. 195–97.

Kraeling, C.H. 1938. *Gerasa: City of the Decapolis*. New Haven: Yale University Press.

Levick, B. 1967. *Roman Colonies in Southern Asia Minor*. Oxford.

Levine, L.I. 1975a. *Caesarea Under Roman Rule*. Leiden: Brill.

Levine, L.I. 1975b. *Roman Caesarea: An Archaeological-Topographical Study*. Jerusalem.

Levine, L.I. and Netzer, E. 1986. *Excavations at Caesarea Maritima, 1975, 1976, 1979: Final Report*. Jerusalem.

Magie, D. 1950. *Roman Rule in Asia Minor*. 2 vols. Princeton: Princeton University Press.

Mazar, B. 1969. *The Excavations in the Old City of Jerusalem: Preliminary Report of the First Season, 1968*. Jerusalem.

Mazar, B. 1975. The Aqueducts of Jerusalem. In *Jerusalem Revealed: Archaeology in the Holy City 1968–1974* (ed. Y. Yadin). New Haven: Yale University Press, pp. 79–84.

Mazar, B. 1976. The archaeological excavations near the Temple Mount. In *Jerusalem Revealed: Archaeology in the Holy City 1968–1974* (ed. Y. Yadin). New Haven: Yale University Press, 1976, pp. 25–41.

Mazar, B., Schwabe, M. and Lifshitz, B. 1973–4. *Beth She'arim: Report on the Excavations during 1936-40*. 2 vols. Jerusalem.

Meshorer, Y. 1976. A hoard of coins from Migdal. *Atiqot*. 11: 54–71.

Meyers, C.L., Meyers, E.M. and Strange, J.F. 1974. Excavations at Meiron in Upper Galilee – 1971, 1972: A Preliminary Report. *BASOR*. 214: 2–25.

Meyers, E.M., Kraabel, A.T. and Strange, J.F. 1976. Ancient Synagogue Excavations at Khirbet Shema', Israel, 1970–1972. *AASOR*. 42.

Meyers, E.M., Strange, J.F. and Groh, D.E. 1978. The Meiron Excavation Project: Archaeological Survey in Galilee and Golan, 1976. *BASOR*. 230: 1–24.

Meyers, E.M., Strange, J.F. and Meyers, C.L. 1981. *Excavations at Meiron, Upper Galillee*. Cambridge, MA.

Mildenberg, L. 1990. Rebel Coinage in the Roman Empire. In *Greece and Rome in Eretz Israel: collected Essays* (eds A. Kasher, U. Rappaport and G. Fuks). Jerusalem: Israel Exploration Society, pp. 62–74.

Netzer, E. 1981. Greater Herodium. *Qedem*. 13.

Paoli, U.E. 1958. *Rome, its people, life and customs*. Harlow: Longman.

Pritchard, J.B. 1958. The Excavation of Herodian Jericho. *AASOR*. 32–3.

Raban, A. (ed.) 1985. *Harbour Archaeology: Proceedings of the First International Workshop on ancient Mediterranean Harbours*. BAR International Series 257. Oxford.

Rajak, T. 1973. Justus of Tiberias. *Classical Quarterly*. 23: 345–68.

Rahmani, L.Y. 1981–1982. Ancient Jerusalem's Funerary Customs and Tombs. *BA*. 44: 171–7.

Rivet, A.L. 1969. *The Roman Villa in Britain*. London.

Roll, I. and Ayalon, E. 1983. Roman Roads in Western Samaria. *PEQ*. 118: 114–34.

Rostovtzeff, M.I. 1935. La Syrie Romaine. *Revue Historique*. 65: 1–40.

Roxan, M.M. 1985. *Roman Military Diplomas 1954–1977*, London.

Safrai, S. and Stern, M. (eds) 1974–6. *The Jewish People in the first Century: Historical Geography*. Compendia Rerum Iudaicarum ad Novum Testamentum: Section 1, in two volumes, Assen.

Saltz, D. 1977. Surveys, Salvage and Small Digs in Israel. *American Schools of Oriental Research Newsletter*, no 10.

Schürer, E. 1979. *The History of the Jewish People in the Age of Jesus Christ (175 BC–AD 135)* (revised and edited by G. Vermes, F. Millar and M. Black). 3 vols. Edinburgh.

Shanks, H. 1979. *Judaism in Stone: The Archaeology of Ancient Synagogues*. New York and London.

Schwabe, M. and Lifshitz, B. 1974. *Beth She'arim, volume II: The Greek Inscriptions*. Rutgers University.

Smallwood, E.M. 1981. *The Jews under Roman Rule from Pompey to Diocletian: A Study in Political Relations*. Leiden: Brill.

Sperber, D. 1978. *Roman Palestina 200–400: The Land*. Ramat Gan.

Stern, E. (ed.) 1993. *The New Encyclopedia of Archaeological Excavations in the Holy Land*. Jerusalem: Israel Exploration Society.

Sukenik, E.L. 1934. *Ancient Synagogues in Palestine and Greece*. London.

Urbach, E.E. 1959. The Rabbinical Laws of Idolatry in the Second and Third Centuries in the Light of Archaeological and Historical Facts. *IEJ*. 9: 149–65; 229–45.

Urman, D. 1985. *The Golan: A profile of a region during the Roman and Byzantine periods*. BAR International Series 269. Oxford.

Waterman, L. 1937. *Preliminary Report of the University of Michigan Excavations at Sepphoris*. Ann Arbor.

Waterhouse, S.D. and Ibach, R. 1975. Heshbon 1973 – The Topographical Survey. *Andrews University Seminar Studies*. 13: 217–33.

Yadin, Y. 1963. *The Finds from the Bar Kokhba Period in the Cave of Letters*. London.

Yadin, Y. 1965. *Masada: Herod's Fortress and the Zealot's Last Stand*. London.

Yadin, Y. 1976. *Jerusalem Revealed: Archaeology in the Holy City 1968–1974*. New Haven: Yale University Press.

Yeivin, Z. 1971. Survey of Settlements in Galilee and the Golan from the Period of the Mishnah in the Light of the Sources. Unpublished doctoral thesis, Hebrew University of Jerusalem.

Chapter 27

Abel, F.M. 1926. Inscription grecque de l'aqueduct de Jérusalem, avec la figure du pied byzantine. *Revue Biblique*. 35: 284–8.

Amit, D., Hirschfeld Y. and Patrich, J. (eds) 1989. *The Aqueducts of Ancient Palestine. Collected Essays*. Jerusalem: Yad Izhak Ben Zvi (Hebrew).

Armstrong, G.T. 1967. Imperial Church Building in the Holy Land in the Fourth Century, *The Biblical Archaeologist*. 30: 90–102.

Aviam, M. 1990. Horvath Hesheq – A Unique Church in Upper Galilee: Preliminary Report. In *Christian Archaeology in the Holy Land. New Discoveries. Essays in Honour of Virgilio C. Corbo* (eds G.C. Bottini, L. Di Segni and E. Alliata). Jerusalem: Studium Biblicum Franciscanum, pp. 351–78.

Avigad, N. 1983. *Discovering Jerusalem*. Nashville: T. Nelson.

Avi-Yonah, M. 1954. *The Madaba Mosaic Map*. Jerusalem: Israel Exploration Society.

Avi-Yonah, M. 1958. The Economics of Byzantine Palestine. *Israel Exploration Journal*. 8: 39–51.

Avi-Yonah, M. 1961. *Oriental Art in Roman Palestine*. Rome: Centro di studi semifici. Instituto di studi del vicino oriente, University of Rome.

Avi-Yonah, M. 1975. *Ancient Mosaics*. London: Cassell.

Avi-Yonah, M. 1981. *Art in Ancient Palestine* (Collected articles). Jerusalem: The Magnes Press.

Bagatti, B. 1971. *The Church from the Gentiles in Palestine: History and Archaeology*. Jerusalem: Studium Biblicum Franciscanum.

Ben Dov, M. 1985. *In the Shadow of the Temple. The Discovery of Ancient Jerusalem*. Tel Aviv: Keter Publishing House.

Ben Pechat, M. 1989. The Paleochristian Baptismal Fonts in the Holy Land: Formal and Functional Study. *Liber Annus*. 39: 165–88, Pls. 27–34.

Bottini, G.C., Di Segni, L. and Alliata, E. 1990. *Christian Archaeology in the Holy Land. New Discoveries. Essays in Honour of Virgilio C. Corbo*. Jerusalem: Studium Biblicum Franciscanum.

Broshi, M. 1977. Standards of Streets Widths in the Roman-Byzantine Period. *Israel Exploration Journal*. 27: 232–35.

Broshi, M. 1980. The Population of Western Palestine in the Roman-Byzantine Period. *Bulletin of the American Schools of Oriental Research*. 236: 1–10.

Chiat, M.J. 1982. *Handbook of Synagogue Architecture*. Brown Judaic Studies 29. Chico, California: Scholars Press.

Chitty, D.J. 1966. *The Desert a City*. Oxford: Basil Blackwell.

Claude, D. 1969. *Die Byzantinisch Stadt im 6. Jahrhundert*. München: C.H. Beck.

Corbo, V. 1955. *Gli Scavi di Kh. Siyar el-Ghanam (Campo dei pastori) e i monasteri dei dintorni*. Jerusalem: Studium Biblicum Franciscanum.

Corbo, V. 1981. *Il Santo Sepolcro di Gerusalemme, I-III*. Jerusalem: Studium Biblicum Franciscanum.

Coüasnon, Ch. 1974. *The Church of the Holy Sepulchre in Jerusalem [The Schweich Lectures 1972]*. London: Oxford University Press.

Crowfoot, J. W. 1941. *Early Churches in Palestine*. London: Palestine Exploration Fund.

Dan, Y. 1984. *The City in Eretz-Israel During the Late Roman and Byzantine Periods*. Jerusalem (Hebrew): Yad Izhak Ben Zvi.

Di Segni, L. and Hirschfeld, Y. 1986. Four Greek Inscriptions from Hammat Gader from the Reign of Anastasius. *Israel Exploration Journal*. 36: 251–68, Pls. 33–5.

Forsyth, G.H. and Weitzmann, K. 1970. *The Monastery of St. Catherine at Mount Sinai – The Church and Fortress of Justinian*, I. Ann Arbor: University of Michigan Press.

Frankel, R. 1992. Some Oil Presses from Western Galilee, *Bulletin of the American Schools of Oriental Research*. 286: 39–72.

Frova, A. (ed.) 1966. *Scavi di Caesarea Maritima*. Milan: Cassa di Risparmio della Provincie Lombarde, Instituto Lombardo-Accademia di Scienze e Lettere.

Grabar, A. 1958. *Ampules de Terre Sainte (Monza-Bobbio)*. Paris: C. Klincksieck.

Green, J. and Tsafrir Y. 1982. Greek Inscriptions from Hammat Gader: A Poem by the Empress Eudocia and Two Building Inscriptions. *Israel Exploration Journal*. 32: 77–96.

Hachlili, R. 1988. *Ancient Jewish Art and Archaeology in the Land of Israel*. Leiden: Brill.

Hirschfeld, Y. 1987. *Dwelling Houses in the Roman and Byzantine Palestine*. Jerusalem: Yad Izhak Ben Zvi (Hebrew).

Hirschfeld, Y. 1992. *The Judean Desert Monasteries in the Byzantine Period*. New Haven and London: Yale University Press.

Hirschfeld, Y. and Birger, R. 1986. Khirbet ed-Deir (désert de Juda) – 1981–1984. *RB*. 93: 276–84.

Hirschfeld, Y. and Briger, R. 1991. Early Roman and Byzantine Estates near Caesarea. *Israel Exploration Journal*. 41: 81–111.

Hohlfelder, R.L. (ed.) 1982. *City, Town and Countryside in the Early Byzantine Era*. Boulder, Colorado: East European Monographs.

Holum, K.G. 1982. Caesarea and the Samaritans. In *City, Town and Countryside in the Early Byzantine Era* (ed. R.L. Hohlfelder). Boulder, Colorado: East European Monographs, pp. 65–73.

Holum, K.G. 1989. The End of Classical Urbanism at Caesarea Maritima, Israel. In *Studia Pompeiana and Classica in Honor of Wilhelmina Jashemski*, II (ed. R. Curtis). New Rochelle, NY: Aristide D. Caratzas, pp. 87–103.

Holum, K., Hohlfelder, R.L., Bull, R.J. and Raban, A. 1988. *King Herod's Dream. Caesarea on the Sea*. New York and London: W.W. Norton and Company.

Humphrey, J. H. 1974. Prolegomena to the Study of the Hippodrome at Caesarea Maritima. *Bulletin of the American Schools of Oriental Research*. 213: 2–45.

Hunt, E.D. 1982. *Holy Land Pilgrimage in the Later Roman Empire, AD 312–460*. Oxford: Clarendon Press.

Hüttenmeister, F. and Reeg, G. 1977. *Die antike Synagogen in Israel*, Teil 1: *Jüdische Synagogen*, Teil 2: *Die Samaritische Synagogen*. Wiesbaden: L. Reichert.

Jones, A. H. M. 1964. *The Later Roman Empire (284–602)*. Oxford: Basil Blackwell.

Kedar, Y. 1967. *The Ancient Agriculture in the Negev*. Jerusalem: The Magness Press (Hebrew).

Kennedy, H. 1985. From *Polis* to *Madina*: Urban Change in Late Antique and Early Islamic Syria. *Past and Present*. 106: 3–27.

Kitzinger, K. 1965. *Israeli Mosaics of the Byzantine Period*. New York: The New American Library, Inc.

Krautheimer, R. 1975. *Early Christian and Byzantine Architecture*. Baltimore: Penguin Books.

Landsberger 1957. The Sacred Direction in Synagogue and Church. *Hebrew Union College Annual*. 28: 181–203.

Levine, I.L. 1975. *Roman Caearea: An Archaeological/Topographical Study*. Qedem. Monographs of the Institute of Archaeology. Jerusalem: The Hebrew University of Jerusalem.

Levine, I.L. (ed.) 1981. *Ancient Synagogues Revealed*. Jerusalem: The Israel Exploration Society.

Levine, I.L. (ed.) 1987. *The Synagogue in Late Antiquity*. Philadelphia: The American Schools for Oriental Research.

Magen, Y. 1990. A Roman Fortress and a Byzantine Monastery at Khirbet el-Kiliya. In *Christian Archaeology in the Holy Land. New Discoveries. Essays in Honour of Virgilio C. Corbo* (eds G.C. Bottini,

L. Di Segni and E. Alliata). Jerusalem: Studium Biblicum Franciscanum, pp. 321–32.

Magen, Y. 1992. Samaritan Synagogues. *Qadmoniot.* 25 (99–100): 66–90.

Magen, Y. 1993. The Monastery of St. Martyrius at Ma'ale Adumim. In *Ancient Churches Revealed* (ed. Y. Tsafrir). Jerusalem: Israel Exploration Society, pp. 170–96.

Magen Y. and Talgam, R. 1990. The Monastery at Ma'ale Adumim (Khirbet el-Murassas) and its Mosaics. In *Christian Archaeology in the Holy Land. New Discoveries. Essays in Honour of Virgilio C. Corbo* (eds G.C. Bottini, L. Di Segni and E. Alliata). Jerusalem: Studium Biblicum Franciscanum, pp. 91–152.

Maoz, Z. 1981. The Art and Architecture of the Synagogues of the Golan. In *Ancient Synagogues Revealed* (ed. I.L. Levine). Jerusalem: The Israel Exploration Society, pp. 98–115.

Maoz, U.Z. and Killebrew, A. 1988. Ancient Qasrin – Synagogue and Village. *The Biblical Archaeologist.* 51: 5–19.

Mayerson, Ph. 1960. The Ancient Agricultural Remains of the Central Negev: Methodology and Dating Criteria. *Bulletin of the American Schools of Oriental Research.* 160: 27–37.

Mayerson, Ph. 1985. The Wine and Vineyards of Gaza in the Byzantine Period. *Bulletin of the American Schools of Oriental Research.* 257: 75–80.

Mayerson, Ph. 1992. The Gaza 'Wine' Jar (Gazition) and the 'Lost' Ashkelon Jar (Askalônion), *IEJ.* 42: 76–80.

Mazor, G. 1981. The Wine Presses of the Negev. *Qadmoniot* XIV (53–54): 51–60 (Hebrew).

Mazor, G. and Bar-Nathan, R. 1987–92. Beth Shean Excavations Project. *Excavations and Survey in Israel.* 6: 7–45; 7–8: 15–32; 11: 33–5.

Meimaris, Y. E. 1986. *Sacred Names, Saints, Martyrs and Church Officials in the Greek Inscriptions and Papyri Pertaining to the Christian Church of Palestine.* Athens: Research Center for Greek and Roman Antiquity, The National Hellenic Research Foundation.

Meimaris, Y.E. 1989. *The Monastery of Saint Euthymius at Khan el-Ahmar (1976–79).* Athens: Eptalophos S.A.

Negev, A. 1974. The Churches of the Central Negev – An Archaeological Survey. *Revue Biblique.* 81: 400–22.

Negev, A. 1989. The Cathedral of Elusa and the New Typology and Chronology of the Byzantine Churches in the Negev. *Liber Annus.* 39: 129–42, Pls 15–20.

Negev, A. 1990. Mampsis – The End of A Nabataean Town. *Aram Periodical.* 2: 337–65.

Nevo, Y. 1991. *Pagans and Herders: a re-examination of the Negev runoff cultivation systems in the Byzantine and Early Arab periods.* Jerusalem.

Ovadiah, A. 1970. *Corpus of Byzantine Churches in the Holy Land.* Bonn: Peter Hanstein Verlag GMBH.

Ovadiah, A. and de Silva, C.G. 1981–84. Supplement to the Corpus of Churches in the Holy Land. *Levant.* 13 (1981): 200–261; 14 (1982): 122–70; 16 (1984): 129–65.

Ovadiah, R. and Ovadiah, A. 1987. *Hellenistic, Roman and Early Byzantine Mosaic Pavements in Israel.* Rome: L'Erma di Bretschneider.

Patrich J. 1994. *Sabas, Leader of Palestinian Monasticism. A Comparative Study in Eastern Monasticism, Fourth to Seventh Centuries,* [Dumbarton Oaks Studies XXXII], Washington, D.C.: Dumbarton Oaks Research Library and Collection.

Peleg, J. 1989. The Water System of Caesarea. In *The Queducts of Ancient Palestine. Collected Essays* (eds D. Amit, Y. Hirschfeld and J. Patrich). Jerusalem: Yad Izhak Ben Zvi (Hebrew).

Rosen, S. 1987. Byzantine Nomadism in the Negev: Results from the Emergency Survey. *Journal of Field Archaeology.* 14: 29–42.

Rubin, R. 1989. The Debate over Climatic Changes in the Negev, Fourth–Seventh Centuries C.E. *Palestine Exploration Quarterly.* 121: 71–8.

Rubin, R. 1990. *The Negev as a Settled Land: Urbanization and Settlement in the Desert in the Byzantine Period.* Jerusalem (Hebrew): Yad Izhak Ben Zvi.

Russell, K. W. 1985. The Earthquake Chronology of Palestine and Northwest Arabia from the 2nd through the Mid-8th Century A.D. *Bulletin of the American Schools of Oriental Research.* 260: 37–59.

Safrai, Z. (ed.) 1986. *The Ancient Synagogue – Selected Studies.* Jerusalem (Hebrew): The Zalman Shazar Center for Jewish History.

Thomsen, P. 1903. Palästina nach dem Onomasticon des Eusebius. *Zeitschrift des Deutschen Palastina–Vereins.* 26: 97–188.

Tsafrir, Y. 1978. Jerusalem, *Reallexikon zur Byzantinischen Kunst* III (eds K. Wessel and M. Restle). Stuttgart: cols. 525–615.

Tsafrir, Y. 1984. *Eretz-Israel from the Destruction of the Second Temple to the Muslim Conquest, II, Archaeology and Art.* Jerusalem: Yad Izhak Ben Zvi (Hebrew).

Tsafrir, Y. 1987. The Byzantine Setting and its Influence on Ancient Synagogues. In *The Synagogue in Late Antiquity* (ed. I.L. Levine). Philadelphia: The American Schools for Oriental Research, pp. 147–58.

Tsafrir, Y. (ed.) 1993a. *Ancient Churches Revealed.* Jerusalem: Israel Exploration Society.

Tsafrir, Y. 1993b. Some Notes on the Settlement and Demography of Palestine in the Byzantine Period: The Archaeological Evidence. In *G. Van Beek Jubilee Volume* (ed. J. Seger). (in press).

Tsafrir, Y. and Hirschfeld, Y. 1979. The Church and Mosaics at Horvat Berachot, Israel. *Dumbarton Oaks Papers.* 33: 293–323.

Tsafrir, Y. and Foerster, G. 1987–92. Beth Shean Excavations Project *ESI.* 6: 7–45; 7–8: 15–32; 9: 120–9; 11: 3–32.

Tsafrir, Y. and Foerster, G. 1992. From Scythopolis to Beisan: Changes in Urban Concepts in Beth Shean in the Byzantine and Arab Periods. *Cathedra.* 64: 3–30 (Hebrew).

Tsafrir, Y., Patrich, J., Rosenthal-Heginbottom, R., Herschkovitz, I. and Nevo, Y.D. 1988. *Excavations at Rehovot-in-the-Negev, Vol. I: The Northern Church.* [Qedem 25]. Jerusalem: The Institute of Archaeology, The Hebrew University of Jerusalem.

Vailhé, S. 1899–1900. Répertoire alphabétique des monastères de Palestine. *Révue de l'Orient Chrétien* 4. (1899): 512–42; 5 (1900): 19–48, 272–92.

Vann, R.L. 1982. Byzantine Street Construction at Caesarea Maritima. In *City, Town and Countryside in the Early Byzantine Era.* (ed. R.L. Hohlfelder). Boulder, Colorada: East European Monographs, pp. 165–99.

Vincent, H. and Abel, F.M. 1914–26. *Jérusalem nouvelle.* Paris.

Warton, A.J. 1992. The Baptistery of the Holy Sepulcher in Jerusalem and the Politics of Sacred Landscape. *Dumbarton Oaks Papers.* 46: 313–25.

Weitzmann, K. 1976. *The Monastery of Saint Catherine at Mount Sinai: The Icons. Vol. I: from the sixth to the tenth century.* Princeton: Princeton University Press.

Wilkinson, J. 1984. Orientation, Jewish and Christian. *Palestine Exploration Quarterly.* 116: 16–30.

Chapter 28

Abu-Lughod, J.L. 1987. The Islamic city – Historic myth, Islamic essence, and contemporary relevance. *IJMES* 19: 155–176.

Alon, D. and Levy, T.E. 1989. The Archaeology of cult and the Chalcolithic sanctuary at Gilat. *Journal of Mediterranean Archaeology* 2: 163–221.

Ashtor, E., 1976. *A Social and economic history of the Near East in the Middle Ages.* London: Collins.

Baly, C. 1935. S'baita. *PEFQ* 62: 171–81.

Banning, E.B. 1986. Peasants, pastoralists and *Pax Romana*: Mutualism in the southern highlands of Jordan. *BASOR* 261: 25–50.

Baramki, D.C. 1969. *The Art and architecture of ancient Palestine.* Beirut: Palestine Research Center.

Ben-Dov, M. 1971. The Omayyad structures near the temple mount. In *The excavations in the old city of Jerusalem near the Temple Mount: Second preliminary report 1969–70 seasons* (ed. B. Mazar). Jerusalem: Hebrew University, pp. 37–44.

Ben-Dov, M. 1976. The area south of the Temple Mount in the early Islamic period. In *Jerusalem revealed: Archaeology in the Holy City 1968–1974* (ed. Y. Yadin). New Haven: Yale University, pp. 97–101.

Ben-Tor, A.B. and Rosenthal, R. 1978. The first season of excavations at Tel Yoqne'am, 1977: Preliminary report. *IEJ* 28: 57–82.

Ben-Tor, A.B., Portugali, Y. and Avissar, M. 1979. The second season of excavations at Tel Yoqne'am, 1978: Preliminary report. *IEJ* 29: 67–83.

Berman, E.K. 1989. Glazed pottery. In *Excavations at Capernaum, vol 1: 1978–1982* (ed. V. Tzaferis). Winona Lake, IN: Eisenbrauns, pp. 115–30.

Blair, S. 1992. What is the date of the Dome of the Rock? In *Bayt al-Maqdis: 'Abd al-Malik's Jerusalem*, part one (eds, J. Raby and J. Johns). Oxford: Oxford University Press, 59–87.

Conrad, K.I. 1981. The *Quṣūr* of medieval Islam: Some implications for the social history of the Near East. *al-Abḥāth* 29: 7–23.

Delougaz, P. and Haines, R.C. 1960. *A Byzantine Church at Khirbat al-Karak*. Chicago: Oriental Institute publication 85.

Dever, W.G. 1987. The Contribution of archaeology to the study of Canaanite and early Israelite religion. In *Ancient Israelite religion* (eds. P.D. Miller et al.). Philadelphia: Fortress, pp. 209–47.

Dever, W.G. 1990. Archaeology and Israelite settlement. *Recent archaeological discoveries and Biblical research*. Seattle: University of Washington, pp. 39–84.

De Vaux, R. and Steve, A.-M. 1950. *Fouilles à Qaryet el-'Enab, Abū Gôsh, Palestine*. Paris: J. Gabalda.

De Vries, B. 1982. *Umm el-Jimal, a tour guide*. Amman: Al Kutba.

Dostal, W. 1984. Towards a model of cultural evolution in Arabia. *Studies in the history of Arabia*, vol. 2: *Pre-Islamic Arabia*. Riyadh: King Saud University.

Elad, A. 1992. Why did 'Abd al-Malik build the Dome of the Rock? A Re-examination of the Muslim sources. In *Bayt al-Maqdis: 'Abd al-Malik's Jerusalem*, part one (eds J. Raby and J. Johns). Oxford: Oxford University Press, pp. 33–58.

Finkelstein, I. 1990. Process of sedentarization in the history of the Sinai and the Negev. *BASOR* 279: 267–88.

Franken, H.J. and Kalsbeek, J. 1975. *Potters of a medieval village in the Jordan valley*. New York: Elsevier.

Geva, H. 1983. Excavations in the citadel of Jerusalem 1979–1980, preliminary report. *IEJ* 33: 55–71.

Gichon, M. (1974. Fine Byzantine wares from the south of Israel. *PEQ* 106: 119–39.

Gil, M. 1992. *A History of Palestine, 634–1099*. Cambridge, Cambridge University Press.

Goitein, S.D. 1967. *A Mediterranean society: The Jewish communities of the Arab world as portrayed in the documents of the Cairo geniza*: vol. 1, *Economic foundations*. Berkeley: University of California Press.

Goitein, S.D. 1980. al-Ḳuds, EI², 322–39.

Goitein, S.D. 1982. Jerusalem in the Arab period (638–1099). *The Jerusalem Cathedra*, vol. 2 (ed. L.I. Levine). Detroit: Wayne State University, pp. 168–96.

Goitein, S.D. 1983. *A Mediterranean society: The Jewish communities of the Arab world as portrayed in the documents of the Cairo geniza*: vol. IV, *Daily Life*. Berkeley: University of California Press.

Goldziher, and Creswell,

Grabar, O. 1990. The Meaning of the Dome of the Rock. *Studies in Arab History: The Antonius Lectures, 1978–87* (ed. D. Hopwood), New York: St. Martin's pp. 51–63.

Grabar, O. et al. 1960. Sondages à Khirbet el-Minyeh. *IEJ* 10: 226–43.

Grabar, O. et al. 1978. *City in the desert: Qasr al-Hayr East*. 2 vols. Cambridge, MA: Harvard University Press.

Hamilton, R.W. 1959. *Khirbat al Mafjar: An Arabian Mansion in the Jordan Valley*. Oxford: Clarendon Press.

Hamilton, R. 1988. *Walid and his Friends: An Umayyad Tragedy*. Oxford: Oxford University Press.

Harrison, T.P. 1992. The Early Umayyad settlement at Ṭabariyah: A Case of yet another *misr*?, *JNES*: 51, 51–59.

Hasson, R., 1979. *Early Islamic glass*. Jerusalem: L.A. Mayer memorial Institute for Islamic Art.

Hauting, G.R. n.d. Apocalyptic and History in the second civil war: The Destruction and rebuilding of sanctuaries. Paper presented to the Bilad al-Sham in the Umayyad period conference, Amman, 1987.

Helms, S. 1982. Paleo-bedouin and transmigrant urbanism. In *Studies in the History and Archaeology of Jordan 1* (ed. A. Hadidi). Amman: Department of Antiquities, pp. 97–113.

Helms, S. 1990. *Early Islamic architecture of the desert. A Bedouin station in eastern Jordan*. Edinburgh: Edinburgh University Press.

Hinds, M. 1971. Kufan political alignments and their background in the mid-seventh century A.D. *IJMES* 2: 346–67.

Holum, K.G. et al. 1988. *King Herod's dream: Caesarea on the sea*. New York: W.W. Norton.

Holum, K.G. 1992. Archaeological evidence for the fall of Byzantine Caesarea. *BASOR* 286: 73–85.

Ibn Hauqal 1938. *Kitāb Ṣūrat al-Ard* (ed. J.H. Kramers). Leiden: Brill.

Kaplan, J. 1959. Excavations at the White Mosque in Ramla. *'Atiqot* 2: 106–15.

Kennedy, H. 1985. From *polis* to *madina*: Urban change in late antique and early Islamic Syria. *Past and Present* 106: 3–27.

Khalidi, T. 1984. Tribal settlement and patterns of land tenure in early medieval Palestine. In *Land tenure and social transformation in the Middle East* (ed. T. Khalidi). Beirut: American University, pp. 181–8.

Knauf, E.A. 1984. Umm al-Jimāl: An Arab town in late antiquity. *Revue biblique* 91: 578–86.

Koren, J. and Nevo, Y.D. 1991. Methodological approaches to Islamic studies. *Der Islam* 68: 87–107.

Lapidus, I.M. 1973. The Evolution of Muslim urban Society, *Comparative Studies in Society and History* 15: 21–50.

Magness, J. 1991. The Walls of Jerusalem in the early Islamic period. *BA*: 208–17.

Magness, J. 1992. A Reexamination of the archaeological evidence for the Sasanian Persian destruction of the Tyropoeon valley. *BASOR* 287: 67–74.

Mayer, K.A., et al. 1950. *Some principal Muslim religious buildings in Israel*. Jerusalem: Government Printer.

Mayerson, P. 1989. Saracens and Romans: Micro-Macro relationships. *BASOR* 274: 71–9.

Melkawi, A. 1992. Pottery kiln in Aqaba. *Newsletter of the Institute of Archaeology and Anthropology, Yarmouk University* 13: 9–10.

Meloy, J.L. 1991. Results of archaeological reconnaissance in west Aqaba: Evidence of the pre-Islamic settlement. *ADAJ* 35: 397–414.

Mez, A. 1937, *The Renaissance of Islam* (trans. S. Khuda Bukhsh and D.S. Margoliouth). London: Luzac.

Miller, K. 1986. *Mappae Arabicae* (reprint ed. H. Gaube). Wiesbaden: Ludwig Reichert.

al-Muqaddasi 1906. *Kitāb Ahsan al-Tagāsīm fī Ma'rifat al-Aqālīm*. (ed. M. de Goeje). Leiden: Brill, BGA 3, 2nd edn.

Negev, A. 1986. Mampsis. In *The Archeological Encyclopedia of the Holy Land*. Nashville: Thomas Nelson, pp. 226–8.

Nevo, Y.D. 1991. *Pagans and herders: A Re-examination of the Negev runoff cultivation systems in the Byzantine and early Arab periods*. Jerusalem: IPS.

Nevo, Y.D. n.d. Sde Boqer and the central Negev, 7th–8th century A.D. Paper presented to the 3rd International colloquium: From Jahiliyya to Islam. Jerusalem: Hebrew University, 1985.

Nevo, Y.D. and Koren, J. 1990. The Origins of the Muslim descriptions of the Jāhilī Meccan sanctuary. *JNES* 49: 23–44.

Oren, E.D. 1971. Early Islamic Material from Ganei-Hamat (Tiberias), *Archaeology* 24: 274–77.

Parker, S.T. 1987. Peasants, pastoralists, and Pax Romana: A Different view. *BASOR* 265: 35–51.

Pringle, D. 1986. *The Red Tower (al-Burj al-Ahmar). Settlement in the plain of Sharon at the time of the Crusaders and Mamluks. A.D. 1099–1516*. London: British School of Archaeology in Jerusalem.

Qedar, Sh. 1980. The dated Islamic coinage of Palestine, *Israel Numismatic Journal* 4: 63–71.

Reitmeyer, E. 1912. *Die Städtegrundungen der Araber im Islam nach den arabischen Historikern und Geographen*. Munich: F. Straub.

Roll, I and Ayalon, E. 1987. The market street at Apollonia – Arsuf. *BASOR* 267: 61–76.

Rosen, S. 1987. Byzantine nomadism in the Negev: Results from the emergency survey. *JFA* 14: 29–41.

Rosen, S. 1992. The Case for seasonal movement of pastoral nomads in the late Byzantine/early Arabic period in the south central Negev. In *Pastoralism in the Levant: Archaeological materials in anthropological perspectives* (eds O. Bar-Yosef and A. Khazanov). Madison, pp. 153–64.

Rosen-Ayalon, M. 1976. The first mosaic discovered in Ramla. *IEJ* 26: 104–119.

Rosen-Ayalon, M. 1989. *The early Islamic monuments of al-Haram al-Sharīf: An Iconographic study*. Jerusalem: Hebrew University Press.

Rosen-Ayalon, M. and Eitan, A. 1969. *Ramla excavations: Finds from the VIIIth century C.E.)*. Jerusalem: Israel Museum.

Rosen-Ayalon, M. and Nevo, Y.D. 1982. *The Early Arab period in the Negev*. Jerusalem: Hebrew University.

Rothenberg, B. 1972. *Timna, valley of the biblical copper mines*. London: Thames and Hudson.

Russell, K.W. 1985. The earthquake chronology of Palestine and northwest Arabia from the 2nd through the mid-8th century A.D., BASOR 260: 37–59.

Sauvaget, J. 1934. Le plan de Laodicée-sur-Mer. BEO 4: 81–114.

Sauvaget, J. 1939. Les ruines omeyyades du Djebel Seis, *Syria* 20: 239–56.

Sauvaget, J. 1941. *Alep. Essay sur le Development d'une grande Ville syrienne, des Origines au milieu du XIXe siècle*. Paris: P. Geuthner.

Schaefer, J. 1989. Archaeological remains from the medieval Islamic occupation of the northwest Neqev desert. *BASOR* 274: 33–60.

Schick, R. n.d. *The Christian communities of Palestine from Byzantine to Islamic rule: A Historical and archaeological study*. Princeton: Darwin.

Serjeant, R.B. 1972. *Islamic textiles: Material for a history up to the Mongol conquest*. Beirut: Librairie du Liban.

Sharon, M. 1966. An Arabic inscription from the time of the Caliph 'Abd al-Malik. *BSOAS* 29: 367–72.

Sharon, M. 1976. Ḳayṣariyya, EI², 841–42.

Sharon, M. 1979, An Inscription from the year 65 A.H., in the Dome of the Rock. In *D.H. Baneth Memorial Volume*. Jerusalem: Hebrew University.

Silberman, N.A. n.d. Thundering hoards: The Image of the Persian and Muslim conquests in Palestinian archaeology. Paper presented to the ASOR meeting, Anaheim, 1989.

Sourdel, D. 1981. La fondation umayyade d'al-Ramla. In *Studien zur Geschichte und Kultur des Vorderen Orients: Festschrift für Bertold Spuler* (eds. H.R. Roemer and A. Noth). Leiden: Brill, pp. 388–95.

Stacey, D. 1988–9. Umayyad and Egyptian red-slip 'A' ware from Tiberias, *Bulletin of the Anglo-Israel Archaeological Society* 8: 21–33.

Tzaferis, V. 1989. *Excavations at Capernaum, vol. I: 1978–1982*. Winona Lake, IN: Eisenbrauns.

Urice, S. 1987. *Qasr Kharana in the Transjordan*. Durham, NC: American Schools of Oriental Research.

van Ess, J. 1992. 'Abd al-Malik and the Dome of the Rock: An Analysis of some texts. In *Bayt al-Maqdis: 'Abd al-Malik's Jerusalem*, part one (eds J. Raby and J. Johns). Oxford: Oxford University Press, pp. 89–103.

Walmsley, A.G. 1987. *The Administrative structure and urban geography of the Jund of Filasṭīn and the Jund of al-Urdunn*. Unpub. PhD thesis, University of Sydney.

Walmsley, A.G. 1988. Convergence of literary and archaeological evidence. *Mediterranean Archaeology* 1: 142–59.

Walmsley, A.G. n.d. Tradition, innovation, and imitation in the material culture of Islamic Jordan: The First four centuries. Paper presented to the Fifth International Conference on the History and Archaeology of Jordan. Irbid, 1992.

Watson, A.M. 1983. *Agricultural innovation in the early Islamic world: The Diffusion of crops and farming techniques, 700–1100*. Cambridge, Cambridge University Press.

Wheatley, P. 1983. *Nagara and Commandery: Origins of the Southeast Asian Urban Traditions*. Chicago: University of Chicago.

Wheatley, P. n.d. The Places where Men pray together: Urban Creation and Adaptation in the early Islamic World, 7th to 10th century. Unpub. ms.

Whitcomb, D. 1985. *Before the Roses and Nightingales: Excavations at Qasr-i Abu Nasr, Iran*. New York: Metropolitan Museum of Art.

Whitcomb, D., 1987. Excavations in Aqaba: First preliminary report. *ADAJ* 31: 247–66.

Whitcomb, D. 1988a. Khirbat al-Mafjar reconsidered: The Ceramic evidence. *BASOR* 271: 51–67.

Whitcomb, D. 1988b. A Fatimid residence in Aqaba, Jordan. *ADAJ* 32: 207–24.

Whitcomb, D. 1989a. Evidence of the Umayyad period from the Aqaba excavations. *The Fourth international conference on the history of Bilad al-Sham during the Umayyad period* (eds. M.A. Bakhit and R. Schick). Amman: University of Jordan, vol. 2, pp. 164–84.

Whitcomb, D. 1989b. Coptic glazed ceramics from the excavations at Aqaba, Jordan. *JARCE* 26: 167–82.

Whitcomb, D. 1989c. Mahesh ware: Evidence of early Abbasid occupation from southern Jordan. *ADAJ* 33: 269–85.

Whitcomb, D. 1990a. Archaeology of the Abbasid period: The Example of Jordan. *Archéologie islamique* 1: 75–85.

Whitcomb, D. 1990b. Diocletian's *misr* at Aqaba. *Zeitschrift des Deutschen Palästina-vereins* 106: 156–61.

Whitcomb, D. 1990–91. Glazed Ceramics of the Abbasid Period from the Aqaba Excavations. *Transactions of the Oriental Ceramic Society* 55: 43–65.

Whitcomb, D. 1992. The Islamic period as seen from selected sites. In *The Southern Ghors and northeast 'Arabah archaeological survey* (ed. B. MacDonald). Sheffield: Sheffield Archaeological Monographs 5, pp. 113–18, 232–42.

Whitcomb, D. n.d. Out of Arabia: Early Islamic Aqaba in its regional context. Paper prepared for the Colloque d'archéologie islamique. Cairo, 1993.

Whitcomb, D. in press. The Misr of Ayla: New Evidence for the Early Islamic City, *Studies in the History and Archaeology of Jordan V*.

Wilkinson, J., 1975. The Streets of Jerusalem. *Levant* 7: 118–36.

Zeyadeh, A.H. 1991. Baysān: A City from the ninth century A.D., *The Fifth international conference on the history of Bilād al-Shām during the Abbasid period*. (eds M.A. al-Bakhit and R. Schick). Amman: University of Jordan. 114–34.

Chapter 30

Abu Bakr Muhammad b. Ahmad al-Wasiti. 1979. *Fadail al-Bayt al-Muqaddas* (ed. Y. Hasson), Institute of Asian and African Studies, The Max Schloessinger Memorial Series, Jerusalem: Hebrew University.

'Akka', *EI²*. In *The Encyclopedia of Islam* (new edition). Leiden: Brill.

Avigad, Nahman. 1983. *Discovering Jerusalem*. Jerusalem: Shikmona.

Ayalon, David. 1967. The Mamluks and Naval Power: A Phase of the Struggle between Islam and Christian Europe. *Proceedings of the Israel Academy of Sciences and Humanities* 1, no. 8: 1–12.

Ayalon, David. 1972. Discharges from Service: Banishments and Imprisonments in Mamluk Society. *Israel Oriental Studies* 3: 25–50.

Ben-Dov, M. Barid, EI² *Excavations of the Temple Mount*. Jerusalem: Keter (in Hebrew).

Ben-Tor, A., Portugali, Y. and Avissar, M. 1978. The Second Season of Excavations at Tel-Yoqneam. *IEJ* 29: 66–83.

Broshi, M. 1976. New Excavations along the Walls of Jerusalem. *Qadmoniot* 9: 75–8 (in Hebrew).

Burgoyne, M.H. 1987. *Mamluk Jerusalem: an Architectural Study*. London: World of Islam Festival Trust.

Clermont-Ganneau, Ch. 1888. Le pont de Baibars a Lydda. *Receuil d'Archeologie Orientale* 1: 262–79.

Cohen, A. 1989. *Economic Life in Ottoman Jerusalem*. Cambridge, MA: Cambidge University Press.

Cohen, A. 1973. *Palestine in the 18th Century*. Jerusalem: Yad Izhaq Ben-Zvi.

Cohen, A. and Lewis, B. 1978. *Population and Revenue in the Towns of Palestine in the 16th Century*. Princeton: Princeton University Press.

Cohen, A. and Simon-Pikali, E., 1993. *Jews in the Moslem Religious Court*. Jerusalem: (in Hebrew).

Cohen-Finkelstein, Joelle. 1991. 'Pottery Distribution, Settlement Patterns and Demographic Oscillations in Southern Samaria in the Islamic Period'. Master's thesis, Hebrew University of Jerusalem (in Hebrew).

Creswell, K.A.C. 1959. *The Muslim Architecture of Egypt*. Oxford: Clarendon Press.

De Vaux, R. and Stève, R.M. 1950. *Fouilles a Qaryat el-'Enab, Abu Gosh, Palestine*. Paris: J. Gabalda.

Elad, A. 1982. An early Arabic tradition about the Jerusalem Markets. *Cathedra*. 31–40 (in Hebrew).

Elad, A. 1991. The History and Topography of Jerusalem during the Early Islamic Period: The Historical Value of Fadail al-Quds Literature – a Reconsideration. *JASI* 14: 41–70.

From the Depths of the Sea. 1985. Israel Museum Catalogue, Jerusalem.

Goitein, S.D. 1967-1988. *A Mediterranean Society*, I–V. Berkeley and Los Angeles: University of California Press.

Haaretz Museum. 1983. *Rashaya al-Fukhkhar*. Catalogue. Tel Aviv: (in Hebrew).

Hasson, Rachel. 1983. Islamic Glass from Excavations in Jerusalem. *Journal of Glass Studies* 25: 109–13.

Hasson, Yizhak. 1987. Jerusalem in the Muslim Perspective: The Qur'an and Tradition Literature. In *The History of Jerusalem: The Early*

Islamic Period (638–1099) (ed. J. Prawer). Jerusalem: Yad Izhaq Ben-Zvi, pp. 283–313 (in Hebrew).

Jacoby, David. 1982. Montmusard, Suburb of Crusader Acre: The First Stage of its Development. In *Outremer* (eds B.Z. Kedar, H.E. Mayer and R.C. Smail). Jerusalem: Yad Izhaq Ben-Zvi, pp. 205–17.

Kaplan, J. 1957. Excavations at the White Mosque in Ramla. *Atiqot* 2: 96–103 (in Hebrew).

'Khatt', *EI²*. In *The Encyclopedia of Islam* (new edition). Leiden: Brill.

Layish, A. 1975. The Sijill of the Jaffa and Nazareth Courts as a Source for the Political and Social History of Ottoman Palestine In *Studies on Palestine during the Ottoman Period* (ed. M.Ma'oz). Jerusalem: Magnes Press, pp. 525–32.

Lehrer Gusta. 1969. *Hebron City of Glassmaking*. Tel-Aviv: Haaretz Museum.

Lewis, Bernard. 1953. An Arabic Account of the Province of Safed. *BSOAS* 11: 477–88.

Lewis, Bernard. 1988. *The Muslim Discovery of Europe*. New York: W.W. Norton and Company.

Makhouly, N. and Johns, C.M. 1946. *Guide to Acre*. Jerusalem: Department of Antiquities.

Mayer, L.A., Pinkerfeld, J. and Hirschberg, J.W. 1950. *Some Principal Muslim Religious Buildings in Israel*. Jerusalem: Committee for the Preservation of Muslim Religious Buildings, Ministry of Religious Affairs, Government Printer.

Mujir al-Dīn. 1866. *Al-uns al-Jalil bi-tarikh al-Quds wa-l-Halil*, 2 vols. Cairo: Bulak.

Nasir-i Khusraw. 1881. *Relations du voyages* (ed. Ch. Shefer). Paris: Shefer.

Prawer, Joshua. 1991. The Jewish Community in Jerusalem in the Crusader Period. In *The History of Jerusalem: Crusaders and Ayyubids (1099–1250)*. (eds J. Prawer and H. Ben-Shammai). Jerusalem: Yad Izhaq Ben-Zvi, pp. 194–212 (in Hebrew).

al-Qalqashandi. 1919. *Subh al-'Asa fi Kitabat al-'insa'*. Cairo: Costa Thomas.

Riis, P.J. and Poulsen, V. 1957. *Hama: Fouilles et recherches, les verreries et poteries, 1931–1938*. Copenhagen: National Muset.

Rosen-Ayalon, M. 1985. On Suleiman's Sabils in Jerusalem. In *The Islamic World from Classical to Modern Times: Essays in Honor of Bernard Lewis* (eds C.E. Bosworth et al.). Princeton: The Darwin Press, pp. 589–607.

Rosen-Ayalon, M. 1990. Art and Architecture in Ayyubid Jerusalem. *IEJ* 40: 305–14.

Rosen-Ayalon, M. (forthcoming). Are there Seljuk Origins for Mamluk Art?

Rosen-Ayalon, M. and Eitan, A. 1969. *Ramla Excavations*. Jerusalem: The Israel Museum.

Sauvaget, J. 1941. *La poste aux chevaux dans l'empire des Mameloukes*. Paris: Adrien-Maisonneuve.

Schein, Sylvia. 1985. Latin Hospices in Jerusalem in the Late Middle Ages. *ZDPV* 101: 82–92.

Sivan, E. 1971. The Beginnings of the Fada'il al-Quds Literature. *Israel Oriental Studies* 1: 263–71.

Toledano, E. 1977. The Sanjak of Jerusalem in the 16th Century: Patterns of Rural Settlement and Demographic Trends. In *Jerusalem in the Early Ottoman Period* (ed. A. Cohen). Jerusalem: Yad Izhaq Ben-Zvi, pp. 61–92 (in Hebrew).

Van Berchem, M. 1922. *Materiax pour un Corpus Inscriptionum Arabicarum – Jerusalem: Ville*. Cairo: Institut Français d'Archéologie Orientale.

Van Berchem, M. 1927. *Materiax pour un Corpus Inscriptionum Arabicarum – Jerusalem: Haram*. Cairo: Institut Français d'Archéologie Orientale.

Vincent, L.H., Mackay, E.J.H. and Abel, F.-M. 1923. *Hebron, le Hamam al-Khalil*. Paris: Ernest Leroux.

Chapter 31

Aaronsohn, R. 1990. *Baron Rothschild and the Colonies, the Beginning of Jewish Colonization in Eretz Israel, 1882–1890*. Jerusalem: Yad Izhak Ben-Zvi (Hebrew).

Aaronsohn, R. 1993 (in press). The beginnings of modern Jewish agriculture in Israel – innovation or diffusion? *Agricultural History*.

Adas, M. 1989. *Machines as the Measure of Men: Science, Technology, and Ideologies of Western Dominance*. Ithaca: Cornell University Press.

Avitsur, S. 1972. The energy basis for the economic development of Eretz Israel. In *Man and His Labor* (ed. S. Avitsur). Tel Aviv: Avshalom Institute, pp. 1–46 (Hebrew).

Avitsur, S. 1974. The Jewish factor in pre-industrial processes in Eretz Israel. In *Shalem* I (ed. J. Hacker). Jerusalem: Yad Izhak Ben-Zvi, pp. 481–99 (Hebrew).

Avitsur, S. 1976. *Man and His Labor, Historical Atlas of Tools and Workshops in the Holy Land*. Jerusalem: Carta (Hebrew).

Avitsur, S. 1977a. Bibliography, writings of Shmuel Avitsur. *Cathedra*. 5: 210–23 (Hebrew).

Avitsur, S. 1977b. *Changes in Agriculture in Eretz Israel 1875–1975*. Tel Aviv: Milo (Hebrew).

Avitsur, S. 1984. Installations and their facilities at Miqve Israel, 'industrial archeology' of the first Hebrew agricultural establishment. Tel Aviv: *Ha-Aretz Museum Yearbook*. 1 (19): 235–46 (Hebrew).

Avitsur, S. 1986. *Inventors and Adaptors*. Tel Aviv: Ha-Aretz Museum (Hebrew).

Avitsur, S. 1989. *The Industrial Revolution in Eretz Israel on the Basis of Energetic Processes*. Tel Aviv: Ha-Kibbutz Ha-Meuchad (Hebrew).

Ben-Artzi, Y. 1988. *Jewish Moshava Settlements in Eretz Israel, 1882–1914*. Jerusalem: Yad Izhak Ben-Zvi (Hebrew).

Blaut, J.M. 1977. Two views of diffusion. *Annals of the Association of American Geographers*. 67: 343–9.

Blech, E.C. 1908. British Consul, Jerusalem to Barclay, H., British Minister, Constantinople, 28 July 1908, British Public Records Office, Record Group 195/2287, pp. 169–70.

Brown, L.A. 1981. *Innovation Diffusion, A New Perspective*. London and New York: Methuen.

Cuno, K.M. 1980. The origins of private ownership of land in Egypt: a reappraisal. *International Journal of Middle East Studies*. 12: 245–75.

Davison, R.H. 1990. The advent of the electric telegraph in the Ottoman Empire. In *Essays in Ottoman and Turkish History, 1774–1923 The Impact of the West* (ed. R.H. Davison). Austin: University of Texas Press, pp. 133–65.

Eliav, M. 1978. *Eretz Israel and Its Yishuv in the 19th Century, 1777–1917*. Jerusalem: Keter (Hebrew).

Finn, J. 1878. *Stirring Times* (2 vols). London: Kegan Paul.

Fischer, C.S. 1985. Studying technology and social life. In *High Technology, Space and Society* [Urban Affairs Annual Review 28] (ed. M. Castells). Beverly Hills: Sage, pp. 284–300.

Fischer, C.S. and Carroll, G.R. 1986. *The Diffusion of the Telephone and Automobile in the United States, 1902 to 1937*. Organizational Behavior and Industrial Relations Working Paper No. OBIR-8. University of California.

Glass, J.B. 1991. The silk industry of Rosh Pinnah. *Cathedra*. 59: 83–94 (Hebrew).

Glass, J.B. and Kark, R. 1991. *Sephardi Entrepreneurs in Eretz Israel. The Amzalak Family 1816–1918*. Jerusalem: Magnes.

Gomulka, S. 1990. *The Theory of Technological Change and Economic Growth*. London and New York: Routledge.

Gottheil, F.M. 1980. On technological change in the 19th century Fertile Crescent: the beginnings of a development path. Paper presented at the International Conference on the Economic History of the Middle East, 1800–1914, A Comparative Approach. University of Haifa.

Graubard, S.R. 1980. Preface to the issue, 'Modern Technology: Problem or Opportunity?' *Daedalus*. 109 (1): v–vi.

Great Britain. 1917. Egyptian Expedition Force. *Military Handbook of Palestine*. Cairo: Government Press (3rd provisional edn).

Greene, K. 1986. *The Archaeology of the Roman Economy*. London: Batsford.

Gross, N. 1977. *Banker to an Emerging Nation: The History of Bank Leumi*. Ramat Gan: Massada (Hebrew).

Hägerstrand, T. 1967. *Innovation Diffusion as a Spatial Process*. Chicago: University of Chicago Press.

al-Hassan, A.Y. and Hill, D.R. 1986. *Islamic Technology*. Cambridge: Cambridge University Press.

Headrick, D.R. 1988. *The Tentacles of Progress, Technology Transfer in the Age of Imperialism, 1850–1940*. New York and Oxford: Oxford University Press.

Issawi, C. 1966. *The Economic History of the Middle East 1800–1914. A Book of Readings.* Chicago and London: University of Chicago Press.

Issawi, C. 1982. *An Economic History of the Middle East and North Africa.* London: Methuen.

Issawi, C. 1988. *The Fertile Crescent 1800–1914, A Documentary Economic History.* New York and Oxford: Oxford University Press.

Kark, R. 1984. Land ownership and spatial change in nineteenth century Palestine: an overview. In *Transition from Spontaneous to Regulated Spatial Organization* (ed. M. Rosciczewsky). Warsaw: International Geographical Union, pp. 183–96.

Kark, R. 1986. The contribution of the Ottoman regime to the development of Jerusalem and Jaffa, 1840–1917. In *Palestine in the Late Ottoman Period* (ed. D. Kushner). Jerusalem: Yad Izhak Ben-Zvi and Leiden: Brill, pp. 46–58.

Kark, R. 1990a. Transportation in nineteenth-century Palestine: reintroduction of the wheel. In *The Land That Became Israel, Studies in Historical Geography* (ed. R. Kark). New Haven: Yale University Press, pp. 57–76.

Kark, R. 1990b. The rise and decline of coastal towns in Palestine. In *Ottoman Palestine 1800–1914. Studies in Economic and Social History* (ed. G.G. Gilbar). Leiden: Brill, pp. 69–89.

Kark, R. 1990c. *Jaffa, A City in Evolution, 1799–1917.* Jerusalem: Yad Izhak Ben-Zvi.

Kark, R. 1994. *American Consuls in the Holy Land, 1832–1914.* Detroit and Jerusalem: Wayne State University Press.

Katz, S. 1982. 'The First Furrow', ideology, settlement and agriculture in Petah-Tiqva in its first decade (1878–1888). *Cathedra.* 23: 57–124 (Hebrew).

Katz, S. 1986. Sociological aspects of the growth and the turnover of agricultural knowledge in Israel: The emergence of extra-scientific systems for the production of agricultural knowledge 1880–1940. Doctoral dissertation. Department of Sociology, Hebrew University, Jerusalem (Hebrew).

Katz, E., Levin, L. and Hamilton, H. 1963. Traditions of research on the diffusion of innovation. *American Sociological Review.* 28: 237–52.

Kroeber, A.L. 1930. Diffusionism. In *Encyclopedia of the Social Sciences* (ed. E.R.A. Seligman). New York: Macmillan, 5: 139.

Landes, D.S. 1969. *The Unbound Prometheus, Technological Change and Industrial Development in Western Europe from 1750 to the Present.* Cambridge: Cambridge University Press.

Landes, D.S. 1980. The creation of knowledge and technique: today's task and yesterday's experience. *Daedalus.* 109 (1): 111–20.

Levy, T.E. (ed.) 1994. Theme guide for authors of *The Archaeology of Society in the Holy Land.*

Lincoln, A. 1915. *Discoveries and Inventions, A Lecture by Abraham Lincoln Delivered in 1860.* San Francisco: Howell.

Lipschitz, N., Lev-Yadun, S. and Biger, G. 1988. The origin of the lumber in the houses of the American Colony in Jaffa. *Cathedra.* 47: 70–8 (Hebrew).

Maddison, A. 1991. *Dynamic Forces in Capitalist Development, A Long-Run Comparative View.* Oxford and New York: Oxford University Press.

Manning, S. 1874. *Those Holy Fields.* London: Religious Tract Society.

Mendel, B. 1984. The diffusion of innovations in Eretz Israel in the nineteenth century as reflected in the local press. Seminar paper. Department of Geography, Hebrew University, Jerusalem (Hebrew).

Merrill, S. 1885. US Consul, Jerusalem to Porter, J., Assistant Secretary of State, Washington, D.C., 10 November 1885, United States National Archives, Record Group 59, T471/5.

Metzer, J. 1982. Technology, labor, and growth in a dual economy's traditional sector: Mandatory Palestine, 1921–1936. *Falk Institute Discussion Papers.* 82.01: 1–23.

Mokyr, J. 1990. *Twenty-Five Centuries of Technological Change, An Historical Survey.* Chur: Harwood.

Mokyr, J. 1992. *The Lever of Riches, Technological Creativity and Economic Progress.* New York and Oxford: Oxford University Press.

Nickoley, E.F. 1924. Agriculture. In *Modern Turkey* (ed. E.G. Mears). New York: Macmillan.

Owen, R. 1981. *The Middle East in the World Economy 1800–1914.* London and New York: Methuen.

Owen, R. 1984. The study of Middle Eastern industrial history: Notes on the interrelationship between factors and small-scale manufacturing

with special references to Lebanese silk and Egyptian sugar, 1900–1930. *International Journal of Middle East Studies.* 16: 475–87.

Pedersen, P.O. 1970. Innovation diffusion within and between national urban systems. *Geographical Analysis.* 3: 203–55.

Penslar, D.J. 1991. *Zionism and Technology, the Engineering of Jewish Settlement in Palestine, 1870–1918.* Bloomington and Indianapolis: Indiana University Press.

Pred, A. 1973. *Urban Growth and City-Systems in the United States, 1840–1860.* Cambridge, MA and London: Harvard University Press.

Pred, A. 1990. *Making Histories and Constructing Human Geographies, The Local Transformation of Practice, Power Relations, and Consciousness.* Boulder, San Francisco and Oxford: Westview Press.

Renfrew, C. and Bahn, P. 1991. *Archeology – Theories, Methods and Practice.* London: Thames and Hudson.

Richards, A. 1981. Growth and technical change: 'internal' and 'external' sources of Egyptian underdevelopment, 1800–1914. *Asian and African Studies.* 15: 45–67.

Rogers, E. 1983. *Diffusion of Innovations.* New York: Free Press (3rd edn).

Rogers, E. and Shoemaker, F.F. 1971. *Communication of Innovations: A Cross-Cultural Approach.* New york: Free Press (2nd edn).

Ruppin, A. 1918. *An Economic Survey.* New York: The Provisional Zionist Committee.

Schölch, A. 1981. The economic development of Palestine 1856–1882. *Journal of Palestine Studies.* 10: 35–58.

Shamir, S. 1986. The beginning of modern times in the history of Palestine. *Cathedra.* 40: 138–58 (Hebrew).

Shva, S. and Ben-Amotz, D. 1973. *Land of Zion Jerusalem.* Jerusalem: Weidenfeld and Nicholson (Hebrew).

Stein, A. 1991. *Fellaheen, Machines and Peasants, The History of Agricultural Technique from the Beginning to the End of the Nineteenth Century.* Tel Aviv: Sifriat Poalim (Hebrew).

Thalmann, N. 1991. The character and development of the farm economy in the Templer colonies in Palestine 1869–1939. Doctoral dissertation. Department of Geography, Hebrew University, Jerusalem (Hebrew).

Wallace, T.R. 1908. US Consul, Jerusalem, to Assistant Secretary of State, Washington, D.C., 14 August 1908, United States National Archives, Record Group 59, T471/10 [Fi 2477/10], pp. 69–73.

Wallace, T.R. 1910a. US Consul, Jerusalem, to Assistant Secretary of State, Washington, D.C., 20 January 1910, United States National Archives, Record Group 59, T471/11 [Fi 2477/11], pp. 54–63.

Wallace, T.R. 1910b. US Consul, Jerusalem, to Assistant Secretary of State, Washington, D.C., 11 July 1910, United States National Archives, Record Group 59, T471/11 [Fi 2477/11], pp. 236–8.

Wallace, T.R. 1910c. US Consul, Jerusalem, to Assistant Secretary of State, Washington, D.C., 8 October 1910, United States National Archives, Record Group 59, T471/11 [Fi 2477/11], pp. 370–5.

Warte, 1912. Die *warte* des Tempels. 12: 96.

Wittfogel, K.A. 1957. *Oriental Despotism: A Comparative Study of Total Power.* New Haven: Yale University Press.

Chapter 32

Adams, Robert McC. 1981. *Heartland of Cities.* Chicago: University of Chicago Press.

Anderson, David 1990. Political Change in Chiefdom Societies: Cycling in the Late Prehistoric Southeastern United States. Unpublished doctoral dissertation, Dept. of Anthropology, University of Michigan, Ann Arbor.

Bawden, Garth 1989. The Andean State as a State of Mind. *Journal of Anthropological Research.* 45: 327–32.

Charpin, Dominique 1982. Marchands du palais et marchands du temple à la fin de la 1re dynastie de Babylone. *Journal Asiatique.* 270: 25–65.

Falconer, Steven 1987. Heartland of Villages: Reconsidering Early Urbanism in the Southern Levant. Unpublished doctoral dissertation, Dept. of Anthropology University of Arizona.

Joffe, Alexander 1993. Settlement and Society in Early Bronze I and II of Southern Levant. Sheffield: Sheffield Academic Press.

Paynter, Robert 1989. The Archaeology of Equality and Inequality. *Annual Review of Anthropology.* 18: 369–99.

Renfrew, Colin and John Cherry (eds) 1986. *Peer-polity Interaction and Socio-political Change*. New Directions in Archaeology. Cambridge: Cambridge University Press.

Sahlins, Marshall 1960. Evolution: Specific and General. In *Evolution and Culture* (eds Marshall Sahlins and Elman Service). Ann Arbor: University of Michigan Press, pp. 12–44.

Stol, Marten 1982. State and Private Business in the Land of Larsa. *Journal of Cuneiform Studies*. 34: 127–230.

van de Mieroop, Marc 1992. *Society and Enterprise in Old Babylonian Ur*. Berlin: Dietrich Reimer Verlag.

Yoffee, Norman 1993a. Too Many Chiefs? or, Safe Texts for the 90s. In *Archaeological Theory: Who Sets the Agenda?* (eds Norman Yoffee and Andrew Sherratt). New Directions in Archaeology. Cambridge: Cambridge University Press, pp. 60–78.

Yoffee, Norman 1993b. The Process of Social Change in Mesopotamia, ca. 2000–1200 B.C.E. In *Bible and the Ancient Near East* (eds J. Hackett et al.) (Forthcoming).

Yoffee, Norman and Cowgill, George L. (eds) 1988. *The Collapse of Ancient States and Civilizations*. Tucson: University of Arizona Press.

Yoffee, Norman and Sherratt, Andrew 1993. Introduction: The Sources of Archaeological Theory. In *Archaeological Theory: Who Sets the Agenda?* (eds Norman Yoffee and Andrew Sherratt). New Directions in Archaeology. Cambridge: Cambridge University Press, pp. 1–9.

INDEX

A

Aaronsohn, Ran 527, 534, 535
Abbott, F.F. 459
Abel, F.M. 474, 475, 504
Acheulean lithic entities 99–100
Acheulo-Yabrudian culture 98
Acre
    mosque 513, 520
    Ottoman khan 520
Adams, George W.J. 533
Adams, Robert McC. 291, 294, 320, 327, 547, 548
Adams, W.Y. 332
Adas, M. 524
Adjeman, Y. 391
advertisements 528, 529, 535
aeolian landscapes 47–51
agrarian society, Early Israel 391–3
agricultural development, Iron Age I 357–8
agricultural specialization, Early Israel 389–91
agriculture
    Byzantine period 483–4
    modern period 533–4
    Negev 485–6
Ahab's palace 420
    carved inlays 426
Aharoni, M. 385
Aharoni, Y. 13, 363, 386, 387, 389, 392, 416
Ahituv, S. 326
Ahlström, G.W. 351, 363, 364, 365, 381, 458
Ain Ghazal figurines 191
Akazawa, T. 117, 119
al- see main part of name
Albright, William Foxwell 416, 437, 501
    antiquity in the Holy Land 9, 13, 17, 18
    highland frontiers 351, 354, 363, 464
    Israel and Judah, kingdoms of 384, 389, 392
    Late Bronze Age 320, 325, 330, 340, 341, 345, 354
    Middle Bronze Age 297, 312, 314
Algaze, G. 228
Alon, David 249, 257, 313, 500
    Chalcolithic period 229, 230, 232, 233, 235–7, 239
    Neolithic 198, 202, 207
Aloni, R. 30
alphabet, Middle Bronze Age 312
Alt, A. 323, 340, 351, 361, 362, 383, 401, 501
Amiel, A. 49
Amiran, D.H.K. 256, 268, 327, 416
Amiran, R. 241, 269, 275, 277, 279, 286, 310, 455
Ammon
    aerial view 400
    Rabbath-Amman 403
    settlement 406–7
    statues 410
    Tell el-Umeiri 412
    tribalism 407–8
Amudian culture 98–9
Anati, E. 60, 210, 229
Anbar, M. 301, 311
Anderson, David 546
Anderson, James D. 9, 240
Anderson, W.P. 372, 379, 380, 381, 544
animal bones 120–1, 197
animal domestication 187, 195–6

animal husbandry 247–9
    Pottery Neolithic to Iron Age 250–5
Annales paradigm 4–8
    change processes 7–8
    innovation and technology 6–7
    major transitions 6
    pattern and process 6
    religion and ideology 7
    social organization 7
Annales school 2–4
    center-periphery 8
Applebaum, S. 449–53, 455–8, 462, 465, 468
Aqaba
    Early Islamic period 498
    excavation plan 498
    kilns 495
arable agriculture 249–50
archaeological exploration 1919-39 15–17
archaeologists, 19th century 14–15
archaeology
    evolutionary process 78–9
    interdisciplinary x–xiv
    social change 79
    space-time approach 86–92
architecture
    Byzantine period
        religious 477–81
        secular 473–7
    Iron Age II 422–3
    Middle Bronze Age 309
    Roman period 454–5
Arensburg, B.
    foragers, Upper Paleolithic 136, 137
    Lower Paleolithic 96
    Middle Bronze Age 301
    Modern Humans, origins of 123
    Neolithic Period 219, 220
    people of the Holy Land 61, 63–8, 71
Ariel, D.T. 437
Armstrong, G.T. 478
Arnold, D.E. 220
Arnon, I. 249
arrowheads, Nahal Hemar 77
Artas, irrigated gardens 533
artifacts, Roman period 461
arts
    Byzantine period 482–3
    Early Neolithic 197–8
    Iron Age II 423–5
    Middle Bronze Age 309–11
Artzy, M. 371
Asaro, P. 334
Ashdod 346
    goddess 333
    offering stand 341
    site plan 340
Asher, Robert 2
Ashkelon 345–6
    aerial view 343
    ramparts 344
    site plan 340
    spools 347
Ashtor, E. 494
Auger, R. 352
Aurenche, O. 141, 190, 193

Aurignacian population 64
Avaris, Middle Bronze Age 308
Avi-Yonah, M.
  Byzantine Period 470, 472, 473, 480, 482, 483, 485
  Persian and Hellenistic Periods 432, 434
  Rome, impact of 450–2, 456, 458, 460–1, 463, 468
Aviam, Mordechai 479, 507
Avigad, Nahman 455, 459, 462, 468, 474, 516, 520
Avitsur, S. 526, 527, 533, 534, 535
Avner, U. 235, 238, 305
Avnimelech, M. 127
Ayalon, David 515, 518
Ayalon, E. 456, 457, 496
Ayla, excavation plan 498
Ayyubid, mosque 515
Ayyubid/Mamluk/Ottoman periods
  innovations and technology 520–2
  major developments 512–14
  religion and ideology 522
  settlement patterns 514–20
  sites 514
  social organization 522–3
Azar, G. 309
Azor, figurines 246

B

Bachdach, J. 148
Baer, Klaus 342
Bagatti, B. 451, 477, 504
Bahat, D. 455
Bahn, P. 226, 301, 372, 376, 405, 409, 524
Baida, U. 42
Bailey, R.C. 87
Baines, J. 234
Bakker-Heeres, J.A. 195, 196
Baly, D. 383
Bankroft, H. 126
Banning, E.B. 193, 386, 468, 500
Bar-Adon, Pessah 229, 233–4, 244, 250, 257–8, 267, 449
Bar-Nathan, R. 474
Bar-Yosef, D.E. 199
Bar-Yosef, Ofer
  approaches to the past 42–5, 47–53
  Chalcolithic Period 234
  chronological framework xiv–xvi
  foragers, Upper Paleolithic 130–5, 137, 139
  hunter/gatherers, end of Paleolothic 141, 144, 148, 152, 153, 156, 161, 162
  Lower Paleolithic of Israel 93, 96, 98, 100–3, 105
  Modern Humans, origins of 110, 112–14, 117–20
  Natufian culture 172, 182, 183
  Neolithic Period, pottery 207, 221
  Neolithic, pre pottery 190, 192–201
  pastoral activity, southern Levant 249, 257, 264
  people of the Holy Land 60, 61, 63, 64, 65
  social change, prehistoric lithic production 78, 81, 82, 83, 85, 86
  southern Levant economy 234
Barag, D. 435
Baramki, D.C. 493, 494
Bard, E. 144, 156
Barid 516
Barkay, G. 416, 435
Barker, G. 2
Barth, F. 404
Bartlett, J.R. 402, 406
Baruch, U. 45, 52, 54, 146, 156, 178
Bate, D.M.
  changing landscape 51
  foragers, Upper Paleolithic Period 124, 127, 128, 129
  Lower Paleolothic of Israel 96, 97, 98, 100

Modern Humans, origins of 117
Natufian culture 171, 176, 177, 180
poeple of the Holy Land 62
Bates, D.G. 290, 291, 293, 405
Baumgarten, Y. 229
Bawden, Garth 545
Beck, P. 301, 302, 371
Be'er Resisim
  domestic shelter 291
  settlement plan 290
Beer Shema, mosaic 483
Beersheva, incense altars 386
Begin, Z.B. 44, 129, 146
Beit-Arieh, I. 241, 243, 384, 386
Belfer, A. 124, 130, 132, 135, 139
Belfer-Cohen, Anna
  foragers, Upper Paleolithic Period 121, 127, 131–5, 137
  hunter/gatherers, end of Paleolithic 141
  Natufian culture 171, 176, 177, 179, 183
  Neolithic Period, pottery 207, 221
  Neolithic, pre pottery 195, 196–201
  people of the Holy Land from prehistory 64, 65, 66, 67
Belitzky, S. 43, 44, 107, 108
Belon du Mans, Pierre 11
Ben Dor, E. 210
Ben Pechat, M. 479
Ben-Amotz, D. 530
Ben-Arieh, Y. 13, 327
Ben-Artzi, Yossi 527
Ben-David, A. 459
Ben-Dov, M. 309, 474, 499, 521
Ben-Tor, A.B. 228, 269, 277, 284, 423, 436, 496, 512, 521
Bennett, C. 407
Bennett, J.W. xii
Bennett, W.J. 436, 438
Benoit, P. 455
Benot Ya'akov Formation 43–4, 45
Benvenisti, M. 504
Beq'ah Valley, aerial view 400
Berekhat Ram
  figurine 101
  strata 98
Bergman, C.A. 115
Berlin, Isaiah 542
Berman, E.K. 494
Besançon, J. 98, 99, 141, 151
Besant, W. 9
Beth Loya
  mosaic 482
  oil press 484
  wine press 486
Beth Shean
  aerial view 476
  plaza 477
  Roman bridge 455
  site plan 475
  stele 329
Betts, A. 181, 199, 272
Biblical Geography 13
Bickerman, E. 461
Bienkowski, P. 314, 322, 324, 325, 326, 402, 406, 408
Bietak, M. 308, 314, 330, 340, 341, 342
Biger, Gideon 380, 382, 527
Binford, L.R. 2, 80, 81, 116, 162, 183, 318, 368
Binford, S.R. 117
Bintliff, John 2, 4, 7, 320
Biran, A. 386
Birger, R. 483, 487
Birnbaum, N. 6, 7
Birsama, mosaic 483
Blair, S. 499
Blakely, J.A. 436, 438
Blalock, H.M. 390

Blaut, J.M. 526
Blech, E.C. 532
Bliss, Frederick 9, 11, 12, 15
Bloch, Marc 2, 7
Bloch-Smith, E. 421
Boardman, J. 436
Boëda, E. 118
bone tools, Upper Paleolithic 133–4
Boraas, Roger S. 290, 412
Bordes, F. 98, 99, 118
Bossut, P. 210
Bottema, S. 45, 52, 128, 129, 146, 178
Bottini, G.C. 477
Bouchud, J. 117
Boutié, P. 119
Boyd, Brian 177
Bradley, R. 239
Braemer, F. 393
Braidwood, R.J. 198, 436
Brandl, B. 277, 355
Braudel, Fernand 351
    Annales school of social historians xii, 2, 4–5, 7, 8, 431
    Chalolithic Period 226, 232, 236
    conclusion 542, 545, 548
    Middle Bronze Age 304, 314
    Sea Peoples, impact of 348
    Transjordan tribalism 411
Braudel, Laura M. 411
Braudelian temporal framework 4
Braun, D. 43, 53
Braun, E. 269, 272
Brawer, A.J. 18
Braziunas, T.F. xiv
Breasted, James 16–17, 22
Bronze Age *see* Early . . .; Late . . .; Middle . . .
Brosch, M. 492
Broshi, M. 280, 349, 355
    Byzantine Period 473, 474
    Early Bronze Age, Canaan 280
    Late Bronze Age 320
    Middle Bronze Age 302, 304, 305
    power, politics and the past 9, 18
    Rome, impact of 455
Brown, L.A. 526
Brown, M.B. 65
Brown, P. 11
Brug, J.E. 335, 342
Bruins, 47
Buccellati, G. 362
Buckingham, John Silk 13
Bull, P.A. 51
Bulliet, R.W. 2, 8
Bunimovitz, Shlomo
    conclusion 544, 547
    highland frontiers 354, 357, 363
    Iron Ages I 363
    Late Bronze Age 320, 322, 323–4, 327, 363
    Middle Bronze Age 300, 302, 304, 314, 315, 317, 356–7
    Sea Peoples 335
Burgoyne, M.H. 518, 522
burial
    Byzantine period 481–2
    cave complex, Nahal Qana 237
    Early Neolithic 197
    EB IV tombs and mortuary practices 282–7
    Gilat 59
    Iron Age II 421–2
    Late Bronze Age 331
    Middle Bronze Age 318–19
    Nahal Zehora 220
    Pottery Neolithic 219–20
    Roman period 459–60, 462
    Shiqmim 239

Tell Abu Hawam 331
    Yarmukian 219
Burian, F. 210
Burkhardt, John 13
Buseirah, aerial view 407
Butzer, Karl xii, xiii
Byrd, B.F. 148, 152, 155, 179, 180, 193, 207
Byzantine period
    agricultural installations 483–4
    architecture
        religious 477–81
        secular 473–7
    art 482–3
    burial practices 481–2
    churches 477–9
    monasteries 487
    Negev 485–6
    sites 472, 507
    synagogues 479–81

C

Caesarea
    aqueduct 456
    coins 471
    pottery 495
    Roman theater 455
Calciform pottery 288
Callaway, J.A. 275, 351, 354, 364, 389
Cameron, D.O. 236
Campana, D.V. 171
Campbell, E.F. 409
Canaan, T. 15
Capernaum
    coins 494
    synagogue 460
Carneiro, Robert L. 226, 294
Carroll, G.R. 526
Casson, L. 458
cattle 258, 267–8
Cauvin, J.C. 195, 198, 199, 207
Cauvin, M.C. 146, 152, 181, 182, 199
Cavanagh, W.G. 331
caves 50–1
    Et-Tabun 50–1
    Kebara 51
    Roman period 453
cemeteries
    Chalcolithic 234–5
    Shiqmim 239
Chalcolithic period
    agro-technology 229–31
    cemeteries 234–5
    climatic factors 241
    collapse of society 241–3
    commercialization 242–3
    craft specialization 232–3, 244
    demographic trends 229
    gift giving 240–1
    ideology 234
    innovation and technology 229–38
    metal production sites 238
    pastoralism 231–2
    population 69
    production and metallurgy 233–4
    public sanctuaries 235–8
    resource competition 239–40
    risk management 238–9
    settlement pattern 229
    sites 228, 230
    social evolution 226–9
    societies 229–38

socio-political organization 241–2
welfare 243
Chambon, A. 392
Champion, T.C. 8
Chaney, M.L. 351, 363, 386
Chapman, R. 331
Charpin, Dominique 547
Chartier, R. 5
Cherry, John 5, 301, 314, 315, 324, 326, 547
Chevaillon, J. 148
Chiat, M.J. 481
Childe, G.V. 141
Chitty, D.J. 487
chronological framework
general historic xvi
prehistoric xiv–xvi
chronological table xvi
chronological uncertainties 110–14
chronology
pottery 339
Sea Peoples 335–6
churches
Byzantine period 477–9
Crusader Palestine 503
cities, Roman period 450–1, 463–4
city planning, Persian and Hellenistic Empires 437–9
Claessen, H.J.M. 326
Clairmont, C. 436
Clark, G.A. 110, 251
Clark, J.D. 93, 101, 110
Clark, S. 5
Clarke, D.L. xiv, 5, 207, 208
Clarke, Edward Daniel 13
class distinctions, Early Israel 376
Claude, D. 474
Clermont-Ganneau, Charles 21, 432, 504, 517
Close, A.E. 79
Clutton-Brock, J. 195, 196, 211, 247, 251, 258
coffins, Deir el-Balah 321
cognitive-spiritual aspects, Upper Paleolithic 136–7
Cohen, A. 519
Cohen, M.N. 200
Cohen, R. 259, 290
Cohen-Finkelstein, Joelle 521, 523
COHMAP 201
Cohn, N. 12
coins
Abbasid 494
Caesarea 471
Capernaum 494
Persian and Hellenistic Empires 435–6
Roman period 458–9, 462
Colledge, S.M. 144
Collon, D. 310
colluvial settings 47
Commenge-Pellergrin, C. 229, 232
commercialization, Chalcolithic 242–3
communications, modern period 536–7
Conder, C.R. 504
Conrad, K.I. 491
Contenau, G. 432
Cook, J. 177
Cooke, G.A. 432
Cooley, R.E. 351
Coote, R.B. 351, 410
Cope, C. 175
Copeland, L. 98, 99, 100, 118, 123, 178
copper implements, Nahal Mishmar 227
copper javelins, Jebel Qa'aqir 288
Corbo, V. 476, 487
Corrucini, R.S. 63
Coüasnon, C. 476
Courty, M.A. 54

Cowgill, George L. 294, 295, 314, 328, 431, 547
Cowley, A. 432
craft specialization, Chalcolithic 232–3, 244
cranial measurements 70, 71
see also skulls
Crawford, 459
Cresswell, K.A.C. 499, 517
Crognier, E. 65
Cross, F.M. 377, 444, 454
Crouwel, J.H. 268
Crowfoot, G.W. 437, 440
Crowfoot, J.W. 210, 426, 450, 477, 479
Crowfoot-Payne, J. 190, 194
Crusader kingdom 11
Crusader Palestine
Frankish manor house 506
Frankish village 505
maisons fortes 505–6
rural burgi 505
St. Anne's church 503
Samaritan sites 508
settlement patterns 506–8
cult objects
Early Neolithic 197–8
Persian and Hellenistic Empires 441–4
cultivation
Early Neolithic 195–6
Late Neolithic 249–50
cults, Middle Bronze Age 313–14
cultural entities
Acheulo-Yabrudian 98
Amudian 98–9
late Acheulean 99–100
Lower Paleolithic 93–6, 97–100
pre-Aurignacian 98–9
Tayacian 97–8
Yabrudian 98
cultures
Late Bronze Age 320
Lodian (Jericho IX) 210–11
Pottery Neolithic 214–15
Wadi Raba 211–14
Yarmukian 209–10
Cuno, K.M. 527
Currid, J.D. 377
Curtin, P.D. 381

D

Dalley, S. 309
Dan, J. 24, 30, 40, 43, 49, 50
Dan, Y. 474, 476, 477
Daniel, G. 76
Danin, A. 24, 26, 28, 30, 33–8, 126, 168, 544
Dar, Shimon 353, 452, 453, 456, 457, 458, 464, 468
Darmon, F. 45
D'Arvieux, Laurent 11–12, 14
Dauvois, M. 108
Davies, G.I. 372
Davies, M.S. 173, 175, 195, 196
Davies, P.R. 351
Davis, S. 378
Davis, Simon J.M. 120
Calcolithic Period 232, 234
Natufian culture 176, 187
Neolithic, pre pottery 195, 196, 201
plough and pasture, southern Levant 251, 253, 257, 258, 259, 267
Davison, R.H. 527
Dayan, T. 199
Dayton, J.E. 384
de Contenson, H. 198, 220, 229, 241

de Geus, C.H.J. 363, 364, 365
De Saulcy, Louis-Félicien 14, 17
de Silva, C.G. 476, 477, 478
de Vaux, R. *see* Vaux, R. de
De Vries, B. 497
Dead Sea, salt deposits 25
Dead Sea Scrolls 21
Dearman, A. 407
Debard, E. 103
Deir el-Balah, coffins 321
Delougaz, P. 494
Demars, P.Y. 130
demography
    Early Bronze Age 280
    Iron Age I 354–9
    Sea Peoples 344
Denyer, S. 240
Dever, William G. 384, 410, 431
    conclusion 544
    Early Bronze IV Period 285, 289, 290, 291, 295
    Early Islamic Period 500, 501
    highland frontiers, conquest of 349, 354, 356, 357, 359, 363–5
    Late Bronze Age 320, 322, 330
    Middle Bronze Age 297, 301, 305, 309, 311, 313–15, 317
    plough and pasture, southern Levant 253, 264
    Sea Peoples, impact of 342
    social change 5, 6, 17, 19, 78
Di Segni, L. 476
Dibble, H.L. 118
Dibon of Moab, aerial view 408
Digard, J.P. 251
Dodu, G. 508
Dollfus, G. 229
domestic economy, Early Israel 386–7
donkeys 258
Dornemann, R.H. 407
Dossin, G. 307, 312
Dostal, W. 497
Dothan, M. 306, 323
    Chalcolithic Period 231
    Persian and Hellenistic Periods 436, 439, 440, 445
    Sea Peoples, impact of 334, 335, 337, 342, 346
    social change 14
Dothan, Trude 14, 332, 334, 335, 340, 341, 342, 343, 346, 347
Doumas, Christos 346
dromedaries 259
Duke, P. 2
Dunand, M. 209, 219, 313
Dupouy-Madre, M. 65
Duri, A.A. 11
Durkheim, E. 234

E

EAEHL 416
Earle, T.K. xiv, 6, 226, 239, 294, 313
Early Bronze IV
    pottery 288, 292
    settlements and settlement patterns 287–93
    sites 284
    social structure 293–5
    socio-economic models 289–93
    tombs and mortuary practices 282–7
Early Bronze Age
    Canaan and Egypt 277–9
    demography 280
    environment 280
    fruit trees 250
    highlands societies 359–60

    population 69
    post-Chalcolithic resettlement 269–72
    settlement disintegration 273–5
    sites 271, 274, 277
    urban settlement patterns 275
Early Islamic period
    Aqaba 498
    innovations and technology 493–6
    kilns 495
    mosque 498
    religion and ideology 496–7
    settlement patterns 488–93
    social organization 497–8
Early Israel
    agrarian society 391–3
    agricultural intensification 391–3
    agricultural specialization 389–91
    centralized state 371–6
    class distinctions 376
    commodity redistribution 393
    commodity storage 393
    domestic economy 386–7
    economic centralization 382–6
    emergence 363
    evolution of wealthy men 376–8
    family contributions 391–3
    House of Omri 382–6
    houses 387–9
    impact of nationhood 386–91
    Israelite settlement patterns 383–6
    Israelites 364
    land alienation 391–3
    professional services 381–2
    regulation 378–9
    residence patterns 391–3
    South Arabian trade 383–6
    transformation from agriculture 376–9
    Tyrian connection 380–1
    urban society 379–82
    wealth distinctions 376
Early Neolithic
    animal domestication 195–6
    art and cult objects 197–8
    chronology 190
    cultivation 195–6
    economy 195–6
    graves and burials 197
    innovation 194–5
    processes of change 200–1
    religion and ideology 197–8
    settlement patterns 190–4
    sites 190–4
    social organization 198–200
    technology 194–5
Echegaray, G.J. 190, 194
economy
    Early Israel 382–6
    Early Neolithic 195–6
    Sea Peoples 344–5
ecosystems, human xii–xiii
Edelman, D. 78, 351
Edelman-Vikander, D. 351
Edelstein, G. 359
Eder, J.F. 80
Edom
    settlement 406–7
    tribalism 408
Edwards, P. 172, 176
Efrat, E. 40
Eickelman, D.F. 404
Eig, A. 24, 26
Ein el Jarba, pottery vessels 213, 214
Ein Gedi, Ghassulian churn 267

Eisenberg, E. 219, 229, 273, 358
Eisenmann, V. 93, 97
Eisenstadt, Shmuel 6, 328
Eisenstein, J.D. 345
Eitan, A. 455, 492, 516
Ekron 346–8
    public building 348
    reconstruction 347
    site plan 340
Elad, A. 499, 522
Eldar, L. 229
Eldridge, N. 371
Elgarvish, J. 438, 439
Eliav, M. 537
'En Besor
    Egyptian building 278
    site 278
Endo, 63
Engberg, R.M. 229, 241
environment
    Early Bronze Age 280
    Iron Age I 352–4
environmental change 255–6
environments, lacustrine 42–5
Enzel, Y. 45
Eph'al, Israel 383, 385, 386
Epipaleolithic
    chronological framework 144
    Early
        cultural sequence 146–8
        environmental background 146
        Kebaran complex 152–3
        Masraqan 148–51
        Nebekian 151–2
        Nizzanan 153–5, 157
        Ohalo II 168
        Qalkhan 152
        tools 150, 151, 154, 155, 157
    food resources 144–6
    Late 166
    Middle
        environmental background 156
        Geometric Kebaran 156–61
        Mushabian 161–4
        Ramonian 164–6
        tools 160, 163, 165
    paradigms and methodology 143–4
    stratigraphic correlation of sites 149
Epstein, C. 219, 229, 232, 238, 250, 258, 265
Esse, Douglas L. 253, 259, 265, 293, 356, 371, 377, 382
Et-Tabun Cave 50–1
Ettema, M.J. 9
Evenari, M. 33
exploration 11–12

F

factory, Jaffa 525
fakes 21
Falconer, Steven 290, 291, 293, 306, 409, 418, 546, 547
farmsteads
    Hirbet Tanurah 454
    Negev 485–6
    Roman period 452–3
Farrand, W.R. 49, 50, 51, 113
Febvre, L. 2, 4, 7
Feinbrun-Dothan, N. 24, 26
Feraud, G. 96, 97
Ferembach, D. 65, 66, 69
Ferring, C.R. 132, 135, 148
fibres 257
field systems, Roman period 453

field tower, Qarawat Bene Hassan 453
figurines
    Ain Ghazal 191
    Azor 246
    Gilat 236
    Middle Bronze Age mould 308
    Netiv Hagdud 198
    Persian and Hellenistic Empires 442, 443
    Pottery Neolithic 218–19
    Yarmukian 222, 223
Filastin, map 490
Finkelstein, Israel 5
    conclusion 544, 546
    Early Bronze Age 280, 282, 292, 293, 294
    Israel and Judah, kingdoms of 371, 373, 377, 383, 386–7,
        389–90, 392
    Late Bronze Age 323, 326, 328
    Late Bronze/Iron Age, Transjordan 406, 409
    Middle Bronze Age 302, 304, 305, 314, 317
    plough and pasture, southern Levant 259
    Sea Peoples, impact of 344, 349, 351, 354–5, 357, 359,
        360–5
Finkielsztein, G. 438
Finn, James 531, 533, 538
Fischer, C.S. 524, 526
Fisher, Clarence 22
Fitzgerald, G.M. 205, 241
Flannery, Kent V. 193, 196, 198, 200, 248, 368
Fleisch, S.J. 119
Fletcher, L. 2, 4
flint tools, Yarmukian 209
flora 24–8
Foerster, G. 455, 460, 462, 474, 477
food animals 248
food producers, early *see* Early Neolithic
food systems, Late Bronze/Iron Age Transjordan 402–3
foraging societies, transport cost model 80–1
forgeries 21
Forster, R. 8
Forsyth, G.H. 482
Forsythe, A.B. 65
fortifications
    Persian and Hellenistic Empires 439–41
    Roman period 453
Foucault, M. 9
founder crops 248
Fowler, D.D. 9
Frankel, R. 441, 442, 483
Franken, H.J. 409, 494
Frankish
    manor house 506
    sites 507
    village 505
Frayer, D.W. 64
Freedman, D.N. 18, 324
Freidel, D.A. 128, 133, 137, 139
Freu, J. 336
Frick, F.S. 405
Fried, M.H. 7, 294
Friedman, E. 210
Friedman, J.D. 334
Friedman, Richard E. 542
Fritz, V. 384, 385, 389
Frova, A. 455, 474, 476
fruit trees, Early Bronze Age 250

G

Gaillard, J.M. 135
Gal, Zvi 304, 380, 383
Galilee skull 60–1, 62
Galili, U. 67, 207, 218, 219

Ganor, E. 47, 49
Garfinkel, Y. 45, 193, 205, 209, 219
Garrard, Andrew N. 124
    hunter/gatherers, end of Paleolithic 141, 146, 152, 155–6, 158, 162
    Natufian culture 179
    Neolithic, pre pottery 193, 199, 201
Garrod, Dorothy A.E. 16, 51, 62
    foragers, Upper Paleolithic Period 124, 129, 130, 138
    hunter/gatherers, end of Paleolithic 141
    Lower Paleolithic of Israel 96–100, 107
    Modern Humans, origins of 113, 117, 121
    Natufian culture 169, 171, 173, 176, 177, 180
Garstang, J.B.E. 205, 210
Gat, J.R. 128
Geary, P.J. 11
Gebel, G.H. 124
Gebel Lagama, case study 139–40
Geertz, C. 313
Geneste, J.M. 118
Gera, D. 445
Geraards, D. 60, 93
Geraty, Lawrence T. 351, 407, 411, 412
Gerstenblith, P. 297, 300, 301, 302, 303, 307, 310
Gesher Benot Ya'akov
    artifacts 100, 108–9
    excavation overview 94
    site 107–9
Geva, H. 459, 499
Gezer
    fortifications 372
    incense altars 386
    Iron Age II houses 424
Ghassulian churn
    Ein Gedi 267
    Gilat 266
Gibeon, water tunnel 428
Gichon, M. 455, 468, 494
Gil, M. 488, 497
Gilat
    figurine 236
    Ghassulian churn 266
    male burial 59
    statuette 240
    tools 235
Gilead, D. 86, 93, 96, 101, 105, 107
Gilead, I. 108, 141, 212
    Chalcolithic Period 229, 232, 241
    conclusion 544, 547
    Early Bronze Age 269, 275
    foragers, Upper Paleolithic period 124, 128–32, 135, 137, 139
    Modern Humans, origins of 114, 117, 120
    plough and pasture, southern Levant 264
Giles, M. 69
Ginzbourg, D. 47
Gisis, I. 98
Gitin, Seymour 5, 16, 335, 342, 345, 346
Gittlen, B.M. 325, 330
Gjerstad, E. 436
Gladfelter, B.G. 129
Glass, Joseph 384, 527, 535, 536, 537
Glock, A.E. 9, 19
Glubb, J.B. 404, 405
Glueck, Nelson 17, 399, 401
Glyptic art 443–4
goats/sheep proportion 263
Goitein, S.D. 493, 496, 497, 499, 523
Goldberg, Paul 5, 146, 193, 241
    changing landscape 44–53
    conclusion 544
    foragers, Upper Paleolithic Period 128, 129
    modern humans, origins of 112, 114, 120, 122
    Natufian culture 178, 181

Goldstein, Lynne 235
Goldwasser, O. 343
Goldziher 499
Gomulka, S. 524
Gonen, R. 324, 325, 331
Goodenough, E.R. 461, 462
Goodfriend, G.A. 46, 52, 128
Goodman, M. 449–52, 455, 459–3, 465, 468
Gopher, Ari 66
    Chalcolithic Period 229, 233, 234, 235
    Neolithic Period, pottery 205, 207–12, 215, 219, 221–2
    Neolithic, pre pottery 195, 197, 199
Gophna, Ram 249, 389
    Chalcolithic Period 229, 235, 242
    conclusion 546
    Early Bronze Age 273, 275–7, 279, 280
    highland frontiers, conquest of 354, 356, 360, 364
    Late Bronze Age 320, 323
    Middle Bronze Age 301, 302, 304, 305
    Neolithic Period, pottery 205, 208, 211, 212
Gordon, C.H. 319
Goren, N. 60, 93, 96
Goren, Yuval 205, 210, 212, 216, 224, 232, 235, 237, 241
Goren-Inbar, Naama
    changing landscape 42, 43, 44
    Lower Paleolithic of Israel 93, 96–7, 100–1, 103, 105, 107, 108
    Modern Humans, origins of 114, 117
Goring-Morris, A. Nigel 64
    changing landscape 45, 46, 47, 48, 49
    conclusion 544
    foragers, Upper Paleolithic Period 124, 132, 134, 135, 136
    hunter/gatherers, end of Paleolithic 141, 143, 146, 148, 155, 158, 161–2, 164
    Modern Humans, origins of 120
    Natufian culture 172, 178, 180, 182
    Neolithic, pre pottery 198, 199
    social change, prehistoric lithic production 82, 83, 85–9, 91
Gosden, Cris 240
Gothman, Johannes 505
Gottheil, F.M. 527, 537
Gottwald, N.K. 324, 363, 364, 402, 501
Gould, Steven Jay 78, 79, 371
Grabar, A. 483
Grabar, O. 491, 496, 499
Grabois, A. 11
Graesser, C. 313
Graf, D.F. 324
Grant, E. 392
Graubard, S.R. 524
graves, Early Neolithic 197
Great Britain 1917 Expeditionary Force 531, 535
Green, J. 476
Greenberg, Raphael 219, 307, 328, 377, 378
Greenblatt, S. 12
Greene, K. 524
Griffeth, R. 326
Grigson, Caroline 52, 120
    Chalcolithic Period 231, 232, 241
    conclusion 544
    plough and pasture, southern Levant 248, 252, 254, 256–59, 264, 267
Gropp, D.M. 432
Gross, N. 535, 536, 537
Grossman, D. 355
Grousset, R. 508
Grün, R. 51, 61, 93, 97, 99, 110, 112
Gubser, P. 404, 405
Gunneweg, Jan 334
Gustavson-Gaube, C. 229
Guy, P.L.O. 22, 309
Gvirtzman, G. 49, 50

H

Haaretz Museum 522
Haas, G. 49, 60, 69
Hachlili, R. 455, 459, 460, 461, 462, 466, 467, 480
Hadidi, A. 19
Hägerstrand, T. 526
Haiman, M. 259
Haines, R.C. 494
Hakker-Orion, D. 259
Halevi, N. 16
Halevy, G. 32, 36
Hall, M. 78, 79, 118, 178
Halstead, P. 81
HaMeshar Formation 45
Hamilton, R.W. 438, 491
Hanbury-Tenison, J.W. 249, 269
Hardin, G. 239
Harding, Gerald Lankaster 18, 384
Harifian, sites 89
Harlan, J.R. 256
Harper, G.M. 459
Harrison, T.P. 491
Harrold, F.B. 110
Hart, S. 406
Harvey, D. 12
al-Hassan, A.Y. 526
Hasselquist, Friedrich 11
Hasson, Rachel 494, 522
Hasson, Yizhak 522
Hauptmann, A. 234, 241, 243
Hauting, G.R. 499
Hayden, B. 220
Hayonim site 175, 176, 179
Hazor 22
    bowls 380
    citadel 425
    gate capitals 421
    Middle Bronze Age 306–8
    plaque 327
    pottery 381
    site plan 371
Headrick, D.R. 524, 529, 530, 537
Heeres, J.A.H. 249, 250
Heichelheim, F. 458
Helbaek, H. 249, 250, 265, 266
Helck 340
Hellenistic Empire *see* Persian and Hellenistic Empires
Hellwing, S. 254, 344, 356, 391
Helmer, D. 195, 196, 201
Helms, Svend 290, 293, 309, 491
Hennessy, J.B. 229, 236, 277, 409
Hennig, G.J. 97
Henry, D.O. 86
    hunter/gatherers, end of Paleolithic 141, 146, 152, 162
    Modern Humans, origins of 112, 114
    Natufian culture 172, 177, 178, 184
Herold, J. 12
Herr, Larry G. 406, 407, 411
Hershkovitz, I. 64, 66, 67, 168, 197, 198, 207, 219, 220
Herzog, Z. 276, 317, 323, 384, 385, 436, 438, 439
Hesse, B. 201, 252, 255, 344
Hexter, J.H. 4
Hiatt, J.M. 404
Hietala, H.J. 117
Higgs, E.S. 82, 85
highlands societies
    Early Bronze Age 359–60
    Iron Age 361–2
    Middle/Late Bronze Age 360–1
Hill, C.F. 451
Hill, D.R. 526
Hill, G.F. 432, 435

Hillman, G.C. 144, 173, 175, 195, 196, 200
Hirbet Najar, olive press 458
Hirbet Tanurah
    farmstead 454
    sites 457
Hirschfeld, Y. 476, 479, 483, 486, 487
Hodder, I. xii, 5, 9, 301, 351
Hoffmeier, J.K. 314, 315, 322
Hoffner, H.A. 336
Hole, Frank 195, 198, 200, 294
Holl, Augustin F.C. xii, xiv, 78, 86, 241, 320, 431, 544
Holloday, John S. 372, 380–2, 386–7, 389, 393, 418, 434, 544
Holocene, population 65–71
Holum, K.G. 474, 477, 488, 495
Homès-Fredericq, D. 406
hominds, Middle Paleolithic 114–15
hominids
    Aurignacian 64
    Kebaran 64
    Lower and Middle Pleistocene 60–1
    Middle Paleolithic 114–15
    Mousterian 61–4
    Upper Pleistocene 61–4
Hopf, M. 195, 211, 249, 250
Hopkins, David C. 352, 382, 386, 402, 403, 406
Hopkins, I.W.J. 451
Hopwood, Derek 14
Horn, Siegfried S. 412
Horowitz, A. 43–7, 49, 103, 107, 113–14, 128, 129
Horowitz, G. 439
horses 258–9
horticulture 250
Horvat Kanaf
    plan 481
    reconstruction 474
Horwitz, Liora Kolska 250–1, 253, 257–8, 268, 287, 356
Hours, F. 93, 96, 97, 99, 141, 148, 153
houses
    Early Israel 387–9
    Gezer 424
    Tell en-Nasbeh 424
Hovers, Erella 45, 117, 120, 137, 153, 156
Howayej, B. Abu 402, 403
Hrdlicka, A. 69, 71
Hublin, J.J. 130
Hufton, O. 5
Hull, D.L. 78
Humphrey, J.H. 476
Hunt, E.D. 11, 470
Hüttenmeister, F. 481
Hütteroth, W. 327

I

Ibach, R.D. 351, 450
Ibrahim, M. 229, 351, 404, 407, 414
ideology
    Ayyubid/Mamluk/Ottoman periods 522
    Chalcolithic 234
    Early Islamic period 496–7
    Early Neolithic 197–8
Ilan, David 241
    conclusion 544
    highland frontiers 357
    Late Bronze Age 323, 325
    Middle Bronze Age 297, 299–301, 310, 311, 319
Iliffe, J.H. 442
imagery, Yarmukian 222–3
incense altars 386, 387
industry, modern period 535–6
Inizan, M.L. 135, 148

innovation
  Ayyubid/Mamluk/Ottoman periods 520–2
  Chalcolithic 229–38
  Early Islamic period 493–6
  Early Neolithic 194–5
  Middle Paleolithic 117–21
  Pottery Neolithic 215–18
  Roman period 454–9
internationalism, Middle Bronze Age 305–8
Irby, Charles 13
Iron Age I
  agricultural development 357–8
  collapse of Late Bronze culture 354
  demographic oscillations 354–9
  dry farming 353
  environment 352–4
  expansion 357–8
  highlands societies 361–2
  material culture 358–9, 365
  pottery 359
  settlement 354–9
  sites 352, 419
  technology 364
Iron Age II
  architecture 422–3
  art 423–5
  biblical evidence 427–9
  burial customs 421–2
  centralization 418–20 421–2
  conquests 431
  ethnic consciousness 420–1
  highlands societies 361–2
  houses 424
  literacy 425–7
  material culture 422–5
  nationalization 418–21
  sites 370, 419
  tombs 421–2
  urbanization 418
Iron Age Transjordan *see* Late Bronze/Iron Age
    Transjordan
irrigation 255–6
  Artas gardens 533
Isaac, B. 449, 450, 453, 456, 457, 464, 468
Isaac, Glynn L. 79, 100, 106
Israel *see also* Early Israel
Israel Exploration Society 18–19
Israel and Judah, kingdoms of 384, 410, 431
Israelite city wall 417
Issar, A. 47, 49, 128
Issawi, C. 526
Isserlin, B.S.J. 259
'Izbet Sartah
  excavation plan 391–2, 392
  strata 378

J

Jackson, K.P. 414
Jacobs, L. 387
Jacobsen, T. 234
Jacoby, David 12, 514
Jaffa
  factory 525
  factory advertisement 529
James, F. 258
James, T.G.H. 234
Jamrah, Mohammed 414
Jebel Mussa, Sinai 543
Jebel Qa'aqir
  cave interior 288
  copper javelins 288

  excavation 283
  tombs 286–7
Jelinek, A.J. 51, 96–100, 106, 110, 113, 117–18, 121
Jericho, seals 311
Jerusalem
  almshouses 533
  Anglo-Palestine bank 537
  Dome of the Rock 489, 499
  fish-eye view xi
  Golden Gate 499
  Holy Sepulchre church 476
  Khan al-Sultan 519
  Mamluk fountain 518
  Mamluk gateway 519
  Ottoman walls 519
  railway station 536
  Western wall 456
jewelry
  Nahal Qana 238
  Tell el-Ajjul 313
Joffe, Alexander H. 291, 295, 546, 547
Joffee, A. 232, 237, 241, 243
Johns, C.M. 520
Johnson, D.L. 415
Johnson, A.C. 459
Johnson, A.W. xiv, 6, 24, 239, 313
Johnson, B.L. 345
Johnson, C. Paul 542
Johnson, G.A. 302, 307, 323, 326
Jones, A.H.M. 449, 450, 451, 463, 464, 474, 485
Jones, Duncan 452
Jones, K. 68
Jones, M. 134
Jones, R. 2
Jordan Valley, landscape 42–5
Josephus 314
Judaism, Roman period 459–62

K

Kadman, L. 459, 463
Kafafi, Z. 66, 68, 209
Kafri, U. 49
Kallai, Z. 361
Kalsbeek, J. 494
Kamp, K.A. 301, 352, 409
Kantor, H.J. 330
Kaplan, J. 205, 209–12, 214, 301, 306, 316, 492, 516
Karageorghis, V. 337, 345, 347
Kark, Ruth 527–8, 530, 532–3, 535–7, 539, 541, 548
Karmeli, A. 49
Katz, A. 44
Katz, S. 524, 527
Kaufman, D. 44, 49, 64, 80, 85, 115, 136, 148, 158,
    166
Kebara Cave
  case study 122–3
  excavation 111
  geology 51
  micromorphology 57
  radial Levallios core 118
Kebaran population 64
Kedar, Y. 486
Keel, Othmar 423
Keeley, L.H. 121, 135
Keita, S.O.Y. 65
Keith, A. 60, 61, 62, 63, 64, 65, 93, 114
Kelm, G.L. 387
Kempinski, Aharon 11, 498
  Early Bronze Age 269, 273, 275, 279
  highland frontiers 355, 365
  Israel and Judah, kingdoms of 384, 385, 389

Late Bronze Age 322, 323, 324, 330
   Middle Bronze age 299, 305, 309, 310, 316
Kennedy, H. 477, 493
Kenyon, K. xvi, 19, 234, 354
   Early Bronze Age 286, 287
   Late Bronze Age 320, 322, 325, 330
   Middle Bronze Age 297, 314, 317
   Neolithic Period, pottery 207, 210, 221
   Neolithic, pre pottery 190, 193, 198
Keshet, M. 28
Key, C.A. 234
Kh. al-Lanza, Frankish manor house 506
Kh. el-Qōm
   inscription 428
   tomb 422
Khalidi, T. 491, 492
Khalil, L. 241
Khan al-Sultan, Jerusalem 519
Khatt, 520
Khazanov, A. 201, 259, 264
Khirbat al-Mafjar
   map 496
   reconstruction 491
Khirbet ed-Deir, aerial view 487
Khuri, F. 405
Killibrew, A. 382, 459, 480
kilns, Aqaba 495
Kimura 63
Kindler, A. 432, 435
King, P.J. 9, 17, 427
Kirkbride, D. 98, 194, 199
Kislev, M.E. 31, 144, 151, 168, 195, 196, 249, 308
Kitchen, K.A. 372, 385, 407
Kitchener, 504
Kitzinger, K. 482
Klein, R. 93
Kloner, A. 439, 440
Knapp, A. Bernard 2, 4, 8, 351, 431
   Late Bronze Age 320, 324, 325, 326
   Middle Bronze Age 305, 306, 307, 308
Knauf, E.A. 402, 406, 408, 497
Kochavi, M. 309, 371, 383, 449
Koeppel, S. 250
Kohl, P. 228
Köhler, I. 259
Köhler-Rollefson, I. 201
Kolska-Horwitz, L. 176
Koren, J. 500, 501
Kotter, W. 305
Kouky, F.L. 156
Kowalewski, S.A. 323
Kozlowski, J.K. 130
Kraeling, C.H. 458, 463
Krahfeld-Daugherty, M. 318
Kramer, Carol 193, 198, 301, 309, 377, 387, 389
Krautheimer, R. 479
Kristiansen, K. 8
Kroeber, A.L. 526
Krogman, W.M. 69, 71
Kuchman, Liza 341
Kuhn, T.S. 78
Kuijt, L. 193
Kuntillet Ajrûd, inscription 428
Kurth, G. 66, 67, 68, 69
Kus, S.M. 294, 319
Kussinger, S. 259
Kutiel, P. 31

L

LaBianca, Ø.S. 5, 291, 355, 402, 404, 407
Lach, D. 12

Lachish
   palace 425
   palace-fort 374
   relief 431
Lacombe, J.P. 69
Ladiray, D. 233, 235
Lagarce, E. 334, 336
Lagarce, J. 334, 336
Lake Lisan 44
Lake Samra 44
Lambert, C. 435
Lamon, R.S. 378, 393
Lancaster, W. 404
Lance, H.D. 384
Landes, D.S. 524, 526
Landes, G.M. 401, 411
landscape
   aeolian 47–51
   Benot Ya'akov Formation 43–4, 45
   caves 50–1
   changes 55–6
   coastal settings 49–50
   colluvial settings 47
   HaMeshar Formation 45
   Jordan Valley 42–5
   Lisan Formation 44
   loess and loessial deposits 47–8
   micromorphology 57
   Negev 45–7
   sandy deposits 48–9
   Shefala 47
   Sinai 46–7
   soil types 43
   temporal distribution 53
   'Ubeidiya Formation 42–3
Lapidus, I.M. 495
Lapp, N. 392
Lapp, P.W. 351, 354, 363
Larkin, J. 9
Larsen, M.T. 8, 9, 17, 383
Late Bronze Age
   see also Late Bronze/Iron Age Transjordan
   burial customs 331
   city states 328
   culture change 320
   culture collapse 354
   demarcation 330
   highlands societies 360–1
   palaces 325
   plaques 327
   politico-economic change 324–6
   population 69–71
   pottery 330
   settlement map 322
   settlement patterns 324
   shifting frontier model 327–8
   social organization 326–7
   temples 325
   transition from Middle Bronze Age 314–15, 320–4
Late Bronze/Iron Age Transjordan
   collapse 411
   environmental risks 403
   food systems 402–3
   ideological roots 408–9
   land use 403
   origin of people 399–402
   settlement 403
   sites 401
   societal changes 406–11
   tribalism 403–6, 408–10, 414–15
   water availability 402–3
Late Pleistocene settlements, Negev and Sinai 88, 90, 91, 92
Lattimore, Owen 327

Laville, H. 50, 51, 53, 122
Layish, A. 520
Le Goff, J. 5
Le Roy Ladurie, E. 2
Le Strange, G. 11
Leakey, M.D. 93, 100, 105
leather 257–8
LeBlanc, S.A. 205
Lechevallier, M. 180, 193, 198
Lederman, Z. 316, 344, 391
Lee, R.B. 126
Lee-Thorp, J.A. 183
Lees, S.H. 290, 291, 293
Lehrer, Gusta 522
Leith, M.J.W. 444
Lemaire, A. 426
Lemche, N.P. 363
Lenski, G. 228
Lenski, J. 228
Leonard, A. 320, 325, 330
Leone, M.P. 9
Lernau, H. 259
Leroi-Gourhan, A. 45, 86
Lev, E. 119
Lev-Yadun, Simcha 280, 527
Lévêque, F. 130
Levick, B. 465
Levine, L.I. 474
    Roman Period 448–51, 455, 458–60, 463, 465, 468
Levy, Leon 342, 344, 345, 346
Levy, Thomas E. xii, xiv, 5, 47, 69
    Chalcolithic Period 229–39, 241, 243
    conclusion 542, 544, 546, 548
    Early Bronze Age 269, 294
    Early Islamci Period 500
    Late Bronze Age 320
    Middle Bronze Age 302, 313
    Modern Humans, origins of 118
    Modern Technology, introduction 524
    Natufian culture 178
    Neolithic Period, pottery 218, 220
    Palestine, Iron II Period 431
    plough and pasture, southern Levant 254, 256, 258, 264
    social change, prehistoric lithic production 82, 83
Lewin, Z. 535
Lewis, Bernard 519, 523
Lewis, N.N. 327, 328, 355
Lieberman, D.E. 117, 133, 158, 180, 181
Lifshitz, B. 462
Lincoln, Abraham 526
Lindly, J.M. 110
linguistic roots 13–14
Liphschitz, Nili 126, 144, 249, 250, 255, 280, 380, 382, 527
Lipkin, Y. 34
Lisan Formation 44
literacy, Iron Age II 425–7
lithic assemblages
    Paleolithic 82–5
    socio-technological structures 85–6
Littauer, M. 268
Lloyd Wright, Frank 393
Lod site, sunken structures 210
Lodian (Jericho IX)
    culture 210–11
    site distribution 216
loess and loessial deposits 47–8
Lombard, M. 2
London, Gloria 286, 287, 324
Long, J.C. 290, 291
Lotter, A.S. 144
Loud, Gordon 22, 314

Lowance, M.I. 12
Lower Paleolithic
    classification schemes 96
    cultural entities 93–6, 97–100
    dating 96–7
    future research 101–2
    research history 96
    technology and innovation 100–1
Lower Pleistocene, population 60–1
Luckenbill, D.D. 337
Luke, J.T. 401
Lydda, bridge 517

M

Maale Adummim, monastery 487
Ma'ayeh, F.S. 407
Mabry, J. 305
Macalister, R.A.S. 9, 15, 384
McCorriston, J. 195, 200
McCowan, C.C. 392
McCown, T.D. 60, 61, 62, 63, 64, 65, 114
McCreery, D.W. 249, 250, 251, 255, 259
MacDonald, B. 210, 229, 232, 351, 406, 407
Macdonald, E. 272
McGovern, P. 308, 402, 406, 407
Madaba Plains Project 412–13
Maddison, A. 524
Madelin, L. 508
Mader, 455
Magaritz, M. 45, 46, 97, 128
Magen, Y. 351, 441, 481, 482, 487
Magie, D. 463
Magness, J. 488, 499
Magness-Gardiner, Bonnie 290, 293, 306, 307
maisons fortes, Crusader Palestine 505–6
Makhouly, N. 520
Malamat, A. 307, 312
Malek, J. 234
Mallaha site 174, 175, 186
Mallon, A. 229, 230, 250
Mamluk
    bridge 517
    fountain 518
    gateway 519
    Khan al-Sultan 519
    minaret 517
    period *see* Ayyubid/Mamluk/Ottoman periods
    pottery 521
Mangles, John 13
Mann, Michael 234
Maoz, U.Z. 480
Maoz, Z. 480
Marcus, E. 301, 302, 308
Marfoe, Leon 228, 291, 327, 351
    Late Bronze Age 297, 300–2, 304, 306–7, 314
Margalit, B. 198
Marks, A.E.
    changing landscape 45, 46, 53, 56
    foragers, Upper Paleolithic Period 128–35, 137, 139
    hunter/gatherers, end of Paleolithic 148
    Modern Humans, origins of 110, 115, 117
    social change, prehistoric lithic production 81–2, 84, 86
Marlowe, J. 12
Marquet-Krause, J. 387
Marshall, D.N. 258
Marx, E. 239, 404
Masada
    aerial view 447
    case study 466–7
    site plan 467

material culture
    Iron Age II 422–5
    Persian and Hellenistic Empires 437–44
    table 300
Matthiae, P. 297, 314
Mauss, Marcel 240
Mayer, Hans 509
Mayer, K.A. 497
Mayer, L.A. 516, 522
Mayerson, P. 484, 486, 500
Mayr, E. 78
Mazar, Amichai xvi, 5, 11, 78
    highland frontiers 351, 359
    Israel and Judah, kingdoms of 371, 373, 377, 385,
        387
    Late Bronze Age 320, 325
    Middle Bronze Age 297, 314
    Palestine, Iron II Period 416
    Sea Peoples, impact of 335, 337, 344, 346–7
Mazar, Benjamin 18, 297, 360
    Roman Period 452, 455, 460, 462
    Sea Peoples, impact of 243, 332, 338, 345
Mazor, G. 474, 486
Meadow, R.H. 117, 196, 200
meat weights 260–2
Mee, C.B. 331
Megiddo 22–3
    non-Israelite housing block 393
    palace plan 311
    palaces 374
    plaque 327
    site 274
    site plan 371
Meignen, L. 51, 114, 118, 119
Meimaris, Y.E. 478, 487
Melkawi, A. 493
Mellaart, J. 205, 211
Meloy, J.L. 495, 496
Mendel, B. 527, 528
Mendenhall, G.E. 324, 351, 363, 402, 501
Mercier, N. 97, 110
Merrill, Selah 532
Mesha Inscription 414
Mesha Stele 21
Meshel, Z. 199, 428
Meshorer, Y. 432, 435, 444, 459
metallurgy, Chalcolithic 233–4
Metzer, J. 537
Meyers, E.M. 449, 451, 452, 465
Mez, A. 497
micromorphology 57
Middle Bronze Age
    alphabet 312
    architecture 309
    arts 309–11
    Avaris 308
    burial practices 318–19
    cults 313–14
    cultural origins 300–1
    definition 297–300
    Egyptian ascendancy 314–15
    Hazor 306–8
    highlands societies 360–1
    internationalism 305–8
    population 69
    pottery 360
    rampart fortifications 316–17
    religious beliefs 313–14
    settlement patterns 301–5
    sites 299, 303, 305
    socio-political disintegration 314–15
    technology 309–11
    trade 306–8

    transition to Late Bronze Age 314–15, 320–4
    urban planning 309
    warfare 311–13
    waterworks 309
Middle Paleolithic
    hominids 114–15
    innovations 117–21
    settlement patterns 116–17
    symbolic behaviour 121
    technology 117–21
    transition to Upper 129–30
    transitions between periods 115–16
Middle Pleistocene, population 60–1
migration, Sea Peoples 336–40
Mi'ilya, village 505
Mildenberg, L. 432, 435
Milik, J.T. 377
milk 256–7, 265–6
Millard, A.R. 372
Miller, D. 20, 326
Miller, J.M. 351, 364, 365, 402, 406, 407, 409
Miller, K. 492
Miller, N.F. 195
Miller, R.G. 65
Miller-Rosen, A. 118
minaret
    Mamluk 517
    Ramla 517
Minor, Clorinda S. 533
Mintz, E. 161, 162
Mitchell, P.J. 85
Mittmann, S. 351
Moab, stelae 411
Mobley, Gregory 337
modern period
    agriculture 533–4
    background 524–6
    communications 536–7
    elements of change 530
    immigrant occupation 531
    industry 535–6
    innovations, source map 528
    international marketing 540–1
    spatial change 538–9
    technological diffusion 533–7
    technology
        nineteenth century 527–37
        pre-nineteenth century 526–7
    transport 536–7
    waterworks 534–5
Mokyr, J. 524, 526
Molist, M. 146
Molleson, 60, 68
monasteries, Byzantine period 487
Monod, T. 33
Montefiore, Moses 533
Moore, A.M.T. 141, 173, 190, 195, 198, 200, 205
Moorey, P.R.S. 9, 15, 78, 228, 233
Mor, D. 97
Moreland, J.F. 2
mortuary practices, EB IV 282–7
mosaics
    Beer Shema 483
    Beth Loya 482
    Birsama 483
    Herodian 459
    Sepphoris 477
Moshkovitz, S. 97
mosques
    Acre 513, 520
    Ayyubid 515
    Early Islamic period 498
    Ottoman 513, 520

Ramla 515
Subeita 498
Mount Carmel
sites 84, 133
Tabun Cave 41
Mount Gerizim, reconstruction 478
Mount Hermon, vegetation 30, 32
Mousterian
chronology 110
population 61–4
Mozel, I. 218
Muheisen, M. 148, 209, 249
Muhly, J.D. 312
Mujir al-Din 515, 516
Munday, F. 114, 117
Munhata
burial 219
Wadi Raba architecture 212
Munhata site 209
Murdock, G.P. 376
Musil, A. 264
Mussi, M. 180

N

Na'aman, N. 301, 311, 320, 323, 326, 327, 351, 361
Nadel, D. 64, 151, 156, 168, 194
Nahal Ein-Gev, female burial 136
Nahal Hemar
arrowheads 77
bone shuttles 203
Cave 202–4
pendants 203
skulls 198
stone mask 204
Nahal Mishmar, copper implements 227
Nahal Qana(h)
burial cave complex 237
gold rings 238
pottery 225
Nahal Zehora
burial 220
flint tools 213
Nahal Zin
cross-section 56
site 55
Nahariya, cultic offerings 308
Nasir-i-Khusraw 516
Nathan, H. 51, 69
Natufian
architecture 172–3
art and decoration 177
bones 172
dogs 187
early phase 178–80
final phase 182–3
flints 172
food 173–6
future research 184–5
Hayonim site 175, 176, 179
industries 169–72
late phase 180–2
Mallaha site 174, 175, 186
mortars 173, 177
mortuary evidence 176–7
necklace 170
population 65–6, 177–8
sedentism 183–4
sites 89, 171
natural history 11
Naveh, J. 428, 432, 437, 445
Naveh, Z. 126, 311

Navon, A. 377
Neef, R. 250, 255, 256, 265
Neev, D. 49
Negbi, M. 250
Negev
agriculture 485–6
alluvial sediments 45–6
Byzantine period 485–6
lakes 45
Northern, landscape 47
revisionism 500–1
sites 87, 88
Western, landscape 46–7
Negev, A. 479, 485, 500
Neolithic
see also Early Neolithic; Pottery Neolithic
population 66–9
pottery jar 206
Nesterhoff, D. 178
Netic Hagdud figurines 198
Netiv Hagdud 193
Netzer, E. 385, 389, 393, 450, 455, 467
Neuville, Rene 64, 96, 97, 117
Chalcolithic Period 229
foragers, Upper Paleolithic Period 124, 129, 138
hunter/gatherers, end of Paleolithic 141
Natufian culture 176, 177, 180
plough ad pasture, southern Levant 250
Nevo, Y. 472, 486, 500, 501
New Archaeology 19–20
Newman, Katherine 376, 378
Nicolis, G. 81
Niebuhr, Carsten 11
Niemeyer, H.G. 436, 437
Noe, S.P. 435
Nora, P. 5
Northover, Peter J. 233, 244
Noth, M. 361, 401, 501
Noy, T. 45, 148, 176, 177, 182, 190, 192, 194, 197, 211
Noy-Meir, I. 35

O

Oakley, K.P. 60
Oates, D. 383
ochre, Upper Paleolithic 134–5
O'Connor, D. 310
Ofer, A. 351, 357, 361
Ohalo II settlement 168
Ohel, M.Y. 82
Ohnuma, K. 115
oil 265–6
oil press, Beth Loya 484
Olami, Y. 82, 83, 84, 93, 131, 210
olive press, Hirbet Najar 458
Olszewski, D.I. 179
Omride dynasty, Early Israel 382–6
Oppenheimer, A. 453
Oren, E.D. 229, 380, 491
Early Bronze Age 269, 272, 277
Late Bronze Age 325, 330
Middlke Bronze Age 309, 319
Persian and Hellenistic Periods 437, 445
Sea Peoples, impact of 335, 341, 343
Orni, E. 40
Orrelle, E. 212, 219, 221, 222
Orshan, 28, 30, 33, 36
Orton, C. xii
Ory, J. 235
O'Shea, J. 81
Otte, M. 121

Ottoman periods
    see also Ayyubid/Mamluk/Ottoman periods
    khan 520
    mosque 513, 520
    walls 519
Ovadiah, A. 476, 477, 478, 482
Ovadiah, R. 482
Ovadya, A. 507
Owen, R. 526, 527
Ozbal, H. 312
Ozbek, M. 69

P

paganism, Roman period 462–3
palaces, Late Bronze Age 325
paleoclimates
    uncertainties 110–14
    Upper Paleolithic 128–9
Paleolithic
    see also Lower . . .; Middle . . .; Upper . . .
    lithic assemblages 82–5
    lithic technology 79–80
    socio-economic dimensions 79–80
Palestine, map 493
Palestine Oriental Society 18
Palumbo, Gaetano 286, 287, 289, 291, 294
Parker, S.T. 500
Parr, P.J. 316, 317, 384
Parrot, A. 436
pastoral systems 264
pastoralism
    Chalcolithic 231–2
    sites 247
Patrich, J. 441, 487
Patterson, T.C. 20
Payne, S. 256, 258
Paynter, Robert W. 323, 545
Pearson, G. 190
Pedersen, J. 416
Pedersen, P.O. 526
Peebles, C.S. 294, 319
Peleg, J. 475
Peltenberg, E.J. 310
Penslar, Derek 527, 530, 534
Perevolotsky, A. 351
Perlman, I. 334
Perrot, J. 134, 197
    Calcolithic Period 229, 231–3, 235
    hunter/gatherers, end of Palelothic 141, 148
    Natufian culture 172, 176, 177
    Neolithic Period, pottery 205, 207, 209, 221–2
Persian and Hellenistic Empires
    administration 432–4
    city planning 437–9
    coins 435–6
    cult objects 441–4
    fortifications 439–41
    Glyptic art 443–4
    material culture 437–44
    pottery imports 436–7
    sites 434
    temples 441
    trade 434–7
    warfare 445
    weights 434–5
Peters, E. 404
Petrie, W.M.F. 15
Pettinato, G. 245, 258, 265, 268
Philip, Graham 306, 308, 312, 313, 319
Phillips, J.L. 82, 85
    foragers, Upper Paleolithic Period 126, 128, 131–2, 134, 139

hunter/gatherers, end of Paleolithic 144, 161–2
phytogeographical analysis 26–7
Picard, L. 42, 43
Pichon, J. 175
Piggott, S. 258, 268
Pignatti 24
pilgrimages 11–13
Pitt-Rivers, Augustus 15
plant cultivation 245–7
    Late Neolithic to Late Bronze Age 249–50
plant geographical territories 26
plant growth forms 26, 28
plants
    human use 38
    potable water indicators 39
plaques
    Hazor 327
    Megiddo 327
Pleistocene xv
    see also Lower . . .; Middle . . .; Upper . . .
Plitmann, U. 24, 26
Plog, F.T. 324
Ploug, G. 436
ploughing 258
Pococke, Richard 12
Poliakov, L. 13
politico-economic change, Late Bronze Age 324–6
Pope, A.O. 435
Popham, M.R. 346
Popper, K. 78
population
    agricultural development 65–71
    Aurignacian 64
    Chalcolithic 69
    cranial measurements 70, 71
    diversity 58–60
    Early Bronze Age 69
    Holocene 65–71
    Kebaran 64
    Late Bronze Age 69–71
    Lower and Middle Pleistocene hominids 60–1
    microevolutionary trends 58–60
    Middle Bronze Age 69
    Mousterian 61–4
    Natufian 65–6, 177–8
    Neolithic 66–9
    recent 69–71
    Terminal Pleistocene 65–71
    Upper Pleistocene hominids 61–4
Porat, N. 97, 277
Porath, Y. 342, 346
Porten, B. 432
Portugali, Y. 229, 235, 242, 273, 280, 302, 320, 323, 436
Postgate, J.N. 258
pottery
    beginnings 224–5
    bowls 380
    Caesarea 495
    Calciform 288
    ceramic types 494
    chronology 339
    Coptic 495
    Early Bronze IV 292
    Hazor 381
    Iron Age I 359, 360
    Late Bronze Age 330
    Mamluk 521
    Middle Bronze Age III 360
    Mycenaean 326
    Persian and Hellenistic Empires 436–7
    Philistine Bichrome 337
    Philistine chronology 338
    Ramat Hanadiv 484

Sea Peoples 334–5
Shechem 330
Shiloh 360
Tel Aphek 330
Tel Dan 326
Tel Dor 436
Yarmukian 225
pottery jar, Neolithic 206
Pottery Neolithic
    belief and ideology 218–20
    burial customs 219–20
    chronostratigraphy 208
    developments in sixth millenium BC 207
    early pottery 207–8
    figurines 218–19
    innovation and technology 215–18
    Lodian (Jericho IX) culture 210–11
    pre-pottery background 205–7
    social organization 220
    subsistence strategies 215–18
    symbolism 218–20
    trade 215–18
    Wadi Raba culture 211–14
    Yarmukian culture 209–10
pottery vessels, cultural aspects 214–15
Potts, T.F. 144
Poulsen, V. 521
Power, W.J.A. 409
Prag, Kay 253, 254, 290
Prausnitz, M.W. 210
Prawer, Joshua 502, 504, 508, 515
pre-Aurignacian culture 98–9
pre-pottery Neolithic *see* Early Neolithic
Pred, A. 526
presses
    Beth Loya 484, 486
    Hirbet Najar 458
    Roman period 458
Price, B.J. 328
Prigogine, L. 78, 79, 81
Pringle, D. 493, 504, 505
Pritchard, J.B. 375, 455
public sanctuaries, Chalcolithic 235–8

Q

Qadesh Barnea, site 140, 161
al-Qalqashandi 516
Qarawat Bene Hassan, field tower 453
Qedar, Sh. 432, 435, 444, 493
Qumran, Roman period 454

R

Ra'anan, U. 14
Raban, A. 302, 338, 450
Rabinovitch, A. 28, 30
Rabinowitz, I. 432
Rahmani, L.Y. 435, 459
Raikes, T. 241
Rainey, A.F. 302, 323
Rajak, T. 451
Rak, Y. 61, 63, 71
Ramat Hanadiv
    pottery 484
    reconstruction 484
Ramat Rahel, palace 425
al-Ramla, gates 492
Ramla
    minaret 517
    mosque 515

Ramonian, sites 89
rampart fortifications, Middle Bronze Age 316–17
Randsborg, K. 331
Ranum, O. 8
Rappaport, R. 313
Rassam, A. 405
Rast, W.E. 272
Rauwolf, Leonhard 11
Raven, 24
Raz, Z. 24
Redding, R.W. 248
Redford, D.B. 320, 326, 331
Redford, D.E. 314
Redman, C.L. 205, 368
Reed, W.L. 406
Reeg, G. 481
Reese, D.S. 384
Rehovot-in-the-Negev
    aerial view 486
    reconstruction 479, 480
Reiner, Elhanan 508
religion
    Ayyubid/Mamluk/Ottoman periods 522
    Early Islamic period 496–7
    Early Neolithic197–8
    Middle Bronze Age 313–14
    Roman period 459–63
religious settlements, Roman period 454
Renfrew, Colin 76, 208, 235, 294, 524, 547
    Israel and Judah, kingdoms of 276, 372
    Late Bronse/Iron Age 405, 409
    Late Bronze Age 320, 324, 326, 329
    Middle Bronze Age 297, 300–1, 313–15
Renger, J. 306
revisionism, Negev 500–1
Reviv, H. 361
Rey, E.G. 504, 508
Richard, Suzanne 269, 290, 291, 293, 294
Richards, A. 527
Riis, P.J. 436, 437, 521
Risden, D.L. 71
Ritter 13
Ritter-Kaplan, H. 436
River, A.L. 452
Rizkana, I. 242
roads, Roman period 456–8
Robinson, Edward 13, 22, 226
Rodinson, M. 11
Roe, D. 113
Rogers, E. 524
Rohrer-Ertl, O. 66, 67, 68, 69
Roll, I. 449, 456, 457, 468, 496
Rollefson, Gary 67, 68
    Neolithic Period, pottery 207, 209, 219, 220
    Neolithic, pre pottery 190, 193–5, 197–9
Roman Empire, map 449
Roman period
    architecture 454–5
    army 468
    artifacts 461
    burial customs 459–60, 462
    caves 453
    cities 450–1, 463–4
    coins 458–9, 462
    farmsteads 452–3
    field systems 453
    fortifications 453
    historical background 446–50
    Judaism 459–62
    map of Palestina 456
    Masada 466–7
    paganism 462–3
    post-First Revolt 448–9

post-Second Revolt 449–50
presses 458
Qumran 454
religion 459–63
religious settlements 454
roads 456–8
Roman army 468
Second Temple Period 446–8
settlement patterns 450–4
social structures 463–4
synagogues 460–2
technological innovations 454–9
trade 458
villages 451–2, 464
Ronen, A. 49, 50, 64, 82
    foragers, Upper Neolithic Period 131–4, 136–7
    hunter/gatherers, end of Paleolithic 158
    Modern Humans, origins of 117, 119
    Natufian culture 180
Rosen, A.M. 230, 241
Rosen, Baruch 259, 377, 391
Rosen, S.A. 47, 210, 232, 241, 486, 500
Rosen-Ayalon, Myriam 492, 499, 517, 519, 521, 548
Rosenthal, R. 496
Rostovtzeff, M.I. 463
Rothenberg, B. 241, 384
Rothschild, Baron 535, 536
Rouse, I. 332
Rowlands, M. 8
Rowton, M.B. 293, 353, 361, 371
Roxan, M.M. 468
Rubin, R. 473, 485, 486
Rudich, D. 34
Running, L.G. 18
Ruppin, A. 532, 533, 535, 536
rural burgi, Crusader Palestine 505
Russel, J.C. 504
Russell, K.W. 488
Rust, A. 98, 148, 151, 152

S

Sabanne, M. 239, 241
Sackett, L.H. 346
Sadeh, M. 254
Safrai, S. 452, 453, 481
Sahlins, Marshall 239, 240, 545
Said, E. 13
St. Catherine's, Sinai 543
Salles, J.F. 319
Saltz, D. 462
Samaria
    Ahab's palace 420
    countryside 350
    intermontane valley 354
    Iron Age I site 357
    olive oil installations 359
    ostraca 428
    royal acropolis 376
    sites 457
    terraces 364
Samaritan, sites 508
Sandars, N.K. 337
Sanderson, Stephen K. 228
Sandler, A. 51
sandy deposits 48–9
Sandys, George 12
Sanlaville, P. 110, 112
Saragusti, I. 108
Sarepta, bowls 380
Sass, B. 311
Sauer, J.A. 229, 406, 411

Sauvaget, J. 491, 492, 516
Saxon, E.C. 49, 148, 155
Schattner, I. 49
Schaub, R.T. 272
Schein, Sylvia 515
Scherer, A. 67, 68
Schick, R. 11, 488, 496
Schild, R. 85
Schliemann, Heinrich 15
Schneider, J. 5
Schölch, A. 534, 537
Schroeder, B.H. 98, 100, 181
Schroer, Silvia 423
Schuldenrein, J. 44, 45, 181
Schulz, M. 67, 68
Schumacher, Gottlieb 15, 22
Schürer, E. 450, 455, 458, 460, 461, 462, 463
Schwabe, M. 462
Schwarcz, H.P. 46, 61, 97, 110, 114
Schyle, D. 148, 152
Scott, T.R 182
Scythopolis
    aerial view 476
    plaza 477
    Roman bridge 455
    site plan 475
Sea Peoples
    chronology 335–6
    demography 344
    economy 344–5
    migration 336–40
    pottery 334–5
    settlements 336
    territories 340–5
    urban imposition 345–8
seals
    Israelite 427
    Jericho 311
    Judean 427
    Tell Beit Mirsim 311
    Tell el-Ajjul 311
Seeher, J. 242
Seetzen, Ulrich 13
Seger, J.D. 241, 275, 314, 315, 323, 330
Seligman, N.G. 35
Sellin, Ernst 15
Sepphoris, mosaic 477
Serjeant, R.B. 494
Service, E.R. 7, 226, 290, 294, 372, 405
settlement disintegration, Early Bronze Age 273–5
settlement patterns
    Ayyubid/Mamluk/Ottoman periods 514–20
    Chalcolithic 229
    Crusader Palestine 506–8
    Early Bronze IV 287–93
    Early Bronze Age 275
    Early Islamic period 488–93
    Early Neolithic190–4
    Early Neolithic 190–4
    Iron Age I 354–9
    Israelite 383–6
    Late Bronze Age 324
    Middle Bronze Age 301–5
    Middle Paleolithic 116–17
    Roman period 450–4
    Upper Paleolithic 131–3
settlements
    Ammon 406–7
    Chalcolithic 242
    Edom 406–7
    Sea Peoples 336
    size 91, 92
Shalev, Sariel 232, 233, 234, 244

Shami, S.K. 405
Shamir, S. 537
Shanks, H. 462
Shapira, Moses Wilhelm 21
Sharon, I. 439, 440, 445
Sharon, M. 493, 495, 501
Shatzman, I. 441, 445
Shavit, Y. 17
Shay, Talia 286
Shea, J.J. 119, 123
Shechem, pottery 330
sheep/goats proportion 263
Shefala, Southern, landscape 47
Shehadeh, N. 402, 403
shells, Upper Paleolithic 135–6
Shennan, S. 390
Sherratt, A. 5, 218, 232, 256, 545
Shiloh, pottery 360
Shiloh, Y. 380, 386, 393
Shipton, G.M. 205, 210, 229, 241, 378, 393
Shiqmim
    animal bones 236
    burial circle 239
    cemetery 239
    cross-section 48
    site 49
    subterranean room 232, 234
    underground village 233
    village site 231
Shoemaker, F.F. 524
Shott, M. 80, 85
Shunera, site 161
Shva, S. 530
Silberman, Neil Asher 9, 12, 14–15, 17, 19, 488, 544, 548
Sillen, A. 183
Simmons, A.H. 67, 68, 164, 207, 209, 210
Simon, H.A. 431
Simon, R. 12
Simon-Pikali, E. 519
Sinai
    Northern, landscape 46–7
    sites 87, 88
Singer, I. 328, 335, 340, 342, 343, 344, 352
sites
    Acheulean 95
    Ayyubid/Mamluk/Ottoman periods 514
    Byzantine 507
    Byzantine period 472
    Chalcolithic 228, 230
    Early Bronze Age 271, 274, 277
    Early Neolithic 190–4
    EB IV 284
    EB Ia 277
    EB Ib 278
    'En Besor 278
    Epipaleolithic 149
    Frankish 507
    Harifian 89, 192
    Iron Age I 352, II 419, 356, 370
    Late Bronze Age 322
    Late Bronze/Iron Age Transjordan 401
    Lodian (Jericho IX) 216
    major urban centres EB II/EB III 276
    Megiddo 274
    Middle Bronze Age 299, 303, 305
    Middle Paleolithic 112, 133
    Mount Carmel 84, 133
    Natufian 89, 171
    Negev 87, 88
    pastoral 247
    Persian and Hellenistic Empires 434
    pigs 256
    Ramonian 89

Samaritan 508
Sinai 87, 88
    Upper Paleolithic 127, 133, 139
    Wadi Raba 217
    western Samaria 457
    Yarmukian 215
Sivan, E. 522
Sivan, R. 445
Skhul IV skull 63
Skhul V skull 62
Skiast, A. 319
Skinner, M. 62
skulls
    Amud cave 116
    cranial measurements 70, 71
    Galilee 60–1, 62
    lateral views 72, 74
    Nahal Hemar 198
    Qafzeh cave 116
    Skhul IV 63, V 62
    Tabun CI 63
Smail, R.C. 502
Smallwood, E.M. 449, 451, 459, 463, 468
Smith, A.B. 79
Smith, Eli 13
Smith, M.E. 2, 4
Smith, Patricia 257, 286, 301, 544
    Lower Paleolithic of Israel 93
    Modern Humans, origins of 114
    Natufian culture 178
    Neolithic, pre pottery 196
    people of the Holy Land from prehistory 61–6, 71, 73
Smith, R.H. 156
Sneh, A. 46, 47
Snodgrass, A. 2, 303
social organization
    Ayyubid/Mamluk/Ottoman periods 522–3
    Early Islamic period 497–8
    Early Neolithic 198–200
    Late Bronze Age 326–7
    Pottery Neolithic 220
social structure, Early Bronze IV293–5
social structures, Roman period 463–4
societies, Chalcolithic 229–38
society, Late Bronze/Iron Age Transjordan 406–11
Society for the Exploration of Eretz-Israel 18
socio-economic models, Early Bronze IV 289–93
socio-political organization, Chalcolithic 241–2
soil types 43
Solar, G. 445
Soliveres, O. 65, 66, 68
Sourdel, D. 492, 520
South Arabian trade, Early Israel 383–6
space-time approach 86–92
Sperber, D. 449
Speth, J.D. 86, 117, 120
Spiegel-Roy, P. 31, 230, 250, 259
Stacey, D. 491
Stadelmann 340
Stager, Lawrence E. xvi, 2, 5, 415
    Chalcolithic Period 239
    conclusion 544
    Early Bronze Age 269, 276, 277, 279
    highland frontiers 351, 360, 364
    Israel and Judah, kingdoms of 370, 380–1, 386–7, 389, 391–3
    Middle Bronze Age 302, 308, 317
    plough and pasture, southern Levant 250, 259, 265
    Sea Peoples, impact of 334–5, 342, 344–6
Stanhope, Lady Hester 14
Stanley 13
state, characteristics 373
statues, Ammon 410
statuette, Gilat 240

Steele, L. 318
Stein, A. 530
Stein, G.J. 257
Stekelis, M. 43, 64
    Chalcolithic period 235
    Lower Paleolithic of Israel 96, 104–5, 107–9
    Modern Humans, origins of 122
    Natufian culture 176
    Neolithic Period, pottery 205, 209, 218, 222–3
stelae
    Beth-Shean 329
    Moab 411
    Tel Gezer 313
Stengers, I. 78, 79, 81
Stern, Ephraim xvi
    Israel and Judah, kingdoms of 372, 379, 380
    Persian and Hellenistic Periods 434–41, 443–5
    Roman Period 450, 452–3, 463–4
    Sea Peoples, imact of 338, 345
Steve, A.M. 229
Stève, R.M. 516, 521
Stevens, D.S. 117
Stiebing, W.H. 341
Stocking, G.W. 13
Stohl, M. 306
Stoianovich, T. 2
Stol, Marten 547
Stone, B. 5, 335
stone objects, Upper Paleolithic 134–5
stone tools
    making 81–2
    socio-technological structures 85–6
Stordeur, D. 171, 199
Stringer, C.B. 50, 61, 63, 99, 110, 112
Strouhal, E. 68
Stuiver, M. xiv, 190
Subeita, mosque 498
Sukenik, E.L. 229, 235, 461
Suzuki, H. 61, 63, 117
synagogues
    Byzantine period 479–81
    Roman period 460–2

T

Tabun CI skull 63
Tabun Cave, Mount Carmel 41
Tadmor, H. 332, 361
Tainter, Joseph A. 294, 295, 314, 431
Takai, F. 61, 63, 117
Talgam, R. 487
Tappy, R.L. 380
Tayacian culture 97–8
Tcherikover, V.A. 436
Tchernov, E. xiv
    changing landscape 42, 43, 45
    foragers, Upper Paleolithic Period 127, 128
    Lower Paleolithic of Israel 93, 103, 105
    Modern Humans, origins of 110, 120
    Natufian culture 176
    Neolithic, pre pottery 199, 200
    people of the Holy Land from prehistoric 60
    plough and pasture 250–1, 257, 268
technology
    Ayyubid/Mamluk/Ottoman periods 520–2
    Chalcolithic 229–38
    Early Islamic period 493–6
    Early Neolithic 194–5
    Iron Age I 364
    Middle Bronze Age 309–11
    Middle Paleolithic 117–21
    nineteenth century 527–37

Pottery Neolithic 215–18
pre-nineteenth century 526–7
Roman period 454–9
Tel Aphek
    Governor's residency
    pottery 330
Tel Beersheva
    aerial view 369
    site plan 420
Tel Dalit, aerial view 270
Tel Dan
    mudbrick gate 298
    pottery 326
Tel Dor
    aerial view 438
    bulla 445
    catapult stones 445
    cross-section 440
    goddess 433
    plan 438, 439
    pottery 436
    reconstruction 439
    stamps 443
    tower 441
Tel Gezer, stelae 313
Tel Hazor, aerial view 317
Tel Masos, site plan 384, 385
Tell Abu Hawam, pit burial 331
Tell Beit Mirsim
    incense altars 386
    seals 311
Tell el-Ajjul
    jewelry 313
    seals 311
    site plan 310
Tell el-Hayyat, temple 307
Tell el-Maskhuta, incense altars 387
Tell el-Mutesellim 22–3
Tell el-Umeiri 412
Tell en-Nasbeh
    houses 424
    plan 375
temples
    Late Bronze Age 325
    Persian and Hellenistic Empires 441
Terminal Pleistocene, population 65–71
territorial ranges, Negev and Sinai sites 88
territorial units, Negev and Sinai 90
territories, Sea Peoples 340–5
Thalmann, Naftali 527, 533, 535
Thomas, C.G. 324
Thompson, T.L. 290, 351
Thomsen, P. 473
Tibawi, A.L. 14
Tilley, C. 9, 326
Tillier, A.M. 61, 62, 110, 114, 115
Tixier, J. 141, 148, 155
Tobias, P. 60, 93
tombs
    EB IV 282–7
    Iron Age II 421–2
    Jebel Qa'aqir 286–7
    Kh. el-Qôm 422
    Middle Bronze Age 318–19
    Shebna 423
tools
    Ahmarian 131
    bone 133–4
    Geometric Kebaran 160
    Gilat 235
    Kebaran 154, 155
    Levantine Aurignacian 132
    Levantine Mousterian 118–19

Masraqan 148–51
Mushabian 163
Nahal Zehora 213
Natufian 172
Nizzanan 157
Ramonian 165
stone 81–2
Upper Paleolithic 131, 132, 133–5
Yarmukian 209
Torrence, R. 80, 81, 84, 85
Toubert, P. 505
towns, Negev 485–6
Toynbee, A.J. 8, 351
trade
Middle Bronze Age 306–8
Middle East 12
Persian and Hellenistic Empires 434–7
Pottery Neolithic 215–18
Roman period 458
transition
Middle Bronze Age to Late Bronze Age 314–15, 320–4
Middle to Upper Paleolithic 129–30
transport
cattle 258, 268
donkeys 258
dromedaries 259
horses 258–9
modern period 536–7
transport cost model 80–1
tribalism
Ammon 407–8
Edom 408
Late Bronze/Iron Age Transjordan 403–6, 408–10, 414–15
Trigger, B. 9, 76, 320, 326, 332
Tringham, R. 294
Trinkaus, E. 61, 62, 63, 93, 110, 114, 115
Tsafrir, Y. 472, 474, 476–7, 479, 480, 482, 485
Tsuk, T. 229, 233
Tubb, J.A. 290, 297, 300
Tufnell, O. 310, 330, 342, 380, 392
Turville-Petre, F. 93, 96, 122, 177
Tushingham, A.D. 406
Tzarferis, V. 491

U

'Ubeidiya
artifacts 103–6
Formation 42–3
site 103–6
Uehlinger, Christoph 423
Uerpmann, H.P. 148, 152, 248
Umm ad-Dananir, aerial view 400
Upper Paleolithic
bone and flint tools 125
bone tools 133–4
climatic phases 129
cognitive-spiritual aspects 136–7
cultural assemblages 130–1
environments 124–9
female burial 136
Levantine sequence 126
non lithic objects 133–6
ochre 134–5
phases 138
settlement patterns 131–3
shells 135–6
sites 127
stone objects 134–5
subsistence resources 124–9
tools 131, 132, 133–4
transition from Middle 129–30

Upper Paleolithic paleoclimates 128–9
Upper Pleistocene, population 61–4
Urbach, E.E. 460
urban centres EB II/EB III 276
urban planning, Middle Bronze Age 309
urban society, Early Israel 379–82
al-Urdunn, map 490
Urice, S. 491
Urkan e-Rubb, incised pebble 142
Urman, D. 451, 452, 458, 460
Ussishkin, D. 236, 267, 316, 324
highland frontiers 358
Israel and Judah, kingdoms of 372, 380, 387
Sea Peoples, impact of 334, 342

V

Vailhé, S. 487
Valla, François 65, 155
conclusion 544
Natufian culture 172, 176, 178–82, 186–7
Social change, prehistoric lithic production 82, 86
Valladas, H. 50, 51, 61, 110, 122
Vallet, J.P. 2
Vallois, H.V. 65
Van Andel, T.H. 129
Van Beek, G.W. 383
Van Berchem, M. 516, 518, 519, 521
van de Mieroop, Marc 547
Van Der Kooij, G. 404, 414
van Ess, J. 499
van Gennep, A. 318
Van Keuren, D.K. 9
van Siclen, C.C. 335
Van Zeist, W. 128, 129, 195, 196, 249, 250
Vandermeersch, B. 93
foragers, Upper Paleolithic Period 129, 134
Modern Humans, origins of 110, 114, 122
people of the Holy Land from prehistoric 61, 63, 64
social change, prehistoric lithic production 82, 85
Vann, R.L. 474
vats 265
Vaux, R. de 516, 521
Chalcolithic period 229
Early Bronze IV Period 277
local kingdoms 381, 416, 454, 494
Neolithic Period, pottery 207, 221
Veenhof, K.R. 383
vegetation 28–37
desert 34
desert savannoid 36
herbaceous 31–2
map 29
maquis and forests 28–30
Mount Hermon 30, 32
mountain forest 30
oases with sudanian trees 35–6
open forests 30–1
sand 34–5
savannoid Mediterranean 32
semi-steppe batha 32
steppe 33
steppes with trees 33–4
swamps and reed thickets 36
synanthropic 36–7
tragacanth 32
wet salines 36
woodlands on basalt 30
villages
Frankish 505
Roman period 451–2, 464
Vilnay, Z. 15

Vincent, H. 474
Vincent, L.H. 522
Vita-Finzi, C. 82, 85
Vogel, J. 44, 153, 161, 162
Voigt, M.M. 198
Volkman, P. 115
Volney, Francois 12

W

Wachsmann, S. 338
Wadi Mujib, aerial view 407
Wadi Raba
    architecture 212
    culture 211–14
    sites 217
Wagstaff, M. 326
Waisel, Y. 126, 144
Waldbaum, J. 341
Walker, A.M. 5
Wallace, T.R. 531, 535, 536
Wallach, J.L. 14
Walmsley, A.G. 488, 493
Wapnish, P. 252, 259
Ward, W.A. 277, 310, 407
warfare
    Middle Bronze Age 311–13
    Persian and Hellenistic Empires 445
Warren, Charles 14
Warton, A.J. 476
Waterbolk, H.T. 44
Waterhouse, S.D. 450
Waterman, L. 450
waterworks
    Middle Bronze Age 309
    modern period 534–5
Watson, A.M. 494
Watson, P.J. 205, 368, 387, 389, 392
wealth distinctions, Early Israel 376
Webley, D. 251, 256
weights, Persian and Hellenistic Empires 434–5
Weiner, S. 51, 102, 122
Weinstein, J.M. 299, 308, 314, 315, 322–3, 328, 342
Weippert, M. 363, 406, 408
Weitzmann, K. 482, 483
welfare, Chalcolithic 243
Wendorf, F. 85, 162
Wente, Edward F. 335, 342
Wertime, T.A. 312
Western, A.C. 255
Wheatley, P. 495, 497, 499
Whitcomb, D. 488, 492–7, 499, 544, 548
White, D. 376
Whitelam, K.W. 326, 351, 374, 410
Wilk, R. 78, 79
Wilken, R.L. 11
Wilkinson, J. 478, 499
Wilkinson, L. 390
Willcox, G.H. 175, 249, 250
Wilson, J.A. 336, 338, 341, 345
Wimmer, D. 406, 407
wine 265–6
wine press, Beth Loya 486
Winnett, F.V. 406
Wittfogel, K.A. 526
Wobst, M. 81
Wolff, S. 19
Wolpoff, M.H. 110
Wood, B.G. 381
Woolley, C.L. 307, 319, 436
Worschech, U.F. 402, 406
Wreschner, E. 117, 135

Wright, G. Ernest 9, 17
    highland frontiers 351, 363
    Israel and Judah, kingdoms of 392, 409, 435
    Late Bronze Age 330
    Sea Peoples, impact of 341–3
Wright, G.A. 184, 185
Wright, G.R.H. 316, 317, 409
Wright, H.T. 302
Wright, K. 169, 196

Y

Yaalon, D.H. 31, 33, 47, 49, 50
Yabrudian culture 98
Yadin, Yigael 11, 18, 22
    Early Bronze Age 287
    highland frontiers 363
    Israel and Judah, kingdoms of 372, 380, 384, 393
    Middle Bronze Age 307, 309, 312, 317
    Persian and Hellenistic Periods 441
    Roman Period 452, 453, 466, 467
Yair, A. 45
Yakar, R. 198
Yannai, A. 337
Yarmukian
    burial 219
    culture 209–10
    figurines 222, 223
    flint tools 209
    imagery 222–3
    Munhata site 209
    pottery 225
    site distribution 215
Yassine, K. 229
Yechieli, Y. 146
Yeivin, E. 210, 218, 277
Yeivin, Z. 452
Yekutieli, Y. 269, 272, 278
Yellin, J. 301, 310
Yener, A.K. 312
Yi, S. 251
Yisraeli, T. 176, 389
Yoffee, Norman 7, 226, 409, 431
    conclusion 545, 546, 547
    Early Bronze Age 294, 295
    Late Bronze Age 320, 352
    Middle Bronze Age 301, 307, 312, 314, 315
Yom-Tov, Y. 31
Yon, Marguerite 336, 337
Younker, Randall W. 406, 407
Yurco, F. 335, 351

Z

Zaccagnini, C. 306
Zaitschek, D.V. 249, 250
Zayadeh, A.H. 496
Zayadin, F. 435
Zertal, A. 304, 323, 351, 357, 359, 364
Zeuner, F.E. 259
Zevulun, U. 306
Ziaei, M. 114
Ziffer, I. 309
Zilberman, U. 62
Zohary, D. 173, 230
    man and the natural environment 24, 26, 31, 36
    Neolithic, pre pottery 195, 196
    plough and pasture, southern Levant 245, 248, 250, 259
Zori, N. 230